HAYDN

OXFORD COMPOSER COMPANIONS

Haydn

EDITED BY DAVID WYN JONES

CONSULTANT EDITOR OTTO BIBA

OXFORD
UNIVERSITY PRESS

OXFORD
UNIVERSITY PRESS

Great Clarendon Street, Oxford, OX2 6DP,
United Kingdom

Oxford University Press is a department of the University of Oxford. It furthers the University's objective of excellence in research, scholarship, and education by publishing worldwide. Oxford is a registered trade mark of Oxford University Press in the UK and in certain other countries

First Edition published in 2002
First published as an Oxford University Press paperback 2009

Published in the United States of America by Oxford University Press
198 Madison Avenue, New York, NY 10016, United States of America

British Library Cataloguing in Publication Data
Data available

Library of Congress Cataloging in Publication Data
Data available

ISBN 978–0–19–955452–2

PREFACE

JOSEPH HAYDN was the last 'great' composer to be adequately served by scholarship. Only within the last 50 years has much of his music become available in reliable editions and a great deal of biographical information too has been discovered. There is now a clearer understanding of Haydn as a composer of symphonies, operas, and masses, for instance, than was possible a generation ago, while the old 'Papa Haydn' view of the man is fast receding, to be replaced with a more realistic and rounded appreciation of the composer's personality. English- and German-language scholarship has never been as active and seems to be building steadily towards a natural high point in 2009, the 200th anniversary of the composer's death. While much of this information and interpretation is to be found in modern biographies and dictionary entries, even more remains inaccessible to the average reader, buried in articles, the three volumes of the standard thematic catalogue of Haydn's music (Hoboken), conference papers, exhibition catalogues, and the prefaces and critical reports to the complete edition of the music (the *Joseph Haydn Werke*). The format of the Oxford Composer Companions allows the full range of modern scholarship on Haydn to be presented in one volume and is the only book to deal comprehensively with the subject in an A–Z guide.

I am grateful to Michael Cox of Oxford University Press who first asked me to prepare the volume, and to his colleagues, Pam Coote, Alison Jones, Wendy Tuckey, and Mary Worthington for their support and expertise. A special word of thanks is due to Joanna Harris who, with tact and firmness, guided the volume through to production.

My indebtedness to the 40 or so contributors and the Consultant Editor, Otto Biba, is obvious and deeply felt; less obvious, but equally valued, is the accommodation they showed with the editorial process. Other individuals who gave freely of their expertise include Malcolm Boyd, Zoltán Farkas, Jane Holland, Angela Lester, Séverine Robitaille, and Christine Trevett. Gill Jones and Judith Hurford of the Music Library, Cardiff University, were unstinting in their professional support. But my greatest debt of gratitude goes to my wife, Ann, who shared the highs and lows of the project and who encouraged it towards completion.

DAVID WYN JONES

Cardiff, December 2001

For this paperback edition, issued in the anniversary year, the material has been up-dated and minor corrections made.

DAVID WYN JONES

Cardiff, December 2008

CONTENTS

NOTE TO THE READER

Entries are arranged in letter-by-letter alphabetical order. Readers new to Haydn and his music, or those who wish to refresh their memories, are encouraged to read the general article 'Haydn, Franz Joseph', which provides an account of his life and music together with an assessment of aspects of his personality and way of life. Entries on Haydn's musical works are broadly of two types. Most vocal works with unique titles (e.g. *The Creation*, *La fedeltà premiata*, and *Missa in tempore belli*) are given individual entries together with a general entry on the genre (respectively oratorio, opera, and mass); songs, however, are discussed in one comprehensive entry. Works with generic titles (e.g. concerto, symphony, and quartet) are discussed under the appropriate genre; in addition individual entries will be found for the many nicknames applied to Haydn's works. For further information on the nature and disposition of entries see the Thematic Overview.

Cross-references. These are indicated by SMALL CAPITALS in the text, with, occasionally, *see* or *see also* at the end of an entry. In cross-references to people, the whole name is set in SMALL CAPITALS, but the person should be looked up under the last part of the name. Cross-references are supplied only when the entry referred to presents further information on, or is closely related to, the article being consulted.

Hob. nos. The standard Hoboken numbers for Haydn's works are used throughout; a few entries will identify individual movements with a supplementary small roman numeral. Symphonies and quartets are referred to using the familiar numbers 1–104 for the former and the customary opus numbers for the latter. No other numbering systems are used in the text but are given in Appendix 1, *List of Haydn's works.* This appendix also contains an explanation of the layout of Hoboken's catalogue. Further information may be found in the entry 'catalogues'.

Bibliographies. The bibliographies appended to certain articles are not intended to be comprehensive; in many cases they contain items which themselves have extensive bibliographies. For exhaustive and up-to-date bibliographical information readers should consult the web pages of the Joseph Haydn Institut (www.haydn-institut-de). The following standard reference works have not been included: L. Finscher, ed., *Die Musik in Geschichte und Gegenwart*, 2nd rev. edn (Kassel, 1994–); S. Sadie and J. Tyrrell, eds, *The New Grove Dictionary of Music and Musicians*, 2nd edn (London, 2001).

Musical pitches are indicated as shown overleaf (with accidentals as required):

Musical pitches

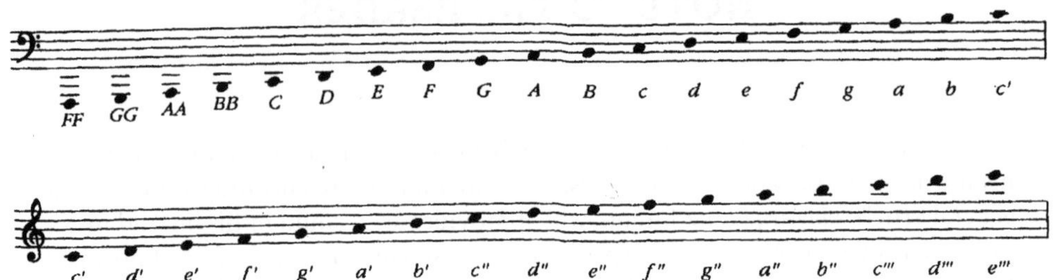

THEMATIC OVERVIEW

[*entries are arranged alphabetically by headword*]

Biography and Background

Authors, librettists, and theorists

Bader, Philipp Georg
Badini, Carlo Francesco
Burney, Charles
Busby, Thomas
Carpani, Giuseppe
Coltellini, Marco
Cramer, Carl Friedrich
Crotch, William
Dies, Albert Christoph
Dlabacž, Gottfried Johann
Framery, Nicolas Étienne
Fux, Johann Joseph
Gellert, Christian Fürchtegott
Gerber, Ernst Ludwig
Goldoni, Carlo
Griesinger, Georg August
Haschka, Lorenz Leopold
Kirnberger, Johann Philipp
Lorenzi, Giambattista
Marpurg, Friedrich Wilhelm
Mattheson, Johann
Metastasio, Pietro
Migliavacca, Giovanni Ambrogio
Pauersbach, Karl Michael von
Porta, Nunziato
Puttini, Francesco
Thomson, James

Aristocratic, royal, and imperial individuals and families

Abingdon, Willoughby Bertie, 4th Earl of
Albert, Prince of Sachsen-Teschen
Apponyi, Count Anton Georg
Erdödy family
Esterházy family
Esterházy, Prince Anton
Esterházy, Prince Nicolaus I
Esterházy, Prince Nicolaus II
Esterházy, Prince Paul Anton
Esterházy, Princess Maria Anna
Esterházy, Princess Maria Elisabeth
Esterházy, Princess Marie Hermenegild
Ferdinand IV, King of Naples
Friedrich Wilhelm II
Fürnberg, Carl Joseph Weber
George III
Grassalkovics, Prince Anton
Harrach family
Haugwitz, Count Friedrich Wilhelm
Joseph II
Lobkowitz, Prince Franz Joseph Maximilian
Maria Theresia
Marie Therese
Morzin family
Ogny, Count Claude-François-Marie Rigoley d'
Osuna, Countess Maria Josefa Alonso Pimentel
Schwarzenberg, Prince Joseph
Wales, George Augustus Frederick Prince of
York, Frederick Duke of

Composers

Albrechtsberger, Johann Georg
Anfossi, Pasquale
Asplmayr, Franz
Aumann, Franz Joseph
Bach, Carl Philipp Emanuel
Beethoven, Ludwig van
Berwald, Johan Fredrik
Boccherini family
Cherubini, Luigi
Clementi, Muzio
Dittersdorf, Carl Ditters von
Eybler, Joseph Leopold
Fuchs, Johann Nepomuk
Gassmann family
Gluck, Christoph Willibald
Gyrowetz, Adalbert
Handel, George Frideric
Hasse, Johann Adolf
Hayda, Joseph
Haydn, Franz Joseph
Haydn, Johann Michael
Heidenreich, Joseph
Hoffmeister, Franz Anton
Hofmann, Leopold
Hofstetter, Roman
Hummel, Johann Nepomuk
Kalkbrenner, Frédéric
Kimmerling, Robert
Kozeluch, Leopold
Kraus, Joseph Martin
Linley, Thomas
Martines, Marianna von
Mozart, Franz Xaver Wolfgang
Mozart, Wolfgang Amadeus
Neukomm, Sigismund
Novotný, Franz Nicolaus
Ordonez, Carlo d'
Pichl, Wenzel
Pleyel, Ignaz Joseph
Porpora, Nicola
Reicha, Antoine
Reutter, Georg
Salieri, Antonio
Sammartini, Giovanni Battista
Seyfried, Ignaz von
Shield, William
Stadler, Abbé Maximilian
Vanhal, Johann Baptist
Vivaldi, Antonio
Wagenseil, Georg Christoph
Werner, Gregor Joseph
Wesley, Samuel
Wranitzky family
Zimmerman, Anton

Family, friends, and acquaintances

Auenbrugger family
Bartalozzi, Gaetano
Fries, Count Moritz Johann Christian von
Genzinger, Maria Anna von
Greiner, Franz Sales von
Hamilton, Emma
Har(r)ington, Henry
Haydn family
Haydn, Johann Evangelist
Haydn, Maria Anna Aloysia Apollonia
Hayes, Philip
Herschel, William
Horn family
Hunter family
Keller, Therese
Kraus, Carl
Latrobe, Revd Christian Ignatius
'Lidley'
Nelson, (Admiral Lord) Horatio
Niemecz, Primitivus
Peploe, Mrs
Polzelli family
pupils
Rahier, Peter Ludwig von
Rosenbaum, Joseph Carl
Schroeter, Rebecca

The Music

folksong settings
insertion aria
keyboard sonata
keyboard trio
keyboard variations
mass
mechanical organ music
notturni for two *lire organizzate*
opera
oratorio
partita
pastorella
quartet
Salve regina
scherzando
song
string trio
symphony
Te Deum
windband music

Structures and style

alternating variations
capriccio
fantasia
folk music
fugue
minuet
rondo
scherzo
sonata form
variation

Individual works

Acide
Ah come il core mi palpita
Alfred oder Der patriotische König
'Applausus' cantata
Arianna a Naxos
Armida
Ave regina
'Berenice, che fai?'
Capriccio: 'Acht Sauschneider müssen sein'
Covent Garden overture
Creation, The
Da qual gioia improvvisa
Der Geburtstag
Der krumme Teufel
Der neue krumme Teufel
Destatevi, o miei fidi
Deutschlands Klage auf den Tod des Großen Friedrichs Borußens König
Dido
Die bestrafte Rachbegierde
Die Erwählung eines Kapellmeisters
Die Feursbrunst
Die reisende Ceres
Dr Harington's Compliment
'Ein' Magd, ein' Dienerin'
English Psalms
'Ens aeternum attende votis'
'Ey, wer hat ihm das Ding gedenkt'
Genovefens vierter Theil
Gioco filarmonico
'God save the King'
'Gott erhalte Franz den Kaiser'
'Harmoniemesse'
'Herst Nachbä, hä, sag mir was heut'
Hexen-Schabbas
'Hin ist alle meine Kraft'
Hungarian National March
Il Maestro e Scolare
Il mondo della luna
Il ritorno di Tobia
'Insane et vanae curae'
Invocation of Neptune
Jacob's Dream
La canterina
La fedeltà premiata
La marchesa nespola
L'anima del filosofo
'Lauda Sion'
Laurette
La vera costanza
Le pescatrici
Libera me, Domine
L'incontro improvviso
L'infedeltà delusa
L'isola disabitata
Lo speziale
'Maria Jungfrau rein'
Miseri noi, misera patria
Missa brevis in F
Missa brevis Sancti Joannis de Deo
Missa Cellensis
Missa Cellensis in honorem BVM
Missa in angustiis
Missa in tempore belli
Missa 'Rorate coeli desuper'
Missa Sancti Bernardi d'Offida
Missa Sancti Nicolai
Missa 'sunt bona mixta malis'
Motetto di Santa Thecla
'Mutter Gottes, mir erlaube'
'Non nobis, Domine'
'Ochsenmenuett'
Orlando paladino
Philemon und Baucis
Pietà di me, benigni Dei
Qual dubbio ormai
Seasons, The
Seven Last Words of our Saviour on the Cross, The
'Solo e pensoso'
Stabat mater
Storm, The
Symphonie concertante
Ten Commandments, The
'Was meine matte Brust'

Nicknames and other given titles

'Alleluja' symphony
'Apponyi' quartets
'Auf dem Anstand'
'Bear' symphony
'Bell' quartet
'Bird' quartet
'Clock' symphony
'Coronation' mass
Der Apotheker
'Derbyshire' marches
'Der verliebte Schulmeister'
'Drumroll' symphony
'Dudelsack'
'Echo' divertimento
'Ein Traum' quartet
'Eisenstädter' trios
'Emperor' quartet
'Erdödy' quartets
'Farewell' symphony
'Festino' symphony
'Fifths' quartet
'Fire' symphony
'Frog' quartet
'gli scherzi' quartets
'Grosse Orgelsolomesse'
'Gypsy' rondo
'Haydn' quartets
'Heiligmesse'
'Hen' symphony
'Hexenmenuett'
'Hornsignal' symphony
'How do you do?' quartet
'Hunt' quartet
'Il distratto' symphony
'Il quakuo di bel'humore'
'Imperial'
'Imperial' mass
'Joke' quartet
'Jungfern' quartets
'Kaffeeklatsch'
'Kleine Orgelsolomesse'
'La Chasse'
'Lamentation' symphony
'La passione' symphony
'La Poule' symphony
'La Reine' symphony
'Largo' quartet
'Lark' quartet
'La Roxelane' symphony
'Laudon' symphony
'Le Matin' symphony
'Le Midi' symphony
'Le Soir' symphony
'Letter V' symphony
'Lobkowitz' quartets
'London' sonata
'London' symphony
'L'Ours' symphony
'Mann und Weib'
Mare clausum

Thematic Overview

'Maria Theresa' mass
'Maria Theresia' symphony
'Mariazeller' mass
'Mass in Time of War'
'Melk' concerto
'Mercury' symphony
'Military' symphony
'Miracle' symphony
Missa Sanctae Caeciliae
Missa Sancti Josephi
'My mother bids me bind my hair'
'National' symphony
'Nelson' mass
'Night Watchman's song'
'Oxford' symphony
'Palindrome' symphony
'Paris' symphonies
'Paukenmesse'
'Philosopher' symphony
'Prussian' quartets
'Razor' quartet
'Recitative' quartet
'Rider' quartet
'Russian' quartets
'Salomon' symphonies
St Antony chorale
Scena di Berenice
'Schöpfungsmesse'
'Schoolmaster' symphony
'Seitenstetten' minuets
'Serenade' quartet
'Symphony mit dem Paukenschlag'
'Symphony mit dem Paukenwirbel'
'Sun' quartets
'Sunrise' quartet
'Surprise' symphony
'Tempora mutantur' symphony
'Teutsche Comedie Arien'
'Theresienmesse'
'Tost' quartets
'Toy' symphony
'Trauer' symphony
un piccolo divertimento
'Weihnachtssymphonie'
'Weinzierler' trios
Windsor Castle overture

Annotations and remarks

'den alten Schmarn'
'Dieses war vor gar zu gelehrte Ohren'
'fatto a posta'
'In Nomine Domini'
'in Schlaff geschrieben'
'Laus Deo'
'nihil sine causa'
'per figuram retardationis'
'sapienti pauca'

Instruments and performance practice

baryton
clavichord
Flötenuhr
fortepiano
horn
lira organizzata
mechanical organ
organ
organisierte Trompete
performance practice
recordings
violone

Scholarship, influence, and reputation

Authors, collectors, conductors, editors, and scholars

Botstiber, Hugo
Brenet, Michel
Carpani, Giuseppe
Deutsch, Otto Erich
Dies, Albert Christoph
Dlabacž, Gottfried Johann
Dorati, Antal
Feder, Georg
Fuchs, Aloys
Gardiner, William
Geiringer, Karl
Gerber, Ernst Ludwig
Griesinger, Georg August
Hadden, James Cuthbert
Hadow, William Henry
Hárich, János
Hoboken, Anthony van
Hughes, Rosemary
Landon, H(oward) C(handler) Robbins
Larsen, Jens Peter
Mandyczewski, Eusebius
Novello family
Nowak, Leopold
Pohl, Carl Ferdinand
Sandberger, Adolf
Schmid, Ernst Fritz
Schnerich, Alfred
Scott, Marion
Tovey, Donald Francis
Weingartner, Felix

Institutions and publications

Handel and Haydn Society
Haydn festivals
Haydn museums
Haydn novels, operas, and plays
Haydn Society
Haydn-Studien
Haydn Yearbook
Joseph Haydn-Institut
Joseph Haydn Stiftung
Joseph Haydn Werke
Münchener Haydn Renaissance

Later composers

Brahms, Johannes
Mahler, Gustav
Schumann, Robert Alexander

Miscellaneous

'Austria' (hymn tune)
catalogues
Der Kapellmeister seiner Durchlaucht
'Deutschland, Deutschland über alles'
'father of the symphony'
'Glorious things of Thee are spoken'
Haydn's skull
Haydntorte
recordings
sources

Technical terms

accompagnato
al roverso
al rovescio
col basso
continuo
contrafactum
dramma giocoso per musica
fausse reprise
Feldharmonie
Fortspinnung
galant
Haydn ornament
monothematicism
Palestrina style
pasticcio
species counterpoint
stile antico
stylus a cappella
thematische Arbeit
veränderte Reprise

Caspar Haydn *m.* Elisabeth [Schalk]
c. 1630–before 1687 — *d.* before 1687

Thomas Haydn *m.* Catharina [Blaiminger]
after 1657–1701 — 1671–1739

Lorenz Koller *m.* Susanna [Siebel]
1675–1718 — 1685–1756

Mathias Haydn *m.* Anna Maria [Koller]
1699–1763 — 1707–54

Anna Maria Franziska
1730–81

Anna Maria

FRANZ JOSEPH
1732–1809

Johann Michael
1737–1806

Anna Maria
1739–1802

Maria Elisabeth
Anna Maria
Anna Katharina
Mathias
Theresia

Anna Katharina
1741–before 1801

Johann Evangelist
1743–1805

Maiden names are given in square brackets.
Siblings (11) and nephews/nieces (13) of Joseph Haydn who did not survive infancy are excluded.

A HAYDN FAMILY TREE

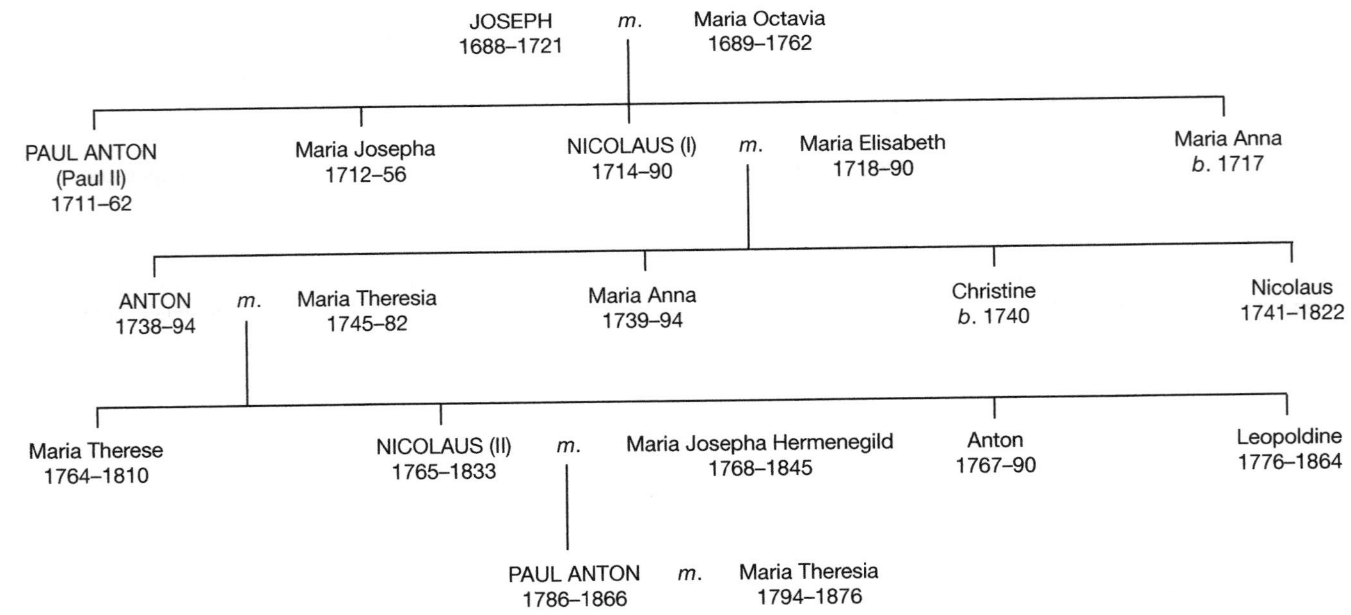

An Esterházy family tree

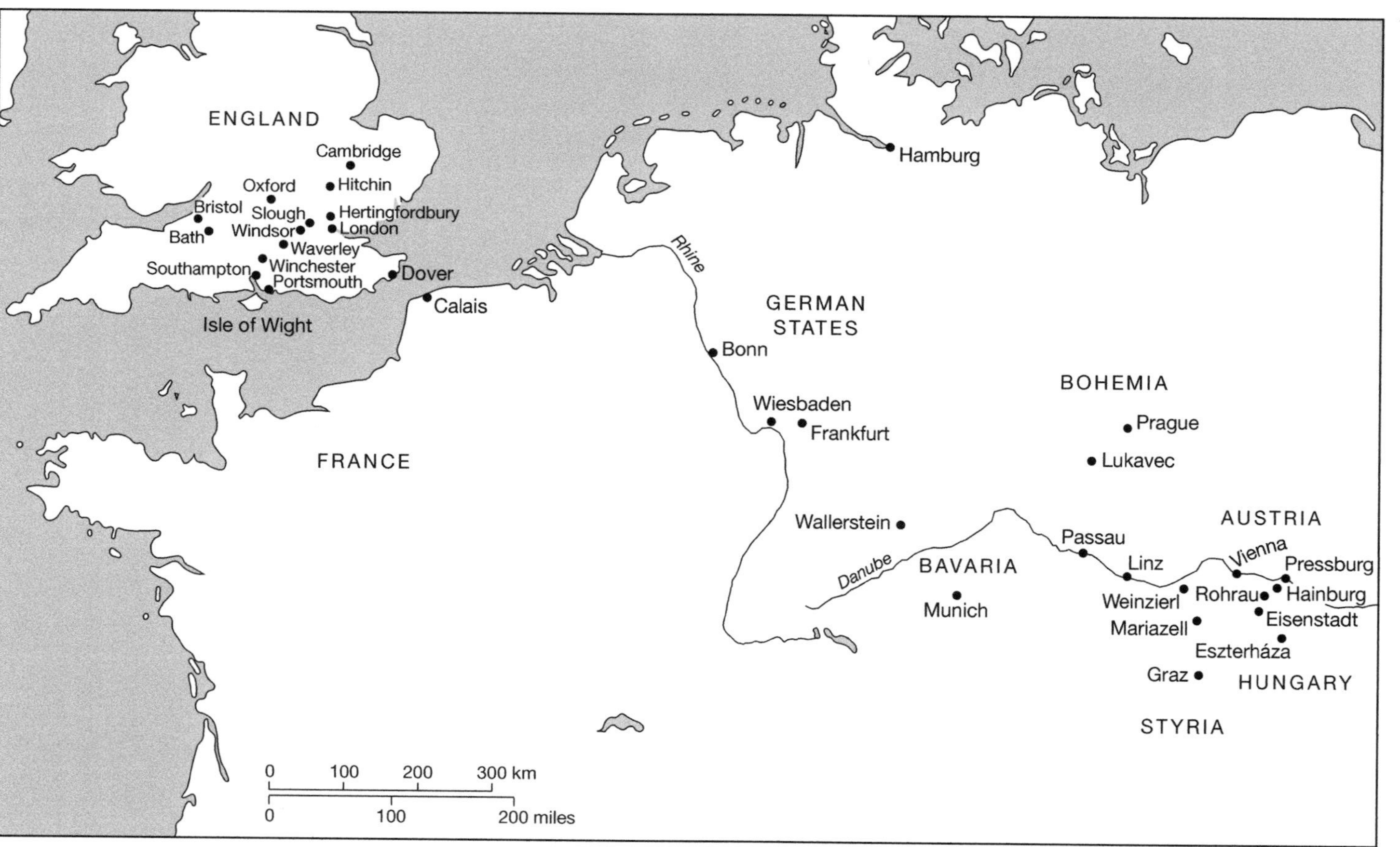

Principal cities, towns, and villages in which Haydn worked or which he visited

CONTRIBUTORS

Unsigned articles, or sections of articles, are the responsibility of the editor.

GA Professor Greger Andersson, University of Lund
ADJB Dr Allan Badley, Artaria Editions, Wellington, New Zealand
MEB Professor Mark Evan Bonds, University of North Carolina, Chapel Hill
PB Professor Peter Branscombe, St Andrews
APB Professor A. Peter Brown, Indiana University
JMB Dr Jenny Burchell, Oxford
DC Dr Derek Carew, Cardiff University
MSC Professor Malcolm S. Cole, University of California, Los Angeles
BARC Dr Barry Cooper, University of Manchester
REC Dr Rachel Cowgill, University of Leeds
JD Dr James Dack, Royal Holloway, University of London
DdV Dr Dorothy de Val, York University, Toronto
RNF Professor Robert N. Freeman, University of California, Santa Barbara
BH Dr Bernard Harrison,† Lancaster University
RH Dr Roger Hellyer, Stratford-upon-Avon
JH Jane Holland, Cardiff
CH Clemens Höslinger, Vienna
DLH Dr David Humphreys, Cardiff University
FJ Dr Friedl Jary, Vienna
LK Lindsay Kemp, BBC, London
ERL Else Radant Landon, Vienna
HCRL Professor H. C. Robbins Landon, Rabastens
AEL Dr Alfred E. Lemmon, New Orleans
SMcV Professor Simon McVeigh, Goldsmiths College, University of London
MSM Professor Mary Sue Morrow, Loyola University, New Orleans
GM Dr Gerda Mraz, Österreichische Nationalbibliothek, Vienna
RM Dr Robert Münster, Munich
DEO Dr Edward Olleson, University of Oxford
TMP Terence M. Pamplin, London Guildhall University
RP Professor Robert Pascall, University of Wales, Bangor
RJR Dr Ronald Rabin, Cornell University, Ithaca, NY
JAR Dr John A. Rice, Rochester, Minnesota
HS-M Dr Helga Scholz-Michelitsch, Vienna
DPS Professor David Schroeder, Dalhousie University, Halifax, Novia Scotia
HS Professor Herbert Seifert, University of Vienna
ES Professor Elaine Sisman, Columbia University
RSte Dr Rita Steblin, Vienna
RS Professor Robin Stowell, Cardiff University
MV Marc Vignal, Paris
GJW Dr Gerhard Winkler, Burgenländisches Landesmuseum, Eisenstadt
SW Dr Susan Wollenberg, University of Oxford

LIST OF ABBREVIATIONS

Bartha and Somfai	D. Bartha and L. Somfai, *Haydn als Opernkapellmeister. Die Haydn-Dokumente der Esterházy-Opernsammlung* (Budapest, 1960)
Dies	A. C. Dies, *Biographische Nachrichten von Joseph Haydn* (Vienna, 1810)
EK	*Entwurf-Katalog*
Geiringer	K. Geiringer, *Haydn: A Creative Life in Music*, 3rd edn (London, 1982)
Griesinger	G. A. Griesinger, *Biographische Notizen über Joseph Haydn* (Leipzig, 1810)
HCRL/1	H. C. Robbins Landon, *Haydn: Chronicle and Works. Haydn: The Early Years, 1732–1765* (London, 1980)
HCRL/2	H. C. Robbins Landon, *Haydn: Chronicle and Works. Haydn at Eszterháza, 1766–1790* (London, 1978)
HCRL/3	H. C. Robbins Landon, *Haydn: Chronicle and Works. Haydn in England, 1791–1795* (London, 1976)
HCRL/4	H. C. Robbins Landon, *Haydn: Chronicle and Works. Haydn: The Years of 'The Creation', 1796–1800* (London, 1977)
HCRL/5	H. C. Robbins Landon, *Haydn: Chronicle and Works. Haydn: The Late Years, 1801–1809* (London, 1977)
HS	*Haydn-Studien*
HV	*Haydn-Verzeichnis*
HYB	*Haydn Yearbook*
JHW	*Joseph Haydn Werke*, ed. Joseph Haydn-Institut (Munich, 1958–)
Larsen	J. P. Larsen, *Three Haydn Catalogues. Drei Haydn Kataloge*, 2nd edn with a survey of Haydn's œuvre (New York, 1979)

A

Abingdon, Willoughby Bertie, 4th Earl of (b. 16 Jan. 1740; d. 26 Sept. 1799). English amateur flautist and composer born in Gainsborough. A peer with radical political views, he was a strong supporter of the modern music movement and a patron of the Bach–Abel concerts. Around 1765 his eldest daughter married JOHN GALLINI, owner of the Hanover Square Rooms. Here Abingdon himself promoted the major subscription series of 1783 and 1784, negotiating with Haydn in an attempt to entice him to LONDON. Haydn did send manuscripts (including Symphonies nos. 76–8), and from this period dates the dominance of the composer's symphonies in concert programmes in London. But Abingdon was not rewarded by financial success; he is said to have lost £1,600 for his pains, blaming the 'illiberality' of the public as he resigned the management. When Haydn eventually arrived in London in 1791, he established a friendship with Abingdon, visiting his estate in the summer of 1794, and accompanying him on a visit to Hertfordshire in November. But the following year Abingdon was involved in a scandalous trial for libel, and on 7 February was sent to prison for three months.

It was Abingdon who encouraged Haydn to set a text taken from the preface to Selden's *Mare clausum* as an ode (Hob.XXIVa:9), although only two numbers were completed. Haydn also presented Abingdon with one of his trios for two flutes and cello (Hob.IV:2). He was an amateur composer of some accomplishment; many of his vocal works were published, including *A Representation of the Execution of Mary Queen of Scots in Seven Views*, a descriptive work for chorus and orchestra. Haydn had a low opinion of Abingdon's skills saying he composed 'miserably'; nevertheless he provided accompaniments for a set of *Twelve Sentimental Catches and Glees* (Hob.XXXIc:16) by Abingdon. SMcV

HCRL/3.

accompagnato. An Italian term applied to recitative 'accompanied' by the orchestra, as opposed to *recitativo semplice* ('simple recitative') or *recitativo secco* ('dry recitative') accompanied by continuo only. In only one of Haydn's operas, *L'isola disabitata*, does the orchestra accompany recitatives throughout. But accompanied recitative plays an important role in his other operas and in his oratorios as well. In the operas accompanied recitatives generally highlight moments of emotional distress: soliloquies in which a major character faces mortal danger or abandonment by a lover. Haydn's accompanied recitatives do, however, tend to slow the pace of his dramas because of their length, preference for slow tempos, and frequent repetition of orchestral material. Accompanied recitatives play a striking part in *The Creation*, encouraging Haydn to highly imaginative depictions of the weather, sunrise, the animal kingdom, and so on. JAR

Acide (Acis) (Hob.XXVIII:1). Opera in 13 scenes (*festa teatrale*) setting a libretto by GIOVANNI AMBROGIO MIGLIAVACCA; it was written for the festivities that accompanied the wedding of Count Anton Esterházy (the eldest son of Prince Nicolaus) to Countess Marie Therese Erdödy in January 1763. It was revised in 1774. Only seven numbers from the two versions survive intact: a three-movement overture, four arias (one for each of the four soloists), an accompanied recitative, and a concluding quartet.

Migliavacca found inspiration for his treatment of the story of Acis and Galatea in Metastasio's *Galatea*. The surviving arias respond to the Metastasian spirit of the libretto with luxuriously long orchestral ritornellos and with da capo forms, both of which were still standard in Italian serious opera in the early 1760s; yet it would be misleading to call *Acide* an *opera seria*. Its brevity, mythological as opposed to historical characters, and pastoral as opposed to courtly setting all place it in the tradition of the *festa teatrale* rather than the *dramma per musica*.

The cyclops Polifemo (bass) lusts after Galatea (soprano). Acide (tenor) expresses his courage in the face of Polifemo's threat in a heroic aria in C major, 'La beltà che m'innamora', whose coloratura suggests that CARL FRIBERTH, who created the role, was a virtuoso of extraordinary skill. With the help of Galatea's friend Glauce (soprano), who pretends to love Polifemo, Galatea escapes his advances. Polifemo's 'Se men gentile' gave Haydn, in his earliest surviving aria for bass, a chance to introduce some comic elements: the repeated quavers sound like patter. The cyclops throws a boulder at Acide, who is thought to have died until the sea nymph Tetide (Thetis, alto) announces that he is alive and well. Everyone except Polifemo joins in a quartet celebrating the happy ending. JAR

D. Heartz, 'Haydn's *Acide e Galatea* and the Imperial Wedding Operas of 1760 by Hasse and Gluck', in E. Badura-Skoda (ed.), *Joseph Haydn. Bericht über den internationalen Joseph Haydn Kongress. Wien, Hofburg, 4–12 September 1982* (Munich, 1986), 332–40.
HCRL/1 and 2.
G. Thomas, 'Anmerkungen zum Libretto von Haydns festa teatrale 'Acide', *HS* 5 (1982), 118–24.

Advent aria. The normal language of the liturgy in Haydn's Austria was Latin. Throughout the 18th century, however, there was a widespread tradition of composing short, vocal numbers setting a German text, sometimes in dialect; they provided a homely contrast to the timeless Latin. Such vernacular music was particularly common at Easter and Christmas. WERNER, Haydn's predecessor at the Esterházy court, wrote several Advent arias in which, naturally, both text and music will often invoke pastoral images. Contemporary usage of the term overlaps with that for the PASTORELLA, which should be more particularly associated with Christmas Eve. Four Advent arias are safely ascribed to Haydn, some composed (or adapted) during the later 1750s when he was in Vienna, some written in the early 1760s for the rogation services in Eisenstadt: 'EIN' MAGD, EIN' DIENERIN', 'MARIA JUNGFRAU REIN', 'MUTTER GOTTES, MIR ERLAUBE', and 'WAS MEINE MATTE BRUST'.

G. Chew, 'Haydn's Pastorellas: Genre, Dating and Transmission in the Early Church Music', in O. Biba and D. W. Jones (eds), *Studies in Music History Presented to H. C. Robbins Landon on his 70th Birthday* (London, 1996), 21–43.

Ah come il core mi palpita (Oh how my heart beats) (Hob.XXIVa:Anh.4). Cantata for soprano and orchestra adapted by the composer from Act 2 Scene 10 of *La fedeltà premiata*. Celia is pining for her lost lover, Fileno. In a vivid accompanied recitative Celia's pounding heart is evoked and her despair when she learns, wrongly, that he is dead. In a brief arioso, 'Ombra del caro', a reflective Celia looks forward to reunion in Elysium, though this consolation is interrupted by several thunderclaps. The arioso theme returns as the main theme of the first section of the following aria, as a kind of motto theme associated with the memory of Fileno. In the subsequent Allegro the music appropriately evokes the self-pity and remorse of Celia.

The revised version of the opera was given at Eszterháza in 1781. Possibly at the instigation of ARTARIA Haydn prepared a version of Celia's scene for concert performance and it was published by the firm in 1782; the principal alterations were the transposition of the music down a semitone to D major and the omission of the original timpani part (particularly missed in the thunder). In this new guise the work was published also in London and performed there at Haydn's benefit concert in 1791.

A lengthy and appreciative review of the cantata appeared in the *Magazin der Musik* in 1783, especially interesting for the many comments it contains on contemporary singing practice.

O. Biba, 'Opernarie, Konzertarie oder Kantate?', *HYB* 22 (1998), 76–88.
HCRL/2.

Albert, Prince of Sachsen-Teschen (b. 11 July 1738; d. 10 Feb. 1822). He was the son of the Elector of Saxony and the King of Poland who in 1766 married Marie Christine, the favourite daughter of Empress Maria Theresia. Until 1780 he was Statthalter (Governor General) in Hungary, living in Pressburg (Bratislava), where he came into frequent political and social contact with Prince Nicolaus Esterházy. He was present at the inaugural opening of the Eszterháza opera house in 1768, when Haydn's *Lo speziale* was first performed, and he had a permanent suite of rooms at his disposal at the palace. He accompanied the empress on her state visit to Eszterháza in the summer of 1773, when Haydn's *L'infedeltà delusa* was given its premiere. From 1781 until 1793 he was Governor General of the Austrian Netherlands, living in Brussels. On his return to Vienna he concentrated on building up a valuable collection of copper engravings, now in the Albertina collection. He was a subscriber to the first printed edition of *The Creation*. ERL

Albrechtsberger, Johann Georg (b. 3 Feb. 1736; d. 7 March 1809). Composer, Kapellmeister at St Stephen's cathedral in Vienna, and pre-eminent organist and pedagogue of his day. His relationship with Haydn spanned over 50 years, grew naturally out of their common provincial backgrounds, training as choirboys, age, and humour, extended to the exchanging of pupils (including BEETHOVEN and KALKBRENNER), and the sharing of sketches and scores. Their initial contacts probably occurred in the years 1757–9 when Albrechtsberger was employed as organist at the church of Maria Taferl because it was around this time he or perhaps his brother Anton (1729–after 1768) played the cello at performances of Haydn's early string quartets at nearby Weinzierl castle. His own chamber music composed shortly afterwards as organist at MELK (from 1759) was patterned after Haydn's opp. 1–2, and at least one of his quartets circulated under Haydn's name (Hob.III:D3). According to STADLER, it was the Haydn brothers who urged him to resign his post at Melk in 1765 and settle in Vienna, which he did permanently by 1767.

Haydn did not agree with Albrechtsberger's

more reactionary theoretical positions, but he did consider him the best teacher of composition in Vienna, and chose to send Beethoven to him for instruction in 1794–5. Later he consented to co-edit with Albrechtsberger and Salieri the first volume of Sonnleithner's *Histoire de la musique depuis les temps les plus reculés*; publication of this anthology of music was thwarted in 1805 when the invading French army melted the plates for munitions. A puzzle canon, 'Solatium miseris', written for Haydn by Albrechtsberger in 1806, was 'composed out of love . . . and dedicated as an old and true friend'. RNF

Griesinger.

HCRL/1.

D. Schröder, 'Albrechtsbergers Beziehungen zu Haydn, Mozart und Beethoven', in *Die geistlichen Vokalkompsitionen Johann Georg Albrechtsbergers* (Hamburger Beiträge zur Musikwissenschaft, 34) (Hamburg, 1987), i, 43–52.

L. Somfai, '"Learned Style" in Two Late String Quartet Movements of Haydn', *Studia Musicologica: Academiae Scientiarum Hungaricae*, 28 (1986), 325–49.

Alfred oder Der patriotische König (Alfred or the patriotic king) (Hob.XXX:5). Incidental music to J. W. Cowmeadow's play *Alfred, König der Angelsachsen, oder Der patriotische König* (Berlin, 1795), adapted from the English of Alexander Bicknell, *The Patriotic King; or Alfred and Elvida* (London, 1788). Haydn's music was first performed when Cowmeadow's play was given at Eisenstadt by the Stadler troupe on 9 September 1796. It consists of an opening chorus of Danes, an aria for the Guardian Spirit ('Ausgesandt vom Strahlenthrone', scored for soprano and pairs of clarinets, bassoons, and horns, plus a spoken part), and a duet for Alfred and Odun ('Der Morgen graut'; written for two tenors, solo violin, strings, and harp, the last only partly scored). The chorus (STB, pairs of oboes, bassoons, trumpets, timpani, and strings) is a stirring if rather static number in C major in which the Danes rejoice in their victory over the Anglo-Saxons. There is a vigorous timpani part and an impressive section in the tonic minor depicting the devastation on the field of battle; a trumpet fanfare anticipates that found at the beginning of the 'Dona nobis pacem' of the *Missa in tempore belli*, composed in the same year. The aria includes spoken text for Queen Elvida in response to the Spirit's words of comfort and hope. The duet breaks off in the dominant with spoken text, and is thus unsuited to concert performance. PB

HCRL/4.

'Alleluja' symphony. Commonly used nickname for Symphony no. 30, originating from the end of the 18th century. At the beginning of the first movement Haydn embeds a reference to the 'Alleluja' plainchant sung in Holy Week in the texture of the music. This seven-note motif figures throughout the subsequent movement. The symphony was composed in 1765, perhaps initially for performance as part of a church service in Holy Week rather than a private concert. The same plainchant occurs in a baryton trio in D major (Hob. XI:64) probably composed for Easter 1768. JH

H. C. Robbins Landon, 'Die Verwendung Gregorianischer Melodien in Haydns Frühsymphonien', *Österreichische Musikzeitschrift*, 9 (1954), 119–26.

al roverso. Retrograde (or crab) motion. Haydn uses the term in the third movement of Symphony no. 47 in G from 1772: 'Menuet al Roverso' and 'Trio al Roverso'. Both movements are palindromes, with the second half playing the first half backwards. The trio also includes palindromic effects on a smaller scale, with the opening four-note figure immediately being followed by its retrograde. A year later Haydn included the same movement, transposed up a tone, in a keyboard sonata (Hob.XVI:26), where it is marked AL ROVESCIO. DLH

al rovescio. This term was normally used by Haydn to indicate the inversion of a fugue subject, though it could also be used to indicate retrograde (or crab) motion. In the first sense it appears in the fugal finales of the quartets op. 20 nos. 2, 5, and 6, an academic conceit to draw attention to a particularly clever passage of contrapuntal writing. DLH

alternating variations. A type of variation form based upon the alternation of mode, from major to minor or vice versa; it is sometimes called double variations. Explored extensively by Haydn as the most important of several kinds of hybrid structures that interested him, it was considered by his contemporaries to be his special contribution to the form, even if he did not invent it, as is sometimes claimed. Variations on a theme in a major key (A) alternate with variations on a theme in a minor key (B), usually arranged so that the movement ends in the major; typically, the resultant form has five parts (ABABA), as in the first movement of the keyboard sonata in G (Hob. XVI:40) and the second movement of Symphony no. 82. Beginning the movement with a theme in the minor key leads to a six-part form ending with a variation on the major theme (ABABAB), as in the first movement of the quartet op. 55 no. 2 and the second movement of Symphony no. 103; notable exceptions are the minor-key conclusions to the slow movement of Symphony no. 70 and the splendid Variations in F minor for piano

(Hob.XVII:6). The B theme may be related to the A theme in melodic profile or rhythm, or it may be unrelated and hence more episodic. In either case, the form suggests a series of antitheses, in which the second element may begin to influence the first before the movement ends. Thus Haydn achieves an overall unity while simultaneously drawing the benefit of the greater contrast implicit in the design in comparison with variations on a single theme.

The prototype for the form was perhaps the sixth of C. P. E. Bach's sonatas with altered reprises (H.140); other composers of the mid-century such as Giovanni Battista Martini (1706–84) and Joseph Anton Steffan (1726–97) alternated mode in sets of variations on a single theme. Stimulated by well-known examples in Haydn's quartets (op. 33 no. 6, op. 50 no. 4, op. 55 no. 2, and op. 71 no. 3) and in Symphony no. 103, later composers were attracted to the design and began to change its shape to include the alternation of groups of variations, contrasting keys as well as modes, and to embrace an increasing sense of climax, especially in slow movements. The following slow movements all build imaginatively on the design as developed by Haydn: Beethoven's piano trio in E♭, op. 70 no. 2, Symphony no. 9 ('Choral'), and quartet in A minor, op. 132; Bruckner's Symphony no. 4; and Mahler's Symphonies nos. 2 and 4. ES

See also VARIATIONS.

E. Sisman, 'Tradition and Transformation in the Alternating Variations of Haydn and Beethoven', *Acta Musicologica*, 62 (1990), 152–82.

André. Music-publishing firm based in Offenbach, south Germany, that played a significant part in disseminating Haydn's music during his lifetime. It was established in 1774 by Johann André (1741–99), who was himself a composer. The following year the firm issued its first publication of music by Haydn, three quartets from the op. 20 set (Hob.III: 31, 35, and 36). It was not until 1785 onwards, however, that the firm printed the composer's music on a regular basis. Haydn never established a direct relationship with André and its publication of symphonies, quartets, sonatas, and many arrangements were variously based on manuscript copies, publications from Paris or from London. From the mid-1790s the firm seems to have been in regular contact with SALOMON in London, who is likely to have furnished the material for André's notable publication of all of the 'London' symphonies, the opp. 71 and 74 quartets, and the symphonie concertante.

Following the death of Johann André in 1799 the firm was taken over by his son, also Johann (1775–1842) and, again like his father, a composer. Over the next few years he attempted to persuade Haydn to allow him to publish some major new works, including *The Seasons*, but the composer preferred to deal with André's principal rival in Germany, BREITKOPF & HÄRTEL. Haydn, however, may well have encouraged the business link between the firm and Mozart's widow, Constanze, that led to André becoming the most important publisher of Mozart's music in the first decades of the 19th century.

B. Constapel, *Der Musikverlag J. André in Offenbach am Main. Studien zur Verlagstätigkeit von J. A. André und Verzeichnis der Musikalien von 1800 bis 1840* (Tutzing, 1999).

W. Matthäus, 'Das Werk Joseph Haydns im Spiegel der Geschichte des Verlages Jean André', *HYB* 3 (1965), 54–110.

Anfossi, Pasquale (b. 5 April 1727; d. ?Feb. 1797). Pupil of Sacchini and Piccinni who became one of the most popular opera composers of the late 18th century, especially in Venice and London. Nearly a dozen of his operas were performed at Eszterháza; several, including *Il matrimonio per inganno*, *Il geloso in cimento*, and *Il viaggiatori felici*, were successful enough to be kept in the repertoire in subsequent seasons. In 1779 Haydn composed a charming insertion aria 'Quando la rosa' (Hob. XXIVb:3) for LUIGIA POLZELLI, marking her debut at court as Nanina in Anfossi's *Metilde ritrovata*; other insertion arias for operas by Anfossi include 'Signor voi sapete' (Hob.XXIVb:7) in *Il matrimonio per inganno* (1785) and 'Dica pura' (Hob.XXIVb:8) in *Il geloso in cimento* (1785). Haydn added wind parts to a number of arias by Anfossi, and occasionally rewrote his melodies.

Haydn, as well as Mozart, made use of librettos previously set by Anfossi. Mozart's *La finta giardiniera* (1775) was performed less than a year after the premiere of Anfossi's opera of the same name, while Haydn's *La vera costanza* (1778) had first been set by Anfossi in 1776. RJR

'Applausus' cantata (Hob.XXIVa:6). Haydn received the commission to compose this *applausus*, a one-act Latin congratulatory cantata, early in 1768 without knowing exactly the occasion or for whom the work was intended. The offer had come through the Zwettlerhof, the Viennese residence of the Cistercian prelates of ZWETTL, and had probably been arranged by Johann Nepomuk Werner, Haydn's likely contact at that abbey. Its performance took place at Zwettl for the golden jubilee of the taking of vows of Abbot Rainer Kollmann on 15 May 1768. Probably because of the unusual circumstances of the commission Haydn felt it necessary to compose an accompanying letter containing detailed performance instructions. This *applausus* letter has long been considered important for the study of 18th-century performance practice, while the music of the *applausus* itself, at least in its original form, has until recently been largely ignored.

As was customary for such monastic productions, the Latin text was probably provided by a member of the monastery. Its allegorical contents recall medieval literary traditions as the four cardinal virtues—Temperance (soprano), Prudence (alto), Justice (tenor), and Fortitude (bass)—express their admiration for 'this house', a not-too-oblique allusion to Zwettl and its chief occupant, Abbot Kollmann, while Theologia (bass) restrains their enthusiasm. Using this quasi-dramatic text Haydn composed eight numbers for his five roles: a quartet, five arias, a duet, and a final chorus, each preceded by recitative, usually of the accompanied variety.

The occasional nature of the work, the large dimensions of the individual numbers, the rich orchestration calling for frequent concertante treatment of solo instruments (violin, divisi violas, bassoon, harpsichord), limited number and types of roles, and the predominance of large da capo structures all prove that Haydn had thoroughly embraced the tradition of the *applausus musicus*, a genre of musical theatre that flourished in the Austrian monasteries up until the third quarter of the 18th century. Consistent with the tradition of such highly occasional, large-scale compositions was the dissection, conversion, and dissemination of individual numbers as contrafacta. As early as 1769 movements from Haydn's work were arranged as offertories or motets in Eisenstadt, apparently with the composer's approval, and thence widely disseminated. The most successful of these was the arrangement of the final chorus 'O Caelites, vos invocamus' as an offertory, hymn, or motet, 'O Jesu, te invocamus'; it was published posthumously by Breitkopf & Härtel in 1812. RNF

I. Becker-Glauch and H. Wiens, foreword to *JHW* 27/2 (Munich, Duisburg, 1969).

R. N. Freeman, 'The applausus musicus, or Singgedicht: A Neglected Genre of Eighteenth-Century Musical Theatre', in D. W. Jones (ed.), *Music in Eighteenth-Century Austria* (Cambridge, 1996), 197–209.

W. A. Kumbier, 'Rhetoric and Expression in Haydn's Applausus *Cantata*', *HYB* 18 (1993), 213–47.

HCRL/2.

F. W. Riedel, 'Joseph Haydns "Applausus" und die Tradition des musikalischen Schultheaters in Österreich', in *Joseph Haydn und die Oper seiner Zeit* (Wissenschaftliche Arbeiten aus dem Burgenland, Bd. 90) (Eisenstadt, 1992), 88–106.

Apponyi, Count Anton Georg (b. 1751; d. 1817). Hungarian aristocrat and music lover. As the Hungarian Chamberlain of the imperial court he lived in a palace in Pressburg (Bratislava). He seems to have become acquainted with Haydn in the early 1780s and following the count's initiation as Freemason in Vienna in 1784 he may well have encouraged the composer to apply for membership; certainly he was one of the composer's sponsors when he was initiated into the 'Zur wahren Eintracht' lodge on 11 February 1784. They remained on friendly terms and Haydn visited the palace in Pressburg on at least one occasion. Their friendship is reflected in the dedication of the six quartets of op. 71 and op. 74, both in the London edition (Corri & Dussek) and in the Viennese edition (Artaria). Apponyi was one of the members of Swieten's Gesellschaft der Associierten who sponsored semi-private performances of oratorios in Vienna in the 1780s and 1790s, including the vocal version of *The Seven Last Words*, *The Creation*, and *The Seasons*. He ordered two subscription copies of the first edition of *The Creation*.

'Apponyi' quartets. Nickname occasionally applied to the six quartets, op. 71 and op. 74, published in 1795–6 and dedicated to COUNT ANTON GEORG APPONYI. JH

Arianna a Naxos (Ariadne on Naxos) (Hob. XXVIb:2). Italian cantata for soprano and piano (sources offer harpsichord as an alternative). It was written by the end of 1789, though very little of any certainty is known about the circumstances of its composition. According to an aside in the *Allgemeine musikalische Zeitung* in 1799 it was written for Bianca Sacchetti, a singer from Venice. The author of the text is unknown; perhaps it was supplied by Sacchetti. Early in 1790 Haydn heard it performed by the 16-year-old daughter of MARIA ANNA VON GENZINGER in Vienna and it was published by ARTARIA in August of that year. He took the music with him to London where it was sung by the castrato Gasparo Pacchierotti accompanied by Haydn at the Ladies' Concert series on 18 February. A couple of weeks later a new edition prepared in London was available from Haydn's residence in Great Pulteney Street and from the publisher BLAND.

The subject matter of the thwarted love of Ariadne for Theseus was one of the most well-known operatic stories of the period. The printed scores contain a summary of the scene: a rocky sea shore on which Ariadne, awakening from a deep sleep, hopes to see her lover Theseus but, instead, sees him on the bow of a departing ship. Unlike a contemporary opera, however, a cantata is allowed to end tragically and Haydn's conclusion strongly suggests that Ariadne has hurled herself from a cliff to her death.

Haydn follows the typical four-part design of a contemporary Italian cantata, as in the works of his mentor HASSE: recitative, slow aria, recitative, and aria, with the last section in the form of a vocal rondò (slow section followed by a concluding Presto). Haydn deals most imaginatively with a rather prolix text. Arianna's gradual awakening is well captured in the opening introduction and her increasing concern in the following aria in B♭ is suggested by a highly unorthodox structural modulation to A♭. The second recitative is more volatile, as Ariadne searches in vain for Theseus, climbs a craggy rock and suddenly sees the departing lover (a bold enharmonic modulation from A♭ major to C♯ minor, something that caught the ear of at least one commentator in London). Two-tempo arias of this kind often move from minor key to major; here Haydn reverses this process so that the work can end with a powerful F minor section, in mood rather like Rosina's aria in Act 2 of *La vera costanza* and the concluding section of the 'Berenice, che fai?' The final *tierce de picardie*, F major chord manages to sound brutal rather than comforting.

In a letter to Bland Haydn told him that he intended to orchestrate the cantata, an attractive proposition that might have elicited even more drama from the work. But whereas orchestrating keyboard music was to become common in the 19th and 20th centuries it was not that common in the 18th century and, in the event, Haydn never orchestrated the work. At least three later orchestrations are known: the first by Haydn's pupil, NEUKOMM, prepared in 1808; the second by Georg Abraham Schneider (1809); the third by Ernst Frank (1885).

Although the work is a comparative rarity today, in Haydn's time it became one of his most admired and popular works. Lady Hamilton sang it to great effect and Rossini regarded the F major section as a prime example of Haydn's gifts as a vocal writer.

J. Rushton, 'Viennese Amateur or London Professional? A Reconsideration of Haydn's Tragic Cantata *Arianna a Naxos*', in D. W. Jones (ed.), *Music in Eighteenth-Century Austria* (Cambridge, 1996), 232–45.

Armida (Hob.XXVIII:12). Opera ('dramma eroico') first performed at Eszterháza on 26 February 1784.

The production of Sarti's *Giulio Sabino* at Eszterháza in 1783 inaugurated a period in which *opera seria* played a crucial role in Prince Nicolaus's theatre. Haydn responded to the success of *Giulio Sabino* by writing a full-length *opera seria*, his first, and for a cast almost identical to the one that had presented Sarti's opera. *Armida* contains occasional echoes of Sarti's music, which Haydn frequently conducted during the months in which he composed his own opera.

Haydn's libretto was one of many derived from Tasso's *Gerusalemme liberata*. Two earlier librettos, Giacomo Durandi's *Armida* and Francesco De Rogati's *Armida abbandonata* (both set to music in 1770), formed the basis of an anonymous hybrid version performed in Venice in 1775 with music by Antonio Tozzi. It was that libretto, with a few minor changes probably made by NUNZIATO PORTA, that Haydn set to music in 1783–4.

A few days after the first performance Haydn boasted to his publisher ARTARIA that *Armida* was his best opera. It remained in the Esterházy repertoire until 1788, performed 54 times.

The Christian knight Rinaldo (tenor, PROSPERO BRAGHETTI) loves the Saracen princess Armida (soprano, METILDE BOLOGNA). At the court of her uncle, King Idreno (baritone, PAOLO MANDINI), Rinaldo declares his willingness to fight against the crusaders. His aria 'Vado a pugnar contento' is colourfully orchestrated with trumpets and timpani. Like most of the arias in *Armida*, this one is in sonata form. Idreno looks forward to Rinaldo's victory in an exuberant aria in a fast tempo, 'Se dal suo braccio oppresso'.

Armida fears for Rinaldo's safety. She sings the first of several scenas with orchestrally accompanied recitative that are among the most compelling features of this opera. Her aria 'Se pietade avete' has some characteristics of the fashionable rondò (an aria in two sections, slow followed by fast), including gavotte rhythms in the slow section.

The scene changes to a mountainside, with Armida's castle in the distance. Ubaldo (tenor, ANTONIO SPECIOLI) leads a group of Christian soldiers in search of Rinaldo. Unexpected modulations in Ubaldo's aria 'Dove son, che miro intorno?' depict his fear and confusion, much as they do in Medoro's aria 'Parto, ma, oh dio, non posso' in *Orlando paladino*. Zelmira (soprano, COSTANZA VALDESTURLA), ordered by Idreno to charm the Christian knights so that they might be led to ambush, is herself charmed by the Christian Clotarco (tenor, LEOPOLD DICHTLER). The simplicity and charm of her aria 'Se tu seguir mi vuoi' reflects the personality of the character who sings it.

Ubaldo finds Rinaldo in Armida's palace and encourages him to rejoin the Christian army. Armida enters; she senses the ambivalence that Ubaldo has stirred up in her lover. He assures her in the duet 'Cara, sarò fedele' that he will never leave her. Haydn derived the brief canonic passages near the end of the duet from the duet in Act 3 of *Il mondo della luna*, but here the canon is much more elaborately orchestrated, with pizzicato strings and solos for oboe, bassoon, and flute.

Act 2 begins with beautiful arias for Zelmira and Clotarco that provide a welcome break from the emotional intensity and musical complexity of the scenes for Armida and Rinaldo. Ubaldo once again urges Rinaldo to abandon Armida. He is about to do so when Armida arrives. She faints; Rinaldo begins a long and elaborately accompanied recitative that culminates in the aria 'Care, è vero, io son tiranno'. The 12-line poem is similar to those normally used as the basis of two-tempo rondòs, and Haydn's setting duly obliges. However, like Sabino's rondò in Sarti's *Giulio Sabino*, 'In qual barbaro momento', this aria is not allowed to conclude in the expected bravura fashion: an orchestral transition inhibits applause and leads directly into the following recitative. Enraged by Rinaldo's rejection, Armida sings a violent aria in D minor, 'Odio, furor, dispetto'.

Ubaldo, welcoming Rinaldo back to the crusaders' camp, sings a lyrical aria, 'Prence amato, in questo amplesso'. The text caused Haydn to reject the sonata form so characteristic of this opera. In response to the second stanza of the text, beginning 'Già dell' armi al chiaro segno', Haydn increased the tempo and introduced trumpets to accompany a melody of distinctly martial character. The opening theme never returns. Armida arrives and the act ends with a trio for Armida, Rinaldo, and Ubaldo.

A large scene complex takes up most of Act 3: a series of recitatives and arias held together by the appearance of the same key at the beginning and end (E♭), by the use of orchestral accompaniment throughout, and by transitions at the ends of arias to the following number that prevent the audience from applauding. Rinaldo finds himself in an enchanted forest. The depiction by the orchestra of murmuring brooks and twittering birds anticipates similar tone-painting in *The Creation*. In response to the indication in the libretto that Rinaldo hears a 'dolce sinfonia', Haydn wrote a fetching melody that returns in several different keys. Zelmira, disguised as a nymph, sings an aria with a similar melody, 'Torna pure al caro bene', in which she tries to persuade Rinaldo to return to Armida. The aria ends with an open cadence.

Rinaldo is about to break the spell by plunging his sword into a great myrtle tree in the middle of the grove when Armida suddenly emerges from the tree. She sings a slow, passionate aria, 'Ah non ferir', which, like Zelmira's aria, leads directly into accompanied recitative. Rejected once again, Armida waves her magic wand, unleashing the furies. As the stage darkens, the orchestra paints a vivid picture of violence and horror. Rinaldo pleads the gods for mercy in the second of his rondòs, again in E♭, 'Dei pietosi, in tal momento'. This great complex of linked numbers ends as it had begun, with Rinaldo alone singing an accompanied recitative. He strikes the myrtle tree; the magic forest disappears, and Rinaldo is transported to the Christian camp.

As the Christians prepare for battle, Armida, Idreno, and Zelmira come to Rinaldo's camp. Armida makes one last attempt to win back Rinaldo, but he rejects her. An infernal chariot appears at her side, and the opera ends with a short ensemble in which Armida curses Rinaldo and he bids her a loving farewell. The trumpets comment ironically with the same fanfare that had accompanied Rinaldo's promise near the beginning of the opera that he would fight on Armida's side.

In the overture two of the most dramatic scenes in the opera are prefigured. The cheerful fast movement in sonata form reaches the development section before it is interrupted by lyrical slow music, the 'dolce sinfonia' that enchants Rinaldo in the magic forest near the beginning of Act 3. A short recitative-like passage gives way to stormy music in the minor mode, the same music with which Haydn depicts Armida's furies in Act 3. JAR

M. McClymonds, 'Haydn and his Contemporaries: "Armida abbandonata"', in E. Badura-Skoda (ed.), *Joseph Haydn. Bericht über den internationalen Joseph Haydn Kongress Wien, Hofburg, 5–12 September 1982* (Munich, 1986), 325–32.

J. A. Rice, 'Sarti's Giulo Sabino, Haydn's Armida, and the Arrival of Opera Seria at Eszterháza', *HYB* 15 (1984), 181–98.

Artaria. Music publisher in Vienna who issued over 300 works by Haydn and played a notable part in promoting a wider knowledge of the composer's music. In comparison with other cities, such as Amsterdam, Berlin, Leipzig, London, and Paris, Vienna did not have a flourishing music-publishing industry until late in the 18th century. The Artaria family had a business in the Kohlmarkt in the city from 1766, selling engravings and maps; ten years later they began importing music editions, especially from Paris. This, inevitably, led to the founding of its own music business, begun in August 1778 with the publication of six trios by one Paolo Bonaga. New publications were regularly advertised in the *Wiener Zeitung* and on 12 April 1780 Haydn's music was first sold, an edition of six keyboard sonatas dedicated to the AUENBRUGGER sisters (Hob.XVI:20, 35–9). As was Artaria's general practice, the firm applied an opus number, in this case op. 30, that followed on from the highest number already applied by a French publisher. Over the following decade a steady stream of works by Haydn followed: quartets, songs, cantatas, symphonies, keyboard trios, variations, and dances. Some of these works were proposed for publication by Haydn while others, such as the songs and the keyboard variations, were solicited by Artaria, naturally keen to print music that was commercially viable. To these original works may be added a third category, arrangements of orchestral works for keyboard or for string quartet; in the case of *The Seven Last Words* Haydn prepared the quartet version and at least sanctioned the keyboard version; although not conclusively documented, other arrangements from the 1780s published by Artaria, including quartet arrangements of the 'Paris' symphonies, may well be equally authentic. That Artaria was willing to be speculative in the case of Haydn's music is suggested by the attitude of the firm to the publication of his symphonies. In general, Artaria was reluctant to incur the costs of printing symphonies—only two by Mozart were published in the 1780s—but it made an exception in the case of Haydn, issuing no fewer than 15 symphonies between 1782 and 1789. In 1786 Artaria purchased the plates of the ailing music publisher, CHRISTOPH TORRICELLA, including those of Symphonies nos. 76–8 by Haydn.

Artaria's ambition as a publisher is evident in the way in which it secured the distribution of its editions by firms elsewhere in Europe. As well as the branch of the family firm in Mainz, Artaria regularly supplied music to LE DUC (Paris), LONGMAN & BRODERIP (London), and Simrock (Bonn), ensuring that these cities too were up to date with Haydn's music.

From 1780, when Artaria issued its first Haydn publication, to 1790, when the composer embarked on his first visit to London, some 60 letters from the composer to Artaria survive, though none from Artaria to the composer. While they provide some insight into the business practice of the firm, they are even more revealing about Haydn's personality. In what was a new phase in the composer's career he is very adept at selling his own music, describing some of the songs, for instance, as surpassing 'all my previous ones in variety, naturalness and ease of vocal execution' (27 May 1781). Music published in sets, such as quartets and sonatas, was often delivered work by work rather than as a complete set. He was paid a single fee for each publication and received a variable number of complimentary copies. Dedications were normally made by the publisher, with Haydn occasionally showing his annoyance at this standard practice. More irritating for the composer was the quality of the music-engraving. Haydn was usually given a proof copy to correct and covering letters show that he was not only punctilious about the accuracy of the text, down to the smallest ornament, but commented too about its general visual appearance. Sometimes Artaria failed to offer proofs and sold the music with many errors; in the disastrous case of three keyboard trios (Hob.XV:6–8) Haydn demanded that the music be re-engraved 'otherwise little honour will accrue to either of us' (10 December 1785). Occasionally there was mutual suspicion that the same piece of music was simultaneously being sold to another firm; in particular, Artaria expressed his annoyance that from 1786 Haydn was often selling the same music to FORSTER in London, undermining the business association between Artaria and Longman & Broderip.

Generally, however, the relationship was a cordial one. Haydn ordered copies of the engraving by Mansfeld of the composer that the firm offered for sale and purchased music by other composers, sometimes asking that payment be set against the next fee. On one occasion Artaria sent him some cheese and sausages. When he was asked to provide some new piano trios (Hob.XV:11–13), Haydn used it as a convenient excuse to order a new piano from Schantz and cheekily asked Artaria to pay the firm directly: 'Please excuse the liberty: it is bestowed on a man who is grateful . . .' (26 October 1788). He promised to pay back the loan by January 1789; a year later Haydn was still in debt to Artaria.

For a variety of reasons, in the 1790s Artaria published fewer first editions of music by Haydn. SALOMON had the publication rights to the 'London' symphonies, while Haydn's two periods of residence in London naturally encouraged him to entrust his music to English publishers including BLAND, Longman & Broderip, and NAPIER. The major large-scale works that Haydn wrote after his return to Vienna, *The Creation*, *The Seasons*, and the six late masses, were not the kinds of work that Artaria would have found commercially viable; in the case of *The Creation*, Haydn was technically the publisher and underwrote all the costs but it was distributed by Artaria. Quartets, however, were a major part of Artaria's catalogue and the first Viennese editions of the op. 76 and op. 77 quartets were issued by the firm; for the op. 76 quartets, issued in two sets of three, Artaria claimed in a newspaper advertisement that 'We may allow ourselves, in recommending our edition of this work, to remark that nothing has ever appeared in our publishing house which—with the exception of the ornamented title page containing a portrait of the composer—can be compared to it in all the diligence and great expense lavished on it'.

By the turn of the century Artaria was no longer a leading figure in music-publishing in Vienna. It remained active until 1858 when it focused its attention once more on art and cartography. As a specialist firm in these areas the firm still survives; as in Haydn's time the shop is in the Kohlmarkt.

During its association with Haydn, Artaria acquired a number of autograph manuscripts of the composer's music. On a visit to Vienna in 1829

VINCENT and MARY NOVELLO were shown the autographs of the *Missa Cellensis* (*Missa Sancti Caeciliae*), the *Missa Sancti Nicolai*, and the *Missa 'sunt bona mixta malis'*. Vincent Novello purchased the last mentioned, the smallest item, for six florins; it was not rediscovered until 1983. Most of the other Haydn material in the collection eventually found its way to the Staatsbibliothek zu Berlin—Preußische Kulturbesitz. Haydn's letters to Artaria, which remained in the archives of the firm until late in the 19th century, are now widely dispersed.

F. Artaria and H. Botstiber, *Joseph Haydn und das Verlaghauses Artaria* (Vienna, 1909).

R. Hilmar, *Der Musikverlag Artaria & Comp. Geschichte und Probleme der Druckproduktion* (Tutzing, 1977).

HCRL/2–5.

R. M. Ridgewell, 'Mozart and the Artaria Publishing House: Studies in the Inventory Ledgers' (diss., University of London, 1999).

A. Weinmann, *Vollständiges Verlagsverzeichnis Artaria & Comp.* (Vienna, 1952).

Ashe, Andrew (b. *c.*1759; d. 1838). Irish flautist born in Lisbon. After serving various patrons around Europe, he settled in Dublin in 1780. Here in the summer of 1791 he was recruited by SALOMON as principal flautist for his concert series in LONDON, making his solo debut on 24 February 1792. In August 1794 Ashe travelled with Haydn to Bath to stay with RAUZZINI; Haydn's last public appearance in London was at Ashe's benefit concert on 8 June 1795. Ashe claimed to have coined the nickname 'Surprise' for Symphony no. 94, advertising it as such on 6 June 1796. In 1810 he succeeded Rauzzini as director of the concerts in Bath. SMcV

HCRL/3.

Ashley, John (b. 1734; d. 14 March 1805). English bassoonist and oratorio manager, probably born in LONDON. A member of the Guards, he played the bassoon at Covent Garden Theatre and the Concert of Ancient Music, but he first came to public prominence through his administrative and entrepreneurial skills. An important figure in the Society of Musicians, he was assistant conductor at the 1784 Handel Commemoration, and in 1789 (in partnership with Samuel Harrison) he restarted the Lenten oratorio season at Covent Garden. These he continued to manage until his death as well as organizing festivals throughout the country, aided by his sons, all talented instrumentalists. Ashley's programmes concentrated on selections of music by HANDEL, and he was sometimes accused of lowering the tone of the oratorio seasons by introducing miscellaneous songs in the pursuit of profit. But this accusation is not entirely justified, for he also promoted major new works. His performance of *The Creation* at Covent Garden on 28 March 1800 anticipated SALOMON's, to the evident annoyance of the latter; in an exchange of newspaper announcements, Ashley answered Salomon's claim to authenticity by asserting that he had received a copy of the printed score from Vienna, signed by the composer. He also gave the first English performance of Mozart's Requiem on 27 February 1801. SMcV

Asplmayr, Franz (bap. 2 April 1728; d. 29 July 1796). Austrian composer born in Graz who became particularly admired for his ballet music in Vienna in the 1760s and 1770s. Earlier, between 1759 and 1761, he was employed as a secretary ('Secretarius') at the court of Count Franz Ferdinand Maximilian Morzin, coinciding with Haydn's period of employment as Kapellmeister. He played the second violin at the likely first performance of Haydn's op. 33 quartets in front of the Russian imperial family in the Hofburg in Vienna in 1781. A number of string trios and one symphony (Hob.I:E♭6) falsely attributed to Haydn are now thought to be by Asplmayr.

D. Heartz, *Haydn, Mozart and the Viennese School 1740-1780* (London, 1995).

Auenbrugger family. Joseph Leopold von Auenbrugger (1722–1809) was a well-known physician in Vienna who had six daughters. Two achieved considerable acclaim as pianists in the emerging salon culture of the city, Maria Katherina and Franziska. Both were admired by the Mozart family and by Haydn. Haydn approved of Artaria's dedication of six keyboard sonatas (Hob.XVI: 29, 35–9) to the sisters, commenting that as players they had 'genuine insight into music equal to that of the greatest masters'. The works are occasionally called the 'Auenbrugger' sonatas.

'Auf dem Anstand'. Nickname used in German-speaking countries in the 19th century for Symphony no. 31. Horn calls feature prominently in the first and last movements. Presumably one of these reminded listeners of a hunting call that indicated 'at ease'. JH

Aumann, Franz Joseph (b. 24 Feb. 1728; d. 30 March 1797). Born in Traismauer, Lower Austria, he became, as composer and music director for the Augustinians at St Florian from 1755 until his death, the most significant composer in Upper Austria in the 18th century. His lifelong friendships with MICHAEL HAYDN and J. G. ALBRECHTSBERGER, which dated back to the early 1750s in Vienna, brought him firmly into the Haydn circle. For St Florian he acquired over the years an almost complete set of masses by Haydn, and many of the symphonies, a few of them in JOHANN ELẞLER'S hand. Numerous works by Aumann circulated in copies under Haydn's name, including half a dozen masses and requiems, and about an equal number of divertimenti and cassations. As late as 1927 his authentic *Requiem solemne* in C minor was published as a newly discovered work of Haydn (Hob.XXIIa:c1). RNF

P. Dormann, *Franz Joseph Aumann (1728-1797): Ein Meister in St. Florian vor Anton Bruckner. Mit thematischem Katalog der Werke*, Studien zur Landes- und Sozialgeschichte der Musik, 6 (Munich, Salzburg, 1985).

'Austria' Name usually given in English hymnals to the hymn tune based on Haydn's anthem 'GOTT ERHALTE FRANZ DEN KAISER'; it has less frequently been titled 'Austrian Hymn', 'Vienna', 'Haydn', and 'Cheadle'. Haydn's melody was known in Britain within a few years of its performance in Vienna in 1797, both in the form in which it is featured in the quartet op. 76 no. 3 ('Emperor'), published by Longman & Broderip in London in 1799, and in the English translation of the Austrian anthem, 'Hymn for the Emperor Francis', made by Charles Burney and probably published the same year. The earliest record of the melody being used in a sacred context occurs in 1801 when the minor London publisher Joseph Dale printed the melody with the already well-known words 'Praise the Lord, ye Heav'ns adore him', a paraphrase of Psalm 148, claiming that it was 'As sung at Durham Cathedral'; the organist at Durham was Thomas Ebden (1738–1811) who, presumably, can be credited with uniting the text and the melody.

From the late 19th century onwards Haydn's melody has been more commonly associated with the text 'Glorious things of Thee are spoken'. Written by John Newton (1725–1807) and first printed in the so-called *Olney Hymns* of 1779, the text is not known to have been used with Haydn's music before the 1860s; they appear together in the seventh edition of *The Parish Hymn Book for the Church, School, and Home* (London, 1867).

Ave regina (Hob.XXIIIb:3). A work for soprano soloist, chorus, strings and continuo. Nothing is known about its inception. Its style, particularly the decorative writing for solo soprano, is very similar to that of the Salve regina in E, which is thought to date from 1756. It may be a work that Haydn composed for church services at the church of the Barmherzige Brüder, the chapel of the Haugwitz residence, or St Stephen's; he was casually employed at all three. The traditional text, an intercession to the Virgin Mary, is divided into three sections: an Andante for solo soprano and strings; a short Allegro for chorus; and a concluding Adagio, mainly for soprano but with telling support from the chorus.

B

Bach, Carl Philipp Emanuel (b. 8 March 1714; d. 14 Dec. 1788). German composer, performer, and writer; son of J. S. Bach (1685–1750). From 1738 he was attached to the court of Frederick the Great as a keyboard player, remaining in Berlin until 1768 when he took the position of Musikdirektor in Hamburg, succeeding Georg Philipp Telemann (1681–1767).

A prolific composer, Bach wrote in most genres (chamber music, concertos, symphonies, songs, larger sacred vocal works, but not opera); however his contemporary and posthumous reputation rests primarily on a large and highly original body of solo keyboard works, in the form of sonatas, fantasias, rondos, and character pieces. Typical of his generation in largely abandoning the formal contrapuntal styles of the Baroque as a primary means of musical argument in favour of thinner *galant* textures, Bach retained and expanded on the complex harmonic language of the late Baroque, recasting it syntactically into one of the most personal musical styles of the 18th century, often referred to as the *empfindsamer Stil* (sentimental style). CHARLES BURNEY commented that Bach 'possesses every style; though he chiefly confines himself to the expressive' (Scholes, *Burney's Musical Tours*, ii. 219). This expressive style relies on a highly rhetorical performance and consequently Bach supplied in his scores remarkably precise instructions to the performer in respect of dynamics (often indicating abrupt contrast), articulation (including an expressive *Bebung*, a vibrato possible only on a clavichord), and elaborate ornamentation that owes much to the French *clavecin* tradition. The clavichord was the instrument par excellence of EMPFINDSAMKEIT, largely because of the reputation of Bach's performances, the emergence in Bach's music of a repertoire written specifically for the clavichord, and the strong advocacy of the instrument in 18th-century treatises.

According to his autobiography (Hamburg, 1773) Bach wrote only a few works 'in complete freedom' and for his own use, and it is, perhaps, the extant fantasias that come closest to his ideal of unhindered expressive freedom. Here one finds Bach's most extreme and frequent changes of mood, most audacious modulations together with strong sectional contrasts between passages of instrumental recitative, fast modulating virtuoso figuration, declamatory melodic sections, and alternating measured and unmeasured sections. Although tempered somewhat in other forms, the spirit of the fantasia informs the best of Bach's music in all genres. In the context of mid-18th-century music, he was an influential voice, protesting against 'present styles', and the declining taste in the composition and performance of contemporary keyboard music.

C. P. E. Bach's *Versuch über die wahre Art das Clavier zu spielen* is one of a number of important treatises on music produced by a circle of theorists based in Berlin. It is the clearest codification of 18th-century practices of ornamentation, fingering, and figured bass, exerting an influence on music pedagogy well into the 19th century, and remaining today a primary source for the interpretation of 18th-century music. In a fundamentally important sense it is also C. P. E. Bach's credo, defining music technique largely in terms of its expressive purpose and meaning. It sketches a dynamic theory of *Affekt* and an expressive chain involving composer, performer, and audience; most striking, it provides one of the most important aesthetic vindications of instrumental music in the 18th century.

The names of C. P. E. Bach and Haydn are frequently linked in both 18th-century and modern criticism. Even though they never met, the two composers admired each other's music; Bach defended Haydn from unjust criticism and in 1795 Haydn called at Bach's house in Hamburg on his return journey from London to Vienna, unaware that the composer had died in 1788. In German writing of the late eighteenth and early nineteenth centuries they are often seen as the foremost representatives of modern German music, the two geniuses who raised instrumental music to a new height, winning for it an aesthetic acceptability which had been denied instrumental music according to the prevalent aesthetic theory that had always privileged vocal music.

The question of the supposed direct influence of C. P. E. Bach on Haydn has also brought their names together; it is mentioned in some accounts from the 1780s, in the first Haydn biographies, and has remained a recurrent topic in modern scholarship. While the references to the influence of Bach's music and his *Versuch* on Haydn in the contemporary biographies of GRIESINGER and DIES provide a documentary basis for this supposed influence, there are problems with their suggestion that it was Haydn's early music that was thus influenced. Recent research by A. Peter Brown and others has established that little of Bach's music was available in Vienna in the 1750s, and the first advertisement for his *Versuch* did not appear in Vienna until 1763. Such matters of documentation, and the general perception of Haydn's early music as largely Austrian-influenced, is supported by the evidence of Haydn's autograph manuscripts from the late 1760s and early 1770s which have distinctively new notational features (in the notation of ornaments and figured bass especially), suggesting that Haydn studied Bach's *Versuch* around 1766. Given this revision of the Griesinger and Dies accounts, A. Peter Brown's suggestion that a number of Haydn works in the fantasia/capriccio tradition were informed by C. P. E. Bach's writings on improvisation have a chronological and stylistic plausibility. The more traditional assertion that Haydn's innovatory variation forms from the late 1760s were influenced by Bach's VERÄNDERTE REPRISEN is also credible, since Bach wrote about the practice in his *Versuch* and his *Sonaten mit veränderten Reprisen* (Berlin, 1760) were available in Vienna from 1767: it is possible that Haydn's characteristic double or ALTERNATING VARIATIONS were modelled specifically on the sixth of Bach's *reprisen Sonaten*. In a more general sense, the way in which, particularly in the keyboard music from the mid-1760s, Haydn controls as a facet of compositional style aspects of performance practice previously left to the performer, mirrors one of the central concerns of Bach's music and his *Versuch*. BH

C. P. E. Bach, *Versuch über die wahre Art das Clavier zu spielen* (Berlin, 1753, 1762); trans. W. J. Mitchell as *Essay on the True Art of Playing Keyboard Instruments* (New York, 1949).

A. P. Brown, *Joseph Haydn's Keyboard Music: Sources and Style* (Bloomington, Ind., 1986).

S. L. Clark (ed.), *C. P. E. Bach Studies* (Oxford, 1988).

B. Harrison, *Haydn's Keyboard Music: Studies in Performance Practice* (Oxford, 1996).

H.-G. Ottenberg, *C. P. E. Bach*, trans. P. Whitmore (Oxford, 1987).

P. Scholes (ed.), *Dr Burney's Musical Tours*, ii (London, 1959).

Bader, Philipp Georg (d. 1779). He was the Esterházy librarian who from February 1778 was entrusted with the administration of the marionette theatre at Eszterháza where he also undertook some of the spoken roles; all musical matters were left in the hands of Haydn. He was assisted by his wife. He was the author of the librettos of two marionette operas, *Dido* and *Die bestrafte Rachbegierde*.

Badini, Carlo Francesco (*fl.* 1769–93). Italian librettist and author, active mainly in LONDON. His first libretto for the King's Theatre was *Nanetta e Lubino*, set by Pugnani in 1769, and his association with the Italian Opera in London lasted over 20 years. In 1785 he was appointed house librettist, responsible for writing and adapting both serious and comic operas. During the 1790–1 season, when the opera community in London was in complete disarray, he retained his allegiance to the King's Theatre, writing the libretto for Haydn's *L'anima del filosofo* but, thanks to the refusal of an opera licence, it was never produced. He was employed for one further season at the reinstated King's Theatre in 1793; he was succeeded by Lorenzo da Ponte.

Badini had a reputation for intrigue and for a vitriolic pen, 'surpassing Aretin in satire and destructive gossip' according to Da Ponte; he certainly kept a noose around the managers of the King's Theatre by virtue of his sharp wit and influence as a newspaper critic. He wrote also the texts for two Italian duets set by Haydn in 1796, 'Guarda qui' and 'Saper vorrei' (Hob.XXVa:1–2). SMcV

C. Price, J. Milhous, and R. D. Hume, *Italian Opera in Late Eighteenth-Century London*, ii *The King's Theatre, Haymarket 1778–1791* (Oxford, 1995).

Bailleux, Antoine (b. *c*.1720; d. 1798–1801). French publisher; also a composer and a violinist. His first publications date from the 1750s and were devoted to his own music. In the following decade the business expanded considerably as Bailleux published music by French composers from the Baroque period alongside modern works by German and Italian composers. By 1793 his total catalogue included some 500 works.

Although Bailleux published Haydn's works intermittently from 1768 (possibly before) to 1792 he never formed a business relationship with the composer but profited from his increasing popularity by issuing editions that were entirely pirated and often knowingly included spurious works. The most notorious example was his publication in 1777, as op. 26, of six quartets by Haydn. Bailleux had already engraved two of the works under the name HOFSTETTER (or had acquired such plates), but proceeded to alter the name to Haydn. These two works plus the other equally spurious four became well known in 18th-century Paris as Haydn, and were included by PLEYEL in his complete edition of the composer's quartets as op. 3. For nearly 200 years the works were regarded as authentic Haydn; Bailleux's deception was uncovered in 1964.

P. Bryan, *Johann Wanhal, Viennese Symphonist: His Life and His Musical Environment* (Stuyvesant, NY, 1997).

C. Johansson, *French Music Publishers Catalogues of the Second Half of the Eighteenth Century* (Stockholm, 1955).

A. Tyson, 'Bibliographical Observations on Bailleux's Edition', in J. P. Larsen, H. Serwer, and J. Webster (eds), *Haydn Studies* (London, 1981), 95–8.
A. Tyson and H. C. Robbins Landon, 'Who Composed Haydn's Op. 3?', *Musical Times*, 105 (1964), 506–7.

Banti, Brigida (b. *c.*1756; d. 18 Feb. 1806). Italian dramatic soprano, specializing in serious roles. She made a sensational appearance in LONDON in Bianchi's *Semiramide* on 26 April 1794, remaining there as prima donna until 1802. Unable to read music and dissolute in behaviour ('a fury, a demon of Hell' in Da Ponte's experience), she was nevertheless unsurpassed for sweetness of cantabile as well as coloratura. She performed with Haydn at the Opera Concerts of 1795, and gave the first performance of the concert aria 'BERENICE, CHE FAI?' at his benefit concert on 4 May. No doubt Haydn had her strong dramatic presence in mind when composing the work but after the performance he noted in his notebook in broken English: 'Mad. Banti (She song very scanty).' SMcV

HCRL/3.

Barmherzige Brüder. A religious order founded in 1534 by St John of God. In English it is often erroneously rendered as Brothers of Mercy, which is a 19th-century religious order; the proper English name is Order of St John of God. Its members were esteemed for their medical services to the community and were noted for their learned understanding of botany and medicine (their hospice next to the church in Vienna, founded in 1614, prepares and dispenses potions to this day). The order also believed strongly in the palliative powers of music which, consequently, played a prominent part in their worship. By the end of the 18th century, in addition to Vienna, over two dozen towns in the Austrian territories had hospices run by the order, including Graz (founded 1615), Pressburg (Bratislava, 1669), Kuks (Kukus, 1743), Linz (1757), and Eisenstadt (1760). Because of their extensive work in the community the order remained unaffected by the religious reforms of Joseph II in the 1780s.

Haydn had direct contact with at least two of these centres. In Vienna, in the late 1750s, he regularly played the violin in services at the church of the Barmherzige Brüder, and some of his early sacred music, perhaps the organ concertos too, were composed for that church. Later, in 1768, Haydn directed a performance of his Stabat mater at the church. Haydn's contact with the order in Eisenstadt was more extended. Founded with the support of Prince Paul Anton Esterházy, it had close links with the court. House officers (the term included Haydn) had a private room at the hospice for any necessary medical care; servants (this term embraced the other musicians) had access to a dormitory. The court also paid the order directly for any medical prescriptions. In 1763, for instance, Haydn was prescribed 'chest powder', 'stomach elixir', and some herbal tea; he seems, too, to have bought his tooth-cleaning powder from the hospice.

It has been conjectured that Haydn's Advent arias and pastorellas, if not first composed in Vienna for the Barmherzige Brüder, were written for the order in Eisenstadt and perhaps Kuks too. In the mid-1770s the composer's *Missa brevis Sancti Joannis de Deo* was written specifically for the order in Eisenstadt.

G. Chew, 'Haydn's Pastorellas: Genre, Dating and Transmission in the Early Church Works', O. Biba and D. W. Jones (eds), *Studies in Music History Presented to H. C. Robbins Landon on his Seventieth Birthday* (London, 1996), 21–43.
M. Freemanová, '"Provincia Germanica" of the Order of Brothers Hospitallers as a Musical Institution, and as a Centre of Circulation of Music and Musicians in the Czech Lands and Central Europe in the 18th and 19th Centuries', *Musicologica Olomucensia*, 4 (1998), 107–9.

Barthélemon family. François-Hippolyte Barthélemon (b. 27 July 1741; d. 20 July 1808) was a French violinist and composer active in London from 1764. He married the soprano and composer Maria (Mary Polly) Young (b. *c.*1749; d. 20 Sept. 1799); their daughter, Cecilia Maria (b. *c.*1770; d. after 1840), also became an accomplished musician.

François led the King's Theatre band and other prominent ensembles in London, and as a soloist was greatly admired for his eloquent playing of slow music. During the 1790s the Barthélemon family befriended Haydn, who spent musical evenings at their home in Vauxhall. Haydn appeared at François's benefit concert on 28 May 1792, accompanying MARA in arias by Sacchini and Handel, and again on 26 May 1794, conducting one of his own symphonies.

The friendship of the two men continued after Haydn's return to Vienna. Haydn promised a violin concerto for François's concert in April 1799 but it has not survived, even if it was composed. The singer and composer C. H. Purday (1799–1885) was to credit Barthélemon with suggesting to Haydn the first chapter of Genesis as a suitable subject for an oratorio. REC

HCRL/3.
S. McVeigh, *Concert Life in London from Mozart to Haydn* (Cambridge, 1993).

Bartolozzi, Gaetano (b. 1757; d. 25 Aug. 1821). Picture dealer. Son of the engraver Francesco Bartolozzi (1727–1815), he married the pianist THERESE JANSEN on 16 May 1795 at St James's church, Piccadilly; Haydn was a witness. He was apparently a good amateur musician. In 1795–6 he had dealings with ARTARIA, sending the firm some of Haydn's works. After selling up his stock in 1797 he left for the continent with his wife and infant daughter. They returned to London in 1800. The couple eventually separated, and Bartolozzi drifted into poverty. DdV

HCRL/3.

A. W. Tuer, *Bartolozzi and his Works* (London, 1882).

baryton. A rare instrument played by Prince Nicolaus Esterházy, for which Haydn and other musicians at the court, such as TOMASINI, were obliged to provide music. Haydn taught himself to play the baryton in the late 1760s.

The instrument probably originated in England in the early 17th century when the characteristics of two instruments, the viola da gamba and the bandora, were combined into one hybrid instrument, the baryton. The gut strings and fretted fingerboard of the gamba were united with the wire strings of the bandora which were strung behind the fingerboard. The lower set of strings produced two effects: they vibrated in sympathy with the bowed notes played on the gamba part of the instrument; secondly, they could be plucked by the thumb of the left hand. The instrument was known at the court of King James I and is mentioned by Michael Praetorius in the second volume of his celebrated treatise, *Syntagma Musicum* (1614–20). Although its peculiar nature ensured that it never became a popular instrument, it acquired a certain cachet in courtly circles, particularly in south Germany and Austria, and survived into the early years of the 19th century. The early repertoire for the instrument is often notated in tablature rather than in staff notation.

The earliest extant baryton, made in 1647 by Magnus Feldlen of Vienna, is owned by the Royal College of Music, London. In its original state it had six strings on the gamba portion and nine sympathetic strings. Six strings remained the norm for the bowed portion but the number of sympathetic strings on occasions reached as many as 24. Prince Nicolaus's instrument was made by Johann Joseph Stadlmann in Vienna in 1750 and was acquired on a visit to Innsbruck in 1765; it had seven bowed strings tuned *A'*, *D*, *G*, *c*, *e*, *a*, *d'*, and ten sympathetic strings tuned *A*, *d*, *e*, *f♯*, *g*, *a*, *b*, *c♯'*, *d'*, *e'*; it is now in the Magyar Nemzeti Múzeum, Budapest. A similar instrument, made *c.*1650 by Andreas Steiner in Absam, was destroyed by fire at Eszterháza in 1945. Two surviving barytons that may have been used at the Esterházy court are owned by the Gesellschaft der Musikfreunde, Vienna (D. Stadlmann, 1732), and the National Museum, Prague (J. J. Stadlmann, 1769); the first is sometimes erroneously referred to as the 'Haydn baryton'.

Haydn wrote the leading line in the treble clef, sounding an octave lower; any plucking of the sympathetic strings was indicated by appropriate numbers placed above or below the notated pitch. However, in three other respects Haydn's baryton-writing is different from that of his immediate predecessors. He occasionally requires the bowed and plucked strings to be played simultaneously, whereas alternation of the two characteristics were much more typical of writing for the instrument. Second, the sympathetic strings are tuned an octave higher than previously, creating more resonance; and, third, instead of numbering them from the highest downwards, he numbered them in the opposite direction, from the lowest note upwards. Since Haydn's music represents the most significant corpus of music for the baryton, this system of tuning and notating the sympathetic strings has become standard in the modern revival of the instrument. TMP

C. Gartell, 'The Baryton: Its History and Music' (diss., University of Surrey, 1983).

baryton music. Haydn's corpus of music for the baryton consists of nearly 200 works, all designed to be played by PRINCE NICOLAUS ESTERHÁZY. They were all composed in the period *c.*1765–*c.*1775. Prince Nicolaus had acquired a baryton on a visit to Innsbruck in August 1765 and seems to have been impatient for some music from his Kapellmeister; a gentle reprimand issued in November 1765 includes the comment that 'Haydn is urgently enjoined to apply himself to composition more diligently than heretofore, and especially to write such pieces for the gamba [baryton], of which pieces we have seen very few up to now . . .'. Ten years later the prince was fast losing his enthusiasm for the instrument, as his musical interests increasingly focused on the new opera houses at Eszterháza. Compared with the bulk of Haydn's instrumental music from the same period—keyboard sonatas, quartets, and symphonies—the baryton music did not circulate beyond the Esterházy court and none of it was published in its original form in Haydn's lifetime. However, many arrangements of the trios, by Haydn and others, have survived and, in some cases, constitute the only extant source.

1. **Works for baryton and another instrument.**
2. **Duets for two barytons.**
3. **Trios for two barytons and cello.**
4. **Trios for baryton, viola, and cello.**
5. **Divertimento in D for two barytons, and two horns.**
6. **Divertimento in F for keyboard, baryton, and two violins.**

7. Quintets for baryton, viola, cello, and two horns.
8. Octets for baryton, two horns, two violins, viola, cello, and double bass.
9. Concertos for baryton and strings.

---

1. Works for baryton and another instrument. Sixteen works for baryton and cello, some possibly for solo baryton, are listed in the ENTWURF-KATALOG, but none survives.

2. Duets for two barytons. Haydn is known to have composed six duets for baryton, perhaps designed to be played by the prince and the composer. Only one, a duet in G major (Hob.XII:4), has survived in its original form. Three works, XII:1, X:11, and XII:5+3, survive only in an inauthentic arrangement for flute, violin, and cello. Part of the finale of XII:5+3 uses a speeded-up version of the trio from Symphony no. 28 composed in 1765; occasional self-quotation, constituting a private joke between Kapellmeister and prince, is a characteristic of the baryton repertoire not shared by other instrumental music from the period. Two duets are lost (Hob.XII:2 and 6).

3. Trios for two barytons and cello. One of the earliest extant compositions by Haydn for baryton is a collection of 12 very short movements (Hob. XII:19), which the composer described as 'cassation pieces'. None lasts longer than a couple of minutes and the collection includes a movement based on the folksong 'A NIGHT WATCHMAN'S SONG' (no. 2) and a polonaise (no. 8). When Haydn began to practise the baryton himself he had to do so at night; the quotation of the song may be a wry reference to this nocturnal habit. The prince's limited technique at this time is suggested by the absence of any sympathetic notes to be played on the second manual, the use of one key (A major) for nine of the 12 movements, and the miniature scale of the music.

4. Trios for baryton, viola, and cello. The most numerous of Haydn's compositions involving the baryton are the 122 extant trios for baryton, viola, and cello; a further four trios have been lost. Haydn seems to have composed them as single works or in groups of three or six. Special presentation copies of the trios were then made for the prince, separate part-books lavishly bound in red leather and each containing 24 works. Five such collections are thought to have been prepared, though only one survives (Book IV).

Book I (Hob.XI:1–24) was bound by January 1767 and contained the 24 trios that Haydn had completed over approximately the previous 15 to 18 months. DIES remarked that the prince, until he was taught otherwise by Haydn, thought that music for the baryton should be restricted to one key, an anecdote confirmed by the content of Book I; as with the 'cassation pieces' for two barytons, A major is, by far, the most frequently used key. Most of the works have three movements in which the opening is as likely to be a slow movement or a set of variations as a binary movement. Such movements have the advantage of having a limited range of modulation in comparison with sonata form, something which suited the limited technique of the prince. One curious result of so many minuets in A major is the number of trio sections in A minor, otherwise a comparatively rare key in Haydn's output. The thematic material of the first movement of XI:5 is based on 'Che farò senza Euridice' from Gluck's *Orfeo*, first performed in Vienna in 1762; other operatic or folk origins to the thematic material may lurk unrecognized in these trios. The trio of the minuet in the same work together with the finale of XI:11 show a rare willingness to think polyphonically in the medium, a characteristic that was to become increasingly common in the later books of trios. None of the trios in Book I requires the sympathetic strings to be plucked.

Book II of the trios (Hob.XI:24–48) was ready to be presented to the prince in October 1767. Although the second book was ready within a year of Book I, the works are much more ambitiously written for the baryton. Three home keys are used: D major (13 works), A major (six works), and G major (five works). In addition, a substantial number of works require the sympathetic strings to be plucked, and the ornamentation of the baryton parts in slow music demands considerable artistry as well as technique. Also indicative of increasing ambition are the three-part fugues that complete XI:33 and XI:40, the latter skilfully picking out the contrapuntal line of the baryton through the use of plucked sympathetic strings. XI:35 is the second baryton trio to refer to the 'Night Watchman's Song', while Haydn bases the first movement of XI:29 on the opening aria from his opera *La canterina*, 'Che visino delicato'. While both of these were surely meant to charm the prince, the transcription in XI:37 of a movement from an earlier keyboard sonata in C (Hob.XVI:3) was probably a convenient way of recycling some forgotten music.

The precise date of composition of individual trios is only occasionally known. Given the technically more ambitious nature of most of the trios in Book II, it is tempting to speculate that all the works post-date Book I. More likely, however, is an overlap in date of composition. Since the two books were meant to honour the prince, maybe Haydn deliberately exaggerated the difference between the two books, consigning the elementary trios to Book I and placing the more difficult ones in Book II.

A similar overlap probably occurred between Book II and Book III (Hob.XI:49–72) which was ready by July 1768. Nicolaus had been playing the baryton regularly for three years and had reached the stage where his technique, if not of the most accomplished, was no longer a constraint on Haydn's compositional imagination. D major, G major, and A major are still the most frequently encountered keys but Nicolaus's increasing dexterity on the two manuals is very evident. The trio sections of the minuets in XI:60 and 66 require the prince to be a one-man band, playing both manuals simultaneously, while the Presto finale of XI:69 is one of several movements that require rapid alternation between plucked sympathetic strings on the beat and bowed notes off the beat. The prince must have been a sympathetic player also in order to partake in the formal polyphony of the fugues in XI:53, 67, and 71, and in the close motivic interaction that features in a movement such as the opening Moderato of XI:53. Although the baryton is always the *primus inter pares*, the relationship between that line and those of the viola and cello often anticipates that practised in the op. 9 and op. 17 quartets, even on occasions, the op. 20 quartets. The many viola solos, especially in trio sections, that appear in Book III are, however, a characteristic not encountered in the three sets of quartets.

The finale of XI:52 is a transcription up a third of the *Menuet alla zoppa* from Symphony no. 58; in the baryton version the trio is headed 'Trio al contrario', not, as usual in Haydn, an indication of some contrapuntal prowess but to point out the obvious, that its simple repetitive rhythms are not like those of the 'limping' minuet.

The first movement of the trio in D major (XI:64) refers to the same Gregorian plainchant, the Easter 'Alleluja', used in the first movement of Symphony no. 30 in C, composed a few years earlier in 1765. But it is an entirely independent composition and, whereas the symphony movement is appropriately celebratory in mood, the baryton trio treatment of the same melody is more witty, even irreverent, as statements of the theme over an old-fashioned walking bass give way to more *galant* textures, including statements in which alternate notes are plucked and bowed.

Book IV (Hob.XI:73–96) of the baryton trios was probably presented to the prince in December 1771, on either his nameday (6 December) or his birthday (18 December). While 17 of the trios are in one of the typical keys of D, G, and A, seven works are in keys not encountered previously in the genre, testimony to Nicolaus's ever-increasing skill: C major (XI:76, 82, 90, and 93), F major (XI:83), B minor (XI:96), and A minor (XI:87). The B minor work has a trio section in B major and while the A minor work must, on the one hand, be seen as a natural development from the many A major works that have sections in A minor, it has the distinction of being the only instrumental work in any genre in this key by the composer. For three of the works (XI:89–91) Haydn replaces the viola with a violin, occasioning a considerable amount of writing in thirds and sixths for the baryton and violin. With only 24 works across three years, compared with the 72 works from the period *c.*1765–*c.*1768, the volume might suggest a waning of interest by the prince and his Kapellmeister. This is unlikely, however, for by this time other musicians at the court, including TOMASINI and, possibly, LIDL, had begun to supply the prince with baryton music, which allowed Haydn to work on the many ambitious operas, liturgical works, quartets, and symphonies written in this extraordinary varied period in the composer's life. Certainly the content of the trios themselves continues to show Haydn's musical curiosity. The third movement of XI:76 is a binary movement in 2/4 that offers balancing five-bar phrases, rather than the normal four-bar phrases, prompting the heading *Scherzo*. Like many other previous finales in the genre that of XI:81 is a fugue, but here the intriguing challenge that Haydn sets himself is to write the fugue using an eight-note theme that ascends in a measured way through the complete major scale. In XI:85 the da capo of the minuet is written out in full so that Haydn can alter the course of the internal repeats, while the trio section of XI:95 is cleverly unsure of its harmonic direction. These and other compositional subtleties obviously intrigued Haydn but they suggest that Prince Nicolaus was anxious to be an initiate too. His patronage was not one merely of vainglory, important though that was, but he shared with his musical employees—to a greater extent, perhaps, than some of them—a willingness to understand the distinctive creativity of the Kapellmeister.

Documentary evidence suggests that Book V (XI:97–126) was compiled by November 1778. As with the previous four books, it probably contained 24 works, which would leave six baryton trios that were not formally gathered together in a presentation volume. From the surviving autographs and manuscript copies of single works it is not possible to state which works were contained in Book V. Thirty works over a period of seven years suggest a continuing decline in interest in new music for the baryton, though of course the prince already had four books of works from which he could pick and choose. As a player, however, Nicolaus had ceased to develop and there are no new demands on his technique in the last 30 baryton trios. The largest baryton trio by Haydn, XI:97 in D, belongs to this period, a seven-movement work specially composed for the prince's birthday on 18 December; the year of composition is not known. An expansive, aria-like Adagio is followed by an Allegro and a minuet, at which point a normal baryton trio would have been complete; Haydn then adds a Polonaise (his second for the baryton), a short Adagio in D minor that leads into a minuet, and a concluding fugue. Trios XI:101 and 114 also end with a fugue, the former proudly labelled in a similar way to the fugues found in the contemporary op. 20 quartets, 'Finale a 3 soggetti in contrapunta doppio' ('fugue on three subjects in double counterpoint'). Haydn found a new way of flattering the prince in XI:101. The trio of the minuet is written for baryton alone, the unusual scoring reflected in the unusual use of two staves for the instrument, one for the bowed line the other indicating the pitch of the plucked sympathetic strings. Two works make use of earlier music by Haydn: XI:103 draws some of its material from a keyboard trio in F (Hob.XV:2), and XI:110 uses material from a divertimento in C for keyboard, two violins, and cello (Hob.XIV:8). A more human indication of the Kapellmeister at work is provided by the autograph of Hob.XI:109 in C. The right-hand side of the first page of the music is disfigured by a large water stain that stretches the entire length of the page, as if a glass of water had been spilt. At the top of the page Haydn wrote, rather cryptically, 'fatto a posta' ('done deliberately') and 'nihil sine causa' ('nothing without cause'). Clearly the spillage was not an accident, and it has been suggested that Haydn's wife, who did not share her husband's devotion to music, was responsible.

5. **Divertimento in D for two barytons and two horns (Hob.X:9).** This quartet, which probably dates from the late 1760s, has not survived and is known only from its entry in the *Entwurf-Katalog*.

6. **Divertimento in F for keyboard, baryton, and two violins (Hob.XIV:2).** Another work from the late 1760s that is known in its original form only from an entry in the *Entwurf-Katalog*. The first two movements were recycled twice: first as the equivalent movements in a later baryton trio (Hob. XI:103), and then as the equivalent movements in a keyboard trio (Hob.XV:2).

7. **Quintets for baryton, viola, cello, and two horns (Hob.X:7, 8).** Two quintets are known to have been composed by Haydn but only the second of the works survives, probably composed *c.*1768. Its scoring consists of the customary baryton trio plus two horns. The additional instruments are heard to maximum effect in the first movement, marked *con sordini* and rising in the first horn to a notated top *e'''*, as found in the baryton octets and in Symphonies nos. 31 and 72. They have a less spectacular solo role in the final minuet and trio.

8. **Octets for baryton, two horns, two violins, viola, cello, and double bass (Hob.X:1–6, 12).** Composed in 1775, these seven octets are very likely the last works that Haydn wrote for the baryton. Unlike the remainder of the repertoire (especially the baryton trios) the prince is here a subordinate member of an ensemble. The music is firmly led by the first violin (presumably the faithful Tomasini) though its line is often doubled by the baryton. Plucked sympathetic strings are not indicated but in an ensemble that has a large number of instruments in the tenor and bass ranges, the freely resonating sound of the sympathetic strings exaggerates an already opaque, even murky sound. A second distinctive feature of the scoring is the writing for horns which exploits both spectacularly high notes and comically grovelling low notes. All seven works are in three movements, but none has a pattern typical of a baryton trio; there are no minuet and trio movements, and the size of the ensemble precludes the intriguing fugues that are found in the trios. Two of the works have the order slow, fast, and fast, the others have the pattern fast, slow, and fast. There are a large number of movements in sectional design, whether variations or rondo, in which members of the ensemble take it in turn to lead the music. As in the baryton trios, sonata forms are restricted in dimensions and scope to accommodate the limitations of the prince and the instrument.

9. **Concertos for baryton and strings (Hob. XIII:1–3).** Haydn composed three concertos for baryton, probably in the late 1760s, all in D major: Hob.XIII:1 and 2 are for one baryton and strings; Hob.XIII:3 is a double concerto for two baryton and strings. None has survived.

See also DEUTSCHLANDS KLAGE AUF DEN TOD DES GROẞEN FRIEDRICHS, BORUẞENS KÖNIG.

S. C. Fisher, 'A Group of Haydn Copies for the Court of Spain: Fresh Sources, Rediscovered Works, and New Riddles', *HS* 4/2 (1978), 65–84.

C. Gartell, 'The Baryton: Its History and Music' (diss., University of Surrey, 1983).

O. Strunk, 'Haydn's Divertimenti for Baryton, Viola, and Bass', *Musical Quarterly*, 18 (1932), 216–51.

'Bear' symphony. *See* 'L'OURS' SYMPHONY.

Beethoven, Ludwig van (b. 16 Dec. 1770; d. 26 March 1827). Composer and pupil of Haydn. The eldest son of a professional singer at the Electoral court in Bonn, Beethoven showed talent at an early age and before long was participating in musical activities at the court. During the 1780s he had the opportunity to become familiar with much of Haydn's music, for one of the court officials, Johann Gottfried von Mastiaux, was a devoted admirer of Haydn and had by 1783 collected many works of his, including 80 symphonies and 30 quartets, according to a report published that year by Beethoven's teacher Christian Gottlob Neefe.

When Haydn's patron Prince Nicolaus Esterházy died in 1790, Haydn at last became free to travel, and was invited to London by the impresario JOHANN PETER SALOMON. Since Salomon was a native of Bonn, the two men inevitably stopped at that city on the way to London, arriving on Christmas Day 1790. The following day, a Sunday, Haydn was introduced to the Bonn musicians, and met Beethoven for the first time. On his return from London, Haydn once more stopped in Bonn, in July 1792, and again met Beethoven, who probably showed him several of his compositions; Gerhard Wegeler specifically mentions that Haydn was struck by a cantata of Beethoven's (perhaps the *Cantata on the Death of Joseph II*, WoO 87), and it was almost certainly at this stage that they agreed that Beethoven should go to Vienna to study with Haydn. (Beethoven had already been to Vienna in 1787 to study with Mozart, but had had to return quickly on hearing that his mother was very ill.)

Shortly before his departure for Vienna in early November 1792, Beethoven received some farewell wishes from his friend and patron Count Waldstein, who wrote prophetically that Beethoven would receive 'Mozart's spirit from Haydn's hands'. Beethoven reached Vienna about 10 November, and proceeded to receive tuition from Haydn until early in 1794, when Haydn left for his second visit to England. During this study, Beethoven completed a large number of exercises in SPECIES COUNTERPOINT, based on Fux's *Gradus ad Parnassum* and using the old church modes. Altogether 245 of Beethoven's exercises for Haydn survive (facsimile in Mann). They were probably completed within a relatively short space of time rather than being spread throughout the year (the manuscript has a very uniform appearance), and many more may be lost.

Despite his considerable talent and experience in composition, Beethoven made quite a large number of technical errors in the exercises. Some were corrected by Haydn, but many were left uncorrected. This has led some people to suppose that Haydn was not a very conscientious teacher, but there is no justification for this conclusion. Haydn probably discussed some of the errors orally, and concentrated on amending those where some interesting technical point had arisen, rather than marking pedantically every single mistake.

Haydn's corrections had little or no effect on Beethoven's style in free composition, and in fact certain musical procedures that were deemed errors in the strict Fuxian style became hallmarks of Beethoven's free style, such as the use of unprepared fourths, or sounding a suspension in one voice at the same time as the resolution in another. Thus when Beethoven told Ferdinand Ries some years later that he had never learnt anything from Haydn, he was correct in one sense.

Not long after Beethoven's death, the composer Johann Schenk claimed to have secretly helped Beethoven with his counterpoint exercises for Haydn because Beethoven had made so little progress in his first few months. Schenk's account, however, contains many details that do not fit with other evidence or known facts, and so although it has been widely reported and discussed by later writers, it is probably entirely fictitious. At best, it should be treated with extreme caution.

Apart from exercises in strict counterpoint, Beethoven's studies with Haydn must also have involved discussing freely written compositions, perhaps those of other composers and certainly Beethoven's own latest efforts. In November 1793, five of the latter were sent by Haydn to the elector in Bonn (who was still nominally Beethoven's patron) as evidence of Beethoven's progress and diligence. In his letter Haydn predicted, on the basis of these works, that Beethoven would in time become one of the greatest musical artists in Europe. The five works completed under Haydn's tutelage were: 'A quintet' (Hess 19, a wind quintet that survives incomplete); 'An eight-voice Parthie' (Octet, op. 103); 'An oboe concerto' (Hess 12, lost apart from incipits); 'Variations for piano' (probably WoO 40, for piano and violin); 'A fugue' (unidentified; possibly Hess 29). The elector replied scathingly that all these works except for the fugue had actually been written before Beethoven's departure from Bonn. The manuscript material of the four works in question indicates otherwise, however, for there are extensive sketches or autograph scores for all four on Viennese paper. Thus all four works were at least revised in Vienna, and the only one that was definitely begun in Bonn is the set of variations on 'Se vuol ballare' (WoO 40). It would appear, therefore, that the elector was misinformed.

All the evidence indicates that, despite any dissatisfaction Beethoven may have felt during the 14 months of study with Haydn, their relationship remained warm and friendly. Beethoven's memorandum book records that they had coffee and chocolate together in November 1793, and Haydn lent Beethoven a considerable sum of money to help with his expenses that year. Beethoven changed teachers (to ALBRECHTSBERGER) only because Haydn left for England, and he dedicated his piano sonatas op. 2 to Haydn when the latter returned in

1795, whereas no such honour was bestowed on Albrechtsberger. Writers who have suggested ill feeling between Haydn and Beethoven at this time have based their speculations on evidence that is now considered unreliable, such as Schenk's account, the elector's claim that Beethoven had deceived Haydn about the newness of four works sent to Bonn, and the incompleteness of Haydn's corrections to Beethoven's exercises.

After Haydn's return the two composers were much less close and probably saw each other only occasionally. There was no outright hostility between them, but a number of anecdotes suggest no great warmth either. Some of these anecdotes are as doubtful as Schenk's claim to have helped Beethoven in counterpoint, but they are sufficiently numerous and widespread to suggest there is some truth in them, especially the accounts of Ferdinand Ries, who is generally reliable. According to Ries, Haydn had wanted Beethoven to put 'Pupil of Haydn' on his title pages but Beethoven refused; and when Haydn heard Beethoven's C minor piano trio (op. 1 no. 3) he advised him not to publish it, which created considerable resentment in Beethoven (the advice must, however, have been retrospective, for Haydn had no opportunity to hear the work until after he had returned to Vienna in August 1795, by which time the trio had already appeared in print). Beethoven's resentment may be the reason why 'Haydn rarely got away without a few digs' when Beethoven discussed his music, according to Ries. Another anecdote, transmitted by Aloys Fuchs, reports that Haydn told Beethoven he had enjoyed a performance of his ballet *The Creatures of Prometheus*, to which Beethoven replied that it was far from being a *Creation*; Haydn agreed that it would never become a *Creation*, and the two men parted slightly embarrassed. Yet they seem to have remained great admirers of each other's music, and Beethoven clearly learnt a great deal from Haydn's, more, perhaps, than he was willing to admit.

Beethoven's debt to Haydn is most evident in the string quartet and the symphony, genres which Haydn had done more than anyone to raise to pre-eminence. Beethoven adopted this pre-eminence, regarding it as axiomatic, and most of his quartets and symphonies have the same overall structure as most of Haydn's: a slow movement and a minuet or scherzo flanked by two fast movements. His whole principle of thematic-motivic manipulation in a multi-movement context, using an often insignificant motif as the basis for extended development and elaboration, owes more to Haydn than to anyone else, as many writers have observed. The motif may be something as small as a single semitone step, which is exploited in a profusion of ways in, for example, both Haydn's Symphony no. 103 and Beethoven's First Symphony. Or it may be a longer melodic fragment of up to six or seven notes, which can in some cases be subdivided into two shorter motifs. One notable motivic technique used by Haydn is to employ the opening figure of a movement again at the very end, as a closing figure, as in his quartets op. 33 nos. 2 and 5, where the first movements both end as they began. Beethoven echoes this procedure in the first movement of his Eighth Symphony, and in his song cycle *An die ferne Geliebte*. The procedure of elaborately developing a short, simple figure was equally effective in generating either sublime or witty effects. Indeed, Beethoven inherited much of Haydn's wit, which is evident even in some of Beethoven's late works such as his last quartet, op. 135.

Many of Haydn's actual melodies anticipate those of Beethoven, notably the slow movement of Haydn's Symphony no. 88, the main theme of which finds echoes in several Beethoven works, right up to the Sonata op. 110 (bar 5). Haydn's interest in exploring remote key relationships in his late works (such as E♭ and E in his final piano sonata, or D and B♭ in his final symphony) was another idea that Beethoven greatly developed. Some of Haydn's most characteristic forms were also adopted by Beethoven, such as sonata RONDO form and ALTERNATING VARIATION form (which finds its most exalted expression in the slow movement of Beethoven's Ninth Symphony). Beethoven's most characteristic movement title is probably the SCHERZO, and it is significant that all six of Haydn's op. 33 quartets replace the traditional minuet with a scherzo movement. Beethoven evidently held this set of quartets in high regard.

Beethoven's love of comical effects in general is also developed from Haydn's. An obvious case is the famous *fortissimo* 'surprise' in Haydn's Symphony no. 94, an effect used more than once by Beethoven, a striking example being the final chord of the slow movement of his Piano Sonata op. 14 no. 2, where a lengthy *diminuendo* to *pianissimo* is terminated by a *fortissimo* crash. Haydn's penchant for rhythmic disruption, often for comical effect, was also inherited by Beethoven, as in the finale of the same sonata. So profoundly and thoroughly did Beethoven absorb elements of Haydn's style, especially in his quartets and symphonies, that almost all aspects of his music show some influence.

Outside the quartets and symphonies, Haydn's direct influence is often more difficult to isolate. There is relatively little of Haydn in Beethoven's vocal works and music for wind, where Mozart's spirit is more strongly in evidence; and in their numerous folksong settings the most striking thing is how different Beethoven's are from Haydn's.

Nevertheless, Beethoven's oratorio *The Mount of Olives* would probably not have been written at all without the inspiration and success of Haydn's two great oratorios composed shortly beforehand, *The Creation* and *The Seasons*. Although Haydn's influence on Beethoven has been well known and recognized from the beginning, the extent of it is not widely appreciated and it has still not been fully documented. When Beethoven remarked that he had never learnt anything from Haydn, he was clearly not referring to the inspiring example of Haydn's music. BARC

G. Feder, 'Stilelemente Haydns in Beethovens Werken', in C. Dahlhaus *et al.* (eds), *Bericht über den Internationalen Musikwissenschaftlichen Kongress Bonn 1970* (Kassel, 1971), 65–70.

A. Mann, *Theory and Practice: The Great Composer as Student and Teacher* (London, 1987).

G. Nottebohm, *Beethoven's Studien* (Leipzig and Winterthur, 1873).

J. Webster, 'The Falling-Out between Haydn and Beethoven: The Evidence of the Sources', in L. Lockwood and P. Benjamin (eds), *Beethoven Essays: Studies in Honor of Elliot Forbes* (Cambridge, Mass., 1984), 3–45.

'Bell' quartet. Nickname formerly in occasional use for the op. 77 no. 2 quartet, prompted by the descending scales (akin to pealing bells) of the main theme of the finale. JH

Bérault, Françoise (*fl.* 1756–84). Although women were often employed as engravers of music in the 18th century, Bérault is a rare instance of a female publisher. Her publications of Haydn's music date from the late 1760s and early 1770s. None was authorized by the composer and of the 33 works printed under his name (mainly symphonies and quartets), only nine were authentic.

'Berenice, che fai?' (Hob.XXIVa:10) Concert aria for soprano and orchestra on a text from Metastasio's *Antigono*, written by Haydn for the soprano BRIGIDA GIORGI BANTI and first performed in London at the composer's benefit concert on 4 May 1795.

This complex and beautiful mad scene falls into two stages. In the opening recitative Berenice expresses despair that her lover Demetrio is dead and imagines his ghost departing for the underworld; in a gorgeous slow arioso, 'Non partir, bell'idol mio', she begs him not to leave. After the arioso gives way to more recitative ('Me infelice!') the scena culminates in a fast aria in the minor mode, 'Perché, se tanti siete', in which Berenice demands that her grief should lead to death.

Berenice's madness is reflected in the unconventional (one might even say irrational) tonal organization with its frequent, abrupt changes of key. After establishing D major at the beginning of the first recitative, Haydn set the arioso in E and the aria in F minor. The listener might be able to perceive the tonic rising by step if it were not for the enharmonic modulations that occur in between. In the opening recitative, for example, a dramatic shift from C♯ minor to B♭ major precedes the words 'Dove son': such harmonic disorientation perfectly depicts Berenice's delirium. The sweet tune in C major played by oboe and bassoon that is heard as she addresses her lover ('Aspetta, anima bella') is Haydn's tribute to the venerable traditions of *ombra* arias in *opera seria*. The simple accompaniment allows the listener to regain a sense of tonal orientation.

For the arioso in E Haydn chose an opening motif almost identical to that with which Euridice begins her first aria in *L'anima del filosofo* ('Filomena abbandonata'); but this melody is nobler and more heartfelt. The gavotte rhythms at 'Per quell'onda all altra sponda' open the possibility that this is the first, slow section of a rondò (a two-tempo aria whose melodies very frequently use gavotte rhythms). But Berenice's madness gets the best of her. Another enharmonic modulation leads to more recitative. She cries out, as if waking from a beautiful dream, 'Me infelice, Che fingo? Che ragiono?' ('Woe is me! What delusions? What am I saying?').

The aria in F minor is reminiscent of Orfeo's aria in the same key in *L'anima del filosofo* ('In un mar d'acerbe pene'); but the tradition to which it belongs goes back much further. It is the last of a great series of Italian arias by Haydn, violent outbursts in the minor mode that he included in almost every one of his Italian operas. JAR

HCRL/3.

Bernardon. *See* KURZ-BERNARDON.

Berwald, Johan Fredrik (b. 4 Dec. 1787; d. 26 Aug. 1861). Swedish violinist, composer, and director; cousin of the composer Franz Berwald (1796–1868). A child prodigy, both as a player and a composer, he undertook a lengthy concert tour with his father from 1795 to 1803. He was in Vienna in 1799 and witnessed the first public performance of *The Creation* at the Burgtheater on 19 March. Even though he was only 11 at the time he left a remarkably vivid and detailed account of the occasion. He also visited the composer in his house in Gumpendorf, providing a rare pen-portrait of Haydn's wife and noting the composer's remark that his minuet movements were 'something between a danced minuet and a presto'.

HCRL/4.

C.-G. Stellan Mörner, 'Haydniana aus Schweden um 1800', *HS* 2/1 (1969), 1–33.

Bianchi, Benedetto (*fl.* 1760–90). Baritone who began his career in Italy in the early 1760s. This fine comedian came to Eszterháza after singing in the Viennese *opera buffa* troupe from 1773 to 1775. During two long engagements (1776–81; 1784–90) he sang in at least 42 operas and created several important roles for Haydn, most of which made full use of his comic talents: Buonafede in *Il mondo della luna*, Villotto in *La vera costanza*, Enrico in *L'isola disabitata*, and Count Perruchetto in *La fedeltà premiata*. JAR

Bartha and Somfai.
HCRL/2.

Billington, Elizabeth (b. *c.*1765–8; d. 25 Aug. 1818). English soprano. She sang in Haydn's vocal trio *Pietà di me, benigni Dei* in London on 25 April 1791. Haydn reported on her singing in Shield's opera, *The Woodman*, on 10 December 1791: 'rather timidly this evening, but very well all the same'. DdV

Birchall, Robert (b. *c.*1760; d. 19 Dec. 1819). London music publisher active from the early 1780s. Although he seems never to have dealt directly with Haydn, his many publications of the composer's music contributed to his fame in England, especially in the first decades of the 19th century. In cooperation with other publishers in the 1780s Birchall issued a number of keyboard sonatas by Haydn. His most significant publications, however, were of the 12 'London' symphonies, which began appearing *c.*1810, the first English edition of these works to appear. Birchall was on friendly terms with SALOMON and Robbins Landon is of the view that these editions include amendments that reflect changes made by Haydn and Salomon during rehearsals and performances of the works; Landon's editions incorporate these changes. There is a contrary view that the Birchall editions were based largely on those of the German publisher ANDRÉ.

Salomon had published his own arrangements of the 'London' symphonies for piano trio and for quintet (flute, string quartet, and piano); after his death in 1814 these were taken over by Birchall. Birchall added arrangements for quintet of earlier Haydn symphonies, plus arrangements of the London symphonies for piano, and for piano duet. Birchall (and his successor Lonsdale) was the publisher of LATROBE's six volumes of sacred music, arrangements in piano score that included over two dozen movements from Haydn's masses and from the Stabat mater.

'Bird' quartet. Nickname for the op. 33 no. 3 quartet, first applied in the early 19th century. It was probably prompted by the many grace notes in the first violin part in the first subject of the opening movement, perhaps, too, by the 'twittering' accompaniment. Less plausibly, some commentators have seen the rapid oscillating thirds of the main theme of the concluding rondo as a parody of cuckoo song. JH

Bland, John (b. *c.*1750: d. *c.*1840). Music publisher who played a notable part in promoting Haydn's music in London in the 1780s and early 1790s. The business was founded in 1776 and the association with Haydn's music started in 1782, when Bland initiated the publication of 12 symphonies that had featured at the private concert series, the Nobility Concert; two years later Bland published a score of the Stabat mater, also performed at the Nobility Concert, part of the remarkable international success of that work. In the winter of 1788–9 Bland became the agent for the Viennese firm of HOFFMEISTER which enabled him to import the small number of Haydn publications issued by that firm, including the D minor quartet (op. 42). In a business environment in which Bland's rivalry with LONGMAN & BRODERIP (Artaria's agent in London) was becoming increasingly rancorous, Bland decided to journey to Vienna in order to negotiate directly with Haydn and other composers such as Kozeluch, Vanhal, Wranitzky, and possibly Mozart. The journey had the secondary purpose of enquiring whether Haydn would consider aligning himself in any future London appearances with SALOMON rather than with Cramer and the Professional Concert series. Haydn was still in Eszterháza in November and Bland made the two-day journey from Vienna to meet the composer. A putative association with Salomon was agreed and Bland secured the right to publish *Arianna a Naxos*, three piano trios (Hob. XV:15–17), and the forthcoming op. 64 quartets. In addition to a fee, Bland also flattered Haydn by later sending him a watch and some razors, the latter occasioning the nickname 'RAZOR' QUARTET.

When, finally, Haydn did arrive in London in January 1791 to be the presiding composer at Salomon's concert, Bland was able to claim some of the credit. The composer stayed overnight at his house in Holborn and Salomon's concerts that season featured the first performance of the op. 64 quartets. Later that year Bland commissioned Thomas Hardy to paint a portrait of Haydn, probably first displayed in his shop in the Holborn. Having realized many of his ambitions as a music businessman Bland played a diminishing role in the artistic life of London during the subsequent course of Haydn's two visits, and in 1795 he sold his publishing business.

I. Woodfield, 'John Bland: London Retailer of the Music of Haydn and Mozart', *Music and Letters*, 81 (2000), 210–44.

Boccherini family. Several members of the Boccherini family from Lucca, Italy, contributed to the musical and theatrical life of Vienna from the late 1750s to the mid-1770s. The double bass player Leopold Boccherini came to Vienna in 1757 with his young son, Luigi, a cellist (b. 19 Feb. 1743; d. 28 May 1805). Both became members of the orchestra in the Kärntnerthortheater. They were soon joined in 1758 by Luigi's sister Maria Ester, a fine dancer who won applause as a prima ballerina in the Burgtheater. Their brother Giovanni Gastone (1742–*c*.1800), a dancer and poet, arrived in Vienna a year later. His tragic libretto *Turno re de' Rutolo*, published in 1767, won praise from Calzabigi.

In Vienna, Luigi soon emerged as a leading soloist in concerts in the Burgtheater and as a talented composer of chamber music. According to the catalogue of his works that he himself compiled, he wrote his first set of string trios in 1760 (at the age of 17) and his first set of six quartets a year later. Although they were later published in Paris (as op. 1 and op. 2), Boccherini's early trios and quartets are products of his intensive engagement with Viennese music. Haydn almost certainly knew them well. Daniel Heartz has pointed out passages in Haydn's early quartets (especially op. 9) that reflect the influence of Boccherini, whose artistic personality, however, was quite different from Haydn's. The prevailing gentleness and sweetness of Boccherini's music led one contemporary, the violinist Giuseppe Puppo, to call him 'Haydn's wife', a description that, however questionable in itself, at least acknowledges the importance of Boccherini's contribution to chamber music.

In 1769 Luigi settled in Madrid, where he continued to produce large quantities of well-crafted instrumental music, especially string quintets. Although Haydn remained familiar with his music and held it in high regard there is no evidence that the two composers corresponded. Giovanni Gastone remained in Vienna until 1775, when he followed his brother to Spain. In Vienna his literary ambitions led to collaboration with Salieri (*Le donne letterate* was the first opera by either man to reach the stage, in 1770) and with Salieri's mentor, FLORIAN GASSMANN. In 1772 Giovanni Gastone succeeded MARCO COLTELLINI as house librettist to the impresario then managing the two court theatres. In 1775, shortly before leaving Vienna, he collaborated with Haydn on a work in a genre that was new to both of them. For the Tonkünstler-Societät they produced an Italian oratorio, *Il ritorno di Tobia*, first performed in 1775. Depending largely on Metastasio's oratorio texts for models, Boccherini provided Haydn with a libretto in two parts, each ending with an extensive chorus, but dominated by dialogue in blank verse (set by Haydn as recitative) and arias. Also typical of Metastasio is the emphasis on religious contemplation at the expense of action. JAR

G. Burchi (ed.), *Atti del convegno internazionale di studi: Luigi Boccherini e la musica strumentale dei maestri italiani in Europa tra Sette e Ottocento, Siena, 29–31 luglio, 1993, Chigiana*, 43 (1993).
G. Biagi Ravenni, 'Calzabigi e dintorni: Boccherini, Angiolini, la Toscana e Vienna', in F. Marri (ed.), *La figura e l'opera di Ranieri de' Calzabigi* (Florence, 1989).
D. Heartz, *Haydn, Mozart and the Viennese School, 1740–1780* (New York, 1995).
D. Heartz, 'The Young Boccherini: Lucca, Vienna, and the Electoral Courts', *Journal of Musicology*, 13 (1995), 103–16.
G. de Rothschild, *Luigi Boccherini: His Life and Work* (London, 1965).

Bologna Porta, Metilde (*fl.* 1768–90). Soprano, and wife of the librettist NUNZIATO PORTA. Born in Rome, she sang *opera buffa* in Italy from 1768. In May 1781 she came to Eszterháza, where she remained until 1790. One of Haydn's most important operatic collaborators, she sang Fillide (Celia) in the 1782 version of *La fedeltà premiata* (Haydn adapted the part for her) and created the role of Angelica in *Orlando paladino*. Her portrayal of Epponina in Sarti's *Giulio Sabino* in 1783, and her performance of the title role in Haydn's *Armida* the following year, helped to establish *opera seria* as a significant part of the Eszterháza repertoire. Although she never completely abandoned *opera buffa*, most of the leading roles that she sang under Haydn were in serious opera. JAR

Bartha and Somfai.
HCRL/2.

Bon, Girolamo (*fl.* 1735–1770). A multi-talented man of the theatre who served two Esterházy princes as impresario and stage designer. He and his wife, Rosa, a singer, had worked for many years in Russia and Germany. Together with their daughter Anna, also a singer, they were engaged several times at Eisenstadt from 1759 onwards. A long-term contract, dated 1 July 1762, made the Bon family Haydn's theatrical collaborators. In that year Bon received payment for various expenses connected with the production of a comedy entitled *Il marchese*, which is probably to be identified with the work known as *Il marchese nespola*, to which Haydn contributed several Italian arias. Bon probably participated in preparations for Haydn's *La canterina*, *Lo speziale*, and *Le pescatrici*. JAR

HCRL/2.

Boßler, Heinrich Philipp (b. 22 June 1744; d. 11 Dec. 1812). German engraver who ran a publishing firm in Speyer, later Darmstadt, from 1780 to 1796. Between 1783 and 1795 he issued 29 works by Haydn, mainly in anthologies. Boßler was in intermittent correspondence with the composer and the authentic single editions include Symphonies nos. 76–8, three piano sonatas (Hob.XVI: 40–2), and three piano trios (Hob.XV:3–5). From 1788 onwards he published the only contemporary music journal in southern German, the *Musikalische Real-Zeitung* (later the *Musikalische Korrespondenz*). In its first year it featured an extensive, laudatory review of *The Seven Last Words*; later issues provided further enthusiastic reviews of music by Haydn, as well as reproducing GERBER's catalogue of his works. MSM

H. Schneider, *Der Musikverleger Heinrich Philipp Bossler 1744–1812* (Tutzing, 1985).

Botstiber, Hugo (b. 21 April 1875; d. 15 Jan. 1942). Austrian musicologist and administrator. Born in Vienna he studied at the Conservatory with Robert Fuchs (1847–1927), and privately with the musicologists, Guido Adler (1855–1941) and Heinrich Rietsch (1860–1927). He first worked for the Gesellschaft der Musikfreunde in 1896. The then archivist was EUSEBIUS MANDYCZEWSKI who had undertaken to complete the third volume of POHL's biography of Haydn, left unfinished at his death. Botstiber became secretary to the Gesellschaft der Musikfreunde in 1905 but left in 1913 to become general secretary to the rival organization, the Konzerthausgesellschaft. He served in the Austrian army in the First World War. Following the invasion of Austria by Hitler's troops in 1938 Botstiber fled the country and at the time of his death he was living in Shrewsbury, England.

Throughout his life there was a tension between his busy administrative career and his work as a scholar. Nevertheless, his contribution to Haydn studies was fundamental. On the centenary of Haydn's death in 1909 an account appeared of the composer's relationship with the publisher ARTARIA, co-written with Franz Artaria. A more formidable challenge was the completion of Pohl's biography of Haydn, willingly undertaken following the death of Mandyczewski. The second volume had appeared in 1882, but the third volume, covering the period 1790–1809, existed only as a collection of disordered notes in Pohl's microscopic handwriting and mingled with material for the earlier volumes; Botstiber described it as 'chaotic disorder'. Although Botstiber's volume did not appear until 1927 it was a fitting conclusion to Pohl's pioneering work and enabled the whole to take its place in the great tradition of multi-volume biographies produced in the 19th century, alongside Spitta's Bach, Jahn's Mozart, and Thayer's Beethoven. Botstiber also wrote on Haydn's relationship with Luigia Polzelli, and made a pioneering study of the composer's settings of Scottish folksongs.

H. Botstiber, 'Mein dritter Band zu Pohls Haydn-Biographie', *Neue Musik-Zeitung*, 49 (1928), 757–9.

Braghetti, Prospero (*fl.* 1774–85). Lyric tenor who sang in comic opera in Italy from 1774. He was engaged at Eszterháza in July 1781, two months after MATILDE BOLOGNA PORTA, opposite whom he frequently sang during the following decade. He created the role of Medoro in Haydn's *Orlando paladino* and went on to demonstrate his abilities as *primo uomo* in *opera seria* in Sarti's *Giulio Sabino* (1783); he sang the heroic title role, originally written for the castrato GASPARO PACCHIEROTTI. A year later he created the role of Rinaldo in Haydn's *Armida*. Although his most important contribution to the Eszterháza troupe was in serious opera, Braghetti also sang many *mezzo carattere* roles in *opera buffa*. JAR

Bartha and Somfai

HCRL/2.

Brahms, Johannes (b. 7 May 1833; d. 3 April 1897). Composer of piano, chamber, orchestral, solo vocal, and choral music. Born in Hamburg, he later settled in Vienna, where he died. He was a notable enthusiast of older music, from the Renaissance to the Classical period. Of the four great composers of the Viennese Classical School —Haydn, Mozart, Beethoven, and Schubert—the first had arguably the least pervasive hold on Brahms's interest, though when he did comment on Haydn's music, it was always enthusiastically, and Haydn was the only one of the four to whom he turned for a theme for variations. Brahms had learnt the core of his compositional technique from modelling movements after Mozart and Beethoven, and his involvement with Schubert's music from the later 1850s on as performer, editor, arranger, and collector brought with it similarly powerful influences on his own creativity.

The year 1855 was an important Haydn year for Brahms. He heard *The Creation* at the Niederrheinisches Musikfest in Düsseldorf in May, and five quartets (including op. 33 no. 2) played by the Joachim quartet in June; after the latter he commented to Clara Schumann, 'These quartets are wonderfully attractive and masterly, with an inconceivable wealth of beautiful and original ideas, especially in the great adagios' (letter of 27 June). That summer he played some Haydn piano trios privately with Joachim, omitting the cello part and sometimes referring to them as violin sonatas. The 'Gypsy rondo' trio (Hob.XV:25) became a firm favourite ('it always makes us quite delirious,' Brahms reported to Clara), and he and Joachim included it in public concerts. On 20 November Brahms heard a Haydn symphony in Bremen, which he described to Clara as 'very beguiling and magnificently fresh'.

By the time of his employment at the court of Detmold (1857–60) Brahms had his own library of Haydn symphonies; he also continued to play trios at court soirées. The Serenade no. 1 from this period is surely one of his most Haydnesque works, beginning with a theme related to that of the finale of Haydn's Symphony no. 104, and returning to motifs from this theme in the fifth movement. Haydn's influence is detectable also in other works from around this time: the fourth movement (*Quasi Menuetto*) from the Serenade no. 2, the finale of the sextet in B♭, the gypsy rondo that concludes the piano quintet in G minor, and the canonic trio in the piano quartet in A. In 1865 Joachim gave Brahms an edition in pocket score of Haydn's complete quartets as a Christmas present, and the two again played trios by the composer on tour in the autumn of 1866. On 14 November 1867 at a concert in Graz Brahms played a Haydn piano sonata, as far as is known for the first and only time in public. On 1 June 1871 he asked his publisher to send him further works by Haydn, commenting 'I really like everything by Haydn'. During his artistic directorship of the Gesellschaft der Musikfreunde in Vienna (1872–5) he conducted two Haydn symphonies, one in C (23 March 1873) and the other in E♭ (19 April 1874). The first of these symphony performances coincided with the inception of his own *Variations on a theme of Haydn* (op. 56*a* and op. 56*b*).

Around November 1870 he had copied the Andante from Haydn's Symphony no. 16 and the 'Chorale St Antoni' (falsely attributed to Haydn) from manuscript sources owned by his friend, the Haydn biographer and archivist of the Gesellschaft der Musikfreunde, CARL FERDINAND POHL; using the latter he composed his *Variations on a theme of Haydn* in the summer of 1873. He broadly retained the original wind-band scoring for the theme (adding cello and double bass), alternated major and minor variations as a structural principle (very probably recalling similar movements in Haydn such as the slow movement of the 'Drumroll' symphony and the F minor variations for piano), and included intricate canons and imitations (he had copied Haydn canons for study purposes). The original idea of the passacaglia finale may have been at least partly suggested by Haydn's variation technique in works like the quartet in E♭, op. 76 no. 6.

Brahms suggested that his friend Bernhard Scholz should programme a Haydn quartet in 1874. He ordered scores of a further ten Haydn symphonies in 1878, around the time he was completing his Second Symphony, and Simrock's edition of the trios in 1880. In 1885 he acquired the autograph manuscripts of the op. 20 quartets. In 1889 Brahms played eight trios privately with Richard Barth and Theoder Engelmann in September in Rüdesheim, and commented that the famous Hellmesberger quartet played too few works by Haydn. In 1894 he recommended playing easy Haydn symphonies in four-hand arrangements as a way of teaching Clara Schumann's daughter to transpose. He continued to lament the neglect of Haydn's quartets in Viennese concerts and in 1896 requested that Joachim programme a quartet during his forthcoming visit. From that year comes Brahms's most extensive recorded remarks on the composer, noted by Richard Heuberger: 'People today understand practically nothing about Haydn any more. No one really considers that we now live in a time where—exactly 100 years ago—Haydn created all our music, where he gave one symphony after another to the world. I myself have for years celebrated these events . . . And Haydn, when he was about my age, after he had seen something of the world and had already composed so much, developed yet further and to immense greatness. What a man; beside him we are just wretches.'

Of the Largo of Symphony no. 88 Brahms famously remarked 'I want my Tenth Symphony to be like this'; presumably this was inspired by a much slower performance of the movement than any Haydn would have heard; perhaps, too, the eloquent cello line of that movement is reflected in the opening of the slow movement of Brahms's Second Symphony. In certain aspects of his structuring of sonata form the later composer was undoubtedly encouraged by Haydn's example: contrapuntal intensification in development sections (as in the first movement of the Second Symphony); pedals in development sections (first movements of the violin sonatas in A and D minor, and in the Clarinet Quintet); inclusion of development within the recapitulation (the second movement of the Fourth Symphony); combination of fugue and sonata form (finales of the first cello sonata and the first string quintet); and canons as second subjects (the first and last movement of the Clarinet Trio, and the first movement of the Clarinet Sonata no. 2). Furthermore, the opening of the Clarinet Quintet has just that ambivalence between D major and the tonic B minor that Haydn had featured in two quartets, op. 33 no. 1 and op. 64 no. 2.

Brahms owned a clavichord by the Viennese maker Ferdinand Hofmann that is said to have been used by Haydn during the last years of his life and is now in the Haydn Museum in Vienna. Brahms's extensive library, including the autograph scores of op. 20, was bequeathed to the Gesellschaft der Musikfreunde in Vienna. RP

O. Biba, 'Haydn-Abschriften von Johannes Brahms', *HS* 4/2 (1978), 119–22.

Breitkopf & Härtel. German music-publishing firm based in Leipzig and Haydn's most important publisher in the last period of his life; it played a major part in the composer's posthumous reputation.

Under the guidance of Bernhard Christoph Breitkopf (1695–1777) and his son Johann Gottlob Immanuel Breitkopf (1719–94) the firm had established itself as the most important music-publishing business in Germany in the 18th century. Like many publishers of the time it also acted as a music shop, selling manuscript copies and music printed by other firms. The BREITKOPF CATALOGUE reveals the extent of this part of the business in the second half of the century, including a substantial quantity of music by Haydn. The firm first wrote to the composer in 1789, enquiring whether he had some music that could be published. Subsequently, the two-movement keyboard sonata in C (Hob.XVI:48) was printed as part of a continuing serial publication of keyboard music and songs entitled *Musikalisches Pot-Pourri*; when Haydn gave his friend MARIA ANNA VON GENZINGER a copy he self-deprecatingly called it a 'Musical Vegetable Pot'. Haydn indicated that he was too busy to compose any further music specifically for Breitkopf.

Over the next six years Breitkopf wrote several letters requesting music from Haydn, but the composer's busy lifestyle in London and Vienna prevented him from replying. From 1796 onwards, however, the firm quickly assumed the role of Haydn's principal publisher, undoubtedly the result of the efforts and ambition of Gottfried Christoph Härtel (1763–1827) who purchased the firm in that year; from now on it was known as Breitkopf & Härtel. At first the revitalized firm dealt directly with Haydn, but from 1799 they used GEORG AUGUST GRIESINGER as an intermediary, which meant that the composer was relieved of a large amount of increasingly wearisome business correspondence. Much of the correspondence between Haydn and the firm, and between Griesinger and the firm, was destroyed in an air raid on Leipzig in December 1943; luckily, over the years various authors had made copies of portions of the material and these afford a full, if occasionally annoyingly incomplete, picture of the relationship.

There were several aspects to the relationship and all were marked by a new spirit of entrepreneurship that not only reflected Haydn's existing popularity but enhanced it. The firm was no longer particularly interested in publishing single small items of instrumental music but preferred large-scale ventures. Between 1799 and 1806, it issued 12 volumes of keyboard music, keyboard trios, and songs, under the general title of *Oeuvres Complettes de Joseph Haydn*, each volume printed with an attractive engraving on the title page. In Haydn's lifetime sacred music for the Catholic liturgy was hardly ever published, for the obvious reason that there was no market for it in Protestant Europe, but from 1802 onwards Breitkopf & Härtel published five of the six late masses, together with the earlier *Missa Cellensis* (*Missa Sanctae Caeciliae*), part of the process that encouraged performances in concert halls as well as churches. Haydn had published *The Creation* at his own expense in 1800, though Breitkopf & Härtel had helped in the process of gathering subscribers. Haydn's increasing faith in the firm is shown by his decision, floated as early as 1800, to entrust the publication of *The Seasons* to Breitkopf & Härtel. It appeared in 1802; the following year the firm took over the publication of *The Creation* too. The firm also published the second Te Deum, the vocal version of *The Seven Last Words*, the Stabat mater, the chorus 'The Storm', and extracts from Haydn's last, unperformed opera, *L'anima del filosofo*.

In 1798 Breitkopf & Härtel founded a new music journal, the *Allgemeine musikalische Zeitung*. While it was not, by any means, the first music journal in Germany, it can fairly be said to have laid the foundations of 19th-century German musical criticism. There were regular reports of musical events in Vienna, including performances of Haydn's music, and lengthy evaluations of the most recent publications of the composer's music which paid due regard to his stature but, as in the review of *The Seasons* that appeared in May 1804, were not afraid to offer criticism. Griesinger's biography of Haydn first appeared in instalments in the journal in 1809, the year of the composer's death, before being published as a book the following year.

The firm continued to flourish in the 19th century, gaining the status of the most important music publisher in the world. More editions of Haydn's music were added to its stock, especially symphonies. It also expanded its publication of books on music and CARL FRIEDRICH POHL's biography of Haydn was entrusted to the firm. Only in one aspect of its distinguished history did the firm fail the composer. During the 19th and early 20th centuries Breitkopf & Härtel published the first collected editions of the music of many composers, including Bach, Beethoven, Mozart, Schubert, Schumann, and Mendelssohn, monumental enterprises that were to underpin the reputation of these composers until after the Second World War, when new collected editions were inaugurated. A Haydn collected edition was not begun until 1907. Between that date and 1933 only ten volumes were produced before the enterprise was abandoned: four volumes of symphonies (nos. 1–49), three volumes of keyboard sonatas, a volume of songs, *The Creation*, and *The Seasons*. The performing parts based on these editions and earlier ones continued to feature in orchestral and choral performances of Haydn's music for much of the remainder of the 20th century and have been supplanted by newer editions only in the last 20 years or so. Alas, Breitkopf & Härtel has not contributed to this most recent phase of making Haydn's music better known and better understood.

O. Biba (ed.), *'Eben komme ich von Haydn . . .' Georg August Griesingers Korrespondenz mit Joseph Haydns Verleger Breitkopf & Härtel 1799–1819* (Zurich, 1987).
R. Elvers, 'Breitkopf & Härtels Verlagsarchiv', *Fontes Artis Musicae*, 17 (1970), 24–8.
H. von Hase, *Joseph Haydn und Breitkopf & Härtel. Ein Rückblick bei der Veranstaltung der ersten vollständigen Gesamtausgabe seiner Werke* (Leipzig, 1909).
HCRL/3, 4, and 5.

Breitkopf Catalogue. Name conveniently applied to the 22 thematic catalogues that were issued separately by the printer and music seller Breitkopf between 1762 and 1787. Developing on the practice of issuing printed catalogues of books and music for the annual trade fairs in Leipzig, the centre of the German book trade, Breitkopf decided to issue specialized catalogues that included the musical incipit of each work. His purpose was to identify more accurately than titles could (particularly genre titles such as concerto and symphony) individual works and their composers, and he encouraged his readers to inform him of any errors. His desire to impose order and consistency on an increasingly international trade was a very modern outlook, as was the explicit aim of relating works to their true authors; his means, the thematic catalogue, was to become fundamental to musical bibliography.

Between 1762 and 1766 Breitkopf issued six catalogues of music (described as Parts), divided according to instrumentation: music for orchestra, music for strings, music for wind instruments, music for keyboard and harp, music for mixed ensembles, and vocal music. Thereafter mainly annual supplements appeared advertising the full range of music; the last supplement, the 16th, covered the years 1785–7. At first most of the music represented was in the form of manuscript copies; gradually music publications, especially from the main centres of Paris and Amsterdam, came to dominate. During the quarter of the century that the catalogues appeared nearly 15,000 incipits representing over 1,000 composers were included. For modern music historians the Breitkopf Catalogue is one of the fundamental resources of the period, providing a clear picture of changing musical fashion, information on patterns of dissemination, and often unique material on authorship and dating.

Haydn's music is first included in Part IV (1763), where two organ concertos (Hob.XVIII:1 and 5) and a keyboard sonata (Hob.XVI:5) are listed. His symphonies and quartets, in particular, were soon regular features in the catalogues with string trios, keyboard sonatas, keyboard trios, and concertos less frequently encountered. Only three vocal compositions are included: the cantata 'Ah come il core' (Supplement XVI, 1785–7), the insertion aria 'Dice benissimo' (Supplement XV, 1782–4), and a score of the Stabat mater (Supplement XIV, 1781). For a few works, such as Symphonies nos. 33 and 34, the orchestral Scherzandos, and the keyboard duet *Il Maestro e Scolare*, their appearance in the Breitkopf Catalogue represents the earliest dated reference, crucially influencing the likely date of composition proposed by modern scholarship.

Haydn was a particular victim of the problem that Breitkopf hoped to eradicate, spurious authorship. From the later 1760s onwards, as his reputation spread beyond Vienna and its environs, the number of inauthentic works ascribed to Haydn in the Breitkopf Catalogue increases noticeably, mainly due to the unscrupulous practices of some publishers in Paris and Amsterdam. The pages of the Breitkopf Catalogue also help with the reverse process, indicating the true composers of works falsely attributed elsewhere to Haydn.

B. S. Brook (ed.), *The Breitkopf Thematic Catalogue. The Six Parts and Sixteen Supplements 1762–1787*, facs. edn (New York, 1966).
P. Bryan, *Johann Wanhal, Viennese Symphonist: His Life and his Musical Environment* (Stuyvesant, NY, 1997).
R. Dearing, 'Annotations to the Breitkopf Thematic Catalogue and Supplements', *HYB* 9 (1975), 256–302.

Bremner, Robert (b. *c.*1713; d. 12 May 1789). Publisher and music seller in Edinburgh and London. Bremner first established himself in Edinburgh in 1754; in 1762 expansion of his business led him to move to London while retaining a branch in Edinburgh. Much of Bremner's success probably derived from his early association with the Edinburgh Musical Society. In London he was called upon with some frequency to act as agent and music supplier for the society, and many of his own publications were angled to its requirements. Bremner made regular trips to Europe to collect new music for both resale and publication, contributing significantly to the introduction of new genres and composers to Britain.

Bremner published a number of Haydn's instrumental works, all of which were copies of previously published works, especially by the firm of HUMMEL. He was responsible for introducing Haydn's music to the British public in 1765 when he sold imported copies of a Hummel edition of six quartets (Hob.II:6, III:1–4 and 6). In the following decade Bremner issued further quartets, as well as string trios and keyboard trios by the composer. Some of these works, like the two symphonies included in his series, *The Periodical Overture*, were spurious. JMB

J. M. Burchell, *Polite or Commercial Concerts? Concert Management and Orchestral Repertoire in Edinburgh, Bath, Oxford, Manchester, and Newcastle, 1730–1799* (London, 1996).

D. W. Jones, 'Haydn's Music in London in the Period 1760–1790', *HYB* 14 (1983), 144–72.

Brenet, Michel (b. 12 April 1858; d. 4 Nov. 1918). Pseudonym of Marie Bobillier, French writer on music born in Lunéville and who died in Paris. She wrote extensively on music from the Middle Ages to the 19th century. Her books on the 18th century include biographies of Grétry (1884) and Handel (1912), and a notable study of concert life, *Les Concerts en France sous l'Ancien Régime* (1900). For the centenary of Haydn's death in 1909 she produced the first life-and-works study in the French language of the composer. Drawing extensively on existing scholarship in the German language, especially the two completed volumes of POHL's biography, it is less fanciful than most writing of the time on the composer. An English translation appeared in 1926 with an appreciative preface by W. H. HADOW.

Burney, Charles (b. 7 April 1726; d. 12 April 1814). English composer, teacher, renowned music historian, and critic; close friend of Haydn.

From the outset of his musical career, Burney's tastes were decidedly Italianate. His experience of German culture was inhibited by a lack of fluency in the language, and the preconception that German music tended to be laboured and over-elaborate when compared with the Italian vocal style. By the early 1780s, however, German instrumental composers had risen steadily in his estimation, particularly Haydn, on whom Burney bestowed laurels in the fourth and final volume of his *General History of Music*, published in 1789: 'I am now happily arrived at that part of my narrative where it is necessary to speak of HAYDN!' he enthused, 'the admirable and matchless HAYDN!' Burney was to idolize Haydn for the remainder of his professional life, drawing tirelessly on his literary talents and influential connections to promote the man and his music in England.

Burney probably first encountered Haydn's music in the early 1770s, when a small crop of Haydn publications—mainly the early quartets—became available in LONDON; by November 1771 he was including Haydn among those 'whose musical productions & performances have given me great delight' (letter to Ebeling, *The Letters of Dr Charles Burney*, vol. i: *1751–1784*, ed. Ribeiro, 102). Further opportunities presented themselves the following summer, when he toured Europe gathering material for the *General History*; while in Vienna Burney heard several symphonies by Haydn and, at a musical party given by the English ambassador, some quartets. His Viennese host offered to introduce him to GLUCK, HASSE, Haydn, WAGENSEIL, and other local musicians worthy of his attention, but Haydn, alas, was at Eszterháza. Hence in the travel journal Burney published in 1773 (*The Present State of Music in Germany, the Netherlands and United Provinces*) there are passing references to Haydn but no detailed assessment. Following his return to England Burney kept abreast of musical developments on the continent via a network of foreign correspondents. News of Haydn's activities and growing reputation came his way, but it was only when rumours of the composer's death began to circulate in 1778 that Burney began to make specific enquiries about him. He wrote to Sir Robert Murray Keith, the British ambassador in Vienna, who scotched the rumours and provided information on Haydn's early life. Details of Haydn's output were gleaned by Burney from German music catalogues dating back to 1763, and from his friend LATROBE, who had lived in Germany until 1784. Opportunities to hear performances of Haydn's orchestral music also multiplied as concert life flourished in London during the 1780s. All this fed into Burney's discussion of Haydn in the *General History*, where he chose in particular to praise the sublimity and expressiveness of Haydn's adagio movements, especially *The Seven Last Words*, and the controversial blending of the comic and serious in his instrumental works.

Dr Burney's grand endorsement of Haydn in his influential history did much to fuel escalating public interest in the composer during the years leading up to his first London visit. Clearly this was Burney's intention. He had already been involved in negotiations to entice Haydn to London, by instigating moves to engage him as opera composer to the King's Theatre for the 1783–4 season; as preparation, he had even encouraged the theatre's *primo uomo* PACCHIEROTTI to perform Haydn's cantata *Ah come il core mi palpita*, a copy of which Burney had received from Vienna. These plans were ultimately thwarted by operatic politics, but Burney remained hopeful, sending Haydn this message via Keith in November 1784: 'if the universal admiration & performance of his works w[oul]d be a temptation to visit us, I can as[s]ure him of that claim to his favour' (*Letters*, ed. Ribeiro, 448). True to his word, Burney made violin and piano arrangements of Haydn sonatas for LONG-

MAN & BRODERIP (Hob.XVI:21–26; 27–32; 35–39, 20) and keyboard arrangements of several Haydn symphonies in 1783–4, recommending these and other Haydn publications to his friends and pupils. Burney claimed to have corresponded with Haydn himself for many years before the composer's English sojourn, although these letters appear not to have survived.

Burney's joy was complete when SALOMON brought Haydn to visit him shortly after his arrival in London: 'I have had the great Haydn here, & think him as *good* a creature as *great a Musician,*' he gushed in a letter to Arthur Young on 16 February 1791 (Lonsdale, *Dr Charles Burney*, 353). He penned a welcoming eulogy, and presented it to Haydn in a German translation by Latrobe, along with his *General History*, handsomely bound. Encouraged by Haydn's gratitude, Burney expanded and published the poem anonymously, intending thereby to 'inform some of our musical folks how great a Man we have at present the good fortune to possess' (letter to Latrobe, 3 March 1791).

For his benefit concert scheduled for 7 April, Haydn asked Burney to translate a chorus from *Il ritorno di Tobia*; Burney gladly agreed, although no chorus was given when the concert eventually took place on 16 May. Haydn became a regular visitor to the Burney household at Chelsea College; at their musical party on 23 April 1791, the composer played second violin in some of his own quartets, and first violin in *The Seven Last Words*, to Burney's delight. Soon Burney was fielding requests for introductions to the great man from friends and associates, including WILLIAM CROTCH and Thomas Twining. In July he engineered a further opportunity for public recognition of Haydn's stature, for it was at Burney's suggestion that Haydn received the honorary degree of Doctor of Music from Oxford University; naturally he accompanied the composer to OXFORD for the ceremony.

Burney's devotion to Haydn continued after the composer's return to Austria. In December 1798, on receiving a copy of 'Gott erhalte Franz den Kaiser', Burney asked Latrobe for a translation of the words which he versified to fit the melody; the resulting *Hymn to the Austrian Emperor* was published by Broderip & Wilkinson around 1799. At some point Haydn also sent him copies of *Armida* and two movements from the 'Grosse Orgelsolomesse' (MISSA IN HONOREM BVM); Burney allowed Latrobe to copy the latter in 1805 and they, in turn, became a source for NOVELLO's edition of the work.

At Haydn's invitation Burney acted as his agent in London for the published edition of *The Creation*, collecting 87 subscribers for which the composer thanked him heartily, if somewhat belatedly in Burney's view. His enthusiasm for this new work is apparent in notes he made after SALOMON's performance on 21 April 1800 (later submitted as an essay to *L'Institut de France* in 1811), and from his staunch defence of it against criticism from London's Handelians, for whom this 'modern' oratorio trespassed on hallowed ground.

As such contretemps suggest, Burney considered it his duty as a historian and critic to guide the public towards a true appreciation of Haydn's worth. Audiences acknowledged this authority, principally because as an eminent man of letters Burney had risen to a social status way above that traditionally allotted to a mere musician: as Burney recalled, his friends Mr and Mrs Crewe 'wished me to tell them how to hear Haydn's music, which the public in general want to be told' (letter to Latrobe, [1800]). It was the same profound sense of historical responsibility that inspired him to chronicle Haydn's London visits meticulously; indeed, had his daughter Fanny not edited his manuscript memoirs so drastically, an almost daily account of Haydn's activities in England would be available.

Burney seems to have been the first in England to link Haydn with Mozart and Beethoven, recognizing the great triumvirate of the Viennese school only a year after hearing his first Beethoven symphony at the age of 77. Among the articles on music he wrote for Abraham Rees's *Cyclopædia; or Universal Dictionary of Arts, Science, and Literature* (London, 1819)—his final contribution to musical scholarship—is an entry on the 'Symphony' drafted around 1804. Here he prophesied that Beethoven 'will be a great man among musicians of the present century, as Haydn and Mozart were of the latter end of the last'. For Burney, however, the symphonies of Haydn still reigned supreme, seeming 'to include every perfection that can render instrumental music interesting and sublime; invention, science, knowledge of instruments, majesty, fire, grace, and pathos by turns, with new modulation and new harmonies, without crudity or affectation'. REC

C. Burney, *A General History of Music*, ed. F. Mercer, 2 vols (New York, 1935).

C. Burney, *The Letters of Dr Charles Burney*, vol. i: *1751–1784*, ed. A. Ribeiro (Oxford, 1991).

K. Grant, *Dr Burney as Critic and Historian of Music* (Ann Arbor, 1983).

HCRL/3–5.

R. Lonsdale, *Dr Charles Burney: A Literary Biography* (Oxford, 1965).

Busby, Thomas (b. Dec. 1755; d. 28 May 1838). English author on music and a composer. His writings include a number of theoretical and reference books on music. In his *A General History of*

Music, from the Earliest Times to the Present Day, published in London in 1819, he hoped to establish himself as a music historian in the tradition of Burney and Hawkins. In the event the work was much criticized for being too dependent on the history of these two authors, though no one could deny that facts and opinion are expressed with a rare abandon. Haydn and Mozart share a chapter and the material on the former obviously draws too on the biographies of GRIESINGER and DIES. Busby's view that Haydn was a much more successful composer of instrumental music than of vocal music was part of a developing critical stance in Britain in the early 19th century. 'Of the present highly improved state of instrumental composition', Busby writes, 'he may indeed, justly be denominated the father . . .', On the other hand vitriol was heaped on *The Creation;* 'A series of attempted imitations of many things inimitable by music, the sudden creation of light happily expressed by an unexpected burst of sound, airs not abundantly beautiful or original, smothered with ingenious accompaniments, and choruses in which the composer toils under his incumbent weight, labours in fugue, copies with a faint pencil the clear lustre of a glorious prototype [Handel], and supplies the absence of true taste and dignity, with the congregated powers of a complicated band . . . In his operas and cantatas, his failure was only partial; in his oratorios, almost total.'

Busby himself had been a prolific composer of vocal music, including many anthems and odes. In about 1789 he had composed an oratorio called *The Creation*, which remained unperformed. The fragments of the work that survive do not suggest a connection with the text of Haydn's work, acquired in London a few years later, but it cannot be ruled out.

C

'Cäcilienmesse'. *See* MISSA CELLENSIS IN HONOREM BVM.

canon. The canon, which involves the total imitation of one part in a continuing polyphonic texture by one or more further parts, is one of the oldest polyphonic forms, dating back to the early 13th century. By Haydn's time canon had come to acquire a wide variety of related associations. Under the name *fuga* it was included in the didactic scheme of counterpoint teaching where canon (as the strictest form of imitation) was traditionally taught after freer forms of imitation, including fugue (in its present-day sense), a didactic scheme found in Fux's *Gradus ad Parnassum* (1725). Canons were often inscribed in commonplace books as a graceful musical tribute by a composer to the owner. Some of Haydn's canons were used for this purpose and Albrechtsberger's four-part canon, 'Solatium miseris', was dedicated to Haydn. Canons in this didactic tradition were revered as examples of the learning acquired by the composers, and were accordingly used for displays of contrapuntal virtuosity involving inversion, retrograde motion, and the simultaneous presentation of several canons. Frequently they were written in enigmatic notation, with the entries of imitating parts indicated by cryptic instructions.

Canons were also extensively used as material for social music-making. Set to texts praising music, drinking, or more basic sensual pleasures, they were a traditional and effective method of recreation in musical company. Unlike canons in the learned tradition of didactic counterpoint, social canons were generally in the form of rounds (perpetual canons at the unison) and were normally supplied with texts, sometimes in several verses (one round per verse).

Both the academic and social canon found their way into art music in the 18th century, though the only example of the latter type that is at all well known is the canon in Act 2 of Mozart's *Così fan tutte* ('E nel tuo, nel mio bicchiero'), where it is used as an inset part of the unfolding drama rather than an integral part of the musical fabric.

As part of the apparatus of STILE ANTICO counterpoint, canon not infrequently appears in works in a minor key, associated by 18th-century musicians with the archaic or learned style in general; as such it makes a number of appearances in Haydn's music. Three symphonies by Haydn, nos. 3, 23, and 44, have minuets constructed as octave canons. The first two are fairly unpretentious—in the major key and on a small scale—but the minuet of symphony no. 44 is in E minor and is a movement of great power and eloquence. The quartet in D minor, op. 76 no. 2, is another work indebted to the 'learned' style and abounds with closely packed contrapuntal ingenuity, including a canonic minuet starkly scored in octaves for two pairs of instruments (violin 1 and 2 versus viola and cello); the gypsy music of the trio section in the major key provides an ironic contrast. Other examples of canonic minuets are found in the second movement of the keyboard sonata in E♭ (Hob.XVI:25) and the baryton trio in A (Hob. XI:94).

Two canons in the six late masses reflect the different traditions of the learned and the convivial. The opening section of the Credo of the 'Nelson' mass (MISSA IN ANGUSTIIS) is a canon at the fifth, its 'learned' severity emphasizing the certainties of the text. For the 'Et incarnatus est' portion of the Credo of the *Missa Sancti Bernardi* Haydn reused an existing social canon, 'Gott im Herzen', its simple melodic style and carefully placed dissonances invoking the beauty of the Virgin Birth.

Little is known of the origin of Haydn's output of vocal canons, which form his contribution to the tradition of recreational canon for singing in convivial company. They include a set of canons on the ten commandments (*Die Heiligen Zehn Gebote*, Hob.XXVIIa:1–10) which were probably composed during the period 1791–5 during one or other of Haydn's two visits to England. A version of the first canon with an English text ('Thy voice, O Harmony') was presented to Oxford University as a thank-offering for the award of the title of Doctor of Music, while the German version was entered in a commonplace book owned by J. C. Falck on 27 June 1792, and a year later in a commonplace book owned by Babette von Ployer. According to one early writer the set was composed for Hans Moritz, count of Brühl-Martinskirchen and the Saxon ambassador in London, during the composer's second visit to the city, but in view of the Oxford version this cannot be true of the set as a whole. The set was published by Breitkopf & Härtel in 1810, rapidly followed by a second edition with a new text; an English version was published by Clementi in London in 1812. The canon on the first commandment ('Du sollst an einen Gott glauben') is an example of mirror-writing, in that it can be read upside down, by reversing the page and reading from the end; the two versions can be combined to form a six-part canon by retrograde motion, though the solution involves the grammatical solecism of consecutive octaves. Short codas are added to the sixth and tenth commandments ('Du sollst nicht Unkeuschheit treiben' and 'Du sollst nicht begehren deines Nächsten Gut').

Forty-six further canons (Hob.XXVIIb:1-46), composed as single items, also probably date from the 1790s. From 1799 (at the latest) Haydn displayed the autograph manuscripts of 40 of them on the walls of his house in Gumpendorf, where they attracted the attention of several visitors. An edition of 42 canons published by Breitkopf & Härtel in 1809 altered all but nine of the original texts, an odd decision since they are mild and inoffensive in comparison with the bawdy texts that the firm had felt obliged to replace in some canons by Mozart.

One of the canons has a text in Italian ('Tre cose'), one in Latin ('Vixi'), and one in English ('Turk was a faithful dog'). The German texts that Haydn set in the remaining canons include some homely proverbs, but others are by distinguished poets, Bürger, Hagedorn, Lessing, and Haydn's favourite, GELLERT. The number of vocal parts ranges from two to eight, with the majority being in three or four. Most are constructed as rounds, but there are some exceptions. 'Das Reitpferd' and 'Das größte Gut' are three-part canons, with the two answering parts entering simultaneously in parallel thirds. 'Das böse Weib' (second version), 'Die Liebe der Feinde', and 'Die Tulipane' are perpetual canons at the fifth, while 'Der Fuchs und der Adler' is a three-part canon at the upper fifth and lower seventh.

Hob.XXVIIb:47 is a seven-part canon in G for which no authentic text has survived. DLH

cantilena pro adventu. Generic title used by Haydn in the ENTWURF-KATALOG for ADVENT ARIA.

canzonetta. Generic title used by Haydn for 12 of his songs in English (Hob.XXVIa:25-36). *See* SONG.

capriccio. A term variously associated with learned contrapuntal pieces of the 17th century and, in 18th-century violin music, with brilliant solo passages often ending with a cadenza. A more general 18th-century usage associates the capriccio with unconventional or idiosyncratic pieces. It is, according to Koch, 'distinguished from ordinary pieces by its freer form, its less fixed character, and a looser connection of its ideas' (Koch, *Musikalisches Lexikon* (Frankfurt, 1802)). In Haydn's music the designation capriccio, used interchangeably with the term fantasia, is associated with movements with a particularly wide harmonic vocabulary, abrupt changes of mood, often cast in a hybrid form (usually owing something to ritornello structures) and in which variation plays an important part. The Capriccio in G (Hob.XVII:1, 1765) and the slow movement of the quartet op. 20 no. 2 (1772), are, according to A. Peter Brown, influenced by the chapter on the 'free fantasia' in C. P. E. Bach's treatise, *Versuch über die wahre Art das Clavier zu spielen*. The Capriccio in Symphony no. 86 (1786) is more regular in structure, but the frequent surprises and upsetting of formal expectation in the movement are very much part of the capriccio tradition. BH

A. P. Brown, *Joseph Haydn's Keyboard Music: Sources and Style* (Bloomington, Ind., 1986).

Capriccio: 'Acht Sauschneider müssen sein' (Hob.XVII:1). A keyboard piece composed in 1765, the authentic title referring to a comical Austrian folksong or, more likely, a song from popular theatre on which the work is based: 'Eight are needed to castrate a boar, two in the front and two behind, two to cut and two to bind.' The work is an early manifestation of a significant change of style in Haydn's keyboard works written in the second half of the 1760s. The 'capricious' nature of the work is evident in a novel structure which fuses ritornello and variation procedures. The theme recurs, in various keys and in full or in shortened form, throughout the work, in the manner of a ritornello, and separated by modulatory episodes. In the process it is elaborated countrapuntally, transferred to the bass, and acquires new accompaniment figurations which, like many strophic sets of variations, have an increasingly active surface rhythm. The notation of a number of left-hand chords in this and two other works (Hob. XVI:47 and Hob.XVII:2) suggests that Haydn may have possessed a harpsichord with a short-octave tuning at this time. BH

A. P. Brown, *Joseph Haydn's Keyboard Music: Sources and Style* (Bloomington, Ind., 1986).

L. Somfai, *The Keyboard Sonatas of Joseph Haydn: Instruments and Performance Practice, Genres and Styles* (Chicago, 1995).

Carpani, Giuseppe (b. 28 Jan. 1752; d. 21/22 Jan. 1825). Italian writer and translator who wrote one of the first biographies of Haydn. Born in the Lombardy region and educated in Milan by the Jesuits, he moved to Vienna in 1796 where he soon established himself as a playwright, poet, librettist, and a translator of literary works and operas from French and German. His poem 'In questa tomba oscura' was set by over 60 composers in the 19th century, including Beethoven. At the instigation of the Empress MARIE THERESE he provided an Italian translation of *The Creation*. When this was performed at the famous concert at the university in March 1808 to celebrate Haydn's 76th birthday, Carpani prepared a dedicatory sonnet for the composer. He also provided the official Italian translation of 'Gott erhalte Franz den Kaiser'.

Carpani's biography of the composer appeared in 1812 and took the form of a series of letters dated from April 1808 to March 1811. He had known Haydn from the later 1790s onwards and claimed that his book also profited from conversations with JOHANN ELßLER, FRIBERTH, GRIESINGER, MARTINES, PICHL, VAN SWIETEN, and others; he seems too to have taken information from the published biographies of Griesinger and DIES. The result is a garrulous account of the composer's life with large digressions on the perceived significance of his music. Since it is much less factually accurate than Griesinger and Dies (especially the former) it has never had the same parity of esteem. Carpani himself had disarmed potential criticism of this kind writing that 'factual information . . . forms the lesser part of my work, which is aimed more at living art than at a dead artist'. The principal fascination of the book is, indeed, the discursive commentary on Haydn's church music and operas, which not only reveals the innate biases of a cultured Italian but begin to chime with the wider perception in the early decades of the 19th century of the relative value of the composer's instrumental and vocal music. While his prose style is certainly a loquacious one he is also capable of formulating a pithy judgement, as in the comment 'Haydn in teatro non è più Haydn' ('Haydn in the theatre is no more Haydn').

The many blatantly incorrect details and the fanciful anecdotes mingle with more plausible information, not found elsewhere. The story that Haydn's rustic complexion caused Prince Paul Anton Esterházy to call him a moor may well be true. Carpani commented on Haydn's early compositions as follows: 'His first productions were some sonatinas for harpsichord, which he sold for a pittance, some minuets, allemandes and waltz tunes for masked balls.' The first part of the sentence is not contentious (except that Haydn would not have used the word sonatina) but the second part of the sentence would have been dismissed as fiction until comparatively recently; in 1993, however, documentary evidence was uncovered that Haydn played the violin at masked balls in the imperial court in the 1750s, making Carpani's statement that he composed dances at this time a wholly believable one.

Carpani's book enjoyed considerable success in the 19th century. Stendhal (pseudonym of Henri Beyle) freely copied large quantities of it in his *Lettres écrites de Vienne en Autriche, sur le célèbre compositeur J. Haydn* (Paris, 1814), which unleashed accusations of plagiarism that went on for several years.

G. Carpani, *Le Haydine, ovvero lettere su la vita e le opere del celebre maestro Giuseppe Haydn* (Milan, 1812); 2nd edn (Padua, 1823), facs. edn (Bologna, 1969).

V. Gotwals, 'The Earliest Biographies of Haydn', *Musical Quarterly*, 45 (1959), 439-59.

H. C. Jacobs, *Stendhal und die Musik* (Frankfurt, 1983).

HCRL/1 and 5.

cassation. Term widely used in Austria and southern Germany in the middle of the 18th century for all kinds of instrumental music, particularly mixed ensembles of strings and wind. It did not normally suggest orchestral music or music with a keyboard. When the *Entwurf-Katalog* was first drawn up *c.*1765 Haydn's copyist Joseph Elßler entered six early quartets with the title 'cassatio' which Haydn changed to the more common and even more catch-all term 'divertimento'. This particular evidence, coupled with the fact that Haydn is never known to have used the title cassation for a work, suggests that he preferred the word divertimento. Nevertheless over a dozen instrumental works from the 1750s and early 1760s circulated under this title and modern editions prepared from these sources will often use it.

Up to nine instruments are required in many of the cassations and unlike Haydn's music for the Esterházy court he often requires two violas, who are given the occasional solo role. Rhythmic energy and instrumental colour rather than any incipient sense of intellectual fascination with form and with thematic and harmonic manipulation characterize the works. As in most of the early quartets a five-movement structure of fast, slow, minuet, slow, and fast is often encountered (e.g. Hob.II:8, 9, 20, 21, 22, D22, G1) though there are examples in four movements (Hob.II:1, 11) and in nine movements (Hob.II:17).

Some of the works were probably first written to be performed outdoors in Vienna in the 1750s when Haydn is known to have played serenades, circumstances that are reflected in the subtitle 'Der Geburtstag' ('The birthday') that was acquired by one work (Hob.II:11). Reminiscing about these early years, Haydn told GRIESINGER that he particularly remembered composing a quintet in 1753 for these purposes. This may be the six-movement work in G major for two violins, two violas, and cello (or double bass) (Hob.II:2); if so, then it is the earliest surviving instrumental work by Haydn. He may have remembered it too for its scoring, a string quintet, a medium that he never again tackled.

The cassations that have horn parts often treat the instrument in the virtuoso manner familiar from some of the later Esterházy symphonies. In particular a cassation in D (Hob.II:D22) for four horns, violin, viola, and bass is a five-movement work whose thematic writing, as well as brazen sonority, recalls Symphonies nos. 31 and 72. It may have been written for the same Esterházy players.

catalogues

1. Catalogues compiled by, or for, Haydn.
2. Modern catalogues.

1. Catalogues compiled by, or for, Haydn. During his lifetime Haydn prepared or caused to be prepared two thematic catalogues of his music that remain a fundamental guide to the authenticity and chronology of his music, though internal inconsistencies and apparent errors and omissions mean that they are not as infallible as might be assumed. The ENTWURF-KATALOG (*EK*) was compiled *c.*1765 and regularly supplemented up to c.1777; thereafter new, additional entries were more haphazardly made. In 1804–5, after Haydn had retired from composition, JOHANN ELßLER prepared a comprehensive catalogue usually referred to as the HAYDN-VERZEICHNIS (*HV*), sometimes as the *Elßler-Verzeichnis*. In addition to these two principal catalogues there are several non-thematic catalogues of Haydn's music or of his musical library, ranging from short summary lists to well-annotated, bibliographically consistent catalogues. Taken as a whole these thematic and verbal catalogues are the product of a proud composer who liked orderliness and was fascinated by data, and these attributes are not diminished by the limitations of any particular one of them. No other major composer has left so many lists or catalogues of his music.

(i) *Catalogue of music composed in and for England.* In the summer of 1795, towards the end of the second visit to London, Haydn compiled a summary list of works he had written during the course of the previous four and a half years, mainly for London, adding for convenience two works written in Vienna in 1793 and intended for that milieu, the F minor variations for piano and 24 dances (Hob.IX:11 and 12). Haydn entered the list in English in the Fourth London Notebook and it was reproduced in German in GRIESINGER's biography and in the original language in DIES's biography; this portion of the original notebook is now lost. As well as summary titles Haydn indicated the number of sheets of manuscript paper utilized for each work, though his figures do not always tally with extant autographs; he added them up to provide a self-satisfyingly grand total of 768 sheets. Headed by the opera *L'anima del filosofo*, the list is a comprehensive one of all the music for London, though some of the summary details do not permit accurate identification of individual works. More tantalizing are indications of works that have not survived: 'Aria for Davide—12 sheets', evidently a major concert aria for the tenor GIACOMO DAVIDE who was to have sung the role of Orfeo in Haydn's opera; 'Maccone for Gallini—6 sheets', probably a catch or glee, or a cycle of such works, written for SIR JOHN GALLINI; 'Aria for Miss Poole—5 sheets'; and an arrangement of the British national anthem, '1 God save the King—2 sheets'.

(ii) *Haydn's chronological list of symphonies prepared for Breitkopf & Härtel.* The ambitious firm of BREITKOPF & HÄRTEL planned to publish a complete edition of Haydn's symphonies with the co-operation of the composer, a project that never came to fruition. To this end, in the winter of 1801–2 the firm sent a list of symphonies it had compiled from various sources, asking Haydn to correct and supplement it as necessary. Haydn duly replied, reducing Breitkopf's list of 123 symphonies down to 108. The Breitkopf list has not survived and Haydn's reply exists only as a copy made by POHL. Careful scrutiny of Haydn's reply reveals that four symphonies were listed twice and three works were inauthentic (by Michael Haydn, Hofmann, and Vanhal). Seven overtures were also included. Haydn himself divided the works into four chronological groups, each occupying a ten-year period: 1757–67, 1767–77, 1777–87, 1787–97. Although some symphonies are listed in the incorrect group and 1797 is the product of mathematical symmetry (Haydn's last symphony was written in 1795), the starting date of 1757 is significant, providing useful corroborative evidence that Haydn's first symphony dates from that time and that he possibly entered the service of Count Morzin in that year, rather than in 1759 as is suggested by other evidence.

(iii) *Catalogue of Haydn's libretto collection.* Between *c.*1799 and *c.*1804. Haydn prepared a catalogue of over 200 printed librettos that he owned. First he listed opera librettos and the wordbooks of oratorios for which he had composed the music, and then, in an alphabetical sequence of titles, the librettos of works by other composers, mainly Italian operas but also oratorios and German operas. Some of this material reflected the repertoire at Eszterháza between 1766 and 1790, but the bulk of it consists of works that were never performed at the Esterházy court, such as Mozart's *Mitridate rè di Ponto* and Salieri's *L'amore innocente.* Indicative of Haydn's enthusiasm for the music of

Handel, and of the growing interest in that composer in general in Austria in the last decades of the 18th century, are the four German-language librettos for *Acis and Galatea*, *Alexander's Feast*, *Hercules*, and *Judas Maccabaeus*.

(iv) *Catalogue of Haydn's music library.* This lengthy and orderly catalogue was prepared by JOHANN ELßLER in *c.*1804–5, possibly slightly later. Its content does not suggest a library accumulated over 40 years, but one that was established after Haydn settled in Vienna in 1795. It would seem that autographs and manuscript copies shared the same sequence of identifying numbers and were placed together on Haydn's shelves, but in this catalogue they are separated. Consequently the catalogue has five sections: printed music by Haydn (95 items), printed music by various authors (160 items), manuscript copies of music by Haydn and others (numerical sequence from 1 to 237 shared with final section), books on music (33 items), and autograph manuscripts (shared numbering sequence with manuscript copies, and supplemented by 40 canons).

The printed music by Haydn in the library contains items published mainly from *c.*1790 onwards with major works from earlier in his career, such as the op. 33 quartets and the 'Paris' symphonies, being conspicuous by their absence. Haydn must surely have at one time owned many more items of printed music; they may have remained at Eisenstadt at the palace. Many items of printed music were acquired in London, and several were of works dedicated to Haydn by former pupils (including Beethoven's piano sonatas, op. 2). The Artaria edition of Mozart's six quartets dedicated to Haydn is to be found in the library, as are printed editions of the Requiem and of *Don Giovanni*. Haydn's curiosity about older music is suggested by the presence of two motets and the '48' by Bach, the 'Utrecht' Te Deum, arias from *Rinaldo* and the oratorio *Jeptha* by Handel, and six overtures by Telemann.

The manuscript copies listed in the library must, likewise, represent only a portion of such material once owned by Haydn. It does not provide a full representation of Haydn's own output and there is not a single manuscript copy of a work by Mozart, for instance. Again various older items catch the attention: an offertorium by his former teacher, REUTTER, 12 oratorios and three settings of lamentation texts by his predecessor, WERNER, Fux's celebrated *Missa canonica*, a harpsichord suite by Rameau, and Bach's B minor Mass.

The books on music contain a number of standard textbooks, including Mattheson's *Der vollkommene Capellmeister*, Marpurg's *Handbuch bey dem Generalbasse*, and Heinichen's *Der Generalbaß in der Composition*; surprisingly there is no copy of C. P. E. Bach's *Versuch über die wahre Art das Clavier zu spielen*. Of later books, a specially bound copy of Burney's *A General History of Music* is conspicuous.

Haydn's collection of his own autograph manuscripts is a small one containing, for instance, only three masses, two quartets, and 19 symphonies. Next to the symphony in F♯ minor and its date 1772, Elßler wrote 'NB: in which one after the other leaves'.

(v) *Summary catalogue for Carl Bertuch.* Carl Bertuch (1777–1815) was the son of a bookseller from Weimar who visited Haydn in 1805 and wrote his impressions in *Bemerkungen auf einer Reise aus Thüringen nach Wien im Winter 1805 bis 1806* (Weimar 1808–10). He was on friendly terms with Griesinger. Haydn prepared a summary list of his works, drawing on the recently completed *Haydn-Verzeichnis*. This hand-written original is lost but its contents were reproduced in Gerber's *Neues historisches-biographisches Lexikon der Tonkünstler*, vol. 1 (1812). Haydn's output is divided into five categories: church music, theatre music, oratorios, part-songs and songs, and instrumental music.

(vi) *Summary catalogue by Haydn.* Hastily written on three pages, this list of the number of works in individual genres was probably written after the autumn of October 1805, possibly for a curious visitor anxious to know more about the celebrated composer. Included in the list is a concerto for bassoon, a lost work for which there is only one further reference, the following catalogue.

(vii) *Summary catalogue by Elßler.* A more orderly and comprehensive catalogue of the number of works in individual genres, reaching a grand total of 925 works, a fair approximation of Haydn's total output. It was prepared sometime after 1805, almost certainly in response to a particular request.

2. Modern catalogues. Musical bibliography proceeded apace in the 19th century and attempts to quantify and order Haydn's output figure in this development, without any single work having the comprehensiveness or the long-term significance that Köchel's catalogue of Mozart's music was to have. ALOYS FUCHS prepared several thematic catalogues of Haydn's music, including two that aimed to cover the entire œuvre, but none of these was published. The first edition of *Grove's Dictionary of Music and Musicians* (London, 1879) contained a worklist of Haydn's music prepared by POHL, and the article on the composer in Fétis's *Biographie universelle des Musiciens* (Paris, 1883) also had a lengthy list of works. Among Pohl's papers in the Gesellschaft der Musikfreunde there is a draft of a thematic catalogue of Haydn's music, evidently prepared for eventual publication as much as an aid to his work on the biography of the composer. EUSEBIUS MANDYCZEWSKI prepared a similar draft catalogue. Also notable was the work of Robert Eitner (1832–1905) whose list of manuscript and printed sources for Haydn's music appeared in the fifth volume of his *Biographisch-bibliographisches Quellen-Lexikon der Musiker und Musikgelehrten der christlichen Zeitrechnung bis zur Mitte des XIX. Jahrhunderts* (Leipzig, 1901).

Draft catalogues, summary catalogues, and catalogues of portions of Haydn's output were prepared in abundance during the 20th century. The rest of this survey restricts itself to the four catalogues that have remained fundamental to Haydn scholarship.

(i) *Mandyczewski's list of symphonies.* Breitkopf & Härtel began its complete edition of Haydn's music in 1907 with the publication of a volume of symphonies that included a complete thematic catalogue in chronological order, prepared by Mandyczewski. This catalogue established the numbering sequence of 1 to 104, numbers that continue to be used and which are unlikely to be replaced. Later scholarship has modified the actual or suggested date of composition of many individual works—Symphony no. 72, which was composed at the same time as no. 31, is the most seriously misnumbered—but Mandyczewski's catalogue was a remarkable achievement. In particular, it managed to avoid including any spurious symphonies by Haydn, unlike the familiar 41 symphonies of Mozart which included three works not by the composer. He could have extended his definition of symphony to include overtures, especially the six overtures that Haydn had published by Artaria as symphonies (Hob.1a: 13, 6, 10, 15, 1, and 2) but his caution here as well as in his proposed dates of composition is understandable. Hoboken extended the sequence of symphony numbers to 108, but these additional four numbers are not commonly used. The standard total is 104 and Mandyczewski's enduring legacy.

(ii) *Hoboken's catalogue.* The three-volume catalogue in German by ANTHONY VAN HOBOKEN was the first to provide a comprehensive bibliographical account of Haydn's music and its individual numbers are the standard means of referring to individual works by the composer. Hoboken's volumes appeared in 1957, 1971, and 1978. The first volume lists the instrumental music, the second the vocal music, and the third is a collection of bibliographical material (including indexes) related to the first two volumes. Hoboken divided Haydn's output into the following 32 sections ('Gruppen'), labelled with a roman numeral and sometimes subdivided.

Contents of volume 1

I	Symphonies
Ia	Overtures
II	Divertimentos for four or more instruments
III	String quartets
IV	Divertimentos for three instruments
V	String trios
VI	Duos for various instruments
VII	Concertos for various instruments
	VIIa violin
	VIIb cello
	VIIc double bass
	VIId horn
	VIIe trumpet
	VIIf flute
	VIIg oboe
	VIIh *lira organizzata*
VIII	Marches
IX	Dances
X	Works for various instruments with baryton
XI	Trios for baryton, viola (or violin) and cello
XII	Duos for baryton, with or without bass
XIII	Concertos for baryton
XIV	Divertimentos for keyboard with three or more instruments
XV	Keyboard trios
	XVa Works for keyboard and one other instrument
XVI	Keyboard sonatas
XVII	Keyboard pieces
	XVIIa Works for keyboard duet and two keyboards
XVIII	Keyboard concertos
XIX	Pieces for mechanical organ (musical clock)
XX/1	*Seven Last Words of our Saviour on the Cross* (Instrumental versions)

Contents of volume 2

XX/2	*Seven Last Words of our Saviour on the Cross* (Vocal version)
XXbis	Stabat mater
XXI	Oratorios
XXII	Masses
	XXIIa Requiem
	XXIIb Libera
XXIII	Small church compositions
XXIVa	Cantatas and choruses with orchestral accompaniment
XXIVb	Arias with orchestral accompaniment
XXV	Multi-voiced songs
	XXVa duets
	XXVb three-part songs
	XXVc four-part songs
XXVIa	Songs with keyboard accompaniment
XXVIb	Cantatas and choruses with the accompaniment of an instrument
XXVII	Canons
XXVIII	Operas
XXIX	Marionette operas and German operas
	XXIXa Marionette operas
	XXIXb German operas
XXX	Incidental music
XXXI	Arrangements of Scottish and Welsh

folksongs, and other arrangements
XXXIa Scottish songs
XXXIb Welsh songs
XXXIc Other arrangements
XXXIc:17 *The Ladies Looking-Glass*
XXXII Pasticcios

Within each section individual works are identified by an Arabic number. In this way, the 'London' symphony becomes Hob.I:104, the trumpet concerto Hob.VIIe:1, and the song 'My mother bids me bind my hair' Hob.XXVIa:27. An asterisk attached to a number indicates a work that Hoboken regarded as doubtful, though it is often omitted by other authors. When Hoboken wants to refer to an individual movement within a work he will add a superscript roman numeral to the main number; thus Hob.I:104^{II} will indicate the slow movement of the 'London' symphony. Appended to most of the sections is a list of works in the same genre that have been attributed to Haydn with, whenever possible, an indication of the likely or possible composer; these are organized by tonality, beginning with C major, with minor following major. Thus Hob.XXII:C47 is a mass in C major falsely attributed to Haydn.

The particular value of the catalogue is that every work, authentic or otherwise, has a unique identifying number and while some of Hoboken's decisions on categorization and authorship have been questioned and modified since the appearance of the catalogue, the utility of the numbers remains. The worklist in Appendix 1 retains the Hoboken classification and gives the reasoning behind the order of works in each section.

Underneath the catalogue number Hoboken gives the title of the work, the date of composition, and the performing forces. All the authentic works and the doubtful works (those with an asterisk) follow this preliminary information with the thematic incipits for each movement; only first-movement incipits are given for spurious works. The number of bars in each movement (or section) is noted above the stave. Incipits are followed by catalogue references, location and description of the autograph, list of manuscript copies, list of printed editions including arrangements, references to the work in Haydn's correspondence, notes on the history of the work, and references to appropriate standard literature. The key to the many abbreviations for instruments, catalogues, libraries, journals, authors, etc. is most conveniently consulted in vol. 3, pp. 237–53; volumes 1 and 2 each have a separately bound booklet inside the back cover that also lists abbreviations.

Hoboken's catalogue is particularly comprehensive and informative on published editions of Haydn's music, both authentic and spurious, and entries will typically reproduce the wording of title pages, give the date of publication, and the source for this date. Hoboken also provides full descriptions of the physical make-up of autograph manuscripts.

Volume 3 is a service volume for the main volumes. Users will most frequently consult it for the addenda and corrigenda to volumes 1 and 2, given on pp. 257–384; this section contains some new Hoboken numbers, applied to works attributed to the composer and discovered after the publication of volumes 1 and 2.

Contents of volume 3

Collections [of printed music]
Collected works
Index of opus numbers
Index of publishers
Catalogue of nicknames and given titles for instrumental music
Dedicatees, commissioners and other individuals associated with single works (including arrangements)
Locus of autographs
Manuscript copies with autograph annotations and alleged autographs
Titles and first lines of vocal works (authentic and inauthentic), including vocal arrangements of instrumental music, alphabetically ordered
Abbreviations
Addenda and Corrigenda for volume 1
Addenda and Corrigenda for volume 2
Index of people, institutions, and places
Afterword

(iii) *RISM catalogue of printed sources.* RISM (Répertoire International des Sources Musicales) is a huge bibliographical project organized by the International Musicological Society and the International Association of Music Libraries that provides catalogues and directories (in printed form and, more recently, electronic form) of musical sources of all kinds. Given the particular strength of Hoboken's catalogue—the extensive and detailed information on printed sources for Haydn's music—it is rather surprising that it does not systematically detail libraries and archives where individual publications can be found. This drawback is rectified by volume 4 of Series A/I, *Einzeldrucke vor 1800*, issued by RISM (Kassel, 1974); volume 12 provides addenda and corrigenda (Kassel, 1991). Prepared by Irmgard Becker-Glauch of the JOSEPH HAYDN-INSTITUT, the entry on Joseph Haydn gives numbers from H 2462 to H 4723 for publications of music by the composer that appeared up to (often beyond) 1800; the catalogue also quotes the appropriate Hoboken number. While the transcriptions of the title-pages are not as literal as the ones in Hoboken's catalogue and no dates of publication are offered, each entry lists all the libraries that are known to have a copy of a particular print. Thus a reader wishing to find information about the first edition of Haydn's op. 33 quartets might first look up volume 1 of Hoboken, III:37–42, where the name of the publisher (Artaria), the date of publication (April 1782, as announced in the *Wiener Zeitung*), and the layout and wording of the title page will be given; Hoboken also supplies the detail that later impressions of the Artaria edition have some additional words on the title page. Turning to the main RISM volume, item H 3476, the reader will be given the names of 20 libraries that have copies of the first version (H 3476) and five libraries that have the later impression (H 3477); the addenda and corrigenda volume gives six additional sources for H 3476 and two additional ones for H 3477.

(iv) *Feder's worklist in the New Grove dictionaries.* While Hoboken will remain the standard catalogue for some time, a more manageable, as well as more up-to-date catalogue of Haydn's music can be found in the *New Grove Dictionary of Music*. This non-thematic catalogue was first prepared for the original edition of the dictionary that appeared in 1980, revised for the separate publication of the Haydn article as a convenient paperback (London, 1982), revised again for a German translation of this paperback (Stuttgart, 1994), and then thoroughly revised for the second edition of the complete dictionary (London, 2001); this latest version is also available separately (London, 2002) and on-line. Feder divides Haydn's output into sections, each labelled with a letter of the alphabet; many sections are followed by a subsidiary section dealing with selected attributed works or arrangements in that genre.

A Masses
B Miscellaneous sacred
C Oratorios and similar works
D Secular cantatas, choruses
E Dramatic
F Secular vocal with orchestra
G Solo songs with keyboard
H Miscellaneous vocal works with keyboard
I Canons
J Symphonies
K Miscellaneous orchestral
L Dances, marches for orchestra/military band
M Concertos for string or wind instruments
N Divertimenti etc. for 4+ string and/or wind instruments—string quartets, works with baryton, *lira organizzata* excepted
O String quartets
P String trios
Q Baryton trios (divertimenti)
R Works for 1–2 barytons
S Miscellaneous chamber music for 2–3 string and/or wind instruments
T Works for 2 *lire organizzate*
U Keyboard concertos/concertinos/divertimenti
V Keyboard trios
W Keyboard sonatas
X Miscellaneous keyboard works
Y Works for flute clock
Z Arrangements of British folksongs

Within each section, individual works are given their Hoboken numbers but are ordered in a new sequence, whenever possible a chronological one, and with new numbers. The 'London' symphony has the unique descriptor J104, the trumpet concerto becomes M17, and 'My mother bids me bind my hair' is G27. These descriptors are obviously much easier to use and less prone to error than Hoboken numbers and it is surprising that they are not more widely applied; they are given in Appendix 1. Feder also routinely gives information on titles, keys, performing forces, dates of composition, principal evidence for authenticity, location in a modern edition (usually that of JHW), and sundry short remarks. As a former director of the Joseph Haydn-Institut, Feder was able to make use of the expertise and resources of that organization. It may well be the case that when the collected edition of Haydn's music is finally completed, Feder's worklist will become the basis of a new comprehensive catalogue prepared by the Institut that will supplant that of Hoboken.

B. Brook and R. Viano, *Thematic Catalogues in Music: An Annotated Bibliography*, 2nd edn (Stuyvesant, NY, 1997).

S. Gerlach, 'Haydns "Chronologische" Sinfonienliste für Breitkopf & Härtel', *HS* 6/2 (1988), 116-29.

A. van Hoboken, *Joseph Haydn Thematisch-bibliographisches Werkverzeichnis*: vol. 1 (Mainz, 1957); vol. 2 (Mainz, 1971); vol. 3 (Mainz, 1978).

I. and J. Kindermann, *Einzeldrucke vor 1800*, RISM Series A/I, vol. 12 (addenda and corrigenda) (Kassel, 1992).

HCRL/3 [includes transcription of 1/i].

HCRL/5 [includes transcriptions of 1/iii–vii].

Larsen.

E. Mandyczewski, [*Thematic Catalogue of Haydn's Symphonies*], *Joseph Haydn Werke. Erste kritische durchgesehene Gesamtausgabe*, series 1, vol. 1 (Leipzig, [1907]).

K. Schlager (ed.), *Einzeldrucke vor 1800*, RISM Series A/I, vol. 8 (Kassel, 1974).

J. Webster and G. Feder, *Haydn* (London, 2002).

Catholicism. The dominant religion in the Austrian monarchy and a fundamental element of Haydn's character. Historically, Catholicism projected two universal characteristics: first, the absolute possession of the truth and the way to salvation; second, the unlimited obligation of preaching the faith.

The claim to have the authentic interpretation of Christ's teaching had caused disputes since earliest Christianity. The first decisive schism occurred in 1054 when the Orthodox Church separated from the Roman Catholic Church. At the beginning of the 16th century legitimate criticism of the deplorable state of the Church, together with nationalist tendencies fuelled by political and economic motives, led to the foundation of national Churches. In the Peace of Augsburg (1555) the followers of Martin Luther were recognized as a separate denomination, though this tolerance was to be governed by the tenet 'Cuius regio, eius religio': individuals had to adopt the religion of the local ruler. Religious tensions in German-speaking Europe led to wider political conflicts that involved the intervention on either side of foreign countries. Only the end of the Thirty Years War (1648) brought a settled accommodation between Catholics and Protestants.

As Holy Roman Emperors, nominally elected by the Empire but in practice usually unopposed, successive members of the Habsburg dynasty had varying influence over the religious persuasion of the people. Within the Austrian monarchy itself the Counter-Reformation led to a successful re-establishing of the Catholic faith. Hungary, however, was not part of the Holy Roman Empire, and its subjects were predominantly Calvinists. To increase its influence on that country the Habsburgs were obliged to cultivate the support of leading Catholics such as the Esterházy family. Security and influence in this part of Europe was affected also by the abiding fear of the territorial ambitions of the Ottoman Empire.

Although the Counter-Reformation was initiated by the Roman Catholic Church it was actively supported and promoted by the Habsburgs. The Jesuit Order played a central role. Summoned to Austria in 1550 by Emperor Ferdinand I, the order soon established itself at the pinnacle of intellectual life. Jesuits became father confessors to the ruling family, advised them on policy, and taught their sons. Soon, schools for the nobility and the universities were entirely controlled by the order, recognized for its modern attitudes to science and education as much as for its religious zeal. Responding to the appeal of Lutheran liturgy in German rather than Latin, the Jesuit Peter Canisius (1521–97) prepared a German catechism that was to remain the foundation of Catholic religious instruction for 200 years.

The consolidation of Catholicism in the Austrian monarchy in the 17th and early 18th centuries provided a unifying force that affected every aspect of society, cultural, educational, economic, health as well as religious. *Pietas austriaca* was a contemporary term that reflected this pervasive piety, and the certainty of belief that is projected in Haydn's personality and which is such a compelling feature of his church music must be considered a particular product of this society. The Habsburg rulers, the members of the nobility, the Jesuits together with the Augustinian and Benedictine orders were the principal agents of this unity, building palaces, abbeys, and churches that were the focal points of local society and filling them with paintings, frescos, sculptures, and lavish music that nurtured the devotion of the people. Through the Church all levels of society were raised, educated, and entertained in the Catholic spirit.

As a young man Haydn made a pilgrimage to Mariazell in the Styrian hills, a journey on foot from Vienna of some 120 km (75 miles). Haydn was one of tens of thousands of pilgrims who visited the small town every year. Prince Paul Esterházy (1635–1713) took part in 58 pilgrimages to Mariazell, on one occasion accompanied by over 11,000 people; the focal point of their veneration, a rustic carving of the Madonna and child, was set on an incongruously opulent altar, partly sponsored by the prince.

Marian devotion was a central feature of Catholic worship. No church was without its image of the Blessed Virgin, though it would be misleading to suggest that people prayed directly to her; rather she functioned as an intermediary to God and was regarded as the advocate of the people. When the Habsburg family won the Battle of the White Mountain (1620) against the Protestant Bohemians at the beginning of the Thirty Years War, the victory was ascribed to the Virgin Mary who subsequently became the patron of the army, Maria della Vittoria. She held the same function in the battles against the Turks at the end of the 17th century. From that time on Mary was frequently depicted crushing the serpent of false teaching, occasionally, and more blatantly, with the disembodied head of a Turk at her feet. More homely depictions reflect the miraculous curing by the Blessed Virgin Mary of ill health and the part she played in mitigating the worst effects of natural disasters. As well as paintings and sculptures in churches, shrines devoted to the Virgin Mary remain a feature of market squares and the open countryside in Austria to this day. Particularly distinctive are the *Schutzmantel Madonnen* in which a crowd of people are gathered under the protective open cloak of the Virgin Mary.

The worshipping of favoured saints was also part of devotion, especially in the countryside where several rites, open-air processions, and ceremonies reveal elements of ancient pagan ritual grafted onto Catholic worship. Every child received at least one saint's name at birth, and the relevant feast day of the saint was celebrated as the person's nameday, an annual occasion more important than the actual birthday. One consequence of this was that many people, such as Haydn himself, were unsure of their birth dates. Haydn's two names, Franz and Joseph, reflect St

Francis of Assisi (founder of the Franciscan Order) and Joseph the father of Jesus; Haydn hardly ever used his first name and would have celebrated his nameday on the Feast of St Joseph, 19 March. Joseph was also the patron saint of the Holy Roman Empire.

The church calendar and, from it, the social calendar were built around the life of Christ, with Christmas (Nativity), and Easter (Resurrection) as high points. Advent (beginning four Sundays before Christmas) provides a period of contemplation and Lent (40 days before Easter) a period of repentance. Epiphany follows Christmas with a particular celebration of the Three Kings, the day when the star first appeared. On 2 February Catholics celebrate Presentation, when, following a Jewish custom, the 40-day-old Jesus is brought into the temple. Lent begins with Ash Wednesday, a strict day of fasting; the mark of the cross made with ash on the forehead signifies the transitory nature of all earthly things. Lent ends with Palm Sunday, the day when Christ entered into Jerusalem, and marks the beginning of Holy Week. Maundy Thursday commemorates the Last Supper, Good Friday the day of crucifixion, and Easter Sunday the Resurrection. Forty days after Easter the Church celebrates the Ascension of Christ, and 50 days after Easter, Whitsun commemorates the day when the Holy Spirit descended on the apostles. On the Sunday after Whitsun, Trinity Sunday celebrates the unity of God the Father, Son, and Holy Spirit, and on the following Thursday Corpus Christi (the celebration of the Eucharist) is marked, now as in Haydn's day, by a public procession of the Host through the neighbourhood. Of the many Marian days, 15 August is the most important, marking the Assumption of the Virgin Mary, a common theme for many church paintings. The memory of the saints is celebrated on 1 November, All Saints' Day, and the following day, All Souls' Day, is a day of remembrance for the dead. GM

Cherubini, Luigi (b. 14 Sept. 1760; d. 15 March 1842). Born in Italy, Cherubini settled in France in 1786 where he enjoyed particular esteem as a composer of opera and, from the age of 50, of church music. He was closely associated with the Conservatoire de Musique from its inception in 1795, becoming its director in 1822. Early in 1805 rumours circulated in France and Britain that Haydn had died. Cherubini composed a commemorative work, *Chant sur la Mort de Joseph Haydn*, for three voices and orchestra to be performed at the Concert dans le Théâtre Olympique. When the report was discovered to be false, the work was hastily withdrawn. It was given its first performance at a concert in Paris in February 1810, nine months after Haydn's death. A keyboard version was published the following year and dedicated to Prince Nicolaus II Esterházy.

Cherubini's operas were first performed in Vienna in 1802 (in German translation) and immediately captured the imagination of the public, including presumably Haydn, though there is no record of him attending a performance. The composer was invited to Vienna and spent nine months there from July 1805. In his capacity as one of the inspectors of the Paris Conservatoire, Cherubini brought with him a medal and a formal report that a monument in Haydn's honour was to be erected in the conservatoire that year, the tenth anniversary of its founding. Haydn told Griesinger that Cherubini was 'an attractive little man, with charming manners', and urged the younger composer: 'Let me call myself your musical father, and you my son.' Continuing in this vein, Haydn presented him with the autograph score of Symphony no. 103 inscribing it 'Padre del celebre Cherubini ai 24tro di Febr. 1805'; the score is now in the British Library. While this mutual admiration was a genuine one, there is little in Cherubini's music that shows the determining influence of his would-be musical father.

Choron, Alexandre Étienne (b. 21 Oct. 1771; d. 29 June 1834). French scholar and composer with a keen interest in music history and theory. From 1807 onwards the Parisian publisher LE DUC offered a series of 27 symphonies by Haydn in score format, prefaced by a biography of the composer prepared by Choron. Together with François Fayolle, he prepared the entry for the composer in the *Dictionnaire historique des musiciens* (vol. i; Paris, 1810).

clavichord. A stringed keyboard instrument, rectangular in shape, with a tangent action, made in fretted (*gebunden*) and unfretted (*Bundfrei*) varieties. The simplest in construction and also the cheapest of keyboard instruments, the clavichord was widely used in 18th-century Germany and Austria as a practice instrument, for composition, for accompanying singers, and, in the appropriate intimate circumstances, as a solo instrument. Although characterized by a relatively small sound, the clavichord has a wide dynamic range and, particularly in North Germany, was regarded as the most expressive of keyboard instruments. In Austria clavichords were built by most fortepiano makers and it was widely used by performers and composers, retaining a role even after the fortepiano had become the principal solo keyboard instrument.

Haydn is known to have played and owned clavichords throughout his career. GRIESINGER mentions a 'worm-eaten Klavier' which the composer owned in his youth in Vienna; documents from 1764 mention 'fürstlichen Klavikordi' at the Esterházy court; and after his return from London Haydn purchased a 1794 clavichord by Johann Bohak (*c.*1754–1805). There are several contemporary references to Haydn improvising at a clavichord, and in the last years of his life he apparently preferred playing the clavichord to other keyboard instruments. Among his solo sonatas the group of works written in the 1760s and early 1770s (Hob.XVI:44–7, 18–20) seem to lend themselves particularly well to performance on a clavichord, although not to the exclusion of other keyboard instruments. The C minor sonata (Hob.XVI:20) (1771) may well have been conceived specifically for clavichord.

The Bohak clavichord of 1794, today in the Donaldson Collection of the Royal College of Music, London, is the only known surviving Haydn keyboard instrument and is typical of the larger Austrian and German clavichords of the later 18th century. It has a five-octave range (FF–f'''), a double-pinned bridge, an undecorated case, and is *bundfrei*. The provenance of the clavichord in the Haydn Museum, once owned by Brahms and said to have been played by Haydn, is less certain. BH

R. Russell, *The Harpsichord and Clavichord*, 2nd edn (London, 1973).

H. Walter, 'Haydns Klaviere', *HS* 25/4 (1970), 256–88.

Clementi, Muzio (b. 23 Jan. 1752; d. 10 March 1832). Born and educated in Rome, Clementi moved to England in 1766–7 where he pursued a highly successful career as a pianist, teacher, composer, and publisher. He visited Vienna in 1781–2 and travelled to Eszterháza to meet Haydn. Clementi no doubt took the opportunity to acquaint himself more thoroughly with the musical life of the city, an acquaintanceship reflected in his *Musical Characteristics* (op. 19), a collection of small piano pieces that deliberately apes the styles of Haydn, KOZELUCH (Koželuh), MOZART, Sterkel (1750–1817), and VANHAL. The two 'Haydn' pieces are not a particularly acute imitation of the composer, though the keyboard sonata in C (Hob.XVI:35) is evoked in the second of them. Back in London, Clementi would have become increasingly aware in the 1780s of the popularity and status of Haydn's symphonies, which may have prompted him to compose his own but, as other composers like GYROWETZ and PLEYEL also found, Haydn's command of the genre made it difficult for him to make his mark as a symphonist in the city. Nevertheless, the works often appeared alongside those of Haydn in Salomon's concerts in the 1790s and were usually received with enthusiasm. In 1795 Clementi, along with Haydn, Bianchi (*c.*1752–1810), and Martín y Soler (1754–1806), was one of the featured composers in the Opera Concert, though Haydn, once more, outshone his colleagues. Clementi always maintained cordial relations with Haydn and invited him to stay at his country house in Evesham.

Clementi had become a modestly wealthy man and from 1798 onwards he was active as a music publisher and piano manufacturer. His contact with Haydn helped ensure that the first London edition of the op. 76 quartets was published by Longman, Clementi & Company, and that of the op. 77 quartets by Clementi, Banger, Hyde, Collard & Davis. Clementi had secured the promise of some new piano music by Haydn but the composer's advancing age ensured that nothing eventuated. Also, Haydn's commitment to Breitkopf & Härtel meant that Clementi had to be content with a peripheral role as a publisher of the composer's music, though the many arrangements (some by Clementi himself) and secondary editions issued by his firm played a part in maintaining the composer's popularity in Britain in the first decades of the 19th century. He helped SALOMON and BURNEY secure subscribers to the first edition of *The Creation*, naturally including himself, and published a keyboard reduction of that work in 1801; a keyboard reduction of *The Seasons* followed in 1813.

M. Clementi, keyboard reduction of *The Creation*, ed. N. Temperley (London: Peters, 1988).

HCRL/3.

L. Plantinga, *Clementi: His Life and Music* (London, 1977).

'Clock' symphony. Commonly used nickname for Symphony no. 101, prompted by the constant tick-tock rhythms of the accompaniment in the slow movement. It originated in the middle of the 19th century. JH

col basso. An indication frequently encountered in 18th-century scores as a form of shorthand. 'With the bass line' means that other denoted instrumental lines are to double the only bass line written fully in the score. Thus in a Haydn symphony the double bass part may be notated and other doubling instruments such as cello, bassoon, and viola may have 'col basso' written in the score. Like his contemporaries Haydn usually used 'basso' in a generic sense meaning 'the bass line', not as an indication of a particular instrument; thus in a quartet 'col basso' next to the viola line would mean that it doubled the cello. Haydn sometimes uses other indications for the same purpose, such as a bass clef (especially if that instrument normally uses a tenor or alto clef) and the sign //.

Coltellini, Marco (b. 13 Oct. 1719; d. 17 Nov. 1777). Librettist who worked in Vienna in the 1760s and 1770s, and later at the Russian court. His most important librettos include those for two *opera seria* by Traetta (1727–79), *Ifigenia in Tauride* (1763), and *Antigona* (1772). He also revised several *opera buffa* librettos, including *La finta semplice* for Mozart (1769) and *La contessina* for Gassmann (1770), both based on GOLDONI. In 1773 Haydn set a heavily revised version of one of Coltellini's comic librettos, *L'infedeltà delusa*. RJR

D. Heartz, *Haydn, Mozart and the Viennese School, 1740-1780* (New York, 1995).

compositional method. See overleaf.

Concertante. *See* SYMPHONIE CONCERTANTE.

Concert de la Loge Olympique. Concert organization founded in Paris in 1781 and which commissioned Symphonies nos. 82–7 from Haydn. *See* PARIS.

concertino. A title that appears on the autograph manuscript of one early work by Haydn and has been used, by extension, for similar works from the same period. Hob.XIV:11 is a three-movement work in C major scored for two violins, cello, and harpischord; a copy of the now lost autograph indicates that it was entitled 'concertino' and that it was composed in 1760. The harpsichord takes the thematic lead for much of the time with the strings offering accompaniment. While 'little concerto' is an appropriate description of the three-movement structure of fast, slow, and fast, and of the texture, the work does not employ the ritornello structures associated with the word concerto; all three movements are in binary form.

These features broadly characterize 12 further works from the same period for which the most common authentic title is divertimento: Hob. XIV:1, 3, 4, 7, 8, 9, 10, 12, 13, C1, C2, and XVIII:F2. As well as standing apart from the concerto these 13 works avoid independent string writing of the kind that is encountered in contemporary keyboard trios by Haydn, and the keyboard technique required is uniformly undemanding. The small scale, the common structure, the nature of the scoring, and the limited keyboard technique required all suggest that the 13 works were composed for the same clientele, perhaps someone like Countess Morzin who did not have the expertise to play Haydn's keyboard trios and the more demanding of his keyboard sonatas.

concerto

---

1. Background.
2. Concertos for organ (harpsichord) and orchestra.
3. Concertos for harpischord or piano and orchestra.
4. Concertos for string instrument and orchestra.
5. Concertos for *lire organizzate* and ensemble.
6. Concertos for wind instrument and orchestra.

---

1. Background. Although Haydn's output of concertos was sizeable, at no stage in his career did the writing of concertos assume a central position in his activities as a composer, and only the very earliest keyboard concertos, most of which were probably conceived for organ, were likely to have been written for his own use. The remainder were either commissioned—as in the case of the concertos for the King of Naples—or composed for specific performers who were usually, although by no means invariably, members of the Esterházy orchestra. Haydn's comparative lack of interest in the genre can be attributed in part to the fact that he did not depend on performing concertos for his livelihood, but it is also a reflection of the professional environment in which he lived and worked. The concerto was a relative latecomer to Viennese musical life and never really attained the level of popularity it enjoyed in contemporary Italy and southern Germany. The symphony was the most prestigious orchestral medium and the proliferation of private orchestras in Vienna in the 1750s and 1760s created an insatiable demand for the new and fashionable form. The concerto, by comparison, was very much the poor relation. One thing is certain: if Prince Nicolaus Esterházy, one of the great musical connoisseurs of the 18th century, had been interested in listening to concertos, Haydn would have composed them in larger numbers.

Like many of his contemporaries, Haydn clearly found the concerto a problematic genre in which to work. Its diffuseness and inherently dualistic nature seemed totally at odds with every other instrumental form of the day, and, to make matters worse, this firmly established and highly successful genre proved unusually resistant to change. The only major structural innovation which occurred during the late 18th century was the change in function of the third ritornello from one of retransition to recapitulation. In every other respect, the ground-plan of four ritornellos enclosing three solos that is standard in the concertos of VIVALDI and Tartini (1692–1770) forms the basis of first movements in Haydn's concertos. More important, however, was the gradual change which occurred in the musical organization of the solo part. From the loose, episodic solos of the Baroque concerto, the solo part in the mid-century concerto began to be organized along sonata-form lines. By the early 1770s both of these structural innovations were reasonably well established but no one, not even Haydn, could have imagined the miraculous trans-

[*cont. on p.45*]

compositional method

Students of Haydn's music are fortunate in having two types of material that reveal a great deal about how the composer conceived and accomplished his musical works. In the biographies of GRIESINGER and DIES there are several passages of direct quotation from the composer or paraphrases of his remarks that discuss his working methods. Of these, only two deal with particular works, both lost, an aria for a *Singspiel* for KURZ-BERNARDON from the 1750s and a keyboard sonata in the unusual key of B major (Hob.XVI:2c) from the mid-1760s. The interest of the majority of the remarks is twofold: the comments can be related to broader aesthetic principles in Haydn's outlook and, more particularly, can be combined with evidence afforded by the second type of material, musical sketches for individual works.

Unlike Beethoven, who prepared sketchbooks for his works which he then usually retained, Haydn worked with single sheets of manuscript paper rather than with loosely assembled books and did not systematically keep the material; once it had served its purpose it was usually discarded. Surviving sketches by Haydn represent, therefore, a very small part of such material and for single works it is not as comprehensive as that typically found in Beethoven's output. Most of the surviving material dates from the 1780s and 1790s and, with the notable exception of sketches for *The Creation*, most of it is for instrumental music. What is striking about the sketches is that they consistently bear out the general comments vouchsafed to Griesinger and Dies and allow a reasonably full picture of Haydn's compositional method to be extrapolated. There is only one pitfall: the working methods revealed are most appropriate to instrumental music. In vocal music, Haydn's working methods must have been slightly different, guided by the given text and not requiring the detailed kind of working out that is apparent in keyboard sonatas, keyboard trios, quartets, and symphonies.

Haydn told Griesinger that he was never a fast writer of music, that everything was composed with deliberation and industry. As a fluent craftsman Haydn could no doubt compose music very quickly, but there is a sense that he deliberately made composition challenging so that the end result would be more individual, an attitude he passed on to his pupil, Beethoven. The beginning of the compositional process occurred at the keyboard, clavichord, harpsichord, or piano.

> I sat down, began to improvise, sad or happy according to my mood, serious or trifling. Once I had seized upon an idea, my whole endeavour was to develop and sustain it in keeping with the rules of art. Thus I sought to keep going, and this is where so many of our new composers fall down. They string one little piece after another, they break off when they have hardly begun, and nothing remains in the heart when one has listened to it.

Sitting down at the keyboard for Haydn was a moment of discipline, unaffected by whether he felt like composing, though there is a suggestion that his mood may have influenced what he improvised. In practice this keyboard-playing might be nothing more than a doodle (such as a perfect cadence) which then became something more formulated as it was explored. 'Once I had seized upon an idea' suggests a point in the exploration when the composer realized that he had discovered something that could form the basis of a single movement. The next stage was typically done at the desk on manuscript paper and was much the most difficult and protracted stage in the process. Haydn's sketches show not only that his melodic ideas could be enhanced through systematic reworking on paper but that sections, even complete movements, were presented in draft form, so-called continuity sketches. Here the essential features of the movement were notated (in short-score format if it was a symphony), that is blocks of significant music in outline form separated by empty staves whose content was more routine. Many sketches approximate a map of a section or movement. It was still a fluid stage and while many extant sketches build recognizably towards the final product, others go up blind alleys with material and 'continuities' that were abandoned. Alongside the continuity sketch Haydn sometimes devoted some staves to the working out of a particularly demanding passage, such as a tricky modulation or an intricate passage of part-writing. Since these sketches are working documents intended for the composer's eyes only they usually do not have clefs (or if they do, they might be incorrect) and omit dynamics and instrumentation. However, comparison of the make-up of individual sketches of quartets and orchestral works with the final product suggests very strongly that Haydn thought habitually in sonority and register. The process of orchestration was never a separate, later stage from composition.

Although these two stages—discovering at the keyboard and composing at the desk—were the norm, common sense indicates that there would often be some toing and froing between the two. Thus the authentic portrait by Ludwig Guttenbrunn that shows Haydn seated at the keyboard with a quill in his right hand, a pot of ink on the keyboard on top of some manuscript pages, and his left hand poised above the keys is not only a conventional pictorial image of a composer waiting for the muse, but bears some resemblance to what was an occasional aspect of his working practice.

A key criterion in the compositional stage is indicated by Griesinger's quotation, the need to ensure a strong sense of logical unfolding: 'my whole endeavour was to develop and sustain it in keeping with the rules of art'. In the narrowest sense these words could be interpreted as a description of monothematic sonata form in which everything in the movement can be related to the opening subject and, from the pre-compositional phase, to something discovered at the keyboard. But whether it was a monothematic sonata form or a structure that allowed contrast, such as a rondo or a minuet and trio, Haydn always sought to integrate or as Geiringer writes 'to keep going'. Mozart and his father more than once talked about 'il filo', the thread of a composition; clearly this was important to Haydn too, though his means of achieving continuity was often quite different.

In the course of 1787 Haydn forwarded the six quartets of op. 50 to his publisher Artaria in instalments, as he completed them. On 12 July 1787 he wrote apologetically, 'I send you herewith the sixth quartet. Because of lack of time I have still not been able to write out the fifth, though it is already composed.' Here Haydn reveals the third stage of composition: converting the continuity sketches ('already composed') into the final, finished score ('to write out'). Dies suggests that Haydn preferred to do this easier task in the afternoons, leaving the mornings to the more challenging second stage of composition. This might suggest that scores were written up in a piecemeal fashion, though Haydn's letter to Artaria and what evidence can be adduced from autograph scores indicates that, in general, the musical work had to be complete before the final score was prepared. Haydn's autograph scores are usually neat and clear with very few crossings out because of errors or because of last-minute changes. However, he did not work from to bar to bar like a scribe. The colour of the ink as well as some anecdotal testimony reveals that the score was built up rather like a jigsaw; important lines first, usually the melody and particularly complex passages, followed by the subordinate parts. Wherever possible Haydn saved himself the trouble of writing out a doubling part with some kind of shorthand indication, easily understood by the copyist. That it was still a mentally absorbing task, the full realization of ideas previously outlined in draft, is suggested by the swift flow of the hand and by the occasional annotation addressed to himself, 'lic.' ('licenza') for an excusable grammatical error, 'DIESES WAR VOR GAR ZU GELEHRTE OHREN', 'PER FIGURAM RETARDATIONIS', and 'SAPIENTI PAUCA'. The whole was usually signed off with a valedictory 'LAUS DEO'.

The part played by 'the rules of art' referred to in Griesinger's account was as crucial here as in the previous stage. In the most basic sense the 'rules' were the common ones of good craftsmanship in a universal musical language, essentially correct musical grammar and syntax. For Haydn, the attitude instilled by studying and teaching SPECIES COUNTERPOINT nurtured a strong sense of part-writing, most keenly felt in the medium of the quartet but evident in many symphonies and often in keyboard music too. Working at the desk clearly encouraged linear thinking in a way that would be difficult if composition were done solely at the keyboard. But Haydn made it perfectly clear that 'rules' were there to be broken and that he was the sole judge of the effectiveness of grammatically or syntactically unorthodox music: 'Art is free, and will be limited by no pedestrian rules. The ear, assuming that it is trained, must decide, and I consider myself as competent as any to legislate here.' It is with this remark that 'rules of art' move to embrace questions of aesthetic judgement.

Very occasionally the completed autograph will reveal a change of content at a late stage in the compositional process. Most well known is the first version of the opening of the slow movement of Symphony no. 94 which was crossed out in favour of a revised version, this time with a new feature, the celebrated surprise. The music leading to the recapitulation in the finale of Symphony no. 98 is another passage that was altered after it had been written out.

Although the glimpses that are afforded of Haydn's compositional method reveal a good deal about the hidden structure of the finished product as well as the process itself, the tenor of Haydn's concluding comment to Griesinger is also instructive, that well-composed music 'remains in the heart when one has listened to it'. In conversation he had been quite willing to expound his views on compositional method, albeit in layman's terms, but his final observation on the merits of a work that had been produced by this process shows his overriding aim: it was not cerebral satisfaction, not something that was merely memorable, but something that stirred in a way that cannot adequately be described in words, even by the composer himself.

G. Feder, 'Joseph Haydns Skizzen und Entwürfe. Übersicht der Manuskripte, Werkregister, Literatur- und Ausgabenverzeichnis', *Fontes Artis Musicae*, 26 (1979), 172–88.

G. Feder, 'Über Haydns Skizzen zu nicht identifizierten Werken', in D. Altenburg (ed.), *Ars musica—Musica scientia. Festschrift Heinrich Hüschen zum 65. Geburtstag* (Cologne, 1980), 100–11.

J. K. Page, 'Wind Instruments in the Music of Joseph Haydn, 1785–1798: Studies in Orchestration, Compositional Process, and Musical Structure' (diss., Duke University, 1993).

H. A. Schafer, '"A wisely ordered Phantasie": Joseph Haydn's Creative Process from the Sketches and Drafts for Instrumental Music' (diss., Brandeis University, 1987).

C. Wolff (ed.), *The String Quartets of Haydn, Mozart, and Beethoven. Studies of the Autograph Manuscripts* (Cambridge, Mass., 1980).

formation the concerto would undergo in the next decade in the hands of Mozart.

In his early concertos Haydn also found himself shackled by stylistic conventions and the limitations of contemporary musical syntax. The musical language of Haydn's youth was characterized by highly articulated phrases (usually in two-bar groupings) alternating with extended periods of self-generating thematic spinning (*Fortspinnung*). The preponderance of short phrases made continuity difficult to achieve and the solution, to employ the sequence a good deal during extended solos, worked well enough in small works but, in large-scale compositions, the practice led all too frequently to prolixity. The best concertos of the period are invariably short, and this rule applies as much to Haydn as to any of his contemporaries. The convention of writing first movements in a leisurely 4/4 with a quaver pulse also posed problems for composers. In order to achieve a sense of momentum it was necessary to write ornate melodic lines which, with their slow harmonic rhythm and frequent cadences, could sound curiously disjointed at times. In stark contrast, the symphony, as a new form, did not suffer these problems to the same degree, and it is interesting to note that nearly every symphony of the period, whether written in Mannheim, Paris, or Vienna, is more lively, vital, and dramatic than any concerto. In fairness, however, the weakness of the mid-century concerto was most apparent in first movements. There were many beautiful and highly effective slow movements written during the middle decades of the 18th century, and a number of exciting finales.

Most of Haydn's concertos were written during the 1750s and 1760s. They are as good as any concertos of the period but not always markedly superior to those of major rivals like HOFMANN, DITTERSDORF, and VANHAL. Their weaknesses are the weaknesses of the prevailing style of the day and not necessarily Haydn's own. It has been fashionable to condemn the mid-18th-century style but even in this much maligned period it was possible to write great music. Haydn's Cello Concerto in C, one of the finest artistic expressions of the age, remains one of the most popular concertos in the repertoire.

After a spate of concerto-writing in the 1760s, largely for members of the Esterházy orchestra, Haydn wrote relatively few concertos. Among these are the Piano Concerto in D (*c.*1780), the Cello Concerto in D (a curiously old-fashioned work for 1783), and his masterpiece in the genre, the Trumpet Concerto in E♭ (1796). Haydn's musical language had changed dramatically during the intervening two decades and many elements of the new style are evident in the later concertos. Gone are the ponderous first movements, except in the case of the stylistically conservative Cello Concerto, and in their place stand lively, vital Allegro movements. The solo parts are tightly organized within the limitless boundaries of sonata form; thematic material is linked organically with the ritornello, or, when new, placed carefully to sidestep the expected; and it is frequently subjected to serious development. There is also a changed relationship between the solo instrument and the orchestra. No longer restricted purely to a limited accompanying role in the solo sections, the orchestra interacts with the solo instrument to carry the musical argument forward. Above all, the thematic material is strongly defined and wholly reflective of Haydn's highly evolved personal style. These concertos are no longer the curiously impersonal works of their early counterparts but compositions worthy to stand alongside the great symphonies and string quartets of the period. It is not just that Haydn has become a better composer. The form itself has matured and he has come to understand its imperatives. Although it is tempting to ascribe some of these innovations to Haydn's knowledge of some of Mozart's concertos, many of them are the logical outcome of his earlier work in the genre. Moreover, the major structural changes are common to the many composers of the period who collectively expanded and refined concerto form.

With the Trumpet Concerto of 1796 Haydn's long, if disjointed career as a composer of concertos drew to a close. Over 40 years separate his first and last works in the genre and, as in every aspect of his work, the technical, stylistic, and expressive gulf between them is almost inconceivable.

The term concerto was sometimes applied rather loosely during the 18th century, in Austria as elsewhere. Small-scale works for keyboard and strings, frequently characterized by binary-form or rounded binary-form first movements, were often styled CONCERTINO or DIVERTIMENTO, as well as concerto. For the purposes of this survey the term concerto is understood to mean a work for solo instrument and orchestra in which the first movement—and generally the subsequent movements—is constructed according to the sonata-ritornello principle.

2. Concertos for organ (harpsichord) and orchestra. During the mid-1750s when Haydn was still eking out a precarious existence in Vienna as a freelance musician, he was employed as leader of the orchestra at the church of the Barmherzige Brüder, and also served as organist at the chapel of Count Haugwitz. It was common practice in Austria, Bohemia, and Bavaria for concertos and symphonies to be performed during the course of a church service, and doubtless both positions afforded Haydn opportunities to compose and perform concertos. A number of Leopold Hofmann's keyboard concertos, for instance, were certainly intended for this purpose. Little detailed information about Haydn's early career survives, and it is difficult to establish a reliable chronology for the six concertos written during these years. Only one autograph score survives (Hob.XVIII:1), and even their designation as organ concertos rests partly on internal evidence (the upper range of the solo part), since the majority of contemporary sources describe the works as concertos 'for the keyboard' ('Per il Clavicembalo').

Concerto in D (Hob.XVIII:2). The present concerto was entered in the ENTWURF-KATALOG around 1765 and found its way into the BREITKOPF CATALOGUE two years later; its actual date of composition is likely to be at least a decade earlier. The work was probably written in connection with one of Haydn's freelance positions in Vienna mentioned above. It is clearly a very early work and, as is to be expected, does not contain many of the composer's distinctive stylistic fingerprints. Without the entry in the *Entwurf-Katalog*, one would be hard pressed to attribute the work to Haydn with any confidence in the light of a conflicting attribution to the popular Italian composer, Baldassare Galuppi (1706–85). The first two movements are highly conventional and strangely impersonal when compared with some of the composer's other early instrumental music; the keyboard-writing is mechanical and generally lacking in invention. The most successful movement by far—and the one most representative of Haydn's growing confidence and personality as a composer—is the finale with its delicate imitative opening and brilliant, vigorous tutti-writing. In spite of the obvious weaknesses of the work it attained a reasonable level of contemporary popularity, and survives in several sources.

Concerto in C (Hob.XVIII:10). The earliest reference to this concerto is in Supplement VI (1771) of the Breitkopf Catalogue where it is listed as the first of 'III. Conc. di Gius. Hayden': the instrumentation is given as 'cemb. conc. 2 Viol. e Basso'. The principal source for the work, a set of manuscript parts preserved in the archive of the Gesellschaft der Musikfreunde in Vienna, also gives the solo instrument as 'clavicembalo', but the range of the part clearly indicates that it was conceived for organ. In many respects the work is far more successful than the Concerto in D (Hob.XVIII:2). Its smaller scale enables Haydn to avoid falling into the trap of writing long, discursive sequences and the kind of aimless mechanical passage-work that mars so many concertos of the period. The slow movement is written in 3/4 time, and is far more personal in style than its rather cold equivalent in the D major concerto. The 3/8 finale, on the other hand, is a good deal more conventional, in spite of its spirited style and taut construction. The scoring of the accompaniment for two violins and basso is not uncommon during the period, particularly in church music. Haydn's employment of such forces may be an indication that the work was composed for a smaller musical establishment than the D major work.

Concerto in C (Hob.XVIII:8). The earliest known copy of this work, dated 1771, carries an attribution to 'Monsieur Hofmann' on the wrapper, which a later hand has cancelled and replaced with 'Haiden'. The attribution to Leopold Hofmann is not unreasonable, but it is unsupported by any other copy of the work. There seems little doubt that this concerto is an authentic work by Haydn.

Although this concerto is larger in scale than Hob.XVIII:10 it is far more tautly organized, notwithstanding a lengthy sequential digression in the first movement. The central Adagio introduces an interesting innovation: the solo instrument launches straight into the movement without the customary opening ritornello, although the ritornello structure is still retained at strategically important places in the movement to underline newly established or re-established areas of tonality. Haydn also succeeds in tightening the finale by using extremely short ritornellos. This movement is remarkable too for the use of unequal phrase lengths which, coupled with its short-breathed thematic cells, propels the music forward with immense vitality.

Concerto in C (Hob.XVIII:5). Although much of the musical language of this concerto is familiar from its companions, there is a growing mastery in the way Haydn manipulates his musical material. His use of a short and seemingly insignificant phrase from the opening ritornello at critical structural points in the movement shows a preoccupation with giving unity to an inherently diffuse form. The slow movement (marked variously Adagio or Andante in the sources) once again opens without the customary ritornello but employs the orchestra to reinforce the dominant at the conclusion of the first solo, and, rather unusually, at the opening of the third part of this simple, ternary movement. The appearance of a closing ritornello is, of course, quite conventional. The finale, once again, is a comparatively brief movement. The solo-writing itself is rather conventional—in one contemporary source a copyist struck out Haydn's name and replaced it with that of GEORG CHRISTOPH WAGENSEIL, the famous Viennese Hofklaviermeister—but it is effective nonetheless and as attractive as any similar movement of the period.

Concerto in C (Hob.XVIII:1). Of all Haydn's early keyboard concertos this is the only work for which the composer's autograph score survives. The date 1756 which appears on the head of the score was added by Haydn as late as *c*.1800. The first two staves of the score are allocated to the trumpets ('clarini') but they have not been filled in. It is possible that the parts were written out for the players at a later date without Haydn entering them into his autograph score. Other auxiliary parts survive, for pairs of oboes, horns, and timpani, but these have either dubious claims to authenticity or are clearly spurious.

After his initial foray into concerto composition Haydn seems to have consciously reduced the length of his works in order to tighten his control over musical structure. In this work, however, the trend is reversed and Hob.XVIII:1 is a good deal larger in scale than its immediate predecessors. It is believed that this concerto was written for the ceremony at which Haydn's youthful love, THERESE KELLER, took the veil. This not only accounts for the work's ceremonial style with trumpets, always such a vital ingredient in Viennese church music of the period, but also for the fact that, like the Salve regina in E of the same year, Haydn took care to preserve the score to the end of his life. As is the case with Hob.XVIII:2 the scale of the work is too large for its musical material. The first movement, invariably the most stilted and prolix in Haydn's early concertos, contains two gigantic sequential passages that, perhaps more than anything else, reveal the composer's inability to infuse the form with life and purpose. The finale, a pacy movement in 3/8, employs double repeats in order to balance the cycle as a whole.

Concerto in F for organ and violin (Hob.XVIII: 6). Late in life Haydn believed that he had written this 'Organ Concerto with one violin' for the ceremony at which Therese Keller, his sister-in-law, took the veil. Like Hob.XVIII:1 it is unusually long, and includes a viola part in the orchestra. Three sets of cadenzas survive for the work and it seems possible that at least one of these is authentic.

Concertos for keyboard and one other solo instrument are not common during this period, although Michael Haydn composed an attractive concerto for organ and viola within a year or two at most of the present work, a concerto that is, in most respects, superior to Hob.XVIII:6. Once again, the fundamental weakness in Haydn's concerto lies in its discursive style, exacerbated by the inclusion of a second solo instrument which demands, according to the conventions of the day, a double announcement of all the principal solo material. This, coupled with full ritornellos and the inevitable sequential wanderings, at times stretches Haydn's attractive, albeit conventional material to the limits. Nevertheless, Haydn's treatment of the two solo instruments, singly and as a pair, is interesting and often highly effective.

3. Concertos for harpsichord or piano and orchestra.

Concerto in F (Hob.XVIII:3). The earliest firm date for this concerto is 1771, the year it appears in the Breitkopf Catalogue; it probably dates from the mid-1760s. Like the earlier organ concertos the Concerto in F major lacks a strong individual profile. Its thematic material is undistinguished and much of the solo-writing is efficient but routine. The work achieved very limited circulation in spite of Breitkopf's advocacy and no sources survive in Austria; it was, however, published with Haydn's authority in Paris in 1787.

Concerto in G (Hob.XVIII:4). This is the second of only three keyboard concertos Haydn wrote during his years in the service of the Esterházy family. Unlike the Concerto in F major, which Haydn probably intended for his own use, this work may have been written specifically for another performer, in this case, Maria Theresia Paradis (1759–1824), the blind Austrian pianist for whom Mozart was later to compose his Concerto in B♭ (K456). Although the work was published in Paris by Boyer in 1784, there are surprisingly few extant manuscript copies, an indication perhaps that Paradis acquired the rights to the work.

The style and range of the keyboard part in this concerto places its date of composition sometime between 1767 and 1770, and it must have sounded rather conservative to Parisian audiences when Paradis performed it there in 1784. Compared with the concertos of Carl Stamitz (1745–1801), for example, or those of the celebrated mulatto violinist, composer, and swordsman Saint-Georges (*c*.1739–1799), the work has a slightly old-fashioned cast to it. Nonetheless, there are some interesting innovations, not least among them the adoption of a consciously popular style in the finale.

Concerto in D (Hob.XVIII:11). This is Haydn's last and incontestably finest keyboard concerto. It is in every respect superior to its predecessors. It has the taut, nervous energy characteristic of Haydn's mature instrumental style; highly distinctive and instantly recognizable thematic material throughout; fluid, inventive keyboard-writing; and a mastery of the sonata-ritornello principle that had hitherto eluded him.

Not surprisingly, it became Haydn's most popular concerto during his lifetime. Between 1784 and 1809, the year of the composer's death, it was published by eight firms in five different countries. Its precise date of composition is unknown although recently, on the basis of a contemporary memoir, it has been suggested that it was played by Fräulein von Hartenstein, a pupil of LEOPOLD

KOZELUCH (Koželuh), at a private concert in Vienna on 28 February 1780. It is unlikely that the work was written for her; it is far more likely that Haydn composed it with a view to publication.

The sprightly first movement is tautly organized and written in a liberating alla breve instead of the customary ponderous moderato. The opening ritornello is packed with interesting thematic material and Haydn's manipulation of these—welding the open-ended themes together in different combinations, interpolating new material and developing the old—is very deft. He even employs a modulating ritornello to introduce the second solo which is a rather rare occurrence. Although the solo part is not formidably difficult, it is highly effective and generally well integrated with the orchestral accompaniment. There are also some delightfully unexpected harmonic twists that remind one of the symphonies composed during the previous decade. The slow movement, which unusually for the period retains the wind instruments, is especially beautiful with its chains of suspensions against long-held notes in the strings. For the finale, Haydn turned to gypsy music, a 'Rondo all'Ungherese', whose main theme contains elements of a Croatian dance, the Siri Kolo, a movement of great pace and originality; drone accompaniments, syncopations, and swirling trills all contribute to the exotic sound of the movement.

4. Concertos for string instrument and orchestra. Haydn's string concertos, like most of his other works in the genre, have survived in only a handful of copies. Moreover, a number of works listed in the *Entwurf-Katalog* have been lost, including two baryton concertos, a concerto for two barytons, and concertos for double bass, violin, and cello. Of the 11 concertos that have survived three are for violin and two for cello. Apart from the Cello Concerto in D major they were all probably written between *c.*1761 and *c.*1771.

Haydn was a competent violinist. He played professionally during the 1750s and later, in Prince Esterházy's employment, he regularly played the violin in chamber music and in the orchestra. Unlike Dittersdorf and Hofmann, both of whom were exceptional violinists, Haydn did not write violin concertos for his own use.

When Haydn took up his duties in Eisenstadt in 1761 as an assistant to Werner, he was specifically entrusted with improving the state of instrumental music at the court. Within the space of year a number of exceptional players had been engaged and under Haydn's direction the orchestra developed into a fine ensemble. Inspired by the calibre of its principal players and, no doubt, by a desire to win over his new colleagues as well as his employer, Haydn composed a series of instrumental concertos, of which barely half survive, and the three programmatic symphonies 'Le Matin', 'Le Midi', and 'Le Soir' which contain concertante writing for all Haydn's principal players. The most important member of the orchestra was its leader, LUIGI TOMASINI, whom Prince Paul Anton Esterházy had brought from Italy to Eisenstadt as a page, perhaps as early as 1752–3. Tomasini was an outstanding violinist, possessed not only of an exceptional technique but also a beautiful tone. There is no doubt that his playing greatly influenced the way in which Haydn wrote for the instrument in all genres.

Concerto for violin in C (Hob.VIIa:1). The entry for the Concerto in C major in the *Entwurf-Katalog* is accompanied by the remark 'fatto per il Luigi'; his strengths as a player are evident throughout the work. His technical prowess is explored in the outer movements, particularly in the 3/8 finale with its rapid passage work in tenths, *spiccato* bowing across the strings and frequent double-stopping. The most immediately appealing movement of the concerto, however, is the graceful Adagio which was clearly tailor-made to show off Tomasini's exquisite Italianate tone. The movement opens and closes with a simple rising scale for the soloist, supported by a semiquaver accompaniment in the orchestra, which encloses a long *crescendo.* These two sections—in reality a brief prelude and postlude—frame a glorious cantilena, artlessly accompanied by pizzicato strings. Its serenade-like quality is a far cry from the plodding slow movements of the organ concertos, and is strongly reminiscent of similar movements in Haydn's earliest string quartets (e.g. in op. 1 no. 1).

Concerto for violin and orchestra in A (Hob. VIIa:3). While there is no firm connection with Luigi Tomasini, the similarity of technique this concerto shares with Hob.VIIa:1 suggests that it was probably written for him. In some respects the work is less immediately attractive than the Concerto in C major although the solo-writing is every bit as demanding. While the central Adagio certainly lacks the charm and spontaneity of its earlier counterpart, it is, as one would expect, well crafted and not without its share of musical subtleties. The finale, on the other hand, is a very fine movement, carefully worked out and sophisticated in its thematic manipulation. The orchestral writing, too, exhibits much of the vigour and contrapuntal ingenuity evident in Haydn's symphonies of the period, and there are even significant instances of thematic interplay between orchestra and solo, something that is exceedingly rare in the mid-century concerto. These important stylistic advances suggest that VIIa:3 may have been composed after the Concerto in C major.

Concerto for violin and strings in G (Hob.VIIa:4). The Concerto in G is generally accepted as a genuine Haydn work, although the case for authenticity largely rests on its appearance, together with the Concerto in C major, in the Breitkopf Catalogue of 1769. The work is not listed in either the *Entwurf-Katalog* or the HAYDN-VERZEICHNIS, and the extant sources are not in the least helpful in establishing its authenticity. Nonetheless, there are enough stylistic fingerprints to allow it to take its place alongside the two undisputedly genuine violin concertos. Judged purely on stylistic grounds the Concerto in G is clearly the earliest of the three in spite of its appearance in the 1769 Breitkopf Catalogue. Structurally, the work is rather old-fashioned, and Haydn's treatment of the solo part, for all its idiomatic deftness, has something of the mechanical quality of the early organ concertos. It is far less technically demanding than either the C major or A major concertos—it hardly goes beyond the third position—and there is no sense of the part having been tailored to suit the soloist in quite the manner of the two concertos associated with Tomasini. While it is possible that Tomasini played the work it seems highly unlikely that it was written for him. Landon's hypothesis that it may may been written for the leader of the Morzin orchestra or one of the Fürnberg groups seems very plausible. Once again, it is the spirited finale, with its driving two-part counterpoint and chain of rising suspensions, that brings the best out in Haydn.

Concerto for cello and orchestra in C (Hob.VIIb:1). The Cello Concerto in C is not only the finest of Haydn's early concertos but it can lay claim to being the greatest and certainly the most popular concerto for any instrument written during the 1760s. Extraordinary though it seems now, the survival of the work hung by a thread. A single set of manuscript parts was discovered in Prague in 1962 by Oldřich Pulkert and at once identified, on the basis of the entry in *Entwurf-Katalog*, as a 'missing' cello concerto by Haydn. The work received its first modern performance in May of the same year and was an instant success. Since then it has established a permanent place in the repertoire of every cellist. But for this chance survival of a single set of parts it would have been lost for ever.

JOSEPH WEIGL, for whom this concerto was written, was a personal friend of Haydn as well as being a respected colleague. He was clearly an extraordinary player whose virtuosity and consummate musicianship inspired Haydn. The language of the first two movements of this concerto is familiar from the composer's other instrumental concertos of the period. The Lombard snaps and sprung rhythms, integral parts of so many mid-century concertos, are here handled with exemplary skill and lend the first movement an air of courtly grace and nobility. The Adagio is beautifully written for the cello, an intimate movement whose gentle lyricism and aura of quiet repose strikes a very personal tone after the almost ceremonial style of the opening Moderato. It is very similar in style to the slow movement of Leopold Hofmann's Cello Concerto in C, one of two concertos Hofmann may have written for Weigl when he was a member of the orchestra of St Peter's in Vienna some time after 1769. Nothing in Haydn's concerto output to date prepares the listener for the finale that follows. He manipulates his thematic building blocks in the ritornello sections in a masterly fashion, and the breathtaking solo cello writing, often lying extremely high, is formidably difficult. Altogether, it is brilliantly laid out, the culmination of Haydn's concerto finales to date.

Concerto for cello and orchestra in D (Hob.VIIb:2). For many years this popular concerto was considered to be the work of ANTON KRAFT, Haydn's principal cellist at Eszterháza during the 1780s. Kraft may have had a hand in the work's composition but only in so far as he possibly advised Haydn on a number of technical aspects in the supremely difficult solo part. Haydn's authorship remained in doubt until the rediscovery of the autograph score in the cellars of the Austrian National Library shortly after the end of the Second World War. It is dated 1783.

After the lean, concentrated style of the Concerto in C, the Cello Concerto in D, written some 20 years later, comes as something of a disappointment. Many of Haydn's old problems associated with the composition of concertos surface once again in this work, whereas the only other concerto of the period, the Piano Concerto in D, reveals a new-found mastery of the genre. All of the thematic material is beautiful, particularly in the gentle central movement, but the work as a whole lacks tension and any sense of drama. The first movement is written once again in a leisurely Allegro moderato with a quaver pulse, and its gentle, unhurried lyricism is curiously undramatic. The lovely Adagio movement is successful but after the driving intensity of the finale of the Concerto in C, the Allegro which rounds off this work, cast in the voguish rondo form of the day, is flaccid and a little dull.

Until the discovery of the Concerto in C major, the Concerto in D major was a staple part of the the cellist's repertoire, usually played from a heavily altered version by F. A. Gevaert, first published in 1890. The third movement featured in the Hollywood film *Deception* (1946), played by one of the central characters, a concert cellist.

5. Concertos for *lire organizzate* and ensemble (Hob.VIIh:1-5). In 1785 or 1786 Haydn received one of the strangest commissions of his life: to compose a series of concertos for KING FERDINAND IV OF NAPLES for two *lire organizzate*, an odd instrument resembling a hurdy-gurdy into which was built a miniature organ. The LIRA ORGANIZZATA was a favourite instrument of native Neapolitans, the *lazzoroni*, and Ferdinand, who had a genuine liking for many of the colourful local customs of his kingdom, had a lifelong interest in this bizarre instrument. The king's *lira*, however, was not the simple instrument of the *lazzaroni*. It had been perfected by the secretary of the Austrian legation in the city, Norbert Hadrava, who had also taught the king to play the instrument to a very high standard. Few foreign composers who visited Naples escaped Hadrava's eagle eye: ADALBERT GYROWETZ, Johann Franz Xaver Sterkel (1750–1817) and IGNAZ PLEYEL, to name three, all received commissions to furnish the king with new works. As the instrument was completely unknown to Haydn, he must have received very specific instructions concerning its capabilities from Hadrava. A similar letter to Sterkel is extant and helps clarify at least two important points in connection with Haydn's concertos: first, that the most practical keys were C, F, and G and, second, that the range of the *lira* was about the same as the contemporary flute.

In composing these works, Haydn did not set out to write true double concertos in the manner of his early concerto for organ and violin. Instead, he wrote ensemble music for two *lire*—the king and Hadrava—with two horns, two violins, two violas, and cello, and in this respect the works resemble the 'Divertimenti a otto voci' (Hob. X:1–6) for baryton, two horns, two violins, viola, violoncello, and double bass written in 1775. Whereas Haydn's mature concertos seek to combine the old ritornello principle with sonata form, the concertos for the King of Naples represent a neat amalgamation of the concerto principle with the divertimento. Perhaps in this sense too they have their counterpart in works like Leopold Hofmann's concertinos, some of which employ up to four solo instruments and a small ripieno group, yet are neither concertos nor symphonies concertantes. Haydn's structures and musical textures are sophisticated ones, particularly in their constant intermingling of solo and tutti.

By the time Haydn wrote these works he was a highly experienced composer and conductor of opera. Many of the works in the repertoire at Eszterháza were of Neapolitan origin, and Haydn had directed performances of several works by one of the most famous composers of the kingdom, Domenico Cimarosa (1749–1801). It is not surprising then that the concertos Haydn wrote for Naples have a strong flavour of Neapolitan opera about them. The slow movement of the second concerto is actually a transcription of the cavatina 'Sono Alcina' (Hob. XXIVb:9) that Haydn composed in 1786 for Gazzaniga's *L'isola d'Alcina*.

6. Concertos for wind instrument and orchestra. Of Haydn's seven known concertos for wind instruments only two survive and somewhat fortuitously, the Horn Concerto in D, and the Trumpet Concerto in E♭. The lost works include concertos for flute, bassoon, horn, and a work for two horns. The lost works were probably composed for members of the Esterházy orchestra. Doubtless these fortunate players jealously protected their 'ownership' of the concertos, ultimately, if unwittingly, contributing to their eventual loss. The two works that survive do so in only a single copy.

Concerto for horn and orchestra in D (Hob. VIId:3). It is not known for whom Haydn wrote this very fine horn concerto in 1762, although it has been suggested that the player concerned was JOSEPH LEUTGEB who was resident in Vienna in 1762–3. Landon believes it possible that Leutgeb received the work as a present from Haydn to mark the birth of his daughter; Haydn's wife was the child's godmother. The autograph score, dated 1762, is the only source for the work and, rather oddly, the concerto does not appear in the *Entwurf-Katalog*. The score shows traces of the speed at which the work was composed. On the last page of the autograph Haydn mixed up the oboe and violin staves and, after correcting his mistake, wrote the comment 'in Schlaff geschrieben' ('written while asleep').

One of the most interesting things about this concerto is that Haydn abandons the old Moderato tempo in the first movement in favour of a sprightly Allegro in common time. This is a significant change and the music gains immeasurably from it in terms of urgency and sense of direction. Perhaps on account of the punishing difficulty of the solo part, which demands sophisticated chromatic alterations through lipping and hand-stopping, the movement is relatively short and lacking in the meandering sequences of the early organ concertos. Haydn exploits the full range of the instrument from dark, sombre pedal notes through to the very highest register. The Largo is one of the most beautiful creations of Haydn's early years. It opens with a lengthy ritornello that contains syncopated patterns common to other works of the period. Although the movement is in A major, Haydn leaves the horn crooked in D and relies on the soloist to negotiate the new accidentals demanded by the change of tonality. The fact that this is done in the lowest range of the instrument provides clear proof that Leutgeb or Haydn's first horn player in Eisenstadt, JOHANN KNOBLAUCH, were capable of hand-stopping at this early period. The finale is another lively movement (in 2/4 and not the ubiquitous 3/8) and even employs a little invertible counterpoint at the octave. Once again the horn part is a very difficult one.

Concerto for trumpet and orchestra in E♭ (Hob. VIIe:1). Haydn's last and greatest concerto was composed in 1796 for the Viennese court trumpeter ANTON WEIDINGER. The instrument for which it was written, the ORGANISIERTE TROMPETE (organized trumpet), was Weidinger's own invention.

The Trumpet Concerto was Haydn's last purely orchestral score. The large-scale scoring of the work is a legacy of Haydn's London visits where the increased orchestral forces at his disposal acted as a spur to creativity. His treatment of the new, experimental instrument is fascinating and characteristically thorough: every single note available on the instrument is employed at one point or another. The thematic material is interesting in itself since Haydn takes care to retain certain familiar trumpet characteristics such as fanfare figures, while taking advantage of the instrument's flexibility to write new kinds of passage-work and genuine cantabile melodies. Haydn's control of musical structure reaches a peak of sophistication and crackles with fire and energy. As in all his finest work no detail is too small to escape Haydn's attention. Structural passages such as transitions are invested with tremendous musical interest, and the recapitulation of material, never a mere structural necessity in Haydn, provides him with endless opportunities to recast, develop, and reinterpret his thematic material. ADJB

H. R. Edwall, 'Ferdinand IV and Haydn's Concertos for the "Lira Organizzata"', *Musical Quarterly*, 48 (1962), 190–203.

G. Feder, 'Joseph Haydns Konzerte: Ihre Überlieferungs- und Wirkungsgeschichte', in R. Evans and M. Wendt (eds), *Festschrift Siegfried Kross zum 60. Geburtstag* (Bonn, 1990), 115–24.

M. Haselböck, 'Die Orgelkonzerte Joseph Haydns', *Musik und Kirche*, 54 (1984), 17–26.

D. Heartz, 'Leutgeb and the 1762 Horn Concertos of Joseph and Johann Michael Haydn', *Mozart-Jahrbuch* (1987–8), 59–64.

H.-C. Mahling, 'Performance Practice in Haydn's Works for lira organizzata', in J. P. Larsen, H. Serwer, and J. Webster (eds), *Haydn Studies* (London, 1981), 297–302.

A. Odenkirchen, 'Die Konzerte Joseph Haydns: Untersuchungen zur Gattungstransformation in der zweiten Hälfte des 18. Jahrhunderts', *Europäische Hochschulschriften 36: Musikwissenschaft no. 106* (Frankfurt, 1993).

continuo. Short for 'basso continuo', literally a 'continuous bass' part that appears through all or most of a musical work, and to which the remainder of the musical fabric relates; this relationship is usually indicated by figures above or below the bass line (hence 'figured bass'). The instruments that perform from this bass line will vary from genre to genre but will normally include at least one bass instrument and a keyboard instrument. The resultant group of players is often called the continuo and the director of performance will usually be the keyboard player. Although the musical thinking embedded in basso continuo is still fundamental to musical composition in the second half of the 18th century, the presence of a continuo in the sense of a core group of players is less pervasive than in the first part of the century. Thus Haydn's church music, oratorios, and operas will have keyboard continuo parts but his quartets, trios, and windband music, for instance, do not. The use of continuo in concertos and symphonies is a more complex matter. *See* PERFORMANCE PRACTICE.

contrafactum. In the broadest sense, a contrafactum is a vocal work in which a new text has been substituted for the original. In accounts of 18th-century music it tends to be associated with substitute sacred texts only, in place of a secular or sacred original. In Catholic Austria, with its unending demand for music to serve the liturgy, substituting alternative texts to make 'new' church compositions was a common practice, particularly for antiphons, graduals, and motets, also for sacred music in the German language. Examples of substitute texts for single movements taken from larger sacred works, such as the mass, the Stabat mater, and the Te Deum, are much rarer.

In Haydn's case attempting to establish the pedigree of many of the contrafacta that circulated at the time is often very difficult. Some were prepared or sanctioned by him, others not. In the typical case of the motet 'O coelitum beati' (Hob. XXIIIa:G9) the awkwardness of the word-setting and the style of the music in the first movement suggest a secular origin to the music, but the sacred version is the only one to have survived; and a newly composed movement ('Alleluia') seems to have been added to that contrafactum to form a two-movement motet.

Haydn's 'APPLAUSUS' CANTATA, written for performance in Zwettl in 1768, was a work that the composer plundered several times for contrafacta items, with no fewer than five movements acquiring sacred texts for performances in Eisenstadt. Two choruses from the later oratorio, *Il ritorno di Tobia*, became more widely known than the original: 'Audi clamorem' (from 'Odi le nostre voci', Part 1) and especially 'Insanae et vanae curae' (from 'Svanisce in un momento', Part 2).

Reflecting essentially 19th-century attitudes to

the integrity of a single work, scholars and performers remain sniffy about Haydn's contrafacta. Ignoring them means not only avoiding the different aesthetic of the period but risks misunderstanding the true nature of Haydn's reputation as a composer of sacred music.

I. Becker-Glauch, 'Neue Forschungen zur Haydns-Kirchenmusik', *HS* 2/3 (1970), 167–241.
HCRL/1.

copyists. The copying of music by hand was a central feature of musical life in the 18th century. The vast majority of manuscript copies was prepared for utilitarian purposes, to serve an immediate performance or to be added to a library for a future performance; they were not to be admired like medieval manuscripts. Although music-printing was becoming increasingly widespread in the 18th century, first performances of all music were invariably played from manuscript parts. In those areas of Europe like Britain, France, and northern Germany where music-publishing was well established, printed copies of instrumental music became the principal means of dissemination once the music had been released by the composer, though large-scale works, such as operas and oratorios, and sacred works whose circulation was naturally confined to Catholic or Protestant areas continued to depend on manuscript distribution. On the other hand, in those parts of Europe, principally the Austrian monarchy, southern Germany, Italy, and the Iberian peninsula, where the printing of music was not well established, copying music by hand remained the principal means of dissemination for all music throughout Haydn's lifetime.

Music-copying in major centres like Vienna was a highly professional business, one that is still only partially and imperfectly understood by scholars. Individuals sometimes worked alone, sometimes as employees for a music shop, and only very few signed their copies. During Haydn's lifetime there were several dozen copyists in Vienna alone, perhaps over a hundred. There is evidence of an apprentice system that encouraged a uniformity of handwriting that often makes it difficult to distinguish one copyist from another. They were trained to work quickly, with legibility for the performer being a more important consideration than an absolutely faultless reproduction of the composer's original. Copies were often prepared from other copies, with consequent decreasing accuracy, particularly as regards dynamics and phrasing. Large-scale works, like operas, were usually prepared by a team of copyists working under central supervision and even in symphonies multiple parts (*Dubletten*), such as those for first violins and second violins, could be prepared by a different hand, perhaps with corrections by the principal copyist. Copyists were paid per page not per musical work which often encouraged them to be generous in the physical layout of the page. While composers naturally tried to gain some income from the sale of manuscript copies, the copyists themselves often undermined the composer or their immediate supervisor by preparing additional copies which they themselves could then sell. In 1788, for instance, Haydn's publisher ARTARIA was preparing an edition of the op. 50 quartets when the firm discovered that manuscript copies of the same works were being offered for sale by the copying shop of Lausch. Artaria evidently felt that Haydn's copyist, in this case probably Peter Rampl, was to blame for the unsanctioned distribution; the composer (who was not above a little double-dealing himself) retorted that it was probably somebody in the employ of Artaria who had prepared an illicit copy. As the correspondence of Mozart and Beethoven as well as Haydn reveals, the integrity and musical accuracy of copyists was an abiding concern and all three were anxious to acquire the regular services of individuals whom they could trust.

Determining the status of copyists in manuscript sources for Haydn's music is an important guide to the authenticity of the work (in the absence of the composer's autograph or other evidence), to the authenticity of the text, and to certain aspects of performance practice. Between 1761, when Haydn first entered the service of the Esterházy family, and 1764 his most important copyist was Anton Adolph, employed by the court. He was succeeded by Joseph Elßler, one of three members of the ELßLER FAMILY that were to assist Haydn until his death in 1809; the first son, Joseph, succeeded his father as a copyist in 1782 and served probably until 1790; the second son, Johann, began copying for Haydn in the late 1780s and gradually assumed the role of a trusted general assistant as well as principal copyist; in this extended capacity he was employed by Haydn personally. At the Esterházy court none of these individuals could be expected to carry out all the copying duties, and orchestral players, singers, and, occasionally, even Haydn himself were called upon to copy parts. With the establishment of a permanent opera company in 1776 at Eszterháza and the consequent need to service operatic performances for up to two-thirds of the year, the demand for efficient copyists increased enormously. Johann Schellinger was engaged primarily to look after the production of operatic material; he was assisted by members of the Elßler family and others. In their study of the manuscript sources for the operatic repertoire at Eszterháza, Bartha and Somfai identified the musical handwriting of no fewer than 81 scribes, labelled, in no particular order, Anonymous 1 to

Anonymous 81. Although some of these were copyists from Vienna, Venice, and elsewhere, whose purchased material could be used unaltered at Eszterháza (or was not used at all), others were employees of the Esterházy court. Rare occurrences of unformed musical handwriting suggest the casual use of an orchestral player or singer anxious to earn some extra money, but other more consistently encountered and/or stylish hands suggest the regular employment of certain individuals to assist Schellinger and the Elßlers. Anonymous 23 has been identified as the singer LEOPOLD DICHTLER and Anonymous 10 is the theatre director NUNZIATO PORTA.

Anonymous 63, who copied also large quantities of instrumental music by Haydn from *c.*1783 onwards, was not an Esterházy employee, but a professional Viennese copyist, Peter Rampl, who was used by the court and the composer on a casual basis. Haydn continued to use him in the 1790s and in large-scale works he sometimes worked in tandem with Johann Elßler. Rampl's son Wenzel was to become one of Beethoven's most trusted copyists.

During the 1780s, especially in the period between the death of Joseph Elßler and the assumption by Johann Elßler of the role of favoured copyist, Haydn frequently used the services of Johann Radnitzky in Vienna, who was sometimes assisted by his brother Peter.

In addition to the Esterházy copyists (regular and casual) and Radnitzky and Rampl, Haydn probably had contacts with further copyists, based in Vienna. Robbins Landon was the first to identify and label individual Viennese copyists, three in number, a sequence that has been extended and modified by later writers. His Viennese Copyist no. 2 may have had the occasional direct contact with Haydn in the 1770s. A collection of early copies of music composed by Haydn in the 1750s and 1760s and once owned by the FÜRNBERG family seems especially reliable which, again, may indicate direct contact with the composer; the music was copied by Viennese Copyist no. 2 and by three copyists that have been labelled Fürnberg 1 to Fürnberg 3.

When Haydn visited London in the 1790s he became part of a new working environment. His symphonies were first performed from manuscript parts—the letters MS on a concert handbill had acquired a certain cachet, indicating that it was not yet published—but no manuscript parts prepared by London copyists have survived. Haydn commented in a letter that copyists in London were no more to be trusted than the ones back home and for his second visit he brought Johann Elßler with him. *See also* DISSEMINATION.

Bartha and Somfai.

A. Peter Brown, *Carlo d'Ordonez 1734–1786: A Thematic Catalog* (Detroit, 1978).

A. Peter Brown, 'Notes on some Eighteenth-Century Copyists', *Journal of the American Musicological Society*, 34 (1981), 325–38.

P. Bryan, *Johann Wanhal, Viennese Symphonist: His Life and His Musical Environment* (Stuyvesant, NY, 1997).

D. Edge, 'Recent Discoveries in Viennese Copies of Mozart's Concertos', in N. Zaslaw (ed.), *Mozart's Piano Concertos: Text, Context, Interpretation* (Ann Arbor, 1996).

S. C. Fisher, 'Haydn's Overtures and their Adaptations as Concert Orchestral Works' (diss., University of Pennsylvania, 1985).

S. C. Fisher and B. H. v. Boer jr, 'A Viennese Music Copyist and His Role in the Distribution of Haydn's Works', *HS* 6/2 (1988), 163–8.

H. Gericke, *Der Wiener Musikalienhandel von 1700 bis 1778* (Graz, 1960).

S. Gerlach, 'Joseph Haydns Sinfonien bis 1774. Studien zur Chronologie', *HS* 7/1–2 (1996), 1–287.

HCRL/1.

G. Thomas, 'Haydn's Copyist Peter Rampl', in S. Brandenburg (ed.), *Haydn, Mozart and Beethoven: Studies in the Music of the Classical Period* (Oxford, 1998), 85–90.

R. von Zahn, 'Der fürstlich Esterházysche Notenkopist Joseph Elßler sen.', *HS* 6/2 (1988), 130–47.

'Coronation' mass (Hob.XXII:11). Nickname formerly used in English-speaking countries for the Mass in D minor ('Nelson') MISSA IN ANGUSTIIS. Dating from the middle of the 19th century, it arose from the mistaken belief that the work had been composed for the coronation of the Austrian emperor. This falsehood also prompted the nickname 'Imperial' mass for the work.

Corri, Dussek & Co. A publishing firm in London and Edinburgh. It was formed in 1794, two years after the marriage of Sophia, the daughter of the violinist and impresario, Domenico Corri, and the pianist Jan Ladislav Dussek.The firm survived until 1800 when it came close to bankruptcy; Dussek hastily left for the continent, but Corri continued on his own until 1804 when he was succeeded by his son.

The connection between the firm and Haydn appears to have been the result of the prior acquaintanceship of Dussek and Haydn which, in turn, was probably fostered by their common friendship with SALOMON. The firm published several works by the composer: arrangements for piano and violin by Dussek of Symphonies nos. 90 and 92, two sets of canzonettas (Hob.XXVIa:25–30 and 31–6), the op. 71 and op. 74 quartets, arrangements for piano trio of the same quartets and, with Salomon, arrangements for piano trio of the 'LONDON' symphonies. JMB

J. M. Burchell, *Polite or Commercial Concerts? Concert Management and Orchestral Repertoire in Edinburgh, Bath,*

Oxford, Manchester, and Newcastle, 1730–1799 (New York and London, 1996).

***Covent Garden* overture.** In his catalogue of music written for London, Haydn noted 'Overtura Coventgarden'. The theatre at Covent Garden in the 18th century was the habitual home of opera in the English language. In April 1795, as part of the celebrations accompanying the wedding of the Prince of Wales and Princess Caroline of Brunswick there was a performance of a new work by Salomon, *Windsor Castle*. According to several newspaper reports the overture was by Haydn. An annotation in the *Entwurf-Katalog* next to the overture to *L'anima del filosofo* (Hob.1a:3) reads, quite inaccurately, 'for an English opera 1994'. Haydn's Italian opera, scheduled for its first performance in 1791 in London, had never been performed but the implication of the faulty annotation in the *Entwurf-Katalog* is that the overture was used in Salomon's stage work four years later. This single-movement overture—a Largo introduction in C minor followed by a Presto sonata form in C major—can, therefore, be given four different titles: *L'anima del filosofo*, *Orfeo* (the alternative name of the opera), *Covent Garden*, and *Windsor Castle*.

In 1796 (perhaps earlier) Salomon provided his own overture to *Windsor Castle*, in D major.

HCRL/3.

Cramer, Carl Friedrich (b. 7 March 1752; d. 8 Dec. 1807). Professor of Greek and Oriental languages at the University of Kiel, and a writer on music. Though he undertook a number of musical projects, he is best remembered for the *Magazin der Musik*, published in Hamburg between 1783 and 1787, with a final volume issued in Copenhagen in 1788. Cramer wrote many of the articles and reviews in the journal himself, including a lengthy, complimentary analysis of 'Ah come il core', and a translation of the biography of Haydn that had appeared in the *European Magazine*; that biography had imputed a conspiracy against Haydn in north Germany, a charge vigorously denied by Cramer in footnotes. Other issues of the journal speak eloquently against such charges, with Cramer and other critics consistently revealing their enthusiasm for the originality of Haydn's music, extolling his genius, and citing him as a model of excellence. MSM

HCRL/2.

M. S. Morrow, *German Music Criticism in the Late Eighteenth Century: Aesthetic Issues in Instrumental Music* (Cambridge, 1997).

'Creation' mass. *See* SCHÖPFUNGSMESSE.

***Creation, The* (*Die Schöpfung*)** (Hob.XXI:2). Oratorio by Haydn, German words by GOTTFRIED VAN SWIETEN after an English original of uncertain authorship; composed 1796–8, and first performed in Vienna on 29 and 30 April 1798. The work owes its most direct stimulus to Haydn's two visits to London. Despite *Il ritorno di Tobia*, written for the Tonkünstler-Societät in Vienna in 1775 and revived, with the addition of two magnificent extra choruses, in 1784, Haydn was previously little concerned with oratorio. He was doubtless aware of the private performances of Handel promoted by Swieten's group of aristocratic sponsors, known as the Gesellschaft der Associierten, for which Mozart prepared arrangements of *Acis and Galatea* (1788), *Messiah* (1789), and the *Ode for St Cecilia's Day* and *Alexander's Feast* (1790). Already in the 1780s Haydn may himself have been involved in them in a small way, and his Storm chorus (Hob. XXIVa:8) was heard in these surroundings in 1793, between the two London visits. By the early 1790s van Swieten was pressing him for a new oratorio of his own. But in the exclusive surroundings of van Swieten's promotions Handel seems to have made little impression on him. It was the popular Handel tradition that he encountered in London, especially the impact of the huge performances that he heard there in 1791, that fired his ambition to compose new choral works.

His first involvement with the subject matter of *The Creation* evidently began with SALOMON, the violinist and impresario who had brought him to London. Doubtless eager to secure another commission from Haydn, perhaps even hoping to persuade him to return to London a third time, Salomon procured for him a book of words which was to become *The Creation*. Given the English taste and Haydn's new enthusiasm, an oratorio must have seemed a particularly attractive prospect. The libretto, moreover, is said to have been originally intended for Handel, although its reputed author, Thomas Linley senior (1733–95) ('Lidley' according to Haydn's biographer, Griesinger), was probably no more than an intermediary on its route to Haydn. Whether this text had anything to do with an oratorio called *The Creation* that Thomas Busby is known to have composed in 1789 cannot be established since very little of that work survives.

Back in Vienna, Haydn had waiting for him in the concerts of van Swieten's group a ready-made platform and financial backing, and in van Swieten himself both an enthusiastic impresario and someone with experience, through his work on Mozart's Handel arrangements, in organizing German versions of English oratorios.

Given Haydn's weak command of English and the ambitions of van Swieten, *The Creation* was inevitably destined for composition in German and first performance in Vienna. But from the start it was clearly designed also to take its place in the English Handelian tradition, at least partly honouring Salomon's commission in the process, although not according him the first performance. This intention explains van Swieten's unusual method of setting about the preparation of the German text from which Haydn worked. Although the original 'Handelian' libretto is now lost, and although adjustments to it were certainly made, it is clear that much of it was left intact and that the German words were for the most part tailored to it, syllable for syllable, in such a way that Haydn's music would fit both languages. When Haydn had finished his German oratorio, the English one was ready as well. In Vienna it was commonly thought to have been 'really written for England'. Its dual nationality was emphasized by the publication of the score with both German and English words underlaid (supposedly the first time that this had been done). Today Haydn would doubtless find it absurd to learn that performances of *The Creation* in English-speaking countries are usually given in German in the mistaken interest of authenticity.

An attractive story concerning Haydn's search for an oratorio subject tells how in London the violinist François Hippolyte Barthélemon handed him a Bible and told him to begin at the beginning. *The Creation* does just that. But before the first words of the biblical account are heard, the scene is magnificently set by the orchestral 'Representation of Chaos', bleakly depicting in uncertain tonalities an earth 'without form and void', until the darkness is triumphantly dispelled by one of Haydn's boldest—and simplest—strokes as the ensuing recitative leads to the choral blaze of pure C major at the words 'And there was light'.

Thereafter the six days of creation that make up Parts 1 and 2 of the oratorio proceed along broadly similar lines, each beginning with narration, continuing with lyrical or descriptive commentary and ending with a hymn of praise. Minor departures from this layout occur, for example when the sixth day, encompassing the creation of most of the animal kingdom (birds and fish having been dealt with the day before) and Adam and Eve, needs to be subdivided, but the overall plan is clear.

The three principal phases of each day correspond in large measure to the three textual sources. The passages of narrative, sung by the three archangels, Gabriel (soprano), Uriel (tenor), and Raphael (bass—like *The Seasons*, Haydn's *Creation* has no alto soloist), show most clearly the origins of the libretto, since they derive directly from the Authorized Version of the English Bible. The more poetic sections that follow, amplifying the objective account, frequently draw on Milton's *Paradise Lost*, which is the origin of the picturesque imagery of the 'serpent error' of the river's course, the stag's 'branching head', and the 'long dimensions' and 'sinuous trace' of the worm. The concluding choral paeans are often paraphrases of psalms.

Haydn responded to this strong but varied scheme with music of incomparable vividness, bringing to bear all the rich resources of his colourful late orchestral style. Raphael's recitative, beginning 'And God made the firmament', portrays in rapid succession a storm, clouds, lightning and thunder, rain, hail, and snow. Graphic depiction of this sort is most readily employed in dramatic, orchestrally accompanied recitative, but it also occurs within closed musical numbers. In 'Rolling in foaming billows' (no. 6) the stormy sea and mountains give way to the quiet river of the plain and the 'purling' of the 'limpid brook'. The splendour of the sunrise in 'In splendour bright' (no. 12) is followed by the mysterious delicacy of the moon. Gabriel's aria 'On mighty pens' (no. 15) has the eagle, the lark, the dove, and the nightingale. In no. 24, the aria 'In native worth', Uriel views as it were from afar the newly created man and woman, before their personification as Adam and Eve in Part 3. Most vivid of all are the delighted portrayals of the animal world in no. 21, 'Strait opening her fertile womb': the rude trombone blast of the 'cheerful' lion; the 'sudden leaps' of the 'flexible' tiger; the placidly grazing cattle; and the 'sinuous trace' of Milton's worm. In Raphael's aria that follows the heavy beasts tread the ground with a *fortissimo* contrabassoon on the lowest note of its compass.

This sort of imagery may owe something to the picturesque depiction occasionally employed by Handel, especially in *Israel in Egypt*, which was among the oratorios performed at the festival witnessed by Haydn in 1791. A more likely direct incentive was the taste of van Swieten, whose manuscript libretto included (probably at Haydn's request) suggestions as to musical treatment and who sometimes urged Haydn further than he might have wished to go in the direction of colourful 'tone-painting', notoriously in his insistence on the depiction of the croaking frog in *The Seasons*.

Most obviously reminiscent of Handel are the magnificent choruses. Often, however, chorus and soloists are not kept apart but interact in the manner so characteristic of Haydn's late masses. In 'The Heavens are telling' (a paraphrase of part of Psalm 19) that closes Part 1 the three archangels play concertino to the tutti of the chorus. Part 2 again ends with a solo and choral complex, 'Achieved is the glorious work' framing another psalm paraphrase, the trio 'On thee each living soul awaits' (no. 27). In the other direction, Uriel's aria 'Now vanish before the holy beams' (no. 2) turns into a chorus. This flexibility in the shaping of dramatic scene complexes makes *The Creation* unlike any earlier oratorio. Conventional Italian oratorio, as most commonly heard in Vienna hitherto and of which *Il ritorno di Tobia* is a representative example, typically proceeded in a succession of static units. Now, in no. 2, Haydn's symphonic mastery can accommodate within a single continuous number both the Miltonic vision of hell's spirits falling in C minor into the abyss, and the serene A major of the 'new created world'.

After the end of Part 2, creation complete, the scene changes, and the remainder of the oratorio is entirely contemplative. Of the three archangels only Uriel remains, and after a magical dawn (quite different from the elemental sunrise in Part 1), opening with three flutes and pizzicato strings, he introduces the soprano and bass soloists in their reincarnation as Adam and Eve. What follows is on the most spacious scale, most of the remainder of the work up to the final chorus being occupied by only two extended numbers. After the greater dramatic urgency of Parts 1 and 2 some have found Part 3 less successful, and in many modern performances (particularly amateur ones) it is sadly cut or even omitted altogether. Certainly the pace has dropped, but in the place of action there is a sense of sublime stillness, rare in any music, which elsewhere in Haydn is most characteristically found in the rapt slow movements of some of the late string quartets. It is in this mood that Adam and Eve begin 'By thee with bliss' (no. 30), originally entitled 'Hymn of praise with alternating chorus of angels', expressing their wonder at the newly created world around them in an encomium reminiscent of the Benedicite or even of St Francis's Canticle of the Sun. Having fulfilled their first duty in giving thanks (as Adam puts it), they then turn to rapturous contemplation of each other in a love duet that is timeless. The oratorio clearly could not end there, but after it the robust concluding chorus, returning to the spirit of choral paean, fine though it is, almost seems to break the spell.

Like the choral version of THE SEVEN LAST WORDS in 1796, *The Creation* was promoted by van Swieten's group of sponsors, the Associierte, who covered all the expenses and paid Haydn a handsome honorarium of 500 ducats (five times the amount that Mozart had received for *Le nozze di Figaro* or *Don Giovanni*, for example). The first performances took place on 29 and 30 April 1798 at the palace of Prince Joseph Schwarzenberg (a member of van Swieten's group) before the cream of Viennese society. The oratorio was immediately an outstanding success. Three further private performances promoted by the Associierte were given within the next few weeks, and there were two more early in March the following year. On 19 March 1799 came the first public performance, in the Burgtheater, but it was still privately sponsored: van Swieten's group met all the costs and made over the proceeds (a record for a Viennese theatre) to Haydn. Finally in December that year it was released to the Tonkünstler-Societät in two performances conducted by Haydn himself, and thereafter it dominated the society's charity concerts.

London had to wait longer for its English oratorio, until the publication of the bilingual score at the end of February 1800. It is said that Salomon had wished to take Haydn to court, presumably because his commission had been hijacked by Vienna. Nothing came of that threat, and in the event he was outsprinted by his rival at the Covent Garden Oratorio, John Ashley, who rushed the work into performance on 28 March, scarcely a month after the appearance of the score in Vienna. Only on 21 April 1800 was Salomon able to present the English oratorio that he believed he had commissioned from Haydn five years earlier. DEO

H. C. Robbins Landon (ed.), *The Creation and The Seasons: The Complete Authentic Sources for the Word-Books* (Cardiff, 1985).

B. MacIntyre, *Haydn: The Creation* (New York, 1998).

E. Olleson, 'The Origin and Libretto of Haydn's Creation', *HYB* 4 (1968), 148–68.

N. Temperley, *Haydn: The Creation* (Cambridge, 1991).

Crotch, William (b. 5 July 1775; d. 29 Dec. 1847). English child prodigy, composer, organist, and teacher. As an eminent public lecturer on music, he significantly influenced the reception of Haydn in England for over 30 years.

As a boy Crotch encountered symphonies and quartets by Haydn while participating at concerts in Cambridge in 1787. His appointment as organist of Christ Church, OXFORD, in September 1790 provided ample opportunity to meet Haydn in person during the composer's doctoral festivities the following summer; on 7 July, according to his memoirs, Crotch played the organ at Christ Church for Haydn, and also performed one of his own 'overtures' for Haydn over dinner.

As professor of music from 1797, Crotch sought to improve public taste with a series of public lectures, which led to prestigious engagements at London's new literary and scientific institutes. During his first season at the Royal Institution in January 1805, however, he angered BURNEY and SALOMON with his remarks on Haydn's *Creation*. His central message was that a composer should always aspire to the Sublime style, particularly in sacred works; in Crotch's view, Haydn and the 'moderns' favoured the lowlier styles—the Beautiful and Ornamental—and this spelt the decline of music as an art form.

According to this argument Haydn's music represented a debilitating aesthetic. Nevertheless, Crotch admired his symphonies for their 'novelty & brilliancy of effect, gaiety of style, & disposition of the score'. Sometimes Crotch emulated these qualities in his own music, for example in the first movement of a symphony in G (1814), and he encouraged domestic performances of Haydn's symphonies by arranging 12 for piano trio, published around 1825.

To mark the first anniversary of Haydn's death, Crotch gave a concert on 28 May 1810 in Oxford; the main item was an anthem based on music from the Stabat mater, the only work of Haydn's to be judged truly sublime by Crotch's criteria. REC

A. P. Brown, 'The Sublime, the Beautiful, and the Ornamental: English Aesthetic Currents and Haydn's London Symphonies', in O. Biba and D. W. Jones (eds), *Studies in Music History presented to H. C. Robbins Landon on his Seventieth Birthday* (London, 1996), 44–71.

H. Irving, 'William Crotch on "The Creation"', *Music and Letters*, 75 (1994), 548–60.

J. Rennert, *William Crotch (1775–1847): Composer, Artist, Teacher* (Lavenham, 1975).

D

dance. Nineteenth-century Vienna, the home of the Strauss family and of the waltz, is often viewed as the time and place where the social dance reigned supreme. In reality dancing had been a favoured social pastime of the lower, middle, and upper classes in the Austrian territories at least as far back as the middle of the 18th century. It is not surprising, therefore, that Haydn composed several sets of dances, from his youth in Vienna in the 1750s through to the 1790s. This is a neglected corner of Haydn's output, partly because many of them were not available in modern editions until the last decades of the 20th century, and partly because very little is known about the precise circumstances in which most of them were composed.

There is some extant documentary evidence that relates Haydn to the pervasive culture of the social dance, but none of it can be directly related to surviving sets of dances. Two of Haydn's earliest biographers, CARPANI and DIES, state that some of the composer's earliest works were dances; in the carnival seasons of 1755 and 1756 Haydn was engaged as a violinist in the orchestra for balls held at the imperial court in Vienna, and he may well have composed dances for these occasions. Certainly as early as 1766, in the profile of the composer that appeared in *Wiener Diarium*, his minuets are described as 'natural, playful and alluring'. (The context makes it clear that the minuets are actual dances, not movements from his instrumental music.) A year after his death, 1810, another commentator remarked that Haydn's dances were 'universally known and danced', from imperial balls to village inns.

As in all aristocratic courts, balls were a feature of the social calendar at the Esterházy court, but it seems that Haydn's many duties as Vice-Kapellmeister and then Kapellmeister did not extend to supplying the necessary music or musicians. Instead, in the 1760s and 1770s, dance orchestras were separately engaged from Vienna, typically 16 to 18 players, an ensemble slightly larger than Haydn's own orchestra at the time. While some of Haydn's extant dances from this period may have been played by these visiting ensembles, the firm impression is that the visiting ensemble came with their own music. At Eszterháza the so-called Chinese Ball Room, a building attached to the main opera house, was a favourite venue for dances, where not only the decor projected the fashionable rococo *chinoiserie*, but the players, too, wore Chinese costumes. Oddly enough the only evidence of Haydn himself directing performances of dances refers to a masked ball organized by Count Anton Grassalkovics in his palace in Pressburg (Bratislava) in November 1772; Nicolaus Esterházy was the count's stepfather and the services of Haydn and the Esterházy orchestra were probably provided as a gesture of friendship. That Haydn's existing dances featured regularly in Viennese circles at the time is suggested by an anecdote, related by Griesinger and Dies, in which Dittersdorf and Haydn entered a dance hall in Vienna, where they heard a Haydn minuet excruciatingly played by some drunk musicians.

Haydn's earliest surviving minuets probably date from the late 1750s (Hob.IX:1), an autograph of 12 minuets now found in the abbey of Seitenstetten in Lower Austria. They are scored for an ensemble of two oboes, two horns, and the standard string forces for dances of two violins and bass. Each dance changes key, moving away from C major, re-establishing it in the fifth dance, and returning to it in the final, twelfth dance. The pivotal role of C major is accentuated by the fact that these three minuets are the only ones to have a trio section, in C minor on each occasion. Further contrast and shaping is provided by the horns, who play in only half the minuets. Some of the melodic and harmonic mannerisms recall minuets in contemporary symphonies, quartets, and other instrumental music by the composer, but the demands of the dance require a consistent and obvious procession of regular four-bar phrases and a more consistent emphasis in the bass part on the pulse of the music than is found in otherwise similar movements in symphonies and quartets. Minuet movements in those genres by Haydn had already attracted adverse comment for their use of octave-writing between the first and second violin; though such writing is occasionally found in these danced minuets, it is not a particularly obvious feature.

The autograph of a single minuet and trio in G (Hob.IX:23) carries the annotation no. 23 and no. 24 in Haydn's handwriting, as well as his customary 'Fine/Laus Deo', indicating that they were the concluding movements in a set of dances that is otherwise lost. The manuscript dates from the same time as the visit of Haydn and his orchestra to Count Grassalkovics's palace in Pressburg, where the complete set may have been played.

The autograph of six minuets (Hob.IX:5) carries the date 1776, but its contents suggest that it is not a complete set: it begins with a minuet and trio in D major for an ensemble of two oboes, two horns, and strings, but the final work is in A major, without a trio section, and is written for strings only. A single flute is used in the trio of the first minuet and presumably would have featured in the later, lost portion of the set. The trio section of the fourth minuet is attractively scored for solo oboe, solo bassoon, and strings, while no. 5 features some duple rhythms in the prevailing triple time, but not in the destructive manner found, for instance, in the minuet of Symphony no. 65 composed a few years earlier.

The next surviving set of minuets by Haydn consists of 14 dances (Hob.IX:7) published by Artaria in 1784 with the title 'Raccolta de Menuetti Ballabili' ('Collection of minuets suitable for dancing'), an unusual title that suggests a heterogeneous collection of single minuets rather than a carefully constructed set. The key structure and instrumentation supports this view: the collection opens with a bracing minuet in D for two oboes, two horns, timpani, and strings, but it ends with a gentle minuet in G for oboes, horns, and strings; also there are two instances of minuets in A major being followed by ones in B♭, a strained juxtaposition of keys that Haydn was usually careful to avoid in genuine cycles of minuets. Artaria seems to have developed an ad hoc plan in the early 1780s of publishing a variety of music by Haydn, divertimenti, sonatas, quartets, symphonies, songs, and cantatas; this collection of minuets may have been initiated by the firm as part of this process. As to the music itself, there are a number of minuets enlivened by scotch snap rhythms, and two that feature melodic lines above a reiterated tonic bass; the trio of no. 8 (in C) doubles the first-violin line with a solo bassoon at the lower octave, a favourite tone colour of the composer from the end of the 1760s onwards.

Early in 1787 Artaria announced the publication of six allemandes by Haydn, works that almost certainly had been circulating in manuscript form for a couple of years. 'Allemande' is not a reference to the old Baroque dance in alla breve time, but an alternative rendering of 'Deutsche Tanz', essentially a minuet but with a propensity towards using up-beats to phrases, and arpeggio motion in the main melody coupled with the repeated yodelling rhythm of four quavers and a crotchet. Although the cycle begins in B♭ and ends in D, adjacent dances are placed a descending third apart, with a fall of a fifth to the final one. There are no trio sections.

Soon after his return from London to Vienna in July 1792 Haydn was asked to write dances for a charity ball to raise money for the dependants of retired or deceased artists and architects, the Pensionsgesellschaft bildener Künstler. The resulting sets of dances, 12 minuets (Hob.IX:11) and 12 'Deutsche Tänze' (Hob.IX:12), were performed on 25 November in a masked ball in the Redoutensaal, the most prestigious venue for public or semi-public dances in Vienna. In comparision to Haydn's other dances, a great deal of information about the circumstances of composition and performance has survived. Haydn provided the dances for nothing, over 2,000 tickets were sold, the orchestra consisted of 47 players, and the occasion made a net profit of over 4,000 gulden. In December, a keyboard arrangement of both sets, prepared by the composer at the express wish of the Empress Marie Therese, was published by Artaria. The dances were repeated at the 1793 ball, when the orchestra was a smaller one of 27 players. Early in 1794, Artaria published an arrangement of the dances for two violins and bass, prepared in-house rather than by the composer.

With a profusion of melodic appeal, the minuets are grandly and imaginatively scored for an orchestra that includes two flutes (with piccolo in the trio of the seventh minuet), two oboes, two clarinets, two bassoons, two horns, two trumpets, timpani, and strings (with occasional separate parts for cellos and double basses). Apart from a brief appearance as part of the windband in *Armida*, this is the first time that Haydn requires clarinets in any of his works; he is cautious in their use, and though they are often given the leading line it is always doubled by the first violins. Every minuet has an associated trio and the proportions of the principal minuet, in particular, are much expanded from Haydn's previous dances. The set begins and ends in D, with the contrast in instrumental colour being complemented by a key scheme that moves to E major on the sharp side and E♭ on the flat side. The 12 'Deutsche Tänze' are less ambitious, of smaller duration, have only one trio section (no. 4), and only gradually permit the full orchestra to make an impact.

Of the circumstances surrounding the composition of Haydn's final set of dances, a set of 24 minuets (Hob.IX:16), absolutely nothing is known, and since it survives only as a set of manuscript parts once owned by the firm of Artaria, some scholars have suggested that the music might not be by the composer. The style of the music points clearly to the 1790s and, apart from the young Beethoven, it is difficult to think of anyone else who could have written music of this quality and appeal. On the other hand, there are certain features that are without precedent in Haydn's dances. All 24 minuets have an associated trio but, apart from four which change to the tonic mode, all are in the same key as the accompanying minuets. The orchestra is the same as the 1792 set, but the solo clarinet writing is more liberated, including, in no. 10, a duet for two clarinets that exploits the contrasting high and chalumeau registers. Also unusual, or progressive, is the number of highly characterized movements in the minor key, including in no. 19 a trio in A minor with optional improvised parts for 'Turkish' instruments (cymbals, triangle, tambourine, and bass drum) and, as no. 22, a *fortissimo* minuet in D minor. Although the order of minuets shows some concern for an appropriate contrast of key from one minuet to the next, the move from the penultimate minuet in B♭ to the final one in A, plus the gentle nature of the latter, suggest that the 24 minuets are a collection rather than a coherent set.

HCRL/3.

G. Thomas, 'Studien zu Haydns Tanzmusik', *HS* 3/2 (1973), 5–28.

Da qual gioia improvvisa (With what spontaneous joy) (Hob.XXIVa:3). One of three extant honorific cantatas that Haydn wrote in the first years of his service at the Esterházy court; he did not use the word cantata for the works but referred to each one as a 'Coro'.

From late January to early April 1764 PRINCE NICOLAUS ESTERHÁZY was in Frankfurt on behalf of the Habsburg family; he was a representative of Bohemia in the election and, subsequently, the coronation of Archduke Joseph (the future Joseph II) as King of the Romans. He gained the approval and gratitude of the Habsburg family for his loyalty, his fabulous display of pomp on behalf of the dynasty, and, not least, for defraying the costs himself. For the Esterházy family it was another crucial step up the ladder of imperial esteem.

Therefore, when Haydn and his fellow musicians greeted the prince on his return with a new vocal and orchestral work, it was not only a beneficent employer that was being honoured but a prince of enhanced political status. The author of the text is unknown but it is likely to have been either GIRALOMO BON or the tenor CARL FRIBERTH, possibly both. Set in the ceremonial key of C major, it does not have the trumpets and timpani often associated with such music and which Haydn uses, for instance, in the Te Deum from the same period. After a lengthy orchestral introduction a solo soprano, representing the assembled Esterházy court, poses the ceremonial question 'What day is this?', subsequently providing the answer that it is the day when the prince has returned from the place 'where the Main washes its banks' and where 'his name will remain for ever known'. The second movement is a chorus with soloists. First the principal singers of the court offer their tribute, echoed by a small chorus; as a composer Haydn's presence has been obvious throughout but here he adds an appropriate element of ostentation by including several short harpsichord solos for himself between the vocal sections. The cantata ends with the repeated exclamation 'Long live the prince, whom the world holds in astonishment'.

As a *pièce d'occasion* the work could not be performed again. The last chorus circulated as a sacred item with the text, 'Plausus honores date', and the three extant sources appropriately add trumpets and timpani to the orchestra. It is doubtful whether Haydn prepared this sacred version.

'Das Ochsenmenuett'. *See* OCHSENMENUETT.

Davide, Giacomo (David) (b. 1750; d. 1820). Italian tenor for whom Haydn conceived the difficult part of Orfeo in *L'anima del filosofo* (London, 1791), with its unusually low register. When the King's Theatre was refused an opera licence, Davide sang at the substitute entertainments there as well as at Salomon's concert series, and Haydn's benefit on 16 May of the same year. For the benefit concert Haydn composed a new concert aria for Davide which has not survived. SMcV

HCRL/3.

C. Price, J. Milhous, and R. D. Hume, *Italian Opera in Late Eighteenth-Century London*, vol. i: *The King's Theatre, Haymarket 1778–1791* (Oxford, 1995).

dedicated works. In Haydn's lifetime the practice of dedicating works to specified individuals followed a certain consistent etiquette. Formal dedications were more likely to be found on published sources than on manuscript copies, and were often initiated by the publisher rather than the composer. Typically the dedicatee was a noble patron, whose perspicacity was thereby flattered and further support ensured. It was comparatively unusual for a published work to be dedicated to a fellow performer or composer. However, the esteem and affection in which Haydn was held prompted several composers to dedicate works to the master, in a way that is not found in the careers of Mozart, Beethoven, and other composers of the time.

Below is given a list of works dedicated to Haydn in his lifetime or shortly afterwards. Following the composer and the work, the date of composition is given for works that exist only in manuscript, and for published works the place, publisher, and date (where known).

The most illustrious dedications to Haydn were those by Mozart, six quartets (1785), and Beethoven, three sonatas (1796), and are particular examples of characteristics evident in many other dedicated works. Mozart was acknowledging Haydn's unprecedented mastery of the quartet medium, and other composers, too, dedicated quartets to him: Eybler, Hänsel, Haigh, Jadin, Mederitsch, Pleyel, Radicati, Romberg, Edmund Weber (Carl Maria von Weber's stepbrother), and Wikmanson. Beethoven was Haydn's most famous pupil, and other pupils likewise dedicated works to their former teacher, including Hänsel, Kalkbrenner, Lessel, Neukomm, Pleyel, Polzelli, Struck, and Edmund Weber. Albrechtsberger's canon and Stadler's musical response to Haydn's printed visiting card, 'HIN IST ALLE MEINE KRAFT', are short, intellectually inventive tributes to the aged composer, while Cherubini's work (initially composed following a rumour that Haydn had died), Kalkbrenner's sonata, Neukomm's canon (inscribed on Haydn's grave in Vienna), and Polzelli's vocal quartet were posthumous tributes. As well as composers who would have known Haydn in Vienna and its environs, the list contains a number of composers, amateur as well as professional, whom Haydn met during his two London visits, Mary Barthelemon, Graeff, Haigh, Hodges, LATROBE, and Tomich.

Albrechtsberger, Johann Georg: canon, 'Solatium miseris' (1806)
Bachmann, Gottlob: quartet, op. 15 (Augsburg, Gombart, 1800)
Barth, Christian Samuel: *Schlesische musikalische Blumenlese* (Breslau, *c.*1804)
Barthélemon, Mary ('Polly'): keyboard sonata, op. 3 (London, *c.*1795)
Beethoven, Ludwig van: three piano sonatas, op. 2 (Vienna, Artaria, 1796)
Benincori, Angelo: six quartets, op. 8 (Paris, Naderman)
Bertini, Benoît-Auguste: three sonatas for piano and violin, op. 1 (London, 1795)
Brandl, Johann: three quartets, op. 17, livre 1 (Heilbronn, Amon, 1799)
Cambini: *see* 'HIN IST ALLE MEINE KRAFT'
Cherubini, Luigi: *Chant sur la Mort de Joseph Haydn* (1805)
Cramer, Johann Baptist: three piano sonatas, op. 23 (Vienna, Artaria, 1799)
Dussek, J. L: three sonatas for piano and violin, op. 16 (London, Longman & Broderip, 1791)
Eberl, Anton: *Grande Sonata caractéristique*, op. 12 (Vienna, Mollo, 1801)
Eybler, Joseph: three string quartets, op. 1 (Vienna, Traeg, 1794)
Graeff, Johann Georg: three flute quartets, op. 8 (London, Linley, *c.*1797)
Grill, Franz: three quartets, op. 3 (Offenbach, André, 1790)
Gyrowetz, Adalbert: six quartets, op. 8 (Paris, Imbault, 1789)
Haigh, Thomas: three piano sonatas, op. 8 (London, Preston, *c.*1795)
Hänsel, Peter: three quartets, op. 5 (Offenbach, André, 1799)
Hodges, Ann Mary: 'When from thy sight I waste' (*c.*1794–5)
Hummel, Johann Nepomuk: piano sonata in E♭, op. 13 (Vienna, Bureau d'Arts et d' Industrie, 1805)
Jadin, Hyacinthe, three quartets, op. 1 (Paris, Magazin de Musique, 1795)
Kalkbrenner: piano sonata, op. 56 (Paris, Pleyel, 1821)
Kospoth, Otto Carl Erdmann: six quartets, op. 8 (Offenbach, André, 1790)
Latrobe, Christian Ignatius: three piano sonatas, op. 3 (London, Bland, 1791)
Leidesdorf, Maximilian Joseph: trio for piano, flute, and viola, op. 14 (Vienna, Bureau d'Arts et d'Industrie, *c.*1804)
Lessel, Franciszek: three piano sonatas, op. 2 (Vienna, Weigl, *c.*1803)
Lessel, Franciszek: variations for piano (before 1804; written for Haydn's nameday; lost)
Mederitsch(-Gallus), Johann: three string quartets, op. 6 (Vienna, Artaria, 1802)
Mozart, Franz Xaver: cantata for Haydn's birthday (1805; lost)
Mozart, Wolfgang Amadeus: six string quartets (K387, K421, K428, K458, K464, K465) (Vienna: Artaria, 1785)
Neukomm, Sigismund: Fantasy in D minor for orchestra (1808)
Neukomm, Sigismund: canon, 'Non omnis moriar' (1814)
Pleyel, Ignaz: six string quartets, op. 2 (Vienna, Graeffer, 1784)
Polzelli, Anton: vocal quartet, 'Nänie' (Vienna, Kunst und Industrie Comptoir, 1810?)
Radicati, Felix: three string quartets, op. 14 (Vienna, Artaria, 1807)
Reicha: thirty-six fugues (Vienna, Chemische Druckerey, 1803)
Romberg, Andreas: three quartets, op. 2, livre 2 (Bonn Simrock, 1802)
Romberg, Bernhard: three quartets, op. 1, livre 1 (Leipzig, Breitkopf & Härtel, *c.*1800; Paris, Pleyel, c.1801)
Salieri, Antonio: 'A un muover sol di sue possenti ciglia' (celebratory sonnet by Carpani that was to be set by Salieri in 1808–9; lost or never set)
Schultesius, Johann Paul: *Riconciliazione fra due amici. Tema originate con delle variazioni analoghe al sogetto* (Augsburg, Gombart, 1803)
Stadler, Maximilian: *Musikalische Abschiedskarte des Herrn Kapellmeister Dr Joseph Haydn beantwortet von Maximilian Stadler* (Vienna, Cappi, 1806)
Struck, Paul: three piano trios, op. 1 (Offenbach, André, 1797)
Tomich, Francesco: three piano trios (London, Longman & Broderip, 1792)
Weber, Edmund: three string quartets, op. 8 (Augsburg, Gombart, 1804)
Wikmanson, Johan: three quartets, op. 1 (Stockholm, Konigl. prieve legierade Not-Tryckeriet, 1801)
Wölfl, Joseph: three piano trios, op. 5 (Augsburg, Gombart, 1798)
Zulehner, Karl: andante and rondo for piano duet, op. 5 (Mainz, Zulehner, *c.*1804)

H. Walter, 'Haydn Gewidmete Streichquartette', in G. Feder, H. Hüschen, and U. Tank (eds), *Joseph Haydn, Tradition und Rezeption* (Regensburg, 1985), 17–53.

'den alten Schmarn'. In June 1803 Haydn wrote from Vienna to Joseph Elßler, an oboist at the Esterházy court in Eisenstadt, asking him to forward a copy of Symphony no. 60, referring to it as 'den alten Schmarn'. 'Schmarn' is a pancake, served in shreds, and a popular dish in Austria and Bavaria; the word is also used colloquially to indicate something worthless. An English equivalent to Haydn's expression would be 'that old tripe'.

Der Apotheker (Hob.XXVIII:3). German title for the opera LO SPEZIALE. It gained particular currency in the 20th century following the publication in 1895 of a one-act version of the opera in German and its subsequent many performances, most famously by the Vienna Boys' Choir.

'Derbyshire' marches. Two marches (Hob. VIII:1–2) written by Haydn in 1794 for the Derbyshire Voluntary Cavalry. *See* WINDBAND MUSIC § 4.

Der Geburtstag (The Birthday). Name given to a divertimento in C (Hob.II:11), composed *c.*1760. Haydn referred to the work simply as 'divertimento a sei' (six-part divertimento) in the *Entwurf-Katalog* but the name is consistently found in contemporary manuscript sources which may indicate that it originated with Haydn, and that the work was originally written to celebrate a birthday. The slow movement is headed 'Mann und Weib', a reference to the melody that is played in octaves throughout (by the 'man and wife'). It is not known whether the melody quotes or alludes to a folksong of that name. The theme of the finale appears also in the slow movement of Symphony no. 14.

The view that the divertimento is linked in some way with a stage work called *Der Geburtstag*, performed in Vienna in 1767, is mistaken.

Der Kapellmeister seiner Durchlaucht. A play based on Haydn's life by the Austrian writer Kurt von Lessen (1877–1960), first performed in Vienna in June 1944. *See* RECEPTION.

Der krumme Teufel (The crooked devil) (Hob. XXIXb:1a). German opera (*opéra-comique*) by KURZ-BERNARDON, presumed to have been set to music by Haydn in *c.*1751. The first recorded performance was at the Kärntnertortheater, Vienna, on 29 May 1753. Text and music are both lost, unless the text is identical with DER NEUE KRUMME TEUFEL. PB

Der neue krumme Teufel (The new crooked devil) (Hob.XXIXb:1b). German opera (*opéra-comique*), setting a text by KURZ-BERNARDON and composed in Vienna *c.*1758; Haydn's music has not survived. The text survives in at least three more-or-less contemporary editions. Haydn's identity as a composer of the work is attested by the original undated printed libretto; it is not known whether Haydn set the intermezzo *Il vecchio ingannato* (The old man tricked) which is contained in the libretto. Both GRIESINGER and DIES relate the story of Kurz's commissioning of the score, and his demonstration to Haydn of swimming so that the ignorant young composer could depict musically Arelquin's escape from a storm at sea. The commission earned Haydn the considerable sum of 24 or 25 ducats. The text is a richly varied farce in a mixture of German and Italian, and packed with spectacle. The score was quite extensive (incidental music, 31 arias, and ten ensembles); its loss is the more surprising in view of its frequent performances in the 18th century. It has been conjectured that Symphony no.1 was originally the overture to *Der neue krumme Teufel.* PB

D. Heartz, *Haydn, Mozart and the Viennese School, 1740–1780* (New York, 1995).
HCRL/1.
O. Rommel (ed.), *Die Maschinenkomödie* (Deutsche Literatur in Entwicklungsreihen: Reihe Barock: Barocktradition im österreichisch-bayrischen Volkstheater, I) (Leipzig, 1935).
G. Thomas, 'Haydns deutsche Singspiele', *HS* 6 (1986), 1–63.

'Der verliebte Schulmeister'. Haydn included the incipit of divertimento in D (Hob.II:10) in the *Entwurf-Katalog* together with the remark 'Der Schulmeister gennant' ('known as the Schoolmaster'). When this incipit was recorded in the *Haydn-Verzeichnis* the remark was amended to 'Der verliebte Schulmeister' ('The Schoolmaster in Love'). The work has not survived. There is no discernible link between this nickname and the similar one, 'Der Schulmeister', given to Symphony no. 55.

Destatevi, o miei fidi (Awake, my faithful ones) (Hob.XXIVa:2). One of three extant honorific cantatas that Haydn wrote in the first years of his service at the Esterházy court; he did not use the word cantata for the works but referred to each one as a 'Coro'.

First performed on 6 December 1763, this was the first of a handful of miscellaneous works that Haydn wrote for the nameday of Prince Nicolaus. It was followed in December 1764 by a second cantata, QUAL DUBBIO ORMAI, in 1766 by a set of baryton trios, in 1767 by Symphony no. 35, and, in 1772, by the MISSA SANCTI NICOLAI. The work consists of three movements (two duets and a chorus) each preceded by a recitative. The author of the text is unknown; it is likely to have been either GIRALOMO BON or CARL FRIBERTH, possibly both.

As in all these cantatas a lengthy orchestral introduction creates a feeling of anticipation. A solo soprano urges her fellow courtiers to celebrate the nameday. The following duet for soprano and tenor is probably the most demanding in Haydn's entire output. The soprano shoots up to a top C in the first phrase and the crucial word 'omaggio' ('homage') sets off six and a half bars of coloratura in parallel tenths. A short unaccompanied recitative leads to a gentler, less demanding duet for two sopranos. In the third recitative the text suggests that whatever treasures the vast sea may contain, serving Prince Nicolaus offers even greater joy. In a rather one-sided response to the text Haydn enthusiastically evokes the sea—the first of several arias in the composer's output to associate D minor and the sea—without emphasizing the pleasures of service. Consequently the music moves rather awkwardly into the final chorus, a da capo movement in 3/8 in which Jupiter is urged to preserve the prince.

With the exception of the short recitative that precedes the second duet and the seascape recitative all the movements circulated with sacred texts in Haydn's lifetime. Although the composer may have known of some of these contrafacta it is unlikely that he was involved in their preparation.

Deutsch, Otto Erich (b. 5 Oct. 1883; d. 23 Nov. 1967). Austrian musicologist. Born in Vienna, he studied art history at the university in the city and in Graz. His early career was as an art historian, and his particular interest in the Biedermeier period led him naturally to a lifelong interest in the biography of Schubert. Following service in the Austrian army in the First World War, he worked as a bookseller before becoming music librarian to ANTHONY VAN HOBOKEN. Following the annexation of Austria by Germany in 1938 Deutsch fled to England, where he lived in Cambridge. He returned to Vienna in 1951.

Although Deutsch's most enduring and influential work was on Handel, Mozart, and Schubert, he wrote also on Haydn. He was the first to study the composer's output of canons, and was entrusted with preparing that volume for the *JHW*. He made a particular study of Admiral Nelson and Austria, including his visit to Eisenstadt in 1800, and of Joseph II's attitude to Haydn. His abiding belief that historical documents and iconographical evidence constituted the essential ingredients of biographical exposition was a strong influence on the work of H. C. ROBBINS LANDON.

O. E. Deutsch, *Admiral Nelson und Joseph Haydn. Ein british-österreichisches Gipfeltreffen* (Vienna, 1982).

O. E. Deutsch, *Wiener Musikgeschichten* [a collection of small essays] (Vienna, 1993).

'Deutschland, Deutschland über alles'. German words written in 1841 by August Heinrich Hoffmann von Fallersleben (1798–1874) as an alternative to the orginal text of Haydn's 'GOTT ERHALTE FRANZ DEN KAISER'; the words were given the title 'Das Lied der Deutschen'. Haydn's music and von Fallersleben's text were officially adopted as the national anthem of Germany in 1922. In 1950 it was decreed that the third verse of Fallersleben's text, 'Einigkeit und Recht und Freiheit', should be sung to Haydn's melody rather than 'Deutschland, Deutschland über alles' which had become forever blighted by Nazi associations.

Deutschlands Klage auf den Tod des Großen Friedrichs Borußens König (Germany's lament on the death of Frederick the Great) (Hob. XXVIb:1). An incomplete work for voice, baryton, and cello; only the vocal part and the bass line survives. CARL FRANZ, a former instrumentalist at the Esterházy court, is known to have performed this work in Nuremberg in 1788, singing the vocal line and playing the baryton simultaneously. There had been a previous performance in Leipzig, when Franz might have been joined by another former Esterházy employee, the soprano COSTANZA VALDESTURLA. Since references to the work are so scanty and Haydn never claimed authorship, its pedigree has been doubted. Frederick the Great had died in August 1786, and the music and the text were almost certainly composed in the following months. The author of the text is not known.

Dichtler family. Leopold Dichtler (d. 15 May 1799) was one of the most long-serving members of the Esterházy court, first as a tenor, later as a double bass player; he occasionally worked as a music copyist and as a singing teacher. He entered the service of the court on 1 March 1763 in readiness for the first performance of *La marchese nespola*. Between that date and the mid-1780s he sang tenor roles in all of Haydn's Italian operas with the exception of *L'isola disabitata*, and, usually, also the leading tenor role in the operas of other composers produced at Eszterháza. As Haydn's favoured tenor he also probably sang in performances of church music, such as the Stabat mater, directed by Haydn. His operatic roles suggest that he had a particularly wide compass, over two octaves reaching up to top C. As he grew older he began to sing the secondary tenor roles and, finally, retired from singing in 1788, when he was given the rare honour of a pension for life. He was re-engaged as a double bass player by Prince Anton in 1792, part of the small ensemble that accompanied church music in Eisenstadt. He was married three times.

Barbara Dichtler, née Fuchs (d. 19 Sept. 1776), was Leopold's first wife. A soprano, she had been at the Esterházy court from 1757. She married Leopold Dichtler in 1764: Haydn was a witness. She sang soprano roles in the composer's *Acide*, *La canterina*, *Lo speziale*, *Le pescatrici*, *L'infedeltà delusa*, and *L'incontro improvviso*, and, like her husband, also took part in performances of Haydn's church music. She died on stage during a performance of Sacchini's *L'isola d'amore*. ERL

J. Harich, 'Das Opernensemble zu Eszterháza im Jahr 1780', *HYB* 7 (1970), 5–46.
HCRL/2.

Dido (Hob.XXIXa:3). A German marionette opera ('eine parodirte Marionetten Operette') in three acts setting a text by PHILIPP GEORG BADER. It was probably written in 1775 and produced at Eszterháza in February or March 1776 in the prince's marionette theatre; it was revived in autumn 1778, from which year a printed copy of the libretto survives. The score is lost, apart from Selene's first aria, 'Jeder meynt, der Gegenstand', which was later published by ARTARIA as a song, Hob.XXVIa:13. *Didone abbandonata* was one of the most frequently set librettos by METASTASIO and Bader's treatment is a lampoon of the story and the characteristics of such librettos; in the preface he writes that 'the poet is permitted to bring into one period Nuremberg, Vienna, Carthage, and Hirschau. The same is true of the dialogue! One presents heroes and kings, queens and princes, as partly tragic figures and immediately thereafter has them talking in low and silly tones, just like the common people.' The libretto indicates that the music consisted of 16 arias, a duet, five choruses, three finales, and at least one piece of instrumental music. It is known that there were ten rehearsals for the one performance of the revival that took place on 15 September 1778. It has been conjectured that the finale of Symphony no. 67 was originally the overture to *Dido*. PB

H. C. Robbins Landon, 'Haydn's Marionette Operas and the Repertoire of the Marionette Theatre at Esterház Castle', *HYB* 1 (1961), 111–97.
G. Thomas, 'Haydns deutsche Singspiele', *HS* 6 (1986), 1–63.

Die bestrafte Rachbegierde (Vengeful desire punished) (Hob.XXIXb:3). Marionette opera ('Singspiel'), setting a libretto by BADER and performed at the marionette theatre at Eszterháza in 1779. The libretto was printed in May 1779; a single copy survives in the library of the University of California. The music, however, is completely lost, probably destroyed in the fire of November 1779. It is clear from the stage directions and the text that the production must have been spectacular; apart from incidental music the libretto indicates at least three recitatives, six arias, a duet, 12 choruses, and several ensembles and melodramas; a number of transformation scenes are also specified. The cast list includes royalty and civic dignitaries, fairies and an evil magician, army officers, courtiers, servants, sailors, spirits, and furies; comedy is most obviously taken care of by Hanswurst as an ambassador. The settings include ruins, a splendid reception hall, an ordinary room, a dark forest, a transparent hall, a castle courtyard with a triumphal arch, a splendid dining hall, a garden overlooking the sea, and a park with fireworks. The libretto indicates that 'The music has been specially written by the princely Kapellmeister Herr Joseph Haiden'; in Act 3 the king, enquiring who wrote the music of an aria that has particularly delighted him, is told 'Haiden is the name of the author'. PB

H. C. Robbins Landon, 'Haydn's Marionette Operas and the Repertoire of the Marionette Theatre at Esterház Castle', *HYB* 1 (1962), 111–97.
G. Thomas, 'Haydns deutsche Singspiele', *HS* 6 (1986), 1–63.

Die Erwählung eines Kapellmeisters (The election of a Kapellmeister) (Hob.XXIVa:11). A cantata for three soloists, SATB chorus, and orchestra, of doubtful authenticity. C. F. POHL maintained that the cantata was written in the mid-1790s for a group of Haydn's friends who met at the White Swan tavern in Vienna. Apart from purely musical reasons for questioning Haydn's authorship, it is totally unlikely that such a meeting in a tavern would include both women and men, and could muster a standard classical orchestra of winds and strings. The music consists of recitatives and arias for Apollo (tenor), Minerva (soprano), and Bacchus (tenor), followed by a recitative for the soloists, a chorus of the followers of Bacchus, a duet for Minerva and Apollo, and a concluding chorus. Given the lack of musical distinction and the fact that all numbers are scored for the same orchestra (pairs of oboes and horns, plus bassoon and strings), it is unlikely that Haydn was the composer. The subject matter is the search for a worthy Kapellmeister, the tone light-hearted. PB

Die Feuersbrunst (The conflagration) (Hob. XXIXb:A). Marionette opera in two acts, probably performed at Eszterháza *c.*1775–8; the spoken text (author unknown) is lost; an anonymous copy of the music was rediscovered in the 1950s, and Robbins Landon convincingly argued that this work was identical with the 'lost' Haydn *Opera comique Vom abgebrannten Haus* (*opéra comique* Concerning the burnt-out house) listed in the ENTWURF-KATALOG. Provided with dialogue reconstructed by Landon and Else Radant Landon the work was published, and has been performed and recorded several times. Though Landon's dating to 1776–8 (the only years when there were clarinets, which occur in some of the numbers of the score, in the Esterházy establishment) is not compelling, the music is of sufficiently high standard for the attribution to Haydn to be convincing, even if stylistically it may be thought to date from a few years earlier. An alternative view is that the work may have been composed by JOSEPH HAYDA.

The plot is close to the typical Viennese Hanswurst farces of one or two decades earlier, with the traditional stock characters of Odoardo (difficult father), Leander (fop), Colombina (resourceful daughter), and Hanswurst himself, a chimney sweep who by swift disguises as a soldier, cavalier, milliner, and beggar-woman manages to win Colombina's hand. The action includes a dragon and a ghost, as well as the fire at the conclusion to Act 1 that gives the work its name. Part of the overture has been identified as the work of Pleyel (who became Haydn's pupil in 1772), 21 of the 26 numbers are arias, which may be due to the requirements of the puppeteers. Six of the arias open in the minor mode; they are mainly short, lively, and tuneful, though there are also some touchingly poignant ones. PB

H. C. Robbins Landon, 'Haydn's Marionette Operas and the Repertoire of the Marionette Theatre at Esterház Castle', *HYB* 1 (1962), 111–97.
HCRL/2.
G. Thomas, 'Haydns deutsche Singspiele', *HS* 6 (1986), 1–63.

Die Jahreszeiten. *See* THE SEASONS.

Die reisende Ceres (The visit of Ceres) (Hob. XXIXb:F Add.). *Singspiel* of disputed authenticity. Haydn's autograph list of German librettos includes 'die Erlösung . . . [von] Jos Haydn' (The deliverance . . . [by] Jos Haydn). Eva Badura-Skoda argues ingeniously in her edition of *Die reisende Ceres* that this entry refers to a work with a text by Maurus Lindemayr (1723–83) that was discovered in the monastery of Seitenstetten in 1970, where the composer is named as Giuseppe Hayden. It is a charming score, consisting of an overture, four arias, a duet, two trios, a quartet, and a finale, as well as two instrumental minuets, though there is no compelling musical reason to attribute the work to Haydn. The story is akin to that of PHILEMON UND BAUCIS; in both works disguised gods visit and test the humanity of a peasant community. In the present work the goddess Ceres and her maid visit a peasant family in which a marriage is only brought to consummation by her intervention in curing the son and bridegroom of his insolence. It has been suggested that the work may have been composed by JOSEPH HAYDA. PB

E. Badura-Skoda (ed.), *Die reisende Ceres* (Vienna, *c.*1982).
A. P. Brown, review, *HYB* 14 (1984), 232–6.

Dies, Albert Christoph (b. 11 Feb. 1755; d. 28 Dec. 1822). Landscape painter who also wrote an early biography of Haydn. Born in Hanover, he studied in Düsseldorf and then travelled to Rome, where he lived and worked as an artist until 1796; his patrons included the Earl of Bristol. After a brief stay in Salzburg in 1796 he settled in Vienna the following year, becoming professor of landscape painting at the imperial academy.

From 1805 onwards he was commissioned to paint a series of landscape views of the Esterházy palace and gardens in Eisenstadt, providing a fascinating visual record of the many changes initiated by Prince Nicolaus II, in particular the fashionable English taste in garden design. Although Dies worked regularly for the prince, he was not, as is sometimes stated, the director of his art collection.

It was a fellow artist, the sculptor Anton Grassi, who suggested that Dies should collect material for a biography of Haydn and, to this end, introduced him to the composer. Between 15 April 1805 and 8 August 1808 Dies visited Haydn in his house at Gumpendorf on 30 occasions. Ten visits were made between April and June 1805, and 14 between November 1805 and August 1806; by this time, Dies had essentially covered Haydn's life to date, and the six more widely spaced visits between December 1806 and August 1808 were to ensure that he remained acquainted with the frail composer, though new stories about the London period, in particular, were vouchsafed too. Had Haydn lived beyond May 1809 no doubt Dies would have made further visits. The accounts of these individual visits constitute the content of his book, supplemented by other material, including information taken from the biography written by GRIESINGER. Dies's volume was published in 1810 and dedicated to Prince Nicolaus II. It was never reprinted in the 19th century.

Dies described his biography as a collection of 'isolated vignettes', implying a crucial distinction between his work and that of Griesinger. Dies provides an engaging, often melancholy picture of Haydn in his old age, alongside a broadly chronological biography. He is less reliable than Griesinger, but comparison of the many incidents and comments that are common to both volumes reveals that Dies is the more animated and enthusiastic storyteller, and, in this respect, he gives a more consistently vivid impression of Haydn's personality.

Die Fürsten Esterházy [Exhibition catalogue] (Eisenstadt, 1995).
V. Gotwals, *Haydn. Two Contemporary Portraits* [An annotated translation of the biographies of Griesinger and Dies] (Madison, 1968).
HCRL/5.

Die Schöpfung. *See* THE CREATION.

'Dieses war vor gar zu gelehrte Ohren' (That was for far too learned ears). An annotation by Haydn in the slow movement of the autograph score of Symphony no. 42. His initial thoughts for the first-violin line from bar 46 onwards would have prolonged and obscured the expected resolution of the previous diminished triad into a cadential six-four chord in E; Haydn thought it too learned—it worked in theory but not in practice—and substituted a more obvious resolution. Typically, however, he cleverly disguised the now routine nature of the progression by having only one note of the chord, a transparent texture that is carefully marked *pianissimo*.

Die Sieben letzten Worte. *See* THE SEVEN LAST WORDS.

Dietzl family. Several members of the Dietzl family served at the Esterházy court from the mid-18th to the early 19th century. Joseph Dietzl (d. 1777) had been employed at the court from 1754 as a tenor and organist; he was also a schoolteacher at the court. He remained part of the small retinue of musicians responsible for church music in Eisenstadt and only intermittently came into contact with Haydn.

His son, Joseph Wolfgang Dietzl (d. 1802), worked at the Esterházy court from 1765 as a horn player. Haydn and his wife were godparents to two of his children. He was to marry a second time and, altogether, fathered 14 children. Following the death of Prince Nicolaus Esterházy, Dietzl worked as a violinist in the small ensemble that accompanied church music in Eisenstadt. In 1801 he moved to an old people's home supported by the Esterházy family, where he died a year later.

Johann Dietzl (b. 31 Jan. 1754; d. 16 Feb. 1806) was the youngest son of Joseph Dietzl the elder. He was first employed in 1775 as a double bass player in the church music ensemble at Eisenstadt, transferring the same year to the main body of musicians under Haydn's direction. He was especially admired by Haydn who, in a document supporting Dietzl's claim for a pay rise, described him as one of the best double bass players in Vienna and Hungary. Following the dismantling of the musical retinue in 1790, Dietzl played the double bass at the principal theatres in Vienna and at the imperial court, returning in 1802 to Eisenstadt to work under the direction of Hummel. Two of his children worked at the court, Elisabeth as an alto from 1804, Nikolaus as a viola player from 1808.

P. Bryan, 'Haydn's Hornists', *HS* 3/1 (1973), 52–8.

J. Harich, 'Das Haydn-Orchester im Jahr 1780', *HYB* 8 (1971), 5–69.

HCRL/2 and 5.

'Die Uhr' symphony. *See* 'CLOCK' SYMPHONY.

dissemination. See opposite.

Dittersdorf, Carl Ditters von [Ditters, Carl] (b. Vienna, 2 Nov. 1739; d. Neuhof, Pilgram, Bohemia, 24 Oct. 1799). Violinist and composer. Carl Ditters (von Dittersdorf from 1772) was one of the most prolific and versatile of the Viennese contemporaries of Haydn and Mozart. Quite apart from his substantial musical legacy Dittersdorf left behind one of the most fascinating and entertaining memoirs of the period. Dictated to his son and completed just two days before his death, it is not only a rich source of information on music and musicians of the period, but it also succeeds in conveying to the reader something of the author's charm, vivacity, and learning. Reading the book one can well understand the warm friendship that Dittersdorf and Haydn struck up early in life. In his last years Dittersdorf was crippled with arthritis and short of money. His music, which had once delighted Europe, was now largely ignored and a subscription offer he sent out in 1799 had no response. In the last pages of his memoirs he appeals to all those who have received pleasure from his works to purchase a copy of the book in the hope that the proceeds will help support his family.

Ditters grew up in comfortable financial circumstances in Vienna and received a good general education at a Jesuit school in addition to private tuition in music, French, and religion. He began violin lessons at the age of 7 and within a few years he was appointed a member of the orchestra at the Benedictine church on the Freyung through the influence of his teacher, Joseph Ziegler. On 1 March 1751 he joined the musical establishment of Prince Joseph Friedrich von Sachsen-Hildburghausen, and began a more disciplined course of violin study with Giuseppe Trani who probably taught LEOPOLD HOFMANN also. His early attempts at composition impressed Trani, who commended him to the composer Giuseppe Bonno (1711–88). Bonno offered him instruction in Fuxian counterpoint and free composition; he seems to have been a generous and kindly teacher. Ditters remained in service until 1761 when the orchestra was dissolved. Along with the other musicians, he was offered employment by the theatre director of the imperial court, Count Giacomo Durazzo (1717–94).

During the early 1760s Ditters was regarded as the finest violinist in Vienna. He appeared frequently as a soloist, generally in his own concertos, and composed prolifically in other genres. When his contract with Durazzo expired in the winter of 1764 he chose to accept the post of Kapellmeister

[*cont. on p.70*]

dissemination

One of the paradoxes of Haydn's career is that, until the age of 58, he lived and worked in comparative isolation, in Vienna, Eisenstadt, and Eszterháza, yet his music was known and appreciated throughout Europe. The two visits to London and the associated journeys through Germany made him directly aware of the nature and extent of his popularity as well as furthering it, and in the last years of his life he was able to draw increasing personal satisfaction from this international status. When he famously told Mozart in 1790 that his 'language was understood all over the world' he was primarily making an aesthetic judgement, pointing out that his music had the ability to communicate regardless of linguistic, religious, and political divisions. More mundanely, the comment was also an acknowledgement that most of his works were widely distributed and that this dissemination had its own dynamic. No other composer before or since has achieved the same degree of popularity in his lifetime.

This entry is concerned with identifying some of the principal means by which Haydn's music was distributed in his lifetime. While a twofold division into manuscript dissemination and printed dissemination is an obvious one, the fact that both were equally important in Haydn's career draws attention to certain distinctive aspects of his musical creativity as well to some contemporary characteristics of musical dissemination. If Haydn had composed only church music or only operatic music, this survey would have concentrated on manuscript distribution; on the other hand, if he had been a composer of symphonies, quartets, sonatas, and trios who lived in Paris or London, rather than in Austria, then the survey would have had to have given primacy to printed sources. These two aspects, the genre of the work and the locality of its distribution, usually determine whether it was made available in manuscript or published form. Since Haydn, to a greater extent than was typical of most composers of the time, composed across the entire range of genres, from sonata to symphony, and from offertory to opera, manuscript and published distribution are bound to feature in equal measure. He lived during a period when the characteristics of music distribution were constantly changing, with greater availability of printed music and increasingly international networks of distribution. The composer's music was an ever-present part of this commercial development.

---

1. Manuscript dissemination. In the narrowest sense the dissemination of Haydn's music began as soon as he had completed the autograph manuscript, often probably as soon as he had completed a single movement. At the Esterházy court it was passed to a copyist who prepared the parts, sometimes (especially for large-scale works such as operas) with the assistance of other copyists. These were then returned to Haydn, who meticulously checked them. Haydn's first contract, signed in May 1761, gave the prince ownership of his musical works and specifically forbade the composer to offer them to anyone else or to allow them to be copied. This was a standard obligation for any court Kapellmeister but it was difficult to enforce, and Haydn, like other composers, did allow his music to be distributed with or without the agreement of the prince. That it was an unrealistic constraint is suggested by the absence of any requests by Haydn for permission to copy his music for distribution elsewhere, whereas there are a number of requests for leave of absence to give performances of works; when Haydn signed a new contract in 1779 this restriction was removed. By this time many aristocratic courts, such as that at Kačina castle in Bohemia, and monastic libraries, such as St Florian near Linz, had acquired performing parts of Haydn's music directly from the composer, identifiable by the handwriting of his principal copyist JOSEPH ELẞLER. In 1765 Haydn had been accused by Werner of allowing church music from the Esterházy library 'to go out to all the world' and it seems that Haydn kept in touch with church musicians in Vienna, regularly supplying them with copies of his music. Of the music that Haydn composed at the Esterházy court his operas were the least widely dispersed, though known performances of *La fedeltà premiata* and *Orlando paladino* in German translation must have been dependent in some way on material acquired from the Esterházy court.

For churches, monasteries, and aristocratic courts, direct contact with Haydn was only one of three ways in which they acquired the composer's music. Bookshops and music copyists in Vienna reqularly sold or hired manuscript parts of Haydn's music, while resident copyists in the various sacred and secular institutions supplemented these by copying their own parts from them or from parts borrowed from neighbouring institutions. The demand for music was an insatiable one, and unravelling the various networks of supply is as difficult as keeping track of illicit photocopies (or photocopies of photocopies) today, but with one additional feature; every time a work was copied outside the composer's jurisdiction, more mistakes would creep in. The errors in some extant manuscript copies of Haydn's music are so grievous as to preclude even a perfunctory performance.

While this dissemination of Haydn's music was a pervasive one in Austria, Bohemia, Hungary, Moravia, and southern Germany, manuscript copies of Haydn's music were also regularly advertised by Breitkopf and by the Hamburg music dealer Westphal, and these merchants supplied Denmark and Sweden, as well as northern Germany. Extant manuscript sources for Haydn's music in Spain are mainly part of an internal network of distribution, although it must have been activated by material purchased from Vienna; from Spain some of these sources crossed the Atlantic to the New World.

The change in terms of employment in Haydn's contract of 1779 allowed him to accept commissions for new music from outside the Esterházy court and to sell his music too. In the 1780s he sold manuscript copies of the op. 33 quartets in advance of their publication by Artaria (extant copies in Melk abbey), he sent a complimentary manuscript score of *L'isola disabitata* to the royal court in Madrid, and regularly supplied PRINCE OETTINGEN-WALLERSTEIN with his latest symphonies. Though these single examples of dissemination afford interesting particular evidence of Haydn's increasing fame, they were a minute part of an active dissemination process, one over which he had little or no control. During the 1780s and 1790s the most important music dealer in Vienna was JOHANN TRAEG whose cumulative catalogue of music issued in 1799 details over 500 works by Haydn that were available in manuscript copies; the composer derived no income from any of these sales.

2. Printed dissemination. Printed copies of Haydn's music began to circulate in the 1760s, when publishers in England, France, Germany, and Holland issued the composer's symphonies, quartets, and trios, later joined by a variety of other instrumental music, but only very occasionally by vocal music. None of these early printed editions was sanctioned by the composer and their musical texts derived ultimately from manuscript copies, though as the market burgeoned publishers also copied from one another; often they attached Haydn's name, knowingly or by accident, to works originally composed by others. For instance, Haydn never composed any flute quartets but a set of six circulated widely under his name, published by Hummel in Amsterdam in 1767, by Bremner in London in 1771, and by Huberty in Paris in 1773; the set contains arrangements of two works by Haydn (Hob.II:1 and 11) plus four entirely spurious works. The Huberty edition was one of a minority of foreign publications known to have been sold by Viennese retailers in the 1770s, where it might have come to the attention of the would-be composer. Since Haydn was powerless to prevent this fraudulent trade he probably would have regarded it with indifference.

Musicians who travelled from one country to another were a regular source for new printed music. The Bohemian composer Antonín Kammel (1730–87) is one of many who may have helped promote Haydn's music. He had settled in London, where his music was regularly published by the firm of Welcker. Early in 1773 The *Public Advertiser* announced the availability of 'Six favourite overtures in eight parts by the most capital masters collected by Kammell'; the 'capital masters' were Mysliveček, the Princess Royal of Saxony, Stamitz, Vanhal, and Haydn. This was the first publication of a symphony by Haydn in London, no. 35, and the musical text 'collected by Kammell' was probably a publication by Venier that had appeared in Paris two years earlier.

The first authentic publication of music by Haydn—that is prepared with the cooperation of the composer—was of six keyboard sonatas (Hob.XVI:21–6), issued by Kurzböck of Vienna in 1774, and dedicated to Prince Nicolaus. But this was an exception and authentic publications of Haydn were not regularly to appear until the 1780s. Haydn's second contract of 1779, which enabled him to accept commissions from publishers, coincided with the founding of the first major music-publishing firm in Vienna, ARTARIA. During Haydn's lifetime Artaria issued over 160 publications of music by the composer. While Haydn was always a shrewd negotiator he was powerless to stop one increasing prevalent aspect of music publication, exploited by Artaria: selling the music to established agents in Bonn, London, Paris, and elsewhere. Haydn himself from the 1780s onwards dealt directly with a number of publishers, Bland (London), Boßler (Speyer and Darmstadt), Boyer (Paris), Breitkopf (later Breitkopf & Härtel, Leipzig), Forster (London), Hoffmeister (Vienna), Kozeluch (Koželuh) (Vienna), Longman & Broderip (London), Napier (London), Sieber (Paris), Thomson (Edinburgh), Torricella (Vienna), and Whyte (Edinburgh). For much of the 1780s and 1790s Haydn attended to the associated correspondence himself, negotiating fees, and sending manuscript copies of parts rather than the autograph scores; these were often written on small-sized paper to facilitate transport. In the 1790s, particularly when he was enlisting subscribers for the published edition of *The Creation* and corresponding with Breitkopf & Härtel, he sought assistance from acquaintances, such as BURNEY, SALOMON, and REBECCA SCHROETER in London, and GRIESINGER in Vienna. Preparing works for publication consumed a great deal of Haydn's time from the 1780s onwards, but the resulting publications constituted only a small part of the total number of editions of music by Haydn in circulation. Unauthorized publications continued to appear in voluminous quantities and there was also a considerable trade in arrangements of Haydn's music. To take one work, the 'Joke' quartet, op. 33 no. 2, this was first published by Artaria in Vienna in 1782, from where it was made available to his agents in other countries; within three years inauthentic editions had been issued by Forster

(London), Guéra (Lyons), Hummel (Amsterdam and Berlin), Kerpen (London), Napier (London), and Sieber (Paris); in addition, publishers in England, France, and Germany issued arrangements (sometimes of single movements) of the work for flute quartet, solo piano, piano duet, piano trio, flute duet, violin and piano, and even as a song (using words from Gray's *Elegy Written in a Country Churchyard*).

Haydn scholarship from the 19th century to the present day has been continually concerned with evaluating the authenticity of this vast amount of material, manuscript and published, making sure that authentic works, authentic manuscripts, and authentic editions are properly ascribed to the composer. While this is a legitimate concern, fundamental to our need to understand individual artistic creativity, it sits uneasily with the practices of Haydn's own time. Modern enthusiasts celebrate Haydn's music, comfortable in the accuracy and authenticity of that experience, but many, if not most, musicians in the composer's own time would have based their own appreciation of 'Haydn' on musical texts that were corrupt, spurious, or not even by the composer in the first place, a rather disquieting truth that scholars have chosen to ignore.

to Prince-Bishop Adam Patachich at Großwardein (now Oradea in Romania), recently vacated by MICHAEL HAYDN, rather than work under the authority of Count Wenzel Spork, Durazzo's successor. In addition to maintaining a steady output of instrumental music he began also to compose vocal works, including several operas and the oratorio *Isaaco*.

Ditters found himself at a loose end when the prince-bishop dissolved his musical establishment in 1769, and undertook a series of travels, presumably in search of a new employer. His next patron, Count Philipp Gotthard Schaffgotsch, Prince-Bishop of Breslau, persuaded Ditters to pay an extended visit to his castle of Johannisberg (Jánský Vrch). Ditters ended up spending much of the next 20 years there, isolated from the mainstream in the same way as Haydn was at Eszterháza. His reputation did not suffer, however, and his instrumental music continued to circulate widely and his vocal music, in particular his operas in Italian and in German, enjoyed great popularity in Vienna and elsewhere. Through the offices of Count Schaffgotsch, Ditters was created a Knight of the Golden Spur in 1770 and, two years later, was granted a certificate of nobility by Empress Maria Theresia, after which he adopted the additional surname von Dittersdorf ('from Dittersdorf', a completely fictitious place).

Among the highlights of Dittersdorf's professional career in the 1770s and 1780s were the highly successful Viennese performances of his oratorio *Esther* (1773); the composition of the 12 symphonies based on Ovid's *Metamorphoses* (completed in 1786), and the huge success of his *Singspiel Doktor und Apotheker* (1786). The success of the work led to commissions for two further German operas (*Betrug durch Aberglauben* and *Die Liebe im Narrenhause*) and an Italian opera (*Democrito corretto*). While still in Vienna late in 1786 Dittersdorf unsuccessfully petitioned Friedrich Wilhelm II of Prussia for a post.

Conditions began to deteriorate at Johannisberg in the late 1780s but Dittersdorf's reputation ensured that external commissions for new works still came his way. Among the most important of these were at least 11 German operas written for the court theatre of Duke Friedrich August of Brunswick-Oels. The death of the prince-bishop in 1795, coupled with Dittersdorf's own declining health, filled his last years with worry. At the time of his death he and his family were living in lodgings provided by Baron Ignaz von Stillfried on his property in Bohemia.

Of Dittersdorf's prodigious output of works a large number survive. His tally of well over 100 symphonies reveals an extraordinary range of styles and musical structures. While much has been made of Dittersdorf's programmatic symphonies, such as the famous Ovid works and the less well-known but cleverly satirical *Il delirio delli compositori, ossia Il gusto d'oggida* (The Delirium of the Composers; or the Taste of Today), his purely abstract symphonies also contain a wealth of strikingly original and at times subversive musical ideas. Dittersdorf's violin concertos were written with himself in mind and they are genial works, full of virtuoso showmanship and infused with a sense of humour. Along with Leopold Hofmann's works in the genre they are the most accomplished violin concertos of their time written in Vienna. While most of Dittersdorf's chamber music lies unpublished and unperformed, his six string quartets, written comparatively late in his career, are beginning to enjoy a modest revival.

Haydn knew Dittersdorf particularly well in the 1750s when both were in Vienna. They remained in contact when Haydn moved to the Esterházy court, and Dittersdorf's symphonies, in particular, were played at the court. When the repertoire of the Italian opera company at Eszterháza was expanded with the establishment of a permanent company in 1776 Haydn encouraged Dittersdorf to forward no fewer than seven operas for possible performance. Four comic operas were performed in 1776 and 1777: *Il finto pazzo per amore*, *Il barone di rocca antica*, *Lo sposo burlato*, and *Arcifanfano, re de' Matti*. According to Michael Kelly, Haydn and Dittersdorf played first and second violin in a quartet party in Storace's residence in Vienna, probably in 1784; Mozart played the viola and Vanhal the cello. Since Dittersdorf was a more expert player than Haydn, it is likely that he played first rather than second violin as indicated by Kelly. An anonymous article on musical taste in Vienna that appeared in the *Wiener Diarium* in October 1766 has been attributed to Dittersdorf. ADJB

C. Ditters von Dittersdorf, *The Autobiography of Karl Ditters von Dittersdorf*, trans. A. D. Coleridge (repr. New York, 1970).

D. Heartz, 'Ditters, Gluck und der Artikel "Von dem wienerischen Geschmack in der Musik"', *Gluck Studien*, 1 (1989), 78–80.

D. Heartz, *Haydn, Mozart and the Viennese School 1740–1780* (New York, 1995).

P. Horsley, 'Dittersdorf and the Finale in Late-Eighteenth-Century German Comic Opera' (diss. Cornell University, 1988).

H. Unverricht (ed.), *Carl Ditters von Dittersdorf (1739–1799): Mozarts Rivale in der Opera* (Wurzburg, 1989).

divertimento. A term in common use in 18th-century Austria for a wide variety of instrumental music, from solo keyboard to windband music; it was not normally applied to orchestral music such as symphonies and concertos. The modern association of the term with light music is not appropriate; also the 18th-century French term *divertissement* is not a synonym, since that term could be used for vocal music, dance, as well as instrumental music. In the last couple of decades of the 18th century the term divertimento became less common, as the increasing internationalization of musical trade encouraged composers, music shops, and publishers towards the use of more specific terms such as sonata, trio, quartet, and so on.

In Haydn's case he used the term for keyboard sonatas, string trios, baryton trios, keyboard trios, quartets, keyboard quartets, baryton octets, and windband music. Usually, it is coupled with an indication of the number of musical parts, 'Divertimento per Cembalo solo' for a keyboard sonata, 'Divertimento a quattro' for a quartet, and 'Divertimento a 8to Stromenti' for a baryton octet, for instance.

The C minor sonata of 1771 is the first keyboard sonata by the composer to use that term rather than divertimento, though the view that it was prompted by the musical ambition of the work is misguided. The early history of the op. 33 quartets shows a mixture of traditional and modern terminology: when Haydn was soliciting subscribers for manuscript copies he called the works quartets; on the other hand manuscript parts delivered to Melk have the heading 'Divertimento a quatro'; the published edition used by Artaria again uses the word quartet. From the early 1780s onwards 'divertimento' was rarely used by the composer for any kind of work; the manuscript copies of the six trios (Hob.IV:1–6) that Haydn sent to Forster in 1784 are a notable exception.

Dlabacž, Gottfried Johann (Dlabač, Bohumir Jan) (b. 17 July 1758; d. 4 Feb. 1820). Czech author, librarian, and musician. He studied philosophy at Prague University and joined the Premonstratensian Order at Strahov in 1778. He conducted the first performance in Prague of Haydn's *Creation*, on 23 April 1800. His broad interest in the development of cultural life in Bohemia led to the three-volume encyclopaedia, *Allgemeines historisches Künstler-Lexikon für Böhmen und zum Theil auch für Mähren und Schlesien* (1815). Although the material on Haydn shows a dependence on GERBER's dictionary and other sources, it does contain the unique information that, as members of the Vienna Hofkapelle in the late 1740s, Haydn and his brother Michael sang in a performance during Holy Week of the Lamentations, in the presence of Maria Theresia and her consort, Franz I.

M. Germer, 'Dlabač's Dictionary and its Place in the Literature', *Fontes Artis Musicae*, 28 (1981), 307–12.

Dorati, Antal (b. 9 April 1906; d. 13 Nov. 1988). Hungarian conductor who settled in America; one of the most important figures in the widening of popular knowledge of Haydn's music from the 1970s onwards. Born in Budapest, he studied at the

Liszt Academy with Bartók, Kodály, and Weiner. After holding a series of conducting posts in opera houses in Hungary, Germany, Monte Carlo, and the USA, he became musical director of the Dallas Symphony Orchestra in 1945, assuming American citizenship two years later. From 1949 to 1960 he was musical director of the Minneapolis Symphony Orchestra before assuming similar positions with the BBC Symphony Orchestra (1963–6), the Stockholm Philharmonic Orchestra (1967–74), the National Symphony Orchestra of Washington (1970–5), and the Detroit Symphony (1977–81).

Dorati's contribution to the Haydn discography is without parallel. Although not a conductor previously associated with the Austro-German repertoire he recorded the complete symphonies with the Philharmonia Hungarica between 1970 and 1973 (Decca), the first and, for nearly 30 years, the only complete cycle of the composer's symphonies; this was followed by recordings of eight operas with first-rate soloists and the Lausanne Chamber Orchestra (Philips). Dorati also recorded *The Creation*, *The Seasons*, and *Il ritorno di Tobia* with the Royal Philharmonic Orchestra, the Twenty-four minuets (Hob.IX:16) with the Philharmonia Hungarica (all Decca), and, with the Bamberg Symphony Orchestra, the complete keyboard concertos with his wife Ilse von Alpenheim as soloist, and the cello concertos with Laszlo Varga (Vox). LK

dramma giocoso per musica (sometimes abbreviated as *dramma giocoso*). A generic term frequently applied to full-length comic librettos in Italian during the second half of the 18th century, and used later by scholars to refer to operas based on such librettos. Most 'comic dramas for music' by CARLO GOLDONI and his immediate successors have three acts, the last of which is shorter than the first two, with finales at the end of the first two acts, and a shorter ensemble at the end of the third. Six or seven characters represent a wide spectrum of social classes. The roles generally fall into three categories—*parti buffe* (comic roles), *parti serie* (serious roles), and *parti di mezzo carattere* (roles that mix the comic and the serious)—that demand substantially different musical treatment.

Of the nine comic librettos in Italian that Haydn set to music, six are called 'dramma giocoso per musica' or 'dramma giocoso' on their title page: LO SPEZIALE, LE PESCATRICI, L'INCONTRO IMPROVVISO, IL MONDO DELLA LUNA, LA VERA COSTANZA, and LA FEDELTÀ PREMIATA (the last-mentioned was also described as a 'dramma pastorale giocoso'). All these librettos deserve their generic designation except *Lo speziale*, a *dramma giocoso* by Goldoni that was drastically shortened through omitting its *parti serie*. JAR

'Dream, The'. *See* 'EIN TRAUM'.

Dr Harington's Compliment (Hob.XXVIb:3). A work for piano, soprano solo, and chorus written in 1794. It was Haydn's own title for an unusual, short composition based on a glee by HENRY HARRINGTON that praised Haydn's gifts as a composer: 'What art expresses and what science praises, Haydn the theme of both raises.' Haydn precedes Harrington's glee with a piano introduction and a setting of the glee melody for soprano and piano, and follows it with three variations for piano, with the soprano singing Harrington's melody and text once more in the third variation. This mutual back-slapping prompted Clementi to observe that 'The first Dr. having bestowed much praise on the 2nd Dr., the said 2nd Dr. out of doctorial gratitude returns the 1st Dr. thanks for all favours recd., and praises in his turn the said 1st Dr. most handsomely'. In 1806 it was published by Breitkopf & Härtel with a German text (a loose translation).

'Drumroll' symphony. Commonly used nickname for Symphony no. 103, first applied during the 19th century, possibly as a translation of the German nickname 'Mit dem Paukenwirbel' which was already in circulation. The symphony opens idiosyncratically with a roll on the timpani. JH

Dudelsack. German word for bagpipes. As a nickname or title it has been associated with three works by, or formerly attributed to, Haydn, prompted in each case by the composer's use of drone basses and a piping melody: Symphony no. 88 (the minuet), a short movement for mechanical organ (Hob.XIX:4) now known to be an arrangement of a Russian dance melody, and the minuet of the quartet op. 3 no. 3 now known to have been composed by HOFSTETTER. It could, in reality, be applied to any number of similar movements in Haydn's output. JH

duets for violin and viola (Hob.VI:1–6). In the ENTWURF-KATALOG Haydn included six duets for violin and viola, describing them, rather oddly, as '6 violin solos with the accompaniment of a viola'. The date of the entry points to *c.*1770, and the formal and stylistic features of the music are reminiscent of contemporary baryton trios and of the op. 9 and op. 17 quartets. Like the vast majority of the baryton trios the duets are in three movements. Most of the opening movements are sonata forms in a moderate tempo with a quaver pulse, and feature the same kind of decorative writing for the violin, including a fondness for double stops, that occurs in op. 9 and op. 17; like the quartets the duets seem to have been written with the capabilities of LUIGI TOMASINI in mind. The third duet opens with a set of four variations, akin to the opening movement of op. 9 no. 5 and of op. 17 no. 3. The slow movement of the first duet is a resourceful Adagio in F minor in which the violin spins out a line over a patterned accompaniment; as in similar movements in op. 9 and op. 17 there is a cumulative cadenza; also reminiscent of the quartets are the siciliano movements found in the third and sixth trios. All the duets conclude with a Tempo di minuet movement.

Haydn's description of the viola part as an 'accompaniment' is an accurate one; the instrument provides unfailingly pointed and rhythmic support but it never enters into thematic dialogue with the violin. While the combination of violin and viola was not as popular as two violins, it was by no means uncommon (Mozart, for instance, wrote two highly resourceful works for violin and viola, K423 and K424). Haydn's simple viola part meant that it could easily be played an octave lower by a cello, and the duets circulated in that scoring, as well as in a version for two violins. Neither of these alternative versions was sanctioned by the composer.

E

'Echo' divertimento (Hob.II:39). An entirely spurious work attributed to Haydn and published several times at the turn of the 18th century. It is written for two ensembles of two violins and a bass, each placed in a different room so that the one can echo the other. Such compositions are by no means uncommon in the period. For instance, Mozart's Notturno (K286) is written for four ensembles, placed in four different rooms.

'Ein' Mag'd, ein' Dienerin' (A maiden, a maid) (Hob.XXIIId:1). An Advent aria, probably composed in the 1770s. This gentle homage to the Virgin Mary in the form of a da capo aria is scored for solo soprano and an orchestra of strings and horns; later sources have parts for oboes too. Haydn probably composed the work for one of the churches in Eisenstadt, possibly that of the BARMHERZIGE BRÜDER.

'Ein Traum'. Nickname for the slow movement of the quartet op. 50 no. 5 that arose in the 19th century. The English 'The Dream' seems to have followed from the German. JH

Eisenstadt. See opposite.

'Eisenstädter' trios. In 1955 Breitkopf & Härtel published five string trios by Haydn, edited by Adolf Hoffmann; they were given the collective title '5 Eisenstädter Trios'. One work is an authentic string trio by Haydn, Hob.V:16; two are editions of inauthentic 18th-century arrangements of baryton trios, Hob.XI:7 and 8; and one work is now thought not to be by Haydn, Hob.V:C7.

Elßler family. Two generations of the Elßler family served at the Esterházy court as copyists and musicians; they were also close friends of Haydn.

1. Joseph Elßler sen.
2. Joseph Elßler jun.
3. Johann Florian Elßler.

1. Joseph Elßler sen. (d. 26 Oct. 1782). Probably born in Kieslingen in Silesia, Joseph Elßler was engaged as music copyist at the Esterházy court on 15 August 1764, replacing Anton Adolph who had left Eisenstadt shortly before because his salary, 12 gulden per month, was insufficient to bring up a family. Apparently, Joseph Elßler thought he could manage on this meagre sum, perhaps because even at this early stage Haydn was already using him independently to provide copies of his music outside Eisenstadt, something that was expressly forbidden in the Kapellmeister's contract. Not only did Haydn use Elßler in a professional capacity but he also became a friend and protector of the family: he was a witness at Elßler's marriage to Eva Maria Köstler at Eisenstadt on 7 October 1766, and was godfather to all seven of their children.

In his role as private copyist, Elßler's work was widely distributed in the Austrian territories, and extant copies can be found in Budapest, Prague, Pressburg (Bratislava), and Vienna, as well as the monasteries of St Florian and Kremsmünster. The copy of the Salve regina in G minor owned by the Gesellschaft der Musikfreunde in Vienna is especially valuable since, unusually, it is signed and dated by Elßler. His hand is fluent and clear, but what Haydn must have especially appreciated was the copyist's accuracy and reliability, as is evident when extant autographs are compared with manuscript copies prepared by him. Elßler was largely responsible for compiling the ENTWURF-KATALOG.

In 1769 Elßler petitioned Prince Nicolaus for a rise in his salary to support his growing family but this was turned down. It seems that he became increasingly dependent on the money given to him directly by the composer.

2. Joseph Elßler jun. Joseph Elßler (b. 7 Aug. 1767; d. 6 Oct. 1843) took over his father's duties a few days after his death in October 1782; he was, however, paid even less money, 10 gulden per month, perhaps because he was still only 15 years old. Although he seems to have worked for about five years at the court as a copyist his handwriting has not been securely identified. He was engaged as an oboe player at the Esterházy court in March 1794, serving first in the Grenadiers Band then in the *Harmonie*, and played second oboe in performances of most of the late masses; he was given a pension in 1813 in recognition of his service to the Esterházy family.

3. Johann Florian Elßler (b. 3 May 1769; d. 12 Jan. 1843). Johann Elßler (he hardly ever used his second name) began working for Haydn as a copyist in his late teens, in about 1787, and within a short period he became his principal copyist. During the first visit to England in 1791–2, Haydn found the local copyists unreliable, and for his second visit he took Johann Elßler with him. As

[*cont. on p.78*]

Eisenstadt

Small town in the Burgenland, 43 km (26 miles) south-east of Vienna, and principal home of the Esterházy family, Haydn's employers for most of his life. The first recorded mention of a settlement dates from 1264, the Latin 'Minor Martin' (to distinguish it from 'Major Martin', the Mattersburg of today). This form was perpetuated in the Hungarian 'Kismarton'. Saint Martin remains the patron saint of the principal church. The German name 'Eysenstatt' ('Iron town') is documented from the year 1388.

Settlements in the area date from much earlier, back to prehistoric times. Celts, Romans, Huns, and the Avarsi have all left some archaeological remains. From the beginning of the 11th century these settlements began to demarcate the boundary between the Holy Roman Empire, that is between the eastern marches ('Ostarrichi', corresponding more or less to modern Austria) and the new Christian territories of the Hungarian kingdom. From the end of the 14th century onwards, much more is known about Eisenstadt. At the time it belonged to the same estate as Hornstein (a village 8 km (5 miles) north-west of Eisenstadt) in the possession of the Kanizsai family. They built a water dam on the present site of the palace. In 1373 Eisenstadt was officially declared a town. From 1445, together with the outlying estates, it belonged to the Habsburg family, who leased out the area to interested parties. In 1622 Count Nicolaus Esterházy (1583–1645) became the lessor of the castle; it was purchased by the family in 1647. The town, on the other hand, was declared a royal free town ('königliche Freistadt') and was responsible to the Hungarian crown. Consequently, successive Esterházy princes, while they were the owners of the castle and its grounds, did not have jurisdiction over the town, a situation that produced regular conflict. Nevertheless, the town flourished precisely because of the splendour and ambition of the Esterházy court.

Count Nicolaus Esterházy founded a knights' academy in Eisenstadt which, as well as the traditional physical and military disciplines, placed emphasis on intellectual development, largely fostered by Jesuit teachers from Tyrnau (Trnava) university. He rebuilt the Minoritenkloster in 1625–9, following its destruction by the Turks, and made it a Franciscan monastery; the Renaissance altars are still extant today. Nicolaus's son, later the first prince, Paul (1635–1713), built a family vault in the monastery. The church of St Martin was also rebuilt in the early 17th century following its destruction by fire, and the town hall in the Markzeile (now Hauptstraße) was extended in the Renaissance style. A hundred years later it was modified to suit the new Baroque style. The extant frescos reveal the original iconography, even though they have been painted over and renovated several times. In various allegorical figures, they portray the virtues of faith, hope, love, justice, wisdom, strength, and temperance; there are also some biblical scenes.

Paul Esterházy established two outlying districts (now part of the town), Oberberg and Unterberg. In Oberberg the prince, with the support of the Franciscans, founded an almshouse and built the Kalvarienberg, a rugged shrine designed to evoke the Mount of Olives, typically Baroque in its extravagant piety, and soon regarded as the 'eighth wonder of the world'. From the Marian chapel pilgrims chartered a course around a grotto, decorated with life-sized carved and colourfully painted figures representing the stations of the Cross, before emerging in the Chapel of the Cross. The many pilgrimages to Oberberg soon made this district a prosperous one. As the Catholic faith strengthened in the region and more Franciscan priests were needed, the old almshouse was taken over by the Franciscans, and a new one erected in 1712, located where the hospice of the Barmherzige Brüder now stands. It was under Prince Paul Anton (1711–62) that the almshouse was rebuilt as a hospital for the Barmherzige Brüder. On 13 June 1760, the prince's nameday, the hospital was officially founded. Out of courtesy to his wife, who was from Lunéville, Paul Anton ensured that a proportion of the clerics spoke French. Haydn wrote his *Missa brevis Sancti Johannis de Deo* ('Kleine Orgelsolomesse') for the church. The Franciscans received a new building alongside the Kalvarienberg; after its dissolution in the 1780s it was used as an inn for pilgrims, Zum Goldenen Engel. Today the building, altered on several occasions, serves as a diocesan office.

Between Oberberg and the palace, a Jewish district was established by Prince Paul on Esterházy land, formally recognized in 1732 as a self-contained community, Unterberg; until 1848 it was under the personal protection of the prince and from then until 1938 enjoyed administrative autonomy. Emperor Leopold I's influential finance minister, Samuel Wertheimer (1658–1724), lived in Eisenstadt and his house now contains the Austrian Jewish Museum of Eisenstadt. The synagogue is one of the few Jewish institutions in Austria to have survived through the Nazi period.

The Esterházy palace is a landmark in Eisenstadt. A fortress was built in the 13th century, and expanded by the Kanizsai family in the following century to incorporate some of the new town wall. It was an imposing square building with four corner towers, two round in shape, two square. During renovation work on the present palace in 1995 the old gate tower was uncovered, a Roman archway with attachments for a drawbridge and a portcullis. Between 1663 and 1672, this medieval fortress was rebuilt as a Baroque palace. The well-known imperial builders and architects, Carlone and Filiberto Luchese, shared responsibility for the project. A moat was dug around the palace (more decorative than functional) and the former drawbridge was replaced by a permanent stone construction. At that time the famous hall was built in which Haydn was to present many of his works and which is now named after him, the Haydnsaal. The frescos were painted by Carpoforo Tencala and narrate the story of Amor and Psyche. On the main façade 18 busts of Hungarian magnates are placed, with an honoured place for the principal instigators of the rebuilding, Princes Nicolaus and Paul.

To the north-west of the palace Prince Paul laid out a cemetery for court employees; Haydn's predecessor as Kapellmeister, GREGOR WERNER, and his brother, JOHANN MICHAEL HAYDN, were both buried there. Alongside the palace (today Joseph Haydn Gasse 1) Prince Paul founded an Augustinian convent for daughters of the aristocracy, including five of his own children. After the dissolution of the monasteries during the reign of JOSEPH II it became an administrative building for the estate.

Prince Paul's pious nature, especially his reverence for the Virgin Mary, permeated the local society. Even today, Eisenstadt and the surrounding areas have a large number of shrines, on the wayside and in eye-level niches on houses and other buildings. Most of the Marian statues are a particular type known as Maria Einsiedeln: rounded shapes, brocade clothing, and with the infant Jesus on Mary's arm. A madonna of this type above the gate of a doctor's house in Eisenstadt so captivated the prince that he arranged for a similar statue to be carved and placed on an Esterházy bathing house in Großhöflein, where it was soon ascribed with miraculous powers. In 1711 the prince transferred the statue to the newly built Kalvarienberg, where it is still to be found. A contemporary reproduction of this statue crowns a column in the square outside.

When the Turks laid siege to Vienna for the second time, in 1683, and the surrounding areas were destroyed, Eisenstadt paid a surety that meant that it was not attacked. Prince Michael (1671– 1721), the eldest son of Paul, wanted to enrich the sanctity of the Oberberg area, so that it became the largest Marian sanctuary in Hungary. What today survives as the so-called Bergkirche was merely the presbytery of a much larger building, planned but never built. Since 1898 (with the sole exception of 1945) Haydn's quartet version of *The Seven Last Words* has been performed on every Good Friday at the church. Under the gallery at the back of the church a memorial stone to Haydn is found. It was erected by Prince Nicolaus II who also built the family vault underneath the church, where Haydn's corpse was laid to rest when it was transferred from Vienna to Eisenstadt in 1820.

Next to the Bergkirche stands a building in which the Esterházy musicians lived, including Haydn until he bought his own house in the Klostergasse (today Haydngasse); the Angel Inn (Engel-Wirthaus) was located in the same building. Also in the Oberberg were the barracks of the Esterházy Grenadiers, no longer extant. As early as 1630 Count Nicolaus had established a company of musketeers, which PRINCE PAUL ANTON ESTERHÁZY expanded into a company of grenadiers in 1736. They were stationed in Eisenstadt and Forchenstein. In their white and blue uniforms (later blue and red) and with distinctive tall hats they served as bodyguards for the prince. Musicians amongst them strengthened the church choir in Eisenstadt and even took part in opera performances.

To the dismay of Haydn and his fellow musicians, PRINCE NICOLAUS ESTERHÁZY preferred his new palace at ESZTERHÁZA to Eisenstadt and spent as much time there as he possibly could. But his commitment to Eisenstadt is shown by the fact that, following the two fires of 1768 and 1776, he paid for the reconstruction of the Franciscan church, the Augustinian church, and many town houses including, on both occasions, Haydn's house.

His son, PRINCE ANTON ESTERHÁZY, in the four years of his rule (1790–4), made the palace at Eisenstadt the focus of Esterházy life once more. The square in front of the castle was partially redesigned in the fashionable Classical style but his death prevented the full realization of the plan. However, the two symmetrical long-drawn-out buildings opposite the palace, whose northern façades unite with the southern façades of the palace to create a stylistic unity, are a legacy of this period. One served as a stable, the other as the office for the princely guard and as a coach house.

The ambitions of PRINCE NICOLAUS II ESTERHÁZY were even more comprehensive. He laid plans for a complete rebuilding of the palace in the Classical style, together with new extensions that were to house a theatre and an art gallery. To this end he engaged the French architect Charles Moreau, whom he had met in Rome. The present garden façade, completed in 1805, gives an impression of what the entire palace would have looked like had his plans been fully realized. Further, partly realized changes concerned the palace gardens. In 1808 the foundations were dug for the art gallery but the invasion of Austria by French forces in the following year halted the work; thereafter, the prince was never able to afford to complete his plans. The changes that were made to the palace brought it to the condition in which it stands today: simple canopy roofs replaced the four onion domes of the corner towers, the moat disappeared, a balcony was built above the main entrance, and a colonnade was built on the garden side.

The palace gardens, however, have changed completely and reflect over 200 years of changing tastes. Originally the ornamental garden had been relatively small, set on the north side of the old castle, with a kitchen garden and the hunting lands marking its boundary. During the time of Prince Paul, the gardens were laid out in the Italian style, with characteristic borders, statues, and fountains. Prince Paul Anton leased out the kitchen garden, but his plans for a garden in the French style were only partly realized. Prince Nicolaus II pursued the latest fashion: an English garden in the manner of 'Capability' Brown, with wandering pathways, copses, lakes, pools, temples, and grottoes, all set in a gently undulating landscape. Beyond the park, on a hill to the north-west of Eisenstadt, Moreau built a hunting lodge, initially called the Marientempel after PRINCESS MARIE HERMENEGILD ESTERHÁZY; it was later renamed the Gloriette.

In 1803 Nicolaus became the first owner in the Austro-Hungarian territories of an English steam engine, designed to pump water around the park. Moreau built a temple in the shape of a Greek cross around the machine, which became known as Maschinenhaus. Also following English fashion several glasshouses were built, housing plants from the orient and elsewhere; they soon became an attraction to visitors from all over Europe.

A modern visitor to Eisenstadt wishing to recreate Haydn's movements around the town can do so with ease. Walking from the palace, where the composer served the Esterházy family for over 40 years, towards the Oberberg, the visitor would first pass the hospice of the Barmherzige Brüder, the Kalvarienberg (with the Bergkirche), and, behind the church, the former living quarters of the musicians (now Wienstraße 1). Following the present Joseph Haydngasse (earlier Klostergasse) in an easterly direction, past the former administrative offices of the Esterházy family (before the fire of 1786 the Augustinian monastery and church were located here), the visitor soon arrives at Haydn's house (now no. 21), built at the beginning of the 18th century and now established as the Haydn Museum. At the end of the street stands the Franciscan church and former monastery (now the Diocesan museum). South-west from here, about 100 m. as the crow flies, Haydn's garden house is to be found, where, local legend has it, the composer used to escape from his quarrelsome wife. GM

Die Fürsten Esterházy. Magnaten, Diplomaten & Mäzene [Exhibition catalogue] (Eisenstadt, 1995).

K. Semmelweis, *Eisenstadt. Ein Führer durch die Landeshauptstadt* (Eisenstadt, 1982).

well as copies of the 'London' symphonies, Elßler prepared and supervised the copying of the parts and scores for *The Creation* and *The Seasons*. In the absence of autograph scores the oratorio sources and the surviving copies of three of the op. 76 quartets (nos. 2, 4, and 6) are particularly valuable. Haydn must have found the same characteristics as in Elßler's father, a flowing, elegant hand, together with astonishing accuracy. Johann Elßler was responsible for compiling the would-be definitive catalogue of his master's music, the *Haydn-Verzeichnis* (1805).

Apart from being his principal copyist Elßler acted in a more general capacity, as the composer's factotum. He and his wife lived with Haydn in his house in Gumpendorf and he was in constant attendance. He left a valuable description of the composer's daily schedule in the last ten years or so of his life. His ability with words is also evident in the touching but dignified description of the composer's death. The single largest bequest in Haydn's will was the 6,000 gulden that he left to his 'true and faithful servant Johann Elßler'; Elßler also received a plain coat, a waistcoat, one pair of knee breeches, an overcoat, and a hat. Although he was only 40 at the time of Haydn's death, Elßler lived comfortably off this legacy for the rest of his life. He had two famous daughters, both dancers and society figures: Theresia (1808–78) and Fanny (1810–84). *See also* COPYISTS. HCRL

R. Hellyer, 'The Wind Ensembles of the Esterházy Princes, 1761–1813', *HYB* 15 (1985), 5–92.

HCRL/2, 3, 4, and 5.

R. von Zahn, 'Der fürstlich Esterházysche Notenkopist Joseph Elßler sen.', *HS* 6/2 (1988), 130–47.

'Emperor' quartet. Nickname given to the quartet in C, op. 76 no. 3; the slow movement is a set of variations on Haydn's anthem 'GOTT ERHALTE FRANZ DEN KAISER'. In early 19th-century Britain the quartet was soon dubbed 'God save the Emperor', later 'Emperor'. As a nickname it seems to have been in circulation before the German equivalent, 'Kaiserquartett'. JH

Empfindsamkeit. Translated variously as sensibility, sentimentality and sensitiveness, *Empfindsamkeit* (and related French terms) are part of a complex semantic web in German, French, and British philosophy and letters of the 18th century. *Empfindsamkeit* denotes an aesthetic, and in the related term *empfindsamer Stil*, a style, associated with north Germany in the mid-18th century. In music the *empfindsamer Stil* is best represented by the intimate and highly original compositions of C. P. E. BACH. The notion of *Empfindsamkeit* is embodied in Bach's musical writings (which posit a dynamic aesthetic of expression), in his performances on the clavichord, and in the contemporary reception of Bach's music in Germany. BH

C. P. E. Bach, *Versuch über die wahre Art das Clavier zu spielen* (Berlin, 1753, 1762); trans. W. J. Mitchell as *Essay on the True Art of Playing Keyboard Instruments* (New York, 1949).

E. Helm, 'The "Hamlet" Fantasy and the Literary Element in C. P. E. Bach's Music', *Musical Quarterly*, 58 (1972), 277–96.

English Psalms (Hob.XXIII: Nachtrag). Six settings by Haydn of metrical psalms by James Merrick, in the collection *English Psalmody*, by the Revd William Dechair Tattersall; Haydn was listed as a subscriber to the volume. Published in three parts in December 1794, the settings of the 75 psalms were mainly for three voices (SAB). Among the contributors were such noted contemporary English composers as Samuel Arnold (1740–1802), John Callcott (1766–1821, William Shield (1748–1829), and Samuel Webbe (1740–1816) as well as some from an older generation. Intended to improve the level of psalmody in parish churches, the settings are primarily homophonic. Haydn set verses from Psalms 26, 31, 41, 50, 61, and 69, using through-composed and strophic settings, and featuring some imitation and word-painting. DdV

P. Holman, 'Haydn and *Improv'd Psalmody*', *Early Music Review* (July 1998).

Enlightenment. See overleaf.

'Ens aeternum attende votis' (Hob.XXIIIa:3). An offertory for chorus and orchestra, thought to have been composed in the 1760s. One early source has an orchestra of strings only; later sources have additional parts for oboes, trumpets, and timpani. It was published posthumously in 1813 by Breitkopf & Härtel with a German text, 'Walte gnädig, ewige Liebe', and in this version was widely performed in the 19th century. Nothing is known about its original circumstances of composition; it may have been written for a church in Eisenstadt or for the BARMHERZIGE BRÜDER. Like many vocal movements of the time it is in da capo form.

Entwurf-Katalog ('Draft catalogue'). A handwritten catalogue of Haydn's music prepared by the composer *c.*1765, regularly updated until *c.*1777, and more haphazardly thereafter. The title, *Entwurf-Katalog*, was not Haydn's own but arose because the volume served as the principal source for the more comprehensive and orderly catalogue of the composer's music that was prepared by Johann Elßler in 1805, the HAYDN-VERZEICHNIS. As originally conceived the *Entwurf-Katalog* was a working catalogue that was to be continually updated and not a draft.

In October 1765 Haydn's superior, Kapellmeister Gregor Werner, wrote an embittered letter of complaint to Prince Nicolaus about Haydn, accusing him of a casual, even negligent attitude to his duties. The prince responded with a sternly written directive to the composer. Following six numbered points that relate directly to issues raised by Werner, the directive concludes with a general instruction, urging Haydn 'to apply himself to composition more diligently than heretofore, and especially to write such pieces as can be played on the gamba [baryton]'. It is thought that the drawing up of a catalogue of his compositions was intended to demonstrate the diligence and orderliness of the Vice-Kapellmeister. While there is no reason to doubt this chain of events, Haydn might have thought too, after four years of stable employment and with some cognizance of his outside reputation, that the time was ripe for a catalogue of his music. He might also have been aware of Breitkopf's suggestion in Part I of the BREITKOPF CATALOGUE (1762) that catalogues compiled by composers would be a useful way of avoiding inaccuracy and piracy in the dissemination of their music.

Under Haydn's supervision Joseph Elßler drew up a volume of 26 pages (sides) divided into nine categories: symphonies, divertimenti, string trios, baryton music, operas, minuets, concertos, sacred works, and keyboard works. Using upright paper of the kind often found in autograph manuscripts of Haydn's music at the time, Elßler drew ten staves on the right-hand side of each page on which the musical incipit of each work was to be written; this allowed the title of the work to be given to the left of the incipit. Elßler himself wrote many of the incipits and titles for existing symphonies, divertimenti, and string trios, with Haydn providing the

[*cont. on p.84*]

Enlightenment

The 18th-century aesthetic and philosophical movement known as the Enlightenment does not lend itself to straightforward definition or the convenience of a unified view. It varied significantly from one country to another, and even within single countries the anomalies outweighed uniformity. With the notable exception of Kant's 'Was ist Aufklärung?' (What is Enlightenment?) the 18th century itself did not attempt to define the term. For Kant the Enlightenment virtually amounted to a new stage in intellectual evolution or human improvement, which suggests that eyewitnesses were not in an ideal position to make pronouncements on the significance of their era. Historians have had to discover its importance from a distance, and that has not proved easy since the century which followed went out of its way to extricate itself from the 18th century. To achieve that, the 19th century labelled its predecessor 'the Age of Reason', almost in a pejorative sense to separate that from its own fondness for the irrational and the mysterious. Throughout much of the 20th century the 18th century continued inappropriately to be called the Age of Reason, a designation much more suited to the 17th century.

A burst of scholarly energy in the past few decades, led initially by Peter Gay, Lester G. Crocker, Ira O. Wade, Theodore Besterman, and others, placed the discussion on a new footing, free of the vested interests of the previous century, treating the extraordinary intellectual ferment of the 18th century as a phenomenon in its own right but with implications for modern times. Their studies tended to focus on the great names of the Enlightenment, such as Diderot, Rousseau and Voltaire, suggesting a community of enlightened thinkers with a broad international influence. The next generation of 18th-century scholars, including Robert Darnton, Dena Goodman, Lynn Hunt, Margaret C. Jacob, Harry Payne, and Pat Rogers, has presented a much more diverse picture, moving away from the famous Frenchmen to include other nations, small societies, salons, issues of gender, and even the hack writers of Grub Street. With the diversity and paradoxes their studies have revealed, it has become still more difficult to arrive at a workable definition.

Paris clearly stands as a focus of enlightened activity, but also as a centre rife with contradiction. The *philosophes* had a strong sense of mission, concentrating their efforts on the *Encyclopedie*, which they saw as a liberator of knowledge. If all people had access to information on all possible subjects, the authority of a repressive state would in fact be broken. During the first half of the century the *philosophes* emerged as champions of a new social order which should move towards freedom and equality, and the salons of Louise d'Épainay, Marie-Thérèse Geoffrin, and Suzanne Necker played no small part in humanizing these often overly acerbic intellectuals. At no time did they become friends of the state, but by mid-century they had become absorbed by the social élite and stood as part of a new establishment. Rousseau, for various reasons (not the least of which was his own irascibility), broke from the group, accusing his former colleagues of social pandering. The new generation of writers felt equally alienated, not only forced to break into the intellectual circle but having to be accepted by polite society as well. It became increasingly questionable which force was the stronger and which direction aspirers should pursue more assiduously.

The intellectual atmosphere of Paris was transmitted abroad by various literary and journalistic means, including the *Correspondance littéraire* of Baron Melchior Grimm, a German who served as the ambassador of Catherine the Great to France. Numerous leading *philosophes* acted as correspondents, and the addressees were heads of state such as Catherine and Frederick the Great, who sought from their vantage points of power to bring about political and social reform. In France itself, where authority remained hostile to this activity, contributors to the *Correspondance littéraire* ran the risk of jeopardizing their own credibility by bringing heads of state into the 'Republic of Letters'. In comparing the relationship between reformers and authorities among France, England, and Germany, conditions could not have been more different. Reform was very much a part of the political process in England throughout the 18th century, and the English were especially appalled by the breakdown of order in France leading to the complete collapse in 1789. Contrary to the intransigence of the French, German monarchs such as Frederick or JOSEPH II attempted to legislate reforms, often over the objections of their subjects.

During a period of exile in England, Voltaire became a strong champion of the achievements of the British, believing they had already accomplished what the French were struggling towards. The leading English and Scottish writers such as Locke, Hume, Berkeley, and Hutcheson similarly did not go unnoticed in the German and Habsburg empires, where a sense of urgency arose about shedding a feudal past and moving into the modern age. The *Spectator* and *Tatler* of Addison and Steele became models for a proliferation of moral weeklies in Germany, one of the first of which was *Der Vernünfftler* (The Rationalist) (1713–14), edited by JOHANN MATTHESON, who would later make his mark as a music critic. A work from the end of the 17th century, the Earl of Shaftesbury's *Characteristics of Men, Manners, Opinion, Times*, had an enormous impact on German moralists such as CHRISTIAN FÜRCHTEGOTT GELLERT and Ignaz von Born. In Germany, unlike England and France, views such as Shaftesbury's on morality, tolerance, improvement of language, and refinement in general, found a home in universities where they were propagated by academics such as Christian Wolff in Halle or Johann Christoph Gottsched and Gellert in Leipzig. From there they spread south into Catholic territories, although the universities in Habsburg lands were very slow to discover reform. In Vienna the salons and Masonic lodges proved much more effective in spreading these ideas.

While the Enlightenment may be amorphous or hard to pin down in France, Britain, and northern Germany, some historians have questioned if it ever existed in the Habsburg domains. German visitors to Vienna as late as the 1780s, such as L. H. Nicolai and Lessing, doubted it, believing the Enlightenment did not mix with the intrusion of the Church in the affairs of the state, as was true of the Catholic Church even during the reign of Joseph II from 1780 to 1790. As co-regent during the final years of the reign of his mother MARIA THERESIA, Joseph, along with ministers of the regime such as Kaunitz, Sonnenfels, and VAN SWIETEN, began to reform Austria's feudal system, economic policy, judiciary, privileged education, and monolithic Church. Not all were pleased by his actions, including peasants, who should have benefited most. The abolition of certain religious holidays not only annoyed the Church but also workers, who had to spend more time in the fields as a result. In spite of the protest, Joseph appeared determined to drag his subjects kicking and screaming into the modern age.

Unlike other parts of Europe, where the Enlightenment had arisen as a type of grass-roots intellectual movement, independent of those in power, in Habsburg lands it came from the top down. Outside observers could certainly be forgiven for not recognizing here what they regarded as enlightened. Austria had no intellectual tradition in its universities, all of which were dominated by Catholic theology and recognized only the most conservative Protestant ideas decades after they had become established thought elsewhere. Germany itself was slower than other nations to develop a literary tradition, but in the Habsburg territories the difficulties were compounded by censorship which did not disappear during Joseph's reign. No group comparable to the academics of Leipzig, to say nothing of the *philosophes* of Paris, existed in Vienna, and the cause of morality, tolerance, and refinement was consequently taken up by scientists and government bureaucrats, many of whom found themselves in the Masonic lodge 'Zur wahren Eintracht' (True Concord) or in the literary salons such as the one in the home of FRANZ SALES VON GREINER. With the dismal state of literature in Vienna, music stood in a particularly advantageous position to take up the cause.

Distinguishing himself as the foremost among Austrian composers in the 1760s and 1770s, Haydn soon found himself sought after by other intelligent people in Vienna. Since Vienna lacked an academy of arts and sciences and its university served no such function, its enlightened intellectuals had to be a little more resourceful in finding means of assembly. Initially they met as small groups in the homes of friends, and these soon developed into salons which focused on specific disciplines such as literature for Greiner or music for van Swieten. Haydn became a regular guest at these salons, although he did not necessarily make a great impression at them, if we take the word of Greiner's daughter Caroline Pichler. Some of the participants of the Greiner salon, led by Born and Sonnenfels, hoped to establish a much larger forum which could include leading representatives from all the arts and sciences. Joseph II found the idea of an Austrian academy unappealing, certainly as an expense and probably as a potential source of political agitation, forcing Born and Sonnenfels to look elsewhere. They hit upon their solution with a Masonic lodge, 'Zur wahren Eintracht', creating it in 1781 as one of a growing number of lodges in Vienna.

In academy-like fashion, the leading scientists and literary figures of the capital were invited to join the lodge. While Masonic rites and rituals were observed, that was of less interest here than in other lodges. In fact this lodge became the focus of the Enlightenment in Vienna, and instead of being secretive about its goals and activities, it made them very public. Numerous members contributed to its literary outreach, the *Journal für Freimaurerer*. Edited by Aloys Blumauer, it espoused views of the importance of scientific advancement and the primacy of virtue. Here was Vienna's answer to the republic of letters, its own small contribution to enlightened goals in a type of journalistic encyclopedia.

Given the nature of the lodge, there was no question that Haydn's membership should be sought, and this it was, although not immediately since Haydn spent little time in Vienna. The invitation came late in 1784, and Haydn eagerly presented himself for initiation early in 1785 at the first opportunity to be in Vienna. Since he never attended another meeting, some have doubted his enthusiasm, but in fact no opportunity arose to attend before Joseph II dissolved the lodge with his *Freimaurerpatent* later in 1785. We have no reason to doubt Haydn's sentiments expressed to the Hofsecretaire von Weber and his sponsor COUNT GEORG APPONYI, to whom he wrote of the highly favourable impression that Freemasonry had made on him and his sincere wish to become a member of the order, with its humanitarian and wise principles. He counted himself privileged to be in a circle of such worthy men.

At the Greiner salon and 'Zur wahren Eintracht', Haydn came into contact with the best minds of the capital and a number of distinguished visitors as well. As a composer and director of opera Haydn already had a fairly sophisticated awareness of Italian literature, and at the Greiner salon his knowledge of German literature surely broadened. Censorship and other factors prevented focus on the new STURM UND DRANG works of Goethe and Klinger; instead, reading and discussion concentrated on mid-century writers such as Gellert, Gleim, Hagedorn, Jacobi, Lavater, and Lessing. It is known from a number of sources, including Haydn's personal library, that the composer shared these preferences. Gellert appealed to Haydn most of all, and he went so far as to call Gellert his hero. With Lavater he had some correspondence in which he commented favourably on the Swiss theologian's works. His choices of opera texts appear to have been influenced by these contacts, and his song texts are frequently from the poets he discovered at this time.

Haydn was no doubt well aware of the dimensions of the international Enlightenment, although he probably knew little of what actually happened in a country such as France. He may have known more about England before he went there in the early 1790s because of the influence of English writers on Germans; not only was Born an enthusiastic supporter of Shaftesbury, but even Haydn owned a copy of the *Characteristics*. It should come as no surprise that enlightened thought would have a critical bearing on Haydn's music; one would be very surprised if it had no effect. This reveals itself more readily in some types of composition than others, and opera is perhaps the most easily accessible. Haydn was active as an opera composer until the mid-1780s, and one notes a distinct shift in his approach during the late 1770s, about the time he came into contact with people such as Sonnenfels. While most of Haydn's earlier operas were comedies, three with librettos by Goldoni, he shifted now to texts that combine comic and serious features (*La vera costanza*, *Le fedeltà premiata*, and *Orlando paladino*) or purely serious librettos (*L'isola disabitata*, *Armida*, and *L'anima del filosofo*). Sonnenfels had waged a pugnacious literary campaign not only against crude Hanswurst comedies but against comedy in general, and Haydn (together with PRINCE NICOLAUS ESTERHÁZY) may have taken this as his cue to shift towards serious works, bringing his operas into line with the more refined types of entertainments Sonnenfels saw as necessary to edify and instruct the public.

Like any 18th-century composer, Haydn at this stage saw himself principally as a writer of vocal music, the music which critics and aestheticians believed was most effective in fulfilling the enlightened purposes of achieving intelligibility, presenting morality, and providing refinement. Refinement itself could be equated to morality, as Shaftesbury had with his notion of the 'moral sense', and overtly moral messages, therefore, need not necessarily be present. That opened the door to instrumental music achieving enlightened ends as well, and here Haydn emerged as the outstanding leader of his age. In his various types of instrumental composition he discovered that he could go well beyond mere refinement, and arouse through purely musical means an awareness of intelligibility, morality, and other tenets of the Enlightenment.

The string quartet, which Haydn refined as a type of composition and brought to extraordinary heights over the course of his long career, provides an excellent case in point. Perhaps his outstanding achievement with the quartet was to take it beyond the musical format of melody, bass, and inner-voice harmony, to a composition which had the potential for equality among all four voices. In this 'democratization' of the voices, he places four intelligent people in an intimate setting in which their sharing and exchanging of the important material allows a sense of unified purpose. The player not only feels his individual importance in the process but the role he plays in creating the whole. As these works were intended more for the enjoyment of the players than public performance, they achieved a goal very similar to that which writers saw for the novel, the moral weeklies, or devotional poetry. Reading material was placed in the hands of individuals who could enjoy it in the privacy of their own homes by themselves, with family members, or in small social gatherings, and, in fact, much of this material focused on intimate situations. In the string quartet, with accompaniments that can be transformed to melodies and vice versa, there is an apparent recognition through the potential for equality of one of highest goals of the Enlightenment.

What the string quartet achieved for intimate society, the symphony did by way of public performance. When his biographer GRIESINGER asked about his motives, feelings, and ideas—in short, what it was he hoped to express through musical language—Haydn replied that on ocassions he had portrayed moral characters in his symphonies. In choosing the term 'moral characters', taken directly from the moral weeklies where such portrayals occurred, he integrated the symphony into the enlightened tradition that had become so important to him. He explains it here in programmatic terms, but one could argue that the music itself functions in a much more sophisticated way in achieving enlightened ends. The process that Haydn follows in many of his late symphonies (especially in first movements), generating opposing musical forces that interact dramatically and arrive at an ultimate sense of coexistence, seems to adumbrate the spirit of tolerance so central to the actions and thinking of Joseph II and Haydn's fellow members of 'Zur wahren Eintracht'.

These features of the symphony appeared prominently in the Paris symphonies, written specifically for a Masonic concert society (the CONCERT DE LA LOGE OLYMPIQUE). They continue in the English symphonies, written for a country which Haydn visited at the prime of his life; here he met such enlightened people as CHARLES BURNEY, Thomas Holcroft, CHRISTIAN IGNATIUS LATROBE, and Thomas Twining. For both countries the works could be a tribute to what Haydn recognized as leadership in the advancement of the Enlightenment. By the time he returned to Vienna from England, the secular thrust of the Enlightenment had penetrated the sacred realm as well, and Haydn could further this spirit in his late masses and oratorios.

DPS

P. Gay, *The Enlightenment: An Interpretation* (New York, 1967).

D. Goodman, *The Republic of Letters: A Cultural History of the French Enlightenment* (Ithaca, NY, 1994).

M. C. Jacob, *The Radical Enlightenment: Pantheists, Freemasons and Republicans* (London, 1981).

R. A. Kann, *A Study in Austrian Intellectual History* (New York, 1960).

R. Porter and M. Teich (eds), *The Enlightenment in National Context* (Cambridge, 1981).

D. P. Schroeder, *Haydn and the Enlightenment: The Late Symphonies and their Audience* (Oxford, 1990).

bulk of the remainder. No date of composition was given and no indication of performing forces.

Within a few years it was obvious that the neat organization of the original would not be able to cope with the composer's burgeoning output. Haydn began filling in the left-hand sides of pages with his own hastily drawn staves and sometimes listed only the title of a work, and many works, especially quartets and baryton trios, had to be included on pages originally intended for other genres. Eventually several pages had a cluttered appearance, containing apparently random works. For instance, a page that was originally intended for operas includes also the first *Missa Cellensis*, two settings of the Salve regina, the Stabat mater, the 'Applausus' cantata, the oratorio *Il ritorno di*

Tobia, the offertory 'Non nobis Domine', and three baryton works. Ironically, the catalogue came to have that very disorderliness that caused to it come into being in the first place.

To compound an already complex situation, two portions were added to the catalogue during Haydn's lifetime: a supplementary list of symphonies prepared in the later 1770s and early 1780s, and a partial copy of the KEES CATALOGUE written in the early 1790s and thereafter updated by Haydn. In addition, modern scholarship has established that the two outer sheets of the catalogue became detached, from constant use, probably during Haydn's lifetime, and subsequently disappeared. The first four pages originally contained as many as 40 symphonies in Elßler's handwriting, and the equivalent sheets of paper at the end of the volume up to 20 keyboard works.

Notwithstanding the complicated structure of the *Entwurf-Katalog* it remains of fundamental value in establishing the authenticity and dating of Haydn's music, particularly for works from the 1760s and 1770s. For many works from the 1750s, such as Symphonies nos. 2 and 4, which do not survive in autograph manuscript or other sources that can be associated with the composer, their inclusion in the catalogue provides the only secure proof of authorship, and the date *c*.1765 (when the catalogue was begun) is the only available date for many works, a crucial *terminus ante quem*. When Haydn began compiling the catalogue he did not have a complete library of his music from the 1750s, so that coverage of that period is not comprehensive, though the missing pages devoted to keyboard music suggests the possibility that many works in that genre have been lost. On the other hand works written and entered in the 1760s include many that have not survived, among them six keyboard sonatas, three operas (*Il dottore*, *La vedova*, and *Il scanarello*), and concertos for flute, double bass, baryton, and horn.

S. Gerlach, 'Haydn's "Entwurf-Katalog": Two Questions', in S. Brandenburg (ed.), *Haydn, Mozart, and Beethoven. Studies in the Music of the Classical Period. Essays in honour of Alan Tyson* (Oxford, 1998), 65–84.
Larsen.

Erdödy family. Hungarian aristocratic family, several of whom were notable patrons of music in the Classical period.

Count Ladislaus Erdödy (1746–86), who was the brother-in-law of PRINCE ANTON ESTERHÁZY, had a musical retinue from at least 1772. It was in that year that he sent PLEYEL to study with Haydn, at a cost of 100 louis d'or per year. After four years of study Haydn was further rewarded with a gift of a coach and two horses. His main residence was Varasdin in Croatia, where Vanhal (1739–1813) too worked on an intermittent basis. Towards the end of his life he spent more time in Vienna. His substantial music library, including several manuscript copies of Haydn operas, was sold by auction in August 1788.

His brother, Count Ludwig (1749–94), also had a musical retinue, based at the old family palace in Eberau, and in a new palace at Kohfidisch. Martin Schlesinger (1754–1818) was the music director and the notable double bass virtuoso and composer Johann Sperger (1750–1812) was a member.

From a different branch of the family, Count Johann Nepomuk Erdödy (1723–89) had his principal palace in Pressburg (Bratislava) where, in 1785, he opened a small opera house for the local nobility and military. An enterprising repertoire of German opera, as well as German translations of Italian and French opera, was given, including four works by Haydn. The vocal ensemble numbered some ten or 11 singers, and the orchestra between 17 and 20 players. Concerts, also, were held in the theatre.

His son was Count Joseph Erdödy (1754–1824). He regularly employed a string quartet ensemble that played in the principal palace at Pressburg and in the summer palace in Freystadtl an der Waag (Gálgocz, Hlohovec) in Slovakia. In 1796 Erdödy commissioned six quartets from Haydn for a fee of 100 ducats; when they were later published as op. 76 by Artaria, the set was dedicated to the count, who sent a letter of thanks to the composer. Neither the letter nor the dedicated copies have survived. In a similar manner quartets by Bernhard Romberg (his op. 25) and Blumenthal (his op. 12) were dedicated to the count.

From yet another branch of the family, Countess Marie Erdödy (1779–1837) figured regularly in Beethoven's life, and was the dedicatee of the composer's op. 70 piano trios. HS

H. Seifert, 'Die Verbindungen der Familie Erdödy zur Musik', *HYB* 10 (1978), 151–63.
H. Seifert, 'Musik und Musiker der Grafen Erdödy in Kroatien im 18. Jahrhundert', *Studien zur Musikwissenschaft*, 44 (1995), 191–201.

'Erdödy' quartets. Name given to the six quartets, op. 76, that were commissioned by Count Joseph Erdödy in 1796. The first edition of the works, published by Artaria in 1799, was dedicated to him. JH

Ernst, Michael (b. 30 Sept. 1760; d. 19 Aug. 1818). Born in Eisenstadt, Ernst spent his entire life working at the Esterházy court. As a gifted young musician he was taken on as a music scholar at the court, where he sang treble in performances of marionette operas, learnt the violin, and, possibly, had composition lessons from Haydn. At the young age of 17 he suffered some kind of stroke that prevented him from fulfilling his youthful promise. He continued to play the violin in the church ensemble based in Eisenstadt and began to devote himself to the composition of sacred music. He was given a pension in 1813.

J. Harich, 'Das Haydn-Orchester im Jahr 1780', *HYB* 7 (1971), 5–69.

HCRL/2.

Esterházy family. A Hungarian aristocratic family in whose service Haydn was employed from 1761 to his death in 1809. The lineage of the 'Esterházy von Galantha' family, to give the full and correct form of the name, can be traced to Salamon (Solomun) who apparently settled with his tribe on the island of Schuett, near the later Pressburg (Bratislava), during the Hungarian occupation at the end of the 9th century. Documentary evidence of the existence of several branches of the family survives from the 12th century onwards. From the beginning of the 15th century the principal line called itself de Zerház (or Zyrhaz), then de Ezterház (with variant spellings) and finally Esztoras (again with variant spellings). One member, Benedickt, married into a family from Galántha in the 16th century, leading to the adoption of the family name Esterházy de Galántha.

Benedickt's son Franz (1553–1601) was a notable military leader in the continuing skirmishes with the Turks. His marriage produced 13 children, which led to three principal Esterházy lineages, named after their main residences: Nicolaus (1583–1645) was the founder of the Forchenstein line, Daniel (1585–1654) the founder of the Csesnek line, and Paul (1587–1616) the founder of the Altsohl line.

The Forchenstein line became the most significant. Although born a Protestant, Nicolaus was educated by the Jesuits at Tyrnau (Travna) and subsequently led a distinguished military career on behalf of the Habsburg court, earning him the titles of first baron and then count. The Hungarian nobility elected him as Palatine, effectively their leader. Count Nicolaus laid the foundation of the wealth of the family, derived from the spoils of the Turkish wars and from two very advantageous marriages; his first wife, Ursula Dersffy, the widow of his commanding officer, owned large estates in the west and north-east of Hungary; his second wife, Christina Nyáry, was another widow, with a large estate in the north of Hungary. These latter territories were even more firmly secured by the Esterházy family when Nicolaus's son married Christina's daughter from her first marriage.

As well as creating the wealth that was to underpin the cultural patronage of later generations of the Esterházy family, Count Nicolaus's ability to maintain the support of fellow Hungarian magnates at the same time as cultivating the favour of the Habsburg dynasty through military service was equally prescient. His son Paul (1635–1713) demonstrated his loyalty to the Habsburgs during the rebellion of Hungarian magnates in 1670 as well as during the continuing wars with the Turks; in 1687 Emperor Leopold I rewarded him with the title of Prince of the Holy Roman Empire. Changes to the family coat of arms reflect the growing status of the Esterházy family. The original coat of arms had showed a bird of prey in blue, crowned in gold and holding three roses in its right claw and wielding a silver sabre in its left claw; marriage with the Nyáry family added a red lion and three red roses; finally, the favour of Emperor Leopold produced the golden letter 'L', the chain of the Golden Fleece, and the crown of a Holy Roman prince.

Prince Paul Esterházy (Paul I) also ensured that the family estates could not be fractured through multiple inheritance by securing permission from the emperor in 1695 to establish an inheritance trust (the *Fideikomissum*); this established beyond contention the principle of primogeniture and safeguarded the wealth of the Esterházy estates against any reckless expenditure by individual members of the family.

Paul was the first to reveal the cultural ambitions of the dynasty. He loved the theatre, dance, and literature, and was a competent composer. Many of his works are devotional, principally the collection of hymns and solo motets for the church year gathered together under the title *Harmonia Caelestis*; it was published in 1711 by the prince's own press in Eisenstadt. Paul established a regular ensemble of church musicians at his court, consisting of some 18 to 20 players, many of whom had been educated at the imperial court in Vienna under Fux.

Prince Paul commissioned Carlo Innocenzo Carlone (1686–1775) to rebuild the castle in EISENSTADT in the Baroque style. The castle at Forchenstein was also rebuilt and an equestrian statue of the prince was erected in the courtyard. Churches, monasteries, chapels, and shrines throughout present-day Burgenland reveal the patronage of the prince.

His son Prince Michael Esterházy reigned from 1712 to 1721, building a new hunting lodge at Süttor, the site of the later ESZTERHÁZA. Since Michael had no heirs he was succeeded by his half-brother Joseph (1688–1721), who ruled for only a few months before dying at the age of 33. He was succeeded by his 10-year-old son, PAUL ANTON ESTERHÁZY (Paul II), who was to be Haydn's first Esterházy patron.

The accumulated estates of the Esterházy family in the 18th century were larger than many German principalities of the time. They were administered in a highly centralized and increasingly bureaucratic manner. At the same time the family embraced newer trends in agriculture, forestry, and, especially, viniculture. Successive members of the family were equally active as commercial entrepreneurs, establishing quarries, sawmills, a paper mill (from where Haydn and other musicians acquired paper for musical manuscripts), brickworks, tanneries, chalk pits, potteries, breweries, dairies, and so on. Although at the end of the 18th century PRINCE NICOLAUS II ESTERHAZY successfully developed a textile industry and his son Prince Paul Esterházy III encouraged coal-mining, the family was not able to manage the new industrial economy to a similarly successful extent. During the first decades of the 19th century the combined effects of comparative mismanagement, an unwieldly bureaucratic structure, two invasions by the French, the enormous expenditure of Nicolaus II on his art collection, and the lavish lifestyle of Prince Paul III, especially as imperial ambassador in London, diminished the wealth of the Esterházy family. Although the family was never to regain the political and cultural prestige it enjoyed in the 18th century, it remained a well-loved local aristocratic family up to the Second World War and the reign of the last prince, Paul V (1901–89). His reign provided a cruel and undignified end to several centuries of beneficent power. After the Second World War Hungary confiscated the family estates in that country and sentenced the prince to 15 years' imprisonment. The Hungarian Uprising of 1956 brought his release, after which he lived in exile in Switzerland. He is survived by his wife, Melinda Esterházy, and their son, Anton. GM

Die Fürsten Esterházy [Exhibition catalogue] (Eisenstadt, 1995).

I. Hiller, *Palatin Nikolaus Esterházy* (Vienna, 1992).

R. Perger, *Das Palais Esterházy in der Wallnerstraße zu Wien* (Vienna, 1994).

G. Schlag, 'Die Familie Esterházy im 17. und 18. Jahrhundert', in *Joseph Haydn in seiner Zeit* [Exhibition catalogue] (Eisenstadt, 1982), 91–104.

Esterházy, Prince Anton (b. 11 April 1738; d. 22 Jan. 1794). Son of PRINCE NICOLAUS I ESTERHÁZY and Maria Elisabeth Ungnad von Weissenwolf, ruling Esterházy prince from 1790 to 1794, and Haydn's third Esterházy patron. In the Seven Years War he served in his father's regiment and was imprisoned by the enemy. In 1763 he was promoted to the rank of captain; in 1780 he became Fieldmarshal Lieutenant and, later, head of the regiment. In 1792, when he was in his mid-50s, he fought in the war against France.

In 1763 Anton married Princess Maria Theresia Erdödy (1745–82). Three years after her death he married for a second time, to Princess Maria Anna Hohenfeld (1767–1848). On his accession to power in 1790 he realized his previously formulated plan to dismiss all the chamber musicians employed by the Esterházy court, except for Haydn and TOMASINI. Undoubtedly the main reason was to cut back on the expenditure of the court; he may also have been more interested at this time in his military career than in music. He certainly would have been aware that other aristocrats in the Austrian territories were disbanding their musical retinues too, and in that sense he was not doing anything that was unfashionable or controversial; indeed his decision to maintain a wind ensemble (*Harmonie*) was very much in keeping with the actions of other artistocrats. For his installation as Lord Lieutenant of Oedenberg (Sopron) in August 1791, Anton mounted a four-day celebration at Eszterháza. He requested that his Kapellmeister should return from London to compose an *opera seria* for the occasion, but Haydn's contract with Salomon obliged him to stay in London. *Venere e Adonis* by Joseph Weigl (1766–1846) was given instead, the last opera to be staged at the palace. Anton never visited the summer palace again.

While music history has not looked favourably on Anton, in other areas of patronage and culture he was very active. He had ambitious plans to restructure the palace at Eisenstadt, plans that were partly realized by his son Nicolaus II. Anton was responsible for the two lengthy, symmetrically placed buildings opposite the entrance to the palace, providing an attractive square. He died before he was able to realize his plans for a summer riding school at the southern end of the new buildings which, again, would have complemented the front of the main palace. He was interested in natural history and founded a notable collection of fossils and minerals. Like his predecessors he took an interest in the welfare of the local population, setting up a school in the Franciscan monastery for 25 children of the poor, taught by two teachers.

Prince Anton had four children from his first wife: Nicolaus (who succeeded him as reigning prince), Anton (who in 1790, at the age of 23, died from wounds received while fighting in the Siege of Belgrade the previous year), Therese (who married a member of the Csáky family), and Leopoldine (who married Prince Anton Grassalkovics). GM

HCRL/3.

Esterházy, Prince Nicolaus I (b. 18 Dec. 1714; d. 28 Sept. 1790). Haydn's second and most important Esterházy patron. He was the second son of Prince Joseph (1688–1721) and Princess Maria Octavia Gilleis. Like his brother, Paul Anton, he studied at the universities in Vienna and Leyden, and journeyed extensively throughout

Europe. Again like his brother, he fought on behalf of Maria Theresia in the War of Austrian Succession (1740–8) and in the Seven Years War (1756–63). As Chief Cavalry Officer, he fought in Bohemia, Bavaria, and in the Netherlands, and took part in the negotiations that led to the Peace of Dresden in 1745. After the War of Austrian Succession he played an active part in the reform of the imperial army. At the beginning of the Seven Years War, in the Battle of Kolin, he had displayed particular valour in the victory over the Prussian forces of Frederick the Great for which he was honoured with one of the first military decorations of the Order of Maria Theresia. As Lieutenant-Field Marshal he ended his military career in 1762 in order to succeed his brother as the reigning Esterházy prince. During the next few years he was the recipient of two of the highest Habsburg honours: in 1764 he represented the Bohemian nobility at the election in Frankfurt of Maria Theresia's son Joseph as Prince of the Holy Roman Empire (Nicolaus's splendour was vividly described by Goethe in *Dichtung und Wahrheit*); and, in the following year, he joined the Order of the Golden Fleece.

For several years Nicolaus and his wife, Maria Elisabeth Ungnad von Weissenwolf, had regularly visited a hunting lodge at Süttör to the south of the Neusiedler See where, as far as the limited facilities allowed, they enjoyed concerts, theatre, and opera performances. When he succeeded his brother as reigning prince, Nicolaus began an ambitious building programme that transformed this modest hunting lodge into a new palace, ESZTERHÁZA, soon dubbed the Hungarian Versailles. A Hungarian writer and member of the Hungarian Guard György Bessenyei (1737–1811) described the palace and grounds as follows: 'Everything that a prince who was anxious to reflect the taste and spirit of the times needed was to be found in the palace and its environs: a large-scale Kapelle, library, picture gallery, armoury, state rooms decorated in white and gold or in the Japanese style, gold leaf, Chinese vases and pagodas, a porcelain room, a belvedere, a winter garden, an orangery, a cafe, an opera theatre, a marionette theatre, cascades, temples dedicated to the Sun, Venus, Diana and Fortune, a hermitage, *champs élysées*, a Dutch pavilion, a park for deer, pheasant and wild boar, a *monbijou*, and a maze.'

At first opera performances were held in the main palace but in 1768 a new and separate opera theatre was completed, an occasion celebrated by the first performance of Haydn's *Lo speziale*. Following the fashion of the day the theatre had a deep perspective of about 18 m, marked by six to eight winged entrances, and was fitted with elaborate stage machinery. When the opera house burnt down in 1779 the prince lost no time in building a new one, completed in 18 months.

For spoken drama the best visiting troupes of actors were engaged, such as that of Carl Wahr, who visited Eszterháza between 1772 and 1777; his plays included translations of Shakespearian tragedies as well as modern plays by German authors such as Gebler, Goethe, and Stephanie. Haydn directed and, on at least one occasion, composed incidental music for these performances. PIETRO TRAVAGLIA worked for ten years for the prince as theatre and costume designer; he, with the occasional assistance of the painter Johann Basilius Grundmann (1726–98), was also responsible for the lavish processions and fireworks that characterized special celebrations at Eszterháza.

The prince cultivated this image of sumptuous luxury, earning him the sobriquet 'Nicolaus the Magnificent' ('der Prachtliebende'). A notable occasion was the visit of Maria Theresia in September 1773. Haydn's *L'infedeltà delusa* was presented on the first evening. A masked ball on the fashionable theme of *chinoiserie* was organized at which the musicians (including Haydn) also were attired in oriental clothing. On the second day, Haydn's *Philemon und Baucis* was given in the marionette theatre, together with an allegorical homage to the Habsburg dynasty. The visit finished with a lavish supper, fireworks, and the sight of 1,000 peasants enthusiastically dancing to Hungarian music. The empress's alleged remark 'If I want to hear good opera, I have to go to Eszterháza' is probably apocryphal; certainly she never made a return visit to the court. Maria Theresia did, however, hire Nicolaus's opera ensemble and the court musicians for a performance at Schönbrunn. Other imperial guests who prompted similarly lavish festivals included Joseph II (Kittsee, 1770), Maria Theresia's favourite daughter, Marie Christine, and her husband, Duke Albert von Sachsen-Teschen (Eszterháza, 1773), and Maria Theresia's son Ferdinand and his wife, Maria Beatrice d'Este (Eszterháza, 1775).

Haydn and his fellow musicians were central to any such display of ostentation and the imperial court, in particular, must have been aware that music played a more central role in the life of Nicolaus than it did in that of the imperial family. That the Kapellmeister Haydn himself recognized the special nature of Prince Nicolaus's patronage is suggested by his remarks to GRIESINGER: 'My prince was pleased with all my work, I received success, I could as head of an orchestra make experiments and observe what made an impression, what weakened it and, in that way, improve, add, delete and experiment. I was cut off from the rest of the world, there was no one in the vicinity to annoy or disturb me, and so I had to become original.' Griesinger commented: 'Haydn had his hands full: he composed, he had to direct musicians, help everyone study, give lessons, even tune the harpsichord in the orchestra. He himself often wondered how it had been possible to write so much.' Like many members of his family Nicolaus was passionately fond of music but without his particular enthusiasm for opera and for an instrument called the BARYTON Haydn would have composed many fewer operas and none of the over 200 works for that instrument. From 1776 there was a regular opera season at Eszterháza that typically began in March or April and regularly went on to October, even November. In 1765, the prince had purchased a baryton in Innsbruck for 172 gulden and for the next decade Haydn was obliged to write music for the instrument.

Prince Nicolaus greatly valued Haydn's services. He listened to the pleas of his Kapellmeister on behalf of musicians who had been unfairly treated, and he twice paid for the rebuilding of Haydn's house in Eisenstadt following fires. In his will, Nicolaus provided Haydn with an annual pension of 1,000 gulden, slightly more than his previous salary.

Nicolaus's patronage of music has tended to obscure his patronage of painting and sculpture, particularly evident when the palace of Eszterháza was being built. Modern knowledge of this aspect of Nicolaus's artistic interest is limited by the fact that much of the rich documentary evidence lies unexamined in family archives housed in the fortress at Forchenstein. Alongside the main building in Eszterháza a new picture gallery was erected and the court painter, Johann Basilius Grundmann (1726–98), was placed in charge. From the travel diaries of many guests who stayed at Eszterháza, it is evident that the prince owned several original works by Dutch and Italian masters. Whether the so-called 'Esterházy Madonna' by Raphael (now in the Szépmüvészeti Múzeum, Budapest) was presented by Pope Clement XI to the prince as a gift cannot be verified. Also unclear is the role of the prince in building up the substantial collection of engravings that has survived. Because his money and his attention were focused on the new palace of Eszterháza there is some evidence to suggest he neglected the other Esterházy collections, such as the extensive one at the small palace at Lackenbach.

Although he preferred the solitude of life at Eisenstadt and, especially, Eszterháza, Prince Nicolaus cultivated the favour of Maria Theresia, attending the court in Vienna and, like his father before him, taking part in balls, masquerades, sleigh rides, and similar amusements. In 1760, in an extravagant ceremony at Pressburg (Bratislava), the empress founded the Hungarian Guard, 120 men financed by the Hungarian counties. Housed in the Palais Trauton in Vienna, they accompanied the empress on public occasions and on journeys beyond Vienna. From 1764 until 1787 Nicolaus was captain of the Hungarian Guard. In 1783, in recognition of Nicolaus's loyalty to the imperial throne, Joseph II granted the male descendants of the prince the automatic right from birth to the title of prince.

As had been his practice for nearly a quarter of a century, Prince Nicolaus spent most of 1790 at Eszterháza. The operatic repertoire that season included Paisiello's *Il barbiere di Siviglia*, Cimarosa's *L'impresario in angustie*, and Martín y Soler's *L'arbore di Diana*. During August, when plans were being made for the performance of Mozart's *Le nozze di Figaro*, the prince was taken ill. In order to receive better care he was taken to the Esterházy palace in Vienna. He died on 29 September. For three days tolling church bells honoured the memory of this faithful servant of the Habsburg dynasty. Haydn always spoke warmly of the prince, and posterity has with complete justice celebrated this partnership of patron and artist as one of the most glorious in the history of music. GM

Die Fürsten Esterházy. Magnaten, Diplomaten und Mäzene [Exhibition catalogue] (Eisenstadt, 1995).

R. Gates-Coon, *The Landed Estates of the Esterházy Princes* (Baltimore, 1994).

M. Horányi (trans. A. Deák), *The Magnificence of Eszterháza* (Budapest, 1962).

HCRL/1 and 2.

Esterházy, Prince Nicolaus II (b. 12 Dec. 1765; d. 15 Sept. 1833). Haydn's fourth and last Esterházy patron. He was the son of PRINCE ANTON ESTERHÁZY and Maria Theresia Erdödy, and grandson of NICOLAUS I ESTERHÁZY. At the age of nearly 18 he married Princess Maria Josepha Hermenegild von Liechtenstein, who had just turned 15. Like most of the Esterházy family he pursued a military career, reaching the rank of General Lieutenant.

He succeeded his father as the reigning prince in 1794. His priorities lay in redesigning the main palace at EISENSTADT and in amassing a substantial collection of paintings. The palace was rebuilt in the Classical style, essentially its appearance today, and the gardens were laid out in the modern English style. He planned to build a gallery to house his collection of paintings, but this plan was never realized. Most of the paintings were collected in 1794 and 1795 when he visited Rome and Naples, and included works by Andrea del Sarto, Correggio, Raphael, and Claude Lorrain. On a journey to Paris he met the Viennese landscape painter and engraver Joseph Fischer and engaged him as director of the collection. While plans for a gallery at Eisenstadt remained unfulfilled, the prince bought and adapted a small palace at Pottendorf to the north-east of Eisenstadt to house the collection, to which were added paintings and other artworks from various Esterházy palaces. Although completed in 1806, this gallery was destined to be a short-term home only. During Napoleon's second invasion of 1809 it was thought prudent to transfer the material by ship to Pest. It returned to Vienna the following year and after two further unsatisfactory locations it was finally housed in the former palace of Prince Kaunitz in the Mariahilf district, which Nicolaus Esterházy had bought in 1814. Here the collection of 542 paintings was displayed in three rooms that were open to the public; it soon became regarded as a major European gallery. Under Joseph Fischer's influence the collection was notable also for its many fine engravings, over 50,000 in number.

Music was a secondary interest for the prince. Although Haydn's position as Kapellmeister was reactivated after his return from London, concerts, church music, and operatic performances in Eisenstadt relied heavily on the engagement of performing musicians on an ad hoc basis, at least initially. Haydn felt that the prince's manner was too severe in comparison with earlier Esterházy princes and one that did not equate with his European status; on one occasion Haydn objected to being addressed in the third-person singular ('Er'), remarking that a Doctor of Music from Oxford University deserved better. Gradually, Nicolaus and Haydn reached a more congenial relationship, though in private the composer bemoaned his master's limited musical knowledge. Nicolaus did, however, build up the library of church music at the court which had been neglected since the middle of the century. He also began the tradition of having a major new mass performed on the nameday of his wife, PRINCESS MARIE HERMENEGILD ESTERHÁZY, beginning with the six late masses of Haydn and continuing with masses by JOHANN NEPOMUK FUCHS, HUMMEL, and BEETHOVEN (his Mass in C, 1807). In Haydn's old age the prince, usually prompted by the princess, regularly ensured that his Kapellmeister led as comfortable a life as possible, giving him the use of a carriage, sending him wine from the Esterházy cellars and, in 1806, granting him an additional yearly allowance of 600 gulden.

The prince figured too as a patron of the arts in Vienna. He was, for instance, a subscriber to Beethoven's op. 1, designed to launch that composer's adult career, and was for a time president of a commission that ran the principal theatres in Vienna. He was even more well known, however, for his debauched lifestyle, keeping what amounted to a private brothel in the Landstraße. Like many other aristocratic families in Vienna in the opening decades of the 19th century, Nicolaus coped poorly with the effects of the hyperinflation unleashed by the Napoleonic Wars. This, together with his continuing expenditure on art and on the pleasures of the flesh, led to an ignominious end to his life. He was the subject of a sequestration order in 1832 and died a year later in Como, Italy. GM

Die Fürsten Esterházy. Magnaten, Diplomaten & Mäzene [Exhibition catalogue] (Eisenstadt, 1995).
HCRL/4 and 5.

Esterházy, Prince Paul Anton (b. 22 April 1711; d. 18 March 1762). Haydn's first Esterházy patron. Eldest son of Prince Joseph (1688–1721) and Princess Maria Octavia Gilleis, he was only 10 years old when he succeeded his father in 1721. During his minority his mother and Count Georg Erdödy acted as guardians and administered the estate. The young prince received a thorough education. He studied jurisprudence in Vienna and Leyden, and in 1731 his thesis of over 200 pages on Hugo Grotius's *De Jure Belli ac Pacis* (1625) was published. Two consuming interests were developed as a young man: music (he was a competent player of the violin, lute, and, especially, flute) and literature (he knew Italian, French, and Latin, as well as German and Hungarian, he founded the Esterházy library and had a particular enthusiasm for French literature).

In 1734 Paul Anton assumed full responsibility for the estates. Following family tradition, he immediately entered military service on behalf of the Habsburg dynasty. While serving in the regiment of Prince Carl von Lothringen he met Princess Maria Anna Louisa Lunati-Visconti. They were married in Lunéville and returned to Eisenstadt in October 1735. She shared her husband's many cultural interests and it was a happy marriage.

On the death of Emperor Karl VI in 1740, his successor MARIA THERESIA was faced with an opportunistic coalition of France, Bavaria, and Prussia, all of whom hoped to capture some of the Habsburg territories. In an astute move, Maria Theresia quickly arranged her coronation as Queen of Hungary and began cultivating the allegiance of the ruling classes of the country. While many of Prince Paul Anton's fellow magnates were hesitant in their support he immediately raised a regiment of hussars, one that was eventually to number between 800 and 1,000 men. Led by the prince it took an active part in the War of Austrian Succession (1740–8), fighting battles in Lower Austria, Bohemia, Netherlands, Moravia, Silesia, Saxony, and in the Rhineland. The prince was accompanied by a retinue of secretaries, servants, pages, and cooks; during the Siege of Prague in 1742, for instance, a lavish table was laid for 12 people with wine forwarded from the Esterházy estates. Prince Paul Anton's military career continued during the Seven Years War (1756–63) when he was given the rank of Field Marshal.

Between these two wars the prince, accompanied by his wife, was an ambassador at the court of Naples (1750–2). A hotbed of political intrigue that fully stretched the prince's diplomatic skills, Naples was also a centre of Baroque culture, especially music. The prince indulged his love of music, presenting the opera *Endimione* (music by Niccolò Conti, text by METASTASIO) on his installation as ambassador in 1750 and the cantata 'Gli orti esperidi' (music by Niccolò Conforti, text by Metastasio) on the birthday of Maria Theresia in 1751. He soon became a leading figure in Neapolitan social life, a typical ball attracting over 1,000 guests who danced through to the morning. Alongside silver, furniture, and a splendid carriage, Prince Paul Anton amassed a substantial collection of music and librettos. On his return to the Esterházy court in 1752 the material was combined with other music collected during his many journeys to France and Germany, an inventory was drawn up, and the whole collection placed under the control of WERNER. It provides a fascinating indication of the range of music that Haydn might have encountered when he joined the Esterházy court in 1761. The prince maintained his enthusiasm for Italian music, in particular building a new theatre at the Esterházy palace and sponsoring periods of study in that country for promising court musicians such as the violinist LUIGI TOMASINI and the singer CARL FRIBERTH; had he lived beyond 1762 he might well have encouraged Haydn to visit the country. GM

H. Benedikt, 'Die Botschaft des Fürsten Anton Esterházy in Neapel', *Mitteilungen des Instituts für österreichische Geschichtsforschung*, 64 (1956), 34–64.
Die Fürsten Esterházy. Magnaten, Diplomaten & Mäzene [Exhibition catalogue] (Eisenstadt, 1995).
R. Gates-Coon, *The Landed Estates of the Esterházy Princes* (Baltimore, 1994).
J. Harich, 'Inventare der Esterházy-Hofmusikkapelle in Eisenstadt', *HYB* 9 (1975), 5–125.
HCRL/1.

Esterházy, Princess Maria Anna (b. 12 Aug. 1712; d. 4 July 1782). Wife of PRINCE PAUL ANTON ESTERHÁZY. Born Countess Lunati-Visconti in Lunéville, her mother was a lady-in-waiting at the court of Princess Charlotte von Lothringen. In 1734–5 Paul Anton was serving in the Austrian army under the command of Prince Karl von Lothringen when he met the young countess. They were married on 21 December 1735. The princess proved a highly congenial partner to the cultured and well-educated prince.

Detailed knowledge of the princess's interests in literature, music, theatre, and, especially, painting is lacking. In July 1773 her nameday was celebrated with the first performance of Haydn's *L'infedeltà delusa*. She had her own library in Eisenstadt and, following the death of Paul Anton in 1762, she lived mainly in her own house in the town, where she assembled a large collection of paintings, porcelain, fine furniture, and shooting rifles. The house and its contents were sold after her death and the proceeds given to charity. She also left money for a new chapel in the Augustinian convent in Eisenstadt, where her heart and that of her husband were entombed. There were no children to the marriage. GM

Die Fürsten Esterházy [Exhibition catalogue] (Eisenstadt, 1995).
HCRL/1, 2.

Esterházy, Princess Maria Elisabeth (b. 21 March 1718; d. 25 Feb. 1790). Born in Linz, Countess Ungnad von Weissenwolf married NICOLAUS ESTERHÁZY in 1737. In the same year the Esterházy family commissioned a portrait of her from Martin von Meytens. The couple had four children: Anton (later PRINCE ANTON ESTERHÁZY), Anna (who married Count Anton Grassalkovics), Christine, and Nicolaus; the last mentioned, who should not be confused with his nephew, PRINCE NICOLAUS II ESTERHÁZY, also married a countess from the Weissenwolf family.

In contrast to the extravagant lifestyle of her husband, Maria Elisabeth seems to have led a more reserved existence. She did not share his enthusiasm for the new summer palace at ESZTERHÁZA, preferring to stay in Eisenstadt. A devout woman, she instigated many architectural changes in the palace chapel. She bought a vineyard near the Kalvarienberg, where she built a two-storey house; she may have spent the last years of her life in this house rather than in the palace. She did, however, take a personal interest in the changes that were executed in the palace gardens in the 1770s and 1780s, including a menagerie, a bird house, and a pheasant reserve. Her death in February 1790 left Nicolaus in deep mourning, a condition that may well have contributed to his own death only eight months later.

Princess Maria Elisabeth Esterházy had little or no direct contact with her husband's Kapellmeister. For her birthday in 1775 Haydn was instructed to prepare a surprise performance of a marionette opera at the palace in Eisenstadt; the identity of the work, which may not have been by Haydn himself, is not known. GM

Die Fürsten Esterházy [Exhibition catalogue] (Eisenstadt, 1995).
HCRL/2.

Esterházy, Princess Marie Hermenegild (b. 13 April 1768; d. 8 Aug. 1845). Daughter of Franz Joseph I, Prince of Liechtenstein. When she married NICOLAUS ESTERHÁZY (II) in 1783 he was 18 and she only 15. The marriage was not a happy one. The prince had a series of affairs, one commentator imputing that he had 200 mistresses and 100 illegitimate children. Maria Hermenegild had three children: Paul III (1786–1866), Leopoldine (1788–1846), who married Moritz Joseph von Liechtenstein, and Nicolaus (1799–1844).

During the Congress of Vienna the salon of Princess Marie (as she was known) was at the centre of Viennese and international society offering a variety of entertainment, including Tyrolean evenings, and balls for the children of the aristocracy and for the crowned heads of European states assembled in Vienna.

Prince Auguste de la Garde, a chronicler of the Congress, described the princess, who was approaching 50, as follows: 'she was still at that time full of grace and charm even though her youth was behind her. She possessed a touching goodness which affected even those who did not possess such a quality.' She reminisced about the *tableaux vivants* that she had organized in the Temple of Leopold in the gardens in Eisenstadt when 'Haydn, her Kapellmeister had improvised an accompaniment that was perfectly matched and contributed distinctively to the illusion'. Although de la Garde is not an altogether reliable witness, there is no doubt that the princess was exceptionally fond of Haydn and liked to demonstrate this affection. It was due to her that Haydn had access to the best wine in the Esterházy cellar, especially Tokay and Malaga wine, was able to use the Esterházy carriage as well as the family's doctor and apothecary, and was given an increase in annual stipend to 600 gulden.

From 1796 to 1802 (with the exception of 1800) Haydn normally presented a large-scale mass on the occasion of the princess's nameday in September, directing the performances, usually in the Bergkirche. The performances attracted music lovers from royalty and the aristocracy to Eisenstadt, including Emperor Franz and the Queen of Naples. Haydn was invited to the celebratory banquets, was treated with respect and his good health toasted. When in his old age Haydn was no longer able to leave his house in Gumpendorf, Vienna, the princess and her son Paul visited the composer. DIES reports that in 1806 the young prince embraced and kissed the composer saying: 'My dearest Haydn, God preserve you for many more years!'

On 27 March 1808 in the Festsaal of the university a performance of Haydn's *Creation* took place to celebrate the composer's 76th birthday. He was taken to the hall in an Esterházy carriage, was led into the hall by Princess Esterházy and Prince Lobkowitz, and was greeted with public cheering. During the performance Haydn sat alongside the princess and when the accompanying doctor thought that the composer was becoming rather cold, the princess loosened her neckerchief and placed it on Haydn's feet; other ladies followed her example. The princess commissioned a miniature painting of the occasion from Balthasar Wigand, which she subsequently had set on the lid of a small box and presented to the composer. It is a measure of her affection for Haydn that after his death she regained possession of the item. It was destroyed during the Second World War.

Humanity and sensitivity made the princess and the Austrian empress, MARIE THERESE, kindred spirits. Their correspondence reveals their shared inclination to be philosophical in adversity, to revel in harmless social gossip, but also on the part of the princess, her frequent disappointment at the actions of her husband and the lack of ambition of her son. Following the princess's persuasion Paul did not assume the customary military career but, instead, became a diplomat. Later, as a widow, the princess continued to be a leading figure in Viennese social life, her existence troubled only by the increasing financial debts of her beloved son.

GM

HCRL/4 and 5.

Eszterháza. See opposite.

Eybler, Joseph Leopold (b. 8 Feb. 1765; d. 24 July 1846). A leading composer in Vienna whose early career was enthusiastically promoted by Haydn. He was distantly related to Michael and Joseph Haydn and like them received his musical education at the choir school in St Stephen's. Later he was a pupil of ALBRECHTSBERGER and received considerable encouragement from Mozart as well as Haydn, though he was never formally a pupil of either composer. In 1787 Haydn warmly recommended three piano sonatas of Eybler to ARTARIA; in the event they were not published. Two years later Haydn was evidently unable to fulfil a commission for three minuets 'for one of my friends' and asked Eybler to forward some of his; the implication is that they were to be dishonestly presented as the work of Haydn. It was from this time that Eybler became friendly with Mozart and it was to Eybler that Constanze Mozart first turned to complete the Requiem following her husband's death in December 1791. Eybler's completion of several movements of the Sequence has survived, and in many ways it is stylistically more convincing than the version subsequently prepared by Süssmayr.

[*cont. on p.96*]

Eszterháza

A summer palace of the Esterházy family built by Prince Nicolaus Esterházy and located 87 km (53 miles) south-east of Vienna in Hungary. Named after the family, it was variously spelt Esterház, Esterháza, Esteraz, and Estoras (Haydn's customary spelling) in the 18th century. The modern correct Hungarian orthography is Eszterháza; during the communist period after the Second World War the hamlet that had grown around the palace was renamed Fertőd.

The Esterházy family had maintained a substantial hunting lodge, named Süttör, on the site from early in the 18th century. It was a favourite residence of Count Nicolaus Esterházy and a detailed description of the estate drawn up in December 1760 shows it to have had 41 rooms on three floors, including two halls and a small chapel, and to be located in extensive gardens. The same document also reveals plans for substantial enlargement of the palace. When Nicolaus became prince in 1762, these plans were made even more ambitious under the supervision of the Viennese builder and architect, Melchior Hefele, and from the mid-1760s through to 1784, the palace and gardens were remodelled to become one of the most striking and sumptuous summer residences in the Habsburg territories, earning the appellations 'the little Versailles of Hungary', 'the Hungarian Paradise', and 'the Hungarian Delight'.

Haydn and his musicians probably visited Süttör to perform at concerts and, possibly, operas from 1762 onwards, and it was from the palace that Prince Nicolaus issued his famous reprimand to the composer in 1765. As the rebuilding progressed the new, central role of the palace in the life of the family was signalled on 3 January 1766 when an instruction was issued that henceforth it was to be known as Eszterháza. Two years later, the principal opera house was completed, celebrated by the first performance of Haydn's *Lo speziale*, followed in 1773 by a smaller theatre for marionette operas; when the main opera house was destroyed by fire in November 1779 instructions were given that it should be rebuilt immediately and fifteen months later, in February 1781, it was reopened with the first performance of Haydn's *La fedeltà premiata*.

The palace is approached from the north and visitors entering through the gates are presented in the middle distance by the central portion of the palace, incorporating the transformed original Süttör palace. From either side two wings project towards the gate, gradually sweeping in a horseshoe shape to converge on the gate. From an original palace of 41 rooms, Eszterháza became one of 126 rooms, on three storeys. Behind the entrance gates were the quarters of the princely guard. The principal room on the ground floor was the Sala Terrena, where concerts were given and, before the opera houses were built, probably operas. The private quarters of the prince and princess were also located on this floor, as were dining rooms, some visitors' quarters, and a chapel with a small organ. The main features of the first floor were a large salon (Paradesaal) and a smaller room specifically designed for the prince's concerts. The second floor was mainly given over to apartments for visitors. Although each room has its character and some, like the prince's quarters and the rooms occupied by Empress Maria Theresia during her visit in 1773, are particularly sumptious, there is a notable uniformity of balancing proportions and consistent use of red marble, gilt, and green fabrics. The prince acquired furniture, porcelain and artwork from China, France, Germany, Japan, and Italy, as well as from Austria, and more than one visitor commented on the number of clocks in the palace. Reaching out at a right angle from both wings were two single-storey buildings, housing an art gallery and a winter garden.

The principal indulgence of the palace was the presence of two purpose-built opera houses. Prince Nicolaus was not alone in having a private theatre, but most other examples in the Austrian territories are contained within the palace and not as separate buildings, and, certainly, there does not seem to have been another palace with two theatres.

The main opera house was built on a site to the south-west of the main building, so as not to impede the views of the gardens from the windows or the palace. It was a building roughly measuring 200′ × 60′ which could hold some 400 people. The prince and his guests sat in a large oval box on the first floor with adjacent rooms for relaxation, private dining, and billiards. Two further boxes on side galleries of the first floor could also be reached by flights of open stairs from the surrounding gardens. The principal seating area was on the ground floor, eleven rows with a central aisle. In the manner of the day the orchestral musicians sat in two parallel rows on benches in front of the stage. As the continuo player responsible for directing the performance, Haydn was seated at one end, where he could keep an eye on the stage and on his players. The stage itself was a notably large one for the size of the auditorium, some 80 feet across and 60 feet deep, raked so that the audience could see to the back. The wings contained six (perhaps eight) sets of flats on castors, each one of which could house as many as four changes of scenery. The flies contained the necessary mechanism for raising and lowering beneficent gods, chariots and clouds, while there was a corresponding trap-door mechanism for devils and the like. The music was kept in a store cupboard between the stage and the auditorium; the changing rooms were underneath the stage towards the back, and the costumes were kept in a large room behind the stage. Light was provided by spirit lamps, deflected and diffused, as necessary, by strategically placed mirrors. As in the main palace, the predominant colours in the auditorium were red, gold, and green. Eight large stoves heated the theatre, some placed in the basement so that the heat could rise through grilles into the main auditorium. Between the opera house and the main palace there was a coffee house with two billiard tables.

On the equivalent site to the south-east of the palace was the marionette theatre. Very little is known about its design. It was built in the form of a grotto, with decorative rock and shell work, and with miniature fountains. There was only one level and no boxes. Although it was much smaller than the main theatre, the stage area was again proportionately large, and certainly large enough for performances of Italian operas to be given when the main opera house was not available following the fire.

The Chinese Ballroom (also called the Bagatelle) stood next to the main opera house, a dance floor overlooked by a gallery, also used as a garden house in the summer. It was an exploding stove in this building that started the fire that destroyed the first opera house, to which it had been attached; when the opera house was rebuilt the two buildings were separated.

To the west of the opera house and Chinese Ballroom were the living quarters allocated to the members of the orchestra, the singers, and visiting troupes of actors. It was habitable from 1768, though changes were still being made in the 1770s. It contained 76 rooms on two storeys built around six courtyards, with communal kitchens. Most employees were allocated one or two rooms but Haydn, like the court apothecary, and court librarian, had a four-room flat. There was also a rehearsal room. When there was insufficient space for all the visiting performers, they were put up in a nearby inn, also newly built by the prince.

This collection of buildings was impressive enough, but many contemporary visitors were even more impressed by the scale of the gardens, laid out in a widening panorama to the south of the palace. While Haydn enthusiasts will always lament the destruction of the opera houses in particular, for the general connoisseur there is no doubt that the absence of these gardens has diminished greatly the sense of grandeur and space of Eszterháza; the palace no longer exists in its proper topographical context. First came the formal gardens, cut, in the French manner, into symmetrical patterns by broad avenues leading into the far distance. Beyond these lay parkland with a game reserve and a swine reserve. So large were the gardens that Prince Nicolaus had a special carriage built, drawn by six to eight horses; rather like a modern touring caravan it had a table, chairs for 12 people, a fireplace, and several closets. In comparative comfort the prince and his guests could survey the parkland, its many statues, fountains, a hermitage, and temples dedicated to the Sun, Diana, Fortune, and Venus.

The Haydn literature often gives a rather isolated picture of the Esterházy Kapellmeister at work in this fabulous summer palace. In truth, it must often have become a community of over 1,000 people, musicians, actors, household staff, princely guard, innkeepers, gardeners, blacksmiths, and, for much of the time, architects and builders too. It had taken some 20 years to create this other world. Sadly, but appropriately, the world disappeared abruptly with the death of its creator, Prince Nicolaus, in September 1790. Shortly afterwards Haydn travelled to Vienna, from where in December he set out for the first visit to London. He revisited Eszterháza only once.

Nicolaus's successor, Anton, was installed as Governor of the County of Oedenburg at Eszterháza in August 1791, the last time the palace was used by the family for a major public occasion, including the opera house and the ballroom. The palace became too costly to maintain and Anton and Nicolaus II preferred Eisenstadt and Vienna. In 1796 Nicolaus ordered that costumes, sets, and stage machinery from Eszterháza be stored, sold, or transferred to Eisenstadt. The buildings in the gardens and the gardens themselves began to fall into increasing decay in the 19th century and by 1832, the centenary of Haydn's birth, the two opera houses were being used to store timber; the main theatre was demolished in 1870. The palace itself, however, was kept in basic good order, though shorn of most of its contents. At the end of the Second World War it was utilized as a hospital by the Russian army, who, with typical cultural brutality, prepared a bonfire of many of the remaining items of furniture and paintings. It was in this fire that Grundmann's portrait of Haydn, executed shortly after he entered the service of the Esterházy family, was destroyed.

From the mid-1950s onwards the main palace has been gradually restored and concerts are often held there. But, whereas the palace at Eisenstadt in the last 20 years has become a major tourist attraction and a focal point for concerts, exhibitions, and conferences associated with the composer, Eszterháza has remained isolated and off the main tourist beat. Just over two centuries after it was first abandoned, there are ambitious plans to rebuild the main opera house.

Rebecca Gates-Coon, *The Landed Estates of the Esterházy Princes* (Baltimore, 1994).
M. Horányi (trans. A. Deák), *The Magnificence of Eszterháza* (Budapest, 1962).
HCRL/2.
M. Mihály, *Eszterháza. Fehéren—Feketén* [with CD Rom] (Budapest, 1998).

Armed with testimonials from Albrechtsberger, Haydn, and Mozart Eybler embarked on a career as a church composer in Vienna, and as a composer at the imperial court. He worked at the Schottenkirche for over 30 years and was Salieri's deputy as Hofkapellmeister, succeeding him to the full post in 1824. Although he wrote substantial quantities of engaging instrumental music up to *c.*1810, he increasingly concentrated on church music and, like Albrechtsberger and Salieri before him, came to represent the most reactionary aspects of Viennese musical life. He was ennobled in 1835.

Eybler acknowledged Haydn's patronage by dedicating his first string quartets to him (Vienna, 1794); in June 1809 he directed the performance of Mozart's Requiem that took place in the Schottenkirche in memory of Haydn. His arrangement of 'Gott erhalte Franz den Kaiser' for windband has not survived. The text of his oratorio, *Die vier letzen Dinge*, prepared by Joseph Sonnleithner, is said to have been originally intended for Haydn.

HCRL/2, 4, and 5.

'Ey, wer hat ihm das Ding gedenkt' (Cor, who'd 'ave thought such a thing) (Hob.XXIIId:G1). A PASTORELLA for soprano, two violins, and organ continuo. As is common in pastorellas it is a setting of an imaginary dialogue between two shepherds who are staring in awe at the infant Jesus in the stable. In vernacular German, the full version has four verses. Typical also of the genre is the use of repetitive drone basses (most noticeable at the end of the instrumental introduction) and the allusion in the vocal line to a popular lullaby, in this instance the Czech 'Hajej můj andílku' ('Sleep, my little angel').

The work has been attributed also to Stephan (1726–97) and Michael Haydn, though there is strong circumstantial evidence to link it with Joseph Haydn. It may date from the late 1750s, and was possibly a product of the composer's association with the BARMHERZIGE BRÜDER.

G. Chew, 'Haydn's Pastorellas: Genre, Dating and Transmission in the Early Church Music', in O. Biba and D. W. Jones (eds), *Studies in Music History Presented to H. C. Robbins Landon on his Seventieth Birthday* (London, 1996), 21–43.

F

fantasia. In the 18th century an instrumental piece, usually for keyboard, associated with improvisation, contrasting moods, formal and harmonic freedom, whether occurring as a prelude to another piece (as in J. S. Bach's Chromatic Fantasy and Fugue, BWV 903) or as an autonomous work (as in C. P. E. Bach's *freien Fantasien*). In his essay on the 'free fantasia' C. P. E. BACH describes how the composer/performer may 'move audaciously from one affect to another', through more keys than is usual in other compositions, and achieve 'the aims of recitative at the keyboard with complete, unmeasured freedom' (*Versuch*, trans. Mitchell, 153). Haydn never wrote a free (unmeasured) fantasia in the manner of C. P. E. Bach, but the Fantasia in C for piano (1789, Hob.XVII:4) and the *Fantasia* in the string quartet op. 76 no. 6 (1797) suggest he associated the term with harmonic adventurousness and hybrid formal types. Twice in extant correspondence Haydn referred to the C major Fantasia by the related term CAPRICCIO.

BH

C. P. E. Bach, *Versuch über die wahre Art das Clavier zu spielen* (Berlin, 1753, 1762); trans. W. J. Mitchell as *Essay on the True Art of Playing Keyboard Instruments* (New York, 1949).

A. P. Brown, *Joseph Haydn's Keyboard Music: Sources and Style* (Bloomington, Ind., 1986).

'Farewell' symphony. Nickname applied to Symphony no. 45, reflecting the progress of the remarkable last movement. A Presto in sonata form is deflected, in the recapitulation, towards a wholly unexpected Adagio, during which instruments of the orchestra gradually drop out in turn, until only two violins are left. The nickname ('Abschied') was known from at least 1794 and performances in London and Paris, for instance, in which the players physically quitted the stage are known from before that, even though there is nothing in the musical sources to suggest that they should do so. Anecdotal information about the circumstances that prompted this unusual conclusion also survives from Haydn's lifetime, the most reliable being that offered by GRIESINGER in his biography.

The living quarters for the musicians at Eszterháza consisted of a single building of 70 rooms, but in 1772 a particularly large theatrical troupe was engaged by the court which meant that the wives and children of most of the musicians had to remain in Eisenstadt. Haydn's players became increasingly restless when their stay lasted well into the autumn. His solution was as diplomatic as it was musically unorthodox. As each instrumentalist finished playing his part in the symphony he blew out the candle and left the room. The prince immediately understood the purpose of the walk-out and gave orders that the musicians be allowed to return to Eisenstadt and their families the following day.

In fact as many as eight players had already been home to Eisenstadt in late August, some because of illness, before returning to Eszterháza. Perhaps it was this return that especially fuelled their disaffection.

'father of the symphony'. From the late 19th century onwards Haydn has frequently been called the 'father of the symphony'. Writers anxious to trace the beginnings of the great symphonic tradition up to Bruckner and Mahler recognized the composer as the begetter of a genre whose broad characteristics and principles lay at the centre of musical culture. When music historians began uncovering earlier symphonies, especially by members of the Mannheim School and by Haydn's predecessors in Austria, the implication that Haydn actually invented the genre became meaningless. That he was the first to appreciate its greatness remains inviolable.

Less occasionally, Haydn has been called the 'father of the quartet' and, more generally, the 'father of instrumental music'. Again these labels reflect the desire of the 19th century to understand the origins of their contemporary culture, and, reflecting notions of creative individuality, the inappropriate wish to nominate an individual.

'fatto a posta'. An annotation on the first page of the autograph of the baryton trio in C (Hob. XI:109). A large water stain disfigures the page and Haydn's remark, 'done deliberately', together with a second comment 'nihil sine causa' ('nothing without cause'), indicates that it was not the result of an accident. It has been suggested that Haydn's wife threw the water.

fausse reprise. A term used more or less interchangeably with 'false recapitulation' or, less common, the German *Scheinreprise*. None of these terms was in use before the 20th century. All three denote a deceptive return to the tonic and opening theme in the course of a development section within a sonata-form movement. Thus, a *fausse* *reprise* causes a listener to think that the moment of recapitulation has arrived when in fact it has not.

Within these broad parameters, there are considerable differences as to the applicability of the term. Some writers reserve it for restatements of the opening theme in the tonic within the development, while others use it more liberally to include well-articulated restatements of the opening theme outside the tonic as well. Instances of *fausse reprise* in the first, narrower sense are found in the first movements of Symphonies nos. 42, 43, 46, 55, 71, and 91; the finale of Symphony no. 48; the first movements of the string quartets op. 17 no. 1, op. 20 no. 4, and op. 77 no. 1; and the finales of the string quartets op. 50 no. 1 and op. 54 no. 3. Instances of *fausse reprise* in the second, broader sense (that is, outside the tonic) are too numerous to list. But the effect of all such deceptive returns is to disorient the listener.

The first movement of Symphony no. 102 in B♭ provides a good example of how such disorientation can work. After 69 bars of development—that is, at a point at which one might well expect a recapitulation to occur—the opening theme returns in C major (bar 185) in an orchestration that is already familiar from the exposition (bars 31 ff.). The average listener, lacking a sense of perfect pitch, is likely to perceive this moment as the onset of the recapitulation. Indeed, it is only in retrospect that one can be certain that this was not in fact part of the 'true' recapitulation.

Haydn explored the possibilities of formal disorientation throughout his career in a variety of forms, including variations, rondo, minuet, etc. Within sonata form alone, he played with the expectations of listeners about transitions and arrivals in the new key area in the exposition, not to mention endings of expositions, recapitulations, and codas. Thus, his interest in the technique of *fausse reprise* is part of a broader approach to musical form that consistently plays with expectations of structural conventions. MEB

M. E. Bonds, 'Haydn's False Recapitulations and the Perception of Sonata Form in the Eighteenth Century' (diss., Harvard University, 1988).

E. Haimo, *Haydn's Symphonic Forms: Essays in Compositional Logic* (Oxford, 1995).

H. C. Robbins Landon, *The Symphonies of Joseph Haydn* (London, 1955).

Feder, Georg (b. 30 Nov. 1927; 11 Dec. 2006). German musicologist and Haydn scholar. After studies at the universities of Tübingen, Göttingen, and Kiel (where he gained his doctorate under Friedrich Blume in 1955) Feder began his long association with the Joseph Haydn-Institut, Cologne, as 'Mitarbeiter' in 1957; in 1960 he took over the direction (Wissenschaftliche Leitung) of the Institut from JENS PETER LARSEN and held the post together with the editorship of the periodical HAYDN-STUDIEN (1965–) until his retirement in 1990. Under his leadership the Institut continued with the primary task of the investigation of the authenticity and transmission of Haydn's works and the accumulation of an archive of sources on film. Feder's report on the distribution of manuscript sources of Haydn's music in Budapest, the then Czechoslovakia and other Eastern European countries, Italy, and the Iberian peninsula ('Die Überlieferung und Verbreitung') is a major document of modern Haydn research that dealt with the most important gaps in what was known at the time about the transmission of the composer's works. The Haydn-Institut had also to develop methods of dealing with the sources in order to achieve its aim of publishing Haydn's complete works in authentic texts (JOSEPH HAYDN WERKE, 1958–). This requires the critical analysis and evaluation of the textual variants transmitted by the sources; here Feder's adoption of classical-philological methods of textual criticism in order to elicit an authentic musical text from the transmitted variants ('Textkritische Methoden') not only provides an explanation of the procedures that underlie the edition but also is one of the earliest attempts to rectify a notable deficiency in musicological literature as a whole.

Feder's editorial activity within the *JHW* has focused on the genres of string quartet (*JHW*/XII) and solo keyboard sonata (*JHW*/XVIII). He has written on a wide range of topics concerning Haydn, in particular on issues of authenticity, both of work and of text (see the cumulative bibliography of Haydn literature in *HS* 3/3–4 (1974); *HS* 5/4 (1985); *HS* 6/3 (1992)). His worklist for the article on Haydn in the revised edition of *The New Grove Dictionary of Music* (2001) is an up-to-date and authoritative listing of Haydn's output, providing many corrections to the Hoboken Catalogue. The discussion begun by Feder in 'Textkritische Methoden' is developed on a broader conceptual and historical basis in his *Musikphilologie*, an introduction to musical textual criticism, hermeneutics, and editing techniques; it presents a systematic account of the philological method as applied to music and evaluates critical issues to do with interpretation and editing; topics range from fundamental questions of the parallels and divergences between music and speech to the various forms of scholarly edition, from facsimile to historical-critical complete edition. JD

G. Feder, 'Die Überlieferung und Verbreitung der handschriftlichen Quellen zu Haydns Werken', *HS* 1/1 (1965), 3–42.

G. Feder, *Musikphilologie* (Darmstadt, 1987).

G. Feder, 'Textkritische Methoden. Versuch eines Überblicks mit Bezug auf die Haydn–Gesamtausgabe', *HS* 5/2 (1983), 77–109.

Feldharmonie. A term often applied to Haydn's early music for wind instruments, usually scored for pairs of oboes, horns, and bassoons; more properly it refers to the ensemble itself, literally the 'field windband', a reflection of the open-air duties often associated with contemporary windbands. The surviving sources for Haydn's works inconsistently label them as 'Parthia', 'Feldparthie', or 'Divertimento', and Esterházy documents, rather confusingly, refer to the performers of this repertoire as the 'Feldmusik' rather than the 'Feldharmonie'. RH

See WINDBAND MUSIC.

Ferdinand IV, King of Naples (b. 12 Jan. 1751; d. 4 Jan 1825). The third son of Carlos III of Spain who became king of Naples at the age of 8. Until his maturity the kingdom was ruled by the first minister, Bernardo Tanucci, who was also responsible for ensuring that Ferdinand received virtually no education. A vulgar, uncouth man, and nicknamed 'Re Nasone' on account of his large nose, the young king loved hunting and playing practical jokes. At the age of 17 he was married to Archduchess Maria Carolina (1752–1814), daughter of Empress Maria Theresia, who had the thankless task of attempting to civilize her husband. Both shared an interest in music. The typical Neapolitan diet of opera was noticeably expanded in the 1770s and 1780s by instrumental music from Austria. The court amassed a large collection of symphonies by Haydn, performed in private concerts and as entra'ctes in French plays, and the Stabat mater was performed during Holy Week in 1788. Ferdinand played the LIRA ORGANIZZATA and commissioned music from Gyrowetz, Haydn, Pleyel, and Sterkel (1750–1817). In 1786–7 Haydn composed six concertos for the king, of which five survive, and in 1788–90 nine notturnos, of which eight survive.

Between September 1790 and March 1791, the king and queen were in Vienna to attend three royal weddings. When Haydn delivered the last of the notturni in December 1790, the king expressed his disappointment that the composer was not able to visit Naples following the recent death of Prince Nicolaus. He did, however, provide Haydn with a letter of introduction to the Neapolitan ambassador in London, Prince Castelcicala, and, later, forwarded a gift of a snuffbox to the composer. Haydn, for his part, promised he would visit Naples on his return from London. This promise was never to be fulfilled not least because Naples became a continuing pawn in the developing Napoleonic Wars. In 1799 it became a republic; Ferdinand returned as king the following year; in 1806 the French reoccupied the city; finally, the Congress of Vienna in 1814 decreed that Ferdinand should have jurisdiction over Naples and Sicily, formally becoming Ferdinand I of the two Sicilies in 1816. Nothing is known about musical life at the court in the Napoleonic period. It may be of significance that neither Ferdinand nor his wife were subscribers to the printed edition of *The Creation* that appeared in 1800. ERL

H. Acton, *The Bourbons of Naples* (London, 1956).

G. Gialdroni, 'La musica a Napoli alla fine del XVIII secolo nelle lettere di Norbert Hadrava', *Fonti Musicali Italiane*, 1 (1996), 75–143.

'Festino' symphony. Nickname occasionally used for Symphony no. 53. This work was especially popular in London in the 1780s, following its performance in 1781 in the concerts promoted by J. C. Bach and Abel and held in the Festino Rooms in Hanover Square. JH

'Fifths' quartet. Commonly used nickname for the quartet in D minor, op. 76 no. 2, first applied in Germany ('Quintenquartett') in the early 19th century. The opening of the first movement and much of the subsequent material is dominated by the interval of a falling fifth; to a less obvious degree the interval of a fifth features in the remaining movements too. JH

'Fire' symphony. Nickname for Symphony no. 59, probably used from the 18th century onwards. It is likely that the symphony (either as a whole or in part) was used as an entr'acte during a performance of the play *Die Feuersbrunst* given at Eszterháza in 1774. The work itself dates from 1769. JH

Flötenuhr. German word for musical clock. *See* MECHANICAL ORGAN.

folk music. Over the past century many writers have observed Haydn's interest in folk music and his use of folk rhythms and melodies in his instrumental music. Some of the earliest studies coincided with late 19th-century nationalism, when researchers in various countries identified national characteristics in art music through its integration of different elements of folk music. In the case of Haydn this resulted in a number of nationalities claiming him as a compatriot because of his use of folk music, which they perceived as distinctively their own. In a somewhat more ominous application of nationalism in the mid-1930s, these earlier claims were rebutted by German researchers whose works were sometimes politically motivated. Other writers have been primarily concerned with the more objective task of identifying Haydn's folk sources or explaining the aesthetic purpose of his application of folk music.

The search for Haydn's melodic sources began in earnest with Franjo (František) Š. Kuhač's *Josip*

Haydn i hrvatske narodne popievke (Joseph Haydn and national folk music) (Zagreb, 1880), which W. H. HADOW popularized in English with his *A Croatian Composer: Notes Toward the Study of Joseph Haydn* (London, 1897). In the spirit of 19th-century nationalism, Kuhač claimed that because of Haydn's use of Croatian folk tunes, the prevalence of Croatians near Haydn's birthplace, and the composer's name itself, Haydn must have been Croatian. As the writer of the article on Haydn in the second and third editions of *Grove's Dictionary of Music and Musicians*, Hadow lent considerable weight to this theory in the English-speaking world. Within a few years other studies sprang up claiming Haydn to be Hungarian, Czech, and even a gypsy, all based on his use of folk music.

In 1934, Ernst Fritz Schmid's *Joseph Haydn: Ein Buch von Vorfahren und Heimat des Meisters*, with its enormously detailed examination of Haydn's genealogy, put all these theories to rest. While all subsequent writers have agreed with Schmid, the timing of this type of study was unfortunate. Only a few years later similar genealogical studies affirming the German (and Aryan) roots of the Germanic musical giants had become a musicological preoccupation as a propaganda service to the National Socialist government; as Germany occupied more territory, justification could be offered by cultural historians in support of the *Lebensraum* doctrine. Schmid's book pre-dates those sponsored by Propaganda Minister Joseph Goebbels and his chief ideologue Alfred Rosenberg, but it is a matter of regret that his proved to be a model for those which followed.

Folk tunes are frequently transmitted beyond national boundaries. The source for a tune in the opening movement of an early cassation for string quintet (Hob.II:2) is identified by Kuhač as a Croatian drinking song, 'Nikaj na svetu', and by Schmid as a German folksong, 'Es trieb ein Schäfer den Berg hinan'. One German writer went so far as to claim the opposite process, that Croatian peasants, having heard Haydn's symphonies, extracted folk tunes from the melodies and rhythms of the symphonies.

Haydn grew up and spent much of his working life in locations that embraced various European folk cultures, and it should come as no surprise that he would be influenced by these cultures. Most later studies have kept this in mind, and view the diversity as a virtue. As the research methodology for folk music identification and transmission has become more sophisticated, so have the attempts to catalogue Haydn's folk music sources. Numerous writers, including Wilhelm Fischer, Walter Deutsch, Dénes Bartha, Bence Szabolcsi, and Stephen Cushman, have made valuable contributions.

The sources for identifying folk music that Haydn may have known are numerous, both in manuscript and printed collections. Some of the more valuable printed sources include *Oesterreichische Volkslieder mit ihren Singweisen* (Budapest, 1819), Franz M. Böhme's *Geschichte des Tanzes in Deutschland* (Leipzig, 1886), and Raimund Zoder's *Altösterreichische Volkstänze* (Vienna, 1937); two of the best manuscript collections are MS Linus, 1786 (Budapest), and the Sonnleithner-Sammlung, 1819 (Vienna). Possible folk sources have been noted in virtually all types of Haydn's instrumental works, from his earliest to his latest, and in various vocal works as well.

The subject becomes more interesting when the possible reasons for the composer's use of folk music are considered. Haydn was neither a folk music arranger nor a composer suffering from a shortage of melodic ideas; he used folk music—or, rather, music in a folk idiom—strategically to achieve certain aesthetic or dramatic ends. Leonard Ratner's work on topoi has been useful in this respect, showing the interpretive possibilities of dance gestures or other sources through specific associations. Here, of course, not only folk sources come into focus; other possibilities include plainchant, hymns, street songs, various types of dances, and opera. If one understands the courtly nature of a minuet, and that Haydn's minuets more often than not approximate the more rustic ländler, one enjoys more fully Haydn's cheeky irony. Similarly, his use of contredanse rhythms in finales places his works in a possibly subversive context, given the provocative nature of the dance itself as described by contemporary dance masters.

This generalized approach to sources proves to be more fruitful than attempts to identify specific tunes, and has implications for Haydn's instrumental first movements as well, especially in late symphonies with slow introductions. One finds distinctive types of sources used in introductions, often of a funereal nature, while subsequent Allegros derive their material from more lively dance sources. The resulting polarities can be at the heart of the dramatic interaction within a movement, and the possible return of material from the introduction, as in Symphony no. 103, can further highlight that dramatic exchange. As a composer who strove in an enlightened way to make his instrumental works more intelligible, Haydn's strategic use of folk music proved extremely useful in achieving this. DPS

P. M. Potter, 'Musicology under Hitler: New Sources in Context', *Journal of the American Musicological Society*, 49 (1996), 70–113.

L. D. Ratner, *Classic Music: Expression, Form, and Style* (New York, 1980).

E. F. Schmid, *Joseph Haydn: Ein Buch von Vorfahren und Heimat des Meisters* (Kassel, 1934).

D. P. Schroeder, 'Melodic Source Material and Haydn's Creative Process', *Musical Quarterly*, 68 (1982), 496–515.

folksong settings. During the course of the 18th century, interest in collecting and performing folksongs grew rapidly. Folksongs became elevated into the realm of art music, either by being incorporated into sonatas and similar works, or by being published with an instrumental accompaniment to make them suitable for performance in the drawing room. Interest was particularly strong in Scotland—probably the only occasion when Scotland has led the way in a European-wide movement in music—and a large number of Scottish songs appeared in print in the late 18th century. The tunes are almost all anonymous, and often the same tune appears in varying versions in different collections. The words of the songs also vary. In many cases older verses were either revised or replaced by newer ones, and Robert Burns (1759–96) was particularly industrious in collecting and reworking a large number of older poems, as well as penning many new ones.

Among the publishers of Scottish songs was WILLIAM NAPIER, a Scotsman working in London, whose first volume of *A Selection of the most Favourite Scots Songs* appeared in 1790. These songs were provided with figured-bass harmony for harpsichord and an optional accompaniment for violin, the settings being by Samuel Arnold, Barthélémon, Thomas Carter, and William Shield. During Haydn's visit to London in 1791 he probably became acquainted with Napier, who was at that time in serious financial difficulty. Haydn agreed to write a hundred settings for him, to be published in a second volume, and according to one report did so without payment as a gesture of assistance. This volume appeared in June 1792 as *A Selection of Original Scot's Songs in Three Parts. The harmony by Haydn.* The melodies Napier used were mostly not very ancient, but as with other contemporary collections their composers are rarely identifiable. Napier also omitted the names of most of the poets, but many can be traced through other publications. Allan Ramsay (1686–1757) and Robert Burns figure prominently, and there are contributions from many lesser poets.

Haydn's settings are scored in the same way as those in Napier's first volume: the 'Three Parts' mentioned on the title page refer to the violin, voice, and figured bass. There are no instrumental introductions or postludes, although in the preface to Volume I it was stated that the air should be played first as an introduction, and the last part of it repeated after each stanza, with the performer varying the melody in these instrumental sections. Most of the settings are marked 'Slow' or 'Moderately slow', the rest being 'Lively' ('O can ye sew Cushions' has a slow first section followed by a lively conclusion). Haydn's accompaniments show considerable variety. The bass line often has running quaver passages beneath a tune that is mainly in crotchets, but sometimes this pattern is reversed. In other settings the accompaniment is mainly chordal, perhaps with short rests, while occasionally Haydn writes semiquaver figuration, as in 'The Bonny Brucket Lassie', where semiquaver scales and Alberti bass patterns are prominent. In a few settings the keyboard accompaniment is silent for two whole bars or more, as in 'The Bonniest Lass', where there is an extended passage for voice and violin alone. Most often the violin helps to fill in the harmony by playing a kind of alto line, but often with passing notes or more decorative figuration. Double-stopping is occasionally required, as in 'The Banks of Spey', and rests or long held notes can also be found. In some passages the violin moves above the voice to provide a kind of descant, reaching a top *f‴* in 'Leader Haughs and Yarrow'. Haydn probably had the texts of at least some of the songs, for there appear to be a few examples of word-painting, such as bird calls in 'Leader Haughs and Yarrow' and perhaps a suggestion of piping in 'Maggy Lauder'.

The success of the second volume of Napier's collection prompted a third volume, containing 50 further settings by Haydn, scored in a similar manner. These settings were composed during his second visit to England and appeared in July 1795, just before his return to Vienna. Meanwhile, however, another folksong collector, GEORGE THOMSON of Edinburgh, had begun an independent series of Scottish songs, the first volume of which was published in 1793 by Preston in London. Thomson aimed to surpass all previous collections in several ways. He was much more rigorous in his choice of texts, rejecting any he found unsatisfactory, and to this end he enlisted the help of Burns, who wrote or adapted over 100 poems for Thomson between 1792 and Burns's early death in 1796. Thomson also passed over minor British composers like Carter and Shield and applied direct to major European figures for harmonizations: first Ignaz Pleyel (formerly a pupil of Haydn), later Leopold Kozeluch, and eventually Haydn himself. Thomson also demanded a fully written-out piano part, accompaniment for cello as well as violin, fully composed preludes and postludes, and occasionally settings for more than one voice. The overall effect was that the melodies were placed in much-enhanced surroundings, especially compared with Napier's volumes.

Thomson first contacted Haydn in October 1799, having had trouble in his dealings with both

Pleyel and Kozeluch. Haydn was offered 2 ducats per setting, and produced his first 32 settings the following June, despite being delayed by illness. More settings quickly followed, with Haydn taking great care to do them well and create works of lasting quality. Soon Thomson was ready to publish a collection of 50, which appeared in July 1802 in Volume III of *A Select Collection of Original Scottish Airs* (Vols. I and II had included settings by Pleyel and Kozeluch). Since Thomson did not give detailed guidelines, Haydn, Pleyel, and Kozeluch each adopted a slightly different approach, so that their settings are nearly always readily distinguishable. Pleyel's accompaniments are rather sparse, so as to place more emphasis on the voice. Kozeluch, unlike Pleyel, virtually always doubles the voice with the right hand of the piano, and he generally adopts a three-part texture, often enlivened by some oscillating figure in the accompaniment. Haydn uses more variable textures for the piano, with more smoothly flowing bass lines, some two-part texture, and occasional rests for the left hand, but the right hand almost always doubles the voice. He also uses interesting chromatic notes in his harmony more often than the other two composers.

Haydn was rarely supplied with the texts, but Thomson did at least give some indication of the character of the music by means of Italian directions such as 'Allegretto scherzando', in contrast to Napier's plain 'Slow' or 'Lively'. The main reason why Thomson did not send texts is that he did not decide until a late stage which texts suited which airs and settings. Moreover he often published a setting with two alternative texts, and did not want a setting tied too closely to a single text, since there had been considerable freedom in the past to replace old texts, or to sing a melody to more than one text. He was particularly likely to provide an alternative text if the traditional one was very strongly Scottish, as in 'An thou wert mine ain thing', for which he published the alternative English words 'Thy fatal shafts unerring move'. Occasionally he even recommends that the song should be performed differently (e.g. slower) if the second set of words is sung. Nevertheless there are occasions when Haydn's setting seems particularly suited to the main text, as in 'Saw ye Johnni cummin', where the accompaniment breaks into semiquavers at the words 'And his doggie runnin'; and for 'Scots wha hae' he was sent the words, for which he composed a suitably martial setting.

Haydn's introductions usually begin by quoting the opening of the song, but often for only a bar or two, after which they proceed with similar rhythms but newly invented motifs and no rigorous development of the material (unlike Beethoven's introductions). In some cases, such as 'With broken words', even the very beginning does not quote the air but is just rhythmically related to it; in 'Scots wha hae', by contrast, the introduction is a straight quotation of the song for practically five bars. The introductions most often end with a clear perfect cadence, but sometimes they end on or even in the dominant, creating more forward thrust. In 'On Ettrick banks', in D major, the prelude even ends with a half-close in B minor, and Haydn harmonizes the opening of the song in that key before returning to the tonic.

The postludes are loosely related to part of the introduction or the song, but often the relationship is rhythmic rather than motivic. Although they are on average a little shorter than the preludes, the postludes are the place where chromaticism is most often found. Both preludes and postludes almost always have a four-square phrase structure (like those of Pleyel and Kozeluch but unlike Beethoven's); four, six, or eight bars are the norm, and ''Twas Even' is one of very few with a three-bar postlude. Haydn treats the violin more or less as in his settings for Napier, rather than in a soloistic manner, while the cello is used merely to reinforce the instrumental bass, as in the manner of a Baroque continuo part.

Although Haydn seems to have found the composition of these settings rewarding, he was increasingly finding all work rather tiring, and he realized the setting of these airs would make a good exercise for his students. Consequently he began subcontracting some of them. Friedrich Kalkbrenner is reported to have composed some, and another of Haydn's pupils, Sigismund Neukomm, composed around 25 settings (perhaps more), which Haydn evidently checked (and perhaps amended slightly) before sending to Thomson. Neukomm's style was not obviously different from Haydn's, and so Thomson published these settings as Haydn's, unaware of the deception, which was only discovered in the 1970s.

In 1804 Thomson reissued his first two volumes of Scottish songs, but replaced some of Pleyel's and Kozeluch's settings with Haydn's (or, in four cases, Neukomm's). Further Haydn (and Neukomm) settings appeared in Volumes IV and V (1805 and 1818), and in a few later editions. Meanwhile Thomson had sent Haydn some Welsh melodies, and these appeared in three volumes of Welsh songs (1809, 1811, and 1817), alongside settings by Kozeluch and Beethoven. There were also one or two Irish ones.

In addition, Haydn supplied some settings for a rival publisher, WILLIAM WHYTE, who published two volumes of Scottish songs in 1804 and 1806. These settings, like those for Thomson, included introductions and postludes, with violin and cello accompaniments. In some cases Haydn provided different settings of the same melody for two or even all three publishers. Little is known about his dealings with Whyte, who paid about twice as much as Thomson, but Thomson thereafter raised his own payments to match Whyte's.

Altogether Haydn produced nearly 400 settings of British folksongs, and they are among his last compositions. Criticisms that they are faulty, on the grounds that Haydn did not have the texts, are misguided, since the texts were not in most cases closely wedded to the airs to which they happened to be sung. The other criticism often encountered is that Haydn's settings are unsuited to the melodies since they belong in a different world from where the tunes originated. The same could be said about Palestrina's adaptations of plainsong, Bach's chorale settings, and Messiaen's use of birdsong. If these works are regarded as acceptable compositions, Haydn's folksong settings must be too. Haydn skilfully absorbed the sometimes strange melodies into his own style to produce thoroughly integrated settings of exceptional quality. It is extraordinary that so many of them have had to wait until very recently for a modern edition.

BARC

K. Geiringer, 'Haydn and the Folksong of the British Isles', *Musical Quarterly*, 35 (1949), 179–208.

C. Hopkinson and C. B. Oldman, 'Thomson's Collection of National Song, with Special Reference to the Contributions of Haydn and Beethoven', *Edinburgh Bibliographical Society Transactions*, 2 (1938–45), 1–64; addenda and corrigenda, 3 (1948–55), 121–4.

C. Hopkinson and C. B. Oldman, 'Haydn's Settings of Scottish Songs in the Collections of Napier and Whyte', *Edinburgh Bibliographical Society Transactions*, 3 (1948–55), 85–120.

D. Johnson, *Music and Society in Lowland Scotland in the Eighteenth Century* (London, 1972).

forged, misattributed, and doubtful works. One consequence of Haydn's popularity was the large number of works in all genres that circulated under his name but which were not composed by him. The Hoboken catalogue lists over 800 such works and this is by no means a comprehensive list. The vast majority of these inauthentic works listed by Hoboken were written by contemporaries of Haydn and the faulty ascription was usually the result of casualness rather than deception. It might be thought that the accumulated skills and thought processes of several generations of scholars from the 19th century to the present day would have allowed the spurious finally to be separated from the authentic, but would-be Haydn continues to tantalize scholars and public alike, and to a greater extent than is the case with any other major composer. In addition there have been a few attempts to forge the music of Haydn.

Forged works. Forgery will be defined as an attempt by an individual, often unknown, to market a specially composed work (or works) as Haydn; it is different from the related practice, common in the 18th century, of taking an existing work and substituting Haydn's name. Using this definition, probably the first instance of a forgery was a minuet in C major, the 'OCHSENMENUETT', that appeared in the last decade of Haydn's life, when it was associated with the tale that the composer had written a minuet as a wedding gift for a butcher's daughter. It was published over and over again in the 19th century, sometimes with an engraving of the alleged transaction, and it featured in an operetta by Ignaz von Seyfried.

From Paris in the 1870s dates a 'Haydn' work with the wholly implausible title of *Concerto de bébe* (The baby's concerto); in reality it is not a concerto, but a work for solo piano in an effete, pseudo Classical style. Perhaps the publisher thought that Papa Haydn had a natural affinity with babies.

Much more substantial is a three-movement concerto in C major for cello and orchestra (Hob. VIIb:5) that was published in Berlin in 1899. It was prepared by David Popper (1843–1913), an Austrian cellist and composer, who claimed that the work was based on sketches by Haydn. These sketches were never made public and the work is almost certainly entirely composed by Popper.

A more malicious fraud was perpetrated in 1993 by a German flautist named Winfried Michel. He noticed that the ENTWURF-KATALOG contained seven incipits of keyboard sonatas written in the 1760s, works that have not survived (Hob.XVI: 2a–e, 2g, 2h). He prepared completed versions of six of these, produced photocopies of the apparent source, and persuaded a number of people of their authenticity; they were even recorded by Paul Badura-Skoda. Suspicion began to mount when Michel steadfastly refused to reveal anything about the 'original' manuscript and when it was pointed out that certain characteristics of the handwriting and of the layout of the manuscript page were more compatible with the 20th rather than the 18th century.

Misattributed works. While a theoretical division of this large category of works into wilful misattribution and accidental attribution would be attractive in theory, in practice only rarely does the available evidence allow an individual work to be placed in one or other sub-category.

The actions of many French publishers, in particular, in the 1760s and 1770s, seem to have been very deliberate in the way they misled purchasers. The most celebrated case was that of the op. 3 quartets, published by BAILLEUX in 1777. Only in 1964 was it discovered that Haydn's name on some of the engraved plates had been superimposed onto that of another composer, ROMAN HOFSTETTER. Op. 3 was quickly removed from the canon of Haydn quartets, including the slow movement of op. 3 no. 5, 'Serenade', which had become one of the composer's most well-known single movements.

Incontrovertible evidence shows that Haydn himself occasionally took the music of other composers and sold it as his own. In 1784 he forwarded three keyboard trios to FORSTER in London, works that were duly published as a set in the following year; but only one was his own (Hob. XV:5), the other two (Hob.XV:3 and 4) were by his former pupil PLEYEL. In 1801 Haydn wrote to the publisher George Thomson in Edinburgh, indicating how congenial he found the work of setting British folksongs: 'I wish that every student of composition would try his hand at this type of music.' Some of Haydn's students did, indeed, try their hand; it is now known that over two dozen (perhaps more) of these arrangements forwarded to Thomson by Haydn were, in fact, the work of another pupil, NEUKOMM.

Works that were more likely to have been misattributed by accident rather than by design are far too numerous to be listed individually. The following Austrian contemporaries of Haydn would figure prominently in a list of true authors of such works: ALBRECHTSBERGER, AUMANN, DITTERSDORF, MICHAEL HAYDN, GASSMANN, GYROWETZ, HOFMANN, ORDONEZ, PICHL, PLEYEL, VANHAL, and WAGENSEIL. The predominantly haphazard nature of misattribution in Haydn's time is proven by the fact that all these individual composers, and others, are similarly affected by problems of authorship, and occasionally one work may be found under the name of as many as three or four different composers. But Haydn's position is different in that some of these 18th-century misattributions were perpetuated and individual works came to form a part of the accepted output of the composer and, thereby, of his musical image. The popular 'TOY' SYMPHONY circulated widely under Haydn's name in the 18th century, accrued ever more fanciful tales about its inception in the 19th, and was still being published as Joseph Haydn in the late 20th century. Similarly, the 'ST ANTHONY CHORALE' was first ascribed to Haydn in the 18th century before it was firmly established in the mind of the public as *echt* Haydn in Brahms's celebrated variations, originally entitled *Variations on a theme of Haydn*.

Many scholars in modern times have been misled by faulty attributions from the 18th century. In 1927 the respected German scholar ERNST FRITZ SCHMID announced that he had discovered a requiem in C minor by Haydn, which turned out to be the work of Aumann; the scrupulous editorial activities of the *JHW* did not prevent them from including a work by Gyrowetz, 'Abschiedslied' (Hob.XXVIa:F1), in a volume of complete songs by Haydn; and Robbins Landon in 1960 issued an edition of a Litany in C (Hob.XXIIIc:C2) that is almost certainly by a composer with the unhelpful name of JOSEPH HAYDA.

Doubtful works. This third category includes works that are known only under Haydn's name but for one reason or another, modern scholars remain doubtful about their authenticity, yet are unwilling to offer the view that they are emphatically not by Haydn. Naturally one scholar's 'definite maybe' can be another scholar's 'definitely not' and it is possible—in a few cases, even likely—that true authorship will never be established. The opera *Die Feursbrunst*, two piano concertos, in F (Hob. XVIII:7) and in G (Hob.XVIII:9), and a Salve regina in E♭ (Hob.XXIIIb:4) are only the largest works of this kind.

J. P. Larsen, *Three Haydn Catalogues*, 2nd facs. edn with a survey of Haydn's œuvre (New York, 1979).
J. Webster, 'External Criteria for Determining the Authenticity of Haydn's Music', in J. P. Larsen, H. Serwer, and J. Webster (eds), *Haydn Studies* (London, 1981), 75–81.
Worklist in J. Webster and G. Feder, *Joseph Haydn* (London, 2001).

Forster, William (b. 5 May 1739; d. 14 Dec. 1808). String instrument maker and music publisher in London. During the 1770s Forster was chiefly known as a violin maker, though he may also have sold music. In 1780 he expanded his business to include the publication of music, and during the following decade became one of the most important publishers in London, playing a central role in the extraordinary growth in popularity of Haydn's music in England in that period. In 1781 he took the unprecedented step for an English publisher of establishing a business connection with a composer not resident in the country; using General Jerningham of the British Embassy in Vienna as an intermediary, Forster signed a contract with Haydn for the supply of new compositions. Between 1781 and 1787 Haydn supplied Forster directly with symphonies, keyboard trios, quartets, and the orchestral version of *The Seven Last Words*.

The arrangement came unstuck in January 1788 when Forster, who believed he had exclusive rights in England to publish the 'Paris' symphonies, discovered that they were being sold in London by his rival LONGMAN & BRODERIP; unknown to Forster, Haydn had sold the music also to ARTARIA in Vienna without realizing that Longman & Broderip acted as Artaria's agent in London and imported much of his music. This tangled web of duplicity was avidly reported in the London newspapers and the composer was forced to provide a public explanation the following month. It exacerbated an already tense relationship between Forster and Longman & Broderip which resulted in legal wrangling over who had the rights over three piano trios (Hob.XV:3–5) that went on for several years. In 1791, a few months after arriving in London, Haydn made two court depositions (using Salomon as a translator) in the latest round of the legal battle. The truth was that copyright law had not yet caught up with international trade in music and the case was finally settled in 1794. The legal arguments between the two publishers forced Haydn to make the shocking admission that two of the piano trios published by both firms had, in fact, been composed by PLEYEL.

Although Forster had ceased to have direct access to Haydn in 1788 he continued to publish his music up to the early 19th century. A great deal of evidence of the relationship has survived, from receipts to manuscript copies of the music as supplied by Haydn; also extant are the proceedings of the legal battle between Forster and Longman & Broderip. Together they paint a rare picture of the vagaries of music publishing at the time and of Haydn's not-so-innocent attempts to exploit them to his own advantage.

N. Mace, 'Haydn and the London Music Sellers: Forster v. Longman & Broderip', *Music and Letters*, 77 (1996), 527–41.

H. E. Poole, 'Music Engraving Practice in Eighteenth-Century London: A Study of Some Forster Editions of Haydn and their Manuscript sources', in O. Neighbour (ed.), *Music and Bibliography. Essays in honour of Alec Hyatt King* (New York, 1980), 98–131.

W. Sandys and S. A. Forster, *The History of the Violin, and Other Instruments Played with the Bow from the Remotest Times to the Present* (London, 1864).

fortepiano. A term widely used in the late 18th and early 19th centuries to distinguish all types of stringed keyboard instruments with a hammered action from the harpsichord or clavichord. It referred equally to smaller domestic instruments ('square' pianos) and the larger, wing-shaped, concert instruments. From the mid-20th century onwards fortepiano has been used loosely as a term to describe historical instruments or reconstructions of them, as distinct from modern pianofortes.

One of the primary characteristics of 18th-century fortepianos is their diversity, in shape, action, touch, and sonority. Haydn was familiar with a number of Viennese and English makers, who from the 1780s represented two quite distinct traditions in manufacture. In 1788 Haydn purchased a fortepiano by Wenzel Schanz and, although no Wenzel Schanz instrument is extant, Haydn's instrument would have shared the distinctive characteristics of Viennese fortepianos of the 1780s. It would probably have had a five-octave range (*F–f'''*), two knee levers (a damper-raising mechanism and a moderator), a Viennese action (possibly with escapement) and with double-stringing throughout. Such instruments were characterized by an extremely shallow dip, light touch, thin soundboards, strings, and hammers, and efficient damping, producing a clear, thin tone. Of the Viennese makers Haydn preferred the instruments of Schanz because they were 'particularly light in touch and the mechanism very agreeable' (letter of 4 July 1790 to Maria Anna von Genzinger).

In England Haydn became familiar with the instruments of Clagget & Stodart and had access to the pianos of John Broadwood, the leading maker of the English tradition. In contrast to Viennese instruments, grand pianos in the Broadwood tradition had a characteristic English grand action, a noticeably heavier and deeper touch, with triple-stringing throughout, a more resonant sound and (purposefully) less efficient damping; two pedals, damper and *una corda*, were standard on English pianos. Haydn brought a five-and-a-half-octave range (*F–c''''*) grand piano by Longman & Broderip to Vienna on his return from London. It has been suggested that an extant Longman & Broderip grand piano from the 1790s (Clinkscale's Longman & Broderip no. 14, now in private possession) may be the instrument once owned by Haydn .

In 1801 Érard sent Haydn a grand piano which was described in the catalogue of Haydn's estate as having a five-and-a-half-octave range (*F–c''''*), with the 'usual pedals', which on Erard pianos of this date would probably have been four in number: bassoon, damper, moderator, and *una corda*.

Although Cristofori had produced the first fortepiano probably around 1698 it was not until the 1770s and 1780s that various types of fortepiano replaced the harpsichord as the principal solo keyboard instrument. Haydn's keyboard music from *c*.1784 onwards would have been written for instruments of the Viennese or English type. His acquisition of the Érard piano post-dates his last keyboard composition. BH

M. N. Clinkscale, *Makers of the Piano 1700–1820* (Oxford, 1993).

K. Komlós, *Fortepianos and their Music. Germany, Austria, and England, 1760–1800* (Oxford, 1995).

R. Maunder, *Keyboard Instruments in Eighteenth-Century Vienna* (Oxford, 1998).

H. Walter, 'Haydns Klaviere', *HS* 25/4 (1970), 256–88.

Fortspinnung A term compiled by the Austrian musicologist Wilhelm Fischer (1886–1962) to describe a type of thematic construction common in the Baroque period, one based on a 'spinning forth' of an idea, usually with recurring rhythmic figures and with an avoidance of obvious phrasing patterns. This technique survives into the early Classical period, particularly in slow movements (e.g. Haydn, Symphony no. 7), occasionally in Allegro movements (e.g. first movement of Haydn's Cello Concerto).

Framery, Nicolas Étienne (b. 25 March 1745; d. 26 Nov. 1810). French writer on music who played a full part in the polemics of musical life in Paris in the 18th century. In the continuing argument over the rival merits of Italian and French opera, he was a supporter of the first, particularly the music of Sacchini (1730–86). But he was also an admirer of German music, especially that of Haydn and Pleyel which came to dominate concert life from the 1780s onwards. He prepared a short biography of Haydn, *Notice sur Joseph Haydn*, published in Paris in 1810, the year of his death. Its content is noticeably independent of GRIESINGER's biography and of earlier German accounts of the composer. It is thought that Framery's principal source was Pleyel, Haydn's former pupil and lifelong friend, who had settled in Paris in 1795; his memories were undoubtedly fond ones, if often rather embroidered and confused.

M. Vignal, *Joseph Haydn—Autobiographie, Premières Biographies* (Paris, 1997).

Franz, Carl (b. 1738; d. 1802). Horn player at Eszterháza, who also occasionally played the violin and the baryton. Born in Silesia, he worked in Olmütz, at the court of Bishop Leopold Eck, before joining the Esterházy court in 1763. His mastery of hand-stopping made him a widely regarded virtuoso, talents readily exploited by Haydn in several symphonies of the time. He left the court in 1776 to join that of Cardinal Batthyani in Pressburg (Bratislava). He had learnt the baryton and soon embarked on a tour of Germany, during which he performed a work that he claimed was written by Haydn, the DEUTSCHLANDS KLAGE AUF DEN TOD DES GROßEN FRIEDRICHS BORUßENS KÖNIG; it has been suggested that Franz himself may have been the composer of this rather inept piece. The final years of his life were spent as a violin player in the Munich court.

S. Gerlach, '"Deutschlands Klage. . ."—Eine Haydn unterschobene Kantate auf den Tod Friedrichs des Grossen', *HS* 8/1 (2000), 39–62.

Freemasonry. Although Haydn was inititated into the first grade ('Apprentice') of the craft of Freemasonry it did not assume an important role in his social and intellectual life, and he never composed any music for its meetings. In both these aspects he was unlike Mozart.

Following its establishment in Britain in 1714 Freemasonry spread quickly across the European mainland. The first Austrian lodge was founded in 1742 and by 1780 the city of Vienna had six lodges with about 200 members. Over the next few years Freemasonry became increasingly vibrant in the city, a distinctive part of the flowering of intellectual and cultural endeavour that characterized the first few years of the reign of JOSEPH II.

Haydn would have met many of the members of the craft during his visits to Vienna in the early 1780s, perhaps especially at the salon of GREINER and applying to join the craft may be seen as a natural part of his widening participation in Viennese life in the decade. While Freemasonry in Vienna was a closed society, it was not a secret society, and in that aspect it took its place alongside aristocratic concerts, private music meetings organized by van Swieten, as well as salon culture. Moreover, at this stage, in the early 1780s, it was not regarded as an organization that nurtured destabilizing political views. Given these characteristics it would have been surprising had Haydn, and indeed Mozart and other musicians, not become members.

In December 1784 Haydn applied for membership of 'Zur wahren Eintracht' (True Concord), a lodge formed in 1781 and whose current Master was the natural scientist, Ignaz von Born. Its membership was less dominated by the aristocracy than other Viennese lodges, and included government officials, military officers, professors, diplomats, court agents, medical doctors, musicians, artists, and Catholic and Protestant clerics; earlier in the same month Mozart had joined the lodge. It often met more than once a week and alongside the standard rituals of Freemasonry had a regular programme of lectures on Masonic and non-Masonic subjects, later published in the *Journal für Freymaurer*. Haydn's application, along with that of Baron Franz von Hallberg from Brussels, was approved on 24 January 1785 and the initiation was set for 28 January. Haydn was at Eszterháza and this information reached him after the appointed date; consequently his initiation was postponed until Friday, 11 February. His sponsors were Count GEORG VON APPONYI, an old acquaintance of Haydn and of the Esterházy family, Franz Philipp von Weber, an imperial secretary, and Heinrich Joseph von Aland Walter, a diplomat in Vienna in the service of the Elector of Trier. The Master of the Lodge, Ignaz von Born, was unable to attend and the ceremony was conducted by Ludwig von Anselm, a member of the imperial army. Mozart, too, was unable to attend because he was taking part in his own subscription concert at the Mehlgrube. Haydn was addressed in a lengthy speech by Joseph von Holzmeister, a civil servant, who outlined the characteristics of the craft and drew the inevitable parallel between its desire for harmony and the work of a composer: 'You, newly elected Brother Apprentice, know especially well the designs of this heavenly gift, harmony; you know its all-embracing power is one of the most beautiful fields of human endeavour; to you this enchanting goddess has granted part of her bewitching power, through which she calms the stormy breast, puts to sleep pain and sorrow, brightens melancholic and cloudy thoughts, and turns the heart of humans to joyful speculation . . .'.

Haydn's duties at the Esterházy court made regular attendance of lodge meetings in Vienna difficult and he is not known to have been present at a single further meeting. While his lifestyle rather than any indifference to the craft explain his apparent lack of interest, Haydn too would have become increasingly aware of the waning status of Freemasonry in Vienna in the second half of the 1780s as a result of Joseph II's reforms. Motivated at first by the all-consuming need to regulate all aspects of society—educational, governmental, legal, military, and religious—the emperor gradually persuaded himself that Freemasonry might be a fertile ground for anti-government views. He restricted the number of lodges in major cities and towns, and required that membership should be scrutinized by the state. In Vienna, Haydn's lodge was merged in December 1785 with two others to form a new one, 'Zur Wahrheit' (Truth). The composer's membership was transferred and he was listed as an absent member until April 1787. Joseph II's reforms had destroyed the intellectual character of individual lodges, and attendance and membership of the new merged lodge declined rapidly, leading to voluntary dissolution in 1789. By 1794 all Viennese lodges had closed. In January 1795 Emperor Franz ensured that Freemasonry could not be reactivated, when all secret organizations were deemed equivalent to high treason.

In London, Freemasonry flourished throughout the century and it is possible that Haydn attended Masonic meetings in the city during his two visits in the 1790s, but relevant records have not survived. JOHANN PETER SALOMON was a member of the Pilgrims Lodge in London, one that included a number of German musicians, and their hall, Freemasons Hall, off Drury Lane, was a frequent venue for concerts, including those of the Academy of Ancient Music.

It is clear that Masonic association played a negligible part in Haydn's career; possibly the most tangible outcome was the commission from the Loge Olympique in Paris for six symphonies, a commission that may have been the consequence of Masonic links between the French capital and Vienna, though, again, there is no direct evidence. Likewise, attempts to find specifically Masonic characteristics in Haydn's music smack of special pleading. The subject matter of *The Creation*, in particular, has many resonances with the characteristics of Freemasonry, particularly the notion of a 'Grand Architect of the Universe', the banishing of Chaos (ignorance) through Light, and the harmonious relationship of each constituent part to the whole, but these are the products of Enlightenment thought in general and there is nothing in the music to suggest a specifically Masonic response by the composer.

J. Hurwitz, 'Haydn and the Freemasons', *HYB* 16 (1986), 5–98.

J. Webb, 'Joseph Haydn—Freemason and Musician', *Ars Quatuor Coronatorum*, 94 (1982), 61–82.

French Revolution. When the Bastille was stormed on 14 July 1789—the single event that marked the beginning of the French Revolution and set in motion a quarter of a century of unrest across the European mainland—Haydn was at Eszterháza in the Hungarian countryside. Because Prince Nicolaus was not in residence it was an unusually quiet month, with only one operatic performance. On the very same day Haydn countersigned a receipt for the scores of three operas, Anfossi's *Le gelosie fortunate*, Cimarosa's *Il pittore parigino*, and Mozart's *Le nozze di Figaro*. That year the opera season lasted until 6 December and Haydn remained at Eszterháza until the end of the year, when he went to Vienna; by early February he was back in Eszterháza preparing for the new season. Throughout this period there is no mention in any of Haydn's correspondence of the momentous events happening in Paris. Oddly enough one of the few letters in which Haydn complains about life at Eszterháza was written in February 1790 to MARIA ANNA VON GENZINGER, but it would be absurd to link this with any incipient sympathy with the ideals of the French Revolution, which at any rate were still rather unformed at this stage. Haydn was from a generation and a background that valued social stability and contentment, and over the remaining 20 years of his life, though he was to become much more aware of contemporary events than he was in 1789, this fundamentally conservative outlook made him the ideal Austrian citizen. If his circumstances and upbringing made him indifferent to the rhetoric of the revolution, he could not avoid its consequences and the course of political events was to influence the rest of his life and, to a certain extent, his output too.

When musical activities at the court were abruptly abolished following the death of Prince Nicolaus in September 1790, Haydn for the first time for over 30 years was able to exercise complete control over the direction of his musical career. Had he been in this situation a couple of years earlier he might well have contemplated visiting Paris; his music was frequently played at the Concert de la Loge Olympique and the Concert Spirituel, he was in contact with a leading figure in musical life, COUNT D'OGNY, and he was in correspondence with Sieber, the musical publisher. Although Count d'Ogny died a month after Nicolaus, musical life in Paris was already too uncertain for any invitation to be issued and, certainly, for Haydn to contemplate accepting. In these circumstances the invitation from Salomon to visit London could not be equalled.

While in London Haydn became much more aware of developments in France than he would have been in Vienna, and certainly in Eszterháza, partly because Paris was closer to London but, more fundamentally, because several daily newspapers freely reported political events from home and abroad in a way that the only newspaper in Vienna, the court-controlled *Wiener Zeitung*, did not. As well as a liberal climate of reporting and debate, Haydn became acutely conscious of the ready patriotism, even jingoism, of the English, a national pride that was to take much longer to emerge in Austria. When he returned for his second visit to London in 1794, newspapers contained sensational stories of the Reign of Terror in France, plus almost daily accounts of those members of the French aristocracy who had managed to escape to Britain. In September 1794 a plot was uncovered to assassinate George III. Haydn recorded some of the details in his notebook: 'The principal murderers were very young, one was a clock-maker, the other a chemist. They constructed a kind of blow-pipe from which a little poisoned arrow was to kill the king in the theatre. The understanding was to start a brawl right under the king's box, during the course of which each of the gang was to raise his stick in the air and threaten to beat the other, whilst the principal rogue was to shoot his arrow at the King.' Although the 1794 season organized by Salomon was a success, the impresario cited difficulties in recruiting singers from the continent as a reason for merging his entrepreneurial efforts with those of the King's Theatre to form the Opera Concert in 1795.

It is hardly surprising that Haydn's willingness to compose music of all kinds in London resulted in some music that reflected directly the spirit of the times. He made an arrangement of 'GOD SAVE THE KING', alluded to the tune at the beginning of the slow movement of Symphony no. 98, wrote two movements of a choral and orchestral work in the typical tradition of the patriotic English ode, INVOCATION OF NEPTUNE, and composed the jingoistic 'Sailor's Song'. The response of the *Morning Chronicle* to a performance of the 'Military' symphony in 1794 shows that Haydn had mirrored to perfection the uneasy, even frightening mood of the time: 'the middle movement [the slow movement] was again received with absolute shouts of applause. Encore! encore! encore! resounded from every seat: the Ladies themselves could not forbear. It is the advancing to battle; and the march of men, the sounding of the charge, the thundering of the onset, the clash of arms, the groans of the wounded, and what may well be called the hellish roar of war increased to a climax of horrid sublimity!'

Just over 200 years later it is difficult for audiences to relate to these emotions stirred up by the slow movement of the 'Military' symphony. In a scaling down of response the march is viewed as an entertaining interlude with percussion instruments in what is otherwise a typical symphony of the time. The reappearance of the percussion instruments in the finale in a wholly jovial context might be viewed as an attempt by Haydn to overcome, in a proto-Beethovenian way, the trauma of the slow movement, but few people—whether conductors, performers, or listeners—would now be persuaded by this grander interpretation.

When Haydn returned to Austria in the summer of 1795 it was to a country that felt quite different from the one he had left 18 months earlier. The previous year a Jacobin revolt had been ruthlessly quashed and the state had doubled its efforts to control and suppress. Although Austria and Britain revealed fundamental differences of approach in dealing with revolutionary activity, the two countries became close allies in the common cause of keeping France in check. For its part Austria admired the easy patriotism of the British and this admiration played a determining part in nurturing the increasing sense of Austrian identity that emerges at the end of the century, as the Holy Roman Empire disappeared and the country concentrated on defending its core territories. It was in this climate that Haydn was commissioned to compose 'GOTT ERHALTE FRANZ DEN KAISER'.

In 1796 Haydn wrote the *Missa in tempore belli*, in which the war-like drumbeats heard in the Agnus Dei are overcome by the jubilation of the 'Dona nobis pacem'. Two years later he composed the 'Nelson' mass (MISSA IN ANGUSTIIS) in which the menacing D minor of the Kyrie and Benedictus is transformed into a life-enhancing D major elsewhere in the work. It is here that Haydn's most personal response to the disquiet and disruption unleashed by the French Revolution is most apparent. Significantly, the work is a mass, a cherished part of Haydn's heritage, and, moreover, an emblem of a religion that Revolutionary France had sought to banish a few years earlier. It is the potency of that religious power that is celebrated in the mass, a vision of society unlike the one that was being crudely fashioned in France and forcibly extended to the rest of Europe. In this work Haydn achieves an integration of the allusive and the visionary in a way that had eluded him in the 'Military' symphony.

Only a handful of works by Haydn concern themselves, directly or indirectly, with the mix of confusion, idealism, patriotism, and militarism that the French Revolution churned up in its wake. But this was also the period when Haydn's music was at its most esteemed throughout Europe, not least in France itself. When, in particular, the popularity of *The Creation* is recalled, maybe Haydn was closer to the true spirit of the times. It is clearly not a 'revolutionary' work; but neither is it an exercise in escapism or other-worldliness. Founded on values that pre-date the Revolution it celebrates them, not as a pretext for nostalgia, but as an alternative vision of social well-being, one that is even more unattainable than that proclaimed by the Revolution.

Friberth family. Carl Friberth (b. 7 June 1736; d. 6 Aug. 1816) was a tenor at the Esterházy court from 1759 to 1776. Haydn composed a number of leading roles for him, including Don Pelagio (*La canterina*), Acide (*Acide*), Sempronio (*Lo speziale*), Frisellino (*Le pescatrici*), Filippo (*L'infedeltà delusa*), and Ali (*L'incontro improvviso*). On the evidence of these parts Friberth possessed a very wide range and was a gifted actor. He also wrote the libretto for Haydn's *L'incontro improvviso* and modified other librettos for Haydn's use. In 1769 Friberth married the soprano Magdalena Spangler (b. 4 Sept. 1750) who had entered Esterházy service the previous year. She made her debut at court as Grilletta in *Lo speziale*; other important Haydn roles include Lesbina (*Le pescatrici*), Vespina (*L'infedeltà delusa*), and Rezia (*L'incontro improvviso*). Husband and wife served as soloists in the first performance of Haydn's *Il ritorno di Tobia* (Vienna, 1775). They left the court on 22 May 1776. Carl subsequently served as Kapellmeister at two Jesuit churches in Vienna. RJR

I. Fuchs and L. Vobruba, 'Studien zur Biographie von Karl Friberth', *Studien zur Musikwissenschaft*, 34 (1983), 21–59.

R. V. Karpf, 'Haydn und Carl Friberth—Marginalien zur Gesangskunst in 18. Jahrhundert', in E. Badura-Skoda (ed.), *Joseph Haydn. Bericht über den internationalen Joseph Haydn Kongress. Wien, Hofburg, 5–12 September 1982* (Munich, 1986), 361–8.

Friedrich Wilhelm II (b. 25 Sept. 1744; d. 16 Nov. 1797). Nephew of Frederick the Great who succeeded him as King of Prussia in 1786. Like his uncle he was a gifted and keen musician. Jean-Pierre Duport (1741–1818) was in charge of chamber music at the court and taught the king the cello. In 1787 Haydn, probably via the Prussian embassy in Vienna, forwarded manuscript copies of the six 'Paris' symphonies to the king, for which he was rewarded with a ring. ARTARIA was also in touch with the Prussian court and it was the publisher who initiated the idea that Haydn's latest quartets, op. 50, should be dedicated to the king. Haydn readily accepted and persuaded Artaria that the dedication should come from the composer rather than from the publisher. However, it is a mistake to suggest that the quartets were written with the royal cellist in mind, notwithstanding three notable passages of solo writing (first movement of no. 1, slow movement of no. 3, and finale of no. 4). The composer intended visiting the court on his return journey from London in 1792 but this plan never materialized and there is no evidence of any further contact between Haydn and the king. Boccherini received a pension from the court and regularly supplied it with music. In 1789 Mozart was commissioned to write a set of quartets for the king (his 'Prussian' quartets, K575, K589, and K590).

Fries, Count Moritz Johann Christian von (b. 1777; d. 26 Dec. 1826). Viennese banker and patron of music. Haydn began to use the services of the bank when he was in London, regularly forwarding money to its offices in Vienna, probably through the intermediary of Coutts. GEORGE THOMSON paid Haydn for the settings of British folksongs in this manner.

Fries was a member of the GESELLSCHAFT DER ASSOCIIERTEN that underwrote the costs of the first performances of *The Creation* in 1798 and of *The Seasons* in 1801; he subsequently purchased four copies of the subscription edition of *The Creation*. At the turn of the century his palace on the Josephplatz, later known as the Palavicini palace, was a regular venue for private concerts. Haydn promised to write some string quintets for Fries but these never materialized. The two completed movements of his final quartet, op. 103, were dedicated to Fries, who approved GRIESINGER's suggestion that the publication include Haydn's visiting card 'Hin is alle meine Kraft'. Fries was a notable patron of Beethoven also.

HCRL 4 and 5.

'Frog' quartet. Commonly used nickname for the quartet in D, op. 50 no. 6, originating in the 19th century. The opening theme of the finale features *bariolage*, alternation of the same pitch on two different strings. Rather oddly, the resultant sound reminded someone of a frog. JH

Fuchs, Aloys (b. 22 June 1799; d. 20 March 1853). Austrian collector of music manuscripts who prepared a number of thematic catalogues of

Haydn's output. After studying philosophy and law at the University of Vienna he became a government official, working for a time with the music historian R. G. Kiesewetter (1773–1850). From the age of 20 he began to amass a library of old music and related material, including manuscripts, printed editions, portraits, and treatises, establishing himself as a musical antiquary of international repute. He compiled a number of thematic catalogues of the output of individual composers, including Beethoven, Corelli, Gluck, Handel, Joseph Haydn, Michael Haydn, Mozart, and Vivaldi. Apart from the Gluck catalogue none of these was published but all of them, including the four devoted to Haydn's output, have proved invaluable to later scholars. The Hoboken catalogue habitually includes references to the Haydn catalogues prepared by Fuchs. Following Fuchs's death the contents of his library were widely dispersed; the majority of the items were acquired by the Staatsbibliothek, Berlin, and the abbey of GÖTTWEIG.

R. Schaal, 'Die Autographen der Wiener Musiksammlung von Aloys Fuchs', *HYB* 6 (1969), 5–191.

R. Schaal, 'Handschriften-Kopien aus der Wiener Musiksammlung von Aloys Fuchs', *HYB* 7 (1970), 255–80.

R. Schaal (ed.), *Thematisches Verzeichnis der sämtlichen Kompositionen von Joseph Haydn*, facs. of 1839 catalogue (Wilhelmshaven, 1968).

Fuchs, Johann Nepomuk (b. 29 June 1766; d. 29 Oct. 1839). Born and bred in Eisenstadt, Fuchs succeeded Haydn as Esterházy Kapellmeister in 1809. He joined the court as keyboard teacher in 1784 and he is probably the same Johann Fuchs who is named as a violinist from 1788 onwards. Following the disbanding of the musical retinue in 1790 it is not clear what happened to Fuchs, but he seems to have carried on his teaching responsibilities and by 1801, at the latest, he had assumed various administrative duties at the court as Haydn's assistant. The following year he was officially appointed to the post of Assistant Kapellmeister, with special responsibility for church music. As Haydn became more infirm and lived most of the time in Vienna, Fuchs's duties increased accordingly; Haydn valued his commitment and their relationship was always a cordial one. When HUMMEL joined the court in 1804 as Concertmeister he succeeded in needling Fuchs at every opportunity; in truth, while Hummel was certainly a temperamental figure, they were from different generations, and perhaps the older man recognized the younger as much the more talented musician of the two. Fuchs was a prolific composer of church music and operas, mostly written for the Esterházy court.

It is thought that Fuchs provided additional wind parts for as many as three of Haydn's masses. The original organ part of the *Missa in angustiis* ('Nelson' mass) was recast, perhaps with Haydn's approval, for flute, two oboes, two clarinets, bassoon, and two horns; these parts are given in the *JHW* edition of the work. Supplementary wind parts for the 'Grosse Orgelsolomesse' MISSA IN HONOREM BVM, the *Missa brevis Sancti Johannis de Deo*, and the 'Theresienmesse' have also been tentatively ascribed to Fuchs.

M. Horányi, *The Magnificence of Eszterháza* (Budapest, 1962).

HCRL/4 and 5.

fugue. Though less central to composers in the GALANT and Classical styles than it had been in the earlier years of the 18th century, fugue still remained an important part of a composer's technique and was respected as a sign of mastery of a hallowed 'learned' style. In church music in particular it was central. Nevertheless, the stylistic changes of the second quarter of the 18th century inevitably meant a change of attitude to fugue and, indeed, counterpoint in general. Fugal technique was increasingly associated with a relatively fixed and increasingly ossified archaism that stood out in opposition to the *lingua franca* of the new lighter musical styles. Fugal writing came to be used to demonstrate compositional mastery, or to impart a special sense of climax or intensification. Specifically, the use of learned devices has a special association with works in a minor key, a small minority in late 18th-century music.

Haydn's formative years in St Stephen's in Vienna would have equipped him with a wide knowledge of the works of Fux, Monn (1717–50), and Wagenseil, which make extensive use of STILE ANTICO counterpoint, and he must also have learnt much from his teacher, Reutter. Haydn made an extensive study of 18th-century counterpoint theorists, including Fux, whose *Gradus ad Parnassum* (1725) he also taught from. Haydn's library also included the writings of J. S. Bach's pupil Johann Philipp Kirnberger (1721–83), whose work he criticized as too constricting 'for a free spirit', and Mattheson (1681–1764). Together with Albrechtsberger and Stadler he is known to have played Corelli's trio sonatas as recreational music, and his library also contained works by Bach (notably the '48' and the B minor Mass), Caldara (*c.*1670–1736), and Fux. Towards the end of his life he assumed (jointly with Albrechtsberger and Salieri) the directorship of a project to produce a history of music in examples, including works from as far back as the late 15th century. Unfortunately, the *Geschichte der Musik in Denkmählern* came to an ignominious end when the plates fell into the hands of the occupying French army in Vienna and were melted down as ammunition, though proof copies have survived.

Most Viennese settings of the mass—other than the most condensed—feature fugal writing at some point, most commonly at the end of the Gloria ('In gloria Dei Patris, Amen'), and the end of the Credo ('Et vitam venturi saeculi'). These conventional culminating fugal sections remained a standard fixture until the early 19th century, continuing to feature in the masses of Beethoven and Schubert. Haydn's own church music, particularly the six late masses, include a number of powerfully argued climactic fugues for the Gloria and Credo. Especially fine examples can be found in the 'Theresienmesse', notably a 6/8 fugue for the 'Et vitam venturi'. The *Missa Sancti Bernardi d'Offida* includes double fugues (that is featuring two recurring themes with associated text) to end the Gloria and the Credo. Of the six late masses only the 'Schöpfungsmesse' contains no full-blown fugues, though it does contain passages of fugal writing. Most of Haydn's earlier settings of the mass use fugue at some or all of the conventional positions. The *Missa Cellensis in honorem BVM* (*Missa Sanctae Ceciliae*) is remarkable for its four fully developed fugues, contributing appropriately to the scale and grandeur of the work as a whole.

Haydn's two oratorios, *The Creation* and *The Seasons*, both contain splendid examples of the composer's powerfully proportioned symphonic fugues. The final chorus of *The Creation* opens with a slow introduction before embarking on a double fugue, with the main subject derived from a fanfare-like figure of three repeated notes and a rising fourth. Towards the end the contrapuntal fabric dissolves and the music swells into a triumphant coda based on motifs from the fugue. Haydn's other major oratorio, *The Seasons*, includes fugal movements in each of its four constituent sections. The best-known is Autumn, which includes the 'drunk fugue' ('Juhe, der Wein ist da') in which the carousing at the harvest supper culminates in a riotous fugal chorus in which the voices drop the subject halfway through the entries (as in a drunken stupor) while the accompanying instruments are left to complete it.

Haydn also made extensive use of fugal technique in his instrumental works, especially in the chamber works. Unlike composers from earlier epochs, for whom fugue was a normal means of expression with no particular expressive significance of its own, Haydn treated fugue as a means of intensification, suitable either for a final climax (as in the sections of the mass mentioned above) or as a means of heightening tension in the middle of a development section of a sonata form. Despite the fact that Haydn was familiar with Bach's '48', his fugal technique has little in common with the knotty complexity of Bach's counterpoint. Rather, it owes much of its character to the Italianate Austrian composers whom Haydn followed as models, including Fux, Monn, Wagenseil, and others. As well as a large number of fugatos (passages of music in a fugal texture), several complete fugues can be found in the quartets, symphonies, and baryton trios.

A key stage in Haydn's development as a fugal composer is marked by the op. 20 quartets, composed in 1772. It contains three of the four quartet fugues composed by Haydn, perhaps with the aim of impressing informed Viennese musical opinion with his contrapuntal learning. It has been pointed out by Warren Kirkendale that in the ENTWURF-KATALOG the six quartets of op. 20 appear in the order 5, 6, 2, 3, 4, and 1, so that the three quartets with fugal finales begin the series and are placed with the number of subjects in ascending order (double, triple, and quadruple). Although they are multiple fugues, it is noticeable that in all cases one subject predominates, possessing a clearer rhythmic profile than the others. The double fugue that ends the F minor quartet (op. 20 no. 5) is perhaps the best known of the three. It is based on a conventional minor key subject involving a falling diminished seventh; it has sometimes been compared with 'And with his stripes' from Handel's *Messiah*, but it is probably more directly associated with Viennese models (including fugues by Birk (1718–63), Caldara, and Gassmann). The treatment of the subject is energetic and concentrated, including a multiplicity of stretto entries (notably a simultaneous stretto entry by inversion and an extended passage in canon). The triple and quadruple fugues in op. 20 no. 6 (A major) and op. 20 no. 2 (C major) are also highly ingenious. Like the F minor quartet, they feature inversion and long pedal points as climactic devices towards the end of the movement after which the contrapuntal texture disintegrates into graceful comedy. Fifteen years later Haydn returned to the complete fugue, in the F♯ minor quartet, op. 50 no. 4, which is based on a version of a diminished-seventh subject, though its austerity is mollified by playful ornamentation and the use of 6/8 metre; despite a brief flurry of stretto towards the end it is shorter and simpler in design than the others. Among the numerous fugatos, special mention should be made of the finale of op. 64 no. 5 in D, and the first movement of op. 76 no. 6 in E♭, where a fugal section ends a set of variations.

Three of Haydn's symphonies (nos. 3, 40, and 70) also have fugal finales. The first of these is based on a conventional four-note tag in semibreves, of the kind used by Haydn himself in Symphony no. 13, and by Mozart in the 'Jupiter' symphony and the G major quartet (K387). The finale of no. 70 is a highly original movement, preceded by an introduction prefiguring the subject. After a powerfully energetic working out, the music turns to the major before dissolving into a coda based on the five repeated notes that open the subject, played unaccompanied by the first violins.

The fugal finales of three of the baryton trios (Hob.XI:97, 101, and 114) are generally simpler in design than the fugues of the op. 20 quartets, which are more or less contemporary, though no. 101 employs three subjects. Nevertheless, many of the same features are to be found, including expositions as double fugues, accompanied opening entries, climactic pedal points (sometimes with stretto), and final relaxation into a non-fugal coda. Haydn also employed fugal technique in the finale of the fifth notturno (Hob.II:29) and one of the pieces he wrote for mechanical organ (Hob. XIX:16).

As an enthralling example of Haydn's fugal technique in action, we may take the final movement from the F minor quartet, op. 20 no. 5. The movement is based on two subjects, one a slow-moving formula that serves as the thematic backbone of the movement, the other a subsidiary idea that provides a sense of movement and much of the material for the episodes. The main subject is given a complete exposition followed by a single, additional entry (a so-called redundant entry) in the second violin, whereupon an episode based on overlapping entries of the countersubject leads the music into A♭ major for the middle group of entries. The first group of entries is in stretto at the octave with an additional false entry of the characteristic descending fifth of the subject (bars 36 ff.). The inversion of the subject enters at bar 92, forming a simultaneous stretto with the direct form of the subject and articulating the return to the tonic. Later features include a number of other stretto entries (mostly at the distance of a bar and the interval of a fourth or fifth), two extended dominant pedal points, and an extended passage in octave canon between the first violin and cello (bars 145–60). The texture is relaxed for the coda, and a single emphatic entry of the final subject rounds off the movement. DLH

W. Kirkendale, *Fugue and Fugato in Rococo and Classical Chamber Music*, rev. and expanded 2nd edn trans. M. Bent and the author (Durham, NC, 1979).

A. Mann, *The Study of Fugue* (London, 1960).

B. C. MacIntyre, *The Viennese Concerted Mass of the Early Classic Period* (Ann Arbor, 1986).

Fürnberg, Carl Joseph Weber (b. *c.*1720; d. 21 March 1767). An important early patron of Haydn. He was an official in the Lower Austrian government and in the imperial government whose country residence, Weinzierl, was near Weissenkirchen in the Danube valley to the west of Vienna. GRIESINGER reports that when the young Haydn had virtually all his possessions stolen in Vienna in the early 1750s, his plight was alleviated by Fürnberg who gave him free board and lodging for two months. More famously, it was a commission from Fürnberg that led Haydn to compose his first quartets, probably from 1757 onwards. It seems that Fürnberg did not have a regular ensemble of musicians and his patronage of Haydn was a casual one. Some of the early string trios may also have been composed for Fürnberg. It was on his recommendation that Haydn was taken on as full-time Kapellmeister by Count Morzin. Fürnberg remained interested in Haydn's music and continued to acquire manuscripts of his music directly from the composer well into the 1760s. This library was bequeathed to his son, Joseph von Fürnberg (*c.*1741–1799), and a substantial portion survives in Keszthely castle, Hungary, a valuable source for Haydn's early instrumental and orchestral music.

Fux, Johann Joseph (b. 1660; d. 13 Feb. 1741). Viennese court composer and musical theorist, of Styrian birth. Fux's career is partly comparable to Haydn's: of humble rural origins, he manifested musical interests from an early age, and later came to Vienna (under Habsburg patronage, serving a succession of three emperors), rising to considerable eminence and gaining an international reputation. But while Haydn's music achieved lasting popularity and status, Fux's compositions remained relatively obscure, and it is chiefly through his theoretical work that his name has been perpetuated. Among his hundreds of compositions in all the main genres then current (including opera) it was the relatively small number of sacred works in STILE ANTICO that continued to attract attention after his death, most notably the *Missa canonica* (K. 7: 1719), a model of 'PALESTRINA STYLE'. Both Michael Haydn and Joseph Haydn had copies of this work.

Besides his direct pupils (who included Wagenseil) Fux influenced the education of many musicians through his didactic work, *Gradus ad Parnassum*, published in 1725. The end of Fux's, and the beginning of Haydn's, period of activity in Vienna overlapped. By the time Haydn came to St Stephen's as a chorister under the direction of GEORG REUTTER, Fux had risen through the ranks at the HOFKAPELLE to the top position of Hofkapellmeister (1715–41). His (unpublished) *Singfundament* would have been used to instruct the choirboys. Through Fux's colleagues and pupils, as well as through his compositions (especially liturgical works) and theoretical teachings, Haydn absorbed the grandiose spirit of late Baroque Viennese music and the living tradition of Palestrina style, which formed part of the foundations of the Viennese Classical style.

At some point, probably early in his studies (during the 1750s) Haydn worked his way through Fux's *Gradus*. Its methodical presentation, based on the system of species counterpoint, and its use of dialogue form (master and pupil), suited self-teaching. Haydn probably enjoyed the dry humour with which Fux imbued the teacher–pupil exchanges. The annotations to the text of the *Gradus* traditionally attributed to Haydn show the critical thoroughness and exegetical zeal with which he studied it. There is evidence that Haydn continued to annotate the text in later years. His annotated copy may have been studied by Mozart in connection with his composition teaching. From Haydn as teacher, the *Gradus* tradition passed directly to his most famous pupil, Beethoven. SW

H. White (ed.), *Johann Joseph Fux and the Music of the Austro-Italian Baroque* (Aldershot, 1992).

S. Wollenberg, 'The Unknown "Gradus"', *Music and Letters*, 51 (1970), 170–8.

G

galant. Term widely used in the 18th century, especially in France and Germany, to denote music that was pleasant and undemanding. Attention was focused on the top line which, typically, unfolded in regular phrases. Although it could be melancholy in mood, more dramatic utterances were shunned. On the other hand, while it was regarded as the prerequisite for civilized music-making, it was never to be mannered. Naturalness was a fundamental watchword. C. P. E. BACH, and no doubt Haydn after him, regarded it as the opposite of the learned style.

In modern historical writing, *galant* is often used to describe the mid-18th-century style that separated the Baroque from the Classical. However preoccupation with the *galant* can be traced back to the 17th century and it remains a vital component of the mature Classical style, alongside other types of music such as the learned and the sublime. The choral tune that greets 'the new created world' in Haydn's *Creation* is an example of the *galant*, heard after the learned ('The Representation of Chaos') and the sublime ('And there was light').

Gallini, John. (b. 7 Jan. 1728; d. 5 Jan. 1805). Italian dancer and impresario, known as Sir John Gallini following a papal knighthood received in 1788. He had first arrived in London around 1753, soon becoming a successful dancer at the theatres and a fashionable dancing master. Ambitious for power within the cultural establishment of London, he married the Earl of Abingdon's eldest daughter and in 1775 joined J. C. Bach and Abel in building the Hanover Square Rooms. He then turned to the Italian Opera and after a troublesome campaign assumed the management of the King's Theatre in 1785. Unsuccessful in his attempts to lure Haydn to London as house composer and forced to rely mainly on imported operas, he nevertheless ran four successful seasons before the King's Theatre burnt down in June 1789.

Another period of uncertainty and legal wrangling ensued. After one season at the small Haymarket Theatre, Gallini joined forces with his former adversary William Taylor at the rebuilt King's Theatre, commissioning a new opera from Haydn, *L'anima del filosofo*, as part of a joint deal with Salomon. But when the opera licence was refused, Gallini could promote only a series of hybrid concerts, many of them directed by Haydn, who contributed a new and very popular catch (subsequently lost). SMcV

HCRL/2 and 3.

C. Price, J. Milhouse, and R. D. Hume, *Italian Opera in Late Eighteenth-Century London*, vol. i: *The King's Theatre, Haymarket 1778–1791* (Oxford, 1995).

Gardiner, William. (b. 15 March 1770; d. 16 Nov. 1853). Leicester hosiery manufacturer, dilettante, and champion of the music of Haydn, Mozart, and Beethoven in England. In 1804, having played Haydn's instrumental music at amateur gatherings, Gardiner sent him a token of his admiration, six pairs of cotton stockings decorated with melodies by the composer. Through the publication of his six-volume collection *Sacred Melodies* (1812–38), Gardiner promoted the singing in Anglican worship of psalms and hymns using melodies by Haydn, Mozart, and Beethoven. He also provided extensive annotations to Berry's translation of CARPANI's biography of Haydn, published in London in 1817. REC

W. Gardiner, *Music and Friends; or, Pleasant Recollections of a Dilettante*, 3 vols (London, 1838–53).

J. Wilshere, *William Gardiner of Leicester (1770–1853), Hosiery Manufacturer, Musician and Dilettante: A Bicentenary Sketch* (Leicester, 1970).

Gassmann family. Florian Leopold Gassmann (b. 3 May 1729; d. 20 Jan. 1774) was one of Vienna's leading composers in the 1760s and 1770s. Born in Bohemia, he received his musical education in Italy. In 1763 he was appointed ballet composer to the court opera in succession to Gluck. On a further journey to Italy he met Salieri and brought him back to Vienna as his pupil. In 1771 he founded the Tonkünstler-Societät, a charitable foundation whose annual concerts raised money for the widows and orphans of deceased musicians and became highlights of the musical season; it was for this organization that Haydn wrote *Il ritorno di Tobia*. Gassmann died at the age of 44 following a fall from a carriage.

Gassmann was a prolific composer of all kinds of music. Two comic operas, in particular, *L'amore artigiano* and *La contessina*, enjoyed international success. The former was presented at Eszterháza in 1777, 1780, and 1790, and Haydn wrote a total of three insertion arias for the work. Gassmann's 33 symphonies provide an interesting context for Haydn's symphonies up to the mid-1770s, especially his occasional fondness for unusual keys

(A♭ and B minor) and for beginning a work with a slow introduction. His quartets frequently include a fugal movement, a clear indication that the three fugues in Haydn's op. 20 would not have been regarded as unusual.

Gassmann had two daughters, both educated by Salieri before assuming brief careers as singers: Maria Anna (b. 1771; d. 27 Aug. 1858) and Therese Josepha (b. 1 April 1774: d. 8 Sept. 1837). The younger sister was a favoured singer of Haydn, taking part in performances of the late masses and in the vocal version of *The Seven Last Words*. He wanted her to be the soprano soloist in the first public performances of *The Creation* in 1799 but was overruled by Swieten and the GESELLSCHAFT DER ASSOCIIERTEN who were paying the expenses. For over a year Therese had been in love with JOSEPH CARL ROSENBAUM, a secretary at the Esterházy court. Haydn lent a sympathetic ear when Therese's mother showed her disapproval. Joseph and Therese were eventually married in 1800. At Haydn's funeral on 2 June 1809 Theresa was the soprano soloist in a performance of Michael Haydn's Requiem. ERL

G. R. Hill, *A Thematic Catalog of the Instrumental Music of Florian Leopold Gassmann* (Hackensack, NJ, 1976).

E. Radant, 'The Diaries of Joseph Carl Rosenbaum', *HYB* 5 (1968).

Geiringer, Karl (b. 26 April 1899; d. 10 Jan. 1989). Musicologist born in Vienna whose special interests included Bach, Brahms, Haydn, and the history of musical instruments. He studied with Guido Adler and Wilhelm Fischer at the university, gaining a doctorate in 1922. After a period working in music-publishing he succeeded MANDYCZEWSKI as archivist of the Gesellschaft der Musikfreunde in Vienna. Following the Nazi invasion of Austria in 1938 he moved first to London, and then to the USA, becoming professor and head of graduate studies in music at Boston University where he remained until 1962. One of his early pupils was H. C. ROBBINS LANDON. From 1962 to 1972 he worked at the University of California, Santa Barbara.

In 1932, the bicentenary of Haydn's birth, Geiringer's short study, in German, of the composer was published. Following his move to the USA this was reworked as *Haydn: A Creative Life in Music* (New York, 1946; London, 1947). Subsequently revised and translated into several languages it became the standard one-volume life and works of the composer, written with the natural empathy and authority of a person with his Viennese background and training. More specialized studies of Haydn's church music and of his settings of British folksongs were also published. For the *JHW* he edited the folksong settings that Haydn prepared for Napier, the opera *Orlando paladino*, and (with Günter Thomas) the fragmentary operas, *Acide* and *La marchesa nespola*.

H. C. Robbins Landon and R. E. Chapman (eds), *Studies in Eighteenth-Century Music: A tribute to Karl Geiringer* (London, 1970).

Gellert, Christian Fürchtegott (b. 4 July 1715; d. 13 Dec. 1769). The fifth son of a poor country parson, he was fortunate to enjoy a good education at St Afra's School, Meißen, and then at Leipzig University (though poverty obliged him to break off his studies for a time and work as a private tutor). He finally graduated in philosophy in 1743, and in the following years he became a lecturer in rhetoric, poetry, and philosophy. He wrote a number of comedies (two volumes appeared in 1747), and a long novel. However, his fame among contemporaries was largely based upon his *Lieder* (1743) and his collection of *Fabeln und Erzählungen* (1746 and 1748); in 1751 a volume of model letters was published, and in the same year he was awarded a chair at Leipzig. His inaugural lecture was in praise of the *comédie larmoyante*. He continued to be productive as a writer, with *Lehrgedichte und Erzählungen* appearing in 1754, and the very influential *Geistliche Oden und Lieder* in 1757. He had never enjoyed good health, and his last years were clouded by physical and mental decline.

Gellert holds an important place in the history of the early Enlightenment. His verses were eagerly set to music by, among others, C. P. E. Bach (55 were included in *Geistliche Oden und Lieder mit Melodien*, 1758 and 1764) and Beethoven (op. 48). Haydn owned several volumes of his writings and regarded him as his favourite poet. He set Gellert's 'Betrachtung des Todes' (Hob.XXVb:3), 'Wider den Übermut' (Hob.XXVc:7), 'Danklied zu Gott' (Hob.XXVc:8), and 'Abendlied zu Gott' (Hob. XXVc:9) as partsongs in the mid- and late 1790s; and from the same period three canons were composed using lines by the poet, 'Der Menschenfreud' (Hob.XXVIIb:7), 'Gottes Macht und Vorsehung' (Hob.XXVIIb:8), and 'Die Liebe der Feinde' (Hob. XXVIIb:26).

The modern reader may wonder at the popularity of Gellert's modest verses in the late 18th and early 19th centuries, but their blend of elegance, wit, musicality, unaffected piety, and directness of utterance, coupled with his contemporaries' sympathetic awareness of the nature of his personal struggle against adversity, and of his willingness to advise those who solicited his help, certainly struck a firm chord in monarchs and peasants alike. It is appropriate, therefore, that Haydn himself was twice compared with Gellert: in an article in the *Wiener Diarium* (Oct. 1766), and by DITTERSDORF in his autobiography. (It has been conjectured that the former, too, was written by Dittersdorf.) PB

genius. A notion central to the Enlightenment understanding of creativity and, as such, a prominent idea in literature, philosophy, and aesthetics of the time. Genius was variously defined, but generally it was understood as an innate quality in the individual, bestowed by nature. As formulated influentially by Immanuel Kant (1724–1804) it is, in many ways, closer in type to the Romantic genius of the 19th century than to earlier notions of divinely inspired genius, and it had as its primary characteristic the capacity for originality. Although, according to Kant, 'every art presupposes rules, which serve as the foundation', genius 'is the talent (natural endowment) which gives the rule to art'; it is 'a *talent* for producing something for which no determinate rule can be given, and not a predisposition consisting of a skill for something that can be learned by following some rule or other; hence the foremost property of genius must be *originality*'. Genius in Enlightenment thought is also exemplary, its 'products . . . must also be models' which must serve 'as a standard or rule by which to judge'; and it is a gift of nature by which the author is enabled to produce a work of genius, although 'he himself does not know how he came by the ideas for it' nor can he 'communicate [his procedure] to others in precepts that would enable them to bring about like products'.

Enlightenment concepts of genius are never systematically articulated in connection with Haydn's music, but with the increasing popularity of his music from the 1780s, the characteristics attributed to his music in contemporary criticism frequently mirror the language and the general concepts of Enlightenment thought on creative genius. The word genius itself, which is not, in general, employed lightly or loosely in the 18th century, is used in many reviews of the later 1780s to distinguish the quality of originality perceived in Haydn's music, particularly his symphonies. The comparisons in such reviews between Haydn and his contemporaries, including those regarded as imitators of the composer's style, are not, from the perspective of today, necessarily supportable in stylistic terms, but it is significant that the reviewers, in insisting on the exemplary quality of Haydn's symphonies, attribute to the composer a characteristic of genius. In terms of 18th-century thinking his symphonies, as the products of genius, may be considered 'fine art', which is, according to Kant, 'possible only as the product of genius'.

In the context of 18th-century concepts of genius the assessment of some symphonies by PLEYEL performed at the Concert spirituel in March 1787 is revealing: 'The novelties which one heard in the last two concerts, were: [firstly] 2 symphonies of M. Pleyel, a pupil of M. Haydn. They were warmly applauded. If M. Pleyel has not all the original genius of his master, because genius does not transmit itself, he owes at least to his lessons [with Haydn] a firm and sure touch and a great knowledge of the effects of harmony' (*Mercure de France*, 7 April 1787). In this and numerous other reviews, the extent to which the genius of Haydn had come to dominate the reception of symphonies in Paris is abundantly clear. Notwithstanding the compositional competency which is granted to Pleyel—the knowledge of rules implicit in Pleyel's 'great knowledge of harmony'—his symphonies do not measure up to the standards of originality and genius attributed to Haydn. It is also clear that Haydn's works are regarded as exemplary and it is implicit that the elusive quality of genius is a gift of nature, since it cannot be transmitted.

While in concert reviews from the later 1780s and 1790s the recognition of Haydn as a genius in these terms emerges piecemeal, writings about the composer from the turn of the century, including the German criticism of Johann Friedrich Reichardt (1752–1814) and the earliest Haydn biographies by GRIESINGER and DIES, are increasingly informed by such concepts. For instance, in a well-known section from Griesinger's biography of the composer, Haydn's view of creativity, his 'theoretical *raisonnements*', are formulated in a way that has much in common with the writings of Kant. Kant's words, 'every art presupposes rules, which serve as the foundation' has a parallel in Haydn's professed aim when composing 'to develop and sustain it [the opening idea] in keeping with the rules of art'. At the same time Haydn's response to Albrechtsberger's rules for strict composition ('his wish to see fourths banished from the purest style') that 'art is free, and will be limited by no pedestrian rules', and his placement of the challenge of writing 'a really *new* minuet' ahead of mere correctness, all closely echo the Kantian precepts that originality is the 'foremost property' of genius and that genius alone 'gives the rule to art'. Similarly, the belief that genius is a 'natural endowment' which cannot be explained scientifically or methodically, nor communicated to another, is mirrored in Haydn's admission that his compositional objectives 'cannot be learned by rules' but depend entirely 'on natural talent and the inspiration of inborn genius'. BH

I. Berlin, *The Magus of the North: J. G. Hamann and the Origins of Modern Irrationalism* (London, 1993).

G. A. Griesinger, *Biographische Notizen über Joseph Haydn* (Leipzig, 1810); English trans. V. Gotwals, *Joseph Haydn: Eighteenth-Century Gentleman and Genius* (Madison, 1963).

I. Kant, *Kritik der Urtheilskraft* (Berlin, 1790); trans. W. S. Pluhar (Indianapolis, 1987).
J. H. Mason, 'Thinking about Genius in the Eighteenth Century', in P. Mattick Jr. (ed.), *Eighteenth-Century Aesthetics and the Reconstruction of Art* (Cambridge, 1993), 210–39.

Genovefens vierter Theil (Genoveve: Part IV) (Hob.XXIXa:5). Marionette opera in three acts, composed in the summer of 1777, libretto by PAUERSBACH. The work was probably first performed on 6 August 1777 in connection with the festivities in honour of the marriage of Count Nicolaus Esterházy to Countess Maria Anna Franziska Weissenwolf; the principal entertainment was *Il mondo della luna*. The music is lost; the text survives only in C. F. Pohl's handwritten copy of the libretto. Doubts as to Haydn's authorship of the music arise both from the absence of any contemporary evidence that he was the composer, and from the fact that he twice listed it in his Libretto Catalogue among works by other composers, and on the last page enters it as 'Genovefens 4^{tr} Theil ii [= two copies] by various masters'. Robbins Landon suggests that Haydn probably compiled the score and was at best one of the composers involved. The long cast list includes Genoveva, Siegfried, and Golo from the 17th-century *Volksbuch von der Pfalzgräfin Genoveva*, but also a motley collection of clowns and soldiers, spirits and ladies, masks and Greek guards. The libretto indicates that there were at least 13 arias, two duets, two trios, and 12 choruses. It has been conjectured that the overture in D (Hob.1a:7) originally prefaced this opera.

The first three parts of the Genoveva story had been performed in 1776 (possibly 1777); the author of the texts was Pauersbach but nothing has survived of the texts or of the music. Again, Haydn's involvement might have been as a compiler rather than a composer. PB

H. C. Robbins Landon, 'Haydn's Marionette Operas and the Repertoire of the Marionette Theatre at Esterház Castle', *HYB* 1 (1962), 111–97.
HCRL/2.

Genzinger, Maria Anna von (b. 1750; d. 20 Jan. 1793). Viennese aristocrat who was on friendly terms with Haydn from 1789 onwards and in whom the composer frequently confided. Her husband, Peter Leopold von Genzinger, was a physician to Prince Nicolaus Esterházy and it was probably through him that Haydn was first invited to the family home in the Schottenhof in Vienna. Maria Anna von Genzinger was a competent amateur pianist and Haydn encouraged her playing and her enthusiasm for arranging his symphonies for keyboard. He recommended that she purchase a piano, probably a square piano, by Wenzel Schantz to replace a harpsichord, encouraged her daughter Josepha and son Franz in their singing, and composed a piano sonata (Hob.XVI:49) specially for her. This entrée into the world of a moderately wealthy, cultured, and stable family in Vienna coincided with a decline in the vibrancy of musical life at the Esterházy court following the death of Prince Nicolaus's wife. Haydn's letters to Maria Anna are amongst the most revealing and eloquent from the composer (certainly in comparison with those to his mistress, LUIGIA POLZELLI) particularly in the way they contrast life in Vienna with that at the Esterházy court. The relationship, although close, was a platonic one; on one occasion, in response to some gossip-mongering, Haydn felt obliged to reassure Maria Anna that his intentions were entirely honourable. Their correspondence continued when Haydn moved to London and again reveal much about the private thoughts of this now very public figure.

HCRL/2 and 3.

George III (r. 1760–1810). The British king was an enthusiastic musician, playing both the flute and the harpsichord. His preference was for older music, especially that of Handel, which he demanded at royal concerts and at the Concert of Ancient Music. He also took a close personal interest in the Handel Commemoration of 1784 and its successors. Unlike the rest of his family, he showed little taste for modern music, and only in 1795 did he acknowledge Haydn's eminence. The PRINCE OF WALES introduced Haydn to the king at a large-scale soirée at the DUKE OF YORK'S, presumably arranged for this sole purpose since only Haydn's music was performed. The king persuaded him to sing a German song, 'Ich bin der Verliebteste' (a version of 'Content', Hob. XXVIa: 36). Subsequently Haydn appeared at other court concerts, on one occasion gratifying the royal taste by playing a Handel psalm on the organ. Nevertheless, the impression remains that George III retained a formal condescension towards the composer and, though the royal family pressed Haydn to remain in England, they did not match this show of enthusiasm with financial reward or attendance at his final benefit in 1795. The statement by Griesinger that a symphony by Haydn was performed at one of the annual Handel charity concerts patronized by the king is unfounded.

SMcV

Gerber, Ernst Ludwig (b. 29 Sept. 1746; d. 30 June 1819). German writer on music who compiled one of the most influential early dictionaries of music. He lived and worked his entire life in Sondershausen, Thuringia, where he held a mixture of musical and administrative posts at the court of Prince Schwarzburg-Sondershausen. He amassed one of the largest private music libraries in Europe, most of which was sold to the Gesellschaft der Musikfreunde in Vienna in 1815. A frequent contributor to the *Allgemeine musikalische Zeitung*, he spent much of his adult life compiling and revising two notable musical dictionaries: *Historisch-biographisches Lexicon der Tonkünstler* (Leipzig, 1790–2) and *Neues historisch-biographisches Lexikon der Tonkünstler* (Leipzig, 1812–14). Although the title of the second dictionary implies a revision it was, in essence, a wholly new, more ambitious work, as the entry on Haydn demonstrates.

The entry in the first dictionary gives a brief outline of Haydn's career up to 1790, followed by an evaluation of his music. Gerber was never to meet the composer but Haydn is already a dominant figure in his estimation, 'great in small things, even greater in large things'. He gives priority to the quartets and symphonies, and, tackling the preoccupation of many north German critics with Haydn's penchant for octave-writing in the quartets, defends the composer.

While the first dictionary devotes two double columns to Haydn, the second dictionary gives lavish coverage of nearly 35 double columns. Fourteen double columns are devoted to a detailed list of Haydn's music, taken first hand from Gerber's library and from his knowledge of the stock held by Breitkopf and by Westphal. Faced with the particular problem of compiling a reliable list of symphonies Gerber suggests the need for a thematic catalogue. The biographical part of the entry was first written in 1808 and though it, naturally, contains more information than the first dictionary it is not very informative on Haydn's time at the Esterházy court or the two visits to London. It does, however, deal extensively with his contemporary European fame, especially as reflected in the many performances of *The Creation*. Two additions were made to the article before the dictionary was printed. The summary catalogue that Haydn gave to Bertuch was added and, following Haydn's death in 1809 and the subsequent appearance of the biography by GRIESINGER, large portions of that biography are summarized in the final section of the article, thereby conveniently plugging gaps in the early part of the entry.

Historisch-biographisches Lexicon der Tonkünstler, facs. (Graz, 1977).

Neues historisch-biographisches Lexikon der Tonkünstler, facs. (Graz, 1966).

Gesellschaft der Associierten Cavaliers. Literally the 'Society of Associated Cavaliers', this organization led by SWIETEN was often referred to as the Gesellschaft der Associierten, sometimes as the Cavaliers. Detailed knowledge of this important body is lacking. It was probably founded towards the end of the 1780s to enable Swieten to mount semi-public performances of oratorios and similar works unfamiliar in Vienna, especially the music of Handel; a consortium of members of the aristocracy was gathered to underwrite the costs. The names of the members varied from year to year, perhaps even from event to event, but the most frequently encountered names were PRINCE NICOLAUS ESTERHÁZY II, COUNT FRIES, COUNT HARRACH, Prince Kinsky (1781–1812), Prince Lichnowsky (1756–1814), PRINCE LOBKOWITZ, and PRINCE SCHWARZENBERG. Swieten was its permanent secretary and the driving force behind its activities. Most of its concerts were held in the palace of Prince Schwarzenberg on the Neuer Markt. Invitations to attend were distributed amongst friends of the aristocratic sponsors, but free admission to rehearsals was often granted to inquisitive listeners. Following Swieten's death in 1803, the Gesellschaft ceased to operate though the idea of a group of aristocrats, rather than one, promoting concerts was to resurface a few years later in the so-called Liebhaber Concerte, whose final concert in March 1808 featured *The Creation* in honour of Haydn's 76th birthday.

In 1793 the society promoted a concert that included the first performance of the German version of the chorus, *The Storm*, and in 1796 it underwrote the costs of the first performance of the vocal version of *The Seven Last Words*. Spurred on by Swieten, who saw Haydn as the new Handel, the society sponsored the first performances of *The Creation* (1798) and of *The Seasons* (1801), all given in the Schwarzenberg palace.

Gherardi, Pietro (*fl.* 1776–92). The only *musico* (castrated male singer) in Prince Nicolaus's opera troupe at Eszterháza. A native of Ravenna, Gherardi languished in obscurity in Italy before his two-year engagement at Eszterháza (1776–7). The initial impetus behind Nicolaus's decision to hire a *musico* (or castrato) was probably a forthcoming production of Gluck's *Orfeo*, in which Gherardi sang the title role. He went on to create the role of the young lover Ernesto in Haydn's *Il mondo della luna*, inspiring some of the composer's most beautiful melodies. On his return to Italy he enjoyed a modest career until 1792, singing mostly secondary roles in *opera seria*. JAR

Bartha and Somfai.

HCRL/2.

Giardini, Felice (b. 12 April 1716; d. 8 June 1796). Italian violinist, composer, and impresario, a prominent figure in the musical life of London for over 40 years. When Haydn called on the aged violinist, Giardini refused to see that 'German dog'; when Haydn attended Giardini's farewell concert at Ranelagh Gardens in May 1792 he apparently relished Giardini's sweet tone but in the privacy of his notebook wrote 'He played like a pig'. SMcV

Gioco filarmonico (Hob.IV, Anhang). A completely spurious musical work for three instruments attributed to Haydn that was issued by the firm of Marescalchi in Naples in the 1780s; the true author was MAXIMILIAN STADLER. With a throw of a dice players are able to construct innumerable minuets from 12 numbered bars, hence 'philharmonic game'. Such publications were common in Haydn's time; there is also one attributed to Mozart.

'gli scherzi' quartets. Name occasionally given to the op. 33 quartets because of their use of the title scherzo rather than the expected minuet. JH

'Glorious things of Thee are spoken'. *See* AUSTRIA.

Gluck, Christoph Willibald (b. 2 July 1714; d. 15 Nov. 1787). Composer of operas and ballets in Italy, London, Vienna, and Paris. Growing up in Vienna during the 1750s, Haydn could hardly avoid contact with Gluck and his French operas (*opéras comiques*), Italian operas, and ballet scores. Even after his engagement by the Esterházy family, frequent visits to Vienna allowed Haydn to hear the great musical dramatist's latest works. He offered Gluck a delightful musical tribute in Symphony no. 8 ('Le soir'), the first movement of which is based on the so-called tobacco song in Gluck's *Le Diable à quatre* of 1759.

Gluck's *Orfeo* was performed at Eszterháza in 1776. Haydn quoted the melody of 'Che farò senza Euridice' in a baryton trio (Hob.XI:5), made fun of the underworld scene in the finale of Act 2 of *La fedeltà premiata*, and quoted 'Che farò' once more in Act 2 of *L'anima del filosofo*. But perhaps the most potent influence of Gluck's genius was on Haydn's orchestral music. Music such as the Dance of the Furies in the ballet *Don Juan* (1761) helped inspire Haydn to create the dark, violent symphonies that are among his greatest achievements in the late 1760s and early 1770s. JAR

B. A. Brown, *Gluck and the French Theatre in Vienna* (Oxford, 1991).

C. Clark, 'Intertextual Play and Haydn's *La fedeltà premiata*', *Current Musicology*, 51 (1993), 59–81.

D. Heartz, 'Haydn und Gluck im Burgtheater um 1760: *Der neue krumme Teufel, Le diable à quatre*, und die Sinfonie "Le soir"', in C.-H. Mahling and S. Wiesmann (eds), *Bericht über den internationalen Kongress Bayreuth 1981* (Kassel, 1984), 120–35.

D. Heartz, 'Haydn's "Acide e Galatea" and the Imperial Wedding Operas of 1760 by Hasse and Gluck', in E. Badura-Skoda (ed.), *Joseph Haydn. Bericht über den internationalen Joseph Haydn Kongress. Wien, Hofburg, 5–12. September 1982* (Munich, 1986), 332–40.

'God save the King'. In 1795, towards the end of his second visit to London, Haydn made a list of the works that he had written for the city. It includes the intriguing entry '1 God save the King—2 sheets'. This arrangement of the British national anthem has not survived, and the question of whether it was written for orchestra or for much smaller forces, such as a piano trio (as in the composer's folksong settings), must remain a matter of speculation. During these early years of the French Revolution performances in London of 'God save the King', sometimes impromptu ones, were common. On 12 February 1792 Haydn heard a windband play the anthem 'in the street during a wild snowstorm' on the express order of Lord Claremont. A month later Haydn's Symphony no. 98 was given its premiere; the allusion to the national anthem that occurs at the beginning of the slow movement was probably intentional. The popularity of 'God save the King' played a determining role in the commissioning of 'GOTT ERHALTE FRANZ DEN KAISER'.

Goldoni, Carlo (b. 25 Feb. 1707; d. 6/7 Feb. 1793). Italian playwright and librettist who did much to fashion comic opera in the middle of the 18th century. Born in Venice he trained as a lawyer at Padua and, until the age of 40, combined or alternated legal work with writing plays and opera librettos. From 1747 he embarked on a series of fully written comic librettos, over 50 in number, that ensured that comic opera thereafter enjoyed the same international prestige as serious opera. Termed DRAMMA GIOCOSO PER MUSICA several of these librettos were repeatedly set and revised by Italian composers working throughout Europe, and one of them *La buona figliuola*, first set by Duni (1708–75) in 1756, became, in the setting made by Piccinni (1728–1800), the most frequently performed comic opera of the century. Together with settings of other Goldoni comic librettos, *Arcifanfano*, *Il mercato di Malmantile*, and *L'amore artigiano*, it figured in the repertoire at Eszterháza. It was only to be expected that Haydn himself should turn to librettos by Goldoni for three of his operas, *Lo speziale*, *Le pescatrici*, and *Il mondo della luna*. *Dramma giocoso* had become a distinct subgenre and its principles were keenly copied by other librettists, including BADINI (the author of the original version of *Orlando paladino*) and Mozart's da Ponte (1749–1838).

Having set an international fashion in motion Goldoni moved from Venice to Paris in 1762, accepting an invitation to write Italian plays for Louis XVI's company of Italian actors. He learnt French and began writing plays in that language. Partial blindness curtailed his activity but the French court continued to support him. This sharp observer of human absurdity and fallibility died in Paris at the height of the French Revolution. ERL

T. Holme, *A Servant of Many Masters: The Life and Times of Carlo Goldoni* (London, 1976).

P. Petrobelli, 'Goldoni at Eszterháza: The Story of his Librettos set by Haydn', in E. Badura-Skoda (ed.), *Joseph Haydn. Bericht über den internationalen Joseph Haydns Kongress. Wien, Hofburg, 5–12. September 1982* (Munich, 1986), 314–18.

'Gott erhalte Franz den Kaiser' (God preserve Franz the Emperor) (Hob.XXVIa:43). Patriotic song composed by Haydn that became the Austrian national anthem, later the German national anthem. It remains the only national anthem written by a major composer.

One of the features of the Austrian state from 1794 onwards was the authoritarian and centralized control it exerted on all aspects of society as it sought to defend itself against the territorial ambitions of France and to foster a fervent sense of Austrian identity to counter the inflammatory rhetoric of the French. The commissioning of a song from Haydn, together with its controlled distribution and performance, was one of many acts in an increasingly oppressive state.

Austria and France had been at war since 1792, largely fought in the Austrian Netherlands and along the Rhine. In 1796 the French escalated its ambitions by signalling an attack on the central Austrian territories. In a pincer movement that was to close on Vienna, troops from the Rhine marched eastwards while troops from Italy (led by Napoleon) captured Austrian territories in that country before advancing northwards. It was in these nervous times that Haydn composed his MISSA IN TEMPORE BELLI. One of the most active state officials of the period was Count Franz Josef von Saurau. He had played a particularly prominent part in suppressing civil unrest in Vienna in 1794 and had formed the idea that Austria needed a national song that would rally patriotism in the way that 'God save the King' did in Britain. Later he remarked, 'we had no anthem fitted to display in front of the whole world the devoted attachment of the people to its wise and good Fatherland, and to awaken in the hearts of all good Austrians that noble pride of a nation, which is indispensable if they are to execute energetically each disciplinary measure considered necessary by the princes of the land.' In 1796 he commissioned the poet LORENZ LEOPOLD HASHKA to write the poetry; four verses were written, each culminating in the same two lines, clear echoes of 'God save our King': 'Gott erhalte Franz den Kaiser, Unsern guten Kaiser Franz (God preserve Franz the Emperor, our good Emperor Franz). It is not known when Haydn received his commission but the music was officially approved by Saurau on 28 January 1797. Haydn was rewarded with a sum of money and with a gold snuffbox decorated with the portrait of the emperor.

Saurau planned an official release of the song on 12 February, the 29th birthday of Emperor Franz. Two different printers were engaged to provide sufficient copies of the words and music to be distributed across the Austrian territories, and theatres and opera houses were instructed to perform the music during the course of the evening. At the Burgtheater in Vienna Dittersdorf's popular opera *Doktor und Apotheker* and Weigl's ballet *Alonzo und Cora* were the routine offerings that night; according to one source the emperor arrived late and the anthem was probably performed during the interval.

The printed version of the anthem consisted of Hashka's text plus a piano score of Haydn's music, a rather unsophisticated setting with no dynamics and with an unevenness of keyboard sonority. For the performance at the Burgtheater Haydn prepared an orchestral version that is much more refined: held notes in the horns emphasize the dominant pedal that precedes the crucial modulation to the dominant; one bassoon picks out a little counter-melody at the same point; trumpets and timpani are kept in reserve for the repetition of the climactic final couplet; and, most unexpectedly, each verse ends quietly, encouraging a feeling of reverence rather than out-and-out splendour.

In 1797 Haydn was busy working on a set of six quartets commissioned by COUNT JOSEPH ERDÖDY, subsequently published as op. 76. For the slow movement of the third quartet he took the theme of 'Gott erhalte Franz den Kaiser'—no title is given—and followed it with four variations. The initial statement of the theme reproduces the string parts of the orchestral version, with some added decoration in the first violin and one telling alteration in the viola line leading into bar 10. Arrangements of themes from operas and oratorios for quartet were a substantial part of the available repertoire, but Haydn's achievement in this quartet is to take this familiar practice, incorporate into one of his most challenging works for the medium, and envelope himself, Erdödy, the players, and any privileged listeners in a warm glow of patriotism. Subsequently Haydn prepared a piano version of this slow movement, adjusting some of the part-writing in order to make it playable on the keyboard.

Saurau's ambition to create a musical rallying point for Austrians had succeeded admirably and, though Hashka and Haydn were nominally equal partners in the enterprise, it was Haydn's contribution, inevitably, that held the continuing affection of the public. Public and private performances, by all kinds of forces, soon became commonplace while Czerny (1791–1857), Matiegka (1773–1830), and Sechter (1788–1867) were only three composers who wrote sets of variations on the melody. Already in 1797 an alternative text praising the emperor's brother, a military leader, was in circulation, 'Gott erhalte Karl den Helden' (God preserve Karl the hero) and this was soon joined by other texts, patriotic, homely, and religious. The anthem held a special significance for Haydn himself. His only musical solace in the last few months of his life was to play it through at the keyboard, including, appropriately, during the bombardment of Vienna by Napoleon's troops in May 1809.

Throughout the 19th century the Austrian government sought to determine the official form of the anthem, particularly the text, occasionally the musical arrangement too. Texts were prepared in all the languages of the empire, Italian, Hungarian, Czech, Slovene, Croatian, Romanian, and Polish. In 1827 the court composer Franz Krommer (1759–1831) was instructed to prepare an arrangement for use by the military bands of the imperial army; described as a march, it marked the transformation of Haydn's slow and dignified melody into something vigorous, potentially bombastic. Hashka's specific mention of 'Franz' in his original version meant that the text was going to have to be altered to accommodate any emperor with a name longer than one syllable. But the changes always went further and for each of the two new emperors in the 19th century—Ferdinand I (from 1836) and Franz Joseph I (from 1854)—entirely new texts were prepared, but always in four verses. Franz Joseph's reign until the First World War produced the most enduring of all the official texts associated with Haydn's melody. Written by Johann Gabriel Seidl (1804–75), it reflects some of the changes that had overtaken Austria in the previous half-century. Franz Joseph's name is not mentioned, but the dignity of his position is indissolubly linked with the welfare of his country, 'Gott erhalte, Gott beschütze, Unsern Kaiser, unser Land' (God preserve, God protect, Our Kaiser, our country), sentiments reinforced in the climactic final two lines, 'Innig bleibt mit Habsburgs Throne, Österreichs Geschick vereint' (Austria's destiny remains intimately bound up with the Habsburg throne).

Following the end of the First World War and the setting up of a republic, an entirely new Austrian anthem was commissioned but it failed to supplant the Haydn in the affection of the people and, in 1929, the old anthem was reinstated, with new words by Ottokar Kernstock (1848–1928), 'Sei gesegnet ohne Ende' (Be blessed beyond measure). Meanwhile the long-standing popularity of the melody in Germany, sung to the text DEUTSCHLAND, DEUTSCHLAND ÜBER ALLES', had led to its official adoption as the national anthem of that country. After the Second World War the Allied Commission refused permission for Haydn's melody to be used as the Austrian national anthem and, apart from performances of the 'Emperor' quartet, Austrian citizens have had to be content with its occasional use as a communion hymn, 'Tantum ergo'. Haydn's music still serves as the German national anthem. *See also* AUSTRIA.

O. Biba, *God Preserve. Joseph Haydn's Imperial Anthem. Facsimile of the First Edition, 1797* (Vienna, 1982).

F. Grasberger, *Die Hymnen Österreichs* (Tutzing, 1968).

HCRL/4.

Göttweig. Benedictine abbey near Krems, 80 km (50 miles) west of Vienna. In the 18th century it was one of the most musically active monasteries in the area, acquiring an extensive collection of Haydn's works. His music was regularly acquired from 1762 to beyond his death, in particular masses, symphonies, and quartets. Many of these copies are very early ones and are written on local paper; their source is unknown, but it has been speculated that the abbey had a direct connection with Haydn, perhaps through its offices in Vienna. The symphonies were often played during church services as well as at concerts held in the refectory and elsewhere in the abbey. The masses include the problematic *Missa 'Rorate coeli desuper'*.

In 1830 the musical director of the abbey, Father Heinrich Wondratsch (1793–1881), compiled a thematic catalogue of the holdings of the library, over 3,000 works. A fascinating and valuable indication of the richness of the musical life of the abbey, the 'Göttweig Catalogue' has proved particularly useful to Haydn scholars. Many of the manuscripts themselves no longer survive but the dates of acquisition given in the catalogue provide rare documentary evidence of the speed of dispersal of Haydn's music. More specifically, in the case of Symphonies nos. 3, 4, 5, 14, 15, 16, 39, Hob.I:107, and the *Missa brevis Sancti Johannis de Deo* the dates in the catalogue are the earliest known ones, unique evidence that has guided scholars to the likely date of composition.

Later in the 19th century Göttweig acquired a portion of ALOYS FUCHS's library, including copies of works prepared by Haydn's principal copyist JOHANN ELßLER.

F. W. Riedel (ed.), *Der Göttweiger Thematische Katalog von 1830*, 2 vols. (Munich, 1979).

Grassalkovics, Prince Anton (b. 24 Aug. 1733; d. 5 June 1794). Along with the ERDÖDY and ESTERHÁZY families, the Grassalkovics family was one of the leading magnates in the Hungarian kingdom in the second half of the 18th century. In

1758 Anton married the daughter of the future Prince Nicolaus Esterházy, Maria Anna, and, for a while, they lived in the Esterházy palace in Pressburg (Bratislava) before moving to their own palace. The two families remained in close contact and in 1772 Haydn directed dance music in the Grassalkovics palace. Anton maintained a small music retinue, which at one time included the horn player JOSEPH LEUTGEB, and in 1790, following the disbandonment of the Esterházy musicians, Haydn was offered the position of Kapellmeister. He declined in order to accept the invitation to travel to London. Two cellists from the Esterházy court, however, Anton and Nicolaus Kraft, did move to the Grassalkovics court.

'Great Organ Solo Mass'. *See* 'GROSSE ORGELSOLOMESSE'; MISSA IN HONOREM BVM.

Greiner, Franz Sales von (b. 1732; d. 1798). Austrian civil servant whose house in the Mehlgrube on the Neue Markt became a favoured venue for salons. Literary figures such as Johann Baptist Alxinger (1755–97), Aloys Blumauer (1755–98), HASCHKA, and Joseph von Sonnenfels (1733–1817) were joined by musicians, including Haydn and Mozart; many of Greiner's guests were also Freemasons. Haydn evidently knew Greiner as early as the winter of 1780–1 and sought his advice when choosing texts for two sets of songs (Hob. XXVIa:1–24). There is no detailed information on the composer's participation in the salons, though he almost certainly performed his songs there. Greiner's daughter, Caroline Pichler (1769–1843), became an author of plays, historical novels, and a fascinating set of memoirs about her life in Vienna. In 1795 she wrote a poem to greet Haydn on his return from London.

Griesinger, Georg August (b. 8 Jan. 1769; d. 9 April 1845). German diplomat and writer on music; his biography of Haydn, first published in 1809, the year of the composer's death, remains a fundamental source. Born in Stuttgart, Griesinger studied theology at the University of Tübingen. He first visited Vienna in 1791, when he attended the premiere of Mozart's *Die Zauberflöte*. The following eight years were spent in Germany and Switzerland as tutor to various sons of the aristocracy. He returned to Vienna in the spring of 1799 to become tutor to the 9-year-old son of Count Johann Hilmar Adolph von Schönfeld, the Saxon ambassador in Vienna. Soon Griesinger began to undertake diplomatic duties for the Saxon court and became a political journalist. His interest in music and his connections with northern Germany led him to function as the Viennese representative for the firm of BREITKOPF & HÄRTEL, ensuring that the music of Haydn and Beethoven, in particular, was published by them. For the journal *Allgemeine musikalische Zeitung*, issued by Breitkopf & Härtel in Leipzig, Griesinger provided regular reports on music-making in Vienna. He continued to advance in his diplomatic career, becoming secretary at the Saxon legation in 1804, later councillor; with the exception of one brief interlude in Berlin in 1814 Griesinger was to represent Saxony in Vienna for over 40 years. In 1823 he married the singer Maria von Lagusius.

On behalf of Breitkopf & Härtel, Griesinger first went to visit Haydn in May 1799; in a letter to Härtel, Griesinger described the composer as 'a cheerful, still well-preserved man and . . . a model of modesty and simplicity'. It was the beginning of a cordial and trusting relationship, one that allowed Breitkopf & Härtel to become Haydn's principal publisher in his old age and one that gave Griesinger privileged access to the composer. Unfortunately, Griesinger's voluminous correspondence with Breitkopf & Härtel was destroyed in the Second World War, but substantial extracts and summaries by POHL and Carl Maria Brand give a vivid picture of Haydn, his dealings with Breitkopf & Härtel, musical life in Vienna, and, not least, Griesinger's own personality; for there is no doubt that his training as a teacher and a diplomat nurtured a dependability and an even-handedness that were valued by composer and publisher alike. More publicly, through the columns of the journal *Allgemeine musikalische Zeitung*, Griesinger ensured that Vienna and Viennese composers assumed an important role in European musical life.

From the beginning the *Allgemeine musikalische Zeitung* had published short biographies and obituaries of composers. Griesinger made himself responsible for the extended biography of Haydn destined for the journal following his death and, it is assumed, carefully amassed material for a number of years, largely based on his conversations with the composer. He was in Störmthal, near Leipzig, when Haydn died in May 1809. Friends in Vienna, including JOHANN ELßLER, kept him informed of the composer's last days and of the funeral arrangements, and the biography appeared in the *Allgemeine musikalische Zeitung* in seven weekly parts between 12 July and 23 August, followed by a postscript on 6 September, an unprecedentedly large article in the journal. The following summer the assembled biography, plus some additions, was published as a book, printed in Leipzig by Breitkopf & Härtel.

In a short preface to the book Griesinger stated that his principal aim was 'to sketch Haydn as faithfully as possible as he lived and as he was, and he thus thought it necessary to resist every temptation to include controversy and artistic notions that people often like to hear themselves talk about'. This is an accurate summary of the virtues of Griesinger's biography. Though clearly a labour of love, it is measured in its tone and not many of the factual details have been found wanting by later scholarship. Within the framework of a biography Griesinger paints a picture of a modest composer, quietly rejoicing in the fame he had earned; it provided a good deal of information on Haydn's period of employment at the Esterházy court up to 1790 and on the London visits; there are also valuable observations on Haydn's method of composition. In 1819 it was printed for a second time. A Swedish translation appeared the same year.

O. Biba (ed.), *'Eben komme ich von Haydn . . .' Georg August Griesingers Korrespondenz mit Joseph Haydns Verleger Breitkopf & Härtel 1799–1819* (Zürich, 1987).

V. Gotwals, *Haydn. Two Contemporary Portraits* [An annotated translation of the biographies of Griesinger and Dies] (Madison, 1968).

E. Olleson, 'Georg August Griesinger's Correspondence with Breitkopf & Härtel', *HYB* 3 (1966), 5–53.

Grießler, Melchior (b. 1727; d. 13 Jan. 1792). Born in Nussdorf, outside Vienna, he entered the service of Prince Paul Anton in June 1761, the same year as Haydn. He worked as a singer in the church choir in Eisenstadt and as a violinist. Only once is he known to have sung in an opera, undertaking the very minor role of the Sultan in *L'incontro improvviso* in 1775. Two of his daughters also worked as singers in the church choir, Elisabeth and Josepha.

'Grosse Orgelsolomesse' ('Great Organ Solo Mass'). Nickname for the MISSA IN HONOREM BVM (Hob.XXII:4), reflecting the many solo passages for the organ and distinguishing it from the 'KLEINE ORGELSOLOMESSE' ('Little Organ Solo Mass') MISSA SANCTI JOHANNIS DE DEO. Occasionally, the work is misleadingly referred to as the 'Grosse Orgelmesse' (Great Organ Mass); strictly speaking the term organ mass refers to a work accompanied by an organ only.

Guéra. French music publisher in Lyons, founded in *c.*1776 and who remained in business until 1788. His editions of Haydn's music were known to the composer since they were available in Vienna through ARTARIA. He published symphonies nos. 44, 55, 56, 57, 60, 66, 80, and 81, as well as some spurious ones, and received a royal privilege in November 1782 to print the op. 33 quartets. The textual value of Guéra's editions of Haydn's music is negligible. APB

A. P. Brown with R. Griscom, *The French Music Publisher Guéra of Lyon: A Dated List* (Detroit, 1987).

'Gypsy' rondo. Nickname for the third movement of the piano trio in G (Hob.XV:25). The first edition of the work, issued under Haydn's supervision in London in 1795, gives the following heading for the movement, 'Finale, Rondo in the Gypsies' stile'. JH

Gyrowetz, Adalbert (b. 19/20 Feb. 1763; d. 19 March 1850). A prolific and long-lived composer who knew Haydn in London, and whose autobiography contains useful information about musical life during the years of Haydn's greatest fame. As a young man Gyrowetz composed many symphonies and a vast array of chamber music: string quartets, piano sonatas and trios, flute quartets, and other works. Some of this music, published in the major centres of music printing, briefly rivalled Haydn's in popularity. Even Haydn's patron, Prince Nicolaus Esterházy, 'derived great pleasure' (according to the autobiography) from a set of symphonies that Gyrowetz wrote during the early 1780s.

Gyrowetz spent the second half of the 1780s and the early 1790s on an extended tour of Europe. In Paris in 1789 he was surprised to hear one of his symphonies (Rice G1) being performed under Haydn's name. He was already in London when Haydn arrived; in his autobiography he claimed for himself an important role in introducing Haydn to London society. The music of Gyrowetz and Haydn often appeared on the same programmes during the following months, and they seemed to have enjoyed cordial relations. Gyrowetz visited Haydn as the latter was writing the 'Surprise' symphony (no. 94), and included in his autobiography a brief account of that visit and of the subsequent first performance.

Gyrowetz learnt much from Haydn's late symphonies, and his adaptation of Haydnesque ideas and techniques earned him an occasional rebuke. In an article on Haydn, the lexicographer GERBER took Gyrowetz to task for imitating Haydn's Symphony no. 86 in a symphony in D major (Rice D7).

Gyrowetz settled in Vienna, where he continued to compose music for publication. In 1804, as the appeal of his instrumental music faded, he joined the staff of the Viennese court theatres. During the next two decades he devoted himself to the composition and performance of ballets and German opera, among the most popular of which were *Agnes Sorel* (124 performances between 1806 and 1816) and *Der Augenarzt* (96 performances between 1811 and 1817). JAR

A. Gyrowetz, *Biographie* (Vienna, 1848); ed. A. Einstein (Leipzig, 1913).

A. Gyrowetz, *Four symphonies*, ed. J. A. Rice in *The Symphony 1720–1840*, Series B, vol. 11 (New York, 1983).

W. E. Hettrick, 'The Autobiography of Adalbert Gyrowetz (1763–1850)', *Studien zur Musikwissenschaft*, 40 (1991), 41–74.

Gyrowetz, Adalbert

HCRL/2 and 3.

J. A. Rice, 'Adalbert Gyrowetz 1763–1850' [thematic catalogue of the symphonies], in *The Symphony 1720–1840*, reference volume (New York, 1986), 284–90.

H

Hadden, James Cuthbert (b. 9 Sept. 1861; d. 2 May 1914). Scottish organist and writer on music. His biography of Haydn published by Dent in the 'Master Musicians' series in 1902 remained the standard life and works of the composer in the English language for 50 years. Drawing heavily on the published work of POHL (and, later, BOTSTIBER) it provided an accurate account of the composer's life and his music, avoiding the sentimentality and fancy of much English writing on the composer at the time. Less widely read, but more original, was his study of GEORGE THOMSON, the Scotsman who had commissioned folksong settings from Beethoven, Haydn, and others.

Hadow, Sir William Henry (b. 27 Dec. 1859; d. 8 April 1937). English scholar, education administrator (he was vice-chancellor of Sheffield University from 1919), and writer on music. Born in Malvern he studied humanities at Worcester College, Oxford, from 1878 to 1882, before seeking a musical education in Darmstadt. He became a tutor in classics at his old college in 1888 but soon became more interested in music education. In 1896 he was appointed editor of *The Oxford History of Music* and subsequently wrote the influential volume, *The Viennese Period* (1904). A more contentious contribution was his well-presented summary of the views of Franjo (František) Š. Kuhač, that Haydn was an ethnic Croat and that his music was heavily influenced by Croatian folk music. Hadow provided some additions to Pohl's article on Haydn in the second and third editions of the *Grove Dictionary of Music*. *See also* FOLK MUSIC.

W. H. Hadow, *A Croatian Composer: Notes toward the Study of Joseph Haydn* (London, 1897).

Hamilton, Emma (b. ?26 April 1765, bap. 12 May 1765; d. 15 Jan. 1815). English actress and admirer of Haydn. Together with her husband, Sir William Hamilton, she visited Eisenstadt from 6 to 9 September 1800 as part of Admiral Nelson's party. In a clear, strong voice she sang to enthusiastic response the cantata *Arianna a Naxos* and a new work, *The Battle of the Nile* (Hob.XXVIb:4), with the composer accompanying. Haydn presented her with manuscript copies (in Johann Elßler's hand) of two songs, one of which was 'The Spirit Song'. DdV

HCRL/4.

O. E. Deutsch, *Admiral Nelson und Joseph Haydn. Ein britisch-österreichisches Gipfeltreffen* (Vienna, 1982).

Handel and Haydn Society. A musical organization in Boston founded in 1815; devoted to the performance of oratorio, it is the oldest of its kind in the USA. In 1818 it presented the first performance of Haydn's *Creation* in America. In recent years the society has departed from its venerable tradition of presenting large-scale choral works, sponsoring a wider spectrum of music, including opera.

Handel, George Frideric (b. 23 Feb. 1685; d. 14 April 1759). German-born composer who, after a sojourn in Italy (1706–10), moved to London in 1711 and over the next 40 years became the leading figure in musical life in the city, especially in opera and, later, oratorio. After his death the popularity of his oratorios and certain of his instrumental works remained and he became a cult figure in English musical taste, seen by many commentators as embodying artistic perfection in contrast to the decline that was apparent in the music of newer composers. As such, Handel and Haydn were often set up as incompatible opposites and only a few commentators, notably CHARLES BURNEY, saw the merits of both. The irony of Handel's posthumous reputation in London was that it was based on an increasingly distorted view of the composer. Performances of his oratorios (or movements from them) and other vocal works were often given by forces much larger than the composer had envisaged, as if his esteem could be measured by the number of people who took part.

In Austria, up to the 1780s, Haydn would have been only dimly aware of Handel's music and it played no part in the formation of his style. As a result of GOTTFRIED VAN SWIETEN's enthusiasm for older music and the performances promoted by the GESELLSCHAFT DER ASSOCIIERTEN Haydn became acquainted in the 1780s and 1790s with several major works by Handel, translated into German and newly orchestrated by local composers (including Mozart): *Judas Maccabaeus*, *Acis and Galatea*, *Alexander's Feast*, *Messiah*, *Ode to St Cecilia*, and *The Choice of Hercules*. But it was during his two visits to London in the 1790s that Handel's music made the most sustained impact on the composer. In June 1791, he attended the Handel Commemoration concerts in Westminster Abbey where forces of over 1,000 gave performances of 'Zadok the Priest', and extracts from *Israel in Egypt, Esther, Judas Maccabaeus, Deborah*, and *Messiah*. Over the next four years Haydn heard many more works by the composer. He was intrigued by the veneration accorded to Handel, from the royal family down to visitors to Vauxhall Gardens who came to look at the statue of the composer. As a token of her estimation of both composers, Queen Charlotte presented Haydn with a manuscript copy of Handel's *Brockes Passion*.

There is no doubt that the experience of hearing performances of Handel's music in London was a major stimulus in the composition of *The Creation* and *The Seasons*, both of which were given public performances in Vienna by forces that numbered 200 or 300, not as extravagant as the Handel tradition in London, but larger than was customary in the city. But beyond this broad stimulus Handel's influence on Haydn's musical style in these oratorios has often been exaggerated. Because of the English pedigree of the texts of Haydn's two oratorios, commentators have tried to see musical influences where none exists. Like Handel, Haydn was an enthusiastic tone painter in his oratorios, and depictions of darkness, animals, and the weather are found in the works of both composers. Haydn's own comment to Griesinger provides a clue to the particular nature of the influence: 'Handel was great in choruses but mediocre in song [i.e. aria].' Handel's many da capo arias in one mood (*Affekt*) and accompanied by strings alone would have struck Haydn as decidedly old-fashioned, and there are no examples of such writing in the late oratorios. On the other hand, the stylistic range of Handel's choral writing, its energy and its ability to evoke the sublime (particularly as performed by large-scale forces) were new to him. The importation of the Handelian sublime into Haydn's musical style is a major development in the music of the last period of the composer's life, evident not only in several choruses in the two late oratorios, but in the second Te Deum and portions of the six late masses.

J. P. Larsen, 'Händel und Haydn', *Händel-Jahrbuch*, 28 (1982), 93–9.

H. Serwer, 'The Coopersmith copy of Handel's *Brockes Passion*. A Haydn connection', *Händel-Jahrbuch*, 38 (1992), 99–107.

Hárich, János (b. 1904; d. 21 July 1990). The last archivist to serve the Esterházy family. Born in Veszprém, as a boy he learnt a variety of musical instruments before studying history at the university in Budapest. In 1928 he became an assistant in the Esterházy archives in Budapest and from 1930 until 1946 was its director. It was during this period that he undertook a reorganization of the family documents into two parts, the Acta Musicalia and the Acta Theatralica. During the early years of the communist era, he was imprisoned for a while, worked in an electricity generating station, and then as a private music teacher. In 1958 Hárich moved to Austria where he resumed his position as director of the Esterházy archives. His detailed and extensive knowledge of their content was unrivalled and he began to publish summaries of his findings in the *Haydn Yearbook* and elsewhere. Modern knowledge of the lives of the instrumentalists and singers employed at the Esterházy court is especially indebted to Hárich's work. Following his death his library was bequeathed to the Gesellschaft der Musikfreunde in Vienna.

O. Biba, 'János Hárich (1904–1990)', *HYB* 18 (1993), 111–14.

Har(r)ington, Henry (b. 29 Sept. 1727; d. 15 Jan. 1816). Physician and amateur composer, especially of glees, resident in Bath. A popular figure in Bath society, he was active in the musical and civic life of the city from his arrival there in 1771, eventually becoming mayor. During Haydn's visit in 1794 he presented him with a new glee that he had composed, 'What art expresses'; Haydn used Harington's glee as the basis for his own composition, called DR HARINGTON'S COMPLIMENT. Along with Haydn and others, Harington was a contributor to the Revd Tattersall's *Improved Psalmody*. DdV

'Harmoniemesse' (Hob.XXII:14). Mass in B♭ composed in 1802. Its nickname did not become current until late in the 19th century and reflects the instrumental forces required, a full wind section as well as strings, the largest orchestra in any mass by Haydn. At the beginning of the 19th century it was still comparatively unusual for a mass to be accompanied by a full wind section and the nickname is more a reflection of this (i.e. the 'mass with the windband') than of the occasional solo passages for wind instruments that occur.

Haydn began composing the mass in April 1802 in Vienna, telling one correspondent that he was 'labouring wearily'. Early in August he moved to Eisenstadt and completed the work in readiness for its performance on Wednesday, 8 September. That date was the Nativity of Mary and marked the celebration of the nameday of PRINCESS MARIE HERMENEGILD ESTERHÁZY. Thanks to the diary of Count Louis Starhemberg (1762–1833), the Austrian ambassador to Britain, an unusually complete picture of the 1802 celebrations is available. He and other invited guests arrived on Tuesday evening, were taken by coaches to the Bergkirche on Wednesday morning for the mass service; Starhemberg noted that Haydn directed the musical forces. After returning to the palace the princess received the congratulations of the assembled company before a lavish dinner was served; background music was provided, probably by the court *Harmonie*; a toast was proposed to the princess, accompanied by trumpet fanfares; further toasts were offered, including one to Prince Starhemberg and one to Haydn. After dinner there was a large ball, consisting mainly of waltzes. Following a break for a supper with 'innumerable' courses, the ball resumed and did not finish until two in the morning. On Thursday the guests were woken by the sound of French horns, summoning them to a hunt. In the afternoon there was a concert directed by Haydn, including movements from the 'Harmoniemesse'. After supper Starhemberg left for Vienna.

The unusually sonorous orchestration of the mass as a whole is coupled in the Kyrie with a slow tempo (Poco Adagio) to produce the grandest setting of the text in Haydn's output, eschewing the tunefulness and the energetic rhythms often found in other masses. Like *the Missa Sancti Bernardi d'Offida* it finds a particular poignancy through the use of an intrusive G♭ in the opening bars. The substantial orchestral introduction leads to a choral entry not at the beginning of a musical phrase but, like some of Haydn's songs, at the end of one. Also unusual is the casual introduction of the text 'Christe eleison', which is not set up as a major contrasting paragraph.

The Gloria is divided into the traditional three stages: an opening fast section (Vivace assai) which, after the opening solo soprano line, is sung by the chorus; a slower section (Allegretto), beginning with the text 'Gratias agimus tibi', that is initially led by the soloists but with some subtle orchestral colouring from the flute and clarinet; and a return to a fast tempo at 'Quoniam tu solus sanctus'. The double fugue associated with 'in gloria Dei Patris' and 'Amen' is notable for its chromatic thematic lines; as the counterpoint dissolves so the harmonic vocabulary becomes more diatonic.

The Credo too has the customary three stages: Vivace, followed by a change of tempo to Adagio at 'Et incarnatus est', and a return to Vivace at 'Et resurrexit'. The central portion in E♭ has extended vocal lines over an accompaniment of triplets, moving effortlessly to the dominant before turning to G♭ major; this mass like its five companions and many numbers in *The Creation* and *The Seasons* finds a good deal of expressive impact in modulations to keys that are a third away from the tonic. Like the equivalent section of the 'Theresienmesse', the Credo ends with a fugue in a brisk 6/8 tempo.

In the Sanctus not only do the exhortations of the chorus become successively louder but the associated harmonies also become more chromatic. More eccentric is the accentuated off-beat beginning to the 'Osanna', likened by one commentator to a hiccup.

Undoubtedly the most unexpected movement is the Benedictus. Rather than the expansive, lyrical movement for soloists that tradition demanded, it is a brisk Molto allegro for chorus, featuring a melody that is sung and played in *pianissimo* octaves over a restless accompaniment; Haydn seems to be evoking the quiet excitement rather than the comfort of a life in Christ. The hiccuping 'Osanna' returns to complete the movement.

Most of the mass is set in the home key of B♭. For the beginning of the Agnus Dei Haydn turns magically to G major, emphasized by extended writing for the soloists and members of the *Harmonie*, creating an optimistic mood that is subtly tempered by chromatic harmony and, later, by a single ominous timpani roll. The modulation pattern too is highly individual: from G to C, to A♭, and, finally, to the dominant of G minor. A brisk fanfare heralds the 'Dona nobis pacem' in the home key of B♭, a section of increasing assurance but with some excitable mirth from the *Harmonie* (especially the bassoon) along the way.

In the months immediately following the first performance of the 'Harmoniemesse' Haydn repeatedly complained of a lack of energy and an inability to concentrate. The mass was destined to be his last major work.

G. Heilingsetzer, ' "Der wahre Sitz eines Souverains." Ein Besuch in der Esterházy-Residenz Eisenstadt (1802)', in *Die Fürsten Esterházy. Magnaten, Diplomaten & Mäzene* [Exhibition catalogue] (Eisenstadt, 1995), 190–8.
HCRL/5.

harpsichord. A stringed keyboard instrument with a plucked quill action, as distinct from the hammered action of the FORTEPIANO or the tangent action of the clavichord. In sources connected with Haydn harpsichords are referred to as *Flügel*, *Cembalo*, *Clavicembalo*, *Clavecin*, *Spinet*, *Clavier*, or simply *Instrument*. *Flügel* refers specifically to a wing-shaped instrument, and spinet to a smaller domestic instrument: other terms, particularly *Clavier*, were commonly used generically to refer to keyboard instruments. For much of the 18th century the harpsichord was the principal keyboard instrument for secular use, domestically, in the theatre and at court, and both as a continuo and a solo instrument. Notwithstanding the early appearances of fortepianos in public concerts (1752 in London; 1763 in Vienna; and 1768 in Paris) and the increasing availability of various types of fortepiano in the 1770s and 1780s, the harpsichord remained in general use. As late as April 1787 a concerto was performed on the harpsichord at the Concert spirituel in Paris, MARIA ANNA VON GENZINGER still owned a *Flügel* in 1790 (when Haydn advised her to purchase a Schanz fortepiano), and according to newspaper accounts from 1791 Haydn directed concerts from the harpsichord during his first London visit.

In the 18th century the harpsichord existed in a variety of dispositions and shapes. It is assumed that in Austria the normal 18th-century harpsichord was, like Italian harpsichords, a single-manual instrument with two eight-foot stops, simpler instruments than in the French or German traditions. However, little is known about 18th-century Austrian harpsichord makers and few instruments have survived. Certainly, more elaborate instruments were known in Vienna and used by Austrian performers. The Mozart family owned a two-manual harpsichord by Friederici of Gera and two extant Stein instruments combine a fortepiano and a two-manual harpsichord (one of which has a 16′ course of strings in addition to the standard two-manual disposition of 2 × 8′, 1 × 4′). The large English instruments of Shudi were also known in Vienna, notably the one sent to the Empress Maria Theresia in 1773 (Shudi no. 691). Another elaborate Shudi instrument (Shudi no. 762), with a five-and-a-half-octave range, a machine stop, and Venetian swell, now in the Kunsthistorisches Museum, Vienna, has been anecdotally connected with Haydn, but there is no documentation to support the claim that Schudi sent this instrument to Haydn from London.

Numerous receipts document the repair of harpsichords at Esterházy establishments throughout the 1760s and 1770s, but no harpsichord connected with Eisenstadt or Eszterháza has survived. Musical evidence in three works (Hob. XVII:1, 2, and XVI:47) suggests that in 1765 Haydn may have used a harpsichord with short-octave tuning. A number of passages in the keyboard sonatas of the 1770s suggest that Haydn calculated the effect of writing for right and left hand on two manuals within a restricted register and these works may have been conceived with a double-manual instrument in mind. BH

D. H. Boalch, *Makers of the Harpsichord and Clavichord 1440–1840*, 3rd edn, ed. C. Mould (Oxford, 1995).

F. Hubbard, *Three Centuries of Harpsichord Making* (Cambridge, Mass., 1965).

R. Maunder, *Keyboard Instruments in Eighteenth-Century Vienna* (Oxford, 1998).

H. Walter, 'Haydns Klaviere', *HS* 25/4 (1970), 256–88.

H. Walter, 'Das Tasteninstrument beim jungen Haydn', in V. Schwarz (ed.), *Der junge Haydn: Bericht der internationalen Arbeitstagung des Instituts für Aufführungspraxis*, I (Graz, 1972), 237–48.

Harrach family. The local ruling family in Rohrau, Haydn's birthplace. Established in the area since the 17th century, the Harrach family were proud of the fame achieved by the composer. Count Carl Anton Harrach (1699–1758) was the ruler in Haydn's youth; at one time the composer's mother was a cook in the palace. The count supported the limited musical activities of the area and in 1757 or 1758 a Prussian military officer captured in the Seven Years War witnessed performances of some cassations by Haydn in the palace. Since the autograph of the divertimento for wind (Hob.II:15) was owned by the Harrach family, it may have been commissioned by Count Franz Anton Harrach (1720–68), who had recently succeeded his father to the title.

In turn, he was succeeded by his son Count Karl Leonhard Harrach (1765–1831) who, because of his age, did not assume the title until 1786. He soon embarked on redesigning the palace gardens. As part of this scheme an obelisk-shaped monument to Haydn was erected in 1793. In the autumn of 1795, following his return from his second London visit, Haydn went to see the monument; it was probably then that he was given a small replica which he kept in his house in Gumpendorf. Harrach was a member of the GESELLSCHAFT DER ASSOCIIERTEN CAVALIERS and remained in friendly contact with the composer. The two evidently discussed how the monument could be maintained for posterity: the count set up a trust fund and the composer bequeathed a sum of money in his will. Haydn also left a commemorative medal from Paris and a bust of the composer to the count. The monument is now located outside Haydn's birthplace in Rohrau.

O. Biba, 'Nachrichten zur Musikpflege in der gräflichen Familie Harrach', *HYB* 10 (1978), 36–55.

HCRL/3.

Haschka, Lorenz Leopold (b. 1 Sept. 1749; d. 3 Aug. 1827). Austrian poet, the author of 'GOTT ERHALTE FRANZ DEN KAISER'. His career was marked by opportunism and several changes of direction. As a young man he was a member of the Jesuit Order, but in the liberal climate of the 1780s left it, became a Freemason, and wrote verses attacking the pope, the Church, spirituality, and, most ironically, sovereignty. With the accession of Leopold II in 1790 Haschka changed tack and even became a police spy. Now a firm member of the political establishment in Vienna he was appointed custodian of the university library and, from 1798, professor of aesthetics at the Theresianum, positions he held until his death. Most of his poetry consisted of odes. It was in the autumn of 1796 that he was commissioned to write the text of a patriotic song that would match the popularity of 'God save the King'. While Haydn must have met Haschka, perhaps as early as the 1780s, they were never close acquaintances.

Hasse, Johann Adolf (bap. 25 March 1699; d. 16 Dec. 1783). A distinguished composer, born in Bergerdorf near Hamburg, whose praise for

Haydn's early sacred music was greatly valued and long remembered by the younger musician.

Although Hasse wrote works in a wide variety of genres, he was most important as a composer of *opera seria*. In Naples during the 1720s he absorbed the stylistic conventions and theatrical flair of young Neapolitan composers such as Leonardo Vinci; and, although he was known as 'Il Sassone' ('the Saxon'), his own early Italian scores show that he subscribed completely to their artistic values.

In 1730 Hasse went to Dresden, initiating a period of four decades in which he rarely stayed in one place more than a few years. Between sojourns in Dresden he made long visits to Vienna, Venice, and Naples. In Vienna in 1733–4 he gave music lessons to the young MARIA THERESIA, who later expressed affection for him and admiration for his operas. In 1743 he began a close collaboration with METASTASIO, most of whose later librettos he set to music for the first time. During the 1760s Hasse contributed greatly to Viennese operatic life with serious operas, *feste teatrali*, and an *intermezzo tragico*, *Piramo e Tisbe*, that is considered to be among his best works. He died in Venice.

By the time Haydn began his career Hasse's music was increasingly viewed as old-fashioned; but that could not keep his praise from strengthening the young composer's reputation. In 1767 Haydn sent his recently composed Stabat mater to Hasse, who, Haydn later boasted, 'honoured the work with inexpressible praise, and wished to hear it performed'. He recalled the compliment proudly in the autobiographical sketch of 1776: 'I shall treasure this testimonial all my life, as if it were gold.' Its precise content is not known and it did not survive Haydn's death.

A performance of a mass by Haydn (perhaps the first *Missa Cellensis*) elicited more praise from Hasse, according to an anecdote related by J. A. Streicher to MARY and VINCENT NOVELLO in 1829. Hasse is supposed to have declared to Empress Maria Theresia 'that Haydn possessed all the qualities that are required for the highest style of writing, viz. beautiful and expressive melody, sound harmony, original invention, variety of affect, symmetrical design, knowledge of the powers of different instruments, correct counterpoint, scientific modulation and refined taste'. Hasse also predicted that Haydn would become 'one of the greatest composers of the age'. JAR

G. Feder, 'Haydn und Hasse', *Analecta Musicologica*, 25 (1987), 305–27.

D. Heartz, *Haydn, Mozart and the Viennese School, 1740–1780* (New York, 1995).

HCRL/2.

F. L. Millner, *The Operas of Johann Adolf Hasse* (Ann Arbor, 1979).

Haugwitz, Count Friedrich Wilhelm (b. 11 Dec. 1702; d. 11 Sept. 1765). An important government official and adviser to Empress Maria Theresia; in the 1750s he had responsibility for finances in Bohemia and the hereditary German territories. At the time he lived in the Bohemian Court Exchequer in Wipplingerstraße. In 1756 the empress endowed a private chapel in the building for the use of its inhabitants, the Theresienkapelle. According to GRIESINGER Haydn regularly played the organ in its services, his second duty every Sunday after playing the violin in the church of the Barmherzige Brüder and before going on to sing in St Stephen's. Haugwitz also had his own palace in the Viennese suburbs to which in 1758 this evidently devout man added a private chapel, the St Anna Kapelle. Haydn may have played there too.

O. Biba, 'Haydns Kirchenmusikdienste für Graf Haugwitz', *HS* 6/4 (1994), 278–87.

R. Steblin, 'Haydns Orgeldienst "in der damaligen Gräfl. Haugwitzischen Kapelle"', *Wiener Geschichtsblätter*, 55/2 (2000), 124–34.

Hayda, Joseph (b. 1740; d. March 1806). Viennese organist and composer, sometimes spelt 'Heyda'. After holding a series of posts in various churches, Hayda became organist at the Michaelerkirche in 1793, working there until his death. He was regarded as one of the best organists in the city, especially renowned for his improvisations. He felt deeply honoured that only one letter differentiated his name from that of the Haydn brothers and he was not alone in regarding MICHAEL HAYDN as the better composer of church music. Inevitably, several of his sacred works were wrongly ascribed to Joseph Haydn. One of these, a Litany in C (Hob.XXIIIc:C2), was published as the work of Haydn in 1960 (Vienna, Doblinger).

G. Thomas, 'Haydns Deutsche Singspiele', *HS* 6/1 (1986), 1–63.

Haydn family. Joseph Haydn's ancestors have been systematically traced back four generations. All lived in the area where the composer was born, all were German-speaking, and were employed as artisans, occasionally serving also as local magistrates.

Grandparents. Thomas Haydn (b. after 1657; d. 4 Sept. 1701) was a wheelwright in Hainburg who in 1687 married Catharina Blaiminger (b. 1671; d. 17 May 1739). The sixth child of this marriage was Mathias Haydn, the composer's father. Following the death of her first husband, Catharina remarried; her fourth child, Juliane Rosina (bap. 15 Feb. 1711), married Johann Mathias Franck, a schoolteacher and choir master in Hainburg; he was to be Joseph Haydn's first teacher.

Lorenz Koller (b. 1675; d. May 1718) was a village magistrate in Rohrau whose second wife was Susanna Siebel (b. 1685; d. 19 Aug. 1756). Their second child was Anna Maria Koller, Haydn's mother. When the grandmother died she left a modest bequest to the composer and his siblings.

Parents. Mathias Haydn (bap. 31 Jan. 1699; d. 12 Sept. 1763). Haydn's father was a wheelwright and magistrate in Rohrau. A self-taught musician who played the harp and sang, he married Anna Maria Koller (bap. 10 Nov. 1707; d. 23 Feb. 1754), a cook at Rohrau castle. His second marriage, to Maria Anna Seeder, took place in 1755. Mathias was killed by a wood fall. Between the two marriages he fathered 17 children of whom six survived infancy.

Haydn's brothers and sisters. The five siblings who survived infancy were Anna Maria Franziska Haydn (bap. 19 Sept. 1730; d. 29 July 1781); JOHANN MICHAEL HAYDN; Anna Maria Haydn (bap. 6 March 1739; d. 27 Aug. 1802); Anna Katharina (bap. 6 Jan. 1741: d. ?before 1801); and JOHANN EVANGELIST HAYDN .

Haydn's first will, drawn up in 1801, leaves substantial sums of money to his surviving brothers and sisters, all of whom, in the event, were to predecease him. In his final will, drawn up in February 1809 several nieces are mentioned. Some are named, suggesting that he remained in regular contact with them; others are unnamed. The nieces mentioned in Haydn's will are: four daughters of Anna Maria, Anna Maria Moser, Elisabeth Böhm, Theresia Hammer, and Anna Loder (the daughter of the last mentioned, Ernestine Loder, was living in the composer's house in Gumpendorf at the time and she, too, was given a bequest); and two unnamed daughters of Anna Katharina.

HCRL 1 and 5.

E. Schmid, *Joseph Haydn. Ein Buch von Vorfahren und Heimat des Meisters*, 2 vols (Kassel, 1934).

Haydn festivals. Unlike Mozart, Haydn has not become the focus of a major international music festival and only in the last 20 or so years has any festival devoted to the music of the composer become firmly established.

In March 1984 the city of Vienna in conjunction with the Gesellschaft der Musikfreunde inaugurated an annual festival devoted to Haydn, the Haydn-Tage (Haydn Days). While performances in the Musikverein by major international artists feature occasionally, the particular appeal of the festival has been the concerts by local musicians (amateur as well as professional) in venues associated with the composer, such as the church of the BARMHERZIGE BRÜDER and the Piaristenkirche. Public lectures and exhibitions, drawing on the holdings of the Gesellschaft der Musikfreunde, also feature. Address: Haydn-Tage, Gesellschaft der Musikfreunde, Karlsplatz 6, Vienna, A-1010 Austria.

From 1989 onwards the town of Eisenstadt has mounted regular concerts devoted to Haydn, in the 'Haydnsaal' of the palace, the Bergkirche, and elsewhere. Between April and October a series of concerts is held in these venues and September presents a concentration of concerts, including chamber, sacred, orchestral, and operatic works. Benefiting from the increasing popularity of Eisenstadt as a tourist destination, the September festival in particular is likely to develop into a major international musical attraction. Address: Burgenländische Haydnfestspiele, Haydn Zentrum, Haydngasse 19–21, Eisenstadt, A-7000 Austria (www.haydnfestival.at).

In England an annual festival devoted to the music of Haydn has been held in June in Bridgnorth (Shropshire) since 1983. Concerts of chamber music and orchestral music are held in churches and in local historic houses. Tel: English Haydn Festival, +44 (0)1952 825235. ERL

Haydn, Franz Joseph. See opposite.

Haydn, Johann Evangelist (bap. 23 Dec. 1743; d. 10 May 1805). Joseph Haydn's youngest brother, who was employed as a tenor at the Esterházy court. As a youth Joseph Haydn would hardly have known his brother since he was already in Vienna when Johann was born. When Johann, in turn, became a choirboy at St Stephen's Joseph may have already left, and Joseph was already in the service of the Morzin family when Johann finished as a treble in St Stephen's. It is not known whether Johann pursued a career as a church singer in Vienna or whether he returned to the family home in Rohrau. In the father's will, dated 1763, Johann is granted a sum of money in advance of the formal division of the estate, which suggests that unlike his brothers, Joseph and Michael, he was not financially independent. Two years later this was evidently still the case because Joseph Haydn secured for him a post at the Esterházy court as an unpaid tenor in the small retinue of musicians responsible for church music in Eisenstadt. From 1771 he was on the payroll. He seems never to have sung in opera performances at Eszterháza but did some teaching and may have acted as an emergency copyist. Following the disbandment of the court in 1790 nothing is known about Johann's existence until the musical retinue was re-established in 1795. As a choral tenor Johann would have sung in performances of the six late masses. He never married.

Haydn, Johann Michael (bap. 14 Sept. 1737; d. 19 Aug. 1806). Haydn's brother and a gifted composer in his own right. His early career mirrored that of Joseph Haydn in its general progress. Born in Rohrau, at the age of 8 he joined Joseph as a choirboy in St Stephen's Vienna; on at least one

[*cont. on p.148*]

Haydn, Franz Joseph

(b. 31 March 1732; d. 31 May 1809). In Haydn's lifetime there was some confusion about his date of birth. He was baptized on 1 April and many sources indicate that he was born that day; Haydn himself, however, was adamant that it was the previous day. As was the custom in a deeply Catholic society the baby was given the name of two saints with proximate feast days: Franz (Francis of Paola; 2 April) and Joseph (husband of the Virgin Mary; 19 March). Haydn hardly ever used his first Christian name and was usually known as Joseph, though in childhood he was often called by the common Austrian diminutive of Sepperl. In his adult life he almost invariably signed autograph manuscripts of his music using the Italian form, Giuseppe Haydn, also in letters that he wrote in that language; presumably Italian acquaintances too, such as the many singers at Eszterháza, would have called him Giuseppe. Formal documents sometimes use the Latin form Josephus. From middle age onwards Haydn was affectionately called 'Papa' by many of his younger friends and colleagues.

---

1. Biographical sketch.

1732–61: youth, Vienna, and the Morzin court. Haydn was born in Rohrau on the west bank of the river Leitha that separated the Austrian monarchy from the kingdom of Hungary. It was a predominantly German-speaking area but with an ethnic admixture of Croats, Hungarians, and Slovaks too. The local magnate was COUNT HARRACH whose family had an imposing palace a few minutes' walk away from the house in which the Haydn family lived. Both sides of the family were long established in the area as artisans and craftsmen. Haydn's father, Mathias Haydn, was a wheelwright who liked to accompany himself singing on the harp. Haydn often reminisced about family evenings spent singing and, in particular, his father's impatience when the two most musical children, Joseph and Michael, would question his rough and ready musicianship. Joseph sang as a treble in the local church and may have begun to learn, if only in a casual way, the harpsichord and the violin. A distant cousin named Johann Mathias Franck, who lived in Hainburg, a small fortress town on the Danube 10 km (six miles) to the north, was a schoolteacher and gave the boy accommodation so that he could attend the school in the town. There, from 1737 or 1738 onwards, Haydn received a basic education, supplemented by a more specialized one at the church where Franck was in charge of the music. After two years Haydn came to the attention of REUTTER, Kapellmeister of St Stephen's, Vienna, who was in the neighbourhood looking for new voices for the cathedral. Following an audition, at which Haydn was bribed by a handful of cherries to sing a trill, it was agreed that the young boy should move to Vienna.

From the age of 7 or 8 until his voice broke at the age of 17 Haydn lived literally in the shadow of St Stephen's, the adjacent Kapellhaus that housed the choirboys (demolished in 1804). His life was governed by the rhythms of the church calendar with its associated music, from Christmas through Lent, Easter, Ascension, and on to Advent once more. Religious observance was closely tied to the ceremonial of the Habsburg court, in private and in public. Haydn was immersed in the music of the principal composers of church music in Vienna, Reutter, Reutter's father (also Georg, 1656–1738), Bonno (1711–88), Caldara (*c.*1670–1736), and FUX; the repertoire also included much older music, by Palestrina (1525/6–1594), Allegri (1582–1652), particularly the famous Miserere, and Alessandro Scarlatti (1660–1725). In the early 1740s musical life at the imperial court in Vienna and at St Stephen's was still one of the most lavishly supported in Europe, though towards the end of the decade an irreversible decline in resources and associated standards was in progress. Reutter was a major administrative figure as well as a musical presence in Vienna, to the extent that he neglected his duties as a teacher of the choirboys. Haydn recalled receiving only two lessons in theory and some dismissive comments when he showed him a juvenile exercise in composition. As well as singing he continued to make progress as a harpsichord player, a violinist, and, possibly, organist too. In his mid-teens he had become one of the choir's regular treble soloists and it was proposed that he should be operated on so that he might have a career as a castrato singer; only a hastily arranged visit by Mathias Haydn prevented the operation from going ahead. Haydn's voice began to break and the new leading treble was his brother Michael. When, finally, in 1749 (possibly earlier) the voice gave way completely Haydn left the choir school. GRIESINGER used the word 'dismissed' as if it was an unprecedented act of cruelty. At the time Haydn (and others) would have regarded it as wholly expected and the fact that he did not go back to his family in Rohrau suggests that he was reasonably confident of his future in Vienna.

The first couple of years were difficult but gradually Haydn established a network of contacts in the city and beyond that provided him with a stable income from playing, singing, teaching, and composition. He moved into a garret room in the Michaelerhaus behind the imperial palace. On the ground floor lived the court poet METASTASIO who was acting as a tutor to MARIANNA VON MARTINES, and Haydn was soon engaged to give her lessons in singing and harpsichord-playing. Through Metastasio, Haydn met one of the leading opera composers of the day, PORPORA, who engaged him to accompany his pupils in singing lessons. Haydn was to credit Porpora with making him a technically assured composer, one who in particular made him familiar with the characteristics of fashionable Italian musical style; Haydn also acquired a good knowledge of the Italian language from the lessons. The Metastasio–Porpora connection introduced Haydn to other leading figures in the Italian operatic world in Vienna, including GLUCK, WAGENSEIL, and, possibly, HASSE.

Haydn maintained his contact with church circles in Vienna, nipping from one service to the next on Sundays and on feast days. According to Griesinger, at one stage Haydn led the orchestra at the BARMHERZIGE BRÜDER church in Taborstraße at eight in the morning, played the organ in the private chapel of COUNT HAUGWITZ in the Bohemian Court Chancellery on the Wipplingerstraße at ten, and sang with his old choir at St Stephen's at eleven. Payment records show that he was employed as an extra singer by the court during Lent in 1754, 1755, and 1756. In 1755 and 1756 the court employed him also as a casual violinist, playing in the special balls arranged for the children of the imperial family and their aristocratic friends during Carnival. In the evenings Haydn often played in outdoor serenades, sometimes in the company of

DITTERSDORF. He recalled composing a quintet in 1753 for this purpose and this work, the Cassation in G (Hob.II:2), may well be his first extant instrumental composition. It was while serenading that he met Kurz-Bernardon, responsible for a troupe of actors and musicians that performed German opera in the Kärntnerthortheater. For him he composed his first opera, DER KRUMME TEUFEL, and its sequel DER NEUE KRUMME TEUFEL. BARON FÜRNBERG was another important patron at this time, commissioning Haydn's first quartets and introducing him to the MORZIN FAMILY.

Haydn's compositions during the 1750s reflect this wide range of musical activity: church music (including organ concertos), string music, mixed ensembles for serenades, harpsichord sonatas and trios for teaching, perhaps dances for the court, and German opera. Despite his contact with the leading figures in Italian opera, however, there is no record of Haydn composing any Italian opera, unless he was the composer of the intermezzo *Il vecchio ingannato* that was performed with *Der neue krumme Teufel*. Court taste in opera had moved decisively in the 1750s from Italian opera towards French opera, with which Haydn had no connection.

In 1757 (possibly later) Haydn was offered his first full-time post, Kapellmeister to the Morzin family, based in Vienna in the winter, and in LUKAVEC in Bohemia in the summer. It was for Morzin's orchestra that Haydn composed his first symphonies, though it is not possible to state how many. When the Morzin family were in Vienna Haydn may have been allowed to supplement his income by continuing some of his freelance activities. Socially, Haydn had kept in contact with one family in particular, the Keller family who lived in the Landstraße to the east of the city. Johann Peter Keller was a professional wig maker who had employed Haydn as a music teacher. Haydn fell in love with the younger daughter, THERESE KELLER, but she was determined to take the veil and entered a nunnery in 1755. Five years later, in November 1760, Haydn married the elder daughter, Maria Anna (MARIA ANNA ALOYSIA APOLLONIA HAYDN).

By this time Haydn's employment at the Morzin court was increasingly insecure. The count's enthusiasm for music had led him to spend far more than he could afford, and to cut his losses he disbanded the musical retinue. In a stroke of good fortune PRINCE PAUL ANTON ESTERHÁZY, who was looking for an assistant to his ageing Kapellmeister, GREGOR WERNER, heard a performance of a symphony by Haydn and engaged him soon afterwards. He began working for the prince in his Viennese residence on the Wallnerstraße in March 1761, signing a formal contract on 1 May. Haydn was to remain with the Esterházy family for the rest of his life, 48 years in total.

1761–90: the Esterházy court. Haydn's contract with the Esterházy court made it clear that he was subordinate to Werner when it came to organizing music for church services, but that he had full responsibility for 'everything else'. Werner had served the court for nearly 33 years and at the age of 68 was no longer at the forefront of musical fashion. His particular expertise, as well as his dignity, was recognized in this division of duties, while a new energy was injected by the engagement of a promising figure from the younger generation. Haydn's contract was for three years and it included the promise that he could expect to assume the senior position in due course.

The Vice-Kapellmeister was involved in selecting a number of new instrumentalists for the court, many of whom he knew from his musical activities in Vienna; it is possible—though, in the absence of documentation, unverifiable—that some of these musicians had served with Haydn at the Morzin court. There was one notable exception, the leader of the orchestra, LUIGI TOMASINI, who was transferred from the domestic payroll of the Esterházy family to the musicians' payroll. Together they were to be the key figures in the musical life of the court for nearly forty years. It is often implied that when Haydn entered the service of the court he moved from Vienna to Eisenstadt, severing his connection with the capital city. But Eisenstadt was the summer palace and the prince spent the winter months in Vienna; indeed in 1761, because of illness, the prince and his new musical ensemble may have spent most of their time in Vienna. Later in the decade Haydn also made regular visits to Esterházy palaces elsewhere, especially Kittsee and PRESSBURG (Bratislava), 55 km (33 miles) to the east of Vienna on either side of the Danube.

One of the earliest compositions by Haydn for his new prince was the trilogy of symphonies, 'Le Matin', 'Le Midi', and 'Le Soir' (nos. 6–8) whose concertante roles for virtually all the instruments of the new Esterházy ensemble diplomatically demonstrated the wisdom of the new appointments. While concertante writing in symphonies by the composer was to feature for several years, formal solo concertos were restricted to the first few years of service at court, when Haydn wrote works for flute, horn, violin, cello, and double bass.

Prince Paul Anton died in March 1762 and was succeeded by his brother, PRINCE NICOLAUS ESTERHÁZY, who was to live until 1790 and be the most lavish of the four Esterházy princes that Haydn served. The duties of the Vice-Kapellmeister did not change radically in the first few years of the prince's service, for he, too, respected the status of Werner. When Werner wrote a vicious letter of complaint about Haydn in 1765, accusing him of a lax attitude to his work, he, publicly at least, sided with Werner, issuing a seven-point directive to Haydn that dealt systematically with the complaints. It was probably as a result of this incident that the younger composer began to keep a catalogue of his own music, the invaluable ENTWURF-KATALOG.

As well as orchestral music, Haydn wrote a number of secular vocal items in these early years of service, including six (possibly seven) rather old-fashioned honorific cantatas for the princes of which three survive (DESTATEVI, O MIEI FIDI, QUAL DUBBIO ORMAI, and DA QUAL GIOIA IMPROVVISA), a serious opera, ACIDE, and four comic operas of which only one survives, in fragments, LA MARCHESA NESPOLA.

On 3 March 1766 Georg Werner died. Despite the reprimand of the previous autumn there was never any real doubt that Haydn would succeed to the position of Kapellmeister. Haydn seems to have viewed this confirmation of his employment as welcome security for, in the same year, he purchased a house with several parcels of land (one with a summer house) in Eisenstadt. More fundamental to Haydn's future, Prince Nicolaus announced that a hunting lodge at Süttör that he was transforming into a new summer palace was henceforth to be known as ESZTERHÁZA. Over the next few years the locus of Haydn's existence was to move from Vienna and Eisenstadt to Eisenstadt and Eszterháza, with eventually the new summer palace being occupied as early as February and as late as November. In a way that Haydn could not have anticipated when he entered the service of the family in 1761, opera gradually came to feature more and more in his duties as a musical director and as a composer. Two opera houses were built at the new summer residence, one for Italian opera, the other for puppet opera.

But this transformation in Haydn's life was a gradual one over a ten-year period from 1766. In those ten years the composer applied himself with unprecedented energy and imagination to writing all kinds of music and no equivalent period witnessed such a broad engagement with musical development, marking out the composer as a commanding figure in the history of music. Five Italian operas were composed, LA CANTERINA, LO SPEZIALE, LE PESCATRICI, L'INFEDELTÀ DELUSA, and L'INCONTRO IMPROVVISO. Approximately two dozen symphonies date from this time, demonstrating an unceasingly experimental attitude to form and content, and yielding a high number of individual works that stand comparison with anything that Haydn was to produce later in his career. Clustered around 1770 are three sets of string quartets, op. 9, op. 17, and op. 20, 18 works that established the genre as a particularly sensitive vehicle for Haydn's abilities as an abstract musical thinker. Less numerous are the keyboard sonatas from this period but, again, individuality of expression in a work such as the C minor sonata (Hob.XVI:20) is increasingly evident. Prince Nicolaus himself played an unusual instrument, the BARYTON, and as Kapellmeister Haydn was obliged to provide the necessary music, over 150 works between 1765 and 1778.

Also during this period Haydn composed a number of major items of sacred music. With Werner's death Haydn had, by implication, taken over responsibility for church music at the court. It was not, however, a musical priority for Prince Nicolaus and over the years its status declined. Only the small-scale *Missa Sancti Nicolai* and the Salve regina in G minor can definitely be associated with the court. More ambitious works like the *Missa Cellensis*, the Stabat mater, and, possibly, the 'Grosse Orgelsolomesse' (MISSA IN HONOREM BVM) were composed as a result of outside commission or, in the case of the second work, from inner compulsion. To these works may be added further large-scale vocal works, the 'APPLAUSUS' CANTATA, written for Zwettl abbey, and the oratorio IL RITORNO DI TOBIA, written for Vienna.

The sheer quantity of music, the range of genres (each with its own stylistic imperatives), and the intellectual mastery of individual works, are compelling and recurring features of this period of extraordinary fertility. Not surprisingly Haydn was seriously ill in 1770–1; the precise nature of the illness is not known—Griesinger writes 'raging fever'—but it could well have been nervous exhaustion. One aspect of this burst of creative energy has caught the imagination of modern commentators, the number of works, principally symphonies but also keyboard sonatas and quartets, plus movements from operas and church music, that are set in the minor key. Given the label STURM UND DRANG such music, however, is only part of a wider expression of musical turbulence at this time.

Prince Nicolaus's musical ambitions reached a high point in 1776, when a permanently constituted opera company gave the first full season of opera performances at Eszterháza. Haydn prepared, rehearsed, and directed six operas, including two of the most fashionable works of the day, Gluck's *Orfeo* and Piccinni's *La buona figliuola*. The marionette theatre, too, had a full season, including the first performance of DIDO, for which Haydn wrote the music (now lost). Over the following years the activity of the opera company at Eszterháza continued to grow, reaching the remarkable figure of 125 performances of 17 different works in 1786. Haydn wrote six further Italian operas, IL MONDO DELLA LUNA, LA VERA COSTANZA, L'ISOLA DISABITATA, LA FEDELTÀ PREMIATA, ORLANDO PALADINO, and ARMIDA. Naturally, this increased emphasis on operatic activity from the mid-1770s meant that fewer works in other genres were composed: no quartets between 1772 and 1781; only one mass, the MISSA BREVIS SANCTI JOHANNIS DE DEO; and a marked decrease in the number of symphonies.

When he was looking back over his life Haydn liked to emphasize the isolation of this period, famously claiming that it helped his originality. His resilience was helped in 1779 by a change in his contract. Previously, the Kapellmeister and his music had been the property of the Esterházy court: Haydn was not allowed to accept outside commissions, to sell his music, or even to perform it elsewhere. There are a handful of occasions when Haydn is known to have asked permission for such activities, and there is no evidence that it was ever refused. Nevertheless, it cannot be established whether Haydn came to regard it as an unwarranted restriction, particularly difficult to enforce when it came to the distribution of his music in manuscript copies, or whether the prince thought that after 18 years of faithful service it was an old-fashioned impediment. For whatever reason, Haydn was given a new contract to sign on 1 January 1779. In four very general clauses it ensured that Haydn gave priority to the Esterházy court but he was no longer prohibited from accepting outside commissions or from selling his music. This single document acted as a catalyst for the next decisive stage in Haydn's career, the achieving of international popularity. By 1790 Haydn was in the paradoxical, if not bizarre, position of being Europe's leading composer, but someone who spent his time as a duty-bound Kapellmeister in a remote palace in the Hungarian countryside.

With a view towards his wider reputation Haydn composed very few works between 1779 and 1790 specifically for the Esterházy court, though many, especially symphonies, sonatas, and other instrumental items, could be performed there also. Most obviously, after *Armida* Haydn did not write a single further stage work for Eszterháza; his operatic writing was restricted to composing insertion arias for the operas of other composers. Also, no music for the baryton was composed in the 1780s. Most of Haydn's symphonies during the decade were written for concert organizations or individuals abroad, particularly in London and Paris (nos. 76–8, 82–92). For the King of Naples he wrote several works for LIRA ORGANIZZATA and, a particular pleasure for a composer who liked to explore his Catholic faith through music, the cathedral in Cadiz asked him to compose a major orchestral work, THE SEVEN LAST WORDS. The only liturgical work of the decade, the 'MARIAZELLER' MASS, was commissioned by a Viennese family in 1782.

Throughout the 1780s the composer was in regular correspondence with publishers in Vienna, London, Paris, Leipzig, and Speyer, their preferences influencing the kind of music that Haydn wrote. Without the likelihood of publication, he would probably not have composed the magnificent series of 25 quartets beginning with op. 33 and ending with op. 64, the two sets of German songs (Hob.XXVIa:1–24), as well as six flute trios, 15 keyboard trios, and various solo keyboard works.

Contact with distant cities must have aroused Haydn's curiosity about visiting them. Throughout the 1780s there were persistent attempts to persuade Haydn to go to London, to compose symphonies and opera, but he was always obliged to turn down invitations because of his duties at court. Apart from one brief visit to Graz in 1787, Haydn's travelling was restricted to the familiar route of Eszterháza, Eisenstadt, Vienna, and back. In the capital city he was able to experience at first hand the burgeoning salon culture of the decade, he became close friends with Mozart, and he joined the Freemasons. The short duration of his stays in Vienna, typically a few weeks in December and January, whetted his appetite for life outside Eszterháza and his correspondence with MARIA ANNA VON GENZINGER at the end of the decade gives a rare picture of a disconsolate person, tired of court routine and lamenting the excitement and occasional luxury that urban Vienna offered.

Soon after the establishing of regular opera seasons at Eszterháza, Haydn had sold his house in Eisenstadt, staying in the accommodation offered by the princely family in Eisenstadt, Eszterháza, and the Wallnerstraße in Vienna. His marriage had never been a happy one. His wife had an affair with the court painter Ludwig Guttenbrunn and Haydn entered an equally open affair with LUIGIA POLZELLI, an Italian singer 18 years his junior who joined the Eszterháza company in 1779.

In 1790 the opera season at Eszterháza began in February and included works by Cimarosa (1749–1801), Martín y Soler (1754–1806), Paisiello (1740– 1816), and Sarti (1729–1802). In August the prince became ill; for a while performances continued in the theatre and preparations were in hand for the first performance at the court of Mozart's *Le nozze di Figaro*. When it became necessary to move the increasingly ailing prince to Vienna, operatic life was suspended. The prince died on 28 September. Haydn and his colleagues already knew that his successor, PRINCE ANTON ESTERHÁZY, had plans drastically to curtail the musical life of the court. With the exception of Haydn and Tomasini, all the chamber musicians and theatrical personnel were summarily dismissed. From now any musical performances were to be one-off occasions which could be organized by the trusted Kapellmeister and the leader. Meanwhile, both were free to accept offers of employment elsewhere.

In Vienna in the three months after the prince's death Haydn would have pondered his future. Since he was in receipt of a pension of slightly more than his previous salary from Prince Nicolaus plus a salary from Prince Anton, and he could rely on continuing, if unpredictable income from selling his music and new commissions, it was not a period of crisis; nevertheless, after three decades of service, he must have been discomfited by the unprecedented freedom. Had the prince died a few years ealier, a visit to Paris, the musical capital of Europe in the 1770s and 1780s, would have been attractive, but the outbreak of the French Revolution in July 1789 now made this a more precarious prospect. KING FERDINAND IV had always hoped that Haydn would visit Naples and such a journey could have been arranged during the king's visit to Vienna in the winter of 1790–1; Haydn also had a standing invitation from PRINCE OETTINGEN-WALLERSTEIN to visit his court. A firm offer of employment came from PRINCE GRASSALKOVICS, the position of Kapellmeister at his court in Pressburg. In December the violinist cum impresario JOHANN PETER SALOMON, who was based in London, arrived in Vienna and presented Haydn with a more challenging opportunity: a visit to the British capital to be the central attraction in two seasons of concerts. For Haydn this was an attractive proposal for several reasons: the variety of musical life in London, especially the vigour of its public concert life, was unequalled in Europe; his music already dominated concert life there; he had long expressed enthusiasm for such a visit; and he was in regular correspondence with the English publisher JOHN BLAND, who was working in close collaboration with Salomon. If he had reservations about not knowing a word of English, then he would have been reassured by the guidance of Salomon, born in Bonn but resident in London for nearly ten years and one of many German-speaking musicians in this cosmopolitan city. On Wednesday, 15 December, at eight in the morning, Haydn and Salomon boarded the diligence coach in Vienna that took them to Linz and Munich, from where they caught a connecting coach to Bonn, Brussels, and Calais. En route, Salomon and Haydn stayed two nights at the electoral court in Bonn, where they were introduced to a promising local composer, LUDWIG VAN BEETHOVEN.

1791–5: London, Vienna, London. Haydn crossed the English Channel on 1 January 1791, arrived in London the following day, and stayed in Salomon's house, 18 Great Pulteney Street; he was also given a studio in the shop of Broadwood, the piano manufacturer, where he could compose. He had been engaged to compose an opera for the newly rebuilt King's Theatre and symphonies for Salomon's concerts. Since Salomon had not yet finalized his arrangements, he was able to give priority to the opera, *L'anima del filosofo*, which was scheduled for performance in March. It was not to be an auspicious beginning to the composer's stay in London for, having completed the work (save for the usual adjustments that would have been made in rehearsals) he was told that it could not be performed because the manager had failed to secure a licence for his new theatre. Salomon's concerts started late in the season, on 11 March; in total, 12 concerts were held in the Hanover Square Rooms on Fridays through to 3 June. In addition, Haydn was given a benefit concert on Monday, 16 May, slotted between the ninth and tenth concerts. Because the visit had been hurriedly arranged and Haydn had given priority to the aborted opera, only two new symphonies were given that season, nos. 95 and 96. The composer was, however, able to present recent works unfamiliar to London audiences, including Symphony no. 92, arrangements of some of the Notturni he had written for the King of Naples, and quartets from the op. 64 set.

Haydn was fascinated by the diversity of musical life in London, in particular the concerts given at the end of May as part of the Handel Commemoration Festival, where works such as *Israel in Egypt* and 'Zadok the Priest' were given with forces of over a thousand, a new and overwhelming experience for the composer.

As the social season drew to a close Haydn's existence became less hectic. He travelled to OXFORD in July to receive an honorary doctorate from the university. For five weeks from early August he lived in the country estate of the Brassey family in Hertingfordbury (Hertfordshire) where he was able to compose, take walks in the wood, improve his English, and observe the sometimes eccentric behaviour of his hosts, a banking family. Back in London his ever-expanding social circle extended to the highly musical PRINCE OF WALES; it was at the prince's instigation that John Hoppner was commissioned to paint a portrait of the composer.

Musical life in London was highly competitive, characterized by factions and petty jealousies, and Salomon's relationship with other violinists and impresarios was not always a cordial one. In 1792 Haydn was dragged into the most recent outbreak of musical politics. The well-established organization, the Professional Concert, first attempted to lure Haydn away from Salomon, and then engaged his former pupil IGNAZ PLEYEL as resident composer. Despite the efforts of the press to whip up a rivalry, master and pupil remained on the most friendly terms and the two series unfolded in parallel. The music of the would-be rivals was played in both series and Haydn was given a complimentary ticket to attend the Professional Concert.

Salomon's 1792 season again consisted of 12 subscription concerts, between 17 February and 18 May, plus a benefit concert on 3 May. Symphonies nos. 93, 94, 97, and 98 were presented for the first time, plus a symphonie concertante for violin, cello, oboe, and bassoon. The success of the season was such that an additional concert was arranged on Wednesday, 7 June, and Haydn duly promised to return for the 1793 season. After an absence of 18 months Haydn was ready to go back to his native Austria, but a year-old friendship with a civilized widow named REBECCA SCHROETER encouraged him to delay his departure until the first week in July. His homeward journey took him once more to Bonn, or rather to Bad Godesberg a few miles south of Bonn, where the electoral court had its own spa. Haydn and Beethoven met for the second time, and it was decided that Beethoven should have lessons with Haydn in Vienna and accompany him on his next visit to London.

Haydn returned to Vienna and to the lodgings on the Wasserkunstbastei that he had occupied in late 1790. Beethoven duly arrived in November and the course of formal instruction began. Prince Anton was reluctant to let his Kapellmeister return so soon to London (even though there was nothing much for him to do) and Haydn may too have become nervous about travelling in Central Europe at a time when France was beginning to realize its designs on surrounding territories. The clinching reason, however, was the composer's troublesome nasal polyp which required an operation. By December Haydn had decided that the second visit should be postponed by a year, to 1794.

In Vienna and, more especially, in Eisenstadt in the summer months Haydn was able to prepare some major works for the second visit, the opp. 71 and 74 quartets, Symphony no. 99, and portions of Symphonies nos. 100 and 101. To make the second journey more comfortable GOTTFRIED VAN SWIETEN lent Haydn a travelling coach; this time, too, the composer took his copyist, JOHANN ELßLER, with him. However, the original intention of taking Beethoven had been quietly forgotten and he was passed on to ALBRECHTSBERGER for further lessons. The journey is known to have taken the two companions to Passau and Wiesbaden, from where they presumably proceeded along the Rhine, through the Austrian Netherlands, to Calais. Haydn and Elßler arrived in London on 4 February 1792 and took up lodgings in 1 Bury Street (St James's), more or less equidistant from the Hanover Square Rooms and Rebecca Schroeter's house in Buckingham Gate.

With the experience of the first visit, Haydn quickly fell into the pattern of the 1794 season, accommodating a change of day from Fridays to Mondays. Twelve concerts were given between 10 February and 12 May, plus a benefit concert on 2 May; but if Haydn was now comfortable in the routine, the reception accorded to the three new symphonies in particular, nos. 99–101, was unprecedentedly enthusiastic. During the summer and autumn of 1794 Haydn remained in London but undertook a number of short visits, to Hampton Court (whose gardens he compared to those at Eszterháza), to Portsmouth and the Isle of Wight, to Bath and Bristol, to Waverley abbey near Farnham, to the Earl of Abingdon's estates near Oxford, and to Preston. During this period Symphony no. 102 was completed in readiness for what Haydn expected would be a fourth season of Salomon concerts. But the impresario was experiencing difficulty securing new singers from the continent and early in January 1795 announced that he had agreed to join a new organization, the Opera Concert, to present a series of nine concerts on Mondays in the concert room that abutted the main stage of the King's Theatre in the Haymarket. Haydn went with him and though he was nominally one of four resident composers—the others were Bianchi (*c.*1752–1810), CLEMENTI, and Martín y Soler—he was undoubtedly the principal attraction. Nevertheless, fewer works by Haydn were played that season than would have been the case if 'Mr Salomon's Concert' had continued. Symphonies nos. 102 and 103 were given their premieres and Haydn's last symphony, no. 104, was given at the composer's benefit concert on 4 May.

Salomon was to reactivate his concert series in 1796 and there was some vague discussion that Haydn might once more be its central attraction. But the composer had already made up his mind that this was to be his last visit to London. Prince Anton had died in 1794 and his successor, PRINCE NICOLAUS ESTERHÁZY II, had indicated that musical life at the court was to be renewed and that the Kapellmeister was expected to fulfil his duties. On 15 August 1795 Haydn left London for the last time. Because of the occupation of the Austrian Netherlands and the Rhineland by French forces, Haydn and Elßler took the lengthy sea crossing to Hamburg and from there travelled via Berlin and Dresden to Vienna, a journey of about two weeks.

1795–1809: Vienna. Unlike his grandfather, the first Prince Nicolaus, Nicolaus II played a full part in the social and cultural life of Vienna, living in the palace in the Wallnerstraße during the winter season and moving to Eisenstadt only during the summer months; he never used Eszterháza as a residence. For the first time since the 1750s, therefore, Haydn's musical activities could be focused on Vienna. The prince had established two ensembles in Eisenstadt, a group of seven or eight string players who were to accompany performances of church music in the palace and a *Harmonie* of two oboes, two clarinets, two horns, and two bassoons. These separately constituted ensembles could be brought together to form an orchestra, as they were in performances of the late masses, but they never became the equivalent of the pre-1790 orchestra and Haydn's career as a composer of symphonies was not to be continued. Although the Kapellmeister had full administrative responsibility for the two ensembles, sustained musical activity was restricted to the months of September and October, the weeks surrounding the nameday of the prince's wife, PRINCESS MARIE HERMENEGILD ESTERHÁZY, when plays and operas were given and a church service held, usually with a new mass by Haydn. The six late masses are in varying degrees associated with these celebrations; Haydn provided incidental music for the play *Alfred, King of the Anglo Saxons*; and the Kapellmeister wrote a march for the *Harmonie* (HUNGARIAN NATIONAL MARCH). At first, Haydn and his fourth Esterházy patron found the relationship difficult—the composer was an international figure who had lived in the liberal society of London while Nicolaus wanted to treat him in much the same way as his predecessors had done—but gradually the prince, prompted by his wife, saw that he could bask in the reflected glory of his Kapellmeister and the relationship became a cordial and supportive one.

In 1793 Haydn had bought a house in the Viennese suburb of Gumpendorf. Extensive building work took three years to complete and in 1796 Haydn and his wife, together with Johann Elßler, his wife, and some domestic staff, moved into the property, Haydn's home for the rest of his life. The GESELLSCHAFT DER ASSOCIIERTEN, a consortium of nobility including Nicolaus II, had become a major force in the musical life of Vienna. In 1796 it sponsored the first performance of the choral version of *The Seven Last Words*. But Haydn had more ambitious plans. He had returned from London with the text of an oratorio, *The Creation*, which he was anxious to set. Van Swieten and the Gesellschaft encouraged Haydn in his ambition and gave him the musical and financial support to realize his greatest single work. It was begun in 1796; the first semi-public performances were given in 1798 at the Schwarzenberg palace; and the first public performance a year later, in the Burgtheater. A second oratorio followed, *The Seasons*, composed between 1799 and 1801, performed semi-privately in the Schwarzenberg palace in April 1801 and publicly in the Redoutensaal the following month. Haydn readily accepted many invitations to direct public performances of both oratorios to raise money for various charities. Performances were given in private too at the imperial court, where EMPRESS MARIE THERESE had developed a particular interest in the music of Haydn; it was the empress who commissioned a new setting of the Te Deum from the composer (Hob.XXIIIc:2). Haydn's growing status within the highest imperial and aristocratic circles and with the public at large was enhanced immeasurably by the success of the national anthem commissioned from the composer, 'GOTT ERHALTE FRANZ DEN KAISER'.

Alongside the composition and direction of masses and oratorio, Haydn was occupied with the very different challenge of composing quartets; a set of six, op. 76, was commissioned by Count Joseph Erdödy and written in 1796–7; Prince Lobkowitz likewise commissioned six works but Haydn was able to complete only two, published as op. 77 in 1802. Haydn's busy schedule in Vienna between 1795 and 1802 meant that there was no time to accept invitations to travel abroad or to write major works for concert bodies or individuals elsewhere in Europe. A residual commitment to provide LONGMAN & BRODERIP with some piano trios was fulfilled in 1796 but, apart from this, new works specifically written for foreign publishers were restricted to the settings of British folksongs commissioned by GEORGE THOMSON and, later, WILLIAM WHYTE. However, the firm of BREITKOPF & HÄRTEL became a major force in consolidating Haydn's European reputation at the turn of the century, publishing recent works such as *The Seasons* and five of the six late masses and ensuring his cooperation in issuing an *Oeuvres complettes* of keyboard music and songs.

Haydn's last major completed work was the 'HARMONIEMESSE' of 1802. His last appearance in public as a conductor of his music was in December 1803, a performance of the vocal version of *The Seven Last Words* held to raise money for the St Marx hospital in Vienna. The composer never fully recovered from the tiredness he felt after composing *The Seasons* and, although he continued to forward settings of British folksongs to Edinburgh for a couple of years and hoped, in vain, to complete a third quartet (in D minor) for Prince Lobkowitz, he had now effectively retired.

Haydn's natural modesty was balanced in his old age by a sense of responsibility to his wider fame. As well as collaborating with Breitkopf & Härtel, he approved of the major venture initiated by PLEYEL to publish the complete quartets; in 1804–5 he instructed Elßler to compile a new thematic catalogue of his music, the *Haydn-Verzeichnis*; and he cooperated with CARPANI, DIES, and GRIESINGER in providing material for their biographies. He was a grateful recipient of honours from abroad, including membership of the Royal Swedish Academy of Music, medals from the Paris Conservatoire and the Philharmonic Society in St Petersburg, and a medal of honour from the city of Vienna for his services to charity. Like the earlier doctorate from Oxford University and the impressive list of subscribers that prefaced the first edition of *The Creation*, these marks of esteem were a great source of pride to the composer.

From 1806 onwards Haydn was virtually housebound, but continued to welcome visitors from all walks of life, amongst them Princess Esterházy, players from the Esterházy court, CHERUBINI, CLEMENTI, HUMMEL, Pleyel, Reichardt (1752–1814), Tomaschek (Tomášek) (1774–1850), and Weber (1786–1826). In March 1808, to mark the end of the first season of a major new venture in the musical life of Vienna, a series of public concerts called the Liebhaber Concerte, there was a special performance of *The Creation*, directed by SALIERI. In a carriage sent by Prince Esterházy the frail composer was taken from his house in Gumpendorf to the venue of the concert, the university, where he was greeted by Beethoven, GYROWETZ, Hummel, and Salieri. Haydn was seated between Princess Esterházy and her two daughters and when he felt cold, the princess covered his legs with a shawl, a gesture copied immediately by a number of other aristocratic ladies. Overcome by hearing the oratorio for the first time in several years and by the adulation of the Viennese, Haydn thought that whole occasion might be too much for him and left after the chorus 'Die Himmel erzählen/ The heavens declare' that ends Part 1.

Haydn spent the last winter of his life witnessing the increasing jingoism of the Austrian people as they prepared to face the invading French. As he had done for several years Haydn consoled himself by repeatedly playing 'Gott erhalte Franz den Kaiser' at the piano. In February 1809 he prepared a second will and on 1 April, the day after his 77th birthday, he sold his piano. Austria declared war on France on 9 April and the order was given to defend the city against Napoleon's troops. In his house in Gumpendorf Haydn was caught in the crossfire between the Viennese and the attacking French; a cannon ball fell in the courtyard and his bedroom door was blown wide open. On 13 May the city surrendered to the French. A few days later a French cavalry officer and admirer of the composer visited him and sang an aria from *The Creation*, 'Mit Würd und Hoheit angethan/In native worth and honour clad'. With Elßler, servants, and a neighbour at his bedside Haydn died peacefully in his sleep at 12.40 a.m. on 31 May. Elßler arranged that a death mask be taken before the composer was buried the next day in the cemetery in Gumpendorf. A day after that a requiem mass was given in the Gumpendorf church, a wretched performance of a setting by Michael Haydn. Since movement around Vienna was restricted following the French invasion, attendance at both these ceremonies was limited. A memorial performance of Mozart's Requiem, given in the Schottenkirche on 15 June, was a grander occasion, attended by French officials and army officers as well as the cream of Viennese society.

2. Appearance and manner. Contemporary writers describe Haydn as being of less than average height, which suggests that he might today be regarded as quite short. He was sturdily built, with brown eyes and a rustic complexion; DIES, with the trained eye of a painter, thought his legs too short for his body. Haydn considered himself ugly, no doubt focusing on his hawk nose, pock-marked skin, enlarged nostrils (aggravated by snuff), and heavy lower lip; Johann Caspar Lavater (1741–1801), the famous physiognomist who prepared a silhouette of the composer, thought the composer's eyes, nose, and forehead distinctive, but the mouth philistine. Even as a boy, Haydn habitually wore a wig and was embarrassed to be seen without one; he was the last great composer to do so. At the Esterházy court he was given a winter and a summer uniform almost every year and he liked to dress early in the day. He valued neatness and cleanliness, occasionally to the point of vanity, and in old age put on a ring whenever he received guests (it can be seen in the portrait by John Hoppner). He spoke in an Austrian dialect. If the conversation was about music he could be intense, but he liked idle chit-chat too, when, it is said, his countenance became animated and smiling. *See also* ICONOGRAPHY.

3. Daily schedule. Haydn's copyist, JOHANN ELßLER, left an account of the composer's working day, typical of the composer in the period from autumn 1795 onwards, when he lived mainly in Vienna; a similar account is given in the biography by DIES.

In summer he rose at half-past six. The first thing he did was to shave, which he did for himself up to his 73rd year. After shaving, he got dressed completely. If a pupil were present, he had to play the lesson he had been assigned on the piano to Haydn as he was dressing. The mistakes were at once corrected, the pupil instructed about the reasons thereof, and then a new task was assigned. For this one and half hours were required. On the dot of 8 o'clock breakfast had to be on the table, and right after breakfast Haydn sat down at the piano and improvised, whereby at the same time he worked out the sketch of the composition: for this, a daily period from 8 to 11.30 in the morning was required. At 11.30 visits were paid or received; or he took a walk until 1.30. From 2 to 3 o'clock was the hour for lunch. After lunch Haydn always concerned himself with some small domestic task, or he went into his small library and read a book. At 4 o'clock Haydn returned to musical affairs. He took the sketch that had been prepared that morning and put it into score, for which task he took three to four hours. At 8 p.m. Haydn usually went out, but came home again at 9 o'clock and either sat down to write scores or took a book and read until 10 o'clock. The hour of 10 o'clock was supper time, which consisted of bread and wine. Haydn made it a rule not to have anything else except bread and wine in the evening, and he broke the rule now and then only when he was invited out for dinner. At table Haydn liked light conversation and altogether a merry entertainment. At 11.30 Haydn went to bed—in old age even later. Winter made no appreciable difference in the daily schedule except that Haydn got up in the morning a half hour later, otherwise everything was as in the summer. In old age, mainly during the last 5 to 6 years of his life, physical weakness and illness disturbed the above schedule. The active man could, ultimately, find no occupation. In this latter period Haydn used to lie down for half an hour in the afternoon.

Haydn must have practised a strict regulation of his time throughout his life, though clearly the pattern would have been different during the heyday of the Esterházy court between 1761 and 1790, and different again during the London visits. Haydn's first contract at the Esterházy court required him to make himself available at midday to receive any orders for music-making, and the schedules surrounding the rehearsals and performances of operas must have imposed their own patterns of work too. Haydn always insisted that he should not be disturbed when composing.

4. Education. Haydn was typical of his generation and class in that his formal education was a casual one. In Hainburg from the age of 5 or 6 he learnt to read and write, studied arithmetic, absorbed the catechism, and indulged a natural ability on a variety of instruments, including the timpani. The language of instruction was German; there is no evidence that Haydn spoke any Hungarian. His particular ability as a singer took him to St Stephen's, Vienna, where basic education in reading, writing, and arithmetic continued, and knowledge of Catholic doctrine was supplemented by the study of Latin; music theory was neglected and Haydn remembered receiving only two lessons from Kapellmeister Reutter. It was during the 1750s and 1760s that Haydn improved his musical education, studying the work of C. P. E. BACH, FUX, KIRNBERGER, and MATTHESON. His contact with METASTASIO and PORPORA led him to learn Italian, which became Haydn's second language. He would have spoken it with the many Italian singers employed at Eszterháza, and all his correspondence with his mistress, Luigia Polzelli, is written in the language. Late in life, Haydn also used Italian when corresponding with Charles Burney and with the publisher George Thomson. His knowledge of French, on the other hand, was virtually non-existent. His correspondence and the occasional annotation on autograph scores suggest that he liked to garnish his broad Austrian dialect with Latin quotations and epigrams.

When he first arrived in England, in 1791, his knowledge of English, too, was very limited, but over the following four years it became fluent, if slightly eccentric. One letter in English by the composer survives.

Haydn's library at his death contained a substantial quantity of non-musical items largely, it is thought, acquired during the 1780s and 1790s. There were English, Italian, and French dictionaries but Haydn's inquisitiveness about the natural world is revealed by the presence of several multi-volume encyclopedias, and books on horticulture, agriculture, medicine, geography, history, meteorology, and astronomy. There are a number of items in English, perhaps given as gifts in London rather than bought there; they include a ten-volume edition of Shakespeare's plays, Pope's *Essay on Man*, Captain Cook's *Voyages*, Sterne's *Sentimental Journey*, and Holcroft's *The Adventures of Hugh Trevor*. His professional work as an opera composer, arranger, and musical director explains the presence of multi-volume editions of the work of Goldoni and Metastasio. As regards German literature, the names of Goethe and Schiller are conspicuously absent. Instead, Haydn had a particular fondness for German lyrical poetry of a sentimental kind, and his favourite author, GELLERT, is well represented; he also owned volumes of poetical works by Alxinger, Bürger, Hagedorn, Kleist, Ramler, and Wieland. There are only three novels by German authors.

Modern literature on music found in Haydn's library included Burney's *History of Music*, Gerber's *Lexicon*, and the first six volumes of the *Allgemeine musikalische Zeitung*. *See also* CATALOGUES §1.

E. K. Borthwick, 'Haydn's Latin Quotations: A Postscript', *Music and Letters*, 75 (1994), 576–9.

E. K. Borthwick, 'The Latin Quotations in Haydn's London Notebooks', *Music and Letters*, 71 (1990), 505–10.

K. Talbot (trans.), 'Maria Hörwarthner, Joseph Haydn's Library: An Attempt at a Literary-Historical Reconstruction', in E. Sisman (ed.), *Haydn and His World* (Princeton, 1997).

5. Finances and personal wealth. Apart from the period following his dismissal from St Stephen's cathedral, when he was earning a living as a jobbing musician in Vienna, Haydn led a comfortable life. As Kapellmeister to the Morzin family and, especially, the Esterházy family he had a regular income, supplemented, as was the practice of the day, by payments in kind for clothing, food, board and lodging, medicines, travel, and even manuscript paper. He was a thrifty person who had known poverty, but by the time of his death he had accumulated a good deal of wealth.

The Austrian currency of the time consisted of two main units, kreutzer (K, Kr, or x) and gulden (G, Gl); there were 60 kreutzer to a gulden; rather confusingly, the latter was also called a florin (fl.). There was a further unit, the ducat, whose precise relationship to the gulden varied from time to time according to imperial decree; in 1786 one ducat was equal to 4½ gulden. From Haydn's youth to the late 1790s there was little inflation, but in the last ten years of the composer's life the cost of living rose steeply as a result of the travails of the Napoleonic Wars. In terms of annual income, a middle-class single person could live comfortably in the city of Vienna in the 1780s on 470 gulden. In 1791, the year when Haydn made his first visit to London, the exchange rate was 9 gulden 45 kreutzer to £1. The following survey cannot claim to list all Haydn's emoluments—an impossible task—but represents the kind of income that the composer received.

As a freelance church musician in Vienna in the 1780s Dies reported that Haydn earned 17 kreutzer per service; more rewarding was the 1 gulden per service that he earned as an extra singer in Easter services at the imperial court and the very generous 4 gulden per evening that he earned as a violinist in court balls. When he began teaching in Vienna he remembered earning 2 gulden per month, later rising to 5 gulden. One of the highest single fees during this early period must have been the 24 ducats he received for *Der krumme Teufel*.

As Kapellmeister to Count Morzin Haydn received a salary of 200 gulden, plus board and lodging, the beginning of a lifetime of stable income. When he moved to the Esterházy court in 1761 to become Vice-Kapellmeister, his official salary was 400 gulden but almost immediately this was supplemented by separate additional payments of 200 gulden, taking his salary beyond that of Kapellmeister Werner. Haydn and his wife lived in the musicians' quarters in the Oberberg and Haydn was entitled to dine at the officers' table or to claim a daily allowance of 30 kreutzer in lieu. In most years he received two new uniforms, one for the winter and one for the summer.

In the 1760s and 1770s, in particular, Prince Nicolaus regularly gave Haydn one-off payments of anything between 12 and 30 ducats for a successful premiere of an opera.

In 1766 Haydn, with the aid of some borrowed money, bought a house with several parcels of land in Eisenstadt. On two separate occasions, in 1768 and 1776, it was damaged by fire and Prince Nicolaus paid for it to be repaired. In 1778 Haydn sold the house for 2,000 gulden, paid debts of 1,000, and invested 1,000 through the offices of the prince; he received an annual income of 50 gulden from this investment for the rest of his life. Meanwhile, Haydn had supplemented his main income from the court by agreeing to be the organist at chapel services in the palace at Eisenstadt in wintertime. For this small extra duty, Haydn joined his fellow musicians in receiving victuals of various kind ('Naturalien') including wheat, corn, lintels, barley, millet, beef, salt, lard, candles, wine, root vegetables, and firewood. The quantities were generous ones: for instance the wine allowance amounted to 504 litres per year. Haydn received these victuals through to 1790.

Following the change in Haydn's contract in 1779, which allowed him to accept commissions for music from outside the court and to sell his music also, the composer's income increased substantially. He was a shrewd salesman, who liked to receive 5 ducats for a published symphony and who negotiated 300 gulden for the op. 50 quartets. The 25 louis d'or per work that he received from the Concert de La Loge Olympique for the 'Paris' symphonies must have been particularly welcome; it converted into 225 gulden per symphony.

The death of Prince Nicolaus might have precipitated unaccustomed financial instability for Haydn but his patron, ever generous and supportive, had left him a pension of 1,000 gulden per annum, slightly higher than the total value of his salary and allowances. Although Prince Anton disbanded the retinue of chamber musicians, he kept Haydn on as Kapellmeister at an annual salary of 400 gulden.

In London for two visits in the 1790s, Haydn earned the largest fees of his life, though there were more expenses than he was accustomed to paying. One source states that Haydn was paid £300 for six symphonies (nos. 93–8), an even larger amount than for the 'Paris' symphonies, and a further £200 for their copyright. He is said to have taken £350 for his first benefit concert in 1791 and the gleeful composer reported that the 1795 benefit concert yielded 4,000 gulden: 'Such a thing is possible only in England.' He received fees for publication of his music and was able to charge one guinea per lesson. Altogether, the London visits yielded a net sum of 15,000 gulden. In 1793 he had bought a house in Gumpendorf, in Vienna, for 1,370 gulden and the modifications to the house, which took three years, must have cost a sizeable amount.

When Prince Nicolaus II reactivated musical life at Eisenstadt in 1795, Haydn's income remained the same (pension of 1,000 gulden plus salary of 400 gulden), but he was given a new allowance, 515 litres of wine per year; in 1797, the salary component was increased to 700 gulden. The Kapellmeister was still given a uniform. Fees from teaching and publishing (especially from Breitkopf & Härtel) remained a steady source of income, supplemented by the occasional fee, such as the 600 ducats Haydn received from Prince Schwarzenberg and the Gesellschaft der Associierten for *The Creation.*

Haydn's withdrawal from composition in 1803 coincided with increasing inflation in the Austrian economy that must have eroded the value of his basic income and his savings. In 1806, following a conversation with Princess Esterházy, Haydn was granted an additional annual sum of 600 gulden. Finally, in December 1808, the Esterházy court agreed to pay all Haydn's apothecary bills, over 1,000 gulden in that year. He continued to live in comfort in Gumpendorf, acquiring, in particular, an expensive wardrobe of clothes (he always liked to dress well). In his will he bequeathed a total of 24,000 gulden but the total value of his estate turned out to be 55,713 gulden.

R. Sandgruber, 'Wirtschaftsentwicklung, Einkommensverteilung und Alltagsleben zur Zeit Haydns', in *Joseph Haydn in seiner Zeit* [Exhibition catalogue] (Eisenstadt, 1982), 72–90.

6. Health. As might be expected from someone who lived to the age of 77, Haydn enjoyed good health, certainly in comparison to Mozart and Beethoven, both of whom were prone to debilitating ailments. As a senior employee of the Esterházy court Haydn was entitled to receive treatment at the hospice of the BARMHERZIGE BRÜDER in Eisenstadt from where he obtained potions for routine ailments. In 1764 Haydn asked for a subsidy from the prince in order to purchase medicines which may suggest a particularly severe, and perhaps costly, bout of illness. Much more serious was an unknown illness that occurred in 1770–1 which led Michael Haydn to contemplate visiting his brother. At the end of the 1780s, when Haydn had served the Esterházy court for over a quarter of a century and when Prince Nicolaus was no longer as fervent a patron, Haydn confided to Maria Anna von Genzinger that he was prone to depression.

Like his mother, Joseph Haydn suffered from a nasal polyp which caused increasing irritation from the 1770s. At one stage a surgeon named Giovanni Alessandro Brambilla (1728–1800) removed some bone from the composer's nose, without any real improvement to the fundamental ailment. By the end of Haydn's first visit to London, July 1792, it was causing him so much discomfort that Dr John Hunter offered to remove it; Haydn—apparently already in the surgeon's chair—refused. While in England Haydn once remarked that he suffered a little from rheumatism. Back in Vienna, continuing nasal pain was given as reason for not returning to London in January 1793; in a letter written in English he told an acquaintance in England: 'I am in so bad circumstances with my poor nose, that I am obliged to undertake an operation.'

In the summer of 1798, following the first performances of *The Creation*, Haydn was exhausted and had to be confined to his rooms for several weeks. His declining physical and mental energy became increasingly apparent and Haydn himself repeatedly blamed the exertion required to compose *The Seasons* for his waning health. From 1803 onwards tiredness, lack of concentration, headaches, hoarseness, and periods of melancholy grew more evident. He began to suffer from bouts of dizziness and his legs became painfully swollen. From 1806 onwards he was virtually housebound and revealed mild symptoms of senility, such as repetitive playing of the same piece of music ('Gott erhalte Franz den Kaiser'), ready weeping, obsession with household accounts, and an exaggerated love of children. He died peacefully in his sleep. The official cause of death was given as 'Entkräftung' (debilitation).

7. Personality. In 1776, when asked to provide information about himself for an Austrian encyclopedia, *Das gelehrte Österreich*, Haydn wrote the following: 'my highest ambition is only that all the world regard me as the honest man I am. I offer all my praise to the Almighty God, for I owe it to Him alone: my sole wish is to offend neither my neighbour, nor my gracious Prince, nor above all our merciful God.' Haydn's Catholicism was an instinctive part of his personality, instilled by his parents when young, never questioned or analysed, and a source of confidence throughout his life. His autograph scores habitually carry the annotation 'IN NOMINE DOMINI' at the beginning and 'LAUS DEO' at the end and, in this regard, Haydn made no difference between sacred and secular music. But he was not a zealot and in the best tradition of Enlightenment thinking sought understanding and tolerance.

When Haydn provided these remarks he was 44 years old. They have an innocence that reflect the very restricted environment in which he had grown up. Over the next couple of decades, as Haydn increasingly engaged with the outside world, spent nearly four years in London, and finally settled in Vienna, he became more worldly wise, occasionally ruthless, but without losing some of the fundamental aspects of his personality revealed in the remarks of 1776.

Evident from Haydn's words is an overwhelming sense of duty. In an age when creative artists were gradually asserting independence and exclusivity the composer saw no conflict between serving a demanding prince, promoting his own musical originality, and seeking popular success. All three were an integral part of his creative personality. At the end of his life Haydn remarked, 'I have done my duty and have been of use to the world. Let others do the same.'

Modesty is also apparent in Haydn's words. He could be self-deprecating about his achievements but this was a mask that hid an inner self-confidence and, although he became a celebrity and welcomed its trappings (keeping newspaper clippings and a box of medals and gifts, for instance), he preferred the company of people he knew: 'I have associated with emperors, kings, and many great gentlemen and have heard many flattering things from them; but I do not wish to live on an intimate footing with such persons, and I prefer people of my own kind.' He had the respect of fellow musicians, also their affection, and his duties at the Esterházy court had nurtured a diplomacy that served his musical integrity. He willingly acted as a godparent to the children of his colleagues, interceded in disputes between his players and the court, and saw the comic side of many situations. When he first arrived in London he had no English but cajoled orchestral players into giving of their best with, according to Dies, many calls of 'mein Schatz' ('my treasure') or 'mein Engel' ('my angel'). By this time he was habitually addressed as 'Papa'; later even his parrot had picked up the word.

Haydn also looked after members of his family. His brother Johann was taken on at the Esterházy court as a singer at Haydn's own expense; Michael Haydn was offered the post of Vice-Kapellmeister at Eisenstadt in 1802; and the names of several nieces are found in the composer's will.

While the 19th century was to ignore the integrity that went with Haydn's genial and stable personality, it also, perversely, chose to ignore less appealing, but no less persistent aspects of his character. Some of his contemporaries accused him of avarice. Certainly in his dealings with publishers he made sure that he was properly paid but he also willingly misled them when it suited him. When he was pushed for time he took two piano trios by PLEYEL and sold them to FORSTER as his own. Equally deceptively he asked another pupil, EYBLER, to provide him with some minuets, enjoining him to keep it a secret. To the surprise of some, he pursued a claim for 100 guineas owed to him by the Prince of Wales; it was eventually paid by Parliament as part of the settlement of the royal bankruptcy.

Haydn's marriage was an unhappy one. He enjoyed female company and even in old age was regarded as something of a flirt. The Italian opera singer LUIGIA POLZELLI was his mistress over a period of a dozen or so years and he may, too, have had an affair with Catherine Csech, a lady-in-waiting to Prince Grassalkovics. His relationships with MARIA ANNA VON GENZINGER and REBECCA SCHROETER were essentially based on companionship and intellectual stimulation, though, in the case of the latter, it probably developed into something more than that; in old age, the composer expressed the regret that he had not been able to marry her. But if this wistfulness is appealing and Haydn's seeking of female company outside his marriage understandable, his often very uncharitable, even bitter remarks about his wife show a different side to his personality. He seems to have despised her. He caricatured her as a religious bigot who liked the company of the clergy, a spendthrift, and someone who was unmusical and parochial; since she was unable to bear children Haydn said he was 'less indifferent to the charms of other ladies'. Writing to his 'cara Polzelli' from London in August 1791 he commiserates with the loss of her husband before anticipating the possible loss of his wife: 'As far as your husband is concerned, I tell you that Providence has done well to liberate you from this heavy yoke, and for him, too, it is better to be in another world than to remain useless in this one. The poor man has suffered enough. Dear Polzelli, perhaps, perhaps the time will come, that we both so often dreamt of, when four eyes shall be closed. Two are already closed, but the other two—enough of this, it shall be as God wills.'

It was during the London period, in particular, that another aspect of Haydn's personality was at its most apparent: his insatiable curiosity and delight in the new. His music bears repeated testimony to this but the LONDON NOTEBOOKS reveal a fascination with the outside world that is rarely evident in the lives of Mozart and Beethoven. He notes the price of coal, the availability of oranges, is shocked by the heavy drinking of the British aristocracy, relishes a visit to the races at Ascot, and is fascinated by Herschel's telescope.

Given his duties as Kapellmeister and his natural diligence as a composer it is difficult to imagine Haydn having time for other pursuits. A fall from a horse on the Morzin estate made him a nervous rider, but he apparently went hunting and fishing, proudly recalling the occasion when three hazel-hens that he had shot were served to Empress Maria Theresia. In old age he sometimes played cards. At this stage of life, too, he read more widely than had been the case in the busiest periods of his life. *See also* HAYDN §6: EDUCATION.

occasion the two boys are known to have sung the solo treble parts in a church service. Michael, like Haydn, was rather scathing about the Kapellmeister Reutter's attitude to his charges, remembering the many thrashings he received rather than anything more positive. When Michael's voice broke, at about the age of 18, he, like his brother before him, was summarily dismissed and for the next few years worked as a church musician in Vienna. Michael Haydn had already established himself as a competent organist and he assisted Albrechtsberger in the Jesuit church. While Joseph was gradually building up a reputation as a composer of instrumental music, Michael's association with the Jesuit Church initiated a lifelong reputation as a composer of church music.

In about 1757 (perhaps later) he moved to Großwardein (Oradea, Romania) to the court of the local bishop, eventually becoming Kapellmeister; as well as church music Haydn was by now composing symphonies, string trios, and some concertos (including an attractive work for the unusual combination of organ and viola). On 2 July 1762 a horn concerto (now lost) was performed by JOSEPH LEUTGEB at the Burgtheater in Vienna; the following day Leutgeb's daughter was baptized in Vienna, with Joseph Haydn and his wife serving as godparents. In September Michael and Joseph returned together to Rohrau in order to settle the inheritance from their late mother.

Michael Haydn's considerable experience as a composer of church music and his abilities as an organist made him a natural candidate for a vacancy at the archiepiscopal court in Salzburg following the death of Eberlin (1702–62). In August 1763 he joined the court, where his colleagues included Leopold Mozart (1719–87), Adlgasser (1729–77), Lolli (1701–78), and, later, Mozart. The correspondence of the Mozart family repeatedly reveals their admiration for Michael Haydn's music, also, less charitably, his occasional terse manner and fondness for drink. While the young Mozart spent much of his youth travelling around Europe, showing increasing signs of dissatisfaction with life in Salzburg, Michael Haydn settled into a comfortable existence in the city, helped by marriage to one of the court singers, Maria Magdelena Lipp (1745–1827); their only child, Aloisia Josepha, died four days before her first birthday.

While it is possible that Michael and Joseph corresponded regularly, no letters have survived from this period; the brothers could have met in Vienna in the autumn of 1767 when Michael was there and there was a lull in Joseph's duties because of Prince Nicolaus's visit to Paris, and Michael is known to have contemplated visiting Joseph in the winter of 1770–1 having heard that he had been seriously ill. For his part, Joseph was never to visit Salzburg, his journeys to London taking him through Passau to the north. Extant sources suggest that Michael Haydn's symphonies were regularly performed at the Esterházy court, while the few known performances of Joseph Haydn's symphonies in Salzburg may have been due to the influence of Michael. However, while Haydn's international reputation blossomed in the 1780s, Michael Haydn's reputation remained restricted to southern Germany and the Austrian territories.

Michael Haydn was probably a more effective teacher of composition than his brother, and his pupils included Diabelli (1781–1858), Weber (1786–1826), and NEUKOMM who later became a pupil of Joseph Haydn. In 1798 Michael travelled to Vienna, hoping to meet his brother whom, according to one source, he had not seen for 27 years. (If this rather precise figure is correct it suggests that the brothers did meet in the winter of 1770–1.) For about ten days in late October, Michael and Joseph were in daily contact, rekindling an affection that was to grow even stronger over the next few years.

Wider political events played some part in this renewed relationship. In 1800 French forces invaded Salzburg and amongst the personal property plundered by the troops were two silver watches and some money owned by Michael Haydn. When Joseph heard of this he forwarded a watch, a snuff-box (possibly for pawning), and promised some money. The unstable environment in Salzburg encouraged Michael to visit Vienna in the autumn of 1801. His church music had come to the eager attention of EMPRESS MARIE THERESE and a new mass, commissioned by her and in which she sang the solo soprano role, was given its first performance in the imperial palace in October 1801. It was during this visit that Michael Haydn, probably at the instigation of his brother, was offered the post of Vice-Kapellmeister at the Esterházy court, where his unrivalled experience as a composer of church music would have been particularly welcome. Despite being offered a salary over twice the size of the one he had in Salzburg, Michael Haydn dithered. Early in 1802 he reported that he would not be able to take up the position until August because he had to complete some new items of church music for Salzburg. Meanwhile, Archduke Ferdinand, who was now the Habsburg ruler of Salzburg, promised him continued and secure employment at the court. Throughout this period of vacillation Joseph remained supportive. In the only letter—a draft—to survive from Joseph to his brother he wrote: 'Both are great, but the Archduke's love and understanding for music are greater than those of my Prince; your heart and your brain must make the decision here, to which of the two you give preference.' In the event Michael Haydn decided to remain in Salzburg, though in a greeting he sent to his brother on his nameday in March 1804 he indicated that he much regretted it.

Michael Haydn continued to receive commissions for new items of church music from the imperial court, but in the winter of 1805–6 his health declined precipitately and he died of consumption in August; a setting of the requiem remained unfinished on his desk. Haydn, already prone to bouts of melancholy, was greatly distressed by the news. In his first will, prepared in 1801, he had left Michael Haydn and his other brother, Johann Haydn, the two largest bequests, 4,000 gulden each. When Haydn prepared his second will, a few months before his death in 1809, he bequeathed 1,000 gulden to his sister-in-law, Maria Magdalene Haydn, who was still living in Salzburg.

Joseph Haydn told Griesinger that the church music of Michael Haydn was of the first rank: 'it was a pity that this category was badly paid, for one could earn more with a bagpipe than with offertories and masses.' Michael Haydn was equally enthusiastic about Joseph's music. He prepared a score from the orchestral parts of *The Seven Last Words* in order to study the work in detail. He directed a performance of *The Creation* in Salzburg in August 1800 and wrote to a friend: 'You may receive this oratorio with awe and devotion! The inserted slips of paper show the places that specially pleased me. You will find none at the arias, and so on, otherwise the score would have looked like a hedgehog. The spot "Und Liebe girrt das zarte Taubenpaar" [bars 93–115 of Gabriel's aria "Auf starkem Fitige"/"On mighty pens"] particularly seems to me to be very successful. Here and there you will be surprised; and what my brother manages in his choruses on eternity is something extraordinary, and so on.' For some time Michael Haydn thought of writing a sequel to *The Creation*. As regards *The Seasons*, he seems to have shared Haydn's reservations, writing rather lukewarmly: 'I have occupied myself with it diligently for many days, and have found some places set in a manner extraordinarily difficult, others, on the contrary, much easier.' On four occasions Michael Haydn arranged music by his brother or took it as the basis for his own composition.

1. Gloria from Haydn's *Missa brevis Sancti Johannis de Deo* (ST 596). Joseph Haydn's movement consists of 31 bars only, with the four choral lines singing four separate lines of the text simultaneously until the concluding 'cum Sancto Spirito in gloria Dei Patris'. To avoid this polytextual setting, Michael Haydn prepared a much-expanded version of the movement, 118 bars in total. The opening 14 bars are based on the original; bars 15–85 are composed by Michael Haydn but with allusions to Joseph Haydn's thematic material; and bars 86–118 reproduce the original. The score, charmingly annotated 'un poco più prolungato dal suo Fratello G. Michele', is dated 16 July 1795. It is given in *JHW* XXXIII/2.
2. Set of six variations for piano on 'Gott erhalte Franz den Kaiser' (ST 771); 1799.
3. 'Zu Dir, o Herr blickt alles auf', a prayer for vocal quartet (ST 791); an arrangement of the trio from Part 2 of *The Creation*; 6 October 1800.
4. 'Dank, O Vater! Deiner Güte', a vocal quartet performed on the election of a new prelate to the abbey of Michaelbeuern (ST 825); an arrangement of 'Gott erhalte Franz den Kaiser'; before 14 August 1803.

It was inevitable that the music of one brother should be ascribed to the other in 18th-century sources, particularly manuscript sources circulating in the Austrian territories. Michael Haydn habitually signed his autograph scores 'G. M. Haydn' and many sources for Joseph Haydn's have 'G. Haydn' or 'Giuseppe Haydn', a situation that would have confused modern tax authorities with their computers, never mind 18th-century scribes. Misattribution of symphonies, string trios, and masses are particularly numerous.

G. Croll and K. Vössing, *Johann Michael Haydn, sein Leben, sein Schaffen, seine Zeit: eine Bildbiographie* (Vienna, 1987).

H. Jancik, *Michael Haydn. Ein vergessener Meister* (Zurich, 1952).

C. H. Sherman and T. D. Thomas, *Johann Michael Haydn (1737–1806). A Chronological Thematic Catalogue of His Works* (Stuyvesant, NY, 1993).

Haydn, Maria Anna Aloysia Apollonia (bap. 9 Feb. 1729; d. 20 March 1800). Haydn's wife. She was the daughter of Johann Peter Keller, a wig maker in Vienna. The little that is known about her is taken from the Haydn literature, much of it unsympathetic. Haydn first fell in love with her younger sister, Therese, but when she entered a nunnery in 1755 his affections turned towards Maria Anna. They were married at St Stephen's on 26 November 1760, a few months before Haydn took up his duties at the Esterházy court. She was unable to bear children and was, apparently, excessively religious (one of her treasured possessions was a relic of the cross) and a spendthrift. She had a love affair in the early 1770s with the court painter Ludwig Guttenbrunn. The unhappy marriage and her difficult personality were widely known, even in the 1780s; for instance, the London newspaper *Gazetteer & New Daily Advertiser* reported, in exaggerated tones, that Haydn was subject to the 'clamorous temper of a scolding wife'. She did not accompany the composer to London on his two visits and had little interest in his musical achievements. It is unlikely, for instance, that she ever attended a performance of *The Creation*. In old age in Gumpendorf they continued to live together in a state of mutual indifference. She regularly visited Baden to take the cure and it is there that she died in 1800. Her will made Haydn residual legatee.

Haydn museums. There are three museums devoted to Haydn in Austria: the house in Rohrau (Lower Austria) where the composer was born; the house he owned in Eisenstadt (Burgenland); and the house in which he lived for the last period of his life, in Gumpendorf, a suburb of Vienna.

The little thatched cottage in the small village of Rohrau has been considerably modified since the 18th century but on the right side of the entrance is the room in which Haydn was born; on the left side there are two further rooms plus a kitchen. The other rooms in the building are later additions. Across the courtyard were once the stables and the workshop used by Haydn's father. A modern wing to the left of the courtyard is now used as a small concert room. The house was in private possession until 1958 when it was purchased by the local government of Lower Austria and restored to its present state. The exhibits consist of engravings, some of the composer's possessions (including a snuffbox), a piano by Walter, a bust of the composer by Grassi, a family tree, and a volume containing the registration of the births of Joseph and Michael Haydn. A small, illustrated catalogue is available. Address: Haydn-Gedenkstätte, Rohrau, A-2471 Austria.

The museum in Eisenstadt is located in Haydn's house in the town and in the adjacent property, which together form a Haydn Centre, established by the JOSEPH HAYDN STIFTUNG in 1993. Haydn's house has been a museum since 1935. In Haydn's time the ground floor consisted of stables; the composer and his wife lived in three rooms on the first floor from 1766 to 1778, when the house was sold. The hayloft was later rebuilt as a separate apartment with its own staircase. The exhibits are numerous, including autographs, manuscript parts, first editions, engravings, paintings, instruments, and period furniture. There is an interesting and well-annotated catalogue while the Centre provides a wide selection of commercial items for the tourist. Address: Haydn Zentrum, Haydngasse 19–21, Eisenstadt, A-7000 Austria. (www. haydnfestival.at)

The museum in Gumpendorf, Vienna, is the one that most faithfully mirrors Haydn's own time. A substantial and well-proportioned house, it has been a Haydn museum since 1904; it was sympathetically restored to its original condition in the 1990s. There are nearly 80 exhibits including engravings, portraits, the composer's death mask, and a pencil owned by him. In 1980 a room on the first floor was converted into a memorial to BRAHMS, a fervent admirer of Haydn; Brahms's last residence in Vienna had been demolished in 1907 and 20 items of furniture and other possessions are attractively displayed in this room in Gumpendorf. There is an informative, if rather severely presented, catalogue. Address: Joseph Haydn-Gedenkstätte mit Brahms-Gedenkraum, Haydngasse 19, Vienna, A-1060 Austria. ERL

Haydn novels, operas, and plays. Along with Mozart and Schubert, Haydn has been the subject matter of several stage works during the 19th and 20th centuries. A list of 19 such works is appended to this article. Apart from a few in English and French, most were written in German for performance in Austria and reflect the image of the composer for that particular audience. Not surprisingly the most recurring feature is the promotion of 'PAPA HAYDN', the caring Kapellmeister and the great patriot. Franz Suppé's operetta, for instance, was particularly suited to creating a feeling of loyalty to the empire at a time of internal political tension following the creation of the dual monarchy in 1867. To promote the benign and wise Haydn, he was often presented as an old man in dramatic situations that were clearly set in the 1760s and 1770s. Most of the works quote freely from Haydn's compositions, especially the 'Farewell' symphony and 'GOTT ERHALTE FRANZ DEN KAISER'. A minority of works deal with Haydn's youth, the 'child in the boys' choir' (an *opéra comique* by Luce and a play by Jessie Elise Gordon) and 'the genius apprenticed to Maestro Porpora' (play by Schubar and an opera by Cipollini). The only work to feature a location in England is the play by Gordon. Musically the most amibitious work is the one-act comic opera by Gaetano Cipollini (1851–1935), entirely written by him and with no quoted material.

Two novels are known. Joachim Kupsch's book paints a reverent picture of Haydn's visit to London, as seen through the eyes of an English gentleman, Percy Lambkin, while Norbert Tschulik's book is aimed at children. FJ

Novels (in chronological order)
1962. Kupsch, *Die Reise nach London. Ein Haydn-Roman*
1982. Tschulik, *Und es ward Licht. Ein Joseph-Haydn-Roman für die Jugend*

Musical Works (in chronological order)
1823. Seyfried/Hoffmann, *Die Ochsenmenuette* (*Singspiel*)
1840. Luce/Vial/Muret, *L'Élève de Presbourg* (*opéra comique*)
1844. Bonnemere, *Joseph Haydn—La Tempête* (operetta)
1846. Hetzel/Dumenil, *La Jeunesse de Haydn* (operetta)
1871. Suppé/Radler, *Joseph Haydn* (*Singspiel*)
1885. Raimann/Philippi, *Haydn's Kaiserlied* (*Singspiel*)
1889. Carissan, *La Jeunesse de Haydn* (operetta)
1889. Soffredini, *Il piccolo Haydn* (melodrama)
1893. Cipollini, *Il piccolo Haydn* (comic opera)
*c.*1900. Renner jun., *Joseph Haydn* (*Singspiel*)
1910. Jarno/Buchbinder, *Das Musikantenmädel* (operetta)

Plays (in chronological order)
1846. Schubar, *Joseph Haydn* (play)
1862. Eberwein, *Vater Haydn* (dramatic poem)
1886. Schlickh, *Joseph Haydn—eine Stunde aus seinem Leben* (play)
1909. Sonuscumt, *Walhall's Haydn Feier* (play)
1909. Hoffmann, *Haydn's letzter Wille* (play)
1934. Gordon, *Scenes from the life of Joseph Haydn* (play)
1944. Lessen, *Der Kapellmeister Seiner Durchlaucht* (play)
1964. Bauer, *Haydn* (microdrama)

Haydn ornament. A term used by some modern authors to describe the Haydnesque symbol +, which occurs in Haydn's autograph manuscripts at all stages of his career. This symbol can, however, indicate a number of different ornaments. Most frequently it represents a *Doppelschlag* (turn) and from the later 1760s Haydn used the symbol interchangeably with the more conventional *Doppelschlag* symbol; in the 1780s especially, the *Doppelschlag* is also indicated by three small notes (Ex. 1).

In certain contexts, in ornamenting the second note of an ascending second interval (e.g. in Hob.XVI:23/ii), or over long notes, particularly at the beginning of a phrase (e.g. in Hob.XVI:46/i and XVI:32/i) the symbol + may also indicate a mordent, since Haydn rarely distinguished between the symbol + and the conventional mordent sign (𝆖), which it resembles (Ex. 2).

In a third usage either of the symbols ~ or + occurs in ornamenting the second note of a legato descending-second interval. In this context a *prallender Doppelschlag* is probably intended, an interpretation suggested by the occurrence of C. P. E. Bach's symbol for this ornament in such a context in Hob.XVI:20/i (Ex. 3). BH

B. Harrison, *Haydn's Keyboard Music: Studies in Performance Practice* (Oxford, 1996).

Ex. 1

Ex. 2

Ex. 3

'Haydn' quartets. The name traditionally given to the set of six quartets by MOZART that were dedicated to Haydn, K387, K421, K428, K458, K464, and K465. Composed between 1782 and 1785, they were in large part stimulated by the appearance in 1781 of Haydn's op. 33 quartets. Haydn's mastery of the genre is acknowledged by Mozart in a celebrated preface to the printed edition issued by ARTARIA in September 1785: 'Here they are then, O great man and my dearest friend, these six children of mine.' It was one of the earliest in a long series of works by a number of composers that were to be dedicated to Haydn. Mozart's effusive letter of dedication refers to Haydn's approval of the works, given during his last stay at Vienna. This had taken place in February, when performances of three of the quartets were given; Mozart's father, Leopold, was visiting Vienna and Haydn told him 'Before God and as an honest man I tell you that your son is the greatest composer known to me either in person or by name. He has taste and, what is more, the most profound knowledge of composition.' This remark was reported back to Wolfgang, paving the way for the subsequent dedication of the works to Haydn.

Haydn Society. An organization founded by H. C. ROBBINS LANDON and others in 1949 to further knowledge and understanding of Haydn's music. Based in Boston and Vienna, it had three complementary aims: first, to issue recordings of the composer's music; second, to promote studies of various aspects of it; and third, to publish a complete edition of his music. As a non-profit organization, the income from the recordings, supplemented by occasional donations, was intended to underwrite the scholarly activities. Although the recordings issued by the society through to 1952 enjoyed considerable commercial success, the income was never enough to subsidize the complete edition. Four volumes, nevertheless, appeared between 1949 and 1951: three devoted to symphonies and one to masses. JENS PETER LARSEN was the General Editor of the Complete Edition and its short-lived example and considerable achievement encouraged the later formation of the JOSEPH HAYDN-INSTITUT also, initially, under the leadership of Larsen. The intention of promoting studies of Haydn's music was never realized, though Robbins Landon's first book *The Symphonies of Joseph Haydn* (1955) was clearly the kind of project the society had in mind.

H. C. Robbins Landon, *Horns in High C: A Memoir of Musical Discoveries and Adventures* (London, 1999).

C. Raeburn, 'H. C. Robbins Landon and the Haydn Society: A Pioneering Musical Adventure', in O. Biba and D. W. Jones (eds), *Studies in Music History presented to H. C. Robbins Landon on his Seventieth Birthday* (London, 1996), 227–33.

Haydn's skull. The story of how Haydn's head was separated from the rest of his corpse shortly after his death, kept as a trophy, and reunited with the body only in 1954 is one of the most bizarre stories in the history of music. It is also a gruesome and duplicitous tale. Those of a sensitive disposition should not read any further.

The principal protagonists were JOSEPH CARL ROSENBAUM and Johann Nepomuk Peter, a fellow civil servant who was in charge of the penitentiary in Lower Austria. They were acquaintances and admirers of Franz Joseph Gall, a Viennese physician interested in phrenology, the later discredited theory that the size and shape of the skull surrounding the brain was related to the nature of a person's intelligence. He examined hundreds of skulls, many of which were collected in nefarious circumstances. Rosenbaum and his friends no doubt felt that an investigation of Haydn's skull would greatly aid this medical study and any doubts they had about the probity of their actions were made subservient to this cause. The necessity for absolute secrecy in their unseemly actions was aggravated in the summer of 1809 by the recent occupation of Vienna by French troops.

Haydn had died on 31 May and was buried in the churchyard in Gumpendorf on the following day. The gravedigger, Jakob Demuth, agreed to sever the head on 2 June and to deliver it on 3 June. However, he was beaten up (possibly by French soldiers) and was not able to meet Rosenbaum until 4 June. Because of the very hot weather the head was already in an advanced stage of putrefaction, and Rosenbaum vomited in the carriage while carrying the head to the hospital for dissection. After an examination of an hour the head was macerated and the skull bleached.

Plans were made for a case to hold Haydn's skull but renewed fighting between French and Austrian forces meant that it was not placed in a case until September 1809. Along with other skulls it was put on display in Peter's home, where it was willingly shown to visitors.

Shortly after Haydn's death Prince Esterházy indicated that he wished Haydn's body to be disinterred and placed in the crypt of the Bergkirche in Eisenstadt. Permission was sought and preliminary arrangements made but then the prince himself seems to have forgotten about the plan and it was not put into action until 1820. When it was discovered that the head had been removed from the coffin the police were informed, and both Peter and Rosenbaum were interviewed. Peter no longer owned his collection of skulls and had passed many of them, including the Haydn skull, to Rosenbaum. He hid the Haydn skull and presented the police with a substitute one which was duly placed in the composer's coffin, now laid to rest in the crypt in the Bergkirche. Mozart's Requiem was performed at the associated service.

When Rosenbaum died in 1829 he bequeathed the true skull to his accomplice, Peter, who, in turn, gave it to the physician Dr Karl Heller. It was then owned by Professor Rokitansky who gave it to the Gesellschaft der Musikfreunde in 1895. As the centenary of Haydn's death approached, the city of Vienna announced that it wished to bury the composer's remains in the Central Cemetery in the city, but the Esterházy family declined to cooperate. The reigning prince (Nicolaus IV) ordered an inspection of the crypt in Eisenstadt that confirmed the presence of a bleached skull. Over the next few decades plans were made to bring the remains together but this was not achieved until 1954. In a well-publicized ceremony a procession of 150 cars escorted a box containing the skull from the Gesellschaft der Musikfreunde in Vienna to the castle in Eisenstadt, where it arrived at midday. From there it was transported by car through a guard of honour of local children; a local choir sang the composer's partsong 'Du bist's, dem Ruhm und Ehr gebührt' (Hob.XXVc:8). In the side chapel of the Bergkirche Haydn's head was ceremonially placed in the coffin by the famous Austrian sculptor, Gustinus Ambrosi, the coffin closed, and slowly lowered into the crypt. ERL

'Documentary Report on the Opening of Haydn's Tomb at Eisenstadt, 1909', *HYB* 17 (1992), 175–80.

O. Plettenbacher, 'Die Odysee des Haydn Schädels', *Mitteilungen der Gustinus Ambrosi Gesellschaft*, 7 (1990), 23–5.

E. Radant (ed.), 'The Diaries of Joseph Carl Rosenbaum 1770–1829', *HYB* 5 (1968).

Haydn-Studien. Periodical founded by the JOSEPH HAYDN-INSTITUT in 1965 for the publication of scholarly enquiry relevant to Haydn's life and works; it is published by Henle Verlag (Munich). Many of the articles present research carried out by the staff of the Haydn-Institut. Four issues (*Hefte*) form a volume (*Band*). The principal language is German. Of fundamental value are the comprehensive bibliographies devoted to the composer: to 1972 in *HS* 3/3–4 (1974); 1973–83 in *HS* 5/4 (1985); 1984–90 in *HS* 6/3 (1992); and 1991–2000 in *HS* 7/2 (2001). A summary of the contents of each volume may be found on the web pages of the Haydn-Institut (www.haydn-institut.de). JD

'Haydn's wife'. The Italian violinist Giuseppe Puppo labelled BOCCHERINI 'Haydn's wife', a casual remark reflecting the popularity of the chamber music of both composers in the 18th century and some perception of the stylistic differences between them.

Haydntorte. A rather dry cake frequently encountered in Austrian cafés and restaurants. Prompted by the opportunistic interest of the Austrian tourist industry in Haydn following the anniversary year of 1982, Johann Altdorfer, a confectioner in Eisenstadt, manufactured a new cake; the basic ingredients include egg white, sugar, hazelnuts, and flour, mixed with the Italian liqueur, *grappa*. There is no suggestion that it was a favourite confectionery of the composer. ERL

Haydn-Verzeichnis. A catalogue of Haydn's music drawn up by JOHANN ELßLER in 1804–5 and for that reason occasionally known as the *Elßler-Katalog*; in the Haydn literature it is often abbreviated as *HV*. Together with the ENTWURF-KATALOG they constitute the most important bibliographical source for Haydn's music. But the *Haydn-Verzeichnis* is by no means infallible. Its preparation was instigated by the composer who looked over its content and the volume was meant to provide a comprehensive listing of his works. The full—but significantly frank—title of the volume was *Verzeichnis aller derjenigen Compositionen welche ich mich beyläufig erinnere von meinem 18ten bis in das 73ste Jahr verfertiget zu haben* (Catalogue of those compositions that I remember approximately to have composed between my 18th and 73rd years). Three copies were prepared. The first was forwarded to PLEYEL and remained unknown until 2007. The second was sent to Breitkopf & Härtel, who owned it until the end of the Second World War when its archives were destroyed. The third copy was retained by Haydn and was acquired by the Esterházy family; it disappeared in 1945.

Haydn did not own anything like a complete library of his compositions and the *Haydn-Verzeichnis* was prepared from a number of sources, of varying reliability. The most important and reliable source was the *Entwurf-Katalog*. This was supplemented by a catalogue of Haydn's symphonies owned by FRANZ BERNHARD KEES; published editions by ARTARIA, BREITKOPF & HÄRTEL, PLEYEL, NAPIER, and THOMSON; any available autographs; and, as the title suggests, imprecise memory. The catalogue is ordered according to genre, with an incipit for all works except operas and oratorios (some of these were added in a later hand). It is not a complete catalogue with dances, marches, music for the *lira organizzata*, and music for the mechanical organ, for instance, being entirely absent. It also includes some works, most notably the op. 3 quartets (from the publication by Pleyel), that are definitely not by the composer. The modern facsimile publication edited by Larsen used the Esterházy copy but did not reproduce the section devoted to Haydn's folksong settings.

Larsen.

Haydn Yearbook. A specialist journal, the first to be devoted solely to the composer, founded in 1962 by H. C. ROBBINS LANDON. Up to 1998, 22 volumes appeared containing major articles on all aspects of Haydn and his music, plus reviews of books and recordings. Many volumes contain extensive documentary material relating to the composer and the Esterházy court. The principal languages are English and German. Vols 1–10 were published by Universal Edition (Vienna); vols 11–16 by UCCP (Cardiff); and vols 17–22 by Robbins Landon (Rabastens; distributed by Thames & Hudson, London).

Hayes, Philip (bap. 17 April 1738; d. 19 March 1797). Oxford-born composer and organist who succeeded his father as Heather Professor of Music in the University of Oxford (1777–97). On the suggestion of Burney (a mutual acquaintance) Haydn was presented for an honorary Oxford degree in 1791; Hayes played a leading role in the proceedings. Notorious for his enormous girth (hence his nickname 'Fill-chaise') and irascible temperament, Hayes nevertheless exerted a beneficial effect on music in Oxford, including promoting Haydn's works. SW

H. D. Johnstone and R. Fiske, *The Eighteenth Century, Blackwell History of Music in Britain* (Oxford, 1990).

J. H. Mee, *The Oldest Music Room in Europe* (London, 1911).

Heidenreich, Joseph (*fl.* 1785–1806). Viola player, organist, and composer in Vienna; perhaps also a copyist. He was a prolific arranger of music for wind ensembles. He is thought to be the author of the additional parts for flute, two clarinets, two bassoons, two trumpets, and timpani that were added to Haydn's early Mass in F in 1805–6; the parts were prepared with Haydn's approval.

'Heiligmesse'. Nickname for the *Missa Sancti Bernardi d'Offida* (Hob.XXII:10) in use since the early 19th century. The opening of the Sanctus conceals the traditional (and appropriate) German melody, 'Heilig, heilig, heilig' (Holy, holy, holy) in the alto and tenor lines. The autograph manuscript draws attention to the quotation. The traditional full text of the hymn is as follows: 'Heilig, heilig, heilig, Heilig über heilig, Jesus Christus ohne End', in dem heiligen Sakrament' (Holy, holy, holy, holy upon holy, Jesus Christ without end, in the holy sacrament). JH

'Hen' symphony. Nickname in common use for Symphony no. 83. It derives from the French equivalent, 'La Poule', in use from early in the 19th century. The dotted note figure in the oboe that accompanies the repetition of the second subject in the first movement (bars 52–6) is reminiscent of a clucking hen. JH

Herschel, (Sir) William (b. 15 Nov. 1738; d. 25 Aug. 1822). German-born musician and astronomer, settled in England during the Seven Years War. Influenced by his family background he contributed with versatility to the English military and provincial musical scene. From the 1780s his professional involvement in astronomy took precedence over his musical activities. In 1782 he was appointed Astronomer Royal, and later in the 1780s he developed his famous 'Forty-foot Telescope', installed at the Observatory House near Slough, where visitors included Burney and (in June 1792) Haydn. SW

F. Brown, *William Herschel: Musician and Composer* (Bath, 1990).

'Herst Nachbä, hä, sag mir was heut' (Oye' mate, tell me what's news) (Hob.XXIIId:3). A PASTORELLA for solo soprano, strings, and continuo. It is a strophic work that enacts a dialogue between two shepherds who are contemplating visiting the infant Jesus. As well as the German dialect of the text, the work is typical of the genre in having arpeggio melodies (the pastoral trumpet), drone basses, and occasional emphasis on sharpened fourths in the melodic material. The circumstances of its composition are not known but it may well have been written for the BARMHERZIGE BRÜDER in the late 1750s. Later, a Latin text was substituted, 'Jesu Redemptor omnium', to convert the work into an Advent aria; this version has additional parts for two horns.

G. Chew, 'Haydn's Pastorellas: Genre, Dating and Transmission in the Early Church Music', in O. Biba and D. W. Jones (eds), *Studies in Music History Presented to H. C. Robbins Landon on his Seventieth Birthday* (London, 1996), 21–43.

'Hexenmenuett'. 'Witches' minuet', a nickname applied to the third movement of the quartet in D minor, op. 76 no. 2, probably from the early 19th century onwards. It is composed as a strict canon, between the two violins and the viola and cello. The remorseless skill of the movement plus its severe sonority prompted the association with witchcraft. JH

Hexen-Schabbas (Witches' Sabbath) (Hob. XXIXa:2). Marionette opera composed in the autumn of 1773. Both text and music are lost, though it is known that the libretto was printed in Vienna in 1773; the author of the text was probably PAUERSBACH or BADER. It was performed at Schönbrunn palace in July 1777 by the Esterházy company. PB

H. C. Robbins Landon, 'Haydn's Marionette Operas and the Repertoire of the Marionette Theatre at Esterház Castle', *HYB* 1 (1962), 111–97.

'Hin ist alle meine Kraft'. The first line of the poem, 'Der Greis' (The old man), by Johann W. Ludwig Gleim (1719–1803) that Haydn set as a partsong (Hob.XXVc:5). In the winter of 1805–6 (possibly earlier) he had the first four bars of the soprano part printed on a visiting card together with the associated text 'Hin ist alle meine Kraft, Alt und schwach bin ich' (Gone is all my strength, Old and weak am I). The composer distributed the card freely and on at least one occasion included it in his correspondence, no doubt taking pleasure in its unsettling combination of sadness and self-deprecation. When in 1806 GRIESINGER forwarded the two completed movements of Haydn's last quartet, op. 103, to Breitkopf & Härtel he enclosed the visiting card, suggesting that it might be printed at the end of the quartet. In the ensuing publication it was wrongly described as a canon. This musical error seems to have prompted MAXIMILIAN STADLER to prepare five canonic versions of the theme for various forces as a tribute to Haydn; he included an added text (presumably by Stadler himself) that changed the sentiments of the visiting card: 'Doch, was sie erschuf bleibt stets, Ewig lebt Dein Ruhm' (Yet, what it produced remains, Ever lives thy fame). The leading part in the canon sings the original text, the answering part the qualifying text. Later, the French composer Cambini (1746–1825) also elaborated the visiting card as a four-part canon for instruments plus figured bass.

Hoboken, Anthony van (b. 23 March 1887; d. 1 Nov. 1983). Dutch collector and bibliographer; compiler of the standard catalogue of Haydn's music. Born in Rotterdam, he trained initially as an engineer in Delft before receiving a musical education at the Hoch Conservatory in Frankfurt and then with Heinrich Schenker in Vienna. A man of private means, in 1919 he began to compile a collection of first editions and early editions of music by composers from Bach to Brahms; eventually this was to number some 5,000 items and is now part of the holdings of the Austrian National Library in Vienna. For that institution in 1927 he established an archive of photographs of autograph manuscripts; this was to prove invaluable after the Second World War when some of the originals had disappeared or been destroyed. In 1934 he began a card catalogue of the 1,000 or so Haydn editions in his possession, the beginning of over 40 years of bibliographical work on the composer. In 1938 he moved from Vienna to Switzerland, where he lived for the rest of his life.

Hoboken's catalogue of Haydn's music, published by Schott of Mainz, appeared in three volumes, in 1957, 1971, and 1978. It was a colossal achievement, the first comprehensive catalogue of Haydn's output compiled—as the author states in the second volume—during a period of momentous historical happenings affecting every aspect of life; 'Hob.' numbers have become a permanent part of musical discourse. The particular bibliographical strength of the first volume, devoted to instrumental music, was its exhaustive coverage of printed sources; apart from autographs, its coverage of manuscript sources was not, however, as comprehensive and as discerning. With the founding of the JOSEPH HAYDN-INSTITUT in 1955, the second and third volumes of Hoboken's catalogue were able to benefit from the resources and expertise of this organization, as well as the general burgeoning of scholarly interest in the composer's music in the 1960s and 1970s. *See also* CATALOGUES § 2 ii.

J. Schmidt-Görg (ed.), *Anthony van Hoboken: Festschrift zum 75. Geburtstag* (Mainz, 1962).

Hoffmeister, Franz Anton (b. 12 May 1754; d. 9 Feb. 1812). Austrian composer and publisher. Although he was particularly active in both areas in the 1780s and 1790s he had little to do with Haydn. A prolific composer of all kinds of instrumental music he set up a music-publishing business in Vienna in 1784, initially to promote his own compositions. Over the next few years the business began to rival that of ARTARIA. Less cautious than Artaria, many of Hoffmeister's plans for subscription series faltered after a few numbers. In the 1780s, rather than issuing works in the traditional set of six or three he issued them singly; Haydn's quartet in D minor (Hob.III:43) was ideally suited to this approach and it was published in 1786. In 1800, in partnership with Ambrosius Kühnel, he founded the Bureau de Musique in Leipzig and, although this firm numbered Beethoven amongst its clients, no new publications of Haydn's music were offered.

H. H. Hausner, 'Franz Anton Hoffmeister (1754–1812): Composer and Publisher', *Mitteilungen der internationalen Stiftung Mozarteum*, 38 (1990), 155–62.

Hofkapelle (sometimes Hofmusikkapelle). Literally 'court chapel' (or 'court music chapel') and, therefore, the retinue of musicians employed by any court. In Haydn studies it is associated with the musical establishment of the Habsburg family in Vienna. When Haydn first went to the city as a boy of 7 or 8, the number of composers, singers, and instrumentalists employed by the court exceeded 120, the largest in Europe. They were responsible for opera, church services, instrumental music, and music for the many private and public ceremonies that were a feature of court life. With the accession of Empress Maria Theresia to the throne in 1740, a period of reorganization and retrenchment began, motivated by the need to save money and a genuine desire to cut back on ceremonial. Over a couple of decades the number of employees was more than halved; ceremonial music was heavily curtailed; the opera was no longer directly managed by the court; and a much smaller retinue of musicians was retained for church services, under the control of Haydn's teacher, GEORG REUTTER.

As a choirboy Haydn was employed at St Stephen's rather than by the Hofkapelle but he would have witnessed this decline in the musical life of the court in Vienna at first hand, as patronage in its most dynamic form was assumed by the aristocracy; the Habsburg court played a negligible part in the development of the symphony, for instance. Even the splendour of church music was curtailed. In the mid-1750s Maria Theresia sought to restrict church music to unaccompanied music of the kind associated with the Sistine Chapel, the so-called 'alla Romana' style. In the Lent seasons of 1754, 1755, and 1756 Haydn was employed as an extra singer by the Hofkapelle to sing such music. After this period he was not to be directly associated with the Hofkapelle until the end of the century, when EMPRESS MARIE THERESE instigated the composition of the second Te Deum. At this time, many of Haydn's later masses, also, were acquired directly from the composer. In one of them, the 'Schöpfungsmesse', Haydn was obliged to revise the passage in the Gloria that quotes a melody from *The Creation* because the empress thought it inappropriate.

L. von Köchel, *Die kaiserliche Hof-musikkapelle in Wien von 1543 bis 1867* (Vienna, 1869).

Hofmann, Leopold (b. 14 Aug. 1738; d. 17 March 1793). Violinist, composer, and church musician who lived his entire life in Vienna. Hofmann has the dubious distinction of being one of only a handful of musicians whom Haydn is known to have disliked. Haydn's antipathy can probably be traced back to his early years in Vienna. Quite apart from his obvious talents as a composer, violinist, and keyboard player, Hofmann enjoyed advantages that the young Haydn might have envied. His father was a highly educated court official whose contacts were wide and varied, and he had the good fortune to be taught by GEORG CHRISTOPH WAGENSEIL, the most progressive and influential musical figure in Vienna during the 1750s.

As a chorister in the chapel of the dowager Empress Elisabeth Christine, Hofmann received an impressive musical education from Wagenseil who instructed him in both keyboard-playing and composition; he also developed into a first-class violinist.

Hofmann's rise to fame was meteoric. A violinist at St Michael's in 1758 and already an established composer, he had six symphonies published in Paris by 1760, and four years later succeeded Johann Nepomuk Boog (d. 1763) as *regens chori* at St Peter's, a major church appointment. In 1769, on Wagenseil's recommendation, Hofmann was named Hofklaviermeister and in 1772 he succeeded GEORG REUTTER as Kapellmeister at St Stephen's cathedral, the most important church music position in Vienna. He declined to apply for Reutter's post at the imperial court (the Hofkapelle) because it was made clear to him that he could not hold this post along with existing ones.

During the 1760s and early 1770s Hofmann was a prolific and popular composer in most genres and clearly one of Haydn's most significant professional rivals in Vienna. His works were disseminated widely throughout Europe, and he was ranked along with Haydn and Gluck as one of the leading composers in Vienna. By the mid-1770s he appears to have virtually ceased composing, and it is unlikely that anything was written during the last 15 years of his life. He continued to serve as Kapellmeister at St Stephen's until his death in 1793; in 1791 Mozart petitioned successfully to be appointed his unpaid assistant. Unlike the vast majority of his professional colleagues, Hofmann died a wealthy man.

In a letter to ARTARIA (20 July 1781) Haydn was scathing about Hofmann, calling him a braggart who slandered him in high society, and castigating three songs of his as 'street songs' in which 'neither ideas, expression nor, much less, melody appear'. To demonstrate his superiority Haydn included his own setting of the same texts in a group of 12 songs (Hob.XXVIa:1–12): 'An Thyrsis', 'Trost unglücklicher Liebe', and 'Die Landlust'.

An attractive flute concerto in D major by Hofmann circulated under Haydn's name in the 18th century, and is still occasionally falsely attributed to him (Hob.VIIf:D1). ADJB

A. D. J. Badley, 'The Concertos of Leopold Hofmann (1738–1793)' (diss., University of Auckland, 1986).
A. P. Brown, 'Joseph Haydn and Leopold Hofmann's "Street Songs"', *Journal of the American Musicological Society*, 33 (1980), 356–83.
D. Heartz, *Haydn, Mozart and the Viennese School 1740–1780* (New York, 1995).
H. Prohàska, 'Leopold Hofmann und seine Messen', *Studien zur Musikwissenschaft*, 26 (1964), 79–139.

Hofstetter, Roman (b. 4 April 1742; d. 21 June 1815). Bavarian composer of instrumental and sacred music; the likely composer of the op. 3 quartets formerly attributed to Haydn. A Benedictine monk, he took vows at the monastery in Amorbach in 1763, becoming its director of music and, for a while, its prior. Following the dissolution of the monastery in 1803 he moved to the town of Miltenberg. He became deaf in old age.

Hofstetter would have remained a footnote in the history of music had it not been for the discovery in 1964 of his name concealed behind that of Haydn on two (Hob.III:13, 14) of the six quartets published by BAILLEUX in Paris in 1777; as op. 3 these six quartets had always been accepted as part of the Haydn canon. This discovery of an alternative composer for two of the works plus the shaky bibliographical evidence for Haydn's authorship for the set as a whole has led to all six works being regarded as inauthentic; however, there is no direct evidence, beyond the circumstantial, that Hofstetter was the composer of the other four works in the set, which may have been written by another composer, or even by several composers. Other quartets by Hofstetter were also attributed to Haydn in the 18th century. Hofstetter was a great admirer of Haydn's music, especially *The Creation*, the masses, and the quartets. With a significance that this completely innocent figure could never have foreseen, he wrote to the Swedish diplomat SILVERSTOLPE in 1802: 'everything that flows from Haydn's pen seems to me so beautiful and remains so deeply imprinted on my memory that I cannot prevent myself now and again from imitating something as well as I can.'

G. Feder, 'Aus Roman Hofstetters Briefen', *HS* 1/3 (1966), 198–201.
'Round Table: Problems of Authenticity—"Opus 3"', in J. P. Larsen, H. Serwer, and J. Webster (eds), *Haydn Studies* (London, 1981), 95–106.
A. Tyson and H. C. Robbins Landon, 'Who Composed Haydn's Op. 3?', *Musical Times*, 105 (1964), 506–7.
H. Unverricht, A. Gottron, and A. Tyson, *Die beiden Hofstetter* (Mainz, 1968).

horn. The horn in use in Haydn's time was the natural horn. The notes of the harmonic series constituted the skeleton of the pitches available to the player, wide apart in the lower register and becoming increasingly close at the top of the register until they eventually merge. The control of embouchure needed to hit the correct note was considerable, particularly in rapid passages in the highest register or, less flamboyantly, in the alternation of registers. In the Austrian territories from the middle of the century onwards many players had developed a further technique, hand-stopping, whereby careful adjusting of the position of the right hand in the bell of the instrument enabled the pitch of the natural note to be changed, filling in the gaps between the harmonic series; part of the skill of hand-stopping was to minimize the difference in tone quality between open notes and stopped notes. In the lower half of the compass many players also cultivated the ability to flatten a particular note of the harmonic series by relaxing the embouchure. The expertise of horn players in these complementary techniques varied a good deal and ambitious horn-writing by composers of the day was invariably prompted by the capabilities of known players. For this reason Haydn's horn-writing in symphonies for the Esterházy court is much more challenging than that found in the 'Paris' symphonies (nos. 82–7) and *The Seven Last Words*.

During the first two years of Haydn's service at the Esterházy court two horn players were employed, specializing (as is still typical of professional players) in the high register and the low register. From 1763 through to 1790 the number of horn players available increased to four on a regular basis, often five, and in the period 1769–72 as many as six. Many of these players had multiple duties, performing in the FELDHARMONIE, accompanying the hunt, as well as playing in Haydn's orchestra. Several of the horn players were also competent violinists and viola players and regularly played those instruments in the orchestra. At least 18 different individuals were employed as horn players between 1761 and 1790 and Haydn responded eagerly to the particular expertise of many of them. JOSEPH LEUTGEB was employed for a few weeks in February 1763 and it was probably for him that he wrote his horn concerto the previous year. Four symphonies, nos. 13, 31, 39, and 72, require four horn players rather than the normal two; given that the Esterházy orchestra as a whole was no more than 16 or 17 players, this amounted to a quarter of the orchestra, a proportion that not even Mahler or Richard Strauss contemplated. (This deliberate imbalance of sonority is often regularized in modern performances, either by increasing the number of strings or by telling the horn players to play down.) The horn is a recurring feature of Symphony no. 31, opening and closing the work with brazen fanfares, providing a principal thematic idea in the first movement, and featuring as a virtuoso ensemble in variation 4 in the finale. Here the first horn is required to play a notated *e'''*, a third higher than the normal upper limit of the register in Haydn's time which, in turn, is another third higher than was to be the norm in the 19th century.

Haydn's orchestra at Esterházy did not have trumpet players, a major drawback for any composer of the time since the sonority of C major coloured by trumpets and timpani was a common orchestral characteristic, exploited in church music, symphonies, and operas. To overcome this deficiency Haydn resorted to a solution unique at the time: whenever he wanted to evoke this distinctive C major world he used horns as substitute trumpets, instructing them to play an octave higher (in C alto) than would normally be the case. The 'Maria Theresia' symphony (no. 48) and Count Errico's aria 'Al trionfar' in *La vera costanza* are good examples of this practice. When horns and trumpets are used in the same work, then the horns revert to their normal, C basso register.

More contentious is the view that horn parts in B♭, in works such as the overture to *La vera costanza* as well as Symphonies nos. 35 and 51, also should be played at the higher octave. The key of B♭ has no history of brightness and jubilation and this, coupled with the fact that Haydn never stipulated B♭ alto in his works, suggests that they should be played in the lower, basso register.

Haydn's music amply demonstrates his eagerness to exploit the capabilities of his players. Occasionally he required them to do something entirely novel, as in Symphonies nos. 45 and 46, in F♯ and B respectively, unusual keys that required the ordering of special half-slides from Vienna so that the normal horn in F and horn in B♭ could be played a semitone higher.

In the chorus 'Hört, hört das laute Getön' from *The Seasons*, Haydn features four horns in a spectacular evocation of a stag hunt, quoting a series of actual horn calls, from the search to the kill.

P. Bryan, 'Haydn's Hornists', *HS* 3/1 (1973), 52–8.

P. Bryan, 'The Horn in the Works of Mozart and Haydn: Some Observations and Comparisons', *HYB* 9 (1975), 189–255.

D. Heartz, 'The Hunting Chorus in Haydn's *Jahreszeiten* and the "Airs de Chasse" in the *Encyclopédie*', *Eighteenth-Century Studies*, 9 (1976), 523–39.

Horn family. Charles Frederick Horn (b. Feb. 1762; d. 3 Aug. 1830) was a teacher, keyboard player, and composer born in Germany but resident in London from 1782. He prepared an arrangement for keyboard and violin of Haydn's Symphony no. 76, published by LONGMAN & BRODERIP in 1786. Between 1789 and 1812 Horn served as music master to Queen Charlotte and the royal princesses. In the 1790s he befriended Haydn, who apparently presented three sonatas to his most deserving pupil, Miss Wetenhall. Horn's son, Charles Edward (b. 21 June 1786; d. 21 Oct. 1849), was a composer and singer who, in his memoirs, recalled sitting on Haydn's knee as a child. REC

[C. E. Horn], 'Biographical notice of the lately deceased Charles Frederick Horn', *Harmonicon*, 34 (1830), 400–1.

'Hornsignal' symphony. A nickname, originally in German ('mit dem Hornsignal'), in use since the middle of the 19th century for Symphony no. 31. The first movement features a series of familiar posthorn, military, and hunting signals. JH

H. Walter, 'Das Posthornsignal bei Haydn und anderen Komponisten des 18. Jahrhunderts', *HS* 4/1 (1976), 21–34.

'How do you do?' quartet. A nickname occasionally encountered in English-speaking countries for the quartet in G, op. 33 no. 5. The opening gesture has been likened to a greeting. For this reason the quartet has sometimes also been called the 'Compliments' quartet. JH

Huberty, Anton (b. *c.*1722: d. 13 Jan. 1791). Engraver and music publisher who worked first in Paris and then in Vienna. In Paris in 1757 he obtained a privilege specifically to print music by foreign composers and his first publications included works by the Viennese composer Wagenseil. Over the next 13 years works by several other Austrian composers were made available, and he may have visited Vienna in 1768–9 to enhance this connection. From 1770 his publications were regularly made available through bookshops in Vienna, and in 1777 he finally moved to the city, with the aim of establishing himself as a major publisher of music. However, he found that he was unable to compete with ARTARIA in particular and was forced to fall back on his skills as a music engraver. He died in poverty.

The number of works by Haydn published by Huberty was not numerous and their textual value is negligible. However, they do include the earliest publication anywhere of Symphony no. 6 ('Le Matin'), which appeared in 1773. The availability of Huberty publications in Viennese bookshops would have provided the composer with some indication of his wider reputation in the 1770s.

P. Bryan, *Johann Wanhal, Viennese Symphonist: His Life and His Musical Environment* (Stuyvesant, NY, 1997).

A. Weinmann, *Kataloge Anton Huberty (Wien) und Christoph Torricella* (Vienna, 1962).

Hughes, Rosemary (b. 26 Nov. 1911). English writer on music. Born in Bromsgrove, she was educated at Somerville College, Oxford (1929–32), and at the University of Toronto (1935). After working at the Royal College of Music from 1936 to 1939 she became a freelance writer on music and occasional broadcaster on the BBC. She was the author of the volume on Haydn in the 'Master Musicians' series. It first appeared in 1950 and in the course of several revisions it has endured as an elegant and skilfully presented account of the composer's life and music; it remains in print. She is also the author of a short study of Haydn's quartets, published in the series 'BBC Music Guides' (London, 1966). Together with N. Medici di Marignano she edited the travel diaries of Vincent and Mary Novello (London, 1955), a major resource for Mozart studies but which contains also some interesting information about Haydn.

Hummel, Johann Julius (b. 17 Dec. 1728; d. 27 Feb. 1798). Music publisher. He established his business in Amsterdam in 1754, opening a branch in Berlin in 1770. Hummel issued his first Haydn opus in 1765, an edition of the op. 1 quartets; by 1785 his catalogue listed more music by Haydn than any other composer. In this way he helped to establish Haydn's European reputation and, in particular, it was through imports of Hummel publications that the composer first became known in England. Hummel's editions eventually reached op. 56 (a publication of Haydn's last quartet, now known as op. 103). However, most of the editions are textually unreliable, full of spurious compositions, unauthorized arrangements, and corrections of perceived irregularities. MSM

G. Feder, 'Die Eingriffe des Musikverlegers Hummel in Haydns Werken', in H. Hüschen (ed.), *Musicae Scientiae Collectanea. Festschrift Karl Gustav Fellerer zum 70. Geburtstag* (Cologne, 1973), 88–101.

C. Johansson, *J. J. & B. Hummel. Music Publishing and Thematic Catalogues* (Stockholm, 1972).

Hummel, Johann Nepomuk (b. 14 Nov. 1778; d. 17 Oct. 1837). Composer and pianist who worked at the Esterházy court in the last years of Haydn's life. Born in Pressburg (Bratislava), the son of a violinist, he became a competent pianist and violinist by the age of 6, and his father's appointment as music director at the Theater auf der Wieden in Vienna in 1786 provided the best possible opportunities for his son. Within months he was taken into the home of the Mozart family as a pupil; after two years, his teacher recommended that he should embark on a performing career. Like Wolfgang and Leopold before them, Hummel and his father set off on a four-year European tour that, in their case, took them to Prague, northern Germany and Copenhagen, reaching Edinburgh in early 1790. Here, they were very successful, attracting many pupils and consolidating their financial position, before moving on to LONDON in the autumn of that year.

As a pianist-composer the teenage Hummel appeared in several concerts in London during Haydn's first visit; on 20 April 1792, in the eighth concert of the 1792 Salomon series, Hummel along with Salomon and the cellist Menel gave a performance of Haydn's piano trio in A♭ (Hob. XVI:14). By the time Hummel left London for Holland the following autumn, he had published several piano compositions in the city.

Back in Vienna Hummel devoted himself to the study of composition with Albrechtsberger and Salieri. Apparently Haydn gave him some organ lessons, with the warning that too much organ-playing would ruin his pianistic ability, and recommended him for several posts. Hummel's piano sonata in E♭ (op. 13) was dedicated to Haydn. When in 1803 it became increasingly clear that Haydn himself would not be able to carry on effectively as Kapellmeister at the Esterházy court he recommended Hummel for the post of Konzertmeister, which he took up in January 1804. With Haydn himself still nominally the Kapellmeister his duties were divided among three people: FUCHS, the Vice-Kapellmeister, had particular responsibility for church music, TOMASINI, Kammermusikdirektor, was responsible for instrumental music, and Hummel as Konzertmeister was placed in charge of secular vocal music, particularly the regular opera season that took place in Eisenstadt in the autumn. In practice, the division of responsibilities was unclear, a situation aggravated by Hummel's occasionally high-handed, even irresponsible actions. In truth, Hummel was both a more gifted composer than Fuchs and Tomasini and belonged to a younger, more independently minded generation; when his music was criticized by Prince Nicolaus, Hummel gave the Beethovenian reply that the prince was not fit to judge music. While serving at the Esterházy court Hummel had three operas performed there, *Die vereitelten Ränke, Das Haus ist zu verkaufen*, and *Mathilde von Guise*. Most of his compositional energies, however, were devoted to sacred music, including five masses performed during, but not in all cases originally specifically composed for, the annual celebrations associated with the nameday of Princess Marie Hermenegild Esterházy. He was also required to update the catalogue of the musical holdings at court and the so-called Hummel Catalogue of 1806 remains an important source of information on the repertoire at the turn of the century. Hummel's casual attitude to his duties led to his dismissal in December 1808, but he was reinstated. He finally left the Esterházy court in 1811.

In the following years he realized his evident potential as one of Europe's leading composers and probably its greatest pianist. He was Kapellmeister at Stuttgart in 1816–18 before moving to Weimar in January 1819, where he came into regular contact with Goethe. A favourable contract enabled him to travel regularly on concert tours, to compose, and to prepare his important treatise on piano-playing. By the 1830s his star was on the wane, as both his playing and his compositions were eclipsed by younger Romantics such as Schumman, Chopin, and Liszt. He died in Weimar.

At the sale of effects that had followed Haydn's death in 1809, Hummel had purchased the older composer's signet ring and walking stick. He also owned a quantity of autograph manuscripts by Haydn which eventually found their way to the British Library. DC

'A Facsimile of Hummel's Catalogue of the Princely Music Library in Eisenstadt, with Transliteration and Commentary', *HYB* 11 (1980), 5–182.
HCRL/5.

Hungarian National March. *See* WINDBAND MUSIC § 5.

Hunter family. John Hunter (b. 13 Feb. 1728; d. 16 Oct. 1793) was a distinguished Scottish surgeon who, from 1790, was Surgeon General and Inspector General of Hospitals. Irascible and blunt, he was a keen, original thinker and an obsessive collector, spending hours each day on dissection and recording his results. He published three medical treatises and numerous papers. In 1783 he acquired a home in Leicester Square, London, and surgical premises in Castle Street, and built a museum devoted to physiology. On his first visit to London in 1791–2 Haydn lodged nearby. Both Griesinger and Dies report that Hunter offered to remove the nose polyp which had long plagued the composer. Shortly before his departure from London in 1792, Haydn was invited to see Hunter who, with several brawny assistants, forcibly tried to persuade him to have the operation; they were not successful. Unfortunately Hunter's surviving casebooks do not record a meeting with Haydn.

Anne Hunter (née Home, b. 1742; d. 7 Jan. 1821) married John Hunter in 1771, and was a published poetess, having been associated with the Scottish national song movement. She was evidently a highly accomplished and sociable woman, and her weekly salon was a forum for discussions of literature and music. She numbered Elizabeth Carter, Mary Delany, Elizabeth Montague, Hester Thrale Piozzi, and Horace Walpole among her friends; she was also an acquaintance of Fanny Burney. She discontinued her salons after her husband's death. Haydn set Anne Hunter's poetry to music in his first set of canzonettas (Hob. XXVIa:25–30), which is dedicated to her, and included one of her poems, 'The Wanderer' in the second set (Hob.XXVIa:31–6), dedicated to Lady Charlotte Bertie. In neither set is Anne Hunter formally identified as the poet. Haydn also set two further poems by her, 'The spirit's song' and 'O tuneful voice' (Hob.XXVIa:41–2). Anne Hunter included the poems set by Haydn in a collection published in 1801, where they are titled merely as 'songs'. Records in the Royal College of Surgeons indicate that other poems in the collection were intended to be set by Haydn. Nine further poems were published as *The Sports of the Genii* in 1804. She also produced a metrical version of the text to *The Creation* after the first English performances in 1800, though it was clearly not meant to be sung. Her poetry was set also by Johann Peter Salomon and commissioned by GEORGE THOMSON for his various collections of national folksongs, including settings by Haydn and Beethoven. DdV

A. Peter Brown, 'Musical Settings of Anne Hunter's Poetry: From National Song to Canzonetta', *Journal of the American Musicological Society*, 47 (1994), 39–89.
HCRL/3 and 4.

'Hunt' quartet. Nickname occasionally encountered for the quartet op. 1 no. 1 by Haydn, prompted by the 6/8 rhythms of the first movement. The French 'La Chasse' is more frequently used and is to be preferred in order to avoid possible confusion with Mozart's 'Hunt' quartet (K458).

I

iconography. Since Haydn became so famous in his lifetime it was only natural that his portrait was sketched, painted, and engraved many times, the likenesses ranging from the profound to the mediocre. Documentary evidence for these portraits, both authentic and spurious, varies a great deal, compounded by the fact that some of the originals are now lost. In the following survey readers are referred to reproductions found in the modern sources cited in the bibliography.

1. **Authentic portraits.**
2. **Spurious representations from the 18th to the 20th centuries.**

1. Authentic portraits. The earliest portrait of Haydn is by Johann Basilius Grundmann (1726–98), who was the official painter at the Esterházy court in the 1760s. Destroyed at the end of the Second World War, when Eszterháza was used as a hospital by the Russian army, the portrait was an oil painted on wood (possibly canvas) (HCRL/1, plate I following p. 352). Oral information provided by the last of the Esterházy archivists, János Hárich, who remembered the painting hanging at Eszterháza, indicates that the uniform was blue with silver braid, which corresponds to descriptions of Haydn's livery as Vice-Kapellmeister at the Esterházy court in the early 1760s. The portrait was probably commissioned by PRINCE NICOLAUS ESTERHÁZY in the period *c.*1762–3. A reconstructed version may be found in Heartz, *Haydn, Mozart*, 261.

Ostensibly, the next portrait of Haydn may be by Ludwig Guttenbrunn (1750–1816), who painted many frescos in the palace of Eszterháza during the two-year period 1770–2. Prince Nicolaus Esterházy then paid for a period of study in Italy (his self-portrait is to be found in the Uffizi Gallery, Florence) but, rather than returning to the court, Guttenbrunn went to England, where he and Haydn again met. He painted the composer's portrait in London in 1792; this became the basis of an engraving by Luigi Schiavonetti (1765–1810) (Somfai, *Haydn*, 224). Two versions of the portrait exist: one, rather like a sketch (reproduced in colour in Robbins Landon, *Essays*, frontispiece), was for some years owned by the Karajan family in Salzburg and is now in the Burgenländisches Landesmuseum, Eisenstadt; the other, which probably formed the basis of the Schiavonetti engraving, is in private possession in London (HCRL/2, plate III following p. 16). Haydn's wife, who had been Guttenbrunn's lover when he was at the Esterházy court, was the owner of the first version, which naturally led to the conjecture that it dated from the early 1770s; it would seem more natural for a painting originating in Austria, rather than one from London, to be owned by Haydn's wife. However, the content of the extant painting points clearly to the 1790s: Haydn is seated at an English square piano (with handstops), an instrument otherwise unknown at the Esterházy court in the 1770s, and the style of his dress is closer to the latter period.

In the early 1980s a previously unknown pastel portrait by an anonymous artist came to light in Bratislava (Galéria hl. mesta SSR). It shows the composer in about 1775 in a blue jacket and is unsigned (Huss, *Haydn*, 81). It might be the ultimate source for the famous engraving by Johann Ernst Mansfeld (1739–96), issued by Artaria in Vienna in 1781 (HCRL/2, plate 1 following p. 160). The engraving was the first portrait of Haydn to be widely distributed; it is mentioned several times in the composer's correspondence and Prince Nicolaus Esterházy ordered copies as gifts. A rather idealized likeness, supported by the words of Horace 'Blandus auritas fidibus canoris ducere quercus' (Blandish the listening oaks with your singing strings, *Odes*, I. xii), it formed the basis of several other engravings (for instance, to accompany a biography of the composer that appeared in the *European Magazine* in October 1784, and in the *Journal für Deutschland* in 1786).

On Christmas Eve 1785 the latest *Österreichisches Nationalkalender* was published in Vienna, featuring silhouettes by Hieronymous Löschenkohl (1753–1807) of, amongst others, opera singers from the Italian company at the Burgtheater, Mozart, and Haydn (Somfai, *Haydn*, 213). It was at this time that some other, excellent miniatures seem to have been executed: the silhouette that Haydn's faithful copyist Elßler owned (Somfai, *Haydn*, 214; Gesellschaft der Musikfreunde, Vienna); a pastel on ivory (HCRL/2, plate I following p. 16) by an unknown artist that, untypically, gives a faithful representation of the composer's rather coarse features (Gesellschaft der Musikfreunde); and the silhouette that appeared on the title page of three keyboard trios (Hob.XV:3–5) published by Boßler of Speyer (HCRL/2, plate 27 following

p. 160). Finally, from this pre-London period there is a rather formal portrait in oils by the north German artist, Christian Ludwig Seehas (1753–1802) (Huss, *Haydn*, 176; Staatlichesmuseum, Schwerin).

The first portrait to appear as a commercial engraving after Haydn arrived in London was by Francesco Bartolozzi (1727–1815), advertised on 4 April 1791 (Somfai, *Haydn*, 116). It was based on a not very successful miniature by A. M. Ott (*fl.* *c.*1790) which was rediscovered in 1995 and is now owned by the Gesellschaft der Musikfreunde, Vienna (*HYB* 20 (1996), 66).

Artistically the most vivid portrait of Haydn was painted in oils by John Hoppner (1758–1810) in December in 1791, commissioned by the Prince of Wales and still part of the Royal Collection (HCRL/3, plate I following p. 16); it was later engraved by G. S. Facius (1807). Also from 1791 is perhaps the most well known of Haydn portraits, by Thomas Hardy (1757–*c.*1805), now in the Royal College of Music, London (HCRL/3, plate II following p. 16, also cover of the present volume). Hardy is known to have painted portraits of a number of musicians for the publisher JOHN BLAND, perhaps to be displayed in his shop in Holborn; maybe the Haydn portrait was part of this continuing series of commissions. Though technically very assured, the oil painting does not capture the rude health of the composer in the way the Hoppner portrait does. Hardy provided an engraving in 1792 (Somfai, *Haydn*, 137).

Towards the end of his first visit to London Haydn recorded in his notebook that Hardy, Ott, Guttenbrunn, and Hoppner had painted his portrait, and someone he described as 'Daßie' had prepared a wax portrait. This turned out to be the Scottish artist James Tassie (1735–99); in 1978 the author located a cameo (a glass-paste medallion) in the National Gallery of Scotland, Glasgow, based on his wax portrait (Landon, 'A New Haydn Portrait', with reproduction).

The composer's favourite portrait of himself dates from his second visit to London, a pencil drawing in profile by George Dance (1741–1825), or rather three similar pencil drawings; one is now owned by the Royal College of Music (HCRL/3, plate 1 following p. 320), a second by the Historisches Museum der Stadt Wien, Vienna (Somfai, p. 148), and a third is in private possession.

On his return to Austria, the Viennese painter Johann Zitterer (1761–1840) made a rather undistinguished portrait of a pensive-looking Haydn seated, as in the Guttenbrunn portrait, at a square piano (Somfai, *Haydn*, 159: Museum der Stadt Wien, Vienna). The music stand shows a keyboard reduction of the beginning of the slow movement of the 'Surprise' symphony. In 1800, Artaria sold an engraving by J. Neidl based on this portrait (Somfai, p. 168). A new miniature by Zitterer or one based on his portrait was formerly in private possession in Leipzig but was destroyed in 1945 (Somfai, *Haydn*, 225).

In 1799 the German artist Johann Carl Rösler (1775–1845) visited Vienna, where he executed oil paintings of Haydn and Luigi Tomasini. The portrait of Haydn shows an ageing composer, tired from the superhuman exertions of composing *The Creation* and *The Seasons*. Its first owner was Johann Rochlitz, the editor of the *Allgemeine musikalische Zeitung*, who later gave it to Mendelssohn; it is now in the Faculty of Music, Oxford University (Landon, *Haydn. A Documentary Study*, 153). At least two different engraved versions are known, by Phillipe Trière (*c.*1801) and Blascke (1802). The Musikbibliothek der Stadt Leipzig owns an unsigned pastel, based on the Rösler (Somfai, *Haydn*, 225).

A more characteristic view of Haydn from the later 1790s is evident in a miniature discovered in 1991 (Pelham Gallery, London; *HYB* 18 (1993), plate 1). Although unsigned, the reverse of the oval miniature has a lock of hair and the indication 'Haydn'. It is a good likeness with a convincingly disfigured nose; the composer is wearing a brown coat and the eyes are, correctly, brown.

There are two extant portraits from 1799 by Vincenz Georg Kininger (1765–1851), a drawing (Somfai, *Haydn*, 224), and a sepia drawing (Somfai, *Haydn*, 172). The latter was prepared for use on the title page of the first volume of Breitkopf & Härtel's *Oeuvres Complettes*, issued in 1800; it was based on the Guttenbrunn portrait which, with some difficulty, had to be borrowed from Haydn's wife.

From the turn of the century date a number of busts of Haydn that, in general, present an authentic image of the composer. A lost life-size bust from 1799, possibly by Anton Grassi (1755–1807), was apparently once owned by the Gesellschaft der Musikfreunde and carried the inscription from Horace 'Tu potes tigres comitesque sylvas ducere et currentes rivis morari' (Thou canst lead beasts and companion forests and still the flowing streams, *Odes*, III xi). It showed the composer without a wig (Somfai, p. 215) and it may have served as the basis for the Artaria engraving of 1808 made by David Weiss (1775–1846) (Somfai, *Haydn*, 216). It is also possible that the intriguing engraving by A. Kunike (HCRL/4, plate 3 following p. 240) published by Steiner & Co. after Haydn's death is based on this lost bust. In 1802 Grassi provided a second bust of the composer, this time with wig, in unglazed porcelain. Two versions were manufactured: a large one, some 40 cm. (15 ins.) high, with a pedestal at first in blue with the same inscription found in the common Mansfeld engraving (HCRL/5, plate 2 following p. 240), later in white with gold lettering, 'J. Haydn'; and a small one, some 15 cm. (6 ins.) high intended for wider distribution, again on a pedestal and with the inscription 'J. Haydn'. Even more honest in its representation of the composer are three wax busts made by Franz Christian Thaller (1759–1817). As well as presenting a realistic view of his pock-marked skin, the clothes and hair of the wig of at least one of these busts were reputed to have been taken from the composer's own clothes and hair. The only surviving version is owned by the Kunsthistorisches Museum, Vienna (see HCRL/4 for colour reproduction and photographs of the second version, plate I following p. 32 and plate 2 following p. 240). An unsigned lead bust of the composer (HCRL/5, plate 1 following p. 240) was once thought to be the work of Grassi but is now ascribed to Thaller. The bust was owned by the composer, who bequeathed it to the HARRACH family in Haydn's birthplace, Rohrau, where it remains; in 1840 the Viennese sculptor Franz Prokop used the bust as a model for the sandstone bust that was added to the Haydn monument in the gardens of the Harrach palace. Finally, from the same period, is a life-size bust in marble by August Robatz (1757–1815) showing the composer in the fashionable, *en antique* pose without his wig (Gesellschaft der Musikfreunde, HCRL/4, plate 5 following p. 240).

While in England Haydn had become acquainted with the well-known artist Philipp Jacob Loutherbourg (1740–1812). In 1801 he provided the engraver Landseer with a hierarchical layout of 27 contemporary composers and musicians with Haydn and Mozart placed at the pinnacle (Landon, *Haydn. A Documentary Study*, 72). The individual images were taken from 'Miniature Cameos by H. de Janvry'.

In 1803 the Viennese sculptor and medallion maker Sebastian Irrwoch (d. 1813) fashioned a wax medallion of Haydn in profile (Somfai, *Haydn*, 188 and 225). An engraving by David Weiss based on this medallion was used as the frontispiece of Dies's biography of Haydn (1810). Also perhaps derived from Irrwoch, alternatively from one of the Grassi busts, is the engraving by Edmé Quenedey (1756–1830) (HCRL/4, plate 6 following p. 240). About this time the Danish artist Christian Hornemann (1765–1844) made a miniature of Haydn, which is now lost. A surviving photograph (HCRL/4, plate 4 following p. 240) shows a rather young-looking Haydn but the famous miniature of the raven-haired Beethoven that Hornemann produced at this time encourages the view that the Haydn portrait may be more vivid than the extant photograph suggests.

The last oil painting of Haydn was commissioned in 1805 by the Esterházy family from Isidor Neugaß (*c.*1780–1847); it remains in the palace in Eisenstadt (HCRL/5, plate I following p. 24). It shows Haydn seated at the desk on which two arias from *The Creation* lie, 'Nun schwanden von den heiligen Strahle' (Now vanish before the holy beams) and 'Nun beut die Flur das frische Grün' (With verdure clad the fields appear). In the background is the Temple of Apollo, while to the right, rather interestingly, a bust of Bach is visible. While the music of Bach had never played a formative part in Haydn's development his presence here is an indication of the increasing historical status being accorded to that composer; the implication is that Haydn is destined to have the same enduring greatness.

A more human indication of Haydn's contemporary fame is represented in the famous miniature by Balthasar Wigand (1771–1846) of a performance of *The Creation* on 27 March 1808, his last public appearance (HCRL/5, plate IV following p. 24). Haydn is seated in the middle awaiting the public greeting of, amongst others, Prince Lobkowitz, Princess Marie Hermenegild Esterházy, and Beethoven. The aquarelle was commissioned by the princess who attached it to a lid of a commemorative box (Somfai, *Haydn*, 203); she gave the box to Haydn as a gift. The box, which was owned at one time by Liszt, disappeared at the end of the Second World War.

The final image of Haydn is the poignantly tranquil death mask, taken by JOHANN ELßLER (Museum der Stadt Wien, Vienna; HCRL/5, plates 5 and 6 following p. 240).

2. Spurious representations from the 18th to the 20th centuries. Although spurious Haydn portraiture is not nearly as extensive as that associated with Mozart, it is often curious, sometimes amusing, and invariably reveals something about the perception of the composer and his music.

The least spurious kind of portrait occurred when originally genuine works of art were copied over and over until such time that true likeness disappeared. This happened notably with the engravings by Mansfeld and by Hardy which were widely copied and gradually became almost unrecognizable as Haydn. But there was a much more sinister way of producing a would-be portrait and that was to claim, with or without some circumstantial evidence, that a particular anonymous figure was Haydn. One engraving purporting to show Mozart being inspired by Haydn (Landon, *Haydn: A Documentary Study*, 106) turns out to be a double misattribution. In 1800 the London publisher Monzani issued a handsome engraving by Rigaud of the EARL OF ABINGDON, Haydn's patron and friend in London. Abingdon is seated and there is an anonymous standing figure playing an archlute. In later editions Abingdon becomes Mozart, and the lute player Haydn.

There have been many other wilful misattributions of which two will be discussed here. In 1932 Joseph Muller published details of a portrait of a musician held by the Brooklyn Museum, New York. He claimed the portrait was by the Venetian painter Alessandro Longhi (1733–1813) and that the musician was the young Joseph Haydn, from his first years of service at the Esterházy court (see photograph in *HYB* 2 (1963/4), 69). While art historians remain unsure about the attribution to Longhi, music historians have decided that the subject is certainly not Haydn. Among other things the red livery does not correspond with any Esterházy livery that Haydn would have used, and the fleshy lips are very unlike those of the composer.

A second misattribution concerns a pair of paintings by Vestier (1740–1824) owned by the Cummer Gallery of Art, Jacksonville, Florida. When purchased they were alleged to show members of the Esterházy family, a seated Haydn with a sword, a violinist identified as 'Simon', and a cleric assumed to be Primitivus Niemecz (the librarian and constructor of mechanical organs at the Esterházy court). The paintings were provisionally dated *c.*1771–4. Subsequent investigation by art historians in the Museum of Fine Arts in Budapest proved that all this was wishful thinking. Vestier never visited Vienna or the Hungarian countryside; the painting was not entered in the extensive catalogues of fine art owned by the Esterházy family; the figures represented in the paintings could not possibly be from the Esterházy family from the early 1770s; Haydn never carried a sword and, moreover, the figure does not look remotely like the composer; finally no 'Simon' ever worked as a violinist at the Esterházy court in the 1770s.

Less harmful have been the many romantic representations of the composer, usually intended to illustrate the composer's life. One is Haydn—the composer of *The Creation* and *The Seasons*—on board ship in the English Channel in a great storm, the composer seated, looking at the lightning, while the women behind him cower in terror. Another is a *gemütlich* scene, in true Viennese tradition: 'Haydn plays string quartets at the house of Peter von Genzinger.' HCRL

O. E. Deutsch, *Mozart und seine Welt in zeitgenössischen Bildern* (Kassel, 1961).

D. Heartz, *Haydn, Mozart and the Viennese School 1740–1780* (New York, 1995).

M. Huss, *Joseph Haydn* (Eisenstadt, 1984).

Joseph Haydn: Zeitgenössische Drucke und Handschriften [catalogue] (Leipzig, 1962).

M. Ladenburger, 'Joseph Haydn in zeitgenössischen Abbildungen', in *Joseph Haydn in seiner Zeit* [Exhibition catalogue] (Eisenstadt, 1982), 301–10.

J. Muller, 'Haydn Portraits', *Musical Quarterly*, 18 (1932), 282–98.

HCRL/1–5.

H. C. Robbins Landon, *The Collected Correspondence and London Notebooks of Joseph Haydn* (London, 1959).

H. C. Robbins Landon, *Haydn. A Documentary Study* (London, 1981).

H. C. Robbins Landon, 'A New Haydn Portrait', *Soundings*, 9 (1979–80), 2–5.

H. C. Robbins Landon, 'The "Loutherbourg" Haydn Portrait', in id., *Essays on the Viennese Classical Style* (London, 1970), 39–43.

J. P. Larsen, 'Zur Frage der Porträtähnlichkeit der Haydn-Bildnisse', *Studia Musicologica*, 12 (1970), 153–66.

L. Somfai, *Joseph Haydn. His Life in Contemporary Pictures* (London, 1969).

'Il distratto'. Nickname for Symphony no. 60. In 1774 Haydn wrote incidental music for a play, *Der Zerstreute*, performed by a visiting troupe of actors at Eszterháza. It was a German translation of one of Regnard's most frequently performed stage works, *Le Distrait* (The absent-minded man). The music was subsequently assembled as a six-movement symphony, reflecting the overture, four entr'actes, and finale of the original incidental music. Although there are no indications of the programmatic content in the score of the symphony, its progress can easily be associated with characters and incidents in the play. The finale, for instance, requires the violins to tune their instruments after the movement has begun, evoking one of the many absent-minded actions of the main character, Leander. Later performances of the play with Haydn's music were given in Vienna and Salzburg. JH

R. Angermüller, 'Haydns "Der Zerstreute" in Salzburg (1776)', *HS* 4/2 (1978), 85–93.

R. A. Green, '"Il Distratto" of Regnard and Haydn: A Re-examination', *HYB* 11 (1980), 183–95.

E. Sisman, 'Haydn's Theater Symphonies', *Journal of the American Musicological Society*, 43 (1990), 292–352.

Il Maestro e Scolare (Master and pupil) (Hob. XVIIa:1). A two-movement work for piano duet consisting of an Andante with seven variations, and a Tempo di Menuetto. It was probably written *c.*1768–70 and was first published in 1780 by Hummel, who gave it its title. The theme of the first movement strongly resembles that found in the first movement of the baryton trio in A (Hob. XI:38) written in the mid-1760s. The master–pupil relationship of the title governs the progress of the first movement with every sub-phrase stated by the second player (the master) being dutifully echoed by the first player (the pupil) two octaves higher; master and pupil join together only during the cadences. This charming conceit retains its freshness through four variations with progressively decreasing note values (from quavers to demisemiquavers), a skipping variation that suggests the plucked strings of a baryton, and a final pair that add expressiveness and vigour to the close. The second movement abandons formal imitation in favour of a euphonious texture with a good deal of doubling in thirds and sixths. ES

Il mondo della luna (The world of the moon) (Hob.XXVIII:7). Opera ('dramma giocoso per musica') in three acts, to a libretto by CARLO GOLDONI, first performed at Eszterháza in August 1777 in celebration of the marriage of Count Nicolaus (1741–1822), Prince Nicolaus's second son, to Countess Maria Anna von Weissenwolf (1747–1822). Several autograph fragments show that Haydn revised the opera extensively, possibly even before it was first performed.

The overture in C major, a single movement orchestrated with trumpets and timpani, is remarkable for its very long development section, which gives it a symphonic character. In 1779 Haydn reused the overture, having reduced its orchestration, as the first movement of Symphony no. 63. In its operatic version the movement ends with an open cadence.

The drama that follows is propelled forward by Ecclitico, a clever man who knows exactly how to take advantage of everyone around him. At the same time, like Don Alfonso in *Così fan tutte*, he shows a philosophical side, using his tricks to teach moral lessons. Haydn wrote the role of Ecclitico for the fine comic tenor GUGLIELMO JERMOLI, who may not, however, have created it, because he apparently left Eszterháza shortly before the premiere. Ecclitico wants to marry Clarice (soprano, created by CATARINA POSCHWA), one of the two daughters of Buonafede (baritone, BENEDETTO BIANCHI). A gullible old man, Buonafede is the perfect victim for Ecclitico's machinations.

Ecclitico, aware of Buonafede's passion for stargazing, pretends to be an astronomer, and in the opening chorus he and his students praise the moon. The key of the chorus, E♭, is identified throughout the opera with the moon, partly because that key was associated during the 18th century with darkness and sleep; Ecclitico refers to the moon as 'la triforme dea' (the goddess who appears in three forms) which may have led Haydn to think of a key with three flats.

Ernesto, a young nobleman, loves Buonafede's other daughter, Flaminia. They are the *parti serie* of the opera: roles featuring the noble feelings, language, and music of *opera seria*. Like many other composers who set Goldoni's librettos, Haydn assigned the male serious part not to a tenor but to a male soprano. He took advantage of the rare presence at Eszterháza of a castrato singer, PIETRO GHERARDI, and the role is the only instance in an opera by the composer of writing for such a voice. MARIANNA PUTTLER sang Flaminia. Ernesto and Flaminia express their love for one another in two serious arias. Ernesto's 'Begli occhi vezzosi' is a love song in the style of a minuet, the first of many numbers in this opera, instrumental as well as vocal, that combine triple metre and a slow to moderate tempo. Flaminia's 'Ragion nell'alma siede', a grand bravura aria with wide leaps and coloratura, begins with a melody with the a–b–b′ form typical of *opera seria*.

Clarice is less noble than her sister, as one can tell from her first aria, 'Son fanciulla da marito', which has much less coloratura than Flaminia's first aria and features comic melodies with two-bar phrases. Ernesto's servant, Cecco (tenor, sung by Leopold Dichtler), loves Lisetta, Buonafede's maid, on whom Buonafede also has designs (the role of Lisetta was originally intended for the soprano Maria Jermoli, before she left with her husband shortly before the premiere).

Ecclitico puts into action a plan to win Buonafede's daughters and maid for, respectively, himself, Ernesto, and Cecco. He tells the old man that he has an elixir that, when drunk, will transport him immediately to the moon. Buonafede begs Ecclitico to share the elixir with him. Ecclitico consents, and Buonafede drinks what is really a sleeping potion. His slumber is so deep that, in the finale of Act 1, Clarice and Lisetta fear that he is dying.

In Act 2 Ecclitico with the help of Ernesto and Cecco put on an elaborate charade to deceive Buonafede into thinking that he is on the moon. The scenery depicts an imaginary world. A slow, dreamy orchestral movement—a kind of tender minuet—is followed by a ballet accompanied by two orchestras: strings in the pit, horns and bassoons offstage; the occasional use of string harmonics adds to the other-worldly effect. Ecclitico's students put fantastic costumes on Ecclitico and Buonafede, who are welcomed by the emperor of the moon (portrayed by Cecco) and the star Hesperus (portrayed by Ernesto).

The 'emperor' announces his intention to marry Lisetta, who quickly figures out what is going on, and joins in the deception. Imagining herself as empress, she sings an aria, 'Se lo comanda', that nicely mixes comic and serious styles. Buonafede, overcoming his jealousy, gives up his beloved Lisetta to the 'emperor'. To the sound of instrumental music Flaminia and Clarice arrive on a movable platform. In the aria 'Se la mia stella' Flaminia declares her love for Ernesto without Buonafede being aware of it. This music, yet another lyrical movement in a slow triple metre, is enlivened by solos for horns and bassoons.

The finale of Act 2 begins with a lunar ceremony in which all but Buonafede speak nonsense ('Luna, lena, lino, lana'). Buonafede is fascinated by what he thinks is the language of the moon, and attempts to speak it himself. He looks on uncomprehendingly as the 'emperor' presides over the wedding of 'Hesparus' to Flaminia, and Ecclitico to Clarice. In a tender passage in moderate tempo and triple metre the newly-weds declare their love, while Buonafede continues to speak gibberish. When Cecco, Ernesto, and Ecclitico announce 'Finita è la commedia', Buonafede at last realizes that he has been duped. The tempo suddenly accelerates and the old man expresses his rage in music that switches dramatically from major to minor and back again.

Act 3 begins with a stormy sinfonia in G minor. Unlike the big sinfonia at the beginning of Act 2 of *L'infedeltà delusa*, this music serves a useful dramatic function: it depicts the anger of Buonafede, who is being held in Ecclitico's house until he forgives his daughters and gives them a dowry. He eventually agrees to do so. Left alone, Ecclitico and Clarice declare their love in an erotically charged duet, 'Un certo ruscelletto'. At the words 'Oh dio, la man levate ch'io moro adesso qua' (For God's sake take your hand away or I'll die) a sudden shift to the minor mode and dissonance vividly emphasize the sexual imagery of the text. The opera ends with a short ensemble of reconciliation and celebration.

Il mondo della luna seems never to have been revived at Eszterháza or performed elsewhere. Because of this it served Haydn as a useful source of material for later works. In addition to the overture, he reused several numbers and parts of numbers. Six pieces reappeared in the trios for flute, violin, and cello (Hob.IV:6–11); the old-fashioned, serious character of Ernesto's 'Qualche volta non fa male' made its transformation into the Benedictus of the 'Mariazeller' mass quite natural; and the canonic passage near the end of the love duet in Act 3 conveys similar amorous excitement in the love duet at the end of Act 1 of *Armida*. JAR

M. Brago, 'Haydn, Goldoni and *Il mondo della luna*', *Eighteenth-century Studies*, 17 (1984), 308–32.

F. Lippmann, 'Haydn e l'opera buffa: tre confronti con opere italiane coeve sullo stesso testo', *Nuova rivista musicale italiana*, 17 (1983), 223–467.

'Il quakuo di bel'humore' (The good-humoured quaker). A title written on a manuscript copy of Symphony no. 49 owned by the Gesellschaft der Musikfreunde, Vienna. It is likely that it refers to the one-act play, *Die Quäcker*, a translation of Chamfort's *La Jeune Indienne*. Haydn's symphony was probably played as incidental music to a local performance, though there is no suggestion that it was first composed with the play in mind. The subject matter of the play is strikingly different from that associated with the familiar nickname to the symphony, 'LA PASSIONE'.

E. Sisman, 'Haydn's Theater Symphonies', *Journal of the American Musicological Society*, 43 (1990), 292–352.

Il ritorno di Tobia (The return of Tobias) (Hob. XXI:1). Oratorio by Haydn, libretto by GIOVANNI GASTONE BOCCHERINI, first performed in Vienna on 2 April 1775; revised version first performed there on 28 March 1784.

Haydn's only oratorio before *The Creation* and *The Seasons* was written for the Tonkünstler-Societät, the musicians' benevolent society in Vienna, founded in 1771, which twice each year mounted a pair of charitable performances. The commission, so soon after the foundation of the society, was a feather in Haydn's cap, indicating the esteem in which he was held in the capital despite his being something of a country cousin, his duties to the Esterházy household permitting him only infrequent periods of residence in the city. He responded to the prestigious occasion and to the large performing forces available by providing his most extended and ambitious composition in any genre up to that time.

The usual repertoire of the Tonkünstler-Societät was the formal Italian oratorio, following closely the conventions of Metastasian *opera seria*. Haydn was not well served by the stiff formality of the dramatic scheme or by his librettist (a brother of the composer Luigi Boccherini), who out of Procrustean deference to the conventional proprieties stifled the freshness of the charming story from the Apocryphal Book of Tobit. The adventures of Tobias, whose opportunities for vivid depiction Haydn, given a different dramatic treatment, would surely have relished, are recounted cursorily in the past tense, in recitative. In the biblical account the climax of the story dramatically tells of the blind Tobit's immediate joy at the restoration of his sight; in the oratorio the event again takes place, without special punctuation, within continuous recitative, and the old man can only complain that the light hurts his eyes. However clinically sound the notion may be of the need for gradual acclimatization after a cataract operation (it also keeps the libretto going for an extra couple of numbers), this was a wasted opportunity: the biblical version might have provoked from Haydn a foretaste of the blaze of light that was to occur, two decades later, in *The Creation*.

For all the musical quality of individual numbers, Haydn's oratorio is stunted by the limitations within which he was working. It proceeds largely in alternation between recitative and aria (there is one duet); the arias are often, as Haydn himself was tacitly to acknowledge, of inordinate length. And it has to be admitted that the limpness of the dramatic scheme of the libretto is matched at times by a leisurely musical pace, already evident in the unusually repetitive overture, that is uncharacteristic of Haydn in general. At the same time, reflective arias without even the distraction of staging to compete for the audience's attention offered great opportunities for purely musical exploration. The most celebrated solo number is the exquisite expression of Sara's quiet ecstasy, 'Non parmi esser fra' gl'uomini', with obbligato wind instruments (including cors anglais, a favourite occasional tone colour in the 1760s and 1770s). But the recitatives too (most of them orchestrally accompanied) show Haydn's meticulous concern for detail and, as far as the conventional scheme would allow, for drama. The episode immediately before the concluding chorus of Part 1, in which Tobias is reunited with his parents and they meet Sara, his new bride, is a masterly scene complex, kept alive by the use of a wide range of keys, its continuity movingly sustained by a recurrent orchestral motif. Remarkable too is the tonal instability of Anna's foreboding in Part 2, her recitative followed by the aria 'Come in sogno un stuol m'apparve', beginning in Haydn's most severe F minor mood but abandoning the usual symmetrical form to finish in a serene F major as her spectral vision clears.

The work was revived for the two Lenten concerts of the Tonkünstler-Societät in 1784 with a cast that featured Nancy Storace (improbably singing the alto part of Anna), Caterina Cavalieri, Theresia Teyber, Valentin Adamberger, and Steffano Mandini, all familiar names from Mozart's operas. The oratorio was substantially revised, cuts in the arias providing a less protracted scheme. The most important alterations, however, were additions. The first version had contained three choruses, which a contemporary reviewer in 1775 already compared to Handel; now Haydn added two more, which make the comparison unavoidable. Each is compellingly linked to the aria of Anna that precedes it, the first picking up her 'Ah gran Dio', the second, the D minor 'Svanisce in un momento', using the F major closing section of her 'Come in sogno' as its principal subsidiary material. Apart from their contrapuntal mastery (which is nothing new in Haydn), these new choruses have an impetus, a taut urgency of harmonic pacing, that belongs more to the age of the 'Mariazeller' mass (1782) MISSA CELLENSIS—even of the 'Paris' symphonies (only a year or two away)—than to 1775 or the methods of Haydn's earlier extended sacred works. The second of them is the only number of the oratorio to remain generally familiar today, as an independent motet to the words 'INSANAE ET VANAE CURAE'.

Further attempts at revival, involving additional pruning and some reorchestration, were undertaken by Haydn's pupil SIGISMUND NEUKOMM with the composer's somewhat reluctant blessing. He successfully performed three of the choruses in St Petersburg in 1807, and in 1808 he conducted his version in Vienna at the two December concerts of the Tonkünstler-Societät, the last performances of an Italian oratorio in this context. The revival was no doubt prompted by the popularity of *The Creation* and *The Seasons*, which by now dominated its programmes, but even with Neukomm's attempts to modernize the work it was understandably found antiquated in comparison, and it was not a success. Attempts by both Haydn and Neukomm to publish the oratorio, even in a cut version and in piano score, came to nothing. The full *Il ritorno di Tobia* appeared in print for the first time in 1963. DEO

HCRL/2.

H. E. Smither, *A History of the Oratorio, III: The Oratorio in the Classical Era* (Oxford, 1987).

Imbault, Jean-Jérôme (b. 9 March 1753; d. 15 April 1832). French violinist and publisher. Until the age of 30 Imbault worked mainly as a violinist. He turned to music-publishing in 1783, initially in partnership with Sieber, gradually becoming one of the leading firms in Paris. He sold his business in 1812 and lived a comfortable existence in retirement. As a publisher of Haydn's music he did not have direct contact with the composer but his edition of the 'Paris' symphonies was prepared from the original material used by the Concert de la Loge Olympique; his edition of the 'London' symphonies likewise is textually reliable. For a short period he was the owner of the autograph manuscript of 13 partsongs by Haydn (Hob. XXVb:1–4; XXVc:1–9).

R. Benton, 'J.-J. Imbault (1753–1832), violoniste et éditeur de musique à Paris', *Revue de Musicologie*, 62 (1976), 86–103.

'Imperial'. A nickname frequently used for Symphony no. 53. It may have originated in France (as 'L'Impériale') but it is not known in any source before the middle of the 19th century; attempts to link it in some way with the Empress Maria Theresia are unfounded. JH

'Imperial' mass. Nickname frequently used in English-speaking countries for the Mass in D minor ('Nelson') MISSA IN ANGUSTIIS (Hob. XXII:11). Dating from the middle of the 19th century it arose from the mistaken belief that the work had been composed for the coronation of the Austrian emperor. This falsehood also prompted the nickname 'Coronation' mass for the work.

'In Nomine Domini'. An annotation (In the name of the Lord) that Haydn habitually wrote on his autograph manuscripts, usually centred above the first system of the music. For Haydn, the devout Catholic, the act of writing out the full score of a work, that is the full realization of something previously only glimpsed in sketches, was the crucial stage of a creative process that was enabled by God. Usually, the final bars of the musical work were followed by the complementary annotation 'Laus Deo' (Praise God).

Since very few autographs from the 1750s survive, it is difficult to state when Haydn got into the habit of annotating his scores in this fashion; certainly by the mid-1760s it is common and remained so, in all genres, up to his final compositions. The autographs of the Cello Concerto in D major and of Symphony no. 89 are two of very few works that do not have the opening inscription, while that of the Trumpet Concerto is unusual in noting it in abbreviated form, 'In N: D'. Rather more works omit the final 'Laus Deo' (e.g. Symphonies nos 28, 50, 56, and 87). From about 1773 (as in Symphony no. 50) Haydn usually coupled the word 'Fine' (or 'Finis') with 'Laus Deo'.

While 'In Nomine Domini' remains unaltered at the beginning of a work the fervour of creativity occasionally encouraged Haydn to be more effusive in his thanks in the concluding annotation, usually evoking the Virgin Mary. *L'infedeltà delusa* has 'Laus omnipotenti Deo et Beatissimae Virgini Mariae'; *L'incontro improvviso* has 'Fine del Drama. Laus Deo et B. V. M. et O. S.'; *Armida* has 'Laus Deo et B. V. M.'; and the *Missa brevis Sancti Joannis de Deo* has the appropriate 'Laus Deo: B. V. M. et Sancti Joanni de Deo'. The only autographs of instrumental music to carry extended final annotations are those of the op. 20 quartets, from which it is reasonable to surmise that they were a particularly gratifying act of creation. Only no. 5 contents itself with the usual 'Fine Laus Deo; no. 1 has 'Soli Deo et Cuique Suum', no. 2 'Laus omnip: Deo' and 'Sic fugit amicus amicam', no. 3 'Laus Deo et B: V: M: cum S° S^{to}', no. 4 'Fine—Gloria in excelsis Deo', and no. 6 'Laus Deo et Beatissimae Virgini Maria'.

'Insane et vanae curae' (Insane and idle cares). A sacred chorus adapted from *Il ritorno di Tobia*. When Haydn prepared a revised version of the oratorio for performance in Vienna in 1784 he added a couple of striking choruses, including 'Svanisce in un momento'. It exploits the familiar metaphor of a storm at sea followed by a calm, the one equated with the tribulations of life, the other with the self-fulfilling hope of the believer. It was probably in 1797 for a performance at Eisenstadt in September that Haydn prepared a sacred version of the movement. A Latin text prepared by an unknown author contrasts, in a similar way to the original Italian of the oratorio, the futility of worldly cares with the seeking of salvation. The structure of the original chorus is maintained, an alternation of two sections, the first in a forceful D minor, the second a more lyrical section, initially in F major and then in D major. For many listeners the highly graphic nature of the original storm music is not matched by the power of the new text. The instrumentation was slightly altered: the original horn parts were replaced with trumpets, and a timpani part was provided. The work was published by Breitkopf & Härtel in 1809 and was widely performed in the 19th century.

I. Becker-Glauch, 'Neue Forschungen zu Haydns Kirchenmusik', *HS* 2/3 (1970), 167–241.

'In Schlaff geschrieben' (written while asleep). An annotation noted by Haydn in the top margin of the last page of the autograph of the Horn Concerto in D. On that page and the preceding one, the composer, coming to the end of the work and, presumably, tired, had mixed up the staves allotted to the oboes and violins.

insertion aria. Late 18th-century Italian opera, whether serious or comic, was orientated towards the performer. Composers tailored their works to the abilities of specific singers, those involved in the premiere. A cast change during a run or revival of an opera, or subsequent performances in a different city with a new cast, often meant that some singers would find certain arias unsuited to their capabilities. In such cases a local composer would be expected to provide viable substitute numbers that would present the singers to best advantage (ensemble numbers were less frequently altered). These new arias might be supplied by the original composer of the opera or, more likely, by another, local composer. Some arias were newly composed specifically for the work in question; others were older arias taken from a different opera altogether.

Although in modern usage the term 'insertion aria' refers to any aria added to an opera after the premiere of the work, it is helpful to distinguish between two types. A replacement aria is a substitute for an aria already present in the earlier version; here the composer uses the same text as the original for the new set piece. An insertion aria, on the other hand, is a new number, for which there is no counterpart in the original score; the text of the aria will be newly written or it may be taken from the libretto of a different opera. Such an aria may also require the composer to add additional recitative, or even an entirely new scene, to prepare the set piece properly.

Haydn prepared and conducted performances of over 100 different operas during his service at the Esterházy court. Only a handful of these operas, those by Haydn himself, were specifically written for the singers at court; the rest were by the leading opera composers of the day, including Cimarosa (1749–1801), Paisiello (1740–1816), Salieri, and Sarti (1729–1802), and were imported from Italy or Vienna. It is therefore not surprising that Haydn usually needed to revise these scores to make them suitable for the Eszterháza company, especially for the modest vocal talents of his mistress, LUIGIA POLZELLI. In addition to composing insertion and replacement arias, Haydn freely altered the scores of his contemporaries; he made a number of alterations to his own operas as well, necessitated by cast changes in later performances or revivals. *La fedeltà premiata*, for example, was given its first performance in February 1781; by the time the opera was revived the following September, the singers of the four principal roles had all left the court, and Haydn was forced to make cuts, transpose arias, and compose two replacement numbers. For a private performance of *Lo speziale* in Vienna in 1770 it appears that he composed a substitution aria for the character of Grilleta ('Caro Volpino'). But the majority of Haydn's insertion and substitution arias were intended for the operas of his contemporaries. (Revisions made before the premiere of an opera, as in the case of *Il mondo della luna*, are not strictly speaking insertion arias.)

It is unclear exactly how many insertion and substitution arias Haydn composed since he did not include any of them in the *Entwurf-Katalog*. Most of these arias were removed, probably by Haydn himself, from the opera scores and parts. Although some autographs and authentic copies survive, the absence of many of the arias from the original performance material has complicated identification and authentication. Another difficulty is that since most of the operas were acquired from other opera houses and not directly from the composers, they arrived at Eszterháza with one or several layers of insertion numbers already present. It is therefore not always possible to determine if an insertion aria pre-dates the arrival of the score at Eszterháza or if it was newly composed by Haydn.

At present just over 20 insertion arias have been authenticated, with another 20 seen as probably the work of the composer. Also of interest are arias and ensembles by other composers that Haydn altered to such an extent that they might be considered new items altogether. RJR

D. Bartha, 'Haydn, the Opera Conductor: An Account of the Newly Disclosed Sources in Budapest', *Music Review*, 24 (1963), 313–21.

Bartha and Somfai.

G. Lazarevich, 'Mozart, Haydn, Cimarosa: Insertion Arias as Reflections of Operatic Customs', in *Internationaler Musikwissenschaftlicher Kongreß zum Mozartjahr 1991 Baden-Wien*, ed. I. Fuchs (Tutzing, 1993), 725–50.

Invocation of Neptune (Hob.XXIVa:9). An incomplete ode composed by Haydn in London in 1794. The autograph of the two movements is in the British Library and carries an annotation (dating from 1821) stating that it was part of a projected oratorio. Many commentators have accepted this suggestion, but one glance at the jingoistic text shows it to be highly untypical of an oratorio. It had previously been set in London by Friedrich Hartmann Graf (1727–95), when it was more appropriately described as an ode, part of a broad English tradition of vocal works on patriotic texts that included Boyce's many odes for the New Year and for the King's birthday, Linley's *Ode to Shakespeare*, and Dupuis's *Ode to the Genius of Britain*.

Haydn's ode was to have consisted of five or six movements of which the two actually composed would have formed the second and third. The text dates back to the 17th century and originally formed the preface by Marchimont Nedham (or Needham) to an edition of a treatise by John Selden, *Mare clausum*, which, as was typical of the time, joined legal argument with romance to justify the expansion of the British Empire. The full title of the ode is 'Invocation of Neptune and his Attendant Nereids to Britannia on the Dominion of the Sea'. In it Neptune suggests that there is a natural alliance between Britannia and himself that makes foreign conquest an entirely natural and laudable ambition.

British audiences in London at the end of the 18th century would not have worried themselves about obscure references in a text that was over 100 years old; in 1794, in particular, they would have been happy to be part of the general wave of patriotism sweeping the country now at war with France. Quite why Haydn never completed the ode is not known. The most likely explanation is a practical one. Choral music featured very infrequently in Haydn's concerts in London, mainly, as the composer himself reported, because of the difficulty of securing boy choristers to perform on prescribed days; there was no opportunity to present the work and it was left unfinished and, subsequently, unperformed. What remains, therefore, is a third of an ode, an imposing aria for Neptune (over an unusual pizzicato accompaniment and with some charming woodwind decoration) and a vigorous chorus that, ultimately, transcends the appalling text.

H. C. Robbins Landon and D. W. Jones, *Haydn: His Life and Music* (London, 1988).

J

Jacob's Dream (Hob.XV:31). In London in 1794 Haydn composed a one-movement work in E♭ for piano trio with the title *Jacob's Dream*. During the Allegro movement several rapid scalic passages played by the violin represent the angels of Jacob's dream, ascending and descending the ladder set between earth and heaven. According to Dies it was written for an amateur violinist who liked to play in the higher register of the instrument; it was first performed at a musical party in Therese Jansen's house. In 1795 Haydn added a first movement, in the extraordinary key of E♭ minor, to make a regular keyboard trio (Hob.XV:30) but erased (not quite successfully) the fanciful title of the second movement. It is the only example in Haydn's keyboard trios of programmatic writing. Some of the documentary evidence wrongly states that the movement was a violin sonata or a piano piece.

Jäger, Eleonora (b. 1721; d. 19 May 1793). A solo and choral singer who served at the Esterházy court for 40 years. She was engaged in 1753 to sing in the church services in Eisenstadt under the direction of Werner, who may have been her teacher. Although she sang in one opera by Haydn (*Acide*) she remained a stalwart of the church choir in Eisenstadt. In 1771 she drew the attention of the prince to the perilous state of that ensemble and ensured that it was maintained. Of the many sacred works by Haydn that she would have performed, the Salve regina in G minor from the same year must have been one of the most gratifying. She is variously described as a soprano and as a contralto. Even though she was nearly 70 years old, she remained an employee of the Esterházy court when Prince Nicolaus was succeeded by Prince Anton in 1790. Her niece Barbara Pilhofer had joined the church ensemble in 1788 and in September 1797 sang the solo soprano part in the performance of Haydn's *Missa in tempore belli*. ERL

HCRL/2.

Jansen, Therese (b. *c.*1770; d. 29 June 1843). Pianist and teacher. Born in Aachen, the daughter of a dancing master, she became a pupil of CLEMENTI, who dedicated his op. 33 sonatas to her. Haydn knew her as a gifted pianist and in 1794–5 composed at least two, probably all three, of his last sonatas expressly for her (Hob.XVI:50–2). In 1797 three piano trios (Hob.XV:27–9) by Haydn were dedicated to her. He was a witness at her marriage to GAETANO BARTOLOZZI at St James's Piccadilly on 16 May 1795. She was also the recipient of a piece for piano trio called JACOB'S DREAM.

In 1797 she left London with her husband and infant daughter. Arriving in Vienna in 1798–9 and discovering that Artaria had published 'her' E♭ sonata (Hob.XVI:52), with a dedication to Magdalena von Kurzböck, she arranged for the sonata to be printed from her autograph by the London publishers Longman & Broderip with a dedication to her. The sonata in C (Hob.XVI:50), for which she owned the copyright, was published by her on her return to London in 1800. Separated from her husband, she supported her two daughters by teaching the piano. The elder daughter became famous as the dancer Madame Vestris. DdV

HCRL/3 and 4.

Jermoli family. Guglielmo (*fl.* 1768–89) was a tenor; his wife, Maria (*fl.* 1777–9), was a mezzo-soprano. Born in Milan, Guglielmo Jermoli sang in most of the principal opera houses in Italy before joining the Eszterháza company in March 1777. His wife, Maria, joined him, but both left for London in July. They returned to the Esterházy court in October 1779 at a handsome joint salary of 1,200 gulden, equivalent to Haydn's own basic salary of 600 gulden. They remained at Eszterháza until the summer of 1781, when they moved to St Petersburg. Maria is not known to have sung in Russia and was probably a less distinguished singer than her husband. It was for this couple that Haydn wrote the central roles of Fileno and Cilea in the first version of *La fedeltà premiata*. ERL

HCRL/2.

C. Sartori, *I libretti italiani a stampa dalle origini al 1800* (Cuneo, 1990–4).

'Joke' quartet. Nickname used in English-speaking countries for the quartet in E♭, op. 33 no. 2, occasioned by the witty manipulation of musical expectations at the end of the finale. It probably arose early in the 19th century. There is no German equivalent. JH

Joseph Haydn-Institut. Established in Cologne in 1955 with the aim of publishing the first historical-critical complete edition of the works of Joseph Haydn (JOSEPH HAYDN WERKE, 1958–), following the collapse of two previous attempts (BREITKOPF & HÄRTEL, 1907–33, and HAYDN SOCIETY, 1949–51). Unlike contemporary 'new editions' of the output of other major composers (for example, the *Neue Bach-Ausgabe*, 1954– and the *Neue Mozart-Ausgabe*, 1955–), where the emergence of important new sources and advances in scholarly and editorial methods were leading to a revision of outputs first defined by the great 19th-century *Gesamtausgaben*, the proposed collected edition of Haydn's works possessed no such fundamental basis in 1955. The problem was exacerbated by the size of the composer's output, the obscurity that enveloped many of his works (particularly from his early years), the numerous unauthorized editions issued during his lifetime, and a degree of misattribution unequalled in the musical works of any other composer.

Broadly defined, the work of the Haydn-Institut is twofold: to establish the extent and chronology of Haydn's output, and to present the musical text as far as possible in its authentic form. At the outset the most urgent task was the separation of authentic works from the mass of misattributions. To this end a comprehensive investigation of all works attributed to Haydn and the acquisition of all relevant sources on film was undertaken on a worldwide basis; to date the photographic archive of Haydn's autographs, 18th- and 19th-century manuscript copies, first editions, and other early editions comprises more than 360,000 frames, from which is derived a further archive of enlargements of the most important sources. Two massive card indexes (the *Werkkartei* of authentic works, cross-referenced to the *Quellenkartei* of sources and their description) lie at the centre of the records of the Haydn-Institut; further files derive from the employment of various codicological and bibliographical specialisms, such as the analysis of handwriting (both Haydn's and that of copyists) and the evidence afforded by paper types and watermarks, to aid the authentication, dating, and clarification of the transmission of Haydn's works. The Haydn-Institut has also accumulated an extensive specialist library. In 1965 it established the journal HAYDN-STUDIEN.

The first president of the Joseph Haydn-Institut was Friedrich Blume (1955–73), succeeded by Karl Gustav Fellerer (1974–7), and from 1977 Klaus Wolfgang Niemöller. The direction of the work of the Institut has been the responsibility of Jens Peter Larsen (1955–60), Georg Feder (1960–90), Niemöller (interim capacity 1990–2), Horst Walter (1992–6), Günter Thomas (1996–7), Marianne Helms (1997–8), and Armin Raab (1998–). International contacts are maintained with Haydn scholars involved in the preparation of the complete edition. The edition is part of a planned programme of publications by a range of learned societies in Germany, coordinated by the Konferenz der deutschen Akademien der Wissenschaften (Mainz) and funded by national and state governments. Further funding is received from the city of Cologne, the Österreichische Akademie der Wissenschaften, the Bundesministerium für Wissenschaft, Forschung, und Kunst (Vienna), and from industry (notably Volkswagen) and commerce. Address: Blumenthalstraße 23, D 50670 Cologne, Germany. Web address: www. haydn-institut.de JD

A. Raab, 'Haydn und Köln. Die Arbeit des Joseph Haydn-Instituts', in *Joseph Haydn und Bonn* [Exhibition catalogue] (Bonn, 2001), 151–63.

Joseph Haydn Stiftung. In 1993 the International Joseph Haydn Foundation of Eisenstadt was founded, initially to secure the purchase of 34 autograph letters by Haydn. It was reconstituted with a wider remit in January 1995. Since 1997 it has been located in newly restored buildings adjacent to the Haydn Museum (Haydn's house in Eisenstadt). There are three principal aims: to establish an international Haydn Centre devoted to archive, audio, and video material; to support Haydn research, conferences, and associated publications; and to promote historically aware performances of music by the composer and his contemporaries. Address: Haydn Zentrum, Haydngasse 19–21, Eisenstadt, A-7000 Austria. (www. haydnfestival.at) GJW

Joseph Haydn Werke. Often abbreviated as *JHW*, sometimes *HW*. The first historical-critical complete edition of Haydn's works, issued by the JOSEPH HAYDN-INSTITUT, Cologne (G. Henle Verlag, Munich, 1958–). The 19th-century zeal to establish canonic *Gesamtausgaben* (for example, those of Bach, Handel, Mozart, and Beethoven) did not embrace Haydn for reasons both critical (his diminution to the status of a genial forerunner of Mozart and Beethoven) and practical (the uncertainty about the content and chronology of his output), quite apart from the problems of the musical texts themselves. These difficulties lay at the root of the failure of two later attempts to produce a complete edition: *J. Haydns Werke*, edited by Eusebius Mandyczewski (Breitkopf & Härtel, Leipzig, 10 vols, 1907–33) and the *Joseph Haydn Gesamtausgabe/The Complete Works*, general editor, Jens Peter Larsen (Haydn Society Inc., Boston and Vienna, 4 vols, 1949–51).

The current *Joseph Haydn Werke* is 'historical' in two fundamental senses. First, because it will present the historical event of Haydn's music (to the extent that it has survived), represented by authentic texts (as far as they can be determined). The historical sequence of composition is reflected in the chronological ordering of works within genres, as far as it is ascertainable. Division into genres cuts across the chronology of Haydn's output as a whole, but corresponds to other historical realities. Second, various aspects of the historical context of works are addressed in the forewords to volumes: for example, the circumstances of composition and first performance; publication and critical reception; the sources and other aspects of verbal texts such as librettos and poetry; matters of historical performance practice; and any other issues that illuminate the music as a historical event.

The edition is 'critical' in its establishment of musical texts that are as authentic as can be determined from transmissions of varying authority. For some works, Haydn's autograph survives, but this does not necessarily put the musical text beyond question, since plausible variant readings in another authoritative source such as authentic performance parts or authorized first edition can raise critical issues of what constitutes a definitive version (or versions); at the other extreme, a transmission that survives only in unauthorized copies or editions calls for the full implementation of the philological method—the chronological relationship of sources, and the determination of a form of the text, its critical scrutiny and revision—in order to arrive at as authentic a text as possible.

The *Joseph Haydn Werke* is arranged by genre into 32 series (*Reihe* I–XXXII), with the chronological subdivision of each series into units of a volume (*Band*); some longer vocal works require further division into a half- or part-volume (*Halbband, Teilband*). Each volume includes a foreword (*Vorwort*), explanation of the layout of the musical text (*Zur Gestaltung der Ausgabe*) and since 1980 the critical report (*Kritischer Bericht*), which presents in concise form the description and evaluation of sources and a list of significant variant readings; this allows the reader to follow the procedure which led to the given musical text, and to engage in a critical appraisal of it. Critical reports for volumes from before 1980 are published separately. Volumes appear as it becomes possible to resolve their peculiar issues; thus many early works and others that are problematic will be among the last to appear. In the following list future volumes are indicated by the absence of editor(s) and date. Series XXXIII (*Supplement*) and XXXIV (*Register*, indexes) will bring the undertaking of some 103 volumes to a close within the next ten years. JD

I/1, Symphonies *c*.1757–60/1, S. Gerlach and U. Scheideler (1998)
I/2, Symphonies *c*.1761–5
I/3, Symphonies 1761–3, J. Braun and S. Gerlach (1990)
I/4, Symphonies 1764 and 1765, H. Walter (1964)
I/5a, Symphonies *c*.1766–9, A. Friesenhage and C. Heitmann (2008)
I/5b, Symphonies *c*.1770–4
I/6, Symphonies 1767–72, C.-S. Stellan Mörner (1966)
I/7, Symphonies 1773 and 1774, W. Stockmeier (1966)
I/8, Symphonies *c*.1775/6, W. Stockmeier with S. Gerlach (1970)
I/9, Symphonies *c*.1777–9, S. C. Fisher with S. Gerlach (2002)
I/10, Symphonies *c*.1780
I/11, Symphonies 1782–4, S. Gerlach and S. E. Murray (2003)
I/12, 'Paris' symphonies, i, H. Nakano (1971)
I/13, 'Paris' symphonies, ii, S. Gerlach and K. Lippe (1999)
I/14, Symphonies 1787–9
I/15, 'London' symphonies, i, G. Gruber and R. von Zahn (2005)
I/16, 'London' symphonies, ii, R. von Zahn (1997)
I/17, 'London' symphonies, iii, H. Walter (1966)
I/18, 'London' symphonies, iv, H. Unverricht (1963)

II, Concertante, S. Gerlach (1982)

III/1, Concertos for violin and orchestra, H. Lohmann and G. Thomas (1969)
III/2, Concertos for violoncello and orchestra, S. Gerlach (1981)
III/3, Concertos for one wind instrument and orchestra, M. Ohmiya with S. Gerlach (1985)

IV, *The Seven Last Words of Our Saviour on the Cross*, orchestral version, H. Unverricht (1959)

V, Dances and marches, G. Thomas (1995)

VI, Concertos with *lire organizzate*, M. Ohmiya (1976)

VII, Notturni with *lire organizzate*, M. Ohmiya (1972)

VIII/1, Divertimenti in five and more parts for string and wind instruments, S. Gerlach (1994)
VIII/2, Divertimenti for wind instruments, six 'Scherzandi' (symphonies), fragment in E flat, S. Gerlach and H. Walter, with M. Ohmiya (1991)

IX, Trios for wind and string instruments, A. Friesenhagen (2004)

X, String duos, A. Friesenhagen and U. Mazurowicz (2004)

XI/1, String trios, i, B. MacIntyre and B. Brook (1986)
XI/2, String trios, ii (attributed to Haydn) B. MacIntyre and B. Brook (1996)

XII/1, Early string quartets, G. Feder and G. Greiner (1973)
XII/2, String quartets 'opus 9' and 'opus 17', G. Feder and S. Gerlach (1963)
XII/3, String quartets 'opus 20' and 'opus 33', G. Feder and S. Gerlach (1974)
XII/4, String quartets 'opus 42', 'opus 50' and 'opus 54/55', J. Webster (2008)
XII/5, String quartets 'opus 64 and 'opus 71/74', G. Feder and I. Saslav, with W. Kirkendale (1978)
XII/6, String quartets, 'opus 76', 'opus 77' and 'opus 103', H. Walter (2003)

XIII, Works with baryton, S. Gerlach (1969)

XIV/1, Baryton trios nos. 1–24, J. Braun and S. Gerlach (1980)
XIV/2, Baryton trios nos. 25–48, H. Unverricht (1960)
XIV/3, Baryton trios nos. 49–72, H. Unverricht (1958)

XIV/4, Baryton trios nos. 73–96, H. Unverricht (1958)
XIV/5, Baryton trios nos. 97–126, M. Härting and H. Walter (1968)

XV/1, Concertos for organ (cembalo) and orchestra
XV/2, Concertos for keyboard (cembalo) and orchestra, H. Walter and B. Wackernagel (1983)

XVI, Concertini and divertimenti for keyboard (cembalo), accompanied by two violins and bass, H. Walter with H. Nakano (1987)

XVII/1, Keyboard trios, i, W. Stockmeier (1970)
XVII/2, Keyboard trios, ii, W. Stockmeier (1974)
XVII/3, Keyboard trios, iii, I. Becker-Glauch (1986)

XVIII/1, Keyboard sonatas, i. G. Feder (1970)
XVIII/2, Keyboard sonatas, ii, G. Feder (1970)
XVIII/3, Keyboard sonatas, iii, G. Feder (1966)

XIX/XX, Keyboard pieces/Works for keyboard for four hands. S. Gerlach (2006)

XXI, Pieces for flute-clock, S. Gerlach and G. Hill (1984)

XXII/1, Stabat mater, M. Helms and F. Stoltzfus (1993)
XXII/2, Smaller sacred works, i
XXII/3, Smaller sacred works, ii

XXIII/1a, Masses nos. 1–2, J. Dack and G. Feder (1992)
XXIII/1b, Masses nos 3–4, J. Dack and M. Helms (1999)
XXIII/2, Masses nos. 5–8, H. C. Robbins Landon with K. Füssl and C. Landon (1958)
XXIII/3, Masses 9–10, G. Thomas (1965)
XXIII/4, Mass no. 11, I. Becker-Glauch (1967)
XXIII/5, Mass no. 12, F. Lippmann (1966)

XXIV/1, *Philemon und Baucis oder Jupiters Reise auf die Erde*, J. Braun (1971)
XXIV/2, Texts of lost *Singspiele*, G. Thomas (1989)
XXIV/3, *Die Feuersbrunst*, G. Thomas (1990)

XXV/1, *Acide* and other Italian opera fragments c.1761–3, K. Geiringer and G. Thomas (1985)
XXV/2, *La canterina*, D. Bartha (1959)
XXV/3, *Lo speziale*, H. Wirth (1959)
XXV/4, *Le pescatrici*, D. Bartha, with J. Vécsey and M. Eckhardt (1972)
XXV/5, *L'infedeltà delusa*, D. Bartha and J. Vécsey (1964)
XXV/6, *L'incontro improvviso*, H. Wirth (1962–3)
XXV/7, *Il mondo della luna*, G. Thomas (1979, 1981–2)
XXV/8, *La vera costanza*, H. Walter (1976)
XXV/9, *L'isola disabitata*, T. Siegert and U. Wilker (2008)
XXV/10, *La fedeltà premiata*, G. Thomas (1968)
XXV/11, *Orlando paladino*, K. Geiringer (1972–3)
XXV/12, *Armida*, W. Pfannkuch (1965)
XXV/13, *L'anima del filosofo ossia Orfeo ed Euridice*, H. Wirth (1974)
XXV/14, Opera librettos in facsimile

XXVI/1, Arias, scenes and ensembles with orchestra, i, R. von Zahn (2000)
XXVI/2, Arias, scenes and ensembles with orchestra, ii
XXVI/3, Arrangements of arias and recitatives of other composers

XXVII/1, Cantatas with orchestra for the princely house of Esterházy, A. Friesenhagen and S. Gerlach (2000)
XXVII/2, 'Applausus', H. Wiens with I. Becker-Glauch (1969)
XXVII/3, Cantatas and choruses with orchestra, dramatic music

XXVIII/1, *Il ritorno di Tobia*, E. Schmid (1963)
XXVIII/2, *The Seven Last Words of Our Saviour on the Cross*, vocal version, H. Unverricht (1961)
XXVIII/3, *The Creation*, A. Oppermann (2008)
XXVIII/4, *The Seasons*, A. Raab (2007)

XXIX/1, Songs for one voice with keyboard accompaniment, P. Mies (1960)
XXIX/2, Various songs with keyboard accompaniment M. Helms (1988)

XXX, Partsongs, P. Mies (1958)

XXXI, Canons, O. Deutsch (1959)

XXXII/1, Folksong arrangements nos. 1–100 (arrangements for Napier, i), K. Geiringer (1961)
XXXII/2, Folksong arrangements nos. 101–150 (arrangements for Napier, ii), A. Friesenhagen (2001)
XXXII/3, Folksong arrangements nos. 151–268 (arrangements for Thomson, i), M. Rycroft with K. McCue and W. Edwards (2001)
XXXII/4, Folksong arrangements nos. 269–364 (arrangements for Thomson, ii), M. Rycroft with K. McCue and W. Edwards (2005)
XXXII/5, Folksong arrangements nos. 365–429 (arrangements for Whyte), A. Friesenhagen and E. Hiller (2005)

XXXIII, Supplement

XXXIV, Indexes

Joseph II (b. 13 March 1741; d. 20 Feb. 1790). From 1765 co-regent with Maria Theresia; 1780–90, emperor. A notable reformer of the state and of public life in Austria, Joseph II was also intimately concerned with the development of musical life in Vienna, especially in the 1780s. Like all members of the Habsburg dynasty, this eldest son of Maria Theresia and Franz Stephan received a basic musical education. He was able to read and play scores with ease, was a competent keyboard player and a cellist, and had a good bass voice. His first teacher was the court organist Wenzel Raimund Birk (1718–63), followed by GASSMANN and SALIERI; Joseph placed considerable value on the advice and opinion of the latter. In his youth Archduke Joseph took part in numerous musical evenings at the imperial court, likewise in the summer palace of Laxenburg (between Vienna and Eisenstadt), his favourite residence. While music was certainly his principal pastime he was interested also in natural science, mathematics, medicine, military science, and technology; he was less inclined towards philosophy and the visual arts.

This theoretical and scientific outlook coloured his attitude towards music, which he liked to discuss as much as he liked to perform and listen to it. It is known that Joseph and his musical friends regularly sat down to assess the latest musical works, especially operas. Even when he was preoccupied with pressing items of state business he maintained the discipline of allotting one hour a day to music. He attended the opera as often as he could, and played a fundamental part in determining its repertoire and choosing its singers.

Given his progressive outlook and his particular interest in music, it is odd that Joseph II should have preferred the music of lesser composers such as Gassmann and Umlauf (1746–96) to that of Gluck, Haydn, and Mozart. The northern German composer and author Johann Friedrich Reichardt (1752–1814) reported that Joseph was reluctant to explore music by composers beyond the immediate Viennese environment. His musical advisers and friends heavily influenced this restricted outlook. As well as Gassmann and Salieri, two court musicians, the violinist Franz Kreibich (1728–97) and KOZELUCH (Koželuh), plus the personal servant Johann Kilian Strack, played a key role. Strack played the cello in quartet performances and was responsible for assembling the parts. Strack and Kreibich together ensured that Haydn's music was not part of the repertoire, not out of personal malice, simply because it did not reflect their own taste. For Haydn's part, he never made any strenuous efforts to promote his music at the imperial court. In essence it made no difference to him if his music was played there or not.

The emperor's indifference to the music of Haydn reflected also his conservative, theoretical outlook on music. Joseph II valued the aesthetic and musical precepts laid out by FUX in his treatise *Gradus ad Parnassum*. He apparently told Reichardt, 'He who has Fux firmly in his head knows everything that can and must be done.' In opera he regarded the works of HASSE and Piccinni (1728–1800) as exemplary, a standard maintained in the 1780s in the stage works of Salieri. Joseph II, with or without his advisers, seems to have convinced himself that Haydn had moved beyond the Fux aesthetic. In particular the musical jesting of the composer he regarded as 'burlesque and unworthy of the highest art'.

Although he never attended a performance of a Haydn opera at Eszterháza Joseph is known to have heard performances in Vienna and Pressburg (Bratislava); he probably misunderstood them in the same way as he did Mozart's stage works, especially the richness of the instrumental accompaniment. In apparent contradiction to this general view of Haydn are the remarks attributed to Joseph II in Dittersdorf's autobiography, where the emperor seems to value both Haydn and Mozart. Like much else in the autobiography the alleged conversation was primarily designed to show Dittersdorf in the best possible light, someone who recognized the superior talents of these two composers: 'I compare Mozart's compositions with a golden snuffbox manufactured in Paris, those of Haydn with one manufactured in London.'

Amongst Joseph's many reforms were those that affected the development of opera. In 1776 he established a German national theatre in Vienna and in 1778 financial support for Italian opera was replaced with that for German opera, an experiment that was reversed a few years later. His aim was to establish Viennese operas and plays in the first rank of German-language theatre, an aim that was never to be realized. CH

D. Beales, *Joseph II, i: In the Shadow of Maria Theresa 1741–1780* (Cambridge, 1987).

D. Beales, 'The Impact of Joseph II on Vienna', in M. Csáky and W. Pass (eds.), *Europa im Zeitalter Mozarts* (Vienna, 1995), 301–10.

O. Biba, 'Kaiser Joseph II. und die Musik', in *Österreich zur Zeit Kaiser Josephs II.* [Exhibition catalogue] (Vienna, 1980), 260–5.

C. Höslinger, 'Zum Musikverständis Josephs II.', in I. Fuchs (ed.), *Internationaler Musikwissenschaftlicher Kongreß zum Mozartjahr 1991 Baden-Wien* (Tutzing, 1993), 33–42.

Josephinism. See opposite.

'Jungfern' quartets. Nickname ('Maiden' quartets) occasionally encountered in German-speaking countries for the op. 33 set. It derives from the publication by Hummel in 1782 in which the title page has the fashionable engraving of a maiden placed in front of a ruin of an ancient column. JH

Josephinism

A concept of political and social reform in the Austrian territories, especially during the 1780s, named after its prime mover, Emperor Joseph II (1741–90). Although it is often seen as the Austrian manifestation of the Enlightenment and, in particular, of Enlightened Absolutism, the process had in truth started much earlier, during the reign (1740–80) of Maria Theresia; indeed, certain elements may be traced even to the reign (1711–40) of Karl VI. Joseph was co-regent with his mother from 1765 and succeeded her in 1780. After his death in 1790, the reforming zeal of the previous decades abated under his successor, Leopold II (1747–92), a change of outlook that gave the notion of Josephinism added legitimacy and lustre.

Josephinism was a complex and multifaceted process. The once prevalent view that it was essentially concerned with restricting the powers of the Catholic Church in the emerging nation state is too confined. All aspects of life were affected, political, social, educational, judicial, commercial, as well as religious.

Although part of a much broader European movement, this reform process was especially influenced in Austria by Jansenism, which spread from Italy northwards in the 1740s, permeating the ruling classes. Its most significant aims were, first, the linking of the Church with the state to form a national Church rather than a Roman Church, and, secondly, the removal of some of the excessively sentimental features of Baroque piety. The Habsburg dynasty had, in truth, long united the sacred and the secular in its projection of power, so that this aspect of Jansenism, though it found fertile soil in Austria, was not especially revolutionary. Jansenists mocked, often with cruel relish, the excesses of homespun piety associated with religious observance, while their questioning of the influence of the Jesuit order in the inner councils of state represented an attack on an order that had held political influence since the Counter-Reformation.

A fundamental element of Josephinism, or rather the reforming period that led up to as well as included Joseph's reign, was the reform of the state. The end of the War of Austrian Succession in 1748 consolidated Maria Theresia's hold on power and saw the beginning of a twofold process: an increasing division between the central Austrian territories (the monarchy) and those of the Holy Roman Empire, and a series of administrative reforms that made the various elements of the former more dependent on central rule from Vienna. Reform of the tax system meant that the aristocracy as well as the Church were required to pay state taxes. A complex administrative structure spread out from Vienna peopled by a new class of loyal and dedicated bureaucrats, while the support of the aristocracy was skilfully harnessed through central patronage. The Esterházy family was one of several dynasties that were happy to provide a bond between local territories—in this case an ethnically and linguistically diverse Hungary—and the supreme ruler in Vienna. However, Hungary was unusual in that it often resisted the increased power of Vienna and during the late 1780s, in particular, this caused PRINCE NICOLAUS ESTERHÁZY, who was caught in the middle, a good deal of discomfort. Decisions to rule Hungary through a commissar and to make German the official language brought the country close to rebellion and had to be revoked.

Agrarian and economic reforms controlled from Vienna also effectively weakened the powers of many local rulers. These reforms aimed to increase the yield of the land and to improve the health of the livestock; simultaneously, peasant farmers saw a gradual decrease in tax duties. Joseph II ended serfdom (though, again, with little success in Hungary), reduced the practice of villainage, and restricted the common obligation to hand over all produce to the landowner to 17 per cent of the total. In order to evaluate ground taxes equitably, Joseph II set up a land registry in Vienna.

Consistent with this policy of centralization was the reform of the legal system. The first stage of a civil justice system, to be applied uniformly throughout the monarchy, was the *Codex Theresianus* of 1766; reforms continued for the next 40 years culminating in the Universal Civil Book of Laws (*Allgemeine Bürgerlichen Gesetzbuches*) of 1811. In the area of criminal law the *Constitutio Criminalis Theresiana* set norms for the state as a whole; torture was abolished in 1776 and, 12 years later, the death penalty was abolished except for crimes against the state.

For society in general the most influential reforms were in the area of schooling and education. Initiated by Maria Theresia in 1760 these reforms brought all schooling under the purview of the state, with the establishing of a general policy for all teaching, and the setting up of training institutions for all teachers. This did not necessarily mean that the traditional influence of the Church on education was diminished, though priests who were also teachers were required to undergo training in state seminaries so that their allegiance to the monarchy could be secured.

While Maria Theresia's reforms mainly concerned primary schooling, Joseph was more occupied with secondary and university education. A pyramid structure that emphasized the value of education for the state encouraged as many people as possible to learn to read and write, a few to attend secondary education (the Gymnasium) and only the most exceptionally talented to study at university; universities themselves were restricted to three in number, Vienna, Prague, and Lemberg (Lvov), the last newly founded.

Although Josephinism is often credited with making the Catholic Church more allied to the state than it was to Rome, in reality this process can be traced back several centuries to the medieval period. Papal influence on the Church in the Austrian territories had always been scrutinized and, likewise, the local power of bishops was rather circumscribed; for instance, all citizens had the right to contest the jurisdiction of the Church using the laws of the state. There is no doubt, however, that reforms in the second half of the 18th century were especially forceful, increasing the secularization of state and society.

Maria Theresia taxed clerics for the first time and restricted their financial dealings; it was forbidden to send money to Rome or, indeed, anywhere outside the country. She reduced the number of holy days and pilgrimages; the age for entering holy service in a monastery was set at 24; church law that allowed, for instance, the holy sacrament to be denied became subject to the approval of the state; and priests were not allowed to preach against the state.

As governor of the Austrian territories in Lombardy, north Italy, Joseph II's brother, Archduke Ferdinand (1754–1814), dissolved numerous monasteries in the 1770s. Under Joseph's reforms a decade later, all monasteries and religious orders that were not deemed to be 'useful', especially for education and for the care of the sick, had their assets confiscated. The resultant empty monastery buildings, some 700, were variously turned into hospitals, prisons, barracks, and warehouses. Diocesan boundaries were made uniform with those of the civil authorities, and every cleric had to swear an oath of allegiance to the state. Direct contact between the churches and monasteries of

Austria and the pope was expressly forbidden. The number of holy days, pilgrimages, processions, communions was further reduced. Even small matters of detail, such as the number of candles to be used during communion services and the construction of coffins, were controlled by the state. More liberal was the Edict of Tolerance (1781) that established equality of status for non-Catholics; Protestants and Jews were allowed freedom of worship, to set up their own schools, to enter the professions, and to hold political and military office.

Alongside religious tolerance Joseph II considerably relaxed the previously harsh rules on censorship, rules that had effectively stifled intellectual and literary debate. During the 1780s there was a virtual explosion of liberal reading and thinking leading to a distinctive, if short-lived, salon culture in Vienna, and to the increasing popularity of Freemasonry amongst the cultural and political elite.

Although church reforms inevitably reduced the prominence of music in worship, the various attempts of the state to control the nature of the music itself were less successful. A papal edict of 1749 had curtailed the use of trumpets and timpani in church services, a measure that Maria Theresia wished to consolidate, but it was so frequently ignored that it was finally repealed. In a series of reforms Joseph II encouraged greater use of the German language in church services, reduced (with mixed results) the number of services that featured instrumental music, and the number and kind of churches that were allowed to perform such music.

Although Joseph Haydn lived through this exciting period of change and many aspects of his career are clearly the product of new forces in Austrian society in general, there is little first-hand evidence of his reaction to Josephinism. The education reforms were begun long after Haydn had finished his formal schooling; his own comments on its haphazard nature suggest that he would have supported the many changes. As a freelance musician who sang and played in church services in the 1750s in Vienna, he would have experienced at first hand the largely futile attempts to reform church music at the time. As for the church reforms of Joseph II in the 1780s the view that they explain why Haydn did not compose much church music at this time is misguided: he was not required to compose sacred music at the Esterházy court, his duties were dominated by the demands of the two opera houses, while his increasing international popularity was based on instrumental music. During occasional visits to Vienna in the 1780s, Haydn experienced at first hand the rapidly changing social and intellectual environment; he was acquainted with the GREINER family, was initiated as a Freemason in 1785, and, in a letter to MARIA ANNA VON GENZINGER contrasted the delights of social life in the capital in comparison with provincial life and duty in Eisenstadt. On the other hand, as a devout Catholic whose own music, sacred and secular, had travelled extensively through the network of Austrian monasteries, Haydn may well have viewed with unease the dissolution of many of them in the 1780s; certainly his reaction to visiting the ruins of Waverley abbey in England in 1794 suggests a real attachment to the old order: 'my heart was oppressed at the thought that all this once belonged to my religion.' GM

D. Beales, 'Was Joseph II an Enlightened Despot', *Austrian Studies*, 2 (1991), 1–21.

H. Hollerweger, *Die Reformen des Gottesdienstes zur Zeit des Josephinismus in Österreich* (Regensburg, 1976).

H. Klueting (ed.), *Der Josephinismus. Ausgewählte Quellen zur Geschichte der theresianisch-josephinischen Reformen* (Darmstadt, 1995).

R. G. Pauly, 'The Reforms of Church Music under Joseph II', *Musical Quarterly*, 43 (1957), 372–82.

F. W. Riedel, 'Liturgie und Kirchenmusik', in *Joseph Haydn in seiner Zeit* [Exhibition catalogue] (Eisenstadt, 1982), 121–33.
E. Wangermann, *The Austrian Achievement 1700–1800* (London, 1973).

K

'Kaffeeklatsch'. Nickname ('coffee party') used by the Viennese Teubner family in the 19th and 20th centuries for one of the pieces on the MECHANICAL ORGAN owned by them. The piece in question, Hob.XIX:6, is an arrangement of the last movement of a baryton trio in C (Hob.IX:76). As with all the items on this particular mechanical organ, Haydn's authorship is doubtful.

Kalkbrenner, Frédéric (b. Nov. 1785; d. 10 June 1849). An early Romantic composer-pianist who studied composition with Haydn. Born in France of German extraction, he was a child prodigy who at the age of 5 played Haydn's Piano Concerto in D in front of the Queen of Prussia. Between 1798 and 1802 he was a student of piano and composition at the Paris Conservatoire. Arriving in Vienna in late 1803 he contacted Haydn, whom he had briefly met seven years earlier, to arrange composition lessons. Haydn gave him some counterpoint exercises but found him deficient and passed him on to Albrechtsberger. He later returned to Haydn, who utilized his now secure musicianship to assist in the setting of Scottish folksongs for Thomson. By 1804 Kalkbrenner was back in Paris, where he soon established himself as a leading performer, teacher, and composer of piano music. Between 1815 and 1824 he lived in England. His entertaining memoir, published in England in 1824, shows clearly his affection for Haydn as does the publication of a piano sonata (op. 56; Paris, 1821) which is inscribed 'dédiée à la mémoire de Joseph Haydn'.
DC

'Memoir of Mr. Frederick Kalkbrenner', *HYB* 12 (1981), 180–91.
H. Walter, 'Kalkbrenners Lehrjahre und sein Unterricht bei Haydn', *HS* 5/1 (1982), 23–41.

Kees catalogue. Franz Bernhard von Kees (1720–95) was one of the most important sponsors of private concerts in Vienna in the second half of the 18th century. Consistent and detailed information on these concerts is not available but it is clear that Haydn's symphonies, in particular, formed a prominent part. In *c*.1790–2 Kees employed a professional copyist to prepare a thematic catalogue of Haydn symphonies owned by him, 'Catalogo Del Sinfonien Del Sig: Giuseppe Haydn', now usually referred to as the Kees catalogue. It contains 90 orchestral works (mainly symphonies) written by Haydn up to 1789 in broad chronological order; two 'London' symphonies (nos. 95 and 96) were later added. Circumstantial evidence suggests that Haydn knew Kees from the early 1760s. The composer was presented with a copy of the catalogue and it was used as the main source for the list of symphonies in the HAYDN-VERZEICHNIS. The year after Kees's death his music library was auctioned. Most of the symphony manuscripts are now owned by the Gesellschaft der Musikfreunde. The catalogue, however, together with some music manuscripts, found its way to the library of the Thurn und Taxis family in Regensburg.

H. C. Robbins Landon, *The Symphonies of Joseph Haydn* (London, 1955).
Larsen.

Keller, Therese (b. 20 May 1732; d. 3 Jan. 1819). Haydn's sister-in-law and first love. Her uncle, Georg Ignaz Keller (1699–1771), was a violinist in St Stephen's when Haydn was a choirboy and introduced him to his brother, Johann Peter Keller, a professional wig maker. He and his wife had seven children of whom Therese was the third daughter. Engaged as a keyboard teacher, Haydn fell in love with the daughter but her religious parents had always planned that she become a nun; in 1755 she joined the Franciscan order of the Poor Clares and entered the convent of St Nicolaus. It is thought that Haydn composed the Salve regina in E and the Organ Concerto in C (Hob.XVIII:1) for an associated ceremony the following year; they are the earliest surviving autographs by the composer, significantly retained by him when others were discarded. The convent was dissolved in the 1780s as the result of Joseph II's reforms. Given the option of joining the order of St Elizabeth, which ran a hospice in the Landstraße, or leading a secular life with an annual pension of 200 gulden, Therese vacillated, eventually deciding in favour of the latter. When Haydn's wife, Maria Anna, died in 1800 she left her sister 200 gulden; in his first will (1801) Joseph Haydn bequeathed the sum of 50 gulden to Therese, raised to 100 gulden in 1809. Therese Keller died of tuberculosis at the age of 86.
ERL

HCRL/1 and 5.

Keyboard sonata. See overleaf.

Keyboard trio. See page 189.

[*cont. on p.195*]

keyboard sonata

A multi-movement work, usually containing from two to four movements, for solo keyboard instrument. Haydn employed the term sonata for the first time in 1771 (for Hob.XVI:20); before that he had randomly referred to similar works by the titles DIVERTIMENTO and PARTITA; these different terms do not imply distinctions of genre or cyclic typology. In the second half of the 18th century keyboard sonatas were often published with the description 'per il clavicembalo o forte-piano' ('for the harpsichord or piano', or its equivalent), although it became an anachronism with the increasing dominance of the fortepiano in the 1770s and 1780s. By the 1790s the harpsichord was no longer an intended vehicle for Haydn's keyboard sonatas.

Haydn's keyboard sonatas span the period from the 1750s, when it is assumed he wrote his first solo sonatas, to 1794–5, when he wrote his three late masterpieces, Hob.XVI:50–2. It is consequently a very diverse repertoire with a range of styles that is representative of Haydn's compositional career as a whole. Very little is known about the precise circumstances for which most of the sonatas were originally composed. Haydn told Griesinger that during the 1750s many of the sonatas that he had written for pupils were presented as gifts. The names of only two keyboard pupils from this time are known, MARIANNA VON MARTINES and THERESE KELLER. When he was employed at the Morzin and Esterházy court, Haydn may well have taught the keyboard to members of the respective families and, indeed, some of the courtiers; for instance, two dwarves, Catharina Kellner and Johann Sidler, lived occasionally in the Esterházy court and both are known to have been taught the keyboard in order to entertain the family and visitors. Haydn may well have taught the keyboard to, and thus written sonatas for, those pupils such as KIMMERLING, Mikysch, and PLEYEL, whose instruction primarily featured theory and composition. As regards sonatas that were given away, the ENTWURF-KATALOG contains the incipits of seven sonatas, now lost (Hob.XVI:2a–e, 2g, and 2h). In the autumn of 1993 six of these sonatas were claimed to have been rediscovered in Westphalia. This proved to be a malevolent hoax perpetrated by the German musician, Winfried Michl.

1. The early sonatas to *c.*1766.
2. Seven expressive sonatas, *c.*1765–71.
3. The Kurzböck and Auenbrugger sets, 1773–80.
4. The late sonatas, 1781–95.

1. The early sonatas to *c.*1766. These works are poorly documented. Of the numerous keyboard sonatas attributed to Haydn that are customarily dated to the 1750s and early 1760s, only one (Hob.XVI:6) survives in an autograph manuscript, and this sonata with only three other extant works (Hob.XVI:3, 4, 14) are listed in the *Entwurf-Katalog* and thus may be reliably regarded as genuine Haydn compositions. Perhaps 11 more early sonatas have, on external and/or internal evidence, strong or relatively strong claims to authenticity, while seven more, although included in one or other of the three important complete editions of Haydn's sonatas (edited by Päsler, Christa Landon, and FEDER) are either of very questionable authenticity (Hob.XVI:5, 11, 16, Es2, Es3) or are now regarded as spurious (Hob.XVI:15, 17). The chronology of these works is equally problematic and, taken with the problems of attribution, it is impossible to speak of the development of Haydn's style in this early repertoire. Such an attempt is probably misguided too, since the scale, technical difficulty, and compositional complexity of these early sonatas were in all likelihood determined more by their intended function as teaching material or simple domestic music-making than by purely compositional or aesthetic considerations. Georg Feder categorized the early sonatas as 'Short early sonatas' and 'Nine early sonatas', two well-founded classifications.

The 'Short early sonatas' are brief, technically simple, and limited in harmonic language, probably intended as pieces suitable for teaching. Texturally they owe much to the continuo sonata and have a predominantly two-part texture with a continuo-like bass line and a fast harmonic rhythm, with the formal articulation relying heavily on the normal repertoire of *galant* cadence figures. They have the same diversity of cyclic structure as the early larger sonatas. Each sonata has a minuet and trio movement—in the short sonatas generally the most polished and inventive movements—and there is a predominance of three-movement sonatas, in which the minuet may occur as a second movement followed by a quick finale, or as a finale preceded by a slow movement. In both groups there is a single four-movement cycle (Hob.XVI:6 and XVI:8), and a single two-movement cycle (Hob.XVI:4 and the probably spurious XVI:Es3).

Taken as a whole the larger sonatas form a very uneven group, which must, at least in part, be due to the high proportion of works in this group with tenuous claims to authenticity, but in comparison with the shorter sonatas they are more expansive in their harmonic vocabulary, technical difficulty, as well as scale. The group contains at least three early minor, though very different, masterpieces. The four-movement cycle of Hob.XVI:6 belongs to the Viennese keyboard tradition and has the most idiomatic keyboard minuet and the most virtuoso finale in these early works. In Hob.XVI:14, particularly in the finale, a characteristically Haydnesque wit is in evidence and the expansive and highly original sonata in B♭ (Hob.XVI:2) foreshadows the expressive depth of Haydn's sonatas from the second half of the 1760s.

2. Seven expressive sonatas, *c*.1765–71. In the remarkable collection of sonatas of *c*.1765 and 1771 (Hob.XVI:44–47, 18–20) Haydn not only established a personal and highly expressive keyboard style but forged a new musical language and explored new formal types, anticipating stylistic changes in other genres. In the second half of the 1760s the keyboard sonata is for the first and perhaps only time in his career a primary vehicle for his compositional experiments.

Elaborate ornamentation and variation is an important characteristic of these sonatas affecting all forms. Of special significance is the integration of variation processes into sonata form movements, and the combination of variations with other formal types to produce new hybrid forms. For instance, a new characteristic of sonata form movements in these sonatas is that counter-statements of first themes are embellished (e.g. in Hob.XVI:45/ii, 19/i, 18/ii) and frequently the recapitulation of the first theme is varied, or the embellished counter-statement is recapitulated in place of the initial form of the theme (again in XVI:45/ii, 18/ii, 19/i, 20/iii). Haydn's characteristic combination of variation and other forms is seen in these sonatas in the rondo variation form of the third movement in Hob.XVI:19 and in the second movement of Hob.XVI:44, a set of double variations with varied reprises. Such combinations were to fascinate Haydn throughout his career.

Haydn's writing for keyboard is notably more idiomatic in these sonatas than in earlier works, particularly in the greater variety of textures, his exploitation of contrasts in register, and the employment of idiomatic keyboard figuration, sometimes of a highly virtuoso nature. In comparison with the neutral continuo sonata textures pervasive in the earlier sonatas, the textures of the 1765–71 sonatas are immensely diverse. Themes employing imitative textures occur in Hob.XVI:18/i and XVI:46/ii and, more generally, within sonata form movements tonal and thematic contrasts are often reinforced by differentiated sections of two- or three-part writing and freer textures. In the Sonata in C minor, for instance, the three-part texture of the first theme is contrasted with the freer texture of the unstable transition, and thematic contrast within the relative major key area is also emphasized through texture. Similarly, the climax in the first movement of the Sonata in G minor at the end of the development section is effected by a stretto-like passage in a four- and five-part texture in the upper register of the keyboard, a sonority unknown in earlier Haydn sonatas.

In the second movement of Hob.XVI:19 the extreme registral contrasts have suggested to a number of writers the opposition of an orchestral ritornello and low-pitched solo instrument in a concerto-like movement; the whole sonata is notable for its exploration of contrasting registers and sonorities. The new virtuosity of these sonatas is particularly evident in Hob.XVI:46, 19, and 20 and the finale of 45. The central section of the development in Hob.XVI:46/i is in the manner of a fantasia, and cadenzas and unmeasured interpolations in a slow tempo articulate structure in Hob.XVI:19/ii, 20/i, and 44/i. The greatest extension of keyboard technique is to be found in Hob.XVI:20, as, for instance, in the finale where, in a remarkable virtuoso passage (bars 90–119), the left hand plays at both extremes of the keyboard, at one point crossing the right to play *f‴*, the highest note on the contemporary five-octave keyboard.

In the Sonata in C minor the expressivity and brilliance of the keyboard-writing is matched by a more complex harmonic language and the grander scale of its structures, qualities that have been widely acknowledged. Yet, the more elaborate modulations and proportionally larger development section of its first movement is representative of this group of sonatas as a whole. Indeed, the extended harmonic language of these sonatas is seen in its most extreme form in the tortuous chromaticism of the slow movement of Hob.XVI:46. These sonatas form a discrete group, Haydn's most personal and experimental keyboard works in a style which he largely abandoned in the 1770s. It is in this group of works that one may suspect the influence of C. P. E. BACH on Haydn. The fantasia-like sections in development sections and the use of varied reprises in Hob.XVI:44/ii may well be inspired by Bach. In a more general sense, the improvisational quality that pervades the sonatas of this period may owe something to the older composer, and Haydn's more direct concern with the rhetoric of performance, especially with expressive and elaborate ornamentation, is reflected in the very precise notation, closer to the north German keyboard tradition than to contemporary Viennese practice.

3. The Kurzböck and Auenbrugger sets, 1773–80. For the keyboard sonata genre the years from 1773 to 1780 constitute the period of greatest productivity. Probably 20 sonatas may be dated to this period, dominated by three important sets of six sonatas intended as public works and widely disseminated. The first set, Hob.XVI:21–6, written in 1773 and published in 1774 by KURZBÖCK, was the first authorized edition of music by Haydn in any genre. Its dedication to PRINCE NICOLAUS ESTERHÁZY suggests that, like first publications by many composers, this was an exhibition set, designed as a musical tribute to his patron. The second set (Hob.XVI:27–32), the '6 Sonaten von Anno 1776' mentioned in the *Entwurf-Katalog*, was also distributed widely, initially in authentic Viennese manuscript copies; and the third set (Hob.XVI:35–9 plus the earlier sonata XVI:20) was published in 1780 in an authentic edition by ARTARIA, marking the beginning of Haydn's long association with the Viennese firm.

The Esterházy sonatas, Hob.XVI:21–6, inhabit a different world from the experimental sonatas of the late 1760s. All are in major keys and, whether a reflection of the musical taste of the prince or with an eye to the commercial market of amateur musicians, they are written in a *galant* style without the extravagant rhetoric and dramatic force of the preceding sonatas. While it is certainly true that in individual movements, such as the first movement of Hob.XVI:21, the thematic material is less distinctive than the 1765–71 sonatas, the *galant* style of the Esterházy set is a polished, sophisticated idiom far removed from the early, pre-1766 sonatas, especially in compositional technique and idiomatic keyboard-writing. In the many sonata forms (favoured in roughly three-quarters of the movements), the more complex handling of structure established in the immediately preceding sonatas remains. Most have elaborate transition sections and/or tonal excursions in the secondary key area, although without the dramatic discontinuities and breaks in texture that characterize the 1765–71 sonatas. The Haydnesque practice of recasting the first theme in some form in the dominant, an occasional occurrence in earlier sonatas, becomes established in the Esterházy set and the increased size and emphasis on the development section found in the 1765–71 sonatas is also characteristic of the Esterházy set, with the development section frequently being of the same proportion as the exposition and recapitulation.

The three-movement cycle also becomes more firmly established as Haydn's norm from the sonatas of 1773 onwards; in the Esterházy set five of the six sonatas are three-movement works, with a decided preference for an Adagio middle movement between fast outer movements (Hob.XVI:21, 23, 24). In Hob.XVI:22 an Andante precedes a Tempo di Menuet finale and in only one work is there a central minuet and trio (Hob.XVI:26). In the Adagio movements the highly decorative keyboard-writing that Haydn developed in these sonatas was to become a hallmark of his style, and the linking of the second movement of Hob.XVI:24 to its finale is the first of a number of experiments with this practice in the sonatas of the 1770s; this practice possibly derives from C. P. E. Bach's example. Minuet and trio and Tempo di Menuet movements are relatively few in these sonatas but three such movements maintain Haydn's lifelong concern for innovation. The canonic Tempo di Menuet (without a trio) of Hob.XVI:25 and the minuet and trio 'al Rovescio' of Hob.XVI:26 (transcribed from Symphony no. 47) introduce into Haydn's keyboard sonatas the Viennese tradition of contrapuntal minuets. The Tempo di Menuet finale of Hob.XVI:22 is a more typically Haydnesque creation, an important model for later experiments, where conventional minuet-and-trio-like movements are extended as a set of double variations with varied reprises.

The Esterházy sonatas are a carefully calculated exhibition set. Stylistically and technically they would hardly have challenged the contemporary listener or performer in the way the more personal preceding sonatas would have done and, perhaps, the inclusion of canonic and 'al Rovescio' minuets may be taken as the token demonstrations of competence in an older strict style that was commonly exhibited in a composer's opus 1. They are not, however, facile or conservative sonatas. At least two of them, Hob.XVI:23 and 26, contain some of Haydn's very best keyboard music, and the set as a whole represents one of the high points in the repertoire of the harpsichord shortly before its demise. Richness in ornamentation and variety in articulation are essential to the style of these works, and Haydn's meticulous notation in four extant autograph fragments are important documents of what may be regarded as his most refined harpsichord idiom. In the finale of Hob.XVI:23, for instance, the variants of the first theme that occur in the dominant are characterized by contrasting articulation, and the practice of varying articulation and/or ornamentation in monothematic sonata forms is one that remained common in Haydn's later works. The keyboard technique in these works, while presenting no extraordinary technical challenges, is finely gauged with many passages of grateful virtuosity that distinguish them from most contemporary sonatas for the amateur market, as in the demisemiquaver passage in the development of Hob.XVI:23/i, perhaps the closest Haydn ever came to the figuration of a free fantasia, and the left-hand octave passages in the chromatic transition and development of Hob.XVI:26/i.

The six sonatas of 1776 reinforce the preference for three-movement cycles in the sonatas of the 1770s. Three have minuet and trio middle movements and two have Adagio movements before Tempo di Menuet finales. Unusually, Hob.XVI:31 has an Allegretto middle movement, ending on the dominant and running directly into the finale, in the manner of Hob.XVI:24 from the Esterházy set. Hob.XVI:30 is a further and more extensive exercise in through composition, in that all three of its movements are run together and the middle Adagio section is scarcely an autonomous movement. There are individual moments in these sonatas that recall the earlier 1765–71 works, but without sustaining the same level of inspiration or achieving a consistency of style throughout a complete work. A *galant*, easy-going style is more pervasive and, while Hob.XVI:28 comes close to attaining the same level of polished sophistication of Hob.XVI:23 and 26 from the Esterházy set, other works lapse into a mundane version of this style, particularly Hob.XVI:27. Two features of the set are, however, remarkable: first, the supreme achievement, which is widely acknowledged, of the Sonata in B minor, Hob.XVI:32, the only minor key work in the set, and, secondly, Haydn's extensive experimentation with new variation forms in five of the six finales of the set.

The two outer sonata-form movements of the Sonata in B minor have distinctive thematic material which, in the first movement, is scrutinized in one of Haydn's most concise and intensely motivic development sections and, in the finale, the B minor and D major themes, highly contrasting in texture but sharing rhythmic features, are elaborated with contrapuntal ingenuity and virtuoso keyboard-writing respectively. The sonata is technically more difficult than any other in the set and has a rich variety of keyboard textures and sonorities, the most remarkable being in the transition section of the finale where the interlocking left- and right-hand octave passage, in similar motion in the exposition and contrary motion in the recapitulation, uses virtually the whole range of the contemporary keyboard in the space of four bars, a memorable instance of virtuosity dramatizing structure.

Of the five variation finales, two (Hob.XVI:29/iii and 30/iii) continue Haydn's practice of combining Tempo di Menuet themes with variation forms. Each of the three variation finales in a fast tempo disrupts the additive structure of strophic variations in a significantly new way. In both Hob.XVI:27/iii and 28/iii the third variation begins as a quasi-recapitulation of the theme before turning to the parallel minor, and the following developmental episode departs from the periodic and harmonic structure of the theme. The third movement of Hob.XVI:31 has a varied reprise in the final variation, and the second and third variations have the character of a central episode in which the melodic and harmonic make-up of the theme is largely abandoned while retaining the phrase structure. These departures from the normal additive structure of strophic variations are significant examples of Haydn's persistent concern with innovation in the most unthinkingly routine of 18th-century formal models, and demonstrate that compositional experimentation was never incompatible with the constraints of writing *galant* sonatas for public distribution.

The set of six sonatas (Hob.XVI:35–9 plus the earlier sonata, XVI:20 of 1771) that Artaria published as op. 30 in 1780 not only marks the beginning of Haydn's long association with the firm, but the launching of a new flourishing music-publishing industry in Vienna. Central to this industry was a large market of amateur keyboard players, especially lady players who were frequently the dedicatees of published keyboard music. Op. 30 is dedicated to the AUENBRUGGER sisters and, as A. Peter Brown has observed, is a publisher's ideal, designed to appeal to both *Kenner* and *Liebhaber*. The complex style of the 1765–71 sonatas is represented by the Sonata in C minor, the first movement of the Sonata in C♯ minor (Hob.XVI:36), and aspects of the Sonata in E♭ (Hob.XVI:38); and a lighter, *galant* style is present in Hob.XVI:35 and 37, especially their first movements and popular rondo finales. The technical demands of Hob.XVI:35 and 37 are also compatible with their lighter style, although none of the set is as simple as the composer's pre-1766 sonatas. On the other hand the technical demands of the Sonata in C minor as a whole, the large cadenza ending with a double trill in the slow movement of Hob.XVI:39, and some difficult passages in thirds in Hob.XVI:39/iii would undoubtedly have tantalized the more ambitious keyboard player.

The thorough exploration of variation forms witnessed in the sonatas of 1776 is represented in the Artaria set by the different treatment of the related themes in Hob.XVI:36/ii and Hob.XVI:39/i to which Haydn rather self-consciously drew attention in a notice published with the set: 'Among these six sonatas there are to be found two movements that begin with a few bars of similar meaning . . . The composer gives notice of having done this on purpose . . .'. Other significant formal features of the set include the use of a varied reprise in a slow movement, a practice found in earlier string quartets, but occurring for the first time in a keyboard sonata in Hob.XVI:38; and the cadenza in the slow movement of Hob.XVI:39, the only extant, authentic, keyboard cadenza by Haydn. The first movement of the Sonata in C♯ minor is Haydn's most extensive essay in monothematic sonata form to date, a particularly sophisticated movement in which the contrasting motifs in the first two bars are expanded independently in the second half of the exposition, and the motivic elaboration and textural contrasts of the development section are on a par with the Sonata in B minor (Hob.XVI:32). In comparison with Haydn's earlier sonatas a significant departure in the Auenbrugger set is the inclusion of more frequent dynamic indications than heretofore, part of Haydn's endeavour to appeal to a broad public of keyboard players, who increasingly played Viennese fortepianos as well as harpsichords and clavichords.

Some movements in these sonatas have no dynamic markings, while in others the changes in dynamic marking denote accents or emphasize textural effects which can be achieved on any keyboard instrument. However, there are also passages where dynamic changes occur independently of textural change and undoubtedly require a touch-sensitive instrument. While for documentary and stylistic reasons it is difficult to sustain the argument that Haydn was writing for the fortepiano in the sonatas up to 1780, the Auenbrugger sonatas mark the tentative beginning of a fortepiano idiom in Haydn's sonatas, albeit in an inconsistent manner, compatible with the ubiquitous description 'Per il Clavicembalo, o Forte Piano' that appeared on the title page of the Artaria edition.

4. The late sonatas, 1781–95. Haydn's production of keyboard sonatas declines considerably after the three sets of six composed between 1773 and 1780. In the first half of the 1780s he wrote only the Sonata in E minor (Hob.XVI:34) and a set of three published in 1784 by BOßLER (Hob.XVI:40–2). From the second half of the 1780s the trio replaced the solo sonata as the keyboard genre of primary concern to Haydn. Two further sonatas, Hob.XVI:48–9, written to commission in 1789–90, were published individually by Breitkopf and by Artaria, and the last three sonatas, at least two of them written for THERESE JANSEN, date from around 1794–5. Haydn's late style is therefore poorly represented quantitatively in the solo sonata genre, but the nine solo sonatas from this period are an estimable body of work containing some of the composer's most famous, technically challenging, and most expansive sonatas, all written in a new idiomatic piano style. At least four sonatas are as sophisticated as any of the mature string quartets, keyboard trios, and symphonies.

After the concentration on three-movement sonatas in the published sets of 1773–80, the Boßler sonatas witness a return to the two-movement sonata cycle, also prominent in the piano trios of the 1780s. All three of the Boßler sonatas are in two movements and are typical of such sonatas in concentrating on an increasingly diverse array of variation forms—double variations, ternary variation form, various hybrid variation forms with developmental episodes, episodes related to the refrain, together with a flexible use of varied reprises in all of these forms—rather than sonata form movements.

The pinnacle of Haydn's attainment in this two-movement sonata type is the Sonata in C major (Hob.XVI:48) of 1789. The Andante con espressione is one of Haydn's most expressive movements, cast in a free (non-strophic) version of his characteristic double variation form, in which the episodes in the minor key are related thematically to the refrain in the major key, but proceed as free developmental episodes. Varied reprises are employed both in the first episode and in the first variation on the major-key theme, and throughout there is subtle thematic and textural cross-referencing between variations and episodes. The finale balances the formal freedom of the first movement with one of Haydn's most economical and tightly constructed rondos, in essence a monothematic sonata-rondo structure with a central developmental episode in the minor key. Thus the improvisatory quality of the first movement is contrasted with a fusion of rondo characteristics and developmental features associated with Haydn's mature sonata style. The ingeniously new ways in which the composer uses variation and rondo forms in this sonata testify to the extent to which he transcended forms that in the 1780s had become tired stereotypes in the works of many of his contemporaries.

In the Sonata in E♭ (Hob.XVI:49) written for MARIA ANNA VON GENZINGER, one of his closest friends, Haydn matches the achievements of Hob.XVI:48. The sonata form of the first movement is rich in thematic and textural contrasts, but the motivic and rhythmic relationships between themes, widely commented on in the literature, make this movement one of Haydn's most coherent sonata form movements, a model of the Classical ideal 'unity in diversity'. The approach to the recapitulation is the most powerful since Haydn's sonatas of the 1760s, but its articulatory function is fused more thoroughly with thematic-motivic argument than in any earlier sonata. Similarly, the conclusion of the movement continues the thematic argument, in the most extensive coda in Haydn's sonatas to date. The Adagio easily matches the sophistication of the first movement and, with the Adagio of Hob.XVI:52, is the apogee of Haydn's keyboard adagios. In a ternary variation form with varied reprises and a contrasting minor-key episode, the decorative treatment of the thematic material is as intense and imaginative as the motivic elaboration of the first movement. Variation occurs not only in the return of the major-key theme after the central episode but within the major-key theme itself, where varied reprises are consistently employed in place of formal repeats. Variation is also central to the finale, which typically also combines an episodic structure with the characteristics of a minuet.

The Boßler Sonatas and Hob.XVI:48–9 are fully committed to a fortepiano idiom and, indeed, in correspondence concerning Hob.XVI:49 Haydn repeatedly advised Frau Genzinger to purchase a Schanz fortepiano. Particularly in Hob.XVI:48 and 49, dynamic, textural, and registral contrasts are intrinsic to the characterization of thematic material as well as structure. The new expressive idiom exploits the contrasting registers of Viennese fortepianos, most originally perhaps in the minor-key section in Hob.XVI:49/ii (bars 57–76) which in a number of ways anticipates Romantic piano sonority. Although extant correspondence between Haydn and Genzinger reveals that this passage stretched her technique, as a whole the sonata is more compatible with the abilities of the talented amateur than the composer's later three-movement sonatas, Hob.XVI:50 and 52.

These sonatas are associated with Haydn's second London visit and were written for the pianist Therese Jansen, a pupil of CLEMENTI, and along with three piano trios written for her (Hob.XV:27–9) they are the composer's most demanding piano music. They represent Haydn's most advanced fortepiano idiom, also a fusion of his mature symphonic style with the keyboard sonata. The weightiest movement in both works is the first. Hob.XVI:50/i is one of Haydn's most rigorous monothematic sonata-form movements, in that the initial thematic idea generates most of the material of the exposition. This idea is subject to manifold variations, occurring in five different guises (that transform the idea texturally, embellish it, and add new counter-melodies in invertible counterpoint), perhaps the most inventive combining of sonata form with elements of variation in Haydn's output. In the development section a new legato version with an 'open pedal' marking (the only pedal marking in Haydn's sonatas) marks the point of furthest tonal remove (A♭ major), and the recurrence of this passage in the tonic in the recapitulation is an indication of the extent to which recapitulations in Haydn's late style may be dramatic reinterpretations rather than restatements. In the first movement of the E♭ major sonata (Hob.XVI:52) the same thematic idea introduces each tonal function in the exposition (tonic, transition, and dominant areas), but the movement is more remarkable for its strong thematic contrasts, constantly changing textures and registers, and profligacy rather than the economy of invention. The emphasis on C and E major in the development is indicative of the broad harmonic range of this movement. Moreover, the prominence of E major in the first movement foreshadows the remote tonal relationship between the three movements (E♭ major–E major–E♭ major), an instance of the cyclic recurrence of remote tonal relationships that is characteristic of Haydn's mature piano trios, string quartets, and symphonies. The slow movement of Hob.XVI:52, and to a lesser extent Hob.XVI:50, is remarkable for the new dense chordal sonorities and elaborate virtuoso flourishes, necessitating complex notation, and a manner also characteristic of the adagios in Haydn's London piano trios. In the finale of XVI:52 the contredanse-type movement, long favoured by Haydn in finales, is enriched by sophisticated harmonic and rhythmic deceptions and the virtuosity characteristic of his London piano music. More so than any other sonata finale it sustains the symphonic weight of the other movements and, as a whole, Hob.XVI:52 represents the most complete realization of Haydn's mature symphonic thought in a solo sonata.

BH

A. P. Brown, *Joseph Haydn's Keyboard Music: Sources and Style* (Bloomington, Ind., 1986).

B. Harrison, *Haydn's Keyboard Music: Studies in Performance Practice* (Oxford, 1996).

L. Somfai, *The Keyboard Sonatas of Joseph Haydn: Instruments and Performance practice, Genres and Styles* (Chicago, 1995).

keyboard trio

A multi-movement work, normally in two or three movements, for keyboard and two other instruments, usually violin and cello. Emerging in the second half of the 18th century the keyboard trio belongs generically to the repertoire of accompanied keyboard music. Before the 1780s, especially, many keyboard trios owe much to the tradition of accompanied sonatas with subordinate, often *ad libitum*, accompaniments to what are essentially keyboard sonatas, a tradition that flourished particularly in London and Paris in the 1760s and 1770s. Other early keyboard trios, especially in Austria and Germany, with more autonomous violin parts, are closer to the textures of the Baroque duo and trio sonatas, or combine such textures with features of the accompanied sonata. From the 1780s the mature keyboard trios of Haydn and Mozart continued to be published with descriptions such as 'Sonata per il Clavicembalo o Forte-Piano con un Violino e Violoncello' although these works largely call for a fortepiano rather than a harpsichord, and the violin part is in true partnership with the keyboard. Although more independent and of greater thematic interest than has often been allowed, the cello part, through to Haydn's late works, is still largely tied to the left hand of the keyboard.

Whereas the mature keyboard trios were written with publication in mind rather than a particular performer, the early keyboard trios were conceived with particular players in mind, though nothing is known about the circumstances of individual works. As with the composer's solo sonatas some of the early trios might have been devised as teaching material initially intended for the composer's pupils, such as MARIANNA VON MARTINES and THERESE KELLER.

---

1. Early keyboard trios, *c*.1760. The early works belong to a relatively small Viennese repertoire of accompanied keyboard music from the third quarter of the 18th century, disseminated largely in manuscript copies. Usually entitled divertimento or partita, all of the extant trios, except Hob.XV:41, are three-movement works with, in the majority of cases, a minuet and trio second movement. Only two works (Hob.XV:36 and 41) depart from the norm of having each movement in the same key. In harmonic rhythm and the patterning of the bass line the early trios show their debt to the continuo sonata, and in the relationship between keyboard and violin parts there are strong reminiscences of the Baroque obbligato duo and trio sonata. Generally the violin part is more integral to the musical argument than in contemporary English or Parisian accompanied keyboard music. There are frequent passages of continuo keyboard-writing accompanying violin solos, of equal sharing of material between a written-out part for the right hand of the keyboard and the violin, and, in one instance (Hob. XV:35/iii), canonic imitation between keyboard and violin. Other Baroque features include the inclusion of a 'Polones' in Hob.XV:36, a sequence of movements reminiscent of a *sonata da chiesa* in Hob.XV:37, and the inclusion of two minuet movements in Hob.XV:33 (only the incipits of this work survive). On the other hand, interspersed within a single movement with conservative textures and particularly characteristic of minuet and trio movements, there are textures closer to accompanied keyboard music in which the violin sustains harmony notes, plays in unison, thirds, or sixths with the right-hand part of the keyboard. Technically these trios are more complex than Haydn's short early solo sonatas and more even in quality than the longer solo sonatas from the same period.

2. Mature keyboard trios, 1784–*c*.1796. The important body of 28 keyboard trios that Haydn wrote in little more than a decade from 1784 reflects the changing external circumstances of his career and constitutes one of the most impressive cycles of instrumental music from the 18th century. Haydn's ever-increasing international reputation from the 1780s meant that he often wrote to commission or specifically for publishers. At a time when his symphonies were beginning to dominate the European symphonic repertoire in terms of public performances and dissemination through the major publishing houses of Europe, the keyboard trio rather than the solo keyboard sonata was the genre in which Haydn appealed to a large international market of amateur musicians.

In the period 1784–*c*.1796, 13 keyboard trios were written, six between 1784 and 1785, and a further seven between 1788 and 1790. Most of the trios from the 1780s were the product of Haydn's close association with the Viennese firm ARTARIA. Documented in an extensive body of correspondence, this association was an important part of the burgeoning music-publishing industry in Vienna in the 1780s. The large market of keyboard players in the aristocratic and bourgeois circles of the city was central to this newly flourishing industry and Haydn's production of keyboard trios at this time is part of the broader popularity of the genre in Vienna. Although the association between composer and publisher was launched by the publication of six solo sonatas (Hob.XVI:35–9, 20) in 1780, between then and 1790 Haydn wrote only six new sonatas, in comparison with 13 trios; later, between *c*.1792 and *c*.1796, only three further solo sonatas were composed in comparison with 15 trios.

Elsewhere in Europe the demand for Haydn's music, including the keyboard trios, was reflected in the fact that the privileged position that Artaria enjoyed for much of the 1780s in issuing first editions of Haydn's music was, especially from the late 1780s, weakened by competition from other publishers who established contact with Haydn and issued equally authentic editions of his music: these include BLAND, FORSTER, LONGMAN & BRODERIP, and PRESTON in London; LE MENU ET BOYER, IMBAULT, LE DUC, Nadermann, SIEBER in Paris; BOßLER, BREITKOPF, HUMMEL, and Simrock in Germany. Appropriately, Haydn's mature series of trios was initiated by his contact with the London publisher Forster, formalized in a contract in 1786, and by the issue of Hob.XV:15–17 in John Bland's series *Le Tout Ensemble* in which the publisher, who had close ties with Haydn between 1789 and *c*.1792, claimed exclusive rights to these works. The English first editions of these works is prophetic of the importance of English publishers in Haydn's trios of the 1790s, which were issued in a series of first editions, by Preston and by Longman & Broderip.

While the number and geographical spread of publishers who sold authentic first editions of Haydn's trios is itself an indicator of his international appeal, the true extent of the popularity of these works in the 1780s and 1790s is emphasized by the number of, mostly unauthorized, editions which almost immediately followed the appearance of a first edition. For instance, the trios Hob.XV:18–20, published by Longman & Broderip in 1794, were issued in at least one new edition per year until 1799, and in several other editions in the early years of the 19th century: the geographical distribution of these editions was a wide one, including Amsterdam, Berlin, Leipzig, London, Munich, Offenbach, Paris, and Vienna.

In fact Haydn was unable to meet all of the requests from publishers for new keyboard works. From his correspondence it seems that promises to Breitkopf, Nadermann, and possibly Sieber, of new sonatas, probably trios, were never fulfilled. The demand for Haydn's music for domestic use was, however, met in other ways, including the issuing of arrangements for keyboard trio of many of his most popular symphonies. In the first two sets of keyboard trios published by Forster in 1785–6 Haydn was unable to supply brand new works. Hob.XV:5 was published alongside two trios actually written by Pleyel (Hob.XV:3–4); and Hob.XV:2 (published with Hob.XV:9 and 10) was an arrangement of an earlier divertimento for keyboard, baryton, and strings.

In writing the 13 trios of 1784–90 Haydn remained acutely aware of his audience. When correcting the proofs of Hob.XV:6–8 he rebuked Artaria for numerous errors (letter of 10 December 1785) and rewrote the trio Hob.XV:13 to include a set of variations as a first movement in accordance with Artaria's, and presumably the public's, taste (letter of 29 March 1789). Technically there are passages of florid embellishment, occasional cadenzas, or embellished pauses and some writing in thirds and octaves that break the usual constraints of 18th-century domestic music; indeed, Hob.XV:14, although written as domestic music, was transferred without discomfort to the public platform when HUMMEL played it in the Salomon concert series at Hanover Square in April 1792.

In the 13 trios of 1784–90 there is an almost equal division between two- and three-movement cycles. Of the seven two-movement works, four end with Tempo di Menuet movements and in the six three-movement cycles five end with rondos or movements with rondo characteristics. In the sets Hob.XV:6–8 and XV:11–13 published by Artaria, Haydn balanced two shorter two-movement cycles with one three-movement work in each set, and in the trios with flute rather than violin (Hob.XV:15–17) two three-movement works ending with rondos are contrasted with a two-movement work ending with a Tempo di Menuet movement. The trios are characterized by diversity in formal types and each of the conventional instrumental forms—sonata form, variations, rondo, and minuet-type movements—is treated with a freedom and variety that distinguish Haydn's trios from contemporary domestic music. Rondo episodes may contain strongly contrasted or developmental material related to the refrain, while the returns of the refrain may be literal, have altered patterns of repetition, or be varied reprises. Similarly, Haydn's extensive experimentation with variation forms in the late 1760s and 1770s is evident in the trios, particularly in the ternary Tempo di Menuetto movements (e.g. XV:6, 8, and 11) and the characteristic double variation set on alternating and related themes in the major and minor key.

Contrasts in scoring are a feature of these variation movements and of other forms in the trios. In ternary and rondo structures, the episodes, particularly those in the minor key, are often scored for violin solo, contrasting with a keyboard-dominated presentation of the refrain or of a Tempo di Menuet theme, and when Haydn employs varied reprises in these movements they, too, feature keyboard and violin in turn. In sonata form movements, also, double statements with changes in scoring are a common feature occurring in the presentation of material in both the tonic and dominant key areas, and broader contrasts in texture and scoring underline different harmonic functions in expositions, as in Hob.XV:11 where the tonic, dominant, and closing sections feature respectively the keyboard, concertante violin-writing, and an imitative texture.

The trios differ from Haydn's solo keyboard sonatas in ways other than the exploitation of contrasts in scoring. In sonata form movements the trios have a more continuous texture without any strong articulation between the tonic area and the transition, while in many solo sonatas the transition is marked by caesuras and breaks in texture. Frequently the continuity in texture and rhythm is uninterrupted for most of the exposition, even when contrasting themes are employed in the tonic and dominant (e.g. Hob.XV:12). Equally, there is a strong tendency in the expositions of trios to have particularly emphatic cadences that articulate the closing theme or group. These are effectively miniature cadenzas, characterized by a slowing of harmonic rhythm, articulating the harmonic patterns Ic–V–I over a number of bars, and the employing of figuration characteristic of cadenza endings including a long cadential trill on the supertonic; such gestures take the trio towards the world of the concerto.

While these features are characteristic of all the 1784–90 trios there is a clear difference in tone between the serious trios of Hob.XV:11–14 and the lighter, *galant* style of the trios with flute (XV:15–17), with Hob.XV:5, 8–10 being closer in style to the former and Hob.XV:6–7 to the latter. Among the serious trios XV:11–14 are Haydn's most outstanding achievements in the genre before the late trios of the mid-1790s, displaying a complexity representative of Haydn's musical language of the late 1780s: a broad tonal range that encompasses remote tonal and enharmonic relationships; harmonic deceptions in development sections; and unorthodox tonal juxtapositions. The remote tonal relationship between the three movements of Hob.XV:14 (A♭ major, E major, and A♭ major) anticipates similar juxtapositions in Haydn's London trios and sonatas of the 1790s , and the joining of the second and third movements of Hob.XV:14 highlights remote tonal relationships that feature in the entire work.

The serious trios Hob.XV:11–14 contain more intense thematic-motivic development than the lighter trios, and a penchant for contrapuntal elaboration, long integrated into Haydn's language in quartets, is also first found in these works. Consisting of a mere 21 bars the development section of Hob.XV:12/i is one of the shortest and most concentrated in the trios (a mere 21 bars), in which the first theme and a motif from a contrasting theme in the exposition (bars 35 ff.) are combined contrapuntally and followed by a series of stretto entries of the first theme. There are also nine bars of stretto based on the headmotif of the principal theme in the development of XV:13/ii, and even the lighter movement types (rondo and Tempo di Menuetto movements) are treated in a more serious manner: thus the developmental second episode in the rondo of Hob.XV:12 contains five bars of strict three-part canon based on the first four bars of the rondo refrain; and the Tempo di Menuetto theme of Hob.XV:11 is written in invertible counterpoint, duly revealed in the reprise when the parts are inverted.

In comparison with this type of sophistication the *galant* style of the trios with flute appears to make more concessions to the amateur public for whom they were intended. Charm and finesse are the primary characteristics. The opening 18 bars of Hob.XV:16 could not be simpler: a clear separation between a tuneful, totally diatonic melody and an accompaniment that is purely harmonic, devoid of melodic part-writing or thematic-motivic interest; the harmonies are limited to the tonic, subdominant, and dominant chords, and their static nature is emphasized by a tonic pedal present for 14 of the 18 bars, interrupted only twice for cadences. The opening themes of Hob.XV:15 and 16 are similar in their tunefulness, and harmonic and textural simplicity. Yet for all the graceful charm of the thematic material in the lighter trios the treatment of this material is contemporary; they could not be mistaken for earlier works by the composer. The first movements of Hob.XV:15 and 16 have significant excursions to minor keys in expositions and recapitulations; the development sections contain numerous harmonic surprises; and first movements and rondos frequently end with extensive codas. These works signify the reinvention of an earlier *galant* style, using the musical language of the late 1780s.

The trios of the 1780s are also significant in that they mark, along with the solo sonatas of 1780–8, Haydn's change from a generalized keyboard style to a committed fortepiano idiom. Dynamic markings, the most obvious indicator of this change, are less frequent in the trios of the mid-1780s than in contemporary solo sonatas (Hob.XVI:40–2) and although some of the trios may be performed on a harpsichord without significant loss, even in Hob.XV:9 (1785) there are occasional dynamic indications which are independent of textural change and which require a touch-sensitive instrument. In the trios of 1784–90 there is a gradual process by which dynamic effects, which make performance on a harpsichord problematic, appear with increasing frequency and it is clear that by 1789 Haydn was committed to writing keyboard music specifically for the fortepiano.

After the intensive production of keyboard trios in the second half of the 1780s, Haydn neglected the genre in the early years of the 1790s. In and around the time of his second London trip, however, the keyboard trio again became a central genre for the composer, and most of the 15 trios of the 1790s were written in a two-year period from 1794 to 1795. Twelve of the 15 were published in sets of three in authentic editions by Longman & Broderip (Hob.XV:18–20 (1794); 24–6 (1795); 27–9 (1797)) and by Preston (Hob.XV:21–3 (1795)), and were very quickly disseminated throughout Europe in reprints derived from the English editions. Of the three other trios published individually, Hob.XV:31 belongs to the same 1794–5 period and, like the composer's last three sonatas (Hob.XV:50–2) and the three trios, Hob.XVI:27–9, is connected with the pianist THERESE JANSEN. Hob.XV:32, published by Bland in 1794, is the earliest of these trios; and Hob.XV:30 is the last of Haydn's trios, probably written in 1796 after his second London trip.

In contrast to the trios of the 1780s there is a preponderance of three-movement works in the later trios: only two of the trios published separately (Hob.XV:31 and 32) retain the two-movement cycle favoured by Haydn in the 1780s. Although the three-movement format is preferred in the 1790s, in the choice of tempo and movement types the trios show more flexibility than contemporary quartets and symphonies. First movements may be sonata form movements (nine examples) or may be slower movements in double variation (three), ternary variation (one) or rondo variation (two) forms. In each of the sets of three, one work begins with a variation movement while two others have first movements in sonata form and in the set Hob.XV:18–20, for instance, the difference between the two movements in sonata form (Hob.XV:18 and 20) signifies the expressive range and compositional diversity of the late trios. In both works variants of the opening themes dominate the movement, but the character of these themes and their treatment is significantly different. In Hob.XV:20 the many passages in thirds or octaves and the innovatory pianistic textures with, for instance, four-octave spacing between the hands at the opening or the thick chordal writing at the climax of the development, contrasts with the lyrical two-part imitative writing in the main thematic idea of Hob.XV:18, which then pervades the movement as a whole. In the second set of trios, Hob.XV:21–3, the first movements of Hob.XV:21 and 22 are similarly contrasted. Hob.XV:21/i is the only work among these trios to borrow Haydn's symphonic practice of beginning with a slow introduction: the Vivace assai is related thematically to the Adagio pastorale and the pastoral character of the introduction pervades much of the first movement, and is echoed in the hunting horn call of the finale. The first movement of Hob.XV:22, on the other hand, has more elaborate pianistic challenges (for instance, frequent passages of semiquavers in thirds), dense contrapuntal textures at the beginning of the development section, and more complex modulations.

The second movements (varying in tempo from Adagio to Allegretto) and those first movements not in sonata form are cast in a variety of structures, but Haydn's characteristic variation procedures are usually in evidence, continuing a long tradition of experimentation that stretches back to the late 1760s. New features include the change of tempo at the end of the double variation first movement of Hob.XV:19; the concluding Presto section is a free expansion of the structure of the major-key theme. Hob.XV:20 and XV:28 are based on passacaglia-like themes, and while these movements have precedents in the composer's solo sonatas, the first mentioned, in particular, is an extraordinary movement, combining archaisms with Classical formal features and two-part counterpoint characteristic of Haydn's late style; as Rosen points out it is 'a passacaglia like no other'.

It is in the finales that one finds the strongest divergence from the trios of the 1780s. Haydn's preference in nine finales for fast movements in 3/4 (from Allegro to Presto) replaces his previous preference for rondos and Tempo di Menuet finales. Of the late trios only Hob.XV:26 has a Tempo di Menuet finale and the famous 'Rondo in the Gipsies' Style' of Hob.XV:25 is the only true rondo form, although a number of other finales have some rondo characteristics. Of the fast finales in 3/4 only that of Hob. XV:20 comes close to the Tempo di Menuet tradition and, certainly, none of the other movements could be mistaken for a minuet in character. It is in Hob.XV:23 that the new finale type is most striking, with new rhythmic experiments added to other features of Haydn's complex late musical language. The main theme, occurring in both tonic and dominant keys, is in characteristic two-part imitative counterpoint with prominent off-beat accents, subjected in the development section to intense contrapuntal and rhythmic treatment, with a number of hemiola passages that have the effect of converting a notated 3/4 to a sounding 4/4. Similar hemiola effects are found in the 'Finale in the German Style' of Hob.XV:29.

The style of the late trios is a radical extension of that witnessed in the trios of the 1780s, giving the impression of a composer relishing the deployment of a highly integrated and complex musical language, explored with even greater freedom in the late trios than in contemporary quartets and symphonies. The infinitely variable textures of the late trios are enriched by the absorption of a contrapuntal language more commonly associated with the quartets and symphonies and serving a variety of expressive and formal functions, including formal fugato sections in development sections, archaic passacaglia-like forms in slow movements, thin two-part contrapuntal writing in the new style of the fast finales in 3/4, and a more lyrical contrapuntal style in some of the slower first movements. Perhaps the most conspicuous aspect of the late trios is their richly expanded harmonic vocabulary; remote tonal relationships between movements are found in seven of the 12 works concerned.

A similar expansion in tonal range operates at many levels within movements. In the trio in E♭ minor (Hob.XV:31) the second episode in the first movement is in B major, and in sonata form movements the process of establishing the secondary tonality is often very complex, involving striking digressions and juxtapositions of tonality. Within the secondary tonal area a degree of digression or instability can also be expected, while development sections in sonata forms and developmental episodes in ternary and rondo structures often contain changes in the notated key signature, a very practical indication of the enormously expanded tonal range of the works.

In comparison with the earlier keyboard trios those of 1794–5 also witness a significant exploration of pianistic technique, texture, and sonority. In London Haydn became familiar with the distinctive heavy sonority of English pianos and had access to Broadwood's instruments. He would also have encountered the virtuoso fortepiano tradition flourishing in the city, represented by performers such as Clementi, Cramer, Dussek, the young Hummel, and Therese Jansen. A direct link between the London pianistic milieu and Haydn's trios is provided by Therese Jansen. The set of trios, Hob.XV:27–9, were written for her and constitute some of Haydn's most difficult keyboard music; for instance, Hob.XV:27 includes octaves in triplet semiquavers, frequent crossing of hands, and, in the third movement, two lengthy passages of uninterrupted semiquaver figuration. More remarkable than the technical difficulties are the brilliantly pianistic themes (such as in Hob.XV:27/i and 28/i), the new richness in chordal writing (such as at the climax of the development in Hob.XV:20/i), and the freer use of contrasting registers of the piano (as in the wide, almost Beethovenian spacing between the hands at the opening of Hob.XV:20). Idiomatic piano-writing and new sonorities are central to Haydn's prodigious transformation of themes: in Hob.XV:28/i the novel combination of staccato and *tenuto* touch in the initial version of the first theme in E major is transformed into the full chordal, forte version of the theme that notably reinforces its appearance in A♭ in the development. In slow movements and variation movements that open a work the decoration of themes is also notably more virtuoso. Such movements are also characterized by embellished pauses, articulating the structure with a flourish. Altogether Haydn's piano-writing is in notable contrast to the rather empty virtuosity of some of his younger contemporaries, fully integrated into his compositional style, and generating idiomatic thematic ideas and new sonorities in the process. BH

A. P. Brown, *Joseph Haydn's Keyboard Music: Sources and Style* (Bloomington, Ind., 1986).

M. Hunter, 'Haydn's London Piano Trios and His Salomon String Quartets: Private vs. Public', in E. Sisman (ed.), *Haydn and His World* (Princeton, 1997), 103–30.

K. Komlós, 'The Viennese Keyboard Trio in the 1780s: Sociological Background and Contemporary Reception', *Music and Letters*, 68 (1987), 222–34.

C. Rosen, *The Classical Style: Haydn, Mozart, Beethoven* (London, 1971).

W. D. Sutcliffe, 'The Haydn Piano Trio: Textual Facts and Textural Principles', in W. D. Sutcliffe (ed.), *Haydn Studies* (Cambridge, 1998), 246–90.

keyboard variations. Unlike his performing contemporaries Mozart and Beethoven, and many others who often improvised sets of variations during private and public concerts to set down and publish later, Haydn wrote relatively few such works for keyboard and there is no evidence that he performed any of them himself. Perhaps because he had no crowd to please, not a single one of the five independent variation sets for solo keyboard and one for keyboard four-hands is on a borrowed theme or popular opera aria. Indeed, he was praised by the theorist and composer Abbé

Vogler (1749–1814) for not needing to have his music 'illuminated by a borrowed glimmer'. Also surprising is the small number of independent sets for keyboard compared with the dozens and dozens of variation movements in all genres that he wrote throughout his long creative life. Only late in his career did he write independent sets on borrowed themes, though neither of the two examples is for keyboard alone: DR HARINGTON'S COMPLIMENT for soprano, chorus, and piano, and 'The Blue Bell of Scotland' (Hob.XXXIa:176) for piano trio. The solo CAPRICCIO: 'ACHT SAUSCHNEIDER MÜSSEN SEIN' is not a variation set per se, but rather a kind of rondo with slightly varied returns of the theme in different keys.

1. **Variations in D for harpsichord (Hob.XVII:7).**
2. **Variations in A for harpsichord (Hob.XVII:2).**
3. **Variations in E♭ for keyboard (Hob.XVII:3).**
4. **Variations in C for piano (Hob.XVII:5).**
5. **Andante in F minor for piano (Hob.XVII:6).**
6. **Variations in G on 'Gott erhalte Franz den Kaiser' for piano.**

1. Variations in D for harpsichord (Hob. XVII: 7). This simple piece exists in a copy dated 1766 and was written as early as the first half of the 1750s; although its authenticity has been in doubt, it was supposedly verified by Haydn late in his life. Its theme is unlike any other by Haydn in its amount of sheer repetition: a single bar is heard four times (bars 3–4 and 12–13). This gives an uncharacteristically static quality to the piece, especially since the bar in question consists of two beats of tonic and one beat of subdominant. The method used to vary the theme is the assignment of a simple rhythmic or figural pattern to each of the five variations, retaining the harmony and occasionally the main melodic notes of the theme.

2. Variations in A for harpsichord (Hob. XVII: 2). Composed about 1765, this lively set of 20 variations was first published by ARTARIA in 1788/9 in a version with only 12 variations. It again uses the constant-harmony type of variation, whereby the harmonies and phrase structure of the theme are maintained in each of the variations but the theme is only occasionally present, in a version either unadorned or decorated; here it appears only once (variation 9, a middle voice). Although the theme is undistinguished, Haydn finds imaginative ways to recast it in variations that seem a virtual compendium of keyboard technique, with hand-crossings (variation 3), consecutive practice in right-hand and left-hand runs (variations 5, 6), repeated notes (variation 8), consecutive thirds (variations 11, 12, 16), trills (variation 18), octaves (variation 20), and many other kinds of dexterity. The piece is thus interesting from both compositional and pedagogical perspectives, and occasionally even puts one in mind of the figurations in Mozart's variations in the sonata in A (K331) (especially variations 3, 10).

3. Variations in E♭ for keyboard (Hob. XVII: 3). Composed in the early 1770s and first published in 1788/9 by Artaria as 'Arietta con 12 Variazioni', the theme of this lovely piece is a minuet from the string quartet op. 9 no. 2, completed in 1770. In the 12 variations, the main notes of the melody are recognizable, especially at the beginning; only variations 5, 6, and 8 significantly depart from it. The cantabile style of several of the variations, in which decorative additions add shading and even poignancy to the melodic line (variations 1, 2), contrasts with those pervaded by an insistent rhythmic figure (variations 6, 8). As in the A major set, a few variations place the melody in a lower register to create an interesting opposition with higher embellishments or runs. Even at this late date, Haydn continues the practice of simple syncopation between left and right hands found in his two earlier sets, but while the D major set devotes an entire variation to it (variation 1), the A major (variation 2) and E♭ major sets (variations 3 and 7) confine it to single phrases.

4. Variations in C for piano (Hob.XVII:5). Nearly 20 years separate the E♭ set from these six variations on an Andante theme, written in late 1790. Although Haydn wrote dozens of variation movements during this time his only other independent keyboard set in the same period was the arrangement of the finale of his G major string quartet, op. 33 no. 5 (1781), published in 1786 by Artaria in Vienna; because two of those variations featured a textural component that the keyboard could not duplicate, the arrangement consists only of the theme, a single variation, and the Presto coda that begins like a variation. The C major variations were published by Artaria as 'agréables et faciles'. The theme is among the most melodically detailed Haydn ever provided for variations, and he adheres very closely to it, even when changing to a march (variation 3) or turning to the minor key (variation 5), the only *minore* in all of Haydn's strophic keyboard variations. Indeed, every variation except the second begins with virtually the identical gesture to that of the opening bar of the theme. In an era when published reviews of keyboard pieces always commented on their degree of difficulty, Artaria's advertised assessment was sound.

5. Andante in F minor for piano (Hob.XVII:6). This most intensely moving of Haydn's keyboard works, indeed one of his greatest works in any genre, was written between the two London visits in 1793. It is Haydn's only independent set for solo keyboard to adopt the special form of

ALTERNATING VARIATIONS on two themes that he had made his own. Moreover, it takes on a shape—ABA¹B¹A¹B²A coda—not shared by any of his other alternating variation movements because of the reprise of the theme and the extraordinary coda. From its first plaintive dotted rhythms, the lengthy and finely etched minor theme sounds more like a character piece than a variation theme. The major theme, in contrast, is more playful and pastoral, more delicately figured and thinner in texture than the *minore*. Every variation employs a more or less standard type of figuration (e.g. syncopation, scales, trills, turning figures).

The work underwent several revisions that affected its structure and level of expression. Indeed, it was called 'Sonata' on the autograph and in his London catalogue and 'Un piccolo Divertimento' on an authentic copy. The original format was an alternating variation set in six sections with a short codetta in F major. Originally Haydn may well have intended to write further movements to make a sonata. But the addition of a thematic reprise and a coda did more than simply create a unique seven-part alternating set; instead, these additions at first match and then surpass the minor theme in intensity. Arising as an emotion-filled interruption of the reprise, the coda gains in power until it propels itself into a cadenza-like outburst. Its insistence upon diminished-seventh chords and intervals associate it unmistakably with the pathetic style. What makes the coda special, beyond its obvious and unprecedented chromaticism, is that it concentrates on the dotted motif of the theme, the single most rhetorically powerful gesture of the piece. It also appropriates from the B theme its frivolous flourish (already used by the A theme to conclude its second variation) for the shocking diminished-seventh chords in bars 190–3. The coda now yields to the close of the reprise, transfigured and fading to a whisper.

6. Variations in G on 'Gott erhalte Franz den Kaiser' for piano. Haydn's final keyboard set was an arrangement of the celebrated slow movement from the string quartet op. 76 no. 3, composed in 1797; the quartets were written in 1797 and published in 1799, with the piano arrangement coming out the same year. Later Viennese editions wrongly attributed the set to Abbé Gelinek (1758–1825), a prolific composer of piano variations. ES

F. Eibner, 'Die authentische Klavierfassung von Haydns Variationen über "Gott erhalte" ', *HYB* 7 (1970), 281–306.

L. Plantinga and G. P. Johnson, 'Haydn's *Andante con variazioni*: Compositional Process, Text, and Genre', *Studies in the History of Music*, 3 (New York, 1993), 129–67.

E. Sisman, *Haydn and the Classical Variation* (Cambridge, Mass., 1993).

Kimmerling, Robert (b. 8 Dec. 1737; d. 5 Dec. 1799). Viennese-born composer and music director at the Benedictine abbey of MELK, Lower Austria, from 1761 until 1777. After he joined the order in 1754, he was sent by his uncle, Abbot Thomas Pauer of Melk, to study composition with Haydn in Vienna from at least November 1760 through to March 1761 when Haydn joined the Esterházy court. Over 60 of his works survive, mostly sacred and composed before 1777, but stylistic and technical characteristics suggest that his teacher had little influence on him. RNF

R. N. Freeman, 'Robert Kimmerling: A Little-Known Haydn Pupil', *HYB* 13 (1982), 143–79.

Kirnberger, Johann Philipp (bap. 24 April 1721; d. 26/7 July 1783). German theorist and composer who studied with J. S. Bach in Leipzig (1739–41) and was dedicated to spreading Bach's teachings. In the 1750s he worked alongside C. P. E. BACH at the Prussian court in Berlin. The majority of his theoretical publications date from the time of his employment as Kapellmeister to Princess Anna Amalia of Prussia (1758–83). Detailed annotations to JOHANN JOSEPH FUX's *Gradus ad Parnassum* traditionally attributed to Haydn include references to Kirnberger's major work, *Die Kunst des reinen Satzes* (1771–9). SW

J. P. Kirnberger, *The Art of Strict Musical Composition*, trans. D. Beach and J. Thym (New Haven, 1982).

F. Sumner, 'Haydn and Kirnberger: a Documentary Report', *Journal of the American Musicological Society*, 28 (1975), 530–39.

'Kleine Orgelsolomesse' ('Little Organ Solo Mass'). Nickname for the MISSA BREVIS SANCTI JOANNIS DE DEO (Hob.XXII:7), reflecting the extended solo use of the organ in the Benedictus and distinguishing it from the 'GROSSE ORGELSOLOMESSE' ('Great Organ Solo Mass'). Occasionally, the work is misleadingly referred to as the 'Kleine Orgelmesse' ('Little Organ Mass'); strictly speaking the term organ mass refers to a work accompanied by an organ only.

Knoblauch, Johann (d. 22 Jan. 1765). A horn player at the Esterházy court from 1761 to 1765. He played first horn in Haydn's earliest works for the court, such as symphonies nos. 6–8; when four horns were employed Knoblauch usually undertook the third horn part (as in Symphony no. 13). ERL

P. Bryan, 'Haydn's Hornists', *HS* 3/1 (1973), 52–8.

Kozeluch, Leopold (Jan Antonín Koželuh) (b. 26 June 1747; d. 7 May 1818). Composer, pianist, teacher, and publisher. Baptized Jan Antonín, Kozeluch adopted the name Leopold around 1773 to distinguish himself from his older cousin and teacher, Jan Evangelista Antonín Tomás (1738–1814), a former pupil of Gassmann and Gluck. Kozeluch received his early musical education in Velvary, later with his cousin (now Kapellmeister at St Vitus's cathedral), and also with Franz Xaver Dussek (František Xaver Dušek) (1731–91), a former pupil of WAGENSEIL. While in Prague Kozeluch experienced enough success as a composer of ballets and pantomimes to abandon the law and concentrate instead on building his career as a musician. He moved to Vienna in 1778 and quickly established a reputation as a fine keyboard player, composer, and teacher. He founded a music-publishing house in 1784, which was later managed by his brother Antonín Tomás Kozeluch (1752–1805), but continued to publish his own music elsewhere with other houses. He maintained close business relations with a number of English publishers, including JOHN BLAND and ROBERT BIRCHALL. Kozeluch's *Huldigungskantata* (Allegiance Cantata), commissioned by the Bohemian Estates, was sung by Josepha Dussek (Josefa Dušek) on 12 September 1791 as part of the festivities for the coronation of Leopold II as King of Bohemia. According to Mozart's early biographer Niemetschek (Nemeček), Kozeluch slandered Mozart villainously in Prague and even attacked his moral character. The cantata, which Niemetschek describes as 'a changeling', was a success and may have been instrumental in securing Kozeluch's appointment in June 1792 as Kammer Kapellmeister and Hofmusik-Compositor, positions he held until his death in 1818.

Kozeluch's career as a composer covers the period *c.*1771 to 1804 after which he devoted most of his time to teaching, activities connected with his court appointment, and arranging Scottish, Irish, and Welsh folksongs for the Edinburgh publisher GEORGE THOMSON. While he composed in a broad range of genres, his most significant work lay in writing for the piano, both as a solo instrument and in combination with other forces. He was an important and influential teacher whose own performing style played a significant role in the evolution of a distinctive piano style. Some of his later works, in particular the Caprices (1798), anticipate a number of stylistic traits that are associated with Schubert. Much of his stage music has been lost.

As a publisher Kozeluch issued the first edition, in 1791, of Haydn's op. 64 quartets. ADJB

O. E. Deutsch, 'Kozeluch ritrovato', *Music and Letters*, 26 (1945), 47.

R.Hickman (ed.), *Leopold Kozeluch. Six String Quartets Opus 32 and Opus 33*, Recent Researches in the Music of the Classical Era, vol.xlii (Madison, 1994).

K. Pfannhauser, 'Wer war Mozarts Amstnachfolger?', *Acta Mozartiana*, 3 (1956), 6.

A. Weinmann, *Verzeichnis der Verlagswerke des Musikalischen Magazins in Wien (1784-1802), Leopold [und Anton] Kozeluch, Beiträge zur Geschichte des Alt-Wiener Musikverlages*, Vol. 2/1a (Vienna, 1979).

Kraft, Anton (b. 30 Dec. 1749; d. 28 Aug. 1820). Cellist and composer who was employed at the Esterházy court from 1778 to 1790. Born in Rokitzan in Bohemia, Kraft studied the cello with Werner, a member of the orchestra at the Kreuzherren church in Prague, where he also attended the university. He joined the Esterházy orchestra as the principal cellist at Prince Nicolaus's personal invitation, and remained a favourite of the prince who became godfather to several of his children. The first child, Nicolaus (1778–1853), may well have been named after Prince Nicolaus; he, too, became a celebrated cellist. Haydn was godfather to Anton's fifth child.

Kraft's abilities as a cellist are reflected in Haydn's concerto in D major written for the player in 1783. A muddled report from the 19th century suggested that Kraft was, in fact, the composer of this work and it was only the rediscovery of Haydn's autograph in 1954 that confirmed the true authorship. Nevertheless, the suspicion remains that Haydn may have used material by Kraft in the work. Kraft had composition lessons from Haydn and his output included trios for baryton and cello, quartets, cello sonatas, and a cello concerto.

Following the disbandment of the Esterházy orchestra in 1790, Kraft joined the orchestra of the Grassalkovics family (Haydn turned down an invitation to become Kapellmeister in favour of the journey to London); he joined the musical retinue of Prince Lobkowitz in 1796; there were also a number of journeys abroad in this period, usually with his son. In 1802 Anton and Nicolaus contemplated rejoining the Esterházy orchestra but they were unable to agree suitable remuneration. According to the often unreliable testimony of Beethoven's early biographer, Schindler, the cello part of Beethoven's Triple Concerto (op. 56) was written for Kraft. In his last years Kraft established a reputation in Vienna as a teacher of the cello, including a position at the conservatory established by the Gesellschaft der Musikfreunde.
TMP

Kraus, Carl (b. 1722/3: d. 3 March 1802). Rector and director of music at the Martinkirche in Eisenstadt from at least the early 1760s. A lifelong friend of Haydn, he copied and borrowed many church compositions from the composer. Given this close connection the textual interest of the material is considerable. Following Kraus's death, part of his library was acquired by the Esterházy archives. He had a blind daughter to whom Haydn bequeathed 100 gulden in his first will (1801).

Kraus, Joseph Martin (b. 20 June 1756; d. 15 Dec. 1792). German composer whose music was greatly admired by Haydn. Born in Miltenberg am Main he received a musical education mainly in Mannheim and a legal one at the universities of Mainz and Göttingen. A speculative visit to Sweden in 1778 resulted in Kraus joining the musical court of Gustav III, becoming assistant Kapellmeister in 1781 and full Kapellmeister in 1788. At Gustav's expense Kraus undertook a four-year tour of Europe in 1782–6. It was in 1783 that Kraus visited Eszterháza, reporting enthusiastically about musical life there, but noting too, with some surprise, an avaricious side to Haydn's nature. Haydn, for his part, came to regard Kraus's instrumental music, especially the symphonies and quartets, as some of the most striking of the age. Kraus was born six months after Mozart, and died just over a year after him. Haydn regarded both as irreparable losses: 'Too bad about that man, just like Mozart! They were both so young.' Many anecdotes suggest that Kraus's fine symphony in C minor was presented to Haydn in Eszterháza in 1783 but other sources suggest that it was composed slightly later.

A. Peter Brown, 'Stylistic Maturity and Regional Influence: Joseph Martin Kraus's Symphonies in C♯ minor (Stockholm, 1782) and C minor (Vienna, 1783?)', in E. K. Wolf and E. H. Roesner (eds.), *Studies in Musical Sources and Style. Essays in Honor of Jan LaRue* (Munich, 1990), 381–418.
HCRL 2 and 4.

Krumpholtz, Jean-Baptiste (b. 3 May 1742; d. 19 Feb. 1790). Harpist and composer. Born in Bohemia he joined the Esterházy court in August 1773, leaving in February 1776. Haydn never wrote any music for the harp in this period, though Krumpholtz would have played the instrument in Gluck's *Orfeo* given at Eszterháza shortly before he left. In his memoirs Krumpholtz stated that Haydn had assisted him in the composition of the ritornellos of a harp concerto subsequently published as op. 6 no. 2.

Kurz-Bernardon, Joseph Felix von (b. 23 Feb. 1717; d. Vienna, 3 Feb. 1784). Austrian comic actor, singer, dramatist, and manager. His name was originally Kurz but became known as Kurz-Bernardon after the stage persona he invented. He was one of the pillars of the Kärntnertortheater from the mid-1730s until 1760 and may be regarded as one of the founders of Austrian *Singspiel*. He toured extensively, and he married wives and fathered children who supported his theatrical endeavours (his second wife, Teresa Morelli, created Amor in Gluck's *Paride ed Elena*). His connection with Haydn is mainly as the author of the farce DER KRUMME TEUFEL. According to an anecdote told by Griesinger, Dies, and Carpani, Haydn came to Kurz's attention when he and fellow musicians serenaded Kurz's first wife; Kurz was so impressed with the quality of the music that he invited Haydn to compose a score for his latest play. Kurz's notoriety and fame extended to royal and imperial displeasure. PB

U. Birbaumer, *Das Werk des Josephs Felix von Kurz-Bernardon und seine szenische Realisierung* (Vienna, 1971).
P. Branscombe, 'Music in the Viennese Popular Theatre of the Eighteenth and Nineteenth Centuries', *Proceedings of the Royal Musical Association*, 98 (1971–2), 101–12.
D. Heartz, *Haydn, Mozart and the Viennese Classical School, 1740–1780* (New York, 1995).

Kurzböck (Kurzbeck), Magdalene von (b. 1767; d. 1845). One of the leading female pianists in Vienna at the turn of the 18th century, especially noted for her retentive musical memory. Haydn dedicated the published edition of his last piano sonata (Artaria, 1798) and of his E♭ minor piano trio (Traeg, 1803) to her. She regularly visited Haydn in his old age and during the bombardment of Vienna by French troops in the days before his death offered to move him to her home in the inner city. She was the daughter of the successful printer and bookseller, Joseph Kurzböck, who in 1774 had published six keyboard sonatas by Haydn (Hob.XVI:21–6).

L

La canterina (The Songstress) (Hob.XXVIII:2). Opera ('intermezzo in musica') in two parts to a libretto derived from Piccinni's *L'Orgille* (1760). The first documented performance was in Pressburg (Bratislava) on 16 February 1767, but it may have been given at Eisenstadt the previous year.

Piccinni's intermezzo, written for Naples, was a late product of the Neapolitan intermezzo tradition that had produced Pergolesi's *La serva padrona* 27 years earlier. *La canterina*, in its amusing depiction of a conflict between a wealthy but gullible old man and a clever, charming young woman, is reminiscent of Pergolesi's opera. Its principal numbers are four arias and two quartets, one at the end of each part. Like many intermezzi it lacks an overture.

In the house of the music teacher Don Pelagio (tenor, sung by CARL FRIBERTH in the Pressburg performance), lives a young student Gasparina (mezzo-soprano, MARIA ANNA WEIGL) and Apollonia, who pretends to be Gasparina's mother. Apollonia was sung by the tenor LEOPOLD DICHTLER; Haydn notated the role in the soprano clef, but whether Dichtler used falsetto throughout or sang the role an octave lower than written is not known. (Even basses occasionally portrayed old women in 18th-century *opera buffa*; Andrea Morigi, for example, created the role of Ortensia in SALIERI's *La finta scema* of 1775.) In another transvestite role, the soprano BARBARA DICHTLER, Leopold's wife, portrayed the young Don Ettore, who flirts with Gasparina.

Pelagio sings a recitative and aria that he has composed in the serious style, with elaborate obbligato parts for oboes and horns. Gasparina repeats the *scena*, with comments by her teacher ('Dolce, dolce'). Apollonia cannot resist giving her own advice, much to Pelagio's annoyance. Later he overhears Gasparina and Ettore talk of plans to cheat him. Enraged, he orders them to leave the house. Part 1 ends with a quartet of anger, alarm and supplication.

In Part 2 Pelagio expresses his resolve to evict Gasparina and Apollonia. Gasparina pleas for mercy; rebuffed, she sings a pseudo-tragic aria in C minor, marked Allegro di molto and including two cors anglais, 'Non v'è mi aiuta'. In an orchestrally accompanied recitative Pelagio begins to relent. He eventually forgives Gasparina, but she, wanting more than forgiveness, pretends to faint. The rest of the cast expresses anguish in an accompanied recitative. A purse full of money from Pelagio and a diamond ring from Ettore finally succeed in placating Gasparina; all four characters join in celebrating the happy ending. JAR

G. Allroggen, '*La canterina* in den Vertonungen von Nicolà Piccinni und Joseph Haydn', *Joseph Haydn: Tradition und Rezeption* (Regensburg, 1985), 100–12.

F. Lippmann, 'Haydn e l'opera buffa: tre confronti con opere italiane coeve sullo stesso testo', *Nuovo rivista musicale italiana*, 17 (1983), 223–46.

'La Chasse'. Authentic title given by Haydn to Symphony no. 73, when it was published by TORRICELLA in Vienna in 1782. The third movement utilizes the overture to *La fedeltà premiata*. 'La Chasse' has also been used as a nickname for Haydn's quartet op. 1 no. 1; as early as 1778–80 a keyboard arrangement of the opening movement of the quartet appeared in London with the title 'The Chase'. JH

La Chevardière, Louis Balthazard de (b. Feb. 1730; d. 8 April 1812). Parisian music publisher active from 1758 to 1784 when the business was sold to LE DUC. He never had a direct relationship with Haydn and approximately a third of the music allegedly by the composer published by the firm was spurious. However, he can be credited with the first publication anywhere of music by Haydn when, in January 1764, he announced the sale of 'Six Simphonies ou Quatuors Dialogues . . . Par Mr Hayden. Maître de Musique a Vienne'; this consisted of four quartets by Haydn (op. 1 nos. 1–4) plus two flute quartets by the Mannheim composer Carl Joseph Toeschi (1731–88). Ten years later, by accident rather than by design, La Chevardière issued the first edition of Haydn's op. 20 quartets, initiating the association of that opus number with the works.

C. Johansson, *French Music Publishers' Catalogues of the Second Half of the Eighteenth Century* (Stockholm, 1955).

La fedeltà premiata (Fidelity rewarded) (Hob. XXVIII:10). Opera ('dramma pastorale giocoso') in three acts, first performed at Eszterháza on 25 February 1781, in celebration of the opening of Prince Nicolaus Esterházy's new opera house. The complicated, well-crafted, and amusing libretto, by the Neapolitan GIAMBATTISTA LORENZI, had recently been set to music by Cimarosa (1749–1801) (as *L'infedeltà fedele*); Haydn had access to Cimarosa's score and learnt much from it.

Several of the singers who created roles in *La fedeltà premiata* left Eszterhàza within a year of the premiere; Haydn revised the opera for a new cast shortly thereafter, transposing several numbers, making cuts and other alterations.

The action takes place at Cumae, near Naples, at some unspecified time in Graeco-Roman antiquity. In its pastoral setting, and rich mixture of comic and serious characters and themes, it resembles Guarini's celebrated play *Il pastor fido*. According to a law imposed by the goddess Diana, every year the shepherds must sacrifice to a monster a man and a woman who love one another faithfully. The imminent sacrifice is to be made under the supervision of Melibeo, Diana's corrupt high priest (bass; the role was created by ANTONIO PESCI in 1781, and sung by DOMENICO NEGRI in 1782). He is attracted to the arrogant Amaranta (soprano; TERESA TAVEGGIA in 1781, MARIA ANTONIA SPECIOLI in 1782). Amaranta's brother Lindoro (tenor, LEOPOLD DICHTLER in 1781 and 1782) previously loved Nerina (soprano, COSTANZA VALDESTURLA in 1781 and 1782), though now seeks the hand of a beautiful woman who goes by the name Celia but whose real name is Fillide (the mezzo-soprano MARIA JERMOLI created the role in 1781; Haydn altered much of the part for the soprano METILDE BOLOGNA PORTA in 1782). Amaranta pretends to return Melibeo's affection in order to persuade him to help Lindoro win Fillide; but her plan is interrupted by the arrival of the ridiculous Count Perrucchetto (baritone; BENEDETTO BIANCHI in 1781, VINCENZO MORATTI in 1782) who flirts with Amaranta.

Long ago Fillide was about to marry Fileno (tenor; GUGLIELMO JERMOLI in 1781, ANTONIO SPECIOLI in 1782) when she was bitten by a poisonous snake. Fileno, believing Fillide dead, left in despair. Now he returns to discover that she is alive. But Fillide pretends not to recognize him because she knows that Melibeo will sacrifice them to the monster if he learns of their love.

Amaranta and Perruccheto are the principal comic characters of the opera. They are counterbalanced by Fillide and Fileno, who sing most of the sincerest and noblest music. The cavatine with which they first appear, Fileno's 'Dov'è, oh Dio' and Fillide's 'Placidi ruscelletti', characterize both lovers vividly with slow, deeply felt music. Rejected by Fillide, Fileno expresses his despair in an aria, 'Miseri affetti miei', which begins with a long orchestral introduction, Allegro di molto; but as Fileno enters the tempo switches to Adagio, as if to portray him as stunned by Fillide's inexplicable behaviour. After he leaves, Fillide sings an elaborate aria, 'Deh soccorri un infelice', whose remarkable bassoon solo Haydn may have originally conceived for horn: it represents Fileno's voice that Fillide, in her distress, imagines she hears.

An enormous, beautifully crafted finale brings all the characters on stage. Fillide once again meets Fileno, who sings one of the most haunting melodies in the opera, 'Se non trova, oh Dio'. Nerina, pursued by satyrs, calls for help, and the act ends with a battle between shepherds and satyrs.

Act 2 is dominated by a hunt in honour of the goddess Diana and by a pair of elaborate solo scenes for Fileno and Fillide in which their predicament is given its fullest and most touching expression. Fillide's scene, published separately by ARTARIA as a cantata, AH COME IL CORE MI PALPITA, became one of Haydn's best-known works. Fileno's scene is equally fine. It begins with a long, orchestrally accompanied recitative featuring a melody very much like one that Mozart later used in the slow movement of the Piano Concerto in B♭ (K595). (*La fedeltà premiata* was performed in Vienna in 1784; Mozart almost certainly knew it.) The tumultuous aria in D minor that follows, 'Recida il ferro istesso', ends with a short, intensely dramatic recitative that anticipates the ending of 'Der Hölle Rache', the Queen of the Night's second aria in *Die Zauberflöte*.

When Perrucchetto and Fillide are discovered together, Melibeo, seeing an opportunity to get rid of the man who stands between him and Amaranta and to punish Fillide for rejecting Lindoro, sentences them to be sacrificed to the monster. In the finale of Act 2 Perrucchetto and Fillide prepare to meet their doom to the sound of sombre music in the minor mode. The other shepherds express horror in an ensemble inspired by the chorus of furies in Gluck's *Orfeo ed Euridice*.

In Act 3 Fillide and Fileno are finally reconciled. Fileno volunteers to face the monster alone. Moved by his selflessness, Diana announces that her harsh law is no longer valid and that she has punished Melibeo with death. She proclaims the engagements of Perrucchetto and Amaranta and of Fileno and Fillide; and the opera ends with a joyful chorus in Diana's praise.

The mixture of heroic and comic in the libretto allowed Haydn to explore a wide variety of musical styles, and to range freely from the sincere expression of serious emotions to hilarious parody. Several delightful comic arias include Melibeo's 'Mi dica, il mio signore', in which he likens himself and Perrucchetto to two bulls fighting over a cow. Unusual five-bar phrases and sudden trumpet blasts enliven Melibeo's aria. In Perrucchetto's entrance aria, 'Salva . . . aiuto', the effect of stormy music in G minor is comically undercut by patter and by the Count's catalogue of wines, which culminates in a request for a bottle of Bordeaux.

Amaranta is a more complex character. While her interaction with other characters is almost always comic, she is capable of tender, even tragic expression (as in her aria near the end of Act 2, 'Del amor mio fedele').

Lorenzi's libretto encouraged Haydn to plan parts of his opera as big scene complexes reminiscent of Gluckian serious opera. In the opening scene a recurring choral melody not only serves to unify the chorus with soloists, 'Bella Dea', but also pulls Melibeo's orchestrally accompanied recitative and Amaranta's lyrical solo 'Prendi, prendi, o Diana' into a single uninterrupted tableau. The reprise of the hunting chorus in Act 2, by integrating Perrucchetto's comic scene with a wild boar into the hunting scene, has a similar effect.

The overture, as concise as it is brilliant, anticipates, with its key of D major and its colourful horn calls, the hunting scene in Act 2 (Haydn reused it as the finale of Symphony no. 73).

Haydn's sense of dramatic pace is unusually astute in *La fedeltà premiata*. Although this is one of his longest operas, it is also one of the few whose length seems fully justified by its musical and dramatic content. Much the same can be said for its individual numbers, many of which leave the audience wanting to hear more. JAR

C. Clark, 'Intertextual Play and Haydn's *La fedeltà premiata*', *Current Musicology*, 51 (1993), 59–81.

D. Heartz, *Haydn, Mozart and the Viennese School, 1740–1780* (New York, 1995).

F. Lippmann, 'Haydns "La fedeltà premiata" und Cimarosas "L'infedeltà fedele"', *HS* 5 (1982), 1–15.

La marchesa nespola (The marchioness of the loquats) (Hob.XXX:1). In 1763 Haydn wrote nine Italian arias for the theatrical troupe of GIRALOMO BON. A note on the autograph score—'Arie per la Comedia *Marchese*'—suggests that the drama for which he wrote the arias was not an opera but a spoken play, which may well have mixed German dialogue and Italian song. The title *La marchesa nespola* is from the ENTWURF-KATALOG. Haydn's fragmentary autograph lacks Arias nos. 5, 6, and parts of 7 and 9.

What is left shows Haydn, in some of his earliest surviving attempts to set Italian poetry to music, already expert at the various styles and aria forms typical of mid-18th-century comic opera, with their threefold division of characters; *parti buffe* (comic roles), *parti serie* (serious roles) and *parti di mezzo carattere* (mixed roles). No. 4, 'Non ho genio con amore', is a good example of a *buffo* aria: very short orchestral introduction (just two bars), patter, and several changes of tempo. In no. 8, 'Se credesse che un visetto', Haydn played cleverly with the normal two-bar units of the *buffo* melodic style by adding an extra bar between a pair of two-bar phrases. Changes of tempo encourage listeners to hear this in the form A–B–A–B, one of the most common forms in comic arias in the third quarter of the 18th century.

The fragmentary no. 7, 'Se non mi credi', is a sincere declaration of love in the melodic style of a tender minuet; this music is reminiscent of that sung by such *mezzo carattere* heroines as Cecchina in Piccinni's *La buona figliuola*. In no. 1, 'Navicella da vento agitata', Haydn responded to *opera seria* imagery of a storm at sea with horns playing syncopated crotchets, while coloratura on the word 'mar' ('sea') depicts waves. No. 3 is a *scena* with accompanied recitative and aria, 'Tema, tiran regnate'. The long orchestral introduction, the opening melody in a–b–b′ form, and the extensive coloratura with large leaps all place this music within the realm of serious opera. JAR

'Lamentation' symphony. Believed to be Haydn's own title for Symphony no. 26. The first and second movements feature Gregorian melodies associated with Holy Week; it is likely that these two movements were first written to be performed at a liturgical service and that the third movement, a minuet, was added to make the symphony suitable for performance in a concert. After an anguished, syncopated opening (with many sighing motifs) a Gregorian melody—Haydn labels it 'Chorale'—enters at bar 17, played by first oboe and second violins. Familiar from many Passion plays of the time the thematic line represents, in turn, the words of the evangelist, 'Passio Domini nostri Jesu', then from bar 26, in a softer dynamic, the words of Christ, 'Ego sum', and, finally from bar 35, the *turba* (the crowd), 'Jesum Nazarene'. In the slow movement a melody (also labelled 'Chorale') associated with the Lamentations of Jeremiah is played by the first oboe and second violins.

J. Dack, 'Haydn's "Lamentation" Symphony and the Lamentations of Gregor Joseph Werner', *Haydn Society of Great Britain Newsletter*, 2 (1980), 5–10.

HCRL/2.

Landon, H(oward) C(handler) Robbins (b. 6 March 1926). American musicologist and leading authority on Haydn. Born in Boston, he studied at Swarthmore College (1943–5) and at Boston University (1945–7) where his teachers included KARL GEIRINGER. Two years' military service in Austria convinced him that his love of Haydn could best be pursued by working in that country rather than following a more conventional academic career in the United States. This distinctive outlook, one that sought to marry scholarly excellence with the wider promotion of Haydn to the general public, was to guide Landon throughout his career. He founded the HAYDN SOCIETY with these aims in mind, to produce much-needed editions of often totally unfamiliar music by Haydn and to record performances of the music.

His first major publication was *The Symphonies of Joseph Haydn* (1955). At 862 pages, it was a typical product of his immense energy and commitment. With great natural authority, he evaluated the source material in detail, established Haydn's contribution to the development of the symphony, introduced aspects of what two decades later would be called 'authentic' performance, and identified the composers of many symphonies falsely attributed to Haydn. The volume marked a decisive step forward in Haydn studies and is one of the major musicological achievements of the 20th century. Four years later Robbins Landon produced the first complete edition of Haydn's correspondence.

Landon's abiding concern that Haydn's music should be widely performed is reflected in his extensive editorial work which often, as in the notable case of opera, presented music unheard since the 18th century or, as in many symphonies and masses, habitually performed from corrupt musical texts. He prepared complete editions (some in collaboration with other scholars) of Haydn's symphonies, quartets, string trios, keyboard trios, many operas, and several items of church music. In a commercially more ad hoc way than Landon had envisaged when the Haydn Society had been founded in 1949, many of these works were given artistically significant recordings, notably the complete symphonies and operas conducted by ANTAL DORATI.

He founded the *Haydn Yearbook* in 1962, then the only scholarly journal devoted to the composer, and began amassing material for a major biography that both reflected the transformation in Haydn studies that had occurred since the Second World War and continued the process. In five volumes, *Haydn: Chronicle and Works* appeared between 1976 and 1980.

H. C. Robbins Landon contributed with distinction also to Mozart scholarship, including an edition of the three last symphonies for the *Neue Mozart Ausgabe* and the widely read account of the composer's last year, *1791 Mozart's Last Year* (London, 1988). As well as a deep love of the music itself, Landon's scholarship is persistently characterized by an affection for the society that produced it, and his enthusiasms have led him to explore the music of minor contemporaries of Haydn and Mozart, most notably Michael Haydn.

Robbins Landon's second wife was the Austrian musicologist Christa Landon (1921–77) who collaborated with him on many projects and who, herself, prepared an edition of Haydn's keyboard sonatas (Wiener Urtext Edition, 1964–6). His third wife (also Austrian), Else Radant Landon (1926–), assisted on many projects, notably documentary material in the *Haydn Yearbook* and in *Haydn: Chronicle and Works*.

J. Agus, 'H. C. Robbins Landon: a Bibliography', in O. Biba and D. W. Jones (eds), *Studies in Music History Presented to H. C. Robbins Landon on his Seventieth Birthday* (London, 1996), 234–53.

H. C. Robbins Landon, *Horns in High C: A Memoir of Musical Discoveries and Adventures* (London, 1999).

L'anima del filosofo (The spirit of philosophy) (Hob.XXVIII:13). *Opera seria* in four acts to a libretto by CARLO FRANCESCO BADINI, composed in London in 1791 but not performed in Haydn's lifetime.

The contract under which Haydn made his first trip to London required him to compose an Italian opera for the King's Theatre, for which he was to receive £300. London audiences enjoyed both comic and serious opera. During 1789, for example, they could attend performances of comic operas by Martin y Soler (1754–1806), Cimarosa (1749–1801), Gazzaniga (1743–1818), Piccinni (1728–1800), and Paisiello (1740–1816); and serious operas by Cherubini (1760–1842), Tarchi (*c*.1760–1814), and Cimarosa. If Haydn had been well known in London as a composer of comic opera he might have been commissioned to write one; but the city knew none of his operatic works. The impresario GALLINI consequently favoured the genre that would bring him and Haydn most prestige and attention, and that would give Haydn the greatest opportunity to display (as a London critic wrote of Cherubini's *Ifigenia in Aulide*), 'all the beauties of the art combined with much science and a variety of striking and elegant songs'.

Shortly after his arrival in London Haydn wrote to Prince Anton Esterházy: 'The new libretto which I am to compose is entitled *Orfeo*, in 5 acts, but I shall not receive it for a few days. It is supposed to be entirely different from that of Gluck . . . The opera contains only 3 persons, *viz.* Madam Lops, Davide, and a castrato, who is not supposed to be very special. Incidentally, the opera is supposed to contain many choruses, ballets and a lot of big changes of scenery.' Haydn worked on *L'anima del filosofo* during the early months of 1791, anticipating its production in May. But Gallini failed to receive permission to use the King's Theatre as an opera house, and Haydn's opera was not performed.

That Haydn referred in letters written in January and March to the opera having five acts has led to the supposition that he left it incomplete. But Badini typically made changes in his librettos while they were being set to music. It is possible that the poet, having started with a five-act plan, compressed the opera into four acts as rehearsals drew near. The four-act work that survives is probably complete; but, of course, it lacks the revisions that Haydn, like any opera composer, would have made as the work went through rehearsals and first performances.

The opera begins with an overture whose slow introduction, in featuring imitative polyphony, anticipates the frequent sound of polyphonic textures later in the drama. King Creonte has promised the hand of his daughter Euridice to Arideo. Euridice, who loves Orfeo, has fled Arideo and now, as the curtain rises, has lost her way at the edge of a dark forest. A chorus warns her to flee its dangers; this is one of several choruses whose identity is unclear, and which sometimes give the opera the character of an oratorio. Euridice, in her two-tempo aria 'Filomena abbandonata', explains that any misfortune is better than that of being married to Arideo. The wild inhabitants of the forest emerge and abduct her.

Orfeo comes to the rescue, charming Euridice's captors with a beautiful harp melody and a two-tempo aria, 'Rendete a questo seno'. (Already here one of the structural problems of the opera is apparent: overuse of the aria in two tempos, slow then fast.) A brief chorus celebrates Orfeo's success. He returns with Euridice to Creonte's palace. The king, whose occasional philosophizing may have given the opera its odd title, approves of their marriage with an aria, 'Il pensier che sta negli oggetti', in which a solo flute plays an important part. Orfeo and Euridice bring Act 1 to a close with a love duet.

About to celebrate their wedding, the lovers are interrupted by a mysterious sound. Orfeo goes off to investigate, and Aride's henchmen take advantage of his absence to capture Euridice. Trying to escape, she is bitten by a snake, whose poison works slowly enough for her to sing a fine aria, 'Del mio core', before she dies. Orfeo returns, expressing anguish in a long accompanied recitative and in a tumultuous aria in F minor, 'In un mar d'acerbe pene'. Creonte vows revenge to the sound of trumpet fanfares.

Act 3 takes place at Euridice's grave. The chorus 'Ah sposo infelice' frames Orfeo's mourning. Creonte meditates on the sorrows of lost love ('Chi spira e non spera'). An otherwise unidentified Genio (Spirit) appears to tell Orfeo that with self-control he will be able to bring Euridice back from the Underworld. To some extent Genio takes over from Creonte the role of *filosofo*; her main teaching tool is coloratura, which she displays in a brilliant aria in C, 'Al tuo seno fortunato'.

A brief imitative passage in the orchestra establishes the dark and dangerous atmosphere of the Underworld. The spirits of the dead sing a lugubrious chorus, 'Infelice ombre dolenti', to which the furies respond with violent, fast music, 'Urli orrendi'. Orfeo, accompanied by Genio, asks for pity; the furies relent with unrealistic and undramatic eagerness ('Trionfi oggi pietà'). A celebratory chorus, 'Son finite le tue pene', reminds the audience of the music sung at the beginning of Act 2 in happy anticipation of the wedding. Warned not to look at Euridice, Orfeo fails this test of self-control. Euridice and Genio disappear; Orfeo, alone, sings a mournful recitative and aria, 'Mi sento languire'.

In the final scene, which Badini possibly initially planned as a separate fifth act, a chorus of bacchantes try to persuade Orfeo to drink poison by pretending that it is an elixir of happiness ('Vieni, vieni, amato Orfeo'). He takes the potion and dies. To the sound of an Allegro in D minor the Bacchantes are destroyed by a storm that gradually fades away as the curtain falls. JAR

W. Dean, 'Haydn's *Orfeo*', in id., *Essays on Opera* (Oxford, 1990), 98–102.

HCRL/3.

S. Leopold, 'Haydn und die Tradition der Orpheus-Opern', *Musica*, 3 (1982), 131–5.

C. Price, J. Milhous, and R. D. Hume, *Italian Opera in Late Eighteenth-Century London*, vol. i: *The King's Theatre, Haymarket 1778–1791* (Oxford, 1995).

'La passione' symphony. Nickname for Symphony no. 49, first found in a manuscript copy of the work dating from *c.*1780 sold by the Leipzig firm of Christian Gottfried Thomas. It was probably meant to suggest that the work was particularly suitable for performance during Passion week. JH

'La poule' symphony. Nickname in common use from early in the 19th century for Symphony no. 83. The dotted-note figure in the oboe that accompanies the repetition of the second subject in the first movement (bars 52–6) is reminiscent of a clucking hen. JH

'La Reine' symphony. Commonly used nickname for Symphony no. 85. It first appears at the top of the first-violin part of the published edition issued in Paris by Imbault in 1788: 'La Reine de France. Mr. Haydn. IIIe Sinfonie.' Whether Marie Antoinette regarded it as her favourite symphony or whether she happened to be present at the first performance cannot be established. The nickname could also reflect the rhythmic figuration of the slow introduction, common in French overtures and frequently used to denote regal authority. JH

'Largo' quartet. Nickname occasionally encountered for the D major quartet, op. 76 no. 5, prompted by the particularly poignant slow movement marked 'Largo e mesto'. JH

'Lark' quartet. Nickname in common use in English and (as 'Lerchen' Quartett) in German for the quartet in D, op. 64 no. 5, occasioned by the initial entry of the first violin high above the rest of the ensemble. It arose in the 19th century. JH

'La Roxelane' symphony. Nickname for Symphony no. 63. The slow movement of the symphony probably originated as incidental music written by Haydn for *Soliman der zweite, oder Die drei Sultaninnen*, a translation of Favart's *Les Trois Sultanes*, given at Eszterháza in 1777. The movement was a portrait of the leading female character, La Roxelane. Authentic parts for the symphony include the title above the slow movement, and it gained wide currency, both as a title for the slow movement and for the symphony as a whole. The Roxelanes were a tribe from the Danube region in the Roman province of Moesia (in present-day Bulgaria).

Larsen, Jens Peter (b. 14 June 1902; d. 22 Aug. 1988). Danish musicologist specializing, primarily, in issues of authenticity in Haydn's output. Born in Copenhagen, he initially studied mathematics and musicology at the university, before concentrating on the latter. During the 1930s he came to international attention for challenging the assertions of ADOLF SANDBERGER that Haydn's output of symphonies, in particular, was much larger than traditionally thought. This sometimes bitter controversy led him to formulate the subject matter of his doctoral thesis, appropriate methodology for determining authenticity in Haydn's œuvre, one that relied on scientific evidence rather than hazy notions of musical style or, worse, wishful thinking. Published as *Die Haydn-Überlieferung* in 1939 it was followed two years later by a facsimile edition of three important thematic catalogues of Haydn's music, the ENTWURF-KATALOG, the HAYDN-VERZEICHNIS, and the KEES CATALOGUE. Because of the Second World War the impact of Larsen's work was delayed by several years. Hoboken and Robbins Landon were only two scholars that acknowledged their fundamental indebtedness to Larsen. He became general editor of the collected edition begun by the HAYDN SOCIETY and the first director of the JOSEPH HAYDN-INSTITUT. Larsen was also an authority on the music of Handel.

Latrobe, Revd Christian Ignatius (b. 12 Feb. 1758; d. 6 May 1836). Gifted amateur composer, organist, pianist, editor, and an influential, though unassuming advocate of Haydn's music in England.

As an ordained minister of the Moravian (United) Brethren, Latrobe's outlook on life was unusually international for an Englishman of his day. Moravian settlements had spread across the world during the 18th century, fostering a simple life based on worship, prayer, and music, shaped by the founding community at Herrnhut in Saxony. Latrobe was born at the Fulneck settlement in Yorkshire, but he moved to Germany in 1771, attending the Moravian schools at Niesky and Barby before returning to Niesky as a music tutor. He played Haydn's string quartets with his Niesky brethren, transcribing several movements from op. 20 into score for private study in 1783; by 1791 he had scored 25 Haydn quartets in this manner, and often played them from memory at the piano. From manuscript parts obtained at Dresden in 1779, he scored up Haydn's Stabat mater which, as he recalled, 'helped to form my taste, and make me more zealous in the pursuit of this noble science' (letter to Vincent Novello, 22 Nov. 1828).

In 1784 Latrobe arrived in London to join the Moravian community at Neville Court and Fetter Lane. His cultivated manners, evangelical principles, and musical abilities won him friends throughout English society, including CHARLES BURNEY, who consulted him on German music during the completion of his *General History of Music*. To Latrobe's delight, Burney reciprocated by introducing him to Haydn in 1791. Detecting a faith in sympathy with his own, Latrobe often discussed spiritual matters with Haydn. They also played their new compositions to each other, and it was at the composer's suggestion that Latrobe published his keyboard sonatas. Haydn's portrait hung in Latrobe's parlour, and he owned scores of two early masses in Haydn's hand (Hob.XXII:6 and 7), presumably a gift from the composer.

From Latrobe's perspective the English were neglectful of church music and blinkered by their loyalty to Handel. He began to circulate his own collection of continental sacred music among friends, replenishing it during his many visits to Germany on church business. He lent manuscripts of masses by Haydn to Burney, CROTCH and Joseph Jowett for example, encouraging Novello to perform them at the chapel of the Portuguese embassy and, later, to edit them for publication. Latrobe's close relations with Breitkopf & Härtel also enabled him to obtain scores of Haydn's *Missa Sancti Bernardi d'Offida* and *Missa in tempore belli* within a year of their publication, despite the disruption caused by the Napoleonic Wars.

Latrobe's six-volume *Selection of Sacred Music from . . . the most eminent composers of Germany and Italy*, published between 1806 and 1826, made Haydn's liturgical music widely available in England for the first time. By compressing the instrumental parts into an accompaniment most amateur pianists could manage, Latrobe encouraged domestic performances by Christian families, a Moravian ideal. His *Selection* kept its appeal for many generations, helping to broaden the musical experience of English amateurs, and establish an interest in Viennese sacred music on which Novello was able to build. REC

J. Boeringer, 'Haydn's Herrn Hutters', *Moravian Music Journal*, 29 (1984), 14–20.

R. Cowgill, 'The Papers of C. I. Latrobe: New Light on Musicians, Music and the Christian Family in late eighteenth-century London', in D. W. Jones (ed.), *Music in Eighteenth-Century Britain* (Aldershot, 2000), 234–58.

'Lauda, Sion' (Praise, Sion). Thirteenth-century text by St Thomas Aquinas written for Corpus Christi. On two occasions Haydn set selected verses in four separate, short movements, designed to be performed as part of the ritual associated with the showing of the Host to the four corners of the earth, represented by either four altars in one church or four altars in different local churches.

Haydn's first setting (Hob.XXIIIc:5) is amongst his earliest extant compositions, possibly dating from as early as 1750 and composed for performance in Vienna, where public processions on Corpus Christi were a major occasion. All the movements are in C major, 3/4, and marked Vivace; the strings of the orchestra (including a viola part) double the voices; oboes and trumpets provide an additional sonority, the latter cutting through the texture with jubilant fanfares in a manner that can be traced back in Austrian church music to at least the early 18th century and one which Haydn was to make distinctly his own. In the *Entwurf-Katalog* Haydn referred to the movements as 'Hymnus de Venerabili'.

The precise date of Haydn's second setting (Hob.XXIIIc:4) is also unknown; it is thought to date from the late 1760s and to have been composed for performance in Eisenstadt. More penitential than the earlier setting, the four movements are all in a slow tempo and offer a contrast of key. While the choral-writing is mainly homophonic the string-writing shows more independence than is evident in the earlier set. In the *Entwurf-Katalog* Haydn described the second set as '4 Responsoria de Venerabili'.

I. Becker-Glauch, 'Neue Forschungen zu Haydns Kirchenmusik', *HS* 2/3 (1970), 167–241.
HCRL/1.

'Laudon' (more correctly 'Loudon') symphony. Nickname for Symphony no. 69 which can be traced back to an arrangement of the symphony (minus the finale) for keyboard, published by Artaria in 1784 and described as 'Sinfonia Loudon'. Ernst Gideon von Loudon (1717–90) was an Austrian military hero who had risen to prominence during the Seven Years War. Haydn wrote to Artaria that having his name on the title page was 'worth more than ten finales'. There is no suggestion that the work is a portrait of Loudon.

Laurette (Hob.XXVIII:8a). An unsanctioned, free adaptation in French of Haydn's opera *La vera costanza*, first performed at the Théâtre de Monsieur, Paris, in January 1791; a further four performances followed that season. Converting Italian comic opera into French *opéra comique* was standard practice in Paris in the second half of the 18th century and Peter Ulric Dubuisson, who prepared Haydn's opera, was a leading exponent, employed by several theatres. It was the only opera by Haydn to be treated in this fashion and was not regarded as a success. As well as numbers taken from *La vera costanza*, Dubuisson used the overture to *Armida* to open the evening, and adapted the second movement of Symphony no. 63 as an ariette for Le Bailli (Ernesto in Haydn's original). Laurette is Dubuisson's name for the central character Rosina.

M. F. Robinson, '*Opera buffa* into *opéra comique*, 1771–90', in M. Boyd (ed.), *Music and the French Revolution* (Cambridge, 1992), 37–56.

'Laus Deo'. An annotation frequently found on Haydn's autograph scores. *See* 'IN NOMINE DOMINI'.

La vera costanza (True constancy) (Hob. XXVIII:8). Opera ('dramma giocoso per musica') in three acts to a libretto by Francesco Puttini, first performed at Eszterháza in April 1779. Pasquale Anfossi's setting of Puttini's libretto (Rome, 1776) had been performed in many European operatic centres, including Vienna, during the decade following its premiere. Haydn paid tribute to Anfossi's opera by incorporating one of its most beautiful scenes into his own work. The original autograph score was destroyed in the fire that destroyed the Eszterháza opera house in 1779; the composer reconstructed the opera for a revival in 1785, and it is this version that is known today.

La vera costanza is one of many sentimental *opere buffe* of the second half of the 18th century—Piccinni's *La buona figliuola* and Mozart's *La finta giardiniera* are two others—in which a virtuous and sincere young woman is the victim of misunderstanding and cruelty. At the centre of the action is Rosina (soprano, the role created by Barbara Ripamonti), the sister of a fisherman. Five years before the action, Count Errico, a headstrong and eccentric young nobleman (tenor, ANDREA TOTTI), fell in love with Rosina, secretly married and then abandoned her; she bore their child. Much later Count Errico's aunt, Baroness Irene (soprano, CATARINA POSCHWA), hearing rumours of Errico's relationship with Rosina, travelled by sea to Rosina's village in order to save her nephew from an unthinkable marriage.

A three-movement overture leads directly to the dramatic action by presenting a depiction of a violent storm at sea as its final movement. As the curtain rises a small boat is seen attempting to reach land. In it are Baroness Irene, Marchese Ernesto (tenor, VITO UNGRICHT), who hopes to marry Irene, Villotto (bass, BENEDETTO BIANCHI), a rich fool to whom Irene hopes Rosina will be married, and Lisetta, the baroness's maid (soprano, ANNA ZANNINI). On shore Rosina and her brother Masino (baritone, LEOPOLD DICHTLER) watch the travellers struggle and help them to safety.

When Irene discovers Rosina's identity she immediately introduces Villotto as the intended husband. Irene cuts off Rosina's attempt to reply by extolling love in an aria, 'Non s'innalza', that conveys her grandeur and nobility through its combination of duple metre, fast tempo, long orchestral introduction, and vocal coloratura. Villotto tries to charm Rosina, but when she runs off, Masino makes fun of him in a comic aria, 'So che una bestia sei'.

Count Errico suddenly appears on the scene, demanding that Villotto renounce Rosina and threatening him with a pistol. While Errico hides, his pistol pointed at Villotto, Irene urges Villotto to ask Rosina for her hand. Caught between Errico's gun and Irene's rage, Villotto sings an amusing aria of indecision, a type of aria that frequently appears in Goldoni's librettos and those of his successors. Like many such arias, it is in the key of E♭. Lisetta and Masino are left alone on stage, and she flirts with him in a gentle, cheerful aria in compound metre, 'Io son, poverina'.

Rosina finds Errico, who tells her that he no longer loves her; but this is apparently a clumsy effort on his part to find out if she really loves him. He encourages Villotto to pursue Rosina, likening courtship to warfare in the aria 'A trionfar t' invita'. This remarkable depiction of Errico's emotional instability alternates unpredictably between fast and slow, comic and serious. The confusion of comedy, heroism, and tenderness culminates at the words 'Oimè! Che smania orribile! | Mi perdo, mi confondo' ('Alas! What dreadful frenzy! | I am lost, I am confused') which prompts Haydn suddenly to shift from major mode to minor. Although the text mentions martial trumpets, no trumpets were available at Eszterháza, and Haydn scored the aria for horns in C alto.

Rosina tells Lisetta of her misfortune, expressing sweetness and sincerity in her aria 'Con un tenero sospiro'. The long finale that follows, however beautiful its music, is largely redundant from a dramatic point of view. Only when Errico and Rosina, alone, enjoy a passionate embrace (represented musically by a brief canon) does the plot begin to advance. But then the Baroness shows Errico a picture of the woman she wants him to marry. He praises her beauty, causing Rosina to give in yet again to despair.

Near the beginning of Act 2 Ernesto tells Rosina that unless she marries Villotto, Irene will not accept his offer of marriage. Irene and Errico overhear Ernesto telling Rosina that she is the only hope and pleads with her in a slow, lyrical aria, 'Per pietà, vezzosi rai'. They come out of hiding and accuse her of treachery. In a quintet reminiscent of the first-act finale of *La buona figliuola* poor Rosina tries in vain to defend herself from angry accusations hurled from every side. She expresses her agony in an outburst of violent F minor, 'Dove fuggo, over m'ascondo'.

Errico's mental instability turns potentially lethal as he demands that Villotto kill Rosina. When Villotto tries to talk his way out of Errico's plans, the count threatens to kill him (for the second time in the opera). Villotto responds with an aria that begins with a slow, mock-serious evocation of death ('Già la morte in mante nero') and ends with comic fast music accompanying his escape from Errico.

When Errico learns from Lisetta that Rosina is still faithful to him, he is overcome by madness, which he expresses in a lovely scene, 'Ah non m'inganno, è Orfeo', that Haydn borrowed from Anfossi's *La vera costanza*. Flutes and pizzicato strings unite to depict Errico's antique world of fantasy: he imagines he is Orpheus in search of Euridice. Frequent changes of tempo and musical style in the aria 'Or che torna il vago Aprile' help to portray Errico's incoherence.

Near a partly ruined tower, Rosina, accompanied by her child, bids farewell to her homeland in a sentimental aria, 'Care spiagge, selve, addio'.

Much of the finale of Act 2 is taken up with the comic interactions of Masino, Lisetta, and Villotto. When the count enters, singing 'Ah, dov' è la mia Rosina', his music as well as his words show that he has regained his sanity. The melody expresses complete sincerity (its resemblance to Gluck's 'Che farò senza Euridice' makes sense in light of Errico's identification with Orpheus during his recent delirium). Rosina appears; he asks for forgiveness. They celebrate their reconciliation with a duet that Haydn neatly incorporated into the finale. The rest of the cast expresses amazement (Masino and Lisetta) or rage (Irene, Villotto, and Ernesto).

In the brief final act, Errico and Rosina confront each other with letters in which each of them has renounced the other. They realize quickly that the letters are forgeries: Irene's last desperate attempt to keep them apart. They sing an elaborate duet that would not have sounded out of place in an *opera seria*. The baroness blesses their marriage and gives her hand to Ernesto. JAR

E. Badura-Skoda, 'Zur Entstehung von Haydns Oper *La vera costanza*', in E. Badura-Skoda (ed.), *Joseph Haydn. Bericht über den internationalen Joseph Haydn*

Kongress. Wien, Hofburg, 5–12. September 1982 (Munich, 1986), 243–55.
M. Hunter, 'Pamela: The Offspring of Richardson's Heroine in Eighteenth-Century Opera', in W. Rempel and U. Rempel (eds), *Music and literature* (Winnipeg, 1985), 61–76.
J. Waldoff, 'Sentiment and Sensibility in *La vera costanza*', in W. D. Sutcliffe (ed.), *Haydn Studies* (Cambridge, 1998), 70–119.

Le Duc, Simon (b. 17 Oct. 1755; d. 18 Oct. 1826). French music publisher who began his business in 1775. He never had direct contact with Haydn but played an interesting role in the dissemination of his music. During the 1780s he acted as an agent for ARTARIA in Paris, importing many works by Haydn and other composers. In 1790 he published the first edition of symphonies nos. 90–2 from the autograph scores owned by the Concert de la Loge Olympique. In 1801 he began publishing a series of miniature scores of the symphonies of Haydn, normally regarded as the first examples in the history of music of this format. In a lengthy preface to the first score, Symphony no. 57, Le Duc indicated that the venture was aimed at amateurs (in the sense of not being performers) who wished to understand the science of Haydn's unsurpassed mastery of music. A total of 27 miniature scores appeared.

C. Johansson, *French Music Publishers' Catalogues of the Second Half of the Eighteenth Century* (Stockholm, 1955).

'Le Matin' symphony. Authentic title ('Morning') for Symphony no. 6, one of a trilogy of symphonies devoted to times of the day, 'Le Matin', 'Le Midi' (no. 7), and 'Le Soir' (no. 8). The title was in widespread use in Haydn's lifetime. There are no further programmatic titles in the work though the slow introduction is commonly held to be an evocation of sunrise. JH

Le Menu. French music publisher active from the 1740s through to the 1780s; reflecting changing business partners it was known at different times as Le Menu & Boyer, Boyer & Le Menu, and Boyer. The firm published a number of inauthentic editions of symphonies, keyboard sonatas, and keyboard trios by Haydn. It tried, in 1783, to become a more authoritative publisher of the composer's music, writing to him requesting autograph scores of recent compositions. Haydn replied that Prince Nicolaus had first claim on his autograph scores, but that he was willing to forward authentic copies of parts of three symphonies, nos. 76–8; these works were duly published by the firm in 1785. No further contact took place.

C. Johansson, *French Music Publishers' Catalogues of the Second Half of the Eighteenth Century* (Stockholm, 1955).

'Le Midi' symphony. Authentic title ('Noon') for Symphony no. 7, one of a trilogy of symphonies devoted to times of the day, 'Le Matin' (no. 6), 'Le Midi', and 'Le Soir' (no. 8). The autograph manuscript of the symphony is the only one of the three to have survived and carries the title. It was in widespread use in Haydn's lifetime. There are no further programmatic titles in the work. JH

Le pescatrici (The fisherwomen) (Hob.XXVIII: 4). Opera ('dramma giocoso per musica') in three acts to a libretto by CARLO GOLDONI; it was Haydn's second setting of a text by the great Venetian dramatist (the first was *Lo speziale*) and his first full-length *opera buffa* (the libretto of *Lo speziale* having been abbreviated and shorn of its serious parts). It received its first performance at Eszterháza on 16 September 1770 as part of festivities surrounding the wedding of Prince Nicolaus's niece, Countess Lamberg. Like Haydn's previous Goldonian opera, *Le pescatrici* survives in a fragmentary state; several recitatives, arias, and portions of arias have been lost.

Le pescatrici is one of many comic operas of the second half of the 18th century in which a woman, believed to have died as a baby, is raised by a man of much lower social status than her real father; the arrival of a nobleman is followed eventually by recognition of the woman's true identity and by marriage. The opera takes place in a fishing village on the coast of southern Italy. Burlotto and Frisellino, two young fishermen (both tenors, created by LEOPOLD DICHTLER and CARL FRIBERTH), love Nerina and Lesbina (sopranos, BARBARA DICHTLER and MAGDALENA FRIBERTH). But Nerina, Frisellino's sister, disapproves of her brother's match; and the resulting quarrel threatens the intended double marriage.

The four comic lovers introduce themselves in arias. Burlotto boasts of his prowess as a fisherman in 'Tra tuoni, lampi e fulmini'. Its long orchestral introduction, three- and four-bar vocal phrases, and coloratura are out of character: this is not the kind of music that one expects of a simple fisherman. Nerina's 'So fa la semplicetta' is a more effective musical characterization: a charming aria in sonata form without development, and with an alternation of tempos (slow-fast-slow-fast) that Haydn exploited frequently in this opera. In 'Fra cetre e cembali ti sposerò', Frisellino sings of the instruments that will play during his wedding. Haydn responded to the text with a large woodwind ensemble (flute, bassoon, and pairs of oboes and horns) that sometimes plays alone, and with a flute solo that is supposed to represent the bagpipe ('la cornamusa'). Lesbina, in 'Voglio amar e vuò scherzare', shows off with an elegant, minuet-like melody and coloratura that ascends to high D.

The old fisherman Mastriccio (bass, Giacomo Lambertini) has raised Eurilda as his own daughter, unaware that she is really a noblewoman. He is a typical Goldonian *buffo caricato*. His only aria to survive complete, 'Son vecchio, son furbo' (Act 2) features many of the favourite devices of mid-century musical comedy, including patter, and abrupt changes of tempo. Eurilda (mezzo-soprano, Gertrude Cellini) has a smaller role in the opera, musically as well as dramatically, than the two comic female roles. Following Goldoni's libretto, Haydn kept her, as a designated serious role (*parte seria*), out of the finales of Acts 1 and 2; and yet in her arias he did not write the kind of splendid, *opera seria*-style music that might have compensated for her marginal role in the drama. Her cavatina in Act 3, which combines 3/8 metre, moderate tempo, and a minuet-like tune, would have been more suitably sung by Nerina or Lesbina.

Prince Lindoro (baritone, Christian Specht) arrives in search of the lost daughter of the Duke of Benevento. In a stormy aria in D minor, 'Varca il mar di sponda in sponda' (unfortunately incomplete) he tells of his dangerous voyage. Constant syncopations in the first violins contrast vividly with rushing semiquavers in the second violins. Nerina and Lesbina, suddenly forgetting about Burlotto and Frisellino, try to persuade Lindoro that they are of noble birth. Lesbina sings plenty of noble coloratura in her aria 'Ti miro fisso' (also incomplete), but this vocal brilliance comes across as false because it makes no sense on the word 'vergognar' ('to be ashamed'). The finale with which Act 1 concludes, in keeping with Goldoni's conception of the finale as a comic ensemble, is limited to the two young fishermen and their newly reluctant fiancées.

Eurilda, feeling the effects of her noble blood, falls in love with Lindoro. He, in a scene reminiscent of an episode in the life of the Greek hero Achilles, leaves gifts for the villagers, including the dagger with which Eurilda's father was killed. Lesbina and Nerina immediately grab jewels; but Eurilda picks up the knife, thus revealing her identity to herself and to Lindoro. In a brief finale the wayward fiancées turn back to their original lovers, who now reject them.

As the noble pair prepare to depart, Lesbina and Nerina try to win back the affection of Frisellino and Burlotto, who test the women's new protestations of fidelity by disguising themselves as noblemen and proposing marriage. Although Lesbina and Nerina fail the test, Mastriccio urges reconciliation. In the chorus 'Soavi zeffiri' the villagers pray that the voyage of Eurilda and Lindoro will be calm; and in a final ensemble, 'Discendi, Amor pietoso', they ask the god of love to bless all three marriages. JAR

HCRL/2.

S. Leopold, '"Le pescatrici": Goldoni, Haydn, Gassmann', in E. Badura-Skoda (ed.), *Joseph Haydn. Bericht über den internationalen Joseph Haydn Kongress. Wien, Hofburg, 5–12. September 1982* (Munich, 1986), 341–9.

'Le Soir' symphony. Authentic title ('Evening') for Symphony no. 8, one of a trilogy of symphonies devoted to times of the day, 'Le Matin' (no. 6), 'Le Midi' (no. 7), and 'Le Soir' (no. 8). It was widely used during the 18th century. Haydn heads the last movement 'La tempesta' ('The storm') which was sometimes used to identify the symphony as a whole. The first movement quotes a song about snuff-taking, taken from GLUCK's opera *Le Diable à quatre*. JH

'Letter V' symphony. Nickname occasionally used in English-speaking countries for Symphony no. 88. The publisher FORSTER issued a sequence of 23 symphonies by Haydn, identifying them with letters of the alphabet rather than numbers: A (no. 71), B (no. 45), and so on to V (no. 88) and W (no. 89). 'V' remained in use.

Leutgeb, Joseph (b. 8 Oct. 1732; d. 27 Feb. 1811). Horn player mainly associated with Mozart who wrote several works for him (including four concertos). Haydn evidently knew Leutgeb in the early 1760s before he joined the Salzburg court. In July 1762, in a church service in Vienna, his wife acted as godparent to one of Leutgeb's daughters and the player was briefly employed at the Esterházy court in February 1763. It has been conjectured that Haydn's horn concerto was written for Leutgeb.

D. Heartz, 'Leutgeb and the 1762 Horn Concertos of Joseph and Johann Michael Haydn', *Mozart Jahrbuch 1987/88* (Kassel, 1988), 59–64.

Libera me, Domine (Deliver me, O Lord) (Hob.XXIIb:1). A short work rediscovered in 1966 by Robbins Landon. Like the *Missa 'sunt bona mixta malis'* and the offertory 'Non nobis, Domine', it is a prime example of the STYLUS A CAPPELLA. In alla breve metre and scored for four-part voices with doubling strings and organ, it is in D minor with a distinctive open fifth on final tonic chords. The words 'Dum venere judicare' (When Thou shall come to judge) elicit some threatening diminished sevenths. The text is the traditional responsory sung at the end of the requiem, immediately before the absolution of the corpse. The extant parts, in the Martinkirche in Eisenstadt, were written by Haydn and his copyist, JOHANN SCHELLINGER, probably sometime in the 1780s for an unknown funeral service. It has been conjectured that Haydn may have merely copied the work rather than composed it.

I. Becker-Glauch, 'Neue Forschungen zu Haydns Kirchenmusik', *HS* 2/3 (1970), 167–241.

H. C. Robbins Landon, 'Haydn's Newly Discovered *Responsorium ad absolutionem* "Libera me, Domine"', *HYB* 4 (1968), 140–7, 228–35.

Lidl, Andreas (d. *c*.1787). BARYTON player at the Esterházy court from August 1769 to May 1774; he also probably played the cello in the orchestra and he may have composed some music for Prince Nicolaus too. After leaving the Esterházy court Lidl travelled to England via Augsburg, arriving in the summer of 1776. Over the next few years he played in concerts in London and Oxford, and published eight sets of chamber music in London. Burney remarked that he played 'with exquisite taste and expression upon this ungrateful instrument'. He may have played a small part in the extraordinary burgeoning in popularity of Haydn's music that occurred in London *c*.1780.

Lidl's baryton, which had been given to him by the Bishop of Salzburg, survived in its original state in London until at least 1862. It was later converted into a cello and is now part of the collection of the Horniman Museum, London.

TMP

'Lidley'. The author of the original English text of *The Creation* is not known. When questioned about this by GRIESINGER Haydn replied that it was 'an Englishman by the name of Lidley'. 'Lidley' sounds suspiciously like a muddled conflation of the names of three people known to Haydn, ANDREAS LIDL, THOMAS LINLEY, and ROBERT LINDLEY. Of these Thomas Linley may have had some association with the text, as the organizer of the oratorio season at Drury Lane.

Lieder. *See* SONG.

L'incontro improvviso (The unexpected encounter) (Hob.XXVIII:6). Opera ('dramma giocoso per musica') to a libretto by CARL FRIBERTH after L. H. Dancourt, *La Recontre imprévue*; first performed at Eszterháza on 29 August 1775 in celebration of the visit of Archduke Ferdinand, Habsburg governor of Milan, and his consort Maria Beatrice d'Este. Gluck's setting of the *opéra-comique* libretto from which Friberth drew his opera had been given its first performance in Vienna in 1764 and was almost certainly known to Haydn, the prince, and the archduke (who had grown up in Vienna). Haydn may have hoped to surpass Gluck, but he did not. Handicapped by a weak libretto, and unwilling or unable to fix it, he produced an opera whose undoubted musical beauties cannot compensate for its dramatic weakness.

Prince Ali arrives in Cairo in search of his beloved Princess Rezia, who has been captured by pirates and now resides in the Sultan's harem. Friberth (tenor) wrote the role of Ali for himself and that of Rezia for his wife, Magdalena (soprano). Ali is accompanied on his travels by a slave, Osmin (tenor, LEOPOLD DICHTLER). Osmin falls in with a dishonest dervish ('calandro'), administrator of the sultan's storerooms and, on the side, a professional beggar (baritone, Christian Specht). Their conversations and songs provide the opera with most of its comedy, but Friberth was unable to integrate their roles effectively into the dramatic action.

The opening scene of the opera presents the comic pair by means of poetic and musical devices that are characteristic of the opera as a whole. Osmin's 'L'amore è un gran briccone' is one of several short, simple songs (Haydn uses the word 'canzonetta') scattered through the opera. Several of the songs, including this one, are in strophic form. Haydn had demonstrated in his opera *Lo speziale* a special aptness for 'Turkish' music. The Middle Eastern setting of *L'incontro improvviso* gave him opportunity to explore Turkish music at much greater length. In setting the mock Turkish text of the calandro's aria, 'Castagno, castagna', Haydn wrote music that is almost as comically incoherent as the words.

The first lines of the opera, 'Che bevanda, che liquore! | La dolcezza ed il sapore | Fanno rallegrar il cor', exemplify a form that Friberth, betraying his weakness as an Italian poet, used to excess throughout the opera: a three-line stanza (usually *ottonari*, as here) with the rhyming scheme of a, a, and b. Haydn managed to think of many different ways to respond musically to this pattern, but the dullness and clumsiness of Friberth's poetry often overwhelm his efforts, especially in the finales of Acts 1 and 2.

With two other girls from the harem, Balkis and Dardane (sopranos, BARBARA DICHTLER and MARIA ELISABETH PRANDTNER), Rezia yearns for happiness in a remarkable trio, 'Mi sembra un sogno'. Inspired by the word 'sogno' (dream) Haydn wove the three soprano lines into an orchestral fabric that includes two cors anglais, and which delicately undulates for nearly ten minutes. Abandoning all concern for dramatic pace and poetic propriety (the text begins with a line containing nine syllables, almost unheard of in 18th-century Italian operatic poetry), the composer surrenders to musical beauty alone.

Rezia sees Ali from a window. Without letting him recognize her, she invites him to the palace. Act 1 ends with a trio for Balkis, Ali, and Osmin in which they look forward to a banquet. The text, in Friberth's favourite three-line stanzas, contains nothing of dramatic interest, and neither does Haydn's music.

In Act 2 Rezia tests Ali's fidelity by having Dardane try to seduce him. She fails, praising his constancy in a big, heroic aria, 'Ho promosso oprar destrezza'. Rezia finally reveals her identity. (Haydn lets the 'unexpected encounter' pass by in simple recitative.) She tells Ali of her misfortunes at the hands of pirates, going so far as to sing a comic canzonetta in which she imitates one of her captors. Then she celebrates her reunion with Ali in a serious aria, 'Or vicino a te, mio cuore', which would make a much stronger impression if it did not follow so soon after Dardane's similarly heroic aria. (In 1783 Haydn detached Rezia's aria from the score and had it published by Artaria.)

The series of brilliant arias continues as Ali rejoices in a noisy aria in which he compares himself to a conquering soldier ('Il guerrier con armi avvolto') and Balkis looks forward to fleeing the harem ('Ad adquistar già volo'). Her opening melody in an a–b–b′ form has a lovely, *galant* character while later off-beat quavers in the strings charmingly depict her heartbeats.

Another comic scene for the calandro and Osmin features a delightful drinking song of welcome brevity, 'Il profeta Maometto', and a long aria in which Osmin discusses the escape by land and sea that he hopes soon to begin. Haydn, never one to ignore an opportunity for tone-painting, evokes the progress of the planned escape: tiptoeing, running, and, finally, rowing.

Rezia and Ali sing a love duet in E major that ends on an open cadence, leading directly to the finale of Act 2. Their celebration is interrupted by news that the sultan is returning. The resulting confusion is vividly described by Haydn's music, though here again the predominance of three-line stanzas and associated rhyme scheme restricted the composer's creativity.

The beginning of Act 3 finds Ali, Rezia, and Osmin hiding in the calandro's storehouse. When he learns that the sultan has offered a reward for Rezia's return, he betrays the lovers. Ali disguises himself as a French painter and, as the sultan's guards enter, describes his paintings in an elaborate aria, 'Ecco splendido banchetto', in which the music evokes images relevant to the canvases held up by Ali; they culminate with a battle scene in which the timpani, hitherto silent, represent the explosion of a bomb.

The disguise fails to deceive the guards, leading the listener to suspect that Friberth introduced it only because it allowed him one last opportunity for a big, colourful aria. The faithful lovers are about to be sentenced to death when the sultan, moved by their devotion, decides instead to pardon them and to punish the calandro for his dishonesty. In the final ensemble (the only number in which the sultan, created by MELCHIOR GRIEßLER, sings) Rezia and Ali ask him to pardon the calandro, which he does. The opera ends in brilliant celebration, enhanced by the sound of 'Turkish' cymbals and drums. JAR

Lindley, Robert (b. 4 March 1776; d. 13 June 1855). English cellist known to Haydn. In 1792, at the age of 16, he made a remarkable solo debut at the Professional Concert in London. Two years later he had become principal cello at the King's Theatre and played in the 1795 series of concerts in the theatre during which Haydn's three last symphonies were first given.

L'infedeltà delusa (Deceit outwitted) (Hob. XXVIII:5). Comic opera ('burletta per musica') in two acts, after a libretto by MARCO COLTELLINI; first performed at Eszterháza on 26 July 1773 in celebration of the nameday of the widowed PRINCESS MARIA ANNA ESTERHÁZY, Prince Nicolaus's mother, and a few weeks later for the visit of EMPRESS MARIA THERESIA to Eszterháza.

Coltellini, active in Vienna from 1763, served as house poet to the Viennese court theatres from 1766 to 1772. He may have written *L'infedeltà delusa* for a performance by children of the Viennese nobility in 1765. But the edition of the libretto that refers to that performance names no composer; and there is no evidence (apart from the libretto itself) that the performance ever took place. Although, in many respects, it follows the precepts of Goldonian *opera buffa*, Coltellini's libretto differs from most of Goldoni's *drammi giocosi per musica* in having two acts instead of three, five characters instead of six or seven, and no serious parts. In these respects it conforms to the conventions of the Roman intermezzo, a subgenre of Goldonian *opera buffa* popular in many parts of Europe (including Vienna) during the 1760s and 1770s.

Clever Vespina (soprano, the role was created by MAGDALENA FRIBERTH) loves Nencio, a rich peasant (tenor, LEOPOLD DICHTLER). Sandrina (soprano, BARBARA DICHTLER) loves the poor peasant Nanni (bass, Christian Specht), but her father Filippo wants her to marry Nencio. (Unlike most comic opera fathers, who are baritones or basses, Filippo is a tenor, CARL FRIBERTH.) Filippo persuades Nencio to marry his daughter, and, in the finale of Act 1, Vespina and Nanni angrily confront Filippo and Nencio.

Vespina wins back Nencio by a complicated plot involving no fewer than four disguises. Pretending to be an old woman, she tells Filippo, in language comically laced with proverbs, that her daughter has been seduced and abandoned by Nencio. Filippo promptly gives up the idea of Nencio as his son-in-law. Vespina reappears, disguised as a German servant and speaking in a mixture of German and Italian. Both her words and her music (a cheerful drinking song, 'Trinche vaine allegramente') may have reminded Haydn's audience of Tagliaferro, the German soldier in Piccinni's *La buona figliuola*. (Piccinni's popular opera was first performed at Eszterháza in 1776.) The fake servant tells Nencio that his master, the Marchese di Ripafratta, intends to marry Sandrina, whom Nencio now gives up hope of marrying.

In her third disguise Vespina impersonates the marchese himself, telling Nencio that he intends that his servant should marry Sandrina. Nencio is happy to think of Filippo's disappointment when he learns of this reversal of fortune. Vespina, disguised as a notary, conducts a fake wedding ceremony at which Filippo believes he is consenting to his daughter's marriage to the marchese, and Nencio believes that he is witnessing Sandrina's marriage to one of the marchese's servants (Nanni in disguise). But when the document is signed, Vespina and Nanni reveal their identity: Nencio agrees to marry Vespina, and the opera ends with a celebration of the double wedding.

Like most of Goldoni's librettos, *L'infedeltà delusa* consists largely of arias, with very few ensembles (an *introduzione*, one duet, two finales). Haydn's arias, mostly in binary and sonata form, express a wide variety of emotional states and explore many musical techniques. His tendency to compose at least one stormy minor-key aria in every opera resulted here in Nanni's 'No v'è rimedio', in which F minor gives way, eventually, to F major and a comic coda. Vespina's 'Ho un tumore in un ginocchio', which she sings while disguised as an old woman, amusingly takes a reference to limping and translates it into a syncopated accompaniment (but the aria is too long, especially if one takes seriously Haydn's tempo marking, Adagio).

Several arias are more memorable for musical invention than for dramatic effect. Nencio sings 'Chi s'impaccia di moglie cittadina' (about the dangers of marrying a woman from the city) with guitar in hand. The text is a pair of *ottave* (a poetic form with eight 11-syllable lines) that Goldoni sometimes used, as Coltellini did here, for the text of a song actually performed by a character on stage (as opposed to an aria). Composers normally responded to such texts with folk-like music in strophic form; and Haydn's librettist probably expected him to set the two *ottave* to the same music. Haydn thwarts expectations, writing a through-composed aria full of striking—and completely unfolk-like—musical ideas: sudden virtuoso runs and high notes in the vocal line, a harsh and surprising dissonance at the line 'perché guai per chi ci casca' (for woe betide him who falls into the trap). Robbins Landon admiringly called attention to this 'deathly serious moment'; but one can legitimately ask whether such a moment belongs in a comic song that a peasant sings to the accompaniment of a guitar.

Taking advantage of the relatively few arias in the libretto (few, that is, in comparison with a typical full-length Goldonian opera), Haydn allowed himself to compose at great length, resulting in a work that is rich with musical delights but sometimes languishes on stage. Act 2 begins with a sinfonia, a fine, substantial orchestral movement in sonata form, but without any apparent dramatic function. The *introduzione*, in which very little happens in the way of plot development, luxuriates in its fourfold statement of a long, lovely minuet-like melody (beginning with Sandrina's 'Ah padre, che tali mi siete') and experiments with an elaborate accompaniment of wind instruments. Many arias likewise unfold at a deliberate pace, giving Haydn opportunity fully to work out the potential of his musical material, but often sacrificing dramatic momentum. The finales, in contrast, move quickly, perhaps because Haydn felt that here, at last, musical and dramatic action had to match one another. JAR

HCRL/2.

Linley, Thomas (b. 17 Jan. 1733; d. 19 Nov. 1795). English composer and impresario. From 1776 he was one the four joint proprietors of the Drury Lane Theatre, where he composed music for a variety of stage works in the English language and organized the annual season (during Lent) of oratorio performances. In this latter capacity he may have been the original owner (not the author) of the libretto to *The Creation*.

lira organizzata. An instrument especially popular with the French aristocracy in the 18th century that combined the older hurdy-gurdy with an organ mechanism, hence 'organized lyre'. A typical hurdy-gurdy of the time was guitar-shaped and held across the body; it had two strings for the melody and four drone strings, all of which were activated by turning a handle that pulled a bow across the strings. The left hand pressed a set of keys that stopped the melody strings to produce the required pitches. A *lira organizzata* added a small organ mechanism to this instrument, with the bellows located inside the hurdy-gurdy and the pipes on the outside. There were usually two small ranks of pipes that doubled both the melody and the drone strings; the bellows were activated by the same handle as the strings. Coupling mechanisms allowed doubling at the unison and/or the octave, and for either the organ or the strings to be played alone, or together. Some instruments had a bellows driven by a foot pedal.

As a Bourbon, FERDINAND IV OF NAPLES was an enthusiastic player of the instrument and commissioned music from GYROWETZ, PLEYEL, Sterkel

(1750–1817), as well as Haydn. His *lira organizzata* has not survived, but to judge from Haydn's music it seems to have been a large instrument. Extant examples of the *lira organizzata* can be found in the Institut für Musikforschung, Staatsbibliothek zu Berlin-Preußische Kulturbesitz, and the Victorian and Albert Museum, London.

See CONCERTOS §5, NOTTURNI FOR TWO LIRE ORGANIZZATE AND ENSEMBLE.

F. Bédos de Celles, *L'art du facteur d'orgues*, iv (Paris, 1778); facs. edn (Kassel, 1996).

S. Palmer, *The Hurdy-Gurdy* (London, 1980).

L'isola disabitata (The deserted island) (Hob. XXVIII:9). Serious opera ('azione teatrale') in two parts on a libretto by PIETRO METASTASIO, first performed at Eszterháza on 6 December 1779 in celebration of Prince Nicolaus Esterházy's name-day.

In this short opera, as different from a three-act *dramma per musica* as it is from comic opera, Metastasio artfully combined heroism and comedy in a pastoral setting. He used a desert island as a setting for the study of human nature, contributing to the 18th-century debate about the relative importance of birth and education in the formation of character. Viewing European civilization from afar, the opera is similar to the many essays and stories in which European intellectuals of the Enlightenment took on the personae of visitors from distant lands in order to comment on contemporary mores.

Haydn responded to the sophistication of the libretto and its seriousness of purpose with music that maintains a high level of craftsmanship and invention. The overture is one of his finest: a single fast movement in G minor into which he incorporated a sombre slow introduction and, within the recapitulation, a lyrical, minuet-like melody in the major mode. To demonstrate that Metastasio's blank verse is an integral part of the drama Haydn wrote orchestral accompaniment for all the recitatives. Most of the arias are relatively short, so that the story moves forward steadily.

Two sisters, Costanza and Silvia, have lived for 13 years alone on an island after Costanza's husband, Gernando, was abducted by pirates. Costanza (soprano, a role created by BARBARA RIPAMONTI), believing that Gernando had abandoned her, bewails her fate much as Ariadne laments her abandonment by Theseus in several 18th-century musical realizations of that ancient story (including one by Haydn, Hob.XXVIb:2). Her first aria, 'Se non piage un felice', resembles Gluck's 'Che farò senza Euridice' in its expressive use of a slow, noble melody in a major mode.

Silvia (soprano, LUIGIA POLZELLI), who was only a little girl when she arrived on the island, remembers nothing of the outside world: she is a child of nature. From Costanza she has learnt that men are wicked beings who cannot be trusted, but from growing up on a beautiful, peaceful island she has a cheerful and generous disposition. Silvia, who provides the opera with its occasional touches of delicate comedy, enjoys playing with her pet fawn. Even before she sings, her lively personality is conveyed by a charming melody in the orchestra that accompanies her entrance.

Gernando (tenor, ANDREA TOTTI), having finally escaped from the pirates, returns to the island in search of his wife. He is accompanied by his friend Enrico (baritone, BENEDETTO BIANCHI), who sings a heroic aria in binary form, 'Chi nel camin d'onore', enlivened with horn fanfares. Silvia sees Enrico from a distance and, not realizing the handsome stranger is one of those men about whom Costanza has warned her, falls in love with him. She expresses her sweet, mysterious feelings in a gentle aria, 'Fra in dolce deliro'.

Gernando, conveying his anguish in violent, tragic music, finds a message inscribed by Costanza on a stone, meant to be read after her death, in which she tells of her abandonment. Believing her dead, he sings a fine aria, 'Non turbar quand'io mi lagno', in which frequent shifts to the minor mode and trenchant dissonances represent his despair.

Enrico and Silvia meet; their conversation is accompanied by a recurring fragment of comic melody. When he tells her that he is a man, she starts to flee in terror. He reassures her; she explains, in a fetching aside, that her heart tells her to trust him. They go off in different directions to find Gernando and Costanza, but not before Silvia innocently reveals her feelings for Enrico. In the long final scene, in which husband and wife are reunited, recitative is given musical coherence by recurring solos for violin, cello, and bassoon. These instruments, together with flute, return for lengthy solos in the festive quartet that brings to an end an opera that some commentators regard as the most perfect that Haydn wrote between 1777 and 1784. JAR

HCRL/2.

'Little Organ Mass'. *See* 'KLEINE ORGELSOLOMESSE' (MISSA BREVIS SANCTI JOANNIS DE DEO).

liturgy. The officially approved form of public worship. In Haydn's Austria the liturgical practices of the Catholic Church reflected the broader worshipping patterns used by Catholics throughout Europe but were modified by local tradition, and, increasingly in Haydn's lifetime, subject to direction by the imperial court. The place of music in the liturgy, likewise, was partly determined by local conventions that often enjoyed considerable popular appeal, and partly by imperial dictate motivated by political and economic principles.

There were two principal services that featured in the daily worship of the Catholic religion, the mass, a ceremonial enactment of the Last Supper, and the Divine Office, a series of prayers. There were also some commonly encountered sacred services and individual musical works that were not part of the prescribed liturgy, so-called para-liturgical services or para-liturgical works that reflected national, even local traditions. The following outline confines itself to the liturgical practice that would have governed Haydn's output of sacred music. Readers wishing broader information on the liturgy are referred to the items in the bibliography.

1. **The mass.**
2. **The Divine Office.**
3. **Para-liturgical music.**
4. **The reforms of Joseph II.**

1. The mass. Modern listeners to the masses of Haydn most commonly encounter them in concerts or on CD where the five movements, Kyrie, Gloria, Credo, Sanctus (with Benedictus), and Agnus Dei, are performed in one unfolding sequence. In their true, liturgical context these movements formed only part of the service, preceded, separated, and followed by other musical movements, Gregorian chant, prayers, and readings. The constant element of the mass service was the Ordinary, the varying element was the Proper. The Proper (in the sense of 'proper' to a particular day) was organized around the liturgical year, which began on the first Sunday in Advent and closed with the last Sunday of Pentecost. Fixed feasts included Christmas (25 December), Epiphany (6 January), and the Annunciation (25 March). In Austria other important fixed feasts included 19 March, the nameday of St Joseph, the patron saint of Austria; 13 May, the birthday of Maria Theresia; 2 September, the nameday of St Stephen of Hungary, the protector of Vienna and its principal church; 15 October, St Theresa, nameday of Maria Theresia; 22 November, St Cecilia, patron of musicians; 6 December, St Nicolaus; and 26 December, St Stephen's. Movable feasts were located between Advent and Epiphany, and, more numerous, between nine weeks before Easter (Septuagesima) and Corpus Christi; they included Ash Wednesday, individual Sundays in Lent, Holy Week, Ascension, and Pentecost. In total, significant movable and fixed feasts numbered in excess of 100. These feasts determined not only the spoken elements within the liturgy but also the type and sophistication of musical contributions.

Masses were broadly of two types: a missa solemnis (more commonly described as 'missa longa') designed for important services; and missa brevis for routine ones. At its most extensive the pattern of Ordinary music, Proper music, prayers and readings (also divided into Ordinary and Proper), and instrumental music was an enriching spiritual experience, supported by the visual splendour of many churches and the olfactory pleasure of incense. The following plan is typical, but not prescriptive in all its features. The main movements of the Ordinary of the mass are shown in capital letters.

Instrumental music: organ music or trumpet and timpani fanfares.
Music (Ordinary): 'Tantum ergo' or 'Asperges me'.
Music (Proper) and spoken prayer (Ordinary): Introit simultaneously with penitential prayers.
Music (Ordinary): KYRIE.
Music (Ordinary): GLORIA.
Prayer (Proper): Collect.
Reading (Proper): Epistle.
Music (Proper): Gradual.
Music (Proper): Alleluja or Tract.
Spoken: Gospel and Homily.
Instrumental music: trumpet and timpani fanfares.
Music (Ordinary): CREDO.
Music (Proper) and Prayer (Ordinary): Offertory simultaneously with prayers over the gifts.
Prayer (Proper): Secret (private prayer).
Prayer (Proper): Preface (public prayer).
Music (Ordinary): SANCTUS and BENEDICTUS.
Prayer (Ordinary): Canon (Eucharist prayer).
Prayer (Ordinary): Lord's Prayer.
Music (Ordinary): AGNUS DEI.
Music (Proper): Communion.
Prayer (Proper): Post-communion.
Music (Ordinary): Dismissal ('Ite, Missa est').
Spoken (Ordinary): Closing blessing.
Instrumental: organ postludium or trumpet and timpani fanfares.

The role of any choral and orchestral setting of the Ordinary of the mass was clearly central; on the other hand, the more optional nature of the Ordinary movements before the Kyrie and after the Agnus Dei meant that they were less regularly set and were often sung as plainchant. Apart from the five principal movements of the Ordinary, substantial musical contributions occurred in the Gradual and Offertory. Movements from symphonies and concertos were played as the former, and motets, usually on appropriate liturgical texts, were performed as the Offertory. Taken as a whole the musical ambition and flamboyance of sacred music by Haydn and his contemporaries encouraged more than one commentator to note that going to the church was like going to a concert. On the most important feast days, particularly those in Vienna that were associated with court ceremonial, trumpet and timpani fanfares added even more drama to the occasion.

Yet more jubilant were the choral and orchestral settings of the Te Deum heard alongside (usually before) that of the mass at certain services on Christmas morning and Easter Sunday. The Te Deum was also sung in special services at coronations, weddings, imperial birthdays, the signing of a peace treaty, the safe return from a lengthy journey, and so on.

The Stabat mater was commonly performed on the Feast of the Seven Dolours, in the middle of Lent, in place of the Alleluja or Tract.

2. **The Divine Office.** The Office consisted of a daily series of prayers, beginning before dawn with Matins and Lauds, and followed by the Hours of Prime, Sext, and None, with Vespers sung before dusk, and Compline shortly after dusk. Much of these services consisted of plainchant and readings from the scriptures and associated texts. Musically, the Vespers were the most ambitious, particularly on Sundays and on the eve of major feasts. Six psalm texts were sung followed by a Hymn (appropriate to the liturgical time of year), a setting of the Magnificat, and an antiphon in supplication to the Blessed Virgin Mary. On important feast days the Litany was also performed: Kyrie and Agnus Dei from the Ordinary of the mass flanking texts in praise of the Virgin Mary or dedicated to the Sacrament. Performances of the Litany were frequently characterized by lavish processions to and from the place of worship.

Unlike Mozart, Haydn did not compose any Vespers or Litanies, but his settings of the Salve regina and Ave regina texts are prime examples of the Marian antiphons featured at the end of Vespers. Instrumental music, such as movements from symphonies and concertos, did not normally feature in Vespers.

3. **Para-liturgical music.** Performances of masses and other liturgical texts in secular surroundings are virtually unknown in Haydn's Austria; indeed in the period of heavy censorship during the Napoleonic era it was explicitly forbidden. However, masses, particularly Votive masses, performed to celebrate the particular achievement of an individual were given outside the normal liturgy. More common were para-liturgical performances of the Te Deum, prompted by any convenient celebration. For instance, during the French occupation of Austria in 1809, the entire populace was required to celebrate Napoleon's birthday; at the abbey of Göttweig, Haydn's first Te Deum (Hob. XXIIIc:1) was performed.

The Stabat mater was often performed para-liturgically as an oratorio, and was the nearest that the Austrian tradition came to the concert performances of that work that were common in London and Paris. Sacred music with texts in the German language, such as Haydn's Advent arias, may also be considered as music outside the liturgy, though there is some evidence that they were sometimes sung as Offertories in mass services too.

Public processions were extremely popular in Austria. In Vienna they often united sacred symbolism with the secular one of the state, while in the countryside they revealed relics of old pagan traditions alongside the central Christian purpose. Haydn's two settings of the text 'Lauda Sion' (Hob. XXIIIc:4 and 5) are typical of the music sung during the procession on Corpus Christi, either in one church or divided between several churches that featured on a standard processional route.

4. **The reforms of Joseph II.** When Joseph II became emperor in 1780, he instigated a period of rapid reform of every aspect of state, its government, finances, laws, education, and religious life. Although the Catholic Church in Austria had long been accustomed to influence and interference from the Habsburg court, during the 1780s Joseph II increased this control considerably and to an unsettling degree. Primarily motivated by the desire to create a centralized, bureaucratic state, Joseph II wished the Church to play a more socially utilitarian role in the religious and educational life of the country. The dissolution of many monasteries and other religious houses in the period was intended to release money that could be used for the broader benefit of the people. Similar economic reasoning, touched with thoughts on the probity of religious music, lay behind a series of decrees on the role that music was to play in the liturgy. In 1782 the emperor proposed that orchestrally accompanied services should be restricted 'so that the bothersome expenses for music and other burdens of the clergy and their assistants might be avoided for the most part, to the benefit of the funds for religious education'. In Vienna, it was subsequently decreed that every parish church should celebrate daily mass with appropriate communal hymns in German; St Stephen's was allowed a choral setting of the mass with or without an organ, but no orchestral participation; on Sundays and feast days high mass in parish churches could be celebrated with orchestral masses if desired, otherwise choral settings would suffice; and that Vespers were henceforth to be sung without orchestral accompaniment, though an organ could be used on feast days. Similar decrees were issued for other parts of the Austrian monarchy. The development of congregational singing of simple German hymns and sacred songs was also systematically encouraged.

The severe curtailment of orchestrally accompanied masses and the complete banning of orchestral settings of the Vespers (and associated Litany) constituted a major change in the role of music in church services and provoked a strong reaction. In Vienna a petition was drawn up, pointing out that up to 2,000 musicians and their dependants were to be consigned to penury as a result. For many composers the effects were equally drastic, though to claim that the reforms were the reason why Haydn did not write any masses between 1782 and 1796 is misleading. He was not required to compose church music at the Esterházy court and his developing wider reputation was based chiefly on instrumental music which became his clear priority in this period. There is no doubt, however, that Haydn's existing sacred music, like that of all composers, was less frequently performed in Austria from the 1780s onwards. The associated tradition of performing symphonies and concertos in church services was similarly dealt a major blow.

The effect of Joseph II's reforms of the role of music in the liturgy was compounded by his reforms elsewhere. Some 700 monasteries and other religious orders were dissolved in the 1780s; public processions and pilgrimages were restricted; and many Brotherhoods that had generously supported the role of music in churches were dissolved. It was the most radical period of change in church music in Austrian history and, though some minor concessions were made and there was some reversion to older ways in the reigns of Leopold II and Franz II, the effects were largely permanent. *See also* CATHOLICISM, JOSEPHINISM, MASS.

J. Harper, *The Forms and Orders of Western Liturgy from the Tenth to the Eighteenth Century* (Oxford, 1991).

H. Hollerweger, *Die Reform des Gottesdienstes zur Zeit des Josephinismus in Österreich* (Regensburg, 1976).

B. MacIntyre, *The Viennese Concerted Mass of the Early Classic Period* (Ann Arbor, 1986).

J. K. Page, 'Music and the Royal Procession in Maria Theresia's Vienna', *Early Music*, 27 (1999), 96–118.

R. G. Pauly, 'The Reforms of Church Music under Joseph II', *Musical Quarterly*, 43 (1957), 372–82.

F. W. Riedel, 'Liturgie und Kirchenmusik', in *Joseph Haydn in seiner Zeit* [Exhibition catalogue] (Eisenstadt, 1982), 121–33.

Lobkowitz, Prince Franz Joseph Maximilian (b. 7 Dec. 1772; d. 15 Dec. 1816). A leading patron of music in Vienna at the turn of the century; Haydn's op. 77 quartets were commissioned by Lobkowitz and dedicated to him. Perhaps because of a physical disability that required him to walk with the aid of a stick throughout his life, Lobkowitz devoted all his waking hours to the cultivation of music. He spoke German, Italian, French, Czech, and a little English, played the violin and the cello, and had a cultivated bass voice. In 1797 he formed a small retinue of court musicians under the leadership of Anton Wranitzky (1766–1820), comprising eight string players (sometimes fewer) and three singers. To this core, additional players and singers were hired as necessary. Moving on a regular annual pattern from Vienna, to Prague, to summer palaces in Eisenberg (Jezeří) and Raudnitz (Roudnice), and then back to Prague and Vienna, the musicians performed at private concerts, birthdays, and nameday celebrations, and balls. Voluminous quantities of music of all kinds were regularly ordered from Vienna, including symphonies, quartets, piano trios, masses, and oratorios by Haydn.

Lobkowitz was a member of the GESELLSCHAFT DER ASSOCIIERTEN and played a leading role in sponsoring the first performances of *The Creation* and *The Seasons*. In 1799 *The Creation* was performed at his country estates in Eisenberg and Raudnitz, and the following year he subscribed to six copies of the first printed edition of the full score. An employee, Johann Kruchina, prepared a Czech translation of the oratorio which was given at Raudnitz in October 1805 with the prince singing the part of Raphael.

In 1798 or 1799 the prince had commissioned six new quartets from Haydn but first the task of composing *The Seasons* and then the composer's declining health ensured that only two works were completed. They were presented to the prince in 1799 and dedicated to him when they were finally published by Artaria in 1802. The prince's main palace in Vienna was a notable venue for private concerts to which Haydn was invited; on one known occasion, in 1804, the prince paid for his coach from Gumpendorf. Lobkowitz regularly gave singers, instrumentalists, and composers gifts of money and gifts in kind. In 1807, for instance, he sent the ageing Haydn six pheasants and four partridges from his Bohemian estates.

Lobkowitz became one of Beethoven's most important patrons, associated with many major works, including the *Eroica Symphony*. His spending on music reached the point of recklessness, exacerbated by the recurring crises in the Austrian economy. Eventually he was declared bankrupt and prevented from further expenditure. An increasingly dejected man, he became seriously ill and died at the age of 44.

HCRL/4 and 5.

J. Macek, 'Franz Joseph Maximilian Lobkowitz. Musikfreund und Kunstmäzen', in S. Brandenburg and M. Gutiérrez-Denhoff (eds), *Beethoven und Böhmen* (Bonn, 1988), 147–202.

'Lobkowitz' quartets. Nickname occasionally used for the op. 77 quartets commissioned and subsequently dedicated to PRINCE FRANZ JOSEPH MAXIMILIAN LOBKOWITZ. JH

London. See opposite.

[*cont. on p.223*]

London

The London that Haydn came to in 1791 was a vast metropolis by comparison with Vienna, brimming with confidence as the centre of world trade, spurred on by a sense of limitless opportunity, and rewarded by seemingly unstoppable wealth creation. It was an ever-expanding city, both in terms of population (approaching a million by the turn of the century) and physically too: westwards towards Hyde Park, as the *haut monde* fought to retain their own exclusive conclaves; northwards towards Hampstead; and (further down the social scale) eastwards past the City and south over London Bridge. It was a city of abundant contrasts, between poverty and riches, between squalor and gentility, between the commercial aspirations of the City bourgeoisie and the gracious living of the landed gentry of the West End. Of course commercial enterprise was not unknown among the aristocracy too, but emerging market opportunities were increasingly coming face to face with the social demands of the old order, in ways that had a significant impact on London's musical life. To judge from his surviving LONDON NOTEBOOKS, Haydn was fascinated by all these contrasts and juxtapositions, and by what he regarded as the eccentricities of English life, from the taciturn naval captain who gave him 50 guineas for a couple of marches, to Quakers who paid their taxes by buying back goods deliberately 'stolen' by a government agent.

Music crossed these boundaries in all manner of ways, and it infiltrated every corner of London's artistic and social life. Songs and instrumental solos formed part of almost every popular entertainment, accompanying the horse shows at Astley's Amphitheatre (forerunner of the modern circus), or interspersed with readings from Shakespeare, or leavening John Cartwright's scientific demonstrations at the Lyceum. Outdoors, bands complete with 'Turkish' instruments could be heard playing military music in the parks, while at the summer pleasure gardens music as varied as Haydn symphonies and Scottish songs beguiled the strolling audience. Music was a vital part of any philanthropic venture, especially at charitable services; Haydn, like Berlioz after him, was intensely moved by the psalm-singing of 4,000 charity children at St Paul's. Similarly it was intrinsic to public ritual, from royal weddings to the formal court celebrations that still required music from the King's Band twice a year; and no major opening ceremony was complete without a newly written ode. At private soirées, songs and keyboard music were equally *de rigueur*, whether performed by nervous daughters or by hired-in opera stars; even gentlemen regarded the ability to sing in an after-dinner glee as a necessary social accomplishment. And all this without mentioning the more direct contribution of music to the cultural life of the city, at the Italian Opera and English playhouses, as well as at the innumerable public concerts and musical societies. Haydn arrived in the middle of a period when London was gripped by intense enthusiasm for music (to which of course his symphonies had already contributed), before the effects of war and a change of national mood dampened the hedonistic spirit.

Much of this musical activity can be attributed to the abundance of wealth in a thriving capital city, for wealth brought leisure, and increasing numbers of well-educated professionals and City folk regarded themselves among the leisured classes. And of course any household of social pretension emulated the pleasures and pastimes of the elite, with the aspirations of wives and daughters—as much social as musical—a decisive factor. The combination of wealth spreading through the upper echelons of the bourgeoisie with energetic entrepreneurialism resulted in an explosion of money-making opportunities, the sale of sheet music, pianos, and concert tickets, even if such things were still way out of reach of most of the population. Just how far music had become a major business can be judged from the ferocity with which publishers like FORSTER and LONGMAN & BRODERIP fought legal battles over Haydn's music in the 1780s.

Not that the artistic results of all this activity were necessarily of the highest: witness Haydn deriding the wretched dance band and 'miserable violins' at a City banquet, or the sleepy orchestra at Covent Garden. The profusion went unregulated, with professional control severely hampered by the interference of patrons and the lack of a professional validating society. British composers were particularly badly situated, denied opportunities for performance at the most prestigious venues, as well as haunted by searching comparison with either HANDEL or Haydn. Artistic aspirations were undoubtedly compromised and tainted by commercial considerations: by the vast sums paid to foreign divas and instrumental stars, attracted by rumours of the flowing wallets of English music lovers, or by publishers' preference for vulgar trivia aimed at amateur pianists, on the lines of Kotzwara's descriptive *Battle of Prague* (even major composers succumbed to this pressure). Concert promoters resorted unashamedly to every possible advertising device, programming curiosities such as the 276-stringed pantaleon or 'double sounds' on the flute.

But at its best this energetic and vital culture did encourage the highest standards of performance and of repertoire. For, if wealth spawned commercialism, it also enabled connoisseurship, whether the leisure of antiquarians expanding the repertoire through manuscript collecting, or that of opera and concert-goers attracted by the finest performers and the latest compositions from the continent. Haydn performed alongside numerous virtuosos of international reputation, some passing through, some resident in London for many years, some refugees from Paris with royalist connections: singers of the calibre of BANTI and MARA, the violinists Giornovichi and Viotti, the pianists Dussek, J. B. Cramer, and CLEMENTI. London's musical culture should not be judged solely by its native composers, nor by its contribution to the canonic repertoire (though with Viotti, Clementi, and Dussek in addition to Haydn the score sheet for 1791–5 is not negligible); the role music played in the life of the time, at every level of society, and its contribution to the cultural and intellectual milieu should also be borne in mind.

A strikingly beneficial example of a symbiotic relationship between commerce and art is provided by developments in piano construction and repertoire. In manufacturing terms London led the world, with Broadwood's pianos a potent symbol of Britain's technological prowess and innovation. In return, pianists like Dussek were able to explore an increasing range and sonority, encouraging an individual London voice that has since been dubbed the London Pianoforte School. The large Broadwood piano (quite unlike the pianos Haydn would have known in Vienna) had a richness and dramatic power ideally suited to the public platform, while the capacity for long-breathed cantabile and sonorous chordal writing could be exploited in profound slow-moving Adagios. Simplicity and pathos were qualities much prized in Handel's England, and now even piano music gained a sense of space, of enlarged time. Of course Dussek's advocacy encouraged more people to buy these large pianos, and turnover was increased by expanding the range from five octaves to six (though in the publications of his music Dussek was careful to provide alternative versions for the smaller instrument).

Debate about commercialism and art within London's musical life was already well under way, partly because the divisions were so hard to demarcate and the stances taken so partisan. In terms of cultural pedigree, music was viewed as ambivalent, not fully accepted into the hierarchy alongside literature and fine art. Instrumentalists, and even composers, were still regarded as highly skilled craftsmen; even Haydn was not much fêted among intellectuals, and music had no equivalent of the Royal Academy of Arts for serious debate on matters of artistic importance. Only the two musical historians, Sir John Hawkins and CHARLES BURNEY, were truly accepted into literary society. Those who did advocate music as an object of study generally regarded the fashionable entertainments of the beau monde as ephemeral amusements. The traditionalist Sir John Hawkins was convinced that J. C. Bach must have retained a more serious musical idiom for his private delectation than he displayed in public. Instead Hawkins venerated the old masters, the revival of 'ancient music', which had gathered pace during the 18th century since the founding of the Academy of Ancient Music (1726) and the Concert of Antient Music (1776). By the 1790s 'ancient' repertoire ranged from Handel back to the Renaissance polyphony of Palestrina (1525/6–94) and Marenzio (1553/4–99), music that demanded close attention, some learning, and an appreciation of less obvious or less superficial qualities. It should be said, however, that this schism between ancient and modern was to some extent ideological, encouraged as propaganda by those (especially those of the threatened aristocracy) who wished to represent themselves as the guardians of continuity and deeper values. Others, like Charles Burney, were beginning to write about modern music (both Italian opera and German symphonies) as equally deserving of serious artistic enquiry. Indeed the complexity of Haydn's symphonic argument was very largely responsible for this change in perception, giving modern German instrumental music a stature previously denied it. Thus in 1796, in a dispassionate survey of ancient and modern music John Marsh suggested, without irony, that a Haydn symphony might require several listenings before its subtleties could be appreciated. And though concerts were still social in tone—patrons arrived late, wandered around, and chatted during the performance—it was not only cognoscenti who listened closely to Haydn symphonies at the Hanover Square Rooms.

Indeed Haydn's music was already regarded by Londoners as music that would outlast its time, something that had never been expected of modern music before. The deepening of expression, even the grandeur of some of Haydn's London music was reflected in the piano music of Clementi and Dussek, and in the violin concertos of Viotti. And certainly much in the newest music—the return of counterpoint and the minor mode, the visionary slow movements, and the awesome changes of vista—allied it in British minds with the Handelian sublime, an important touchstone for English audiences; while the expressive intensity and exploration of instrumental sonority can be seen as pre-Romantic traits that undoubtedly influenced Beethoven.

London's musical taste was still heavily influenced by an elite patronage, despite the commercial nature of much of its activity. The 'ancient' cause was adopted by the nobility as a rallying point with GEORGE III at their head. The rest of the royal family, on the other hand, favoured modern music, not only in their own private concerts but also through their patronage of public concert life. The king's brothers and sons, especially the PRINCE OF WALES, were undoubtedly among the leaders of taste who contributed to the success of Haydn's music (and Pleyel's) during the 1780s, and prepared the ground for their arrival in the 1790s. Another was the EARL OF ABINGDON, who himself promoted concert series in 1783 and 1784, and was personally involved in negotiations with Haydn. The vigour of London's concert life did not, therefore, originate from a desire by a middle-class public to share in aristocratic delights or from direct efforts by musician-impresarios to tap an expanding market. Though a broadening musical public must have attended Hanover Square concerts, there is little sign that they were regarded as leaders of fashionable taste at prestigious West End venues. Indeed the City, the commercial centre of London, sustained musical institutions of its own such as the Academy of Ancient Music and the Anacreontic Society, both organized by wealthy merchants and bankers. Haydn's own patrons came from both the aristocracy and the upper levels of the bourgeoisie; during the out-of-season summer months, he associated with (amongst others) the Prince of Wales, the Duke of York, Abingdon himself, Lord Pembroke, the merchant banker Nathaniel Brassey, and the captain of an East India merchant ship. Through his connection with the poet ANNE HUNTER, wife of a prominent surgeon, he was introduced also to the 'blue-stocking' community that included Fanny Burney, Elizabeth Carter, and Horace Walpole. But perhaps he was most comfortable with musicians and others from the artistic community, travelling with ASHE and Cimador to visit RAUZZINI in Bath, dining with Burney (and with Boswell and Holcroft), witnessing the marriage of THERESE JANSEN to GAETANO BARTOLOZZI, son of the engraver.

It was during the winter season that everything of artistic moment took place. The season extended broadly from September to early June (this was when the theatres were open), but the height of the social calendar was in the spring, and few concerts of any importance took place before Christmas. As ever the Italian Opera—expensive, fashionable, and exclusive—dominated the social calendar, despite a series of disputes over management, and the burning down of the Opera House (perhaps deliberately) in 1789. When Haydn arrived in 1791, London's opera establishment was in as much turmoil as it had ever been. Taylor and GALLINI had a theatre (the rebuilt King's Theatre) but no licence, resulting in Haydn's new opera, *L'anima del filosofo*, being replaced by a season of unstaged arias and ballets (as Walpole described it, 'a sort of opera in *déshabillé*'). Their rival, O'Reilly, was a frontman for a powerful group of nobles intent on building a new opera house in Leicester Fields, as a subsidized court theatre; when the plan folded, they were reduced to putting on operas at the hastily converted Pantheon. The situation was resolved the following season, when after behind-the-scenes deals and a mysterious fire at the Pantheon, the licence was returned to the King's Theatre. London's opera managers imported many of the best serious and comic Italian operas, to be sung by the outstanding Italian singers of the day: PACCHIEROTTI, Marchesi, and Banti. A few distinguished opera composers were invited to London; and in their knowledge of the theatre and the Italian cabal on their side Bianchi (*c.*1752–1810) and Martín y Soler (1754–1806) would have proved formidable opponents to Haydn's operatic aspirations. The Italian Opera was sustained too by innovations in other areas, beginning in the 1780s with the dramatic ballet of Noverre and with evocative, romantic scenery inspired by De Loutherbourg, while no less a figure than William Turner was a scene painter at the Pantheon in 1791.

Music was also a major attraction at the two main English playhouses, Covent Garden and Drury Lane, where the cheaper range of tickets and the English fare were designed for a quite different clientele (noisy and impertinent, according to Haydn). Even straight plays, from Shakespeare to Sheridan, always included a few songs, and characteristic music was essential to the pantomimes that typically formed the closing 'afterpiece'. But the playhouses also put on English opera in its many different guises. Ballad operas such as *The Beggar's Opera* still held the stage, as did Arne's full-length English opera *Artaxerxes*. Modern English operas typically had spoken dialogue in the ballad opera tradition, often using exotic or picturesque settings such as Shield's *The Mysteries of the Castle* and Storace's *The Siege of Belgrade*. Such works could be something of a patchwork, their own songs interspersed with Scots ballads and 'borrowings' from Paisiello and Grétry, but Storace also lavished attention on substantial operatic finales, reflecting his friendship with Mozart during the 1780s. When Haydn attended Covent Garden in 1791, he saw Shield's *The Woodman*; and for the same theatre in 1795 SALOMON wrote his WINDSOR CASTLE in honour of the Prince of Wales's wedding.

London's concert life had been steadily increasing in importance during the three decades before Haydn's arrival, to the point that the various weekly subscription series were regarded as major events, both socially and artistically. They were widely reported in the press and almost rivalled the Italian Opera for attention; indeed the high-priced subscription system was designed to retain similar social exclusivity and prestige. Modern music was at the forefront of these concert programmes, the latest German symphonies alternating with Italian arias by the top opera stars, a potent mix that appealed to snobbery and an avaricious search for novelty and sensation in equal measure. The Hanover Square Rooms, built for the Bach–Abel concerts in 1775, was the principal venue; it was an elegantly decorated room, with gilded ornament and elaborate chandeliers, seating no more than 500 comfortably. A larger room, seating 800, was built on to the back of the stage of the new King's Theatre, providing the venue for the Opera Concerts of 1795.

The late 1780s were dominated by the Professional Concert, formed by London's top instrumentalists in 1785, which, through adroit manipulation of taste and patronage of the highest class, became a formidable operation, with a highly disciplined orchestra. Reliant on Haydn sending over new music during the 1780s, they were largely responsible for the frenzy of anticipation before Haydn's arrival in person; so Salomon's coup in recruiting Haydn for his own series of concerts was a bitter blow. In this context should be viewed their much-reviled subsequent attempts to blacken Haydn's name, then to bribe him, and finally to rival him by recruiting PLEYEL in 1792. In the same year the Vocal Concerts, promoted by Harrison and Knyvett, surprised everyone by making English songs and glees suddenly fashionable, and the Professionals eventually wilted after the 1793 season. A year later Salomon, in turn, proved unwilling to shoulder the burden of continental recruitment alone, and 1795 saw a pooling of resources in the Opera Concert, in effect a coalition between Salomon, the Professionals, and the King's Theatre.

The 'ancient' cause provided the other regular feature in London's concert season. The Lenten oratorio series founded by Handel persisted, but in altered and more populist guise. In 1791 two rival series took place at the playhouses, but the promoters presented hardly any complete oratorios apart from *Messiah*, following instead a general trend towards selections of favourite songs and choruses from Handel oratorios, and even other miscellaneous items. Working to a quite different agenda, though the programmes were not dissimilar, was the Concert of Ancient Music, the figurehead of the opposition to modern music. Founded by noblemen with a genuine zeal for fine older music, the society was patronized by the king and a high proportion of the aristocracy; and the concerts were a self-conscious reassertion of conservative artistic and social values. The directors were heavily involved in the gigantic Handel Commemoration of 1784 and in succeeding festivals at Westminster abbey most years until 1791, when Haydn attended a performance of *Israel in Egypt.* By this date the elevated ranks of the orchestra and choir numbered well over a thousand, while the royal box housed the entire royal family and other dignitaries in a powerful assertion of tradition and continuity. For Haydn it was a formative experience, which led eventually to his own metamorphosis of the Handelian idiom in *The Creation.*

Many other societies met on a regular basis in London, ranging from amateur glee clubs and instrumental societies to more formal institutions like the Noblemen and Gentlemen's Catch Club. Some were distinctly casual: John Marsh visited one tavern society where the audience was engulfed in a fog of pipe smoke, though the president did request gentlemen to lay down their pipes when Mrs Goodban was singing. On the other hand, the Anacreontic Society, a bourgeois dining and glee club, prefaced its meetings with a full-scale concert by leading instrumentalists. Meeting early in the season, the society functioned partly as a proving ground for new music and musicians, and indeed it was here that the new celebrity, Haydn, made his first official appearance in 1791. He had already been fêted at another society with similar clientele, the Academy of Ancient Music, which had long lost its antiquarian mission in favour of programmes mixing older music with modern glees and even symphonies by Haydn himself.

The end of every season was filled with benefit performances of operas, plays, and concerts promoted by charities or more usually by performers themselves as a reward for good service. Some 25 benefit concerts took place each year, and by a combination of inventive programming, assiduous marketing, and pressure on patrons, it was possible to make substantial profits. Haydn specified in his contract with Salomon that his 1791 benefit should be guaranteed at £250 (with expenses paid by the promoter); in the end it brought in as much as £350, which would have been a handsome annual income for a lawyer. In return, Haydn generously took part in benefits for Salomon's performers and indeed for many other musicians.

Music formed an essential part of private entertaining, especially as the *haut ton* began to turn away from the increasingly mixed company at the public venues. The two main 'private' series, the Nobility Concert and the Ladies Concert, hired full-scale orchestras for regular formal concerts; in 1791 the latter actually clashed directly with Salomon's series. Ladies of fashion vied with each other in putting on elaborate concerts, reported (of course) in the press, though an ostentatious salon culture was not to develop before the next century. Less grandiosely, songs and piano music figured at private parties of all kind at all social levels, jostling for attention with conversation, flirting, card-playing, and all the usual diversions of the social round. This was assuredly the milieu for which Haydn's London piano music was destined, as were his English canzonettas with their very typical sentiment and pastoral imagery. Sometimes, though, music was the central focus of private parties, such as those of Charles Burney, or the Prince of Wales's morning concerts, intimate chamber music sessions, where the prince played the cello alongside invited virtuosos and a dignified silence was maintained. Haydn appeared 26 times at the Prince's request at both formal and informal concerts, though he did not receive due payment until Parliament agreed to settle the prince's many debts.

Outside the winter season, when most patrons retired to their country seats, and many leading musicians accompanied them, or else went on provincial tours, London was starved of serious music-making. The main theatres were dark, and the only concerts of any moment were those at the pleasure gardens, outdoors in the bandstand at Vauxhall, a self-conscious *rus in urbe*, carefree and sentimental, and a touch risqué; or indoors in the great rotunda at the more expensive Ranelagh, where guests perambulated in sober procession. Haydn himself visited Ranelagh in 1792, the unusual venue for Giardini's farewell concert, but it would have been out of the question for him to have performed at the pleasure gardens himself despite the popularity of his symphonies.

The 1790s were not a fruitful period for native English music. Even the finest composers, such as Storace (1762–96), were excluded from the musical elite at the King's Theatre or Hanover Square, and there was little demand for new oratorios either. But in compensation there was a rich harvest of continental composers, widely appreciated in London. Haydn reached both the broad spectrum of casual listeners at Vauxhall Gardens and those connoisseurs at Salomon's concerts in the Hanover Square Rooms who recognized that here, at last, was modern music of more than passing ephemerality. He even managed to break through the oratorio barrier when *The Creation* (as much an English work as German) reached London in 1800 to immediate and lasting acclaim. Some three decades after Handel's death, London was ready for Haydn, in the same way as it was to take Mendelssohn to its heart a further 30 years on. SMcV

R. Fiske, *English Theatre Music in the Eighteenth Century*, 2nd edn (Oxford, 1986).
HCRL/3.
S. McVeigh, *Concert Life in London from Mozart to Haydn* (Cambridge, 1993).
C. Price, J. Milhous, and R. D. Hume, *Italian Opera in Late Eighteenth-Century London*, vol. i: *The King's Theatre, Haymarket 1778–1791* (Oxford, 1995).

London Notebooks. During his two visits to London Haydn compiled four notebooks of random jottings, anecdotes, and reminiscences. Only the first three survive. Each is roughly equivalent in size to the modern A6 and was designed to be carried in the pocket for easy access. Most of the entries are written in ink with the occasional one in pencil. Two books were used interchangeably in the first visit (1791–2), with the entries being written on any convenient page; some pages are left empty and the occasional space suggests that some entries were to be completed later. The third and fourth notebooks cover the second visit (1794–5); the contents of the fourth notebook are known only from the extracts, probably incomplete, quoted in GRIESINGER's biography of Haydn.

The notebooks provide a fascinating glimpse of the impact which London and England made on Haydn and are testimony to his insatiable curiosity. Alongside lists of musicians and some of the concerts and operas that he attended are descriptions of visits to the provinces, sometimes cryptic references to scandal, and, a characteristic concern, notes on the cost of living. Of particular documentary value are the copies of REBECCA SCHROETER's letters to the composer which he included in the second notebook and the list of works written in and for London that were entered in the fourth notebook.

D. Bartha (ed.), *Joseph Haydn. Gesammelte Briefe und Aufzeichnungen* (Kassel, 1965).
E. K. Borthwick, 'The Latin Quotations in Haydn's London Notebooks', *Music and Letters*, 71 (1990), 505–10.
H. C. Robbins Landon (ed.), *The Collected Correspondence and London Notebooks of Joseph Haydn* (London, 1959).

'London' sonata. Nickname occasionally used for Haydn's piano sonata in C (Hob.XVI:50) written in London in 1794–5. Two other sonatas, in D (Hob.XVI:49) and in E♭ (Hob.XVI:51), equally deserve the nickname. The C major sonata is sometimes called the 'English' sonata. JH

'London' symphony. Commonly used nickname for Symphony no. 104, first performed in London in May 1795. In use since the middle of the 19th century, it is not a particularly sensible nickname since 11 other symphonies (nos. 93–103) also were written for London. Indeed the 12 are often collectively referred to as the 'London' symphonies. JH

Longman & Broderip. Music publishers, distributors, and instrument makers in London. During its heyday in the 1780s and early 1790s the firm played a vital part in promoting Haydn's music in London. It can be traced back to the 1760s, and already in 1772 (as Longman, Lukey & Co.) it had issued the first edition in London of Haydn's op. 9 quartets. As part of a more general expansion of the business in the 1780s, Longman & Broderip became ARTARIA's agent in London, gaining access to the many editions of Haydn's music issued in Vienna in that decade. Some of Artaria's publications were simply sold with a gummed label attached ('Imported and Sold by Longman & Broderip . . . who have a regular Correspondence with all the most eminent Professors and Publishers of Music in every part of Europe'), while others were used as the basis of new editions. In these complementary ways many Haydn symphonies, piano sonatas, and piano trios, in particular, were made available in London. Longman & Broderip's confidence in the market can be judged by the fact that the firm published Haydn's 24 German songs (Hob.XXVIa:1–24), based on the Artaria edition, but with new, English texts.

In the fiercely competitive atmosphere between rival music publishers that existed in London, the productive relationship between Longman & Broderip and Artaria resulted in a bitter dispute with FORSTER who negotiated directly with the composer. In 1788 matters came to a head when it was discovered that two editions of the recent 'Paris' symphonies became available in London: one published by Forster, based on manuscript material forwarded by the composer, the other by Longman & Broderip, based on the relationship between that firm and Artaria to whom Haydn had also sold the works. It became something of a scandal, avidly reported in the newspapers. Another dispute, concerning three piano trios (Hob.XV: 3–5), was the subject of a lengthy court dispute that was not finally resolved until 1794.

Longman & Broderip enjoyed an increasingly close working relationship with the concert organization the Professional Concert who were attempting to attract Haydn to London. The composer forwarded manuscript copies of the six quartets of opp. 54 and 55 to the Professional Concert; the works were played in the 1789 and 1790 seasons and duly published by Longman & Broderip. By this time another publisher, JOHN BLAND, had entered the fray; he established himself as the London agent for the Viennese publisher HOFFMEISTER and allied himself with Salomon, rather than the Professional Concert. Longman & Broderip regained some prestige in 1794–7 when Haydn entrusted the firm with the publication of three sets of piano trios (Hob.XV:18–20, 24–6, and 27–9).

Longman & Broderip went bankrupt in 1795 but was reactivated by the presence of a new energetic partner, CLEMENTI. As Longman & Clementi, the firm published the first edition in London of the op. 76 quartets (1799), based on material forwarded by the composer.

As was often the case in the 18th century, Longman & Broderip was also active in a more general way in the musical market. It had a circulating library, sold tickets for concerts, had agents as far afield as India, and manufactured or sold instruments of all kinds. Its pianos, in particular, were well regarded. Haydn acquired a Longman & Broderip grand piano in 1795 which may have been given to him by the firm in order to promote its instruments in Vienna.

N. Mace, 'Haydn and the London Music Sellers: Forster v. Longman & Broderip', *Music and Letters*, 77 (1996), 527–41.

I. Woodfield, 'John Bland: London Retailer of the Music of Haydn and Mozart', *Music and Letters*, 81 (2000), 210–44.

Lorenzi, Giambattista (b. 1719: d. Dec. 1805). Italian librettist, associated with the Teatrino di Corte and Teatro San Carlo in Naples. Cimarosa set Lorenzi's *L'infedeltà fedele* in 1779. Haydn owned a copy of this score and made his own setting of the libretto two years later, renaming the work *La fedeltà premiata* in order to avoid confusion with his earlier opera *L'infedeltà delusa*. The anonymous arranger of the libretto for Haydn made a number of changes to Lorenzi's work, including eliminating the Neapolitan dialect and the passages of crude humour. RJR

F. Lippmann, 'Haydns "La fedelta premiata" und Cimarosas "L'infedeltà fedele" ', *HS* 5 (1982), 1–15.

Lo speziale (The apothecary) (Hob.XXVIII:3). Opera ('dramma giocoso') in three acts after CARLO GOLDONI, first performed at Eszterháza during September 1768 in celebration of the opening of Prince Nicolaus's opera house. The opera survives incomplete; two scenes in Act 3 have been lost.

Goldoni created *Lo speziale*, one of his most amusing librettos, for two of the leading comic singers in Italy, Francesco Baglioni and Francesco Carattoli, who performed the drama frequently during the 1750s with music by Domenico Fischietti (*c*.1725–*c*.1810) and Vincenzo Pallavicini (*fl.* 1743–66). Haydn, or whoever revised the libretto for him, omitted the *parti serie* and one minor comic character, but in other respects stayed close to the original.

Haydn's music, consisting largely of exit arias separated by long stretches of simple recitative, enters fully into the spirit of Goldonian comedy, despite its use of vocal types that an Italian composer would have found strange. Sempronio, an old apothecary, is addicted to newspapers and to following current affairs in distant lands; but he wants also to marry his ward, Grilletta. His is the type of comic role that was normally sung by a bass or baritone, such as Carattoli, who sang Sempronio in the settings by Fischietti and Pallavicini. But Haydn did not apparently have a good comic bass available when composing *Lo speziale.* He assigned Sempronio to the tenor CARL FRIBERTH. Conventionally, Volpino, Grilletta's suitor, would have been a tenor; but Haydn reacted to a libretto that contained only one female role by having Volpino sung by his resident soprano, BARBARA DICHTLER, who otherwise would have been idle.

Sempronio's assistant, Mengone (LEOPOLD DICHTLER), loves Grilletta (Magdalena Spangler), and she returns his affection. Haydn brought the activities of the apothecary's shop to musical life in Mengone's first aria, 'Tutto il giorno pista, pista'. The orchestra depicts Mengone's clumsy use of pestle and mortar as he explains that his heart beats just as vigorously for Grilletta.

Here and elsewhere in *Lo speziale* Haydn found more comedy in tone-painting than is typical of mid-18th-century comic opera. Repeating an item of news Sempronio illustrates the word 'lunghezza' ('length') by holding a note for two bars and then extending it into a scale up to a high C, and 'larghezza' ('width') by leaping from a high note down two octaves. Haydn exploited a coarser kind of comedy in his musical setting of Mengone's 'Per quel che ha mal il stomaco'. He depicts stomach ache with a number of augmented seconds in the melody; and descending coloratura runs are used to represent runs of a different kind.

Grilletta gently rejects Volpino's advances in 'Caro Volpino amabile', which uses the moderate tempo and triple metre typical of many arias sung by women from the lower and middle classes in settings of Goldoni's librettos. But Haydn once more ignores convention by including coloratura, normally reserved by contemporary Italian composers for *parti serie.* (A second setting of the same text, composed by Haydn for a revival of *Lo speziale,* is sometimes performed in place of the original aria.)

During the later 1760s and early 1770s Haydn liked to combine a fast tempo with the sound of the minor mode in his operas as well as in his symphonies. Volpino's anger at being rejected by Grilletta gave him an opportunity to write an aria in G minor, Presto, 'Amore nel mio petto'. Three-bar phrases in the opening melody suggest that Volpino belongs to a social level higher than the rest of the characters and tempt the listener to take his anger seriously; but the music becomes more comic as short, *parlante* phrases and bits of patter remind the listener that Volpino is not a serious role.

Lo speziale comes to its comic climax in the finale of Act 2, in which Sempronio thinks he is getting married to Grilletta. In a delightful variation of the well-worn ruse of the fake notary, Goldoni has both Volpino and Mengone disguise themselves as notaries. They both individually make copies of the marriage contract, naming themselves as the bridegroom.

Act 3 is likewise dominated by disguises. Grilletta and her young suitors take advantage of Sempronio's obsession with distant lands by dressing themselves up as Turks. In one of only two numbers that survive from what was, in any case, a short act, Volpino greets Sempronio with amusing mock-Turkish words and music, 'Salamalica, Semprugna cara'. It features several musical elements that, in combination, were perceived in the 18th century as typically Turkish: 2/4 time, fast tempo, repeated alternation of the first and third degrees of the scale, and references to the Lydian mode. Haydn, however, does not here use the triangle, cymbals, and bass drum associated with Turkish music, drawing attention to the fact that *Lo speziale,* in general, is less imaginatively scored than later operas. JAR

'L' Ours' symphony. Nickname for Symphony no. 82, originating in the late 18th or early 19th centuries. The opening of the finale, with its exaggerated drone bass line and four-square melody, was thought to resemble a bear dance. JH

Lukavec (Unter-Lukavec) (Dolní Lukavice). A village 15 km. (10 miles) south of Pilsen (Plzen) in Bohemia (Czech Republic). The MORZIN FAMILY, for whom Haydn worked between 1757 (possibly slightly later) and 1761, had a summer palace there. Built early in the 18th century it had a chapel in a contiguous wing and was set in extensive pleasure and ornamental gardens. It still survives, though now empty and in a state of decay.

M

Mahler, Gustav (b. 7 July 1860; d. 18 May 1911). Like many of his contemporaries Mahler regarded Haydn and Mozart as important precursors of Beethoven rather than as significant composers in their own right. Nevertheless, his international career as a conductor did include reasonably frequent performances of a few works by Haydn. During his second season in charge of the opera house in Vienna, 1898–9, he directed six performances of *Der Apotheker* (a German version of *Lo speziale*), apparently accompanying the recitatives on an upright piano. As an overture he used the 'London' symphony (no. 104). The renowned Viennese critic Eduard Hanslick (1825–1904) found the production delightful, remarking that the symphony was performed 'in an unforgettable manner, perhaps never equalled anywhere in the world'. Mahler also conducted other London symphonies and a string orchestra version of the variations on 'Gott erhalte Franz den Kaiser' from the quartet op. 76 no. 3. Dissatisfied with the recitatives in *The Creation* he provided his own. Press reports of the time suggest that Mahler was able to create an appropriate lightness of texture in his performances of Haydn despite using large forces, a notable characteristic of his own symphonies.

Mandini, Paolo (*fl.* 1777–90). Baritone who began singing comic opera in Italy in 1777 and five years later joined the Eszterháza troupe on a one-year contract (November 1783–October 1784). Although he created the role of Idreno in Haydn's *Armida*, most of his roles were in comic opera. After contributing intensively but briefly to operatic life at Eszterháza he sang for a year in Vienna and then returned to Italy. He later sang in Paris and St Petersburg. JAR

Bartha and Somfai.
HCRL/2.

Mandyczewski, Eusebius (b. 18 Aug. 1857; d. 13 July 1929). Austrian musicologist of Romanian birth. At the University of Vienna he studied with Hanslick and Nottebohm, and later acted as an amanuensis to Brahms. In 1887 he succeeded Pohl as archivist of the Gesellschaft der Musikfreunde, a position he held until his death. He contributed notably to scholarship on Haydn, Beethoven, Schubert, and Brahms. For the complete edition of Haydn's works published by Breitkopf & Härtel he prepared *The Creation*, *The Seasons*, and three volumes of symphonies (nos. 1–12, 13–27, and 28–40). His most familiar scholarly contribution are the numbers 1 to 104 given to Haydn symphonies, part of a thematic catalogue of orchestral music composed and attributed to Haydn that appeared in 1907 in the complete edition (Series 1, vol. 1).

'Mann und Weib'. *See* DER GEBURTSTAG.

Mara, Gertrud Elisabeth (b. 23 Feb. 1749; d. 20 Jan. 1833). German soprano, renowned for her commanding style, the agility of her voice, and the expressive intelligence she brought to cantabile singing. Despite her temperamental nature she was constantly in demand in London from 1784 as a concert and oratorio singer, as a prima donna in Italian opera, and even on the stage of the English playhouse. In 1792 and 1794 she appeared alongside Haydn at Salomon's series, and the following year Haydn attended her benefit, where he witnessed an unpleasant altercation with her estranged husband. Haydn never wrote anything for her to sing. SMcV

HCRL/3.
C. Price, J. Milhous, and R. D. Hume, *Italian Opera in Late Eighteenth-Century London*, vol. i: *The King's Theatre, Haymarket 1778–1791* (Oxford, 1995).

March for the Prince of Wales. *See* WIND-BAND MUSIC §4.

Mare clausum. Title misleadingly given to Haydn's INVOCATION OF NEPTUNE, the text of which comes from a preface to a 17th-century treatise called *Mare clausum*.

'Maria, Jungfrau rein' (Mary, chaste maiden) (Hob. deest). An ADVENT ARIA for soprano, two violins, and continuo. A lengthy aria in a da capo structure in which the occasionally rather awkward word-setting strongly suggests that the text is not the original one. It has been conjectured that the work is a contrafactum of an aria from one of the three lost comic operas or three lost secular cantatas that Haydn composed in the early 1760s. Whether Haydn himself was responsible for the change of text cannot be established; also the date is not known.

I. Becker-Glauch, 'Neue Forschungen zu Haydns Kirchenmusik', *HS* 2/3 (1970), 167–241.

'Maria Theresa' mass. *See* 'THERESIENMESSE'.

Maria Theresia (b. 13 May 1717; d. 29 Nov. 1780). Queen of Bohemia and Hungary, Archduchess of Austria, etc. Eldest daughter of Emperor Karl VI and Elisabeth Christine von Braunschweig-Wolfenbüttel; they had looked forward in vain to the birth of a son. Through the arrangement known as the Pragmatic Sanction a woman's right to succeed to the imperial throne was established and made known to the leading European powers. Nevertheless, when the 23-year-old princess succeeded her father after his unexpected death in 1740, she was faced with a dangerous front of enemies, France, Prussia, and Bavaria. In the following War of Austrian Succession (1740–8) she was able to defend her inheritance with considerable success, aided by the support of George II who was particularly anxious to limit the influence of France. Her subsequent disillusionment with this traditional alliance led to an alliance with France in the Seven Years War (1756–63). This culminated in the reluctant handing over of Silesia to Prussia.

Away from these two wars Maria Theresia pursued the peaceful strategy of diplomacy through dynastic marriage. Of the 16 children she bore her beloved husband, Franz Stephan (1708–65), six died in infancy or childhood, three remained unmarried, but no fewer than five were married to members of the Bourbon dynasty in France, Spain, and Italy. The Habsburg presence in Italy was to be a continuing facet of Austrian politics with notable consequences, too, on the development of music (especially opera) in Austria.

Within Austria itself the empress introduced largely successful measures to stimulate the economy, commerce, and to improve the finances of the state. However, the centralizing nature of various administrative reforms was counter-productive, as were the attempts to break the power of the Hungarian nobility. The reforms of the legal system and of the education system, the creation of a loyal bureaucracy with a pronounced middle-class element, an equally loyal and dependent clergy, and, not least, the influence of the empress's own deeply religious views on the reform of the Church all reveal the influence of the Enlightenment and paved the way for the more radical reforms of her son, JOSEPH II.

As countless letters and marginalia in documents demonstrate, Maria Theresia was a tireless administrator, but she was also a high-spirited woman. She loved banquets, balls, carousels, masquerades, sleigh-rides, fireworks, target-shooting, but not hunting. Like her ancestors she was highly musical. Her teacher was WAGENSEIL and her art instructor was Daniele Bartoli. In poetry she was instructed by METASTASIO, as were her children. She liked dancing and had a pleasant voice. According to Burney, at the early age of 5 she was already singing an aria in the court theatre and regularly took part in the private performances of opera that occurred at court.

As a choirboy in St Stephen's Haydn would have sung at many church services in the presence of the empress and, according to DIES, she was familiar with Haydn's solo voice. Haydn himself in old age recalled being caught clambering on scaffolding in Schönbrunn by Maria Theresia and being beaten for his impudence. During the mid-1750s, when Haydn was leading the life of a jobbing musician in Vienna, he was several times engaged to play the violin in fancy dress balls given at the court for Maria Theresia's many children.

In 1746 the musical personnel of the imperial court had been divided into two, church music and opera. At the time Italian opera was the preferred form of theatrical music but during the 1750s, in response to the closer political ties between Austria and France that were being fashioned by Kaunitz, opera in French by Gluck and Starzer largely displaced Italian opera. By 1772 operatic taste had swung back; Maria Theresia wrote to her sister-in-law Maria Beatrix in Modena that 'Gluck and the others can occasionally make a good piece or two, but overall I prefer always the Italians. In instrumental music there is a certain Haydn, who has unusual ideas, but he is just a beginner.' These are altogether rather jaundiced comments from someone who was a keen lover of music; Gluck was Vienna's leading opera composer and Haydn at the age of 40 was hardly a beginner. Perhaps this remark reflected the increasingly introverted nature of musical life at court, which until the accession of Franz II in 1792 was to regard Haydn's music with indifference.

Nevertheless in 1773, only a year after her dismissive remark, Maria Theresia made a three-day visit to Eszterháza during which she heard Haydn's *L'infedeltà delusa* and *Philemon und Baucis*. Symphony no. 48, which has the nickname 'Maria Theresia', was once thought to have been composed specially for the empress but there is no foundation to the story, though she may, of course, have heard it at some time. Equally apocryphal is the comment attributed to the empress that in order to hear good Italian opera she had to travel to the Esterházy court. GM

A. von Arneth, *Geschichte Maria Theresias*, 10 vols (Vienna, 1863–79).

P. Dickson, *Finance and Government under Maria Theresia 1740–1780* (Oxford, 1987).

W. Koschatzky (ed.), *Maria Theresia und ihre Zeit in Bildern und Dokumenten* (Munich, 1979).

HCRL/1 and 2.

G. and G. Mraz, *Maria Theresia. Ihr Leben und ihre Zeit in Bildern und Dokumenten* (Munich, 1979).

'Maria Theresia' symphony. Nickname traditionally given to Symphony no. 48, first found in 1812 in GERBER's dictionary. It was subsequently assumed that the symphony was specially composed for the visit of Maria Theresia to Eszterháza in 1773. However, in the 1960s a manuscript copy from Martin in Slovakia was discovered with the date 1769, a new *terminus ad quem* for the symphony. It could, of course, have been played during the 1773 celebrations. JH

Mariazell. A small town, nestling at an altitude of 850 m (2,800 ft) in the Styrian hills, 50 km (30 miles) to the south of the Danube. To this day the church is a favoured place of pilgrimage. A Benedictine priory was founded in 1157 and work on the church began in 1200. In the 14th century a shrine to the Madonna was built, probably at the instigation of Ludwig I and Elizabeth of Hungary. The centrepiece was a rustic carving, some 47 cm (20 in.) high, of the Virgin Mary and the infant Jesus. Early in the 18th century the carving, usually clothed, was placed in an ostentatious setting of solid silver designed by Fischer von Erlach. Already by the end of the 14th century Mariazell had become a favoured destination for pilgrims; by the middle of the 18th century the number of pilgrims who visited the town from all over the Austrian territories regularly numbered over 100,000 a year, and from all ranks of society. The Esterházy family had a close connection with Mariazell and were regular benefactors.

Haydn made the journey from Vienna in 1750, walking with his fellow pilgrims for five or six days. According to Griesinger and Dies he wanted to sing in the choir at the church but the music director refused permission; undaunted, Haydn sneaked into the choir during a service, waited for a solo section, deftly snatched the part from a chorister, and proceeded to sing the solo to everybody's delight and surprise. It is entirely likely that Haydn made more than one pilgrimage to Mariazell.

Haydn was to write two masses associated with pilgrimages to Mariazell, both entitled *Missa Cellensis* (literally the 'mass for Zell'). Both were likely to have been performed in Vienna at services associated with the pilgrimages, rather than at Mariazell itself.

'Mariazeller' mass. *See* MISSA CELLENSIS.

Marie Therese (b. 6 June 1772; d. 3 March 1807). Wife of Emperor Franz II (I), daughter of KING FERDINAND I OF NAPLES and the two Sicilies (from the House of Bourbon) and of Maria Carolina, and granddaughter of EMPRESS MARIA THERESIA. Franz and Marie Therese were first cousins. As the wife of the Holy Roman Emperor she was, from his accession in 1792, the empress. In 1804, following Napoleon's assumption of the title of Emperor of France, Franz II became the first emperor of Austria (hence Franz I) and Marie Therese the first empress.

It was a happy marriage that produced 12 children. Of the daughters, Marie Louise (1791–1847) became the wife of Napoleon in 1810 following the humiliating defeat of Austria, Leopoldine (1797–1826) was Empress of Brazil from 1822, and Karolina Ferdinanda (1801–1832) married Crown Prince Friedrich August of Saxony in 1819. Between the years 1800 and 1805 emperor and empress were often apart because of the Napoleonic campaigns; they wrote affectionate daily letters to each other, sometimes twice a day. Marie Therese cursed the 'loathsome French', her longing for her 'beloved violinist' (as she liked to call her husband) was 'beyond words', and the day when a temporary truce in the war came to an end was a 'day of death'.

Marie Therese was a high-spirited, happy woman. She loved dancing, masquerades, *tableaux vivants*, shadow puppetry, conjuring tricks, carnival balls, and travelling with her husband when circumstances allowed. Particularly treasured were the times spent in the summer palace at Laxenburg where there was a romantic fortress and where the couple could wander in a virtually boundless park. She had endless imagination for inventing cheerful games, although they did not always please the more stuffy courtiers and earned her some rebuke; they felt she did not take the difficult times seriously enough. Another accusation was more grievous: that she interfered in political decisions and aggravated the often strained relationship between the emperor and his brother, Archduke Karl (1771–1847), who was in overall charge of the war against the French.

Maria Therese shared a love of music with her husband, who played the violin and occasionally the xylophone at musical house parties. The empress played the piano and had a pleasant, well-trained soprano voice. From two musical diaries she kept between 1801 and 1803 it is evident that Haydn's music was performed at private concerts at the Viennese court on several occasions, with professional singers performing alongside the empress (in *The Creation*, for instance) and her brother-in-law, Ferdinand, Archduke of Tuscany. Her estate included an Italian version of the *The Creation* prepared in 1798 (three years before the published version by CARPANI) and two drafts of a libretto for an oratorio entitled *Guidizio finale* (Last Judgement) which the empress originally hoped Haydn would set and which she then passed on to CHERUBINI. Divided into three parts and with three angels as interlocutors the libretto was expressly modelled on that of *The Creation*. Haydn wrote his second Te Deum (Hob.XXIIIc:2) for the empress; a copy of the Mass in B♭ (Hob.XXII:12) owned by the empress occasioned the nickname 'Theresienmesse', even though the work was written for PRINCESS MARIA HERMENEGILD ESTERHÁZY; and her name headed the list of subscribers to the published edition of *The Creation*. When she objected to the quotation of a theme from the oratorio in the Gloria of the 'Schöpfungsmesse', Haydn felt obliged to provide an alternative setting of the passage for use in the imperial court. Marie Therese was also the dedicatee of Beethoven's Septet, op. 22.

The empress remained an uncompromising enemy of Napoleon. Fortunately for her she was not to live to witness the politically sacrificial marriage of her eldest daughter, Marie Louise, to the beast (as she called him). Towards the end of her 12th pregnancy she contracted pleurisy. The baby was born prematurely and died; a week later at the age of only 35 the mother, too, died. GM

HCRL/4 and 5.

E. Wertheimer, *Die drei ersten Frauen des Kaisers Franz* (Leipzig, 1893).

Marpurg, Friedrich Wilhelm (b. 21 Nov. 1718; d. 22 May 1795). German writer on music and composer. Based in Berlin his musical allegiances were firmly rooted in the first half of the century and he was discomfited by newer trends. While Haydn would have thought his views on musical taste old-fashioned he valued his books on music theory. He owned copies of the *Anleitung zum Claiverspielen der schönen Ausübung der heutigen Zeit gemäss* (Berlin, 1755) and the *Handbuch bey dem Generalbasse und der Composition* (Berlin, 1755–8).

D. A. Sheldon, *Marpurg's Thoroughbass and Composition Handbook: A Narrative Translation and Critical Study* (New York, 1989).

Martines, Marianna von (b. 4 May 1744; d. 13 Dec. 1812). Haydn's first known pupil who later became a respected composer, pianist, and musical hostess in Viennese society. Her family was well connected at the imperial court and Metastasio was her tutor. It was through him she was sent, at the age of 7, to have keyboard and singing lessons from Haydn, which lasted three years. She studied counterpoint with Giuseppe Bonno (1711–88) who was in the service of the imperial court. In adulthood she composed keyboard concertos, sonatas, chamber cantatas, several items of church music, and an oratorio. No further contact between her and Haydn is known.

A. P. Brown, 'Marianna Martines' Autobiography as a New Source for Haydn's Biography During the 1750's', *HS*, 6/1 (1986), 68–70.

I. Godt, 'Marianna in Vienna: A Martines Chronology', *Journal of Musicology*, 16 (1998), 136–58.

Mass See overleaf.

Mass in Time of War. *See* MISSA IN TEMPORE BELLI.

Mattheson, Johann (b. 28 Sept. 1681; d. 17 April 1764). German composer and writer based in Hamburg. His early training in music bore fruit in a series of publications reflecting his varied and prolific career and showing his modernist musical sympathies, sparking a professional dispute with JOHANN JOSEPH FUX. According to GRIESINGER and DIES, Mattheson's encyclopedic treatise *Der vollkommene Capellmeister* (1739) was one of two important works studied by Haydn in the 1750s, the other being Fux's *Gradus ad Parnassum*. SW

G. J. Buelow and H. J. Marx (eds), *New Mattheson Studies* (Cambridge, 1983).

E. C. Harriss, *Johann Mattheson's "Der vollkommene Capellmeister": A Revised Translation with Critical Commentary* (Ann Arbor, 1981).

mechanical organ. An organ with an attached facility for storing music and mechanically reproducing it. With the advances in clockwork technology in the 18th century came a similar advance in the precision and reliability of mechanical organs; such instruments often constituted the base of a clock, whose mechanism could be made to activate the organ. This association lies behind the term musical clock. The more neutral term mechanical organ is preferred by many authorities for three reasons: first, the organs could usually be activated independently of any clock; second, mechanical clocks were sometimes attached to other kinds of furniture such as mirrors and writing desks; and third, the music produced by musical clocks was not always from a mechanical organ.

Musical clocks were fashionable in Haydn's lifetime. Prince Nicolaus Esterházy, who was fascinated by clocks in general (he owned some 400 timepieces), is known to have had six musical clocks at Eszterháza in the 1780s. A viola player in Haydn's orchestra, Christian Specht (1742–1808), was entrusted with their care. The Esterházy librarian, PRIMITIVUS NIEMECZ, began to build mechanical organs as a hobby in the 1780s, at least initially assembling them from parts ordered from Vienna, and it was Niemecz who asked Haydn to provide music for some of his instruments. Three mechanical organs by Niemecz have survived that play music by Haydn. Although they differ in size, they were all probably originally attached to a clock and they all share the same basic mechanism. A clockwork mechanism activated a bellows and the turning of a single permanent cylinder; pins carefully placed on the cylinder guided the air to the appropriate flute pipes which sounded at four-foot pitch. Recordings of all three mechanical organs have been made and provide a unique aural

[*cont. on p.* 232]

mass

Haydn composed 14 settings of the Ordinary of the mass, all designed to be performed liturgically. For a man who was a committed and unquestioning Catholic and whose formative years were spent as choirboy in Hainburg and in Vienna, it is appropriate that his first and last major compositions were masses. Otherwise, biographical circumstances that led the composer to devote most of his adult life to other genres meant that Haydn's masses are not distributed evenly across his life but are clustered in certain periods.

Two short settings date from about the time of his dismissal from St Stephen's in 1749, the MISSA 'RORATE COELI DESUPER' and the MISSA BREVIS, both of which reflect the ecclesiastical music circles in which the teenage Haydn moved. Gradually over the next few years Haydn came to be associated more with instrumental music, even though he continued to earn some of his freelance income as a violinist, organist, and singer in church services. It was because of his prowess as a composer of instrumental music that Haydn was engaged by the Morzin family and then by the Esterházy court. Consequently no masses were composed by Haydn in the 1750s and early 1760s. When Haydn became full Kapellmeister at the Esterházy court in 1766, assuming additional responsibility for church music, he might have expected to devote himself extensively to sacred music, including the composition of masses. Between 1766 and 1772 Haydn did, indeed, compose four masses but at least one work, the MISSA CELLENSIS IN HONOREM BVM, was composed independently of his duties at the court and nothing is known about the circumstances that led to the composition of the MISSA 'SUNT BONA MIXTA MALIS' and the MISSA IN HONOREM BVM; they could have been intended for the court, or for performance in a church in Eisenstadt, or even performance in Vienna, since circumstantial evidence suggests that Haydn kept in touch with his church friends in the capital. Only the *Missa Sancti Nicolai*, presumed to have been performed on 6 December 1772, the nameday of Prince Nicolaus, can be associated unequivocally with the Esterházy court.

Between 1772 and 1790 Haydn composed only two masses, neither for the court. The MISSA BREVIS SANCTI JOANNIS DE DEO was written for the church of the BARMHERZIGE BRÜDER in Eisenstadt and the MISSA CELLENSIS (a second work with this title) was commissioned by Anton Liebe von Kreutzner, a retired military officer living in Vienna.

Haydn's most productive period as a composer of masses occurred in the years after his second visit to London. Between 1796 and 1802 he composed six works of great individuality, generally recognized as one of the enduring achievements of sacred music in this period: MISSA SANCTI BERNARDI D'OFFIDA, MISSA IN TEMPORE BELLI, MISSA IN ANGUSTIIS ('Nelson' mass), 'THERESIENMESSE', 'SCHÖPFUNGSMESSE', and 'HARMONIEMESSE'. Scholarship has traditionally linked these six masses with the annual celebrations, in September, of the nameday of PRINCESS MARIE HERMENEGILD ESTERHÁZY. However, actual evidence for such an association exists for only the last three masses. The *Missa in tempore belli* and the *Missa in angustiis*, which share references to warfare, may have been composed for a movable feast in September associated with commemorating the defeat of the Turks in 1683, and the *Missa Sancti Bernardi d'Offida* had as another focus, the feast of St Bernard (11 September). Since September was a high point in the social calendar of the Esterházy family, the performance of a new mass by the court Kapellmeister at this time of the year became a tradition even if not all six works were directly connected to the princess's nameday.

The musical ambition of each mass was determined by its function within the liturgical practice that governed the initial performance. Broadly there were two types of masses. The missa brevis was intended for routine services, and musical settings would typically be very short, require small musical forces (two violins, bass, and organ would be a routine minimum), be musically constrained (avoiding elaborate fugues, for instance) and, most perfunctorily, in the two longer movements of the Ordinary, the Gloria and the Credo, set several clauses of the text simultaneously in an incomprehensible babble. Haydn used the title missa brevis for two works, the early F major mass and the *Missa brevis Sancti Joannis de Deo*; the *Missa 'Rorate coeli desuper'* is a third prime example. The other kind of mass, designed for more important feast days, was termed a missa solemnis or, more prosaically, missa longa. Haydn himself never used either of these titles for any of his masses, though manuscript sources in various religious institutions in Austria often applied them to their copies as an appropriate indication of scale and scope. Lasting over an hour, the *Missa Cellensis in honorem BVM* most obviously warrants the label, but the six late masses and the *Missa in honorem BVM* could also be regarded as being of the 'solemnis' type.

The degree of celebration associated with a particular mass was also, in part, a matter of sonority, governed in particular by the presence or absence of trumpets and timpani. The three missa brevis masses do not have trumpets and timpani while the *Missa Cellensis in honorem BVM* and the six late masses do; in their original scoring the *Missa in honorem BVM* and the *Missa Sancti Nicolai* do not have trumpets and timpani but additional, authentic parts for the instruments do exist, probably designed for performance on a more festive occasion than the first one. Even the shortest mass could be dressed up with trumpets and timpani for an important service; for instance many churches and monasteries in Austria had copies of Haydn's *Missa brevis Sancti Joannis de Deo* with supplementary parts for trumpets and timpani.

Strongly associated with sonority was the choice of key for a mass. Church masses in Haydn's Austria were overwhelmingly in C major, the most common key for trumpets at the time. However this broad characteristic can only be partly perceived in Haydn's masses. Only three works from the 14 are in C major, an unusually low proportion. The most common key is B♭ major, used in five masses of which four are from the period 1796–1802. In these late masses in B♭ Haydn created a new association of trumpets, timpani, and key, which a writer in the *Allgemeine musikalische Zeitung* described as 'of the greatest strength, dignity, and gravity'.

Only a minority of Haydn's masses were called simply 'missa' on the autograph, the variety of titles reflecting a range of common practices. The name of a saint (Nicholas, John, and Bernard) whose feast day was commemorated in the first performance is found in three masses; a further two refer to the Blessed Virgin Mary, reflecting performance on one of the many Marian feast days in the church calendar, and two refer to a place, Mariazell (Cellensis), associated with the first performance. As these masses circulated elsewhere they tended to lose their original titles, replaced by more generic ones such as 'Missa in G' or 'Missa solemnis in G'. Occasionally, however, individual works acquired a second, even third specific title as a result of a particular performance. Until the partial autograph of Haydn's *Missa Cellensis* was rediscovered in 1975 that mass was usually known as the *Missa Sanctae Caciliae*, from a performance on St Cecilia's day. The original title of the *Missa in honorem BVM* indicates that it was one of the ones first performed on a Marian day but in the *Entwurf-Katalog* Haydn called it *Missa Sancti Josephi*, probably recalling a performance on St Joseph's day, 19

March, his own nameday. Many of the masses in the 19th century acquired a further layer of ascriptions, nicknames that reflected in some measure a musical feature or the circumstances of some performance, such as the use of a full wind section in the 'Harmoniemesse' or a musical quotation from *The Creation* in the 'Schöpfungsmesse'.

In the same way as Haydn's own religious beliefs were part of pervasive culture, his settings of the mass were particular manifestations of a wide repertoire and a long tradition. Generic practice plays a more determining part in the composition of a Haydn mass than it does in the composer's symphonies, quartets, operas, and other works. For Haydn and his listeners recurring formal and stylistic features, such as fugues at the end of the Gloria and Credo, expansive lyrical settings of the Benedictus, and starting the Agnus Dei in a minor key, were welcome and comfortable characteristics, and no matter how often Haydn used the many local clichés of word-painting, such as the juxtaposition of energetic *forte* and slow moving *piano* for 'Gloria in excelsis Deo' (Glory to God in the highest) and the succeeding 'Et in terra pax' (And peace on earth) or chromatic writing for 'Crucifixus' in the Credo, the music had an appeal that was as timeless as the surroundings in which it was performed. But Haydn's masses are distinguished by an individuality of expression that reflects his own committed belief and musical imagination. The full drama and resonances of the text are realized in a way that generally eluded him in his operas.

Compared with the composer's symphonies, quartets, keyboard sonatas, keyboard trios, operas, and songs, the number of masses composed by Haydn is small. As extant copies and catalogue references show, however, they were widely distributed in Catholic areas in Haydn's lifetime, from Bavaria to Romania, Italy to Poland, and Spain to Mexico. As a consequence of the composer's general popularity at the turn of the century, musicians in Protestant areas too became interested in this music, which they saw as transcending its Catholic origins. In England LATROBE and NOVELLO began the process of making individual works well known in that country while Breitkopf & Härtel's publication of seven masses nurtured the curiosity of all Germans, whether Protestant or Catholic. *See also* LITURGY.

O. Biba, 'Die Kirchenmusikalischen Werke Haydns', in *Joseph Haydn in seiner Zeit* [Exhibition catalogue] (Eisenstadt, 1982), 142–51.

C. M. Brand, *Die Messen von Joseph Haydn* (Würzburg, 1941).

W. Kirkendale, 'New Roads to Old Ideas in Beethoven's *Missa Solemnis*', *Musical Quarterly*, 56 (1970), 665–701.

H. C. Robbins Landon and D. W. Jones, *Haydn: His Life and Music* (London, 1988).

J. W. McGrann, 'Of Saints, Name Days, and Turks: Some Background on Haydn's Masses Written for Prince Nikolaus II Esterházy', *Journal of Musicological Research*, 17 (1998), 125–210.

B. MacIntyre, *The Viennese Concerted Mass of the Early Classic Period* (Ann Arbor, 1986).

J. Webster, 'Haydn's Sacred Vocal Music and the Aesthetics of Salvation', in D. Sutcliffe (ed.), *Haydn Studies* (Cambridge, 1998), 35–69.

record of music at the Esterházy court. The three instruments and their repertoire are described below; many of the Haydn pieces appear on more than one organ.

The first is an instrument made by Niemecz in 1792. Formerly owned by Hanz Urban in Vienna, it was sold to an unknown purchaser in 1962 and its present location is unknown. Attached to a clock it had 17 pipes covering a range of two octaves, and played 12 pieces of music. Five were provided by Haydn: Hob.XIX: 9, 10, 17, 18, and 24.

A second mechanical organ survives without its clock and is owned by the Teubner family in Vienna. The organ is undated. According to a family tradition it was thought to date from 1772 and is still sometimes referred to as the '1772' instrument. It is certainly later than 1789 and probably dates from 1796. It has 25 pipes, covering a range of two octaves and a tone, and plays 16 pieces. Eight were provided by Haydn: Hob.XIX:9–16.

The third mechanical organ also survives without its clock and is on loan to the instrument collection of the Stadtmuseum, Munich. It is dated 1793 and is thought to have been the property of Prince Paul Anton Esterházy. It has 29 pipes, covering a range of two octaves and a fifth, and plays 12 pieces. Ten were provided by Haydn: Hob.XIX: 11–16 and XIX:27–30.

Since the three mechanical organs provide direct aural evidence of performances from Haydn's time, modern musicians have been tempted to use them as evidence for performance practice, particularly tempo and the realization of ornaments. This exercise is fraught with problems since the musical clocks probably played the music much faster than live instrumentalists, for this was part of their charm, and consistency in matters of ornamentation was not a priority for Niemecz, to judge from the transcriptions of the performances that have been made.

A. W. J. G. Ord-Hume, *Joseph Haydn and the Mechanical Organ* (Cardiff, 1982).
JHW XXI.

mechanical organ music. Seventeen short movements by Haydn were composed for three mechanical organs built by NIEMECZ. Haydn seems to have received the first request in 1788, and perhaps as many as 12 pieces were written in that and the following year. The remainder were probably written in 1793, in the period between the two London visits. Haydn wrote the music in the treble clef on a single stave; manuscript sources in the hand of Niemecz and the aural evidence provided by the mechanical organs themselves show that some alterations were made to Haydn's original music.

Three types of movements are found more than once: minuets (though Haydn does not label them as such), binary movements in 2/4; and short rondo-like structures. As well as incorporating more decoration than would be possible or deemed tasteful in equivalent movements in quartets, sonatas, and symphonies, the structural repeats are always written out so as to provide even more embellishment; passages in parallel thirds and cadential flourishes are highly characteristic. One of the earliest pieces is a fully-fledged fugue in three parts (Hob.XIX:16) complete with several stretto entries and a climactic pedal point; maybe this apparently inappropriate music, played as the clock struck the hour, was prompted by the common inscription on clocks of 'tempus fugit'.

Five pieces are Haydn's own arrangements of movements from other works: the minuet from the quartet op. 54 no. 2, the finale of op. 64 no. 5, the finale from op. 71 no. 2, the finale from Symphony no. 99, and the minuet from Symphony no. 101. The last-mentioned work was partly composed by Haydn in 1793 in readiness for his forthcoming, second visit to London. Its most celebrated movement turned out to be the slow movement, whose ticking accompanying patterns gave rise to the nickname 'Clock'. Perhaps the idea for the movement was prompted in some way by Haydn's contemporary concern with providing music for Niemecz's latest musical clock.

Melk. Benedictine abbey located 80 km.(50 miles) west of Vienna on a promontory overlooking the Danube. Its wealth, influence, and the strong musical patronage of its 18th-century prelates, particularly that of abbots Thomas Pauer (1746–62) and Urban Hauer (1763–85), made the abbey fertile ground for the cultivation of Haydn's music. A group of talented performing composers, later known as the Melk Circle—J. G. ALBRECHTSBERGER, Rupert Helm (1748–1826), ROBERT KIMMERLING, Marian Paradeiser (1747–75), Franz Schneider (1737–1812), MAXIMILIAN STADLER, and others—were all zealous students of Haydn's music, as were the abbots themselves. Haydn's early patron, CARL JOSEPH VON FÜRNBERG, who had close ties with the abbey and whose country estate of Weinzierl lay only a few miles to the south-east, could have been one of the conduits through which Haydn's early music was introduced to Melk. Perhaps it was also through his acquaintance with Fürnberg that Abbot Pauer was encouraged to send his nephew Kimmerling to Haydn in Vienna for compositional instruction in 1760–1. The moment Kimmerling returned to Melk to assume the music directorship in 1761, Haydn's music was assured a substantial place in the abbey's repertoire. Valuable copies of the church compositions were acquired, but it was Haydn's instrumental music that drew the greatest attention. The symphonies were diligently collected, so that by 1787 the abbey owned at least 44 of them. Most categories of his works are still represented at Melk in large numbers of 18th-century manuscript copies or prints, many of which have proven invaluable in past and current scholarly editions of Haydn's music. RNF

R. N. Freeman, *The Practice of Music at Melk Abbey: Based upon the Documents, 1681–1826* (Vienna, 1989).
HCRL/1.

'Melk' concerto. Nickame occasionally used to identify the violin concerto in A (Hob.VIIa:3) which was discovered in the abbey of MELK in 1950 by Robbins Landon and colleagues. JH

'Mercury' symphony. Nickname for Symphony no. 43 which arose in the 19th century for no discernible reason. Using the names of Classical gods to identify individual works, rather than to suggest a programmatic content, was an occasional practice in the 18th century, as in symphonies by Pichl (1741–1805) and Anton Wranitzky (1761–1820).

Metastasio, Pietro (Antonio Domenico Bonaventura) (b. 3 Jan. 1698; d. April 1782). Poet and one of the most influential opera librettists of the 18th century; from 1729 until his death he was imperial court poet in Vienna. Many of his nearly 30 librettos for serious opera were set dozens of times in the century; in particular *Alessandro nell' Indie*, *Artaserse*, *Didone abbandonata* were each set over 70 times by various composers. When the young Haydn was in Vienna in the 1750s he lived in the same building as Metastasio (the so-called Michaelerhaus); the court poet introduced him to PORPORA, from whom Haydn had some informal lessons, and to MARTINES. Haydn set his texts less frequently than might be expected. In 1779 he set the poet's *L'isola disabitata* and, in London in 1795, he chose a scene from Metastasio's *Antigono* for a concert aria, 'BERENICE, CHE FAI?' To these might be added the marionette opera, *Dido*, which is a parody of Metastasio's well-known text. JAR

Migliavacca, Giovanni Ambrogio (b. *c.*1718; d. after 1787). Italian librettist and amanuensis to PIETRO METASTASIO in Vienna in the 1750s. From 1752 he worked at the Dresden court. Haydn set Migliavacca's libretto *Acide e Galatea* in 1762. Only fragments survive of the opera, retitled *Acide.* RJR

D. Heartz, *Haydn, Mozart and the Viennese School* (New York, 1995).

'Military' symphony. Nickname for Symphony no. 100. It arose almost immediately after the first performance, given at the Hanover Square Rooms on 31 March 1794, and reflects the sensational slow movement, a march with percussion instruments and, towards the end, an army bugle call. JH

minuet. In conversation with his first biographer, Griesinger, Haydn was asked his view about a knotty issue of theory in the STYLUS A CAPPELLA. He was not particularly interested, dismissing it as pedantic affectation: 'I would rather someone tried to compose a really *new* minuet.' The vast majority of Haydn's instrumental music—symphonies, quartets, keyboard trios, keyboard sonatas, baryton trios, string trios, and miscellaneous divertimenti —contain a minuet movement, over 400 examples in total; the solo concerto is the only genre not to have a minuet movement. In addition Haydn composed over 80 minuets for dancing. His comment to Griesinger shows his fascination for the form and reflects a lifelong interest in probing its musical possibilities.

Initially, the listener might be tempted to regard a minuet movement in a typical symphony or quartet as a pleasant interlude alongside the more weighty concerns of Allegro movements in sonata form or the eloquence of slow movements. Minuets are certainly the shortest movement in a typical symphony or quartet but within this confined space there is mastery of language that is as impressive as that found elsewhere in an instrumental cycle. The mastery is different not only because it is on a small scale—a miniature as opposed to a portrait or landscape—but because it invariably relies on the listener's experience of a familiar set pattern, a dance minuet, to an extent not evident in any other movements.

As a social dance in aristocratic and royal society, the minuet can be traced back to the middle of the 17th century, to the court of Louis XIV. By the middle of the following century, it was the most common social dance in Austria, at all levels of society. Danced by couples who weaved the characteristic Z-shaped pattern, the music had certain standard features necessary for its successful realization as a dance: a steady crotchet pulse in 3/4, usually in the bass; a succession of four-bar phrases (sometimes two-bar phrases); an uncomplicated homophonic texture; and a binary structure of eight bars repeated, followed by a second set of eight bars also repeated. Sometimes the formal units were increased in multiples of four (to 12, 16, etc.) but the essential binary form was maintained. Usually (but not always), there was a contrasting minuet, called variously trio, *alternativo*, or minuet II, which was heard after the main minuet; the main minuet then returned to form an overall form of A, B, and A. Typically in dance halls, single minuets and (if present) associated trios were strung together to form larger additive structures, providing music for dancing sequences that lasted as long as 15 or 20 minutes, even longer on occasions. A typical dance band could be as small as two violins and a bass, or, on the grandest occasion, could involve the fullest available orchestra (including trumpets and timpani).

Given that the minuet was such a familiar feature of social life it is not surprising that it should be included as a major point of attraction in instrumental music that was not composed for dancing. In principle, composers could have taken existing dances and simply incorporated them into instrumental cycles, but there is little evidence to suggest that this happened on any appreciable scale. In the case of a highly imaginative composer like Haydn, someone who was always fascinated by the syntax and grammar of musical language, using one of his dances would have been to risk presenting a movement that was too simple for its context, one that would have, indeed, sounded like an interlude. Nevertheless, the dance background is a determining one, since minuets in Haydn's instrumental music invariably function as gentle distortions of the dance, sometimes fulfilling expectations, sometimes thwarting or undermining them. Living in a dance culture that included the minuet, it was certainly much easier for Haydn's players and listeners to appreciate this intriguing tussle between form and content than it is for modern players and listeners, but the rewards of rekindling such an awareness are considerable.

This creative friction between reality and implied model is present in minuets throughout Haydn's career. The second minuet in the B♭ quartet, op. 1 no. 1, is a good example. It has the overall ternary shape of minuet, trio, and minuet, with each section in binary form. In the main minuet there is a steady emphasis on crotchet beats all the way through and, if one were to focus on the first and second violins, most of the phrases are four-bar phrases. The element of disruption is provided by the viola and cello, which contradict the standard flow by entering before or after the violins. As often in Haydn's minuets and trios, the trio draws attention to the essential character of the minuet, by doing the exact opposite, here a series of obvious four-bar phrases with no disruptive elements at all, a section that could, in fact, be danced.

Haydn's probing of the expectations of the dance involves all aspects of the music, especially phrase patterns, metre, rhythm, and texture. The minuet of Symphony no. 65 is a hilarious mixture of the expected regular phrase patterns in triple metre mixed with music that effectively sounds in 2/2 (though still notated in 3/4). In Symphony no. 84, Haydn evokes a particular kind of minuet, characterized by an exaggerated emphasizing of a regular beat (the minuet in Mozart's Symphony no. 39 is a more familiar example); it is a foot-tapper's and head-nodder's delight until Haydn throws in an empty bar to disrupt the flow and embarrass the listener.

Both these minuets feature a strong sense of reprise when the main melody returns approximately halfway through the second half of the binary structure, akin to the sense of recapitulation in a sonata form. Owing much to Haydn's habitual thought process that sought to exploit qualities inherent in the main theme, the section after the double bar often has the character of a short development section, sometimes, as in no. 104, settling expectantly on the dominant before returning to the main theme.

While contrast is the main function of trio movements, Haydn will sometimes, paradoxically, feature a characteristic in common with the main minuet. The trio of Symphony no. 65 refers hesitantly to the disruptive duple rhythms of the minuet, while the minuets of quartets op. 20 no. 2, op. 50 no. 4, and op. 76 no. 3 take their melodic cue from the minuet before demonstrating a completely different usage for it.

Minuets in quartets show Haydn at his most inventive, exploiting the medium of four single players in a way that would not be possible in a minuet in a symphony. The minuet in op. 54 no. 1 opens with a pair of balancing five-bar phrases, with a deliberately gauche extension to each of the constituent four-bar phrases. The end of a first phrase is often a critical moment in the design, the point where Haydn has to decide whether to provide the obvious expected cadence, hint at it, or completely avoid it in favour of a larger unit. While the phrase patterns, the steady crotchets, and the overall binary structure of the C major minuet in op. 50 no. 2 are recognizably those of a minuet, the texture is so sparse, the harmonies so chromatic, and the tonal pattern so unorthodox (it never modulates to the dominant and the only firm modulation is to D minor) that the movement has a feeling of being a severe exercise in testing the principles of minuet composition; but, in a way that is wholly typical of Haydn's art, it does not sound studied.

More obviously learned, in a formal way, are those minuets by the composer that use CANON: a severe and unrelenting minuet in op. 76 no. 2, a playful one in Symphony no. 23 (making use of the decorative triplets of the old rococo minuet), and a more subdued one in Symphony no. 44. The minuet and the trio in Symphony no. 47 are headed 'Menuet al Roverso' and 'Trio al Roverso', respectively; the music is first read in the normal way and then backwards to provide the second half of the binary structure, a tease for the players and an elegant display of learning by the composer.

As well as minuets that form the third (sometimes second) movement of a four-movement cycle Haydn used movements headed 'Tempo di Menuetto' as finale movements, especially if the instrumental cycle had three or fewer movements. They are reasonably common in string trios, keyboard sonatas, and keyboard trios; some early symphonies have them too (nos. 4, 18, and 30). Such movements have the gait of a minuet but the customary compact structure of minuet and trio is replaced with other approaches, for instance a set of variations in a sonata in A major (Hob.XVI:30) and an expanded ternary form of 135 bars in the piano trio in F♯ minor (Hob.XV:26).

Rather than the Italian word 'minuetto' Haydn, for most of his life, used the French spelling of 'menuet', a habit begun *c.*1760 and a small reflection of the importance of French culture in Austrian society at that time. The occasional alternative of 'menuetto' (e.g. Symphony no. 93) does not necessarily indicate a less ambitious movement, either in size or scope. The minuet movements of the op. 33 quartets were headed 'scherzo' but they are no different from movements headed 'menuet'; certainly they should not be regarded as precursors of the Beethovenian one-in-a-bar scherzo. However, four movements from late in Haydn's career are, indeed, one-in-a-bar movements though the composer continues to use the term minuet: 'Menuet. Presto' in op. 76 no. 1 and op. 77 nos. 1 and 2, and 'Menuetto ma non troppo Presto' in op. 103.

Occasionally in vocal works Haydn will invoke the minuet as a topic that communicates subliminally, the style and certain elements of the structure being sufficient to remind listeners of the dance without the particular title being used. The orchestral introduction to Autumn in *The Seasons* is essentially a minuet, setting the scene for the celebration of the harvest. The 'Osanna' section of the 'Harmoniemesse' with its prominent Scottish-snap figure in triple time recalls a number of minuets by Haydn, such as the ones in Symphony nos. 75 (trio section) and 85. In Symphony no. 46 in B major, Haydn combines both approaches: the third movement is a minuet and trio and then, shortly before the end of the Presto finale, part of the music is played once more, as if it were a quotation, before the movement resumes as a Presto. Given its unfamiliar context it does not here register as a minuet and trio, but, as one authority has suggested, a reminiscence of one, 'a re-experiencing, tinged with nostalgia or regret'.

As the use of the word 'presto' and especially 'ma non troppo Presto' in four of the late quartets indicates, the speed of Haydn minuets varied considerably from a leisurely three-in-a-bar (reflecting the aristocratic origins of the dance) to a brisk one-in-a-bar. Evidence from metronome markings applied to some of Haydn's works early in the 19th century by Czerny (1791–1857) and Crotch suggests that many minuets were performed at a quicker tempo than is customary today. Against this evidence is the cautionary comment made by Haydn to JOHAN FREDRIK BERWALD and his father in 1799 about performances that were too brisk: 'they will ruin my minuets . . . for these minuets are a cross between minuets for dancing and prestos.' The appropriate tempo in many cases is a contentious issue, with some modern performances being three times (or more) as fast as others. It is clear that Haydn and his musicians understood instinctively from their broader experience of the dance what the correct tempo for a particular minuet was and only through much fuller acquaintance with the dance culture of the period will modern interpreters acquire the same easy authority. In the process they will certainly uncover many more of the allusions and ambiguities that inform the minuet in Haydn's instrumental music. *See also* DANCE and SCHERZO.

W. Malloch, 'The Minuets of Haydn and Mozart: Goblins or Elephants?', *Early Music*, 21 (1993), 437–44.

S. Reichart, 'The Influence of Eighteenth-Century Social Dance on the Viennese Classical Style (diss., City University NY, 1984).

G. Wheelock, *Haydn's Ingenious Jesting with Art: Context of Musical Wit and Humor* (New York, 1992).

'Miracle' symphony. A nickname commonly used for Symphony no. 96 in English-speaking countries. It arose *c*.1800 in England, reflecting a performance of a Haydn symphony at the Opera Concert on 2 February 1795 when, during an encore of the finale, a chandelier crashed to the ground; by a 'miracle' no one was hurt. Modern research has shown, however, that the work in question was Symphony no. 102. It was performed in the second part of the concert, which is when the incident took place. The concert had opened with another, unidentifiable symphony by Haydn; it could well have been no. 96, which later wrongly acquired the nickname. When Dies reported the incident and the nickname to Haydn, the composer replied that he knew nothing about either.

JH

Miseri noi, misera patria (Wretched are we, wretched is our country) (Hob.XXIVa:7). A cantata for soprano and orchestra, composed no later than 1786 but not published in Haydn's lifetime; it is possible that it was written as a concert aria, since no suitable operatic context has been found. The text, by an anonymous poet, is an eyewitness account of the horror caused by a fire in a city being attacked by an unspecified conqueror, a typical *opera seria* situation reminiscent of the burning of the Capitol in Metastasio's *La clemenza di Tito*. The leading singer of serious roles at Eszterháza in the 1780s was METILDE BOLOGNA PORTA and the cantata may have been written for her. Haydn took the work with him to London where, almost certainly, it was performed in Salomon's concerts. It has the typical structure of an accompanied recitative followed by a rondò aria (that is a slow section followed by a fast section). The recurring triplet figuration of the Largo is Haydn's frequent response to dejection, but is too underpowered for the powerful images of this particular text. In standard fashion the aria moves from melancholic passivity to a forceful display of valour. Unusually Haydn returns during the course of the Allegro to the text of the Largo section, recalling some of the earlier music too.

Missa brevis in F (Hob.XXII:1). According to Haydn's testimony of 1805/6, when he inscribed the words 'di me Giuseppe Haydn mpria 1749' on the organ part of a late copy, this is his earliest authenticated work, composed in all likelihood in his 18th year while still a chorister in St Stephen's in Vienna, or shortly after his dismissal. Haydn's entry around 1798/9 in the *Entwurf-Katalog* ('Missa brevis in F. a due Soprani') emphasizes the peculiar scoring for two solo sopranos with choral parts for alto, tenor, and bass; only in late sources is a choral soprano part abstracted from the unison of the two sopranos in the tutti sections. The instrumental accompaniment comprises the essential church ensemble of two violins and organ continuo (with violone). On coming across the work again in 1805 the aged Haydn was delighted to discover 'a certain youthful fire' that prompted him to begin the addition of wind instruments, apparently with a view to updating the mass for publication. The parts for flute, two clarinets, two bassoons, two trumpets, and timpani in the expanded orchestration, however, appear to be the work of someone else, perhaps incorporating Haydn's sketches; the most likely author is JOSEPH HEIDENREICH. The mass remained unpublished in Haydn's lifetime.

This early work displays some blemishes of technique that Haydn, swayed by its 'youthful fire', later ignored. It follows procedures characteristic of a missa brevis whereby each item of the Ordinary is set as a single movement, the 'Dona nobis pacem' repeats the music of the Kyrie, and different lines of the text are set simultaneously in the Gloria and Credo. JD

D. McCaldin, 'Haydn's First and Last Work: The "Missa Brevis" in F Major', *Music Review*, 28 (1967), 165–72.

Missa brevis Sancti Joannis de Deo (Hob. XXII:7). Although the autograph of this short mass is extant, rather unusually Haydn did not date it. It was composed in the mid-1770s and certainly no later than 1778. The 'John of God' of the title is a reference to the patron saint of the BARMHERZIGE BRÜDER, a holy order represented in many towns and cities in the Austrian monarchy including Eisenstadt; the feast day of John of God is on 8 March which, presumably, was when the mass was first performed. The Eisenstadt church of the order is much smaller than the Bergkirche, associated with the late masses, and Haydn's mass is scored for the small forces of SATB chorus (from which a solo soprano is detached), two violins, and continuo; both the vocal forces and the instrumental forces could have been performed with one person per part.

Designed for a routine service rather than an important holy day Haydn's missa brevis follows the frequent practice of setting the two longest movements of the Ordinary polytextually, that is several clauses are sung simultaneously so as to proceed through the text in approximately a quarter of the time. Elsewhere, however, Haydn adopts an imaginative and artful approach that overcomes the imposed constraints. The opening and closing movements are both in an adagio tempo, providing a contemplative frame for the work with, in the last movement, the standard division into 'Agnus Dei' and 'Dona nobis pacem' being avoided in favour of one, comparatively expansive movement. To encourage a sense of musical coherence the 'amen' sections at the end of the Gloria and Credo are the same. But it is the Benedictus that offers the spiritual and musical highlight of the setting. It is a luxurious aria for solo soprano accompanied by obbligato organ and strings; the use of the organ gave rise to the later nickname of 'KLEINE ORGELSOLOMESSE'.

As a very useful mass, one that could be performed with limited musical forces, it was widely distributed in manuscript copies in Haydn's Austria, often with added instruments provided by a local composer. MICHAEL HAYDN provided an extended version of the Gloria and this version circulated too.

Missa Cellensis (Hob.XXII:8). Haydn's second mass with this title referring to MARIAZELL; it is sometimes called the 'Mariazeller' mass. It had been commissioned by Anton Liebe von Kreutzner, a retired military officer who was raised to the nobility in 1781. Traditionally it has always been thought that he commissioned this mass from Haydn as part of the celebrations surrounding his ennoblement and that it was performed at a church in Vienna associated with pilgrimages to Mariazell; it is unlikely to have been performed in Mariazell itself since the church had very limited musical resources. There is an alternative view. Kreutzner may have been involved with the Viennese brotherhood responsible for honouring the tradition of Mariazell pilgrimages and the mass could, instead, have been commissioned by the brotherhood for a performance that was unrelated to Kreutzner's ennoblement. Haydn's autograph has the annotation 'Missa Cellensis Fatta per il Signor Liebe de Kreutzner', that is a 'Cellensis mass prepared for Mr Liebe de Kreutzner'. It was composed in 1782 and nothing is known about its first performance.

In C major, the most popular key for Austrian masses, it is an assertive forthright work, though on a smaller scale than the first *Missa Cellensis*. Following a short slow introduction the Allegro of the Kyrie is set out as a monothematic sonata form, with the text 'Christe eleison' constituting the development section (bars 74–99). The Gloria has the standard approach of two fast sections for full forces enclosing a slower section; the latter, beginning with the clause 'Gratias agimus tibi' and ending with 'miserere nobis', has reduced orchestration and is initiated by an extended solo for the soprano. A short but intricate passage of polyphony is used for the concluding 'Amen'.

The Credo, too, has a broad ternary design, brisk sections enclosing a central Largo for 'Et incarnatus est'. That Haydn may have been given a time limit for his setting of the mass is suggested by the return to a fast tempo, where 13 bars are set polytextually, reverting to one, clear text for the important 'et unam sanctam catholicam'. More individual is the character of the concluding fugue, a jaunty 6/8 that is prone to chromaticism, a response that Haydn was to use at a similar point in two of the late masses, the 'Theresienmesse' and the 'Harmoniemesse'.

The generally homophonic progress of the Sanctus appropriately evokes the mystery and the grandeur of the text. Haydn's response to the ensuing Benedictus is more idiosyncratic. Instead of the customary extended lyrical movement in a major key, it begins in G minor with dotted rhythms, trills, and suspensions over a descending bass line, as if it were a Baroque aria. The movement was taken, with some minor adjustments, from Ernesto's aria 'Qualche volte non fa male' from *Il mondo della luna*, where it expressed the rueful sentiment that the course of true love does not run true.

For the threefold statement of the text in the Agnus Dei Haydn turns to C minor and Adagio. The ensuing 'Dona nobis pacem' is a Vivace fugue, the most extensive in the work.

Missa Cellensis in honorem BVM (Hob. XXII:5). From the turn of the 18th century this mass was widely known by the inauthentic title 'Cäcilienmesse' (*Missa Sanctae Caeciliae*), until the discovery in 1975 of an autograph fragment comprising the title page, first Kyrie and Christe. The abbreviated title *Missa Cellensis* that links the mass with the pilgrimage church of MARIAZELL had been entered by Haydn in the *Entwurf-Katalog* (later transferred to the *Haydn-Verzeichnis*) but was ignored by scholars because it was believed that Haydn had confused the mass with another *Missa Cellensis*, from 1782.

The 1766 autograph of Kyrie and Christe, however, is at odds with two other autograph fragments that date from 1769–73, containing part of the Benedictus and the 'Dona nobis pacem'; other documentary evidence together with certain stylistic features suggest that these movements were composed around 1773. Thus this work seems to have been completed in two stages, several years apart. The nature of the work offers one explanation for this unusual state of affairs: the *Missa Cellensis* is a missa solemnis in the Italian manner—Haydn's only mass of this type—in which the text is set as a number of separate solo and tutti movements; such elaborate settings often comprised the Kyrie and Gloria only. Haydn therefore could have considered the earlier part of the mass (the Kyrie and Gloria) as a finished work and eligible for entry in the *Entwurf-Katalog* in 1766/7; the remaining movements were added later for some unknown occasion that required a full setting of the Ordinary. The Cecilian nickname might indicate a performance at one of the celebrations of the Cecilian Congregation in Vienna, held annually on St Cecilia's day (22 November).

Haydn's promotion to full Esterházy Kapellmeister with responsibility for both secular and sacred music on the death of Werner in 1766 and a tradition of Esterházy pilgrimages to Mariazell may have first given rise to this mass. It was Haydn's largest undertaking to date, on a scale, incidentally, that argues against an original performance at Mariazell which had a very limited musical tradition; more likely would have been a performance in one of the larger Viennese churches before or after a pilgrimage.

The mass was published by Breitkopf & Härtel in 1807 in an inauthentic version that omitted the first Kyrie after the opening slow introduction and the movements 'Laudamus te', 'Gratias agimus', and 'Domine Deus' from the Gloria. The *Allgemeine Musikalische Zeitung* judged the work 'indisputably the most serious, the purest, and the most appropriate to the Church' of Haydn's masses that had so far appeared in print and praised in particular the many fugal sections, the 'Qui tollis', the 'Et incarnatus est', and the Benedictus. JD

O. Biba, 'Die Kirchenmusikalischen Werke Haydns', in *Joseph Haydn in seiner Zeit* [Exhibition catalogue] (Eisenstadt, 1982), 142–51.

J. Dack, 'The Dating of Haydn's *Missa Cellensis in Honorem Beatissimae Virginis Mariae*: An Interim Discussion', *HYB* 13 (1982), 97–112.

D. Heartz, *Haydn, Mozart and the Viennese School 1740–1780* (New York, 1995).

Missa in angustiis ('Nelson' mass) (Hob. XXII:11). Mass in D minor composed in 1798 and the third in the series of six late masses performed in Eisenstadt in September and associated with the celebration of Princess Marie Hermenegild Esterházy's nameday. Unusually Haydn's autograph records the date on which he began composing the mass, 10 July, and the day on which he finished it, 31 August. This was a remarkably short period of 53 days compared with the three months that Haydn normally took to compose one of the six late masses. He had started late because of the exhaustion he had felt after the first performances of *The Creation* in April and May. As well as composing against the clock Haydn was faced with another restriction. Prince Esterházy was attempting to reduce expenditure at court and had dismissed the windband (*Harmonie*) that Haydn had been able to call upon for previous masses. His solution was to make a virtue of this situation and to score the mass for strings (always available in Eisenstadt), organ (played by the composer himself), three trumpet players (specially hired for the occasion), and timpani (a local player). The resulting sonority—sparse yet capable also of great theatricality—is a highly distinctive feature of the mass.

The mass is known to have been performed on Sunday, 23 September, but this was not a day associated with the nameday of Princess Marie Hermenegild. The actual nameday, a fixed feast, was 8 September and the alternative, the movable feast of the Most Holy Name of Mary (*Maria Namen*) occurred on the following Sunday, which in 1798 would have been the next day, 9 September. According to the diaries of ROSENBAUM Princess Marie did, indeed, commemorate her nameday that year on the 9th, but there is no mention of a church service. Haydn's evident haste in composing the work suggests a deadline; that the deadline was, in fact, 9 September is borne out by the musical characteristics of the mass. The feast of the Most Holy Name of Mary was also the day when Austrians commemorated the defeat of the Turks in 1683 and Haydn's mass in D minor, with its vivid images of war and victory, would have been particularly suited for that liturgical day. Even though Haydn finished the work nine days before the putative deadline, there was precious little time to copy the parts and rehearse the singers (the solo soprano part is especially demanding) and orchestra; and it seems that the performance was delayed by a fortnight. This postponement might explain, too, why it was not in the usual venue of the Bergkirche, but in the Martinkirche.

When Haydn entered the work in the *Entwurf-Katalog* he called it *Missa in angustiis*, an unusual title which literally means 'Mass in straitened times'. This was never the formal title of the work—Haydn elsewhere used only the word 'missa'—and it may have been a parody title, like the earlier *Missa 'sunt bona mixta malis'*, referring, in this case, to the pressing circumstances in which it was composed. The alternative view that it refers to the difficult political climate in Europe generally at that time is also possible and would tie in with the intended performance on a liturgical day associated with the commemoration of the defeat of the Turks. When, in the 19th century, the work acquired the nickname 'NELSON' MASS commentators began to look for more specific events that could be linked to the composition of the mass and alighted, conveniently, on the stunning victory of the British fleet under Nelson's command over Napoleon's fleet in the Battle of Aboukir in the summer of 1798. But the news of this victory did not reach Austria until September, after Haydn had finished the mass. It is therefore a mistake to make a direct link between the mass and Nelson, and to associate 'straitened times' with specific events in contemporary European history.

What remains is the extraordinary tension and drama of Haydn's mass, one that makes the final resolution into unalloyed joy so uplifting. The first movement is in D minor, the only time in an orchestral mass that Haydn sets the text in a minor key. The unusual orchestral forces make their threatening impact immediately, joined later by the chorus and a particularly theatrical part for the solo soprano.

The Gloria is in a strongly contrasting D major, divided conventionally into three sections, two Allegro sections enclosing an Adagio in B♭ for 'Qui tollis'. The opening motif, declaimed by the solo soprano, recurs in both fast sections (sometimes modified) to provide a strong sense of focus. The 'Qui tollis' beautifully integrates a leading role for the bass soloist, the occasional support of the soprano, short homophonic utterances from the chorus, and an instrumental accompaniment that features solo-writing for the organ. The movement ends with the customary fugue on 'in gloria Dei Patris, amen'.

The opening section of the Credo is layed out as a strict canon at the fifth, sopranos and tenors followed a bar later by altos and basses: an unremitting statement of the first sentences of the creed. The following 'Et incarnatus est', dealing with the mystery of the Virgin Birth, could not be more different. In G major the richness of the harmonic language, the sophistication of the bass line and associated spacing of the chords, together with detailed dynamic indications reveal the kind of mastery developed over the years in the composer's quartets. When the text mentions Pontius Pilate trumpets and timpani enter with ominous fanfare figuration, a foretaste of their appearance in the Benedictus. A fast tempo returns, conventionally, at 'Et resurrexit', but, beginning in B minor, the music modulates widely before magically realighting on the tonic when the solo soprano announces the text 'et vitam venturi saeculi. Amen'. Rather than the expected concluding fugue Haydn allows the soloist and chorus to expand on this material.

The two opening statements of the word 'Sanctus' are each accompanied by an exaggerated *messa di voce*, with trumpets, timpani, and organ marking the apex of the sound, a cleverly calculated realization of the reverence of the word. A change of tempo from Adagio to Allegro occurs at the expected point, 'Pleni sunt coeli'.

Tradition would have led the congregation to expect a Benedictus movement in the major key, characterized by grace and lyricism. Instead Haydn returns to D minor, presenting a nervous movement, simmering with latent power that is finally unleashed when the three trumpets play an insistent fanfare against the contradictory text of 'Blessed is he who comes in the name of the Lord'. Haydn's response to this overwhelmingly dramatic movement is, initially, to ignore it, opting for the customary repeat of the 'Osanna' music from the Sanctus.

In the key of G major, the same as the 'Et incarnatus est', Haydn begins a setting of the Agnus Dei that is comfortingly reassuring, but the second of the three statements, led by the soprano, nearly collapses into accompanied recitative, before regaining its composure. Only in the final Vivace in D major, with its overlapping vocal entries on the text 'Dona nobis pacem' and scurrying violins, is the memory of the D minor of the Benedictus finally dispelled.

The unusual, though highly effective, orchestration of Haydn's mass was born of necessity. A few years later, Haydn's colleague JOSEPH FUCHS provided a more regular orchestra, broadly assigning the role of the organ to one flute, two oboes, two clarinets, one bassoon, and two horns. It is thought that Haydn, at the very least, sanctioned this version.

HCRL/4.

J. W. McGrann, 'Of Saints, Name Days, and Turks: Some Background on Haydn's Masses Written for Prince Nikolaus II Esterházy', *Journal of the Musicological Research*, 17 (1998), 195–210.

Missa in honorem BVM ('Grosse Orgelsolomesse') (Hob.XXII:4). The work belongs to an Austrian tradition of masses with obbligato organ, including works by Dittersdorf, Mozart, and Reutter, as well as Haydn's *Missa brevis Sancti Joannis de Deo*. The key of E♭, however, was unusual for a mass, as was the use of two cors anglais and two horns; the cor anglais was a favourite alternative tone colour in Haydn's music at this time, found in Symphony no. 22, *Acide*, *La canterina*, *Le pescatrici*, *L'incontro improvviso*, and, especially relevant, the Stabat mater.

The surviving fragment of the autograph comprises the Sanctus, Benedictus, and most of the Agnus; Haydn's dating, which according to his usual practice would have been given on the title page and at the head of the Kyrie, is therefore lost. The evidence of the watermarks in the autograph gives 1767–9 as the period of composition; Haydn's entry in the *Entwurf-Katalog* directly follows that for *Missa 'sunt bona mixta malis'* which suggests that it dates from 1768 or 1769.

This mass was therefore among the earliest sacred works which Haydn composed at the Esterházy court after becoming full Kapellmeister following the death of WERNER in 1766; it was obviously intended to be a substantial setting and, in all likelihood, Haydn himself played the organ.

Additional parts for trumpets (clarini) and timpani are transmitted by copies of the mass from the mid-1770s and later, including one made by Haydn's copyist Joseph Elßler senior, which suggests that these parts might be authentic. Other variations in instrumentation, such as the substitution of oboes, clarinets, or violas for the cors anglais, have no authentic basis.

As the unusual key and instrumentation suggest, this is a very individual mass. The plangent sound of cors anglais is complemented by a melodic style that draws on the interval of a rising fourth throughout and often, as in the opening Kyrie, produces a ruminative quality. To counter this, the solo contributions of the organ are highly decorative. It is heard immediately at the beginning of the work, at the end of the Gloria and the Credo, and, most extensively, as an obbligato instrument in the Benedictus; its interjections in the 'Dona nobis pacem' are frivolous rather than decorative, though this is a very characteristic emotion, a defensive nervousness that Haydn was to evoke again, most notably in the concluding moments of the *Missa in angustiis*. JD

D. Heartz, *Haydn, Mozart and the Viennese School 1740–1780* (New York, 1995).

Missa in tempore belli (Mass in time of war) ('Paukenmesse') (Hob.XXII:9). Mass in C major composed in 1796. The title was Haydn's own, appearing on the autograph score, in the *Entwurf-Katalog*, and the *Haydn-Verzeichnis*. During the summer and autumn of 1796, four years into the European war that followed the French Revolution, Austrian forces were under attack on two fronts: the Italian territories were being conquered by French troops under the inspired leadership of the young Napoleon, while on the western front French and Austrian troops were fighting for control of southern Germany. For the first time since the Turkish threat in 1683, Austria sensed an imminent invasion of its heartland. The resonance of 1683, when the infidel was repulsed, was a strong one in Austrian folk memory, commemorated every September in Vienna by a public procession and associated church service. Church music, especially masses and settings of the Te Deum that have unusually prominent parts for trumpets and timpani, sometimes invoked the threat and the triumph of war. Haydn's *Missa in tempore belli*, his *Missa in angustiis*, and Beethoven's *Missa Solemnis* are three well-known examples of this mingling of the bellicose and the religiously triumphant, sentiments reignited during the Napoleonic period.

The *Missa in tempore belli* was first performed in the Piaristenkirche in Vienna on 26 December 1796 as part of a service celebrating the admission to the priesthood of Joseph Franz von Hofmann. His father almost certainly commissioned the work and his post as Imperial Royal Paymaster for War may have encouraged Haydn to write this 'war mass' (as one contemporary report described it). Haydn himself directed the performance.

Haydn also directed a performance on Friday, 29 September 1797, in Eisenstadt. Although this was part of a series of events—church services, concerts, plays, and banquets—that surrounded the celebration of Princess Marie Hermenegild Esterházy's nameday, it was not the actual nameday; that had occurred on 10 September (a movable feast) when a new mass by JOHANN FUCHS had been performed.

'In tempore belli' first suggests itself, very subtly, in the Benedictus. Traditionally, the text of this movement was set indulgently, with an expansive, lyrical style and an atmosphere that was gently ecstatic. Here, however, the opening orchestral introduction in C minor, with its short phrases leading to a powerful climax, suggests an entirely different mood; when the four solo voices enter it is not with expansive melodies but with a comparatively short motif, nervously shared between all four voices. Later, the music turn to C major, yet the memory of the unsettling C minor remains.

In the following Agnus Dei the menace is more explicit: the three traditional statements of the prayer are undermined by ominous drumbeats and insistent fanfares on wind instruments. In an interview with his first biographer, Griesinger, Haydn said the drumbeats should sound 'as if one heard the enemy approaching in the distance'. The drumbeats gave rise to the later German nickname for the work of 'Paukenmesse'.

The opening movements of the mass—Kyrie, Gloria, Credo, and Sanctus—provide a more conventional background to the 'tempore belli', but one that is informed with the full range of techniques and emotions typical of Haydn's six late masses: easy integration of soloists and chorus, simple melodies as well as intricate fugues, and great vitality alongside sections of exquisite beauty (such as the 'Qui tollis' with its obbligato part for cello). When, after the Agnus Dei, wind instruments herald the 'Dona nobis pacem' with a forceful flourish, it is not merely peace that is granted but a victory that transcends the 'tempore belli': a secure vision delivered with irresistible joy. Griesinger's comments on the *Missa in tempore belli* also draw attention to the contrasting passage immediately after the initial flourish of the 'Dona nobis pacem' (bars 57–68) where Haydn 'all at once pathetically interrupts all the voices and instruments'.

The mass was scored for an orchestra of two oboes, two clarinets, two bassoons, two horns, two trumpets, timpani, strings, and organ; Haydn later expanded the contribution of the clarinets and added a part for one flute.

HCRL/4.

J. W. McGrann, 'Of Saints, Name Days, and Turks: Some Background on Haydn's Masses Written for Prince Nikolaus II Esterházy', *Journal of Musicological Research*, 17 (1998), 196–210.

Missa 'Rorate coeli desuper' (Hob.XXII:3). Around 1798–9 Haydn noted in the *Entwurf-Katalog* a 'Missa Rorate coeli desuper in G' with a brief violin incipit, later given in extended form, without title, in the *Haydn-Verzeichnis*. The title derives from a text ('Drop down, ye heavens, from above') found throughout the liturgy for Advent and identifies the work as an Advent 'Rorate' mass. It remained unknown until the 20th century when it was discovered as a work ascribed to Haydn's teacher, GEORG REUTTER. Later, a source attributed to Haydn was discovered, several further sources naming it as a work of Reutter, and two claiming it as the work of Ferdinand Arbesser (c.1719–94). To aggravate an already complicated situation the musical beginning recorded by Haydn is not quite the same as that in the rediscovered sources.

The mass is scored for voices, two violins, and continuo, and displays extreme brevity of setting, with four lines of the text being set simultaneously in the Gloria and the Credo. The many apparently authentic errors of technique suggest an early essay in composition by Haydn, written while still a chorister under Reutter at St Stephen's in Vienna and before the Missa brevis in F. That the errors occur chiefly in the vocal parts above a competent figured bass raises the possibility that Haydn added voices and then accompanying violins to a bass by Reutter, which might explain the contradictory indications of authorship. The unambitious nature of the work itself is not necessarily a reflection of Haydn's inexperience; such apparently perfunctory settings of the Ordinary are characteristic of the period. JD

Missa Sanctae Caeciliae. *See* MISSA CELLENSIS IN HONOREM BVM .

Missa Sancti Bernardi d'Offida (Hob.XXII:10). Mass composed in the summer of 1796 and first performed at the Bergkirche in Eisenstadt in

September. The saint referred to in Haydn's title is Bernard of Offida, a 17th-century Capuchin monk who had been beatified by Pope Pius VI in 1795. The Capuchins celebrated the feast of St Bernard on 11 September, which in 1796 coincided with the movable feast of the Most Holy Name of Mary (Maria Namen). Princess Marie Hermenegild Esterházy usually celebrated her nameday on that day and, though actual evidence is not forthcoming, Haydn's mass was almost certainly first performed on that date.

The celebrations surrounding Princess Esterházy's nameday in 1796 also included a season of plays and operas in the palace in Eisenstadt, given by a visiting theatrical troupe. The repertoire included *Das rotte Käpchen* by Dittersdorf, *Zauberflöte* by Mozart, and a play *Alfred* for which Haydn wrote incidental music.

As the Kyrie of the mass suggests, this is the most openly tuneful of Haydn's late masses. At the beginning of the Sanctus Haydn wrote in the margin next to the tenor line 'Heilig', drawing attention to a well-known German hymn tune 'Heilig, Heilig' (Holy, Holy) that is concealed, like a favoured keepsake, in the middle of the texture. This musical reference occasioned the later nickname for the mass, 'HEILIGMESSE'. A particularly poignant melody, also borrowed, is that in the 'Et incarnatus' section in the Credo. It was first composed as a three-part canon, 'Gott im Herzen' (Hob.XXVIIb:44) that dwells on the homely view that all that is required in life is God and a wife, one for the soul, the other for the body. In the mass the initial presentation of the canon is associated with the mystery of the Virgin Birth, high treble voices, pizzicato strings, and the sound of clarinets. For the ensuing 'Crucifixus' Haydn changes the mood completely, though still using the same melody: male voices and low, bowed strings, and commencing in a minor key.

A distinctive feature of the mass—certainly in comparison with a work like the *Missa in angustiis* ('Nelson' mass)—is the comparatively small role given to the vocal soloists. Most of the setting is led by the choir, and it is they who invariably transform the tunefulness into a radiant energy that is equally captivating. Even the Benedictus movement, traditionally the place where soloists are given an extended role, is set for the chorus. In sonata form largely drawn from the opening theme, it is a remarkable movement in its harmonic control, decoration, as well as lyricism. Unusually, instead of repeating the music of the 'Osanna' at the end of the movement—an awkward corner even in the best of works—Haydn incorporates the text into the continuing music of the Benedictus. Beethoven was to use this same technique in the Benedictus of the *Missa Solemnis*.

The performers are required to negotiate the five flats of B♭ minor in the Agnus Dei, a moment of so-called *Augenmusik* (eye music) as they ask for mercy. The following 'Dona nobis pacem' juxtaposes the customary jubilant response with brief interpolations in a *piano* dynamic and, before the final phrases, a wholly unexpected interrupted cadence.

The orchestra in the *Missa Sancti Bernardi d'Offida* originally consisted of pairs of oboes, clarinets, bassoons, trumpets, and timpani, plus strings and organ; later Haydn added parts for horns and extended those for the clarinets.

HCRL/4.

J. W. McGrann, 'Of Saints, Name Days, and Turks: Some Background on Haydn's Masses Written for Prince Nikolaus II Esterházy', *Journal of Musicological Research*, 17 (1998), 195–210.

Missa Sancti Josephi. An authentic alternative name, hardly ever used, for the *Missa in honorem BVM* ('Grosse Orgelsolomesse'). When Haydn entered the work in the ENTWURF-KATALOG he first wrongly labelled it *Missa Sancti Nicolai*. He amended this to *Missa Sancti Josephi*, perhaps recalling a performance on St Joseph's day, 19 March, his own nameday.

Missa Sancti Nicolai (Hob.XXII:6). Composed in 1772 and almost certainly first performed in that year on 6 December, the Feast of St Nicholas and the nameday of Prince Nicolaus Esterházy. This nameday was customarily celebrated by the performance of a solemn mass in the Eisenstadt castle chapel, although this is the only known occasion when Haydn provided a new mass. It has been suggested that he composed a new mass in 1772 in grateful acknowledgement of the Prince's compliance with the musicians' request to end an unusually extended season at Eszterháza and to return to Eisenstadt, a difficult set of circumstances that had given rise to the 'FAREWELL' SYMPHONY. If this was so, then Haydn, who appears to have been at Eszterháza as late as 20 November, would have had little time for the composition (even if already begun) and preparation of a new mass. Some haste on the part of the composer and his copyist, Joseph Elßler senior, seems to be indicated by Haydn's unusual participation in the preparation of the parts for the first performance, and his adoption of time-saving procedures characteristic of a missa brevis: the simultaneous setting of different lines of text in the Credo and, most obviously, the repetition of the music of the Kyrie for the 'Dona nobis pacem'. The latter procedure is not uncommon in masses by Austrian composers of the time and the fact that the music and the text were not written out for the 'Dona' and had to be improvised would not have posed particular problems for the performers. Subsequently someone (not Haydn, as has been thought) added the notes of the Kyrie and an underlay of the 'Dona' text to the Eisenstadt vocal parts, a completion which occurred no later than 1782 since it is also contained in another copy made by Joseph Elßler, who died in that year. In the autograph Haydn notated a part for viola in the 'Et incarnatus est' and the Benedictus, and directed 'col Basso' thereafter for the second 'Osanna'. The extension of a 'col basso' viola part to all other movements as in the first edition (Simrock, 1806, unauthorized) and some modern editions appears not to have been Haydn's intention, since the original performance parts and the two further authentic copies made by Joseph Elßler conform strictly to the autograph.

The work belongs to a distinct type of mass associated with Advent, often separately catalogued in 18th-century sources as *missae pastorales*, pastoral masses. Traditional musical techniques designed to conjure up the familiar intermingled images of the loving Shepherd, the birth of Christ in a stable, and the shepherds in the field characterize the work, as they do any number of contemporary pastoral masses: gently lilting metres (the opening and closing movements are in 6/4, an unusual metre in the Classical period), simple melodies, and a propensity for the top of the texture to move in parallel thirds, especially downwards. Even the choice of key, G major, is characteristic; it was often favoured for pastoral masses to distinguish them in sonority from the large number of masses in C. Since the main aim is to comfort rather than to uplift, Haydn's time-saving ploy of repeating the music of the Kyrie for the 'Dona nobis pacem' is appropriate. The final impression is the same as the initial one. JD

B. C. MacIntyre, 'Johann Baptist Vanhal and the Pastoral Mass Tradition', in D. W. Jones (ed.), *Music in Eighteenth-Century Austria* (Cambridge, 1996), 112–32.

Missa 'sunt bona mixta malis' (Hob.XXII:2). Haydn's longest essay in the STYLUS A CAPPELLA, composed in 1768. Until the discovery in 1983 of the autograph of the Kyrie and the first part of the Gloria, this mass was known only by Haydn's entry of the title and incipit in the *Entwurf-Katalog* (thence transferred to the *Haydn-Verzeichnis*) and the report of Vincent Novello (not published until 1955) that in 1829 he had bought what was clearly the autograph of the work from Haydn's publisher Artaria in Vienna. Haydn's entry in the *Entwurf-Katalog* implies a finished work; in the autograph, however, the section of the Gloria ('Et in terra' to 'propter magnam gloriam tuam') is followed by five blank pages, which suggests that Haydn took the work no further. One explanation of the contradiction is that the autograph is the beginning of a fair copy of a complete draft; for some reason (the loss of the draft in the fire which destroyed Haydn's house in Eisenstadt in August 1768?) Haydn did not bring the fair copy to completion.

In turning to the *stylus a cappella* for this mass, voices, and organ continuo, Haydn followed a tradition of the imitation of late Renaissance vocal polyphony, albeit with a later sense of harmony and rhythm, as the style particularly suited to sacred music, especially for the periods of Advent and Lent; the inclusion of the Gloria suggests that the mass was intended for Advent. It is possible, however, that Haydn was engaging in a more abstract exercise in composition, exploring a contrapuntal style accorded high status by tradition and theory, at a time of intensive experimentation in his career.

The significance of the title of the mass is unclear. It derives from the proverb 'Sunt bona mixta malis, sunt mala mixta bonis' ('the good mixed with the bad, the bad mixed with the good'), apparently something of a commonplace in Haydn's day: his predecessor at Eisenstadt, GREGOR JOSEPH WERNER, also wrote a *Missa 'sunt bona mixta malis'* (which, however, is not in the *stylus a cappella*); and Haydn himself, according to Griesinger, laconically assessed his own works with the second half of the maxim. Whether with the first part he likewise passed judgement on the finished or unfinished attempt to compose a mass in the strict contrapuntal style remains an open question. JD

D. W. Jones, 'Haydn's *Missa sunt bona mixta malis* and the *a cappella* tradition', in D. W. Jones (ed.), *Music in Eighteenth-Century Austria* (Cambridge, 1996), 89–111.

monothematicism. A term used to describe a technique found in many of Haydn's sonata-form movements in which the first theme in the secondary key area of the exposition is more or less the same as the opening theme of the movement, the only essential difference being that of key. Differences of register, texture, or instrumentation do not alter the readily perceptible relationship of this theme with the initial idea.

Although widely used today, the term monothematicism is in fact both misleading and anachronistic. Few so-called monothematic movements are actually based on a single theme. Theories of sonata form in the 19th century placed great emphasis on the contrast between a movement's opening ('masculine') theme and its 'second' ('feminine') theme, that is, the first theme in the secondary key area. The inherent tension between these two opposing themes was seen as an important source of dialectic. Later theorists dealing with Haydn's monothematic sonata-form movements thus felt the need for a special term to describe movements in which no such overt thematic contrast was present.

For 18th-century composers like Haydn, however, contrast between 'first' and 'second' themes was simply not an issue. Most of Haydn's sonata-form movements do in fact feature such thematic contrast, but many others do not. Thematic contrast, moreover, can occur almost anywhere in the course of a sonata-form exposition. The first movement of the quartet in F Minor, op. 20 no. 5, for example, although nominally monothematic in that the first idea heard in A♭ (bar 20) is a version of the opening, incorporates considerable thematic contrast by virtue of a subsequent thematic idea that is entirely new (bar 28).

The technique of monothematicism is by no means unique to Haydn. Mozart used it on occasion as well, although not nearly as frequently. On the whole, Haydn's greater propensity for writing monothematic sonata-form movements can be attributed to his characteristic tendency of elaborating and varying an opening idea not only in the development section, but already within the exposition itself. *See also* SONATA FORM. MEB

Moratti, Vincenzo (*fl.* 1760–85). Comic tenor-baritone, born in Bologna. He first appeared on the professional stage in Venice in 1760. He must have been in his early 40s when he joined the opera troupe at Eszterháza, creating the roles of Pasquale in *Orlando Paladino* and singing Perruchetto in the 1782 revival of *La fedeltà premiata*. In his musical portrayal of the timid servant Pasquale, Haydn took full advantage of Moratti's talents. The nonsense syllables 'tra la ra la' in Pasquale's first song ('La mia bella') suggest that Moratti danced while he sang. In 'Ho viaggiato in Francia', an amusing catalogue aria, he showed off his patter, and, just before the end, his ability to whistle. In a second catalogue aria ('Ecco spiano') Pasquale lists his abilities as a violinist, a big aria that offered Moratti a chance to show off his falsetto. JAR

Bartha and Somfai.
HCRL/2.

Morzin family. Haydn went to work for Count Morzin in 1757 (possibly later) and left in 1761 when the count was forced to disband his musical retinue to save money. Haydn's earliest biographers, Griesinger, Dies, and Carpani, all fail to identify which member of the Morzin family Haydn served and next to nothing is known about the composer's time at the court. Almost certainly the patron in question was Franz Ferdinand Maximilian (b. 1693; d. 22 Oct. 1763) who had a summer palace in LUKAVEC in the Bohemian countryside and, perhaps, a small palace in Prague; in Vienna, however, he apparently stayed at the Batthyany palace. He was a widower whose wife had died in 1736. Their son was Carl Joseph Franz von Morzin (1717–83) and it is possible that he, rather than his father, was Haydn's employer. The countess, whose inadvertent display of cleavage distracted the young Haydn when he was playing the harpsichord, was probably his wife, Wilhelmine, whom he had married in 1749. Apart from the cleavage, the only incident from this time that Haydn recalled in his old age was falling off a horse.

Similarly little of certainty is known about Haydn's duties at court. He composed his first symphony there but how many more is educated guesswork, perhaps upwards of 15. Some keyboard sonatas, keyboard trios, string trios, and works for harpsichord and ensemble are likely to have been written for the Morzin family. Musical life at court does not seem to have included church or operatic music.

In his desire to provide further information on the Morzin period CARL FERDINAND POHL perpetrated an error that is still common in the literature. He suggested that the composer Johann Friedrich Fasch (1688–1758) was Haydn's predecessor as Kapellmeister. In fact Fasch worked for another member of the family, Count Wenceslas, who lived in Prague; it was this count who also received the dedication of Vivaldi's op. 3.

C. F. Pohl, *Joseph Haydn*, vol. i (Berlin, 1875).
M. Poštolka, 'Haydn, Fasch and Count Morzin', *Musical Times*, 129 (1988), 78.

Motetto di Sancta Thecla (Hob.XXIIIa:4). A work for soprano, chorus, and small orchestra from the early 1760s whose precise original form is difficult to establish. The St Thecla of the title, written on a set of manuscript parts signed by Haydn, was a native of Iconium converted to Christ by St Paul and subsequently much persecuted. She is commemorated on 23 September, which was, presumably, when the motet was performed. However, the text in the source has strong secular sentiments, suggesting that it does not belong to a motet in praise of St Thecla. A short recitative for soprano praises the splendour of the star that gladdens the pious heart; a lengthy da capo aria notes that melancholy events have given way to those requiring celebration; and the short final chorus praises virtue. It has been suggested that the work was originally a cantata composed to celebrate the accession of Prince Nicolaus in May 1762 to the Esterházy title following the death of his brother, Prince Paul Anton, in March, and his mother, Maria Octavia, in April. Two further texts (plus variants) are known.

I. Becker-Glauch, 'The Apparently Authentic Version of the *Motetto de Sancta Thecla* (Hob.XXIIIa:4)', in J. P.

Larsen, H. Serwer, and J. Webster (eds), *Haydn Studies* (London, 1981), 82–4.
HCRL / 1.

Mozart, Franz Xaver Wolfgang (b. 26 July 1791; d. 29 July 1844). Youngest son of Wolfgang Amadeus Mozart who pursued a successful career as a pianist and a composer. Under Constanze's watchful eye—she added Amadeus to his first names when he was 2—he studied with the leading musicians of the day including Haydn's pupil Neukomm, Streicher (1761–1833), HUMMEL (a pupil of Mozart and Haydn), SALIERI, Vogler (1749–1814), and ALBRECHTSBERGER. His debut as a pianist and composer took place at the Theater an der Wien in Vienna on 8 April 1805, when the programme included a piano concerto in C by his father (probably K503), six numbers from *Idomeneo*, and the Symphony in G minor (K550) (no. 40). At the heart of the concert was a new composition by him, a cantata for three soloists and orchestra, dedicated to Haydn on the occasion of his recent 73rd birthday; apart from the opening chorus the text was by GRIESINGER. Unfortunately the cantata has not survived. In a symbolic gesture, Haydn was to have led the 13-year-old Mozart onto the stage, but he had to decline because of increasing frailty.

Most of Franz Xaver's life was spent in and around Lemberg (Lvov), as tutor in several important houses and later as freelance teacher, pianist, and choirmaster. He embarked on a widely flung tour in 1819, taking in Russia, Poland, Bohemia, Austria, Germany, Italy, Switzerland, and Denmark. For the last six years of his life he lived in Vienna, travelling to Salzburg for the unveiling of his father's memorial in 1842. DC

R. Angermüller, '"Des Vaters Name war es eben, was deiner Tatkraft Keim zerstört". Franz Xaver Wolfgang Mozart—Wie lebte er mit dem Erbe seines Vaters?', *Mitteilungen der Internationalen Stiftung Mozarteum*, 43/3–4 (1998), 29–48.

Mozart, Wolfgang Amadeus (b. 27 Jan. 1756; d. 5 Dec. 1791). Mozart's friendship with Haydn is one of the most famous in the artistic world, comparable perhaps to that of their near contemporaries Goethe (1749–1832) and Schiller (1759–1805). It is not known where and when Haydn and Mozart first met. They would have had some opportunities during the 1770s and early 1780s when both were visiting Vienna, Haydn from Eisenstadt and Eszterháza, and Mozart from Salzburg. The two Christmas concerts of the Tonkünstler-Societät on 22 and 23 December 1783 have been suggested as a likely first meeting; Mozart had been living in Vienna for two years and Haydn, with no commitments at Eszterháza, probably spent the Christmas period in Vienna. The concerts contained works by Haydn (a symphony and a chorus, both probably from *Il ritorno di Tobia*) and Mozart (a new concert aria, probably 'Misero! o sogno!' (K431), and, on the first night, a piano concerto). Haydn could have heard one of Mozart's greatest vocal pieces, in which intensity, passion, and personal involvement with the text clearly distinguish the treatment of the libretto, compared to Haydn's more detached, sometimes more cynical approach. As to the Mozart piano concerto, perhaps it was the brilliant and martial concerto in C (K415), suited to a large audience and the large orchestra that characterized the concerts of the Tonkünstler-Societät.

The first known meeting between Haydn and Mozart took place in 1784 when, in a much-quoted account by the Irish tenor Michael Kelly, the two composers played in a quartet party given by Stephen Storace. According to Kelly, Haydn played the first violin, Dittersdorf the second violin, Mozart the viola, and Vanhal the cello. By this time Mozart was at work on six quartets stimulated by the publication of Haydn's op. 33 in 1782. He took nearly three years to compose these works, testimony to his determined attempt to absorb the unparalleled intricacy that Haydn had demonstrated in his op. 33 quartets, and a particular lie to the notion that Mozart found composition easy.

On 11 February 1785, Leopold Mozart (1719–87) arrived in Vienna to visit his son and daughter-in-law in their large flat in the Domgasse, in the shadow of St Stephen's. On the next day Wolfgang gave a quartet party in honour of Haydn, newly initiated as a fellow Freemason. The report of the party that Leopold wrote to his daughter, Nannerl, in Salzburg contains the most quoted remark that Haydn ever made: 'I tell you before God, and as an honest man, that your son is the greatest composer I know, either personally or by reputation. He has taste and, apart from that, the greatest knowledge of composition.' When the quartets were published by Artaria the following September they were dedicated to 'Giuseppe Haydn' and contained a fulsome and lengthy letter of dedication written in their mutual musical language of Italian.

> To my dear friend Haydn:
> A father having resolved to send his sons into the great world, finds it advisable to entrust them to the protection and guidance of a highly celebrated man, the more so since this man, by a stroke of luck, is his best friend.—Here, then, celebrated man and my dearest friend, are my six sons.—Truly, they are the fruit of a long and laborious effort, but the hope, strengthened by several of my friends, that this effort would, at least in some measure, be rewarded, encourages and comforts me that one day, these children may be a source of consolation to me.—You yourself, dearest friend, during your last sojourn in this

capital, expressed to me your satisfaction with these works.—This, your approval, encourages me more than anything else, and thus I entrust them to your care, and hope that they are not wholly unworthy of your favour. Do but receive them kindly, and be their father, guide, and friend! From this moment I cede to you all my rights over them: I pray you to be indulgent to their mistakes, which a father's partial eye may have overlooked, and despite this, to cloak them in the mantle of your generosity which they value so highly.
From the bottom of my heart I am, dearest friend,
Your most sincere friend,
W. A. Mozart.

Although Haydn was a great admirer of Mozart's operas, famously turning down a commission from Prague for a new opera partly because 'no man can brook comparison with the great Mozart', none was performed at the Esterházy court; a score of *Le nozze di Figaro* was ordered and parts prepared for performance in 1790 but the death of Prince Nicolaus in September forced the abandonment, for ever, of this production. Earlier that year Haydn, along with Michael Puchberg, had been Mozart's guests at a rehearsal of *Così fan tutte* and in the same season Haydn heard the revised version of *Le nozze di Figaro*.

In the last few months of 1790 Haydn and Mozart seem to have met almost daily. According to Maximilian Stadler, Mozart, Haydn, and Stadler played in performances of three of Mozart's string quintets, K515 in C, K516 in G minor, and K593 in D major. Salomon arrived in December to lure Haydn to London. He seems also to have made a gentleman's agreement with Mozart to appear in 1792, alongside Haydn, in what would have been the most celebrated concert series in the history of music. Mozart was a much more experienced international traveller than Haydn and expressed his concern that the 58-year-old would not be able to cope: 'You have no education for the great world, and you speak too few languages.' Haydn's reply reflected the fact that his music was much better known than Mozart's: 'Oh, my language is understood all over the world!'

Haydn was in London when he heard of Mozart's premature death in December 1791, at first refusing to believe the newspaper reports. He wrote to Maria Anna von Genzinger: 'I look forward tremendously to going home and to embracing all my good friends. I only regret that the great Mozart will not be among them, if it is really true, which I trust it is not, that he has died. Posterity will not see such a talent again in 100 years.'

Haydn continued to proclaim Mozart's greatness and to bemoan his loss. In 1798, only seven years after Mozart's death, a Czech teacher Franz Xaver Niemetschek (Nemeček) wrote the first biography of Mozart, which he dedicated to Haydn. It contains several anecdotes, some derived from Constanze Mozart, of Mozart's admiration for the older composer.

While the question of the precise nature of the influence of one composer on the other has often been discussed casually or, in the obvious case of quartets dedicated by Mozart to Haydn, in considerable detail, the full story of their musical relationship has yet to be written. One of the earliest pieces of documentary evidence, as opposed to plausible supposition, is a set of parts of the op. 17 quartets apparently copied in 1771/2 but with some additional dynamic markings in Mozart's hand, probably written *c.*1780. HCRL

M. E. Bonds, 'The Sincerest Form of Flattery? Mozart's "Haydn" Quartets and the Question of Influence', *Studi musicali*, 22 (1993), 365–409.

A. P. Brown, 'Haydn and Mozart's 1773 Stay in Vienna: Weeding a Musicological Garden', *Journal of Musicology*, 10 (1992), 192–230.

C. Eisen, 'The Mozarts' Salzburg Music Library', in C. Eisen (ed.), *Mozart Studies 2* (Oxford, 1997), 85–138. HCRL/2.

H. C. Robbins Landon, *Mozart: The Golden Years. 1781–1791* (London, 1989).

F. Niemetschek, *The Life of Mozart*, English trans. H. Mautner (London, 1956).

Münchener Haydn Renaissance. A publication series from the 1930s, edited by ADOLF SANDBERGER, that presented newly discovered works by Haydn. The series gained a certain notoriety because of its uncritical attitude to sources, and most of the works printed under Haydn's name have proved to be inauthentic. Moreover, the editions themselves were heavily edited.

Sandberger planned the series in five parts: symphonies; other orchestral works (including dances and marches); concertos and concertante symphonies; chamber, keyboard, and organ music; and vocal music. Only a few works had appeared before the onset of the Second World War forced the abandonment of the project. All the symphonies published under Haydn's name in the series are spurious: Hob.I:C27 is by ANTON ZIMMERMANN; Friedrich Witt (1770–1836) is the likely composer of Hob.I:D14, a work obviously modelled on Haydn's London symphonies; Hob.I:D19 is attributed also to Antonio Rosetti (Franz Anton Rößler) (*c.*1750–92); Hob.I:Es11 is by Theodor von Schacht; and Hob.I:B11 is by VANHAL. APB

musical clock. *See* MECHANICAL ORGAN.

'Mutter Gottes, mir erlaube' (Grant me, mother of God) (Hob.XXIIId:2). A short ADVENT ARIA, actually in this case a duet for soprano and alto accompanied by two violins and continuo. A surviving manuscript copy from the mid-1770s suggests that Haydn composed the work for performance in the chapel of the Esterházy palace in Eisenstadt.

I. Becker-Glauch, 'Neue Forschungen zu Haydns Kirchenmusik', *HS* 2/3 (1970), 167–241.

'My mother bids me bind my hair'. First line and commonly used title of a song that Haydn called 'A Pastoral Song' (Hob.XXVIa:27), the first of six canzonettas published in London in 1794. The words are by ANNE HUNTER. *See* SONG §3.

N

Napier, William (b. ?9 Aug. 1740; d. 9 July 1812). Publisher and acquaintance of Haydn. Napier was probably born in Edinburgh, where he first became prominent as a violinist before moving to London about 1765. There he set up as a music publisher in 1772, and published works by many composers in the following decades. In 1790, following the example of several other publishers, he issued a volume entitled *A Selection of the most Favourite Scots Songs*, in which the melodies were set for voice, violin, and figured bass by Samuel Arnold, François Barthélemon, Thomas Carter, and William Shield. Although there were numerous subscribers, Napier's financial position was at that time precarious, for he had a large family to support; he was declared bankrupt the following year. About that time he probably met Haydn, who composed a hundred settings of Scots songs for publication in a second volume, apparently without payment, at least initially. This volume appeared in June 1792 as *A Selection of Original Scots Songs in Three Parts. The harmony by Haydn*, and from about that time Napier's financial fortunes improved, helped in part by the sales of Haydn's volume. The success of this volume prompted a third volume, for which Haydn wrote 50 further settings during his second visit to England, and it appeared in July 1795. Napier continued as a music publisher until 1809. BARC

C. Hopkinson and C. B. Oldman, 'Haydn's Settings of Scottish Songs in the Collections of Napier and Whyte', *Edinburgh Bibliographical Society Transactions*, 3 (1948–55), 85–120.

'National' symphony. In August 1789 Haydn wrote to the French publisher, SIEBER, confirming that he would compose four symphonies for him, one of which would be called a 'National' symphony. Haydn never fulfilled this promise. A 'National' symphony would probably have invoked national musical styles, as Dittersdorf had done in a symphony in A (*Sinfonia nel Gusto cinque Nazioni*) from before 1766.

Negri, Domenico (*fl.* 1760–95). A Bolognese bass-baritone active in comic opera from the early 1760s; he is not to be confused with Giovanni Domenico Negri, who sang mostly in serious opera during the 1740s and 1750s. On 3 September 1782 he was engaged to sing for two years at Eszterháza, where he created the role of Rodomonte, the boastful soldier, in *Orlando Paladino* and sang Melibeo in the 1782 revival of *La fedeltà premiata*. Haydn wrote brilliant, heavily orchestrated arias for him, such as 'Temerario! senti e trema' and 'Mille lampi d'accese faville' from *Orlando Paladino*, that depend for their effect on a powerful voice. In 1784 Negri returned to Italy, where he continued to sing until the mid-1790s. JAR

Bartha and Somfai.
HCRL/2.

Nelson, (Admiral Lord) Horatio (b. 29 Sept. 1758; d. 21 Oct. 1805). In 1800 Nelson and an entourage that included Sir William and Lady Hamilton, Mrs Cadogan (Emma Hamilton's mother) and the poetess Ellis Cornelia Knight travelled from Naples to Austria en route to London. On arriving in Laibach (Ljubljana) on 18 August they attended a concert given by the Philharmonic Society that included Haydn's 'Military' symphony (no. 100). In Vienna, Nelson, the hero of the Battle of Aboukir and, more recently, the man responsible for recovering Naples from the French, was fêted by all sections of society. As part of the social whirl the entourage made a four-day visit to Eisenstadt (6–9 September) as guests of the Esterházy family. Emma Hamilton (b. ?1765; d. 15 Jan. 1815), Nelson's mistress for two years, was a keen amateur musician with a clear, strong singing voice. She and Haydn apparently performed ARIANNA A NAXOS and Haydn was encouraged to set some verses by her companion, Ellis Cornelia Knight (1757–1837), the *Battle of the Nile*. Haydn also presented Lady Hamilton with a manuscript copy of 'The Spirit's Song' (now in the British Library). Nelson himself was rather reserved but he would have been well aware of the composer's popularity in England and accepted a used quill from the composer, giving him a watch in return. Nelson was a hero in Austria and, like many of his countrymen, Haydn owned an engraving of the Englishman and of the Battle of Aboukir.

O. E. Deutsch, *Admiral Nelson und Joseph Haydn. Ein britisch-östereichisches Gipfeltreffen*, ed. G. Deutsch and R. Klein (Vienna, 1982).
HCRL/4.

'Nelson' mass (Hob.XXII:11). Commonly used nickname for the MISSA IN ANGUSTIIS, arising early in the 19th century. It is generally thought to have originated when Haydn's mass was performed during NELSON's visit to Eisenstadt in September 1800, but actual evidence is lacking. Nelson was in Eisenstadt from Saturday, 6 September, to Tuesday, 9 September. The nameday of Princess Mary Hermengild was on Monday, 8 September (the fixed feast of the Nativity of Mary), but there is no record of a mass service that day; more likely, given the usual practice of the Esterházy family, was a liturgical performance the following Sunday, 14 September, on the movable feast of the Most Holy Name of Mary; by this time Nelson and his entourage had left Eisenstadt. Whatever the truth about this supposed performance, by the middle of the century the association between the work and Nelson was so persistent that it led to the view that its composition two years earlier was directly influenced by Nelson's celebrated victory at the Battle of Aboukir. News of that event, however, did not reach Austria until after Haydn had completed the mass.

One unfortunate consequence of the prevalence of the nickname and associated stories is that many conductors have sought a Beethovenian heroism in the work, exaggerated by large forces and slow tempi, that is wholly at odds with Haydn's conception.

Neukomm, Sigismund (b. 10 July 1778; d. 3 April 1858). After spending his early life in Salzburg, where he was a pupil of Michael Haydn, Neukomm moved to Vienna in March 1797 to study composition with Joseph Haydn. He remained Haydn's pupil for seven years, and greatly admired his teacher for the rest of his life, dedicating several works to him. With the composer's approval Neukomm also made arrangements of several of Haydn's works, including *The Creation* and *The Seasons*. During this period Haydn was engaged in composing settings of Scottish and Welsh folksongs for GEORGE THOMSON of Edinburgh, and he was so impressed by Neukomm's ability that Neukomm was allowed to write some on Haydn's behalf. Altogether Neukomm made at least 25 settings, which Haydn duly sent to Thomson as if they were his own, and Thomson published them as Haydn's without realizing the deception. Neukomm's settings are indeed very similar to Haydn's, and distinctly different from those of PLEYEL and KOZELUCH (Koželuh), who had also contributed to Thomson's collection.

Neukomm moved to St Petersburg in May 1804, and remained there until 1808, when he returned to Vienna. There he was in daily contact with Haydn from November 1808 to February 1809. He then settled in Paris, although he continued to travel widely, visiting Britain, Italy, North Africa, and South America, always promoting Haydn's music. BARC

R. Angermüller, 'Neukomms schottische Liedbearbeitungen für Joseph Haydn', *HS* 3 (1973–4), 151–3.

R. Angermüller, *Sigismund Neukomm: Werkverzeichnis, Autobiographie, Beziehung zu seinen Zeitgenossen* (Munich, 1977).

M. Vignal, 'A Side-Aspect of Sigismund Neukomm's Journey to France in 1809', *HYB* 2 (1963–5), 81–7.

Niemecz, Primitivus (b. 9 Feb. 1750; d. 9 Jan. 1806). Librarian at the Esterházy court, and a keen builder of mechanical organs. Haydn composed music specifically for three instruments built by him. Born Joseph Niemecz in Vlašim in Bohemia he studied philosophy before joining the Order of the Hospitallers of St John of God (BARMHERZIGE BRÜDER) in Prague in 1769; it was then that he took the first name of Primitivus. He was consecrated as a priest in Königgrätz in 1776. He joined the Esterházy court in 1782 as librarian and court chaplain. He apparently played the gamba, baryton, violin, piano, and harp, and studied composition with Haydn, though none of his music has survived.

His interest and expertise as a builder of musical automata of all kinds grew quickly and, in 1795, he was given an assistant, Joseph Gurk, who helped Niemecz in the library and in the workshop. His instruments were sold and displayed regularly in Vienna, and even exported to England. Mozart's Fantasy in F minor (K608) was probably written to be played on a mechanical organ built by Niemecz. Following his death from tuberculosis the well-established business was carried on by Gurk. *See* MECHANICAL ORGAN.

A. W. J. G. Ord-Hume, *Joseph Haydn and the Mechanical Organ* (Cardiff, 1982).

'Night Watchman's song'. A well-known folksong that can be traced back to Bohemia in the 16th century and which by the 18th century was known (with inevitable local variants) throughout Central Europe. It is sung by the watchman to greet the dawn. Amongst its distinctive features are the fall of a fourth at the end of the first phrase and, often, a prominent sharpened subdominant. It was quoted by Haydn in several works, sometimes for an illustrative purpose (as in Symphony no. 60 and the vocal canon, 'Wunsch'), on other occasions, apparently gratuitously (as in the divertimento in E♭) though it may have been prompted by particular circumstances now unknown. The following list of its appearances in Haydn's music could be supplemented by more casual, even unintentional references (e.g. the theme of the second movement of Symphony no. 103). *See also* FOLK MUSIC.

Symphony no. 60 ('Il distratto'): 6th movement, bars 61–71.
Divertimento in C (Hob.II:17): 8th movement, opening.
Divertimento in E♭ (Hob.II:21): 5th movement, trio.
Baryton trio in A (Hob.XI:35): 3rd movement, trio.
Baryton duet in A (Hob.XII:19): 2nd movement, opening.
Keyboard sonata in C♯ minor (Hob.XVI:36): 3rd movement, opening.
Canon, 'Wunsch' (Hob.XXVIIb:43).

G. Chew, 'The Night-Watchman's Song Quoted by Haydn and its Implications', *HS* 3/2 (1974), 106–24.

Nigst, Franz (d. 29 Oct. 1773). Initially engaged as a grain steward in 1752 Nigst eventually became chief bursar in the complex court administration of the Esterházy family. Between 1760 and 1768 he supplemented his income by playing the violin in the orchestra. This dual role became more difficult as the musicians spent more of their time at Eszterháza, and he was relieved of his playing duties in 1768; his plea that he be allowed to keep his musician's uniforms was rejected. He continued to play in church services in the palace in Eisenstadt, receiving some income for this duty from 1771.

ERL

U. Tank, *Studien zur Esterházyschen Hofmusik von etwa 1620 bis 1790* (Regensburg, 1981).

'nihil sine causa'. *See* FATTO A POSTA.

'Non nobis, Domine' (Not unto us, O Lord) (Hob.XXIIIa:1). An offertory in D minor, scored for SATB choir and organ continuo, and written in the STYLUS A CAPPELLA. The text, from Psalm 115, is an unusual one for a Catholic offertory and was probably taken by Haydn from MATTHESON'S treatise, *Der vollkommene Kapellmeister*, which quotes a celebrated canon on the text, falsely attributed to William Byrd. Nothing is known about the date and circumstances of Haydn's composition; in terms of performance, music in this style was most frequently encountered during Lent. Three versions of the musical text are known but whether all three are by Haydn cannot be established for certain. In its musically most ambitious version, the characteristic polyphonic apparatus of the style builds up to a powerful conclusion featuring two extended dominant pedals. The work was copied into a choirbook in the El Escorial, Spain, in 1786 which provides the earliest *terminus ante quem*; it may originally have been composed up to 20 years before this.

D. W. Jones, 'A Spanish Source for Haydn's "Non nobis, Domine"', *HYB* 17 (1992), 167–9.

Notturni for two *lire organizzate* and ensemble (Hob.II:25–32). In 1786 Haydn had received a commission from FERDINAND IV, King of Naples, for some ensemble music featuring the LIRA ORGANIZZATA, and five concertos were subsequently delivered. They were evidently well received, since they were followed in the period 1788–90 by nine notturni, of which eight have survived. The details of both commissions are not known.

The eight notturni are scored for an ensemble of nine players: two *lire*, two clarinets, two horns, two violas, and bass (cello). The king's *lira* could play effectively in only three keys, C, F, and G; consequently four of the notturni are in C, two in F, and two in G. The parts are written as single lines; presumably the drones of the *lira organizzata* would provide a continuous background. All the works originally had three movements in the order fast, slow, and fast, except Hob.II:25 which prefaces the cycle with a march; the finale of Hob.II:30 has not survived.

During Haydn's first visit to London, 1791–2, he revised at least five of the works for presentation at Salomon's concerts: Hob.II: 27–9, 31, and 32. This involved substituting a flute and oboe for the two *lire* parts (two flutes in Hob.II:32) and two violins for the two clarinets; Haydn also strengthened the bass line with a part for the double bass, and, for Hob.II:27, whose opening Allegro begins quietly, the composer added a slow introduction. Performances at Salomon's concerts took place on 5 April 1791, 20 May 1791, 27 April 1792, 11 May 1792, and 18 May 1792. Haydn never regarded them as mere filler items in the concerts. In all cases they constituted the only new work in the programme in the absence of the first performance of a symphony or a quartet.

Haydn's regard for the music is fully justified. Though on a smaller scale than the symphonies alongside which they were composed and performed (nos. 88–98), they have a good deal of the same energy and charm; the lyrical slow movements and rondo movements, in particular, provide many echos of movements in contemporary symphonies. Especially striking is the finale to Hob.II:29, a sonata form Allegro in which a fugal texture is maintained throughout the movement, making it both an updating of the fugal finales found in some of the earlier baryton trios, and a movement to be set alongside the finales of Mozart's 'Jupiter' symphony and Haydn's own Symphony no. 95. Coupled with the unusual variety of tone colours (especially in the orginal version), these qualities mark the works as the most sophisticated of Haydn's music for mixed ensembles. *See also* CONCERTO §5.

Novello family. Influential English family of musicians and music publishers, who did much to circulate and popularize the sacred works of Haydn and Mozart in the 19th century.

Vincent Novello (b. 6 Sept. 1781; d. 9 Aug. 1861) was an organist, conductor, choirmaster, music editor, and composer. He was a Roman Catholic, the son of a pastry cook from Piedmont who had settled in London with his English wife. Religious intolerance by the British state obliged Catholics resident in London to worship at the chapels of foreign embassies. Novello studied the organ with Samuel Webbe (1740–1816) whilst a chorister at the Sardinian embassy, and from 1797 until 1824 he served as organist in the chapel of the Portuguese embassy, where his brother Francis sang principal bass.

It was probably through SAMUEL WESLEY that Novello met CHRISTIAN IGNATIUS LATROBE, who lent him manuscript copies of liturgical works by Haydn and Mozart. Novello began to include this music in services at the Portuguese chapel where musical amateurs of all denominations soon flocked to hear it. To meet demand for copies Novello prepared a two-volume selection of the music in vocal score (*A Collection of Sacred Music*, 1811), issuing it himself by subscription after failing to attract a publisher; a version of Haydn's Salve regina in G minor (Hob.XXIIIb:2) appeared alongside movements by Mozart, Webbe, Wesley, Novello himself, and others.

As restrictions on Catholic worship in Britain relaxed, new churches were built and the burgeoning market for liturgical music was supplied with further publications by Novello, usually featuring adaptations of secular music by Haydn. These included *A Collection of Motetts for the Offertory, & other Pieces principally adapted for the Morning Service* (1818–24) and *The Evening Service* (1823–8). Novello sought to bring this music to the widest public by encouraging amateur and domestic performances. He therefore followed Latrobe's practice of supplying each piece with a full but undemanding accompaniment for organ or piano instead of the usual figured bass.

Novello's most significant contribution to Haydn's reputation in 19th-century Britain was the editing and arrangement of 16 masses in vocal score with organ accompaniment, published by William Galloway between 1822 and 1825. Only eight masses had been published in Europe by that time, so Novello gathered further, manuscript sources from fellow enthusiasts including Latrobe, Domenico Dragonetti (1763–1846), and Edmund Harris of Bath. Even though four of the 16 masses were spurious, Novello took pains to establish authenticity where possible, seeking the assistance of Prince Nicolaus Esterházy II. From January 1829 instrumental parts were also published, with cues facilitating performance by reduced orchestras; Novello also reworked selected movements as organ voluntaries during the 1830s.

In 1828, building on his earlier forays into music publishing, Novello established his eldest son, Joseph (Alfred) Novello (b. 12 Aug. 1810; d. 16 July 1896), in business at the family home, 67 Frith Street. True to his father's ideals and his own entrepreneurial instinct, Alfred cut the price of popular vocal works by reviving the practice of printing music from movable type; Novello & Co.'s cheap octavo editions of Haydn's sacred works were thus brought within reach of most parish churches, choral societies, amateur musicians, and even schools, helping to fix Haydn's place in the canon of 'classical works' during the 19th century. REC

R. Darby, 'The Music of the Roman Catholic Embassy Chapels in London' (diss., University of Manchester, 1984).

M. Hurd, *Vincent Novello and Company* (London, 1981).

N. Medici di Marignano and R. Hughes (eds), *A Mozart Pilgrimage: being the Travel Diaries of Vincent and Mary Novello in the year 1829* (London, 1955).

Novotný, Franz Nicolaus (b. 6 Dec. 1743; d. 25 Aug. 1773). At the age of 20 Novotný entered the service of the Esterházy family as a bookkeeper. His father, Johann Novotný, had been the organist in the chapel of the palace since 1736 and on his death in 1765 Franz assumed this additional duty. As the organist he may well have played the instrument in any performances of Haydn's 'Grosse Orgelsolomesse' (MISSA IN HONOREM BVM) that took place in Eisenstadt, unless the composer himself took that role. A promising career as a composer of church music was cut short when he died a few months before his 30th birthday. After a search for a replacement organist proved futile, Haydn assumed responsibility for playing the organ in Eisenstadt in the winter months. ERL

U. Tank, *Studien zur Esterházyschen Hofmusik von etwa 1620 bis 1790* (Regensburg, 1981).

Nowak, Leopold (b. 17 Aug. 1904; d. 27 May 1991). Austrian musicologist noted mainly for his work on the musical texts of Bruckner's symphonies. He studied with Guido Adler and Robert Lach at Vienna University. He became director of the music collection at the Österreichische Nationalbibliothek in 1946 and held the position until his retirement in 1969. Two articles on Haydn refer to manuscript material in the Nationalbibliothek. In 1954 he drew attention to the autograph manuscript of the Cello Concerto in D, signed by the composer, at a time when the increasingly prevalent view was that the work was by Anton Kraft, and he wrote a detailed study of the sketches for the finale of Symphony no. 99. A substantial one-volume study of Haydn's life and work appeared in 1951 and was, for many years, the standard modern study in German.

O

'Ochsenmenuett' ('Oxen minuet') (Hob.IX:27). An entirely spurious minuet in C attributed to Haydn that spawned pictorial representations and operettas in the 19th century. The earliest reference to the minuet is as a movement for piano issued by Hummel in the first years of the 19th century. It is accompanied by the story that Haydn composed the dance for the wedding of a butcher's daughter; as payment in kind the butcher gave Haydn his best ox. It is possible that the minuet was composed by someone to fit a story that was already in circulation, for as early as 1805 there was a stage work (now lost) performed in Verdun, France, with the title *Le Menuet de Bœuf ou Une Leçon de Haydn.* In 1812 a vaudeville, *Haydn, ou le Menuet de Bœuf,* was performed in Paris. The text of this work formed the basis of the most widely performed operetta based on the story, *Das Ochsenmenuett.* First given at the Theater an der Wien in Vienna on 13 December 1823, it subsequently received performances in Berlin, Hamburg, Hanover, Prague, New York, and (in Swedish) Stockholm, contributing to the increasingly prevalent image of the genial Haydn. The music had been prepared by IGNAZ VON SEYFRIED and, as well as the spurious minuet, included arrangements of several movements from *The Seasons,* from the quartet in D, op. 20 no. 4, and, inevitably, 'GOTT ERHALTE FRANZ DEN KAISER'.

O. Deutsch, 'Curious Title-Pages of Works by Haydn', *Musical Times,* 73 (1932), 516–18.

B. von Seyfried, *Ignaz Ritter von Seyfried. Thematisch-Bibliographisches Verzeichnis. Aspekte der Biographie und des Werkes* (Frankfurt, 1990). *See also* HAYDN NOVELS, OPERAS, AND PLAYS.

Oettingen-Wallerstein. One of the most musically active courts in central Germany in the second half of the 18th century, noted especially for the quality of its orchestra and for the range of its repertoire. Set in the rolling hills of Swabia, the court had two palaces, at Wallerstein and Hohenaltheim. Prince Kraft Ernst Oettingen-Wallerstein (1748–1802) was a highly educated man who had private music lessons in Vienna while attending the Savoyan Ritterakademie in the city, studied at the universities of Göttingen and Strasbourg, and, to complete his formal education, visited France, England, and Italy. Under his direction the musical life of the court was transformed in the 1770s and 1780s. As elsewhere there was a Kapellmeister, successively Joseph Reicha (1752–95), uncle of ANTON REICHA, and Antonio Rosetti (*c.*1750–1792), but there was, in addition, a musical intendant, Ignaz von Beecke (1733–1803), whose duties were to ensure that the repertoire of the court orchestra was as diverse and as modern as possible. He travelled regularly on behalf of the court, spending a considerable amount of time in Vienna in the 1770s. From the music shops in the city Beecke regularly ordered manuscript copies of symphonies by Haydn who, next to the Wallerstein composers, gradually became the best represented in the court repertoire. Much of this material is now in the library of Augsburg University.

In 1781 Prince Kraft Ernst was one of several individuals to whom Haydn wrote offering manuscript subscription copies of the op. 33 quartets in advance of publication by Artaria. The prince accepted but was later to complain about the delay in delivery. In 1788 the prince enquired whether Haydn would compose three new symphonies for the court; the composer was too busy to oblige but sent a copy of *Il ritorno di Tobia.* Towards the end of the following year he forwarded copies of Symphonies nos. 90–2, commissioned by COMTE D'OGNY, and twelve minuets (lost or unidentified) that were to be played at the wedding celebrations of the prince. Although he was disappointed to receive manuscript parts of the symphonies rather than a set of scores in Haydn's handwriting the prince forwarded a gold snuffbox as well as the agreed fee. In December 1790, en route to London, Haydn stayed overnight at the court of Oettingen-Wallerstein, but a promised second visit, on his return journey, never materialized. The prince remained an avid collector of Haydn's music; for instance, his name appears in the subscription list for the first edition of *The Creation,* published in 1800.

A. Diemand, 'Josef Haydn und der Wallersteiner Hof', *Zeitschrift des Historischen Vereins für Schwaben und Neuburg,* 45 (1920–2), 1–40.

S. E. Murray (ed.), *Seven Symphonies from the Court of Oettingen-Wallerstein 1773–1795,* in *The Symphony 1720–1840,* editor-in-chief B. S. Brook, Series C, vol. 6 (New York, 1981).

Ogny, Count Claude-François-Marie Rigoley d' (b. Sept. 1757; d. 4 Oct. 1790). Born in Dijon, Count d'Ogny became one of the leading musical patrons in Paris in the 1780s. After military training he became intendant general with responsibility for the postal service, but his real passion, inherited from his father, was music. At about the age of 20 he began amassing a private library of music that was to include some 2,000 works, including 34 symphonies by Haydn. As a leading Freemason he was a prime mover in the setting up in 1781 of the CONCERT DE LA LOGE OLYMPIQUE, a concert series promoted by the Freemasons. The count played the cello in the orchestra. It was at his instigation that Haydn was commissioned to write six symphonies, nos. 82–7 (the 'Paris' symphonies). Their success encouraged d'Ogny to commission a further three works, Symphonies nos. 90–2; two of the forwarded autographs carry dedications from Haydn to the count.

B. S. Brook, *La Symphonie française dans la second moitié du XVIIIe siècle* (Paris, 1962).

Oliva, Joseph (b. ?1731: d. 25 Oct. 1806). Born in Bohemia he was employed from 1764 to 1769 at Großwardein (Oradea Mare) where Dittersdorf was the Kapellmeister. Together with his colleague, Franz Pauer, he transferred to the Esterházy court on 1 June 1769. This brought the complement of available horn players to six and Oliva, like the others, was probably required to play in public ceremonies that requred a windband, in the hunt, as well as in the court orchestra. He also played the violin and, as his ability on the horn declined with age (an occupational hazard for horn players), he played that instrument rather than the horn. When the court orchestra was disbanded in 1790 he was transferred to church music duties at the Eisenstadt palace and was granted a pension in 1794. He moved to Vienna where he played the violin in the court opera. He died of dropsy. At Eszterháza his children had often worked as extras in opera performances, and a son, Wenzel Oliva, was briefly employed as a violinist in 1789–90. ERL

P. Bryan, 'Haydn's Hornists', *HS* 3/1 (1973), 52–8.
HCRL/2.

opera. See overleaf.

oratorio. See page 260.

Ordonez, Carlo d' (b. 19 Apr. 1734; d. 16 Sept. 1786). Viennese composer and violinist; unusually, he did not have a musical post but worked as a clerk in the Lower Austrian court. He was especially noted as a composer of symphonies (over 70) and quartets (over 30).

In 1772 CHARLES BURNEY heard Ordonez, together with Starzer (1726/7–87), WEIGL, and Count Brühl perform quartets by Haydn, probably from op. 20. He was the leader of the second violins in the two performances of *Il ritorno di Tobia* presented by the Tonkünstler-Societät under Haydn's direction in March 1784.

On 30 August 1775, as part of the celebrations that accompanied the visit of Archduke Ferdinand and Beatrice d'Este to Eszterháza, Ordonez's marionette opera, *Alceste*, was performed; it was later repeated by the Esterházy company at Schönbrunn, eliciting the praise of Maria Theresia. Haydn kept the autograph score of the opera in his personal library. Of the many instrumental works by Ordonez that were falsely attributed to Haydn, a symphony in A (Hob.I:A6) is particularly interesting. As late as the early 1950s several Haydn authorities, including Robbins Landon and Jens Peter Larsen, were willing to accept that this work might have been composed by Haydn; later research revealed Ordonez to be the undisputed author. APB

A. P. Brown, *Carlo d'Ordonez (1734–1786): A Thematic Catalog* (Detroit, 1978).

A. P. Brown, 'The Unknown Viennese Composer Carlo d'Ordonez', in T. L. Noblitt (ed.), *Music East and West: Essays in Honor of Walter Kaufmann* (New York, 1981), 243–59.

H. C. Robbins Landon, 'Problems of Authenticity in Eighteenth-Century Music' in D. G. Hughes (ed.), *Instrumental Music: a Conference at Isham Memorial Library May 4, 1957* (Cambridge, 1959), 31–56.

D. Young, 'Karl von Ordonez 1734–1786: A Biographical Study', *Royal Musical Association Research Chronicle*, 19 (1983–5), 31–56.

organ. Haydn was a competent organist who played the instrument from his youth until old age. At the Esterházy court from 1773 onwards he was required to play the organ at church services in the chapel of Eisenstadt castle during the winter months. He wrote several organ concertos in Vienna during the 1750s and included obbligato parts for the instrument in four masses: *Missa in honorem BVM*, *Missa brevis Sancti Joannis de Deo*, *Missa in angustiis*, and the 'Schöpfungsmesse'. The notated organ parts in these works indicate the nature of the instrument in Austria. Unlike the glorious tradition in north Germany, most organs in Austria did not have a pedal board and Haydn, like other composers, wrote the music on two staves only. Large instruments that did have a pedal board usually replaced a full compass with only the most commonly encountered notes, the so-called short octave.

The organs with which Haydn was associated can be divided into three groups; first, the very small chamber organs that typically would have been used in the St Anne's chapel in the HAUGWITZ residence and in the Esterházy palace in the Wallnerstraße; second, the medium-sized organs found in the churches of the BARMHERZIGE BRÜDER in Vienna and Eisenstadt; and third, the larger organs found in the Bergkirche and the Martinkirche (now cathedral) in Eisenstadt. Of these only the latter two have survived and been

[*cont. on p.262*]

opera

Opera featured in Haydn's output for much of his life and in the period 1776–90, when there was a permanent operatic company at Eszterháza, it dominated his existence. He could fairly be said to have become one of the most experienced opera composers of his day. But in comparison with opera composers such as Anfossi, Cimarosa, Gluck, Paisiello, Piccinni, and Sarti, many of whose works he directed at Eszterháza, he was not an international figure. Indeed, although his very earliest operas were written for Vienna and there were occasional performances of later works there, he never made an impact as an opera composer even in that city.

1. German opera.
2. Italian opera.

1. German opera. As many as nine operas in German (*Singspiel*) have reasonably been attributed to Haydn. However, accurate discussion of his contribution to the genre is inhibited both by the loss of most of the scores and by doubts about the attribution of three of the works (one of which is lost, two of which survive). Haydn's first *Singspiel* setting was almost certainly DER KRUMME TEUFEL of *c.*1751, the last was DIE BESTRAFTE RACHBEGIERDE of 1779, by when he was an experienced composer of Italian operas at the Esterházy court. Whether or not DER NEUE KRUMME TEUFEL, the printed libretto of which survives, was identical with, or, more likely, was a revision of, the totally lost *Der krumme Teufel*, it is improbable that this work, which was performed quite widely in German-speaking Europe, was Haydn's only commissioned *Singspiel* before he began to write marionette operas for Prince Nicolaus Esterházy some 20 years later. Moreover, it is possible that Haydn also composed miscellaneous songs and ensembles for unknown German operas in Vienna in the 1750s, such as the numbers that survive in a couple of anonymous manuscript volumes entitled 'TEUTSCHE COMEDIE ARIEN'.

The Kärntnerthortheater, the institution for which Haydn wrote his first known stage work, *Der krumme Teufel*, has a history going back to *c.*1710, when it became home to Joseph Anton Stranitzky's company. From the mid-1720s the troupe was led by Stranitzky's successor Gottfried Prehauser, and particularly after KURZ-BERNARDON joined them, music played an important part in the extemporized comedies and ballets. No music has survived earlier than the 'Teutsche Comedie Arien', likely to have been composed in the mid-1750s.

Judgement of Haydn's achievement in operatic composition in his native language has to be based on the highly inadequate evidence of extant musical and textual sources: PHILEMON UND BAUCIS (1773; incomplete), DIE FEUERSBRUNST (if authentic, and if identical with the *Opera comique Vom abgebrannten Haus*, *c.*1775–78); and DIE REISENDE CERES (doubtful authenticity). The word-books survive for *Der neue krumme Teufel*, DIDO (?1776; the libretto from the revival of 1778 is extant), GENOVEFENS VIERTER THEIL (1777; it is likely that Haydn was at most the compiler of the score, though he perhaps contributed numbers to it), and DIE BESTRAFTE RACHBEGIERDE (?1779). Entirely lost are *Der krumme Teufel* (if distinct from *Der neue krumme Teufel*), HEXEN-SCHABBAS (?1773), and *Opéra comique Vom abgebrannten Haus* (unless identical with *Die Feuersbrunst*, if authentic). German adaptations of Haydn's Italian operas such as *La vera costanza*, *La fedeltà premiata*, and *Orlando* *paladino*, can be excluded from consideration since they were not made by the composer himself.

There is, then, insufficient evidence for a proper assessment of Haydn's contribution to the development of *Singspiel.* While it is very likely that in the years of his early adulthood in Vienna he wrote more theatre scores than *Der krumme Teufel*, thereafter he was not regularly in contact with an urban theatre company or tradition. The bulk of his German-language operatic settings were written for the marionette theatre opened by Prince Nicolaus at the time of Empress Maria Theresia's visit in September 1773. The previous year the prince had purchased a *Marionetten Theater* (that is puppets and associated theatrical props) from KARL MICHAEL VON PAUERSBACH, a former civil servant in Vienna who wrote plays; from *c.*1776 he directed the marionette performances at Eszterháza.

It is clear from contemporary reports that the standard of performances in the marionette theatre at Eszterháza was high, but commentators say more about the sets, puppets, and staging than about the music. The extant librettos show that, though the arias were naturally the most numerous musical items, a surprising number of choruses was called for, together with a sprinkling of duets, trios, and larger ensembles. This runs contrary to what one might expect of a marionette theatre, where solo scenes would naturally be easier to handle, both for the puppeteers and the singers, than large ensembles. The texts contain many local references, including in *Die bestrafte Rachbegierde*, one to Haydn himself. It would be dangerous to attempt to draw conclusions on the basis of the paucity of the surviving authentic music as to the principles that dictated the scope of Haydn's scores. For instance, *Die Feuersbrunst* consists mainly of arias ('songs' would be a more appropriate general term), whereas *Die reisende Ceres* and *Dido, Genovefens vierter Theil* and *Die bestrafte Rachbegierde* contain quite a high proportion of vocal numbers for more than one singer. There was plenty of opportunity for word-painting, particularly of physical movement and natural phenomena, and the librettos call for a number of trumpet fanfares, instruments that Haydn did not normally have at his disposal.

On the basis of the slender evidence available, one may hesitantly suggest that in his *Singspiel* settings of his native language Haydn showed a more direct and uninhibited response to the drama than is usually evident in his Italian operas with their leisurely and generally much longer musical numbers. It can only be hoped that in the course of time some at least of the lost scores will come to light, thus permitting a more thorough and better informed summing-up of his contribution to this vernacular genre. PB

E. Badura-Skoda, '"Teutsche Comoedie-Arien" und Joseph Haydn', in V. Schwarz (ed.), *Der junge Haydn* (Graz, 1972), 59–73.

P. Branscombe, 'Germany and Austria: The Singspiel', in S. Sadie (ed.), *History of Opera* (Basingstoke, 1989), 86–94.

H. C. Robbins Landon, 'Haydn's Marionette Operas and the Repertoire of the Marionette Theatre at Esterház Castle', *HYB* 1 (1962), 111–99.

G. Thomas, 'Haydns Deutsche Singspiele', *HS* 6 (1986), 1–63.

2. Italian opera. Although he never visited Italy, Haydn absorbed the principles and practices of Italian opera from an early age; they helped to shape his artistic personality and are reflected in his works as composer in all genres, and as an arranger and conductor.

Haydn received some musical education from REUTTER at St Stephen's but in the autobiographical sketch of 1776 he credited a later experience as being more important for his development as a composer. After his voice broke he served PORPORA—formerly an important composer of Italian opera, later a singing teacher in Vienna—as accompanist and assistant. That Haydn absorbed the values implicit in Italian opera is clear from a recommendation that he made to one of his own students, ROBERT KIMMERLING, to study Galuppi's *Il mondo alla rovescia* 'because of its fine cantabile'.

As a freelance musician in Vienna during the 1750s Haydn also came into contact with GLUCK, HASSE, and WAGENSEIL; undoubtedly he heard Italian operas by them and others. At Eszterháza Haydn maintained contacts with Viennese musicians. Through manuscript scores of operas performed in Vienna and visits to the capital he kept himself up to date with developments in Italian opera to which the operatic establishment at Eszterháza (and Haydn with it) responded either by imitation or by doing exactly the opposite.

Viennese Italian opera of the 1750s was for the most part serious. In the few full-length Metastasian *drammi per musica* performed in Vienna during the decade, such as Andrea Adolfati's *La clemenza di Tito* (1753), most of the musical interest was concentrated in a series of brilliant exit arias in da capo form. Like the characters in most of Metastasio's full-length operas, those of *La clemenza di Tito* were all of noble rank and include a ruler. They took part in a drama based on historical events rather than the mythological subject matter preferred by composers of *tragédie lyrique*.

Several other serious operas in Italian, such as the pasticcio *Euridice* of 1750 and Gluck's *L'innocenza giustificata* of 1755, anticipated the revolutionary amalgamation of French spectacle and Italian singing that produced Gluck's *Orfeo* and *Alceste* in the 1760s. Short *feste* and *azioni teatrali* represented a third kind of Italian serious opera that Haydn probably heard during the 1750s. In Giuseppe Bonno's *Il re pastore* (1751) he could admire an exquisite example of the cantabile vocal style that he later praised in Galuppi's music. In Gluck's *Le cinesi* (1754) he could enjoy colourful orchestral writing and spectacular coloratura.

With the arrival in Vienna of Giacomo Maso's travelling troupe in 1763 Goldonian *opera buffa* began to rival serious opera and *opéra comique*; and for most of the last third of the 18th century *opera buffa* dominated the Viennese operatic repertoire. In structure *opera buffa* of the 1760s and 1770s did not differ greatly from Metastasian *dramma per musica*: exit arias predominated in dramas laid out in three acts; but the finale, popularized if not invented by GOLDONI, represented an innovation quite unlike anything in Metastasian serious opera. Probably inspired by the success of such finales, librettists and composers of *opera buffa* wrote ensembles with increasing frequency. Characteristic of Goldoni's librettos is the incorporation of noble, serious characters into largely comic plots and the subdivision of the rest of the characters into *parti buffe* (comic roles) and *parti di mezzo carattere* (roles midway between comic and serious). Each category required special treatment, resulting in stylistic diversity much greater than that normally encountered in *opera seria*.

From his engagement by Prince Paul Anton Esterházy in 1761 to his first trip to London in 1790, Haydn devoted enormous energy and effort to the production of Italian opera, whether his own works or those of other composers. He composed 13 operas in Italian for Eisenstadt, Eszterháza, and London; he edited, rehearsed, and conducted the operas of ANFOSSI, Cimarosa (1749–1801), Gazzaniga (1743–1818), Paisiello (1740–1816), SALIERI, and many others. This editing included transposing, shortening, and in many other ways rewriting; it involved also composing new arias, a task that he undertook with special eagerness when reshaping roles for his mistress, the Neapolitan soprano LUIGIA POLZELLI.

Haydn's works as composer-director of Italian opera at Eisenstadt and Eszterháza can be divided into three phases. In the first (up to 1776), Prince Nicolaus seems to have been more interested in playing the baryton than in supervising the production of opera; there was no regular opera season, and the opera troupe consisted mostly of local singers. CARL FRIBERTH, a tenor who had some knowledge of Italian poetry, dominated the production of opera as librettist and singer.

By the mid-1770s Prince Nicolaus's participation in chamber music had begun to wane and he focused more attention on the theatre, thus initiating the second phase of Haydn's operatic career (1776–84). Perhaps partly in reaction to a decision by JOSEPH II to give German spoken drama a privileged place in his newly founded Nationaltheater at the expense of *opera buffa*, the prince established a regular season of Italian opera at Eszterháza and increased the number of Italian singers to the point where, by 1780, the troupe was almost entirely Italian (several of its members had previously sung in Vienna). Friberth departed, replaced by Italian tenors, and there was an Italian poet, NUNZIATO PORTA. Haydn's activity as an arranger of operas written by other composers became increasingly intense.

In the third and final phase (1784–90) Haydn gave up the composition of opera, limiting his theatrical activity to the arrangement and conducting of his earlier operas and those of other composers.

During the first phase Haydn wrote occasional works in a wide variety of genres. These included a *festa teatrale*, ACIDE (1762), that belongs closely to the tradition, cultivated in Vienna during the 1750s and 1760s, of short serious opera in Italian. In its reliance on long orchestral ritornellos, coloratura, and da capo structure, *Acide* shows Haydn re-creating the sound of Viennese Italian opera for his new Hungarian patron. Two full-length *opere buffe* (LE PESCATRICI, 1769, and L'INCONTRO IMPROVVISO, 1775), an intermezzo in two parts (LA CANTERINA, 1766), a *burletta per musica* much like an intermezzo (L'INFEDELTÀ DELUSA, 1773) and a *dramma giocoso per musica* shortened and shorn of its *parti serie* (LO SPEZIALE, 1768) reflect the increasing popularity of *opera buffa* in Vienna during the 1760s. That three of these comic operas are settings of librettos by Goldoni illustrates the importance of the Venetian's librettos in the triumph of *opera buffa* not only at Eszterháza but all over Europe. Several of the early operas survive incomplete, in most if not all cases because of the fire that destroyed the Eszterháza theatre in 1779; the most tragic loss was that of about a third of *Le pescatrici*.

In the absence of a good comic bass or baritone, Haydn made Carl Friberth, a tenor, his principal comic singer. He evidently combined ability as an actor with a penchant for coloratura and for displaying his high notes. The combination was completely foreign to Goldonian comic opera, where comic singing was almost always *parlando* and comic males were mostly baritones. If Don Pelagio (in *La canterina*), Sempronio (in *Lo speziale*), Frisellino (in *Le pescatrici*), and Filippo (in *L'infedeltà delusa*) do not convey in modern performances all the comedy that is expected of them, it may be because Haydn was forced to adapt their music to suit Friberth's abilities.

Many features of these early operas are typical of Haydn's operatic output as a whole. His favouring of slow dramatic pace is especially evident in *L'infedeltà delusa*, the text of which is shorter than a normal, three-act *dramma giocoso per musica*. But by allowing several arias and ensembles to expand far beyond the requirements of their musical and dramatic content, he turned the concise libretto into a long, somewhat languorous opera. Another characteristic feature of Haydn's operatic style is the fast aria in a minor mode. Although such arias are very rare in comic operas by Italian composers, there is one in almost all of Haydn's *opere buffe*. Among the earliest are 'Non v'è chi mi aiuta' from *La canterina*, and 'Amore nel mio petto' from *Lo speziale*.

After Prince Nicolaus's establishment of a permanent Italian troupe in the mid-1770s Haydn wrote only one short opera, L'ISOLA DISABITATA, a delightful *azione teatrale* on an unconventional libretto by METASTASIO. The rest of his output consists of full-length works, of which only IL MONDO DELLA LUNA is a setting of a libretto by Goldoni. During this phase of his career Haydn abandoned Goldoni's librettos in favour of more modern ones in which serious elements play an increasingly prominent role. In LA VERA COSTANZA he explored the troubles of a sentimental heroine abandoned by a mad lover. In LA FEDELTÀ PREMIATA and ORLANDO PALADINO he artfully combined the worlds of *opera seria* and *opera buffa*, achieving a delicate balance between the heroic, the epic, and the comic. The dramatic action of *La fedeltà premiata* moves forward with admirable energy; here Haydn faced and solved the problems of dramatic pacing that mar some of his other operas.

From an emphasis on serious drama within comic operas to the performance of a completely serious full-length opera was a small step, which Prince Nicolaus took in 1783 with the production of Giuseppe Sarti's *Giulio Sabino*. A work that in most respects adheres to the musico-dramatic principle of Metastasian *dramma per musica*, *Giulio Sabino* was the first of several *opere serie* performed at Eszterháza during the 1780s. In giving *opera seria* such an important role, the prince's repertoire differed markedly from that of Vienna, where *opera seria* was almost completely absent during the 1780s. In this respect Eszterháza followed Italy, where *opere serie* such as *Giulio Sabino* were frequently and widely performed. As if in response to the success of *Giulio Sabino* Haydn wrote his own serious opera the following year, ARMIDA, which received more performances at Eszterháza than any other of his operas.

After *Armida* Haydn withdrew from the composition of opera. Heavily burdened with his responsibilities as operatic music director, he may have preferred to devote his limited compositional energy to instrumental music. His awareness of the extent to which Mozart's skills as an operatic composer exceeded his own may also have discouraged him from writing operas. (It may be no accident that Haydn wrote only one opera for Eszterháza after *Die Entführung aus dem Serail*, the first opera by Mozart that Haydn can be assumed to have been familiar with, began its triumphant progress through Germany.) In 1787 Haydn refused an invitation to have one of his Eszterháza operas performed in Prague 'because all my operas are too closely connected with our personal circle, so that they could never produce the proper effect, which I have calculated in accordance with the locality' (letter to Franz Rott, Prague, December 1787). He went on to express reluctance even to write a new opera for Prague 'for scarcely any man could brook comparison with the great Mozart'.

But Haydn did not refuse an opportunity to write an Italian opera during his first trip to London, in part because there was a long-standing obligation to do so, in part because the fee was too large to turn down, and, perhaps after the success of *Armida*, because he felt more confident writing a serious opera than a comic one; moreover, Mozart's operas were unknown in London. *L'anima del filosofo* is a big, elaborate treatment of the story of Orpheus and Eurydice, with impressive choral tableaux and virtuoso arias for the great singers who were to create the principal roles, but it never came to the stage because the impresario who commissioned it was unable to obtain permission for its performance.

Haydn's work on *L'anima del filosofo* was his last intense involvement with Italian opera. In London he experienced for the first time not only the excitement of collaborating with Europe's leading operatic singers, but also the power and popular appeal of Handelian oratorio performed in the native language of the audience. For Haydn the Handel Commemoration concerts of 1791 laid the conceptual foundation for his later success as a composer of German oratorio in Vienna, which replaced Italian opera as the most important musico-dramatic genre of his old age. JAR

Bartha and Somfai.

D. Heartz, *Haydn, Mozart and the Viennese School, 1740–1780* (New York, 1995).

M. Hunter, 'Haydn's Aria Forms: A Study of the Arias in the Italian Operas Written at Eszterháza 1766–1783' (diss., Cornell University, 1982).

H. C. Robbins Landon and D. W. Jones, *Haydn: His Life and Music* (London, 1988).

oratorio

Until the arrival of Haydn's *Creation* in 1798 the extended treatment of a sacred or moralizing subject in a semi-dramatic (though normally unstaged) setting occupied a relatively minor role in the music of the later 18th century. In England Handel's oratorios enjoyed an unbroken tradition of performance after his death, giving rise to many imitations but producing nothing of the first rank, and they were occasionally heard elsewhere. In Catholic Europe oratorio was predominantly in Italian and closely followed the practices of Italian opera, but it was unable to keep up with the developments that produced the operatic masterpieces of the second half of the century. Oratorio in German, largely the preserve of the Protestant north but increasingly in Catholic regions as well, maintained a more robust tradition but impinged little on Haydn. His native familiarity was with the Italian genre, but it was HANDEL who inspired the two great oratorios composed after his second return from London.

The history of Italian oratorio is for the most part the history of Italian opera, with which it shared the same musical and dramatic principles. In the early 18th century it was to all intents and purposes *opera seria* apart from its sacred subject. The action was played out by a cast of dramatic characters (the old tradition of a narrator role was long dead) in a poetic libretto that decorously observed the Aristotelian unities of time, place, and action. Apostolo Zeno (1668–1750) and PIETRO METASTASIO were among the leading librettists of oratorios, as they were of operas. Musically the oratorio was consequently, like opera, a solo genre, proceeding essentially in alternation between recitative and aria. Choral movements had their place, especially as finales, but sometimes the chorus made only a token appearance or none at all.

Different though the formality of such a scheme is from the vividness of Handel's choral dramas, at its best Italian oratorio could compare favourably with contemporary opera. In the absence of staging, the music was the sole medium for dramatic expression and was often weighted accordingly. A work such as *La conversione di Sant'Agostino* (Dresden, 1750) by HASSE, perhaps the most successful composer of *opera seria* of his generation, can hold its own with his finest stage works. But Italian oratorio had nowhere to go. It was never the subject of the concern for greater dramatic cogency that took serious opera in the direction of Gluck's *Orfeo* (1762) and *Alceste* (1767) or Mozart's *Idomeneo* (1780), and its subject matter precluded its joining the growing preference for *opera buffa* as the most effective vehicle for musical drama. By the beginning of Haydn's composing career it was already looking antiquated.

If, in southern Germany and Austria, Italian oratorio was aristocratic and formal, Protestant oratorio in the north tended to be earthier and more direct, with important choral parts and features that aimed (in the vernacular) at a wider audience. Full-blooded melodrama rather than Metastasian refinement is characteristic of works within the strong tradition of dramatic oratorio in Hamburg such as *Der Tag des Gerichts* (The Day of Judgement, 1762) by Georg Philipp Telemann (1681–1767). Telemann's successor was CARL PHILIPP EMANUEL BACH, who after almost 30 years at the court of Frederick the Great moved to Hamburg in 1769 as municipal director of music and responded to the broader horizons there with music on a public scale including the fine oratorios *Die Israeliten in der Wüste* (1769) and *Die Auferstehung und Himmelfahrt Jesu* (1774–80). The increasingly popular devotional, rather than dramatic, type of oratorio included what was probably the most frequently performed oratorio during the later 18th century, *Der Tod Jesu* (Berlin, 1755) by Carl Heinrich Graun (1703/4–59), whose libretto by Carl Wilhelm Ramler was the source of part of the text of the choral version of Haydn's *Seven Last Words*.

Under the patronage of a succession of musical Habsburg emperors, Vienna was a leading centre of late Baroque Italian oratorio and of its particular Passiontide branch the *sepolcro*, shorter and normally at least semi-staged. But after the death of Karl VI in 1740 music at court declined. The splendid sacred works, including numerous oratorios, of FUX and Antonio Caldara (*c.*1670–1736) had few worthy successors, and oratorio became a matter of occasional patronage by aristocratic households. It came into the public domain in 1772, following the foundation of the Tonkünstler-Societät the year before. The exceptional forces that took part in the twice-yearly charitable performances of the society would have been well suited to the grandest Handelian manner, but the repertoire, initially at least, consisted predominantly of Italian oratorio of the conventional sort, opening with two Metastasian settings, *La Betulia liberata* (also composed by Mozart, K118/74c, a year earlier) by the society's founder, GASSMANN, and Hasse's *Sant'Elena al Calvario*. It was for this series of concerts, and within this conventional genre, that Haydn composed *Il ritorno di Tobia*, first performed on 2 April 1775.

Quite exceptional in the programmes of the Tonkünstler-Societät was the performance in 1779 of Handel's *Judas Maccabaeus*, given in German in an adaptation by Joseph Starzer (1726/7–87). Thereafter choral excerpts (never again a complete oratorio) by Handel were occasionally heard, and Handelian grandeur may have something to do with the two magnificent extra choruses that Haydn added to *Il ritorno di Tobia* for its revival in 1784. Also splendid in its choral writing, alongside solo numbers in the most operatic manner, is Mozart's *Davidde penitente* (K469) arranged for the society the following year from the unfinished C minor mass (K427). From the end of the 1770s works in German became increasingly common, but between the society's foundation and its adoption in 1799 of Haydn's *Creation* as its chief standard bearer Italian oratorio outnumbered other types by about two to one.

Occasional performances of a wider variety of oratorios were heard in Vienna under different auspices. Works that from time to time received a public hearing included Graun's *Der Tod Jesu*, but ultimately more fruitful were occasions under private patronage. Although isolated instances can be found earlier, regular performances of Handel began at some time in the 1780s with the organization by Baron Gottfried van Swieten of a group of aristocratic patrons, known as the Gesellschaft der ASSOCIIERTEN, brought together specifically to sponsor oratorios. Probably among the first works mounted by the group was C. P. E. Bach's *Auferstehung und Himmelfahrt Jesu*, in February 1788, but thereafter the diet consisted almost exclusively of Handel, and it was for this series of essentially private concerts before an invited audience (although repeat performances in public sometimes followed) that Mozart prepared his arrangements of *Acis and Galatea* (1788), *Messiah* (1789), and the *Ode for St Cecilia's Day* and *Alexander's Feast* (1790). The sponsorship of van Swieten's group continued through the 1790s, reaching its peak with the promotion of the choral version of Haydn's SEVEN LAST WORDS, THE CREATION, and THE SEASONS.

Oratorio apparently played no part at any stage of Haydn's employment by the Esterházys, despite the existence of a long series of oratorios, all performed in Eisenstadt and extending as late as 1762, by his predecessor WERNER. He may have been involved in a small way in the activities of the Associierte in Vienna, and it is known that van Swieten was pressing him for an oratorio, going so far as to procure from the poet Johann Baptist von Alxinger (1755–79) a libretto entitled *Die Vergötterung des Hercules*, which Haydn was to set 'in the spirit and manner of Handel'. It was indeed Handel that was to inspire Haydn's return to oratorio, not, however, as heard in the exclusive private surroundings of van Swieten's group but as experienced in the popular English tradition that he encountered on his visits to London.

When Haydn returned from England the second time in 1795 with ideas for choral works, all the machinery (and finance) for their realization were waiting for him in Vienna, not in the Tonkünstler-Societät but in the Associierte. His choral arrangement of *The Seven Last Words* was carried out by a process remarkably similar to the methods employed by Mozart in augmenting Handel's scores, and its first performance in 1796 took place before an invited audience as part of the series sponsored by van Swieten's group. The arrangements for promoting *The Creation* in 1798 and *The Seasons* in 1801 were similar. But once released into the public domain they immediately achieved a popular following for oratorio in Vienna comparable to that enjoyed by Handel's works in England.

The Creation may have closer Handelian connections than pure inspiration, since the English libretto (now lost) that Haydn brought back from London is said to have been originally intended for Handel. In any event, the finished work has nothing to do with the Viennese tradition of oratorio and everything to do with the English which, indeed, it was clearly intended to join, being designed in English as well as German from the outset. In Vienna *The Creation* and *The Seasons* were the death-blow to the Italian oratorio and established a new tradition of their own.

For about 18 months after the first performance of *The Seasons* in April 1801 Haydn contemplated writing another oratorio, *The Last Judgement*; he was encouraged, in particular, by EMPRESS MARIE THERESE. He wanted the German poet and author Christoph Martin Wieland (1733–1813) to provide the libretto and envisaged a work in three parts dealing with death, resurrection, and hell and heaven. However, Wieland's apparent reluctance to take on the project and Haydn's advancing old age together ensured that the work never proceeded beyond the planning stage. Ludwig Spohr (1784–1859) was to compose an oratorio with the same title, setting a text by Rochlitz, but there is no direct link between his work and Haydn's projected oratorio.

DEO

H. E. Smither, *A History of the Oratorio*, iii: *The Oratorio in the Classical Era* (Oxford, 1987).

restored to their 18th-century state. Both were built by the Viennese maker Gottfried Malleck and have the same specification. It is on these instruments that Haydn would have played in performances of the six late masses and Beethoven in the performance of his Mass in C in 1807.

Hauptwerk
(main manual)

Principal	8′	Fleten	4′
Copl	8′	Fugura	4′
Quintadena	8′	Quinte	3′
Octave	4′	Superoctave	2′
		Mixtur	(IV–III) 1 1/3′

Rückpositiv
(positive organ)

Copl	8′
Principal	4′
Fleten	4′
Octave	2′
Mixtur	(II) 1′

Pedal

Subbaß	16′
Posaunbaß	16′
Principalbaß	8′
Bourdonbaß	8′
Octavbaß	4′

Pedal coupler, manual coupler (handstops)

Both organs had a short-octave pedal board of 12 notes. The Martinkirche instrument had the customary range from notated *C* to c'''; the Bergkirche organ had an extra tone, up to *d'''*. Only on one occasion did Haydn indicate a choice of registration. In the 'Et incarnatus' section of the 'Schöpfungsmesse' the organ, which is otherwise a continuo instrument in this work, has a fully notated part including the instruction 'flauto' for the right hand, to simulate the traditional association of the holy spirit with a dove. The 18th-century console of the Bergkirche organ is now on display in the Haydn Museum, Eisenstadt.

H. Dreo, 'Die Musiktradition der ehemaligen Stadtpfarrkirche in Eisenstadt', in *Joseph Haydn in seiner Zeit* [Exhibition catalogue] (Eisenstadt, 1982), 134–41.

organisierte Trompete (literally 'organized trumpet'). The name given by ANTON WEIDINGER to a modified form of trumpet for which Haydn composed his concerto. The notes available on the 18th-century trumpet were restricted to those of the harmonic series; consequently, there were wide gaps in the lower register which gradually became narrower towards the highest register. From the *c.*1770s onwards various players and inventors sought to devise ways of filling in the gaps between the notes. The most successful instrument of this kind was developed in Vienna in the 1790s by Weidinger and remained in use in Austria and Italy until well into the 19th century, when it was superseded by valved instruments. Starting near the bell, four to six holes were bored that altered the pitch by a semitone, a tone, a tone and a half, and so on; pads on these holes were activated by keys played by the fingers of the left hand. Although the trumpet lost some of its innate brilliance—one contemporary reported that it sounded like an oboe—it gained a new melodic fluency in the middle register, resourcefully exploited by Haydn in his concerto. The instrument has been revived in modern times for performances of the concerto and works by other composers of the time.

R. Dahlqvist, *The Keyed Trumpet and its Greatest Virtuoso, Anton Weidinger* (Nashville, 1975).

Orlando paladino (Knight Roland) (Hob. XXVIII:11). Opera ('dramma eroicomico') in three acts setting a libretto by NUNZIATO PORTA, first performed at Eszterháza on Prince Nicolaus Esterházy's nameday, 6 December 1782. The librettist CARLO FRANCESCO BADINI had used an episode from Ariosto's *Orlando furioso* as the basis for an extraordinary operatic parody, *Le pazzie d'Orlando*, performed in London in 1771 with music by Guglielmi. Described as a 'new comic opera' it alludes to, and makes use of, French *opéra comique*, Metastasian *opera seria*, and Gluckian music drama. Porta heavily revised the libretto for a production of Guglielmi's opera in Prague in 1775 (under the title *Orlando paladino*), and two years later a similar version was performed in Vienna. Porta came to Eszterháza as director of opera in 1781. He probably brought *Orlando paladino* with him, which Haydn (after further revisions by Porta) set to music the following year.

Porta's various reworkings made Badini's libretto closer, in some respects, to a conventional *opera buffa* by Goldoni; most of the characters fit more easily than Badini's into the conventional types exploited by Goldoni. The large-scale structure of the work is identical to that found in many settings of Goldoni: three acts, with an *introduzione* at the beginning of Act 1, finales at the end of Acts 1 and 2, and a short, simple ensemble at the end of the opera. But Porta and Haydn preserved many of Badini's allusions to other kinds of opera and added some of their own. *Orlando paladino*, like Guglielmi's *Pazzie d'Orlando*, is very much an opera about operatic conventions.

After a cheerful overture the *introduzione* presents the shepherdess Eurilla (soprano, role created by MARIA ANTONI SPECIOLI), her father Lincone (tenor, LEOPOLD DICHTLER), and Radamonte (baritone, DOMENICO NEGRI), the violent King of Barbary. Lincone disappears awkwardly from the opera after this scene (one of Porta's lapses in craftsmanship); Eurilla and Radamonte go on to contribute much to the comic scenes in the opera, together with Orlando's servant Pasquale (baritone, VINCENZO MORATTI). The flirting of Eurilla and Pasquale, and the boasting of the two men are in keeping with the comic conventions of Goldonian opera. Especially characteristic of Goldoni are Pasquale's two catalogue arias; in one ('Ho viaggiato in Francia, in Spagna') he tells of his travels, in the other ('Ecco spiano, ecco il mio trillo') of his musical talents.

Like many *opera buffa* heroines Angelica (soprano, Matilde Bologna) makes her first appearance in a cavatina ('Palpita ad ogni istante'). Fearing the mad Orlando, and worrying for the safety of her timid lover Medoro, she calls on the enchantress Alcina (mezzo-soprano, COSTANZA VALDESTURLA) for help. Alcina's appearance, to the sound of a stormy interlude in C minor, is a major departure from Goldonian *opera buffa* where supernatural events and characters rarely occur. Alcina introduces herself in an aria, 'Ad un guardo', that begins as a rather old-fashioned *opera seria* aria (with a long-breathed melody in a–b–b′ form) but comically switches to a simple, *parlante* style at the line 'e Minosse a mio favore' (and Minos, at my pleasure, often judges on earth).

Haydn explored other kinds of juxtapositions of serious and comic in his portrayal of Medoro and Orlando. Medoro (tenor, PROSPERO BRAGHETTI), in the words he sings, is timid to the point of comedy, yet the composer consistently takes his fear and indecisiveness seriously; in 'Parto, ma, o

Dio, non posso', for example, the minor mode, sudden *forte* outbursts in the accompaniment, and the striking modulations unite to form a memorable picture of emotional turmoil. On the other hand, Orlando (tenor, ANTONIO SPECIOLI), whose words seem to express a hero's tragic predicament, sometimes comes across in Haydn's music as comic. Orlando sings 'Cosa vedo! cosa sento!' ('What do I see? What do I perceive?') after being confronted by monsters (not products of his fevered imagination but real monsters); Haydn, by combining the major mode, fast tempo, and relentless two-bar phrases, characterizes him as a comic figure and invites the audience to laugh at his plight.

Alcina answers Angelica's plea for help, but does not easily succeed in curing Orlando. At the climax of the finale of Act 1 she imprisons him in an iron cage, but by the beginning of Act 2 he is free, and just as mad as before. In the finale of Act 2 Alcina turns Orlando into a stone and back into a man; when this does not cure him she takes him to the underworld (beginning of Act 3), and commands Charon (bass, Dichtler in a second role) to wash his memory clean in the river Lethe. Thus freed from his love for Angelica and from his madness, Orlando joins the other characters in the opera in celebrating (in a delightful ensemble) the forthcoming weddings of Angelica and Medoro, and of Eurilla and Pasquale.

Orlando paladino unfolds at a leisurely pace, calculated to take up a long, quiet evening at Eszterháza. Neither poet nor composer was overly concerned about establishing and maintaining forward momentum. Awkwardly placed comings and goings bring the action almost to a halt in Act 2, when Angelica's aria 'Aure chete' is followed by her exit and the simultaneous entrance of Alcina. After Alcina's recitative, she exits as Angelica returns to declaim yet more recitative. The many orchestrally accompanied recitatives are heavily laden with instrumental commentary that, while often very beautiful, slows down the declamation of the text. The forward progress of Haydn's finales is delayed by several long, slow melodies sung by Angelica and Medoro, passages more remarkable for their musical charm than their dramatic interest. JAR

B. A. Brown, '*Le pazzie d'Orlando*, *Orlando paladino*, and the Use of Parody', *Italica*, 64 (1987), 583–605.

K. Geiringer, 'From Guglielmi to Haydn: The Transformation of an Opera', in *International Musicological Society Congress Report XI. Copenhagen 1972*, 392–5.

H. Geyer-Kiefl, 'Guglielmi's *Le pazzie d'Orlando*', in E. Badura-Skoda (ed.), *Joseph Haydn. Bericht über den internationalen Joseph Haydn Kongress. Wien, Hofburg, 5–12 September 1982* (Munich, 1986), 403–15.

A. van Hoboken, 'Nunziato Porta und der Text von Joseph Haydns Oper "Orlando paladino"', in F. W. Riedel and H. Unverricht (eds), *Symbolae historiae musicae: Festschrift für H. Federhofer* (Mainz, 1971), 170–9.

Osuna, Countess Maria Josefa Alonso Pimentel (*fl.* 1780–90). Member of the Benavente y Osuna family in Madrid who in 1783 arranged via an agent in Vienna (Carlos Alejandro de Lelis) that Haydn forward on a regular basis at least 12 recent compositions per annum, of which eight should be symphonies. Between that date and 1790, when the contract probably lapsed when Haydn left Vienna for London, the composer forwarded music regularly to Madrid. None of these Spanish sources is extant. In April 1784 Haydn reported to Artaria that he was working on three quartets for Spain; they may have been part of the Osuna contract but nothing has survived; in 1789 he apparently wrote two sets of dances for Osuna (Hob.IX:9d,e) that, likewise, have not survived.

N. A. Solar-Quintes, 'Las relaciones de Haydn con la casa de Benavente', *Anuario musical*, 2 (1947), 81–8.

Oxford. University and cathedral city, 91 km (57 miles) north-west of London. The medieval college buildings, churches, and fortifications (still visible today) would have impressed Haydn in 1791, when he visited Oxford. Concert life was centred from 1748 on the Holywell Music Room; surviving programmes from the Musical Society's subscription series and individual benefit concerts show that Haydn's symphonies—sometimes billed as 'overtures'—featured regularly from at least the 1780s onwards, typically within a chronological *mélange* including Handel and Corelli, as well as Haydn's continental and British contemporaries.

Haydn's first appearance in Oxford was scheduled for 18 May 1791, at a benefit concert in the Music Room for Mr Hayward, a member of the Holywell Band. When Haydn was prevented by a rehearsal in London from coming to Oxford, the audience broke into a riot. Haydn's apology, printed in Jackson's *Oxford Journal*, promised that 'as the University of Oxford, whose great Reputation I heard abroad, is too great an object for me not to see before I leave England' he would endeavour to take 'the earliest Opportunity of paying it a Visit'. Between May and July, it seems, possibly at Burney's instigation and certainly with Hayes's approval, it was arranged that Haydn would receive the honorary Oxford D.Mus. (then rarely awarded) during the Encaenia celebrations on 8 July. The Sheldonian Theatre (designed by Wren and built 1664–7) was the assembly room for the public degree ceremonies; the summer festivities typically included three 'Grand Concerts' in the theatre. Haydn arrived late for the first concert on 6 July, leaving no time to rehearse his 'new' symphony, the 'Oxford' (no. 92); it was heard, to great acclaim, in the second programme on 7 July. Another work associated with Oxford is the riddle-canon 'Thy voice, O harmony is divine' (Hob.XXVIIb:46) which Haydn presented to the university.

On 16 June 1801 'The Creation: a Sacred Oratorio composed by Doctor Haydn' was performed at the Music Room with MADAME MARA among the soloists, conducted by WILLIAM CROTCH, the professor of music. Of the works recurring in the Holywell programmes, 'La Roxelane' symphony (no. 63) and 'Military' symphony (no. 100) were favourites; symphonies (often unidentified) were billed as 'MS', or designated with reference to publishers' numberings, while other genres such as quartets and songs were also occasionally represented. There was clearly a Haydn cult in Oxford. In the 19th century the university acquired the Rösler portrait of the composer which now hangs in the Faculty of Music.

The enthusiasm of one person is probably responsible for a curious token of Haydn's association with the city. Above the bar of the the Royal Oak Pub, on the Woodstock Road, there is a round, plate-sized stained glass image of Haydn. Although the pub itself dates back to the 1770s the image included in the stained glass became popular only in the 19th century. SW

R. Hughes, 'Haydn at Oxford: 1773–1791', *Music and Letters*, 20 (1939), 242–9.

J. H. Mee, *The Oldest Music Room in Europe* (London, 1911).

S. Wollenberg, 'Music and Musicians', in *The History of the University of Oxford*, v (Oxford, 1986).

'Oxford' symphony. Nickname for Symphony no. 92 that became current in the 19th century. The work was performed under Haydn's direction in July 1791 at a concert in Oxford that coincided with the award of an honorary doctorate by the university. The symphony itself had been composed in 1789. JH

P

Pacchierotti, Gasparo (bap. 21 May 1740; d. 28 Oct 1821). Italian male soprano, one of the last outstanding castrato singers, renowned for the affecting pathos of his singing. From 1778 he was a frequent visitor to London and, in 1791, he was engaged as principal singer at the Professional Concert, rivals to Salomon's concerts. Despite this, he joined Haydn in a performance of *Arianna a Naxos* at the Ladies Concert on 18 February, which was rapturously received, and he also appeared at Haydn's first London benefit on 16 May 1791. SMcV

HCRL/3.

Palestrina style. One of the two principal elements in musical pedagogy during the 18th century, the other being figured bass. The chief theorist of the Palestrina style was JOHANN JOSEPH FUX, whose *Gradus ad Parnassum* (1725) set a standard for the teaching and study of strict counterpoint. Its chapters on practical composition are in the form of a dialogue between master (Aloysius, identified by Fux as Palestrina) and pupil (Josephus, for Johann Joseph Fux). Palestrina is described as the 'light of music', and the pupil is advised to imitate his style, with special reference to the STYLUS A CAPPELLA.

Within his lifetime and immediately after, Palestrina (*c.*1525–94) had become a legendary model of 16th-century contrapuntal style; his compositional language lent itself to theoretical codification, and was crystallized by Fux's *Gradus* in the system of SPECIES COUNTERPOINT.

The music of Palestrina was also a living part of Viennese sacred choral tradition. The HOFKAPELLE owned, and regularly performed, his works during the 17th and 18th centuries. As well as imbibing the Palestrina style through his study of Fux's *Gradus*, Haydn, as a choirboy in Vienna, would have heard and sung works in the a cappella style of which Palestrina was still considered the leading representative. Haydn composed two, possibly three, works that reflect this continuing tradition: *Missa 'sunt bona mixta malis'*, 'Non nobis, Domine' and, possibly, *Libera me*. SW

D. W. Jones, 'Haydn's *Missa sunt bona mixta malis* and the *a cappella* tradition', in D. W. Jones (ed.), *Music in Eighteenth-Century Austria* (Cambridge, 1996), 89–111.

F. W. Riedel, *Kirchenmusik am Hofe Karls VI. (1711–1740). Untersuchungen zum Verhältnis vom Zeremoniell und musikalischem Stil im Barockzeitalter* (Munich and Salzburg, 1977).

S. Wollenberg (trans. and intro.), 'Johann Joseph Fux, Gradus ad Parnassum (1725): Concluding Chapters', *Music Analysis*, 11 (1992), 209–43.

'Palindrome' symphony. Nickname occasionally used for Symphony no. 46. In the third movement both the minuet and the trio are written as palindromes, the second half of each being an exact reversal of the first half. JH

'Papa Haydn'. Haydn is the only major composer who acquired a nickname during his life that has figured also in his posthumous reputation. Three aspects of 'Papa Haydn' are evident. First, 'Papa' arose as a term of affection, commonly used by the Esterházy players, later others (including Mozart) for a father figure, somebody who willingly gave advice and who was generally respected as a musician. As such it was not an uncommon appellation; Schubert, for instance, called Salieri his 'Großpapa' ('grandad'). Gradually in the 19th century, as the sense of reverence for older composers increased, 'Papa' in Haydn's case transformed itself into 'pater omnipotens', the begetter of the whole symphonic tradition, the composer of the oratorio *The Creation*, and of the Austrian national anthem. Predominantly a German image, more specifically a nationalist Austrian, even Viennese one, it informs the term 'father of the symphony' in English writing.

The third aspect of 'Papa Haydn', common from the middle of the 19th century, is a more patronizing, even dismissive one. In comparison with Romantic artists and Romantic music, Haydn and his output was seen as genial, but naive and superficial. It is in this pejorative sense that 'Papa Haydn' remains in use to this day. CH

Paris. Although Haydn never visited Paris, the French capital played an important part in developing his reputation. As the major centre for music-publishing in Europe, the city from the mid-1760s onwards issued the composer's instrumental music in substantial quantities, and its active concert life featured his music prominently from the late 1770s through the Revolutionary period into the First Republic.

At first the publication of Haydn's music by firms such as BAILLEUX, BÉRAULT, HUBERTY, LA CHEVARDIÈRE, LE MENU & BOYER, SIEBER, and VENIER did not lead to an appreciable number of public performances. During the 1770s a few symphonies were played at the two leading concert series, the Concert spirituel and the Concert des amateurs, but it was only from 1781 that Haydn's music, especially the symphonies and, rather unexpectedly, the Stabat mater, began to feature regularly in concert programmes. Between 1781 and 1790 of the 335 concerts presented by the Concert spirituel under the direction of Joseph Legros, Haydn's music featured in 191 of them. From 1788 onwards two Haydn symphonies, sometimes even three, were performed at each concert. In comparison Mozart's symphonies were performed on only about a dozen occasions in the 1780s.

Given this background, it is not surprising that another concert organization, the Concert de la Loge Olympique, commissioned six new symphonies from the composer at the end of 1784 or the beginning of 1785. Founded in 1781, this concert series, sponsored by a Masonic lodge, had proved so popular that it had moved its venue from the Hotel de Bouillon in the rue de Coq Héron to the guard room at the Palais des Tuileries; at the last concert in the old venue, on 13 April 1784, Haydn's 'Farewell' symphony was given. With a total complement of 67 players the orchestra of the Loge Olympique was over three times the size of the orchestra at Eszterháza and its members included amateurs as well as professionals. In order to boost the quality of music-making leading performers were made nominal Freemasons, and a lodge of Adoption, that is a lodge of lady Freemasons, was established in order to provide female singers. Members paid an annual subscription of 120 livres which entitled them to attend 12 concerts, Masonic meetings, and to use the premises of the lodge as a meeting place. This wealthy organization paid Haydn 25 louis d'or for each of the 'Paris' symphonies (nos. 82–7), five times the going rate (as reported by Mozart in 1778), plus a further 5 louis d'or for the publication rights. No correspondence between the Concert de la Loge Olympique and Haydn survives; it is possible that initial contact with the composer was made through Freemasons in Vienna.

For the first eight years of the Revolution, concert life in Paris was rather sporadic. Between 1798 and 1805, however, Haydn's music, in particular the symphonies, became a major attraction in a new concert series, the Concerts de la rue Cléry. These years also saw the first performance in Paris of *The Creation*, on 24 December 1800 at the Théatre des arts; Napoleon attended, famously the victim of an assassination attempt on his way to the theatre. Paris gave Haydn several honours. Following the performance of *The Creation* the musicians forwarded a commemorative medal to the composer (1801); he was elected to the Institut National des Sciences et des Arts in the same year; in 1805 he was presented with a diploma by the Conservatoire de France; and, two years later, he was made an honorary member of the Société Académique des Enfants d'Apollon. At the end of 1802 Haydn intimated that he might write a new symphony for the Concert des amateurs and it was even rumoured that the composer himself would attend.

Haydn's employer, Prince Nicolaus Esterházy II, spent the winter of 1802–3 in Paris and in January attended a concert at the rue de Cléry that included two of the 'London' symphonies; the finale of one of them was encored. In honour of the prince and of Haydn, a portrait of the composer was put on display while the prince, for his part, presented autograph manuscripts of three items by the composer, including the 'Schöpfungsmesse'.

In December 1804 a rumour spread round Paris that Haydn had died. Cherubini composed a reflective new work, the *Chant sur la mort d'Haydn*. When the rumour was discovered to be false the performance was diplomatically cancelled; it was subsequently first performed on 18 February 1810, eight months after the composer's death. Haydn's status in Paris may be gauged by the remark of a French diplomat who attended the Congress of Vienna in 1814: 'That Vienna has not yet put up a monument to Haydn is absolutely scandalous. In Paris it would have been done long ago.' MV

V. Della Croce, *Cherubini dei Musicisti Italiani del Suo Tempo* (Turin, 1983).
B. Harrison, *Haydn: The 'Paris' Symphonies* (Cambridge, 1998).
J. Mongrédien, *French Music from the Enlightenment to Romanticism 1789–1830* (Portland, Ore., 1996).
C. Pierre, *Histoire du Concert Spirituel 1725–1790* (Paris, 1975).
J.-L. Quoy-Bodin, 'L'Orchestre de la Société Olympique en 1786', *Revue de musicologie*, 70 (1984), 95–107.

'Paris' symphonies. Name traditionally given to a group of six symphonies, nos. 82–7, commissioned by the Concert de la Loge Olympique in PARIS. Symphonies nos. 90–2 also were commissioned by the organization but are not usually referred to as the 'Paris' symphonies. JH

Parke, William Thomas (b. 15 Feb. 1761; d. 26 Aug. 1847). English oboist and memoirist, for many years principal oboe at Covent Garden Theatre and Vauxhall Gardens. Parke and his brother were leading figures at the Professional Concert in opposition to SALOMON; but Haydn was affectionate towards Parke's niece (a singer) and appeared at her benefit in 1794. In 1830 Parke published his memoirs; garrulous and unreliable, they nevertheless paint a lively picture of London's music life in the 1790s, with first-hand descriptions of concerts at which Haydn performed. SMcV

HCRL/3.
W. T. Parke, *Musical Memoirs* (London, 1830).

partita (partitta, parthia, parthie). A term used at various times in the 18th century to describe variations, suites, and sonatas. In the transmission of Haydn's early music it occasionally occurs as the title of symphonies, but it is mainly associated with multi-movement chamber music works, irrespective of genre, and without the earlier associations of the term with suites and variations. In sources for Haydn's early keyboard sonatas and trios the terms partita and DIVERTIMENTO are used interchangeably and there is no basis for believing that they described a genre or indicated sub-generic classifications; for instance the incipit of Hob.XVI:6 is labelled 'Divertimento' in the *Entwurf-Katalog* while the autograph of the second movement is headed 'Partitta'. From the late 1760s and 1770s onwards Haydn's terminology became more specific. In *Entwurf-Katalag* entries and/or autograph manuscripts he referred to Hob.XVI:20–32 as sonatas rather than divertimenti or partitas (though, exceptionally, the autograph of Hob.XVI:29 reverts to the term divertimento). In the 1780s Haydn's keyboard trios and string quartets are called sonatas and quartetti (or quatuors) respectively. With the emergence of this more specific terminology for the more common genres, the earlier usage *Feld-Parthie*, referring specifically to outdoor music, was retained. BH

J. Webster, 'Towards a History of Viennese Chamber Music in the Early Classical Period', *Journal of the American Musicological Society*, 27/2 (1974), 212–47.

partsong. During Haydn's two visits to London in the 1790s he experienced the convivial English tradition of singing catches and glees, a national tradition that can be traced back to the 16th century. In honour of SIR JOHN GALLINI Haydn wrote such a partsong, now lost. DR HARINGTON'S COMPLIMENT also belongs to the same tradition. Finally, for the EARL OF ABINGDON, Haydn added a keyboard or harp part to nine catches and three glees for three male voices composed by the earl; they were published in 1795 as *Twelve Sentimental Catches and Glees* (Hob.XXXIc:16).

Back in Vienna in 1796 Haydn embarked on a project to write a set of 24 partsongs in German, a relaxing diversion from the challenges of the two late oratorios, the six late masses, and the final quartets. Although nine partsongs were written that year Haydn managed to complete only a further four over the next three years and, with increasing old age, he eventually gave up the project, entrusting BREITKOPF & HÄRTEL with the publication of the completed partsongs, which appeared in 1803 (Hob.XXVc:1–9 and XXVb:1–4). Although the English tradition may be sensed in some of the comic partsongs, particularly in their witty use of silence and brisk antiphony, Haydn's works soon joined the distinctive German tradition of partsongs that flourished in the 19th century.

At first Haydn seems to have set out to compile a set based on texts taken from a collection of poetry assembled by Karl Wilhelm Ramler, *Lyrische Blumenlese* (Lyrical Flower Harvest), that he had in his library; later he sought texts outside this collection, turning in particular to his favourite German poet, CHRISTIAN FÜRCHTEGOTT GELLERT, for four texts. Composed mainly for four-part voices, a few three-part, Haydn provided a figured bass for the first nine songs which was realized in the publication by Breitkopf & Härtel, probably by a local musician in Leipzig, August Eberhard Müller (1767–1817); for the final four songs Haydn provided a fully written-out piano part.

The first song, 'Der Augenblick' ('The Moment', text by Johann Nikolaus Götz), jokingly warns that it takes only a 'weak moment' to fall in love; as in many of the partsongs the text is repeated several times. 'Die Harmonie in der Ehe' ('Marital harmony', text by Götz) is a lively portrayal of domestic compatibility, though the frequent slightly contorted harmony that accompanies 'Harmonie' adds a touch of irony; as always in this repertoire such jokes are more for the performers—here as they concentrate hard on harmonizing—than for the listeners. No. 3, 'Alles hat seine Zeit' ('A time for everything', text translated from the Greek of Athenaeus), is a drinking song in which snatches of thematic material are tossed between the participants, the singers coming together for the crucial phrase 'ich bin wider klug mit dir' ('Now I'm sensible with you again'); the clause 'wenn ich schwärme' ('when I revel') is set in imitative bursts of semiquavers. 'Die Beredsamkeit' ('Eloquence', text by Gotthold Ephraim Lessing) contrasts the tongue-loosening qualities of Rhenish wine with the dumb silence that comes from drinking water; Haydn indicates that the last word 'stumm' (dumb), on an implied tonic, should be mouthed rather than sung.

No. 5, 'Der Greis' ('The old man', text by Johann Ludwig Wilhelm Gleim), is a touching portrayal of declining powers and the welcome release of death; Haydn was to use the opening four bars of the soprano line as a musical inscription on his visiting card, 'HIN IST ALLE MEINE KRAFT'. The following partsong, 'An den Vetter' ('To the cousin', text by Christian Felix Weisse), is a spirited warning from three singers (soprano, alto, and tenor) that love and folly are the same thing. In no. 7, 'Daphnens einziger Fehler' ('Daphne's only fault', text by Götz), two tenors and a bass skilfully build a winning picture of Daphne's peerless beauty and charm, and an equally wistful one of her only failing: she doesn't know how to love. In no. 8, 'Die Warnung' ('The Warning', text from Athenaeus), the music warns of the scorpions of deceit that lay hidden under every stone. No. 9, 'Betrachtung des Todes' ('Contemplation of death', text by Gellert) is written for soprano, tenor, and bass and is a rather one-dimensional setting of a grim text, with no sense of comfort and no apparent irony.

No. 10, 'Wider den Übermut' ('Preserve me from insolence'), one of three partsongs with a sacred text, has an eloquent piano introduction to a prayer that seeks deliverance from pride and insolence. In typical Austrian fashion (as in the juxtapositions of the sacred and the secular in 'Winter' in *The Seasons*), the following partsong returns to women, 'An die Frauen' ('To the ladies', text from the Greek by Anakreon), in particular their distinctive quality, beauty. The last two songs have sacred texts by Gellert, a sonorous song of praise to God ('Aus dem Danklied zu Gott') and an evening hymn to God ('Abendlied zu Gott'). The vocal writing in the latter is especially well judged in texture and sonority, making use, as often in the contemporary late masses, of gently rhetorical pauses.

HCRL/4.

pasticcio. Italian word for a pie; used pejoratively it signifies a mess or a jumble. Applied to opera, mainly of the 18th century, it denotes a work, usually an *opera seria*, consisting of numbers from different sources and by different composers. It is useful to distinguish a true pasticcio from an opera by a single composer in which, following normal contemporary practice, an arranger has introduced one or more substitute or additional numbers by another composer. While Haydn very frequently replaced arias in the operas that he arranged for performance at Eszterháza, true pasticcios formed a negligible part of the repertoire of Haydn's opera company. *La circe ossia L'isola incantata*, performed at Eszterháza in 1789, is a rare example of a pasticcio with some comic characters and scenes. It included music by Johann Gottlieb Naumann (1741–1801), Haydn, and other, unidentified composers. In preparing Niccolò Zingarelli's serious opera *Montezuma* for performance in 1785 Haydn inserted no fewer than eight arias; but enough of Zingarelli's music survived for the work to be performed under his name. JAR

pastorella. A church composition for Christmas that relates, either in whole or in part, the narrative of the shepherds in the fields, the appearance of the angels, and the offering of gifts to the infant Jesus. Typically set in dialect German, the music often alludes to folksong and uses standard images of the pastoral, such as drone basses and exotic melodies; the total effect is often delightfully comic as well as edifying. Usage of the term overlaps with ADVENT ARIA. Two pastorellas are safely attributed to Haydn, 'EY, WER HAT IHM DAS DING GEDENKT' and 'HERST NACHBÄ, HÄ, SAG MIR WAS HEUT', though he may have composed further examples.

G. Chew, 'The Austrian pastorella and the *stylus rusticanus:* Comic and Pastoral Elements in Austrian Music, 1750–1800', in D. W. Jones (ed.), *Music in Eighteenth-Century Austria* (Cambridge, 1996), 133–93.

G. Chew, 'Haydn's Pastorellas: Genre, Dating and Transmission in the Early Church Music', in O. Biba and D. W. Jones (eds), *Studies in Music History Presented to H. C. Robbins Landon on his Seventieth Birthday* (London, 1996), 21–43.

Pauersbach, Karl Michael (Joseph) von (b. Feb. 1737; d. 17 Oct. 1802). A civil servant in Vienna who turned to a career as an author, playwright, and puppeteer. In July 1772 he sold a set of puppets and associated props to Prince Esterházy for the new marionette theatre that was formally opened the following year. For a while, Pauersbach was its part-time director before moving permanently to Eszterháza *c.*1776. As an author he was responsible for the texts of four works entitled *Genoveva*, the last of which was possibly set by Haydn; he also wrote librettos for German operas by Ordonez, Pleyel, and Purksteiner. As well as managing the company and writing librettos he undertook some spoken parts. In 1778 he married the court singer Maria Anna Tauber; the couple left at the end of the year for Russia where Tauber hoped to pursue her singing career. From 1781 they lived in Regensburg where Pauersbach was employed in the postal service of the local Thurn und Taxis family. He continued to work occasionally as an author and adapter. ERL

HCRL/2.

K. M. Pollheimer, 'Karl Michael (Joseph) von Pauersbach (1737–1802). Das Leben und Werk des Begründers und Direktors des Marionettentheaters in Eszterháza', in *Beiträge zur Theatergeschichte des 18. Jahrhunderts* (Eisenstadt, 1973), 34–78.

'Paukenmesse' (Hob.XXII:9). Nickname for the MISSA IN TEMPORE BELLI arising in the mid-19th century and occasioned by the unusual and evocative writing for timpani (*Pauken* in German) in the Agnus Dei. JH

Peploe, Mrs (*fl.* 1795–1805). A travelling amateur British singer and pianist who transmitted some of the works of Haydn and Mozart to England. During two visits to VIENNA (Nov.– Dec. of 1796 and 1797), Peploe obtained manuscript copies from Haydn of 'Berenice, che fai?', Orfeo's recitative and aria 'Perduto un altro volta' from *L'anima del filosofo*, and two new vocal duets (Hob.XXVa:1–2). She is listed among the subscribers to *The Creation* as a resident of Curzon Street, Mayfair. REC

'per figuram retardationis'. An annotation written by Haydn above bars 53–4 of the slow movement of the F minor quartet, op. 20 no. 5. The traditional view of the remark is that it indicates that the florid line of the first violin should be held back in tempo, a view that can be traced to Joachim (1831–1907): 'It means that the figures of the violin are always a step behind the chords; it must be played dreamily and tenderly, not stiffly and coldly.' However, Haydn's remark referred to an aspect of 18th-century musical theory and was not in itself a performance indication. Retardation was the delayed resolution of a dissonance. Haydn's florid line for the first violin features a number of dissonances that are not immediately resolved and the annotation is a typically wry remark of self-justification in the same category as the *licenza* ('licence') that the composer noted next to a grammatical solecism in the slow movement of the E♭ quartet, op. 71 no. 3.

performance practice. See opposite.

Pesci, Antonio (*fl.* 1763–83). Bass singer who worked in the Italian opera house at Eszterháza from March 1779 to July 1782. Born in Bologna he was primarily a singer of comic roles, appearing in various theatres in Italy and in Lisbon before joining the Esterházy court towards the end of his career. During his time at court he sang no fewer than 18 roles, including the part of Melibeo in Haydn's *La fedeltà premiata*. From Eszterháza he returned to Italy, to Gorizia, where his career seems to have ended. ERL

Philemon und Baucis oder Jupiters Reise auf die Erde (Philemon and Baucis or Jupiter's journey to the Earth) (Hob.XXIXa:1). Haydn's first marionette opera ('Kleines Schauspiel mit Gesang'), setting a libretto by Gottlieb Konrad Pfeffel, and first performed at Eszterháza on 2 September 1773 during the visit of Empress Maria Theresia. Of the music of the prologue, *Der Götterrath* (The council of the gods), only the overture and a brief orchestral movement survive, though the text is extant; the overture was reused as the first two movements of Symphony no. 50. The opera itself consists of an overture in D minor, four arias, a duet, and two choruses. As Jupiter and Mercury are spoken roles and the arias, for all their charm, are in moderate or slow tempos, there is little tension in the music once the opening storm chorus gives way to a song of thanksgiving. The plot tells of the gods' search for generous-spirited mortals; the disguised Jupiter and Mercury are given shelter by Philemon (tenor) and Baucis (soprano), despite their poverty and the fact that they are mourning the deaths of their son, Aret (tenor), and his betrothed, Narcisa (soprano), both killed by a thunderbolt. Jupiter, moved by their story, brings the young couple back to life; the old couple's hut is transformed into a temple and they themselves are made priests; the villagers who had declined to give hospitality to the gods are admonished; and Jupiter and Mercury return to the heavens. A final scene, for which no music survives, is an apotheosis of the House of Habsburg. PB

HCRL/2.

'Philosopher' symphony. Nickname in common use for Symphony no. 22. It arose in the 18th century ('Le Philosophe'), reflecting the earnest mood of the opening slow movement. The symphony may have been performed as incidental music to a play by Goldoni, *Il filosofo inglese*, when, as *Die Philosophinnen*, it was given at the Kärntnerthortheater in Vienna in December 1764. JH

E. Sisman, 'Haydn's Theater Symphonies', *Journal of the American Musicological Society*, 43 (1990), 292–352.

piano music. *See* KEYBOARD SONATA, KEYBOARD TRIO, KEYBOARD VARIATIONS.

Pichl, Wenzel (b. 25 Sept. 1741; d. 23 Jan. 1805). Born in Bohemia, Pichl received a broad education in law, philosophy, and theology, as well as music. He played the violin in Dittersdorf's orchestra in Großwardein (Oradea), moved to Prague, and then to Vienna. On the personal recommendation of Empress Maria Theresia, in 1777 he became musical director for the governor of Milan, Archduke Ferdinand, a position he held for the rest of his life. From Milan he frequently sent his own compositions (including baryton trios, string quartets, and symphonies) to the Eszterházy court which seems to have retained him as an unofficial agent in the city. The French invasion of 1796 caused the Habsburg court in Milan to return to Vienna. From that time on Pichl and Haydn became casual acquaintances. He died while playing in a concert at the Lobkowitz palace.

Pichl's symphonies were played throughout Europe, including at Salomon's concerts in London in the 1790s. Among their characteristic features, replicated to a greater or lesser extent in Haydn's symphonies, are slow introductions, canons, and descriptive titles. A few works were falsely ascribed to Haydn. ERL

Pietà di me, benigni Dei (Benign gods, have pity on me) (Hob.XXVb:5). Trio for two sopranos and a tenor, solo cor anglais, bassoon and horn, and orchestra. Apart from being highly unusual in scoring it has an unclear history. For these reasons doubts have been cast on its authenticity. It can, however, be identified with the new 'terzetto' by Haydn performed at the Professional Concert in London on 25 April 1791, with soloists Elizabeth Billington (soprano), GASPARO PACCHIEROTTI (male

[*cont. on p.286*]

performance practice

The conditions in which Haydn's music was performed and the traditions that informed its realization were very different from those generally encountered today. For convenience the following survey of the main issues is divided into six areas. Some of the material mentioned in one area applies with equal validity to others and readers are encouraged to read the entire entry for the fullest picture.

---

1. Chamber music. Haydn's chamber music spans a period of change in the construction of string instruments and bows that significantly affected playing techniques and resulting sonority. Modern players with historical performance as their goal must, therefore, decide whether to use short-necked instruments with lighter fittings and pre-Tourte bows or, as may be the case say for Haydn's op. 50 (1787) and later quartets, to use Tourte-model bows and instruments designed to produce greater volume.

For Haydn's chamber music up to *c.*1770—quartets, trios, miscellaneous divertimenti, and ensembles with keyboard—a decision needs to be taken regarding the appropriate string instrument for the bass line. Haydn used the generic term 'basso' to mean 'the bass part' and not a specific instrument and it is clear that while the progressive trend was towards a cello on the bass line, a double bass (violone) was often used instead.

For the most part Haydn's performers are fortunate in being able to establish musical texts based on sources that either derive directly from the composer or were approved by him. Although such sources are often incomplete in their performing directions (as in the extreme instance of the autograph manuscripts of op. 64), or are ambiguous or inconsistent, they, nevertheless, furnish invaluable information regarding expression, articulation, phrasing, accentuation, ornamentation, and other aspects of interpretation. Thus, the performer's traditional role of conveying faithfully, yet personally, the composer's intentions according to the mood, character, and style of the music can be fulfilled.

The 18th century witnessed the culmination of the 'doctrine of the affections', the central aim of which was the musical expression of specific human emotions. Simple descriptive words at the beginning of a piece, movement, or section suggested broadly its mood and approximate tempo; additional words, as increasingly found in Haydn's later music, are used to qualify or to make even more specific the required mood. In his celebrated treatise on violin-playing Leopold Mozart characterized 'Grave' as sad and earnest, 'hence very slowly', while 'Adagio' is simply slow (not extremely slow as in the 19th century). Within the affect of one movement Haydn often achieves remarkable variety by varying themes on their recurrences whether in scoring, phrase rhythm, or tonal direction.

Individual movements (apart from variations) were generally performed with a uniform pulse, although some flexibility of the prescribed melodic rhythm was regarded as desirable even if not specifically indicated. A flexible approach to rhythm, especially dotted rhythms, was also common, a dotted note often being lengthened and its complementary note shortened and played in 'lifted' style.

Leopold Mozart consistently stressed expressive playing and the development of a 'singing' style of performance, favouring a 'strong, masculine bow stroke'. He divided bow strokes into four 'divisions', characterized by a differently placed swelling or diminishing of tone: division 1 = <>; division 2 = >; division 3 = <; and division 4 = <> <>. These became so widely practised that sustained strokes without nuance were comparatively rare. In his early works Haydn indicated dynamic markings sparingly; however, his basic markings of *forte*, *piano*, and, occasionally, *mezza voce* call not for sudden, 'terraced' leaps between extremes, but for a graduated approach to expression. *Sforzando* is much more commonly encountered than in music of his contemporaries and is variously employed to emphasize chromatic alterations of notes, to accentuate cross-rhythms, and as an accent. Broadly speaking Haydn's later works incorporate more detailed dynamic markings.

The fundamental stroke of pre-Tourte bows was non-legato. Staccato bowing involved even greater articulation and was generally conveyed by lifting the bow from the string after each stroke, tempo permitting. True legato bowing was achieved only by slurring; traditionally the first note under a slur was emphasized slightly and the convention of slurring appoggiaturas and other such dissonances to their resolutions was tacitly understood. Haydn's sometimes quite complex phrasing patterns are not indicated as such and need to be articulated by pausing briefly on the last note of one phrase and starting anew on the first note of its successor, by reducing slightly the tonal volume of the last note and re-establishing it with the first of the next phrase, or by shortening the last note of one phrase, when necessary, to separate it from the first note of the next.

Eighteenth-century musicians observed the three categories of accent used in everyday speech, grammatic, rhetorical, and pathetic. Grammatic accents, which occurred regularly on the beats of the bar, were not given equal length and emphasis. The first accent in the bar was reproduced in string-playing by the traditional 'rule of the down bow': a long-standing principle that required such notes to be played with the stronger down bow and the unaccented ones with the weaker up bow. Rhetorical and pathetic accents were distinguished from grammatic accents not only by the more pronounced manner in which they were executed but also by the fact that they were not restricted to any part of the bar. A note that is longer, or markedly higher or lower than its predecessor, or is dissonant are all common instances when emphasis through prolongation of the note beyond its written length provided a flexible, musicianly solution.

According to Leopold Mozart, necessity, convenience, and elegance were the reasons for using left-hand positions on the fingerboard other than the first. Until at least the end of the 18th century shifts were generally made when the punctuation of the music allowed: on the beat or on repeated notes, by the phrase in sequences, after an open string, on a rest or pause between staccato notes, or after a dotted figure where the bow was generally lifted off the string. Leopold Mozart's 'elegant' shifts were associated with uniformity of timbre within a phrase; Haydn draws attention to such passages with the indication 'sopra una corda' ('on one string') or similar, by long slurs, or by specific fingerings.

In the quest for an even tone, open strings were generally avoided when stopped notes were technically viable, but they nonetheless appeared in certain scale passages, figurations, and double stops to facilitate shifting and for special effect. In the first movement of the quartet in F, op. 77 no. 2, for example, Haydn specifies 'das leere A' (literally 'empty A') as a particular point of emphasis in the development section. Haydn also occasionally makes an open string function as a pedal simultaneously with a moving part; an unusual instance of harmonics is indicated in the third movement of a string trio in D (Hob.V:21). Haydn's keenness to assist performers in music that is grammatically very tortuous is demonstrated by his annotations in the first movement of op. 77 no. 2, where he recommends cello fingering for the enharmonic notes E♭ and D♯ as well as helpfully writing 'l'istesso tuono' ('the same pitch').

Portamento (sliding from one note to the next) was rejected outright by some 18th-century writers but was, nevertheless, employed by many performers, especially in solo contexts. Haydn's fingerings sometimes indicate its use, especially for humorous purposes; the trio of op. 33 no. 2 is an extended, deliberately vulgar case.

Details of ornaments and their realization are given in the following section, on keyboard music. String players should consider the sparing, expressive use of vibrato, applied at a speed and intensity appropriate to the dynamic, tempo, and character of the music. More challenging is the introduction of apparently spontaneous improvisation, principally in the form of melodic variation and decoration of pauses and cadences, using models from vocal repertoire as well as instrumental repertoire. Finally, the optimum placement of individuals in ensembles is an important matter about which there has never been unanimity. It is quite likely that many chamber ensembles performed on their feet (apart from the cellists); on the other hand, the survival of elegant quartet desks from the period—four reading stands mounted on a table top—suggests that quartets played seated and facing each other. RS

2. Keyboard music. Given that Haydn's keyboard music was written over a period of approximately 50 years the performance practices associated with it are, understandably, quite diverse and cannot be reduced to a single set of conventions that operate throughout the entire period. In the first instance the keyboard instruments for which Haydn wrote, and consequently the keyboard idiom, changed considerably. Haydn wrote for harpsichords and clavichords in his early keyboard music; it is one of the happy historical coincidences of the 1780s that the later keyboard music of Haydn and Mozart was written at a time when the level of craftsmanship of makers like Stein, Schanz, and Walter brought a particular tradition of Viennese fortepiano manufacture to perfection; and in the 1790s Haydn became familiar with the sonorous qualities of the very different English tradition of piano-making, in the instruments produced by Longman & Broderip and Broadwood. The early works are written in a generalized keyboard idiom that relies in performance on the expressive potential of articulation, touch, ornamentation, agogic accentuation, etc., rather than specifically on the peculiarities of individual instrument types (such as the registration on a harpischord, the expressive *Bebung* possible on a clavichord, and the touch-sensitive control of dynamics on clavichords and fortepianos). This music requires no less an expressive performance than later works, but the keyboard idiom is not reliant on any particular type of instrument.

The date at which the harpsichord was displaced by the fortepiano varied from place to place, and from composer to composer. Certainly by 1788, when Haydn bought a Schanz fortepiano, his music is no longer compatible with performance on harpischord. Increasingly in the 1780s Haydn notated dynamic markings in his keyboard music and, on internal evidence, the sonatas of 1784 (Hob.XVI:40–2) mark Haydn's irreversible commitment to a fortepiano idiom. (The earlier C minor sonata, Hob.XVI:20, which contains detailed dynamic markings in the autograph manuscript, was, arguably, conceived with a clavichord in mind when written in 1771, but when it was published in an authentic first edition by Artaria in 1780 further dynamic markings were added to appeal to a broader public, including an increasingly large number of players who owned Viennese fortepianos.) The sonatas and trios from 1788 onwards are particularly rich in their notation of dynamic nuance and accentuation which, with a sophisticated exploitation of the sonorities and contrasting registers of late 18th-century pianos, are integral to Haydn's compositional ideas and underline structural features of the music.

Apart from dynamics, Haydn's notation of ornaments, articulation, and other facets of performance practice changes significantly in the course of his career and, on the evidence of his autograph manuscripts and other good sources, phases of notational revision can be identified in the mid-1760s and again in the early 1780s. Haydn's early works from before *c.*1766 are, stylistically and in respect of their notation, in the Austrian tradition. They contain few ornament signs or indications of articulation and generally such refinements are left to the good taste of the performer. The ornaments that are given are often notated generically (the ***tr*** symbol does not, for instance, distinguish between different types of trill and, arguably, sometimes merely indicates that any appropriate ornament should be played); the notation of appoggiaturas is conventional, in the sense that their duration is contingent on context rather than on the literal meaning of the notation since, in all autograph manuscripts until 1763, Haydn uniformly indicated appoggiaturas with a small note, a quaver in value.

From 1766, however, there is a fundamental change in Haydn's notation of ornaments, as from that date, and for more than a decade, he employed an array of specialized diacritic symbols, more often associated with the French–north German tradition, to distinguish different ornament types. Between 1766 and the late 1770s Haydn distinguishes notationally between long and short trills, uses a variety of means to indicate trills ending with a turn (*Nachschlag*), those beginning with a lower auxiliary note (*Triller von unten*), and those beginning with an appoggiatura. In the notation of appoggiaturas he employs small notes that vary in value from demisemiquaver to minim, suggesting that, when transmitted in reliable sources, these small notes represent the actual duration of the appoggiaturas in performance, a notational practice described by C. P. E. BACH and termed 'real' notation.

Even at its most precise, Haydn's notation of ornament signs advises the performer which ornaments to play, not precisely how to play them and there are many matters relating to the interpretation of ornaments that were controversial in the 18th century and remain so today. Since C. P. E. Bach influenced the revision of Haydn's notation in the mid-1760s, his treatise, *Versuch über die wahre Art das Clavier zu spielen* (Berlin, 1753, 1762) together with Marpurg's *Anleitung zum Clavierspielen* (Berlin, 1755; Haydn owned two copies), and Türk's *Klavierschule* (Leipzig, 1789), a later treatise but, like Marpurg's, belonging to the same tradition as Bach's *Versuch*, are the most valuable starting point for the interpretation of Haydn's ornaments. The principal lesson to be learnt from Haydn's notation is the diversity of ornaments that is requisite in his music; the table below gives conventional and approximate suggestions for the realization of ornament signs found in Haydn's keyboard music, and, less frequently, elsewhere, based on contemporary treatises and the evidence of his notation.

From the 1780s Haydn's notation of ornaments is simplified and, in general, ornaments indicated by diacritic symbols are less prominent in his fortepiano idiom of the late 1780s and 1790s than in the keyboard music of the 1760s and 1770s. In other respects Haydn's notation from the 1780s is more precise (dynamic markings and distinctions between dotted and double-dotted rhythms are, for instance, more frequent). Two important aspects of performance practice, embellishment and articulation, which were notated with a new precision in the keyboard music of the 1760s and 1770s, continue to be indicated in meticulous detail in the 1780s and 1790s. From *c.*1766 Haydn frequently embellished phrase repetition, counter-statements in expositions, and sometimes recapitulations in sonata form movements, and wrote out varied reprises in Tempo di Menuet movements, rondos, and, occasionally, slow movements, in place of formal repeats. Comparisons of the original state of themes and their embellished forms provide sophisticated models for the reconstruction of practices of improvised embellishment and inform the player of the contexts in which embellishment was appropriate in Haydn's music (see, for instance, the second movements of Hob.XVI:45, 19, 18, 44, 38, and XV:23). At the same time such passages suggest that restraint may be more appropriate than lavish improvisation in works that Haydn has already embellished heavily and provide a stringent standard for the criticism of improvisation.

Beginning also in the mid-1760s and continuing through to his last keyboard works, Haydn provided, at times, remarkably precise indications of articulation that reward careful study. These indications include the careful notation of slur lengths (which are characteristically short slurs that do not, in general, cross the barline, except as special contra-metric effects), and, in good sources, careful distinctions between staccato (indicated by vertical dashes), and *portato* (for which he used, interchangeably, dots, and the normal indication of dots covered by a slur). Characteristically Haydn gave precise instruction for the articulation in important thematic material in a movement. This is not to say that his notation of articulation is ever complete: on the contrary it remains an essential taste in performance to complete the composer's articulation markings. This involves the selection of appropriate touches to characterize themes, effect expressive accents, and articulate metre, even in the later fortepiano music where accentuation may be reinforced by dynamic nuance. The practice of eliding characteristic patterns of short slurs into long flowing lines, widely advocated by influential 19th- and 20th-century authors, is not supported by the evidence of 18th-century theory and by Haydn's notation.

The numerous works in which Haydn varied the articulation of a theme in subsequent recurrences or transformations are especially worthy of close scrutiny (e.g. Hob.XVI:23/iii, 20/i, XV:18/i, and 28/i). They caution both the editor and performer that Haydn's purposeful variation in articulation should not be reduced to uniformity and also provide the best possible models for the development of varied and lively articulation in the performance of his keyboard music. BH

Table of Ornaments

Haydn's Notation | **Suggested Realization**

(i) Trill Types

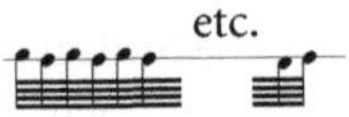

etc.

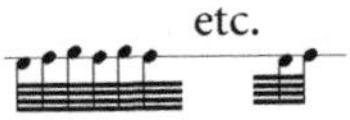

etc.

or

Praller

or

or

Schneller

Haydn's Notation	Suggested Realization
(ii) Doppelschläge	
	or
prallender Doppelschlag	
	or
geschnellter Doppelschlag	
(iii) Mordent	
(iv) Schleifer	
(v) Anschlag	

(vi) Appoggiaturas
Before *c.*1765/6 the duration of appoggiaturas indicated by small notes must be decided by context alone. Generally, in Haydn's keyboard music, most such appoggiaturas seem to require a realization half, or less than half, the value of the main note.
After *c.* 1765/6 Haydn used a variety of values for small notes (from demisemiquaver to minim) indicating appoggiaturas. When transmitted in good sources these notated values suggest plausible durations in performance.

3. Opera. During Haydn's first 15 years of service at the Esterházy court, from 1761 to 1775, operas were performed sporadically, often as part of a wider programme of diversion for a festive occasion such as a wedding or a royal visit. The year 1776 marked the beginning of regular opera seasons at Eszterháza, with an average of between 90 and 100 performances every year; these performances, prepared and directed by Haydn, continued until the death of Nicolaus Esterházy in 1790. The repertoire consisted of works by the most popular opera composer of the day, such as Anfossi, Cimarosa, Paisiello, and Salieri, as well as operas by Haydn himself. In its heyday Eszterháza was a major operatic centre and, within Austria, a worthy rival to the Viennese court theatre.

Compared to the period after 1776, when the large number of performances produced a substantial quantity of associated paperwork, there is considerably less documentation concerning the earlier productions. Nicolaus's predecessor, Prince Paul Anton, had ordered that a theatre be constructed in the garden at Eisenstadt, but he died before its completion. The theatre was abandoned, and operas were subsequently performed in the hall of the palace itself or perhaps in the garden. No details or contemporary accounts survive of what must have been a makeshift operation.

It was at Eisenstadt that Haydn's first operas composed for the court were performed, *La marchesa nespola*, *Acide*, and three lost works, *Il dottore*, *La vedova*, and *Il scanarello*. GIROLAMO BON, a distinguished painter and architect as well as an impresario, furnished the sets. Although none of this original scenery survives, two elaborate paintings dated 1762—a grove with ruins and a deep-perspective interior—are likely to be his work. Bon also provided the decorations for *La canterina*.

In 1768, with the completion of the main theatre and musicians' quarters, Eszterháza became the centre of operatic activity. There are few descriptions of the first theatre, which was destroyed by fire in 1779; an account of the disaster in the *Pressburger Zeitung* mentions a grand box for the prince and two side boxes for his guests. It seems that the rebuilt theatre, completed in just 14 months, closely resembled the one that was destroyed.

There is a sizeable amount of archival material concerning both the players and the singers who performed at Eszterháza. The ensemble that otherwise performed Haydn's symphonies was used in the pit. When Haydn first arrived in Eisenstadt in 1761 the orchestra consisted of 14 members: six violinists, one viola player, one cellist, one bass player (who could also play the bassoon), one flautist, two oboists, one bassoon player, and two horn players. These could be expanded to 16 players, if necessary. Over time the orchestra increased in size; in 1772 the string complement was probably 4–3–2–1–1, and from 1776, with the beginning of regular opera performances, it remained more or less fixed at 5–5–2–2–1. From 1776 to early 1778 two clarinet players were available and, on occasions, trumpets and timpani were present as well; at other times Haydn was forced to cut or rewrite clarinet and trumpet parts. Descriptions of operatic performances from 1774 and 1783 number the ensemble at 24, while another from 1778 mentions 30 people, suggesting the presence of extra, occasional players.

The orchestra played directly in front of the stage; the pit was sunken slightly so that the heads of the musicians were just below stage level. Haydn directed from the harpsichord, probably assisted by his leader, Tomasini. A cello, possibly double bass too, played with the harpsichord in recitatives; they read off a single part. Arpeggiated chords notated in recitatives in *Lo speziale* suggest that the cellist was expected to play multiple stops occasionally, a practice that led in 1769 to a dispute between Küffel and Weigl as to who was the better player. That the harpsichord played not only in the recitatives but in the set pieces as well seems clear from the indication 'cembalo solo' in one of Buonafede's arias in *Il mondo della luna*; no doubt Haydn would play in the tutti sections but drop out during softer passages, a practice suggested as late as 1792 in Türk's *Kurze Anweisung zum Generalbaßspielen*.

Most of the players were seated on two long rows of benches and used a single long music stand. Haydn probably sat to one side where he could be seen easily by both the singers and the players. The often reproduced *gouache* picture (now in the Deutsches Theatermuseum, Munich) that supposedly shows a performance of *L'incontro improvviso* has no connection with Eszterháza or Haydn, but as a contemporary depiction of an opera performance it gives some idea of the likely placement of the musicians relative to the stage and the audience.

The singers at Eszterháza were mostly Italians. Although small in number (rarely more than a dozen were employed at one time), they were frequently excellent in quality. Only one castrato singer was ever employed, PIETRO GHERARDI, who was engaged for Gluck's *Orfeo* in 1776 but stayed only two years. There was no Italian opera chorus at Eszterháza. If a chorus could not be performed by the soloists, it was either cut from the production or extra singers were recruited from the church choir in Eisenstadt. It is likely that choral numbers were performed with only two or three people per part. However, there were no limits on non-musical 'extras', freely drawn from the prince's grenadiers (standing at a minimum height of 2 metres (6 feet)), their wives and children, and, sometimes, other employees. A performance of Traetta's *Ifigenia in Tauride* in 1786 had over 50 personnel on stage in one scene.

No contemporary depictions of an operatic performance at Eszterháza is known. Nevertheless, some idea of the splendour of the costumes and sets can be gleaned from the detailed documents that have survived. The tailor from the court opera in Vienna was brought in to make the costumes for *Le pescatrici*; extant bills and memoranda show that the fishermen and fisherwomen of the opera all sported costumes with silver fringes, taffeta ribbons, and blue atlas (an Eastern fabric of silk and satin). Costume bills for other operas show that the women often wore a short-sleeved bodice, over which was fastened an outer garment and sometimes an apron, supported by a hooped skirt frame; hats and gloves were standard. Men often wore a vest, knee breeches, stockings, and a hat. Costumes and scenery were sometimes modified for reuse in different operas.

The designer of the costumes was PIETRO TRAVAGLIA, who was both costume and stage designer at Eszterháza from 1777; he supervised the lighting (provided by lead-lined alcohol lamps and refracting mirrors) and special effects like fire, thunder, and lightning (flash powder, obtained from the court pharmacy). None of Travaglia's sets survives. (The sketchbook often mentioned in the Haydn literature has nothing to do with Travaglia or Eszterháza.)

The theatre contained 30 benches and 24 seats in the parterre, and benches and a special box for the prince in the gallery; it could seat over 400. (In comparison, the surviving 18th-century theatre at Drottningholm, near Stockholm, has a capacity of 350, while the Burgtheater in Vienna, where Mozart's *Le nozze di Figaro* and *Così fan tutte* were premiered, accommodated about 1,300 people.) The Eszterháza theatre was equipped with stage machinery that allowed nearly instantaneous changes of sets to take place before an open curtain. The scenery was painted on canvas mounted on a wooden frame; six to eight such frames would be placed in tracks on either side of the stage and quickly slid into place on casters, while a back-wall decoration could be unfurled from a cylinder. Several of Travaglia's designs suggest that the use of perspective painting could give an illusion of great depth.

Despite the wealth of detail about certain aspects of operatic performance at Eszterháza, a number of practical considerations remain for those who wish to stage Haydn's operas. Directors, composers, and performers of Italian opera in the 18th century were flexible and pragmatic in their approach to the repertoire, and there is little to suggest that opera at Eisenstadt or Eszterháza was untypical in this respect. Haydn frequently transposed arias to make them suitable for the singers he had available; occasional transpositions by modern singers do not violate 18th-century practice and might be permitted. Singers should be well acquainted with contemporary ideas about ornamentation and the performance of unwritten appoggiaturas. As few opera houses today can reproduce the intimacy of the theatre at Eszterháza, an orchestra somewhat larger than Haydn's may be required in order to fill the hall. It is essential that the text of the opera be understood by the audience. Many productions of Haydn's operas given outside Eszterháza during the composer's lifetime were performed in German; that the composer himself did not object to the practice may be gathered from his careful emendations to a German translation of *Orlando paladino*. Today, a performance in the original Italian with projected subtitles is a successful way of involving the audience in the comic repartee or the serious pronouncements of the operas, especially if it allows them to appreciate works that have all too often been the victim of unsatisfactory productions. RJR

4. Oratorio. In this section five works will be considered, the so-called 'Applausus' cantata, the Italian oratorio *Il ritorno di Tobia*, the oratorio version of *The Seven Last Words*, *The Creation*, and *The Seasons*.

The 'Applausus' cantata was written for a place and occasion unfamiliar to Haydn; for the 18th-century composer of vocal music a knowledge of the performance circumstances was absolutely essential so that the arias, in particular, could be tailored to performers. As a result of these unusual circumstances, Haydn wrote the so-called 'Applausus' letter to his remote patrons, at the abbey of Zwettl. In it Haydn makes ten numbered points, ranging from the practical to the expressive. He requests that the tempos reflect the character of the texts; that an Allegro and Andante of an overture be used to introduce the opening Allegro chorus; that the cadences at the end of recitatives wait until the singer has finished the text; that the distinctions between contrasting dynamics be faithfully observed and that dynamics be uniform in all the parts; that the notated articulation—particularly the ties—be played as written; that two violas be employed since 'you will find in all my compositions that the viola rarely doubles the bass'; that the page turns and the da capo signs are placed differently in the string parts to avoid a weakening of sonority; that the text be clearly declaimed and the appoggiaturas of the recitatives be properly rendered; that the bass section should normally include a bassoon since Haydn prefers 'a band with three bass instruments—

cello, bassoon, and double bass—to one with six double basses and three cellos, because certain instruments stand out better that way'. This document tells the modern musician more about Haydn the performer than any other from the period; from it, it is especially apparent that he valued clarity of texture and of musical line. The 'Applausus' cantata was probably performed by an ensemble of three to four violins per part, two violas, a bassoon, cello, double bass, and single wind instruments. A complementary chorus would have consisted of two to three voices to a part, perhaps more depending on the availability of trebles at Zwettl.

In direct contrast, Haydn's four remaining oratorios were all conceived for public occasions in Vienna, where, traditionally, much larger forces were used, as revealed in contemporary documents and surviving performance materials. For the revival of *Il ritorno di Tobia* in March 1784 there were no fewer than 20 first violins and 20 second violins (seated on benches of six or seven players), six violas, five cellos, six basses, two flutes, seven oboes, two cors anglais, six bassoons, six horns, two trumpets, two trombones, and timpani; flute and cor anglais players were less numerous because their parts were concertante ones. The listed choral forces included 15 tenors and 15 basses, as well as two male altos, complemented by some 30 boys for the treble and alto parts. Tobia's aria 'Quando mi donna un cenno' exists in two versions: the original, probably sung by FRIBERTH in 1775, and a highly embellished one written for Adamberger who took the role in one of the performances in 1784. It is an instructive example of what Haydn considered to be appropriate vocal decoration.

Haydn's final three oratorios—*The Seven Last Words*, *The Creation*, and *The Seasons*—were performed by an even larger body of performers, particularly the wind group which had six of each woodwind instrument and six horns; the two trumpet parts, the timpani, and the first and second trombones were doubled, perhaps the contrabassoon too; the bass trombone part was not doubled. From a description of the first public performance of *The Creation* in the Burgtheater in March 1799, provided by Johan BERWALD, comes a reasonably clear indication of the layout of the forces. The performers were on the stage in an amphitheatre arrangement. In the pit (that is the ground floor of the auditorium) stood the chorus, the soloists, and the continuo group (fortepiano, cello, and double bass). On the stage, Haydn as the conductor was placed in the middle with the first violins to his left and the second violins to his right; violas and cellos were situated in the middle, and double basses were divided equally left and right; woodwind and horn players sat on the next level; and, at the highest level, sat the trumpets, timpani, and trombones. Although Berwald estimated the total number of performers at about 400, there is more persuasive evidence that the total strength was somewhere between 180 and 200, with a chorus of 60 to 80 voices. Compared with modern performances, the most striking difference is the placing of the chorus, in front of rather than behind the orchestra; this was standard practice throughout Europe until well into the second half of the 19th century.

While large-scale performances constituted a special tradition in Vienna they should not be regarded as the only authentic way of presenting the works. In Vienna, Eisenstadt, Budapest, and elsewhere, smaller-scale performances without doubling instruments, including ones directed by Haydn, proved to be equally compelling.

The use of embellishments and ornaments in the late oratorios has been a matter of some controversy. One might reasonably surmise that ornaments would be inappropriate in *The Seven Last Words*. In the surviving performance material for *The Seasons*, there are no added ornaments or embellishments in the solo vocal parts, perhaps a reflection of the social standing of the characters, who are three peasants. The material for *The Creation*, however, does contain some ornaments; many of these enhance the music, while others seem more gratuitous. In his old age Haydn said that he preferred that there be no additions, but whether he meant decoration at pauses and cadences or more extensive embellishment (as in the aria from *Il ritorno di Tobia*) is not clear.

Haydn died before the invention of the metronome but two composers closely associated with him in the last few years of his life recorded metronome markings for *The Creation*. SALIERI, apparently, wrote metronome markings on a manuscript score which, unfortunately, has not survived; the four markings mentioned in a contemporary journal, the *Allgemeine musikalische Zeitung*, seem erratic. Much more plausible is the complete list of metronome markings provided by NEUKOMM for a keyboard reduction issued in London in 1832, the centenary of the composer's birth.

It appears that Haydn wished *The Creation* and *The Seasons* to be performed in the language of the audience. The first edition of *The Creation* was a bilingual one, English and German, and he later sanctioned translations into French and Italian. Parallel first editions of *The Seasons* were issued, in German and English, and in German and French. APB

5. Orchestral music. Performance practice in Haydn's orchestral music has focused on two major issues: the size of Haydn's ensemble during more than 40 years of composing symphonies, concertos, and dances; and the presence or absence of a harpsichord continuo.

Nothing is known about Haydn's orchestra during his time as Kapellmeister at the Morzin court. It is generally acknowledged that Haydn composed symphonies and, possibly, other orchestral works during this time and Morzin probably maintained an orchestra of rather small proportions, perhaps eight or nine strings plus pairs of oboes and horns, and a single bassoon. Whether Haydn played the violin or the keyboard is not known.

When Haydn came into the service of the Esterházy family in 1761 the orchestra was reconstituted, eventually including six violins (some or all of the players could play the viola), one cello, one double bass, one flute (also a violin player), two oboes (doubling flute, if necessary), two horns, and a bassoon. Surviving performance material from the Esterházy archive does not include a continuo part and much of the anecdotal evidence suggests that Haydn played the violin rather than the harpsichord in performances of symphonies. However, the autograph of Symphony no. 7, one of a trilogy of symphonies that he wrote in 1761, specifically mentions 'basso continuo', suggesting that a harpsichord might well have been present in this symphony at least.

The size of the Esterházy orchestra between 1761 and 1774 fluctuated between 14 and 18 players. The standard disposition was three first violins, three second violins, one viola, one cello, one double bass, one bassoon, and pairs of oboes and horns. A flute player was occasionally added and the horns sometimes numbered four. In a letter that accompanied the delivery of the 'Applausus' cantata in 1768 Haydn indicated that he liked to have two viola players, something that the documentary evidence suggests was not possible at the Esterházy court at the time; also he specifically mentions that a bassoon should double the bass line in the absence of a written-out part. From 1775 onward the orchestra increased in size. By 1781 it consisted of nine or ten violins/violas, two cellos, one double bass, one flute, three oboes, three bassoons, and five horns; some of the wind players could play string instruments also.

If, as seems likely, Haydn played the violin rather than the harpsichord in performances of symphonies, there is ample evidence that performances with harpsichord continuo were familiar to him and, in the absence of any evidence to the contrary, acceptable also. Indeed, when he directed his own orchestral music in the theatre or in the church, he might well have played the harpsichord or even the organ. (During his visit to Vienna in 1772 Burney heard some symphonies by Hofmann in St Stephen's accompanied by an organ.) In sum, it is unwise to be authoritarian about the presence or otherwise of a keyboard continuo in modern performances.

Outside the Esterházy court and similar musical establishments, Haydn's symphonies from the 1780s onwards were often played by much larger orchestras. They were frequently included in programmes of the Tonkünstler-Societät in Vienna when the orchestra numbered more than 100 players, though whether all the players took part in the orchestral music as opposed to the main choral item is unknown. The nine symphonies that Haydn wrote for the Concert de la Loge Olympique in Paris (nos. 82–7, 90–2) were performed by an orchestra of over 60 players, but they were also performed at the Esterházy court and many scholars have opined that there is no evidence that Haydn had the larger orchestra in mind.

For the 12 'London' symphonies (nos. 93–104) Haydn took time to become acquainted with the personnel of the orchestra. Salomon's orchestra in the 1791, 1792, and 1794 seasons consisted of about 40 players: nine first violins, eight second violins, four violas, four cellos, four double basses, pairs of woodwind, horns, and brass, plus timpani. Contemporary accounts enable a broad picture of the layout of the orchestra to be given. The players sat in an amphitheatre arrangement that focused attention on two individuals, Haydn at the fortepiano (with his back to the audience) and, on a raised dais and probably standing, Salomon; the two shared direction of the performance. To the immediate left of Haydn and the fortepiano were first violins and violas, then further upstage more first violins; to his immediate right were second violins and some more violas, with the remaining second violins further upstage. On the first tier, going from Haydn's left to right, were cellos, bassoons, horns, oboes, flutes, and further cellos. On the second tier, again from left to right, were double basses, trumpets, timpani (directly facing Haydn), and double basses. In comparison with modern layouts, which separate the harmonic voices very clearly, the layout in use in London makes a clear separation between first and second violins but the sound of lower strings emanated from both sides of the stage.

When in 1795 Salomon joined forces with Viotti to form the Opera Concert the orchestra was a larger one: the string section consisted of 12 first violins, 12 second violins, six violas, four cellos, five basses; the woodwind section was doubled; but horn, trumpet, and timpani parts were not doubled.

There are some secondary issues that might be considered when performing Haydn's symphonies. In the many concertante movements found in symphonies up to the mid-1770s some judicious ornamentation might be appropriate (e.g. in the second movements of Symphonies nos. 8 and 13). Trio sections might be performed with one player per part and in those movements where the leading lines are doubled it might be appropriate to vary the instrumentation on the repeat, as in the trio of Symphony no. 22 which could be played by cors anglais the first time, by horns the second time.

For Haydn's concertos, many of the same issues are pertinent. For the early concertos for organ, violin, and cello, the bass line ('basso') may have been performed without a cello. Very little is known about the specific performing circumstances surrounding Haydn's dance music. It is likely that the ensemble could have been as small as three players (two violins and a bass) or, as is reported for the Redoutensaal in Vienna in the 1790s, as large as 40 or so players; there is no evidence of the presence of a keyboard continuo.

Metronome markings supplied by pupils or associates of Haydn have not survived for any of the orchestral music. Among the most interesting supplied in the 19th century were those by Carl Czerny (1791–1857) for a piano arrangement of symphonies nos. 93–104 published in London in *c.*1845. APB

6. **Sacred music.** Since Haydn's sacred music was functional music, designed to adorn services in Catholic churches, the performance circumstances were governed fundamentally by two factors: the demands and tradition of the LITURGY and, second, the musical resources of a particular institution. While his sacred music could be performed in richly endowed churches with skilled singers and players, at the other end of the scale it was also performed in the most circumscribed of circumstances by barely competent local amateurs. Modern performances, which are more likely to be in the concert hall rather than as part of a Catholic service, have evolved a more uniform approach to this repertoire than would have been apparent in Haydn's Austria.

In Vienna many ecclesiastical institutions such the Hofkapelle and St Peter's had exclusively male choirs, boy trebles and altos alongside adult tenors and basses; castrato singers were still employed in the 1780s but were becoming increasingly rare. Some other churches in Vienna had mixed choirs of female and male voices, and, apart from monasteries, this was a practice that was common in churches in the provinces, including Eisenstadt. There is little or no evidence of choirs with both boys and women. Statistically, most performances of liturgical music were given by a choir of one person per part, with better-off institutions, particularly on important days of the church calendar, expanding their vocal forces to 12 or 16, that is three or four singers per part.

The instrumental support was correspondingly small. A minimum complement, widely used, was two violins, double bass, and organ; even when the instrumental forces were larger it was common up to *c.*1780 for there to be no violas or cellos in the string section. To add an element of awe and ceremony, trumpets and timpani were often added, even to the smallest forces. In Vienna and Salzburg, but not in Eisenstadt, alto and tenor parts could be doubled by trombones and, though Haydn himself never specified the instruments in his sacred music, there are many contemporary manuscript sources of his music with these supporting trombone parts.

The performing forces were usually located in a gallery at the back of the church. Minimalist forces of three instrumentalists and four singers were clustered around the organ; larger forces would be more formally arranged across the gallery with, usually, the vocal forces at the front. Supervision of the performance was shared between the organist, the first violinist, and a senior member of the choir. In multi-voiced works in which Haydn required a distinction between soloist and chorus, the soloists would normally be taken from the choir. Although there is evidence of increasing use of specialist soloists towards the end of the century, modern performances of the six late masses that physically separate soloists from the chorus frequently distort the texture of the music and misrepresent the function of the solo line as a representative of the choir.

Today, works like the Mass in F, the Salve regina in E, the *Missa Sancti Johannis de Deo*, and the early Te Deum in C, could be performed with single singers and single instrumentalists (and without cellos), though some doubling of forces (and adding of cellos) up to a complement of 16 or so would not be inappropriate. In the case of the Salve regina in G minor, this was specifically written for four voices, organ, and strings, following the petition in 1771 of the Esterházy court singer ELEONORA JÄGER, for the restitution of the church ensemble in Eisenstadt to a complement of four singers, two violinists, and an organist; additional string players were taken from Haydn's orchestra, normally based in Eszterháza. More fully scored works from the early Esterházy period, such as the 'Grosse Orgelsolomesse' (MISSA IN HONOREM BVM) and the *Missa Sancti Nicolai*, start from a higher minimum complement of players and singers, *c.* 20, and both have the option of using authentic trumpet and timpani parts.

For the early 1800s the likely forces for the performances of masses during the festivities associated with the nameday of Princess Marie Hermenegild Esterházy can be reconstructed from extant documents. The two works with the largest instrumental forces, the 'Schöpfungsmesse' and the 'Harmoniemesse', were likely to have been performed with an orchestra of six violins, two violas, two cellos, one double bass, plus single wind players and timpani (a total of 11 in the 'Schöpfungsmesse', 12 in the 'Harmoniemesse') as well as organ continuo; the mixed chorus numbered about 27, divided into nine sopranos, eight altos (all female), five tenors, and five basses. The first four works in the series of six late masses have a smaller orchestra, and could therefore have been performed with a commensurably reduced choir.

In 1771, on Good Friday, Haydn directed a performance of his Stabat mater in the Piaristenkirche in Vienna with 60 performers. Although occasions like these were exceptional, they do suggest that the composer regarded such performances as viable; similarly when, in old age, he added (or sanctioned) supplementary wind parts to the Mass in F and the Stabat mater this, too, suggests that he was comfortable with the notion of expanded numbers of performers for his sacred works.

Nothing of certainty is known about pronunciation practice in the liturgy. A widely held principle for all periods and localities is that the Latin was influenced by the local vernacular. Given the Italianate nature of musical life in Vienna in general, it is likely that this language rather than German was the dominant influence. Thus words such as 'unigenite' and 'pacem' were sung with soft consonants rather than hard consonants, and German pronunciation (e.g 'patzem') was probably the exception rather than the rule.

C. P. E. Bach, *Versuch über die wahre Art das Clavier zu spielen* (Berlin, 1753, 1762); trans. W. J. Mitchell, *Essay on the True Art of Playing Keyboard Instruments* (New York, 1949).

E. Badura-Skoda, 'Haydns Opern: Anmerkungen zu Aufführungspraktischen Problemen der Gegenwart', *Österreichische Musikzeitschrift*, 3–4 (1982), 162–7.

Bartha and Somfai.

O. Biba, 'Beispiele für die Besetzungverhältnisse bei Aufführungen von Haydns Oratorien in Wien zwischen 1784 und 1808', *HS* 4/2 (1978), 94–104.

O. Biba, 'Die Wiener Kirchenmusik um 1783', *Jahrbuch für österreichische Kulturgeschichte*, 1/2 (1971), 7–79.

A. P. Brown, *Performing Haydn's The Creation: Reconstructing the Earliest Renditions* (Bloomington, Ind., 1986).

A. P. Brown, 'Options: Authentic, Allowable, and Possible in Performing Haydn's *The Creation*', *Musical Times*, 131 (1990), 3–6.

C. Brown, *Classical and Romantic Performing Practice 1750–1900* (Oxford, 1999).
W. Drabkin, 'Fingering in Haydn's String Quartets', *Early Music*, 16 (1988), 50–7.
G. Feder and G. Thomas, 'Dokumente zur Ausstattung von *Lo speziale, L'infedeltà delusa, La fedeltà premiata, Armida* und anderen Opern Haydns', *HS* 6/2 (1988), 88–115.
S. Gerlach, 'Haydns Orchestermusiker von 1761 bis 1774', *HS* 4/1 (1976), 35–48.
S. Gerlach, 'Haydns Orchesterpartituren. Fragen der Realisierung des Textes', *HS* 5/3 (1984), 169–83.
J. Harich, 'Das Opernensemble zu Esterháza im 1780', *HYB* 7 (1970), 5–36.
B. Harrison, *Haydn's Keyboard Music: Studies in Performance Practice* (Oxford, 1996).
M. Horányi, *The Magnificence of Eszterháza* (Budapest, 1962).
'Part Three: Performance', in J. P. Larsen, H. Serwer, and J. Webster (eds), *Haydn Studies* (London, 1981), 183–326.
H. C. Robbins Landon, *The Symphonies of Joseph Haydn* (London, 1955).
W. Malloch, 'Carl Czerny's Metronome Marks for Haydn and Mozart Symphonies', *Early Music*, 16 (1988), 72–82.
L. Mozart, *Versuch einer gründlichen Violinschule* (Augsburg, 1756); trans. E. Knocker, *A Treatise on the Fundamental Principles of Violin Playing* (London, 1948).
L. Somfai, *The Keyboard Sonatas of Joseph Haydn: Instruments and Performance Practice, Genres and Styles* (Chicago, 1995).
R. Stowell, *Violin Technique and Performance Practice in the Late Eighteenth and Early Nineteenth Centuries* (Cambridge, 1985).
N. Temperley, 'Haydn's Tempos in *The Creation*', *Early Music*, 19 (1991), 235–45.
D. G. Türk, *Klavierschule* (Leipzig, 1789); trans. R. H. Haggh, *School of Clavier Playing* (Lincoln, Nebr., 1982).
J. Webster, 'The Bass Part in Haydn's Early String Quartets', *Musical Quarterly*, 63 (1977), 390–424.
J. Webster, 'On the Absence of a Keyboard Continuo in Haydn's Symphonies', *Early Music*, 18 (1990), 599–608.
J. Webster, 'The Significance of Haydn's String Quartet Autographs for Performance Practice', in C. Wolff and R. Riggs (eds), *The String Quartets of Haydn, Mozart, and Beethoven. Studies of the Autograph Manuscripts* (Cambridge, Mass., 1980), 62–98.
J. Webster, 'Violoncello and Double Bass in the Chamber Music of Haydn and his Viennese Contemporaries, 1750–1780', *Journal of the American Musicological Society*, 29 (1976), 413–38.

soprano) and Gustavo Lazzarini (tenor). English sources suggest that it was specially written for Mrs Billington; on the manuscript copy in the British Library Vincent Novello noted that William Shield had received it from Haydn 'on purpose to be sung by Mrs Billington', though why he should have written such an ambitious work for the Professional Concert, a rival organization to Salomon's concerts, is unclear. It also survives in a manuscript copy, probably from the 1790s, by Johann Schellinger, a former copyist at the Esterházy court, as part of a pasticcio entitled *Alessandro il Grande*. Whatever its history, the trio is a work on a grand scale and, if genuine, unique in Haydn's output. A single movement, it contains fine cantabile writing for all the vocal and instrumental soloists, yet the dominant impression is of breathtaking virtuosity: the singers in heroic bravura and the three obbligato instrumentalists matching them for extreme technical demands. All three unnamed characters share the same text, a plea to the gods to have pity on them in their plight, coupled with the hope that love might ameliorate their suffering. SMcV

HCRL/3.

Pleyel, Ignaz Joseph (b. 18 June 1757; d. 14 Nov. 1831). Violinist, composer, music publisher, and instrument manufacturer. At the beginning of the 19th century Haydn's former pupil Ignaz Pleyel was the most popular composer in Europe. He was also a leading music publisher, and, from 1807, his firm in Paris began manufacturing instruments. The latter and the Salle Pleyel, the concert hall he founded in 1830, survive to this day.

Born in Ruppersthal, near Vienna, Pleyel lodged with Haydn in Eisenstadt as his pupil from the age of 15 to 20. His patron, Count Ladislaus Erdödy, was so satisfied with his progress that he presented

Haydn with a carriage and two horses as a measure of his gratitude. Although nothing is known about Pleyel's studies it is safe to assume that it featured a systematic course of contrapuntal studies based on FUX's *Gradus ad Parnassum* together with exercises in free composition. During his time with Haydn, Pleyel's marionette opera *Die Fee Urgele* received its premiere at Eszterháza (November 1776); it was performed also at the Nationaltheater in Vienna. Haydn's marionette opera *Die Feuersbrunst* (Hob.XXIXb:A), which was performed in 1776 or 1777, has an overture now thought to be largely by Pleyel.

Pleyel's first professional position was probably as Kapellmeister to Count Erdödy although there is no extant documentation to confirm this. In appreciation of his 'generosity, paternal solicitude and encouragement', Pleyel dedicated his string quartets op. 1 to Erdödy, and, in a similar vein, his highly accomplished op. 2 quartets were dedicated to Haydn.

Pleyel travelled to Italy in the early 1780s and while in Naples he secured commissions to write pieces for *lira organizzata* for the king, and an opera, *Ifigenia in Aulide*, which received its premiere at the Teatro San Carlo on 30 May 1785.

Around this time Pleyel was appointed assistant to Franz Xaver Richter (1709–89) at Strasbourg cathedral. He succeeded to the position on Richter's death, shortly after the Revolution broke out. Before long, religious services and Pleyel's public concerts were forcibly abandoned. With his professional circumstances in Strasbourg so uncertain in the aftermath of the Revolution, Pleyel accepted an invitation to direct the Professional Concert series in London, and stayed there from December 1791 until May 1792. To his surprise and embarrassment he found himself in direct competition with his former teacher, Haydn, who was the star of the rival concert series organized by JOHANN PETER SALOMON. Pleyel and Haydn resumed their easy relationship in London. They met frequently, dined together, and even played each other's music. While Haydn was clearly the man of the moment, Pleyel's concerts were well attended and his symphonies, concertantes, and quartets in particular received generous praise in the press. Their cordial relationship even managed to survive the long-continuing legal battle between FORSTER and LONGMAN & BRODERIP over the publication rights of three piano trios by Haydn; the previous year Haydn had been forced to admit in a sworn statement that two of the trios had actually been written by his former pupil.

With the establishment of his music business in Paris in 1795 Pleyel began to scale down his activities as a composer. Much of his later output seems to have been tailored to Parisian tastes, although his music proved phenomenally popular everywhere. The urgent, taut athleticism of his early works written in the shadow of Haydn is rarely to be heard. As early as 1789, however, CHARLES BURNEY had commented that Pleyel's music was becoming cliché-ridden and too dependent on Haydn's example.

Pleyel's legacy as a publisher is immense. In the course of its 39-year life Maison Pleyel issued over 4,000 works, including compositions by Boccherini, Beethoven, Clementi, and Haydn. Among the historically most important publications issued were the first miniature scores (including symphonies by Haydn) and, in 1801, the first complete edition of Haydn's quartets. Prepared with the composer's cooperation, this edition laid the foundation of his posthumous reputation as a master of the medium, although it did mistakenly include the spurious six quartets of op. 3, now attributed to HOFSTETTER. ADJB

R. Benton, 'Pleyel as Music Publisher', *Journal of the American Musicological Society*, 32 (1979), 125–40.

M. Hornick, 'Ensemble and Solo Works of Ignaz Pleyel Originally Composed for Keyboard: A Style-Analytical Review' (diss., University of New York, 1986).

J. Kim, 'Ignaz Pleyel and his early string quartets in Vienna' (diss., University of North Carolina, Chapel Hill, 1996).

E. Radant (ed.), 'Ignaz Pleyel's Correspondence with Hoffmeister & Co.', *HYB* 12 (1981), 122–74.

Ployer, Barbara (Babette) (b. Sept. 1765; d. before 1811). Brought up in Upper Austria, from the age of 15 she lived with her uncle, Gottfried Ignaz von Ployer, a court official in Vienna. In the burgeoning salon culture of the city she soon established a reputation as a sensitive pianist. Mozart composed two piano concertos for her (K449 and K453) and Haydn copied the canon 'Du sollst an einen Gott glauben' (Hob.XXVIIa:1) into her autograph album. Haydn's piano variations in F minor were written for Gottfried von Ployer's wife, Antonia von Ployer.

W. Senn, 'Barbara Ployer. Mozarts Klavierschülerin', *Österreichische Musikzeitschrift*, 33 (1978), 18–26.

Pohl, Carl Ferdinand (b. 6 Sept. 1819; d. 28 April 1887). German music historian who in a monumental biography of Haydn set the secure foundations of scholarship devoted to the composer. Born in Darmstadt he did not attend university but trained as a music engraver. In 1841 he moved to Vienna where he studied composition with Simon Sechter (1788–1867), an esteemed teacher whose previous pupils had included Schubert. Between 1848 and 1853 he was organist at the new Protestant church in Gumpendorf, the suburb of Vienna where Haydn had lived in the last period of his life. Some compositions date from this period.

Ill health forced Pohl to give up this worthy career as an organist, teacher, and composer, and he devoted himself, instead, to a career as a scholar and occasional music critic. For three years, from 1863 to 1866, he lived in London where he amassed material relating to the visits of Mozart and Haydn to the city. *Mozart und Haydn in London* was published in 1866; the part devoted to Haydn includes a survey of the major musical institutions in London, a biography of Salomon, and an account of Haydn's two visits and was not to be surpassed in its coverage for over a century.

Pohl had become acquainted with the Mozart scholar, Otto Jahn, and it was through him, Köchel, and others that he was recommended for the post of archivist at the Gesellschaft der Musikfreunde in Vienna, a position he held from 1866 to his death. Having completed a four-volume biography of Mozart Jahn had been asked to turn his attention to Haydn. He declined and instead recommended Pohl, who proceeded to devote 20 years to the task: the first volume, covering the period up to 1766, when Haydn became full Kapellmeister at the Esterházy court, appeared in 1875 and was dedicated to Jahn; the second volume dealt with the period 1766–90 and appeared in 1882, the 150th anniversary of Haydn's birth; a large amount of material had been prepared for the third and final volume but Pohl had barely started writing his text when he died at the age of 67; the task of completing the volume was first entrusted to MANDYCZEWSKI and finally accomplished by BOTSTIBER in 1927. Pohl was a scrupulous scholar and archivist who, at the same time, revealed a natural warmth for his subject without sentimentalizing him. Indeed, of all the major 19th-century biographies—Spitta on Bach, Thayer on Beethoven, and Jahn on Mozart—Pohl is arguably the most dispassionate. It was particularly unfortunate that, unlike the volumes by Spitta, Thayer, and Jahn, Pohl's biography was never translated into English, though many readers would have savoured Pohl's work in his article on Haydn in the earliest editions of *Grove's Dictionary of Music*.

As well as working on the biography, Pohl published a valuable history of the Tonkünstler-Societät in Vienna and of his own institution, the Gesellschaft der Musikfreunde. His library and papers are owned by the Gesellschaft, and are a staggering testimony to his industry in an age before photocopies and word processors. As well as notes for his various books, they included a draft of a thematic catalogue of Haydn's music, copies of many of Haydn's letters and of documents from the Esterházy archive, transcribed scores of works by Haydn, and handwritten copies of opera librettos set by the composer. In some cases the originals from which Pohl worked have disappeared or been destroyed, making his copies invaluable.

Polzelli family. Luigia Polzelli, née Moreschi (b. 1750; d. 1832) was a soprano of mediocre talent and Haydn's mistress from shortly after her arrival at Eszterháza in 1779 to her departure in 1790. Haydn wrote only one role for her, Silvia in L'ISOLA DISABITATA, but in preparing the operas of other composers for performance he allowed his emotional life and his work as Kapellmeister to become inextricably mixed. He devoted countless hours to the adjusting of Polzelli's vast number of mostly minor roles to her limited abilities. This labour of love included the composition of several delightful substitute (or insertion) arias. Polzelli certainly played an important role in Haydn's life and music during the 1780s; but Geiringer surely attributed too much influence to the relationship when he remarked that 'It seems doubtful that Haydn ever could have achieved the artistic maturity that his works of the 1780s reveal so splendidly if his passion for the Italian singer had not opened to him new vistas of life'.

Of Polzelli's career before she came to Eszterháza it is known only that she sang (under the name Luisa Moreschi Polzelli) in a production of Paisiello's *La frascatana* in the small town of Correggio in 1778. On 15 March 1779 Prince Nicolaus Esterházy engaged Polzelli and her husband Antonio, a violinist, for a combined salary so low that it is obvious that he was the more talented musician. The prince dismissed them in 1780 but the order was rescinded through Haydn's intercession; it was doubtless on account of his protection that the couple remained in the employ of the Esterházy family until 1790.

Polzelli made her debut in Anfossi's *L'incognita pereguitata* (under the title *Metilde ritrovata*) in July 1779. In addition to subjecting Anfossi's score to the kind of revision that every Italian opera underwent before performance at Eszterháza, Haydn also composed an entirely new aria, 'Quando la rosa' (Hob.XXIVb:3), for the 29-year-old Neapolitan soprano. This was the first of several arias that Haydn wrote for Polzelli to sing in the operas of other composers, including 'Signor voi sapete' (Hob.XXIVb:7, for Anfossi's *Il matrimonio per inganno*), 'Chi vive amante' (Hob.XXIVb:13, for Bianchi's *Alessandro nell' Indie*, one of the few serious operas in which Polzelli sang), and 'Il meglio mio carattere' (Hob.XXIVb:17, for Cimarosa's *L'impresario in angustie*). Robbins Landon has written of Polzelli and her arias: 'She had a kind of soubrette voice, and Haydn wrote very characteristic music for her—light, ironic, charming.'

Haydn probably spent much more time and effort rewriting arias so as to make the most of Polzelli's abilities than composing new ones. In Anfossi's *La giardiniera* (performed at Eszterháza in 1780) Polzelli sang the role of Arminda. Haydn completely reworked her aria 'Si promette facilmente', transposing it down from A major to G, adding oboes and horns, and reshaping the opening melody in order to avoid its highest notes. He performed a similar operation on 'Deh frenate i mesti accenti', sung by Polzelli in Anfossi's *Il curioso indiscreto* (Eszterháza, 1782). Indicative of his personal involvement with Polzelli's performances is his practice of writing out the orchestral parts for the music that he had composed for her, rather than entrusting the task to a copyist in the normal way.

After the dispersal of the opera company in 1790 and Haydn's later departure for London, he kept in touch with Polzelli by post, expressing the wish that he should see her again (he seems never to have done so), sending her money on several occasions, and even promising to marry her; he left her an annuity of 150 gulden in his final will. Luigia remarried and attempted to resume her career in Italy with little success (her advancing age undoubtedly compounded other disadvantages). She eventually returned to Hungary.

Polzelli's sons Pietro (1777–96) and Antonio (1783–1855) enjoyed the composer's paternal affection—he may have been the actual father of Antonio—and benefited from his musical instruction; both became violinists. Pietro died in Vienna at the age of 19. Antonio, after serving for several years in the orchestra of the Theater auf der Wieden in Vienna, joined the Esterházy orchestra at Eisenstadt in 1803; he was also active as a composer. His daughter openly maintained that she was Haydn's granddaughter. JAR

Bartha and Somfai.

H. Botstiber, 'Haydn and Luiga Polzelli', *Musical Quarterly*, 18 (1932), 208–15.

HCRL/2, 3, and 5.

Porpora, Nicola (Antonio) (b. 17 Aug. 1686: d. 3 March 1768). Singing teacher and composer of vocal music from whom the young Haydn gained important musical and linguistic insights.

Trained in Naples, Porpora achieved his first big operatic success in 1708. He won prestigious positions at conservatoires in Naples, where among his singing students was the great castrato singer Farinelli (1705–82), and Venice. During the 1730s he worked in London as principal composer to the Opera of the Nobility and Handel's rival. From 1747 to 1751 he served in Dresden as singing teacher to Princess Antonia of Saxony; from 1752 (or 1753) he was in Vienna, in great demand among the aristocracy as a singing teacher.

Born one year after Handel (1685–1759), four years before Vinci (1690–1730), and eight years before Leo (1694–1744), Porpora found a stylistic path somewhere between that taken by his older and younger contemporaries. He did not fully accept the operatic language adopted in the 1720s by Vinci and Leo and although one of his pupils, HASSE, was to become one of the leading opera composers of the mid-century, Porpora's music only infrequently anticipates that of his pupil.

During Porpora's stay in Vienna, Haydn became his valet and keyboard accompanist, polishing his shoes, repairing his wig, and assisting at singing lessons. That Haydn received any formal instruction from Porpora is doubtful, but he nevertheless learnt much from the old Neapolitan master. According to CARPANI, Porpora 'gave him some good advice and rules both for singing and for accompaniment'. In his autobiographical sketch of 1776 Haydn remembered: 'I wrote diligently, but not entirely correctly, until I had the good fortune to learn the true foundations of composition from the celebrated Porpora.' To GRIESINGER he mentioned another important benefit that a musician who was never to visit Italy gained from the grumpy old man, knowledge of Italian. 'There was no want of *Asino*, *Coglione*, *Birbante* and pokes in the ribs; but I put up with all of it because I greatly profited from Porpora in singing, in composition, and in the Italian language.' JAR

A. Mayeda, 'Nicola Antonio Porpora und der junge Haydn', in V. Schwarz (ed.), *Der junge Haydn* (Graz, 1972).

Porta, Nunziato (*fl.* 1770–95). Librettist and director of Italian opera at Eszterháza from July 1781 until the company was disbanded in the autumn of 1790. Porta's duties included purchasing opera scores and librettos for the Eszterháza theatre, copying music, and writing new texts for INSERTION ARIAS. He was more widely known, however, for his librettos, among them an early operatic treatment of the Don Juan story, *Il convitato di pietra o sia Il dissoluto* (set by Righini, Vienna 1777; performed at Eszterháza in 1781), *Il contratempi* (Sarti, Vienna 1784; Eszterháza 1785) and *L'incontro inaspettato* (Righini, Vienna 1785; Eszterháza 1786). Some of these were poorly received and he was more successful reworking the librettos of others. His libretto for Haydn's *Orlando paladino* was ultimately based on one by FRANCESCO BADINI, set by Guglielmi in London in 1771. It is likely that Porta adapted the libretto for Haydn's last opera for Eszterháza, *Armida*. RJR

M. Horányi, *The Magnificence of Eszterháza* (London, 1962).

HCRL/2.

Poschwa, Catarina (*fl.* 1776–9). A soprano who, with her husband, Anton, an oboe player, worked at the Esterházy court between January 1776 and August 1779. She had a light voice and undertook many secondary roles, including Clarice in *Il mondo della luna*, Baroness Irene in *La vera costanza*, and

Euridice in Gluck's *Orfeo*. During a performance of Dittersdorf's *Il finto pazzo* in 1776 she was the victim of an injudicious prank when her colleague, BENEDETTO BIANCHI, repeatedly raised her clothing with a walking stick. He was confined to quarters for a fortnight and had to read out a public apology. Nothing is known about Poschwa's career before or after her employment at the Esterházy court. ERL

Prandtner, Maria Elisabeth (b. 1758?; d. 28 Oct. 1780). A singer, possibly of Viennese origin, who in 1774 joined the choir based in the palace in Eisenstadt that sang in the church services. She received singing lessons from LEOPOLD DICHTLER and made such progress that she made the unusual move from the church choir to the opera troupe based at Eszterháza. She made her debut as Dardana in Haydn's *L'incontro improvviso* in 1775 and in the following years undertook roles in operas by Anfossi, Dittersdorf, Gassmann, Paisiello, Piccinni, and Sacchini. This flourishing career was halted by an illness of several months that led to her death. ERL

Pressburg (Bratislava). City located on the Danube, 55 km (33 miles) east of Vienna. Presently the capital of Slovakia, Pressburg was the capital of the kingdom of Hungary in the 18th century; its Hungarian name was Pozsony. Its status as the administrative centre for Hungary and its proximity to Vienna ensured that Pressburg was one of the most important cities in the Austrian territories. The Esterházy family had a palace there, in the Pfaffengasse (now Kapitulská ulica 13), and a country residence across the Danube at Kittsee. In the 1760s and 1770s, before Eszterháza became the favoured residence together with Eisenstadt, the Esterházy court frequently visited Pressburg and, especially, Kittsee. Nicolaus Esterházy's daughter Maria Anna (1739–94) married ANTON GRASSALKOVICS and they lived for a while in the Esterházy palace in Pressburg before occupying their own palace. The two families remained in regular contact.

As Vice-Kapellmeister Haydn spent the summer and autumn of 1764 at Kittsee; it is possible that the opera *Acide* was performed then. Independently of the Esterházy court, Haydn's German opera *Der neue krumme Teufel* was performed in the town the same year. Two months were spent in Pressburg in 1767 during which *La canterina* was presented. In 1770, Empress Maria Theresia and the future Joseph II were guests at Kittsee when the entertainment is known to have included music performed by Haydn and his colleagues. Other shorter visits are assumed to have taken place in this period.

When Joseph II moved some of the Hungarian government administration to Buda (Budapest), Pressburg began to lose some of its status and social allure. Musical life, however, continued to flourish, especially as sponsored by members of the ERDÖDY family. In the 1780s several operas by Haydn were performed in Pressburg and, at the turn of the century, the oratorio version of *The Seven Last Words* together with *The Creation* and *The Seasons* were presented. Founded in 1768, the local newspaper, the *Pressburger Zeitung*, reported, often in considerable detail, on musical events in the city and elsewhere, including Eszterháza and Vienna.

HCRL/1 and 2.

M. Pandi and F. Schmidt, 'Music in Haydn's and Beethoven's Time Reported by the *Pressburger Zeitung*', *HYB* 8 (1971), 267–93.

Preston & Son. London firm of music publishers active from the mid-1780s to 1834. It issued two first editions of Haydn's music: a piano trio in G (Hob.XV:32) in 1794 and, the following year, a set of three piano trios dedicated to Princess Marie Hermenegild Esterházy (Hob.XV:21–3). Beyond this Preston published numerous arrangements of quartets or symphonies (or movements from them) for keyboard or small ensemble.

'Prussian' quartets. Nickname frequently given to the six quartets of op. 50, first published by ARTARIA in December 1787. Haydn had readily agreed to Artaria's suggestion that they should be dedicated to King FRIEDRICH WILHELM II of Prussia. The title page carries the coat of arms of the family. JH

pupils. Haydn was an active and enthusiastic teacher all his life, from the earliest, freelance years in Vienna in the 1750s through to the first years of the 19th century. He taught the clavichord and the harpsichord, perhaps the piano too, and told Griesinger that many of his sonatas were written for pedagogical purposes; gradually the teaching of theory and composition became more important, especially from the 1780s onwards. BEETHOVEN was certainly his best-known pupil but in his lifetime PLEYEL also achieved international pre-eminence as a composer. It is from Beethoven's extant exercises for Haydn that a picture of the teacher's methods and concerns can be established. Pupils were weaned on species counterpoint as laid out by FUX in *Gradus ad Parnassum*, then moved on to canon and fugue; free composition seems to have been taught alongside rather than after the formal instruction.

It is impossible to compile a full list of Haydn's pupils since it is sometimes difficult to distinguish between informal advice given to figures such as EYBLER, REICHA, and TOMASINI and a planned course of instruction. Also the extent of any keyboard lessons given to members of the Morzin and Esterházy households and others such as THERESE KELLER cannot be established. In his correspondence with MARIA ANNA VON GENZINGER Haydn referred to himself as her teacher, though it is clear that the relationship was based on unstructured conversations and the occasional observation in a letter rather than a series of lessons. The eighth clause of Haydn's contract with the Esterházy family signed in May 1761 required him 'to instruct the female singers, in order that they do not forget (when staying in the country) that which they have been taught with much effort and at great expense in Vienna'; with the later establishment of a full and active opera company such coaching duties became routine.

The following list restricts itself to individuals who are known (or are thought) to have followed a formal course of instruction in theory and composition with Haydn. Many of them subsequently showed their gratitude to the composer by dedicating works to him. *See* DEDICATED WORKS.

Beethoven, Ludwig van (1770–1827)
Callcott, John Wall (1766–1821)
Destouches, Franz Seraph von (1772–1844)
Feodorovna, Archduchess Maria (1759–1828)
Haigh, Thomas (1769–?1808)
Haensel, Peter (1770–1831)
KALKBRENNER, FRIEDRICH (1785–1849)
KIMMERLING, ROBERT (1737–99)
KRAFT, ANTON (1749–1820)
Kranz, Johann Friedrich (1752–1810)
KRUMPHOLTZ, JOHANN BAPTIST (1742–90)
Lessel, Franz (*c.*1780–1838)
Magnus, F. C. (*fl. c.*1790)
MARTINES, MARIANNA VON (1744–1812)
NEUKOMM, SIGISMUND (1778–1858)
NIEMECZ, PRIMITIVUS (1750–1806)
PLEYEL, IGNAZ (1757–1831)
POLZELLI, ANTONIO (1783–1855)
POLZELLI, PIETRO (1777–96)
Spech, Johann (1767–1836)
Struck, Paul (1776–1820)
Weber, Edmund von (1766–1828)
Weber, Fritz von (1761–1833)
WRANITZKY, ANTON (1761–1821)
WRANITZKY, PAUL (1756–1808)

'Haydns Schüler, in *Joseph Haydn in seiner Zeit* [Exhibition catalogue] (Eisenstadt, 1982), 546–53.
H. Walter, 'On Haydn's Pupils', in J. P. Larsen, H. Serwer, and J. Webster (eds), *Haydn Studies* (London, 1981), 60–3.

Purksteiner, Joseph (b. 1739; d. 1797). Violinist and composer at the Esterházy court. In 1766 he joined the church music ensemble in Eisenstadt as a violinist, but later regularly played the viola in operatic performances at Eszterháza. A competent composer, his marionette opera *Das ländliche Hochzeitsfest* was written for the court in 1778 and he is also known to have written baryton trios for the prince. Some of his instrumental music falsely circulated under Haydn's name. Following the dissolution of the musical retinue in 1790, Purksteiner resumed his duties as a violinist in church services in Eisenstadt. In 1792 he was given the job of caretaker at Deutschkreuz (Németkeresztúr), a small castle owned by the Esterházy family. He was unmarried. ERL

HCRL/2.

Puttini, Francesco (*fl.* 1776). Italian librettist about whom very little is known. His libretto *La vera costanza* was first set by ANFOSSI in Rome in 1776, and then, in revised form, by Haydn (Eszterháza, 1779). Although Anfossi's setting was extensively performed throughout Europe it did not lead to an extended career for Puttini himself; only two other librettos by him are known, *La frascetana* (Genoa, 1776) and *Il trionfo della costanza* (possibly a version of *La vera costanza*, London, 1783). RJR

Puttler (Buttler), Marianna (d. Oct. 1778). A soprano who joined the opera troupe at Eszterháza in January 1776 and sang many leading roles, including the taxing role of Flaminia in *Il mondo della luna*. Nothing is known about her career before she joined the Esterházy court. She may have been related to the Viennese harpsichord player, Joseph Buttler. ERL

Q

Qual dubbio ormai (With humility, my friend) (Hob.XXIVa:4). One of three extant honorific cantatas that Haydn wrote in the first years of his service at the Esterházy court; he did not use the word cantata for the works but referred to each one as a 'Coro'.

First performed in December 1764, this was the second of two consecutive cantatas designed to celebrate the nameday of Prince Nicolaus, following the success of DESTATEVI, O MIEI FIDI the previous year. The work consists of two movements, an aria and a chorus, the first preceded by an accompanied recitative, the second by a short *secco* recitative. The author of the text is unknown; it is likely to have been either GIRALOMO BON or CARL FRIBERTH, possibly both.

Following a lengthy orchestral introduction a solo soprano, a loyal representative of the Esterházy court, announces the particular reason for this festive work: to celebrate a recent honour bestowed on 'our prince'. This is a reference to the formal installation in Vienna on 6 December 1764 of Prince Nicolaus as captain of the Hungarian Guard, an integral part of Habsburg court life and a symbol of the link between Hungary and the imperial court. Given that the ceremony was in Vienna, perhaps the cantata was also performed in the city, in the Esterházy palace in the Wallnerstraße. Alternatively the nameday celebrations may have been delayed until the prince returned to Eisenstadt. Later that month, on 18 December, Nicolaus celebrated his 50th birthday. Maybe the cantata served to commemorate both occasions.

The centrepiece is a large da capo aria with a prominent and dashing part for solo harpsichord, played by Haydn, that vies with a virtuoso vocal line reaching up to d'''. The concluding chorus is also in da capo form, but is more measured in its delivery. Unlike the two other extant cantatas, movements from this work did not subsequently circulate with sacred Latin texts.

Quartbuch (kleine Quartbuch). An 18th-century thematic catalogue in two volumes, containing about 750 entries for symphonies and chamber music by Haydn and dozens of his contemporaries. At one time it was believed to have represented the instrumental repertoire of the Esterházy orchestra under Haydn; later it was thought to have some connection with MELK abbey. However, its precise purpose and place of origin, although undoubtedly Austrian, remains a mystery. It has been established that the catalogue was compiled around 1775 by Johann Nepomuk Weigl, possibly a bookbinder active in Lower Austria, and that it was later acquired by Haydn before it was purchased by the Esterházy family from Haydn's estate. The original manuscript has been missing from the Esterházy archives in Budapest since the end of the Second World War, but fortunately a handwritten copy prepared by Hoboken is preserved in Vienna. Because it includes virtually a complete list of Haydn's symphonies written up to 1775 and because it was annotated by Haydn himself, the *Quartbuch* (so named by Pohl because of its small quarto format) counts as one of the most valuable thematic listings of Haydn's early instrumental works. RNF

R. N. Freeman, *The Practice of Music at Melk Abbey: Based upon the Documents, 1681–1826* (Vienna, 1989).

J. P. Larsen, 'Evidence or Guesswork: The "Quartbuch" Revisited', *Acta Musicologica*, 49 (1977), 86–102.

quartet. See opposite.

quartet

Haydn's mastery of the quartet genre is one of the most telling and celebrated achievements in the history of Western music. His innate understanding of the grammar and syntax of musical style in the second half of the 18th century was unrivalled and his quartets are a continual exploration of this mastery of language, all the more effective because it is articulated by four players. In a celebrated comment Goethe once said that 'a good quartet was like listening to a stimulating conversation between four intelligent people'. This was not a fanciful observation but one that was firmly rooted in 18th-century musical aesthetics. Music was hardly ever compared with art or architecture; on the other hand comparison with speech was common and, in an age when social conversation was esteemed and people read aloud to each other, a good string quartet shared similar qualities of narrative, proposition, debate, argument, and consensus. A figure like Samuel Johnson was highly prized for his wit and, in many ways, Haydn was his musical equivalent, though in a language that wonderfully lacked concrete meaning: he was fascinated by its properties and displayed inexhaustible inventiveness in its use.

Haydn wrote 68 original quartets. Having to all intents and purposes invented the genre in the 1750s with ten early works, he was unable to return to the medium for a while, until, around 1770, three sets of six were composed, op. 9, op. 17, and op. 20. Another break of similar duration followed before Haydn once more returned to quartet-writing, completing the op. 33 set in 1781. Between that date and 1799 Haydn was more consistently occupied with the genre, especially in the period 1788–90, when three sets of six were composed in as many years, op. 50, opp. 54 and 55, and op. 64.

Haydn's mastery of the quartet was widely recognized in his own lifetime. As particular testimony to this esteem PLEYEL, his former pupil, prepared a complete edition of Haydn's quartets with the composer's approval. Dedicated to Napoleon, it first appeared in Paris in 1801. In his edition Pleyel referred to the works using many of the opus numbers that had been current in the 18th century; these opus numbers have remained in use to this day. However, Pleyel's edition was more complete than it should have been in that it included six quartets, labelled op. 3, now known to be the work, either wholly or in part, of HOFSTETTER.

---

1. **Op. 1, op. 2, and 'op. 0'.**
2. **Op. 9.**
3. **Op. 17.**
4. **Op. 20.**
5. **Op. 33.**
6. **Op. 42.**
7. **Op. 50.**
8. **Op. 54 and op. 55.**
9. **Op. 64.**
10. **Op. 71 and op. 74.**
11. **Op. 76.**
12. **Op. 77.**
13. **Op. 103.**
14. **Arrangements for quartet.**

---

1. Op. 1, op. 2, and 'op. 0'. In old age, when interviewed by Griesinger for a biography of the composer, Haydn implied that he had written his first quartets by accident.

Baron Fürnberg happened to be the host for a regular meeting of a quartet ensemble of his pastor, manager, Albrechtsberger, and Haydn; the composer duly obliged by writing his first quartets. Between them, Griesinger and Haydn managed to exaggerate the novelty of the occasion since it was an invention waiting to happen; music in four harmonic parts was already common in concertos and symphonies and quartets would have happened by accident when such works were performed by one player per part. Griesinger's biography states explicitly that Haydn was 18 years old at the time, which implies 1750, shortly after his dismissal from St Stephen's. The craftsmanship of the music as well as circumstantial evidence suggests that this is far too early and a period between 1757 and 1762 is now generally accepted as the likely time of composition.

Griesinger does not state how many works Haydn composed for Fürnberg. By the first decade of the century Griesinger (and perhaps Haydn too) would have understood his first quartets to mean the two sets of six that had been published in the mid-1760s, op. 1 by La Chevardière of Paris and op. 2 by Hummel of Amsterdam. But these have no integrity as individual sets and were merely assembled, without Haydn's knowledge, by publishers from manuscript parts already in circulation. They, in fact, include three works that are not genuine quartets: op. 1 no. 5 was a symphony (Hob.I:107, a particular instance of converting symphonies into quartets) and op. 2 nos. 3 and 5 were sextets for quartet plus two horns. When, quite independently of La Chevardière, Hummel issued his own op. 1, he included six genuine quartets, including a work in E♭ (Hob.II:6) and omitting the spurious version of the symphony. This quartet in E♭ was rediscovered only in the 1930s when it was—not altogether helpfully—dubbed 'op. 0'. In total, therefore, there are ten early quartets. All were entered by Haydn in the *Entwurf-Katalog* and there is no evidence of any lost quartets from this period.

Given the pre-eminence that Haydn's quartets were to achieve in his lifetime it is understandable that he and Griesinger should wish to present the first quartets as a novel invention. What is remarkable, however, is the high level of resourcefulness the works exhibit; in no sense are they orchestral music that happens to be written for single players. In fast movements and minuets, in particular, the music is firmly led by the first violin but the contribution of the second violin, viola, and cello is unfailingly pertinent in the way that they highlight, contradict, or support the first violin; at this stage their contributions do not have the symphonic import evident in later works but the pointed vitality of the ensemble is a constant marvel. Although Haydn had already demonstrated this ability to think in rhythmic polyphony in some of the early cassations and, fleetingly, in the string trios, these ten quartets reveal a new level of mastery.

Particularly engaging is Haydn's imaginative way with phrase rhythms and the recasting of material. Op. 2 no. 1 in A opens with two three-bar phrases before moving on to the norm of two-bar phrases; at the beginning of the development four staggered entries that refer to this opening theme disturb the flow of two-bar phrases; at the beginning of the recapitulation (bar 71) the phrase patterns are again disguised when the constituent threads of the texture are reworked to form an apparently new theme. The consequence on phrase rhythms of thinking in imitative or quasi-imitative part-writing is also present in minuet movements, with a movement like the second minuet of op. 1 no. 1, for instance, being some way from the danced minuet as exemplified in the contemporary 'Seitenstetten' minuets.

If fast movements and minuets show a ready engagement with the self-imposed challenge of writing absorbing music for all four players, then the slow movements are much less inventive, revealing an indebtedness to the Baroque violin concerto, in their spinning out of melodic lines over a repetitive accompaniment, a reminder that Vivaldi's music was reasonably well known in mid-18th-century Austria. In the slow movement of op. 1 no. 4 the second violin provides an occasional echo (marked *con sordino*) of the first violin, a technique that Haydn was to employ again in the Andante molto of Symphony no. 38.

All ten quartets have five movements, as in some contemporary cassations and music for wind instruments. For eight of the works the rather schematic approach of two outer movements enclosing two minuets which, in turn, surround the central slow movement does succeed in making the slow movement the emotional core of the work, despite the undemocratic scoring. Two works, op. 1 no. 3 and op. 2 no. 6, reverse the position of the opening first movement and slow movement. Rather than a concertante movement, the opening Adagio of op. 2 no. 6 is a set of four variations on a theme, the first of many in his quartets.

2. Op. 9. None of the autograph manuscripts of these six quartets has survived, but the integrity of the works as a set rather than six individual works is suggested by their entry in the *Entwurf-Katalog*. They circulated in manuscript and were first published, without the composer's cooperation, by Huberty in Paris in 1772; the associated opus number, 9, derives from this publication. Huberty had visited Vienna on business in 1770 where he probably acquired the manuscript copies for his edition. It is thought that the works were composed between *c.*1768 and 1770 and the unchallenged assumption is that they were written for Haydn's colleagues at the Esterházy court; the florid first-violin part recalls some of the mannerisms in the violin concertos written for TOMASINI and it is likely that these quartets too were composed with that particular player in mind.

Rather than the five-movement format of the early quartets, Haydn now opts for a cycle of four movements. His symphonies in the 1760s, too, show a preference for a four-movement structure, but whereas they tend to favour the order fast, slow, minuet, and fast, the op. 9 quartets place the minuet second in the design: fast, minuet, slow, and fast. The likely reason for this difference is the moderate pace of five of the opening movements in the quartets ('Moderato' in nos. 1 and 2, 'Allegro moderato' in nos. 3 and 4, and 'Poco Adagio' in no. 5), a new movement type in Haydn's quartets, though previously evident in many concertos from the 1750s and 1760s; to have followed such movements with a slow movement ('Adagio' or 'Largo' in all cases) would not have afforded the direct contrast provided by a minuet. Five of the quartets move from a steadily paced opening movement to a Presto conclusion (Allegro moderato in no. 3). The exception is op. 9 no. 6 in A which moves from a Presto to a final Allegro of only 53 bars, the very brevity of the latter compensating for its speed.

One of the features of the ten early quartets that aroused repeated criticism in Haydn's lifetime was the composer's fondness for doubling minuet melodies at the octave, like 'father and son begging' as one north German writer put it. The prevalence of the criticism, however, is out of all proportion to the number of occurrences in Haydn's quartets. There are only two instances in op. 9, the minuets of nos. 3 and 5, and in neither case can it be said to be an instance of dumbing down. In op. 9 no. 3, in G major, it carefully draws attention to a distinct harmonic colouring in the third bar

(V^7/IV), while in op. 9 no. 5 it is coupled with a turn figure to produce a gentle dislocation of the beat. The trio of op. 9 no. 3 with its reckless cross-rhythms was cited by the theorist Heinrich Koch (1749–1816) as a prime instance of *imbroglio* (controlled confusion); for its part the trio of op. 17 no. 5 is an early instance of that section offering an apparent contrast but taking its thematic cue from the preceding minuet.

Viewed against the background of Haydn's musical development in general during the 1760s, the most curious and disappointing aspect of op. 9 is the nature of the slow movement. Whereas Haydn symphonies had developed a variety of approaches in their slow movement, the six quartets of op. 9 cling to the practice established in the early quartets: a concertante movement featuring the solo violin over a persistent accompaniment. Several movements towards the end move to a six-four chord and a pause, inviting a cadenza; some cadenzas by unknown contemporary musicians survive. The main portion of the slow movement of op. 9 no. 2 is appropriately headed Cantabile and is preceded by a written-out improvisation of the kind that keyboard players referred to as 'preluding'.

With this first set of six quartets, Haydn establishes the practice of including one work in the minor key. The choice of key in op. 9 no. 4, D minor, is also prophetic, the first of four striking quartets in that key, the others being op. 42, op. 76 no. 2, and op. 103. D minor often encourages Haydn to an earnestness and intensity of endeavour, characteristic of symphonies nos. 26, 34, and 80, the piano trio (Hob.XV:23), the 'Nelson' mass (MISSA IN ANGUSTIIS), as well as the four quartets. Apart from the resourceful use of rhythmic decoration, which is hardly ever gratuitous, what especially impresses in the first movement of op. 9 no. 4 is the new power Haydn associates with harmonic reorientation; in the development section the first subject is presented twice, in G minor and A minor, with the insistent semiquaver figuration of the third bar of the subject leading to a different continuation on both occasions. To encourage this feeling of intensity the 34 bars of the exposition are compressed into 20 in the recapitulation.

Unusually, the minuet of op. 9 no. 4 is a through-composed movement, omitting the pleasantry of the thematic recall that is a standard feature of such movements. The trio is the only music in the entire quartet that is set in D major. For once, it is a genuine trio, in that there are three harmonic voices, but the obvious scoring of first violin, second violin, and viola is replaced by first violin, playing in double stops throughout, and second violin.

Although the texture and style of the following Adagio in B♭ are disappointingly conventional ones, the repeat of the opening 22 bars is written out so that Haydn can vary the accompaniment as well as the leading line, the first instance of a VERÄNDERTE REPRISE in the composer's quartets. The Presto finale returns to D minor and, though the rhythmic figurations of the movement are those of a gigue, the fabric of the music is built out of two contrapuntal fragments initially played by second violin and viola and then by the remaining instruments, a glimpse of the process featured more ambitiously in the finales of op. 20 nos. 2 and 6.

3. Op. 17. These six quartets are the earliest to survive in autograph form. Bound together as a set of six they were owned by the Neuwirth family in Vienna before they were acquired by the Gesellschaft der Musikfreunde. Apart from an annotation that states that Haydn played the viola in quartet parties in the Neuwirth household, nothing is known about his relationship with the family. They are unlikely to have been associated with the commissioning of the works, if only because the music of op. 17 was clearly designed as a complementary set to op. 9, and therefore almost certainly intended for Tomasini and his Esterházy colleagues. Composed in 1771, immediately after op. 9, they have so many features in common with the earlier set that it makes sense for the two opuses to be regarded as a double set, in a way not apparent elsewhere in Haydn's ouput of quartets. As Georg Feder has pointed out, both sets have four works that open with a Moderato in common time, one work that opens with a set of variations in a slow 2/4, and one that begins with a Presto in 6/8; furthermore, one of the slow movements in both sets is a siciliano and there is one work in the minor key. With the exception of E♭ major, used in op. 9 no. 2 and op. 17 no. 3, no key is duplicated in the later set and between them, the 12 works cover the eight most common major keys, from C to E major in a sharp direction and E♭ in a flat direction, plus works in two of the most familiar minor keys, D and C.

Again, it is the work in the minor key, op. 17 no. 3 in C minor, that has drawn most attention from commentators. Although it shares many broad characteristics with its predecessor, it has its own individuality. Harmonic ambiguity is a particularly fascinating feature of its first movement, the opening rising arpeggio figure leading to a different continuation on virtually every occasion; this kind of figure had already become a favoured one in the composer's symphonies (e.g. finales of nos. 13, 25, and 29) and as a catalyst to invention it was never to lose its potency.

Most of the slow movements continue to rely on the simple charms of the 'aria without words' format, but the addition of an 'orchestral' introduction and a recitative in the expressive G minor slow movement of op. 17 no. 5 is a notable extension of the format and a foretaste of the overly dramatic evocation of opera in the slow movement of op. 20 no. 2. More prophetic of future slow movements in general is that of op. 17 no. 3 which mixes concertante passages over a persistent accompaniment with a more varied scoring that is alive to the euphony of the medium in a slow tempo; the harmonic range of this movement is also unusually broad, its opening section moving from A♭ to E♭ via G♭ major.

Manuscript copies of three quartets, op. 17 nos. 2, 5, and 6, were owned by the Mozart family, the scrupulous notation of additional dynamics by Wolfgang suggesting that he was intimately familiar with the music.

The works were published within a year of their composition, in May 1772 and without Haydn's knowledge, by Hummel of Amsterdam and with the addition of a figured bass. Exactly a year later Sieber issued them in Paris, also with figured bass. The musical texts of both editions are of no value but both played a part in the posthumous history of the works; the familiar order of the works was taken from both publications and the opus number, 17, from the Sieber edition.

4. Op. 20. Op. 20 has earned the status of Haydn's first mature quartets for two complementary reasons: they are the first works to involve all four instruments in the dialogue; and each work is strongly characterized, ranging from the lighthearted to the profound. Mozart deeply admired the works, Beethoven copied them out in order to study their craftsmanship, and, at the end of the 19th century, Brahms was the proud owner of the autograph manuscripts, later bequeathed to the Gesellschaft der Musikfreunde. When, in 1801, a new edition of the quartets was advertised in the *Wiener Zeitung*, the publisher ARTARIA remarked that it was with these works that

'Haydn so decisively founded his fame', a sentiment echoed by GERBER 11 years later in his dictionary entry on the composer.

Back in 1772, Haydn had no sense that he was initiating a tradition. For him they were his latest quartets, like op. 9 and op. 17, probably composed for Tomasini and other colleagues at the Esterházy court. The first, unsanctioned edition was issued by La Chevardière in 1774, initiating the use of op. 20. A second unsanctioned edition was advertised by Hummel of Amsterdam and Berlin in 1779, and it was this publication that established the familiar order. It has an attractive title page with an engraving of a midday sun, prompting the nickname 'Sun' quartets for the set.

The Allegro moderato which opens op. 20 no. 1 in E♭ immediately shows the greater sense of democracy in the part-writing evident throughout the set. Much of the writing is in three parts, but is cleverly distributed between four players. Coupled with a much reduced role for routine repeated quavers, this produces a texture that creates its own self-sufficiency. Although the first violin is the first among equals, each instrumental line contributes pointedly to the texture and changes harmonic function within it: every instrumentalist must be prepared to be the 'soprano', 'alto', 'tenor', and 'bass', and to partake in duets and trios of varying combinations as well as the full quartet.

With its strong melodic quality and regular phrases, the minuet of op. 20 no. 1 has a strong sense of identity. The trio, on the other hand, is deliberately vague in both these aspects; like many trio sections in op. 17, it includes an anticipation of the return of the minuet, but this return, rather eccentrically, prepares for F minor rather than the home key of E♭.

The slow movement is equally striking. Marked 'Affettuoso e sostenuto' it unfolds in a smooth three beats to a bar, with a consistently full four-part texture and with little discernible articulation. Mozart was fascinated by this movement and used it as a model for the slow movement of his E♭ quartet (K428). Beethoven is known to have copied out the op. 20 quartets in 1793–4, but this tranquil movement seems to prefigure late rather than early Beethoven. The finale is of a kind familiar from Haydn's two previous sets: a binary Presto movement in 2/4. Notwithstanding bouts of persistent syncopation it provides an undemanding conclusion to an otherwise probing work.

Haydn's use of a three-part musical texture to enforce equality between three players is pointedly evident at the beginning of op. 20 no. 2. The distribution can only be described as perverse: the bass is in the viola, the middle line is in the second violin, and the melody is played by the cello; in the repetition the three-strand texture is divided between violins and viola. While this variety of part-writing is at its most extreme in these opening bars it is present throughout the movement.

For the slow movement in C minor, headed *Capriccio*, Haydn takes the structure of a vocal number as a model: an accompanied recitative leading to an aria, with the ensemble playing all the usual clichés of orchestral punctuation in recitative and the three 'soloists' (cello and violin in the recitative, violins in the aria) doing their best to act as distraught figures in an imaginary *opera seria*. In an opera one would expect the aria to lead into a fast section (to form a so-called rondò); here Haydn links the music into the expected third movement of a string quartet, a minuet. But it is not an abrupt change from the theatre to the salon. At a time when operatic arias availed themselves of dance rhythms to communicate a particular dramatic point, Haydn's minuet still manages to sound very vocal. It is known that the composer sometimes conceived his music in terms of images; perhaps there was a hidden programme behind these two middle movements.

As part of the conscious process of encouraging the full use of the ensemble, three of the finales in the op. 20 quartets are set as fugues. This was not a self-conscious return to the lost glories of the Baroque but a lively demonstration that Haydn's up-to-date style could be as polyphonic as the most impressive fugue by Bach. The composer proudly heads the finale of op. 20 no. 2 'Fuga a 4^{tro} soggetti' (fugue on four themes) and the movement is a continuous buzz of counterpoint. To encourage a sense of mystery and admiration, Haydn instructs that three-quarters of the movement be played 'sempre sotto voce'; the last section is in a confident *forte*.

One particular indication of deepening expressive content in op. 20 is the presence of two works, rather than one, in the minor key, no. 3 in G minor and no. 5 in F minor. The years around 1770 saw a general increase in the use of minor keys in Haydn's music altogether. In symphonies, operas, and church music it usually produces a flamboyant, agitated mood. In these two quartets, however, the seriousness is more thoughtful. In op. 20 no. 3 the opening to each of the four movements offers a variant on the same thematic profile and two movements, the first and the minuet, take delight in balancing phrases of unusual lengths, seven and five bars respectively. These two movements and the finale are in G minor, while the rich textures of the slow movement, with its eloquent cello part, are heard in G major. When, however, G major returns at the very end of the finale it is with a feeling of poignancy rather than optimism.

The first movement of op. 20 no. 4 in D major is in a gently ambling triple time but, rather like the first Allegro of Mozart's Symphony no. 39 in E♭, this easy delivery belies its extreme sophistication. The first subject is a large leisurely paragraph: five six-bar phrases over a held bass note establish three repeated notes as a generating motif and, in the last phrase (marked by a drop from *piano* to *pianissimo*), a propensity for gentle harmonic surprise (unsupported C♮s). Later, apparently contrasting melodic material is all brought within the orbit of this first subject through combination and juxtaposition.

The slow movement in D minor (Un poco adagio e affettuoso) is a set of variations on the opening theme, meticulously controlled in harmony and instrumental layout. One technique that Haydn learnt very early in quartet-writing was how best to space (or voice) chords and how well-shaped individual lines can enhance such spacing. After three variations the theme returns in its original form so that its conclusion can be deflected into an expansive paragraph that impressively realizes the latent harmonic power of the theme.

The *Menuet alla Zingarese* (Gypsy Minuet) is a thrilling evocation of Eastern folk music which must have delighted Brahms, the one-time owner of the autograph manuscripts of op. 20. Though notated in the required triple time, the violins sound in duple time throughout the minuet; the viola and cello also effectively play in duple time but their accents are a beat later. This lusty conflict of both metre and accent is exaggerated by liberal *sforzando* markings. The trio, in contrast, could not be more straightforward: scalic cello passages with the simplest of accompaniments, and in an endless parade of four-bar phrases.

The final movement takes on the exhilaration of the minuet, but in a sonata form in which, once again, all the thematic material arises naturally from the opening phrase.

The atmosphere of the fifth quartet in F minor (op. 20 no. 5) could not be more contrasting, a world of pathos rather than comedy. Much of the emotional power of the opening Moderato is due to the long span of the principal melody which exerts an influence on the entire movement; if one of the commonly understood aims of mid-18th-century music, especially chamber music, was a feeling of conversation then this is akin to an eloquent speech with supportive comment, rather than dialogue. The minuet stays in the minor key but very cleverly avoids lyricism, allowing the slow movement to make maximum impact and anticipating the finale. The gentle siciliano rhythms of the Adagio in F minor and its well-placed, gently dissonant harmonies might well have caught the attention of Mozart, the slow movement of whose 'Linz' symphony (K425) echoes it. The web of decoration spun by the first violin is also a special quality, contributing to a movement that manages to sound even sadder than the surrounding movements in a minor key.

The finale is a fugue on two themes, 'Fuga a 2 soggetti'. The principal one will remind modern listeners most readily of the chorus 'And with His stripes' from *Messiah*. At this stage in his life Haydn would not have known Handel's chorus, but there was no need for him to know it because the theme was a common one, used on literally dozens of occasions by composers from the 17th century through to the early 19th century; Haydn was to use it again in another quartet, op. 55 no. 1 (finale). As in the other two fugues in op. 20, Haydn instructs that the music be played 'sempre sotto voce', in this case until the very last phrase.

The first movement of the final quartet in the set, op. 20 no. 6 in A, is headed 'Allegro di molto e scherzando', a description that might with equal validity apply to the complete work, one of Haydn's most 'playful' quartets. Of the six works in the set it is the one that most consistently looks back to opp. 9 and 17, as in the many double stops in the thematic material of the first movement (a Tomasini speciality) and, more extensively, the concertante scoring of the slow movement.

Individual instruments make a pointed, yet slight, contribution to the minuet, even more so to the trio, which is a genuine trio for first violin, viola, and cello, all of whom are instructed to play on the lowest string of their respective instruments.

Up to this point, the lack of ambition in the work might tempt the unwary listener to label the quartet a disappointment. But this turns out to be a complete misjudgement, as the finale shows Haydn at his most brilliantly inventive. The 'Fuga con 3 soggetti' (fugue with three subjects) involves all four players and, though it contains some very learned moments (Haydn draws attention to an inversion of one of the themes by labelling it 'al rovescio'), it is entirely 'scherzando'.

5. **Op. 33.** After op. 20, nine years were to elapse before Haydn had the opportunity to return to the composition of string quartets. By December 1781 he had completed six works which were published the following April by Artaria in Vienna. Before publication Haydn sent a number of letters—three have survived, probably more were sent—to potential patrons offering pre-publication manuscript copies. In these letters the quartets are described as being 'written in a new and special way'. On one level this is sales talk, but there are, nevertheless, several novel features that give the set a distinctive sense of identity. Haydn's overriding aim was to make the quartets as appealing as possible to potential purchasers without in any way compromising his art.

Op. 33 no. 1 offers a challenge and a tease immediately. By 1781 purchasers of quartets in 18th-century Vienna had long expected to find one work in the minor key.

A glance at the music would show it to be in B minor, itself something of a shock since it is a rather unusual key in the 18th century; Haydn never wrote a symphony in the key and, before this quartet, only one other major work uses it, a keyboard sonata from 1774 (Hob.XVI:32). Haydn plays on this element of surprise because the actual opening of the quartet, played by two violins, pretends to be in D major. It requires some highly rhetorical harmony to force the music into the correct key of B minor. Haydn then proceeds to demonstrate that this opening in the wrong key can send the music in all kinds of directions and can appear at every level of the texture.

Those movements in op. 33 that might have been expected to carry the headings 'Menuet' and 'Trio' bear the title 'Scherzo' and, for the separate enclosed section no title at all, an obvious 'new and special' feature, though the musical consequences are less fundamental than the changes of title imply. The scherzo in B minor encloses a trio section in B major, the well-articulated phrases of the former (featuring some quivering *bariolage* from the first violin) contrasting with the smooth movement of the latter.

Taking its cue from the scherzo, the Andante of op. 33 no. 1 (in D major) uses the same upward rising figure as the main feature of its melody, gradually shared by all the instruments. The figure appears too in the main theme of the finale, a brilliant yet severe conclusion to the work.

The combination of accessibility and high art that is the hallmark of op. 33 in general is immediately apparent in the opening of the second work, in E♭. Nothing could be simpler than the tune plus accompaniment of the opening, but, gradually, Haydn draws the listener into a very intricate discussion of the properties of this theme, especially the figure at the cadence. The number of bars in this movement that do not relate directly to the main theme can be counted on the fingers of one hand.

The scherzo in op. 33 no. 2 is particularly daring. The main section alludes to the 'Deutsche Tanz', a peasant dance that involved a good deal of hopping, stamping, fast circular motion, and close physical contact. The middle section is even more rustic, invoking a one-finger peasant fiddler who drunkenly glides about his instrument. (The 19th century thought this section too vulgar and omitted Haydn's careful instructions for sliding from one note to the next; astonishingly, it was not until 1974 with the appearance of the relevant volume in *JHW*, that Haydn's original text was restored.)

Following the high jinks of the scherzo Haydn needs to restore composure. This he does in the Largo by announcing the main theme not in full four-part harmony (as, for instance, in the slow movement of op. 33 no. 3) but in two parts, viola and cello. Gradually, the whole ensemble becomes involved as the lyricism embraces rhetoric too.

The finale is one of Haydn's 'new and special' features, a rondo rather than the binary or sonata form that had usually ended his earlier quartets. With its simple structure of a recurring theme alternating with contrasting sections that draw on the characteristics of the theme, it is irresistibly easy listening. It concludes with one of Haydn's most celebrated jokes (hence the nickname of 'Joke' for this quartet): a portentous Adagio halts the progress of the Presto and then, after a pause, the constituent phrases of the main theme are played, each separated by a bar's silence, and followed, after three bars' rest, by the first phrase, *pianissimo*. However many times the joke is told, ending a work with a beginning ('There was an old woman . . . ') always unnerves listeners, such is the power of Haydn's musical language.

For this ability to manipulate musical language Igor Stravinsky was a great admirer of Haydn's music, at a time when it was not fashionable to admit to such an enthusiasm. The first movement of op. 33 no. 3 ('Bird') may well have attracted Stravinsky's careful scrutiny because of the way it takes a cliché of the Classical style, repeated quavers underpinning a melody in C major, in order to re-examine its possibilities, precisely the same process that occurs in the first movement of Stravinsky's Symphony in C (1938–40). Every time the chattering quavers occur the music takes a different and, sometimes, wholly unexpected course; these quavers gave rise to the irritating nickname 'Bird'.

Part of the essential character of the first theme of the Allegro moderato is the way it spreads out from the middle register to first the top, and then the bottom of the ensemble. The scherzo formalizes this division, the main section exploiting the sonority of the lower strings of the instruments while the middle section is scored for two violins only.

The Adagio ma non troppo in F is a *locus classicus* of string quartet-writing in a slow tempo, with its beautifully judged chordal spacing, easy sense of forward movement, and well-paced harmonic climax; the melody too is distinctive, one of the earliest examples in Haydn's œuvre of a hymn-like theme, a new warm dimension to his melodic style.

The main theme of the concluding rondo uses some of the 'Bird' figuration from the first movement while the main contrasting section alludes to the 'Turkish' style that was so popular in Vienna in the 1770s and 1780s. As in three of the six quartets of op. 33, Haydn avoids a bravura conclusion in a *forte* dynamic in favour of something much less emphatic. Haydn was always concerned that his dynamic markings should be scrupulously observed and on the manuscript copies that were sent to Melk abbey he wrote in Italian 'Prego umilmente d'osservare il piano, e forte' (Please pay attention to the *piano* and *forte*).

Op. 33 no. 4 has always been the least often performed work of the set, with players, listeners, and commentators alike recognizing its appealing light-heartedness without discovering anything more individual. When all six quartets were entered in the *Entwurf-Katalog*, this quartet was placed sixth in the sequence, suggesting that it was the least favoured by the composer. Perhaps one reason is that the quartet has less variety in the scoring than its companions; Haydn seems to be content with a full four-part texture throughout. Nevertheless it has two of the 'new and special' features that Haydn talked about when trying to sell pre-publication manuscript copies of op. 33, a scherzo instead of a minuet, and a rondo finale. It is these movements that seem the most original. The dotted rhythms of the scherzo are akin to those found in the minuet of Mozart's Symphony in A (K201); both movements probably refer to a particular kind of German dance. The switch to B♭ minor for the trio section accompanies a theme that has the same profile as that of the main section. The finale is a sectional rondo, ABACA, with a catchy main theme. Haydn pretends to be unsure how to end the movement in order to spring a charming surprise, a simplified version of the main theme played pizzicato and *pianissimo*.

One trivial indication of how successful Haydn was in his intention to give op. 33 a popular appeal is that three of the six works acquired nicknames. In English-speaking countries op. 33 no. 5 in G has sometimes been called the 'How do you do?' (sometimes 'Compliments') because the first phrase sounds like a greeting. But, as several commentators have pointed out, it sounds more like an adieu. As always with such whimsical moments in Haydn's quartets the musical function of the phrase is more complex than can be communicated by one nickname. At one level, it has the practical purpose of settling the players and allowing them to begin the subsequent phrase absolutely together; it also unostentatiously draws attention to a rhythmic pattern that is to become more and more important in the movement; finally, it breaks up what otherwise might be a rather simplistic phrase structure (like a short-breathed verse) at the beginning of the movement.

The second movement, Largo e cantabile, sees a switch from G major to G minor, and from high comedy to high tragedy, as Haydn returns to the concertante format standard in his quartets up to op. 17. After the opera house the listeners are taken to the dance hall in the scherzo, but the players are particularly mischievous and refuse to play the music with the correct musical accents; with complete innocence the middle section demonstrates that they can play properly when they want to. The last movement is a set of three variations on the opening theme, a siciliano but marked Allegretto; a presto coda ends the movement.

When op. 33 was first published by Artaria in 1782, one person who eagerly studied the music was Mozart. Three years later Mozart completed six quartets dedicated to the older composer. Mozart's quartets are naturally very individual but single movements often have their direct equivalent in Haydn's op. 33, as if Mozart, having studied a particular Haydn movement, set himself the challenge of writing a considered response. One such case is the finale of op. 33 no. 5 which is echoed in the finale of Mozart's Quartet in D minor (K421). Another is the first Allegro of Mozart's quartet in B♭ (K458) which seems to have been stimulated by the first movement of op. 33 no. 6. Mozart's quartet gained the nickname 'Hunt', which would have been an appropriate one for Haydn's quartet too. The first movement is built entirely out of 'hunting' rhythms, the prevalent topic as much as the particular thematic properties of the music providing a sense of unity.

Another topic or image underlies the following Andante in D minor, that of an aria. The first violin is the 'soloist'; the second violin, viola, and cello constitute a very attentive 'string orchestra'. Towards the end there is even an opportunity for a brief cadenza for the 'soloist'. The scherzo is Haydn at his most mischievous. The music seems to want to settle into a regular series of phrases but imitative entries undermine the sense of regularity. The finale is a typical hybrid between variations and rondo of a kind that was to become increasingly common in the composer's quartets in the 1780s and 1790s. Two themes are announced, one in D major (the key of the first movement and scherzo), the other in D minor (the key of the slow movement). Both themes are then varied in turn, but every time the music switches to the major key there is first a statement of the theme in its original form. Interestingly, this mixing of rondo and variations was one aspect of Haydn's craft that was never taken on board by Mozart. Beethoven, however, was fascinated by it.

6. Op. 42. With one exception Haydn's mature quartets were composed—or, in the case of the final three, intended to be composed—in sets of six. The exception is this single quartet in D minor which Haydn completed in 1785. Apart from the date of composition nothing is known about its inception. The following year it was published by the firm of HOFFMEISTER in Vienna; the publishing practice of the firm may explain why the work is an isolated one. Instead of issuing works in sets of six, the normal practice, Hoffmeister preferred to print works singly; Mozart's single 'Hoffmeister' quartet (K499) is another work published by the firm. Hoffmeister, who was a popular composer of quartets himself, may well have asked Haydn to write the work.

There is an alternative explanation. In 1784 Haydn casually mentioned in a letter to Artaria that he was working on 'three very short' quartets 'of three movements only; they are intended for Spain'. These works have not survived and it is possible that the D minor quartet has some relationship with these Spanish works. It is certainly 'short' compared with other Haydn quartets from the 1780s, but it has four movements, not three as mentioned in the letter.

It may be less ambitious than other works, but it is beautifully shaped and immaculate in its scoring. In contrast to the relaxed dialogue of the first movement (D minor) and the minuet (D major), the Adagio (B♭ major) has a rich sonority; its thematic progress too is notable, the main theme being followed by an elaboration of its constituent phrases. The quartet ends with a taut finale in D minor, featuring two-part invertible counterpoint. An entire musical personality is enshrined in this deceptively simple work. The opus number, 42, was not applied until late in the 19th century.

7. Op. 50. The year 1787 was a typically busy one for Haydn. As Kapellmeister at the Esterházy court he spent most of his time rehearsing and directing opera, 96 performances of 14 different works. His 'Paris' symphonies were successfully performed the same year and he was now involved in selling them to publishers in Vienna and London. In the middle of such a busy schedule it is difficult to imagine how Haydn found time to compose. He turned down a request from Prague for a new opera mainly because 'no man can brook comparison with the great Mozart'. Paris had asked for further symphonies and nos. 88 and 89 probably date from this year. In the early part of the year he also composed six quartets, works that were published as op. 50. The autograph manuscripts of the work were lost until three, nos. 3–6, unexpectedly emerged in Melbourne, Australia, in 1982.

Haydn had completed two of the quartets and sounded out his Viennese publisher, Artaria, about publishing them when he heard that FRIEDRICH WILHELM II of Prussia was anxious to receive new music from him. With the composer's approval Artaria dedicated the quartet to 'Sa Majesté Frederic Guillaume II, Roi de Prusse'. The king was a keen and accomplished cellist who was a regular purchaser of music by Boccherini and Dittersdorf and who later commissioned Mozart's three 'Prussian' quartets (K575, K589, and K590). Though Haydn approved the dedication to the royal cellist, he—unlike Mozart—did not set out to flatter the king with lengthy passages of solo-writing.

Like op. 33 no. 3, but on an extended basis, the first quartet of op. 50 opens with an ending: the repeated tonic notes of the cello and the wisps of cadential phrases in the upper instruments could have been taken from a relaxed conclusion to a work, except that the general direction of the melodic material is upwards rather than downwards to an actual ending. With this crucial difference and the injection of faster, triplet rhythms, Haydn skilfully turns an ending into a beginning, and a cliché into something unique.

Haydn's quartets and symphonies were so popular that individual movements were often arranged for different forces, such as keyboard solos, keyboard trios, and even songs. The theme of the slow movement of op. 50 no. 1 is the subject of three variations, followed by a coda. Later the theme achieved a rather unusual distribution through being engraved on a monument in Haydn's birthplace, Rohrau. In 1793 the local aristocrat, Count HARRACH, erected a column in tribute to the village's greatest son; the lilting tune of the slow movement of this quartet was set to a text that begins 'Ein Denkmahlstein für Haydns Ruhm' (A stone monument for Haydn's glory).

Whereas in the slow movement most of the thematic lead is taken by the first violin, the cello shares the lead in the minuet, a reminder, perhaps, that it had initiated the entire quartet. The finale is a highly sophisticated comedy in sonata form in which, as in the best farce or *opera buffa*, everything depends on pacing and timing. The opening theme features throughout, but Haydn toys with the expectations of listeners as if he were a master actor. In the development an exaggerated 'wait for it' leads only to the shortest of reprises; then another lengthy preparation occurs in readiness for a full return; finally, there is reluctance to end the movement before yielding once more to a statement of the theme, but *piano*.

Op. 50 no. 2 is a hugely challenging work. Its key, C major, may be the most routine of keys but Haydn produced at least five quartets in C that are undoubted masterpieces: op. 20 no. 2, op. 33 no. 3, the present work, op. 54 no. 2, op. 74 no. 1, and op. 76 no. 3. No other single key elicited the same number of unique works.

Monothematicism, creating diversity out of unity, is particularly suited to the quartet genre. In the first movement of op. 50 no. 2, however, Haydn sets himself the opposite challenge, creating a focused movement out of quite diverse thematic material. The argument in the first movement is based on two contrasting main subjects, the first characterized by chromaticism and rhythmic strength, the second by a rich harmonic digression (bars 58–83). The process of making the music integrated rather than disparate is largely associated with the first subject which, having started life as a tune above an accompaniment, reveals an amazing ability to encourage the texture into four-part counterpoint.

Profundity is the last word one would use to describe the Adagio and, for that reason, it has puzzled some commentators. In his youth Haydn would have disdained the plodding accompaniments and the short-breathed phrases; in his middle age he seems to welcome them. It emerges as a parody of a serenade, an ironic interlude in the middle of so much cerebration.

The third movement, a minuet and trio, is, once again, a tough one, testing accepted premises of musical continuity and structure, to the extent that the minuet avoids a conventional modulation to the dominant. Haydn preserves the typical contrast of complex minuet and simple trio and, in the process, provides the turning point in the work, the minuet itself referring back to the serious-minded first movement, the trio anticipating the lighthearted energy of the finale. Marked Vivace assai, the last movement is a sonata form of incessant bravura, involving all four players in fast-moving repartee covering the total span of the ensemble, from the bottom C of the cello to a climactic top C, five octaves higher, on the violin.

In complete contrast to the first movement of the C major quartet, the content of the first movement of op. 50 no. 3 in E♭ is derived from the opening figure featuring a turn. Haydn makes use of this material in elaborate contrapuntal paragraphs as well as in simple theme-plus-accompaniment textures. Working with this pervasive motif prompted the composer into a radically reworked recapitulation section, one in which a formal presentation of the first subject in the tonic is not heard until 20 bars from the end. The 6/8 rhythms together with the very argued content results in an Allegro con brio of considerable forward momentum. The slow movement (Andante o più tosto Allegretto) provides a complete contrast, something that is essentially static: a set of variations on the opening theme, presented by the cello.

Using the steady phrase patterns of the minuet Haydn subtly returns the music to the very reasoned atmosphere of the first movement; the trio offers some contrast, though its thematic material arises naturally out of that of the minuet.

The finale of the quartet is another monothematic sonata form. One senses that it could become something much more unbuttoned but Haydn resists this temptation—there is very little virtuosity, for instance—and the quartet ends quietly.

Two features of op. 50 no. 4 would have struck contemporary listeners immediately, the key of F♯ minor and the use of a formal fugue as a finale rather than the expected rondo or sonata form. As Dean Sutcliffe has pointed out, the interaction of these two features provides a fundamental clue to the severe nature of the work in general. There is a distinct tendency for music in the minor key to be associated with polyphonic textures (the opening of the first movement, the second theme in the slow movement, the trio of the minuet, and the concluding fugue) while simpler, homophonic textures tend to be associated with the major key (second subject in the first movement, the opening theme in the slow movement, and the minuet itself). One might have expected this creative friction between minor and major, severe and positive, to resolve itself into the major. But Haydn's emotional journeys in his quartets are often much more varied and idiosyncratic than they are in public works such as symphonies. The work ends in the minor key.

The first movement of op. 50 no. 5 in F reveals Haydn at his most constructively perverse. The gait of the material is folksy but the first entry of the viola and cello on a 'wrong' note (C♯) ensures that the movement never becomes routine, as all the participants cash in on the potential of this disruptive tactic. The slow movement (Poco adagio) could not be more contrasting, leisurely, *legato* rather than staccato, and with no disruption. Haydn's interest in thematic economy often led him to write minuets that were extremely concise; the minuet of this quartet together with that in op. 50 no. 2 are particularly good examples of this concision. Everything in the minuet arises out of the opening line in the first violin; rather than offering the conventional contrast of thematic material and texture, the trio section continues the process. Following this concentration the sonata form finale is much less argumentative relying, rather like the finale of no. 6, for much of its effect on the unusual sonority of the main theme: trills and 'sul una corda' (on one string, producing a controlled scoop between notes). The occasional harmonic discolouration is produced by the very note (C♯/D♭) that had produced so much of the narrative in the first movement and in the minuet. Here, however, it has no long-term influence; it is completely absorbed into the discourse.

Interviewed by his biographer Griesinger, Haydn said of the process of composition: 'Once I have seized upon an idea, my whole endeavour was to develop and sustain it in keeping with the rules of art.' The first movement of op. 50 no. 6, like the others in the set, is a good example of Haydn basing everything on the opening 'idea'. The 'idea' itself is typically memorable: the first violin begins alone, away from the tonic, with the other three instruments joining in the second bar, and is another instance of music that sounds more like an ending than a beginning. Through repeated and varied reference to this central 'idea' Haydn creates a lively discussion. On occasions, it becomes forceful too (including two passages in the flattened sixth), but the movement ends quietly, in careful anticipation of the Poco adagio.

The middle movements—the slow movement and the minuet—are also strongly focused on their respective opening ideas, the lilting rhythms of a siciliano in the Poco adagio (D minor), and the dotted note figure that characterizes the main theme of the minuet. The unifying feature of the finale (Allegro con spirito) is not so much a thematic profile or a particular rhythmic pattern, but an instrumental effect. The main theme of the sonata form features *bariolage*, that is rapid sounding of the same pitch on two adjacent strings to create a quivering effect. In the last few moments of the quartet the *bariolage* is comically extended to all four instruments. For Haydn 'developing' and 'sustaining' an 'idea' is as likely to produce whimsy as it is sustained intellectual discourse.

8. Op. 54 and op. 55. In 1788, only a year after op. 50, Haydn composed a further set of six quartets, entrusting their sale to a violinist from the Esterházy orchestra, JOHANN TOST, who was travelling to Paris. They were published there in June 1789 by the firm of SIEBER, divided into two sets of three, op. 54 and op. 55, an increasingly common trend towards the end of the century.

The repeated quavers of the accompaniment to the first subject provide much of the energy of the first movement of op. 54 no. 1 in G but, as often in Haydn's quartets, this apparently simple background allows the first subject to take a different direction almost every time it occurs. Repeated notes figure too in the accompaniment of the following Allegretto in C, but here they underpin a movement that is tuneful rather than energetic. Just when the listener is lulled into complete security Haydn interpolates a wholly mysterious passage in attenuated harmonies: held together by a thread of repeated notes the music moves to completely uncharted territory (B♭ major and D♭ major). It was the experience of composing passages like this that Haydn was to draw on when he wrote the orchestral introduction to *The Creation*, 'The Representation of Chaos'.

There is something very gauche about the question-and-answer phrases of the opening of the minuet; they are slightly too long for dancing, five plus five. The trio section, led throughout by the cello, points out this oddity by sticking rigidly to regular four-bar phrases. The finale is a foot-tapping rondo of the kind Parisian audiences had recently enjoyed in Symphony no. 85 ('La Reine'), the first in his quartets since op. 33. Haydn encourages listeners to think that the quartet, too, is going to reach a rousing 'orchestral' conclusion, then changes his mind at the last possible moment and substitutes a *pianissimo* ending.

Op. 54 no. 2 in C has one of the most dramatic openings in the whole of Haydn's quartets: two balancing five-bar phrases separated by a general pause; following a second general pause, the music explodes into A♭ major and the third clause of the first subject. In the recapitulation Haydn deflates the abruptness of this opening by filling in the general pauses with *pianissimo* crotchets in the first violin. But despite this nervous gesture, the turbulent energy of the Vivace is not to be subdued until the finale.

The second movement is a dark Adagio in C minor in which the melody is smothered with rhapsodic decoration by the first violin; it moves directly into the minuet. The C major minuet encloses a C minor trio that is an anguished compression of the material of the minuet, including an anticipation of Wagner's 'Tristan' chord (third beat of bar 66).

All the intensity and power of the first three movements are then distilled in the finale. Rather than the expected C major movement in a brisk tempo it is another Adagio, in which a gentle melodic line is heard over the simplest of accompaniments, a movement of touching simplicity which, had it been late Beethoven, would have been labelled 'cantante e tranquillo'; a Presto interruption suggests a conventional unbuttoned ending, but the Adagio returns to form the most appropriate resolution to this spellbinding work.

Everything that occurs in the first movement of op. 54 no. 3 in E can be related to the first phrase, begun by second violin and viola, joined by first violin and cello. The legato contours of this thematic material feature throughout the movement and lead naturally to a second main feature: the propensity for the music to sit on a sustained note in the cello. To counterbalance this almost dangerously inactive music Haydn has bursts of animated triplets, usually in the first violin.

The Largo cantabile is in ternary form: a lyrical main section in A major; a more severe section in A minor that draws its material from the cello figure that had ended the first section; and the return of the opening section, now lavishly ornamented.

For the first time since op. 17 (apart from briefly in op. 33 no. 3) Haydn returns in the minuet to octave scoring between first and second violins; he makes the minuet even more plebeian by constantly using a syncopated 'Scottish snap' figure. The tempo indication of the sonata form finale, Presto, together with the lively rhythms, suggest a movement that is going to be very animated, rather like the finale of op. 54 no. 1, but the influence of the first movement is still felt in the frequent long sustained notes in the accompaniment.

It is well appreciated that the key of A major always elicited a particular kind of music from Mozart; a number of major masterpieces, such as the Piano Concerto (K488), the Clarinet Quintet (K581), and the Clarinet Concerto (K622) share a warmth of sonority that is not evident in works in other keys. The key of A major in Haydn's music, on the other hand, is less consistently characterized and, indeed, in statistical terms, it is not that common in his output. There are four quartets: op. 2 no. 6, op. 9 no. 6, op. 20 no. 6, and the only work after 1772, op. 55 no. 1.

It is possible that Haydn recalled op. 20 when writing this work, because the finale includes fugal passages rather like those found in three quartets from the earlier set, including the A major. But the context is entirely different. In a compositional *tour de force* Haydn sets out to compose a rondo in a completely non-fugal manner with music that is completely self-sufficient, but at the first reprise of the rondo theme (bar 61) he adds a new slower-moving line to this material to convert it into what the composer could have labelled a 'Fuga a 3 Soggetti' (Fugue on three subjects). The new theme is from the same family of fugal themes as that heard in the finale of op. 20 no. 5 in F minor. Subsequently, the fugal texture disappears, as naturally as it had first appeared.

The Adagio cantabile, too, contains an unexpected feature. Towards the end of the movement there is a written-out cadenza for the four instrumentalists, heralded in the customary fashion by a six-four chord and concluded by a trill on the dominant. Haydn may well have taken this attractive idea from the quartets of Vanhal, where it is common.

Op. 55 no. 2 in F minor ('Razor') shows Haydn experimenting with the conventions of emotional balance and movement types. For the first time in his quartets he interchanges the position of slow movement and sonata form Allegro in a four-movement scheme; some symphonies from the 1760s have this pattern and the key of the last example, no. 49 in F minor, may have prompted Haydn to think of the pattern in this quartet. Within the work itself two complementary reasons for this change can be suggested. The first is that the slow movement (Andante o più tosto allegretto) is particularly imposing; it is a set of variations on two alternating themes, one in F minor and the other in F major, with the second theme being a paraphrase of the first. The second movement (Allegro), in turn, is a particularly uncompromising movement in F minor, dominated by its opening theme and featuring several stark contrasts of key; the recapitulation turns to the major key but its content is compressed from an expected 76 bars or so to only 36. Had the slow movement followed this tough movement it might have been overshadowed by it. As it is, the slow movement is allowed to make its own considerable impact first: an impressive beginning followed by a compelling continuation.

The second reason is that the variations introduce some harmonic and tonal characteristics that are to feature in later movements; in that sense the movement is an introduction to the rest of the quartet. The opening theme reaches a harmonic and melodic peak on a Neapolitan chord (bar 20); shortly after the beginning of the Allegro two bars of silence are followed by a switch to precisely the same chord. The oscillation between F minor and F major featured in the first movement also remains fundamental to the rest of the quartet: the Allegro begins in F minor and ends in F major; the minuet is in F major, the trio in F minor; the finale in sonata form resolves the conflict by being in F major.

Op. 55 no. 3 in B♭ lacks the restless creative energy of the 'Razor' quartet and is the least characterful work in the set of six. But it is certainly not superficial. The apparently straightforward melodic flow of the first movement is constantly undermined by a nagging chromaticism. The Adagio ma non troppo in E♭ consists of two variations on an unusually lengthy and already quite elaborate theme. In the first variation, the decorative descant offered by the first violin gradually spreads to all the instruments, while the second begins contrapuntally. The sliding chromatic lines that are heard towards the end of the slow movement return in the minuet where they do their best to destabilize what is otherwise a rather jaunty movement. They appear, too, in the Presto finale, where they are more comfortably contained within the general sweep of the sonata form.

9. Op. 64. This set of quartets was completed during that unsettled period between September and December 1790 that Haydn spent in Vienna, before leaving for his first visit to London. Although the set was dedicated to Johann Tost, their composition was perhaps instigated by another musician, LEOPOLD KOZELUCH (Koželuh). As well as being a successful composer, especially of piano music, Kozeluch had started a music publishing firm in Vienna, the Magazin de Musique, designed, at least initially, to promote his own career. Gradually, publishing became more rewarding than composing as towards 1790 Kozeluch sought to expand his business and began publishing music by other composers. In Vienna, Artaria had always been Haydn's principal publisher. Perhaps to help Kozeluch's fledgling business, Haydn agreed that the new firm should publish his latest quartets. The composer also took manuscript copies of the works with him to London, where three of them were played at Salomon's concerts in 1791, and where the local firm of John Bland published a second authentic edition. The opus number of 64 was first used in a later edition by Pleyel.

The key of C major in Haydn's music is often associated with the sound of the march, either obviously, as in the slow movement of the 'Military' symphony (no. 100), or sublimated, as in the first movement of the Cello Concerto in C. The monothematic first movement of op. 64 no. 1, marked Allegro moderato, relies heavily on this association, and allows the music to incorporate a number of unexpected events en route, including a deflection to D♭ major in the recapitulation.

In the trio sections of his quartets Haydn often entrusts the thematic lead to the cello; here, for the first and only time in the quartets, the cello takes the lead at the beginning of the minuet, perhaps because the preceding movement had spotlighted the first violin. The trio turns to C minor but its thematic material is based on the opening motif of the minuet, an opaque view of a melody that had been so self-confident.

The third movement, Allegretto scherzando, is a set of three variations on the opening theme in F major. The instruction 'scherzando' (playful) is designed to ensure a light, gently nimble account, but it is also a warning that the theme and, consequently, each variation contains an unorthodox and very strenuous sounding modulation to A♭. Haydn is to revisit this musical sore thumb in the finale. That movement, a sonata form marked Presto, is one of great strength and vitality. At the beginning of the development the music drops to a *piano* dynamic and the cello initiates a bizarre passage of imitation in A♭ major, a moment that would have excited the unlikely attention of Berlioz (one thinks of the fugue in the 'Witches' Sabbath' in the *Symphonie Fantastique*). Gradually, through ruthless imitation, this unorthodoxy is normalized and incorporated within the energy of the movement.

If the move to A♭ major in op. 64 no. 1 suggests that Haydn was forcing himself to be exploratory—a 'Let's see what I can do with this' attitude—then the second quartet in the set seems to look for inspiration in a different way, to the op. 33 quartets. It is set in the same unusual choice of key, B minor, as in op. 33 no. 1; even more striking, Haydn repeats the trick of pretending to begin in D major. In any direct comparison the first movement of op. 64 no. 1 emerges as a more angular sounding work, a product of the widening of the composer's harmonic palette that took place between 1781 and 1790.

As in all Haydn's quartets that begin with a brisk first movement, the slow movement comes second. In this Adagio ma non troppo in B major, the continuous sound of stopped strings creates a warm sonority that contrasts with the sharply etched sonority of the first movement. The principle of the movement is that of variations but, in order to present a strong sense of unfolding, Haydn avoids the regular, variation-by-variation approach, if only through the psychological means of not providing regular double bars in the score. The minuet too turns to op. 33 for inspiration, to the disruptive phrase patterns of the scherzos in that set. It opens with a five-bar phrase, the extra bar being the third (a sticking repetition of the second bar). This distinctive bar then figures prominently in the unpredictable unfolding of the remainder of the minuet. The B major trio, in contrast, could not be more constructively uneventful. The quartet ends with a sonata form in two beats per bar (Presto), rather studiously focused on the main theme. A late switch from B minor to B major promises a grand conclusion, but, quite enigmatically, Haydn makes the music disappear into thin air.

In the opening Vivace assai of op. 64 no. 3 in B♭, Haydn sets aside his preferred monothematic approach in favour of an almost Mozartian generosity of melodic ideas, except that Mozart would never have used such a simple idea as the side drum figure that follows the first theme. It returns in the finale, also in sonata form, where it proceeds to play a harmonically more creative role than in the first movement. Between these outer movements there is a ternary shaped Adagio and a minuet whose trio section uses the same syncopated rhythms found in the equivalent movement of the 'Oxford' symphony (no. 92), composed the previous year.

A Mozartian profusion of thematic material is a feature also of the first movement of op. 64 no. 4 in G. Four themes can be identified: the opening idea, an altered version (bar 16, after some *bravura* passage-work in the first violin), a syncopated melody in the dominant minor (bar 23), and a cadence theme played on the lowest string (bar 33). But Haydn was too individual a composer to write pastiche Mozart and the remainder of the movement, including the part that is nominally the recapitulation, is a continuous exploration of the properties of these themes.

The minuet also warrants the label Mozartian, in the sense that it sounds much more like a social dance written by that composer in the last years of his life than it does a typical minuet from a quartet by Haydn. Simplicity is the hallmark of the Adagio too, a ternary movement in C major that turns to C minor in the middle section. The quartet ends with a 6/8 sonata form, full of energy and, in the middle section, unexpected changes of direction.

Mozart's influence, whether in technique or spirit, is not evident in op. 64 no. 5 ('Lark'). The opening Allegro moderato begins with the second violin, viola, and cello playing a crisp, march-like theme that is apparently self-sufficient. Then the first violin enters way above this material which turns out to be the accompaniment to the melody. This initial soaring entry gave rise to the nickname 'Lark', but the whole passage is a particularly neat demonstration of how Haydn can transform foreground into background, theme into accompaniment. Out of these two complementary ideas and the later, apparently casual outburst of virtuoso triplets in the first violin, Haydn builds an entire first movement.

The structure of the Adagio in A major is the same as that found in four slow movements in op. 64: ternary with the middle section in the minor and drawing its thematic material from the principal sections. But this favoured structure here produces one of the composer's most heart-warming slow movements, anticipating some of the slow sections of the late masses in its rapt simplicity.

Throughout the course of the minuet there is a tendency for the music to feature a rising scale figure; the trio takes its melodic cue from the minuet but, because of the minor key, it now sounds much more austere. Contrast between major and minor underlines the ternary structure of the finale too where, reinforced by a switch from *piano* to *forte*, it underpins an exciting *moto perpetuo*, marked Vivace.

The final work in op. 64 is in E♭, a key that often encourages Haydn towards lyricism, not a quality, one would have thought, that readily submits itself to the searching procedures of a typical Haydn sonata form. In the opening Allegro of this quartet, however, the composer quite unostentatiously proceeds to base the entire movement on this warming melody. Nothing occurs twice in exactly the same way, not even in the recapitulation.

Eloquence is a feature of the Andante in B♭ too, as each instrument in turn enters with a sweeping arpeggio figure that gradually produces more and more expressive dissonances. The middle section is a stormy interlude, beginning in B♭ minor.

The minuet is a careful staging post on the way to the finale, in that it has the eloquence of the first two movements as well as the humour of the finale. Again Haydn seems to be referring back to op. 33, this time to the scherzo of the 'Joke' quartet: the main section wilfully avoids an obvious phrase and cadence structure, while the trio is the complete opposite, another evocation of peasant dancing with violin *portamenti*.

The Presto finale sets out as a completely uninhibited ABACA rondo. Halfway through the C section Haydn proceeds to demonstrate that he can be vastly learned and uninhibited at the same time, as all four instruments vie with each other in contrapuntal ingenuity and virtuosity. They resolve their differences by playing the main theme once more. As well as looking back to the 'Joke' quartet of 1781, this movement anticipates many of the comic antics found in the finales of the 'London' symphonies.

10. Op. 71 and op. 74. Only after observing London's concert life for two seasons did Haydn begin his next set of quartets. Written in Vienna during late 1793, they were first publicly performed by Salomon's quartet at his London subscription series in 1794, and published by Corri, Dussek & Co. with a dedication to COUNT ANTON GEORG APPONYI in 1795–6. Though clearly intended as a single group of six, they appeared in two sets of three each. The familiar opus numbers, however, derive from a 1797 edition by Pleyel.

In many ways radically different from their predecessors, these quartets have been both misunderstood and under-appreciated: indeed, some commentators have viewed them an aberration from which Haydn retreated as soon as he left London. The principal misconception has been that Haydn was himself responsible for inventing a public concert idiom for the medium; in fact the composer was responding, rather late, to what had become the norm for string quartet-writing in the 1790s.

As early as the 1770s, London concert programmes featured vivid, attention-grabbing chamber music, works that matched the Parisian *quatuor concertant* for soloistic character, variegated textures and loose-limbed structure. This penchant peaked in the late 1780s, so that in 1788 every London subscription programme included a chamber work. Clearly they provided a showcase for orchestral principals, a symbol of corporate virtuosity essential to a cooperative like the Professional Concert. An essentially private genre was thus transferred into the concert hall, flattering the taste of aristocratic connoisseurs like the Prince of Wales (who himself played the cello at serious morning quartet parties), and at the same time forming modern music's strongest artistic claim against the ancient music cause. It also satisfied publishers as part of a web of international business relations: Haydn's set was published more or less simultaneously by Corri, Dussek & Co. in London ('as performed at Mr. Salomon's Concert') and by Artaria in Vienna, although the intended amateur market was no doubt put off by comments in the press about their technical difficulty.

Haydn was not in fact the dominant composer of chamber music in London's concert programmes before 1791. Chamber works by Pleyel, his former student, outnumbered those by Haydn by a considerable margin at subscription concerts, as high as 12 to one in 1790. Wilhelm Cramer, Salomon's rival, became particularly identified with Pleyel quartets, and Pleyel dedicated one set to the Prince of Wales as early as 1788, four years before his arrival in London. His concert quartets and quintets have little in common with Haydn's intricate and intimate discourses of the 1780s. Rather they typify a general European trend towards a more arresting version of the *quatuor concertant*, with ostentatious solo breaks, brilliant interplay of instruments and a sectionalized structure articulated by changes of texture. Strenuous orchestral writing recalls the contemporary symphony, especially in minor key works, and often Pleyel refers directly to the concerto and operatic scena. Another London visitor, GYROWETZ, dedicated an even more flamboyant set to the Prince of Wales, in which solos are replaced by a concertante use of the entire texture, stretched both horizontally and vertically, together with excitable contrasts, exaggerated tonal plunges, and so on. Clearly this was a very different world from the urbane subtleties of Haydn's op. 64, introduced to London with only limited success in 1791.

That Haydn transformed his approach to quartet-writing for London audiences is familiar; less so that this reflected the forthright and dramatic idiom of Pleyel and Gyrowetz, with its sectionalized drama and vivid concertante textures, albeit modified by a more symphonic integration. Most interesting of all is the change of perspective this engendered, for Haydn actually contrives to make texture the main element of his discourse, rather than motivic or tonal questions, seizing a prime chance to write about the very nature of the quartet medium.

A striking example of such enquiry is provided by the introductions, not mere noise-killers but a systematic exploration of how one might begin a quartet. Op. 74 no. 2 begins with a unison Allegro fanfare that introduces the main thematic material, while op. 74 no. 3 actually integrates the bizarre opening gesture into the structure itself. Other introductions are brief and apparently unconnected: op. 71 no. 3 begins ironically with just a single E♭ chord. This turns out, however, to be not merely a gesture or sonority, but a paradigm for the movement itself: action, followed by suspenseful stasis. The coda finally reconciles this inherent tension by reversing it, as a striking passage of inert frustration is followed by an exultant extravaganza stressing the sonority of that opening chord.

Textural argument can be seen more elaborately in op. 71 no. 2. The apparently unrelated introduction again embodies the main dialectic of the movement: arresting chord or arpeggio versus linear, contrary-motion counterpoint. This duality is immediately played out in the succeeding Allegro, but especially interesting is the treatment of the contrasting melody in popular style (bar 39). As the movement progresses this gradually assumes an alter ego: a linear version in species counterpoint. First suggested in the development section, this returns just where the simple melody is expected in the recapitulation; and finally, in its most stable form, it provides the ultimate resolution in the coda.

In the C major quartet, op. 74 no. 1, Haydn confronts head on the problem of exceptional contrast and discontinuity posed by Gyrowetz's London set. There is, for example, a complete syntactical breakdown at bars 34–5 of the first movement. But this lack of coherence turns out to be part of an overall strategy. The opening melody, an anonymous tag, proves unable to develop melodically, its increasing impotence symbolized by shortening phrases and a loss of textural stability on each reappearance (the reassuring drum bass gradually fades away). Only in the recapitulation, as so often in this set, is coherence and continuity achieved, resolving the textural problems posed by the exposition. First Haydn introduces an ostentatious polyphonic working in learned style (more species counterpoint), releasing the potential of the melodic tag (bar 105); and then he reorders the exposition material so that the brilliant violin semiquaver passage gains a comprehensible closing function, and the *forte* version diverts dramatically to A♭ major (bar 132), by this date a conventionalized sign of impending resolution in Haydn's music. In the coda, the tag regains its most bold persona, a unison *forte*, its contrapuntal dress now reduced to a single voice—a forthright, if faintly ironic confirmation of the textural transformation.

Haydn does not alternate soloists in the manner typical of the concertante quartet, although he does write parts worthy of Salomon's virtuoso technique; indeed in one passage in the first movement of op. 71 no. 1 he deliberately recast the first violin part with a more flashy string-crossing effect (bars 103–8). More typical, though, is his exploitation of the corporate virtuosity of the string quartet. The opening of this same quartet may serve as an example. After an abrupt chordal introduction, the Allegro immediately announces the new sonority, a high-lying first-violin line detached from a vivid but transparent accompaniment. To emphasize the move to the dominant, an extrovert variant of this texture ensues: the melody is now transformed, aspiring to the heights of the violin register and imitated by the sonorous open C string of the cello, while the sedate inner accompaniment is enlivened into frenetic arpeggio patterns. The 'second subject' area typically returns to the opening motif, but in yet another textural variant, this time a sensuous contrapuntal fabric, reinforcing the sense of textural variation as a leading component of the argument. The closing material is more or less a quartet cadenza, with concerto-style motifs tossed around all four instruments, an effect reinforced in the recapitulation, when all four instruments trill on the cadential dominant chord.

A related feature of the set is the oft-remarked orchestral sonority that Haydn explores. Certainly there are powerful passages where the quartet asserts its presence by strong chordal gestures and full sonorities, by assertive unisons reinforced with trills, by the most vivid contrasts of dynamic and register, all characteristics that are designed to capture attention in a public concert hall. But if orchestral in derivation they are placed in the service of a strongly virtuosic character to the quartet medium as a whole (as often with Pleyel too). The first movement of op. 71 no. 2 in D major, with its leaping octave figures invading every layer of the texture and its strenuously brilliant passage-work for all four players together, is particularly effective.

For the London audience, therefore, Haydn built on a new idiom derived from his pupil Pleyel, adding a new dimension to his quartet-writing, that of textural debate and resolution. These quartets may not have the subtle motivic interplay of op. 64 and earlier sets, but they have subtleties on different levels that have been insufficiently appreciated. Yet it would be a mistake to dwell only on the vivid and often extrovert features of the quartet texture, for in many other ways these are remarkable and often experimental works. Elements of the 'popular' style remain: the rustic finale themes, the exotic folk chromaticism over a drone at the end of op. 74 no. 1, and the gentle ländler that forms the second subject in the first movement of op. 74 no. 3. But even in these cases Haydn integrates the effects into a serious and often intense contrapuntal discourse; and elsewhere he uses counterpoint in unexpected situations, as in the finale of op. 74 no. 1 where instead of a relaxing second subject we get a complex fugato working of the opening motif. In the first movements, too, Haydn seems deliberately to have eschewed attractive melody in favour of anonymous tags capable of textural and contrapuntal working; certainly some of the most involved thematic development occurs in op. 74 no. 2, based on a simple rising triad.

Striking too is Haydn's exploration of variation techniques, with reprises varied in many unusual ways. The Adagio of op. 71 no. 1 returns with decorative grace notes in all four parts, perhaps evoking the spread chords of a harpsichord; while in the remarkable trio of op. 71 no. 3 the initial dark-hued harmonies gradually evaporate as the movement unfolds. One particular device Haydn uses to avoid a direct repeat is the mechanistic staccato, as in the finale of op. 74 no. 1 (compare the minuet of symphony no. 97). It also occurs in one of the most remarkable sonorities in Haydn's quartet output: the very high variation without cello (marked 'staccato assai e piano') in the Andante con moto of op. 71 no. 3.

This experimental quality is evident in the finales of op. 71. That of the second quartet, in D major, begins as a teasing Allegretto in 6/8, but after an intricate central section (beginning and ending in D minor but mainly in F) and a lightly decorated return, it is transformed into a boisterous allegro dance; at the end a torrent of semiquavers transforms the music into an apparent presto at double the speed. Something of the same effect occurs in the Vivace of op. 71 no. 3, which starts in a raunchy 6/8, but soon becomes a much more complex and demanding movement; first there is a counter-melody in a disruptive cross-rhythm, then another intricate contrapuntal exploration that later disrupts and diverts the recapitulation. The mood of uncertainty returns towards the end of the movement, with moments of hesitancy that go a long way towards undermining the exultant final bars.

Haydn continues to experiment, too, with tonal relations, both within movements and between them. The first movement of op. 71 no. 3 contains a fascinating development section, where, as László Somfai has observed, the tonality moves down by major thirds from the tonic E♭, so that the recapitulation is strictly speaking in F♭♭ major (though of course Haydn does not notate it thus). Several trio sections are placed in remote third-related keys (a preoccupation of Haydn at this time); the key of A major in the case of the C major quartet (op. 74 no. 1) and D♭ major in the F major quartet (op. 74 no. 2).

But the most richly romantic tonal shifts are to be found in the slow movements, often the emotional heart of these quartets and among the most deeply felt in Haydn's quartet output. From op. 71, the Adagio of no. 2 is one of Haydn's most sensual: though essentially a long-breathed first-violin melody in the manner of the 'Lark' quartet (op. 64 no. 5), there is a richness of imagination in the weaving of the accompanying lower parts. The harmonic diversions to flat keys (F major, C major) recall the vivid contrasts of Haydn's symphonic slow movements, but with the drama of full orchestral interruptions replaced by the warmth and sonority of the quartet texture. Haydn is clearly reluctant to let go his extremely beautiful chromatic cadence, which he repeats with rare indulgence (compare the similar loving repeats of a sensuous exchange in the minuet of op. 71 no. 3). By general acknowledgement, though, the outstanding movement of the set is the unusually titled Largo assai of the 'Rider' quartet (op. 74 no. 3). Perhaps the finest of Haydn's hymn-like slow movements, the rapt contemplative mood is emphasized by the key, E major within a G minor quartet. It was a key often used by Haydn for such profound contemplations, while for English audiences it inevitably brought to mind the reverence and restrained ecstasy of 'I know that my Redeemer liveth' from *Messiah*. After the serenity of the first few bars, Haydn opens up bold harmonic vistas and awesome dynamic contrasts, summoning up through his most personal medium, the string quartet, the very same images of the vastness of the sublime that Handel achieved in his great oratorios.

SMcV

11. **Op. 76.** Haydn began work on the six quartets of op. 76 in 1796, composing them at the same time as *The Creation*, and probably finishing them by the autumn of 1797. They were not published until 1799, by Longman & Broderip in London (as op. 76) and by Artaria in Vienna (as op. 75). The latter publication dedicates the set to Count Joseph Erdödy, who had commissioned the works. From London, in 1799, Charles Burney wrote an enthusiastic letter to Haydn. 'I had the great pleasure of hearing your new *quartetti* (*opera 76*) well performed before I went out of town, and never received

more pleasure from instrumental music: they are full of invention, fire, good taste, and new effects, and seem the production, not of a sublime genius who has written so much so well already but of one of highly-cultivated talents, who had expended none of his fire before.'

Like some of the quartets from op. 71 and op. 74, the first work in the op. 76 set, in G major, begins with a preliminary gesture, in this case three chords. But here the purpose is not to silence an audience—op. 76 were intended, initially at least, for the salon culture of aristocratic Vienna—but to set off the simplicity of the following main theme. Only a composer of Haydn's confidence could risk a theme of such devastating simplicity; it is almost like a nursery rhyme. At the beginning of the development the single line is enlivened by a running quaver accompaniment, a scoring that is repeated at the beginning of the recapitulation. The ability to see inner strength in the apparently charming is a characteristic of the entire movement.

Simplicity is the hallmark of the Adagio sostenuto too. But here it is the simplicity of structure that allows the content to make maximum impact. Haydn was never to write 'late period' music in the sense that Beethoven was, that is, initially difficult music that only gradually releases its profundity; yet there is a parallel to be made, since both composers in their old age favoured increasingly simple formal patterns and sought new inspiration in inner lyricism. The German word *Innigkeit* is an untranslatable formulation of the resulting atmosphere. Here four statements of simple, hymn-like theme contrast with four sections that muse rather than sing.

The minuet is a Beethoven scherzo some time before he wrote one: fleeting staccato crotchets in a *piano* dynamic followed by a rude *fortissimo*.

An equally startling innovation occurs in the finale. Listeners and players accustomed by the 1790s to dozens of quartets by the master of the genre would have expected him to turn to high comedy for the conclusion of a work. Instead, Haydn greets the listener with the sound of the minor key, G minor, and a new sense of drama that seems a long way from the mood of the first three movements. When G minor does eventually give way to G major at the beginning of the recapitulation, it is a moment of complete surrender; and Haydn's supreme powers of assimilation even allow him to end with a flippant coda, featuring a derivation of the main theme over a pizzicato accompaniment.

The rigour of the D minor quartet, op. 76 no. 2, is encouraged by the pervasive use of the motif of a fifth: omnipresent (usually falling) in the opening Allegro movement, it features in the remaining three movements too, delineating the contours of the melodic material.

Equally fundamental to the uncompromising nature of the work is the opposition of D minor and D major. After a first movement in D minor, one of Haydn's most radical essays in sonata form, the Andante o più tosto allegretto is in D major and begins with a 15-bar (!) theme played by first violin over an alternating accompaniment of pizzicato and arco. The design of the movement is Haydn's personalized form of ABA, in which the return of A is varied and a coda added, and B turns to the tonic minor but derives its thematic material from A. The keys of D minor and D major are brought into even closer proximity in the following minuet: a ruthless canon in D minor is succeeded by a trio that begins in D minor and switches to D major, a moment of brutal conflict that encapsulates the tension of the work as a whole. The D minor finale, Vivace assai, is given added spirit and rigour by the many 'Hungarian' inflections, sharpened fourths in the melody, *glissandi,* drone harmonies, and double stops. The music finally turns to the major after the beginning of the recapitulation.

There is ample circumstantial evidence that Haydn in the 1790s often conceived symphonies and quartets around a slow movement, and that the process of composition was finding a suitable home for the slow movement. It is entirely possible that this was the case with op. 76 no. 3 ('Emperor') which features Haydn's anthem 'Gott erhalte Franz den Kaiser', first performed in February 1797, as the theme for a set of variations. Unfortunately, the autograph manuscripts of op. 76 have not survived; they may well have included some clues to the order of composition, both within works and within the set.

The first movement of the quartet is richly scored, with textures that have an orchestral power and sonority. This allows the still beauty of the national anthem, marked Poco adagio, cantabile, to make maximum impact. Each player in turn, first violin, second violin, cello, and viola, plays the complete melody while the other instruments weave an increasingly elaborate accompaniment around it. In this way the movement becomes an individual as well as a collective statement.

Behind the elegant progress of the minuet lies a knowledge and experience derived from 40 years of writing symphonies and quartets. Every note counts and every inflection (even in the quizzical trio) contributes to the debate. Bluster and rhetoric mark the opening of the Presto finale which, as in the equivalent movement in the G major quartet, begins in the minor key. Haydn delays the return of C major until the recapitulation of the second subject (bar 152), when it emerges not so much in triumph as with a sense of fulfilment.

The nickname 'Sunrise' (used in English-speaking countries) or 'L'Aurore' (used in French-speaking countries) was prompted by the nature of the opening theme of op. 76 no. 4: still chords above which the first violin projects a rising melody. But, as Haydn's direction Allegro con spirito suggests, this is not a relaxed, sunny work. Indeed, it shares many features with the D minor quartet (op. 76 no. 2) and it is only the major key that makes it a more welcoming work. All the thematic material in the quartet draws on the collection of intervals first presented in the 'sunrise' and, were it not so clumsy, a nickname of 'Thirds and Semitones', to parallel the 'Fifths' of op. 76 no. 2, would be entirely appropriate. As in the D minor quartet Haydn gives the entire work a sense of unity through consistently employing these same intervals.

In the Adagio in E♭ the pause marks seem designed to draw attention to this feature; even the later filigree decoration is spun from the same intervals. The minuet is of the lively, German dance variety with heavy accents; the trio, like several such sections in the social dances of Mozart and Haydn, evokes the exotic East, with its held drones and primitively hypnotic tune.

The last movement, too, seems to be inspired by an East European dance; it even has the characteristic shout and clap on off-beats. At first, the dance is rather measured (Allegro, ma non troppo) but it becomes increasingly unruly as Haydn ups the tempo, first to più allegro and then più presto.

Neither of the last two quartets in the op. 76 set begins with a sonata form, both substituting a variations movement. The one in op. 76 no. 5 is much the less formal of the two. Marked Allegretto, the lilting main theme is a Haydn speciality, found in the English canzonettas ('My mother bids me bind my hair', for instance), the aria 'With verdure clad'/'Nun beut die Flur' from *The Creation*, and in the slow movement of the Trumpet Concerto. Like the last two examples the melody in op. 76 no. 5 features some beautifully judged ornamentation. The central section of the movement is an extended commentary in the minor key on the rhythmic and melodic contours of the main theme. The return of the main theme is followed by an extended final section in a faster tempo (Allegro) that transforms the mood from lyricism to a sort of bright agitation.

Haydn does not follow the first movement with a minuet (as he might have done early in his career in op. 9 and op. 17) or with a sonata form Allegro (as in the 'Razor' quartet) but with a second lyrical movement. The lengthy tempo indication, Largo ma non troppo, cantabile e mesto, is a guide to its special nature, a full sonata form and one of the composer's most moving slow movements in any genre. The key, F♯ major, produces a richness that also has a soft edge, mainly because the bright sound of open strings (as heard in the surrounding movements) is absent. From this distinctive sonority Haydn moves to C♯ minor, E major, G major, and F♯ minor in the development, all the while musing on the constituent phrases of the theme.

The minuet constitutes an immaculately judged transition from the slow movement to the finale. Reticent at first, it gradually becomes more animated; the trio is in D minor. Along with the finales of op. 76 nos. 2 and 4, the finale of the fifth quartet is another movement that draws inspiration from folk music, in this case a helter-skelter dance in sonata form (but without double bars) with snatches of melody over an insistent accompaniment. Some preliminary cadences call the dancers to attention.

It would seem to be a grossly unfair question to ask how Haydn might have continued to develop the quartet had he lived into his 80s, but his own relentlessly inquisitive musical intellect invites such a question. Op. 76 no. 6 in E♭, in particular, provides some clues. Haydn retains the idea of a work in four movements that moves towards a light-hearted conclusion. But, rather than opening with a sonata form, Haydn begins with a set of variations. Maybe this would have become an increasingly standard alternative for Haydn. Would this, in turn, have encouraged Beethoven to be more questioning than he was of the convention of beginning a four-movement work, like a symphony or a quartet, with a fast movement in sonata form? Certainly Beethoven knew op. 76 intimately. He would have noticed that the salient characteristic of the theme in the first movement is not its melodic appeal but a sturdy harmonic framework; as James Webster has pointed out, the movement acted as a direct model for a similar movement in Beethoven's 'Harp' quartet, op. 74, also in E♭. The conclusion to the movement is novel too in that it is a fugue (marked by a change of tempo from Allegretto to Allegro). Again this was a summative technique that Beethoven came to favour in variation movements.

The slow movement of op. 76 no. 6 is even more audacious. Headed 'Fantasia' it is divided into two complementary parts. The first is notated without a key signature and consists of successive statements of the main theme, announced in regular phrase lengths and traversing an enormously wide tonal terrain: B major, C♯ minor, E major, G major, B♭ major, B major, and A♭ major. In the second half of the movement, notated in B major, the texture is more polyphonic, which makes the phrase structure less obvious, but there is, in compensation, a stronger sense of the tonality being rooted to a key. This movement was written at the same time as *The Creation* and, like the 'Representation of Chaos'/'Vorstellung des Chaos' in that work, it is at the very cutting edge of stylistic development. It was to take the history of music over a hundred years to catch up with the grammatical and syntactical issues raised by this movement. After the warmth of B major in the slow movement it takes a particularly energetic minuet to re-establish the home key of E♭, though Haydn takes care to end the slow movement with the third at the top of the tonic (D♯) providing an enharmonic link into the tonic (E♭) of the minuet. The movement is one of three in Haydn's late quartets marked Presto, clear forerunners of the Beethovenian scherzo. Beethoven seems to have made a strong mental note of the content of the trio, which marches up and down, or rather down and up the E♭ major scale in a way that is reproduced in the minuet of his First Symphony.

While the opening movement could be said to be a set of variations on a harmonic grid rather on a melody, the last movement is a typically light-hearted Haydnesque finale featuring all the familiar features except the most obvious one, a catchy tune. The very beginning promises one, but, instead, the listener is given a continuous series of up-beats that proceed to permeate the entire texture. Haydn has transformed his comic instrumental language into a parody that challenges as well as entertains, yet another Beethovenian characteristic.

12. Op. 77. In 1799 PRINCE LOBKOWITZ commissioned a set of six quartets from Haydn. The composer accepted the commission and embarked enthusiastically on the project. But the composition of the oratorio *The Seasons* drained his musical and mental resources and he managed to complete only two quartets, works that were published as op. 77 by Artaria in 1802. Two movements of a third quartet were also composed; these were eventually published by Breitkopf & Härtel.

Although Haydn was unable to fulfil the commission the completed quartets show no sign of weariness; in his late 60s Haydn was as confident and assured as he had ever been. Only a composer of his experience and confidence could have begun a quartet in the simple manner of op. 77 no. 1; its tramping rhythms and echo phrases permeate the entire Allegro moderato, giving it a mood that is almost Schubertian.

Another technique that Schubert was to make his own occurs at the beginning of the slow movement; instead of being in C major or D major it is in E♭ major. Following this bold initial contrast, this movement too uses repetitive accompaniment patterns and easy dialogue (especially between cello and first violin), but the result is much more impassioned than the first movement; it offers an intensification of mood rather than a relaxation, the opposite pattern to the norm. Following a minuet in G major marked Presto, the trio plunges once more into E♭ and again features tramping rhythms, this time in the prevailing presto tempo. The sonata form finale, too, is marked Presto, but with its quirkily accented main theme it strikes a balance between the bluster of the minuet and the more considered nature of the first movement.

Although the F major quartet, op. 77 no. 2, is the last completed quartet from Haydn's pen, there is nothing valedictory about the work. This positive outlook is nowhere more apparent than in the quiet confidence and lyricism of the opening theme; its opening rhythm crops up regularly, including in the nominally contrasting second subject (bar 37). But it is from the anacrusic quaver figure first heard in the transition that Haydn builds up the character of the development including a passage that manages to move from E♭ minor to E minor in ten bars.

The minuet has reminded many commentators of Dvořák. Its presto tempo and skilful balancing of subdivisions of the beat into threes and twos are characteristic of the *Furiant*, a dance often evoked by the Czech composer in his music. Dvořák was fond of plunging his listeners into distant keys at the beginning of contrasting sections and Haydn anticipated him in this too, as the trio enters in D♭ major. At the end of the trio a *pianissimo* link passage to the return of the minuet is another pre-echo of a technique that Dvořák was to make his own.

The Andante is placed in another third-related key, D major, and begins as a gently ambling duet for violin and cello. The simplicity of this opening belies the complexity of the structure, a mixture of rondo and variations.

Dvořák comes to mind once more in the finale which combines the jostling rhythms of a peasant dance with the rigour of a monothematic sonata form; in a constantly full texture the flamboyance of the former is matched by the intellectual energy of the latter.

13. Op. 103. Originally intended to form the two middle movements of a work in D minor in the set for Prince Lobkowitz, the Andante grazioso and the Menuet ma non troppo presto were published as an unfinished two-movement work by BREITKOPF & HÄRTEL in 1806. After the second movement the publisher reproduced Haydn's visiting card with the text 'HIN IST ALLE MEINE KRAFT, ALT UND SCHWACH BIN ICH', a gesture that was copied by several other publishers of the work. The opus number of 103 derives from an edition by André that appeared in 1808. Apart from the two completed movements there are some extant sketches for a first movement in D minor and for a finale, also in D minor.

The completed two movements show Haydn at his most concentrated and unyielding, a step further on the road he had explored in his last quartet in D minor, op. 76 no. 2. The slow movement is in ternary form, the first and last sections in B♭ framing an unnerving and unstable middle section that begins in G♭ major, moves to C♯ minor (the enharmonic equivalent of D♭ minor), and concludes on the dominant of G minor in readiness for the return of B♭. Harmonic asperity characterizes the minuet too, but in a local compressed manner. The falling bass line that underpins the chromatic harmony is derived from the age-old pattern of a descending fourth but it never reaches its appointed conclusion as a means of affirming the tonic; instead later chromatic lines in the bass move mainly upwards. At first, the trio in D major seems more welcoming, but soon it too becomes harmonically restless. According to GRIESINGER, the last movement was to have been a rondo. Would it have remained in the severe mood cultivated in the Andante and in the main portion of the minuet or would it have moved to D major and the more positive mood glimpsed in the trio?

14. Arrangements for quartet. The market for quartet music in Vienna from the 1780s through to the early decades of the 19th century was an extensive one and alongside original works for the medium players could purchase arrangements of anything from overtures by Handel to movements from operas by Paisiello. Haydn's music formed a considerable part of this additional repertoire. Most of the arrangements were prepared and sold without his consent but as many as nine works were adapted by the composer himself, though evidence of his direct involvement varies.

The quartet arrangements of *The Seven Last Words* (Hob.XX/1B) were prepared by Haydn in 1787; together with the original orchestral version it was published by Artaria that year. Haydn's task was a relatively straightforward one since for most of the work he was able to use the orchestral string parts without any alteration. In 'Hodie mecum' the doubling of the melody at the lower octave by a solo cello in the orchestral version had to be sacrificed and in 'Sitio' the woodwind solos associated with the musical realization of that word are incorporated into the string parts. Apart from the varied colours and textural weight of the orchestral version, the most telling difference is the omission in the quartet version of the long-held note played by flute and horns at the end of 'In manus tuas Domine', signalling the moment of Christ's death.

The quartet version was widely distributed in Haydn's lifetime and when Pleyel prepared his collected edition of the quartets he included the arrangement alongside original works for the medium. Two hundred years later, audiences are still much more likely to encounter the arrangement than the original work.

In 1788 Artaria issued three of the Paris symphonies (nos. 84, 85, and 86) as quartets, claiming on the title page that the arrangements had been prepared by Haydn; a similar claim was made by Artaria for an arrangement of three of the 'London' symphonies (nos. 99, 102, and 104) that appeared in 1800. No further verification of Haydn's alleged involvement is forthcoming and these six arrangements have never been accepted as part of the Haydn canon.

The case for the authenticity of quartet arrangements of over 30 numbers from two of Haydn's operas, *La vera costanza* and *Armida*, is more persuasive since they survive in copies prepared under Haydn's jurisdiction.

W. Drabkin, *A Reader's Guide to Haydn's Early String Quartets* (Westport, Conn., 2000).

G. Feder, *Haydns Streichquartette. Ein musikalischer Werkführer* (Munich, 1998).

D. Heartz, *Haydn, Mozart and the Viennese School 1740–1780* (New York, 1995).

M. Hunter, 'Haydn's London Piano Trios and His Salomon String Quartets: Private vs. Public', in E. Sisman (ed.), *Haydn and His World* (Princeton, 1997), 103–30.

H. Keller, *The Great Haydn Quartets: Their Interpretation* (London, 1986).

H. C. R. Landon and D. W. Jones, *Haydn: His Life and Music* (London, 1988).

C. Rosen, *The Classical Style* (London, 1971).

C. Rosen, *Sonata Forms* (New York, 1980).

L. Somfai, 'The London Revision of Haydn's Instrumental Style', *Proceedings of the Royal Musical Association*, 100 (1974), 159–74.

W. D. Sutcliffe, *Haydn: String Quartets, Op. 50* (Cambridge, 1992).

D. F. Tovey, 'Franz Joseph Haydn', in W. W. Cobbett (ed.), *Cyclopedic Survey of Chamber Music* (London, 1929), i. 514–48.

J. Webster, 'Traditional Elements in Beethoven's Middle-Period String Quartets', in R. Winter and B. Carr (eds), *Beethoven, Performers, and Critics* (Detroit, 1980), 94–133.

C. Wolff and R. Riggs (eds.), *The String Quartets of Haydn, Mozart, and Beethoven: Studies of Autograph Manuscripts* (Cambridge, Mass., 1980).

D. Young (ed.), *Haydn The Innovator: A New Approach to the String Quartets* (Todmorden, Lancs., 2000).

R

Radnitzky. *See* COPYISTS.

Rahier, Peter Ludwig von (d. 1791). A former military man who had seen active service in the Seven Years War, he was appointed estates director by Prince Nicolaus Esterházy in November 1763. He ran the administration like a military machine and was feared because of his short temper. His peremptory manner brought him into occasional conflict with the court Kapellmeister who had to defend his musical colleagues, including in 1775 his own brother, Johann, who had been dismissed by Rahier for some minor infraction. HCRL

Rauzzini, Venanzio (bap. 19 Dec. 1746; d. 8 April 1810). Italian castrato singer, composer, and teacher. A flamboyant figure in his adopted city of Bath, he was Haydn's host when the composer visited Bath from 2 to 5 August 1794. After a career in Italy and Munich he had moved to London in 1774, where he had several of his operas performed between 1774 and 1792; he was also a featured singer in the first four years. He made his first appearance in Bath in March 1776. With the violinist Lamotte (1751–81) he managed and conducted subscription concerts, becoming sole director from 1780 to 1810, during which time he dominated the musical scene in Bath. He composed string quartets, piano sonatas, and vocal music. Noted and loved as a teacher, he numbered among his pupils such famous singers as Nancy Storace and John Braham. Haydn stayed at Rauzzini's summer residence, which was in the south-eastern part of the city, in Perrymead Road. Haydn was much struck by an epitaph on the grave of Rauzzini's dog, Turk, and composed a round on its concluding lines: 'Turk was a faithful dog; and not a man' (Hob. XXVIIa:45). DdV

HCRL/3.

M. Sands, 'Rauzzini at Bath', *Musical Times*, 94 (1953), 15–19, 108–11.

'Razor' quartet. Nickname traditionally applied to the quartet in F minor, op. 55 no. 2. According to an anecdote, the London publisher JOHN BLAND, during a visit to Vienna, chanced upon Haydn one morning shaving with a blunt razor; the composer remarked that he would exchange one of his best works for a sharp razor. Seizing his chance Bland rushed to his inn to collect some razors and gave them to the composer who duly presented him with the manuscript of a quartet that was later dubbed the 'Razor' quartet. Although this charming story circulated quite widely in England in the 19th century, scholars gave it little credence until, in 1982, a letter from Haydn to Bland was discovered in which the composer thanked him for two gifts, a watch and some razors. Bland, however, never published the six quartets of op. 54 and op. 55 and the nickname should be more appropriately applied to one of the op. 64 quartets published by the firm in London in 1791. However, conclusive evidence about which of the six quartets should be labelled 'Razor' quartet is not forthcoming—op. 64 no.1 and op. 64 no. 5 are the most likely—and in these circumstances it seems sensible not to change the identity of the work from op. 55 no. 2.

I. Woodfield, 'John Bland: London Retailer of the Music of Haydn and Mozart', *Music and Letters*, 81 (2000), 210–44.

reception. See opposite.

'Recitative' quartet. Occasional nickname, arising in the 19th century, for the quartet in G, op. 17 no. 5. The slow movement has two passages in recitative style, though not labelled as such. In truth the nickname could be applied with equal validity to two other quartets, op. 9 no. 2 and op. 20 no. 2. JH

recordings. There can be little doubt that the enormous revival in public interest in Haydn's music that has occurred since the end of the Second World War owes much, on the one hand, to the increased and improved publication of his music and, on the other, to the growing involvement of the recording industry. Nor can there be much question that the two have fed off each other. For the first decades of the 20th century, Haydn was as ill served by gramophone recordings as he was by reliable published editions. Some important recordings were made: in England, HMV's Walter Legge founded the Haydn Quartet Society, which issued eight volumes of quartets performed by the Pro Arte Quartet between 1932 and the outbreak of war; and Parlophone produced several recordings of piano trios featuring Lili Kraus, Szymon Goldberg, and Anthony Pini during the 1940s. Elsewhere there were isolated recordings of certain popular works: keyboard sonatas were recorded by the likes of Violet Gordon Woodhouse and Wanda Landowska on the harpsichord, and

[*cont. on p.338*]

reception

The first paragraph of Griesinger's biography of Haydn, published a few months after the composer's death, gives a vivid impression of the widespread popularity of the composer's music. 'Haydn was the founder of an epoch in musical culture, and the sound of his harmonies, universally understood, did more than all written matter together to promote the honour of German artistic talent in the remotest lands. Haydn's quartets and symphonies, his oratorios and church pieces, please alike on the Danube and on the Thames, on the Seine and on the Neva, and they are treasured and admired across the seas as in our part of the world.' Griesinger's specific mention of rivers in Austria, England, France, and Russia, could have been supplemented by any number of rivers in America, Germany, Italy, Scandinavia, Spain, and elsewhere. Perhaps no other composer before or since has enjoyed such widespread popularity in his own lifetime. It remains a fundamental weakness in Haydn scholarship that this popularity has not been fully chartered and evaluated. While the enormous advances in the last 50 years in the control of contemporary sources for Haydn's music has, at long last, enabled his musical output to be properly appreciated, the reception of his music, both in his own life and posthumously, has been less thoroughly explored. The following survey, devoted to reception in Haydn's own lifetime and, in section 11, to a review of some aspects of his posthumous reception, can serve only as an introduction to the topic and, by omission, an indication of what remains to be done.

---

1. **Austrian territories.**
2. **England and Scotland.**
3. **France.**
4. **Italy.**
5. **Latin America and the United States of America.**
6. **The Netherlands and North Germany.**
7. **Russia.**
8. **Scandinavia.**
9. **South Germany and Switzerland.**
10. **Spain and Portugal.**
11. **Posthumous reputation.**

---

1. Austrian territories. One of the earliest indications of Haydn's reputation in Austria appears in the Viennese newspaper, the *Wiener Diarium* (forerunner of the *Wiener Zeitung*), in October 1766. After only five years as Kapellmeister at the Esterházy court Haydn's name appears in an article entitled 'Viennese Taste in Music'. Along with DITTERSDORF (who may well have been the author of the piece), GLUCK, HOFMANN, REUTTER, and WAGENSEIL, Haydn emerges as an important figure. He is described as the 'darling of our nation' and his cassations, quartets, trios, and symphonies are given special mention as, more oddly from a modern perspective, are his dance minuets. Even odder is the mention of 'cantatas', described as 'charming, fetching, flattering', which can only mean the works written for the Esterházy court during the previous three years (*Da qual gioia improvvisa*, *Destatevi, o miei fidi*, and *Qual dubbio ormai*). In no sense does this account suggest that Haydn is the most important figure in contemporary Austrian music but the emphasis on his instrumental music is significant; there is no mention of the German opera, *Der krumme Teufel*, and of the limited number of items of church music already in circulation.

As the supply of new instrumental works by the composer steadily increased over the next couple of decades so this image of Haydn became stronger. Extant manuscript sources in the Austrian territories, in monasteries such as Göttweig, Lambach, Melk, Osek, and the archives of the Clam Gallas family in Friedland (Frydlant), the Schwarzenberg family in Krumau (Český Krumlov), and the prince-archbishop in Kremsier (Kroměříž) point to an extensive dissemination of Haydn's music in the Austrian territories from the 1760s onwards. However, Haydn scholarship has sometimes managed to give the impression that the composer was a commanding figure whereas he was one of many composers contributing to a musical culture of unprecedented vibrancy.

Haydn begins to stand apart from his fellow composers in the Austrian territories in the 1780s, as his own career became more international. In Vienna the biannual concerts of the Tonkünstler-Societät regularly included performances of his symphonies and initiated a close association between the composer and charity performances that was to remain for the rest of his life. No other composer (certainly not Mozart) rivalled Haydn in this respect in the 1780s, though it would be a mistake to claim that the symphony as a genre was at the centre of musical life, since the main event in these concerts was usually a large-scale choral work by composers such as Albrechtsberger, Dittersdorf, and Haydn himself (*Il ritorno di Tobia*). Haydn's pre-eminence is reflected too in the catalogue of the major music publisher in Vienna, ARTARIA.

Haydn's music had never featured prominently at the Habsburg court, which had its own group of favoured composers, and since the court continued to influence the running and, consequently, the repertoire of the main theatres in Vienna, the Burgtheater and the Kärntnerthortheater, Haydn's operas, the most important element of his duties at Eszterháza, were conspicuous by their absence; performances of the German version of *La fedeltà premiata*, given in the Kärntnerthortheater in December 1784, were a rare exception. Outside Vienna a German version of *La vera costanza* enjoyed some success with performances in Brunn, Pest, and Pressburg. The rather conservative and circumscribed imperial taste extended to church music too where, again, Haydn's music at this stage of his life hardly figured at court.

During the 1790s a transformation in Haydn's reputation in the Austrian territories occurs, partly a reflection of fundamental changes in musical life in general, partly the product of the equally fundamental changes in Haydn's own circumstances. As a result of the reforms of Joseph II, musical life in the Austrian monasteries was not as active as it had previously been and, although many continued to acquire new music by Haydn, they no longer represented a major force in the market for music. The steady decline in the number of orchestras supported by aristocratic families represented another change that affected all composers and their works. After his return from London Haydn, for the first time since the 1750s, resided regularly in Vienna and his limited duties at the Esterházy court allowed him to interact with its musical life. It is in this last period that Haydn becomes recognizably a Viennese composer. His contact with Gottfried van Swieten led to the composition of two oratorios, *The Creation* and *The Seasons*, that dominated musical taste in the capital for over a decade. While concert life in Vienna did not have the range and vigour that Haydn had experienced in London, the symphonies that he had composed for that city were given in public concerts in Vienna. Particularly notable was the ambitious Liebhaber Concerte of the 1807–8 season in which a group of aristocratic patrons promoted the music of Haydn, Mozart, and Beethoven as the very best which the city had to offer.

There was, too, a change in the attitude of the imperial court to Haydn; his church music was favoured by Empress Marie Therese and the whole court drew sustenance from the patriotic fervour aroused by the national anthem composed by Haydn, 'GOTT ERHALTE, FRANZ DEN KAISER'. As well as imperial patronage and the continuing support of the aristocracy (especially the Erdödy and Lobkowitz families), Haydn became a revered national figure who was honoured repeatedly: in 1797 the Tonkünstler-Societät made him an honorary life member; in 1803 he was given a civic medal of honour; and in 1804 he was made an honorary citizen of Vienna. A venerable man and, in an age that was rapidly changing, someone who personified an older period, his perceived musical importance was different from that outlined early in his career in the 1766 newspaper article and from that which he was to acquire in later decades. It was firmly led by two very public works, *The Creation* and *The Seasons*, featured his sacred music to a greater extent than it did in other countries, while in the area of instrumental music his quartets were performed more frequently than his symphonies.

V. Cosma, 'Zur Verbreitung der Musik der Brüder Haydn in Rumänien vor 1810', in E. Badura-Skoda (ed.), *Joseph Haydn. Bericht über den internationalen Joseph Haydns Kongress. Wien, Hofburg, 5–12. September 1982* (Munich, 1986), 513–18.

HCRL/1, 2, 4, and 5.

M. S. Morrow, *Concert Life in Haydn's Vienna: Aspects of a Developing Musical and Social Institution* (Stuyvesant, NY, 1989).

2. **England and Scotland.** Haydn's name is first encountered in England in an issue of *St James's Chronicle* dated 25–7 June 1765. ROBERT BREMNER, the leading music publisher in London, regularly imported music editions from HUMMEL of Amsterdam and the latest advertised batch consisted of Haydn's quartets op. 1. Further Hummel publications of Haydn's music were not imported into London until the early 1770s and gradually over that decade the number of works by Haydn that were available in London increased steadily, including the quartets of opp. 2, 17, and 20, and four symphonies (nos. 10, 20, 35, and 41). During the first few years of the following decade, however, Haydn suddenly became the leading figure in the musical life of London, a position that was not be relinquished for over 15 years. Two factors encouraged this sudden surge in demand for his music. With the death of J. C. Bach (1735–82) on New Year's Day, 1782, London concert life lost a commanding figure who, with his friend Carl Friedrich Abel (1723–87), had dominated public concert life for nearly 20 years. A new organization, the Professional Concert, gave a much-needed shot in the arm to the concert life of the city, which was soon dominated by the music of Haydn, to the extent that hardly a concert did not feature a work by him, usually a symphony. Publishers, too, played a newly invigorated role in publishing Haydn's music in London in the 1780s with FORSTER establishing a direct link with the composer and LONGMAN & BRODERIP acting as an agent for Haydn's principal publisher in Vienna, Artaria. As early as 1782 there were attempts to persuade Haydn to visit London, invitations that finally came to fruition in January 1791 when Haydn arrived in London to be the resident composer at a concert series organized by JOHANN PETER SALOMON.

Although Haydn's compositions written in and for London included all manner of works, from arrangements of Scottish folksongs to opera, and from keyboard sonatas to symphonies, it was in London that he would have personally experienced the primacy that posterity was to accord to his symphonies. In that sense London with its active concert life deserves a place in a historical narrative that is usually dominated by Vienna.

Despite a general decline in the number and quality of concerts in London following Haydn's second visit, his symphonies continued to be performed well into the 19th century. *The Creation* was eagerly awaited and was given four performances in March and April 1800 by two rival organizations, one led by John Ashley, the other by Salomon. Its reception, however, was a mixed one as diehard Handelians resented Haydn's attempts to conquer a medium that lay at the core of Handel's reputation. Nevertheless, the appeal that Haydn's music in general held for the English can be judged by the large number of English people who subscribed to the first edition of the work, including GEORGE III, the PRINCE OF WALES, the Duchess of York, DR CHARLES BURNEY, CLEMENTI, and REBECCA SCHROETER. *The Seasons*, however, fared less well and was not performed in England until 1817 when a few numbers from 'Spring' were performed in a concert in Birmingham.

Outside London, too, Haydn's music had formed a significant part of the repertoire. Few, if any, of Haydn's symphonies seem to have been heard before 1770, when several performances were given in Manchester. In this and other provincial centres further performances in the 1770s are sporadic. In the early 1780s, however, Haydn's symphonies suddenly achieved universal popularity with nos. 53, 63, and 73 enjoying particular esteem. Haydn's compositions seem to have been introduced to Bath relatively late: a 'favourite' symphony was advertised in 1781, quartets in 1782, and a keyboard sonata and a keyboard concerto in 1789. While the variety of advertised works performed in Bath is perhaps greater than elsewhere, only Haydn's symphonies were performed more frequently than similar works by other composers; Pleyel's quartets, for instance, were heard considerably more often in Bath than those of Haydn.

Edinburgh presents another picture. The earliest documented performance in Edinburgh of a Haydn quartet was given in a benefit concert for Thomas Pinto in 1772. The programmes of the Edinburgh Musical Society show regular performances of quartets from at least as early as 1778 (gaps in documentation do not permit a true picture of the situation before that year); in that city, at least, Haydn's quartets seem to have been more popular than those of Pleyel. The first documented performance of a symphony by Haydn did not take place until 1780, but numbers increased rapidly thereafter. Few concerts did not include at least one work by Haydn, and correspondence in 1791 over the management and future of the Musical Society describes his compositions—not without an element of Scottish caution—as 'some of the *best* of the New Music'. *See also* LONDON. JMB

J. Burchell, *Polite or Commercial Concerts? Concert Management and Orchestral Repertoire in Edinburgh, Bath, Oxford, Manchester, and Newcastle, 1730–1799* (New York, 1996).

D. W. Jones, 'Haydn's Music in London in the Period 1760–1790: Part One', *HYB* 14 (1983), 144–72.

S. McVeigh, *Concert Life in London from Mozart to Haydn* (Cambridge, 1993).

T. Tolley, 'Music in the Circle of Sir William Jones: A Contribution to the History of Haydn's Early Reception', *Music and Letters*, 73 (1992), 525–50.

3. France. Haydn never visited Paris and he set foot on French soil only on his way to and from England. The country, nevertheless, played a vital part in his career, disseminating his works, commissioning new ones, and, in the last years of his life, recognizing with various honours his pre-eminence as a composer. The first editions of Haydn's works to be published in Paris were in 1764, coincidentally the year of Rameau's death, when three publishers, HUBERTY, LA CHEVARDIÈRE, and VENIER, issued symphonies and quartets. France had already shown a predilection for the newer kinds of instrumental music, as shown by the many publications of music by Stamitz and other composers from the Mannheim School. The only Viennese composer to make any kind of impact in the 1750s and 1760s was WAGENSEIL and the acquisition of music by Haydn may be viewed as building on this foundation.

Soon Haydn's instrumental music became a mainstay of the published repertoire in Paris. Before the 1780s it is unlikely that the composer had direct contact with French publishers though a number of links, mainly indirect, can be conjectured. Huberty made several visits to Vienna *c.*1770 when he may have come into contact with the composer; Prince Nicolaus Esterházy and TOMASINI visited the French capital in 1767 and the publication the following April of six 'Simphonies ou Quatuor dialogués' (actually five symphonies and a divertimento) may be connected with the visit; and the music by Haydn published in Lyons by GUÉRA in the 1770s may owe something to the fact that a former violinist in Haydn's orchestra, Franz Garnier, had settled there. Practically all of Haydn's symphonies and quartets were published in Paris, some several times over. More sinister, between 1765 and 1775 nearly as many apocryphal works were published in France as authentic ones, and from 1775 to 1780 the number of apocryphal works exceeded the genuine ones. One of the most popular works was Symphony no. 56 in C. It was played at the Concert des amateurs and the Concert spirituel in 1777 and was soon printed by three different firms, de Silly, Guéra, and SIEBER. This success signalled an increase in known performances of Haydn's music in Paris, at the Concert spirituel in particular, to the extent that he became the most frequently performed composer in Paris in the 1780s. It was against this background that the Concert de la Loge Olympique commissioned new symphonies from the composer, nos. 82–7. Pergolesi's Stabat mater had long been a favourite of audiences at the Concert spirituel; during the 1780s it was rivalled by Haydn's setting of the text, published by Sieber in 1785.

The only stage work by Haydn to be performed in France was *La vera costanza*, reworked into an opera comique entitled LAURETTE. When it was first performed in 1791 concert life in Paris, and with it Haydn's popularity in France, was in temporary abeyance, but from 1798 onwards it was revitalized with again the symphonies of Haydn at its core. To a certain extent the success of Haydn's symphonies in France during the Napoleonic period stifled the ambitions of native composers; Méhul (1763–1817) was the only composer of significance in France to tackle the genre in this period. In March 1809, a couple of months before Haydn's death, Méhul responded to some inevitable criticism of his symphonic ambitions by François Sauvo, critic of the *Moniteur universel*: 'As a passionate admirer of Haydn's music I realize the dangers of my undertaking, but, little by little, I shall try to accustom the public to the idea that a Frenchman can follow Haydn and Mozart from afar.'

Before the Revolution France had done much to promote Haydn as a leading composer of instrumental music and, in the process, establish the credentials of the symphony and quartet, in particular, as genres that rivalled the long-standing dominance of opera. During the Napoleonic period in particular, French musical life emphasized another element in the historical narrative: the primacy of German composers in the new genres. *See also* PARIS. MV

L. de La Laurencie, 'L'Apparition des œuvres d'Haydn à Paris', *Revue de musicologie*, 13 (1932), 191–205.

J. Mongrédien, *French Music from the Enlightenment to Romanticism 1789–1830* (Portland, Ore., 1996).

4. Italy. Haydn's music was relatively little known in Italy during his lifetime. This was partly because Austro-German music in general held little appeal for most Italian music lovers. Nevertheless Italians were willing to patronize northern composers if they came to Italy and wrote music specifically calculated for Italian tastes and musical conditions. Unlike Hasse, Mozart, Naumann (1741–1801), Mysliveček (1737–81), PICHL, and other northerners who achieved success in Italy, Haydn never crossed the Alps. Many parts of Italy were linked to Austria by strong political connections. Sons of Maria Theresia ruled Tuscany and Lombardy, and Trieste was part of the Habsburg Monarchy. The Viennese court composers Gassmann and Salieri benefited from these political and dynastic ties: several of Gassmann's Viennese operas were performed in Italy; and Salieri won commissions to compose operas for the inaugurations of La Scala in Milan and the Teatro Nuovo in Trieste. As someone who was outside Habsburg circles Haydn could not take advantage of such connections.

However, as a composer of instrumental music Haydn seems to have achieved some degree of popularity in Italy by 1780, when he was elected a member of the Philharmonic Academy of Modena. Norbert Hadrava, secretary to the Austrian ambassador in Naples, reported in 1788 that Haydn's 'instrumental music is greatly prized' (letter to Johann Paul Schulthesius, Lutheran minister in Livorno and an amateur composer). That is no doubt why Hadrava, himself an amateur musician who taught KING FERDINAND OF NAPLES how to play the LIRA ORGANIZZATA, commissioned Haydn to compose works for his royal pupil to play. The king was so pleased with Haydn's concertos that he invited the composer to Naples, an invitation that he might have accepted had he not received a more lucrative offer from London.

The music library assembled by the Ricasoli family of Florence during the late 18th and early 19th centuries (now at the University of Louisville) is probably representative of the musical taste of Florentine nobility. It contains many instrumental works by Austrian and German composers, including Haydn.

While Italians learnt to appreciate Haydn's instrumental music, most remained ignorant of his large-scale vocal works. Thus the opera composer Giuseppe Sarti, who visited Eszterháza in 1784, was 'curious to see a man whose many works, especially his symphonies, had made him famous throughout Europe'; but 'he knew nothing of Haydn's dramatic music' (Framery, *Notice sur Joseph Haydn*). Writing at the beginning of the 19th century, Benedetto Frizzi, a music lover resident in Trieste, acknowledged the primacy of Austro-German instrumental music: 'In truth Haydn, Mozart, and Pleyel . . . are among those who have immortalized the Germanic name. But as for dramatic music for the voice, the Italian has carried off the palm.'

Some of Haydn's arias and dramatic *scene* were popular in Italy. Several manuscript copies of 'Ah come il core' from *La fedeltà premiata* survive in Italian libraries. The publication of the text of the cantata *Arianna a Naxos* in Verona in 1798 (under the title *Arianna abbandonata*) suggests that a performance of Haydn's cantata took place there. A report in the *Allgemeine musikalische Zeitung* suggests that it had been composed for the Venetian singer Bianca Sacchetti. Manuscripts of the work circulated widely in Italy.

Of Haydn's large-scale vocal works, *Il ritorno di Tobia* was probably the most frequently performed in Italy during the late 18th century. Librettos document performances of the oratorio in Rome on the third Sunday of Lent in 1783, and in Modena during Lent in 1784. One of the very rare productions of an opera by Haydn in Italy during his lifetime was that of *Armida* in Turin in 1804, a production that may have owed something to Masonic links between Vienna and Turin.

As part of his efforts to advance the appreciation of Austro-German music in Italy, Hadrava arranged a performance of Haydn's Stabat mater in Naples in 1788. According to his report of the occasion, four great opera singers took part; the sopranos Girolamo Crescentini and Giuseppe April, the tenor Giacomo David (for whom Haydn was to write the role of Orfeo in *L'anima del filosofo*), and the bass Giuseppe Trabalza. A Neapolitan music lover, 'charmed and delighted by this masterpiece', asked Hadrava, 'Why have you hidden such a treasure for so many years?' He replied, 'Because you have boasted too much of your riches, and disdained our poor Germans.'

Hadrava's cultural campaign had little long-term effect. The subscription list for the first edition of *The Creation* testifies to the anticipation with which Haydn's oratorio was awaited in England, Germany, and Russia but it contains the name of only one subscriber resident in Italy; he, ironically, was Hadrava's German correspondent, Schulthesius. JAR

A. Basso, 'Un' iniziativa della massoneria: la rappresentazione dell'*Armida* di Haydn a Torino nel 1804', *Analecta musicologica*, 22 (1984), 383–404.

G. Gialdroni, 'La musica a Napoli alla fine del XVIII secolo nelle lettere di Norbert Hadrava', *Fonti musicali italiane*, 1 (1996), 75–143.

J. A. Rice, 'Benedetto Frizzi on Singers, Composers and Opera in Late Eighteenth-Century Italy', *Studi musicali*, 23 (1994), 367–97.

5. Latin America and the United States of America. During his lifetime Haydn's music circulated extensively in the Spanish and Portuguese Americas, and in North America, the first largely dependent on transmission from the Iberian peninsula, the second from Britain and Central Europe.

In 1785 the well-known Venezuelan political figure, Francisco de Miranda, visited Eszterháza, where he attended an opera performance and, the following day, discussed musical matters with Haydn. Also in 1785, Iriarte's lengthy poem *La música*, first published in Madrid in 1779, was issued in Mexico; celebrating Haydn as the leading figure in 'German' music it contributed greatly to the composer's increasing fame in the Spanish Americas. Caracas was one of several cities in Venezuela that had substantial collections of Haydn's music, usually in printed parts, assembled in the composer's lifetime; as well as symphonies, *The Seven Last Words*, the Stabat mater, and some of the late masses are represented too. In Chile, Santiago has a number of 18th-century sources for Haydn's music, especially in the archive of the cathedral. Haydn's popularity in Mexico City is attested by several articles on the composer's life and music published in the *Diario de México* between 1806 and 1810. In Brazil, while a few sources suggest that Haydn's music was played in Rio de Janeiro in the last decades of the 18th century, it was not until NEUKOMM resided in that city between 1816 and 1821 that the composer's music was frequently performed; *The Creation* was given for the first time in 1820.

The reception of Haydn's music in the United States has been chartered in detail by Irving Lowens. As well as manuscripts and published editions imported into the country from London, Paris, Leipzig, and other centres, 60 editions of Haydn's music appeared in the United States during the composer's lifetime, principally songs. Not a single symphony or quartet was published, and only one keyboard sonata (Hob. XVI:21). Performances of Haydn's music in public concerts were relatively small, a reflection of the largely rural population of the country. New York City has the largest number of documented concerts and a Haydn Society was formed there in 1798, followed in 1809 by one in Philadelphia. Music played an important part in the lives of the many Moravian communities in the United States. The settlement of Nazareth in Pennsylvania boasted a Collegium Musicum that held regular concerts, including symphonies and quartets by Haydn. It is presumed that the largest communities, in Bethlehem (Pennsylvania) and Old Salem (North Carolina), also organized concerts but no documentary evidence has survived. Thomas Jefferson, president of the United States from 1800 to 1809, was an accomplished musician. He is known to have prepared a list of compositions by Haydn that he wished to purchase and his library does, indeed, contain music by the composer, though many of these were acquired by Jefferson's daughter, Martha ('Patsy'). AEL

I. Lowens, *Haydn in America* (Detroit, 1979).

I. Lowens, 'Haydn in America', in J. P. Larsen, H. Serwer, and J. Webster (eds), *Haydn Studies* (London, 1981), 35–48.

L. Merino, 'An 18th-century Source of Haydn's Music in Chile', in E. Badura-Skoda (ed.), *Joseph Haydn. Bericht über den internationalen Joseph Haydns Kongress. Wien, Hofburg, 5–12. September 1982* (Munich, 1986), 504–10.

L. Merino, 'Presencia de Joseph Haydn en Latinoamérica colonia y decimonónica: "Las Siete Ultimas Palabras de Cristo en la Cruz", y Dos Fuentes en Chile', *Rivista Musical Chilena*, 30 (1976), 135–6.

D. N. Nichols, 'A Mexican Tribute to Haydn', *HYB* 13 (1983), 231–2.

R. M. Stevenson, 'Haydn's Iberian World Connections', *Inter-American Music Review*, 4 (1982), 3–30.

6. The Netherlands and North Germany. Modern scholarship has generally held that Haydn's music did not fare well in northern Europe and has dwelt on the adverse reaction of some humourless critics who failed to recognize his wit and originality. As music historians have begun to explore the broader cultural context in which the composer lived and worked, however, a less entirely negative picture of his reception has emerged.

Haydn's works circulated widely in northern Europe beginning in the 1760s. In particular the Dutch firm of HUMMEL (with shops in Amsterdam and Berlin) published one or two opuses a year; by Haydn's death the firm had reached op. 56, a number exceeded in its catalogues only by the works of Pleyel. As well as publishing the music, Hummel publicized and marketed it in an effective manner, as is shown by the frequency with which the publications were reviewed in late 18th-century German periodicals. Hummel's role as a major distributor of Haydn's music was rivalled by the Leipzig firm of BREITKOPF, whose extensive offering of music manuscripts (as documented in successive thematic catalogues issued between 1762 and 1787) contained more works by Haydn than any other composer, including most of the early symphonies and quartets. No publisher from Hamburg issued works by Haydn until the turn of the century, but the principal music dealer in the city, Johann Christoph Westphal, regularly advertised and sold manuscripts and published editions of music by him. Thus, from the early stages of Haydn's compositional career, his works found a market in all the major cities in the Netherlands and north Germany. Just how frequently these works received performances as a result of this distribution is, at present, a matter of conjecture. Available evidence—such as the report of a performance of the op. 33 quartets in Hamburg in August 1782, a few months after their publication—suggests an eager public.

There may well have been a gulf between the reaction of the wider public to the music and the pronouncements of writers on music. That Haydn had his detractors was clear from the late 1760s, when the Hamburg periodical *Unterhaltungen* published a series of disparaging remarks, calling his string trios and quartets 'truly bad music' and objecting to his 'strange mixture of pranks with the affect-laden'. A few years later, in 1776, Carl Ludwig Junker repeatedly attacked Haydn's use of musical humour in his biographical sketches of 20 composers (*Zwanzig Componisten, eine Skizze*). Then, in 1784, the *European Magazine* in London published an article alleging a conspiracy against Haydn by jealous north German composers. Though Carl Friedrich Cramer in his journal *Magazin der Musik* dismissed the allegation as ridiculous, the damage had been done, and the notion of a vendetta was securely established. Haydn himself had contributed to this perception by complaining in 1776 about 'Berliners' who praised him to the skies one minute and dashed him to the ground the next.

Thus the theory of a reserved northern reception to Haydn's music has a basis, but the existence of some negative remarks should not lead to an exaggerated view of such critical remarks, especially as no one has yet identified the 'Berliners' mentioned by Haydn. Moreover, there is a good deal of written evidence from the area of a positive reaction. North German writers found that Haydn's music embodied those characteristics most valued in the late 18th century, his originality, the novelty of his ideas, the sublimity of his sacred works, his inexhaustible genius, and, more technically, his unexpected modulations, which led listeners into 'hidden romantic regions', as one critic put it. Often Haydn's name was linked with the revered C. P. E. BACH. While northern critics disliked the lighter, comic style, they did not damn Haydn for exploiting it. Nor did most critics seem to notice, or care about, the mixing of serious and comic affects; in fact one of the most persistent advocates of the old, single-affect approach, Johann Friedrich Reichardt (1752–1814) specifically absolved C. P. E. Bach and Haydn from adhering to it, because they required all possible means in the 'representation of their original humour'. MSM

O. Landmann, 'Die Dresdener Haydn-Quellen im Hinblick auf ihre Provenienzen', in E. Badura-Skoda (ed.), *Joseph Haydn. Bericht über den internationalen Joseph Haydns Kongress. Wien, Hofburg, 5–12. September 1982* (Munich, 1986), 519–25.

M. S. Morrow, *German Music Criticism in the Late Eighteenth Century* (Cambridge, 1997).

G. A. Wheelock, *Haydn's Ingenious Jesting with Art. Contexts of Musical Wit and Humor* (New York, 1992).

7. Russia. Haydn's music was advertised for sale in Moscow and St Petersburg from the mid-1780s onwards and performances of symphonies and quartets from editions prepared in Paris and Vienna occurred with increasing regularity from that time. Count Sheremetev, who had palaces in both cities, received regular consignments of music from his former cello teacher, Hyvart, now living in Paris. *The Seven Last Words* (probably in the quartet version) together with other works by Haydn were given in the Masquerade Hall of the Petrovsky theatre in Moscow in March 1789. Known performances of symphonies, in particular, increased steadily during the 1790s. Evidently, the empress, Catherine the Great, was familiar with Haydn's music since she was presented with a portrait of the composer in 1796. The previous year the German writer Johann Daniel Gerstenberg, who had established a music and bookshop in St Petersburg, published a short biography, in Russian, of the composer in a pocket-book of similar articles.

In September 1798, a few months after the first performance of *The Creation* in Vienna, an advertisement appeared in a Moscow newspaper soliciting subscribers for the edition that was being prepared by Haydn. The violinist and teacher Johann Dengler acted as agent and collected over 30 subscribers from Russia. The oratorio was performed for the first time in St Petersburg on 14 February 1801 and in Moscow on the following day. The Moscow performance was given in a Russian translation prepared the previous year by N. M. Karamzin. To further the appeal of the work in Russian polite society Tsar Paul I commissioned a French translation of the oratorio. Following the example of the Tonkünstler-Societät in Vienna, musicians in St Petersburg founded a charity for musical orphans and widows, launching its fund-raising with a performance of *The Creation* in March 1802.

In Russian translation Thomson's poem *The Seasons* was already well known in intellectual circles in the country and the first performance of Haydn's oratorio was, consequently, eagerly awaited. A translation of the libretto was commissioned and the first performance was given in Moscow on 25 February 1803; 12 days later, on 9 March, a performance was given in St Petersburg, this time in French.

It was with these two oratorios and the occasional performances of instrumental works that Haydn's fame was ensured in Russia in the first decade of the century. In 1808 the composer was made an honorary member of the St Petersburg Philharmonic Society, writing a warm-hearted letter of thanks. In the steady stream of musicians who journeyed from Vienna to Russia, Haydn's former pupil NEUKOMM played a particular part in promoting his music, especially the version of *Il ritorno di Tobia* reorchestrated by him.

B. Steinpress, 'Haydns Oratorien in Rußland zu Lebzeiten des Komponisten', *HS* 2/2 (1969), 77–112.

8. Scandinavia. In Haydn's lifetime there were two kingdoms in Scandinavia, Denmark (including Norway) and Sweden (including Finland), and it is in the capital cities of these kingdoms, Copenhagen and Stockholm, that Haydn's music is most extensively documented.

As early as 1767 newspapers in Copenhagen advertised music by Haydn, alongside works by Abel, Cannabich (1731–98), and Pugnani (1731–98), probably English or French editions imported from London or Paris. In 1771–2 a Swedish scientist, Samuel Heurlin, was permitted to join the Music Society in Copenhagen, having successfully taken part in a performance of Haydn's op. 2 quartets. In the 1780s, as in contemporary London and Paris, music by Haydn came to dominate concert life in Copenhagen. The Stabat mater was performed in 1785, and in 1787 the publisher Søren Sønnichsen advertised no fewer than 14 symphonies, 40 quartets, and 15 string trios and divertimenti, alongside a Danish translation of some of Haydn's songs published by Artaria in 1781 and 1784. *The Creation* was given its first performance in Copenhagen in the winter of 1799–1800.

Musicians in Sweden would have encountered Haydn's works in 1773 when he is mentioned, along with Wagenseil and Dittersdorf, in the first history of music written in Swedish, by Abraham Hülphers. During the remainder of the decade music dealers in Stockholm regularly advertised the availability of quartets and symphonies by the composer; in 1781 an unidentifiable symphony by Haydn was played in a public concert in Stockholm for the first time. Haydn's music also reached the Finnish part of the kingdom through a remarkable musical amateur named Erik Tulindberg. A civil servant by profession, he lived in Turku and then in Uleåborg (about 600 km (375 miles) north of Helsinki). In both places he was active as a musician and organized performances of quartets and symphonies by Haydn (including the op. 9 quartets and Symphonies nos. 79–81).

In Stockholm public performances of Haydn's symphonies became more numerous in the 1780s; the first performance of the Stabat mater in Sweden took place in 1784. Many keyboard arrangements of popular movements from Haydn's symphonies were published in Sweden in the latter decades of the century and the poet Carl Michael Bellman (1741–95) united his poetry with melodies from Haydn's symphonies to create songs that also became very popular. Haydn's reputation in Sweden was considerably enhanced by the diplomat FREDRIK SAMUEL SILVERSTOLPE. As the Swedish chargé d'affaires in Vienna between 1796 and 1807 he became acquainted with Haydn and it was at his instigation that the composer was elected as a foreign member of the Royal Academy of Music in Stockholm in 1799.

The first performance of *The Creation* in Sweden took place in Stockholm on 3 April 1801, at the traditional Good Friday concerts organized by the Freemasons. The text was translated into Swedish by Silverstolpe and Jakob Gustaf De La Gardie. Performed with combined choral and orchestral forces of about 190 the performance was a notable success and for many years the oratorio was regularly performed on Good Friday in the city. GA

H. Glimstedt, 'Haydn och Sverige', *Ord och Bild*, 41/3 (March 1932), 129–44.

C. F. Hennerberg, 'Det första uppförandet i Stockholm av Haydns oratorium skapelsen', *Svensk Tidskrift för Musikforskning*, 3 (1921), 37–51.

O. Kongsted, 'Haydn og Danmark', in *Joseph Haydn 1982* [Exhibition catalogue] (Copenhagen, 1982), np.

C.-G. S. Mörner, 'Haydniana aus Schweden um 1800', *HS* 2/1 (1969), 1–33.

9. **South Germany and Switzerland.** Haydn never visited Switzerland and travelled in south Germany only in the 1790s on his journeys to and from London. One of Haydn's earliest works, the divertimento in G for string quintet (composed no later than 1754), has an intriguing, though doubtful, connection with Elector Carl Theodor, best known for developing musical life at the Mannheim court in the middle decades of the 18th century before moving to Munich in 1778. According to the title page of an edition of the work issued by Simrock in the 19th century, it had been composed for the elector. In Munich, in December 1790 Haydn met Cannabich, the director of music at the court. Performances of symphonies by Haydn at the Liebhaberkonzerten in Munich are known from 1787 and in 1795 the cantata *Arianna a Naxos* was performed. Between 1800 and 1811 *The Creation* was performed every year, in 1801 on the express wish of General Jean Victor Moreau, the commander-in-chief of the occupying French forces. *The Seasons* was performed for the first time in Munich on 27 February 1802 on the occasion of the birthday of Elector Maximilian IV. Known performances of Haydn's operas in Munich include *Der neue krumme Teufel* in January 1783 and *Ritter Roland* (a translation of *Orlando paladino*) in December 1800. In the early decades of the 19th century Haydn's pre-eminence as a composer of symphonies and quartets is reflected in concert programmes of the time and in 1828 a bust of the composer was unveiled in a new concert hall, the Odeon.

The free city of Augsburg also had a flourishing public concert life in the final decades of the 18th century, held in the Gasthof zur goldenen Traube and at the palace of Prince Fugger-Babenhausen; Haydn's symphonies featured in both series. In Nuremberg Haydn's symphonies had featured in the programmes of a winter concert series held in the Roten Roß since 1785. Particularly notable was Haydn's close contact with the court of PRINCE KRAFT ERNST OETTINGEN-WALLERSTEIN which amassed one of the largest collections of Haydn's music outside the Esterházy court, including 76 symphonies, 20 quartets, seven masses, 17 songs, and *Il ritorno di Tobia*. The court of Thurn and Taxis in Regensburg also had a large collection of symphonies and quartets by Haydn and in the 1790s regularly shared music and musicians with the Oettingen-Wallerstein court. Other princely courts in the area that are known to have owned and performed music (especially symphonies) by Haydn from the 1760s onwards include those of Hohenzollern-Sigmaringen, Hohenlohe-Bartenstein, Hohenlohe-Langenburg, and Fürstenberg.

To judge from extant sources Haydn's music was not frequently performed in monasteries in Bavaria, though his output is better represented than that of Mozart. Copies of *The Seven Last Words* (in the orchestral and in the vocal versions) and the Stabat mater are common, the composer's masses surprisingly rare. In the Benedictine abbey of Heilig Kreuz at Donauwörth the last abbot, Cölestin Königsdorfer, was an enthusiast for keyboard music and the library includes copies of sonatas by Haydn. Since instrumental music was usually the private property of monks it was not listed in official inventories, so the full extent of any private music-making (including performances of music by Haydn) cannot be judged. For many of the abbeys themselves their dissolution in 1803 resulted in considerable loss of material. Surviving sources in cathedrals and churches, such as those in Landshut, Munich, Passau, Straubing, and Wasserburg, suggest that Haydn's music formed part of the available repertoire, but did not dominate it.

The Creation was performed at the Benedictine monastery in Ottobeuren in 1801 and at the Premonstratensian abbey of Schussenried the following year under the direction of Justin Heinrich Knecht (1752–1817).

In Switzerland many civic music societies performed Haydn's music. The Musikkollegium in Winterthur first purchased symphonies by the composer in 1783; likewise the Academie de Musique in Neuchâtel first purchased symphonies in *c.*1790. In Lucerne, the Theater- und Musik-Liebhabergesellschaft, active from 1806 until 1813, owned no fewer than 64 symphonies and overtures by Haydn. Even more active was musical life in Zurich which from the 1780s regularly featured performances of symphonies, masses, and oratorios by Haydn. In abbeys in Switzerland, such as Einsiedeln and Engelberg, Haydn's music does not figure until the end of the 18th century and then only in insignificant quantities.

Music-publishing in south Germany in Haydn's lifetime was not as ambitious as that found in major centres in the north and most editions of Haydn's music consisted of arrangements. RM

W. Jerger, *Die Haydn-Drucke aus dem Archiv der 'Theater- und Musik-Liebhabergesellschaft zu Luzern' nebst Materialien zum Musikleben in Luzern um 1800* (Freiburg, Switzerland, 1959).

G. Walter, *Katalog der gedruckten und handschriftlichen Musikalien des 17. bis 19. Jahrhunderts im Besitze der Allgemeinen Musikgesellschaft Zürich* (Zurich, 1960).

L. Wilss, *Zur Geschichte der Musik an den oberschwäbischen Klöstern im 18. Jahrhundert* (Stuttgart, 1925).

10. Spain and Portugal. Musical life in Spain in the 18th century was a largely self-sufficient and independent one, dominated by music for the Catholic Church and less willing to feature musical influences and characteristics from abroad; Italian opera, for instance, had a much more chequered history in Spain than in any major European country. In the second half of the century, however, there were some signs of increasing internationalism in which, not surprisingly, the music of Haydn features prominently. The royal court in Madrid, more specifically that of the Prince of Asturias, the future Carlos IV, had an active musical life, focused on the music of the violinist and composer Brunetti (1744–98). Since, apart from Brunetti and BOCCHERINI, there were no composers of instrumental music in Spain, the court imported the rest of its repertoire from abroad. From as early as *c.*1770 Haydn's latest symphonies were acquired by the court, some of them directly from the composer, until by the 1790s some 50 orchestral works formed part of the repertoire. Haydn also forwarded a manuscript score of *L'isola disabitata* for which he was rewarded with a snuffbox, delivered to Eszterháza by a member of the Spanish legation in Vienna in the autumn of 1781.

Between 1783 and, at least, 1789 Haydn regularly forwarded copies of his music to the Countess Osuna y Benavente in Madrid and to the Duke of Alva; none of these sources survives but the documents rather imprecisely mention symphonies, quartets, sextets, concertos, dances, masses, and operas. Haydn himself in a letter to Artaria in 1784 said that he was working on a set of three-movement quartets for Spain; these, too, have not survived. In 1786 Haydn composed *The Seven Last Words* for the cathedral of Cadiz in southern Spain, and copies of it were distributed elsewhere in the country. Also frequently encountered in church and monastic libraries are manuscript copies of Haydn's Stabat mater.

Two unusual aspects of the reception of Haydn's music in Spain should be mentioned, a poem and a painting. Tomás de Iriarte (1750–91) was a government official, a poet, and an amateur musician. In 1779 he published a poem in five cantos entitled *La música*. A didactic work, it first outlines the elements of music, gives a discourse on aesthetic matters, and then explains the social purpose and value of music. In the fifth canto the music of Haydn, especially the quartets, is praised. It was Iriarte who represented and probably advised the Countess Osuna y Benavente when she was acquiring the composer's music. The Duke of Alba's fondness for the music of Haydn is evident from a portrait of the duke painted by Goya in 1795, in which he is seen holding a manuscript of a musical work by Haydn.

Haydn seems to have lost direct contact with his Spanish patrons in the early 1790s, when he was in London, and there is not a single Spaniard in the subscription list for the first edition of *The Creation* issued in 1800.

Musical life at the Portuguese court in Lisbon during the reign (1777–92) of Queen Maria I occasionally featured music by Haydn but there is no evidence of direct contact. String trios and quartets (mainly publications by Hummel) were acquired during the 1780s; the Stabat mater was performed in the Palácio da Ajuda on 21 March 1782; *Il ritorno di Tobia* in the same venue on 19 March 1784; and a benefit for the royal violinist Pierre Gervais held in the Rua dos Condes theatre on 23 May 1792 opened with a symphony by Haydn.

M. C. de Brito, *Opera in Portugal in the Eighteenth Century* (Cambridge, 1989).

S. C. Fisher, 'A Group of Haydn Copies for the Court of Spain: Fresh Sources, Rediscovered Works, and New Riddles, *HS* 4/2 (1978), 65–84.

N. A. Solar-Quintes, 'Las relaciones de Haydn con la casa de Benavente', *Anuario musical*, 2 (1947), 81–8.

11. Posthumous reputation. The last years of Haydn's creative life and the few that preceded his death in 1809 were a period of political and social upheaval. The Napoleonic Wars brought not only continuing and, eventually, fundamental political changes in Europe, but influenced the artistic life of the period as well. Avid patriotism that manifested itself in Austria, Britain, Germany, as well as France brought a new aesthetic consciousness, full of energy and rampant enthusiasm. Just as Friedrich Schiller's poetry seemed to express the mood of the time to a new generation, Ludwig van Beethoven's music was felt to be the harbinger of fundamental change. In comparison Haydn's music was soon seen as innocent, old-fashioned, and enervated. He belonged to an older, obsolete epoch. Indeed, to a certain extent this image of Haydn the man had overtaken any objective view of his art. Nevertheless, it is not entirely correct to view the 19th century as an era that was unsympathetic to the composer, though it is undeniable that Haydn of all the composers of the Viennese Classical period was the least cherished. Part of the reason for this is that, increasingly in the 19th century, opera, whether new or old, assumed a dominant role in cultural life: Haydn, unlike Gluck and, especially, Mozart, had not left a stage work that claimed a central place in the repertoire. Also the virtuoso concert of the 19th century, designed primarily to demonstrate the capabilities of instrumentalists and singers rather than the creativity of composers, was inimicable to regular performances of Haydn's music. Only the two late oratorios, *The Creation* and, to a lesser extent, *The Seasons*, became regular items in the repertoire; even this was to the composer's disadvantage since it led in the second half of the 19th century to a certain ossification in performance tradition and, consequently, the image of the composer.

In Catholic areas of German-speaking Europe Haydn's church music was regularly performed in the 19th century, surviving the ambitions of the Cecilian movement to substitute a cappella church music modelled on Palestrina in the affections of the public and, more directly injurious, the many, often cack-handed, arrangements that were made of Haydn's sacred music.

Haydn's symphonies played an insignificant role in public concert life in the early part of the 19th century, with the notable exception of Paris, which regularly performed them well into the 1820s. When they did feature in concerts, often single movements were given and, in Vienna, they were as likely to be heard as incidental music performed during the intervals of theatrical works. Oddly enough it was in Vienna, with the founding of the Philharmonic Orchestra in 1842, directed by Otto Nicolai, that the central importance of the symphonic tradition in Western cultural life began to be impressed on musical audiences. Performances were prepared with great care and with esteem for the composer. Nicolai was the first conductor who nurtured this outlook, creating in the process a quasi-mystical role for the conductor himself, an aspect of public concert life that was to remain apparent for over 150 years. Beethoven's symphonies were central to this new seriousness of endeavour and they dominated the symphonic repertoire. For Haydn, however, this fortuitously led to more frequent performances of the 'London' symphonies, appreciated for their proto-Beethovenian qualities. In German-speaking Europe, in particular, this perceived relationship between the symphonic output of these two composers is still current.

The years 1882, 1909, and 1932, marking, respectively, the 150th anniversary of Haydn's birth, the centenary of his death, and the 200th anniversary of his birth, were each celebrated with great enthusiasm but with little resultant change in the composer's status. Scholars and performing musicians were aware of Haydn's broader contribution but the increasingly contented, self-perpetuating nature of concert life meant that there was no incentive to explore the full range of his symphonic output, while performances with orchestras that were four or five times the size imagined by the composer and with tempos and articulation suited to Wagner, Bruckner, and Strauss did nothing to whet the appetite. It was partly for these reasons as well as the innate scholarly complexities of the task itself that the symphonies remained unpublished in their entirety until the 1960s. After nearly 200 years of obscurity the full range of Haydn's achievement in the genre is only now becoming embedded in the public's view of the composer.

In the medium of the quartet, the situation has always been a wholly different one. As a result of Pleyel's complete edition, all the music has always been available. Haydn's quartets featured prominently in the move in the early 19th century from salon to concert life. In Vienna, Ignaz Schuppanzigh (1776–1830), closely associated with Beethoven, was the first leader of a quartet ensemble to present public concerts and to undertake international concert tours. In later decades chamber music concerts became an established part of musical life throughout Europe and Haydn's quartets played a full part.

In his lifetime Haydn was twice compared to the poet GELLERT, an indication of esteem, as was the occasional remark in England that he was the 'Shakespeare of music' and a musician worthy of comparison with the great Handel. Haydn liked to call himself Dr Haydn and in the last years of his life, when he was given awards by France, Sweden, as well as Vienna, he was widely recognized as an estimable figure. Over time 'PAPA HAYDN' became an ambiguous appellation, sometimes patronizing, sometimes referential. As the 19th century proceeded, the known biographical differences between Haydn's life and that of Beethoven worked, inevitably, to the older composer's disadvantage: Beethoven was free, emancipated, the modern artist, while Haydn, who had always worked in an aristocratic court in a subordinate position, was tantamount to a lackey and represented the old order.

Beethoven's music—and, later, that of Wagner—was regarded as the unsurpassable peak of musical endeavour, and composers like Haydn (to a lesser extent Mozart too) occupied a historical position as worthy forerunners. The narrative of a genial Haydn whose style was then given some depth by Mozart and perfected by Beethoven is a common one throughout the 19th century, and, in the eyes of the general public, it lasted well into the second half of the 20th century. While most writers and musicians willingly paid Haydn the compliment of founding the symphonic tradition, some were openly dismissive of his music. For ROBERT SCHUMANN Haydn was one of the 'old wigs' of music, someone who had no relevance to contemporary music. Perhaps because he was closer to Haydn's generation, the German poet Jean Paul (1763–1825), ironically a major influence on Schumann, frequently expressed his admiration for Haydn while BRAHMS, a close friend of Schumann, was a lifelong enthusiast for his music; his musical thought processes are strongly marked by those of Haydn.

A rather strange re-evaluation of Haydn's music was sometimes apparent in popular reaction to the music of Richard Strauss (1864–1949), MAHLER, Schoenberg (1874–1951), Berg (1885–1935), and Webern (1883–1945). Those commentators who regarded their music as a betrayal rather than an enhancement of tradition occasionally evoked the 'healthy' and 'sensible' Haydn as a stick with which to beat the 'confused' and 'morbid' modernists. Although this was yet another misrepresentation of Haydn, it is undoubtedly true that the collapse of the ever-progressive modernist agenda in the decades after the Second World War, or at least its marginalization, has enabled Haydn, along with any number of other composers, to figure more prominently and more widely in performance, aided by the availability of reliable editions, the enterprise of the recording industry, and the wider discovery of early music. *See also* 'GOTT ERHALTE FRANZ DEN KAISER'; HAYDN NOVELS, OPERAS, AND PLAYS; RECORDINGS. CH

L. Botstein, 'The Consequence of Presumed Innocence: The Nineteenth-Century Reception of Joseph Haydn', in W. D. Sutcliffe (ed.), *Haydn Studies* (Cambridge, 1998), 1–34.

C. Höslinger, 'Der überwundene Standpunkt. Joseph Haydn in der Wiener Musikkritik des 19. Jahrhundert', *Jahrbuch für österreichische Kulturgeschichte*, 1/2 (1971), 116–42.

C. Höslinger, 'Joseph Haydn—Das Nachleben', in *Joseph Haydn in seiner Zeit* [Exhibition catalogue] (Eisenstadt, 1982), 316–23.

HCRL/5.

Vladimir Horowitz and Ignacy Paderewski on the piano; concertos were recorded by musicians such as Landowska, Goldberg, and Emanuel Feuermann; Charles Lautrop recorded the choral version of *The Seven Last Words* in Tokyo in the 1930s; and both Vittorio Gui and Clemens Krauss conducted recordings of *The Seasons* during the war. What symphonies had been recorded were those with easily remembered nicknames, with Thomas Beecham and Bruno Walter prominent among their exponents. It was a situation that reflected fairly accurately the state of affairs then prevailing in the concert hall, and which, on the whole, did little to advance Haydn's reputation.

The foundation of the HAYDN SOCIETY in 1949, however, was a landmark in Haydn's fortunes on record. H. C. Robbins Landon's famous remark in the published prospectus of the society that 'barely one-seventh of Haydn's music has ever been printed' preceded a further observation that 'with the single exception of the string quartets, only a tiny fragment of his compositions have been recorded'. The use of gramophone recordings to promote a greater public awareness of Haydn was seen as a main priority alongside that of the preparation of good published editions, and within a year the society had issued its first commercial record, 500 copies of the 'Harmoniemesse' in a 1947 Salzburg Festival performance in which the Munich Cathedral Choir was conducted by Ludwig Berbreich. This had been purchased from Austrian Radio, who also provided wartime tapes of *The Creation* and *The Seasons*, both with Krauss conducting the Vienna Philharmonic Orchestra and the chorus of the Vienna State Opera. *The Creation*, amazingly, was the first complete recording, while other Haydn choral works recorded for the first time included the 'Nelson' mass (MISSA IN ANGUSTIIS) under Jonathan Sternberg, the 'Mariazellermesse' (MISSA CELLENSIS) under Hans Gillesberger, and a number of symphonies in which various Viennese orchestras were conducted by Sternberg, Anton Heiller, Fritz Litschauer, and Hans Swarowsky, and the Danish Radio Chamber Orchestra by Mogens Wöldike.

Over five years the Haydn Society issued around 40 recordings with a definite bias towards 'unknown' works by the composer. It had had to get by, however, on limited funds, and attracted few major artists. Haydn's profile had been raised but, despite some successes (a recording of the Trumpet Concerto with Helmut Wobisch as soloist sold 30,000 copies in its first year) sales were only moderately encouraging. For the moment, the bigger record companies, who could employ a Beecham, a Backhaus, or an Amadeus Quartet, continued only to dabble in Haydn, offering largely 'named' symphonies and quartets plus the occasional piano sonata or well-known concerto.

The next important impetus came, once again, from the world of publishing. In 1958, the first complete edition of the symphonies was initiated in Vienna, and two years later a plan was put into operation to record them. The performances were by the orchestra of the Vienna State Opera conducted by Max Goberman, and the recordings were issued by Goberman's own label, the Library of Recorded Masterpieces. In the event, only 45 symphonies were issued before the project was halted by Goberman's death in 1962, but a precedent had been set. From then on, the continuing re-emergence of much of Haydn's music—more often than not for the first time in reliably edited texts—was to prove a constant source of inspiration to the 'completist' proclivities of record companies, performers, and public alike. Thus, the 1960s and 1970s witnessed the appearance of complete cycles of the keyboard sonatas (no fewer than six followed the appearance of the Wiener Urtext edition of 1963–4), the symphonies, the quartets, the keyboard trios (in the wake of the Doblinger edition, completed in 1978), the operas, the masses, the songs, and so on.

The effect of this flood of newly recorded material on public appreciation of Haydn cannot be overestimated. Few people are likely to hear every one of the composer's symphonies, sonatas or quartets in concert in a lifetime, let alone get the chance to know them well. Chances to hear his church music or operas in public remain relatively rare, and the prospects for such areas of his output as the baryton trios or the orchestral dances are scarcely less bleak than they ever were. With these pieces on record, not only have they become more familiar, but a more knowledgeable and discerning approach to them has also become possible. Alongside the blanket coverage of the complete cycles, more selective recordings have appeared—of *Sturm und Drang* symphonies, of 'great' masses, or of 'English' piano sonatas—based on an increased awareness of Haydn's life and musical development. While almost all of Haydn's music has now been recorded at least once, not the least important of the functions of the 'completist' approach has been to help people decide which of his works are most worth listening to.

---

1. **Symphonies and other orchestral music.**
2. **Chamber music.**
3. **Keyboard music.**
4. **Operas.**
5. **Oratorios and songs.**
6. **Sacred music.**

---

1. Symphonies and other orchestral music. Following Goberman's attempt at a complete symphony cycle in the early 1960s, two more were instigated towards the end of the decade, both of which made it to the finish. Ernst Märzendorfer's cycle with the orchestra of the Vienna State Opera (the same ensemble that Goberman had used) was issued as an essentially non-commercial operation by the American Musical Heritage Society. It was swamped, however, by the conspicuous commercial and artistic success of the Decca cycle (1970–3), surely one of the major achievements in the history of recording, in which ANTAL DORATI conducted the Philharmonia Hungarica. More recently, Adám Fischer began a cycle with the Austro-Hungarian Orchestra in 1987, a project now in its final stages.

The post-war rise of the chamber orchestra can also be seen as having contributed to the growth in Haydn symphony recordings, and so, more recently, has the emergence of orchestras playing on period instruments. In the early 1990s two symphony cycles were initiated on period instruments. Christopher Hogwood's project with the Academy of Ancient Music for Oiseau-Lyre (begun eight years after the completion of their groundbreaking Mozart series) was rigorously planned so that each of the 15 boxed sets contains a coherent chronological grouping, but with about two-thirds of the symphonies recorded the rate of production noticeably slowed and eventually stopped; Roy Goodman's cycle with the Hanover Band on Hyperion foundered sooner, but not before it, too, had nearly half the symphonies recorded. The coincidence of these two cycles was given added spice at their outset by a musicological dispute concerning Haydn's use of a keyboard continuo instrument. Goodman used a harpsichord for his performances; Hogwood, following the advice of James Webster, used no keyboard instrument at all.

Away from the intended complete cycles, certain areas of Haydn's symphonic output have inevitably received more attention than others. Most popular by far are the 'London' symphonies, with the named works among them topping the list and attracting quite a few big-name conductors. Among those who have recorded all the 'London' symphonies are Thomas Beecham with the Royal Philharmonic, Hermann Scherchen with the Vienna Symphony, Georg Solti and Eugen Jochum (both with the London Philharmonic), Leonard Bernstein with the New York Philharmonic, Herbert von Karajan with the Berlin Philharmonic, Colin Davis with the Amsterdam Concertgebouw Orchestra, Jeffrey Tate with the English Chamber Orchestra, Nikolaus Harnoncourt with the Concertgebouw, and Frans Brüggen with the Orchestra of the Eighteenth Century. Others to have shown a strong interest but not recorded them all include George Szell with the Cleveland Orchestra, Antonio de Almeida with the Rome Symphony Orchestra, and Sigiswald Kuijken with La Petite Bande. Neville Marriner has also recorded several as part of a larger overall series of 'named' symphonies with the Academy of St Martin in the Fields.

Next in frequency are recordings of the 'Paris' symphonies, which have been recorded complete by Bernstein, Brüggen, Karajan, Kuijken (with the Orchestra of the Age of Enlightenment), and Davis, and also by Ernest Ansermet with the Suisse Romande, Yehudi Menuhin with the Menuhin Festival Orchestra, Daniel Barenboim with the English Chamber Orchestra, Neville Marriner with the Academy of St Martin in the Fields, Libor Pešek with the Slovak Philharmonic, Charles Dutoit with the Montreal Sinfonietta, Hugh Wolff with the St Paul Chamber Orchestra, Leslie Jones with the Little Orchestra of London, Denis Vaughan with the Naples Orchestra, and Bruno Weil with the Canadian period-instrument orchestra Tafelmusik.

Also popular with record-buyers in recent years have been the *Sturm und Drang* symphonies, although those with names (notably the 'Farewell' and 'La passione') still attract more interest than the others. Weil has recorded a number with Tafelmusik, while two period-instrument sets from Britain have covered similar ground: Trevor Pinnock's English Concert recorded 18 symphonies for the Archiv label (Deutsche Grammophon) during the 1980s; and, a few years earlier, Derek Solomon's L'Estro Armonico produced several recordings of symphonies from this period as a follow-up to their earlier recordings of the 'Morzin' symphonies.

The orchestral version of *The Seven Last Words* has been disappointingly neglected on record compared to the less interesting quartet version: the most notable exceptions are those by the Academy of St Martin in the Fields under Marriner and the Berlin Philharmonic under Riccardo Muti, plus the only period-instrument version, that by the Concert des Nations conducted by Jordi Savall.

The concertos include some of the best-represented works on record in Haydn's entire output. A significant number of these recordings go right back to the 78 era: Guilhermina Suggia (1928), Feuermann (1935), and Fournier (1951) all made 78s of the Cello Concerto in D major, Landowska the keyboard concerto in D major (on harpsichord), Goldberg and Isaac Stern the Violin Concerto in A major, and Harry Mortimer the Trumpet Concerto. Indeed, the Trumpet Concerto is one of Haydn's most popular single works on record: the nearly 60 versions include four by Maurice André plus one which he conducts, but there are also recordings by John Wilbraham, Wynton Marsalis (twice), John Wallace, Håkan Hardenberger, and Crispian Steele-Perkins. At least three recordings use a keyed trumpet (the ORGANISIERTE TROMPETE): Friedemann Immer with Hogwood and the Academy of Ancient Music, Mark Bennett with Trevor Pinnock and the English Concert, and Reinhold Friedrich with the Vienna Academy under Martin Haselböck.

On the same level of popularity is the Cello Concerto in D major, followed not far behind by its companion in C major, discovered in 1961. Perhaps no area of Haydn's recorded output is so well populated with great names: Mstislav Rostropovich (with Benjamin Britten conducting), Jacqueline Du Pré, Paul Tortelier, Pierre Fournier, Janos Starker, Lynn Harrell, Yo-Yo Ma, Mischa Maisky, and Heinrich Schiff have all recorded both concertos, and there are strong period-instrument versions as well from Christophe Coin, Anner Bylsma, and Pieter Wispelwey.

The violin concertos have held less interest for the big names than those for cello. Apart from Isaac Stern, Salvatore Accardo has recorded all three concertos, Pinchas Zukerman, and Arthur Grumiaux the C major and the G major, and Yehudi Menuhin the C major. Violinists to have recorded all three concertos include Christian Tetzlaff, Rainer Kussmaul, Mayumi Seiler, Gérard Jarry, Gilles Colliard, Andrea Cappelletti, and the period player Simon Standage.

Recordings of the keyboard concertos are dominated by the D major, whose long history includes not only Landowska but also Emil Gilels, Alfred Brendel, Arturo Benedetti Michelangeli, Tatyana Nikolayeva, and Martha Argerich on piano, Pinnock and Steven Lubin on fortepiano, and George Malcolm, Sylvia Marlowe, and Ton Koopman on harpsichord. There is a formal complete cycle of piano concertos, with Ilse von Alpenheim as soloist and husband Antal Dorati conducting the Bamberg Symphony Orchestra, but among the others to have recorded a substantial proportion of keyboard concertos are Koopman (harpsichord and organ), Philippe Entremont (piano), Christine Jaccotet (harpsichord), and the organists Franz Lehrndorfer, Daniel Chorzempa, Albert de Klerk, and Gebar Lehotka.

2. Chamber music. The string quartets have long been well represented on record, though only three complete cycles have so far been achieved. That by the Aeolian Quartet for Decca, recorded between 1972 and 1976, was another of the great landmarks of recording, while the 1990s saw both the Kodály (Naxos) and Angeles (Philips) quartets complete further cycles. As with the symphonies, several ensembles have embarked in more or less determined fashion on complete cycles: the Pro Arte Quartet intended to record them all before the Second World War intervened, while other quartets to have recorded large numbers include the Tátrai, Dekany, Amadeus, Schneider, Vienna Konzerthaus, Festetics, and Lindsay quartets, and on period instruments the Salomon and Mosaïques quartets.

Distribution across the canon not surprisingly centres on the works from op. 20 onwards. Only the Aeolian, Dekany, Tátrai, Kodály, Schneider, Festetics, and Vienna Konzerthaus quartets have shown much interest in those up to op. 17. (An exception of sorts are the numerous recordings, some orchestral, of the famous 'Serenade' from the spurious op. 3 no. 5.) Recordings of the remaining quartets, however, reflect the long-uncontested position of these works at the heart of the quartet repertoire, and there are few major modern ensembles who have resisted them; indeed, it is almost more interesting to note those ensembles who have shown little or no interest in Haydn—such as the Borodin and Kronos quartets—than those who have. Again 'named' quartets have tended to attract the greatest attention. Op. 33 no. 2 ('Joke'), op. 33 no. 3 ('Bird'), op. 50 no. 6 ('Frog'), op. 64 no. 5 ('Lark'), op. 74 no. 3 ('Rider'), op. 76 no. 2 ('Fifths'), op. 76 no. 3 ('Emperor'), and op. 76 no. 4 ('Sunrise') have all received more recordings than others from the same sets. In general, however, it is the quartets of opp. 76, 77, and 103 that have appeared on record most.

The other main area of Haydn's output of chamber music, the piano trio, has also received a complete recording, although this one is unusual in that it benefits from the participation of a genuinely front-rank ensemble. Issued by Philips, the recording by the Beaux Arts Trio was inspired by the completion of the Doblinger published edition in 1978. Nearly a quarter of a century on it is unlikely that such a project would be undertaken on modern instruments rather than period ones, but the lack of established 'fortepiano trio' ensembles has meant that recording patterns by period performers have had a somewhat random look. The largest number comes on Harmonia Mundi from the fortepianist Patrick Cohen with two members of the Mosaïques Quartet, Erich Höbarth and Christophe Coin (with Konrad Hünteler for the flute trios). Elsewhere there has been little systematic application to this repertoire, with just a few famous trios receiving a significant number of recordings, often by 'celebrity ensembles'. The trios of the 1790s are the most recorded, the most popular single work being the 'Gypsy' rondo, with recordings reaching back to one made in 1927 by Alfred Cortot, Jacques Thibaud, and Pablo Casals. Other notable musicians to be heard playing these trios down the years include the Kraus–Goldberg–Pini trio in the 1940s, David Oistrakh with Lev Oborin and Sviatoslav Knushevitsky in 1961, Pierre Fournier with brother Jean and Jacques Février, Emil Gilels with Oleg Kagan and Mstislav Rostropovich, Isaac Stern with Leonard Rose and Eugene Istomin, and András Schiff with Yuuko Shiokawa and Boris Pergamenshchikov.

3. Keyboard music. Although some of Haydn's keyboard music made it onto record during the 78 era, none of it became part of the pianistic mainstream. The Haydn Society issued a number of (mainly later) sonatas performed by Virginia Pleasants, but it was the Wiener Urtext edition of 1963–4 that really precipitated a flood of recordings, including several complete cycles. Of these, some offer a variety of artists and instruments—the series issued by Vox employs Fritz Neymeyer on harpsichord, clavichord, and fortepiano, and Rena Kyriakou, Walter Klien, and Martin Galling on piano, while the Hungaroton cycle features Zsusza Pertis and János Sebestyén on harpsichord and a host of pianists including Deszö Ränki and Zoltán Kocsis—while others use a single artist on piano throughout. John McCabe's set for Decca is the most celebrated of these, but there are others from Emma Contestabile (Cetra), Arthur Balsam (American Musical Heritage Society), Monique Mercier (Monodiodis), and Rudolf Buchbinder (Teldec). The piano sonatas have been able to attract some of the biggest stars as well. Horowitz, Backhaus, Gould, Richter, and Brendel have all recorded several, while others who have shown more intermittent interest include Solomon, Serkin, Gilels, Pogorelich, Kissin, and Ax. More recently, the rise in the number of committed performers on the fortepiano (and the improved reliability of modern copies of early pianos) has given a new impetus to the recording of Haydn's piano music. Paul Badura-Skoda and Malcolm Bilson were notable pioneers here, but the field is growing, with Andreas Staier's recordings for Deutsche Harmonia Mundi and Ronald Brautigam's for BIS among recent entries.

4. Operas. The operas are probably the single area of Haydn's output to have benefited most from recordings, since they remain unlikely to find a place in the regular repertoires even of minor opera houses. Once again the influential figure is Dorati: his set of the eight Eszterháza operas (*L'infedeltà delusa*, *L'incontro improvviso*, *Il mondo della luna*, *La vera costanza*, *L'isola disabitata*, *La fedeltà premiata*, *Orlando paladino*, and *Armida*) is another great recording monument, and has inspired a number of staged productions. A joint project between Philips and the European Broadcasting Union, it was recorded during the late 1970s and features singers of the calibre of Jessye Norman, Edith Mathis, Elly Ameling, Ileana Cotrubas, Frederica von Stade, Margaret Marshall, Arleen Auger, Anthony Rolfe Johnson, Samuel Ramey, and Benjamin Luxon. The orchestra throughout is the Lausanne Chamber Orchestra and, like Dorati's symphony series, it is an achievement that seems unlikely to be surpassed for many years.

Other recordings of Haydn operas are thin on the ground. *L'infedeltà delusa* is the most popular. As well as Dorati's, there are recordings conducted by Antonio de Almeida in the late 1960s with the Rome Chamber Orchestra, Kuijken with La Petite Bande and a cast that includes Nancy Argenta and Christoph Prégardien, and by Frigyes Sándor. This last is one of a Hungaroton series that also includes *Lo speziale* (conducted by György Lehel) and *La fedeltà premiata*, recorded at Eszterháza with the Franz Liszt Chamber Orchestra and a strong Hungarian cast. Philips also supplement their Dorati cycle with an abridged *Lo speziale*, with Rolf Maedel conducting. The London opera, *L'anima del filosofo*, received its first recording (under the title *Orfeo ed Euridice*) in 1952 when the Haydn Society issued an Austrian Radio recording featuring the Vienna State Opera conducted by Swarowsky, with Walter Berry among the soloists. Since then Richard Bonynge conducted a performance featuring Joan Sutherland and Nicolai Gedda in 1967, but no more followed until the 1990s, and

Leopold Hager's performance with Bavarian Radio, Hogwood's with the Academy of Ancient Music (featuring Cecilia Bartoli), and Michael Schneider's with La Stagione, Frankfurt.

5. Oratorios and songs. The two late oratorios, despite their late start, have both been recorded several times. *The Creation* started out in 1949 with the notable Haydn Society premiere, and since then it has been recorded over 30 times, sometimes by conductors not usually associated with Haydn. Among the major names to have tackled it are Bernstein (twice), Kubelík, Karajan (twice, the first of which, with the Berlin Philharmonic, featured a de luxe cast of Gundula Janowitz, Christa Ludwig, Werner Krenn, Fritz Wunderlich, Dietrich Fischer-Dieskau, and Walter Berry), Solti, Dorati, Jochum, Markevitch, Horenstein, Levine, Harnoncourt, Rilling (twice), Jordan, Münchinger, Willcocks, Rattle, and Robert Shaw (the last three in English). The first period-instrument performance was Kuijken's on Accent in 1982, and this has been followed by others from Hogwood (in English), Brüggen, Weil, and Gardiner.

The Seasons has been less well served, though it too has attracted some unusual names. Karl Böhm's performance features Janowitz, Schreier, Talvela, the Vienna Singverein, and the Vienna Symphony Orchestra, and in 1990 Gardiner conducted one of the few period-instrument versions with Barbara Bonney, Anthony Rolfe Johnson, Andreas Schmidt, the Monteverdi Choir, and the English Baroque Soloists. This version, on Archiv, uses the longer original versions of the orchestral preludes to each season, as did Dorati's recording for Decca with Cotrubas, Krenn, Hans Sotin, the Brighton Festival Chorus and the Royal Philharmonic. Others to have recorded the work include Ferenc Fricsay, Harnoncourt, Kuijken, Marriner, Karajan, Davis (in English), Beecham, Solti, and Rilling.

The Seven Last Words has also been recorded in its choral version several times following Lautrops's premiere in the 1930s. They include Scherchen and the Vienna Symphony, Ferencsik and the Hungarian State Philharmonic, Bernius and the Württemberg Chamber Orchestra, Rilling and the Stuttgart Bach Collegium, and Almeida (with Russian forces), and, on period instruments, Harnoncourt with the Vienna Concentus Musicus. *Il ritorno di Tobia* has not fared so well; Dorati's 1979 recording for Decca features Barbara Hendricks, Linda Zoghby, Della Jones, Philip Langridge, and Benjamin Luxon, while Ferenc Székeres conducted an all-Hungarian cast for Hungaroton.

Haydn's songs were recorded as a set by Elly Ameling with the pianist Jörg Demus on Philips in 1981. Otherwise they are to be found scattered to the winds in a number of assorted recital discs, including notable ones by Peter Pears with Britten, Fischer-Dieskau with Gerald Moore, and Anne Sofie von Otter with Melvyn Tan on fortepiano.

6. Sacred music. Before 1949, Haydn's masses were virtually unknown outside the churches of Austria and southern Germany, where they were regularly encountered serving the liturgy. The Haydn Society helped to rescue them from their undeserved obscurity (apart from the first recordings listed above, there were also releases of the *Missa in tempore belli* and of the 'St Cecilia' mass, under Gillesberger) and they now represent one of the more respected —if not yet over-recorded—areas of the composer's output. A complete cycle of sorts was put together by Decca, in which masses from 'Kleine Orgelsolomesse' (MISSA BREVIS SANCTI JOANNIS DE DEO) onwards feature in almost all the cases the Choir of St John's College, Cambridge, and the Academy of St Martin in the Fields under George Guest (originally on Argo), while the earlier ones (on Florilegium) were given to the Choir of Christ Church Cathedral, Oxford, with the period instruments of the Academy of Ancient Music conducted by Simon Preston. A more integrated cycle, including the fragment *Missa 'sunt bona mixta malis'* and a number of attractive filler items, has been issued by Chandos, with the period instrument forces of CM90 conducted by Richard Hickox. Otherwise, the six late masses have, unsurprisingly, grabbed the lion's share of the recordings. Marriner and Harnoncourt have both been busy here, while another, perhaps unexpected figure to have shown an interest in them was Bernstein, who recorded all except the *Missa Sancti Bernardi d'Offida* and the 'Schöpfungsmesse' with the London Symphony Orchestra and the New York Philharmonic; one of Bernstein's recordings of the *Missa in tempore belli* was of a live concert for peace held outside Washington cathedral in 1973. The 'Nelson' mass (MISSA IN ANGUSTIIS)has been easily the most recorded of the late masses; apart from the conductors mentioned above, Swarowsky, Willcocks, and Pinnock are among those who have been attracted to it. Pinnock has also conducted the 'Theresienmesse' and the early *Missa Sancti Nicolai* with the choir and orchestra of the English Concert. Next in popularity is the *Missa in tempore belli*, which has brought recordings from Kubelík, Levine, Harnoncourt and Weil among others.

Of the earlier works, the 'Kleine Orgelsolomesse' has been relatively frequently recorded (twice by Gillesberger, for instance, and also by Marriner and Münchinger), while the first *Missa Cellensis* has brought fourth accounts from Jochum, Kubelík, and Michel Corboz.

Three other sacred works by Haydn have a respectable history on record: the Stabat mater has been recorded by the Vienna Boys' Choir under Gillesberger, by the London Chamber Choir and orchestra under Laszlo Heltay, the Stuttgart Chamber Choir directed by Bernius, and on period instruments by Harnoncourt and Pinnock. Pinnock has also been prompted into action by the late Te Deum, along with Gillesberger, Weil, Kuijken, Karl Forster, Fricsay, and Corboz. The Salve regina in G minor has been recorded by Heltay, Weil, Harnoncourt, Ferencsik, and Harry Blech, and on period instruments by the Parlement de Musique under Martin Gester. LK

Reicha, Antoine (-Joseph) (b. 26 Feb. 1770; d. 28 May 1836). Composer, theorist, and teacher who worked mainly in Paris. Born in Prague, he joined the court orchestra at Bonn in 1785, where he was a colleague of his exact contemporary Beethoven. He and Haydn first met when the latter called in on the town on his way to and from London. In 1794 Reicha moved to Hamburg where, the following year, he met the composer for a third time. From 1802 to 1808 Reicha lived in Vienna, becoming a close friend of Haydn. He was never formally a pupil but in his autobiography Reicha remarked that Haydn's 'discourses on composition in general were a revelation and of great help to me'. In 1803 he completed a set of 36 fugues for piano which he dedicated to Haydn. Described as being 'composed according to a new system', they reveal a curious musical mind that borders on the eccentric, with experiments in modality, unusual cadences, and simultaneous use of different metres. Haydn would have been fascinated by the thought processes even if he had reservations about the musical results. In his autobiography Reicha claimed to have introduced the French Secretary of State, Hugues Maret, the violinist Baillot (1771–1842), and Cherubini to Haydn. As professor of counterpoint and fugue at the Paris Conservatoire from 1818 to his death his pupils included Berlioz, Franck, and Liszt.

Reutter, (Johann Adam Joseph Karl) Georg (von) (bap. 6 April 1708; d. 11 March 1772). Austrian composer and Haydn's teacher at St Stephen's, Vienna. Reutter grew up in musical circles at the imperial court where his father, also Georg Reutter (1656–1738), worked as an organist and Kapellmeister. Following lessons from Caldara (*c.*1670–1736) the son was sent to Italy for a period of study, returning to Vienna in the autumn of 1730. Early in the following year he successfully applied for a post as court organist, the formal beginning of a lifetime of service at the Habsburg court. He succeeded his father in 1738 as first Kapellmeister at St Stephen's; in 1747 he became second Kapellmeister at the imperial court; in 1756 he assumed the duties of second as well as first Kapellmeister at St Stephen's; and in 1769 he formally became court Kapellmeister. For nearly 30 years in the middle of the century, therefore, Reutter was the single most influential church musician in Vienna. His duties at court also included the supervision of instrumental performances.

Reutter's duties as Kapellmeister at St Stephen's required him to audition new members for the choir and he was given a yearly allowance for the instruction and the boarding of six choirboys. It was during a visit to Hainburg in 1739 or 1740 that Joseph Haydn was recruited. Looking back on his musical training at St Stephen's, Haydn was not particularly complimentary, telling Griesinger that he remembered receiving only two lessons from Reutter who, in other respects, was a stern disciplinarian; he was also rather dismissive of Haydn's juvenile attempts at composition. But Haydn's less than fond memories of his teacher should not be allowed to detract from the enormous influence that Reutter's music had on the formation of his style. Neither should the emphasis that Haydn himself gave to C. P. E. Bach, whose music he discovered later, be allowed to obscure the importance of Reutter who together with Porpora and Wagenseil were the key figures in Haydn's early musical development.

Reutter wrote over 500 church compositions, many of which Haydn as a boy treble would have known intimately. They cover the complete spectrum of contemporary sacred composition: masses with elaborate orchestral accompaniment, a cappella masses designed for Advent and Lent (Haydn's *Missa 'sunt bona mixta malis'* is part of the same tradition), and about 300 motets, offertories, and psalm settings. The disposition of solo and choral-writing, the choice of texture and style, and the characteristics of word-painting and instrumental colouring are to be found repeatedly in Haydn's sacred music, even in the six late masses and the second Te Deum.

Although Reutter was much less prolific as a composer of instrumental music the orchestral works that he was required to provide for occasional performance during banquets in the imperial palace are an important source for a recurring sonority in the symphonies of Haydn and other Austrian composers: C major works brilliantly coloured by trumpets and timpani.

D. Heartz, *Haydn, Mozart and the Viennese School 1740–1780* (New York, 1995).

HCRL/1.

B. MacIntyre, *The Viennese Concerted Mass of the Early Classic Period* (Ann Arbor, 1986).

rhetoric. The appeal of rhetoric for the 18th century may not have been as overwhelming as it was for previous centuries, but it nevertheless remained strong. Successive generations tended to find their own distinctive approaches to the Classical rhetoric of Quintilian and Cicero, and the early 18th century focused on the oratorical principles of persuasion and how these could be applied to modern literature. For writers whose primary goal was a moral one, as was true of many in the 18th century, persuasive language became the critical element. A writer such as the Earl of Shaftesbury mapped out the possibilities before the end of the 17th century, and influenced other writers throughout Europe for the better part of a century.

While England and France had established literary traditions in place, Germany did not, and those who attempted to shape a national literature consequently relied heavily on rhetorical principle to achieve their end. Most notable early in the 18th century were Christian Wolff and Johann Christoph Gottsched, whose efforts to instil morality in writing resulted in a simpler, more direct style which sought to communicate effectively. One notes rhetorical devices in sentences as well as larger formal levels in the attempt to achieve this.

The 18th-century focus on rhetoric concerned itself less with the specifics of grammar or the direct application of the classical principles than with power to move a reader or an audience. While the devices are not necessarily abandoned, they play as direct a role as possible in reaching the audience. Morality itself could be cultivated through a process of refinement, and writing styles which sought simplicity and effectiveness were therefore necessary. This applied not only to professional writers but to the general public as well. Manuals on letter-writing and conversation, such as those by CHRISTIAN FÜRCHTEGOTT GELLERT and Adolf von Knigge (both of which Haydn owned), placed these objectives in the public domain, and relied heavily on principles of rhetoric to achieve their ends.

The active discussion on rhetoric during the century extended well beyond literature to include music as well, and some writers on music had their feet firmly planted in both areas. JOHANN MATTHESON for one, whose *Der vollkommene Capellmeister* (1739) exerted a profound influence on the next generation of musicians, had earlier in the century been involved in purely literary ventures, such as his editing of the moral weekly *Der Vernünfftler* (The Rationalist). As much of this journal consisted of translations of material from the *Tatler* and *Spectator*, he played a strong role in popularizing English thought in Germany. His musical treatises, like those of numerous other writers on music such as Daube, Forkel, Kirnberger, Koch, MARPURG, and Vogler, emphasized the connection between music and oratory, involving the persuasive or moral capacity of music as well as rhetorical principles concerning periodicity, rhythm, melody, and form that would allow the effect on the audience to be realized.

Since the 18th century placed a higher value on vocal music than instrumental, often doubting the capacity of instrumental music to be intelligible, critical writing tended to focus on vocal music. The aria in opera or oratorio was generally seen as reaching the greatest heights of language and eloquence, most capable of moving the listener and achieving refinement. By the end of the century lagging theory began to give instrumental music its due, taking notice of the potential for a new type of wordless rhetoric. Instrumental composers themselves had recognized this much earlier: C. P. E. BACH in his *Versuch über die wahre Art das Clavier zu spielen* had spoken of avoiding the error of orators who try to place an impressive accent on every word. The keyboard player could be compared to the orator, and as Gottsched or Gellert argued, he should strive for effective simplicity and refinement.

The essentially self-taught Haydn had cut his compositional teeth on the treatises of Mattheson and Bach. Proclaiming that his isolation had forced him to be original, he surpassed his contemporaries in absorbing enlightened, rhetorical principles into both his vocal and instrumental music. Various comments made to his biographer Griesinger confirm his intentions: he believed he had done his duty and been of use to the world through his works, he said he worked out his ideas in keeping with the rules of art, and he claimed to portray moral characters in his symphonies.

The realizations of these remarks can be seen in numerous ways. His use of melody as a reference point, his compositional process of working from motivic units or expansions of periodicity, or his effective use of rhythm all suggest applications of rhetorical principles to music. In some instrumental works, by using material that the listener would recognize as having a text, such as the first two movements of Symphony no. 26 ('Lamentatione'), he makes a direct application of oratorical principles. He goes even further in some late symphonies with slow introductions, applying what he had learned from Gottfried van Swieten and others: giving the work the appropriate oratorical tone of gravity and dignity before moving on to the main 'arguments'. As in classical rhetoric, the introduction (exordium) should be divided into two parts, the first to make the listener attentive and the second to steal into the listener's mind by dissimulation. The introduction to Symphony no. 102 fits the model especially well, beginning slowly and quietly with a melodic passage which is followed by an elaborate and destabilizing contrapuntal passage. Rather than applying rhetoric consciously, he may, in the pursuit of moral goals, have inadvertently used a procedure which was well tried in the past and honoured throughout his own century. DPS

E. A. Blackall, *The Emergence of German as a Literary Language 1700–1775* (Cambridge, 1959).

M. E. Bonds, 'The Symphony as Pindaric Ode', in E. Sisman (ed.), *Haydn and His World* (Princeton, 1997), 131–53.

L. Ratner, *Classic Music: Expression, Form, and Style* (New York, 1980).

'Rider' quartet. Nickname for the quartet in G minor, op. 74 no. 3, that arose in the 19th century, probably first in Germany ('Reiterquartett') and then in England. The incessant energy of the last movement in G minor appealed to the Romantic image of a horseman riding recklessly into the dangerous unknown. JH

Ringmacher, Christian Ulrich (b. 30 June 1743; d. 7 June 1781). The owner of a book- and music-selling business in Berlin, active from 1770 to 1781. Following the example of Breitkopf he issued several thematic catalogues of instrumental music available from his shop, of which only one has survived. Dating from 1773 it contains 38 works by Haydn. The particular value of the Ringmacher catalogue for Haydn scholarship is that its pages reveal the likely authors of works wrongly attributed elsewhere to the composer.

C. U. Ringmacher, *Catalogo de' Soli, Duetti, Trii . . . Berlin 1773*, facsimile edn with concluding essay by B. S. Brook (Stuyvesant, NY, 1987).

Rohrau. A village 40 km (25 miles) east of Vienna and Haydn's birthplace. Situated in Lower Austria near the Leitha river that marked the boundary of Austria and Hungary, it was a part of a rural economy that profited also from the trade plied along the Danube river, 17 km (11 miles) to the north. From the 16th century the local aristocratic rulers were the HARRACH family whose castle is still a notable landmark. Although the basic layout of the village remains unaltered, successive floods and fires have meant that most houses and buildings have been rebuilt several times over the centuries. Haydn's birthplace, on the southern side of the village, was twice flooded and once burnt in the 19th century. Now extended and rather sanitized in appearance, it houses a museum devoted to the composer. In the local church, where Haydn first flexed his musical talents, the font at which he was baptized can be seen as can the memorial statue to his parents. *See also* HAYDN MUSEUMS.

rondo. In the 18th century lexicographers and theorists defined rondo as a musical form in which an opening section (refrain) regularly recurs in the tonic key between contrasting sections (couplets or episodes) before returning to conclude the composition. Although most commonly encountered in instrumental music the form was found also in vocal music. From the early 1770s there was a remarkable upsurge in the use of rondo patterns, especially in instrumental music. Haydn's own rondo output dramatically increased at this time and he proceeded to cultivate the form steadily and imaginatively for the remainder of his career. The form is found across the full range of his output, most frequently in the symphony, quartet, keyboard trio, and keyboard sonata, but also in other genres such as concerto, divertimento, opera, oratorio, and mass.

A rondo can appear anywhere in a multi-movement instrumental cycle by the composer, occasionally as a first movement in small-scale works such as keyboard sonatas and trios (e.g. Hob. XVI:48 and Hob.XV:25), more often as internal slow movements (quartets op. 50 no. 3 and op. 77 no. 2), and most frequently as a finale, where it becomes the standard alternative to sonata form. Surviving autographs suggest that, unlike Mozart, Haydn never used the word rondo as a heading to a movement, preferring a simple tempo marking, sometimes preceded by the word 'Finale'. With the striking exception of the first movement of the keyboard trio in E♭ minor (Hob.XV:31), Haydn rondos do not exceed keys of four sharps or four flats. Like his contemporaries, he rarely chose the minor mode, in keeping with the prevailing attitude that a rondo should be pleasant, agreeable, and charming. With rhythms that often allude to dances, such as the minuet, the gavotte, the contredanse, and the gigue, the metres selected for rondos include 3/8, 6/8, 2/4, ¢, and 3/4.

To an even greater extent than in sonata form, or even in a set of variations, the impact of a rondo depends on the quality of the opening theme. Early in his career Haydn favoured themes that feature gestures associated with opera overtures, especially wide leaps and rushing scales (e.g. Symphony no. 15/iv), or, more gracefully, themes that allude to the minuet (e.g. Symphony no. 18/iii). Gradually Haydn came to favour themes that had many features taken from the contredanse: duple metre, steady motion in quavers, small leaps, and regular phrase structure (e.g. Symphony no. 55/iv). Songs and folk music occasionally provide the thematic material (e.g. Symphony no. 73/ii, based on the song 'Gegenliebe', Hob.XXVIa:16; and the finale of the keyboard concerto in D major, based on an East European folk tune). Haydn customarily shapes his refrains as closed structures with internal repetitions; often he lavishes attention upon subsequent returns, imaginatively varying and rescoring them.

While the couplet/episode material may be new, more characteristically it is derived in some fashion from the refrain. Couplets usually unfold in keys other than the tonic: tonic minor, submediant minor, and subdominant are the areas of choice early in Haydn's career; later, under the influence of sonata form, the dominant becomes a favoured goal. Structurally, first couplets range from closed units to extended paragraphs analogous to the transition, second subject, and closing sections of a sonata form. Similarly, second and third couplets range from closed units to full, sonata-like development sections. At times, stormy minor-key episodes, with their atmospheric string tremolos, jagged pitch contours, and dynamic extremes, disrupt the prevailing mood of cheerfulness (Symphonies no. 51/iv and no. 102/iv).

As regards the overall structure of a rondo movement, four basic designs are used, carefully shaped in a way that is appropriate to the potential of the musical material of that particular movement. First are movements that are based on a ternary pattern, whether on a small scale (e.g. keyboard sonatas Hob.XVI:8/iv and 9/iii) or at greater length (e.g. Symphony no. 78/iv). Second are those movements that have a two-couplet design, ABACA, a design that can be obvious in its outlay, as in the finale of the keyboard sonata Hob.XVI:37, or wonderfully organic, as in Symphony no. 97/iv. Third, multi-couplet designs are sometimes found, particularly ABACADA, as in Symphony no. 68/iv. Fourth are movements in so-called sonata-rondo form, in its fullest manifestation ABACAB′[A], as in Symphonies nos. 85/iv, 102/iv, and 103/iv; in this structure, the first couplet (B) unfolds like the transition, second subject, and closing section of a sonata-form exposition, while the third couplet (B′) functions as a recapitulation in the tonic.

To combat the restricted expressive range, obviously sectional progress, and frequent returns to the tonic of a rondo pattern Haydn uses other structural principles and compositional techniques. Particularly favoured are rondo movements that use elements taken from VARIATION form; the returns of the refrain in the following finales are altered as if they were a single variation in a set, Symphonies nos. 61, 66, 68, 69, and 75. (This was a two-way process. Movements in variation form sometimes include contrasting couplets/episodes, as in Symphony no. 42/iv.)

Through a blend of rondo and SONATA FORM, Haydn achieved highly sophisticated accommodations between sectionalization and continuity, and between popular appeal and intellectuality. Concentrated in symphonic finales, such fusions challenged 20th-century scholars brought up on definitions of sonata-rondo form that were based on the more restricted patterns found in the keyboard music of Mozart and Beethoven. The debate has concentrated on which and how many of the following formal elements should be present to warrant the label sonata rondo as opposed to simple rondo: a tonal plan analogous to sonata form; a first couplet with the sonata-form components of transition, second subject, and closing theme; a central couplet that is akin to a development section; and a repetition of the first couplet in the tonic, akin to a recapitulation. The most appropriate minimum criterion would seem to be whether the refrain and first couplet demonstrate features taken from a sonata-form exposition. Thus, Symphony no. 64/iv from the early 1770s marks the beginning of Haydn's experimentation with the combination of rondo and sonata elements, followed by the finales of symphonies nos. 66, 69, 85, 88, 93–5, 97, and 99–103. The overture in (Hob.Ia:4), dating from 1782–4, becomes his first sonata rondo with recapitulation. While useful to indicate the overall structure of the movement, letter schemes, such as those utilized in this article, cannot convey the carefully constructed proportions of Haydn's sonata-rondos, with their often lengthy first couplets and their breathtaking drive to closure. In these effervescent finales, Haydn attains an ever closer rapprochement with sonata form, including monothematic sonata form, without sacrificing the basic sense of a periodic return to a favoured theme. As in some of the composer's sonata form, textures in Haydn's rondo form occasionally reach out and embrace polyphony, including canon, invertible counterpoint, fugato, and contrapuntal combination (the first three variously in the couplets of Symphony no. 95/iv, the last in the refrain of Symphony no. 103/iv).

The utilization of the form varies a little from genre to genre. In the composer's symphonies the few examples of rondo form in internal movements (e.g. no. 73/ii and no. 101/ii) are far outnumbered by the 31 rondo finales: nos. 2, 15, 18, 20, 30, 34, 42, 51, 53A, 55, 61, 64, 66, 68, 69, 75, 78–9, 85, 88–9, 93–7, and 99–103, plus the overture in D (Hob.Ia:4). Much of this output is concentrated in two periods: five years in the mid- to late 1770s (ten rondos); and the years 1791–5 (ten rondos). The regular use of rondo in the final movements of Haydn's mature symphonies contrasts markedly with Mozart's preference for sonata form in his mature symphonies.

Similarly, in the quartets, interior rondo movements such as op. 50 no. 3/ii and op. 77 no. 2/iii are outnumbered by rondo finales: op. 1 nos. 3–4, op. 33 nos. 2–4, op. 54 no. 1, op. 55 no. 1, op. 64 nos. 5–6, op. 71 nos. 2–3, op. 74 no. 2, and op. 76 nos. 2 and 4.

None of Haydn's concertos from the 1750s and 1760s uses rondo form; from *c.*1780 onwards all his concertos end with a rondo, the keyboard concerto in D major, the Cello Concerto in D major, the five concertos for *lire organizzate*, and the Trumpet Concerto. To these may be added the finale of the symphonie concertante.

The domestic genres of the keyboard sonata and the keyboard trio reveal a more flexible attitude to the placing of any rondo form. Often its presence as a first movement is designed to avoid using the more taxing sonata form (e.g. Hob.XVI:11/i and Hob.XV:25/i). Elsewhere, in the cycle, however, its appearance unleashes a compositional imagination that is fully the equal of any rondo in a symphony or quartet. Of the many rondos in the sonatas the one that forms the second movement of the two-movement sonata in C (Hob.XVI:48) is particularly engaging, while the keyboard trios reveal a greater diversity of approaches, including highly imaginative transitions and retransitions, and rhapsodic couplets (Hob.XV:7, 10, 16, 18, 25, and 28).

From time to time, well-made rondos appear in Haydn's operas and sacred music. For example, Act 2 of *Lo speziale* concludes with the quartet 'Colla presente scrittura privata', a dramatically conceived, multi-tempo variation-rondo with accelerated coda. Similarly, the vaudeville finale 'Son' confuso e stupefatto' brings *Orlando paladino* to a rousing close; the assembled cast declaims the moral in the refrain and the seven individual characters comment in the couplets, producing an overall structure of ABACDBABA. *The Creation* includes the duet and chorus 'By thee with bliss, o bounteous Lord'/'Von deiner Güt', o Herr und Gott', an extended rondo of unprecedented design: an introduction followed by the pattern ABACBADBAEFE, plus a coda. The 'Qui tollis' from the *Missa in tempore belli* and the Benedictus from the 'Schöpfungsmesse' illustrate further the expressive potential of the form. Scored for bass solo, chorus, cello obbligato, and orchestra the 'Qui tollis' has a powerful second couplet that moves to the mediant minor to evoke the text 'suscipe deprecationem nostram' (receive our prayer) and, most tellingly, the final refrain is in the tonic minor, prompted by the clause 'miserere nobis' (have mercy upon us).

GRIESINGER wrote that Haydn's 'allegros and rondeaux are especially often planned to tease the audience by wanton shifts from the seemingly serious to the highest level of comedy, and to be tuned to an almost wild hilarity'. Because of its anticipated simplicity and regularity, the rondo form often served as a perfect foil for musical humour, realized with Haydn's full array of melodic, rhythmic, harmonic, dynamic, colouristic, textural, and formal devices. One of the most celebrated examples is the finale of the quartet op. 33 no. 2 ('Joke'), a game of second-guessing about when and how the piece will end that crucially depends on exploiting the normal expectations of rondo form. In contrast, the apparently understated beginning to the rondo finale of Symphony no. 101 is later followed by a second couplet that is highly forceful, and a final return of the refrain that is clothed in contrapuntal finery of the most delicate kind. Haydn's ability to unveil unsuspected potential for development and textural complexity from seemingly artless tunes challenges the listener constantly to adjust predictions about the direction, design, and mood of a movement. On another, aesthetic level recent writers, investigating the parallels made in the composer's lifetime between Haydn's music and Laurence Sterne's prose, find a comparable subversion of aesthetic illusion that leads to a sense of ironic distance between the artist, his work, and his audience.

Haydn's rondos are a highly characteristic part of the composer's musical make-up that only Beethoven, of later composers, was able to comprehend and fully exploit. Certainly the finales of Beethoven's Symphonies nos. 2 and 8 owe a great deal to Haydn's consummate mastery of the form.

MSC

M. S. Cole, 'Haydn's Symphonic Rondo Finales: Their Structural and Stylistic Evolution', *HYB* 13 (1982), 113–42.

S. C. Fisher, 'Further Thoughts on Haydn's Symphonic Rondo Finales', *HYB* 17 (1992), 85–107.

E. R. Sisman, *Haydn and the Classical Variation* (Cambridge, Mass., 1993).

G. A. Wheelock, *Haydn's Ingenious Jesting with Art. Contexts of Musical Wit and Humor* (New York, 1992).

Rosenbaum, Joseph Carl (b. 5 July 1770; d. 26 Dec. 1829). Administrator in the service first of the Esterházy family and then of a pension foundation in Vienna; friend of Haydn who kept a fascinating diary of life in Vienna over a period of 32 years. He was the son of an Esterházy employee, Georg Rosenbaum, who had worked his way from porter to senior administrator. Following in his father's footsteps, Joseph Carl Rosenbaum entered the service of the family at the age of 15; within ten years he was in charge of the stabling accounts. In 1796 he met the singer THERESE GASSMANN, who was in Eisenstadt to take part in the festivities associated with the nameday of Princess Marie Hermenegild Esterházy. They fell in love but Therese's mother was bitterly opposed to the match. As an employee of the Esterházy family Rosenbaum needed the approval of the prince to marry; Haydn tried to intercede on his behalf, but to no avail. Rosenbaum left the service of the court and moved to Vienna. After three years of difficult courtship the couple finally married on 11 June 1800; Rosenbaum wrote in his diary that his mother-in-law 'wept appallingly' during the service and afterwards. Rosenbaum and Therese remained in friendly contact with Haydn and visited him regularly in Gumpendorf. Less honourable was the leading part Rosenbaum played in stealing HAYDN'S SKULL to assist the medical research of Franz Joseph Gall.

Despite the Napoleonic Wars Rosenbaum managed to amass a considerable fortune, and when he died in 1829 he left his wife several houses and a suburban villa. His diaries are a valuable source of information on Haydn in the last period of his life, musical life in general, and the tribulations of daily existence in Vienna during the two periods of occupation by French forces. His musical tastes were conservative ones. A close friend of Salieri as well as Haydn, he preferred the music of that epoch and his comments on Beethoven's works are largely unsympathetic. ERL

E. Radant (ed.), 'The Diaries of Joseph Carl Rosenbaum 1770–1829', *HYB* 5 (1968), 1–158.

'Roxelane' symphony. *See* 'LA ROXELANE' SYMPHONY.

'Russian' quartets. Nickname occasionally used to describe the op. 33 quartets because of their association with Grand Duke Paul Petrovich, later Tsar Paul I. Some or all of the quartets were played in a private concert on 25 December 1781 during the grand duke's visit to Vienna. Haydn, who was present along with the quartet ensemble of TOMASINI, ASPLMAYR, WEIGL, and Huber, was given an enamelled gold box encrusted with diamonds. Haydn may have suggested that the quartets would be dedicated to the grand duke. The autograph manuscripts of the quartets are lost (perhaps they were forwarded to the grand duke) and the first published edition, issued by Artaria in April 1782, carries no dedication. When, 14 years later, in 1796 Artaria reissued the set as part of a complete edition of the composer's quartets it carried a dedication to the grand duke.

S

Saal family. Family of singers active in Vienna and, in Haydn's case, particularly associated with performances of *The Creation* and *The Seasons.* Ignaz Saal (1761–1836) was a bass who sang in Munich and Pressburg before making his debut at the Burgtheater in Vienna in 1782 in Umlauf's *Die Bergknappen.* He sang comic and serious roles, and occasionally took spoken roles too; he sang the part of Raphael in the first, semi-private performances of *The Creation* in 1798. His wife, Maria Anna Saal (1762–1808), was a soprano and the couple were often engaged in the court theatres as a pair. Of five children, three pursued careers as musicians. Franz Saal (b. 1804) was a teacher of music and Karl Saal (b. 1800) sang at the theatre in Brünn, but the most talented was the eldest, Therese Saal (1782–1855). At the age of 17 she sang the part of Gabriel alongside her father (Raphael) in the first public performances of *The Creation* in 1799 (nobody seems to have remarked on the propriety of father and daughter singing the parts of Adam and Eve in Part 3). Father and daughter also undertook the parts of Hanne and Simon in the first performances of *The Seasons* in 1801. As well as singing opera at the court theatres Therese and Ignaz became stalwarts of the biannual concerts of the Tonkünstler-Societät, including several performances of Haydn's oratorios. In 1805, Therese married a well-to-do furrier, Johann Gawet, and retired from the stage. Her father, however, continued to perform until at least 1814 when he sang the role of Don Fernando in the first performance of Beethoven's *Fidelio.* He had been a member of the Hofkapelle since 1795 and probably sang in the choir in church services until his death. ERL

HCRL/4 and 5.

O. Michtner, *Das alter Burgtheater als Opernbühne* (Vienna, 1970).

'St Anthony Chorale'. BRAHMS composed his orchestral work, Variations on a theme by Haydn (op. 56a) in 1873, later arranging it for two pianos (op. 56b). He found the theme, entitled 'Chorale St. Antoni', in a manuscript score in the Gesellschaft der Musikfreunde (VIII 41541). The score, in the handwriting of POHL, contains six divertimenti for windband, the title page claiming Haydn as the composer, though stylistic evidence makes this most unlikely. Three works are for pairs of oboes, clarinets, horns, and bassoons, and three are for two oboes, two horns, three bassoons, and serpent; the 'Chorale St. Antoni' forms the second movement of the sixth work (Hob.II:46).

Haydn's association with these divertimenti derives from their listing in the BREITKOPF CATALOGUE of 1782–4 ('VI Divertimenti da Gius. Haydn'); parts from the Breitkopf shop survive in Zittau from which Pohl made his score. No other musical source, in Haydn's name or anyone else's, has ever been discovered. The occasional modern attribution to Pleyel is pure speculation.

'St Anthony Chorale', like two other melodies in the set of divertimenti, 'Dolcema l'amour' and 'La vierge Marie', were popular tunes incorporated by the unknown composer into his divertimenti.

RH

St Stephen's. The metropolitan cathedral church in Vienna. Built originally in the Romanesque style in the 12th century, it was rebuilt as a large Gothic edifice in the following 300 years. It became the seat of the Archbishop of Vienna in 1723. It remained largely untouched by the taste of the Baroque period so evident elsewhere in Vienna, and Charles Burney was only one person to comment on its unfashionably dark and gloomy interior. After some 150 years of comparative neglect it was thoroughly restored in the second half of the 19th century, work that was completely undone by its virtual destruction in the final weeks of the Second World War; it was then, too, that a good deal of the old music library was lost. The cathedral has been rebuilt and still dominates the central skyline of the city.

Although officially part of the city rather than of the court, St Stephen's was frequently visited by the imperial court, particularly on grand state occasions. REUTTER, Haydn's teacher, was the imperial Kapellmeister but was also responsible for music at St Stephen's. Haydn sang as a choirboy there from 1739 (or 1740) to 1749 and in his 20s he continued to sing as an 'extra' in church services; on 26 November 1760 he married Maria Anna Keller in the cathedral. Thereafter Haydn had little direct contact with the cathedral though his sacred music was performed there. Like all Viennese, he would have been aware that its spire acted as a convenient watchtower for fires in the city and, during Napoleonic times, for sighting the advancing French armies. *See also* VIENNA.

C. F. Pohl, *Joseph Haydn*, vol. i (Berlin, 1875).

Salieri, Antonio (b. 18 Aug. 1750; d. 7 May 1825). Italian musician resident in Vienna, a contributor to Viennese musical life of crucial importance during 35 years of activity as an operatic composer and conductor. As a 16-year-old orphan Salieri was brought to Vienna from Venice in 1766 by FLORIAN GASSMANN, who served as his teacher and mentor. He won the patronage of Joseph II, under whose protection his career flourished. From 1770 to 1804 he wrote many operas for the Viennese court theatres; he also fulfilled commissions in Italy, Munich, and Paris. In 1788 JOSEPH II appointed him Hofkapellmeister, a position he occupied for the rest of his career.

The court theatres influenced the operatic repertoire at Eszterháza; not surprisingly Salieri's operas were performed under Haydn's direction and subjected to adaptation for the Esterházy forces. Haydn heavily revised *La scuola de'gelosi* (first performed in Venice during Carnival 1779) and conducted frequent performances of it during 1780 and 1781. He presented *La fiera di Venezia* (Vienna, 1772) in 1782 and probably *Axur re d'Ormus* (Vienna, 1788) in 1790. A production of *La grotta di Trofonio* (Vienna, 1785), planned for the same year, was cancelled on the death of Prince Nicolaus.

Salieri played the fortepiano in the first performance of *The Creation* in April 1798. Ten years later, on 27 March 1808, a few days before Haydn's 76th birthday, Salieri conducted a performance of *The Creation* in Italian translation. The author of the translation, GIUSEPPE CARPANI, recalled: 'The two celebrated composers embraced tenderly. Salieri wrung Haydn's hand and flew to the orchestra. A general enthusiasm possessed the players, the singers, and the audience.' JAR

J. A. Rice, *Antonio Salieri and Viennese Opera* (Chicago, 1998).

Salomon, Johann Peter (bap. 20 Feb 1745; d. 28 Nov. 1815). German violinist and impresario, mainly resident in London. The son of a court musician in Bonn, he was himself appointed to the court at the age of only 13; by 1764 he had moved to Rheinsberg as musical director to Prince Heinrich of Prussia. During this period he wrote a number of stage works and oratorios; he also met C. P. E. Bach, who introduced him to his father's solo sonatas and partitas, which he later performed 'in exemplary fashion' in London.

Salomon left Rheinsberg in 1780, travelling via Paris to London. On 23 March 1781 he made his public debut at Covent Garden Theatre, playing a concerto at an oratorio performance: 'He was not handsome nor of an imposing figure, but the animation of his countenance, and the great elegance of his manner, soon caught the public eye. Having bowed [tuned up], he so placed the desk that not the smallest particle of his violin was hidden, and the "Tutti" of his favourite concerto, by Kreutzer, commenced rather mezzo-piano, and increased to a crescendo that drew down volumes of applause. Now came the solo; a repetition of the melody an octave higher, which he played with an effect perfectly sublime. It was in the minor key, and the cadence he introduced was a long shake [trill], with the melody played under—something new, which put Fischer almost into fits . . . Such a *début* has scarcely ever been experienced. We were jumping from our seats' (Papendiek, *Court and Private Life*). The author of this graphic (if not entirely trustworthy) account was Charlotte Papendiek, wife of a German valet and flautist in the royal household, suggesting that Salomon quickly become involved with the German community in London. Furthermore it was at the German-speaking 'Pilger Loge' ('Pilgrim Lodge') that he was initiated into Freemasonry on 24 April 1782. But his relationship with London's musical establishment, represented by Wilhelm Cramer and the Hanover Square performers, proved uneasy. In 1783 he was a regular performer at Abingdon's series there (on the viola), but only after the collapse of another series at the Freemasons Hall which he was to have led. His professional rivalry with Cramer was amusingly represented by a concert promoted by J. F. Klöffler on 26 May 1783, at which Cramer and Salomon led two opposing orchestras in a battle symphony. The following year he set himself up in opposition, leading a major series at the Pantheon featuring the soprano Madame Mara. Though he did occasionally perform at the Professional Concert he preferred to cultivate an independent role: at the Pantheon series of 1785, at a short series of his own in 1786, and at Madame Mara's series in 1787. He could not rival Cramer (leader at the Italian Opera, the Professional Concert, the Concert of Ancient Music, and the Handel festivals), but his prestige was rising through his association with Mara and because of the special qualities of his playing. Thomas Twining offered a direct comparison after hearing both Cramer and Salomon at Cambridge in 1785: Cramer he found rather mechanical, while Salomon showed finer taste, 'more tone, more glow', and, above all, a human touch. Salomon was increasingly in demand at provincial festivals, and in 1789 he took over the leadership at the Academy of Ancient Music in London, a body that had sacrificed its early ideals and now included modern music such as Haydn's symphonies. In the same year, he put on show his abilities as a vocal composer when his chorus 'on the happy recovery of His Majesty' (following George III's first serious mental illness) was performed at the New Musical Fund benefit on 13 April 1789.

However, in this period, there is little to foreshadow his celebrity in the next decade: he was not a major concert promoter; he had shown no unusual partiality to the music of Haydn, and none towards that of Mozart; and he was less of a specialist in chamber music than Cramer. Late in 1790 his fortunes were turned round as a result of a new association with JOHN GALLINI, owner of the Hanover Square Rooms and the artistic manager of the planned Italian Opera at the rebuilt King's Theatre. Their exact relationship during this unsettled period of London's musical history remains unclear, but it presumably revolves round the employment of the orchestra of the Professional Concert at the rival Pantheon Opera. Salomon may have been journeying on the continent in search of singers for Gallini, or he may have already had ideas of an orchestral series of his own. Everything changed as soon as he heard in Cologne of the death of Prince Nicolaus Esterházy. He went immediately to Haydn in Vienna, introducing himself with the decisive and famous greeting: 'I am Salomon of London and I have come to fetch you. Tomorrow we will arrange an *accord*.' In a letter from Vienna, dated 8 December and sent to several London newspapers, Salomon announced his first major subscription series; at the same time Haydn agreed to write an opera for Gallini. Shortly before their departure from Vienna, Salomon and Haydn dined with Mozart (to whom Salomon extended a future invitation), and they travelled via his native Bonn to England, arriving on New Year's Day 1791.

Salomon acted as Haydn's guide during his first weeks in London, introducing him to London music lovers at the Academy of Ancient Music, and to the Prince of Wales at a court ball. Yet his coup in luring Haydn to London was not rewarded by immediate success. First there were delays when the King's Theatre insisted that their star singer, GIACOMO DAVIDE, should appear there before he made his concert debut and, second, despite frenzied advertising and an avalanche of enthusiastic publicity, Salomon was not overwhelmed with subscribers. Though Mrs Papendiek wrote in rapturous terms of the long-awaited first concert on 11 March 1791, even she was forced to admit that the room was not full. This must, in part, be attributed to the established reputation of the Professional Concert. Often vilified in the Haydn literature for its intrigues against Salomon, Cramer's organization still remained the dominant partner in London's concert life, with an orchestra far superior to anything that Salomon could assemble. The reviews, however, leave one in no doubt of the artistic triumph of Salomon's first season.

In 1792 Salomon weathered the opposition provided by the arrival of PLEYEL at the Professional Concert, and began to experiment with more varied programmes introducing, for example, Haydn's short choral work, *The Storm* (Hob.XXIVa:8). Salomon was himself honoured with prominent solos, not only in the Symphonie concertante but also in Symphonies nos. 97 and 98 (the former wryly marked 'Salomon ma piano'). Nevertheless artistic kudos and popular acclaim for Haydn's 'Surprise' symphony (no. 94) were still not matched by financial returns; ironically it was not until 1793, when Haydn decided to remain in Vienna, that Salomon began to reap his rewards. The arrival of Viotti (1755–1824), unquestionably the finest violinist of the age, contributed to the overwhelming success of Salomon's series, effectively destroying the Professional Concert in the process.

Salomon's own playing was clearly highly individual to judge from reviews like the following: 'Whose violin-playing approaches nearer the human voice? On the whole Salomon is a mannerist, but he has much originality—he is very susceptible—he is a genius.' He had frequently performed concertos during the 1780s and during his career he published a handful of pleasing if not especially distinguished violin pieces: a set of sonatas, some variations, a romance, and a concerto. During the 1790s he began to turn away from the public platform, no doubt recognizing the superior skills and grander manner of violinists such as Viotti. Yet he still retained two outstanding qualities: as a leader he improved his orchestra beyond recognition by skilful recruitment and effective rehearsal, while as a player of quartets his refinement was unsurpassed.

The later quality was clearly recognized by Haydn, who returned to London in 1794 with a set of six brilliant quartets for Salomon's concerts, op. 71 and op. 74. With performances of these and of three new symphonies, including the 'Military' (no. 100), 1794 was surely Salomon's most alluring concert season. But despite this heady success he decided to bow out of concert promotion in 1795, pleading difficulties with recruitment during wartime; he eventually pooled resources with the Opera Concert (and in effect with his long-standing rivals, the Professional Concert whose players constituted the opera orchestra) for Haydn's last series. With Viotti in command, Salomon himself played an inconspicuous role, leaving time for a change of direction. His setting of William Pearce's text *Windsor Castle*, in honour of the Prince of Wales's marriage, was performed at Covent Garden on 6 April. Haydn, whose overture to *L'anima del filosofo* was pressed into service as the *Windsor Castle* overture, was not over-enthusiastic about Salomon's music ('quite passable', he wrote in his notebook), and this proved Salomon's only major venture on the English playhouse stage.

After Haydn's departure, Salomon promoted one further series in 1796, another in 1801 (at which he gave the London premiere of Beethoven's Septet, op. 20), and a final series in 1808; he also led at the Italian Opera from Viotti's departure in 1798 until 1802. He continued to make the most of his connection with Haydn. With the British rights to the 12 'London' symphonies, he kept careful control over the performing material, hiring it out to the Opera Concerts and delaying publication of the orchestral parts in London; instead he published his own admirable arrangements, for piano trio and for quintet (flute, string quartet, and optional piano). And having provided Haydn with the original text on which *The Creation* was based, he certainly intended to give the first London performance in 1800. But in this he was outwitted by JOHN ASHLEY, having to resort to the lame rejoinder that he had received from Haydn himself 'particular directions on the stile and manner in which it ought to be executed'. Salomon's performance took place in the concert room of the King's Theatre on 21 April, with Mara as principal soprano, and Samuel Wesley at the organ.

Salomon increasingly preferred private concerts to the public stage, and in his later years he maintained the persona of a cultivated gentleman, keeping a wide circle of distinguished friends and attending a musical club that included William Shield, Clementi, and the playwright Thomas Holcroft (1745–1809). He was a successful teacher who encouraged young talent (a notable pupil was the prodigy George Frederick Pinto, 1786–1806). In 1813 he was one of the founder members of the Philharmonic Society and was honoured with the distinction of leading their first concert on 8 March. Two years later he died after a long illness following a riding accident; he was buried in the south cloister of Westminster abbey. His death prompted a brief but eloquent tribute from Beethoven in a letter of 28 February 1816 to Ferdinand Ries: 'I am greatly distressed at the death of Salomon, for he was a noble-minded man, whom I well remember since my childhood.' SMcV

A. Peter Brown, 'Musical Settings of Anne Hunter's Poetry: From National Song to Canzonetta', *Journal of the American Musicological Society*, 47 (1994), 39–89.

C. Hogwood, 'In Praise of Arrangements: The "Symphony Quintetto"', in O. Biba and D. W. Jones (eds), *Studies in Music History Presented to H. C. Robbins Landon on his Seventieth Birthday* (London, 1996), 82–114.

HCRL/3.

S. McVeigh, *Concert Life in London from Mozart to Haydn* (Cambridge, 1993).

C. Papendiek, *Court and Private Life in the Time of Queen Charlotte* (London, 1887).

A. Tyson, 'Salomon's Will', *Studien der Musikgeschichte des Rheinlandes*, 3 (1965), 43–5.

'Salomon' symphonies. Name occasionally used to identify Symphonies nos. 93–104 because of their association with the violinist and impresario JOHANN PETER SALOMON. They are more frequently referred to as the 'London' symphonies. 'Salomon' symphony is very occasionally encountered as a nickname for no. 104. JH

Salve regina. Settings of the Salve regina, a prayer to the Virgin Mary, are numerous in Catholic Austria in the 18th century. MICHAEL HAYDN composed 17, REUTTER 19, and WERNER at least 44. Joseph Haydn set the text on two occasions. The first Salve regina (Hob.XXIIIb:1) is in the unusual key of E major, always an emotive one for the composer, and was probably written in 1756. Rather unusually for a work from this earliest period Haydn kept the autograph manuscript, adding the date of composition in the 1790s; it has been suggested that it was written for a service in 1756 at which his first love, THERESE KELLER, took the veil, though there is no evidence for this. But there is no doubt about the quality of the work, beautifully crafted and evocative, and certainly his first composition of stature. As well as revealing an acquaintance with the standard responses to the text, the Salve regina in E reveals in its writing for solo soprano a sure command of several Italianate tricks of the trade picked up during Haydn's association with PORPORA: the *messa di voce* beginning (a long held note) to draw attention to 'Salve' (Hail), the affecting rests in the middle of phrases, and the agile decoration. As in many contemporary settings, the work is scored for soprano soloist, chorus, and a small orchestra, in this case two violins and continuo. The alternation throughout of elaborate writing for the soloist and more homophonic writing for the choir is highly effective. It is the chorus that ends the work with a quiet, contemplative plagal cadence on the word 'Maria'.

Haydn's second setting of the text dates from 1771 and is in G minor (Hob.XXIIIb:2). Given the date of composition and the minor-key, commentators have sometimes inappropriately associated the work with the so-called *Sturm und Drang* symphonies of the period. In fact, minor key settings of the text are quite common, including two in G minor by Reutter. More unusual is Haydn's explicit remark on the autograph score that the work is for a quartet of singers not a chorus: 'Salve Regina a quattro voci ma Soli'. The vocal forces available for the church services at the palace in Eisenstadt had been allowed to fall to the bare minimum of four singers and Haydn made a virtue out of necessity; later in the century, the vocal parts were divided into solo and tutti by an unknown musician, disturbing the subdued melancholy of the work.

Texturally, the work is bound together by a concertante part for organ, supported by two violins, viola, and bass.

Whereas in the E major setting the six verses of the text were reshaped into five musical movements, in the G minor setting they are condensed into a more focused three-movement structure, one that skilfully elides one movement into the next: an Adagio that moves from G minor to E♭; an Allegro in C minor; and, finally, an accompanied recitative (beginning with a diminished seventh) that moves towards an Allegretto in G minor. Many of the features of the word-painting are replicated from the earlier setting but, here, the more rhetorical harmonic gesture that accompanies the initial exclamation 'Salve' (an augmented sixth moving to the dominant, that is an end of a musical phrase rather than a beginning) resurfaces several times during the work. As in the first Salve regina the work concludes with a contemplative cadence, here in the previously unheard key of G major.

Twenty years after the composition of the Salve regina in G minor Haydn told the Moravian minister CHRISTIAN IGNATIUS LATROBE that he had once been very ill ('seized with a violent disorder') and had vowed to compose a work of thanks 'in honour of the blessed Virgin' on recovery. Latrobe's written account of this conversation identifies the work as the Stabat mater, composed in 1767. Since Haydn is known to have been ill in 1770–1 rather than 1767, the work in question must have been the Salve regina in G minor.

B. MacIntyre, 'Wiener Salve-Regina-Vertongungen und Haydn', *HS* 6/4 (1994), 261–77.

J. Webster, 'Haydn's Sacred Vocal Music and the Aesthetics of Salvation', in W. D. Sutcliffe (ed.), *Haydn Studies* (Cambridge, 1998), 35–69.

Sammartini, Giovanni Battista (b. 1700/1; d. 15 Jan. 1775). Italian composer who spent his entire career in Milan, writing over 70 symphonies (68 are extant), many string quintets, quartets, and other kinds of chamber music, three operas, and a considerable amount of sacred music. In his *Le Haydine* CARPANI recalled that the Bohemian composer Mysliveček (1737–81), on hearing the performance of a symphony by Sammartini around 1780, exclaimed: 'I have found the father of Haydn's style.' Haydn acknowledged to GRIESINGER that he knew some of Sammartini's music, but that he did not value it: 'Sammartini was a scribbler [Schmierer].' He further denied the influence of Sammartini's music on the formation of his own style: 'He laughed heartily when I came out with Mysliveček's supposed discovery, and said he recognized only Emanuel Bach [C. P. E. BACH] as his prototype.' JAR

Sandberger, Adolf (b. 19 Dec. 1864; d. 14 Jan. 1943). An influential German musicologist who taught at the University of Munich from 1900 to 1930. He wrote on a wide variety of subjects including Haydn. His essay on Haydn quartets, published in 1900, influenced the perception of these works for the following century and laid the foundation of some of the characteristics associated with the term 'Classical style'. Sandberger viewed Haydn's op. 33 quartets from 1781 as a decisive point in the history of music, in which the composer realized the full potential of the Classical style with his powers of thematic development ('THEMATISCHE ARBEIT'). His view was based on Haydn's own assertion that op. 33 were composed 'in a new and special way'. Coupled with the fact that in the same year, 1781, Mozart moved to Vienna, this interpretation led naturally to the view that the Classical style had truly begun in that year, and that everything composed in the immediately preceding decades was in some way a preparation for it.

Sandberger also wrote extensively about the 18th-century thematic catalogue known as the QUARTBUCH, which he believed to be a list of the repertoire at the Esterházy court; since it contained a number of unknown works attributed to Haydn, Sandberger made the sensational claim that the canon of 104 symphonies should be supplemented by a further seven–eight works. These claims and the counter-claims of the young Haydn scholar, JENS PETER LARSEN, were argued in a number of issues of the journal *Acta Musicologica* between 1935 and 1937; it encouraged Larsen to write a dissertation, *Die Haydn-Überlieferung*, which firmly established the methods and principles for judging the authenticity of Haydn's music. For his part Sandberger presented many of the 'new' works in a series entitled MÜNCHENER HAYDN RENAISSANCE. APB

J. P. Larsen and A. Sandberger, [Larsen–Sandberger controversy], *Acta Musicologica*, 7–9 (1935–7).

A. Sandberger, *Ausgewählte Aufsätze zur Musikgeschichte* (Munich, 1921).

A. Sandberger, 'Neue Haydniana: zu Haydns Repertoire in Eisenstadt und Esterhaz', *Jahrbuch der Musikbibliothek Peters*, 40 (1933), 28–37.

A. Sandberger, 'Zur Einbürgerung der Kunst Josef Haydns in Deutschland', *Neues Beethoven-Jahrbuch*, 6 (1935), 5–25.

A. Sandberger, 'Zur Geschichte des Haydnschen Streichquartetts', *Altbayerische Monatshefte* (1900), 1–24.

'sapienti pauca'. Latin expression used on two occasions by Haydn; an English equivalent would be 'a word to the wise'. At bar 150 on the autograph of the first movement of the 'Farewell' symphony the composer writes 'sapienti pauca' underneath the second-violin line. It is probably an acknowledgement of the unorthodox harmony in this and the following bar, a moment of real intensification in the music: essentially a diminished chord but with a clashing D♯ in the bass. Haydn also used the expression in the LONDON NOTEBOOK as a comment on a meal he had spent on 3 June 1792 in the company of MARA, the tenor Michael Kelly (1762–1826), the soprano Nancy Storace (1766–1817), and her brother the composer Stephen Storace (1763–96). Although the significance of the expression here is not quite clear it probably indicated approval of a convivial occasion.

E. Kerr Borthwick, 'The Latin Quotations in Haydn's London Notebooks', *Music and Letters*, 45 (1990), 505–10.

***Scena di Berenice*.** Modern title for the concert aria 'BERENICE, CHE FAI?'

Schellinger, Johann (*fl.* 1776–93). Music copyist at the Esterházy court, mainly responsible for providing material for the Italian opera house at Eszterháza. He may have worked in Vienna before joining the court in 1777 (possibly 1776). His duties as opera copyist soon became all-consuming and, not surprisingly, in 1786 he suffered a bout of illness; following a petition to the prince his medical expenses were paid by the court. He also worked as a stage prompter. With the sudden closure of the opera houses at Eszterháza in September 1790 Schellinger returned to Vienna where he seems to have continued his career as a copyist. Some symphonies by Haydn were also copied by Schellinger and his hand is to be found in the ENTWURF-KATALOG.

Bartha and Somfai.
HCRL/2.

scherzando. Part V of the BREITKOPF CATALOGUE, issued in 1765, contains a set of six 'scherzandi' by 'Sigr. Gius. Hayden'. Although the works were widely distributed in manuscript copies in Haydn's lifetime there are no surviving sources that can be related to the composer. Almost certainly the title was not Haydn's own; each work is more likely to have been termed a 'sinfonia'. However their coherence as a set of works is clear. The key scheme (as given in the Breitkopf Catalogue) of F, C, D, G, E, and A is characterized by a fifth relationship between pairs of works; they are scored for two oboes, two horns, first and second violins, and 'basso' (but not violas); every trio section uses a solo flute; all have four movements in the order fast, minuet, slow, and fast; with one exception (the trio of no. 5) the trio sections and slow movements are in the tonic minor; each of the opening movements is an energetic Allegro, mainly in 2/4 time; and the finales are Presto movements in 3/8.

The string scoring without viola, the small dimension of the works, and their clear organization as a set distinguishes them from the symphonies of the early 1760s. Nothing is known about the circumstances of their composition. It is conjectured that they date from the first years of service at the Esterházy court.

Haydn occasionally used the word *scherzando* ('playful') to qualify a tempo heading of a fast movement in 2/4 (alternatively ¢ or 6/8): keyboard sonata in E (Hob.XVI:36/ii), quartets op. 20 no. 6/i, and op. 64 no. 1/iii, symphonies nos. 42/iv, 46/iv, and the wind divertimento in E♭ (Hob.II:41/iv). It is related to Haydn's usage of the word SCHERZO.

scherzo. Up to *c.*1770 Haydn occasionally used the word scherzo ('jest') as a heading for a brisk finale in 2/4: baryton trio in D (Hob.XI:43), baryton trio in C (Hob.XI:76), keyboard sonata in F (Hob.XVI:9), wind divertimento in F (Hob.II:44), and string trio in E♭ (Hob.V:6, a 6/8 movement). The movements are in binary form and do not have an associated trio section. In the op. 33 quartets Haydn used the word in place of the expected term minuet, though all six movements have the formal and stylistic characteristics associated with the latter. Haydn never used 'scherzo' in the familiar, later sense of a brisk, one-in-a-bar movement, typically encountered between the slow movement and the finale of a 19th-century symphony. However, the minuets in four late quartets by Haydn (op. 76 no. 1, op. 77 nos. 1 and 2, and op. 103) are all marked Presto and are effectively scherzos in the familiar sense of the word.

Schiringer, Carl (d. 1802). Double bass and violone player at the Esterházy court; he also played the bassoon in the windband. He was engaged on Haydn's recommendation in March 1767 and served until the musical retinue was disbanded in September 1790. He was also a competent composer, chiefly of church music. The following music has survived: *Missa Sancti Antoni di Padua* (1787), two Advent arias, five settings of Ave regina, Te Deum (1776/77?), Regina coeli (no later than 1783), and Salve regina (1783). A church sonata and two lost symphonies complete his known output. JD

J. Dack, 'The Church Music of Karl Schiringer, Double-bass Player in the Esterházy "Kapelle" 1767–1790', *HYB* 9 (1975), 329–40.
HCRL/2.

Schmid, Ernst Fritz (b. 7 Mar. 1904; d. 20 Jan. 1960). German musicologist who published valuable essays on a variety of aspects of Haydn's life and output including studies of his early life, his relationship with C. P. E. Bach, and the music for mechanical organ. He studied at universities in Munich, Freiburg, Tübingen, and Vienna. After working as a freelance conductor and musicologist in Vienna he returned to his native town, Tübingen, as a professor in the university. After the Second World War he was based in Augsburg, becoming general editor of the *Neue Mozart Ausgabe* in 1954. His work on Haydn continued and he edited *Il ritorno di Tobia* for the *JHW*. His most impressively painstaking work was on Haydn's ancestors and musical life in Rohrau and Hainburg. Completed in 1934 as a doctoral dissertation, the methodology was inevitably tainted by its association with that practised in Nazi Germany to demonstrate purity of Aryan descent. It remains, however, a fundamental documentary resource for Haydn's childhood and background.

E. F. Schmid, *Joseph Haydn: ein Buch von Vorfahren und Heimat des Meisters* (Kassel, 1934).

Schmitt, Joseph (bap. 18 Mar. 1734: d. 28 May 1791). Composer and publisher. A Cistercian monk at Eberbach im Rheingau, he moved to Amsterdam where in 1772 or 1773 he set up his own publishing business. As well as original publications he sold many editions from other countries, including several by FORSTER of London. His publications of Haydn, while textually unimportant, did much to promote the composer's music in the Low Lands and Scandinavia. They include symphonies, quartets, keyboard sonatas, keyboard trios, and the keyboard concerto in D. Some of Schmitt's own music falsely circulated under Haydn's name.

A. Dunning, *Joseph Schmitt. Leben und Kompositionen des Eberbacher Zisterzieners und Amsterdamer Musikverlegers* (Amsterdam, 1962).

Schnerich, Alfred (b. 22 Oct. 1859; d. 29 April 1944). Austrian musicologist. After studying theology at Graz University and art history at Vienna University he worked in the library of the latter institution from 1889 to 1923. He had a particular interest in sacred music and published a number of studies of Haydn's church music. He also published two, more general books on the composer, extensively read in German-speaking countries between the two world wars: *Joseph Haydn. Leben und Wirken des grossen Meisters* (Vienna, 1921) and *Joseph Haydn und seine Sendung* (Zurich, 1922).

'Schoolmaster' symphony. Nickname for Symphony no. 55 already in circulation early in the 19th century; it is mentioned in GERBER's second lexikon of 1812–14. Its significance is not clear. The favoured explanation is that the slow insistent rhythms of the slow movement reminded a listener of the wagging finger of a schoolmaster. The ENTWURF-KATALOG contains an incipit of a lost divertimento in D (Hob.II:10) with the title 'Der Schulmeister' (The Schoolmaster); when it was entered into the HAYDN-VERZEICHNIS the title was changed to 'Der verliebte Schulmeister' (The schoolmaster in love). It is possible that the theme in the divertimento and the one in the slow movement of the symphony refer to a folksong or a song from popular theatre.

'Schöpfungsmesse' ('Creation' mass). Mass in B♭ (Hob.XXII:13) composed in 1801 and first performed on 13 September in the Bergkirche in Eisenstadt. Unusually Haydn noted on the autograph manuscript the precise date when he began work on the mass, 28 July; towards the end of August he indicated to GRIESINGER that he was rather pushed for time. Nevertheless the mass was ready for performance on Sunday, 13 September, the Feast of the Holy Name of Mary (Maria Namen), at a church service associated with the annual celebration of the nameday of PRINCESS MARIE HERMENEGILD ESTERHÁZY. Apart from one general report that mentions a banquet, a ball, and the firing of cannon, very little is known about the 1801 celebrations and the performance of Haydn's mass.

From 1800 onwards a reasonably full complement of wind instruments was available to Haydn at the Esterházy court and this mass is scored for oboes, clarinets, bassoons, horns, trumpets, timpani, strings, and organ. Only the 'Harmoniemesse' from the following year has a larger orchestra. In the section of the Credo dealing with the mystery of the Virgin Birth, the 'Et incarnatus est', Haydn had it in mind to depict the Holy Spirit in the centuries-old manner, as a dove. In music such an image was often represented by a flute. Since Haydn did not have a player at his disposal he gave the line to the organ indicating that it should be played on a flute stop, the only time in his career that the composer indicated an organ registration. According to one anecdote Haydn 'darted like a weasel' to the organ to play the part himself, much to the amusement of the performers.

The vocal forces are the customary SATB choir and four soloists (momentarily expanded to six towards the end of the Gloria). As is immediately apparent in the Adagio introduction, instruments and voices are integrated into one seamless texture: the instruments are as much vocalists declaiming the text as the singers are instrumentalists projecting a complementary musical argument. As well as unconscious manipulation of forces, Haydn shows, too, how easily his mature musical language can move between melody with accompaniment and the most intricate contrapuntal writing. The latter never sounds stolid or spuriously authoritative, the fugue at the end of the Gloria, for instance, featuring a delightfully unorthodox chromatic theme.

The nickname of the mass, 'Schöpfungsmesse', which became current in the 19th century, was prompted by one of Haydn's most incautious musical pranks. In the Gloria listeners and performers steeped in Austrian church music would have expected a change of tempo from fast to slow at either the clause 'Gratias agimus tibi' or 'Qui tollis peccata mundi'. Haydn does neither. Instead the orchestra carries blithely on in a fast tempo, quoting Adam and Eve's music from *The Creation*, music associated with the text 'The dew-dropping morn, Oh how she quickens all!'/'Der thauende Morgen, o wie ermuntert er!'; the instrumentation, including the very secular-sounding horns, is the same. In the mass the bass soloist then enters and repeats the tune with the liturgical text 'Qui tollis peccata mundi' ('Who takest away the sins of the world') before the choir in an abrupt change of tempo from allegro to adagio asks for mercy, 'Miserere nobis'. The joke is a multi-layered one: the salacious innuendo of the quotation, the sudden realization that the composer has 'forgotten' to change the tempo (Haydn's score does not have the usual double bar between the sections but moves directly from one to the other with the indication 'attacca subito'); and the mock contrition of the choir.

At least one person was offended. EMPRESS MARIE THERESE was an avid collector of the composer's music, but Haydn had to recompose this passage in her copy. The offence is mitigated rather than removed since the wrong tempo and the abrupt change at 'Misere nobis' remain; only the quotation of the theme from *The Creation* is removed.

Elsewhere in the mass Haydn adheres more closely to the conventions of word-setting, though always with striking freshness and energy. The luminous G major of the 'Et incarnatus est' section returns at the beginning of the Agnus Dei before yielding to the home key, B♭, in the 'Dona nobis pacem'; the chromaticism of the fugal theme in this final section is another unifying remembrance, this time of the end of the Gloria.

Schroeter, Rebecca (née Scott; b. 13 May 1751; d. April 1826). Amateur pianist and widow of the composer Johann Samuel Schroeter (1750–88). A young woman from a wealthy family, she had been Schroeter's pupil, later marrying him against the wishes of her family. They settled in London in 1786. Rebecca Schroeter befriended Haydn on his first visit to London in 1791 and asked him to give her lessons. Her letters to the composer, which date from 29 June 1791 to 26 June 1792, are full of solicitude and admiration, with frequent invitations to dine. It seems that Haydn returned her affection, as he confided to DIES that he would have married her had he been free to do so. Haydn's recollection that she was aged 60 was wildly inaccurate.

There are no letters from her to Haydn during his second visit, perhaps because they lived near each other. She was the dedicatee of three piano trios (Hob.XV:24–6), completed in the summer of 1795. The Adagio cantabile of the third trio is a reworking of the slow movement of Symphony no. 102, possibly a favourite of hers. In July 1796 Mrs Schroeter was a witness to a contract between the music seller Frederick Augustus Hyde and Haydn.

DdV

HCRL/3.
T. Scull, 'More Light on Haydn's "English Widow"', *Music and Letters*, 78 (1997), 45–55.

Schumann, Robert Alexander (b. 8 June 1810; d. 29 July 1856). The youngest son of a bookseller and publisher, Schumann's musical career was strongly marked by literature and writing, and his diaries attest to his daily preoccupation with both creative fields. His law studies at the universities of Leipzig and Heidelberg came to nothing, but afforded him the opportunity to develop his musical knowledge and talents, and he became a serious piano pupil of the well-known Friedrich Wieck whose daughter Clara was to become his sweetheart and, eventually, his wife. Schumann combined his love of literature and music to perfection in two forms, the small piano piece (usually programmatic) and the song. Schumann spent the last two years of his life in an asylum, where he died.

As a leading critic of music in the Romantic era, Schumann's attitude to Haydn was ambivalent and, in general, suffered from his profound admiration for Mozart. In 1841, in a review of some concerts at the Leipzig Gewandhaus, he wrote of Haydn: 'One can no longer learn anything new from him; he is like a familiar friend of the house who is always greeted with pleasure and respect, but is of no further interest for the present day.' The Turkish music in Symphony no. 100 he thought 'somewhat childish and tasteless'. He was more complimentary about the composer's quartets, perhaps recognizing that Haydn's pervasive motivicism had a parallel with his own musical thought processes; it has also been suggested that the hybrid forms that are occasionally found in Schumann's music owe something to Haydn's particular mixing of variation, ternary, and rondo forms. DC

Schwarzenberg, Prince Joseph (Johann Nepomuk Anton Carl) (b. 27 July 1769; d. 19 Dec. 1833). A notable patron of music in Vienna at the end of the 18th and the beginning of the 19th centuries. The country estate of the family at Krumau (Český Krumlov) in Bohemia and the town palace in Mehlmarkt (now Neuer Markt) in Vienna were regular venues for private concerts. As a young man Schwarzenberg became an enthusiastic member of van Swieten's GESELLSCHAFT DER ASSOCIIERTEN CAVALIERS, designed to promote concerts of oratorios during the Lenten season in Vienna. The palace in central Vienna was soon the preferred venue for its concerts, including the first performance of the oratorio version of *The Seven Last Words* in 1796, *The Creation* in 1798, and *The Seasons* in 1799. While van Swieten busied himself with the artistic side of the ventures, Schwarzenberg, by now a successful banker, assumed the role of business manager. As a member of van Swieten's consortium he paid his due share of the costs, but in addition made several ad hoc additional payments to Haydn and seems to have taken on the responsibility for arranging and paying for sentries-cum-policemen to guard the palace on concert evenings and compensating the flour traders in the market for the inconvenience caused by the habitually large crowds that attended the public rehearsals and performances. Not surprisingly, he ordered six copies of the first edition of *The Creation*. After van Swieten's death in 1803, Schwarzenberg remained active as a patron of music, playing a leading part in the consortium of noblemen that ran the court theatres from 1807 to 1811.

The Schwarzenberg town palace in Vienna was demolished in 1894 but the summer palace in Český Krumlov, including the 18th-century theatre with all its stage apparatus, has survived and is open to the public. The large family archives in the palace contain a substantial quantity of manuscript copies of Haydn's music.

G. Croll, 'Mitteilungen über die "Schöpfung" und die "Jahreszeiten" aus dem Schwarzenberg-Archiv', *HS* 3/2 (1974), 85–92.

HCRL/4 and 5.

Scott, Marion (Margaret) (b. 16 July 1877; d. 24 Dec. 1953). English violinist and writer on music. She studied the violin at the Royal College of Music and for many years was a professional player, turning to musicology in her 50s. She developed a particular interest in Haydn's quartets and in unearthing material about the composer's visits to London. She drew attention to a 'lost' early quartet in E♭ (Hob.II:6) by Haydn and issued an edition of the work in 1931. Her studies of Haydn were to have led to a book on the composer but only three chapters were completed by the time of her death. She was the author of the well-regarded volume on Beethoven in the 'Master Musicians' series.

Seasons, The (*Die Jahreszeiten*) (Hob.XXI:3). Oratorio by Haydn, words by GOTTFRIED VAN SWIETEN after JAMES THOMSON; composed 1799–1801, and first performed in Vienna on 23 and 24 April 1801.

Its origins were similar to those of *The Creation*, whose spectacular success in 1798 inspired van Swieten to seek another oratorio for his group of sponsors, the GESELLSCHAFT DER ASSOCIIERTEN, and persuaded Haydn, despite some misgivings, to persevere with the project. Its text was again the responsibility of van Swieten, following an English model, but the manner of its working out was substantially different. In *The Creation* van Swieten's model was already an oratorio libretto, around which he could hang his German words, leaving the original largely intact as the English version of Haydn's bilingual oratorio. James Thomson's huge epic poem, in grandiloquent blank verse, could not be handled in the same way; for reasons of style as well as of scale, van Swieten had much to do to shape it into an oratorio. Once again the work was designed for an international audience, except that this time, even more ambitiously, the score was published in two alternative versions, with not only German/English words but also German/French. As in *The Creation*, the wording of the original model sometimes survives in the English text of the bilingual score, but this is relatively rare. Even when Thomson's images were retained, they required abbreviation and adaptation to such an extent that usually no more than faint echoes of them can be discerned, and the libretto often loses all touch with the poem which was its starting point. Increasingly during the course of the oratorio, the words are essentially van Swieten's own or even imported from foreign sources. For the English text he consequently had himself to provide a re-translation, with often grotesque results. If today performances of *The Creation* in English-speaking countries should be given in English, as Haydn intended, *The Seasons* is better served by the decent obscurity of a foreign language than by the English of its first edition.

This would have been of little concern to Haydn, who naturally worked from the German libretto, which, if undistinguished as verse, at least makes sense on its own terms. But he was often unhappy about its content. He was feeling his age and found it particularly difficult to rouse himself to compose music in praise of such an abstract concept as industry (in the sense of industriousness). The subject matter is often undeniably prosaic, and it obviously lacks the grand purpose of *The Creation*: as Haydn himself put it, 'In *The Creation* angels speak and tell of God, but in *The Seasons* it is only Simon speaking.' The three peasant characters, Hanne/Jane (soprano) and Lucas (tenor) as well as Simon (bass—as in *The Creation*, there is no alto soloist), have no true identity except in the duet between Jane and Lucas in 'Autumn' (no. 22), which is the only occasion on which any of them speaks to another as a person. There is little dramatic or narrative coherence between or even within the four seasons. But if this results in a work that is more in the nature of a series of cantatas than a continuous oratorio, it did provide a succession of tableaux which Haydn brought to life with characteristic vividness, and, for a man approaching 70, extraordinarily youthful freshness.

The oratorio opens with an orchestral introduction depicting 'the passage of winter to spring', which, except for its elision into Simon's recitative, amounts to Haydn's last great purely symphonic movement, but it stands apart from the sonority of any of the symphonies proper in its use of trombones, whose tone colour is vital to much of *The Seasons*. The ensuing chorus is one of the few passages explicitly to reveal its origins, quoting directly Thomson's opening line, 'Come, gentle spring, ethereal mildness, come'. The general lack of dramatic tension may be reflected here, as in other movements, in the ternary outline of the tonal scheme, the first main section remaining stably in the tonic rather than rising to the dominant. The ploughman too, in no. 4, cheerfully whistling the Andante theme of Haydn's 'Surprise' symphony, works contentedly within the home key, digressing only as far as the tonic minor and closely related tonalities, and the same is true of the serene 'Sei nun gnädig' (Be gracious) (no. 6), the first of the solo and choral complexes, until the concluding fugue introduces a wider range. Elsewhere, however, there is the greatest tonal boldness. The 'Song of joy, with alternating chorus of girls and lads' (no. 8) that closes 'Spring', having begun in A major, reaches a quiet close on D before the dramatic tutti interruption of B♭ for the 'Ewiger Gott' (Endless God) of the chorus, and the movement remains there, ending a semitone higher than its opening. This is an instance where Haydn's treatment corresponds closely to the suggestions as to musical effects that van Swieten provided in the margins of his libretto of *The Seasons*, as he had in *The Creation*. One may already suspect van Swieten's liking for the picturesque earlier in the movement, at the graphic depiction of, for example, 'lambkins', fish, the bees, and the birds; now he noted: 'a key strikingly different from that of the preceding Song of Joy would create a good effect and would greatly enhance the solemn and devotional nature of the [choir's] cry.'

As in Thomson's poem, 'Summer' follows the course of a single summer's day, beginning with cock-crow and dawn (Simon's awakening horn calls clearly inhabit the same F major part of the country as Beethoven's *Pastoral Symphony*, only some seven years away) and leading to an almost pantheistic hymn to the sun. Jane finds shady refreshment from the torpid noonday heat in an aria, 'Welche Labung für die Sinne' (How refreshing for the senses) (no. 15), in which time stands still, but thunder, pizzicato raindrops, and forked lightning from the flute (essentially the same as had occurred 40 years before in the 'La tempesta' finale to Symphony no. 8, 'Le Soir') introduce the thunderstorm. The two remaining numbers together make up one of Haydn's great scene complexes. The C major close of no. 17 does not truly dispel the violence of the C minor storm but acts as a dominant up-beat to the tranquil F major of the evening. The country scenes described by the soloists are illustrated by the orchestra: the lowing cattle, the quail, the cricket, and, notoriously, the croaking frog, in respect of which van Swieten's insistence on the picturesque provoked from Haydn the angry protest, 'This Frenchified trash was forced upon me'. The key sinks soporifically from F to end in E♭, and the women's voices innocently accept the men's invitation to follow them to bed.

'Autumn' combines dutiful solemnity and exuberance. It begins with 'the husbandman's satisfaction at the abundant harvest', leading to the Thomsonian hymn to industry (no. 20), whose moralizing tone Haydn found so uninspiring but which he turned into a fine solo and choral movement. Once the harvest festival thanksgiving is over, everyone can relax. The duet between Lucas and Jane (no. 22) could be a parody of Rousseau in its preference for the 'daughters of Nature' over the painted ladies of the town, and it closes with sentiments that seem to echo *Die Zauberflöte*: 'Lieben und geliebet werden ist der Freude höchster Gipfel, ist des Lebens Wonn' und Glück' (To love and be loved is the highest peak of joy, life's rapture and felicity). The two remaining scenes are perhaps the most vivid of any in *The Seasons*. Both the hunt and the drinking festivities have their origins in Thomson, but they are transformed by their transference to the Austrian countryside. The English poem has nothing of van Swieten's and Haydn's gleeful relish for blood sports. Shooting is depicted with detailed realism, the bird scented by the gundog, put to flight, and brought down with a single shot. After frantic attempts at escape, hare-coursing is soon over, to give place without a break to the baying of four horns in unison for the extended stag hunt, rising from D to E♭ in the excitement of the chase. Only a short recitative separates this from the celebration of the wine harvest, a chorus of cheerful intoxication instead of Thomson's puritanical portrayal of sordid drunkenness. The scene develops into a village barn dance to pipe and drum, fiddle, and bagpipe, and culminates in what Haydn himself called his 'sozzled fugue'. In one of his most brilliantly imaginative inventions the fugue is played out in the orchestra, while the chorus, too inebriated to follow its syncopated counterpoint, can only interject disjointed snatches until they find a simpler, homophonic version in which they can all lustily join.

The 'thick fogs' of the 'pale declining year' begin 'Winter' in sombre mood, and the overall message of the final season is allegorical and serious. Yet when the traveller, lost in the snow, eventually finds a safe haven, he is greeted by a convivial scene in which the assembled company entertain themselves with a spinning song and a narrative ballad. Both of these numbers are interpolations into the general scheme of the text. The spinning song, no. 34 (in the same D minor and sharing similar figuration with Schubert's 'Gretchen am Spinnrade' of 1814), is to words by Gottfried August Bürger. The immediate derivation of Jane's pert 'Ein Mädchen, das auf Ehre hielt' (A lass who guarded her honour) (no. 36) was a *Singspiel* song, translated by Christian Felix Weisse from the French original by Mme Favart, from Johann Adam Hiller's *Die Liebe auf dem Lande* (1768); but the *opéra comique* from which it was taken, *Annette et Lubin*, had been arranged in German by Johann Joachim Eschenburg as *Lukas und Hannchen*, curiously prefiguring the names of Haydn's tenor and soprano soloists. At this point Simon's fine aria 'Erblicke hier, betörte Mensch' (Look on this, deluded man) (no. 38) dispels the atmosphere of frivolity; the year becomes an allegory of life, and winter of man's old age. The first section of the final trio and chorus is a moving catechism whose Masonic flavour is again reminiscent of *Die Zauberflöte*: 'Wer darf durch diese Pforten gehn? Der Arges mied und Gutes tat' (Who may pass through these gates? He who eschewed evil and did good). The closing fugue might have served as the motto for Haydn's increasingly enfeebled later years: 'Uns leite deine Hand, o Gott! Verleih' uns Stärk' und Muth' (May your hand lead us, God. Grant us strength and courage).

In circumstances identical to those of *The Creation* before it, *The Seasons* was promoted by van Swieten's group of sponsors. Its first performances, again at the town house of Prince Joseph Schwarzenberg, took place in an open rehearsal on 23 April 1801 and the gala premiere the following day; further private performances followed. More quickly than *The Creation*, it was released for public performance by the Tonkünstler-Societät at their two December concerts in 1801, and the published score appeared in May 1802, scarcely a year after the first performance. It was generally well received, but negative criticism was soon to be heard. COUNT KARL VON ZINZENDORF, an invaluable observer of the social scene but musically insensitive, remarked laconically in his diary, having listed the various episodes that caught his attention, 'Cela est long'. The high-minded were condescending, to a greater extent than they had been in the case of *The Creation*, about the oratorio's delightful use of colourful depiction (a patronizing attitude that was surely the cause of Beethoven's defensiveness about his *Pastoral Symphony*). Gradually emerging stories of Haydn's own dissatisfaction at some aspects of the text and even of its musical treatment added to growing misgivings, and the oratorio has never established itself to match the perennial success of *The Creation*. DEO

H. C. Robbins Landon (ed.), *The Creation and the Seasons: The Complete Authentic Sources for the Word-Books* (Cardiff, 1985).
HCRL/5.

'Seitenstetten' minuets. Nickname arising in modern times to identify the first set of minuets by Haydn to have survived, Hob.IX:1; the autograph manuscript is owned by the Benedictine abbey of Seitenstetten in Lower Austria. JH

'Serenade' quartet. Nickname for the quartet in F, op. 3 no. 5 (Hob.III:17), formerly attributed to Haydn. It refers to the slow movement, which has often been played alone and as a piece for string orchestra. HOFSTETTER is the likely composer.

Seven Last Words of our Saviour on the Cross, The. A penitential work that exists in two versions: the original orchestral version composed in 1786 (Hob.XX/1), and a choral version composed in 1795–6 (Hob.XX/2). In addition Haydn prepared an arrangement of the orchestral version for quartet (Hob.III:50–6), published by Artaria in 1787, and sanctioned a keyboard arrangement by an unknown musician, again published by Artaria in 1787.

The work was the product of a distinctive Spanish tradition of sacred music and reflected the esteem in which Haydn was held in that country in the 1780s. The Stabat mater, in particular, was widely distributed in Spain and the locus of that work, the foot of the cross, as well as its masterly evocation of contemplation across thirteen, mainly slow movements may well have encouraged the commissioning of *The Seven Last Words* from Haydn. A full account of the origins of the work is given by Griesinger, Haydn's earliest biographer, which must reflect details of the circumstances of performance forwarded to the composer at the time of the original commission.

> A canon in Cadiz [on the southern coast of Spain] requested Haydn, about the year 1785, to make an instrumental composition of the Seven Words of Jesus on the Cross which was to be suited to a solemn ceremony that took place annually during Lent in the cathedral [actually the grotto of Santa Cueva] at Cadiz. On the appointed day the walls, windows, and piers of the church were draped with black, and only a single lamp of good size, hanging in the middle, illuminated the sacred darkness. At an appointed hour all doors were locked, and the music began. After a suitable prelude the bishop mounted the pulpit, pronounced one of the Seven Words, and delivered a meditation upon

> it. As soon as it was ended, he descended from the pulpit and knelt down before the altar. The music filled in this pause. The bishop entered the pulpit a second, a third time, and so on, and each time the orchestra came in again at the end of the oration.
>
> It was indeed one of the most difficult tasks to make out of thin air, with no text, seven adagios following one another that would not weary the listener but would stir all the feelings inherent in each of the Words uttered by the dying Saviour. Haydn many times declared this work to be one of his most successful.

Apart from a meditation on each of the seven words, called sonatas, Haydn provided an introduction (*Introduzione*: Maestoso ed Adagio) in D minor and, to conclude, *Il terremoto*, a depiction of the earthquake that convulsed Calvary according to the Gospel of St Matthew (28: 2). Haydn's task of encouraging contemplation and veneration in a way that would not, as Griesinger put it, 'weary the listener' was a supremely challenging one. Though *The Seven Last Words* does not have a text, the 'Words' themselves (taken variously from the gospels of Matthew, Luke, and John) are strongly suggested in the music, in that each opening theme is a musical realization of the rhythms of the spoken Latin. When the music was published by Artaria, Haydn went to great pains to ensure that the text was underlaid correctly in the first violin part; for the listener the association registers subliminally in the main, more consciously in the fifth and sixth sonatas, 'Sitio' ('I thirst') and 'Consummatum est' ('It is finished'). These 'leitmotifs' occur through the course of each respective slow movement.

The musical language of the work has a resourcefulness not previously encountered in large-scale compositions by Haydn, sacred or secular, and was not to be surpassed until the late masses and oratorios. Rather like the Stabat mater, the work alternates minor and major throughout: D minor, B♭, C minor, E, F minor, A, G minor, E♭, and C minor. The power and anguish of Calvary are evoked by the many passages of diatonic harmony, routine accompaniment, and easy cantabile. There is some telling graphic detail too: the pizzicato accompaniment in the fifth sonata to suggest Christ's thirst, the final moments of life at the end of the seventh sonata, and the concluding earthquake, the only fast music in the work, marked to be played 'Presto con tutta la forza' and, in the last few bars, an unprecedented *fff*. It is in this movement that the power of the orchestra of flute, two oboes, two bassoons, two horns, two trumpets, timpani, and strings is most keenly felt; elsewhere there is an equally unprecedented variety of orchestral colour and density, with four horns, rather than two, being used in the second and fourth sonatas. The whole is a masterly aural equivalent to the paintings and sculpture of rococo churches throughout Catholic Europe, inducing penitence and peace of mind in equal measure.

The orchestral version was published in London and Paris, as well as Vienna, and manuscript copies were found all over Europe, the work becoming as well known as any symphony by the composer. It was perhaps inevitable that such an articulated musical text should encourage someone to add a verbal one, making apparent that which registers subconsciously. Late in August 1795, on his return journey from London, Haydn spent the evening in Passau, a town on the Danube, where he heard a vocal version of his work. It had been prepared by Joseph Friebert, Kapellmeister to the local prince-archbishop, Count Franz Anton Auersperg. According to the later testimony of NEUKOMM Haydn was pleased with the performance but felt that the arrangement could have been better done. Friebert was probably the author of the German text which amplifies the sentiment of the Latin headings of the original; for *Il terremoto* (the Italian title was retained) the text was taken from the cantata text 'Der Tod Jesu' written in 1756 by Karl Wilhelm Ramler (1725–98), well known from the setting by Carl Heinrich Graun (1703/4–59). Back in Vienna Haydn found a natural ally in van Swieten who was anxious to include a work by the composer in the Lenten concerts presented by the GESELLSCHAFT DER ASSOCIIERTEN CAVALIERS. Van Swieten edited the text while Haydn set about improving Friebert's musical work. The adaptation was ready by early 1796 and was first performed on 26 March at the Schwarzenberg palace under the aegis of the Gesellschaft. It soon became a favoured Lenten oratorio in Vienna and following its publication by Breitkopf & Härtel in 1801 began to usurp the position of the original version in performances throughout Europe. Orchestral music of the 19th and 20th centuries was not notable for religious subject matter, even though Haydn's work fulfilled many of the reiterated criteria of the symphonic poem and was a telling demonstration of an abiding concern of many writers in the 19th century, the superior power of instrumental music over vocal music; the vocal version, however, found a natural home in the rich oratorio tradition.

As well as making the content of the work a more literal one, the choral writing, with its many passages of syllabic delivery (and little counterpoint), undermines the rapt mood of the original. The text required Friebert and Haydn occasionally to alter the profile of the violin line in order to make it comfortable for sopranos, to add up-beats to the melody of the fifth word (the heading 'sonata' is not used in the vocal version), and to provide long note values in the previously busy texture of *Il terremoto*. The orchestration is adjusted a little: only two horns are needed, clarinets are added to most movements, and two trombones are used to double the alto and tenor lines in *forte* passages. In order to affirm the importance of the choir and to relate the work to sonorities frequently heard in church services during Lent in Vienna, Haydn precedes six of the movements with short, four-part a cappella introductions declaiming, in German, the title of each movement. Before the fifth word, 'I thirst', Haydn provides a new movement, again in a slow tempo: a chilling *Introduzione* in A minor scored for wind instruments only. To add extra depth to the sonority of this movement Haydn requires a contrabassoon.

Seyfried, Ignaz von (b. 15 Aug. 1776; d. 27 Aug. 1841). A leading composer of theatre and church music in Vienna in the early decades of the 19th century. After studying with Mozart, Kozeluch, and Hayda he became Kapellmeister at the Freyhaustheater in 1797, the beginning of a long life of composition of German operas, both complete works and arrangements of existing music by other composers, including Dittersdorf, Haydn, Mozart, and Salieri. In 1799 he sent Haydn a complimentary ticket to attend *Der Wundermann am Rheinfalle*; following the performance Haydn sent Seyfried a letter of congratulations and thanks, now lost. In 1800 Seyfried was a subscriber to the printed edition of *The Creation*. His most popular stage work was *Das Ochsenmenuett*, based on a spurious incident in Haydn's life and illustrated by arrangements of his music. From 1822 onwards Seyfried's life was marred by bouts of illness. Most of his church music dates from this time onwards; as well as original works it includes some arrangements and reorchestrations of liturgical works by Haydn. A rather bizarre arrangement of 'Gott erhalte Franz den Kaiser' for choir and orchestra begins in the minor key before moving, triumphantly, to the major. *See* OCHSENMENUETT.

B. von Seyfried, *Ignaz Ritter von Seyfried. Thematisch-Bibliographisches Verzeichnis. Aspekte der Biographie und des Werkes* (Frankfurt, 1990).

Shield, William (b. 5 March 1748; d. 25 Jan. 1829). English composer with whom Haydn was on friendly terms in London. Haydn attended a performance of his stage work, *The Woodman*, at Covent Garden in 1791 and both provided settings for Tattersall's *English Psalmody*. They shared an admiration for the music of Handel and when Haydn gave Shield a copy of his oratorio *Il ritorno di Tobia*, Shield reciprocated with a score of Handel's *Jephtha*, which remained in the composer's library. According to Shield Haydn was particularly taken with the harmony of the accompanied recitative 'Deeper and deeper still'.

HCRL/3.

Sieber, Jean-Georges (b. 2 Feb. 1738; d. 13 Jan. 1822). French music publisher who issued substantial quantities of instrumental music by Haydn, especially keyboard trios, quartets, and symphonies. The business was essentially founded in 1771 and it continued until Sieber's death just over 50 years later. As a young man Sieber played the horn, the trombone, and the harp and was a member of the Concert spirituel orchestra, enabling him to develop an ad hoc relationship between the repertoire of the concerts and his activities as a publisher. In addition to many Haydn symphonies, Sieber published the Stabat mater in 1785, reflecting and promoting the extraordinary popularity of the work in Paris. Later, he published the orchestral and quartet versions of *The Seven Last Words* and the *opéra comique* version of *La vera costanza*, entitled LAURETTE. Three extant letters from Haydn written in 1789 show that he had entrusted the violinist TOST with negotiating the sale of two symphonies and the op. 54 and op. 55 quartets. Symphonies nos. 88 and 89 joined Sieber's successful serial publication of symphonies by various composers, *Simphonie périodique*, as nos. 29 and 28 respectively; the quartets were also published.

A. Devriès, 'Les Editions musicales Sieber', *Revue de Musicologie*, 55 (1969), 20–46.

Silverstolpe, Fredrik Samuel (b. 1769; d. 1851). Swedish diplomat whose correspondence and reminiscences of Haydn provide a valuable picture of the composer at the time of the composition of *The Creation* and *The Seasons*. From a gifted and musical family, Silverstolpe's career as a diplomat took him to Vienna as chargé d'affaires from 1796 to 1803. He soon immersed himself in the musical life of the city, meeting Constanze Mozart (with whom he apparently played billiards), Schwarzenberg, van Swieten, and leading composers such as Albrechtsberger, Beethoven, Kozeluch (Koželuh), and Salieri. He visited Haydn several times in Gumpendorf, his letters containing details about the composition (and later, performances) of *The Creation* and *The Seasons* and their mutual admiration for the music of JOSEPH MARTIN KRAUS amongst many other topics. Silverstolpe was instrumental in making Haydn an honorary member of the Royal Swedish Academy of Music in 1799 and translated the libretto of *The Creation* into Swedish.

HCRL/4 and 5.

C.-G. Stellan Mörner, 'Haydniana aus Schweden um 1800', *HS* 2/1 (1969), 1–33.

Smart, George (b. 10 May 1776; d. 23 Feb. 1867). Conductor, organist, and composer. Haydn and Smart met in 1794 when Haydn was directing an orchestral rehearsal. As the timpanist was absent Smart, who was only 17 and normally a violinist and violist, volunteered his services. Haydn, noting his lack of technique, demonstrated the correct use of the drum stick, using an oblique stroke. Smart apparently never attempted to play timpani again, but wrote affectionately of Haydn's 'lesson'. A quarter of a century later Smart became a leading champion of Beethoven's music in London. DdV

HCRL/3.

'Solo e pensoso'. Concert aria for soprano and orchestra (Hob.XXIVb:20), composed in 1796 and first performed on 22 December at one of the biannual concerts of the Tonkünstler-Societät held in the Burgtheater in Vienna. The aria has an unusual text for this kind of work, Petrarch's 28th sonnet, one of many inspired by his love for Laura; it was apparently suggested, if not requested, by an unidentifiable Russian prince resident in Vienna. Haydn's aria is the customary rondò, a two-stage design, Adagio and Allegretto, the change of tempo occurring at the end of the octave of Petrarch's sonnet. The poem is a dignified picture of a lonely figure 'bereft of joy' but inwardly aflame and who finds solace in solitude. Although the sonnet concludes in resolution, Haydn's ebullient, conventionally operatic ending is rather at odds with the deep personal mood of the words. The setting is accompanied by a small orchestra of clarinets, bassoons, horns, and strings.

sonata form. One of the enduring misconceptions about Haydn the composer is that he 'followed established forms'—like sonata form—more or less strictly, in contrast to Beethoven, who 'broke the rules'. Anyone who makes such a statement does not know very much about either sonata form or Haydn's music (or, for that matter, Beethoven's). The framework of sonata form is extremely flexible, and Haydn manipulated the basic elements of the form with astonishing ingenuity throughout his career as a composer. There were no 'rules' of sonata form in the 18th century, only conventions, and Haydn was a master at following these conventions even while violating them, usually to great effect.

The term sonata form refers to the structure of an individual movement, not to the structure of a multi-movement sonata as a whole. Sonata form is by far the most important movement-length formal convention of the Classical period, and it figures in a great variety of genres (principally instrumental genres such as sonatas, symphonies, quartets, and trios, but also in operas and masses), and in movement types (first movements, slow movements, finales, and to some extent even minuets).

Sonata form is in some respects bipartite and in some respects tripartite. The form is bipartite in that it falls into two distinct reprises, usually marked by repeat signs. This two-reprise structure reflects the historical origins of sonata form in the binary movements that were so prevalent in dance music of the 18th century. In the tradition of these dances, the first reprise of an 18th-century sonata-form movement typically moves from the tonic to the dominant (I to V) if the movement is in the major mode, or from the tonic to relative major (i to III) if the movement is in the minor mode. The second reprise, in turn, usually begins away from the opening key but brings the music back to the tonic by its end.

Sonata form can also be viewed as a tripartite structure. The first of its three sections—the exposition—is congruent with the first reprise of binary form. The function of the exposition is to 'expose' the principal tonalities and thematic ideas of the movement. The second section, known as the development, occupies the first portion of the second reprise. Its purpose is to take the music through various keys other than the tonic and to manipulate the themes that were introduced in the exposition. In the development section, themes are often fragmented, extended, or combined, and the order of their appearance is in no way predictable. Only rarely is there an entirely new thematic idea here.

The third section of a sonata-form movement, occupying the second portion of the second reprise, is known as the recapitulation. Its purpose is to establish a strong sense of harmonic stability and closure, and to reiterate the thematic ideas of the exposition. The return to the tonic at the beginning of the recapitulation is usually reinforced by a simultaneous return to the opening theme. This simultaneous double return—both harmonic and thematic—provides an important signpost to the listener, signalling an end to the instability of the development and a return to the familiar. The sequence of ideas presented in the recapitulation follows more or less the course of the exposition, with the important difference that the material heard outside the tonic in the exposition is now transposed to the tonic; thus, a theme or group of themes presented in the dominant or relative major in the exposition will now be heard in the tonic. Occasionally, the recapitulation is followed by another section, a coda (from the Italian word for tail), which functions as a brief closing section.

Schematically, the basic outline of sonata form can be represented as shown in the figure opposite.

The hypothetical sonata-form movement outlined here sets out two different themes in the tonic (1 and 2), another theme within the modulatory transition from the tonic to the secondary key area (3), and two themes in the new, secondary key area (4 and 5). The development begins with the transition theme (3), but in a new key, and goes on to manipulate other themes in keys that are relatively

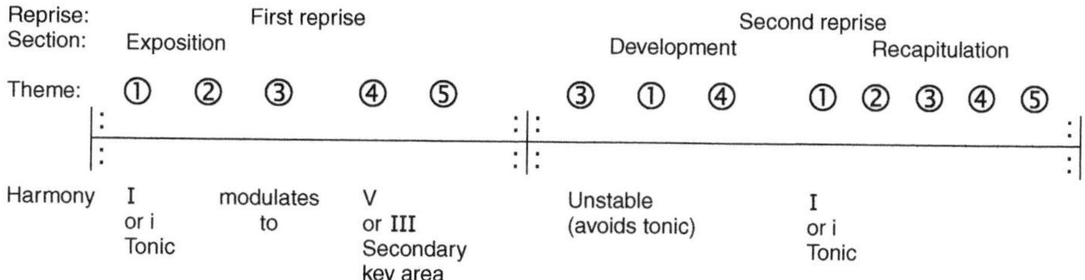

remote from the tonic. In the recapitulation, all the themes of the exposition are heard once again and in their original order; but this time, the music does not modulate, remaining instead in the tonic. The absence of a modulation, after all, is what distinguishes a recapitulation from an exposition; thematically they are identical, at least in theory.

But only in theory. In practice, no two manifestations of sonata form are entirely alike. The only constant elements are the modulation from a primary to a secondary key area in the exposition; a departure from these harmonic areas in the development; and a return to the primary key area in the recapitulation. The thematic content of the various sections can be extremely flexible.

Within this basic outline, Haydn's sonata-form movements invariably exhibit idiosyncratic elements of rhythm, harmony, thematic design, or structure. (The inquisitive listener will frequently be reminded of Haydn's celebrated remark to GRIESINGER that in his isolation at Eszterháza, with an excellent orchestra at his disposal and no one to pester him, he was 'forced to become original'.)

Indeed, the very terms exposition, development, and recapitulation are to a certain extent misleading, for in a very real sense, Haydn's sonata-form movements develop ideas in every section, including even the exposition. In the first movement of the string quartet in E♭, op. 33 no. 2 ('Joke'), for example, the opening statement of the first theme is followed not by its repetition (as one might well expect at this early point in the movement), but rather by a developmental passage that begins to elaborate a small fragment of the theme, the two-semiquaver figure derived from the up-beat to bar one. This unexpectedly early elaboration of an unlikely motif is a portent of things to come, for the up-beat figure will in fact play a central role throughout the entire movement.

The exposition of this particular work provides other useful examples of how Haydn plays with our expectations of sonata form. Having heard the opening theme twice, and with a cadence on the tonic in bar 12, there is every reason to expect that the modulatory transition beginning in bar 13 will move directly to the dominant. The extended pedal point on F in the cello reinforces this expectation, and sure enough, B♭ is reached at bar 21. In this respect, Haydn is following the conventions of sonata form quite predictably. But the sense of having truly arrived in the new key area at bar 21 turns out to be highly tenuous: the urgency of the rhythm and the lack of any memorable theme at this point preclude a sense of true arrival in the new (secondary) key area. Although nominally in B♭, the music sounds as if it is still in the process of moving towards that key. The figurations of the first violin in bar 21 place the music in a kind of holding pattern, and the unexpected virtuosic eruptions in bars 25–7 delay the anticipated moment of arrival still further. It is almost as if Haydn himself has forgotten both his theme and his goal. There is no real sense of having finally arrived in B♭ until the middle of bar 28—a mere five bars before the end of the exposition!

Another example of this kind of play with listeners' expectations of formal conventions can be found in the first movement of Symphony no. 102 in B♭. Here, the music modulates through a relatively long transitional section to the dominant (F major), with an emphatic cadence squarely in the new key at bar 80. All this is quite conventional: the music has moved from the tonic to the dominant. But when the music resumes in bar 81 rather than a theme in the expected new key of F there is, instead, a loud unison 'A', which in turn leads to a figure that implies D minor rather than the expected key of F major. Haydn finally delivers the anticipated tonality at bar 92 with a new theme, and in this sense, the movement conforms to the broad outlines of sonata form. But, in practice, the events are far from predictable.

Not all expositions were meant to be repeated literally. Composers of the late 18th century (including Haydn) would occasionally write out an embellished version of the entire exposition, moving from tonic to dominant once again with the same thematic ideas, but now with melodic variants, different accompaniment, altered harmonies, new orchestration, or some combination of these or still other devices. The VERÄNDERTE REPRISE ('varied reprise', the name by which it was known already in Haydn's time) might be thought of as a kind of variation on the opening exposition. Examples of this procedure are found in a number of slow movements throughout Haydn's career: in the quartets op. 9 nos. 2 and 4; op. 17 no. 4; op. 20 no. 6; and op. 33 no. 3, as well as in the late Symphony no. 102 (first section = bars 1–16; varied 'reprise' = bars 17–32).

Each of the three sections of sonata form is susceptible to comparable permutations, although surprises are harder to generate in the development section for the simple reason that this is the most unpredictable stretch of any sonata-form movement. Thematic fragmentation, manipulation, a reordering of themes, and modulation to remote key areas are all typical of this section. On rare occasions, Haydn introduces a new theme here: the most celebrated instance occurs in the first movement of the Symphony no. 45 in F♯ minor ('Farewell'). But on the whole, Haydn prefers to manipulate ideas and processes already heard in the exposition. When asked by GRIESINGER late in his life about the manner in which he went about composing any given piece, Haydn declared that once he had 'seized on an idea', his 'whole endeavour' then went toward 'developing and sustaining' that idea. This sense of continuous elaboration is particularly evident in Haydn's sonata-form movements, in which sometimes the smallest scrap of an idea—such as the two-semiquaver up-beat at the beginning of op. 33 no. 2—provides the basis for virtually every subsequent idea in the movement.

Development sections can nevertheless have their share of surprises. From time to time, in a procedure often labelled FAUSSE REPRISE, Haydn lulls unwary listeners into thinking that the recapitulation has already begun, only to remind them quite forcefully that the development is still in progress. Within recapitulations, in turn, Haydn was almost never content to take the lazy way out and simply transpose the second half of an exposition to the tonic. Instead, he seems to have relished the challenge of re-presenting familiar material in a new guise by varying thematic development, small-scale harmonic direction, instrumentation, and (occasionally) the actual sequence of ideas.

Proportionally, the coda is much briefer than any of the three sections discussed above, and indeed is often absent entirely. When present, however, it almost always functions as something more than a merely cadential close. In the first movement of the string quartet op. 20 no. 5, for example, Haydn takes the music through some remarkable remote tonal regions before finally bringing things to a close in the tonic. There is an intensification of mood here that rivals that of the development section.

It is important to remember that sonata form is manifested and perceived in time, through sound, and that 18th-century audiences routinely heard each of the two halves of a sonata-form movement twice. Performers nowadays generally observe the repeat of the first reprise (the exposition) but all too often ignore the second (the development and the recapitulation). Haydn himself was sensitive to the need for such repetition. In the first movements of his symphonies, for example, he would occasionally dispense with the repeat of the second reprise (nos. 26, 50, 61, 80). This non-reprise became more common later in his career: only one of the first movements of the 'London' Symphonies (1791–5) calls for a repeat of the second reprise. It is precisely Haydn's concern for such matters of proportion that argues in favour of honouring his intentions on those occasions when he did in fact indicate a repeat of the second reprise.

In spite of the widespread use of sonata form throughout the Classical period, theorists of the time had no accepted term to identify it, and there are only a few descriptions of the form, by Koch and Galeazzi, that make any pretensions to real substance. After demonstrating how to join discrete phrases of music into increasingly larger units, composition manuals would rarely illustrate the principles of movement-length form with anything larger than a simple minuet. The construction of large-scale forms was considered as much an aesthetic challenge as a mechanical one, and for this reason, aspiring composers were urged to study and emulate exemplary movements by acknowledged masters. Not until the 19th century did these manuals actually begin to describe large-scale structures like sonata form in detail and give their respective elements distinctive names. As a result, 'textbook' accounts of sonata form have tended to be based on 19th-century conceptions of the form, in which thematic contrast between 'first' and 'second' themes (that is, between a movement's opening theme and the first theme presented in the secondary key area) were of fundamental importance. No such distinction existed in Haydn's time. A sense of strong thematic contrast might or might not be present in any given work, but the absence of such strong contrast caused many later theorists and critics to see Haydn's sonata-form movements as somehow deficient.

In truth, Haydn's sonata forms operate more on a principle of variation than of contrast. From this perspective, sonata form constitutes a kind of framework in which composers could present a central theme—the movement's opening idea—and then elaborate that theme by means of harmonic and thematic variety. It is for this reason that so many critics of Haydn's time conceived of musical form (and not merely sonata form) as a kind of large-scale rhetorical structure whose purpose was to allow composers to convey musical ideas, and, at the same time, enable listeners to grasp more readily the essence and trajectory of those ideas. *See also* FAUSSE REPRISE and MONOTHEMATICISM. MEB

M. E. Bonds, *Wordless Rhetoric: Musical Form and the Metaphor of the Oration* (Cambridge, Mass., 1991).
M. Broyles, 'Organic Form and the Binary Repeat', *Musical Quarterly*, 66 (1980), 339–60.
W. E. Caplin, *Classical Form: A Theory of Formal Functions for the Instrumental Music of Haydn, Mozart, and Beethoven* (New York, 1998).
B. Churgin, 'Francesco Galeazzi's Description (1796) of Sonata Form', *Journal of the American Musicological Society*, 21 (1968), 181–99.
L. G. Ratner, *Classic Music: Expression, Form, and Style* (New York, 1980).
C. Rosen, *The Classical Style: Haydn, Mozart, Beethoven*, rev. edn (London, 1997).
C. Rosen, *Sonata Forms* (New York, 1988).

song. See overleaf.

sources. The raw material that informs biographical studies of Haydn and editions of his music is vast and includes letters, documents, newspaper and journal reports, diaries, reminiscences, biographies, musical sketches, autograph manuscripts, manuscript copies, catalogues, and printed editions. This entry surveys the primary sources for the composer's life and for his music, that is material that emanated directly from Haydn or was sanctioned by him.

1. Biographical sources. In 1776, at the age of 44, Haydn was asked to provide material for inclusion in *Das gelehrte Oesterreich*, a dictionary devoted to the arts and professions issued in Vienna. The so-called 'Autobiographical Sketch' is a document of four sides that was subsequently reworked in the dictionary. Written with almost naive humility Haydn begins with a couple of paragraphs that outline the course of his life to date. He thought that he had been born in 1733 not 1732, and draws particular attention to the importance of Porpora, Fürnberg, Morzin, and the Esterházy family 'in whose service I wish to live and die'. He then lists his most significant music, the three largest operas to date (*Le pescatrici*, *L'incontro improvviso*, and *L'infedeltà delusa*), the oratorio *Il ritorno di Tobia*, and the Stabat mater. Not a single symphony or quartet is mentioned. Haydn, however, reveals his disappointment and concern that his instrumental music has not found favour in north Germany (Haydn's word is 'Berliners', which is clearly a synecdoche). The sketch mentions Hasse's approval of the Stabat mater, suggests that Haydn was in friendly contact with Dittersdorf, and that he had met Gottfried van Swieten, the future librettist of *The Creation* and *The Seasons*, in the winter of 1775–6.

Although Haydn was never again asked to provide a biographical account, he did cooperate fully with three writers who issued biographies within three years of the composer's death, GRIESINGER, DIES, and CARPANI. All three based their accounts on knowledge of the composer in the last ten years of so of his life and each one purports to quote Haydn directly, though there may, naturally, be an element of poetic licence; as the most rhapsodic, Carpani is also the most unreliable. The biographies of Griesinger and Dies, in particular, have always provided the basic information on Haydn's career and have guided perception of his personality too. Although confined to a particular period, the LONDON NOTEBOOKS, four small volumes of random impressions of life in London written by the composer during his two visits in the 1790s, reveal much about his character and, in the summary list of works composed for the city, his musical output at this time.

Some 300 letters written by Haydn have survived, either in their original form or in copies. None has survived from the 1750s including Haydn's period of employment at the Morzin court, but from 1762 onwards letters survive through to December 1808 when Haydn thanked Prince Nicolaus for paying his medical bills. Letters to ARTARIA in Vienna form by far the largest group, over 60 from 1780 through to 1805, especially numerous in the first ten years. They provide a full account of the relationship between the composer and his principal publisher and though by nature they are business letters, they do reveal aspects of Haydn's personality not evident in the deferential biographies of Griesinger, Dies, and Carpani. The letters (along with many by other composers of the time) were kept by the firm of Artaria and were published as a collection in 1909, the centenary of the composer's death.

Apart from the Artaria letters, there is no other recipient who received substantial numbers of letters over a sustained period of time. Unlike the Mozart family, there are no letters by Haydn to his family (except for a draft of a letter to Michael Haydn). From London he wrote to his mistress, Luigia Polzelli, but there are no extant letters to his wife (if she did receive any she presumably disposed of them soon after). Also disappointing is the negligible correspondence between Haydn and Salomon (one letter from 1799), and the complete absence of correspondence between Haydn and Mozart, and Haydn and Beethoven. Among the most subtly revealing, ranging from the tender to the frustrated, are the 25 letters Haydn wrote to MARIA ANNA VON GENZINGER between 1789 and 1792. Haydn's collected correspondence was first assembled by Robbins Landon and published in English in 1959; an edition in the original language

[*cont. on p.371*]

song

Haydn composed original songs in two languages, German and English, making a small if often distinctive contribution to the two traditions. Domestic music-making throughout Europe in Haydn's own lifetime would have featured many more 'songs' by the composer, manuscript and printed arrangements in English, French, and German of melodies from the composer's instrumental and operatic music, inauthentic arrangements that both reflected his popularity and promoted it.

The majority of Haydn's original songs appeared in published sets. His German songs ('Lieder') were published in two sets of 12 songs each, in 1781 and 1784, while his English songs ('Canzonettas') appeared in two sets of six, in 1794 and 1795. In addition, there are seven further songs in German, and two in English. Although these sets were composed for rather specific and different local markets, when the English songs were published with German texts (all in Haydn's lifetime) they were able to take part in the central development of the German lied from the late 18th century through to the early 19th. Indeed, Haydn anticipated many of the devices for which Schubert (1797–1828) and Schumann (1810–56) have been so highly extolled. At their very best Haydn's songs deserve to be placed alongside those of the acknowledged masters of German lied.

---

1. **Twelve lieder (Hob.XXVIa:1–12); twelve lieder (Hob.XXVIa:13–24).**
2. **Single lieder (Hob.XXVIa:37, 38, 39).**
3. **Six canzonettas (Hob.XXVIa:25–30); six canzonettas (Hob.XXVIa:31–6).**
4. **Single English songs (Hob.XXVIa:41–2).**

---

1. Twelve lieder (Hob.XXVIa:1–12); twelve lieder (Hob.XXVIa:13–24). Haydn's German songs must have been among the first works that the Viennese publisher ARTARIA requested from Haydn following the establishment of the firm in 1778. They can be seen as part of a broader cultural movement in Austria at the time that aimed to promote the German language. In 1778 Emperor Joseph II had established the German National Theatre, which offered plays and opera in the German language to challenge the traditional dominance of French spoken theatre and Italian opera. Between 1778 and 1782 a series of *Deutsche Lieder* by Joseph Anton Steffan (1726–97), CARL FRIBERTH (formerly a tenor at the Esterházy court), and LEOPOLD HOFMANN was published by the firm of Kurzböck. Haydn's songs were clearly meant to take their part in this developing market, which by the end of the decade was to include printed sets by Sterkel (1750–1817), GLUCK, STADLER, MOZART, and others. Haydn knew the songs of Steffan, Friberth, and Hofmann well; he took texts from them and directly criticized Hofmann's songs as 'street songs' ('Gassenlieder'). This personal antipathy between Haydn and Hofmann was probably the partial result of the rivalry of the two publishers Kurzböck and Artaria, since Haydn's first printed set also contains three songs on texts previously set by Hofmann ('Das strickende Mädchen', 'Der erste Kuß', and 'An Thyrsis').

Haydn's taste in German poetry has sometimes been belittled but this does not mean that he was not particular about the nature of the poems he set. He wanted his texts to provide a variety of affects, so that the songs in their published order could alternate between the gentle and the vigorous, between slow and fast tempos, and between keys on the sharp side and on the flat side of the tonal spectrum, though these principles are less evident in the second set. Haydn sought advice from FRANZ VON GREINER on choosing texts but his tardiness ensured that the second set was not completed immediately after the first. The first set together with the first three songs of the second set were finished by 23 June 1781, a further three were completed by October 1781, but the final six were not finished until March 1784.

While there is no hint of a song cycle in the Schubertian sense, Haydn's 24 German songs do form loose internal cycles, in that texts were selected for the musical contrast they would elicit and the responsive musicianship and wide sympathies that could be demonstrated by the composer. All the songs are strophic with the right hand of the piano doubling the voice part throughout to aid the intended clientele of the amateur singer. Haydn himself sang many of these songs in private music parties.

No. 1, 'Das strickende Mädchen' (Knitting maiden) deals with unrequited male love: Phyllis prefers knitting to the attention of a suitor. The suitor presses his case in an adagio tempo; Phyllis's indifference is reported in the third person in a contrasting allegro. Her ceaseless knitting is suggested by the Alberti figuration found in the slow section, and in the postlude of the fast section. No. 2, 'Cupido' (Cupid), also mirrors the text in its keyboard part; a recurring figure that begins with a *sforzando* suggests Cupid's darting arrows. No. 13, 'Der erste Kuß' (The first kiss), begins in a mock solemn way; the union of the two lovers is suggested in the eventual move to parallel thirds. No. 4, 'Eine sehr gewöhnliche Geschichte' (The usual story), is a saucy narrative that deals with the initial rejection of a lover's plea to enter the house; the rapid change of mind is 'the usual story'. No. 5, 'Die Verlassene' (The forsaken one), is a powerful evocation of rejection; set in G minor, the voice and keyboard are motivically linked and the diminished chords are tellingly placed. Taken in sequence, therefore, the first five songs, though drawing on five different poems, constitute a progression of love songs, moving from rejection, through consummation, to abandonment.

A similar narrative can be seen in the last seven songs of the first set: no. 6, 'Der Gleichsinn' (Mutual feeling), is the equivalent of no. 1; no. 7, 'An Iris' (To Iris), is a coy expression of love; no. 8, 'An Thyrsis' (To Thyrsis), is the female reaction; no. 9, 'Trost unglücklicher Liebe' (The solace of unhappy love), is the male reaction; no. 10, 'Die Landlust' (Country pleasure), represents a quick recovery from the fickleness of love; no. 11, 'Liebeslied' (Love song), revives disappointment; and no. 12, 'Die zu späte Ankunft der Mutter' (Mother arrives too late), replays the consummation of no. 4.

Three of the best songs in the first set, nos. 8–10, were those Haydn composed to texts already used by Hofmann. In every way he displays his superiority. Hofmann's melodies are eminently forgettable, Haydn's memorable; Hofmann's harmonies are bland, Haydn's colourful; Hofmann slavishly follows the accentuation of the text, Haydn modifies it; and Hofmann has no grasp of poetic structure, Haydn understands its potential. 'An Thyrsis' and 'Die Landlust', in particular, are fine examples of Haydn's ability to compose effective miniatures using the simplest of means. In the former, after a diatonically straightforward opening in contredanse rhythms, Haydn explores more expressive harmonies before returning to the opening; the keyboard plays an introduction, an interlude, and a postlude for each of the three verses. 'Die Landlust' is even simpler, with virtually no expressive harmonies and a short postlude; its simple but attractive melody is carefully shaped in arching lines, drawing on the typical rhythms and thematic shapes of pastoral music. 'Trost unglücklicher Liebe' is a gentle song of deep expression. Set in F minor, it has a melodic line characterized by piercing *sforzandi* on the sixth degree of the scale and careful chromaticism. Although the texture is mainly a two-part one, there is some wonderful burgeoning into three parts with calculated part-writing. At the text 'Schmerz und Wunden und tötet mich einmal' (pain and wounds that would at one time kill me) the surface activity of the music slows as a rising chromatic line intensifies the expression before resolving to the relative major. Rosemary Hughes rightly heard this as 'strangely Schubertian in its tranquil sadness'.

The songs that did not use the same texts as Hofmann also show some special felicities of expression, such as the momentary sharing of the melodic line between singer and keyboard, and the expressive leap of a tenth on the word 'gefühlvolles' (tender) in 'An Iris'. 'Liebeslied' utilizes some of the expressive means of 'Trost unglücklicher Liebe' but with an added sense of declamation. The obvious strophic structure of 'Die zu späte Ankunft' is cleverly contradicted by the unexpected progress of the internal phrase patterns.

Haydn considered the texts of the second set of German songs, published in 1784, to be less satisfactory and, certainly, the implied wider narratives found in the first set are absent. Although eight of the texts again deal with various aspects of love, four deal with other topics: no. 17, 'Geistliches Lied' (Sacred song), sets an anonymous devotional text of a kind Haydn was soon to favour, especially in the partsongs of his old age (Hob.XXVb:1–4 and Hob.XXVc:1–9); no. 20, 'Zufriedenheit' (Contentment), speculates on what the life of a king would be like; no. 22, 'Lob der Faulheit' (In praise of indolence), is self-explanatory; and no. 24, 'Auf meines Vaters Grab' (At my father's grave), is a song of mourning with an element of religious consolation; the feeling of a miscellany is further suggested by the opening song, no. 13, 'Jeder meint, der Gegenstand' (Everybody means the opposite), which Haydn adapted from his marionette opera *Dido*.

Surprisingly, it is the four songs that do not have the subject matter of love that convince the most. 'Geistliches Lied' deals with man's unworthiness compared to the sacrifice of Christ; the anguish is readily suggested by the many *sforzandi* and rich harmonic texture, especially when the music invokes the 'throne of highest majesty' ('dem Thron der höchstens Majestät'), and the death of Christ ('mein Jesus Christus starb dafür'). No. 22 is Haydn at his most ironic. When, nearly two decades later, Haydn was composing *The Seasons* he complained wrily that he had to set the word 'industry'. Here it is the opposite quality that is praised, laziness. With a text by Lessing, the song has no parallel in Haydn's output. The music, in A minor, can hardly muster any movement. Thirty-three bars of an Andante in common time have only four semiquavers in total; the melodic line rises slowly, frequently fails to reach its expected destination, descends in failure, and is broken by rests. The powerful chords at the end that lead to a final *tierce de picardie* provide a comforting sanction of indolence. Nobody would claim that 'Gegenliebe' (Mutual love) is a particularly strong song, but it has wider interest in that the text was set also by Beethoven (WoO 118), using a melody that was later to be transformed into the 'Ode to Joy' theme in the finale of the Ninth Symphony. While Beethoven would have known Haydn's setting there is no musical link between the two songs.

2. Single lieder (Hob.XXVIa:37, 38, 39). Nothing is known about the earliest of the single German songs, 'Beim Schmerz, der dieses Herz durchwühlet' (With the pain that this heart churns), including the author of the text. The manuscript paper on which it survives suggests that it was written in the late 1760s, and the nature of the text points to it having been part of a theatrical work. The complicated, if charming circumstances surrounding the composition of 'Der schlaue und dienstfertige Pudel' (The sly and ever-faithful poodle) were recorded by Griesinger and Dies. About 1780 an officer's daughter from Coburg wrote to Haydn enclosing 20 verses that related the story of how, in order to win a bet, a captain deliberately hid a coin in order to demonstrate how effectively his poodle could recover it. The young girl hoped that Haydn would set the verses as a song and, though she was poor, enclosed some money. Haydn set the shaggy poodle story, returned the money and suggested that the young girl should, instead, knit him a pair of garters. She did, and Haydn kept them into old age. 'Trachten will nicht auf Erden' (I will not endeavour on earth) is a cosy religious homily on the good life, composed, probably as a gift, on the eve of Haydn's departure for London in December 1790.

About ten years later Haydn completed three single songs: 'Als einst mit Weibes Schönheit' (As once with wifely beauty) is a tongue-in-cheek discussion of the rival merits of beauty and honour in a wife; 'Ein kleines Haus' (A little house) is a cosy picture of domestic bliss, and 'Antwort auf die Frage eines Mädchens' (Response to a girl's question) is a declaration of love unto death. All three of these songs draw on the experience earlier in the decade of writing English songs, in that they are through-composed and, like many of the canzonettas, repeat the final line of the text several times, in a kind of musical musing.

3. Six canzonettas (Hob.XXVIa:25–30); six canzonettas (Hob.XXVIa:31–6). Apart from their language, Haydn's English canzonettas differ from the German songs of the 1780s in several noticeable ways: they are consistently written on three staves, are longer and musically more elaborate, and the piano part is more demanding. Haydn retains the notion of organization of songs in alternative stylistic pairs that can be related to a larger overall narrative. In both sets of canzonettas, Haydn begins with a sea song, a favourite English type. This is followed by two pairs of melancholy and pastoral songs, and the set is concluded by a finale. 'Fidelity', the final canzonetta of the first set, is a through-composed song coming after five strophic songs, a minor-mode piece after five in the major, and is altogether the most expressive in the set. 'Content', the final song in the second set, is a less striking conclusion; it was a reworking of an earlier German song 'Der verdienstvolle Sylvius' (The worthy Sylvius). The set was completed just before Haydn returned to Vienna in July 1795. Perhaps, in order to save time, he took the old song and adapted it to a new text.

The first set of canzonettas, published by Haydn himself in London in June 1794, used poems by ANNE HUNTER. Married to the famous surgeon, Dr John Hunter, Mrs Hunter (as she called herself) had established an enviable reputation as a poetess. She had the knack of creating lyrics that were specially suited for song-setting. It seems that Haydn depended on her literary expertise not only for the first set, but also for the selection of texts that constituted the second set of canzonettas, published by Corri, Dussek & Co. in October 1795. Only one of these later texts is known to be by Anne Hunter herself, 'The Wanderer'. 'The Sailor's Song', 'Piercing Eyes', and 'Content' remain unattributed; 'She never told her love' is from Shakespeare's *Twelfth Night*; 'Sympathy' is usually credited to Metastasio, from *Olimpiade* (Act 3, Scene 3), though it comes from John Hoole's translation of the opera rather than from the original Italian of Metastasio.

In the first canzonetta of the 1794 set, 'The Mermaid's Song', Haydn's more expansive attitude to song composition, in comparison with the German songs of the previous decade, is apparent immediately, with many internal repetitions of lines and of individual words. In the accompaniment Haydn suggests the waves as well as the mermaid splashing in the water. According to Anne Hunter's obituary the text was freely translated from an unspecified Italian original.

It has been speculated that Hunter wrote the poignant text of 'Recollection' shortly after the death of her husband on 16 October 1793; Haydn set it a few months later at the beginning of his second visit. Even though the strophic song is in the major key, its mood is projected by an appealing melodic line with carefully placed appoggiaturas and falling intervals. The most famous canzonetta of all, 'A Pastoral Song', is better known by its opening line, 'My mother bids me bind my hair'. In the 19th century it was made particularly popular by the soprano Jenny Lind (1820–87). Here, there seems to be a deliberate creative tension between the text and the music, the former representing the sad protagonist, the latter those who dance and play. 'Despair' uses some of the same resources as 'Recollection' (adagio tempo, triple metre, major key, and strophic form) to convey a melancholy mood, but the greater number of interruptions in the delivery of the poetry intensify that mood. The many repetitions of the text in 'Fidelity', especially of the key phrase 'fixed on me', produce the largest song in the set, an appropriate culmination; the common sequence of a storm in the minor and a calm in the major is a common 18th-century conceit, and can be viewed as a wider resolution of the melancholy of many of the previous songs in the set.

'The Sailor's Song', which begins the second set, represents the ever-present dangers of being a patriotic British sailor, storms at sea and battle, both reflected in the 'hurly, burly' of life on the ocean waves. Haydn accompanies 'The Wanderer', the most melancholy song of the second set, with a walking bass to represent the wanderer, one of the most favoured topics of the Romantics. 'Sympathy' recalls 'A Pastoral Song' in metre, sharp key, and atmosphere; but here Haydn provides a through-composed song with a particularly dramatic beginning to the second verse. 'She never told her love', from Shakespeare's *Twelfth Night*, encourages Haydn to a heightened dramatic setting, suggested by the tempo marking of 'Lento assai e con espressione'. With a more than usually prominent part for the piano, it is akin to an arioso and is a strong candidate for the most effective song written in the 18th century. The following canzonetta, 'Piercing Eyes', is a disappointment, an unremarkable, through-composed pastoral setting. The text of the final song, 'Content', is, in fact, the third text associated with the music. As 'Der verdienstvolle Sylvius' it was composed in the mid-1780s and may even have been intended for one of the sets published by Artaria. Haydn had a copy of the song with him in London during his second visit and sang it at two soirées given by members of the royal family; it was later published by Traeg in Vienna. When Haydn was completing the second of the canzonettas in the summer of 1795, he took this German song, transposed it up a semitone to A major, and gave it the text 'Transport of Pleasure'. It was published by Corri, Dussek & Co. as part of the first edition of the second set, but a few months later, in what would now be termed a second edition, the text was changed to a completely new one, 'Content'. Certainly the amorous nature of 'Transport of Pleasure' is more explicit than that in 'Content', and this may have been the reason why a new text was substituted; Haydn probably had nothing to do with this third version.

4. Single English songs (Hob.XXVIa:41–2). Two single songs in English were composed to texts by Anne Hunter. 'The Spirit's Song' seems to have been composed when Haydn was in England and may have been intended for the second set of canzonettas, but was perhaps rejected because it duplicated the mood of 'The Wanderer' and, to a certain extent, 'She never told her love'. This evocative poem inspired Haydn to a high romantic style. According to Griesinger, Haydn was given the text of 'O tuneful voice' before he left England in 1795, but it is not known when he set it to music. It, too, anticipates the 19th century in its striking entry of the voice, the colouristic use of the piano, and its telling harmonic language. APB

A. P. Brown, 'Joseph Haydn and Leopold Hofmann's Street Songs', *Journal of the American Musicological Society*, 23 (1980), 356–83.

A. P. Brown, 'Musical Settings of Anne Hunter's Poetry: From National Song to Canzonetta', *Journal of the American Musicological Society*, 47 (1994), 39–89.

W. Kumbier, 'Haydn's English Canzonettas: Transformations in the Rhetoric of the Musical Sublime', in P. Barker, S. W. Goodwin, and G. Handwerk (eds), *The Scope of Words: In Honor of Albert S. Cook* (New York, 1991), 73–93.

M. Scott, 'Some English Affinities and Associations of Haydn's Songs', *Music and Letters*, 25 (1944), 1–12.

(mainly German) was prepared by Dénes Bartha and appeared in 1965. Since that date a number of new letters by Haydn have emerged and a new complete edition, in English and in the original language, is much needed.

The archives of the Esterházy family are probably the largest surviving source of material relating to the activities of an 18th-century aristocratic family in the Austrian territories. Over 5,000 known documents relate in some way to the cultural life of the court in the 18th century and beyond and a few are signed by the Kapellmeister himself, covering everything from the purchase of manuscript paper to the seeking of permission to travel to Vienna. Several contracts and payrolls also survive. Haydn's two wills, prepared in 1801 and 1809, have survived together with a catalogue of his library.

2. Musical sources. Approximately 40 per cent of Haydn's total output of music has survived in autograph. The largest single collection is in the National Széchényi Library, Budapest, acquired from the Esterhazy archives, and includes many symphonies, baryton trios, operas, and masses written for the court. Remaining autographs are widely dispersed. The British Library in London, for instance, possesses the autograph scores of Symphonies nos. 95, 96, and 103, the keyboard sonata in E♭ (Hob.XVI:45), a portion of *Orlando paladino*, the Ode to Neptune, and some folksong settings; and the Gesellschaft der Musikfreunde in Vienna owns the autograph scores of the op. 17 and op. 20 quartets, the Horn Concerto, the Trumpet Concerto, the 'Applausus' cantata, part of *Il ritorno di Tobia*, and the *Missa brevis Sancti Joannis de Deo*. Surviving autographs of smaller items of church music, baryton music, keyboard sonatas, and especially keyboard trios are few but the most grievous loss are the autograph scores of *The Creation* and *The Seasons*; van Swieten had them in his possession when he died intestate in 1803, but nothing is known about their subsequent history. During the Second World War many valuable autographs of music by Bach, Beethoven, Mozart as well as Haydn owned by Preußischen Staatsbibliothek in Berlin were sent elsewhere for safe keeping; their whereabouts became known only in 1976, a small library in Kraków. The following year they were returned to Berlin. The Haydn autographs include Symphonies nos. 98, 99, and 101.

Music manuscripts prepared under Haydn's direct supervision, such as those by the ELßLER FAMILY, have survived in appreciable quantities, whether as copies of the original score or manuscript parts prepared from it; often they will contain minor corrections or amendments by Haydn. The surviving sources for the *Missa Sancti Nicolai* are indicative of the number of such sources and their distribution. The original performing parts, still at the palace in Eisenstadt, were mainly written by Joseph Elßler but Haydn helped with the underlay of the text in the vocal parts and the figuring of the organ part; other sets of parts prepared in Eisenstadt for the same work subsequently found their way to libraries in the abbey of St Florian near Linz, the church of St Michael in Sopron (Hungary), the Piaristenkirche in Vienna, and the Luigi Cherubini Conservatory in Florence. Naturally the

National Széchényi Library, Budapest, owns a large collection of such material, especially valuable for the manuscript scores and parts associated with Haydn's operas since these did not receive the same degree of distribution as his other music. Authentic parts for instrumental music and church music abound in the principal libraries in the Austrian territories but occasionally they have found their final resting place elsewhere. The loss of the autograph scores of *The Creation* and *The Seasons* is partly compensated by the survival of material prepared by Johann Elßler and colleagues: scores of both works plus an associated set of parts (Stadtbibliothek, Vienna) plus a further set of parts for both works (National Széchényi Library, Budapest). Such scores and parts not only provide the essential basis for scholarly editions but also reveal a good deal about performance practice.

Haydn's many dealings with publishers in Vienna, London, and Paris yielded substantial quantities of authentic editions that were sold in the immediate locality and distributed further afield. Thus musically valuable editions of Haydn's music can be found all over the world. Since print runs of the time could be very small, as few as 50 (even smaller on occasions), some authentic editions of music by the composer are extremely rare and a few have not survived at all.

A substantial corpus of musical sketches by Haydn exists though, in comparison with Beethoven, they reflect only a small proportion of his output. Also they reveal less about the compositional process of individual works than they do in the case of Beethoven. The sketches for *The Creation*, now found in London (British Library), New York (Public Library), and Vienna (Österreichische Nationalbibliothek), are the most extensive for any Haydn work.

Of inestimable value in establishing the authenticity, dating, and chronology of Haydn's music are two catalogues of his music that were prepared under his supervision, the ENTWURF-KATALOG from *c.*1765 onwards and the HAYDN-VERZEICHNIS from 1804–5. *See also* CATALOGUES.

G. Feder, 'Joseph Haydns Skizzen und Entwürfe. Übersicht der Manuskripte, Werkregister, Literatur- und Ausgabenverzeichnis', *Fontes Artis Musicae*, 26 (1979), 172–88.

G. Feder, 'Manuscript Sources of Haydn's Works and their Distribution', *HYB* 4 (1968), 102–39.

G. Feder, 'Nachricht über die Krakauer Haydn-Autographen', *HS* 5/2 (1983), 135–6.

F. K. Grave and M. G. Grave, *Franz Joseph Haydn. A Guide to Research* (New York, 1990).

species counterpoint. A system of teaching strict counterpoint in the PALESTRINA STYLE, codified by JOHANN JOSEPH FUX in his *Gradus ad Parnassum* (1725). Although the system existed already, it was refined by Fux in the form that became standard for counterpoint teaching.

The five 'species' as formulated by Fux were based on the rhythmic character of a contrapuntal part set against a cantus firmus (a given part in long notes). An important feature was the increase in complexity from the simplest (note-against-note: first species) to the most elaborate (mixed note values against the cantus firmus: fifth species). Between these extremes were intermediate values (two or four notes against one: second and third species), and syncopated (with suspensions: fourth species). Although an artificial reduction of Palestrina's style to a method bearing little precise relation to the actual music of the composer, species counterpoint was an effective pedagogical tool.

Rhythmic patterning in late 18th-century counterpoint owes much to species counterpoint, as does the systematic use of suspended dissonances. Linear models of species counterpoint can often be derived from the surface texture of the Viennese Classical style; alternatively it was sometimes used in deliberate contrast to the modern style. Much of Haydn's work in symphonic, chamber, and sacred genres contains fugal or contrapuntal writing suggestive of this training; bar 32 onwards in the finale of Symphony no. 95 is a particularly flamboyant example. SW

D. M. Arnold, 'Haydn's Counterpoint and Fux's Gradus', *Monthly Musical Record*, 87 (1957), 52–8.

S. Wollenberg, 'Haydn's Baryton Trios and the "Gradus"', *Music and Letters*, 54 (1973), 170–8.

Specioli family. Antonio Specioli (*fl.* 1774–91) was a tenor who joined the opera troupe at Eszterháza in August 1782. He was one of the most experienced singers at the court having sung in 11 different opera houses in Italy. At Eszterháza he took the leading tenor roles in Haydn's *La fedeltà premiata*, *Orlando paladino*, and *Armida*, as well as in operas by Anfossi, Cimarosa, Guglielmi, and Sarti. His wife, Maria Antonia Nicetti (*fl.* 1782–98), whom he seems to have met when they were both working in Bologna in 1782, came with him to Eszterháza. She undertook secondary soprano roles in Haydn's *La fedeltà premiata* and *Orlando paladino* and in operas by other composers. The couple left Eszterháza in August 1785 to return to Italy, where they resumed their careers as itinerant singers. ERL

HCRL/2.

C. Sartori, *I libretti italiani a stampa dalle origini al 1800* (Cuneo, 1990–4).

Stabat mater (Hob.XXbis). Haydn's only setting of this liturgical text, composed in 1767; it became the composer's most frequently performed and most widely disseminated work in his lifetime, performed as part of the liturgy and as a concert work. Musical settings of the Stabat mater in the 18th century are comparatively rare. Haydn was probably familiar with the famous setting by Pergolesi (1710–36) and the one by Alessandro Scarlatti (1660–1725); in addition Palestrina's Stabat mater was a standard part of the repertoire in the Hofkapelle in Vienna and, as a boy, Haydn almost certainly would have sung it on several occasions. Liturgically the Stabat mater, a prayer written in the first-person singular that draws sustenance from the crucifixion, was designed to be performed on Good Friday and on the Feast of the Seven Sorrows in September, though para-liturgical performances in Lent are also known. In Eisenstadt, Haydn's predecessor as Kapellmeister, WERNER, had contributed to an abiding local tradition of providing sacred oratorios and so-called *Grabmusik* (literally 'Tomb music') for performance on Good Fridays, usually in the chapel of the Esterházy palace, though he never set the text of the Stabat mater. Following Werner's death in 1766, Haydn, who was now in charge of church music, may have been eager to continue this local tradition; if so the likely first performance of his Stabat mater would have taken part on Good Friday, 1767 (17 April). Haydn was evidently pleased with the work, sending a copy to HASSE for his approval; the venerable composer replied with a generous letter of praise, proudly retained by Haydn for the rest of his life. Two performances directed by Haydn are known to have taken place in Vienna in the following years, the first at the church of the BARMHERZIGE BRÜDER in March 1768, the second in the Piaristenkirche in March 1771.

Hasse was no doubt impressed by the depth of expression in Haydn's setting, unprecedented in any sacred work by the young composer. No fewer than six complete movements and a portion of a seventh (the opening section of the final chorus, 'Quando corpus morietur') are in the minor key. Only one of these minor-key movements can justly be compared with the so-called *Sturm und Drang* movements in symphonies of the period, a blustering bass aria in C minor ('Flammis orci ne succendar'). The other minor-key movements evoke a more individual realm of expression. Haydn also rose admirably to the challenge of writing so much music in a slow tempo, with eight movements having a tempo marking between Largo assai and Andante. (Two unusual markings are further evidence of the composer's expressive ambitions: Lento e mesto for 'Vidit suum dulcem natum' and Lagrimoso for 'Fac me vere tecum flere'.)

The orchestral forces include two oboes, bassoon, strings, and continuo; in the two movements in E♭ major, 'O quam tristis' and 'Virgo virginum', the oboes are replaced by the more doleful sound of cors anglais. Whereas Haydn's symphonies of the time often feature extensive solo passages for wind instruments there are no such solos in the Stabat mater since contemplation rather than ostentation is the dominant concern. The four vocal forces of soloists and chorus are likewise carefully disposed. The work is built around five choruses, separated by seven arias and one duet. In the opening movement the chorus reaffirms the response of the solo tenor; in the third movement it assumes the role of onlookers as they comment on the image of the weeping Virgin Mary, at first rhetorically and then more comfortingly. The chorus next appears in the seventh movement, 'Eia mater', a crucial moment in the text as it turns from depicting the sorrow of Calvary to the hope it offers mankind. In 'Virgo virgininum' the solo quartet unfolds a leisurely fugue, later supported by the chorus. In the final movement it is left to the chorus, now in an unprecedentedly bright G major, to establish the vision of 'Paradisi gloria' (the glory of heaven).

Contemporary manuscript copies of the Stabat mater exist not only in Catholic countries such as Austria, southern Germany, France, Italy, Portugal, Spanish Americas, and Spain, but also in Protestant north Germany and Holland. A reflection of its fame as a concert work is that the score was published no fewer than three times: by Bland in London in 1784, Sieber in Paris in 1785, and by Breitkopf & Härtel in 1803. In 1803, under Haydn's guidance, NEUKOMM provided additional parts for flute, two clarinets, two bassoons, two horns, two trumpets, three trombones, and timpani for a performance in Eisenstadt.

Stadler, Abbé Maximilian (b. 4 Aug. 1748; d. 8 Nov. 1833). Keyboard player, composer, church administrator, and music historian whose life spanned the entire Viennese Classical period. He became a prominent and influential, if somewhat conservative, figure during the life of Beethoven. His relationship with Haydn can be viewed in three dimensions. First, as an acquaintance of his from at least the early 1760s, Stadler on occasion offered advice on certain compositional matters, such as suggesting a programmatic approach to the individual movements of the original, orchestral version of the *Seven Last Words*. Second, as director of the imperial music archive from 1815 to 1826, he collected, copied, and otherwise took interest in Haydn's music, notably the early works (e.g. Symphony no. 1, and the capriccio for keyboard, Hob.XVII:1). He supplemented the text to Haydn's visiting card ('Hin ist alle meine Kraft'), working its four-bar melody into canons at the unison, third, fifth, and seventh for various combinations; the string quartet version of these canons was published in 1807, dedicated to Haydn, and Stadler hoped it would serve as the finale to op. 103. Thirdly, as a music chronicler he helped formulate Haydn's historical position within the Viennese School in the material he gathered for a projected history of music in the Austrian lands. RNF

O. Biba, 'Nachrichten über Joseph Haydn, Michael Haydn und Wolfgang Amadeus Mozart in der Sammlung handschriftlicher Biographien der Gesellschaft der Musikfreunde in Wien', in O. Biba and D. W. Jones (eds.), *Studies in Music History Presented to H. C. Robbins Landon on his Seventieth Birthday* (London, 1996), 152–64.

V. and M. Novello, *A Mozart Pilgrimage in the Year 1829*, ed. R. Hughes (London, 1955).

K. Wagner, *Abbé Maximilian Stadler: seine Materialien zur Geschichte der Musik unter den österreichischen Regenten* (Kassel, Basle, 1974).

stile antico. Term used for music from the 17th century onwards that purports to imitate the 'old style' of Palestrina (1525/6–94), typically (but not exclusively) polyphonic music for voices without independent instrumental support. A more familiar term in Haydn's Austria was STYLUS A CAPPELLA.

Storm, The (Hob.XXIVa:8). A single movement for SATB (solo and chorus) and orchestra setting words by John Wolcot (pseudonym: Peter Pindar); following the poet Haydn called his work a 'madrigal'. The first performance in London on 24 February 1792 was well received, with one reviewer noting Haydn's felicitous setting of English words. A heavily revised version was given as *Der Sturm* in Vienna in December 1793, with a German translation probably by VAN SWIETEN. It was published by Breitkopf & Härtel in German and Italian translations in 1802. With its colourful orchestration, vivid harmonies, and alternating stormy and calm sections, this short vocal work is an interesting harbinger of Haydn's later oratorios, *The Creation* and *The Seasons*. DdV

HCRL/3.

string trio. Haydn's string trios are an obscure corner of his output. They are early works composed in the 1750s and 1760s and nothing is known about the circumstances of their composition. Twenty-one trios were entered in the *Entwurf-Katalog*, and perhaps as many as 12 to 15 other works from the 1750s have some kind of claim to be regarded as authentic. The string trio was a popular medium in mid-18th-century Austria with composers such as Asplmayr (1728–86) and Wagenseil (1715–77) contributing prolifically to it. Haydn followed these composers in writing most of his trios for two violins and bass instrument; only Hob.V:8 in B♭ is scored for violin, viola, and bass. Haydn also followed contemporary practice in calling the works divertimenti.

While there was a ready market for such music in the 1750s and 1760s, there is no anecdotal evidence from GRIESINGER and DIES about Haydn's string trios. CARPANI, however, suggests that the composer began writing them in the early 1750s and that some were composed for BARON FÜRNBERG, associated with Haydn's early quartets. The mistaken view that the medium of the string quartet evolved out of the string trio, through the simple addition of a viola, encouraged the view that Haydn stopped composing trios as soon as he had 'discovered' the quartet; the *Entwurf-Katalog* makes it clear that trios were composed until the mid-1760s, as many as ten years after the earliest quartets. It was the baryton trio that replaced the string trio in Haydn's output as a composer. It is disappointing that he never returned to the medium, particularly in its later favoured form of violin, viola, and cello; the single string trio by Mozart (K563) and the five by the young Beethoven (two single works and a set of three, op. 3, op. 8, and op. 9) show what a challenging and rewarding medium it could be for a questing composer.

In comparison with Haydn's early quartets, his string trios are oddly unimaginative in their scoring with very little interplay between the instruments. Perhaps the reason for this is that the texture of two treble instruments and a bass was so ingrained in Haydn's musical imagination—and that of his players and listeners—that he found it difficult to escape from it. The same texture is consistently found in all manner of mid-18th-century genres: church music, symphonies, keyboard trios, and even, occasionally, Haydn's quartets. Passages such as the trio section of Hob.V:15, where all three instruments engage in shared thematic material are very rare. As in other genres in the mid-century in Haydn's Austria, the bass instrument was as likely to have been the violone as the cello, an instrumentation that would have emphasized the polarity between the top and the bottom of the texture. However, it would be a mistake to state that the scoring in these trios is equivalent to a standard Baroque trio sonata minus the keyboard, since most of the time the first violin takes the thematic lead and the often very formal distribution of thematic outlay between the two treble instruments that characterizes the older genre is not a feature.

The sources do not permit any secure attempt to place the works in chronological order and it is difficult also to provide wholly convincing evidence that the works were conceived in sets of three or six though, given contemporary practice, that is very likely. By far the most common movement pattern is a sequence of three movements, slow, Allegro, and a finale in minuet style, found in nine trios (Hob.V:1, 2, 3, 10, 12, 13, 15, 19, and 21).

Sharp keys predominate with three works in E major (Hob.V:1, 12, and 19). Two works (Hob.V:3 and V:14, the latter lost) are in B minor which, taken with the baryton trio (Hob.XI:96), the keyboard sonata (Hob.XVI:32), and the two quartets op. 33 no. 1 and op. 64 no. 2, reveal a fondness for the key not evident in the composer's symphonies and operas, for instance. Four works (Hob.V:16, 17, 18, and 20) have a three-movement pattern of fast, minuet, and fast; in all cases they move to a 2/4 Presto (6/8 in Hob.V:20) in binary form, of the kind regularly found in Haydn's quartets up to op. 17. Other shared characteristics in these four works suggest that they were composed together, including trio sections that turn habitually to the minor key and first-violin writing that is very reminiscent of that associated with LUIGI TOMASINI, first violinist at the Esterházy court.

Although for Haydn the genre of the string trio was one that he left behind, the works themselves, authentic and inauthentic, continued to be widely distributed in his lifetime. As late as 1799 the Viennese music dealer Johann Traeg advertised manuscript copies of no fewer than six sets of six string trios each by Haydn; as well as spurious trios Traeg's material probably included also many arrangements for two violins and bass of Haydn's baryton trios. Publishers in Amsterdam, Bonn, London, Paris, and Vienna likewise published string trios by Haydn, though none of these publications was prepared with the cooperation of the composer. In the 19th and 20th centuries Haydn's string trios were almost entirely neglected, totally eclipsed by the composer's contribution to the string quartet and the historical status of that genre in general. Only in the last 20 years have reliable editions of the music become available but the works still lag behind the rest of Haydn's instrumental output in popular appeal. While baryton trios, keyboard trios, keyboard sonatas, and miscellaneous divertimenti have attracted the attention of performers and recording companies, the string trios are hardly ever encountered.

B. S. Brook, 'Determining Authenticity through Internal Analysis: A Multifaceted Approach (with Special Reference to Haydn's String Trios)', in E. Badura-Skoda (ed.), *Joseph Haydn. Bericht über den internationalen Joseph Haydn Kongress. Wien. Hofburg, 5–12. September 1982* (Munich, 1986), 551–66.

B. S. Brook, 'Haydn's String Trios: A Misunderstood Genre', *Current Musicology*, 36 (1983), 61–77.

S. Fruehwald, *Authenticity Problems in Franz Joseph Haydn's Early Instrumental Works: A Stylistic Investigation* (New York, 1988).

H. Unverricht, *Geschichte des Streichtrios* (Tutzing, 1969).

Sturm und Drang (Storm and Stress). A German literary movement which flourished briefly in the 1770s, named after Maximilian Klinger's play of 1776. Characterized by emotional intensity and revolt again social and artistic conventions, Shakespeare was the artistic hero of the movement and other sources of inspiration included the cult of nature in Rousseau, the irrationalism of Hamann, and Macpherson's Ossian forgeries. The young Goethe of *Götz von Berlichingen* (1773) and *Die Leiden des jungen Werthers* (1774) was the focus of the movement, and Schiller's *Die Räuber* (1781) marks its zenith.

Parallels with the literary movement have been found in the painting of Fuseli (1741–1825), in music for the theatre of the 1770s, and in Austrian instrumental music from *c.*1765 to *c.*1775. In particular a conspicuous group of works in the minor key by Haydn, notably a number of symphonies (nos. 26, 39, 44, 45, 49, and 52), have been seen as analogous to the literary aesthetic, even though they largely pre-date it. These works make distinctive use of the sonority of the minor key together with syncopated rhythms, abrupt accents, sudden changes in dynamics, daring modulations, rhetorical pauses, strongly profiled unison themes, and contrapuntal textures. Other authors, doubting a direct connection between such music and the literary movement, have explained the musical phenomenon in a purely musical context and questioned the strong focus on a minority of works in this period. BH

B. S. Brook, 'Sturm und Drang and the Romantic Period in Music', *Studies in Romanticism*, 9 (1970), 269–84.

HCRL/2.

R. Pascal, *The German Sturm und Drang* (Manchester, 1953).

R. L. Todd, 'Joseph Haydn and the Sturm und Drang: A Revaluation', *Music Review*, 41 (1980), 172–96.

stylus a cappella (literally 'in the style of the chapel'). A technical term traditionally used (under the influence of 19th-century ideals) for unaccompanied choral singing; this usage derives from the practice at the Sistine Chapel. By extension it has been applied to 16th-century sacred choral style in general, and as a synonym for PALESTRINA STYLE and *stile antico*. In practice much 16th-century sacred vocal music was probably accompanied by organ and instrumental ensembles, doubling the voice parts. By Haydn's time many authors defined a cappella in this latter sense.

JOHANN JOSEPH FUX in his *Gradus ad Parnassum* (1725), the composition treatise which Haydn studied and used in teaching, demonstrated the strict contrapuntal foundations of the style, then in his final chapters gave a more practical demonstration ('De Stylo à Capella') with musical examples from his own Latin sacred vocal works. 'A capella' style is here defined in both its unaccompanied and accompanied forms (the latter used more 'in modern times'), and is characterized as possessing 'ecclesiastical dignity'. Its use was associated with Lent and Advent; this tradition was kept up at the Vienna HOFKAPELLE. The music typically looks antiquated, using mainly alla breve metre with predominantly 'white-note' values; in sound its archaic quality derives from modal tendencies and contrapuntal structure (the voices taking up in turn a series of short imitative points). Haydn's use of the style, most notably in his *Missa 'sunt bona mixta malis'* (characteristically titled 'Missa a 4tro voci alla Cappella') reflects both his *Gradus* training and his experience as a choirboy, as well as conforming to the tendency of his Austrian contemporaries to achieve a mixture of old and new styles. SW

D. W. Jones, 'Haydn's Missa sunt bona mixta malis and the a cappella tradition', in D. W. Jones (ed.), *Music in Eighteenth-Century Austria* (Cambridge, 1996), 89–111.
S. Wollenberg (trans. and intro.), 'Johann Joseph Fux, *Gradus ad Parnassum* (1725): Concluding Chapters', *Music Analysis*, 11 (1992), 209–43.

sublime. The sublime was an aesthetic obsession of the 18th century. Early in the century it was fuelled by a revived interest in RHETORIC, but by mid-century the term had freed itself from that association. Initially Longinus's classical treatise *On the Sublime* had sparked discussion, but it moved in a very different direction when taken up by writers such as Edmund Burke and Immanuel Kant. For those concerned with oratory and rhetoric, the sublime was thought of as a device for persuading through the emotions. The sublime could therefore give a certain quality to works of art, focusing on objects or phenomena of nature such as rivers, oceans, storms, volcanoes, and mountains, awakening a sense of grandeur and vastness. The emotions aroused were terror, horror, and ecstasy; through this effect of nature one could better approach the incomprehensible greatness of the divinity.

In his *Philosophical Enquiry into the Origin of our Ideas of the Sublime and Beautiful* (1747), Burke continued to emphasize emotion and terror, but now as an aesthetic theory rather than a device of rhetoric. For him the sublime lay in qualities such as vastness, darkness, obscurity, solitude, and power, and he shared the fascination of some of his contemporaries with ruins, melancholy, and tales of terror. In the end the effect should not be one of physical pain, but a type of pleasurable sensation. Through the influence of the *Enquiry* (of which Haydn owned a copy), the discussion extended beyond literature to include all the arts.

Going even further than Burke, Kant, in his *Beobachtungen über das Gefühl des Schönen und Erhabenen* (Observations on the feeling of the beautiful and the sublime, 1764), focused on the observer instead of the object. In his theory the aesthetic experience itself, or the capacity of the person to have the imagination aroused, supersedes the object. Like others who wrote of the subject, he elaborates a careful distinction between the sublime and the beautiful. With beauty, limits are in place, limits that can be defined by form and comprehended through understanding. The sublime lacks any such limits and reaches towards an unconditioned totality. In the experience of beauty positive pleasure exists, while that of the sublime is in a sense negative since ultimately the limitless phenomenon cannot be grasped by the imagination. Beauty achieves its effect through harmony, while in the sublime, harmony between object and subject will be lacking.

In critiques of *Paradise Lost* in the *Tatler* and *Spectator* by Addison and Steele, Milton emerged as the leading writer associated with the sublime, and this view quickly spread throughout Europe. The works of other writers linked with the style include Young's *Night Thoughts* (1742–6, Haydn owned a translation of it), Macpherson's *Ossian* (1760–3), and Thomson's *Seasons* (1726–46). Thomson, for one, sought to arouse terror by representing the destructive forces of nature, through the horrifying descriptions of sharks, a shepherd struck by lightning, the spread of the plague, or the ravaging of starving wolves ('Cruel as Death, and hungry as the Grave! Burning for Blood, bony, and gaunt, and grim!', that 'tear the screaming Infant from [the Mother's] breast').

The term sublime arises often in contemporary descriptions of Haydn's music, and Haydn himself used it. While it applies most aptly to his late oratorios, there are implications for his symphonies and masses as well. Haydn's practice of interweaving melodic or formal beauty with complexity and instability met with derision from some English writers, such as William Jackson (1730–1803), whose *Observations on the Present State of Music in London* appeared in print in 1791, the year Haydn first set foot on English soil. Without naming names but clearly implying Haydn, Jackson complained that 'later Composers, to be grand and original, have poured in such floods of nonsense, under the sublime idea of *being inspired*, that the present Symphony bears the same relation to good Music, as the raving of a Bedlamite do to sober sense. Sometimes the Key is perfectly lost, by wandering so from it, that there is no road to return.' Unlike Jackson's ranting, the opinions of WILLIAM CROTCH were more difficult to counter. He could accommodate the opposition of simplicity and complexity, as he does in his *Substance of Several Courses of Lectures on Music* (London, 1831): 'Simplicity, and its opposite, intricacy, when on a large scale (such an intricacy as, from the number of its parts, becomes incomprehensible), are sublime.' His application of this idea was in fact useful, as he equated the breadth of symphonies to undefined vastness, major chords to a blaze of light, and unintelligible discords to darkness.

For Crotch, discord remained extraneous and unintelligible, and failed, as did Haydn in his opinion, to achieve the level of the sublime. It was left to CHARLES BURNEY to set things straight. He argued vigorously that music was a language as durable and intelligible as classical Greek, and that instrumental music was capable of being sublime and having a stronger effect on our feelings than an opera air combined with poetry. Similarly after Haydn's death he answered detractors of 'The Representation of Chaos' at the opening of *The Creation*, defending the logic of chaos when chaos was called for, calling this the most sublime idea in Haydn's works. Even Haydn came to the defence of this work against those who objected to the secular presentation of something sacred, pointing out that the creation story had always been regarded as most sublime, inspiring the utmost awe in mankind.

While the term sublime may be appropriate for Haydn, he clearly did not think of it in the terror-arousing way that some literary figures did. Unlike the deeply disturbing and pessimistic aspects of Milton's *Paradise Lost*, Haydn's *Creation* moves from chaos to light, emphasizing human ascendency. Further, his adaptation of Thomson's *Seasons* sheds the gruesome aspect of nature and becomes a celebration of creation, even in the graphic hunting chorus in Autumn ('Hört das laute Getön'). While the work may inspire awe and a sense of boundlessness, it does that without inciting horror. Contrary to where literature had gone with the sublime by the first decade of the 19th century, Haydn remained much more comfortable with a mid-18th-century notion of the term. DPS

P. de Bolla, *The Discourse of the Sublime: Readings in History, Aesthetics and the Subject* (Oxford, 1989).

A. P. Brown, 'The Sublime, the Beautiful and the Ornamental: English Aesthetic Currents and Haydn's London Symphonies', in O. Biba and D. W. Jones (eds), *Studies in Music History Presented to H. C. Robbins Landon on his Seventieth Birthday* (London, 1996), 44–71.

S. H. Monk, *The Sublime: A Study of Critical Theories in XVIIIth Century England* (Ann Arbor, 1960).

J. Webster, 'The *Creation*, Haydn's Late Vocal Music, and the Musical Sublime', in E. Sisman (ed.), *Haydn and His World* (Princeton, 1997), 57–102.

T. E. B. Wood, *The Word 'Sublime' and its Context, 1650–1760* (The Hague, 1972).

'Sun' quartets. Nickname occasionally used for the op. 20 quartets. It derives from the publication of the works by HUMMEL in 1779 that has a title page that features the sun. JH

'Sunrise' quartet. Nickname in common use in English-speaking countries from the 19th century onwards for the quartet in B♭, op. 76 no. 4, and prompted by the slowly rising first subject that is heard above a sustained chordal background. The French refer similarly to the work as 'L'aurore' ('dawn') but there is no German equivalent in use. 'Tannhäuser' quartet is occasionally encountered in German-speaking countries because of the similarity to Haydn's theme of 'Freudig begrüßen wir die edle Halle' from Wagner's opera. JH

'Surprise' symphony. Commonly used nickname for Symphony no. 94, occasioned by the unexpected loud chord that disturbs the course of the opening theme of the slow movement. The nickname originated during Haydn's time in London, the flautist Andrew Ashe claiming that he had coined it. However, details of the circumstances that prompted Haydn to include the surprise vary from one source to another. In his autobiography, GYROWETZ, who was in London in 1792 at the time of composition and first performance, wrote that Haydn pointed to the score and said 'There the ladies will jump'. DIES gave a more extended account, indicating that Haydn had noticed that some people fell asleep in concerts in London and the chord was designed to wake them from their slumbers. The continuation of Dies's story has not, however, become part of the folklore, presumably because it is not in keeping with the image of the genial Haydn: a young lady fainted during a performance of the movement and 'some used the incident to find fault, and said that Haydn had always surprised us up to now in a courteous fashion but this time he had been very coarse'. When GRIESINGER asked Haydn whether the loud chord was designed to wake up sleeping members of the audience, the composer rejected the idea saying merely that it was his wish to surprise with something new. The surprise was a comparatively late addition to the score. The first version requires the first eight bars to be repeated exactly with no loud chord; Haydn cancelled this in favour of a written-out repeat so that he could include the surprise. Connoisseurs of Haydn's symphonies might have recalled that he had included a similar surprise in the final tranquil moments of the slow movement of Symphony no. 85.

Swieten, (Baron) Gottfried (Bernhard) van (b. 29 Oct. 1733; d. 29 March 1803). Viennese statesman and patron of music, closely associated with the composition and first performances of Haydn's oratorios, *The Creation* and *The Seasons*. Born in Leiden in the Austrian Netherlands, he was the son of the distinguished doctor Gerhard van Swieten (1700–72), and in 1745, on his father's appointment as personal physician to Empress Maria Theresia, the family moved to Vienna, which was to remain his home until his death.

The early part of his career was spent in training for the diplomatic service and he lived for short periods in Brussels, Paris, London, and Warsaw; his most significant posting was as ambassador to the court of Frederick the Great in Berlin (1770–7). Returning to Vienna as Prefect of the Imperial Library (which he remained for the rest of his life), he was during the 1780s a leading figure in Austrian internal affairs, his position as president of the Court Commission on Education and Censorship placing him at the forefront of the liberal policies of JOSEPH II. But his prominence in public affairs ended in 1791 when he fell victim to the political retrenchment of Leopold II.

From his youth he was active in musical matters. Two slight but not unattractive *opéras comiques* of his own survive, together with several symphonies, of which three appeared in print under Haydn's name, and one is known to have received a performance in Vienna as late as 1782 in the company of a symphony by Mozart. But Haydn was hardly unfair when he described them as being 'as stiff as [the man] himself'. Van Swieten's significance is not as a composer but as a champion of the music of others, both living and dead. Crucial were the years in Berlin, since it was there that he developed his enthusiasm for music of the past, especially the works of J. S. Bach and Handel.

Back in Vienna he quickly made his musical presence felt. The performance by the Tonkünstler-Societät in 1779 of Handel's *Judas Maccabaeus* (in German, in an arrangement by Joseph Starzer (1726/7–87)) was surely due to his influence. He amassed an enviable collection of old music and subscribed to English publications of HANDEL. Mozart in his letters of 1782–3 reported his excitement at his discovery of the music of Bach (1685–1750) and Handel at the regular informal gatherings on Sundays at van Swieten's lodgings. Another northern contact was C. P. E. BACH, from whom van Swieten had commissioned a set of six string symphonies (H.657–62) in 1773, and whose published works he now promoted in Vienna, receiving in return the dedication of the third set of *Sonaten für Kenner und Liebhaber* (1781).

At some time in the 1780s van Swieten established a group of aristocratic sponsors, known as the GESELLSCHAFT DER ASSOCIIERTEN CAVALIERS to promote performances of oratorios. Probably among the first works performed was C. P. E. Bach's *Auferstehung und Himmelfahrt Jesu*, conducted by Mozart, in February 1788, but thereafter the repertoire consisted almost exclusively of Handel, and it was for this series of concerts that Mozart prepared his arrangements of *Acis and Galatea* (1788), *Messiah* (1789), the *Ode for St Cecilia's Day*, and *Alexander's Feast* (1790). These were essentially private occasions, although repeat performances in public sometimes followed. The Associierte bore all the costs, and the oratorios were heard by an invited audience in the residence of one of the members. Van Swieten himself coordinated the operation, including the preparation of performing parts, and in particular made himself responsible for the German texts, normally drawing on already existing translations.

Haydn had long been acquainted with van Swieten, his close contemporary. His autobiographical sketch of 1776 suggests that the latter had championed his music in the face of general indifference in Berlin. Even in the 1780s Haydn may have been involved in a small way with the Associierte, although in view of his duties to the Esterházy household he is unlikely to have undertaken the direction of Handel oratorios 'in alternation with Mozart', as GRIESINGER was to claim. The series of concerts continued through the 1790s, and in one of them in 1793, between Haydn's two visits to London, his chorus *The Storm* was performed; van Swieten may have been the author of the German translation of the text. In any event, he was already pressing Haydn for another oratorio of his own, going so far as to commission from the poet Johann Baptist von Alxinger no later than about 1790 a libretto entitled *Die Vergötterung des Hercules*, which the composer was to set 'in the spirit and manner of Handel'. Nothing came of that project, and Handel in the context of van Swieten's exclusive performances seems to have made little impact on Haydn. But when in 1795 he returned from England the second time, inspired to new choral works by the popular Handel tradition that he had experienced in London, a platform was ready for him in Vienna. Van Swieten was still trumpeting, 'Haydn, we're still waiting to hear another oratorio from you', and he was happy to put all the organization and financial backing of his group at Haydn's disposal.

The concert series of the Associierte reached their climax with the choral version of THE SEVEN LAST WORDS (1796), THE CREATION (1798), and THE SEASONS (1801). In each case van Swieten's group paid Haydn a handsome honorarium and looked after the costs and organization of the first performances, which took place before an invited audience in the town house of PRINCE JOSEPH SCHWARZENBERG. Van Swieten himself again took personal responsibility for the texts, and this resulted in his increasingly close involvement in the genesis of the three works. In the case of *The Seven Last Words* his task amounted to little more than minor revisions to the words of the earlier arrangement by Joseph Friebert, but *The Creation* was a different matter. Haydn had brought back from London an old English libretto, supposedly intended in the first place for Handel, and van Swieten's aim was (as he himself put it) to 'clothe the English poem in German garb'. The result was a remarkable exercise in providing, as it were, a German version of a Handelian oratorio that did not yet exist. Although the English libretto from which he worked is now lost, and although cuts and alterations were certainly made, it is clear that for the most part the German text was designed so that Haydn's music would fit the original English words as well, thus creating an oratorio that would take its place within the Handelian tradition, and as at home in London as in Vienna. This intention was emphasized by the publication of the score with words in both languages. The process was similar in principle for *The Seasons*; but working from James Thomson's extended poem rather than a source already to the scale of a libretto meant that van Swieten had a greater part to play in shaping the oratorio, with less happy results (as Haydn himself complained), especially in the English back-translation he was then obliged to provide from his German words.

His involvement with the composition of the oratorios went beyond the words, however. His manuscript librettos also contained marginal suggestions for musical treatment. Patronizing though these annotations may seem (and blatantly obvious though some of them are), they probably arose at Haydn's request, and many left their mark on the music. Particularly characteristic was van Swieten's desire for local colour, and at times he clearly pressed Haydn further than he would have wished to go, most famously evident in Haydn's protest (concerning the croaking frog in *The Seasons*), 'This Frenchified trash was forced upon me', which caused some friction between the two men.

From the time of their collaboration on the oratorios onwards, van Swieten also acted as adviser to Haydn in financial and other matters. He was closely involved with the publication of the choral works, and Haydn would agree to nothing without his approval. There is little doubt that, as Haydn's pupil SIGISMUND NEUKOMM observed, he was 'not so much a friend as a very self-opiniated patron of Haydn and Mozart', but he provided valued support during Haydn's later years. Sadly, he was also unwittingly involved in the loss of Haydn's autographs of *The Creation* and *The Seasons*; on his death the scores disappeared from his desk and have not been seen since.

Beethoven during his early years in Vienna was another composer who received support and stimulation in the direction of old music from van Swieten, to whom he dedicated his First Symphony. In recognition of his promotion of the music of J. S. Bach, van Swieten was also the dedicatee of Johann Nikolaus Forkel's prophetic Bach biography (1802). DEO

H. C. Robbins Landon (ed.), *The Creation and The Seasons: The Complete Authentic Sources for the Word-Books* (Cardiff, 1985).

E. Olleson, 'Gottfried van Swieten, Patron of Haydn and Mozart', *Proceedings of the Royal Musical Association*, 89 (1962–3), 63–74.

E. Olleson, 'Gottfried, Baron van Swieten and his Influence on Haydn and Mozart' (diss., University of Oxford, 1967).

Symphonie concertante (Hob.I:105). Haydn's only work in the genre—he used the frequently encountered shortened title of 'Concertante' on the autograph—was given its first performance on 7 March 1792 at the fourth Salomon concert that season. Scored for four soloists, violin, cello, oboe, and bassoon the leading parts were played by Salomon, Menel, Harrington, and Holmes. The genre of the symphonie concertante, a work for multiple soloists and orchestra, was especially associated with public concert life in Paris. But it enjoyed some success in London too. J. C. Bach (1735–82) composed over a dozen examples and from the late 1780s a symphonie concertante in E♭ (Benton 111) by Pleyel scored for oboe, violin, viola, and cello was performed several times at the Professional Concert in London. On 27 February 1792, eight days before the premiere of Haydn's work, a new symphonie concertante in F (Benton 113) by Pleyel for flute, oboe, bassoon, violin, viola, and cello was presented at the rival Professional Concert. Haydn was, therefore, tapping into a minor but consistent aspect of the concert repertoire in London. He might, too, have been encouraged by the reception given in the 1791 season to the notturni originally written for an ensemble led by two *lire organizzate* that he had rescored for performance in London. The same easy-going interplay of instruments is to be found in the symphonie concertante.

The language and gestures of the three movements are not those of Haydn's 'London' symphonies, with repetition of appealing melodic lines and ready virtuosity being the prime concern rather than evolutionary symphonic thinking and drama. Inevitably the violin tends to assume the leading role, particularly in the finale, but the cello part is probably the most taxing. The first movement concludes in an ensemble cadenza, while the third avoids a cadenza in favour of a mock-serious recitative passage.

A forgotten work in the 19th century the symphonie concertante gained considerable popularity from the 1930s onwards. Prompted by Haydn's work the Czech composer Bohuslav Martinů (1890–1959) wrote a symphonie concertante for similar forces and in the same key.

HCRL/3.

'Symphonie mit dem Paukenschlag'. German nickname for Symphony no. 94, literally 'symphony with the timpani stroke', prompted by the same, famous loud chord that gave rise to the nickname 'Surprise'. JH

'Symphonie mit dem Paukenwirbel'. German nickname for Symphony no. 103, literally 'symphony with the drumroll'. JH

symphony. See opposite.

symphony

Joseph Haydn has long been considered the 'father of the symphony'. Such an appellation should not be taken to mean that he invented the genre, rather that he was the first composer to propagate and develop it into what came to be regarded as the ultimate test of a composer's mettle. It was with Haydn's 'Paris' and 'London' symphonies (nos. 82–7, 93–104), as well as the symphonies of Mozart from the 1780s, that the status of the symphony was established.

Two central issues have affected the historiography of Haydn's symphonies: authenticity and chronology. While today it is generally acknowledged that Haydn composed 106 symphonies, 148 further symphonies were attributed to him during his lifetime. For the authentic works, the numberings used today (1–104) are from the catalogue (1907) by MANDYCZEWSKI that accompanied the symphony volumes of the complete edition initiated by Breitkopf & Härtel. Despite the claim of SANDBERGER that he had discovered further symphonies, Mandyczewski's list has not been challenged, except for the addition of two early symphonies, Hob.I:107 and Hob. I:108. In addition, Hob.I:106, listed by Haydn in the ENTWURF-KATALOG, is now thought to be the overture to *Le pescatrici*. Chronology was not so well settled by Mandyczewski's catalogue; some works that carry a rather high number are actually earlier (e.g. no. 72) and the order of symphonies within the 'Paris' and 'London' sets is faulty. There have been a number of attempts to settle details of chronology, by Landon, Larsen, and Gerlach, using both source and stylistic evidence. The most recent, Gerlach's essay (1996) covering Haydn's symphonies up to 1774, is the most scientific, but has not yet been subjected to the debate it inevitably will engender.

Despite the modern preoccupation with definitions of the genre and Haydn's contribution to it, for the composer himself what exactly comprised a symphony was less rigidly conceived. From the authentic catalogues (the *Entwurf-Katalog*, the HAYDN-VERZEICHNIS, and the KEES CATALOGUE) and titles on authorized publications, it is clear that the composer might well have included several overtures. In 1782, for instance, Artaria published 'Sei Sinfonie' (op. 35), six overtures culled from Haydn's operas and from the oratorio *Il ritorno di Tobia*, some with altered endings and others with added finales. Overall these works are shorter than contemporary symphonies, particularly in their slow movements and finales. They are symphonies in miniature. Also to be considered miniature symphonies are the SCHERZANDI, four-movement works contemporary with Haydn's earliest extant symphonies.

---

1. Symphonies composed before 1761 (nos. 1, 2, 4, 5, 10, 11, 15, 18, 20, 27, 32, 33, 37, and Hob.I:107). Although Haydn himself identified Symphony no. 1 in D as his first and said it was written for Count Morzin, it may not actually be the first. For instance, no. 37 is dated 1758 on an old manuscript copy, preceding by a year the earliest documented date for no. 1 (25 November 1759). During this first period there are symphonies in the style of the contemporary overture (nos. 1, 4, 10, and 27); works that belong to the distinctive Viennese tradition of C major music coloured by trumpets (nos. 20, 32, 33, and 37); so called *da chiesa* symphonies, that is, works that begin with a slow movement (nos. 5, 11, and 18); and what might loosely be considered as chamber symphonies (nos. 2, 15, and Hob.1:107).

The overture-styled symphonies are all in three movements and in sharp keys, with the opening fast movement being the most substantial; this is followed by a slow movement scored for strings only and a finale in 3/8 time. First movements are marked by characteristics usually associated with the Italian operatic overture: forceful opening chords ('hammerstrokes'), *crescendo* passages based on gradually rising melodic lines, tremolos, active surface rhythms, and a generally bustling impression. For some scholars these traits derive from the Mannheim style associated with Johann Stamitz (1717–57) but this is a mistaken view of stylistic development at the time. Rather than a line of influence from Italy, to Mannheim, and on to Vienna, both Stamitz and Haydn (indeed others too) were affected by a shared Italian tradition. That Haydn takes over such traits is not significant, but what he does with them is. In the first movement of no. 1 the opening *crescendo* is activated by more than a rising line; Haydn also decreased the size of the module from single bars to single beats. Later, some polyphony is added. Even in silences the music pushes forward in anticipation, while full cadences tend to be overridden with surface activity. Nos. 4/i and 10/i imaginatively manipulate hammerstroke exclamations, while no. 27/i begins with a simple rhythmic idea of broadly striding minims that encourages all kinds of later manipulation. As is the case in the early symphonies in general, the slow movements are moderate rather than extremely slow in tempo. Particularly notable is that of no. 4 with its singing line for first violins, walking bass lines in quavers, and *alla zoppa* ('limping') second violins. Even the 3/8 finales display Haydn's imagination; that of no.1, for instance, refuses to settle down into a routine procession of phrases and sentences, yet ultimately forms a compact and complete sonata form.

Of the four symphonies in C major that are part of a broad Viennese tradition of works in that key, the first movement of no. 37 seems to reflect the particular influence of a *Servizio di Tavola* by REUTTER, Haydn's teacher. The trio of the minuet, as in many of the early symphonies, provides an expressive peak with its minor mode and mixing of 3/4 and 6/8. No. 32/i reveals Haydn's unorthodox sense of structure, emphasizing the second subject in the development to such an extent that it is omitted from the recapitulation. Nothing is known about the particular circumstances surrounding the composition of these C major symphonies but these jubilant works with their brilliant sound in the outer movements and more subdued slow movements and trio sections could well have been designed for noble celebrations or certain festive dates in the liturgical year.

Those symphonies often categorized as *da chiesa* have acquired that description following the standard textbook definition of *sonata da chiesa*, a cycle of instrumental movements that opens with a slow movement. However, there is no evidence in Haydn's case that such symphonies were more likely to have been performed in church than those that open with an Allegro. The first movement is followed by an Allegro, a minuet, and, often but not always, a finale. Each of the opening slow movements has a distinct character: no. 5 features high horn-writing in a delicate orchestral fabric;

no. 11 has a trio-sonata texture with rudimentary horn parts; and no. 18 is another trio texture but with unexpected *fortissimo* outbursts, after which the music continues as if nothing had happened. The fast movements and minuets of nos. 5 and 18 are comparable in style to equivalent movements in contemporary symphonies by the composer.

Among the three chamber symphonies, no. 15 opens with an Adagio, reminiscent of the first movement of no. 5. Of sufficient duration to make the listener believe that it is a full slow movement, it is interrupted by a Presto in a full sonata form before the Adagio returns. Haydn returns to this idea of a frame for the main portion of a movement in later symphonies. For the 3/8 finale the usual sonata form is replaced by an unusual structure in three sections (ABC, plus coda) but with a good deal of internal repetition. No. 2/iv is a more conventional simple rondo (ABACA). Its first movement has no repeats and shows Haydn mixing sonata with ritornello forms and homophony with counterpoint. The central Andante, saturated with semiquavers, is one of Haydn's most continuous and homogeneous products. Hob.I:107 in B♭ is easily one of his weakest works in any genre.

The 14 symphonies in this first period of composition are evenly divided between works in three movements and those that have four. The emotional focus lies in the first two movements, leaving the minuets and most of the finales to be less weighty. The scoring is mostly for two oboes, two horns, and strings with three (possibly four) symphonies adding trumpets and timpani. In all slow movements, the winds are omitted and, sometimes, the strings use mutes. A full scoring returns for the minuet, while the trio section is again either reduced or features solo-writing. Haydn's first movements are sonata forms that often take a single idea and refer to it consistently. This does not preclude the appearance of a contrasting second subject which, typically, may be characterized by reduced orchestration, a softer dynamic, a completely new texture, or a brief turn to the minor mode. The structure of the slow movements is usually that of sonata form, though the typical tempo of Andante ensures a less obviously eventful content. Minuets are consistently aristocratic in their feel, in the sense that they have dotted rhythms, rolling triplets, fanfare rhythms, and bass lines marking the beat. The most consistent aspect of the finales is the combination of a Presto tempo and a 3/8 pulse, found in nine symphonies. Two finales are in the tempo of a minuet (3/4), one is in 2/4, one in 6/8, and one in alla breve.

2. Symphonies from *c*.1761 to *c*.1763 (nos. 3, 14, 16, 17, 19, 25, 36, and Hob.I:108). Like the symphonies in the first group, these eight symphonies do not survive as autographs and their date of composition is conjectural. As a group they tend to be more homogeneous: all are scored for two oboes, two horns, and strings, and they consist of the customary three- or four-movement patterns. No. 25 has a lengthy slow introduction leading to an Allegro, followed, not by a slow movement but by a minuet, and a concluding Presto in 2/4; partly because of its unusual movement structure, some scholars have cast doubt on the authenticity of the work. Slow movements are mostly in 2/4 and marked Andante, while the finales are variously in 3/8, 6/8, 2/4, and alla breve.

Hob.I:108 in B♭ is a miniature four-movement symphony lasting no more than 12 minutes (even with all its repeats). The outer movements are highly energized, the two middle ones deeply original. Horns lend a brilliance to the first, third, and fourth movements, while the minor mode and the contrapuntal textures of the slow movement provide a strong contrast. The trio of the minuet provides the first instance of solo bassoon-writing in Haydn's symphonies.

Symphonies nos. 17 and 19 are comparatively unremarkable, while no. 3 in G is among Haydn's most distinctive efforts, with different types of contrapuntal activity defining the individual movements. The first movement begins with two-part SPECIES COUNTERPOINT: long notes in the oboes and violins against running quavers in the bass. Every time this theme returns its contrapuntal make-up changes. At times the long notes disappear and a new environment is composed for the running quavers, while at other times the long-note idea finds a new counterpoint or accompaniment. At the recapitulation, two intensified versions of this subject are heard. The Andante moderato is also highly thematic in its texture with very little orchestral padding. The minuet is canonic, part of a Viennese tradition that continues from the mid-18th century through to Brahms in the 19th century. The finale is a double fugue in alla breve metre with the second subject (bar 39) providing a new counterpoint to the opening theme.

A preoccupation with counterpoint is also apparent in no. 16/i. Instead of being associated with the first subject, it is heard five times during the course of the exposition of the sonata form. Haydn enriches the string sonority in the Andante, where a solo cello doubles at the octave the muted violins. No. 14/ii replicates the enriched sound of no. 16/ii, but this time it is based on material from the divertimento in C (Hob.II:11); in the divertimento the theme is used for variations, here it is enlarged to produce a sonata form. The finale is a polyphonic movement based on a descending scale.

The opening theme of Symphony no. 36 in E♭ is a distinctive one, resting on a tonic chord for three bars; the lengthy development, divided into three stages, is also striking. The Adagio could have been taken from a concerto, or rather a double concerto for violin and cello, an association made even more marked by the strings-only sonority and the strong octave unison writing that heralds the solo passages.

3. Early Esterházy symphonies, 1761–5 (nos. 6, 7, 8, 9, 12, 13, 21, 22, 23, 24, 28, 29, 30, 31, 34, 40, and 72). Haydn officially entered the service of the Esterházy family as Vice-Kapellmeister on 1 May 1761, when he signed his contract. He had explicit responsibility for instrumental music and a virtually new orchestra was established. Of the 17 symphonies written during the first five years of service, half feature concertante movements (first movements, slow movements, and finales) designed to display the talents of Haydn's colleagues; the number would be even higher if trios from minuets were added.

Dating from 1761 and thought to be Haydn's first works as Vice-Kapellmeister are Symphonies nos. 6–8, given the titles 'Le Matin', 'Le Midi', and 'Le Soir'. At the suggestion of Prince Anton, Haydn composed three programmatic works, which he combined with concertante writing. Not only is there compelling external support for these symphonies to be regarded as a trilogy, but the internal factors are equally persuasive. Nos. 6 and 7 begin with slow introductions (the first proportionate introductions in Haydn's œuvre) and no. 8 begins with a 3/8 movement, a metre normally associated with a finale and here initiating the 'finale' to the trilogy. The slow movements all present concertante writing that is almost operatic in its character: no. 6 is a duet for violin and cello; no. 7 presents a recitative that leads into another duet for the same instruments; and no. 8 is a quartet for two violins, cello, and bassoon.

All the trio sections feature the double bass as a solo instrument. Symphonies nos. 6 and 7 have contredanse finales, while that to the Symphony no. 7 is a storm (*La tempesta*).

As regards their character, 'Le Matin' begins with a slow introduction representing a sunrise, while the Allegro features a standard pastoral melody, moving around the tonic triad; later there are some imitations of birdsong (bars 35–9) and some dark patches of orchestral and harmonic colour (bars 58–65). At the same time this movement is a hybrid of sonata and ritornello principles, especially the alternation of solo and tutti. Many people have commented that the false start to the recapitulation, played by the horn, anticipates a similar moment in the first movement of Beethoven's *Eroica Symphony*. The slow movement is an Andante for solo violin and cello framed by an adagio *exordium* and *conclusio*. The trio features a truly bizarre combination of solo instruments, double bass, bassoon, viola, and cello, all over a pizzicato accompaniment. The finale includes solo passages for flute, violin, and cello in a structure similar to that of the first movement.

No. 7 in C ('Le Midi') also begins with a slow introduction in the style of a festive slow march followed by another ritornello-cum-sonata form. Some have heard this as the entry of the prince and his guests for the midday meal, Haydn's own *Servizio di Tavola*. The second movement is an accompanied recitative that presents a series of contrasting moods; it leads into a pastoral movement featuring solo violin and cello, plus a pair of solo flutes; it concludes with a cadenza for the two solo string instruments.

The first movement of no. 8 in G ('Le Soir') quotes a song about snuff-taking from Gluck's *Le Diable a quatre*, which Prince Anton (and obviously Haydn) must have heard at the Burgtheater in Vienna. No doubt the square phrasing of the song must have determined the initial stretch of 32 bars before an irregular phrase occurs, probably a record in Haydn's instrumental music. Two ideas dominate the slow movement: the melodic material, well suited to ornamentation, is given to the four soloists while the dotted rhythms and staccato quavers are played by the tutti. The trilogy, and the day, ends with a storm, as Haydn evokes raindrops, heavy rain, and lightning.

Nos. 6, 7, and 8 must have found favour at the Esterházy court, for Haydn continued to write concertante and characteristic symphonies both separately and in combination, though he never repeated the idea of a set of symphonies on a programmatic idea. Among the most famous of the symphonies of the early 1760s is no. 31 in D, the 'Hornsignal'. A quartet of horns (perhaps physically separated into two pairs in a performance) feature as commanding solo instruments alongside every other instrument in Haydn's orchestra except the viola. Symphony no. 72 in D is an obvious twin to no. 31 with its use of four horns and many soloistic passages. No. 13 is the third symphony in D with four horns, but here they are deployed in a much less ostentatious manner. For modern listeners the finale is notable for its governing motif, the same one as Mozart was to use in his 'Jupiter' symphony (K551) exactly a quarter of a century later. It is a thematic commonplace and there is no suggestion that Haydn's symphony influenced Mozart; indeed Mozart may not have known the work.

Nos. 21 and 22 from 1764 begin with a slow movement, both marked Adagio. No. 21/i cannot be explained by any formal stereotype; Haydn alternates two ideas, one for strings and one for winds. Played at a subdued dynamic throughout, the movement drops to a *pianissimo* for some polyphonic writing (bar 49) before briefly bursting into an unprecedented *forte*. The second movement, marked Presto, and the finale, marked Allegro molto, are interrelated not only in their extreme hyperactivity but also by a rhythmic pattern and the omission of the first subject at the beginning of the recapitulation. With justification many commentators have regarded the symphony as one of Haydn's finest.

However, no. 22 in E♭ has tended to overshadow no. 21 because of its nickname 'Philosopher' and its unusual use of two cors anglais rather than oboes, the only symphony by Haydn (indeed the only symphony in the entire history of the genre) to do so. The first movement is less freely conceived than no. 21/i. Robbins Landon has compared it to a chorale prelude with the 'chorale' in the wind instruments and walking quavers in the strings; the antiquated stance is further underlined by suspensions and appoggiaturas. In a sense, the following Presto is a rewrite of the second and fourth movements of no. 21: the same rhythmic motif dominates. Yet the movement does not achieve the raw energy and brilliance of the movements in no. 21. The minuet begins with a motif that recalls the first movement. Though Haydn writes a Presto finale in 6/8, it is neither a gigue nor a hunt. Overall, no. 22 is a mixed success with the cors anglais, so effective in the first movements, being an awkward presence in the last three movements.

Symphony no. 34 in D minor also begins with a slow movement, but greater consideration for performance in a church should be given to no. 30 in C whose Allegro first movement is built out of the Alleluja plainsong associated with Holy Week. A march dominated by dotted rhythms and flute solos comprises the central movement. The finale has the unusual marking 'Tempo di Menuet, più tosto Allegretto' and consists of three couplets (A, B, and C) with a final return to A (without repeats) plus a coda. But is the apparent structure of ABCA the way Haydn intended the movement to be performed or are the couplets to be formed into a rondo, with A returning after B to form the standard pattern of ABACA? The latter makes more sense tonally as well as thematically. Haydn reformulated the first movement in the baryton trio in D (Hob.XI:64).

Of the remaining eight symphonies from this period, no. 9 in C is thought to have started life as an overture, perhaps to *Vivan gl'illustri sposi*, a lost work written for Count (later Prince) Anton's wedding, not only because of its jubilant key, but also because of its brevity, three-movement structure, and overture style in the first movement. No. 24 in D also displays some of the bustling traits of an overture, alongside more intricate qualities; the concerto-like slow movement spotlights the flute and includes a cadenza. Symphonies nos. 12 and 40 are excellent examples of the Austrian chamber symphony with all the compositional polish a listener could desire, including a fugue to conclude no. 40.

The other two chamber symphonies, nos. 23 and 29, are notable for their slow movements. In no. 23/ii the demisemiquaver runs in the viola and bass lines are deliberately obtrusive rather than merely decorative, almost certainly prompted by a visual image. A close parallel in Viennese music is to be found in a set of keyboard variations by Alessandro Poglietti (d. 1683) in which one of the variations with a similar rhythmic character is entitled 'Französische Baiselmens' (French kisses). Robbins Landon has drawn attention to another possible allusion to Poglietti in symphony no. 57/iv. Perhaps Haydn knew his music quite well.

At first the Andante of Symphony no. 29 in E, scored for strings alone, appears to be a familiar type. But, very eccentrically, the melody is shared, bar-by-bar, between the first and second violins, as if it were a musically illiterate solution to a demarcation dispute. Only in the coda do first and second violins come together to present the melody together in an appropriately musical way. The north German critic, Johann Adam Hiller (1728–1804), completely missed the joke when he complained in 1770 about the 'ridiculous' division of the melody. Had Hiller noticed the following minuet, he would have found another joke: Haydn presents only an accompaniment to a theme; the would-be soloist, the oboe, is entirely silent.

No. 28 is another compelling symphony in A major, marked by a high level of rhythmic energy (Allegro di molto, minuet: Allegro molto, and Presto assai), leaving only the second movement (Poco Adagio) as a contrast. The opening movement is among Haydn's most hyperactive with its mixing of 6/8 and 3/4. The slow movement alternates *con sordino* lyricism with march-like rhythms in a different register; Robbins Landon has suggested that this movement and the symphony as a whole was conceived as incidental music. The minuet brings to mind a peasant fiddler who amuses his listeners with *bariolage* (repeating the same pitch on two different strings). The finale is a gigue in 6/8.

The symphonies of the period from 1761 to the end of 1765 demonstrate Kapellmeister Haydn's increasing individuality as a composer as well as his skills as a musical diplomat in the Esterházy court. Programmatic allusions flattered and amused the prince while the many concertante movements gratified the players and proved to the prince how wise his investment had been.

4. Esterházy symphonies *c.*1766–72 (nos. 26, 35, 38, 39, 41, 42, 43, 44, 45, 46, 47, 48, 49, 52, 58, 59, and Hob.I:106). With the death of Werner in March 1766 Haydn assumed responsibility for the full range of musical activity at the Esterházy court. Although sacred music and opera engaged his interest, often to striking effect, it was in the area of instrumental music that he continued to make his most pointed and potent contributions. Having used the minor mode as colouration within movements and within three- and four-movement cycles, Haydn now composes symphonies in which the minor becomes the principal mode. Of the 17 symphonies listed above, six are in the minor key. Another symphony, no. 46, is in the unusual key of B major. Many have referred to the years *c.*1766–72 as Haydn's STURM UND DRANG period; it is better, however, to talk of a *Sturm und Drang* style utilized in certain passages and movements but only occasionally in complete works. Apart from the minor mode, the style is characterized by driving rhythms in a brisk tempo including strong surface movement with anacrustic gestures, syncopation, and persistent quaver activity, as well as polyphony, unusually wide melodic leaps, sudden accents, and abrupt changes in dynamic.

Symphony no. 39 in G minor is one of the first to display these tendencies. Yet, it is not consistently of a *Sturm und Drang* character; the first and final movements fit the profile, but the Andante and the minuet are decidedly *galant*. Indeed, the 3/8 Andante is a prime example of that style with its triplets, cadences on weak beats, echoes, and generally thin texture. Given the character of this movement, the symphony as a whole fails to cohere as a unit. The first movement is a homogeneous piece in which most of the principal paragraphs begin with the same driving and impetuous theme. Its initial statement is interrupted by silence that transforms what would have been a reasonably regular phrasing pattern of 4+6+4 into an irregular one of 5+7+4. Each time this material returns, the pattern changes. After the central *galant* movements, the finale is even more densely packed with *Sturm und Drang* features: leaping first subject accompanied by tremolos and, after a silence, an electrifying burst of semiquavers. As in other *Sturm und Drang* movements, the development contains a contrasting passage of lyricism.

Symphony no. 49 in F minor is another *da chiesa* cycle. It acquired its nickname 'LA PASSIONE' because someone thought it appropriate for performance during Holy Week. Certainly the character of the first two movements seems appropriate to Christ's final moments on the Cross, a contemplative Adagio followed by an Allegro di molto that suggests the earthquake that convulsed Calvary. Each of the first three movements features the thematic profile of C, D♭, B♭; less obviously it features in the finale too, helping to create a symphony that is more consistent in purpose than no. 39.

No. 26 in D minor, known as 'LAMENTATION', is no doubt a symphony intended for Passiontide. As in no. 30, Haydn embeds chants in the first movement (bar 17 onwards), here associated with the telling of Christ's Passion and, in the following Adagio, the chant of lamentation. The opening subject of the symphony is like a ritornello with its stark texture, division into discrete sections, and strong tonic cadence at the end. In the presentation of the chant Haydn distinguishes between the sections sung by the Evangelist and Jews, which are declamatory, and those by Christ, sung in minims.

The influence of ritornello form is evident in the Adagio too, in that the chant (labelled 'Chorale') alternates with episodic interludes. As in the first movement, the point of recapitulation is emphasized by horns supporting the presentation of the chant. The finale is a severe minuet in D minor, notable for its silences and, towards the end, imitative writing. The trio turns to D major, alludes to the theme of the main minuet, but several times disturbs the tranquillity with *forte* chords on the third beat. It is possible that both the minuet and trio allude to aspects of the Passion story.

The high point of this remarkable series of symphonies in the minor key is no. 44 in E minor. Something of the intensity of the first movement may be sensed in Haydn's tempo heading 'Allegro con brio'. Thematically, the first subject is constructed as a statement–response phrase; a decisive cadence follows. Nearly every subsequent statement has a new response. It also becomes the subject of polyphony which, in turn, provides a different response (bar 44). The closing theme (bar 47) has a driving lyricism rare in Haydn's sonata forms. The development section further exploits the polyphonic potential of the first subject and intensifies the rhythmic drive of the exposition. Haydn attaches an unusually lengthy coda to the first movement during which the main subject yields yet more expressive possibilities.

The minuet, still in E minor, is placed second in the cycle, and is the last use in Haydn's symphonies of a canonic minuet. Again the trio section affords the first extended view of the tonic major, underlined by the first horn climbing into its highest register. The Adagio is also in E major and sustains a serene effect, carefully delineated by the appearance of the wind instruments to close the first subject, the exposition, and the movement.

A statement–response pattern figures at the beginning of the Presto finale too. But it is soon embroiled in strongly profiled counterpoint. The development takes a different approach and is largely an enormous sequence that rises and falls over nearly 36 bars. As the movement returns to the tonic, polyphony returns but Haydn avoids a decisive moment of recapitulation in order to keep the momentum going. Only in the last few bars does the theme come once more into focus.

The accomplishment of no. 44 is not evident in no. 52 in C minor which seems altogether less focused. For example, in the first movement there are a number of thematic ideas and a double statement of the second subject surrounded by less stable ideas. The second subject dominates the development and in the recapitulation it is again heard twice.

Much has been written about Symphony no. 45 in F♯ minor ('FAREWELL') not only because of the circumstances that led to its composition, but also because of the unusual layout of movements (ending with a slow section), its key (the only known appearance in the 18th-century symphonic repertoire), its *Sturm und Drang* character, and its two-stage finale ending with two solo violins. During the 19th century and up to the Haydn renaissance of the last third of the 20th century, the 'Farewell' was the only early symphony by the composer that remained in the repertoire; Mendelssohn (1809–47) conducted it at the Gewandhaus in Leipzig and Koussevitzky (1874–1951) at Symphony Hall, Boston. The American scholar James Webster (b.1942) has devoted an entire book to the symphony and views it as one of the composer's highest accomplishments.

Sturm und Drang features saturate most of the first movement. There is no second subject; Haydn uses a three-stage exposition of first subject, transition, and closing material that allows for no relaxation. Haydn maintains the tension for the beginning of the development. Then, after a pause, comes the most discussed passage in the movement, where the music relaxes in preparation for the recapitulation. Robbins Landon describes this as a delayed second subject, Charles Rosen draws parallels with a trio section in a minuet or the middle section of a da capo aria, Judith L. Schwartz thinks it to be a minuet, and Webster calls in an 'interlude'.

The Adagio, in A major, is remarkable for its quietude; there is no dynamic louder than *pianissimo*, the violins are muted, and the wind instruments are used sparingly. The beginning of the minuet is tentative with a scoring (two violins) and a key (F♯ major) that anticipates the very end of the symphony. The trio, also in the major key, begins with a theme played by horns which Robbins Landon hears as an allusion to the lamentation chant.

Some commentators have viewed the symphony as having five movements but Haydn makes it clear by heading the Presto as *Finale* that the fourth movement is in two complementary stages, Presto followed by Adagio; they are not separate movements. Following a nearly full sonata form in F♯ minor the movement is diverted into a serene Adagio in F♯ major. The concertante texture of the earlier Esterházy symphonies is evoked as each instrument plays a solo before departing, leaving two muted violins to end this unique symphony.

The 'Farewell' is the last symphony in the minor mode in this period and none was to be composed until no. 78, ten years later. However, these minor-key symphonies represent a little more than a third of Haydn's output from this time. Those symphonies in a major key also contain some remarkable works, though with a different expressive ambience. But, just as *Sturm und Drang* symphonies have passages and movements in the *galant* style so do major-key symphonies include *Sturm und Drang* features when appropriate.

The first of the major-key symphonies in this period is no. 35 in B♭, which displays both styles. Haydn begins in his most *galant* manner: melody in thirds and sixths over a bass line of repeated quavers. A large central section (bars 17–39) in the exposition displays much of the drive and agitation—though not the minor key—of *Sturm und*

Drang, followed by a statement of an amended version of the opening theme as a second subject. Intensive thematic action characterizes the development section during which the main theme is stripped of its *galant* proprieties and moves firmly towards the *Sturm und Drang* idiom, including the sound of minor keys.

The Andante (E♭) too manipulates themes and motifs to great effect including variation, development, compression, and expansion. In the finale, Haydn plays his favourite game of beginnings and ends. He begins with three assertive cadential chords that can function as a beginning or an ending. At the onset of the movement they form the first component of the standard statement–response pattern; in the development they form the second component. Even at the end of the movement the fact that the highest note of the repeated chords is a mediant and not a tonic makes the listener question whether the movement has, indeed, ended, an ambiguity that is emphasized if the second repeat (development and recapitulation) is taken.

Symphony no. 38 in C can be rather precisely dated because of its elaborate writing for the oboe in the third and fourth movements (including a cadenza). A particularly fine player, Vittorino Colombazzo, was employed for four months at the end of 1768 and it is thought the symphony was composed then. But the first two movements are notable for the absence of solo-writing for the oboe; perhaps they were composed before Colombazzo arrived. The result is a rather disjunct work.

Symphony no. 59 in A ('FIRE') is a much more intriguing work. The opening movement, marked Presto, makes particularly effective use of the rhythmic characteristics of the opening theme but it is the distribution of more relaxed passages that is unorthodox. At the end of the first subject (bar 6) one might expect an increase in surface tension; instead there is a marked decrease. Conversely, the second subject at bar 34, instead of providing relaxation, increases the tension with a passage of fast-moving triplets.

The Andante più tosto Allegretto, in A minor, is a new kind of slow movement in Haydn's symphonies. Rather than unfolding with undifferentiated material, the contrasts of the paragraphs are ones associated with first movements. At the same time the scoring is apparently conservative, for strings alone, until in the recapitulation when the music turns to A major and the second-subject oboes and horns magically enter. The minuet and trio alludes to both subjects of the previous slow movement. Looking back over the whole of Haydn's symphonic output the finale of no. 59 invites comparison with that of the 'Drumroll' symphony (no. 103) in that it is based on the opening horn call and answering phrase. A short development again avoids preparing for a strongly signalled return of the first subject, preferring to defer it to near the end of the movement.

The 'Fire' symphony has much of the *brio* atmosphere and originality associated with its *Sturm und Drang* companions. The 'Maria Theresia' symphony, no. 48 in C, belongs to the older tradition of brilliant C major works. The horns, pitched in C alto, are used as substitute trumpets, there are fanfare rhythms, and impressively emphasized single chords are used to galvanize the music into action. The Adagio in F major and 6/8 time offers a contrast, evoking the pastoral. The minuet interrupts its strongly tuneful course with a fanfare, simultaneously notated in quavers, triplets, and semiquavers; Haydn obviously wanted a blur of sound not clarity. Most striking about this 'trumpeting' symphony is that its ceremonial character is occasionally interrupted by stretches of *Sturm und Drang* material: the minor-key passages in the first movement, the trio in C minor, and the high agitation of the transition and development sections of the finale. Such contrasts are difficult to find elsewhere in this broad tradition of C major symphonies, whether by Haydn himself or others.

Symphony no. 58 in F is a potent refutation of the notion of a *Sturm und Drang* period. From the second half of the 1760s nearly every bar, except for the trio, is *galant* in its expression. It was entered into the *Entwurf-Katalog* next to Symphony no. 49 in F minor and it is possible that they form a contrasting pair. Of particular interest are the last two movements, *Menuet alla zoppa*, a 'limping minuet', and a 3/8 finale that includes some unexpected chromatic passages.

Symphony no. 41 is another festive work in C major that includes some *Sturm und Drang* passages, but the contrasts are not as heavily drawn as in no. 48. The high point is the slow movement whose lyricism is enhanced by muted violins and extended use of solo flute.

Robbins Landon characterized Symphony no. 43 in E♭ ('MERCURY') as an 'Austrian chamber symphony *par excellence*', prompted by its leisurely gait and unobtrusive emphasis on expressive and technical subtleties. The finale, for instance, begins almost reticently with two balancing five-bar phrases, as if based on a discarded sketch for a string quartet. The second subject (bars 49–52) is even more elliptical, four chords. Only in the lengthy coda (41 bars) does Haydn relate the one to the other. This is music for the connoisseur.

Symphony no. 42 in D was composed in 1771. Here, for the first time for a decade, Haydn evokes the style of an Italian overture. Indeed, he seems to be satirizing it, beginning with a string of clichés: hammerstroke chords, a singing allegro theme over a bass of repeated quavers, a rising scale passage that invites a *crescendo*, fanfare-like figures, measured tremolo, and a contrasting second subject. Unlike a genuine overture for an Italian opera, however, it is a very long movement, 224 bars. The Andante cantabile in A major caught the attention of the theorist Heinrich Koch (1749–1816) who cited it in his treatise *Versuch einer Anleitung zur Composition* (1782–93) as an example of sonata form. The finale is headed 'Scherzando e presto' and is the first rondo in a symphony to vary the repeats of the main theme.

The year 1772 was a remarkable one for symphonies. As well as the 'Farewell', two further symphonies of great individuality were produced, no. 46 in B and no. 47 in G. Apart from its key, no. 46 is notable for the way Haydn links the minuet with the finale; towards the end of the finale he quotes the minuet, revealing a thematic relationship between the movements. To help this feeling of overall coherence Haydn uses B as a tonic throughout, major in the first movement, minuet, and finale, minor in the slow movement and the trio of the minuet. The first subject of the opening movement reveals a kinship with that of no. 44, and both movements too are permeated with sighs. The potential of the first subject is drawn out by species counterpoint, imitation, canon, and inversion which results in an ever-increasing sense of complexity as the movement unfolds. A *fausse reprise* in the tonic occurs in the development (bar 70) after which a secondary theme in the first subject area is extensively explored. Shortly after the recapitulation proper (bar 105) it is the turn of the first subject to be developed, having received little attention in the development section. In contrast to nos. 44 and 45, this symphony has a leaner and more piercing sonority, largely the result of the use of horns in B alto; but, by emphasizing two-part and octave textures, the string-writing too contributes to this mood.

For the Poco adagio in B minor, the horns are required to change from B alto to D, producing a mellower sound which together with the muted violins and the generally fuller texture creates a wholly different atmosphere. The frequent semiquavers, carefully marked 'staccato assai', foster a mysterious rather than a melancholy mood. The minuet returns to the key and sonority of the first movement; however it is nearly obliterated from memory by the sparse, deadpan trio in B minor, scored for strings alone.

The finale with the unusual marking Presto e scherzando begins quietly, without asserting the tonic; its singularity might prompt the attentive listener into noting a resemblance between the material and that of the minuet. During the course of the movement the various implications of 'scherzando' become evident: the character of the melodic material, the use of pauses, and the generally driven nature of the movement. All this prepares for the return of the second strain of the minuet near the end of the movement, making explicit what had been implicit throughout. Symphony no. 46 is a special work but to emphasize its historical significance is probably a mistake. Most commentators draw a parallel between the work and the last two movements of Beethoven's Fifth Symphony. Putting to one side the fact that Beethoven is unlikely to have known this work, it should be noted that the effect of the return of the third movement in the two works is completely different. Each should be appreciated on its own terms.

Symphony no. 47 in G has four discrete, seemingly unrelated movements, each with its peculiarities. The march topos of the opening is shared between horns and strings in such a way that when it returns at the beginning of the recapitulation it can be played in G minor not G major. The theme and variations of the slow movement are informed by invertible double counterpoint of the kind Brahms was to admire. More contrapuntal artifice follows in the *Menuet al Roverso* and associated *Trio al Roverso* in which the first eight bars of each are played backwards to provide the second half of the respective movements. The purely homophonic finale is best viewed as a monothematic sonata form, relieved by a Hungarian episode heard three times (exposition, bar 45; development, bar 154; and recapitulation, bar 206). Its function is to provide some exotic contrast to the otherwise bland diatonicism. Mozart evidently knew the work; he wrote down its incipit in April 1782, together with those of symphonies nos. 62 and 75, perhaps with a view to performing them at his concerts in Vienna.

5. Esterházy symphonies from *c*.1772 to *c*.1781 (nos. 50, 51, 53, 54, 55, 56, 57, 60, 61, 62, 63, 64, 65, 66, 67, 68, 69, 70, 71, 73, 74, and 75). As the first person to survey in detail the whole of Haydn's symphonic output Robbins Landon was also the first to suggest that these symphonies were less worthy of attention than those in the previous group because they turn away from the *Sturm und Drang* idiom. Recently, commentators have come to regard the works positively, appreciating the broadening of symphonic style evident in this period, responding to the individuality of certain works, and recognizing their relationship to later, and greater, symphonies. All commentators have noted the evidence of Haydn's experience as a composer of opera. Accordingly subdivision into two periods, marked by the establishment of a full season of opera at Eszterháza, is appropriate: *c*.1772 to *c*.1774–5, and *c*.1775 to *c*.1781.

At first glance Symphonies nos. 65 and 51 are standard works in the major mode. Yet, both have eccentric slow movements. That of no. 65, an Andante in 3/8 time in D, is wholly unpredictable in its course, leading Robbins Landon to characterize it as of 'almost lunatic irrationality'; Elaine Sisman suggests that it might have started life as incidental music to Shakespeare's *Hamlet*. A different kind of eccentricity features in the slow movement of no. 51, an Adagio in E♭: in a concertante movement featuring one oboe and two horns the first horn rises to an unprecedented (notated) *f'''* and the second horn descends to a similarly unprecedented (notated) *FF*♯. Most notable in the first movement of no. 65 is the failure of the opening hammerstrokes to return in their original form, though a three-note figure that is derived from them features throughout. The recapitulation begins in the subdominant and with the second subject. The first movement of no. 51 is an unusually expansive one with large areas of tonal stability for the first and second subjects. The minuet has two trio sections, one for strings and one for wind instruments. The rondo finale (ABACA) contains a gypsy episode (C) and a fanfare to herald its close.

'Tempora mutantur' is possibly Haydn's own title for Symphony no. 64 in A, more specifically the slow movement, which manipulates expectations of passing musical time in the unusual tempo for this period of Largo. The finale is another ABACA rondo, with B referring back to the material of A, and C a *Sturm und Drang* interlude.

The first two movements of Symphony no. 50 in C originated as the overture to the lost marionette opera *Der Götterrat*, performed during Maria Theresia's visit to Eszterháza in 1773. Two movements were added to make it an attractive addition to the tradition of C major symphonies. The slow introduction is particularly prophetic of similar sections in later works with its dotted figuration for full orchestra and darkening of harmonic colour before settling on the dominant in preparation for the Allegro di molto.

As well as the nickname 'IL DISTRATO' the unusual six-movement structure of Symphony no. 60 in C is explained by its origins as incidental music to a play by Regnard performed at Eszterháza. In Haydn's lifetime it became his most widely performed symphony, probably to the composer's embarrassment since in 1803 he referred to it as 'DEN ALTEN SCHMARN'.

Symphony no. 54 in G is another work with a notable slow movement, an Adagio assai in C and one of Haydn's longest and most deeply felt pieces. The music unfolds with a series of almost improvisatory gestures culminating in a notated cadenza for the first violins. In the recapitulation the cadenza is written for first and second violins and is much longer. Exceptionally for this period, the finale is not a rondo but a sonata form.

One of the most consistently impressive works of the period is no. 55 in E♭ ('SCHOOLMASTER'), even though its slow movement does not match the expressivity of no. 54/ii. If this work is another example of an Austrian chamber symphony then no. 56 is yet another work in the C major tradition, this time scored for trumpets and horns in C alto. Haydn lays out the Allegro di molto in broad paragraphs that reveal his sense of large-scale structural balance. The Adagio bears comparison with that of no. 54, though its expressive means are different: lyrical with a sure sense of orchestral colour including two extended solos for bassoon.

Symphony no. 57 in D is a fourth work from 1774. The first movement begins with a slow introduction followed by an unremarkable Allegro, the slow movement is once more quite quirky (with its alternation of pizzicato and arco), and the finale, like no. 56/iv, is a Prestissimo sonata form that effectively sounds in 12/8; the thematic material of the finale belongs to a broad tradition of birdsong, that includes works such as Poglietti's *Capriccio über das Hennengeschrey* (Capriccio on the noise of a clucking hen) and Haydn's own evocation of the cockerel in *The Seasons*.

No. 68 in B♭ is another fine example of a chamber symphony, though unusual in having two movements in triple time followed by two movements in duple time. On the whole the minuet, placed second, is rather old-fashioned, but the trio section (also in B♭) is prophetic, featuring exaggerated emphasis on the up-beat in a way that Haydn was to find endlessly amusing and stimulating (e.g. the trio sections in the quartet op. 64 no. 3 and in symphonies nos. 62 and 92, and the 'Osanna' in the 'Harmoniemesse'). The Adagio cantabile in E♭ simultaneously looks back to the serenade-like movements from early in Haydn's career and forward to the slow movement of the 'Clock' symphony with its persistent (though very fast) ticking rhythms. The gratuitous decoration of the first-violin line that occurs towards the end of the movement has caused one commentator to draw a parallel between it and the forest scene in Act 3 of *Armida*. The finale is an extended rondo (ABACADA); the first episode draws attention to the two bassoons, available for the first time at the Esterházy court in 1774–5; the second episode features the oboes; and the third episode is in the minor key. The coda is the first instance in the composer's instrumental music of a burlesque ending of a kind featured in Symphony no. 90 and the quartet op. 33 no. 2. The texture disintegrates to nothing, as if the performers had completely lost their way. In turn, seven hesitant instrumental lines (marked 'echo') try to give the impression of continuity before the full orchestra enters with a rousing conclusion.

During the three years from 1775 to 1777 Haydn was successively preoccupied with the composition of two large-scale works, both major challenges, the oratorio *Il ritorno di Tobia* and the opera *L'incontro improvviso*, and with preparing for the first full seasons of operas at Eszterháza. Consequently, according to Sonja Gerlach's careful reasoning, only three symphonies were composed in *c.*1775–6, one in 1776, and probably none in 1777. These four symphonies and the eight composed between 1778 and *c.*1781 often show Haydn working quickly, recycling music from other works (typically one movement, sometimes more) to form symphonies. The most complex work is no. 53 in D, which exists in four different versions, that is, four different works for four different occasions; three have a common slow introduction, one does not; and three use a finale derived from an operatic overture (possibly the one to the lost marionette opera *Genovefens vierter Teil*). When Haydn came to write his next symphony in D, no. 62, he used one of the finale movements from no. 53 as the basis of the first movement. The first movement of no. 63 is based on the overture to *Il mondo della luna* and the second movement is taken from incidental music to *Soliman der zweite*; while the slow movement of no. 73 uses the song 'Gegenliebe' and the finale reutilizes the overture to *La fedeltà premiata*. It is likely that other works, too, contain reused material. For instance Symphony no. 67 in F has a Presto first movement in 6/8 that could well be a reworking of a previous finale and a fourth movement whose structure of Allegro di molto, Adagio e cantabile, and altered repeat of the Allegro di molto, is a common format for an overture (the so-called da capo overture). The unexpected appearance of *col legno* (with the wood of the bow) and the peasant drones of the trio (in which a solo violin is required to tune the lowest string down to *f*) suggests that this music, at least, had a programmatic origin.

Symphony no. 69 is one of Haydn's weakest works in the genre with uncharacteristically straightforward use of sonata form in the first movement and a lacklustre slow movement and minuet. The finale almost seems to be pastiche Haydn, prompting the speculative thought that PLEYEL, who was his pupil at this time, may have had something to do with its composition.

The slow movement and minuet of no. 66 capture the attention, the first for its effective contrast of lyrical and articulated material and the trio section for its solo use of oboe and bassoon doubling the first violin, a new timbre in Haydn's symphonies. The rondo finale, also, looks to the future; its broad structure is ABACA but all the material is in some way related to the opening of the movement, each of the returns of A is varied, and there is an extended closing section.

During the fire that engulfed the Eszterháza palace in November 1779 Haydn lost many autograph manuscripts of symphonies; that of no. 61 in D is one of the few to survive from this period. Once more it is the slow movement that catches attention, an instrumental evocation of a pastoral scene in Italian opera reminiscent of moments in Haydn's *La fedeltà premiata*. The finale is a rondo in ABACA design but, in a reversal of normal practice, section B is in the minor key and C is in a major key; the returns to the main theme are charmingly protracted but not with the sense of suspense that is associated with such passages in the 'London' symphonies.

Although Symphony no. 71 is set in one of Haydn's favoured keys for a symphony in the 1770s, B♭, the sonority of many passages in this work is unlike that of a typical symphony in the key. Wind instruments are not heard until the transition (bar 29) and the slow introduction has an introspective quality generated by octave unison-writing; throughout the horn-writing is particularly cautious, never rising above a notated *e''*. The slow movement is a set of three variations plus a coda on an adagio theme. The trio section in the minuet imports a texture from dance music, two solo violins playing in octaves over a persistent accompaniment. But Haydn thwarts any would-be dancers by having a very irregular phrase structure of seven bars in the first section followed by 4+3+4+7. Rather than a rondo in 2/4 the finale is a sonata form in common time. At the beginning of the development Haydn plunges without any preparation into D♭ major, a favoured relationship later in the composer's development but here unusual enough for someone (not the composer) to write 'per licentiam' ('with permission') on an early set of parts.

Written for a concert associated with the laying of the cornerstone of a new opera house at Eszterháza in December 1779, Symphony no. 70 in D is a neglected masterpiece. The special occasion explains the disposition of the orchestra, one flute, two oboes, one bassoon, two horns, two trumpets, timpani, and strings but alongside the flamboyance that is to be expected from such an ensemble there is a good deal of learnedness too. The opening of the development section is even more of a 'licence' than that in no. 71/iv, a bare repeated C♮ after the A major of the end of the exposition. The recapitulation includes a new passage of close polyphony, anticipating the formal counterpoint of the second movement and the finale. The Andante is a set of variations on two alternating themes, one in D minor, the other in D major. The D minor theme is headed 'Specie d'un canone in contrapunto doppio' ('an example of invertible counterpoint') and, like no. 47/ii, announces a theme in two-part counterpoint which is turned upside down from bar 9 onwards. In contrast, the D major theme is entirely devoid of formal counterpoint. The minuet returns to the mood of the first movement, with its rhythmic simplicity and harmonic surprise (the intrusive A♯ in bar 27), but the following movement is wholly unexpected, Haydn's first fugal finale since Symphony no. 40 from 1763. In the tradition of spoken rhetoric it is flanked by an *exordium*, outlining the principal ingredients of the movement (in particular a repeated five-note figure), and by a large *conclusio* that promises a stirring ending in D major but, instead, returns to the repeated five-note figure. The main section is intensely serious, even fierce, a fugue on three themes in invertible counterpoint, again proudly labelled by the composer ('a 3 soggetti in contrapunto doppio').

In general the remaining symphonies in this group are less impressive, though they do contain some remarkable movements, again often slow movements. That of no. 75 in D is a new kind, featuring a hymn-like theme in triple time; the slow movement of no. 63, headed 'LA ROXELANE', is a set of variations on two alternating themes that became even more popular in an authorized keyboard transcription. Perhaps the most unorthodox is no. 62/ii which might be characterized as an accompaniment in search of a theme; only towards the end of the movement do the undulating 6/8 accompaniment patterns support a plausible theme.

No. 74 in E♭ is presumed to be the last symphony composed in 1780. From its opening of three hammerstroke chords and quiet response one might think that it is a routine essay in the Italian style but once more these commonplace procedures are cleverly integrated into the unfolding of the movement in a way no other composer of the time could rival. The slow movement, Adagio cantabile in B♭, is a mixture of rondo and variations, marked by beauty of melody and sonority. Unfortunately the remaining movements, a minuet and a sonata form finale in 6/8, are not equal to the first two.

Although it is always assumed that the slow movement of no. 73 in D ('LA CHASSE') was based on the existing song 'Gegenliebe', it is possible that the song was adapted from the symphony, an increasingly common practice in Vienna and elsewhere in the 1780s. The slow introduction to the work, like that found in another D major symphony, no. 75, has a thematic kinship with the following Allegro. In the Allegro itself, striking harmonic juxtapositions are highlighted by the almost complete concentration on a single motif, a three-quaver up-beat and following down-beat. The development is even more intense, both motivically and harmonically, and Haydn marks the moment of recapitulation in a proto-Beethovenian manner, *fortissimo* and full orchestra, a real landmark in the structure. Assuming that the song 'Gegenliebe' came first, then the symphony is a telling reworking, yielding a more melancholy atmosphere than the song. This kind of movement, built around a simple theme in 2/4 time and in an Andante tempo (sometimes Allegretto), was to become common in Haydn's later symphonies (nos. 82, 85, 90, 91, 94, and 100). The heavily emphasized appoggiaturas of the minuet provide a link back to the introduction. The overture to *La fedeltà premiata* had ended quietly and its unaltered inclusion here makes it one of only four symphonies by Haydn to end quietly; the others are nos. 23, 26 and the 'Farewell' symphony.

6. Symphonies from 1782 to 1784 (nos. 76, 77, 78, 79, 80, 81). While the twelve 'London' symphonies of the 1790s (nos. 93–104) are celebrated works written for the English capital, they were preceded in 1782 by a neglected set of three symphonies, nos. 76–8, composed for an intended visit to London that never came to fruition. Haydn's knowledge of English music, composers, and public taste was obviously rather limited. Nevertheless, they possess a certain polish and élan that is reminiscent of the music of the two leading composers in London, Carl Friedrich Abel (1723–87) and Johann Christian Bach (1735–82). Haydn, too, might have been aware that one of the versions of Symphony no. 53 was frequently played in London in the early 1780s, gaining the nickname 'FESTINO', and this set of three seems to capitalize on the geniality of that work.

This was the first set of symphonies whose publication was authorized by Haydn; they were published in 1784 by FORSTER in London and TORRICELLA in Vienna, and in the following year by Boyer in Paris. In a letter to the last-named, Haydn had described the works as 'all very easy, and without too much *concertante*' (15 July 1783). Indeed, there are few instances in the works where the wind instruments are not doubled by strings, though Haydn's sense of colour is still evident. As for the character of the symphonies, the opening movements and slow movements are highly individual, the minuets and finales less so. No. 76 is in a mellow E♭, no. 77 in a brilliant B♭, and no. 78 is in a dark C minor. Given its key, the last-mentioned has always attracted the most attention. Its first and last movements are essentially in a *Sturm und Drang* idiom, while the middle movements are in major keys, E♭ and C. The very opening of the work seems to have made an impact on several later composers; most well known is the opening of Mozart's Piano Concerto in C minor (K491) and it can be sensed too in the finale of Schubert's quartet in C (D32) and Spohr's double quartet in D minor, op. 65. As all these composers must have observed, Haydn's first subject is not only rhythmically highly recognizable but has great potential for motivic development and contrapuntal imitation. The sonata rondo finale (ABACAB) in a Presto tempo draws on Haydn's experience of writing variations on two alternating themes that are related. The main theme (A) is in the tonic minor and the first episode (B) is in the tonic major, but they are thematically close enough for the C major conclusion to the movement to seem a synthesis of both.

Although Haydn's next three symphonies, nos. 79, 80, and 81, were all completed in 1784, they were never formally distributed as a set, though there is some evidence to suggest that they were conceived as such. Like the 1782 'London' symphonies two are in the major key (no. 79 in F and no. 81 in G) and one is in the minor (no. 80). The programme for the traditional pair of concerts given by the Tonkünstler-Societät in March 1785 was originally advertised as having three symphonies by Haydn, including no. 80 in D minor, to be performed alongside Mozart's *Davidde penitente*; in the event the number of Haydn symphonies was reduced to two. It seems likely that the three symphonies, nos. 79–81, were originally to have been presented at these concerts.

The D minor symphony is another unrecognized masterpiece that skilfully mixes *Sturm und Drang* and *galant* idioms. In the first movement the former mood, as is suggested by the marking Allegro spiritoso, is evident for virtually all the exposition; as a closing theme and almost as an afterthought Haydn presents a *galant* theme, a Ländler over pizzicato accompaniment, except that no true *galant* composer would have used the phrase rhythms of 4+3. This surprising juxtaposition is played out in the development as the two styles alternate and are underlined by an equally surprising modulation pattern. In the wonderfully recomposed recapitulation the *galant* theme is given its expected phrasing pattern of 4+4. The Adagio in B♭ also contains some effective contrasts: a lyrical opening, a pastoral continuation, and a theme in restless dotted rhythms. The atmosphere of the first movement is recalled in the minuet, not only in its key, D minor, but the fact that the opening seems a thematic compression of the beginning of the symphony. Much of the finale consists of a syncopated figure that denies the listener the pleasure of regular down-beats; it also must have been quite a novel challenge to players in the 1780s. *Galant* in style but highly sophisticated in technique, the movement also briefly refers to the more heightened emotions of earlier movements. The overall result is an extraordinary symphony that finds coherence in its diversity.

Nos. 79 and 81 have the same essential style and ambience: there are no surprising or dramatic gestures, little use of the minor mode, no overt displays of learnedness, and all is accessible at first hearing. The slow movement of no. 79 is unique. Set in B♭ it has two clear stages: an Adagio cantabile in 3/4 followed by an Un poco Allegro in alla breve time featuring a melody that, consciously or otherwise, alludes to the first movement of Symphony no. 39 in G minor. The first movement contains at least one element that would have appealed to the connoisseur. A strong opening in G major veers towards the subdominant in a manner normally associated with the end of a piece. The ramifications of this beginning are exploited in the development. Significantly, the first subject does not return until the end of the recapitulation, where it can assume its appropriate role as a theme that closes a movement.

Taken together the symphonies from 1782 and 1784 can be seen as a conscious effort by Haydn to cultivate a European audience and to seek a synthesis between the *galant* and the *Sturm und Drang* idioms. In no. 78 the accommodation is less convincing than in no. 80. But the achievements of these two works should not be allowed to overshadow the attractions of the four works in a major key, which represent Haydn at his most sophisticated. It is inevitable that modern listeners will find the 'Paris' and 'London' symphonies more enthralling but a very particular world is encapsulated in the symphonies of 1782 and 1784. APB

7. Symphonies nos. 82–7 ('Paris' symphonies), 1785–6. The 'Paris' symphonies were commissioned at the end of 1784 or the beginning of 1785 by CLAUDE FRANÇOIS MARIE RIGOLEY D'OGNY, a leading light in the concert organization Concert de la Loge Olympique in Paris. They were probably first performed during the 1787 concert season. The following year the Paris publisher IMBAULT issued the six works in the order 83, 87, 85, 82, 86, and 84. Haydn had recommended to ARTARIA that the works should be published in the order 87, 85, 83, 84, 86, and 82 which may reflect the actual order of composition. In the event Artaria ignored this request and issued them in two sets of three in the order 82–7, the sequence chosen by Mandyczewski in his catalogue.

Symphony no. 82 ('L'OURS') in C, though commissioned by Paris, is clearly another instance of the Austrian tradition of C major symphonies; the parts for two horns in C alto (designed primarily for performance at the Esterházy court) may be replaced by two trumpets. As in many previous examples by Haydn of symphonies of this kind, the first movement (Vivace) is in 3/4. The first subject has three distinct components: a *fortissimo* rising arpeggio, a melodic response in *piano*, and a rousing fanfare. Alongside the bustle of the music the harmonic language too contributes to the tension, especially towards the end of the transition (bar 51 onwards) where it has an asperity that has been compared to that found in the first movement of Beethoven's *Eroica Symphony*. The ensuing second subject, new and distinct, provides a momentary contrast. The development section brings these contrasting elements into closer contact. The following movement, Allegretto, is a set of variations on two alternating themes, the first in F major, the second in F minor. With several brief oboe solos the minuet is less grand than might have been predicted, but the woodwind writing neatly prefigures that found more extensively in the trio section; after a pause the music plunges into E♭ major, the kind of progression that elicited the comment 'per licentam' in Symphony no. 71 but with which players and listeners were becoming increasingly familiar in the 1780s. The finale is a sonata form whose opening theme seems, at first, to be a whimsical allusion: drone bass with a piping melody. Out of this commonplace material Haydn fashions a movement of striking power.

The opening theme of Symphony no. 83 in G minor ('LA POULE') contains many of the essential ingredients of the movement: a four-note motif used extensively in the exposition and, even more forcefully, in the development, and a dotted-note motif that binds this theme with the later, apparently contrasting second subject. The minor key yields to the tonic major in the recapitulation and, indeed, never returns in the work. The Andante is a spacious movement in E♭, another instance of a 'licensed' contrast of key, and incorporates a variety of thematic material. The finale is a 12/8 gigue of the kind that Haydn had last used in Symphony no. 65/iv. But the prominent horn-writing found in that movement is not evident here; instead the thematic writing is strongly characterized and instantly memorable.

Symphony no. 84 in E♭ opens with a striking slow introduction, marked Largo, though without that darkening of harmonic colour that habitually features in later slow introductions. This is in keeping with the predominant mood of the following Allegro, a *galant* movement updated to the 1780s. The main theme is heard repeatedly during the movement but only once in a *forte* dynamic: in F major in the development (bar 148). The Andante is a set of three variations on a 6/8 theme; the coda section expands into a wholly unexpected ensemble cadenza for wind instruments supported by pizzicato strings. The third movement contrasts a leisurely and expansive minuet with a short trio, though both are in E♭. The finale is a monothematic sonata form in which Haydn reveals his developing sense of dramatic timing, teasing the listener who is eagerly awaiting the return of the main theme at the beginning of the recapitulation and then interrupting its continuation.

Prompted by its nickname, 'LA REINE', commentators have seen Symphony no. 85 as the most French of the six 'Paris' symphonies, a picture of the *ancien régime.* Certainly the slow introduction, with its unisons, dotted rhythms, and upward scalic flourishes, is much closer to the old French overture tradition than the introductions found in Symphonies nos. 84 and 86. It is followed by a Vivace in triple time that begins quietly, precisely the contrast that Mozart was to employ in his Symphony no. 39 in E♭ (K543). The sudden move to F minor at bar 62 coincides with a quotation of the opening of the 'Farewell' symphony, a well-known work in Paris in the 1780s; it recurs in the development section but is omitted from the recapitulation. The slow movement is a set of variations on a French song 'La gentille et jeune Lisette' (Kind, young Lizzy). The minuet is Haydn at his most courtly while the trio invokes a musette. The outline of sonata rondo may be perceived in the finale though disguised by the composer's habitual sense of offering thematic unity rather than a profusion of melodic contrast; he also avoids an exact repetition of the main theme and makes the episodes of uneven length.

While no. 85 has always been a popular work, no. 86 in D has been unjustly neglected; in truth it may be regarded as the finest of the six 'Paris' symphonies. To the standard orchestra of flute, two oboes, two bassoons, two horns, and strings Haydn adds two trumpets and timpani. Haydn's last two symphonies in D major, nos. 73 and 75, had opened with probing slow introductions; the one to no. 86 seems to build on those achievements. The following Allegro spiritoso begins off-key, on the dominant of the supertonic which makes the emphasis on the tonic in the following *fortissimo* a necessary, rather than an empty, series of gestures. There is a contrasting second subject and an intensive development that deals with all of the thematic material. The slow movement, in G major and 3/4, is headed *Capriccio*. In a Largo tempo its opening material is used four times, each subtly altered and eliciting different continuations. At 62 bars the minuet is one of the largest in Haydn's symphonies, exceeded only by four in the 'London' symphonies (nos. 97, 99, 101, and 102), and is laid out as a sonata form including a coda. The trio offers a complete contrast in style as well as scale.

Symphony no. 87 in A is the most cautious of the six 'Paris' symphonies; apart from the occasional detail it contains nothing that would have startled Prince Esterházy. The first subject of the Vivace includes a repeated-note figure that is skilfully integrated with the normal accompaniment pattern of repeated quavers to maintain the momentum, also the dynamic level, a continuing *forte*. The second subject is *piano* but includes a rising and descending figure in quavers that is clearly related to the rest of the material. The second movement, Adagio, is in full sonata form with increasingly prominent parts for the woodwind instruments, culminating in the second subject which is framed like a cadenza by a tonic 6/4 and a dominant (with associated cadential trill). In the recapitulation the melodic lines also become more decorative. Like many trio sections in the 'Paris' symphonies the one in no. 87/iii features a solo instrument, the oboe, but unlike most solo wind passages in the 'Paris' symphonies it is entirely unsupported and, more spectacularly, rises to a top *e'''*, the highest note that Haydn ever wrote for the instrument. The finale is a monothematic sonata form in which, rather like the finale of no. 44, the return of the tonic does not coincide with a statement of the main theme; instead it is heard towards the end of the movement.

8. Symphonies nos. 88–92, 1787–9. In September 1788 the Esterházy violinist JOHANN TOST travelled to Paris. Haydn had entrusted him with manuscript copies of the opp. 54 and 55 quartets and two recently composed symphonies, nos. 88 in G and 89 in F. They were subsequently published by SIEBER in his *Simphonie périodique* series. Although there is no suggestion that they had been commissioned by anyone in Paris, it is clear that Haydn had publication rather than performance at the Esterházy court as his principal aim; quite independently he arranged for them to be published in Vienna also, by Artaria.

No. 88 has always been recognized as one the composer's greatest works, rich and powerful in its orchestration, harmony, and dynamics, and remarkably focused in its thematicism, with each of the four movements warranting the lable monothematic. Apart from the ancruses that end the slow introduction, there is no obvious link between it and the following Allegro. The short motif that opens the Allegro is combined at the first tutti with a brusque semiquaver figure in the bass; these two elements, continually transformed and interchanging roles as theme and accompaniment, are the essential ingredients of the movement. It is a measure of Haydn's inventiveness that the recapitulation is almost entirely recomposed. Although not labelled as such, the slow movement is another capriccio as found in Symphony no. 86, with statements of the eloquent main theme leading to different continuations on each occasion. To add to the sublime drama of the movement Haydn includes trumpets and timpani for the first time in a symphony slow movement. Instrumental colour features in the following minuet too, especially the timpani (imitating a peasant drum) and the prominent drones of the trio (deliberately marked *forte assai* against the prevailing *piano*), but it has some of the harmonic adventurousness of the previous movement too, as in the central modulation in the minuet to B♭ major. The finale is a sonata rondo.

In Symphony no. 89 in F, vigour is tempered by elegance. Like some of the later quartets of opp. 71 and 74 the Vivace opens with a set of introductory chords followed by a flowing melody. Procedurally the movement is remarkable in that it reverses the traditional functions of the development and recapitulation sections. While modulating extensively (C minor, E♭, F minor, and D minor) the development presents the themes of the exposition in virtually the same order and with little alteration. The recapitulation, however, remains—as it should be—in F major but reworks the themes and presents them in a different order. A concerto in F for LIRA ORGANIZZATA (Hob.VIIh:5), written for KING FERDINAND OF NAPLES, provides the material for two of the remaining movements. The Andante con moto, in ternary form, is based on the slow movement of the concerto while the finale is an expanded version of the equivalent movement in that work; returns of the main theme are to be played 'strascinando', an unusual indication which literally means dragging or drawling; an exaggerated *glissando* into the opening of the theme seems to be what Haydn intended. Between the two borrowed movements is an unremarkable, though attractively scored, minuet and trio.

Symphonies nos. 90–2 were composed as a set of three in 1788 and 1789 and were probably commissioned by Count d'Ogny for the Concert de la Loge Olympique, following the success of nos. 82–7; certainly the autograph manuscripts were all owned by the count. Haydn also sent the three symphonies to PRINCE OETTINGEN-WALLERSTEIN. No. 90 is Haydn's penultimate example of a flamboyant C major symphony and can be played either with horns in C alto or horns in C basso with trumpets and timpani. The deceptively obvious repeated quavers that appear in the slow introduction provide the boundless energy of the following Allegro assai which in other respects is a sonata form based on two contrasting themes; in the exposition the second subject is announced by the flute and repeated by the oboe; in the recapitulation it is the other way round. The Andante is a set of variations on two alternating themes, one in F major and one in F minor. Initially the coda sits uneventfully on a long dominant pedal in readiness for the expected fall to the tonic but then shifts up to D♭ (emphasized by a drop in dynamic to *pianissimo*) before returning to the expected cadential patterns. In the minuet of no. 89 wind instruments had opened the movement, answered by full orchestra; here Haydn does the reverse, full orchestra, then wind instruments. The finale shows the composer at his most outrageous, setting up expectations and then completely undermining them. In 2/4 the opening theme seems to be that of a rondo but it turns out to be a monothematic sonata form. A lengthy development leads to a shortened recapitulation which makes its way to an exaggeratedly grand conclusion that invites applause. But after four bars of silence (except for the applause) the orchestra carries on in a hesitant D♭ before moving round, eventually, to the real ending in C. Modern audiences, in particular, become even more disorientated if Haydn's instruction to repeat the development and recapitulation is observed—common in many finales in the 1780s but abandoned in the two symphony finales in sonata form in the 1790s (nos. 98 and 104).

A more private, subtle side of Haydn's musical personality is evident in no. 91 in E♭. The gentle slow introduction reaches a melodic peak on B♭″, the descent from which anticipates the character of the main theme of the ensuing Allegro assai. The theme is presented in two-part counterpoint; later appearances add further, decorative elements. The Andante is a set of three variations on a theme in B♭ that has the quirkiest harmonic structure of any in a set of variations by the composer: the first phrase ends in F minor, not F major; the third phrase ends on the dominant of F minor and the third one in F minor; this is followed by a deflection to D♭ before a forceful cadence in B♭. In the coda a sustained emphasis on the dominant of B♭ (with endless trills) is required in order to make that key a convincing tonic. Like the equivalent movement in the last E♭ symphony (no. 84) both the minuet and trio are in the same key and feature pleasingly regular phrasing patterns; associations with the dance are even more obvious in the trio of no. 91, a waltz in all but name. The influence of no. 84 hangs over the finale too, a genial sonata form.

Combining the subtlety of no. 91 with some of the flamboyance of no. 90, the third work in this set, no. 92 in G, stands above the other two; indeed many commentators regard it as fully equal to the 'London' symphonies. Scored for flute, two oboes, two bassoons, two horns, and strings, Haydn later added trumpets and timpani; still later and for an unknown occasion he made a version of the second and fourth movements for flute, two oboes, two horns, and strings. Frequently, as already in the second bar, the cello line is separated from its normal companion, the double bass line. Tinged with melancholy the introduction outlines the thematic profile of the first subject of Allegro spiritoso which dominates most of the exposition; an apparently contrasting cadence theme turns out to be able to share its opening and closing feature of emphasized first and second beats with the first subject. The proportions of the movement are strikingly irregular. The exposition has 62 bars, the development has 42, but the recapitulation has 108, revealing still more potential in the material presented in the exposition; in the final stages of the movement (bar 220 onwards) the first theme and closing theme are brought into a balancing relationship of dominant (first theme) falling to tonic (closing theme).

The deeply moving Adagio in D major is in ternary form (ABA) with, as in many of the 'London' symphonies, a noisy interlude (with trumpets and timpani) in the minor key providing a completely contrasting middle section. The main theme itself also has a ternary shape but at the point where Haydn might have been expected to repeat the opening phrases exactly, the oboe (later the flute) and first violins offer the kind of expansive decoration that Haydn had learnt from writing quartets. At the return of the main theme after the contrasting interlude, the decoration encourages a rhapsodic departure, with even more prominent roles for woodwind instruments. The theme of the minuet has a strong kinship with thematic material in the first movement (emphasized first and second beats and rising scales, initially in the bass) but the movement has its own sense of drama too: a few bars into the second section the music suddenly stops, before continuing its sequential progress down the scale to land on a dominant pedal. The trio certainly offers a contrast, but its dimensions are much larger than those in nos. 89 and 90 with the second half seizing the opportunity to exploit the syncopation pattern of the main theme. The finale is a sonata form that offers a contrasting second subject but brings the music back to the first subject in the form of a peroration to the exposition. Both themes are featured separately in the development before, as in the first movement, the two are brought together in a dominant to tonic relationship in the final pages. But if this is the hidden craft then the brilliance of the orchestration in this movement is irresistibly obvious. MV

9. Symphonies nos. 93–104 ('London' symphonies), 1791–5. Haydn's last 12 symphonies were written for his two visits to London between 1791 and 1795: the first six for the subscription series organized by SALOMON at the Hanover Square Rooms in

1791 and 1792; nos. 99–101 for Salomon's 1794 series; and the final three for the Opera Concerts in the concert room of the King's Theatre.

Enthusiasm for Haydn's symphonies had been well nurtured in London during the previous decade. Though all attempts by concert promoters during the 1780s to entice Haydn to London had failed, in lieu the composer had sent manuscripts of his latest works and he was also in direct contact with publishers such as Forster. From 1783 hardly a programme at the Hanover Square subscription concerts (from 1785 the Professional Concert) lacked a Haydn symphony, and particular works such as 'La Chasse' (no. 73) were already established as favourites. By 1791 London was familiar with all his most recent works, including the 'Paris' symphonies, and anticipation was therefore at fever pitch when he brought forward his new symphonies at Salomon's concerts.

Under this weight of expectation, Haydn made a clear decision to adapt his style for London audiences, writing in a letter to Vienna that his earlier Symphony no. 91 would have to be altered 'for I have to change many things for the English public'. Never does he specify exactly what he meant (and in this particular case there is no extant evidence), but he evidently intended to build on the more public idiom of the 'Paris' symphonies for the relatively large Hanover Square Rooms and its enthusiastic but demanding audience, an audience that required to be entertained, entranced, and challenged according to very varied levels of musical sophistication.

In some respects Haydn seems to be appealing to a still more popular taste than before, exaggerating the simple charm of *faux naif* andantes and trios in ländler style, favouring rounded second subjects with light accompaniment and pizzicato bass, and exploiting rustic imagery and dance rhythms in minuets and finales. The English had always shown a taste for breezily direct diatonic melodies like James Hook's mock folksong 'The Lass of Richmond Hill': perhaps Haydn was parodying this taste in his most ostentatiously naive andante, the 'Surprise' (no. 94). Certainly such melodies from earlier symphonies by Haydn had already become allied to the English tradition as a result of their adaptation by local musicians and poets as simple songs, often with cosily pastoral verses.

Haydn also ensured that each symphony had a single identifying tag, such as the drumroll of no. 103, that subsequently prompted a nickname for the work. The London symphonies are permeated by easily understood pictorial topics, allying them clearly in the wider public mind with familiar images from Handel and from Vauxhall songs; and also with the faintly exotic colourings they would have heard in 'oriental' pieces at the playhouses. Haydn uses every resource to capture and sustain attention, from brilliant orchestral colours and alluring combinations of timbres to the most vivid contrasts of sonority. It was often remarked that the English, for all their supposed sophisticated taste for Italian melody, were best pleased by grand effects: as CHARLES BURNEY wrote, 'The English, a manly, military race, were instantly captivated by the grave, bold, and nervous styles of Handel, which is congenial with their manners and sentiment.'

Yet, at the same time, Haydn reaches directly towards the connoisseur, synthesizing extremes of contrast through the most sophisticated play with counterpoint and thematic transformation, delighting in displays of wit and allusion, experimenting constantly with form and genre. If the early 'London' symphonies (especially nos. 96 and 95) in some respects play safe, Haydn felt free to experiment on his second visit with daring formal designs, and ever more complex and ingenious narratives, that demand concentrated listening across a whole symphony, not just a single movement. Haydn's typical strategy—positing a destabilizing problem to be resolved in the course of a musical argument—can now revolve around any musical idea, a theme or harmony or tonality, even an abstract concept such as the role of the introduction. Haydn's experiments with tonality, especially unusual third relationships between movements, provide a clear example of this, the apparent dislocations ultimately proving part of a larger and yet more coherent design. Often this investigation involves cross-referencing throughout a whole symphony, though Marx's detailed analysis of germ cells unifying whole symphonies has yet to find universal support. In Schroeder's view, Haydn intends in each 'London' symphony not only a musical but also a moral journey (in both senses achieving 'enlightenment'), in the early symphonies leading the listener along this path with direct signposts, later leaving more subtle arguments to be appreciated with less guidance. Certainly listeners in London were aware that they were being treated to an elaborate disquisition on the material, and thus on the nature of instrumental music itself: 'A new composition from such a man as HAYDN is a great event in the history of Music. – His novelty of last night was a grand Overture [no. 94], the subject of which was remarkably simple, but extended to vast complication, exquisitely modulated, and striking in effect. Critical applause was fervid and abundant' (*Morning Herald*, 24 March 1792).

Haydn also forces the listener to think about movement genres (an opening movement may begin like a finale and vice versa); and he experiments with the balance between movements by putting the weight on slow visionary Adagios or even on long rondo finales, where some of the most complex counterpoint and tonal arguments are to be found. And he shows a marked reluctance to repeat sections literally, instead rewriting or reorchestrating reprises, and continuing thematic development through the recapitulation section until the term itself seems an irrelevance. This process of continuous growth through a symphonic movement often involves a radical shift in the stress laid on the material, so that an apparently incidental motif or closing melodic idea assumes an ever-greater role through the development and into the 'recapitulation'.

Haydn's use of surprise as a compositional device crosses all these boundaries: if sometimes the unexpected is blatantly humorous or deliberately crass (the 'Surprise' or the bassoon joke in the slow movement of no. 93), at other times its full understanding depends on a sophisticated knowledge of norms of formal and tonal procedure. Certainly Haydn exploits every layer—unexpected juxtaposition, discontinuity and dislocation, metric distortion—for humorous effect. In the 'London' symphonies the incongruities are theatrically highlighted, and all the more appreciated by the London public, with their love of unaffectedly good-humoured quirkiness and eccentricity. Wit and musical argument prove one and the same, as Haydn leads the audience teasingly through his debate, the musical transformations and deceptions requiring active listening in just the same way as an *opera buffa* ensemble. Sometimes he draws explicit attention to his procedures, whether in the extravagant fugal transformation of the finale of no. 95, or the exaggerated self-parody of excessive motivic repetition before a delayed reprise; at other times the layers of irony lie much deeper. The intrusion of the author in this way has a clear parallel with the novels of Laurence Sterne; and it was as much their perception of intellectual play, of symphony as commentary on the nature of the symphony, as their eccentricities and oddities, that led Londoners repeatedly to compare Haydn's work with *Tristram Shandy*.

The London critics were acutely aware of Haydn's extraordinary combination of the sublime and the naive, of direct effect and sophisticated argument, of high seriousness and jesting comedy. An oft-quoted review of the premiere of Symphony no. 93 will bear repetition: 'Novelty of idea, agreeable caprice, and whim combined with all Haydn's sublime and wonten grandeur, gave additional consequence to the soul and feelings of every individual present' (*The Times*, 20 February 1792).

A striking example of Haydn revelling in this dichotomy is found in the minuet of no. 103, where a rustic yodel on the wind instruments is immediately transformed into an elegant 'art' melody on the strings in a remote key. The quirkiness of the juxtapositions, the rude low-life interpolations, raised an aesthetic debate comparable to that about piquant peasant scenes in landscape painting. Unable to reconcile these characteristics with the traditional categories of the sublime and the beautiful, aestheticians eventually turned to a new concept, the picturesque. The recurrent pictorial and pastoral allusions of the 'London' symphonies were certainly regarded in this light. There is also a connection with the value placed by London commentators on 'simplicity', whether the simple pathos of an unadorned folksong, or the noble simplicity of a Handel chorus, the true embodiment of the sublime. This alliance between rustic nature and the sublime underpins Rosen's magisterial assessment of Haydn's late symphonies: 'Pastoral is generally ironic . . . But Haydn's pastoral style is more generous, with all its irony: it is the true heroic pastoral that cheerfully lays claim to the sublime, without yielding any of the innocence and simplicity won by art.'

Another issue for London critics was the implicit claim of these symphonies to be regarded as more than mere entertainment. Many of London's artistic arbiters had appropriated 'ancient' music as the real yardstick, classic, elevated, and requiring a measure of learning for its understanding. Despite their rustic allusions and their winning melodies, Haydn's symphonies were regarded as the flagship of modern music, an answer to those critics who asserted the triviality of the symphonies of J. C. Bach and the Mannheim composers. This aspiration is asserted immediately in the slow introductions that preface every symphony except the one minor-key work (no. 95). These impose a sense of scale and sonority, and at the same time they are increasingly integrated into the overall musical design, through thematic, harmonic, or tonal connections: indeed the very presence of an introduction subtly alters the balance of a work. The 'London' symphonies are not necessarily longer, but they achieve a sense of grandeur through sonority and vivid contrasts, the emotional depth of slow movements enhanced by the use of full orchestra. Grandeur was a term frequently used at the time: coloured as the modern view is by the *Eroica Symphony* of Beethoven, written only a decade later, we should not forget that J. C. Bach had been dead less than ten years when Haydn arrived in London. The imposing stature and the contrapuntal argument of the late symphonies were easily associated with the sublimity and broad-brush contrasts of Handel's choral style, thereby validating them as music worthy of serious artistic attention. Equally related was the deepening and intensifying of Haydn's emotional world, especially in slow movements and introductions, where one particular image of the sublime is recurrent: that of sudden enlightenment. One chorus in Handel's *Samson*, 'O first created beam', directly foreshadows the contrast between chaos (dark and unformed) and light (coherent and 'knowledgeable') that was to be expressed most directly in *The Creation*. It is also foreshadowed in many of the 'London' symphonies, most simply in the characteristic switch from brooding minor-key introduction to bright major-key Allegro. More subtly, the 'Drumroll' (no. 103) starts with unformed timpani, then moves up from the depths of the orchestra into the light of day, in a striking gesture of transcendence. Certainly such awesome contrasts of sonority recapture the unmistakable voice of the Handelian sublime; and Haydn's distant key relationships, at the same time as they present a tonal argument, contribute metaphorically to this sense of mystical remoteness.

For London, too, Haydn develops further the fascination with orchestral colour seen in the Paris symphonies. Most striking is his inventive ear for unusual combinations of timbre, not only sections for woodwind alone, but all kinds of innovative textures involving solo strings, brass, and even timpani. Certainly colouristic instrumental combinations, especially wind instruments, were a common feature of the English repertoire, from large works by J. C. Bach or Arne, to Hook's Vauxhall songs. Now the very fabric of the symphony orchestra begins to condition musical material and structure, as flexible changes in texture become part of the musical narrative in a way more associated with Mozart.

Salomon's orchestra numbered around 40: a report of 1793 noted 12 to 16 violins, four violas, five cellos, and four double basses, plus standard winds but no clarinets; a trombone was also used this season to strengthen the bass line. Since Salomon could not draw on the best players in London (who were employed at the Professional Concert), standards were at first not high, but by assiduous training Salomon and Haydn built up an orchestra of impeccable ensemble and musical understanding; certainly the composer made no concessions in the difficulty of the first-violin parts. He himself was always listed as directing Salomon's concerts, in 1791 at the harpsichord, thereafter at the piano; it was a system of dual direction with the leader that persisted in London well into the 19th century. In 1795 the Opera Concert used the full 60-strong orchestra of the King's Theatre, its doubled woodwind including clarinets. In 1791 clarinettists were still not regularly employed in London's concert orchestras, though they had been used at the Opera House since the 1760s, and J. C. Bach made idiomatic use of the instrument in concert music too. Haydn incorporated clarinets in five of the later symphonies (nos. 99–101, 103, 104), but though he provides occasional solos, his use of the instrument remains somewhat tentative and reliant on the instrument's military heritage.

The first six symphonies formed part of a contract (now lost) whereby Haydn would appear at Salomon's concerts and compose six symphonies for £300 plus a benefit (with profits guaranteed at £200). He was also to receive £200 for their copyright; a subsequent agreement handing over the copyright to Salomon was signed on 13 August 1795. Contractual arrangements for the later symphonies are not known, but Salomon again received the copyright by an agreement dated 27 February 1796.

Both manuscript and publishing history of the symphonies is complex. Two main lines of transmission can broadly be distinguished: one continental, one English. Haydn took most of the autographs back with him to Vienna, initiating the continental line of manuscript copies and publications such as those by Artaria. The autographs of symphonies nos. 95 and 96 must have remained in Salomon's possession, for they eventually became part of a complete set of manuscript scores owned by London's Philharmonic Society, a set rediscovered in its entirety only in 1981. The remaining ten scores in this collection were apparently copied from Salomon's performing material, and they include a number of corrections and variants which may derive from Haydn's own work with London orchestras. These versions show many similarities with the London edition eventually published by BIRCHALL around 1810. Salomon also published in London his own remarkably successful arrangements for piano trio and for quintet of flute and strings, with optional piano. The traditional numbering reflects neither the original printed sources, nor the true order of composition and performance, which will be followed here.

After the success of the 'Oxford' symphony at the first Salomon concert of 1791, Haydn brought forward two genuinely new symphonies: nos. 96 and 95. Symphony no. 96 in D (the so-called 'MIRACLE') is not a particularly challenging work, referring instead to earlier D major symphonies such as the popular no. 53 (D major was also a favourite key of J. C. Bach). The introduction contains many of the hallmarks to be explored and extended in later works: the majestic fanfare on the tonic chord, answered by a delicate melody with decorative turns; the shift to the minor and gradual subsidence onto a hesitant dominant chord, here decorated by a plaintive oboe solo. This open-ended note prepares for the resolution of the triple-time Allegro, beginning softly in the strings with a brief inconclusive melody, before the full splendour of an orchestral tutti with trumpets and timpani is heard for the first time. Two features of the opening subject prefigure later developments. One is the play with structural elements, the scoring and regular harmony suggesting the idiom of a 'second subject': and indeed when one might expect a contrasting theme later in the exposition, Haydn markedly avoids the opportunity. Another is the skewed rhythm and phrasing, caused by the accompaniment beginning before the melody; furthermore the three quaver up-beats (themselves derived from the end of the introduction) are immediately then transferred to a down-beat. But this posing of ambiguities to be 'worked out' in the course of a movement is little more than a foretaste of what is to come in later symphonies.

Another foretaste is to be found in the graceful G major Andante: the juxtaposition of light and dark, of pastoral serenity against minor mode angst, of clear transparent textures against full orchestral drama or counterpoint. The movement begins in pastoral vein, overlaid with delightful woodwind filigree, but a darker side gradually insinuates itself, with a central section building up in stern fugal minor mode. The return to light is emphasized by flute doubling at the higher octave, over pizzicato strings: but this time culminating in a radiant orchestrated cadenza, featuring two solo violins and woodwind, recalling the sinfonia concertante tradition of J. C. Bach. The need to show off individuals in Salomon's orchestra inspired a soloistic emphasis rare in Haydn's symphonies since the 1760s, while the modulation to E♭ is one of Haydn's most glowingly seductive moments.

Both the minuet, with its delectable ländler for solo oboe, and the exuberantly monothematic finale are clouded by minor-mode interruptions, recalling the D minor arpeggios that similarly passed across the face of the introduction and the end of the first movement. But the lasting impression is of the brilliant fanfare rhythms of the first movement, whose close is directly recalled in a windband version of the rondo theme near the end of the finale.

Symphony no. 95 has never achieved the popularity of the other 'London' symphonies. It was a bold step for Haydn to write a minor-key symphony at this stage in his campaign: perhaps he intended a more explicit statement of artistic seriousness, or an alliance with those people in London who preferred the older Handelian style (for there is some ostentatious contrapuntal working). Not that London was resistant to the minor mode, which contributed to the expressive seriousness of the piano works of Clementi and Dussek, and of Viotti's violin concertos; Haydn also explored turbulent minor-mode agitation in his London opera, *L'anima del filosofo*, as well as *The Storm* and 'Berenice, che fai?' But this symphony does not attempt to work out the drama implied by its stern unison opening gesture and the challenging uncertainties that follow: indeed Haydn immediately undermines these tragic implications, rapidly escaping to E♭ major for a charming second-subject melody of luxuriant length. The development section hints at the contrapuntal drive inherent in the main motif, but the moment of recapitulation is diversified, so that the true resolution is only felt with the generous second subject, now in C major. Minor and major are simply juxtaposed rather than explored or resolved, and there is little of the symphonic drive of Symphony no. 44, for example, which starts similarly.

This dichotomy between C minor and C major (the keys of darkness and light in *The Creation*) permeates the symphony as a whole. The minor-mode minuet recalls the hesitant silences and chromatic unease of the opening, in sharp distinction to the continuous and diatonic trio in C major, a fully-fledged cello solo. The finale is in pure C major, beginning unassumingly over a tonic pedal, and giving no hint that the main thrust of the movement will be vigorous fugal working in exuberant species counterpoint. Counterpoint evaporates towards the end, however, and the last statement of the rondo theme is harmonized with valedictory chromaticism, before another confident fanfare conclusion. The symphony is articulated by various interlocking connections in addition to tonal changes: the cello solos in the inner movements; a link of two notes across the gap between these two movements; and the rush of counterpoint in the finale that fulfils the contrapuntal leanings of the first movement. But it remains an emotionally ambiguous work.

Four symphonies were premiered in the 1792 season, and all show a renewed adventurousness. No. 93 (17 February 1792) represents an early return to the D major symphony, revisiting some of the ideas of no. 96, but in a much grander and more ambitious way. The introduction starts similarly but this time diverts into rich harmonic regions, a romantically coloured excursion into Neapolitan E♭ major giving a hint of the velvet flat-side keys that colour every movement. The Allegro assai is again in triple time, but this time in warmer string textures, allowing for a true second subject later—not a common feature of Haydn's symphonies, but one which the English public, with their knowledge of J. C. Bach and Abel, must have appreciated. The charming melody is stated at length, though characteristically cut off halfway through its repetition; and it dominates the long contrapuntal development section. Variants of it recur in both the minuet and the finale.

The slow movement is better known for its flatulent 'bassoon joke' near the end than for its beauty of material and the subtlety of its hybrid construction, a continuous exploration of the possibilities suggested by the opening passage scored for string quartet. Again the minor key provides the first interruption, this time with the full force of brass and timpani reinforcing the dotted rhythms, a clear suggestion of Handelian idiom. Martial fanfares return in the trio section, this time representing stability against the soft string interpolations in every key but the one expected. Immediately after the first performance, Haydn wrote that he needed to revise the finale, as he and the audience alike had found it unsatisfactory. While there is no evidence that he did revise the movement, it is hard to imagine a negative response to the existing one, for it is one of Haydn's wittiest and most ingenious rondo variants, making great play with audience expectations. After so many switches of key and mode, and the substitution of new melodies, the listener is totally confused about the structure, and the expected full reprise is put off so long that it never takes place at all. Again instrumental colour provides an essential feature of the compositional process, not perhaps with the warmth of Mozart's orchestration, but for sharply defined picturesque episodes. Windband interpolations are by turns pastoral, rustic, and military, with the timpani often providing the bass line.

As if Haydn had reached the limits of this particular path, Symphony no. 98 in B♭ (2 March 1792) represents a major new challenge and the most substantial symphony of the first two seasons. Less overtly alluring in its orchestral sound-world, it is nevertheless weightier in tone and deeper in emotional impact. The portentous unison of the opening is uncompromisingly set on strings alone, now beginning in the minor mode for the first time. The listener is immediately pulled into a discourse about openings, the Allegro explicitly based on the melody of the introduction, and likewise scored for strings in unison. It is clearly an idea destined for contrapuntal elaboration, which indeed dominates this exhilarating movement. There is also a particularly striking and wide-ranging tonal excursion near the end. This can only be resolved by yet more contrapuntal working and a final *fortissimo* distillation of the theme into a trumpet fanfare.

The Adagio, said to be a memorial to Mozart who had died the previous December, is one of Haydn's most profound, returning to the hymn-like mode of some of the 'Paris' symphonies, and beginning with a quiet allusion to 'GOD SAVE THE KING'. Early harmonic richness gives a foretaste of profundities to come, including the now customary central minor episode, in which stormy development surrounds an enchanting A♭ section. The reprise is beautifully rescored with obbligato cello and an increasingly sensuous role for the woodwinds.

The final two movements do not attempt to maintain the same intensity, but the spry 6/8 Presto is a long and ambitious movement with two memorable instrumental tricks: a development section for Salomon's solo violin, whimsical in tone, but highly controlled in structure; and an arpeggiated 'cembalo solo' that Haydn added for himself in the coda.

Discussion of Symphony no. 94 (23 March 1794) has always been overshadowed by debate about the 'SURPRISE' in the slow movement, debate that has cast doubt on the traditional anecdote ('there the ladies will jump', in the version relayed by Gyrowetz). In fact it is clear from a surviving sketch that the disruptive chord was added only at a late stage. Perhaps more deeply shocking is the extraordinary risk Haydn took in building a movement on such a child-like melody. A contemporary critic allied this directly with pastoral imagery: 'The surprise might not be unaptly likened to the situation of a beautiful Shepherdess who, lulled to slumber by the murmur of a distant Water-fall, starts alarmed by the unexpected firing of a fowling-piece' (*Oracle*, 24 March 1792). The pastoral musical tradition in England was strong, from Corelli's Christmas Concerto, through Handel's *Acis and Galatea* and *L'Allegro, il Penseroso ed il Moderato*, to sentimentally rustic songs for Vauxhall Gardens. And there is indeed a pastoral vein throughout the symphony, evident both from the key and from the way oboes and horns are used, beginning with the unprecedented woodwind opening. In the Vivace, tonic pedals underpin suggestions of a musette; the minuet is a rustic romp in a very fast tempo; and the finale has an unmistakably open-air *joie de vivre*.

With these direct and appealing qualities the symphony was the outstanding public success of the season. Yet there were compositional subtleties for the connoisseur, too.

The slow movement has delightful variations, the theme unusually turning into a bass for a flute and oboe duet, and later reharmonized with autumnal chromatic chords once again. It is easy to miss the structural subtleties of the first movement in the easy-going mood: the opening melody, starting off-key and brusquely truncated, is revisited throughout the movement, only achieving rounded stability towards the end of the recapitulation.

In Symphony no. 97 (3 or 4 May 1792), Haydn's last C major symphony, the normal process is reversed. The Vivace begins in an arresting manner with bold fanfares for full orchestra; but the introduction is surprisingly restrained, an achingly beautiful cadence on an ambiguous diminished-seventh chord (inevitably reminding the modern listener of Schubert's String Quintet). It is surely the richest example of one of Haydn's favourite paradoxes: opening a movement with closing material. The cadence returns to lead straight into the Vivace, and once again it has a direct connection with the main body of the movement: in this case reappearing in its 'true' position, rounding off both exposition and recapitulation. In the latter case, however, a new structural ambiguity ensues, for the diminished seventh is now used to divert C major to more distant harmonic regions that require further resolution. The development section also contains one of Haydn's most remarkable orchestral passages, a contrapuntal trio for upper winds alone, punctuated by apparently random interjections from *pianissimo* strings.

The remainder of the symphony is just as full of instrumental delights, such as the extraordinary reprise in the slow movement, where a soulful adagio is transformed in character into a *forte* tutti, the strings playing *sul ponticello* (at or near the bridge of the instrument). Such emotional transformation may be derived from variation technique, but it is unusual at points of structural reprise before Beethoven. The minuet also includes transformations, this time *staccato* variants replacing the *legato* melody in written-out repeats. The enchanting trio section introduces a kind of glottal effect to the melody and to the horn accompaniment, ending with a violin solo at the upper octave, cheekily annotated 'Salomon solo ma piano'.

Haydn started to write the second set of 'London' symphonies in Austria during 1793, so that when he returned to London, no. 99 was ready for performance early in the 1794 season. The symphony has long been a special favourite with musicians, including Sir Thomas Beecham. The first of two late symphonies in Masonic E♭ major, its fuller sonority is announced in the initial chord, two notes only (E♭ and G) richly spaced with the new sound of clarinets. The introduction explores yet more distant harmonic territories, arriving by pillars of descending thirds (E♭, C♭ = B♮, G) back to E♭ for the ensuing Vivace. This preparation of E♭ by a G chord is a technique familiar from the Baroque; and returning by chords other than the expected dominant is not new in Haydn either (compare the comic effect in the finale of no. 93), but here the third relationship becomes an intrinsic part of the musical argument. Most obviously G is the key of the slow movement, but it is also used to prepare the reprise within the minuet and to return from the C major trio. Within the slow movement, the G major return is preceded by B major, thus fulfilling one of the implications of the slow introduction. Beyond this, no. 99 is one of Haydn's most lovable symphonies, with a powerful symphonic drive and energy in the fast movements. The lilting second subject of the first movement is constantly redirected, the continuing explorations taking over the extensively rewritten recapitulation. Once again the woodwinds are used in a most individual, but no longer sensationalist way, notably a beautiful intertwining wind quartet passage in the Adagio, and some quick-fire exchanges in the finale (for which a substantial sketch survives).

Symphony no. 101 (3 March 1794) is known as the 'CLOCK' from the gentle ticking accompaniment figure that accompanies the melody of the slow movement, another Andante with a vehement episode in the minor. Once again this outburst suggests the pastoral image of a storm, which clears as suddenly as it had arrived for a return of the main theme in a delightfully lucid orchestration: one part of the clock accompaniment moves into the flute above the melody, and then joined by the oboe it turns into a tracery above the melody, as in the 'Surprise' (no. 94). This idyll is characteristically supplanted by normality, when a third statement of the theme is given out rumbustiously by full orchestra. The flute returns to a pastoral role in the trio section, a celebrated passage mistakenly 'corrected' by 19th-century editors, as the strings gently repeat the same chord over 12 bars in harmonic conflict with the top note of the flute line. Apart from these moments of pastoral reflection, the general mood is of exuberant energy. The opening returns to the dichotomy of darkness and light, now directly posited as a transformation: the upward scale of the brooding D minor Adagio becomes a brilliant D major Presto, once again in 6/8 finale style and taxing the agility of the orchestra to the utmost. Here it is the second subject that provides a long-term strategy. Originally in the first violins, its development is begun by the second violins, but most unusually it is recapitulated in the cellos before further contrapuntal working; and the second half of the tune only arrives in the ensuing tutti. But the weightiest movement is surely the finale, a massive rondo that explores its three-note tag in ever more contrapuntal textures, culminating after a massive build-up of tension in a complex string fugato: but in ironic *pianissimo*, which fizzles out before a dynamic tutti conclusion from which all counterpoint is eventually banished.

The greatest popular success of the entire series was Symphony no. 100 (31 March 1794), the 'MILITARY'. In truth there is not much military about most of the music; but the triangle, cymbals, and bass drum introduced in the slow movement were familiar from the Duke of York's band playing at St James's Park and Vauxhall. Modern commentators have quite rightly pointed out that the instruments reflect the same Turkish or janissary tradition found in Mozart's *Die Entführung aus dem Serail*, but in Britain the instruments were played by black Africans in fancy dress. Whatever the association, they certainly provided a colourful and ear-catching sound that captured the public imagination shortly after the declaration of war against France; other 'military' works were to achieve great popularity in London, notably Dussek's Piano Concerto in B♭, op. 40.

Haydn's slow movement is in fact based on a rather simple Allegretto from a concerto for two *lire organizzate* and ensemble (Hob.VIIh:3), dedicated to King Ferdinand IV of Naples. The pastoral idiom appears to represent peace and tranquillity, for the percussion instruments are first added in a stormy C minor interruption, although this distinction is not clearly maintained. For a coda Haydn tacked on an overtly warlike evocation: a solo trumpet playing the Austrian General Salute leading to a tumultuous catastrophe, a cloud which quickly passes in favour of a somewhat chastened return of the pastoral. The passage was clearly far more threatening than we can recapture today, for it was allied in extravagant terms with the sublime once more: 'It is the advancing to battle; and the march of men, the sounding of the charge, the thundering of the onset, the clash of arms, the groans of the wounded, and what may well be called the hellish roar of war increased to a climax of horrid sublimity!' (*Morning Chronicle*, 9 April 1794). This contrast of warlike sounds with pastoral contentment would have been very familiar to Londoners from popular battle pieces, most obviously Kotzwara's ubiquitous *The Battle of Prague*. It was also mirrored in evocations of storms: Haydn himself had written a storm chorus (Hob.XXIVa:8) for Salomon in 1792, and later in the decade the pianist Daniel Steibelt (1765–1823) achieved great success in London with his 'Storm' concerto.

The work as a whole retains the outdoor confidence of another G major symphony, no. 94, and it has likewise suffered in modern critical appreciation. But again Haydn dissects and develops the beguiling tunes with a sophistication that can easily be missed. The finale, for example, subjects an unpretentiously catchy melody to exhaustive analysis, which by the end has linked all the separate strands into a single unity. Haydn makes explicit his thematic working: the descending four quavers of the second bar are later demonstrated to be the origin of a slower scalic descent, which is then inverted and used for a mysterious fugato in a very distant C♯ minor.

The last three symphonies were written for the Opera Concert with its larger orchestra and venue, and Haydn was eventually to exploit the new grandeur and variety of sonority at his disposal. Not so much, however, in no. 102 in B♭ (2 February 1795), whose high reputation has never been matched by the popularity of its neighbours. Here Haydn appears almost to disdain catchy melodies and superficial effects in the service of one of his most intricately woven symphonic fabrics. Of course there are memorable orchestral sonorities, especially the subtly unobtrusive solo cello and muted trumpets and timpani in the Adagio, which is suffused with warmth and romantic yearning. But much of the argument is carried by the strings, often in contrapuntal textures, and the omission of clarinets now emphasizes a certain cragginess: the very first note of the symphony was originally scored only for strings, brass, and timpani. The first movement is certainly one of Haydn's most intense symphonic edifices, especially the rising sequences interlocking between the violins and the driving development section, that includes a relentless canon between the outer parts. The finale, too, is a *tour de force* of thematic manipulation, witty yet strongly intellectual, at one point tossing a single motif between the instruments in string quartet style (it was an idea Beethoven was to take up in his quartet in E minor, op. 59 no. 2).

The 'Drumroll' symphony (no. 103) is built on themes of disarming simplicity. The melodic ideas of both the slow movement and the finale are closely related to Croatian folk tunes (the former spiced with 'exotic' sharpened fourths), while the minuet suggests an Austrian yodel. The first movement is once again based on a 6/8 rondo-type melody, with an enchanting second-subject melody for oboe and strings. Yet Haydn transforms this approachable material into the most expansive musical structures. The first movement begins after the celebrated drumroll with a lugubrious melody in the bass instruments, formless and metreless, once again suggesting the void before the Creation (a similarity—probably coincidental— to the 'Dies irae' plainchant has been observed). Yet even this is integrated into the lively Allegro, the ingenuity of the connection only gradually becoming apparent: the melody (now in Allegro tempo) is first mentioned unobtrusively at bar 73, then again more explicitly in the development section, before it returns in the recapitulation at one of the most dramatic moments in all Haydn's output. After a catastrophic breakdown in the middle of the cheerful second subject, a cataclysmic turn to the minor is emphasized by stabbing accents and menacing timpani rolls (all attributes of Haydn's storm music), finally collapsing in a total loss of nerve. This breakdown is only resolved by a return of the slow introduction, which turns immediately into its Allegro transformation for a triumphant close based on E♭ horn calls.

The finale begins with another horn call, which then accompanies the folk tune, and from these two insignificant scraps of material Haydn builds up a fascinating web of contrapuntal ingenuity and orchestral colour, a full sonata rondo of nearly 400 bars. As in that other fine E♭ symphony, no. 99, the clarinets add a warmth of sonority unusual in Haydn's output, and indeed they take centre stage in the trio section of the minuet.

Haydn's final symphony (4 May 1795), the 'London', is another large-scale D major work beginning in the minor mode, though this is not immediately apparent from the opening, an imperious unison archetype, featuring the notes D and A, which form the thematic basis for the symphony. The Allegro, by contrast with the 'Clock' symphony, is in common time, and the moderate-tempo finale is unusually cast in sonata form, suggesting a more weighty aspiration. Its finale character is, however, secured by the D drone which underpins the melody (fancifully claimed either as another Croatian tune or as a London street-cry, 'Live cod'). Perhaps the most remarkable feature of the finale is the retransition. A visionary soft chordal passage diverts harmonically to a C♯ pedal, which then slips unobtrusively into D, reworking a comic device in Symphony no. 93 but now with profound emotional impact. The C♯ has itself been prepared earlier in a remarkable passage within the slow movement, yet another *faux naïf* Andante with dramatic and unsettling episodes. An apparently stable G major return teases out a harmonic ambiguity to arrive on a mysterious D♭ chord, a moment of hushed sublimity. Then a still but poignant passage for woodwinds alone gently leads back to a more orthodox restatement, this time, however, extended and embellished with woodwind counter-melodies and chromaticism, as if the moment of awestruck revelation could not so easily be swept aside. SMcV

M. E. Bonds, 'The Symphony as Pindaric Ode', in E. Sisman (ed.), *Haydn and His World* (Princeton, 1997), 131–53.

A. P. Brown, 'The Sublime, the Beautiful and the Ornamental: English Aesthetic Currents and Haydn's London Symphonies', in O. Biba and D. W. Jones (eds), *Studies in Music History presented to H. C. Robbins Landon on His Seventieth Birthday* (London, 1996), 44–71.

S. Gerlach, 'Die chronologische Ordnung von Haydns Sinfonien zwischen 1774 und 1782', *HS* 2/1 (1969), 34–66.

S. Gerlach, 'Joseph Haydns Sinfonie bis 1774: Studien zur Chronologie', *HS* 7/1–2 (1996), 1–287.

E. Haimo, *Haydn's Symphonic Forms: Essays in Compositional Logic* (Oxford, 1995).

B. Harrison, *Haydn. The 'Paris' Symphonies* (Cambridge, 1998).

D. Heartz, *Haydn, Mozart and the Viennese School 1740–1780* (London, 1995).

H. C. Robbins Landon, *The Symphonies of Joseph Haydn* (London, 1955).

H. C. Robbins Landon and D. W. Jones, *Haydn: His Life and Music* (London, 1988).

C. Rosen, *The Classical Style* (London, 1971).

D. P. Schroeder, *Haydn and the Enlightenment: The Late Symphonies and their Audience* (Oxford, 1990).

E. Sisman, *Haydn and the Classical Variation* (Cambridge, Mass., 1993).

E. Sisman, 'Haydn's Theater Symphonies', *Journal of the American Musicological Society*, 43 (1990), 292–352.

J. Webster, *Haydn's 'Farewell' Symphony and the Idea of Classical Style: Through-Composition and Cyclic Integration in his Instrumental Music* (Cambridge, 1991).

J. Webster, 'Haydn's Symphonies between *Sturm und Drang* and "Classical style": Art and Entertainment', in W. D. Sutcliffe (ed.), *Haydn Studies* (Cambridge, 1998), 218–45.

G. A. Wheelock, *Haydn's Ingenious Jesting with Art: Contexts of Musical Wit and Humor* (New York, 1992).
R. Will, *The Characteristic Symphony in the Age of Haydn and Beethoven* (Cambridge, 2001).

T

Taveggia, Teresa Amelia (*fl.* 1769–81). Soprano who worked briefly at the Eszterháza court where she created the role of Amaranta in Haydn's *La fedeltà premiata*. She sang at opera houses in Genoa and Milan in 1769 and 1770 respectively, but nothing else is known about her career before she arrived at Eszterháza in August 1780. She was joined by her husband, Anton Eckhardt, a horn player, in October. Both left the employ of the court the following July. ERL

Te Deum. Haydn composed two settings of the Te Deum, the first dating from the early years at the Esterházy court, the second from the last period of his life in Vienna. While the second setting has great power and resourcefulness, both settings exploit long-standing characteristics of such works in 18th-century Austria: C major coloured by trumpets and timpani, and a three-part design in which brisk outer sections frame a contrasting slow section for the words 'Te ergo quaesemus' ('We therefore pray to Thee').

As Vice-Kapellmeister at the Esterházy court under Werner, Haydn was primarily responsible for instrumental music but he could be called upon to assist the Kapellmeister in the area of church music if required. The composition of the first Te Deum (Hob.XXIIIc:1), Haydn's only original item of sacred music from this time, might well have been such an occasion, possibly prompted by the steadily worsening health of Werner. It was certainly composed by 1765 but there is no clear information about when and why it was first written. The most likely event was the celebrations that accompanied the wedding of Count Anton Esterházy (the future Prince Anton, 1790–4) and Countess Therese Erdödy in January 1763. The couple were married in the Hofburg in Vienna, travelled to Eisenstadt where they were greeted in front of the palace by a flourish of trumpets and timpani, and attended a church service (with Te Deum) in the palace chapel. As often in contemporary performances of the Te Deum, the sound of trumpets and timpani provided a clear link between praising God and dignifying princes. If Haydn's setting shows that he was fully aware of such traditions and associations it is notable in that it contains his first fugue in a vocal genre, an early instance of an increasing preoccupation in the 1760s with polyphonic textures.

According to a letter from Griesinger to Breitkopf & Härtel that initiated the publication of the second Te Deum (Hob.XXIIIc:2) the work had been commissioned by EMPRESS MARIE THERESE, almost certainly in 1799. Its first known performance took place in Eisenstadt in September 1800, probably on 14 September at a service to celebrate the nameday of Princess Marie Hermenegild Esterházy. Whereas the first Te Deum was scored for two trumpets, timpani, and strings, this setting indulges wonderfully in three trumpets, timpani, and strings, plus one flute, two oboes, two bassoons, and two horns, the result having a splendour matched in the composer's output only by a few choruses in *The Creation* and *The Seasons*. Its raw energy seems to sum up not only Haydn's long experience as a composer but the entire heritage of Austrian C major music. A vital component is the basing of the main theme on the strongly profiled plainchant associated with the Te Deum, sung boldly by the chorus in octave unison. The unflinching determination of the concluding fugue ('In te Domine speravi', 'In Thee O Lord have I trusted') is remarkable, Haydn's use of syncopation and would-be unsettling harmonies (particularly diminished sevenths) for 'non confundar in aeternum' ('let me never be confounded') even more so.

'Tempora mutantur' symphony. A possibly authentic nickname for symphony no. 64. Haydn's autograph has not survived and the words occur on the title page of a set of parts prepared at the court. The Latin is part of the well-known epigram by the Welshman John Owen (*c.*1565–1622): 'Tempora mutantur, nos et mutamur in illis' ('Times are chang'd, and in them chang'd are we'). A favoured interpretation of the annotation is that it refers to the very deliberate pace of events in the slow movement. The alternative, that the text fits the opening theme of the finale, is not musically convincing. It may, of course, have a completely unmusical, even trivial significance that cannot be guessed, whether applied by Haydn or someone else.

Ten Commandments, The. A set of canons, *Die Heiligen Zehn Gebote* (Hob.XXVIIa:1–10), by Haydn. *See* CANON.

'Teutsche Comedie Arien'. A title ('German comedy arias') that appears on two manuscript volumes of songs and ensembles held in the Austrian National Library; none of the composers is named. The volumes were copied *c.*1770, perhaps later, and include material that was very likely performed in German opera in Vienna in the 1750s. Since Haydn is known to have composed such works and the music is often strikingly reminiscent of extant music by the young Haydn, it has been speculated that some of the anonymous material was composed by him. Peter Eder and Joseph Ziegler have been identified as the composers of five of the numbers.

E. Badura-Skoda, '"Teutsche Comoedie-Arien" und Joseph Haydn', in V. Schwarz (ed.), *Der junge Haydn* (Graz, 1972), 59–73.

Denkmäler der Tonkunst in Österreich, 64 (Vienna, 1926).

Denkmäler der Tonkunst in Österreich, 121 (Graz, 1971).

HCRL/1.

G. Thomas, 'Haydns deutsche Singspiele', *HS* 6 (1986), 1–63.

thematische Arbeit (thematic working, or development). A term of especial significance in the Haydn literature since SANDBERGER identified *thematische* (or *motivische*, motivic) *Arbeit* with the 'entirely new and special way' that Haydn claimed for his op. 33 quartets (1781). For Sandberger *thematische Arbeit* was a new type of entirely thematic texture, the synthesis of polyphony and homophony, the invention of which makes op. 33 epochal. Sandberger's idea was most influentially recast in Charles Rosen's argument that op. 33 represents the invention of a new Classical counterpoint. BH

C. Rosen, *The Classical Style*, 3rd edn (London, 1997).

A. Sandberger, 'Zur Geschichte des Haydnschen Streichquartetts', *Altbayerische Monatsschrift*, 2 (1900), 41–64.

J. Webster, *Haydn's 'Farewell' Symphony and the Idea of Classical Style* (Cambridge, 1991).

'Theresienmesse'. Mass in B♭ (Hob.XXII:12), composed in 1799. This is the fourth in the sequence of six late masses. There is no particular evidence about when Haydn began its composition or indeed about its first performance, but the customary celebrations of the nameday of PRINCESS MARIE HERMENEGILD ESTERHÁZY are known to have taken place in 1799 on Saturday, 7 September, and Sunday, 8 September (the feast of the Nativity of Mary), and, if the usual practice was followed, then the mass would have been performed at the Bergkirche in Eisenstadt on the Sunday morning. The Austrian empress, MARIE THERESE, was especially fond of Haydn's music and soon acquired the mass for her library. From this association grew the view that the work had been composed for the empress, hence the misleading nickname. The issue was further confused because two years later Haydn's brother MICHAEL HAYDN composed a mass for the empress, *Missa Sancti Theresa* (MH 796).

The vocal forces of Haydn's mass are the customary soprano, alto, tenor, and bass soloists plus chorus, written in such a way that there is continual interweaving of single and massed voices; the soprano part, in particular, is much less demanding than that found in the *Missa in angustiis* ('Nelson' mass) from the previous year. Like that mass, however, the 'Theresienmesse' has a unique orchestral sonority, in this case clarinets (rather than the customary oboes), bassoons, trumpets, timpani, and strings, plus organ continuo.

These varied orchestral hues, from the brilliant to the soft, are apparent in the slow introduction, encouraging a mood that is lyrical and then dramatic. Unostentatiously the section hints at the shape of the themes that are to be used in the subsequent Allegro: the fugue subject associated with the text 'Kyrie eleison' and the secondary, more lightly scored idea associated with the text 'Christe eleison'. The Allegro is set out as a sonata form, but since the second idea with its associated text cannot, for liturgical reasons, conclude the movement the recapitulation moves with great resolution into a repetition of the slow introduction, the *fons et origo* of the music.

The Gloria is divided into the customary three sections: Allegro for chorus; a change of tempo to Moderato at 'Gratias agimus tibi' for a section initially led by the soloists and later joined by chorus; and, at the text 'Quoniam tu solus sanctus', a Vivace mainly for chorus. Unusually, however, Haydn does not have a fugue for the text 'in gloria Dei patris, amen'. The Credo, likewise, is in three stages. Following an Allegro in which the chorus declaims the text in the home key, B♭, there is change of tempo to Adagio, a change of key to B♭ minor, and change of sonority to soloists for the 'et incarnatus est'. The close of this section is one of many passages in the six late masses to make telling use of trumpets and timpani in a soft dynamic. The chorus re-enters in G minor and in Allegro tempo, reaching B♭ at the dramatic moment 'judicare vivos et mortuos' ('to judge the living and the dead'). At the end of the Credo Haydn has a fugue, as was the norm, to draw the lengthy movement to a climactic conclusion. But Haydn's fugue is not a dry-as-dust, dutiful conclusion; like the one at the equivalent point in the 'Harmoniemesse' it is set in a jaunty 6/8, proclaiming the joy as well as the certainty of eternal life.

The Benedictus movement in the 'Theresienmesse' is one of the most captivating in Haydn's output of masses. After four movements anchored in B♭—some 25 minutes of music—the Benedictus switches magically to a luminous G major. The orchestral introduction leads to an extended setting of the text culminating in a central climax where the music swings round to B♭, the home key of the mass, so that the composer can feature trumpets and timpani to punctuate a martial declamation of the text.

The traditional three statements of 'Agnus Dei, qui tollis peccata mundi' are set in an Adagio tempo and in G minor. This mood of severity is swept aside by the return to B♭ and a fast tempo for the final section, 'Dona nobis pacem'. As always, Haydn is not merely asking for peace and deliverance, but also rejoicing in the fact that they are to be granted. There is no anguish or doubt, just a wonderful certainty.

HCRL/4.

Thomson, George (b. 4 March 1757; d. 18 Feb. 1851). Scottish amateur musician and publisher, responsible for commissioning over 200 settings of Irish, Scottish, and Welsh folksongs from Haydn. Born in Fife, at the age of 17 he moved to Edinburgh where he was employed as a clerk at the Board of Trustees for the Encouragement of Arts and Manufactures, a post he held until his retirement in 1839. He became involved in the lively musical scene in the city and in the 1780s embarked on what was to become a consuming hobby, issuing printed settings and arrangements of Scottish folksongs. Rather than using local musicians, Thomson contacted many of the leading composers in Europe, Beethoven (1770–1827), Hummel (1778–1837), Kozeluch (1747–1818), Weber (1786–1826) as well as Haydn. For the new texts that Thomson wanted to supply alongside these high-quality musical settings he turned to leading literary figures such as Robert Burns (1759–96) and Walter Scott (1771–1832). The many collections of folksongs were printed in attractive volumes with sometimes lengthy prefaces and with appropriate engravings. Many were reprinted more than once or their content reassembled into other collections.

Thomson first contacted Haydn in October 1799. Over the next five years they were in regular correspondence, sometimes using an intermediary in the British Embassy in Vienna. Haydn's first extant letter to Thomson, dating from April 1801, is written in German but in a PS the composer wrote accommodatingly, 'I understand and love the English language.' Despite this invitation, most of the subsequent correspondence was in Italian, with one letter by Haydn written in French. Thomson was always very sure what he wanted from his composers and did not hesitate to complain if a setting was not to his satisfaction; on the other hand he knew how to flatter Haydn and, as well as paying him an average fee of one guinea per song, sent him gifts of silk handkerchiefs and, on one occasion, a snuffbox. The correspondence also reveals some projects that never materialized, settings of English folksongs and a 'sonatine' for piano and harp (which was probably, in the fashion of much drawing room music of the day, intended to feature one or more folksongs). *See* FOLKSONG SETTINGS.

J. C. Hadden, *George Thomson, the Friend of Burns: His Life and Correspondence* (London, 1898).

Thomson, James (b. 7 Sept. 1700; d. 27 Aug. 1748). Scottish poet, author of *The Seasons*. Born in the Scottish borders he studied divinity at Edinburgh University. At the age of 25 he moved permanently to London, earning a living as a poet, occasional tutor to the aristocracy, and, from 1733, Secretary of Briefs in the Court of Chancery, a sinecure post that paid £300 per annum. He lived in Kew Lane, Richmond, a mile or so away from his friend Alexander Pope (1688–1744), who lived in Twickenham. With David Mallet (?1705–65) he was the author of the masque *Alfred* and is usually credited with writing the words of its most enduring number, 'Rule, Britannia'.

The Seasons was his most ambitious work and enjoyed considerable success in his lifetime and well into the 19th century. Often described as the first poetical work to take nature as a subject, it was initially issued in four books, one for each season ('Winter', 1726; 'Spring', 1727; 'Summer', 1728; and 'Autumn', 1730), followed by a final 'Hymn' (1730). The text was revised several times and in its final version consisted of 5,541 lines of blank verse. In 1745 a German translation by Barthold Heinrich Brockes (1680–1747) was published in Hamburg. GOTTFRIED VAN SWIETEN knew this translation and made use of it when preparing his libretto for Haydn's oratorio. There is no evidence that Haydn owned or, indeed, knew the Thomson poem, either in English or in German translation.

Tomasini, Aloisio Luigi (Aloys) (b. 22 June 1741; d. 25 May 1808). Italian violinist and composer, born in Pesaro, who became first violin at the Esterházy court, and later director of instrumental music (Kammermusikdirektor); a lifelong friend of Haydn.

Nothing is known about Tomasini's youth and training in Italy, but he was brought to Austria by Prince Paul Anton as a page. This move has usually been dated 1757, but it is likely to have occurred as early as 1752–3 when the prince relinquished his position as Austrian ambassador in Naples and returned to Vienna. The prince paid for a period of instruction in Venice in the summer of 1759. According to the correspondence of Leopold Mozart, Tomasini studied with him in Salzburg in 1760; in 1763 Tomasini undertook a concert tour in southern Germany, including a performance at the court of the Elector of Bavaria in Munich.

In 1761, Tomasini appears for the first time as a violinist in the payroll lists of the Esterházy court, coinciding with the appointment of Haydn as Vice-Kapellmeister. From an initial stipend of 12 florins 20 kreutzer, his pay moved quickly to 200 gulden, plus the customary victuals. It is not known when

Tomasini assumed the position of leader, though it must have been almost immediately; he later referred to himself as the concertmaster (Concertmeister). When most of the musical retinue of the court was disbanded by Prince Nicolaus in 1790, Tomasini, along with Haydn and LEOPOLD DICHTLER, was granted an annual pension of 400 gulden. When musical life at the court was reactivated by Prince Nicolaus II in 1794 Tomasini was employed once more as concertmaster, now with a salary of 600 gulden. From 1802, in the absence of Haydn, he became responsible for the direction of instrumental music at the court and for the maintenance of the music library. By 1803 his salary had climbed to 1,100 gulden. Tomasini was buried in the Bergkirche, Eisenstadt.

Tomasini's name is frequently encountered in musical life outside the Esterházy court. At the first performance of Haydn's *Il ritorno di Tobia* in Vienna in April 1775, Tomasini played a violin concerto during the interval, probably one of his own. On Christmas Day 1781 at the imperial palace in Vienna, he played first violin in quartets by Haydn, probably from op. 33, at a concert given by the Russian Grand Duchess, Maria Feodorovna (1759–1828), who was visiting the city. Each player was presented with a golden snuffbox. In 1792, in Frankfurt, Tomasini played in a concert as part of the celebrations accompanying the crowning of Franz II as Holy Roman Emperor.

He married twice. His first wife, Josepha, died in 1793; in April 1799, at the age of 58, he married the 20-year-old Barbara Feichinger (1779–1821) from Pressburg. There were 11 children from the two marriages, of whom four were to pursue a musical career. The most notable was a son, Aloiso Luigi (1779–1858), also a violin virtuoso, who joined the Esterházy establishment in 1796 before moving to the court at Neustrelitz in 1808, becoming concertmaster in 1825, and opera director in 1835. Anton Eduard Tomasini (1775–1824) played the viola at the Esterházy court. Two daughters, Josepha (1773–1846) and Elisabeth (b. 1788), were employed as sopranos.

Tomasini must be counted as one of the most important musicians in the court of Prince Nicolaus, forming with Haydn and Leopold Dichtler an inner circle of influential and respected figures. As well as being an admired violin player, Tomasini's personality endeared him to the prince, the Kapellmeister, and the various officers of the court. His friendship with Haydn was particularly close. The composer was godfather to several Tomasini children, and supported their petitions for financial assistance. He referred to Tomasini as 'my brother, Luigi' (letter of 5 June 1803) and remarked that no one played his quartets better. When Haydn entered the Violin Concerto in C major into the *Entwurf-Katalog*, he wrote alongside the incipit 'fatto per il luigi' ('made for Luigi'). Other music from the period, such as solo passages in several symphonies, the A major Violin Concerto, string duos, string trios, and, especially, the op. 9 quartets can also justifiably be regarded as 'made for Luigi'. He was the particular means by which Haydn was made aware of the distinctive tradition of Italian violin-playing. Tomasini also played the cello, the viola da gamba, and the BARYTON, Prince Nicolaus's favourite instrument.

As a composer Tomasini, not surprisingly, concentrated on music that reflected his training as a violinist. His output included concertos, string quartets, violin sonatas, duo concertantes for two violins, and 24 baryton trios. The last were written for Prince Nicolaus but differ from Haydn's works in their cyclic structure and instrumentation: baryton, violin, and cello rather than Haydn's typical ensemble of baryton, viola, and cello. A Salve regina by Tomasini also survives. GJW

E. Fruchtman, 'The Baryton Trios of Purksteiner, Tomasini, and Neumann' (diss., University of North Carolina, 1960).

F. Korcak, 'Luigi Tomasini, Konzertmeister der Fürstlich Esterházyschen Kapelle in Eisenstadt unter Joseph Haydn', *Burgenländische Heimatblätter*, 36 (1974), 91–6.

E. Schenk (ed.), *Komponisten der Fürstlich Esterházyschen Hofkapelle. Luigi Tomasini 1741–1807. Denkmäler der Tonkunst in Österreich*, 124 (Vienna, 1972).

Torricella, Christoph (b. *c.*1715; d. 4 Jan. 1798). Owner of a music-publishing business in Vienna that flourished briefly in the early 1780s. Born in Switzerland he arrived in the city in the early 1770s, setting himself up as an engraver and importer of musical editions. From 1781 onwards he began to issue his own editions, including Symphonies nos. 73, 76, 77, and 78 by Haydn. He lacked the business acumen and energy of his rivals Artaria and Hoffmeister and by 1784 his financial difficulties were such that three further symphonies by Haydn, nos. 79–81, that he started to engrave were sold on to Artaria. The business came to an end in 1786 and, following a public auction, Artaria acquired most of his stock, including the published symphonies of Haydn. There is no extant correspondence between Haydn and Torricella.

Tost, Johann (bap. 27 April 1759; d. 27 March 1831). Violinist at the Esterházy court; later a businessman in Vienna. Born in Iglau (Jihlava) in Moravia, where his father was a church organist, Tost worked at the Esterházy court as leader of the second violins from March 1783 to March 1788. While at the court his business ambitions began to emerge when he set himself up as a part-time copyist and music distributor. Haydn, who must have been sympathetic to these ambitions, gave him the authority to sell two symphonies (nos. 88 and 89), the six quartets of op. 54 and op. 55, and, later, the six quartets of op. 64. During a speculative visit to Paris, Tost sold the two symphonies and the op. 54 and op. 55 quartets to Sieber; in addition, he passed off a symphony by GYROWETZ as a work of Haydn (Hob.I:G3) and this, too, was published by the firm.

In December 1790 Tost married Maria Anna Gerbischek (1765–96) to whom six months earlier Haydn had dedicated the keyboard sonata in E♭ (Hob.XVI:49). A moneyed lady, her wealth was bequeathed on her death to her husband, enabling him to finance his business ambitions. For 15 years or so Tost prospered, selling amongst other things equipment to the Austrian army. However, he was one of many people who suffered from the hyperinflation in the Austrian economy in the latter years of the Napoleonic Wars and, in order to earn a living, he started to play the violin again. There is no evidence of any contact between Tost and Haydn in the last period of the composer's life; he was not, for instance, a subscriber to the printed edition of *The Creation*.

S. Gerlach, 'Johann Tost, Geiger und Grosshandlungsgremialist', *HS* 7/3–4 (1998), 344–65.

'Tost' quartets. A nickname rather confusingly given to two sets of quartets by Haydn because of their association with JOHANN TOST. In 1788 Haydn entrusted Tost with selling the six quartets of op. 54 and 55 and they were duly issued by Sieber in Paris in 1789–90; the publication was not dedicated to Tost. The sale of Haydn's next set of quartets, op. 64, also seems to have been entrusted to Tost since Haydn was about to leave Vienna for London. They were published by Kozeluch (Koželuh) in Vienna in April 1791 and carried a dedication to 'Monsieur Jean Tost'. The view that both sets of quartets were composed with the playing capabilities of Tost in mind is mistaken.

Totti, Giovanni Andrea (b. *c*.1751). Born in Siena, Totti began his career in his native city in 1768, later singing roles in opera houses in Livorno, Pisa, Lucca, Palermo, and Venice. He joined the opera troupe at Eszterháza in June 1778 and stayed for four years. As well as creating the roles of Count Errico in *La vera costanza* and Gernando in *L'isola disabitata* he sang leading tenor roles in over ten operas by other composers. His wish that he be re-engaged in 1783 was declined because there were sufficient tenors at Eszterháza, and Totti returned to Siena where he is known to have sung until 1784. Nothing is known of his career thereafter. ERL

Tovey, Sir Donald Francis (b. 17 July 1875; d. 10 July 1940). English pianist, composer, and writer on music. Born in Eton, he studied Classics at Balliol College, Oxford, but was simultaneously developing into a pianist of stature under the guidance of Sophie Weisse. From 1894 to the outbreak of the First World War he pursued an international career as a pianist and a composer, and was particularly associated with the violinist Joachim (1831–1907). In 1914 he was appointed to the Reid Chair of Music at Edinburgh University. He founded the Reid Orchestra and the Reid Concerts that became central to the musical life of the city. It was for these concerts that Tovey wrote lengthy explanatory programme notes, later collected into several published volumes entitled *Essays on Music*. Works by Haydn that were covered included Symphonies nos. 88, 92, 94, 95, 98, 99, 100, 101, 102, 103, and 104, the Cello Concerto in D major, the keyboard sonata in E♭ (Hob.XVI:52), *The Creation*, and *The Seasons*. Written with great style and erudition they show deep sympathy for Haydn's music and a disdain for those who were not similarly persuaded. Even more compelling was his coverage of the composer's quartets for Cobbett's *Cyclopedic Survey of Chamber Music* (London, 1929), which, despite the discoveries of the last 70 years, remains a central contribution to Haydn studies. Tovey's magisterial opening pronouncement is unforgettable: 'In the history of music no chapter is more important than that filled by the life-work of Joseph Haydn.'

M. Grierson, *Donald Francis Tovey* (London, 1952).

'Toy' symphony. A work falsely attributed to Joseph Haydn (Hob.II:47) and which enjoyed widespread popularity in the 19th and 20th centuries. In its most familiar version it has three movements in C major scored for strings and seven toy instruments (cuckoo, quail, trumpet, drum, rattle, hen, and cymbals). Musical works with toy instruments were not uncommon in the second half of the 18th century and were sometimes, singly and collectively, known as Berchtesgaden music after the small town south of Salzburg where the instruments were manufactured and were especially popular. Haydn was credited with the 'Toy' symphony as early as the late 1780s and it was even performed in Vienna in the 1790s as the work of the composer. Modern scholarship has at various times put forward the names of Edmund Angerer (1740–94), Michael Haydn (1737–1806), and Leopold Mozart (1719–87) as the true composer. Evidence derived from the manuscript sources of the time together with some circumstantial material point to Michael Haydn as the likely composer.

R. Illing, *Berchtolds Gaden Musick: A Study of the Early Texts of the Piece popularly known in England as Haydn's 'Toy' Symphony and in Germany as 'Kindersinfonie' and of a Cassation attributed to Leopold Mozart which embodies the 'Kindersinfonie'* (Melbourne, 1994).

Traeg, Johann (b. 20 Jan. 1747; d. 5 Sept. 1805). The most important music dealer in Vienna in the last 20 years of the 18th century. He had established himself as a copyist in the city in the early 1780s and he soon became a central figure in its commercial musical life. He built up a vast store of manuscript copies of all kinds of music which could be purchased or hired and, for musical evenings, he even offered a package deal of players and music. As well as acquiring music by local composers he gradually built up a significant library of music from abroad, including works by composers such as Bach and Handel that were little known in Vienna. It was as an agent for Breitkopf of Leipzig that Haydn seems to have first dealt with Traeg; in 1789 he acted as intermediary between the composer and Breitkopf concerning the publication of the keyboard sonata in C (Hob.XVI:48).

In 1794 he began to be active also as a printer of music, his first publication being of Eybler's quartets, op. 1, dedicated to Haydn. Most of his publications of Haydn's music consisted of arrangements of single movements, especially from quartets and symphonies, but in 1803 Haydn entrusted him with the first edition of the keyboard trio in E♭ minor (Hob.XVI:31).

In 1799 Traeg issued a cumulative catalogue of all the music, manuscript and published, that was available from his shop, followed in 1804 by a supplement. Over 500 works by Haydn are listed. Alongside genuine works there are a number of inauthentic ones and many arrangements; the vast majority of the material was acquired independently of the composer. These were characteristics of contemporary musical life that Haydn would have accepted but in 1803 it led to a quarrel between composer and dealer. Traeg had acquired from a member of the ERDÖDY family several autograph scores of Haydn's operas, including *L'isola disabitata.* Breitkopf & Härtel had expressed an interest in publishing the opera and Haydn borrowed the autograph score from Traeg; after a while Traeg asked that either the score be returned or purchased. Haydn did neither and gave the dealer a dressing down in front of several mutual acquaintances.

O. Biba (ed.), *'Eben komme ich von Haydn . . .' Georg August Griesingers Korrespondenz mit Joseph Haydns Verleger Breitkopf & Härtel 1799–1819* (Zurich, 1987).

HCRL/2, 4 and 5.

A. Weinmann, *Die Anzeigen des Kopiaturbetriebs Johann Traeg in der Wiener Zeitung zwischen 1782 und 1805* (Vienna, 1981).

A. Weinmann, *Johann Traeg: Die Musikalienverzeichnisse von 1799 und 1804* (Vienna, 1973).

'Trauer' symphony. Nickname ('Mourning' symphony) for Symphony no. 44 that came into use in the 19th century. It may have originated from a performance of the work given at a commemorative concert in Berlin in 1809 following Haydn's death. There is no basis to the story that the composer wanted the slow movement to be played at his funeral. JH

Travaglia, Pietro (*fl.* 1770–90). Principal designer of costumes and scenery for the Italian opera and the puppet theatre at Eszterháza; he also supervised the lighting. Travaglia had studied with the brothers Bernadino and Fabrizio Galliari in Milan before entering the service of the Esterházy court in 1777. The sketchbook of seven watercolours attributed to him and often reproduced in the Haydn literature have nothing to do with Travaglia or Eszterháza. They relate to a production of Salieri's *Armida* in Vienna in 1771. In 1791 Travaglia was commissioned to design three sets for Mozart's *La clemenza di Tito.* RJR

M. Horányi, *The Magnificence of Eszterháza* (Budapest, 1962).

U

Ungricht, Vito (*fl.* 1764–94). A singer who worked with DITTERSDORF from 1764, first at Großwardein (Oradea in Romania) and then in Johannisberg (Jánský Vrch). He moved to Eszterháza in June 1776 where he sang roles in the marionette theatre and in the main theatre, including the part of Ernesto in Haydn's *La vera costanza.* As his voice declined he turned to playing the violin and viola in the court orchestra until it was disbanded in 1790. He later worked as a violinist in the Kärntnerthortheater in Vienna. ERL

un piccolo divertimento. The self-deprecating title that Haydn used on the manuscript copy of the Andante in F minor (Hob.XVII:6) that he gave ANTONIA VON PLOYER in 1793. It may be 'a small divertimento' in that it has only one movement but it is without doubt one of Haydn's greatest keyboard works. *See* KEYBOARD VARIATIONS.

V

Valdesturla, Costanza (b. *c.*1758; d. 1809). Soprano who worked at Eszterháza from July 1779 to July 1785, undertaking the roles of Nerina in *La fedeltà premiata*, Alcina in *Orlando paladino*, and Zelmira in *Armida*. Born in Pisa she seems to have made her debut in Siena in 1776, thereafter singing in opera houses in Florence, Pisa, Bologna, and Faenza. At Eszterháza she sang some 30 different roles. On leaving the court in 1785 she contemplated joining the court opera in Vienna but changed her mind when she was invited to Leipzig by Johann Gottlieb Schicht to sing at the Gewandhaus concerts. They subsequently married. Valdesturla continued to sing in public in Leipzig until 1805. ERL

HCRL/2.

Vanhal, Johann Baptist (Wanhal) (b. 12 May 1739; d. 20 Aug. 1813). Composer. Born into bondage in the small town of Nechanicz in Bohemia (Nové Nechanice), Johann Baptist Vanhal succeeded through a combination of ability, determination, and courage to carve out an impressive reputation for himself as a composer in Vienna.

Little is known about Vanhal's early musical training beyond the fact that he was evidently an excellent violinist and organist. Even the circumstances of his move to Vienna *c.*1760 are uncertain, although it was possibly at the invitation of one of his earliest patrons, Countess Schaffgotsch. Once in Vienna, Vanhal quickly made an impression and within the space of a few years was regarded as one of the city's leading composers, particularly of symphonies. Haydn acquired several of them for Prince Esterházy's orchestra, and directed performances of them on a number of occasions. Baron Riesch, who intended to appoint Vanhal Kapellmeister of his newly assembled orchestra, sent him to Italy for further training (May 1769–September 1771). On his return Vanhal signalled his intention to decline Riesch's offer—a move many of his colleagues must have considered unwise—and settled down into the life of a freelance composer and teacher. He did, however, enjoy the occasional patronage of Count Ladislaus Erdödy (1746–86).

Like any artist of the time, Vanhal's professional circumstances exerted a powerful influence on his output. When economic changes in Vienna caused the market for new symphonies to dry up in the 1780s, Vanhal, like many others, simply stopped composing them. Particularly interesting are a number of symphonies in the minor key composed *c.*1770, the same time as Haydn's so-called *Sturm und Drang* symphonies; he may even have anticipated Haydn as a composer of such works. Together with his quartets, Vanhal's symphonies were distributed throughout Europe. According to Michael Kelly he once played the cello in a quartet ensemble that included Haydn (violin), Dittersdorf (violin), and Mozart (viola).

In his latter years he concentrated for the most part on the production of chamber works, particularly works based around the keyboard. If there is one anomaly in his output it is the large corpus of church music, which includes around 46 masses. For a man who was not employed as a church musician this figure is remarkably high and can be understood best, perhaps, in terms of his deep and unshakeable religious faith. ADJB

P. Bryan, *Johann Wanhal, Viennese Symphonist: His Life and His Musical Environment* (Stuyvesant, NY, 1997).

B. MacIntyre, *The Viennese Concerted Mass of the Early Classic Period* (Ann Arbor, 1986).

variation. A compositional principle and a musical form central to Haydn's creative imagination. Indeed, the variation principle vied with the sonata principle in shaping his larger musical structures and became more and more important to his style during his long and productive life. By the 1770s Haydn had emerged as a profound innovator in variation form itself, by using it in weighty slow movements and by transforming its repetitive shape in hybrid mixtures with rondo and ternary forms. It was Haydn's innovations—placing the variation set in every movement of the multi-movement cycle, broadening its array of theme types, and transforming its larger shape—that created the Classical variation. He was recognized for these achievements by contemporary writers: Koch (1749–1816) claimed he was the first to write slow-movement variations among his 'pre-eminent masterpieces in this form'; Vogler (1749–1814) called him 'a true Phoebus . . . [who] showed us in symphonies how we should vary'; BURNEY credited him with saving the world from the 'dull and unmeaning variations to old and new tunes' that had 'overwhelmed' the world at mid-century, turning them into 'the most ingenious, pleasing, and heart felt of his admirable production' by means of 'richness of imagination, by double counterpoint, and inexhaustible resources of melody and harmony'; and E. T. A. Hoffmann (1776–1822) asserted that Haydn had invented the form of variations on two themes on which Beethoven drew.

1. The variation principle in other forms.
2. Strophic variations.
3. Hybrid variations.
4. Other late trends.

1. The variation principle in other forms. Haydn applied variation techniques within sonata-form movements to the repeats of large sections, to expand phrases, and to create relationships between themes and modulatory or developmental areas. This was especially true of slow movements. The following paragraphs deal with each of these aspects in turn.

Drawing on C. P. E. Bach's idea of providing sonatas with written-out 'varied reprises' (VERÄNDERTE REPRISE) of each of the two reprises of an Allegro, Haydn wrote a number of movements, mostly in the 1770s, in which the entire exposition is given a varied repetition with ornaments and passage-work. However, he never repeated the second section the way Bach did, perhaps because Bach's varied-reprise movements were all outer-movement Allegros and Haydn's were all slow movements. Examples are string quartets op. 9 no. 2, op. 9 no. 4, op. 17 no. 4, op. 20 no. 6, op. 33 no. 3, and the keyboard sonata in E♭ (Hob.XVI:38). In the only varied-reprise movement in his symphonies, the slow movement of no. 102, the exposition is varied by a striking change of tone colour.

In the slow movement of Symphony no. 42, every phrase and sub-phrase is subjected to varied repetition, and the units to be varied are reduced from eight-, to four-, to two-bar segments; after the repetition of the opening phrase, the smaller variations act like interpolations in the flow of melodic events, expanding phrases from their centres. Koch used this movement as a prime example of variation as expansion technique in the third volume (1793) of his composition treatise *Versuch einer Anleitung zur Composition*.

In the slow movement of Symphony no. 87, one of the 'Paris' symphonies, the main theme is expanded by varied repetition and also gives rise to the subsidiary melodic sections (the theme in the dominant, its reiterations and subsequent expansion in the development section). A similar procedure appears in the first movement of Symphony no. 85 ('La Reine'), but with added tuttis between the varied repetitions, in keeping with the symphonic style characteristic of Allegros. Perhaps the most 'paratactic' of Haydn's sonata forms (that is, the most repetition-based and hence the most perceptibly influenced by variation principle) is the first movement of Symphony no. 88. Here, a pair of rhythmic figures—a theme in quavers followed by a semiquaver counterfigure—comprises each of the four principal thematic segments of the exposition (first subject, transition, second subject, and closing theme). Each segment sounds like a melodic, rhythmic, and structural variant of the preceding one.

2. Strophic variations. These appear in Haydn's works from the beginning to the end of his career, in every instrumental genre except the concerto. The earliest and latest are independent sets, respectively the keyboard variations in D (Hob.XVII:7) and the variations for piano trio on 'The Blue Bell of Scotland' (Hob.XXXIa:176). Of the 87 sets, 81 are movements in larger works and the earliest and latest of these are in string quartets: op. 2 no. 6/i and op. 76 no. 6/i. Many of the variations movements appear in chamber-music genres that Haydn cultivated during the earlier part of his Esterházy career (or even earlier) such as string trios, baryton trios, violin–viola duos, and divertimenti; these sets are all first movements or finales. In string quartets and symphonies variation movements were introduced as slow movements in 1772, with considerable deepening of expression and complexity of technique; the slow movement of op. 20 no. 4, Haydn's only strophic variations in the minor key, has an extraordinary coda after the reprise of its powerful theme, and Symphony no. 47/ii sets its opening section in two-part invertible counterpoint which returns after a beautifully orchestrated middle section with the parts inverted. Only two later strophic sets in these genres are not cast as slow movements (the finale of op. 33 no. 5 and the first movement of op. 76 no. 6), whereas the keyboard sonatas never use variations in their slow movements. Among Haydn's theme types are serene hymns (Symphony no. 75/ii, which may have influenced the equivalent movement in Mozart's concerto in B♭ (K450)), ethereal chord progressions (op. 64 no. 2/ii), and character pieces (the Andante for piano in F minor, a set of alternating variations).

Perhaps as part of his professional interest in demonstrating the abilities of the first-rate Esterházy musicians, Haydn often turned to the overt display of concertante textures during the 1760s. When this technique came to the fore during variation movements, it meant that the instruments in the ensemble took turns to revel in figuration, normally one kind per variation; for example, in the finale of Symphony no. 31 ('Hornsignal') the variations on the string theme feature in turn wind instruments, cello, flute, horns, violin, tutti, and double bass. The decorated line may migrate from instrument to instrument in a string quartet (as in op. 20 no. 4/ii). Later in his career, concertante display might be localized to a single variation or to such novelties as a cadenza for wind instruments (slow movements of Symphonies nos. 84 and 87, the latter a monothematic sonata form with variation technique).

In his earliest variations of the 1750s and 1760s, the bass line remains constant throughout, and the melody may or may not resemble that of the theme; such variations might be termed 'constant bass variations'. When the bass line itself then became subject to change, the result is 'constant-harmony variations'. Finally, in a process most evident in the baryton trios, the principal melodic notes of the theme are present and recognizable in nearly every variation ('melodic-outline variations'). These three approaches may be mixed in a single set. Sometimes 'melodic-outline' variations appear to add new notes to the clear thematic framework, while at other times they seem to dissolve the melody into figuration.

In none of Haydn's variation sets and movements is the stereotyped pattern found in Mozart's variations evident: a variation in the opposite mode, and a final adagio–allegro pair with the fast section in a different metre. Only eight sets by Haydn have a *minore* variation, primarily in symphonies, quartets, and sonatas, perhaps because his interest in alternating mode more often took the form of ALTERNATING VARIATIONS on a major and a minor theme. After 1776, Haydn never included more than four variations in a movement, so that any *minore* has the power to reorganize the whole series, by acting like a kind of middle section; for this reason the *minore* is most often the second variation. Rarely decorative, Haydn's minor-key variations normally do not retain the harmonic structure of the theme, tending instead toward a simple first reprise closing in the relative major, then an intensified second reprise. A characteristic example is the slow movement of the 'Surprise' symphony (no. 94), in which the first period restates the quiet theme in a *forte* unison before the second phrase, paradoxically more like the theme in dynamics and texture, is diverted to the relative major. The second reprise becomes sequential and polyphonic, almost developmental in its extensions, dominant pedal, and the retransition to the next variation rather than a cadence. In the first movement of the D major sonata (Hob.XVI:42) the improvisatory nature of the theme, deriving from its frequent rests, gives way in the *minore* (variation 2) to a powerful contrapuntal and suspension-laden development of its opening dotted rhythm in overture or preludial style. An astonishing climax in the second period at the point of return also bursts the bonds of the double bar. It is likely that the *minore* provided the impetus for Haydn's later slow movements in ternary (ABA) form in which the B section in the parallel minor varies or develops material from A (e.g. op. 76 no. 2/ii).

3. Hybrid variations. Beginning in the late 1760s, Haydn combined variation procedures with forms based on contrast and recurrence rather than immediate repetition, often in conjunction with the alternation of mode. While quite a few composers varied one or more refrains in a rondo movement, Haydn's rondos are often systematically rather than incidentally varied, to the point where they can be called rondo variations or variations with episodes (e.g. $ABA^1\ CA^2$). The 13 movements of this type consist of five finales, five slow movements, and three first movements. The latter include two keyboard trios (Hob.XV:25 and 31) and the movement that furnishes the prototype for Hob.XV:25, namely the sonata in G (Hob.XVI:39). The well-known G major keyboard trio (Hob.XV:25) is particularly delightful in that it unites a charming theme and variations with the rare feature of two episodes in the minor key (G minor and E minor), the first of which sounds like a variation, the second like an episode.

Only Haydn was drawn to the idea of alternating variations on a major and minor theme ($ABA^1B^1A^2$ or $ABA^1B^1A^2B^2$), and he made that form his own in 21 movements and one independent set. One element of this design that might have appealed to Haydn is the often close relationship between the two themes: when they share melodic contours or rhythmic patterns, the second seems to be a reaction to, or interpretation of, the first. Thus, by the end of the movement two themes of opposite character will have found common ground. Haydn was also drawn to juxtaposing tonic major and minor in successive movements and between minuets and their companion trios. Symphony no. 70 in D exemplifies this trait with alternating variations in the slow movement (the austere minor theme in invertible counterpoint is here unrelated to the two playful *maggiore* sections, and has the last word) and a finale that alternates chordal and fugal passages first in minor, then in major. Moreover, the alternation of *galant* and learned styles in the slow movement is writ large in the symphony as a whole, which alternates *galant* style (accessible sonata form and minuet) in the first and third movements with the learned style (strict counterpoint and fugue) in the second and fourth. A unique five-part alternating variation structure forms the first movement of the keyboard trio in G minor (Hob.XV:19) in which the fifth section is not a variation of the first theme but rather a Presto sonata-form expansion of the second theme. Haydn's richest six-part alternating variations, found in the slow movement of the 'Drumroll' symphony (no. 103), offer themes with contrasting scoring but with similar opening bars. In the course of the movement each takes on some aspects of the scoring of the other, while the coda, based on the second theme, alludes to the first as well. The only seven-part example of the form is the celebrated Andante in F minor for piano (Hob.XVII:6), a revision of the original more typical six-part form ending in the major. Haydn added a thematic reprise and a lengthy, extraordinarily expressive and chromatic coda to an already powerful piece. The dark-hued minor theme with its inexorable dotted rhythms, registral shifts, and bruising syncopated Neapolitan chord towards the end, is varied with syncopations and figurations that elaborate but cannot intensify it. The sweet, even frivolous, major theme, on the other hand, with its ascending chromatic thirds and arpeggiated flourishes, becomes even more so during the variations featuring trills and triplets. Haydn's later reassertion of the power of the minor theme shows his desire to have the movement end not merely with melancholy but with tragedy. The flippant flourish of the second theme, already heard at the end of the second minor variation, comes back as an agent of the disorienting chromaticism in the coda (bars 190–3), chords which also overthrow the Neapolitan climax in bars 212–14. Although the piece fades to a whisper, it contains some of Haydn's most dynamically vibrant piano music.

4. Other late trends. After 1780, having already developed nearly every variation format to a high degree, Haydn began to infuse variation into his ternary movements as well (28 examples) and, indeed, into most of his slow movements. Of the symphonies from the Paris set on, only the slow movements of nos. 83, 98, and 99 are without significant variation. In the Andante of his last symphony, no. 104, Haydn adapts a ternary variation form that he had first introduced in keyboard sonatas and trios in 1784 and thereafter employed in quartets and symphonies. While many of his ternary variations feature varied repetition, even in the B sections, by 1795 the B sections were more fluid, developmental, and sometimes even contrapuntal, and in Symphony no. 104/ii the varied repetitions set off considerable phrase expansion in both the first and second A sections. Because the B sections are most often in the minor key, they can sometimes, as here with the wind choir, sound like a variation until their structures become too expanded.

Haydn's last strophic variation movement in a quartet, the first movement of op. 76 no. 6, explores a variation-type found in three other quartet movements of the 1790s: a melody that migrates nearly unchanged from voice to voice in the manner of a cantus firmus or 'constant melody'. When 'Gott erhalte Franz den Kaiser' was treated in the same manner in the slow movement of op. 76 no. 3, it made sense to hear the national anthem again and again. The theme of op. 76 no. 6, however, is repetitive, circular, and rhythmically static, so there is a touch of amusement in the exaggerated way it is repeated: in overture style in variation 2, and with a mocking echo in variation 3. The movement even ends with a wonderful Allegro fugato. But this repetitive presentation has important consequences for the rest of the quartet. In the slow movement, headed *Fantasia*, a series of repetitions of the same hymn-like theme in different keys connected by improvisatory transitions gives way, once more, to a fugato, while in the *Alternativo* to the minuet, the theme is an E♭ major scale stated over and over again in successive instruments, either ascending or descending, with new counterpoints and accompaniments every time. The latter piece has never been described as theme and variations but it clearly derives from the 'constant-melody' approach of the first and second movements. Finally, the last movement uses a scalic theme metrically displaced to different parts of the bar. Repetition, variation, counterpoint, and humour form the underlying 'plot' of the entire work. No better example could be found of the central importance of variation principle in Haydn's musical thinking. *See also* ALTERNATING VARIATIONS, KEYBOARD VARIATIONS.

ES

R. U. Nelson, *The Technique of Variation: A Study of the Instrumental Variation from Cabezón to Reger* (Berkeley and Los Angeles, 1948).

E. Sisman, *Haydn and the Classical Variation* (Cambridge, Mass., 1993).

E. Sisman: 'Tradition and Transformation in the Alternating Variations of Haydn and Beethoven', *Acta Musicologica*, 62 (1990), 152–82.

Venier. Publishing firm in Paris that flourished from 1755 to 1784. It was particularly notable for its many publications of symphonies, though works by Haydn were comparatively under-represented. Haydn never had any contact with the firm. It had the distinction of being the first in Paris to issue a symphony by the composer, no. 2 in 1764. Many subsequent publications were of spurious works. They include an intriguing version of Symphony no. 22 that uses the second and fourth movements of the authentic version to enclose a short Andante grazioso in A♭ (Hob.I:22bis); the true composer of the slow movement has yet to be established.

veränderte Reprise (varied, or altered, reprise). A term describing the practice in which embellished repeats replace (literal) formal repeats, as for instance in C. P. E. Bach's *Sechs Sonaten mit veränderten Reprisen* (Berlin, 1760). Haydn, very probably under Bach's influence, began to notate varied reprises from the late 1760s or early 1770s, and they feature consistently in his later works, particularly in rondos, hybrid variations, Tempo di Menuet movements, and slow movements. An example of the latter is the adagio of the quartet op. 33 no. 2, where bars 30–58 constitute a varied reprise of bars 1–29. The term varied reprise is sometimes employed more loosely to describe any decoration, however brief, of a thematic return.

BH

B. Harrison, *Haydn's Keyboard Music: Studies in Performance Practice* (Oxford, 1996).
E. Sisman, *Haydn and the Classical Variation* (Cambridge, Mass., 1993).

Vienna. See opposite.

violone. Although this term (literally 'large viol') may indicate the cello or any viol, it most commonly refers to the lowest member of the viol family, which doubled the bass viol at the octave below. The direct ancestor of the double bass, it had a fretted fingerboard and its size, stringing, and tuning varied: for instance, Quantz (1752) stipulating five or six strings and Leopold Mozart (1756) between three and five. A particularly common instrument in Austria in Haydn's time was a five-string instrument tuned F, A, d, f♯, and a, for which several composers wrote concerted works. Haydn himself wrote a Concerto in D for the violone in the early 1760s (Hob.VIIc:1) which has not survived. Symphonies that feature the violone as a solo instrument include nos. 6, 7, 8, 31, 45, and 72; it is also found in the baryton octets (Hob.X:1–6). Its focused, light sound—certainly in comparison with the modern double bass—meant that it was almost certainly also used as an alternative to the cello in Haydn's early divertimenti, string trios, quartets, and keyboard trios. RS

F. Baines, 'What exactly is a Violone?', *Early Music*, 5 (1977), 173–6.
J. Webster, 'The Bass Part in Haydn's Early String Quartets', *Musical Quarterly*, 63 (1977), 390–424.

Vivaldi, Antonio (b. 4 March 1678; d. 27/8 July 1741). Italian composer whose instrumental music was published extensively in Europe. In his native Venice and Italy generally, he was also well regarded as a composer of church music and of opera. In 1740 he travelled to Vienna where he hoped the court opera would present one or more of his stage works, but the death of Karl VI in October thwarted these plans. He stayed on in Vienna, living in the Kärntnerstraße, where he died on 28 July 1741. He was given a pauper's funeral including a short service at St Stephen's; six choirboys were present including, almost certainly, the young Joseph Haydn.

Vivaldi's music was not especially well known in Austria. The first edition of *The Seasons* was dedicated to Count Wenceslas Morzin, a relative of Haydn's patron, and the library of the Esterházy family, for instance, contained a few sets of concertos, including *The Seasons*, but in the 1760s the music would have been regarded as increasingly dated. Its presence, however, does remind listeners that the whole tradition of Italian Baroque music, of which Vivaldi was a leading exponent, figures strongly in Haydn's early stylistic development, most obviously in his violin concertos, but also in the many slow movements in symphonies and quartets that appropriate the texture of the Baroque concerto.

Vienna

In 1739 or 1740, when the boy Haydn arrived in the imperial royal city of Vienna, this original outpost of the Roman Empire, once known as Vindobona, had already served as the residence of the Habsburg court for nearly five centuries. Thus, it had already developed into the rich, imposing capital of a vast domain, the Holy Roman Empire, one of the most powerful empires on earth.

Vienna is situated on the southern bank of the Danube river, which branches out here on its long journey from the Black Forest to the Black Sea into many arms. The north-west view from the city is dominated by the verdant, rolling hills of the Vienna Woods (Wienerwald), the end of a spur of the eastern Alps. These green hills include the Kahlenberg and Leopoldsberg, both crowned with churches and which provide magnificent views over the whole city and the alluvial plains to the east. Between these hills and the inner city lie the wine-growing villages of Nussdorf, Heiligenstadt, and Grinzing, long since incorporated into the city, but still country retreats in Haydn's day. A few miles further north, on the west side of the Danube, the low hills descend to Klosterneuburg, an important Augustinian monastery. The Viennese countryside is justly famous for the variety of its beauty.

Vienna's climate has four distinct seasons. In the long, cold winter (December through to March), with the temperatures swinging above and below freezing, the grey days stretch on forever and carnival festivities become a psychological necessity. The occasional heavy snowfall can turn the streets into sheets of ice. When spring finally arrives, nothing on earth matches the musical quality of the birdsong or the perfumed smells of the flowering lilacs and lime (linden) trees. Summers can be unbearably hot and dry with occasional violent thunder storms, and those who can afford it have always tried to escape to the countryside. The plagues of dust (fine chalk from the surrounding plains) irritate the eyes and lungs. Autumn is windy and wet, but the chestnut trees provide splendid colours, and nuts for roasting.

Vienna itself is dominated physically and spiritually by St Stephen's cathedral, standing in the middle of the old medieval town centre. The single steeple, rising to a height of 137 m (450 feet), still forms the most important landmark in the city. Begun in the mid-12th century in Romanesque style, the cathedral was later transformed into a magnificent Gothic edifice. For the whole of the 1740s, Haydn's life as a choirboy revolved around this huge building with its high, gloomy interior. He even lived in its shadow, boarding with Kapellmeister Georg Reutter in the Kantorei, a five-storey building (demolished in 1804) at the south side of the cathedral. This house was attached to the Magdalenenkapelle (its outline now marked on the square by red pavement), which was destroyed by fire in 1781 and never rebuilt. An underground chapel (Virgilkapelle), recently discovered when the subway was built, is now open to view. St Stephen's was also where Haydn was married in 1760.

Vienna's other principal building is the imperial residence or Hofburg, which was progressively enlarged over the centuries, thus juxtaposing different architectural styles. It includes not only the Spanish Riding School, housing the trained Lippizaner horses, but also such 18th-century buildings as the Prunksaal of the court library (constructed 1723–6) and the Albertina (built 1742–5). The Hofburg is located next to the Herrengasse, the middle section of a crooked narrow street that runs north from the Albertina, past the Josephsplatz and Michaelerplatz, ending at the Schottentor. Many of the city palaces built by the upper aristocracy as their winter residences line this central street. The Esterházy palace, where Haydn probably stayed when visiting Vienna from Eisenstadt, was in the Wallnerstraße, just a block away from the Herrengasse. In the later 1790s, Haydn was frequently invited to the Hofburg by Emperor Franz and his musical wife Marie Therese, and he conducted his oratorios in private performances there.

The face of Vienna changed in accordance with its political history. When the young Maria Theresia inherited the Habsburg empire on the death of her father Karl VI in 1740, she found the treasury drained and the army weak. She was soon forced into war by Frederick the Great of Prussia, who aggressively invaded the rich industrial province of Silesia. This war dragged on with interruptions until 1763, but Silesia was never recovered. At the same time, the War of Austrian Succession (1740–8) established general acceptance of the Pragmatic Sanction (guaranteeing the right of a female heir to reign over the Empire), and in 1745 Maria Theresia's husband, Franz Stephan of Lorraine, was elected Holy Roman Emperor. The Hungarian nobility continued to support the empress, and in return were granted special privileges. On the advice of her new Chancellor, Wenzel Kaunitz, Maria Theresia struck up an alliance with France and Russia, causing England to side with Prussia to maintain Europe's balance of power. Frederick II's invasion of Saxony led to the Seven Years War (1756–63), which resulted, for example, in France's loss of Canada to the British. All these years of war further drained Austria's economy, no doubt affecting Haydn's early struggles to earn a living. They also meant that Maria Theresia no longer had the financial means to continue her ancestors' generous support of music. This role was now taken over by wealthy aristocrats such as the Esterházy family.

In 1765, on the death of Maria Theresia's husband, their son Joseph became co-regent. Joseph soon asserted himself, winning the large province of Galicia in the first partition of Poland in 1772 and starting to make social changes in line with his enlightened ideas. The empress had already instituted some administrative and financial reforms, and since she herself always insisted on duty, conscience, and morality, she gained the lasting love and respect of her subjects. After her death, when Joseph II was in sole command (1780–90), he decided to speed up the reforming process. However, his excessive zeal in wanting reason to prevail over any sense of tradition produced much opposition. His drastic religious reforms (closing over 700 monasteries and confiscating their property, and eliminating 118 brotherhoods in Vienna alone) even antagonized the pope, Pius VI, who travelled to Vienna in 1782 to try to undo some of the damage. One unfortunate result of these reforms was that much Baroque sacred music was destroyed and many church musicians lost their positions. In the end, Joseph saw many of his well-intentioned, benevolent projects miscarry.

After the death of Joseph's short-lived successor Leopold II (1790–2), the new Emperor Franz began his long reign (1792–1835). The French Revolution (including the beheading of Marie Antoinette in 1793), produced a conservative reaction among her Austrian relatives, and Joseph's liberal ideas were gradually replaced by the iron-fisted control of an intrusive and overbearing state. The Napoleonic Wars brought renewed hardships, including two occupations by French troops, in 1805 and 1809, and in 1806 Franz, having previously declared himself Emperor of Austria, renounced the crown of the Holy Roman Empire, ending this historic institution. The constant inflation during wartime meant that most of the private orchestras maintained by the Austro-Hungarian nobility were disbanded. However, a growing middle class interested in music provided new audiences for concerts, and increased markets for the distribution and sale of music, including printed copies of Haydn's works.

In Haydn's day, Vienna's old inner city—approximately identical with today's First District—was still fortified. This walled city was shaped in a semicircle bounded on the north-eastern side by the Danube canal, a regulated arm of the river, and on the south-western side by the river Wien, which flows into the canal. The city wall and outer dry moat, called respectively Bastei and Glacis, dated back to the Middle Ages and served as a protection against the repeated attacks by the Turks, but not against the French. (This fortification no longer exists, having been replaced after 1857 by the Ringstraße with its monumental buildings. A remnant of the wall can still be seen at the Mölker Bastei, near the Schottentor.) In 1704, the fortified area had been expanded to include the suburbs (much of which had been burned down in the 1683 siege of the city by the Turks), and an outer ring of trenches and walls, the Linienwall, was constructed. This larger semicircle (now replaced by the Gürtel or belt—some 32 km (20 miles) in length) joined onto the main Danube itself and contained toll booths to control and tax imported goods.

In the 18th century, the city could be circumnavigated by foot on the Bastei in about an hour. During Maria Theresia's reign, commoners still required special permission to walk on the wall, a restriction later removed by Joseph II. The dirt-covered Glacis was 600 paces in width and was originally used for military exercises. It also served as an area for selling produce in stands, and as an open workplace for certain trades (carpentry, stonemasonry, etc.). In 1770 Joseph ordered footpaths and roads to be laid out connecting the city with the suburbs. Grass was also planted to cut down on the continual problem of dust blowing into the city. In 1776 lanterns were installed and in 1781 the Glacis was planted with 3,000 chestnut and acacia trees. The area soon developed into a favourite promenade. In the early 1790s Haydn lived for several periods in the Hamberger House on the Wasserkunstbastei, where he was visited by Mozart in 1790, and by Beethoven in 1793. Demolished in 1891, the building had its main entrance at Seilerstätte 21. From this house Haydn would have had a fine view to the south, overlooking the Glacis (where the Stadtpark now lies) and the Landstraße suburb beyond (today's Third District). There were 12 gates in the wall through which roads radiated out to the numerous suburbs, one of which, Gumpendorf (actually Obere Windmühle, in today's Sixth District), contained the house Haydn purchased in 1793 (now a Haydn Museum). This house was just inside the outer wall, near the Mariahilfer Linie, at that time surrounded by gardens and fields.

The suburb of Leopoldstadt to Vienna's north-east, between the river and the canal, was largely unfortified and often subject to flooding. This extensive suburb (today's Second District) includes the two separate wooded retreats known as the Prater and the Augarten. The Prater's immense green space was once a private hunting reserve for the royal family. In 1766, Joseph opened up the area to the general public, and the section nearest to the city (Wurstelprater) soon developed into a famous amusement park with refreshment stands and popular games, especially bowling and ring-throwing. The wealthier segment of society found it fashionable to take a daily ride in the Prater in their carriages, and a favourite destination was the Lusthaus, a two-storey café house at the end of the 5 km (3 mile) long main avenue. In 1774, the fireworks artist Johann Georg Stuwer set off the first of his immensely popular pyrotechnic displays on the meadow here, and in 1791 Jean-Pierre Blanchard's successful balloon flight across the Danube was initiated here. In 1775, Joseph also opened up the

Augarten, with its restaurants and performance hall, for public use. Concerts were held here, at 7 o'clock on Saturday mornings, and Haydn was known to attend.

In 1740, the 8-year-old Haydn would have experienced Vienna at the height of its Baroque splendour. The victory over the Turks in 1683 had inspired a period of intense building to repair the devastation caused by the siege and to restore the glory of the Habsburg Empire. The numerous aristocratic palaces, garden villas, and city buildings, decorated with monumental figures from antiquity, formed Vienna's architectural character. Important new buildings included the Karlskirche (begun in 1715, consecrated in 1737), a unique structure combining two ornamented columns, a Roman portico and a Baroque cupola, designed by one of the country's greatest architects, Johann-Bernhard Fischer von Erlach. Vivaldi, at whose funeral in 1741 Haydn probably sang, was buried in the 'Burgerspital' cemetery next to this church, located to the south just outside the city walls, across the river Wien.

From 1744 to 1749 construction work was completed on Schloß Schönbrunn, the Habsburg summer palace (with 1,200 rooms), built to replace a hunting lodge destroyed by the Turks, and intended to rival Versailles. Marie Antoinette spent her childhood here, surrounded by Rococo white and gold, and this is where Mozart, at the age of 6, astonished the court with his prodigious talents. The formal Baroque gardens combine straight alleys of trimmed trees and flower beds with allegorical statues and fountains. Haydn delighted in relating how Empress Maria Theresia had caught him as a teenage boy climbing the scaffolding and personally ordered his punishment. In 1747 a theatre, designed by Johann Ferdinand Hetzendorf von Hohenburg, was opened in the palace. It would be used for private royal entertainments, including marionette operas. Europe's first zoo was founded at Schönbrunn in 1752 and housed lions and monkeys and even an elephant (which died of a throat infection in 1784). In 1776 the Gloriette was built on top of a hill overlooking the palace, and in 1778 artificial Roman ruins were constructed in the gardens as a fashionable attraction.

In the 1750s, Haydn served as first violinist for the eight-o'clock morning service at the church of the Barmherzige Brüder in the Taborstraße (a street dating from 1409, now Second District). This church and its adjoining hospital still flourish today, honouring Haydn with special celebrations. He then reportedly had to rush from the Leopoldstadt to play the organ at ten o'clock at Count Haugwitz's chapel, and then to St Stephen's to sing at eleven o'clock. In this period, Haydn was also involved in writing and performing serenades, and he recounted how he had played a cacophonous joke on residents of the Tiefer Graben, a few blocks north-west of the cathedral. Once the bed of the Alser stream, this 'deep ditch' was later lined with houses.

An area of the inner city that played a major role in Haydn's life was the Kohlmarkt, a street running north from St Michael's church to the Graben. Next to the church (its present classical façade was erected only in 1790) was the large Michaelerhaus (Kohlmarkt 11) where Haydn spent the early 1750s lodged in a miserable garret. After a fire in 1704 had destroyed the previous structure, a new building was constructed by the Barnabite owners (finished in 1710) to provide rented accommodation. Among the famous tenants were the MARTINES family, PIETRO METASTASIO, and NICOLA PORPORA. The house still exists, but the attic was removed in 1848 and replaced with an additional storey. Next to it (from 1789 on) were the offices of Haydn's preferred Viennese publisher, Artaria & Co. (The firm is still there today at Kohlmarkt 9.)

In 1753 construction work was begun on the Aula of the Old University, a festive hall with elaborate frescos on the ceilings. This hall served as the venue for the gala celebration of *The Creation* in honour of the composer's birthday in 1808. In 1754 the Dutch botanist Nikolaus von Jacquin began planting the Botanical Garden, next to the Belvedere palace (just south of the inner city), with exotic plants and trees collected on scientific expeditions to foreign lands. This was the era of intensive scientific enquiry that led, for example, to new developments in music instrument construction.

Two main theatres dominated Haydn's Vienna. Across from St Michael's church and attached to the Hofburg was the Burgtheater, founded in 1741, the building being completed in 1759. Although this was a small court theatre, Maria Theresia also opened it up to the paying public, thus providing a new exposure to the arts for a wider public. Haydn's *Creation* and Trumpet Concerto received their premieres at this theatre. On 12 February 1797, the birthday of Emperor Franz II, Haydn's anthem 'Gott erhalte Franz den Kaiser' was performed at the Burgtheater for the first time.

The second theatre, originally built for Italian players in 1709 and known as the Komödienhaus, burnt down in 1761. The court then constructed a new Kärntnerthortheater (standing approximately where the Hotel Sacher is located today). It was designed by Nicolà Pacassi, dedicated in 1763, and demolished only in 1870 after the new State Opera had opened the previous year. These two theatres were used for operas, ballets, and plays, and could also be rented for benefit concerts. The decade of Joseph's liberal reforms, including the freeing of censorship regulations, gave birth to several important suburban theatres: the Leopoldstädter Theater in 1781, the Theater auf der Wieden in 1787, and the Theater in der Josephstadt in 1788. The year 1748 saw the opening of the Redoutensäle, two elegant ballrooms in the Hofburg, where masked balls and concerts were held. Haydn later composed dances for the court balls here. In 1793, Haydn gave a public performance of three of the 'London' symphonies in the small Redoutensaal.

The 1780s also saw the construction of such buildings for the public good as the expanded Allgemeine Krankenhaus (General Hospital) and the Narrenturm (Lunatic Asylum, 1783). In an attempt to improve health conditions, Joseph ordered in 1784 that all cemeteries within the inner city be closed and that burials subsequently take place in outlying graveyards. This included the Hundsturmer Friedhof where Haydn was first buried (now the site of the Haydn Park, in the Twelfth District).

The burgeoning Industrial Revolution also helped change the face of Vienna. Porcelain and silk manufacturing boomed in the suburbs, and engravers (Jakob Schmutzer) and book printers (Thomas Trattner) began to flourish. In 1780 the latter employed about 200 typesetters and printers. Living quarters and workshops, which had often been combined in one room, were now increasingly separated. In 1770 a new law expressly allowed women to be employed. Later, in 1795, Emperor Franz banished all factories to the suburbs for fear of having too many working-class people in the inner city. In 1774 the school system was reformed, improving standards of education for the common people. New methods for controlling security in the city were instigated, and in 1791 a civil police system was formed in the suburbs. Haydn had already suffered in the mid-1750s through lax security when all his possessions were stolen after he had moved from the Michaelerhaus to an unknown location in the Seilerstätte.

The population of Vienna grew rapidly from a figure of about 80,000 at the beginning of the 18th century to 175,609 (for city and suburbs) in 1754, when the first census was conducted. By 1788 this number had reached 270,000, and Vienna had become the largest German-speaking city in the world. The birthrate was high, but so was the child mortality rate. Typhoid and tuberculosis were endemic diseases. There was no running water and the well-water was often contaminated. Standards of hygiene were, in general, deplorable. At the beginning of the 19th century, for every 100 births in Vienna there were 50–70 deaths of children in their first year of life. Diseases especially increased during periods of war and, at the time of the Napoleonic invasions, the population declined temporarily to 230,000.

The inner city contained 127 streets and alleys (often crooked and narrow) and 1,200 houses (excluding churches). About 1750 this included 22 apothecaries, 21 coffee houses, 45 inns and 111 beer parlours. In 1788 the city together with its suburbs had 6,500 dwelling houses, each with 40–50 inhabitants. Owing to the large influx of immigrants from the Habsburg lands, and an ordinance passed in 1767 allowing buildings constructed on empty ground to remain untaxed for 20 years, much new housing was constructed in the suburbs: solid buildings built of sturdy brick or stone, with roofs made of tile or copper. Most apartments consisted only of one large room and a small kitchen with an open hearth. Rents there were about a third cheaper than in the inner city, but none of the streets was paved. City houses were usually five to six storeys high, while those in the suburbs, with simpler façades influenced by the new Classicist style, were one to two storeys lower. When Haydn purchased his house in Gumpendorf in 1793, it consisted only of the ground floor, with two rooms and a kitchen, to which he was allowed to add a second storey.

In Haydn's Vienna, the principal currency was the gulden, abbreviated fl. (for florin), with 60 kreuzer making one gulden. Wages varied drastically from the standard 15 kreuzer per day earned by a hard labourer (much less for spinners), amounting to a theoretical 75 gulden per year, to the high salaries of certain court officials, which at the uppermost end reached 100,000 gulden yearly. In contrast to this, Prince Esterházy's annual income amounted to 700,000 gulden. Haydn's income ranged from the 60 Gulden he made as a violinist at the church of the Barmherzige Brüder in the 1750s to the Esterházy pension of 2,300 gulden he received in 1806. Because the wages for servants were so low, many artists and musicians could afford one, if not two. At his house in Gumpendorf (assessed later at 5,100 gulden), Haydn employed both a cook and a valet. According to Johann Pezzl's tally of living expenses for a single man of middle-class status living in Vienna in the mid-1780s, rent would cost 60 fl., firewood and light 24 fl., clothing and laundry a total of 170 fl., and food 180 fl. To live comfortably, he would need an annual income of 500–50 gulden.

The characteristic street life in Haydn's Vienna is visible in various pictures from the time that depict workers at their occupations, in particular the plump market women at their stalls, the young parlour maids in their pretty outfits, the water sellers, the sedan chair carriers, etc. There were also young dandies strolling along the fashionable Graben and Kohlmarkt, replaced at night by the street ladies, the so-called Graben nymphs. The city was a continuous bustle of people from all European nations (in their various native costumes) walking, on horseback, or riding in carriages. The Viennese in general loved spectacles, but most of the Baroque-era processions, with their pompous ceremonies and fine uniforms, fell victim to the religious reforms. Animal-baiting drew enormous crowds, but when the popular Hetz Theater in the Landstraße suburb (where lions, tigers, bears, etc. had been baited since 1755) burnt down in 1796, Emperor Franz would not allow its reconstruction.

Since the land surrounding Vienna was very fertile, its inhabitants were generally better-fed than the populations of other large European cities. Haydn in particular enjoyed the fine food that was available in Vienna. The main meal of the day, held at noon, began with soup and contained several courses of meat dishes. The growing fashion for drinking coffee led to the opening of numerous coffee houses, where newspapers could be read at leisure. Over the century, wine consumption declined from *c.*160 litres annual consumption per person (*c.*1730) to only 100–120 litres per person (*c.*1800). At the same time beer consumption increased from 65 to 145 litres. (In 1795 Haydn was allotted 515 litres of wine.) At the end of the century, drinking hot chocolate and eating sweets were signs of luxury, and Haydn was able to afford both. He also possessed numerous snuffboxes and a pipe.

Haydn's experience of Vienna spanned almost 70 years and encompassed both the dark side of bitter poverty, crime, and a struggle to earn a living, and the glorious, bright side of wealth, house-ownership, and the delights of full recognition at the highest level. It is to Vienna's credit that, through talent and hard work alone, such a stunning rise in social position was possible. RSte

I. Ackerl, *Die Chronik Wiens* (Dortmund, 1988).

M. Huss, *Joseph Haydn* (Eisenstadt, 1984).

Joseph Haydn in seiner Zeit [exhibition catalogue] (Eisenstadt, 1982).

H. C. Robbins Landon, *Mozart and Vienna* [including translation of extensive extracts from J. Pezzl, *Skizze von Wien*, 1786–90] (London, 1991).

A. Schusser (ed.), *Wien zur Zeit Joseph Haydns* (Vienna, 1982).

Wagenseil, Georg Christoph (b. 29 Jan. 1715; d. 1 March 1777). A leading composer in Vienna in the middle of the century, and one of the most formative influences on Haydn's stylistic development. His instrumental output included over 100 symphonies, over 100 concertos (especially for keyboard), and over 200 works for solo keyboard. A favoured pupil of FUX he entered the service of the imperial family at the age of 24 as court composer and keyboard teacher to Maria Theresia and, later, to her daughters (including Marie Antoinette). His keyboard sonatas, composed largely as teaching pieces, influenced Haydn's own early sonatas, and Leopold Mozart (1719–87), too, used them to educate his children. He was also esteemed as a performer on the harpsichord. His 16 Italian operas, composed for Florence and Venice as well as Vienna, were, in general, less well received, the imperial poet, Metastasio, for instance, suggesting that he did not have an innate understanding of the genre. On the other hand his church music, which numbered over 100 works, constituted an ever-present part of the Viennese repertoire in the period.

Unlike his contemporaries, and in notable anticipation of Haydn, Wagenseil achieved international distribution for his instrumental music, including publication in Paris and London, and manuscript distribution in German-speaking Europe. The Esterházy court owned manuscript parts of symphonies and operatic extracts by Wagenseil, and Haydn's earliest symphonies, in particular, have many characteristics in common with those of the older composer: C major symphonies with trumpets and timpani, three-movement structures, thematic material that is predominantly rhythmic rather than melodic, second subject areas that include a passage in the dominant minor, slow movements for strings alone, and finales in 3/8 time. Wagenseil's concertos, likewise, provide an important stylistic background to Haydn's concertos from the 1760s. HS-M

D. Heartz, *Haydn, Mozart and the Viennese School, 1740–1780* (New York, 1995).

J. Kucaba (ed.), *G. C. Wagenseil. Fifteen symphonies*, in *The Symphony 1720–1840*, editor-in-chief B. S. Brook, B/III (New York, 1981).

H. Scholz-Michelitsch, *Georg Christoph Wagenseil, Hofkomponist und Hofklaviermeister der Kaiserin Maria Theresia* (Vienna, 1980).

Wales, George Augustus Frederick Prince of; later George IV (b. 12 Aug. 1762; d. 26 June 1830). An avid patron and supporter of music, especially in the period 1783–95. As a young boy he learnt the cello and, already in his teens, began organizing private concerts at which he would play alongside leading instrumentalists of the time. His regular morning concerts at Carlton House came to favour the string quartet, especially the works of Gyrowetz, Haydn, and Pleyel, which had to be listened to in absolute silence; the more occasional evening concerts were the first in London to feature Haydn's 'Paris' symphonies. He was a patron of the Professional Concert, a friend of the impresario JOHN GALLINI, and regularly influenced the course of musical politics in London. There is no doubt that the prince's enthusiasm for new music in general helped create a receptive climate for Haydn's music in particular.

Haydn first met the prince at a court ball at St James's Palace on 18 January 1791. Speaking in fluent German, he invited him to participate in a private concert at Carlton House the following day, the first of many during Haydn's two visits to London. Haydn usually played the piano and presided at the instrument in performances of his symphonies. Evening concerts were sometimes delayed by the prince's late arrival and, if the mood took him, could be protracted affairs before supper was served. In a letter to MARIA ANNA VON GENZINGER Haydn wrote: 'The Prince of Wales is the most handsome man on God's earth; he has an extraordinary love of music and a lot of feeling, but not much money. *Nota bene*, this is between ourselves. I am more pleased by his kindness than by any financial gain.' Haydn's private reservations became public in 1795–6 when he submitted a bill for 100 guineas to the Parliamentary Commissioners who were settling the enormous debts accumulated by the prince; he received the money in April 1796. Part of this debt had no doubt been incurred in 1791 when the prince commissioned John Hoppner (1758–1810) to paint a striking portrait of the composer, still in the royal collection. In 1792 Haydn wrote a march for the Prince of Wales (Hob.VIII:3). He is listed as a subscriber to the first edition of *The Creation* alongside several other members of the British royal family.

HCRL/3.

S. McVeigh, *Concert Life in London from Mozart to Haydn* (Cambridge, 1993).

C. F. Pohl, *Haydn in London* (Vienna, 1867).

'Was meine matte Brust bekränket' (What ails my faint heart) (Hob. deest). An ADVENT ARIA in G major for tenor, two violins, and bass. It survives in one source only which may be a contrafactum of a lost work, possibly a PASTORELLA.

Weidinger, Anton (b. 9 June 1766; d. 20 Sept. 1852). Viennese trumpet virtuoso and contributor to the development of the keyed trumpet. With the ORGANISIERTE TROMPETE he was able to play a full chromatic scale, but apparently at the cost of some of the natural distinctive sonority and power of the instrument. For Weidinger and his keyed trumpet Haydn wrote the Trumpet Concerto in E♭. Although Haydn dated the autograph 1796, the first known performance was in a concert given by Weidinger in the Burgtheater on 22 March 1800. Several other leading composers in Vienna, including HUMMEL, KOZELUCH (KOŽELUH), and WEIGL, also wrote works for Weidinger, but none of them surpassed Haydn's resourceful exploitation of Weidinger's instrument and technique. JAR

R. Dahlqvist, *The Keyed Trumpet and its Greatest Virtuoso, Anton Weidinger* (Nashville, 1975).

A. Lindner, 'Anton Weidinger (1766–1852)' (diss., University of Vienna, 1993).

Weigl, Joseph (Franz) (b. 19 May 1740; d. 25 Jan. 1820). Cellist at the Esterházy court. Born in Bavaria, Weigl joined the orchestra at the Esterházy court on 1 June 1761, a few weeks after Haydn, and remained there for eight years. Clearly a fine player, Weigl must have stimulated Haydn to write the Cello Concerto in C and the many extended solo passages in his symphonies. The surviving performance material for *Lo speziale* suggests that Weigl realized chords on the cello when playing continuo. In 1764 he married Anna Maria Scheffstoß, daughter of Anton Scheffstoß, an official at the Esterházy court. She was a soprano who took leading roles in Haydn's *Acide* and *La canterina*, as well as singing the solo part in the Stabat mater. In 1769 Weigl joined the orchestra of the Kärntnerthortheater in Vienna and from 1792 he is listed as a cellist in the Hofkapelle. The subscription list for the first edition of *The Creation* includes the name Joseph Weigl but with the annotation 'wholesale merchant' next to it. Whether this indicates another person of the same name or that the 60-year-old Weigl was now also a businessman of some sort cannot be established.

Haydn and his wife were godparents to two of Weigl's children. The first of these, also Joseph Weigl (1766–1846), became a successful composer of stage works (ballet, German opera, and Italian opera) in Vienna from the 1790s onwards. Following a performance of *La Principessa d'Amalfi* in January 1794 Haydn sent his godson a glowing letter of congratulations that was subsequently made public in the *Wiener Theater Almanach für das Jahr 1795*.

HCRL/1, 2, and 3.

J. A. Rice, *Antonio Salieri* (Chicago, 1998).

'Weihnachtssymphonie'. A completely inappropriate nickname ('Christmas' symphony) first applied to Symphony no. 26 by Mandyczewski in his edition of that work for the Breitkopf & Härtel complete edition. The more familiar nickname 'LAMENTATION' is entirely appropriate. JH

Weingartner, Felix (b. 2 June 1863; d. 7 May 1942). Austrian conductor, composer, editor, and writer on music. In 1908 he succeeded Mahler as musical director of the court opera in Vienna. He relinquished the post three years later but maintained his association with the Vienna Philharmonic Orchestra until 1927. Beethoven was at the centre of his musical universe as a conductor, a viewpoint reflected in his writings on music where Haydn, if mentioned at all, is a peripheral figure. However, Weingartner was interested in exploring unfamiliar music. He was involved with the projected complete edition of Berlioz's music and with the first three volumes (Symphonies nos. 1–40) in the aborted complete edition of Haydn's music published by Breitkopf & Härtel (1907–33).

'Weinzierler' trios. In 1938 the German publisher Kallmeyer issued an edition of six string trios (Hob.V:C4, V:D3, II:38, II:33, V:D4, and V:Es9), giving them the title 'Weinzierler Trios' because of their putative association with Weinzierl, the home of BARON FÜRNBERG for whom Haydn wrote his first quartets. They are no more or less likely to have been associated with Weinzierl than any number of other string trios. JH

Werner, Gregor Joseph (b. 28 Jan. 1693; d. 3. Mar. 1766). Austrian composer and Haydn's predecessor as Esterházy Kapellmeister. His engagement on 10 May 1728 opened a new era for music at the court after seven years of retrenchment under Princess Maria Octavia Esterházy during the minority of Prince Paul Anton Esterházy. On taking up his appointment Werner brought new church music from Vienna in order to improve the outdated stock at Eisenstadt and began the tireless production of his own works; over nearly four decades of service he composed a vast quantity of church music (masses, requiems, litanies, vespers, settings of the Te Deum, Marian antiphons, and numerous other pieces), instrumental music for church use (organ concertos, pastorellas, and trio sonatas), and a smaller amount of secular instrumental music (symphonies and various chamber works). A few pieces reached publication, notably a set of orchestral suites evoking the 12 months of the year (*Neuer und sehr curios-Musicalischer*

Instrumental-Calender, Augsburg, 1748), and the comic portrayal of a Viennese flea market and the election of a peasant judge that form the two movements of *Zwey neue und extra lustige musicalische Tafel-Stücke* (Augsburg, after 1748). In 1729 Werner composed the first of a series of over 20 Lenten oratorios which, in imitation of the custom of the Viennese imperial court, were performed on Good Fridays in the Esterházy castle chapel and elsewhere in Eisenstadt. The tradition lasted until 1762 and together with Werner's settings of the Lamentations of Jeremiah (performed in the castle chapel as part of the liturgy for Holy Week) imparted a gravity to this period of the year that was doubtless part of Haydn's early experience at Eisenstadt; this finds an echo in the composer's 'Lamentation' symphony (no. 26) and the Stabat mater.

By the end of his career Werner's fundamentally contrapuntal style of church music had become outmoded through the general turn to a more melodic style of sacred music. However, a distinction is to be drawn between, on the one hand, the bulk of his output, weighty works with Latin texts and the German-language oratorios, and, on the other, pieces with German texts often in dialect for Advent and the Nativity (with associated instrumental pastorellas) that employ a distinctly homespun idiom, invoking elements of Austrian and indeed Eastern European folk music. This 'rustic style' retained its currency, as comparable pieces such as 'Ey, wer hat ihm das Ding gedenkt' and 'Herst Nachbä, hä, sag mir was heut' by Haydn show, while Werner's mastery of the severe a cappella style lies behind the composition of Haydn's *Missa 'sunt bona mixta malis'*. Werner's other instrumental music likewise displays a differentiation between conservative trio sonatas in the traditional four-movement format of the *sonata da chiesa* and modern three-movement symphonies, as in the *Symphoniae sex senaeque sonatae* (Augsburg, 1735).

From 1761 to 1766 the careers of Werner and Haydn coincided at Eisenstadt. An attitude of embittered jealousy on the part of the Kapellmeister has usually been inferred from a long letter of complaint against his young deputy sent to Prince Nicolaus Esterházy in October 1765, a few months before Werner's death. Yet some justification can be found for the increasingly infirm composer who, incapable of overseeing his designated preserve of the church music, had received reports of a disordered choir loft and negligent musicians. The new prince's musical interests lay with Haydn and the development of instrumental music: it must have appeared to Werner that the efforts of 37 years of assiduous service were being set at nought. His criticisms of Haydn as a mere 'song writer' ('G'sanglmacher') and 'fashion follower' ('Modehansl') imply as much a sense of isolation from current musical tastes as antipathy towards Haydn. For his part, Haydn maintained a discreet silence on his relationship with his superior. It seems, however, that he esteemed the solid worth of Werner's music, for late in life he organized the publication for string quartet of introductions from six of Werner's oratorios, in each case a slow opening followed by a quick fugue (Artaria, 1804). The title page states that the publication was 'edited by his successor J. Haydn out of particular esteem towards the famous master'. Haydn's editing was restricted to selecting the music, changing a few tempo headings, and omitting the figures above the bass line. JD

HCRL/1.

L. Somfai, 'Haydns Tribut an seinen Vorgänger Werner', *HYB* 2 (1964), 75–80.

Wesley, Samuel (b. 24 Feb. 1766; d. 11 Oct. 1837). English organist, composer, conductor, and teacher. In his reminiscences he recalls Haydn playing the unexpected piano solo in the finale of Symphony no. 98 and relates an anecdote that Prince Paul Anton Esterházy suggested that Haydn write a work for several ensembles placed in different rooms. The latter story has been linked with the 'ECHO' DIVERTIMENTO (Hob.II:39), a spurious work. Samuel's brother, Charles Wesley (1757–1834), was a subscriber to the first edition of *The Creation* and later arranged four melodies by Haydn as hymn tunes ('Albion Chapel', 'Embden', 'Otaheita', and 'Otranto'), published in a collection entitled *The Seraph. A Collection of Sacred Music Suitable to Public or Private Devotion* (London, [1818]).

Whyte, William (b. 1771; d. 1858). Whyte flourished as a bookseller and music publisher in Edinburgh from *c.*1799 to 1858. He published a large number of songs individually, but is most noted for engaging Haydn to set 65 Scottish songs with accompaniments for piano, violin, and cello. Little is known about the arrangements between the two men, but Haydn reported to GEORGE THOMSON in June 1803 that Whyte had been paying him two guineas per setting, twice what Thomson had paid in the past. Thomson objected to Haydn doing work for a rival publisher, but Haydn pointed out that he could not refuse any reasonable offer from other publishers. He also claimed that the airs he set for Whyte were quite different from those he had done for Thomson. Although there are actually a few examples where essentially the same melody appears in both collections, for example 'Maggy Lauder' and 'The Lass of Patie's Mill', the settings are quite different. All of Haydn's settings for Whyte were apparently composed about 1802–3, and were published in two volumes, in 1804 and 1806, as *A Collection of Scottish Airs harmonized for the Voice & Piano Forte....*

BARC

C. Hopkinson and C. B. Oldman, 'Haydn's Settings of Scottish Songs in the Collections of Napier and Whyte', *Edinburgh Bibliographical Society Transactions*, 3 (1948–55), 85–120.

windband music. Music for wind instruments forms a small, comparatively insignificant part of Haydn's musical output, which is perhaps surprising given the prevalence of such works in his musical environment, especially at the Esterházy court. As well as self-standing works the following survey includes windband music that is included in larger dramatic and choral works.

1. Music for Count Morzin and/or Prince Paul Anton Esterházy (*c.*1760). Haydn was appointed Vice-Kapellmeister to Prince Paul Anton Esterházy on 1 May 1761. One of his earliest duties was the reorganization of the instrumental personnel at the court, including the appointment of new young wind players to form the *Feldmusik* (literally 'field-music'), an ensemble of pairs of oboes, horns, and bassoons whose duties included playing out of doors; these players were also members of the regular orchestra and received an extra 17 kreuzer per day for their services in the *Feldmusik*. Haydn had recently written, or was in the process of writing, several divertimenti that probably formed part of their repertoire. But it remains uncertain when or for whom Haydn originally wrote this music. Haydn's first employer, Count Morzin, may have retained a windband at Lukavec, but there is no direct evidence of this beyond the suggestive date of 1760 that appears on the autograph manuscripts of two of the divertimenti for windband (Hob.II: 15, 16). Haydn may have already left Morzin's employment when he wrote them, or had a commission from elsewhere. It is certainly possible that some if not all of these divertimenti were written for the new *Feldmusik* of Prince Esterházy.

Eight works have survived (Hob.II:3, 7, 15, 16, and 23; Hob.II:D18, D23, and G9). Seven are scored for the typical *Feldmusik* ensemble of pairs of oboes, horns, and bassoons; Hob.II:16 is rather oddly scored for two violins, two cor anglais, two horns, and two bassoons. They are all largely unsophisticated pieces, typically comprising five short movements in a symmetrical movement pattern around a slow movement, rather like the composer's earliest quartets. Haydn's scoring is always colourful, if sometimes eccentric, as in the high parts for horns or the low, divided parts for bassoons.

2. Windband music with clarinets (1761–*c.*1768). Haydn also wrote some divertimenti in the 1760s that included parts for clarinets. His reasons for doing so are unclear, since there were no clarinettists in Esterházy employment at the time of their composition. Four works are documented. The only one to have survived is a divertimento in C (Hob.II:14) scored for two clarinets and two horns. Haydn dated his autograph manuscript 1761, and it is reasonable to suppose he composed it for the same or a similar occasion as a divertimento (cassation) in C (Hob.II:17), scored for the same four instruments plus strings. Perhaps he was asked to compose music for some visiting clarinettists. The diaries of Count Karl von Zinzendorf bear witness to one such occasion: on 6 October 1761 he dined with Prince Paul Anton Esterházy in Vienna, after which Michael Casimir Oginski performed some clarinet pieces of his own composition. Oginski (1731–1803) was a Polish count and dilettante clarinettist who travelled extensively, apparently with a companion who would play second clarinet.

3. Music for Count Marschall and Prince Nicolaus Esterházy (*c.*1770–1784). A single manuscript source, originally from Friedland castle in Bohemia, exists for a work with the title 'Marche Regimento de Marshall'. The person in question, Count Ernst Dietrich Marschall (1692–1771), was the founder of an imperial regiment of that name. The commandant of the regiment from 1767 to the beginning of the 1770s was Count Anton Esterházy, son of Prince Nicolaus and from 1790 the reigning prince. It was almost certainly through him that Haydn received a request to compose this short march for pairs of oboes, horns, and bassoons.

At the Esterházy court, even though the *Feldmusik* continued to function to at least 1780 Haydn was not, apparently, required to compose music for it. The probability is that the orchestral wind musicians had less and less time for such activities, and what evidence there is suggests that by the end of the 1770s Prince Esterházy had established a separate regimental band of clarinets, horns, and bassoons for the parades and other ceremonies featuring his personal guard of grenadiers. An anonymous visitor to Eszterháza in 1784 described a grenadier parade as follows: 'The musical march is precisely executed, very harmonious, and a composition by Haydn.' Two surviving marches, both scored for pairs of clarinets, horns, and bassoons, may have been for the grenadiers' band. One is a march in E♭ (Hob.VIII:6) and the other is a march in B♭ that is played by a stage band in Act 1 of Haydn's opera *Armida*, first performed in February 1784. It is known that the grenadiers regularly acted as extras in opera performances at Eszterháza; on this occasion they brought their instruments and music with them.

4. Windband music written in London (1791–5). In London, Haydn would have become exposed to English military bands, perhaps particularly active in this period of imminent and actual war with France. Most of Haydn's windband music from this time consists of the staple item of such bands, marches. In all cases Haydn follows the English practice of using clarinets rather than oboes.

During his first visit to London, Haydn wrote the March for the Prince of Wales (Hob.VIII:3). This masterly composition demonstrates the remarkable ear that Haydn had developed when writing for a wind instrument ensemble. The intricacy of his scoring is apparent in every bar: the interplay between tutti and solo textures, the constant variation in the instrumental colouring of the melodic line that is sometimes supported by parallel writing (even at the double octave), and the variety in the accompanying textures including some delicious Alberti figuration in the chalumeau register of the second clarinet.

When later in 1792 Haydn was commissioned to compose a march for the Royal Society of Musicians, he had the Prince of Wales march copied and added parts for strings, flutes, and a second trumpet, while omitting the serpent.

During his second visit to London (1794–5) he made an arrangement of the popular second movement of Symphony no. 100 ('Military') for a windband of one flute, two oboes, two clarinets, two horns, two bassoons, trumpet, serpent, and percussion. It may well have been commissioned by an individual who supported such a band and who admired the symphony. Unlike the movement in the symphony the idiomatic arrangement carries the self-evident title of 'March'.

Haydn wrote two marches for the Derbyshire Voluntary Cavalry, raised in 1794 by Sir Henry Harpur (Sheriff of Derbyshire) and others. Dies gave a protracted account of how the music was commissioned by an extremely reserved unnamed officer for a generous fee of 50 guineas, and played by Haydn on the piano a day before the officer left for America. This anonymous person is now known to have been Charles Francis Greville, brother of Sir Henry, though he is not known to have been a member of the regiment himself; the details of Dies's story are, as often, unreliable. The autograph of the first is signed, and dated London 1795. In order to avoid piracy both marches were privately published in an edition printed for Sir Henry Harpur by William Simpkins, Clement Inn, London; the publication also includes a piano arrangement, presumably by the composer. The march in E♭ was probably intended for mounted troops, the slower second one in C for dismounted troops.

5. Windband music written in Vienna (1796–1802). Haydn returned to Vienna in September 1795. One of his first tasks was to revise *The Seven Last Words* for choir and orchestra, subsequently given its first performance in the palace of Prince Schwarzenberg on the Mehlmarkt on 26 March 1796. A new movement, entitled *Introduzione* was added before the Fifth Word, 'I thirst', a magnificent Largo e cantabile in the cold and curiously rare key of A minor, scored for a windband of one flute, two oboes, two clarinets, two horns, two bassoons, contrabassoon, and two trombones.

There could be no more potent evidence of Haydn's total mastery over the medium than a comparison between the austerity of this *Introduzione* and the warmth and sensuality of the 'Aria des Schutzgeistes', composed only six months later as part of his incidental music to *Alfred*. Haydn accompanied a soprano soloist and a spoken part with a sextet of clarinets, horns, and bassoons.

Between 1790 and 1794 a full windband (*Harmonie*) was employed at the Esterházy court but Haydn is not known to have written anything for the ensemble. It was reconstituted in 1800 and it was for this ensemble that the composer was asked to write the Hungarian National March (Hob.VIII:4) in 1802. Haydn composed it in Vienna and forwarded it to Eisenstadt on 27 November. He had omitted some alternative passage-work in the first oboe part, and this formed the substance of a letter to the oboist Jacob Hyrtl the following day. Haydn's fee, for what proved to be his last completed instrumental composition, was a paltry one florin. Rather than an indication of musical style the 'Hungarian' element in the title is a reflection of the political standing of the Esterházy family as leaders of the Hungarian aristocracy; the march may well have been played at some local political ceremony in 1802.

Although Haydn's output of windband pieces is a small one his mastery of its sonorities is evident in the oratorios and many of the masses from this late period, nowhere more so than in the vocal trio 'On thee each living soul awaits/'Zu Dir, o Herr, blickt alles auf' from Part 2 of *The Creation*. RH

K. Haas, 'Haydn's English Military Marches', *The Score*, 2 (1950), 50–60.

R. Hellyer, 'The Wind Ensembles of the Esterházy Princes', *HYB* 15 (1985), 5–92.

***Windsor Castle* overture.** *See* COVENT GARDEN OVERTURE.

Wranitzky family. Two brothers, Paul and Anton, who studied with Haydn and became leading figures in Viennese musical life at the turn of the 18th century.

Paul Wranitzky (b. 30 Dec. 1756; d. 26 Sept. 1808) was an excellent violinist, who from 1790 was the chief orchestra director ('Director bei der Violine') of the Viennese court theatres, an accomplished composer whose stage works enjoyed considerable success in the city and elsewhere, and a conductor who enjoyed the confidence of both Haydn and Beethoven. At Haydn's insistence he directed the first performances of *The Creation* (1799 and 1800); he also directed the premiere of Beethoven's First Symphony on 2 April 1800.

After receiving his initial education at Nová Rise, Wranitzky studied at Jihlava (1770–1), and he later entered the theological seminary at Olmütz (Olomouc) where he served as choirmaster. He continued his musical studies in Vienna with Haydn, and possibly also with Joseph Martin Kraus, who spent several months in Vienna in 1783. Prior to his appointment to the directorship of the court theatre orchestras, Wranitzky served as music director to Count Johann Baptist Esterházy (1748–1800), a distant cousin of Haydn's employer who maintained a court orchestra at his palace in Pressburg (Bratislava) and at various country residences.

Wranitzky acquired a considerable reputation as a composer of symphonies and chamber works. His 51 symphonies were written between *c.*1786 and 1805, and exhibit many of the hallmarks of the mature Classical style. Although his reputation stood high at the imperial court, a public performance of his *Grande sinfonie caractéristique pour la paix avec la République françoise* (1797) was forbidden by imperial decree on the grounds that its title was politically provocative.

Like his elder brother, Anton Wranitzky (b. 13 June 1761; d. 6 Aug. 1820) was a friend of both Haydn and Beethoven. He was a fine violinist who numbered among his pupils Ignaz Schuppanzigh (1776–1830) and Joseph Mayseder (1789–1863). His most important works include 15 violin concertos, 15 symphonies, and a substantial corpus of chamber music.

Anton Wranitzky studied law and philosophy at Brno but moved to Vienna sometime before December 1783, when he is known to have been employed as choir master at the chapel of the Theresianisch-Savoyische Akademie, one of many positions that disappeared as a consequence of Joseph II's reforms. He studied composition with Mozart and Albrechtsberger, and by 1790 he had entered the service of PRINCE LOBKOWITZ as a composer and music teacher, later becoming Konzertmeister and, in 1797, Kapellmeister. When, in 1807, Prince Lobkowitz became a leading figure in the management of the principal theatres in Vienna, he moved swiftly to appoint Wranitzky orchestra director of the two court theatres, a position he held until his death. In 1814 he also became orchestra director at the Theater an der Wien. ADJB

HCRL/4 and 5.

M. Poštolka, 'Thematisches Verzeichnis der Sinfonien Paul Vranickýs', *Miscellanea musicologica*, 20 (1967), 101–28.

Y

York, Frederick Duke of (b. 16 Aug. 1763; d. 5 Jan. 1827). Second son of George III and a notable patron of music. In 1791 he married Princess Friedericke Charlotte Ulricke (1774–1820), the eldest daughter of the Prussian king, FRIEDRICH WILHELM II. In November of the same year Haydn was a guest at their country residence, Oatlands, near Weybridge in Surrey. No doubt Haydn relished the opportunity to converse in German and he gave a vivid account of his stay in the First London Notebook and in a letter to Maria Anna von Genzinger. In February 1795 Haydn was a guest at a concert in their palace on Piccadilly. The young duchess was the only member of the royal family to attend Haydn's benefit concert the following May. Five years later she is listed as one of several subscribers from the British royal family to the first edition of *The Creation*.

C. F. Pohl, *Haydn in London* (Vienna, 1867).

Z

Zannini, Anna (*fl.* 1779). Soprano who worked for only nine months at Eszterháza, from December 1778 to August 1779, during which time she undertook the role of Lisetta in Haydn's *La vera costanza.* The evidently more capable VALDESTURLA replaced her. Nothing is known about Zannini's career before and after her time at Eszterháza. ERL

HCRL/2.

Zimmermann, Anton (b. 25/6 Dec. 1741; d. 8–14 Oct. 1781). A rather elusive, but talented figure in the history of 18th-century Austrian music. The place and date of his birth are uncertain, and little or nothing is known of his early career. He must have achieved more than local prominence, however, since a bassoon concerto of his is listed in the BREITKOPF CATALOGUE as early as 1769 and his several sets of chamber works were published as far afield as Lyons and Paris by the middle of the 1770s. The *Pressburger Zeitung* names him as being active in Pressburg (Bratislava) by 1772, the year in which his *Singspiel Narcisse et Pierre* was performed there, and the following year he composed works for the St Cecilia festivities. In 1776 Zimmermann was appointed Kapellmeister and court composer to Prince Joseph Batthyány, Archbishop of Hungary (cardinal from 1778). Based in the capital of Pressburg, Zimmerman developed the orchestra into an outstanding ensemble of about 20 players. Among its members were the double bass virtuoso, Johannes Sperger (1750–1812), for whom Zimmermann presumably composed his concerto in D, and two clarinet players, unusual instruments in Austria before the 1780s. When the orchestra was disbanded in 1783 some of its members entered the service of Prince Nicolaus Esterházy. A fine symphony in C major by Zimmerman circulated under Haydn's name in the 18th century (Hob. I:C27); it was published in 1939 by SANDBERGER as one of a series of newly discovered symphonies by Haydn.

ADJB

M. Jurjevich, 'Anton Zimmermann's chamber music for strings' (diss., University of Illinois, Urbana, 1987).

A. Meier, 'Die Pressburger Hofkapelle des Fürstprimas von Ungarn, Fürst Josef von Batthyány', *HYB*, 10 (1978), 81–9.

Zinzendorf, Count Carl von (b. 5 Jan. 1739; d. 5 Jan. 1813). Austrian government official whose diaries are an invaluable source of factual information about musical life in Vienna. Born in Dresden, he studied law at the University of Jena before moving to Vienna in 1761 to take up a government position in commerce. He converted to Catholicism and in 1764 embarked on a period of international duty that took him to Switzerland, Italy, Malta, Germany, the Netherlands, France, Spain, Portugal, Britain, and Belgium. Between 1776 and 1781 he was governor of Trieste. From 1781 to his retirement in 1809 he worked in Vienna, becoming a Councillor of State under Franz II.

Zinzendorf began keeping a diary at the age of 8 and by his death there were 57 volumes, written in French. He was particularly fond of the theatre, including opera, and he usually notes the work and the presence of important guests. He was not musical and most of his comments are prompted by the text or reproduce the views of others. Waxing eloquent did not come easily to him and there are no extended remarks on Haydn or his music, even though he was clearly an admirer of the composer. Zinzendorf seems to have been on particularly friendly terms with Prince Paul Anton Esterházy and visited him in Eisenstadt in 1761. In May 1772 he visited Eszterháza where at a post-dinner concert Haydn played the violin. Unusually for a man in his position Zinzendorf had no family wealth and he was not, consequently, active as a financial patron of music. ERL

D. Link, *The National Court Theatre in Mozart's Vienna; Sources and Documents 1783–1792* (Oxford, 1998).

E. Olleson, 'Haydn in the Diaries of Count Karl von Zinzendorf', *HYB* 2 (1964), 45–63.

Zmeskall, Nikolaus Paul (b. 20 Nov. 1759; d. 23 June 1833). Secretary of the Hungarian Chancellery in Vienna from 1784 to 1825 and a notable patron of music, particularly private concerts of chamber music held in his apartment near the Kärntnerthortheater. He was a competent cellist and composed 14 quartets himself. Haydn seems to have first met Zmeskall in 1792. Eight years later, in May 1800, a new edition of the op. 20 quartets issued by Artaria was dedicated by the composer to Zmeskall. Zmeskall also subscribed to the printed edition of *The Creation*. He was a close and long-standing friend of Beethoven who showed his gratitude by dedicating the quartet in F minor, op. 95 to him.

Zwettl. A Cistercian abbey, located in the Waldviertel, Lower Austria, that has influenced the area culturally and spiritually since its founding by

Hadmar I in 1138. Music reached a zenith here during the decades corresponding to the first half of Haydn's career, when Zwettl was under the leadership of Abbot Rainer Kollmann (1747–76), Vicar General of the Austrian Cistercians and adviser to Empress Maria Theresia. Haydn's principal contact at the abbey was very likely Johann Nepomuk (Paul) Werner (1734–99), a son of GREGOR JOSEPH WERNER, Haydn's predecessor as Kapellmeister in Eisenstadt, who himself emanated from Ybbs near Zwettl. As a member of the convent since 1754, a gifted organist, and prefect of choirboys (music director) until 1766, Werner was probably responsible for arranging for Haydn to provide the music for a golden jubilee that Kollmann celebrated at the abbey in 1768, the so-called 'Applausus' cantata. This work was just one in a series composed anonymously and performed for the abbot at the rate of about one every three or four years up until 1775. Even before he received this commission, however, Haydn's output was most likely well represented in the abbey's music collection, just as it is today with over 40 extant compositions. RNF

HCRL/1.

APPENDIX 1

LIST OF HAYDN'S WORKS

Presentation and numbering

The list is based on the standard catalogue of Haydn's music, by Hoboken, divided into thirty-two groups according to genre. For each group Hoboken's methodology is explained. Doubtful and spurious works have been omitted but authentic works missing from Hoboken's catalogue are added to the appropriate group.

To the immediate right of each Hoboken number the numbers allocated by Georg Feder and presented in the Haydn worklist in various editions of *The New Grove Dictionary of Music* are given. For further information on the Hoboken and Feder catalogues see CATALOGUES §2, ii and iv.

Dates

Single dates without qualification indicate that the item was composed (or almost certainly composed) in that year. Where such precise information is not known two dates will normally be given, the first a proposed date of composition (e.g. *c.*1768), the second, in brackets, reflecting the earliest known reference, e.g. (1786).

Editions

For works that have already appeared in the standard collected edition of Haydn's music, the *Joseph Haydn Werke* (*JHW*), the appropriate volume number is given. Under 'Other edn(s)' the reader is referred to other modern editions of a particular work that are reliable, also to facsimile editions of music autographs and printed librettos; dates of publication are given. The following abbreviations for the names of publishers are used.

ADV	Akademische Druck- und Verlagsanstalt, Graz
Bä	Bärenreiter, Kassel
BH	Breitkopf & Härtel, Wiesbaden
Bö	Böhm und Sohn, Augsburg
Br	Broude Brothers, New York
C	Coppenrath, Altötting
CV	Carus Verlag, Stuttgart
D	Doblinger, Vienna and Munich
E	Eulenburg, London
EM	Editio Musica, Budapest
EMB	Éditions Mario Bois, Paris
F	Faber Music, London
H	Henle Verlag, Munich
HMP	Haydn-Mozart Presse, Salzburg
IMC	IMC Music Corporation, New York
MP	Music Press, New York
MV	Musikwissenschaftlicher Verlag, Leipzig (now Bärenreiter)
N	Novello (now Music Sales Group, Bury St Edmunds)
NM	Nagels Musik Archiv, Kassel
OUP	Oxford University Press, Oxford
S	Schirmer, New York
Sch	Schott, London
UCCP	University College Cardiff Press (now William Elkin Music Services, Norwich)
UE	Universal Edition, Vienna
VEB	Deutscher Verlag für Musik, Leipzig
VUAW	Verlag der Ungarischen Akademie der Wissenschaften
WUE	Wiener Urtext Edition, Vienna

Appendix 1

Abbreviations

The following abbreviations and contractions are used:

A	solo alto
B	solo bass
b	basso
bary	baryton
bn	bassoon
ca	cor anglais
chor	chorus
cl	clarinet
cont	continuo
db	double bass
dbn	double bassoon
facs	facsimile
fl	flute
hn	horn
hpd	harpsichord
kbd	keyboard
lib	libretto
lira	lira organizzata
ob	oboe
org	organ
perc	percussion
pic	piccolo
pf	pianoforte
S	solo soprano
serp	serpent
str	string orchestra
T	solo tenor
timp	timpani
tpt	trumpet
trbn	trombone
va	viola
vc	cello
vn	violin

Hoboken I: symphonies

The numerical order, 1–104, established by MANDYCZEWSKI is used, extended to 108 for further works (including the symphonie concertante).

Hob.I	*Title/nickname*	*NG*	*Key*	*Date*	*Scoring*	*JHW*	*Other edn(s)*
1		J1	D	?1757 (1759)	2 ob, 2 hn, str	I/1	UE 1964
2		J2	C	*c.*1760 (1764)	2 ob, 2 hn, str	I/1	UE 1964
3		J3	G	*c.*1761 (1762)	2 ob, 2 hn, str	I/2	UE 1964
4		J4	D	*c.*1760 (1762)	2 ob, 2 hn, str	I/1	UE 1964
5		J5	A	*c.*1760 (1762)	2 ob, 2 hn, str	I/1	UE 1964
6	Le Matin	J6	D	1761	fl, 2 ob, 2 hn, str	I/3	UE 1964
7	Le Midi	J7	C	1761	fl 2 fl/ob, bn, 2 hn, str	I/3	UE 1964 facs. EM 1972
8	Le Soir	J8	G	1761	fl, 2 ob, bn, 2 hn, str	I/3	UE 1964
9		J9	C	1762	2 fl/ob, bn, hn, str	I/3	UE 1964
10		J10	D	*c.*1760 (1766)	2 ob, 2 hn, str	I/1	UE 1964
11		J11	E♭	*c.*1760 (1766)	2 ob, 2 hn, str	I/1	UE 1964
12		J12	E	1763	2 ob, 2 hn, str	I/3	UE 1964
13		J13	D	1763	fl, 2 ob, 4 hn, (timp) str	I/3	UE 1964
14		J14	A	*c.*1762 (1764)	2 ob, 2 hn, str	I/2	UE 1964
15		J15	D	*c.*1760 (1764)	2 ob, 2 hn, str	I/2	UE 1964
16		J16	B♭	*c.*1763 (1766)	2 ob, 2 hn, str	I/2	UE 1964
17		J17	F	*c.*1762 (1765)	2 ob, 2 hn, str	I/1	UE 1964
18		J18	G	*c.*1760 (1766)	2 ob, 2 hn, str	I/1	UE 1964
19		J19	D	*c.*1762 (1766)	2 ob, 2 hn, str	I/1	UE 1964
20		J20	C	*c.*1760 (1766)	2 ob, 2 hn, 2 tpt, timp, str	I/1	UE 1964
21		J21	A	1764	2 ob, 2 hn, str	I/4	UE 1964
22	Philosopher	J22	E♭	1764	2 ca, 2 hn, str	I/4	UE 1964
23		J23	G	1764	2 ob, 2 hn, str	I/4	UE 1964
24		J24	D	1764	fl/2 ob, 2 hn, str	I/4	UE 1964
25		J25	C	*c.*1760 (1766)	2 ob, 2 hn, str	I/1	UE 1964
26	Lamentation	J26	d	*c.*1768 (1768)	2 ob, 2 hn, str	I/5	UE 1964
27		J27	G	*c.*1760 (1766)	2 ob, 2 hn, str	I/1	UE 1964
28		J28	A	1765	2 ob, 2 hn, str	I/4	UE 1965
29		J29	E	1765	2 ob, 2 hn, str	I/4	UE 1965

Hob.I	Title/nickname	NG	Key	Date	Scoring	JHW	Other edn(s)
30	Alleluja	J30	C	1765	fl, 2 ob, 2 hn, str	I/4	UE 1965
31	Hornsignal	J31	D	1765	fl, 2 ob, 4 hn, str	I/4	UE 1965
32		J32	C	*c.*1760 (1766)	2 ob, 2 hn, 2 tpt, timp, str	I/1	UE 1965
33		J33	C	*c.*1760 (1767)	2 ob, 2 hn, 2 tpt, timp, str	I/2	UE 1965
34		J34	d	*c.*1765 (1767)	2 ob, 2 hn, str	I/2	UE 1965
35		J35	B♭	1767	2 ob, 2 hn, str	I/6	UE 1965
36		J36	E♭	*c.*1763 (1769)	2 ob, 2 hn, str	I/2	UE 1965
37		J37	C	*c.*1758	2 ob, 2 hn (or 2 tpt, timp), str	I/1	UE 1965
38		J38	C	*c.*1767 (1769)	2 ob, 2 hn, (2 tpt, timp), str	I/5	UE 1965
39		J39	g	1765 (1770)	2 ob, 4 hn, str	I/2	UE 1965
40		J40	F	1763	2 ob, 2 hn, str	I/3	UE 1965
41		J41	C	*c.*1768 (1770)	fl, 2 ob, 2 hn (2 tpt, timp), str	I/5	UE 1967
42		J42	D	1771	2 ob, 2 bn, 2 hn, str	I/6	UE 1967
43	Mercury	J43	E♭	*c.*1771 (1772)	2 ob, 2 hn, str	I/5	UE 1967
44	Trauer	J44	e	*c.*1771 (1772)	2 ob, 2 hn, str	I/5	UE 1967
45	Farewell	J45	f♯	1772	2 ob, 2 hn, str	I/6	UE 1967 facs VUAW 1959
46		J46	B	1772	2 ob, 2 hn, str	I/6	UE 1967
47		J47	G	1772	2 ob, 2 hn, str	I/6	UE 1967
48	Maria Theresia	J48	C	*c.*1768 (1769)	2 ob, 2 hn (or 2 tpt, timp), str	I/5	UE 1967
49	La passione	J49	f	1768	2 ob, 2 hn, str	I/6	UE 1967
50		J50	C	1773	2 ob, 2 hn, 2 tpt, timp, str	I/7	UE 1963
51		J51	B♭	*c.*1772 (1774)	2 ob, 2 hn, str	I/5	UE 1963
52		J52	c	*c.*1772 (1774)	2 ob, bn, 2 hn, str	I/5	UE 1963
53	Imperial	J53	D	*c.*1778	fl, 2 ob, bn, 2 hn, timp, str	I/9	UE 1963
54		J54	G	1774	2 fl, 2 ob, 2 bn, 2 hn, 2 trpt, timp, str	I/7	UE 1963
55	Schoolmaster	J55	E♭	1774	2 ob, bn, 2 hn, str	I/7	UE 1963
56		J56	C	1774	2 ob, bn, 2 hn, 2 tpt, timp, str	I/7	UE 1963
57		J57	D	1774	2 ob, 2 hn, str	I/7	UE 1963
58		J58	F	*c.*1767 (1774)	2 ob, 2 hn, str	I/5	UE 1967
59	Fire	J59	A	*c.*1767 (1769)	2 ob, 2 hn, str	I/5	UE 1967
60	Il distratto	J60	C	1774	2 ob, 2 hn, (2 tpt), timp, str	I/5	UE 1967
61		J61	D	1776	fl, 2 ob, 2 bn, 2 hn, timp, str	I/8	UE 1967

Hob.I	Title/nickname	NG	Key	Date	Scoring	JHW	Other edn(s)
62		J62	D	*c.*1780 (1781)	fl, 2 ob, 2 bn, 2 hn, str	I/10	UE 1967
63	La Roxelane	J63	C	*c.*1778 (1781)	fl, 2 ob, bn, 2 hn, str	I/9	UE 1967
64	Tempora mutantur	J64	A	*c.*1773 (1778)	2 ob, 2 hn, str	I/5	UE 1967
65		J65	A	*c.*1772 (1778)	2 ob, 2 hn, str	I/5	UE 1967
66		J66	B♭	*c.*1776 (1779)	2 ob, 2 bn, 2 hn, str	I/8	UE 1967
67		J67	F	*c.*1776 (1779)	2 ob, 2 bn, 2 hn, str	I/8	UE 1967
68		J68	B♭	*c.*1775 (1779)	2 ob, 2 bn, 2 hn, str	I/8	UE 1967
69	Laudon	J69	C	*c.*1776 (1779)	2 ob, 2 bn, 2 tpt, timp, str	I/8	UE 1967
70		J70	D	1779	fl, 2 ob, bn, 2 hn, 2 tpt, timp, str	I/9	UE 1967
71		J71	B♭	*c.*1779 (1780)	fl, 2 ob, bn, 2 hn, str	I/9	UE 1967
72		J72	D	*c.*1764 (1781)	fl, 2 ob, bn, 4 hn, (timp), str	I/2	UE 1967
73	La Chasse	J73	D	1781 (1782)	fl, 2 ob, 2 bn, 2 hn, (2 tpt, timp), str	I/10	UE 1967
74		J74	E♭	*c.*1780 (1781)	fl, 2 ob, bn, 2 hn, str	I/10	UE 1966
75		J75	E♭	*c.*1780 (1781)	fl, 2 ob, bn, 2 hn, (2 tpt, timp), str	I/9	UE 1966
76		J76	E♭	1782 (1783)	fl, 2 ob, 2 bn, 2 hn, str	I/11	UE 1966
77		J77	B♭	1782 (1783)	fl, 2 ob, 2 bn, 2 hn, str	I/11	UE 1966
78		J78	c	1782 (1783)	fl, 2 ob, 2 bn, 2 hn, str	I/11	UE 1966
79		J79	F	(1784)	fl, 2 ob, 2 bn, 2 hn, str	I/11	UE 1966
80		J80	d	(1784)	fl, 2 ob, 2 bn, 2 hn, str	I/11	UE 1966
81		J81	G	(1784)	fl, 2 ob, 2 bn, 2 hn, str	I/11	UE 1966
82	L'Ours	J82	C	1786	fl, 2 ob, 2 bn, 2 hn (or 2 tpt), timp, str	I/13	UE 1963
83	La Poule	J83	g	1785	fl, 2 ob, 2 bn, 2 hn, str	I/12	UE 1963
84		J84	E♭	1786	fl, 2 ob, 2 bn, 2 hn, str	I/13	UE 1963
85	La Reine	J85	B♭	1785	fl, 2 ob, 2 bn, 2 hn, str	I/12	UE 1963
86		J86	D	1786	fl, 2 ob, 2 bn, 2 hn, 2 tpt, timp, str	I/13	UE 1963
87		J87	A	1785	fl, 2 ob, 2 bn, 2 hn, str	I/12	UE 1963
88		J88	G	1787	fl, 2 ob, 2 bn, 2 hn, 2 tpt, timp, str	I/14	UE 1965
89		J89	F	1787	fl, 2 ob, 2 bn, 2 hn, str	I/14	UE 1965
90		J90	C	1788	fl, 2 ob, 2 bn, 2 hn, (2 tpt, timp), str	I/14	UE 1965
91		J91	E♭	1788	fl, 2 ob, 2 bn, 2 hn, str	I/14	UE 1965
92	Oxford	J92	G	1789	fl, 2 ob, 2 bn, 2 hn, (2 tpt, timp), str	I/14	UE 1965
93		J93	D	1791	2 fl, 2 ob, 2 bn, 2 hn, 2 tpt, timp, str	I/15	UE 1966

Hob.I	Title/nickname	NG	Key	Date	Scoring	JHW	Other edn(s)
94	Surprise	J94	G	1791	2 fl, 2 ob, 2 bn, 2 hn, 2 tpt, timp, str	I/16	UE 1966
95		J95	c	1791	fl, 2 ob, 2 bn, 2 hn, 2 tpt, timp, str	I/15	UE 1966
96	Miracle	J96	D	1791	2 fl, 2 ob, 2 bn, 2 hn, 2 tpt, timp, str	I/15	UE 1966
97		J97	C	1792	2 fl, 2 ob, 2 bn, 2 hn, 2 tpt, timp, str	I/16	UE 1966
98		J98	B♭	1792	2 fl, 2 ob, 2 bn, 2 hn, 2 tpt, timp, hpd, str	I/16	UE 1966
99		J99	E♭	1793	2 fl, 2 ob, 2 cl, 2 bn, 2 hn, 2 tpt, timp, str	I/17	UE 1968
100	Military	J100	G	1793-4	2 fl, 2 ob, 2 cl, 2 bn, 2 hn, 2 tpt, timp, perc, str	I/17	UE 1968
101	Clock	J101	D	1793-4	2 fl, 2 ob, 2 cl, 2 bn, 2 hn, 2 tpt, timp, str	I/17	UE 1968
102		J102	B♭	1794	2 fl, 2 ob, 2 bn, 2 hn, 2 tpt, timp, str	I/18	UE 1968
103	Drumroll	J103	E♭	1795	2 fl, 2 ob, 2 cl, 2 bn, 2 hn, 2 tpt, timp, str	I/18	UE 1968
104	London	J104	D	1795	2 fl, 2 ob, 2 cl, 2 hn, 2 tpt, timp, str	I/18	UE 1968 facs VEB1983
105	[Symphonie] concertante	J105	B♭	1792	solo vn, vc, ob, bn, fl, 2 ob, 2 bn, 2 hn, 2 tpt, timp, str	II	UE 1965
106		J106	D	?1769	2 ob, 2 hn, str	XXV/4	
107		J107	B♭	*c.*1759 (1762)	2 ob, 2 bn, str	I/1	UE 1965, as Symphony 'A'
108		J108	B♭	*c.*1761 (1765)	2 ob, bn, 2 hn, str	I/2	UE 1965, as Symphony 'B'

Hoboken Ia: overtures

This section includes overtures by Haydn, many of which were published separately for concert use and two of which cannot be associated with absolute certainty with dramatic works.

Hob.Ia	*NG*	*Key*	*Scoring*	*Origin*	*JHW*	*Other edn(s)*
1	K8	C	2 ob, 2 hn, timp, str	L' infedeltà delusa	XXV/5	
2	K9	C	2 ob, 2 bn, 2 hn, 2 tpt, timp, str	Il ritorno di Tobia	XXVIII/1	
3	—	C	fl, 2 ob, 2 hn, 2 tpt, timp, str	L'anima del filosofo	XXV/13	HMP 1952
4	K10	D	fl, 2 ob, 2 bn, 2 hn, str	not identified	I/10	D 1959
5	—	D	2 ob, 2 hn, str	Acide	XXV/1	D 1959
6	K5	D	2 ob, 2 hn, str	L'incontro improvviso	XXV/6	D 1964
7	K3	D	2 ob, 2 bn, 2 hn, str	not identified	I/9	D 1959
8	—	d	2 ob, 2 hn, str	Philemon und Baucis	XXIV/1	
10	K6	G	fl, 2 ob, 2 hn, str	Lo speziale	XXV/3	D 1959
13	K4	g	fl, 2 ob, bn, 2 hn, str	L'isola disabitata	XXV/9	E 1959
14	—	B♭	fl, 2 ob, 2 bn, 2 hn, str	Armida	XXV/12	
15	K7	B♭	2 ob, bn, 2 hn, str	La vera costanza	XXV/8	
16	—	B♭	2 ob, bn, 2 hn, str	Orlando paladino	XXV/11	D 1960
17	—	D	fl, 2 ob, bn, 2 hn (or tpt), timp, str	La fedeltà premiata	XXV/10	D 1963

Hoboken II: divertimenti for four or more instruments

This is one of the least coherent groupings in Hoboken. It includes the works listed as divertimenti in the HAYDN VERZEICHNIS to which are added the notturni for *lire organizzate* and ensemble (II:25–32), the six scherzandos (II:33–8), and various other works. The early string quartet in E♭, op. '0', is also included here, as II:6.

Hob.II	*NG*	*Key*	*Scoring*	*Date*	*JHW*	*Other edn(s)*
1	N13	G	fl, ob, 2 vn, vc, db	*c.*1760 (1764)	VIII/1	D 1984
2	N6	G	2 vn, 2 va, b	*c.*1753 (1763)	VIII/1	D 1988
3	N24	G	2 ob, 2 hn, 2 bn	(1766)	VIII/2	D 1960
6	O5	E♭	2 vn, va, vc	*c.*1758 (1764)	XXII/1	D 1979
7	N23	C	2 ob, 2 hn, 2 bn	*c.*1760 (1765)	VIII/2	D 1959
8	N9	D	2 fl, 2 hn, 2 vn, b	(1767)	VIII/1	
9	N1	G	2 ob, 2 hn, 2 vn, 2 va, b	(1764)	VIII/1	
11	N11	C	fl, ob, 2 vn, vc, db	(1765)	VIII/1	D 1961
14	N30	C	2 cl, 2 hn	1761	VIII/2	D 1959
15	N21	F	2 ob, 2 hn, 2 bn	1760	VIII/2	D 1959 facs *HYB* 1
16	N27	F	2 ca, 2 hn, 2 vn, 2 bn	1760	VIII/2	
17	N3	C	2 cl, 2 hn, 2 vn, 2 va, b	(1765)	VIII/1	D 1960
20	N2	F	2 ob, 2 hn, bn, 2 vn, 2 va, b	*c.*1757 (1763)	VIII/1	D 1962
21	N11	E♭	2 hn, 2 vn, va, b	*c.*1761 (1763)	VIII/1	
22	N12	D	2 hn, 2 vn, va, b	*c.*1760 (1764)	VIII/1	
23	N22	F	2 ob, 2 hn, 2 bn	*c.*1760 (1765)	VIII/2	D 1959
24	N5	E♭	fl, 2 ca, bn, 2 hn, solo vn, 2 vn, vc, db	?1761	VIII/1	
25	T6	C	2 lire, 2 cl, 2 hn, 2 va, b	(1790)	VII	D 1961
26	T7	F	2 lire, 2 cl, 2 hn, 2 va, b	(1790)	VII	D 1979
27	T13	G	2 lire, 2 cl, 2 hn, 2 va, b	(1790)	VII	D 1980
28	T12	F	fl, ob, 2 hn, 2 vn, 2 va, vc, db	(1792)	VII	D 1980
29	T10	C	fl, ob, 2 hn, 2 vn, 2 va, vc, db	(1792)	VII	D 1979
30	T11	G	2 lire, 2 cl, 2 hn, 2 va, b	(1790)	VII	D 1980
31	T9	C	2 lire, 2 cl, 2 hn, 2 va, b	(1790)	VII	D 1979
32	T8	C	2 lire, 2 cl, 2 hn, 2 va, b	(1790)	VII	D 1979
33	N15	F	fl, 2 ob, 2 hn, 2 vn, b	*c.*1763 (1765)	VIII/2	D 1961
34	N16	C	fl, 2 ob, 2 hn, 2 vn, b	*c.*1763 (1765)	VIII/2	D 1961

Hob.II	*NG*	*Key*	*Scoring*	*Date*	*JHW*	*Other edn(s)*
35	N17	D	fl, 2 ob, 2 hn, 2 vn, b	*c.*1763 (1765)	VIII/2	D 1961
36	N18	G	fl, 2 ob, 2 hn, 2 vn, b	*c.*1763 (1765)	VIII/2	D 1961
37	N19	E	fl, 2 ob, 2 hn, 2 vn, b	*c.*1763 (1765)	VIII/2	D 1961
38	N20	A	fl, 2 ob, 2 hn, 2 vn, b	*c.*1763 (1765)	VIII/2	D 1961
D22	N10	D	4 hn, vn, va, b	*c.*1763		D 1960

Hoboken III: quartets (2 violins, viola, and cello)

Hoboken used the familiar sequence of opus numbers for this section, though the internal order of some sets is not that commonly encountered. Nine works from Hoboken's list are omitted here: op. 1 no. 5 (III:5) which is a symphony (see I:107) and op. 2 nos. 3 and 5 which are sextets (see II:21 and 22). Hoboken also included the six spurious quartets of op. 3 (III:13–18) now thought to have been composed by HOFSTETTER.

Hob.III	*NG*	*Op. no./title*	*Key*	*Nickname*	*Date*	*JHW*	*Other edn(s)*
1	O1	op. 1 no. 1	B♭	La Chasse	*c.*1758 (1762)	XII/1	D 1979
2	O2	op. 1 no. 2	E♭		*c.*1758 (1762)	XII/1	D 1979
3	O2	op. 1 no. 3	D		*c.*1758 (1762)	XII/1	D 1979
4	O4	op. 1 no. 4	G		*c.*1758 (1762)	XII/1	D 1979
6	O6	op. 1 no. 6	C		*c.*1758 (1762)	XII/1	D 1979
7	O7	op. 2 no. 1	A		*c.*1761 (1763)	XII/1	D 1977
8	O8	op. 2 no. 2	E		*c.*1761 (1765)	XII/1	D 1977
10	O9	op. 2 no. 4	F		*c.*1761 (1762)	XII/1	D 1977
12	O10	op. 2 no. 6	B♭		*c.*1761 (1762)	XII/1	D 1977
19	O12	op. 9 no. 1	C		*c.*1770 (1771)	XII/2	D 1977
20	O14	op. 9 no. 2	E♭		*c.*1770 (1771)	XII/2	D 1977
21	O13	op. 9 no. 3	G		*c.*1770 (1771)	XII/2	D 1977
22	O11	op. 9 no. 4	d		*c.*1770 (1771)	XII/2	D 1977
23	O15	op. 9 no. 5	B♭		*c.*1770 (1771)	XII/2	D 1977
24	O16	op. 9 no. 6	A		*c.*1770 (1771)	XII/2	D 1977
25	O18	op. 17 no. 1	E		1771	XII/2	D 1988
26	O17	op. 17 no. 2	F		1771	XII/2	D 1988
27	O21	op. 17 no. 3	E♭		1771	XII/2	D 1988
28	O19	op. 17 no. 4	c		1771	XII/2	D 1988
29	O22	op. 17 no. 5	G		1771	XII/2	D 1988
30	O20	op. 17 no. 6	D		1771	XII/2	D 1988
31	O28	op. 20 no. 1	E♭		1772	XII/3	D 1981
32	O25	op. 20 no. 2	C		1772	XII/3	D 1981
33	O26	op. 20 no. 3	g		1772	XII/3	D 1981
34	O27	op. 20 no. 4	D		1772	XII/3	D 1981

Hob.III	NG	Op. no./title	Key	Nickname	Date	JHW	Other edn(s)
35	O23	op. 20 no. 5	f		1772	XII/3	D 1981
36	O24	op. 20 no. 6	A		1772	XII/3	D 1982
37	O31	op. 33 no. 1	b		1781	XII/3	D 1988
38	O30	op. 33 no. 2	E♭	Joke	1781	XII/3	D 1988
39	O32	op. 33 no. 3	C	Bird	1781	XII/3	D 1988
40	O34	op. 33 no. 4	B♭		1781	XII/3	D 1988
41	O29	op. 33 no. 5	G		1781	XII/3	D 1988
42	O33	op. 33 no. 6	D		1781	XII/3	D 1988
43	O35	op. 42	d		1785	XII/4	D 1988
44	O36	op. 50 no. 1	B♭		1787	XII/4	D 1985
45	O37	op. 50 no. 2	C		1787	XII/4	D 1985
46	O38	op. 50 no. 3	E♭		1787	XII/4	D 1985
47	O39	op. 50 no. 4	f♯		1787	XII/4	D 1985
48	O40	op. 50 no. 5	F		1787	XII/4	D 1985
49	O41	op. 50 no. 6	D	Frog	1787	XII/4	D 1985
50–6	Oapp1:1	Seven Last Words			1787		E 1956
57	O42	op. 54 no. 2	C		1788	XII/4	D 1986
58	O43	op. 54 no. 1	G		1788	XII/4	D 1986
58	O44	op. 54 no. 3	E		1788	XII/4	D 1986
60	O45	op. 55 no. 1	A		1788	XII/4	D 1987
61	O46	op. 55 no. 2	f	Razor	1788	XII/4	D 1987
62	O47	op. 55 no. 3	B♭		1788	XII/4	D 1987
63	O53	op. 64 no. 5	D	Lark	1790	XII/5	D 1986
64	O52	op. 64 no. 6	E♭		1790	XII/5	D 1986
65	O48	op. 64 no. 1	C		1790	XII/5	D 1986
66	O51	op. 64 no. 4	G		1790	XII/5	D 1986
67	O50	op. 64 no. 3	B♭		1790	XII/5	D 1986

Hob.III	*NG*	*Op. no./title*	*Key*	*Nickname*	*Date*	*JHW*	*Other edn(s)*
68	O49	op. 64 no. 2	b		1790	XII/5	D 1986
69	O54	op. 71 no. 1	B♭		1793	XII/5	D 1978
70	O55	op. 71 no. 2	D		1793	XII/5	D 1978
71	O56	op. 71 no. 3	E♭		1793	XII/5	D 1978
72	O57	op. 74 no. 1	C		1793	XII/5	D 1978
73	O58	op. 74 no. 2	F		1793	XII/5	D 1978
74	O59	op. 74 no. 3	g	Rider	1793	XII/5	D 1978
75	O60	op. 76 no. 1	G		1797	XII/6	D 1982
76	O61	op. 76 no. 2	d	Fifths	1797	XII/6	D 1982
77	O62	op. 76 no. 3	C	Emperor	1797	XII/6	D 1982
78	O63	op. 76 no. 4	B♭	Sunrise	1797	XII/6	D 1987
79	O64	op. 76 no. 5	D		1797	XII/6	D 1984
80	O65	op. 76 no. 6	E♭		1797	XII/6	D 1982
81	O66	op. 77 no. 1	G		1799	XII/6	D 1984 facs EM 1972
82	O67	op. 77 no. 2	F		1799	XII/6	D 1982 facs EM 1972
83	O68	op. 103	d		1803	XII/6	D 1982

Hoboken IV: trios (other than keyboard or string trios)

Works are grouped according to scoring and are not in chronological order.

Hob.IV	*NG*	*Key*	*Scoring*	*Date*	*JHW*	*Other edn(s)*
1	S14	C	2 fl, vc	1794	IX	P 1959
2	S15	G	2 fl, vc	1794	IX	P 1959
3	S16	G	2 fl, vc	1794	IX	P 1959
4	S17	G	2 fl, vc	1794	IX	NM 1954
5	S7	E♭	hn, vn, vc	1767	IX	D 1957
6	S8	D	vn or fl, vn, vc	1784	IX	D 1989
7	S9	G	vn or fl, vn, vc	1784	IX	D 1989
8	S10	C	vn or fl, vn, vc	1784	IX	D 1989
9	S11	G	vn or fl, vn, vc	1784	IX	D 1989
10	S12	A	vn or fl, vn, vc	1784	IX	D 1989
11	S13	D	vn or fl, vn, vc	1784	IX	D 1989

Hoboken V: string trios (except baryton trios)

The first twenty-one works are taken from the entries in Haydn's *Entwurf-Katalog*. Hoboken consigned other string trios to the doubtful category; many of the latter are now considered to be authentic and are given below.
The numbers given in the Doblinger edition by Robbins Landon have not attained common currency.
All the works are scored for two violins and bass, except V:8 which is scored for violin, viola, and bass.

Hob.V	*NG*	*Key*	*Date*	*JHW*	*Other edn(s)*
1	P1	E	*c.*1757 (1767)	XI/1	D 1982, as no. 1
2	P2	F	*c.*1757 (1767)	XI/1	D 1982, as no. 2
3	P3	b	*c.*1757 (1767)	XI/1	D 1985, as no. 3
4	P4	E♭	*c.*1757 (1767)	XI/1	D 1981, as no. 4
6	P6	E♭	*c.*1757 (1764)	XI/1	D 1985, as no. 6
7	P7	A	*c.*1757 (1765)	XI/1	D 1982, as no. 7
8	P8	B♭	*c.*1757 (1765)	XI/1	D 1982, as no. 8
10	P10	F	*c.*1757 (1767)	XI/1	D 1982, as no. 10
11	P11	E♭	*c.*1757 (1763)	XI/1	D 1981, as no. 23
12	P12	E	*c.*1757 (1767)	XI/1	D 1981, as no. 11
13	P13	B♭	*c.*1757 (1765)	XI/1	D 1984, as no. 12
15	P15	D	*c.*1757 (1762)	XI/1	D 1981, as no. 14
16	P16	C	*c.*1763 (1765)	XI/1	D 1981, as no. 15
17	P17	E♭	*c.*1763 (1766)	XI/1	D 1982, as no. 16
18	P18	B♭	*c.*1763 (1765)	XI/1	D 1984, as no. 17
19	P19	E	*c.*1763 (1765)	XI/1	D 1982, as no. 18
20	P20	G	*c.*1763 (1766)	XI/1	D 1982, as no. 19
21	P21	D	*c.*1765 (1768)	XI/1	D 1982, as no. 22
D3	Papp1	D	*c.*1760	XI/2	D 1981, as no. 20
F1	Papp2	F	*c.*1760	XI/2	D 1981, as no. 28
G1	Papp3	G	*c.*1760	XI/2	D 1981, as no. 21
A2	Papp4	G	*c.*1760	XI/2	D 1985, as no. 34
A3	Papp5	A	*c.*1760		
D1	Papp6	D	*c.*1760	XI/2	D 1981, as no. 24
B1	Papp7	B♭	*c.*1760	XI/2	D 1981, as no. 27
G3	Papp8	G	*c.*1760		D 1985, as no. 33
G4	Papp9	G	*c.*1760		D 1984, as no. 26
C3	Papp10	C	*c.*1760		D 1985, as no. 25

Hoboken VI: duets for violin and viola

Hob.VI	*NG*	*Key*	*Date*	*JHW*	*Other edn(s)*
1	S1	F	c.1770 (1773)	X	D 1957
2	S2	A	*c.*1770 (1773)	X	D 1957
3	S3	B♭	*c.*1770 (1773)	X	D 1957
4	S4	D	*c.*1770 (1773)	X	D 1963
5	S5	E♭	*c.*1770 (1773)	X	D 1963
6	S6	C	*c.*1770 (1773)	X	D 1963

Hoboken VII: concertos for various instruments (excluding keyboard and baryton)

Eight subdivisions are given, a–h, according to the solo instrument(s); the concertos for two *lire organizzate* and ensemble are included in this group. The lost and spurious concertos listed by Hoboken are omitted here.

Hob.VIIa	*NG*	*Key*	*Date*	*Scoring*	*JHW*	*Other edn(s)*
1	M1	C	*c.*1763 (1769)	solo vn, str	III/1	E 1953
3	M3	A	*c.*1763 (1771)	solo vn, str	III/1	HMP 1952
4	M4	G	*c.*1761 (1769)	solo vn, str	III/1	E *c.*1960

Hob.VIIb	*NG*	*Key*	*Date*	*Scoring*	*JHW*	*Other edn(s)*
1	M5	C	*c.*1763 (1765)	solo vc, 2 ob, 2 hn, str	III/2	IMC 1967
2	M6	D	1783	solo vc, 2 ob, 2 hn, str	III/2	UCCP 1984

Hob.VIId	*NG*	*Key*	*Date*	*Scoring*	*JHW*	*Other edn(s)*
3	M15	D	1762	solo hn, 2 ob, str	III/3	E *c.*1960

Hob.VIIe	*NG*	*Key*	*Date*	*Scoring*	*JHW*	*Other edn(s)*
1	M17	E♭	1796	solo tpt, 2 fl, 2 ob, 2 bn, 2 hn, 2 tpt, timp, str	III/3	UE 1982

Hob.VIIh	*NG*	*Key*	*Date*	*Scoring*	*JHW*	*Other edn(s)*
1	T1	C	1786	2 lire, 2 hn, 2 vn, 2 va, vc	VI	D 1959/60
2	T3	G	1786	2 lire, 2 hn, 2 vn, 2 va, vc	VI	D 1959/60
3	T5	G	1787	2 lire, 2 hn, 2 vn, 2 va, vc	VI	D 1959/60
4	T2	F	1786	2 lire, 2 hn, 2 vn, 2 va, vc	VI	D 1959/60
5	T4	F	1787	2 lire, 2 hn, 2 vn, 2 va, vc	VI	D 1959/60

Hoboken VIII: marches

The order in this group is a random one.

Hob.VIII	*NG*	*Key*	*Title/nickname*	*Date*	*Scoring*	*JHW*	*Other edn(s)*
1	L22	E♭	'Derbyshire'	1795	2 cl, 2 bn, 2 hn, tpt, serp	V	D 1960
2	L22	C	'Derbyshire'	1795	2 cl, 2 bn, 2 hn, tpt, serp	V	D 1960
3	L17a	E♭	'Prince of Wales'	1792	2 cl, 2 bn, 2 hn, tpt, serp	V	D 1960
3a	L17b	E♭	Grand March … Royal Society of Musicians	1792–5	2 fl, 2 cl, 2 bn, 2 hn, 2 tpt, str	V	D 1961
4	L23	E♭	Hungarian National March	1802	2 ob, 2 cl, 2 bn, 2 hn, tpt	V	D 1960
6	L15	E♭		*c.*1785 (1793)	2 cl, 2 bn, 2 hn, tpt, serp	V	D 1960
7	L16	E♭		?	2 cl, 2 bn, 2 hn, tpt, serp	V	D 1960
deest	L4	G	Marche Regimento de Marschall	(1772)	2 ob, 2 hn, 2 bn	V	D 1960
deest	K12	C	March (from I:100/ii)	1794–5	fl, 2 ob, 2 cl, 2 bn, 2 hn, tpt, serp, perc	I/17	

Hoboken IX: dances

Hob.IX	*NG*	*Title/Nickname*	*Date*	*Scoring*	*JHW*	*Other edn(s)*
1	L1	12 'Seitenstetten' minuets	*c.*1757	2 ob, 2 hn, str	V	D 1988
5	L6a	6 minuets	1776	fl, 2 ob, bn, 2 hn, str	V	
7	L9	14 menuetti ballabile	(1784)	fl, 2 ob, 2 bn, 2 hn, timp, str	V	D 1970
9	L11	6 allemandes	1785	fl, 2 ob, bn, 2 hn, 2 tpt, timp, str	V	D 1970
11	L18	12 minuets	1792	pic, 2 fl, 2 ob, 2 cl, 2 hn, 2 tpt, timp, str	V	
12	L19	12 deutsche Tänze	1792	2 fl, 2 ob, 2 cl, 2 bn, 2 hn, 2 tpt, timp, str	V	
16	L14	24 minuets	*c.*1798	pic, 2 fl, 2 ob, 2 cl, 2 bn, 2 tpt, timp, perc, str	V	D 1974
23	L5	Minuet and trio	*c.*1773	2 fl, 2 hn, str	V	

Hoboken X: works for various instruments and baryton

Hoboken included a number of lost works in this section, here omitted.

Hob.X	*NG*	*Key*	*Scoring*	*Date*	*JHW*	*Other edn(s)*
1	R31	D	bary, 2 hn, 2 vn, vc, b	1775	XIII	
2	R27	D	bary, 2 hn, 2 vn, vc, b	1775	XIII	
3	R29	a	bary, 2 hn, 2 vn, vc, b	1775	XIII	
4	R30	G	bary, 2 hn, 2 vn, vc, b	1775	XIII	
5	R28	G	bary, 2 hn, 2 vn, vc, b	1775	XIII	
6	R32	A	bary, 2 hn, 2 vn, vc, b	1775	XIII	
10	R26	D	bary, 2 hn, va, b	*c.*1768	XIII	
11	R17	D	2 bary	*c.*1766	XIII	
12	R33	G	bary, 2 hn, 2 vn, vc, b	1775	XIII	

Hoboken XI: baryton trios

All are scored for baryton, viola, and cello except XI:89–91 which substitute a violin for the viola. The broadly chronological order is taken from the *Haydn-Verzeichnis*. Though preserved as single works the order and content reflect that of five bound volumes presented to Prince Nicolaus Esterházy, indicated below in the third column.

Hob.XI	*NG*	*Book*	*Key*	*Date*	*JHW*	*Other edn(s)*
1	Q1	1	A	1765–6	XIV/1	
2	Q2	1	A	1765–6	XIV/1	
3	Q3	1	A	1765–6	XIV/1	
4	Q4	1	A	1765–6	XIV/1	
5	Q5	1	A	1765–6	XIV/1	
6	Q6	1	A	1765–6	XIV/1	
7	Q7	1	A	1765–6	XIV/1	
8	Q8	1	A	1765–6	XIV/1	
9	Q9	1	A	1765–6	XIV/1	
10	Q10	1	A	1765–6	XIV/1	
11	Q11	1	D	1765–6	XIV/1	
12	Q12	1	A	1765–6	XIV/1	
13	Q13	1	A	1765–6	XIV/1	
14	Q14	1	D	1765–6	XIV/1	
15	Q15	1	A	1765–6	XIV/1	
16	Q16	1	A	1765–6	XIV/1	
17	Q18	1	D	1765–6	XIV/1	
19	Q19	1	A	1765–6	XIV/1	
20	Q20	1	D	1765–6	XIV/1	
21	Q21	1	A	1765–6	XIV/1	
22	Q22	1	A	1765–6	XIV/1	
24	Q24	1	D	1766	XIV/1	
25	Q25	2	A	1765–7	XIV/2	
26	Q26	2	G	1765–7	XIV/2	
27	Q27	2	D	1765–7	XIV/2	
28	Q28	2	D	1765–7	XIV/2	
29	Q29	2	A	1765–7	XIV/2	
30	Q30	2	G	1765–7	XIV/2	

Hob.XI	*NG*	*Book*	*Key*	*Date*	*JHW*	*Other edn(s)*
31	Q31	2	D	1765–7	XIV/2	
32	Q32	2	G	1765–7	XIV/2	
33	Q33	2	A	1765–7	XIV/2	
34	Q34	2	D	1765–7	XIV/2	
35	Q35	2	A	1765–7	XIV/2	
36	Q36	2	D	1765–7	XIV/2	
37	Q37	2	G	1765–7	XIV/2	
38	Q38	2	A	1765–7	XIV/2	
39	Q39	2	D	1765–7	XIV/2	
40	Q40	2	D	1765–7	XIV/2	
41	Q41	2	D	1765–7	XIV/2	
42	Q42	2	D	1767	XIV/2	
43	Q43	2	D	1765–7	XIV/2	
44	Q44	2	D	1765–7	XIV/2	
45	Q45	2	D	1765–7	XIV/2	
46	Q46	2	A	1765–7	XIV/2	
47	Q47	2	G	1765–7	XIV/2	
48	Q48	2	D	1765–7	XIV/2	
49	Q49	3	G	*c.*1767–8	XIV/3	
50	Q50	3	D	*c.*1767–8	XIV/3	
51	Q51	3	A	*c.*1767–8	XIV/3	
52	Q52	3	D	*c.*1767–8	XIV/3	
53	Q53	3	G	1767	XIV/3	
54	Q54	3	D	*c.*1767–8	XIV/3	
55	Q55	3	G	*c.*1767–8	XIV/3	
56	Q56	3	D	*c.*1767–8	XIV/3	
57	Q57	3	A	1768	XIV/3	
58	Q58	3	D	*c.*1767–8	XIV/3	
59	Q59	3	G	*c.*1767–8	XIV/3	
60	Q60	3	A	*c.*1767–8	XIV/3	
61	Q61	3	D	*c.*1767–8	XIV/3	
62	Q62	3	G	*c.*1767–8	XIV/3	
63	Q63	3	D	*c.*1767–8	XIV/3	

Hob.XI	*NG*	*Book*	*Key*	*Date*	*JHW*	*Other edn(s)*
64	Q64	3	D	*c.*1767–8	XIV/3	
65	Q65	3	G	*c.*1767–8	XIV/3	
66	Q66	3	A	*c.*1767–8	XIV/3	
67	Q67	3	G	*c.*1767–8	XIV/3	
68	Q68	3	A	*c.*1767–8	XIV/3	
69	Q69	3	D	*c.*1767–8	XIV/3	
70	Q70	3	G	*c.*1767–8	XIV/3	
71	Q71	3	A	*c.*1767–8	XIV/3	
72	Q72	3	D	*c.*1767–8	XIV/3	
73	Q73	4	G	*c.*1768–71	XIV/4	
74	Q74	4	D	*c.*1768–71	XIV/4	
75	Q75	4	A	*c.*1768–71	XIV/4	
76	Q76	4	C	*c.*1768–71	XIV/4	
77	Q77	4	G	*c.*1768–71	XIV/4	
78	Q78	4	D	*c.*1768–71	XIV/4	
79	Q79	4	D	1769	XIV/4	
80	Q80	4	G	*c.*1768–71	XIV/4	
81	Q81	4	D	*c.*1768–71	XIV/4	
82	Q82	4	C	*c.*1768–71	XIV/4	
83	Q83	4	F	*c.*1768–71	XIV/4	
84	Q84	4	G	*c.*1768–71	XIV/4	
85	Q85	4	D	*c.*1768–71	XIV/4	
86	Q86	4	A	*c.*1768–71	XIV/4	
87	Q87	4	a	*c.*1768–71	XIV/4	
88	Q88	4	A	*c.*1768–71	XIV/4	
89	Q89	4	G	*c.*1768–71	XIV/4	
90	Q90	4	C	*c.*1768–71	XIV/4	
91	Q91	4	D	*c.*1768–71	XIV/4	
92	Q92	4	G	*c.*1768–71	XIV/4	
93	Q93	4	C	*c.*1768–71	XIV/4	
94	Q94	4	A	*c.*1768–71	XIV/4	
95	Q95	4	D	*c.*1768–71	XIV/4	
96	Q96	4	b	*c.*1768–71	XIV/4	

Hob.XI	*NG*	*Book*	*Key*	*Date*	*JHW*	*Other edn(s)*
97	Q97	5	D	*c.*1771–8	XIV/5	
98	Q98	5	D	*c.*1771–8	XIV/5	
100	Q100	5	F	*c.*1771–8	XIV/5	
101	Q101	5	C	*c.*1771–8	XIV/5	
102	Q102	5	G	*c.*1771–8	XIV/5	
103	Q103	5	A	*c.*1771–8	XIV/5	
104	Q104	5	D	*c.*1771–8	XIV/5	
105	Q105	5	G	1772	XIV/5	
106	Q106	5	D	*c.*1771–8	XIV/5	
107	Q107	5	D	*c.*1771–8	XIV/5	
108	Q108	5	A	*c.*1771–8	XIV/5	
109	Q109	5	C	*c.*1771–8	XIV/5	
110	Q110	5	C	*c.*1771–8	XIV/5	
111	Q111	5	G	*c.*1771–8	XIV/5	
112	Q112	5	D	*c.*1771–8	XIV/5	
113	Q113	5	D	*c.*1771–8	XIV/5	
114	Q114	5	D	*c.*1771–8	XIV/5	
115	Q115	5	D	*c.*1771–8	XIV/5	
116	Q116	5	G	*c.*1771–8	XIV/5	
117	Q117	5	F	*c.*1771–8	XIV/5	
118	Q118	5	D	*c.*1771–8	XIV/5	
119	Q119	5	G	*c.*1771–8	XIV/5	
120	Q120	5	D	*c.*1771–8	XIV/5	
121	Q121	5	A	*c.*1771–8	XIV/5	
122	Q122	5	A	*c.*1771–8	XIV/5	
123	Q123	5	G	*c.*1771–8	XIV/5	
124	Q124	5	G	*c.*1771–8	XIV/5	
125	Q125	5	G	*c.*1771–8	XIV/5	
126	Q126	5	C	*c.*1771–8	XIV/5	

Hoboken XII: baryton duets

Hoboken included a number of lost works in this group, here omitted.

Hob.XII	*NG*	*Key*	*Scoring*	*Date*	*JHW*	*Other edn(s)*
1	R19	A	2 bary	*c.*1766	XIII	
4	R18	G	2 bary	*c.*1766	XIII	
5 (+3)	R20	D	2 bary	*c.*1766	XIII	
19	R23	A, A, D, A, A, D, A, A, D, A, A, A	2 bary, b	*c.*1766	XIII	

Hoboken XIII: baryton concertos

The three concertos listed in this section are lost.

Hoboken XIV: divertimentos for keyboard plus two or more instruments

Hob.XIV	*NG*	*Key*	*Scoring*	*Date*	*JHW*	*Other edn(s)*
1	U1	E♭	hpd, 2 hn, vn, b	(1766)	XVII	
3	U10	C	hpd, 2 vn, b	*c.*1760 (1771)	XVI	
4	U9	C	hpd, 2 vn, b	1764	XVI	
7	U11	C	hpd, 2 vn, b	*c.*1760 (1766)	XVI	
8	U13	C	hpd, 2 vn, b	*c.*1770	XVI	
9	U12	F	hpd, 2 vn, b	*c.*1760 (1766)	XVI	
10	U8	C	hpd, 2 vn, b	*c.*1765	XVI	
11	U7	C	hpd, 2 vn, b	1760	XVI	D 1959
12	Uapp4	C	hpd, 2 vn, b	*c.*1765 (1772)	XVI	D 1969
13	Uapp5	G	hpd, 2 vn, b	*c.*1765	XVI	Sch 1956
C2	Uapp7	C	hpd, 2 vn, b	*c.*1765	XVI	D 1969

Appendix 1

Hoboken XV: keyboard trios

Much of this group (XV:5 to XV:32) is in broad chronological order, from 1784 to *c.*1796, preceded and followed by earlier works. XV:3 and 4 are now known to be by Pleyel. The trios are scored for keyboard, violin, and cello but XV:15 and 16 replace the violin with a flute, and XV:17 offers it as an alternative. In the Doblinger edition Robbins Landon provided a new chronological numbering, given below in the third column.

Hob.XV	*NG*	*Landon*	*Key*	*Date*	*JHW*	*Other edn(s)*
1	Vapp9	5	g	c.1757 (1766)	XVII/1	D 1977
2	V6	17	F	*c.*1772	XVII/1	D 1976
5	V1	18	G	1784	XVII/2	D 1976
6	V2	19	F	1784	XVII/2	D 1976
7	V3	20	D	1785	XVII/2	D 1976
8	V4	21	B♭	1785	XVII/2	D 1975
9	V5	22	A	1785	XVII/2	D 1975
10	V7	23	E♭	1785	XVII/2	D 1975
11	V8	24	E♭	1788 (1789)	XVII/2	D 1974
12	V9	25	e	1788–9	XVII/2	D 1974
13	V10	26	c	1789	XVII/2	D 1973
14	V11	27	A♭	1789–90	XVII/2	D 1973
15	V13	29	G	1790	XVII/2	D 1970
16	V12	28	D	1790	XVII/2	D 1970
17	V14	30	F	1790	XVII/2	D 1970
18	V16	32	A	1793–4	XVII/3	D 1970
19	V17	33	g	1793–4	XVII/3	D 1970
20	V18	34	B♭	1793–4	XVII/3	D 1970
21	V19	35	C	1794–5	XVII/3	D 1970
22	V20	36	E♭	1794–5	XVII/3	D 1970
23	V21	37	d	1794–5	XVII/3	D 1970
24	V22	38	D	1795	XVII/3	D 1970
25	V23	39	G	1795	XVII/3	D 1970
26	V24	40	f♯	1795	XVII/3	D 1970
27	V25	43	C	*c.*1796 (1797)	XVII/3	D 1970
28	V26	44	E	*c.*1796 (1797)	XVII/3	D 1970
29	V27	45	E♭	*c.*1796 (1797)	XVII/3	D 1970

Hob.XV	*NG*	*Landon*	*Key*	*Date*	*JHW*	*Other edn(s)*
30	V29	42	E♭	1796 (1797)	XVII/3	D 1970
31	V28	41	e♭	1795	XVII/3	D 1970
32	V15	31	G	1793–4 (1795)	XVII/3	D 1970
34	Vapp5	11	E	*c.*1757 (1771)	XVII/1	D 1977
35	Vapp10	10	A	*c.*1757 (1771)	XVII/1	D 1977
36	Vapp1	12	E♭	*c.*1760 (1774)	XVII/1	D 1977
37	Vapp3	1	F	*c.*1757 (1766)	XVII/1	D 1977
38	Vapp4	13	B♭	*c.*1757 (1769)	XVII/1	D 1977
40	Vapp8	6	F	*c.*1757 (1766)	XVII/1	D 1977
41	Vapp7	7	G	*c.*1757 (1767)	XVII/1	D 1977
C1	Vapp2	2	C	*c.*1757 (1767)	XVII/1	D 1977
f1	Vapp6	14	f	*c.*1760	XVII/1	D 1977

Appendix 1

Hoboken XVI: keyboard sonatas

Hoboken used the numbers originated by Carl Päsler in 1918 for the complete edition prepared by Breitkopf & Härtel. A more thoroughgoing attempt at chronology was made by Christa Landon for her edition published by WUE; these numbers are often used and are given below in the third column.

Hob.XVI	*NG*	*C. Landon*	*Key*	*Date*	*JHW*	*Other edn(s)*
1	Wapp8	1	C	*c.*1753	XVIII/1	WUE 1966
3	W3	14	C	*c.*1765	XVIII/1	WUE 1966
4	W4	9	D	*c.*1765	XVIII/1	WUE 1966
6	W1	13	G	*c.*1760 (1766)	XVIII/1	WUE 1966
7	Wapp9	2	C	*c.*1758 (1766)	XVIII/1	WUE 1966
8	Wapp10	1	G	*c.*1758 (1766)	XVIII/1	WUE 1966
9	Wapp11	3	F	*c.*1758 (1766)	XVIII/1	WUE 1966
10	Wapp12	6	C	*c.*1758 (1767)	XVIII/1	WUE 1966
11	Wapp13b	5	G	*c.*1760 (1767)	-	WUE 1966
13	Wapp4	15	E	*c.*1761 (1767)	XVIII/1	WUE 1966
14	W2	16	D	*c.*1761 (1767)	XVIII/1	WUE 1966
18	W17	20	B♭	*c.*1771 (1788)	XVIII/1	WUE 1966
19	W14	30	D	1767	XVIII/1	WUE 1966
20	W36	33	c	1771	XVIII/2	WUE 1966
21	W19	36	C	1773	XVIII/2	WUE 1964
22	W20	37	E	1773	XVIII/2	WUE 1964
23	W21	38	F	1773	XVIII/2	WUE 1964
24	W22	39	D	1773	XVIII/2	WUE 1964
25	W23	40	E♭	1773	XVIII/2	WUE 1964
26	W24	41	A	1773	XVIII/2	WUE 1964 facs H 1958
27	W25	42	G	1774–5 (1776)	XVIII/2	WUE 1964
28	W26	43	E♭	1774–5 (1776)	XVIII/2	WUE 1964
29	W27	44	F	1774 (1776)	XVIII/2	WUE 1964
30	W28	45	A	1774–5 (1776)	XVIII/2	WUE 1964
31	W29	46	E	1774–5 (1776)	XVIII/2	WUE 1964
32	W30	47	b	1774–5 (1776)	XVIII/2	WUE 1964
33	W38	34	D	*c.*1773 (1778)	XVIII/3	WUE 1964

Hob.XVI	NG	C. Landon	Key	Date	JHW	Other edn(s)
34	W39	53	e	*c.*1782 (1784)	XVIII/3	WUE 1964
35	W31	48	C	*c.*1779 (1780)	XVIII/2	WUE 1964
36	W32	49	c♯	*c.*1778 (1780)	XVIII/2	WUE 1964
37	W33	50	D	1779 (1780)	XVIII/2	WUE 1964
38	W34	51	E♭	1779 (1780)	XVIII/2	WUE 1964
39	W35	52	G	1779–80 (1780)	XVIII/2	WUE 1964
40	W40	54	G	1783 (1784)	XVIII/3	WUE 1964
41	W41	55	E♭	1783 (1784)	XVIII/3	WUE 1964
42	W42	56	D	1783 (1784)	XVIII/3	WUE 1964
43	W37	35	A♭	*c.*1775 (1783)	XVIII/3	WUE 1966
44	W18	32	g	*c.*1770 (1788)	XVIII/1	WUE 1964
45	W13	29	E♭	1766	XVIII/1	WUE 1964
46	W16	31	A♭	*c.*1768 (1788)	XVIII/1	WUE 1964
47	W12a	19	E	*c.*1765 (1788)	XVIII/1	WUE 1964
48	W43	58	C	1789	XVIII/3	WUE 1964
49	W44	59	E♭	1789–90	XVIII/3	WUE 1964 facs ADV 1982
50	W46	60	C	1794–5	XVIII/3	WUE 1964
51	W47	61	D	1794–5	XVIII/3	WUE 1964
52	W45	62	E♭	1794	XVIII/3	WUE 1964
G1	Wapp13a	4	G	*c.*1757	XVIII/1	WUE 1966

Hoboken XVII: miscellaneous keyboard works

Hoboken gave numbers only to those works originally composed for keyboard. Elsewhere in the catalogue keyboard arrangements of music by Haydn are listed. Those now thought to have been prepared by the composer are appended to the following list as keyboard works in their own right.

Hob.XVII	*NG*	*Title*	*Date*	*JHW*	*Other edn(s)*
1	X1	Capriccio: 'Act Sauschneider müssen sein'	1765	XIX	WUE 1975
2	X2	Variations in A	*c.*1765 (1771)	XIX	WUE 1975
3	X3	Variations in E♭	*c.*1772 (1774)	XIX	WUE 1975
4	X4	Capriccio/Fantasia in C	1789	XIX	WUE 1975
5	X5	Variations in C	1790	XIX	WUE 1975
6	X6	Andante in f	1793	XIX	WUE 1975
7	Xapp7	Variations in D	*c.*1753 (1766)		H 1969
9	X9	Adagio in F	(1786)	XIX	WUE 1975
deest	Xapp1	12 minuets (IX:3)	*c.*1764	V	WUE 1989
deest	Xapp2	Allegretto in G (op. 33 no. 5/iv)	1786	XII/3	WUE 1975
deest	Xapp3	12 minuets (IX:8)	(1785)	V	WUE 1989
deest	Xapp4	12 minuets (IX:11)	1792	V	WUE 1989
deest	Xapp5	12 deutsche Tänze (IX:12)	1792	V	WUE 1989
deest	Xapp7	2 marches (VIII:1 and 2)	1795	V	
deest	Xapp8	Variations: 'Gott erhalte'	1797–9		WUE 1975

Hoboken XVIIa: keyboard duet

Hob.XVIIa	*NG*	*Title*	*Date*	*JHW*	*Other edn(s)*
1	X8	Il Maestro e Scolare	*c.*1768–70 (1780)	XX	WUE 1975

Hoboken XVIII: concertos for keyboard

Works for organ (or harpsichord) and harpsichord (or piano) are mingled indiscriminately in this section with no attempt at chronology.

Hob.XVIII	*NG*	*Key*	*Date*	*Scoring*	*JHW*	*Other edn(s)*
1	U1	C	1756	solo org/hpd, 2 ob, (2 tpt, timp), str	XV/1	BH 1986
2	U2	D	*c.*1753 (1767)	solo org/hpd, (2 ob, 2 tpt, timp), str	XV/1	D 1978, as no. 1
3	U4	F	*c.*1766 (1771)	solo hpd, (2 hn), str	XV/2	
4	U5	G	*c.*1769 (1781)	solo hpd/pf, (2 ob, 2 hn), str	XV/2	
5	Uapp1		*c.*1753 (1763)	solo org/hpd, (2 tpt, timp), str	XV/1	NM 1959
6	U3	F	*c.*1756 (1766)	solo vn and org/hpd, str	XV/1	Bä 1959
8	Uapp2	C	*c.*1753 (1771)	solo org/hpd, (2 tpt, timp), str	XV/1	D 1962, as no. 2
10	Uapp3	C	*c.*1753 (1771)	solo org/hpd, str	XV/1	H 1969
11	U6	D	*c.*1779 (1784)	solo hpd/pf, 2 ob, 2 hn, str	XV/2	
F2	Uapp6	F	(1767)	hpd, 2 vn, b	XVI	D 1969

Hoboken XIX: music for mechanical organ

Hoboken lists all the music contained on the three extant instruments. Later scholarship has established that a number of these pieces did not originate with the composer. They are omitted here.

Hob.XIX	*NG*	*Key*	*Title*	*Date*	*JHW*	*Other edn(s)*
9	Yapp1:1	C	Menuet	*c.*1789 (1792)	XXI	
10	Y1	C	Andante	*c.*1789 (1792)	XXI	
11	Y5	C	—	*c.*1789 (1793)	XXI	
12	Y6	C	Andante	*c.*1789 (1793)	XXI	
13	Y7	C	—	*c.*1789 (1793)	XXI	
14	Y8	C	—	*c.*1789 (1793)	XXI	
15	Y9	C	—	*c.*1789 (1793)	XXI	
16	Y4	C	Fuga	1789	XXI	
17	Y1	C	—	*c.*1789 (1792)	XXI	
18	Y3	C	Presto	*c.*1789 (1792)	XXI	
24	Yapp2:1	C	Presto	*c.*1789 (1792)	XXI	
27	Y11	C	Allegretto	1793	XXI	
28	Yapp1:2	C	Allegro	1793	XXI	
29	Yapp1:3	C	—	1793	XXI	
30	Yapp1:4	G	Presto	1793	XXI	
31	Y10	C	Presto	1789	XXI	
32	Yapp1:5	F	Allegro	1793	XXI	

Hoboken XX/1: instrumental music on The Seven Last Words

In this subgroup the orchestral and quartet versions of the work are given separate numbers, the latter an alternative to the one in Group III, III:50–6. Hoboken lists a version for keyboard too (XX/1:1 C) which was not prepared by Haydn. Because instrumental and vocal music are separated into volumes 1 and 2 respectively, the vocal version of the work is placed in a separate subgroup (XX/2).

Hob.XX/1	*NG*	*Title*	*Date*	*Scoring*	*JHW*	*Other edn(s)*
1 A	K11	The Seven Last Words of our Saviour on the Cross	(1787) 1786	2 fl, 2 ob, 2 cl, 2 bn, 4 hn, 2 tpt, timp, str	IV	
1 B	Oapp1:1	The Seven Last Words of our Saviour on the Cross	1787	2 vn, va, vc		E 1956

Hoboken XX/2: vocal music on The Seven Last Words

Hob.XX/2	*NG*	*Title*	*Date*	*Scoring*	*JHW*	*Other edn(s)*
	C4	The Seven Last Words of our Saviour on the Cross	1795–6	S, A, T, B, chor, 2 fl, 2 ob, 2 cl, 2 bn, dbn, 2 hn, 2 tpt, 2 trbn, timp, str	XXVIII/2	

Hoboken XXbis: Stabat mater

Hob.XXbis	*NG*	*Title*	*Date*	*Scoring*	*JHW*	*Other edn(s)*
	C1	Stabat mater	1767	S, A, T, B, chor, 2 ob/ca, str	XXII/1	F 1977

Hoboken XXI: oratorios

The three works are listed in chronological order; the 'Applausus' cantata is to be found in Group XXIVa.

Hob.XXI	*NG*	*Title*	*Date*	*Scoring*	*JHW*	*Other edn(s)*
1	C3	Il ritorno di Tobia	1774–5	2S, A, T, B, chor, 2 fl, 2 ob, 2 ca, 2 bn, 4 hn, 2 tpt, 2 trbn, timp, str, cont	XXVIII/1	
2	C5	The Creation/Die Schöpfung	1796–8	S, T, B, 3 fl, 2 ob, 2 cl, 2 bn, dbn, 2 hn, 2 tpt, 3 trbn, timp, str, cont	XXVIII/2	OUP 1995
3	C6	The Seasons/Die Jahreszeiten	1799–1801	S, T, B, chor, 2 fl, 2 ob, 2 cl, 2 bn, dbn, 4 hn, 3 tpt, 3 trbn, timp, perc, str, cont	XXVIII/3	E *c.*1960

Hoboken XXII: masses

Hoboken placed the masses in presumed chronological order; later discoveries have undermined this sequence.

Hob.XXII	*NG*	*Title/Nickname*	*Key*	*Date*	*Scoring*	*JHW*	*Other edn(s)*
1	A2	Missa brevis	F	1749	2S, chor, str	XXIII/1	CV 1979
2	A4	Missa 'sunt bona mixta malis'	d	1768	chor, cont	XXIII/1	EMB 1992
3	A1a	Missa 'Rorate coeli desuper'	G	c.1749	chor, str	XXIII/1	CV 1982 HMP 1957
4	A5	Missa in honorem BVM 'Grosse Orgelsolomesse'	E♭	*c.*1768 (1774)	S, A, T, B, chor, 2 ca, 2 hn, (2 tpt, timp), solo org, str	XXIII/1	D 1957
5	A3	Missa Cellensis in honorem BVM. 'Cäcilienmesse'	C	1766 *c.*1773	S, A, T, B, chor, 2 ob, 2 bn, 2 hn, 2 tpt, timp, str	XXIII/1	HMP 1952
6	A6	Missa Sancti Nicolai	G	1772	S, A, T, B, chor, 2 ob, 2hn, (2 tpt, timp), str	XXIII/1	F 1969
7	A7	Missa brevis Sancti Joannis de Deo. 'Kleine Orgelsolomesse'	B♭	*c.*1775 (1778)	S, chor, solo org, str	XXIII/2	Bä 1962 OUP 1989 S 1972
8	A8	Missa Cellensis 'Mariazellermesse'	C	1782	S, A, T, B, chor, 2 ob, bn, 2 tpt, timp, str	XXIII/2	Bä 1963 CV 1986 S 1974
9	A10	Missa in tempore belli. 'Paukenmesse'	C	1796	S, A, T, B, chor, fl, 2 ob, 2 cl, 2 bn, 2 hn, 2 tpt, timp, str	XXIII/2	Bä 1962 S 1965
10	A9	Missa Sancti Bernardi d'Offida 'Heiligmesse'	B♭	1796	S, A, T, B, chor, 2 ob, 2 cl, 2 bn, 2 hn, 2 tpt, timp, str	XXIII/2	Bä 1962 S 1972
11	A11	Missa in angustiis 'Nelson' mass	d	1798	S, A, T, B, chor, 3 tpt, timp, solo org, str	XXIII/3	Bä 1966 E *c.*1964 OUP 1996
12	A12	'Theresienmesse'	B♭	1799	S, A, T, B, chor, 2 cl, bn, 2 tpt, timp, str	XXIII/3	Bä 1970 S 1971
13	A13	'Schöpfungsmesse'	B♭	1801	S, A, T, B, chor, 2 ob, 2 cl, 2 bn, 2 hn, 2 tpt, timp, solo org, str	XXIII/4	CV 1989 S 1975 facs H 1957

Hob.XXII	*NG*	*Title/Nickname*	*Key*	*Date*	*Scoring*	*JHW*	*Other edn(s)*
14	A14	'Harmoniemesse'	B♭	1802	S, A, T, B, chor, fl, 2 ob, 2 cl, 2 bn, 2 hn, 2 tpt, timp, str	XXIII/5	Bä 1967 S 1966

Hoboken XXIIa: settings of the requiem text

Since Haydn never composed a requiem the works listed in this group are all spurious.

Hoboken XXIIb: settings of the Libera me

Hob.XXIIb	*NG*	*Key*	*Date*	*Scoring*	*JHW*	*Other edn(s)*
1	B16	d	*c.*1778	chor, 2 vn, cont	XXII/3	HMP 1968 facs *HYB* 4

Hoboken XXIII: small church compositions

Four subdivisions are used: XXIIIa, graduals, offertories, and motets; XXIIb, marian antiphons; XXIIIc, settings of the Te Deum and other choruses; and XXIIId, arias. There is also a significant addendum (*Nachtrag*), Haydn's setting of six English psalm texts.

Hob.XXIIIa	*NG*	*Title*	*Key*	*Date*	*Scoring*	*JHW*	*Other edn(s)*
1	B15	Non nobis Domine	d	*c.*1768 (1786)	chor, cont	XXII/2	D 1978
2	B7	Animae Deo gratae	C	*c.*1765 (1776)	2S, T, chor, 2 ob, 2 tpt, timp, str	XXII/3	
3	B6	Ens aeternum	G	*c.*1765 (1772)	chor, str	XXII/3	
4	B4	Motetto di Sancta Thecla	C	*c.*1762	S, chor, 2 tpt, timp, str	XXII/3	
G9	Bapp2: 15	O coelitum beati	G	*c.*1763	S, str		CV 1996
deest	Bapp1: 4	Insanae et vanae curae	d	*c.*1797	chor, 2 fl, 2 ob, 2 bn, 2 tpt, timp, str		N [nd]

Hob.XXIIIb	*NG*	*Title*	*Key*	*Date*	*Scoring*	*JHW*	*Other edn(s)*
1	B3	Salve regina	E	1756	S, chor, str	XXII/2	D 1990
2	B11	Salve regina	g	1771	S, A, T, B, solo org, str	XXII/2	D 1964
3	B2	Ave regina	A	*c.*1756 (1763)	S, chor, str		Bö 1970

Hob.XXIIIc	*NG*	*Title*	*Key*	*Date*	*Scoring*	*JHW*	*Other edn(s)*
1	B5	Te deum	C	1763 (1765)	S, A. T, B, chor, 2 tpt, timp, str	XXII/2	D 1966
2	B23	Te deum	C	1799 (1800)	chor, fl, 2 ob, 2 bn, 2h, 3 tpt, timp, str	XXII/2	D 1959 OUP 1992
3	B9	Alleluja	G	*c.*1768 (1771)	S, A, chor, str	XXII/2	
4	B8	Lauda Sion	B♭, d, A, A♭	*c.*1765	chor, 2 hn, str	XXII/2	H 1956
5	B1	Lauda Sion	C	*c.*1750 (1776)	chor, 2 ob, 2 tpt, str	XXII/3	D 1996

Hob.XXIIId	*NG*	*Title*	*Key*	*Date*	*Scoring*	*JHW*	*Other edn(s)*
1	B13	Ein' Magd, ein' Dienerin'	A	*c.*1773	2 hn, str	XXII/2	HMP 1957
2	B14	Mutter Gottes, mir erlaube	G	*c.*1775	S, A, str	XXII/2	
3	B10	Herst Nachbä	D	*c.*1758	S, str	XXII/2	C 1975
G1	Bapp2:6	Ey, wer hat ihm das Ding gedenckt	G	*c.*1758 (1764)	S, str		C 1975
deest	Bapp2:14	Was meine matte Brust	G	*c.*1758	T, str		

Hob.XXIII Nachtrag	*NG*	*Title*	*Key*	*Date*	*Scoring*	*JHW*	*Other edn(s)*
a	B17	How oft, instinct with warmth divine	F	1794	chor	XXII/2	Br 1980
b	B18	Blest be the name of Jacob's God	E♭	1794	chor	XXII/2	Br 1980
c	B19	Maker of all!	D	1794	chor	XXII/2	Br 1980
d	B20	The Lord, th'almighty Monarch spake	C	1794	chor	XXII/2	Br 1980
e	B21	Long life shall Israel's king behold	E♭	1794	chor	XXII/2	Br 1980
f	B22	O let me in th'accepted hour	A	1794	chor	XXII/2	Br 1980

Hoboken XXIVa: cantatas and choruses with orchestral accompaniment

This heterogeneous collection of works, from concert arias to multi-movement works with chorus, is arranged in chronological order.

Hob.XXIVa	*NG*	*Title*	*Key*	*Date*	*Scoring*	*JHW*	*Other edn(s)*
2	D2	Destatevi, o miei fidi	G	1763	2S, T, chor, 2 ob, 2 hn, str	XXVII/1	
3	D4	Da qual gioia improvvisa	C	1764	2S, A, 2T, B, chor, fl, 2 ob, bn, 2 hn, hpd, str	XXVII/1	
4	D3	Qual dubbio ormai	A	1764	S, chor, 2 ob, 2 hn, hpd, str	XXVII/1	D 1971
6	C2	Applausus	C	1768	S, A, T, B, 2 ob, bn, 2 hn/tpt, timp, hpd, str	XXVII/2	D 1969
7	F7	Miseri noi, misera patri	E♭	(1786)	S, 2 fl, 2 ob, 2 bn, 2 hn, str	XXVI/2	D 1960
8	D8	The Storm	d	1792	S, A, T, B, chor, 2 fl, 2 ob, 2 bn, str	XXVII/3	D 1969
9	D9	Invocation of Neptune	F, D	1794	B, chor, fl, 2 ob, 2 cl, 2 bn, 2 hn, 2 tpt, timp, str	XXVII/3	D 1990
10	F25	Berenice, che fai?	f	1795	S, fl, 2 ob, 2 cl, 2 bn, 2 hn, str	XXVI/2	D 1965
deest	D11	Gott erhalte Franz den Kaiser	G	1797	chor, fl, 2 ob, 2 bn, 2 hn, 2 tpt, timp, str		HCRL/4

Hoboken XXIVb: arias with orchestral accompaniment

Most of the arias are insertion arias; XXIVb:1 is now thought to be part of a lost opera by Haydn; and XXIVb:20 is a concert aria. The sequence is broadly chronological.

Hob.XXIVb	*NG*	*Title*	*Role; opera*	*Date*	*JHW*	*Other edn(s)*
1	E4	Costretta a piangere	Dorina (S); Haydn, unknown	*c.*1761	XXV/1	HMP 1961
2	F2	D'una sposa meschinella	Donna Stella (S); Paisiello, La frascatana	1779	XXVI/1	HMP 1961
3	F4	Quando la rosa	Nanina (S); Anfossi, La Metilda ritrovata	1779	XXVI/1	HMP 1961
5	F5	Dice benissimo	Lumaca (B); Salieri, La scuola de' gelosi	1780	XXVI/1	HMP 1964
7	F6	Signor, voi sapete	Rosina (S); Anfossi, Il matrimonio per inganno	1785	XXVI/1	HMP 1961
8	F3	Dica pure chi vuol dire	Modesta (S); Anfossi, Il geloso in cimento	1785	XXVI/1	
9	F8	Sono Alcina	Lesbia (S); Gazzaniga, L'isola di Alcina	1786	XXVI/1	HMP 1961
10	F9	Ah tu non senti … Qual destra omicida	Oreste (T); Traetta, Ifigenia in Tauride	1786	XXVI/1	HMP 1964
11	F10	Un cor sì tenore	Ormondo (B); Bianchi, Il disertore	1787	XXVI/1	HMP 1964
12	F11	Vada adagio, signorina	Cardellina (S); Guglielmi, La quakera spiritosa	1787	XXVI/1	HMP 1961
13	F12	Che vive amanta	Erissena (S); Bianchi, Alessandro nell'Indie	1787	XXVI/1	HMP 1961
14	F13	Se tu mi sprezzi	Il Cavaliere (T); Sarti, I finti eredi	1788	XXVI/1	HMP 1964
15	F14	Infelice sventurata	Beatrice (S); Cimarosa, I due supposti conti	1789	XXVI/1	HMP 1961
16	F16	Da che penso	Titta (T); Gassmann, L'amore artigiano	1790	XXVI/1	HMP 1964
17	F18	Il meglio mia carattere	Merlina (S); Cimarosa, L'impresario in angustie	1790	XXVI/1	HMP 1961

Hob.XXIVb	NG	Title	Role; opera	Date	JHW	Other edn(s)
18	F19	La moglie quando è buona	Giannina (S); Cimarosa, Giannina e Bernardone	1790	XXVI/1	HMP 1961
19	F17	La mia pace, oh Dio	Costanza (S); Gassmann, L'amore artigiano	1790	XXVI/1	
20	F26	Solo e pensoso	[concert aria]	1798	XXVI/2	HMP 1961
22	F20	Tornate pur mia bella	T; unknown	(1790)	XXVI/2	
23	F21	Via siate bonino	S; unknown	*c*.1790	XXVI/2	

Hoboken XXV: songs for two, three, or four voices

This group is subdivided into three: XXVa, duets; XXVb, trios; XXVc, quartets. One consequence of this decision is that the late partsongs, conceived and published as a collection, are divided between two subgroups (b and c). XXVb:5 is a concert work rather than a domestic work.

Hob.XXVa	*NG*	*Title*	*Date*	*Scoring*	*JHW*	*Other edn(s)*
1	H5	Guarda qui che lo vedrai	1796	S, T, kbd	XXIX/2	D 1960
2	H4	Sapper vorei	1796	S, T, kbd	XXIX/2	D 1960

Hob.XXVb	*NG*	*Title*	*Date*	*Scoring*	*JHW*	*Other edn(s)*
1	H11	An den Vetter	1796	S, A, T, cont	XXX	
2	H7	Daphnens einziger Fehler	1796	T, T, B, cont	XXX	
3	H14	Betrachtung des Todes	1796	S, T, B, cont	XXX	
4	H16	An die Frauen	1796	T, T, B, kpd	XXX	
5	Fapp1:1	Pietà di me, benigni Dei	1791	2 S, T, solo ca, solo bn, solo hn, 2 bn, str		D 1982

Hob.XXVc	*NG*	*Title*	*Date*	*Scoring*	*JHW*	*Other edn(s)*
1	H6	Der Augenblick	1796	S, A, T, B, cont	XXX	CV 1988
2	H7	Die Harmonie in der Ehe	1796	S, A, T, B, cont	XXX	CV 1988
3	H8	Alles hat seine Zeit	1796	S, A, T, B, cont	XXX	CV 1988
4	H9	Beredsamkeit	1796	S, A, T, B, cont	XXX	CV 1988
5	H10	Der Greis	1796	S, A, T, B, cont	XXX	CV 1988
6	H13	Die Warnung	1796	S, A, T, B, cont	XXX	CV 1988
7	H15	Wider den Übermut	1796	S, A, T, B, cont	XXX	CV 1988
8	H17	Danklied zu Gott	1796	S, A, T, B, cont	XXX	CV 1988
9	H18	Abendlied zu Gott	1796	S, A, T, B, cont	XXX	CV 1987

Hoboken XXVIa: songs with keyboard accompaniment

This group is ordered according to the four published collections, two German and two English; single songs in the two languages are placed at the end of the sequence.

Hob.XXVIa	*NG*	*Title*	*Date*	*JHW*	*Other edn(s)*
1	G1	Das strickende Mädchen	1780–1	XXIX/1	
2	G2	Cupido	1780–1	XXIX/1	
3	G3	Der erste Kuss	1780–1	XXIX/1	
4	G4	Eine sehr gewöhnliche Geschichte	1780–1	XXIX/1	
5	G5	Die Verlassene	1780–1	XXIX/1	
6	G6	Der Gleichsinn	1780–1	XXIX/1	
7	G7	An Iris	1780–1	XXIX/1	
8	G8	An Thyrsis	1780–1	XXIX/1	
9	G9	Trost unglücklicher Liebe	1780–1	XXIX/1	
10	G10	Die Landlust	1780–1	XXIX/1	
11	G11	Liebeslied	1780–1	XXIX/1	
12	G12	Die zu späte Ankunft der Mutter	1780–1	XXIX/1	
13	G13	Jeder meint, der Gegenstand	1780–1	XXIX/1	
14	G14	Lachet nicht, Mädchen	1780–1	XXIX/1	
15	G15	O liebes Mädchen	1780–1	XXIX/1	
16	G16	Gegenliebe	1781–4	XXIX/1	
17	G17	Geistliches Lied	1781–4	XXIX/1	
18	G18	Auch die sprödeste der Schönen	1781–4	XXIX/1	
19	G19	O fliess, ja wallend fliess	1781–4	XXIX/1	
20	G20	Zufriedenheit	1781–4	XXIX/1	
21	G21	Das Leben ist ein Traum	1781–4	XXIX/1	
22	G22	Lob der Faulheit	1781–4	XXIX/1	
23	G23	Minna	1781–4	XXIX/1	
24	G24	Auf meines Vaters Grab	1781–4	XXIX/1	
25	G25	The Mermaid's Song	1794	XXIX/1	
26	G26	Recollection	1794	XXIX/1	
27	G27	Pastoral Song	1794	XXIX/1	
28	G28	Despair	1794	XXIX/1	
29	G29	Pleasing Pain	1794	XXIX/1	

Hob.XXVIa	*NG*	*Title*	*Date*	*JHW*	*Other edn(s)*
30	G30	Fidelity	1794	XXIX/1	
31	G31	Sailor's Song	1794–5	XXIX/1	
32	G32	The Wanderer	1794–5	XXIX/1	
33	G33	Sympathy	1794–5	XXIX/1	
34	G34	She never told her love	1794–5	XXIX/1	
35	G35	Piercing Eyes	1794–5	XXIX/1	
36	G36	Transport of Pleasure/Content	1794–5	XXIX/1	facs UCCP 1983
37	G37	Beim Schmerz, der dieses Herz durchwühlet	*c.*1768	XXIX/1	
38	G38	Der schlaue und dienstfertige Pudel	*c.*1784	XXIX/1	
39	G39	Trachten will ich nicht auf Erden	1790	XXIX/1	
41	G41	The Spirit's Song	*c.*1795	XXIX/1	
42	G42	O Tuneful Voice	*c.*1795	XXIX/1	
43	G43	Gott erhalte Franz den Kaiser	1796–7	XXIX/1	facs D 1982
44	G44	Als einst mit Weibes Schönheit	*c.*1800	XXIX/1	
45	G45	Ein kleines Haus	*c.*1800	XXIX/1	
46	G46	Antwort auf die Frage eines Mädchen	*c.*1800	XXIX/1	
47	G47	Bald wehen uns des Frühlings Lüfte	?	XXIX/1	

Hoboken XXVIb: cantatas and choruses with the accompaniment of one [or more] instrument

Hob.XXVIb	*NG*	*Title*	*Scoring*	*Date*	*JHW*	*Other edn(s)*
2	H1	Arianna a Naxos	S, kpd	1790	XXIX/2	HMP 1965
3	H3	Dr Harington's Compliment	S, chor, pf	1794	XXIX/2	
4	H19	The Battle of the Nile	S, pf	1800	XXIX/2	D 1981
deest	H20–5	6 Scottish airs with variations	S/T, vn, vc, kbd	1800–3	XXXII/3	

Hoboken XXVII: vocal canons

This group is divided into two: XXVIIa, sacred canons, that is *Die Heiligen Zehn Gebote*; and XXVIIb, secular canons, all single works. In fact a few of the canons in the second subgroup are sacred in their sentiments. The order in the second section follows that in the *Haydn-Verzeichnis* and has no discernible logic.

NG does not allocate numbers to individual canons.

Hob.XXVIIa	*NG*	*Title*	*Parts*	*Date*	*JHW*	*Other edn(s)*
1	I	Du sollst an einen Gott glauben	3/4	1791–5	XXXI	
2	I	Du sollst den Namen Gottes nicht eitel nennen	4	1791–5	XXXI	
3	I	Du sollst Sonn- und Feiertag heiligen	4	1791–5	XXXI	
4	I	Du sollst Vater und Mutter verehren	4	1791–5	XXXI	
5	I	Du sollst nicht töten	4	1791–5	XXXI	
6	I	Du sollst nicht Unkeuschheit treiben	5	1791–5	XXXI	
7	I	Du sollst nicht stehlen	5	1791–5	XXXI	
8	I	Du sollst kein falsch Zeugnis geben	4	1791–5	XXXI	
9	I	Du sollst nicht begehren deines Nächsten Weib	4	1791–5	XXXI	
10	I	Du sollst nicht begehren deines Nächsten Gut	4	1791–5	XXXI	

Hob.XXVIIb	*NG*	*Title*	*Voices*	*Date*	*JHW*	*Other edn(s)*
1	I	Hilar an Narziss	3	1790s	XXXI	
2	I	Auf einen adeligen Dummkopf	3	1790s	XXXI	
3	I	Der Schuster bleib bei seinem Leist	8	1790s	XXXI	
4	I	Herr von Gänsewitz zu seinem Kammerdiener	4	1790s	XXXI	
5	I	An den Marull	5	1790s	XXXI	
6	I	Die Mutter an ihr Kind in der Wiege	3	1790s	XXXI	
7	I	Der Menschenfreund	4	1790s	XXXI	
8	I	Gottes Macht und Vorsehung	3	1790s	XXXI	
9	I	An Dorilis	4	1790s	XXXI	
10	I	Vixi	3	1790s	XXXI	
11	I	Der Kobold	4	1790s	XXXI	
12	I	Der Fuchs und der Marder	4	1790s	XXXI	
13	I	Abschied	5	1790s	XXXI	

Hob.XXVIIb	*NG*	*Title*	*Voices*	*Date*	*JHW*	*Other edn(s)*
14	I	Die Hofstellungen	3	1790s	XXXI	
15	I	Aus Nichts wird Nichts (Nichts gewonnen, nichts verloren)	5	1790s	XXXI	
16	I	Cacatum non est pictum	4	1790s	XXXI	
17	I	Tre cose	3	1790s	XXXI	
18	I	Vergebliches Glück	2	1790s	XXXI	
19	I	Grabschrift	4	1790s	XXXI	
20	I	Das Reitpferd	3	1790s	XXXI	
21	I	Tod und Schlaf	4	1790s	XXXI	
22	I	An einen Geizigen	3	1790s	XXXI	
23	I	Das böse Weib	3	1790s	XXXI	
23bis	I	Das böse Weib	2	1790s	XXXI	
24	I	Der Verlust	3	1790s	XXXI	
25	I	Der Freigeist	3	1790s	XXXI	
26	I	Die Liebe der Feinde	2	1790s	XXXI	
27	I	Der Furchtsame	3	1790s	XXXI	
28	I	Die Gewissheit	4	1790s	XXXI	
29	I	Phöbus und sein Sohn	4	1790s	XXXI	
30	I	Die Tulipane	2	1790s	XXXI	
31	I	Das gröste Gut	2/3	1790s	XXXI	
32	I	Der Hirsch	5	1790s	XXXI	
33	I	Überschrift eines Weinhauses	4	1790s	XXXI	
34	I	Der Esel und die Dohle	8	1790s	XXXI	
35	I	Schalksnarren	6	1790s	XXXI	
36	I	Zweierlei Feinde	3	1790s	XXXI	
37	I	Der Bäcker und die Maus	5	1790s	XXXI	
38	I	Die Flinte und der Hase	4	1790s	XXXI	
39	I	Der Nachbar	4	1790s	XXXI	
40	I	Liebe zur Kunst	4	1790s	XXXI	
41	I	Frag und Antwort zweier Fuhrleute (Die Welt)	5	1790s	XXXI	
42	I	Der Fuchs und der Adler	3	1790s	XXXI	
43	I	Wunsch	4	1790s	XXXI	
44	I	Gott im Herzen	3	1790s	XXXI	

Hob.XXVIIb	NG	Title	Voices	Date	JHW	Other edn(s)
45	I	Turk was a faithful dog	4	1790s	XXXI	CV
46	I	Thy voice, o Harmony, is divine	3/4	1791	XXXI	
47	I	[no text]	7	1790s	XXXI	

Hoboken XXVIII: Italian operas

Thirteen extant Italian operas are listed in chronological order. *La marchesa nespola* is included in Group XXX.

Hob.XXVIII	NG	Title	Libretto	Date	JHW	Other edn(s)
1	E2	Acide	Migliavacca	1762	XXV/1	
2	E8	La canterina		1766	XXV/2	MP 1947
3	E9	Lo speziale	after Goldoni	1768	XXV/3	lib facs *HYB* 20 HMP 1969
4	E10	Le pescatrici	after Goldoni	1769	XXV/4	lib facs *HYB* 21 UE 1965
5	E11	L'infedeltà delusa	Coltellini	1773	XXV/5	lib facs *HYB* 20 HMP 1961
6	E14	L'incontro improvviso	Friberth	1775	XXV/6	MV 1939
7	E17	Il mondo della luna	Goldoni	1777	XXV/7	Bä 1958
8	E19	La vera costanza	Puttini	1778 1785	XXV/8	UE 1975
9	E20	L'isola disabitata	Metastasio after Lorenzi	1779	XXV/9	Bä 1976
10	E21	La fedeltà premiata		1780	XXV/10	UE 1970
11	E22	Orlando paladino	Badini, Porta	1782	XXV/11	
12	E23	Armida		1783	XXV/12	
13	E24	L'anima del filosofo	Badini	1791	XXV/13	Bä 2000 UE 1951

Hoboken XXIX: marionette and other German operas

This section is rather artificially divided into two: XXIXa, marionette operas; and XXIXb, German operas. *Philemon und Baucis* is given a number in both groups (XXIXa:1 and XXIXb:2). Unlike the group devoted to Italian opera (XXVIII) Hoboken allocates numbers to lost works. Those whose texts only have survived are included here.

Hob.XXIXa	*NG*	*Title*	*Libretto*	*Date*	*JHW*	*Other edn(s)*
1	E12	Philemon und Baucis		1773	XXIV/1	Bä 1959
3	E15	Dido	Bader	1775	XXIV/2 facs lib	
5	Eapp1	Genovefens vierter Theil	Pauersbach	1777	XXIV/2 lib	

Hob.XXIXb	*NG*	*Title*	*Libretto*	*Date*	*JHW*	*Other edn(s)*
1[b]	E1b	Der neue krumme Teufel	Kurz-Bernardon	*c.*1758	XXIV/2 facs lib	
3	E18	Die bestrafte Rachbegierde	Bader	1779	XXIV/2 facs lib	
A	E16b	Die Feuersbrunst		*c.*1776	XXIV/3	Sch 1963

Hoboken XXX: incidental music

La marchesa nespola is misleadingly included in this section.

Hob.XXX	*NG*	*Title*	*Title of play, author*	*Date*	*JHW*	*Other edn(s)*
1	E3	La marchesa nespola		1763	XXV/1	
4	E26	Fatal amour				
5a	E25	Triumph, dir Haldane (chor)	Alfred, König der Angelsachsen (Cowmeadow)	1796	XXVII/3	
5b	E25	Ausgesandt von Strahlenthrone (aria)	Alfred, König der Angelsachsen (Cowmeadow)	1796	XXVII/3	HMP 1961
5c	E25	Der Morgen graut (duet)	Alfred, König der Angelsachsen (Cowmeadow)	1796	XXVII/3	

Hoboken XXXI: arrangements

This very large group is divided into three: XXXIa, settings of Scottish folksongs; XXXIb, settings of Welsh folksongs; and XXXIc, other arrangements by Haydn. The division and order of the settings of folksongs derive from the published editions by Napier, Thomson, and Whyte. However, duplicate settings of the same melody are incorporated in the numerical sequence following the first setting, thereby undermining the broad chronological order. The vast majority of settings are for solo voice; the occasional larger forces are here indicated following the title. The third subgroup consists mainly of revisions by Haydn of Italian arias sung at the opera house in Eszterháza.

Hob.XXXIa	*NG*	*Title*	*Accompaniment*	*Date*	*JHW*	*Other edn(s)*
1	Z217	Mary's dream	vn, cont	1791–2	XXXII/1	
1bis	Z218	Mary's dream	vn, vc, kb	1801	XXXII/3	UCCP 1984
2	Z165	John Anderson, my Jo	vn, cont	1791–2	XXXII/1	
2bis	Z166	John Anderson, my Jo	vn, vc, kbd	1802–3	XXXII/5	UCCP 1984
3	Z155	I love my love in secret	vn, cont	1791–2	XXXII/1	
4	Z379	Willie was a wanton wag	vn, cont	1791–2	XXXII/1	
4bis	Z380	Willie was a wanton wag	vn, vc, kbd	1801	XXXII/3	
5	Z295	Saw ye my Father?	vn, cont	1791–2	XXXII/1	
5bis	Z296	Saw ye my Father?	vn, vc, kbd	1800	XXXII/3	
5ter	Z297	Saw ye my Father?	vn, vc, kbd	1804	XXXII/5	
6	Z343	Todlen hame	vn, cont	1791–2	XXXII/1	
6bis	Z344	Todlen hame	vn, vc, kbd	1802–3	XXXII/5	
7	Z109	Fy! gar rub her o'er wi' strae	vn, cont	1791–2	XXXII/1	
7bis	Z110	Fy! gar rub her o'er wi' strae	vn, vc, kbd	1801	XXXII/3	
8	Z123	Green grow the rashes	vn, cont	1791–2	XXXII/1	
8bis	Z124	Green grow the rashes (with chor)	vn, vc, kbd	1801	XXXII/3	
9	Z356	The waefu' heart	vn, cont	1791–2	XXXII/1	
9bis	Z357	The waefu' heart	vn, vc, kbd	1802–3	XXXII/5	
10	Z275	The ploughman	vn, cont	1791–2	XXXII/1	
11	Z16	Barbara Allen	vn, cont	1791–2	XXXII/1	
11bis	Z17	Barbara Allen	vn, vc, kbd	1800	XXXII/3	UCCP 1984
12	Z336	Thou'rt gane awa'	vn, cont	1791–2	XXXII/1	
12bis	Z337	Thou'rt gane awa'	vn, vc, kbd	1802–3	XXXII/5	
13	Z120	Gramachree	vn, cont	1791–2	XXXII/1	
13bis	Z121	Gramachree	vn, vc, kbd	1801	XXXII/3	
13ter	Z122	Gramachree	vn, vc, kbd	1802–3	XXXII/5	

Hob.XXXIa	*NG*	*Title*	*Accompaniment*	*Date*	*JHW*	*Other edn(s)*
14	Z333	This is no mine ain house	vn, cont	1791–2	XXXII/1	
14bis	Z334	This is no mine ain house	vn, vc, kbd	1802–3	XXXII/5	
15	Z112	Galla water	vn, cont	1791–2	XXXII/1	
15bis	Z113	Galla water	vn, vc, kbd	1802–3	XXXII/5	
15ter	Z114	Galla water	vn, vc, kbd	1803	XXXII/4	
16	Z255	O'er Bogie	vn, cont	1791–2	XXXII/1	
16bis	Z256	O'er Bogie	vn, vc, kbd	1801	XXXII/3	
17	Z152	I had a horse	vn, cont	1791–2	XXXII/1	
17bis	Z153	I had a horse	vn, vc, kbd	1804	XXXII/5	
18	Z236	My boy Tammy	vn, cont	1791–2	XXXII/1	
19	Z321	St Kilda Song	vn, cont	1791–2	XXXII/1	
20	Z31	The blythesome Bridal	vn, cont	1791–2	XXXII/1	
20bis	Z32	The blythesome Bridal	vn, vc, kbd	1801	XXXII/3	
21	Z302	The shepherd Adonis	vn, cont	1791–2	XXXII/1	
22	Z374	The white cockade	vn, cont	1791–2	XXXII/1	
23	Z183	The lass of Livingston	vn, cont	1791–2	XXXII/1	
24	Z170	John of Badenyon	vn, cont	1791–2	XXXII/1	
24bis	Z171	John of Badenyon	vn, vc, kbd	1801	XXXII/3	
25	Z42	The bonniest lass in a' the world	vn, cont	1791–2	XXXII/1	
26	Z87	Duncan Davison	vn, cont	1791–2	XXXII/1	
27	Z189	Leader haughs and yarrow	vn, cont	1791–2	XXXII/1	
28	Z352	Up in the morning early	vn, cont	1791–2	XXXII/1	
28bis	Z353	Up in the morning early	vn, vc, kbd	1802–3	XXXII/5	
28ter	Z354	Up in the morning early	vn, vc, kbd	1801	XXXII/3	
29	Z102	Fife and a' the lands about it	vn, cont	1791–2	XXXII/1	
30	Z156	I'm o'er young to marry yet	vn, cont	1791–2	XXXII/1	
31	Z190	The lea-rig	vn, cont	1791–2	XXXII/1	
31bis	Z191	The lea-rig	vn, vc, kbd	1800	XXXII/3	
31ter	Z192	The lea-rig	vn, vc, kbd	1802–3	XXXII/5	
32	Z73	Dainty Davie	vn, cont	1791–2	XXXII/1	
33	Z273	Pentland Hills	vn, cont	1791–2	XXXII/1	
34	Z88	Duncan Gray	vn, cont	1791–2	XXXII/1	
35	Z207	Maggie Lauder	vn, cont	1791–2	XXXII/1	

Hob.XXXIa	*NG*	*Title*	*Accompaniment*	*Date*	*JHW*	*Other edn(s)*
35bis	Z208	Maggie Lauder	vn, vc, kbd	1800	XXXII/3	UCCP 1984
35ter	Z209	Maggie Lauder	vn, vc, kbd	1804	XXXII/5	
36	Z141	How can I be sad on my wedding day	vn, cont	1791–2	XXXII/1	
37	Z245	My nanie, O!	vn, cont	1791–2	XXXII/1	
37bis	Z246	My nanie, O!	vn, vc, kbd	1802–3	XXXII/3	
37ter	Z247	My nanie, O!	vn, vc, kbd	1803	XXXII/4	
37^{quater}	Z248	My nanie, O! (duet)	vn, vc, kbd	1801	XXXII/3	
38	Z386	Woo'd and married and a'	vn, cont	1791–2	XXXII/1	
38bis	Z387	Woo'd and married and a' (with chor)	vn, vc, kbd	1801	XXXII/3	
39	Z38	Blue bonnets	vn, cont	1791–2	XXXII/1	
40	Z362	The wauking of the fauld	vn, cont	1791–2	XXXII/1	
41	Z167	John, come kiss me now	vn, cont	1791–2	XXXII/1	
42	Z229	Mount your baggage	vn, cont	1791–2	XXXII/1	
43	Z391	Ye Gods! was Strephon's picture blest	vn, cont	1791–2	XXXII/1	
44	Z317	Sleepy bodie	vn, cont	1791–2	XXXII/1	
45	Z115	The gard'ner wi' his paidle	vn, cont	1791–2	XXXII/1	
46	Z52	The brisk young lad	vn, cont	1791–2	XXXII/1	
46bis	Z53	The brisk young lad	vn, vc, kbd	1801	XXXII/3	
47	Z71	Cumbernauld house	vn, cont	1791–2	XXXII/1	
48	Z254	O can ye sew cushions	vn, cont	1791–2	XXXII/1	
49	Z134	Here's a health to my true love	vn, cont	1791–2	XXXII/1	
50	Z221	Merry may the maid be	vn, cont	1791–2	XXXII/1	
50bis	Z222	Merry may the maid be (duet)	vn, vc, kbd	1804	XXXII/5	
51	Z230	The mucking of Geordie's byer	vn, cont	1791–2	XXXII/1	
51bis	Z231	The mucking of Geordie's byer	vn, vc, kbd	1801	XXXII/3	
52	Z340	Tibby Fowler	vn, cont	1791–2	XXXII/1	
53	Z203	Love will find out the way	vn, cont	1791–2	XXXII/1	
54	Z18	Be kind to the young thing	vn, cont	1791–2	XXXII/1	
55	Z59	Cauld Kail in Aberdeen	vn, cont	1791–2	XXXII/1	
55bis	Z60	Cauld Kail in Aberdeen (duet)	vn, vc, kbd	1801	XXXII/3	
56	Z298	Saw ye nae my Peggy?	vn, cont	1791–2	XXXII/1	
57	Z14	The banks of Spey	vn, cont	1791–2	XXXII/1	
58	Z24	The birks of Abergeldie	vn, cont	1791–2	XXXII/1	

Hob.XXXIa	*NG*	*Title*	*Accompaniment*	*Date*	*JHW*	*Other edn(s)*
58bis	Z25	The birks of Abergeldie	vn, vc, kbd	1801	XXXII/3	
59	Z46	The bonny brucket lassie	vn, cont	1791–2	XXXII/1	
60	Z318	The soger laddie	vn, cont	1791–2	XXXII/1	
60bis	Z319	The soger laddie	vn, vc, kbd	1801	XXXII/3	
61	Z193	Let me in this ae night	vn, cont	1791–2	XXXII/1	
61bis	Z194	Let me in this ae night	vn, vc, kbd	1801	XXXII/3	
62	Z370	When she came ben she bobbit	vn, cont	1791–2	XXXII/1	
63	Z128	Hallow ev'n	vn, cont	1791–2	XXXII/1	
64	Z396	Young Jockey was the blythest lad	vn, cont	1791–2	XXXII/1	
64bis	Z397	Young Jockey was the blythest lad	vn, vc, kbd	1801	XXXII/3	
65	Z215	Margret's ghost	vn, cont	1791–2	XXXII/1	
66	Z28	The black eagle	vn, cont	1791–2	XXXII/1	
67	Z142	How long and dreary is the night	vn, cont	1791–2	XXXII/1	
68	Z30	Blink o'er the burn, sweet Betty	vn, cont	1791–2	XXXII/1	
69	Z360	Wat ye wha I met yestreen?	vn, cont	1791–2	XXXII/1	
69bis	Z361	Wat ye wha I met yestreen?	vn, vc, kbd	1801	XXXII/3	
70	Z243	My mither's ay glowran o'er me	vn, cont	1791–2	XXXII/1	
70bis	Z244	My mither's ay glowran o'er me	vn, vc, kbd	1800	XXXII/3	
71	Z395	Young Damon	vn, cont	1791–2	XXXII/1	
72	Z287	Robin quo' she	vn, cont	1791–2	XXXII/1	
72bis	Z288	Robin quo' she	vn, vc, kbd	1804	XXXII/3	
73	Z200	Logie of Buchan	vn, cont	1791–2	XXXII/1	
74	Z90	Eppie Adair	vn, cont	1791–2	XXXII/1	
75	Z376	Widow, are ye waking?	vn, cont	1791–2	XXXII/1	
75bis	Z377	Widow, are ye waking?	vn, vc, kbd	1804	XXXII/5	
76	Z372	Whistle o'er the lave o't	vn, cont	1791–2	XXXII/1	
76bis	Z373	Whistle o'er the lave o't	vn, vc, kbd	1801	XXXII/3	
77	Z239	My heart's in the Highlands	vn, cont	1791–2	XXXII/1	
78	Z320	Steer her up and had her gawin	vn, cont	1791–2	XXXII/1	
79	Z159	Jamie come try me	vn, cont	1791–2	XXXII/1	
80	Z149	If a body meet a body	vn, cont	1791–2	XXXII/1	
80bis	Z150	If a body meet a body	vn, vc, kbd	1801	XXXII/3	
81	Z219	McGrigor of Rora's lament	vn, cont	1791–2	XXXII/1	

Hob.XXXIa	*NG*	*Title*	*Accompaniment*	*Date*	*JHW*	*Other edn(s)*
82	Z382	Willy's rare	vn, cont	1791–2	XXXII/1	
83	Z196	Lizae Baillie	vn, cont	1791–2	XXXII/1	
84	Z210	The maid's complaint	vn, cont	1791–2	XXXII/1	
85	Z262	Oh onochrie	vn, cont	1791–2	XXXII/1	
86	Z206	Maggie's tocher	vn, cont	1791–2	XXXII/1	
87	Z148	I dream'd I lay	vn, cont	1791–2	XXXII/1	
88	Z118	The glancing of her apron	vn, cont	1791–2	XXXII/1	
89	Z253	O bonny lass	vn, cont	1791–2	XXXII/1	
90	Z104	The flowers of Edinburgh	vn, cont	1791–2	XXXII/1	
90bis	Z105	The flowers of Edinburgh	vn, vc, kbd	1801	XXXII/3	
91	Z164	Jockie and Sandy	vn, cont	1791–2	XXXII/1	
92	Z223	The mill, mill O!	vn, cont	1791–2	XXXII/1	
92bis	Z224	The mill, mill O!	vn, vc, kbd	1802–3	XXXII/5	
93	Z303	Shepherds, I have lost my love	vn, cont	1791–2	XXXII/1	
93bis	Z304	Shepherds, I have lost my love	vn, vc, kbd	1802–3	XXXII/5	
94	Z48	Bonny Kate of Edinburgh	vn, cont	1791–2	XXXII/1	
95	Z151	If e'er ye do well it's a wonder	vn, cont	1791–2	XXXII/1	
96	Z272	Peggy in Devotion	vn, cont	1791–2	XXXII/1	
97	Z66	Colonel Gardner	vn, cont	1791–2	XXXII/1	
98	Z342	To daunton me	vn, cont	1791–2	XXXII/1	
99	Z162	Jenny was fair and unkind	vn, cont	1791–2	XXXII/1	
100	Z132	Her absence will not alter me	vn, cont	1791–2	XXXII/1	
101	Z40	The bonnie gray ey'd morn	vn, cont	1794–5	XXXII/2	
101bis	Z41	The bonny gray ey'd morn	vn, vc, kbd	1801	XXXII/3	
102	Z43	Bonnie wee thing	vn, cont	1794–5	XXXII/2	
102bis	Z44	Bonnie wee thing	vn, vc, kbd	1802–3	XXXII/5	
102ter	Z45	Bonnie wee thing	vn, vc, kbd	1801	XXXII/3	
103	Z293	Roy's wife of Alldivaloch	vn, cont	1794–5	XXXII/2	
104	Z371	While hopeless	vn, cont	1794–5	XXXII/2	
105	Z108	Frae the friends and land I love	vn, cont	1794–5	XXXII/2	
106	Z305	The shepherd's son	vn, cont	1794–5	XXXII/2	
106bis	Z306	The shepherd's son	vn, vc, kbd	1802–3	XXXII/5	
106ter	Z307	The shepherd's son	vn, vc, kbd	1804	XXXII/4	

Hob.XXXIa	*NG*	*Title*	*Accompaniment*	*Date*	*JHW*	*Other edn(s)*
107	Z64	A cold frosty morning	vn, cont	1794–5	XXXII/2	
108	Z261	O, for ane-and-twenty Tam!	vn, cont	1794–5	XXXII/2	
109	Z168	Johnie Armstrong	vn, cont	1794–5	XXXII/2	
110	Z147	I do confess thou art sae fair	vn, cont	1794–5	XXXII/2	
111	Z252	Now westlin winds	vn, cont	1794–5	XXXII/2	
112	Z125	Green sleeves	vn, cont	1794–5	XXXII/2	
112bis	Z126	Green sleeves	vn, vc, kbd	1801	XXXII/3	
113	Z280	The posie	vn, cont	1794–5	XXXII/2	
114	Z7	As I cam down by yon castle wa'	vn, cont	1794–5	XXXII/2	
115	Z225	The minstrel	vn, cont	1794–5	XXXII/2	
115bis	Z226	The minstrel	vn, vc, kbd	1801	XXXII/3	
116	Z95	The ewie wi' the crooked horn	vn, cont	1794–5	XXXII/2	
116bis	Z96	The ewy wi' the crooked horn	vn, vc, kbd	1800	XXXII/3	
117	Z97	Fair Eliza	vn, cont	1794–5	XXXII/2	
118	Z375	The widow	vn, cont	1794–5	XXXII/2	
119	Z394	Yon wild mossy mountains	vn, cont	1794–5	XXXII/2	
120	Z238	My goddess woman	vn, cont	1794–5	XXXII/2	
121	Z312	She's fair and fause	vn, cont	1794–5	XXXII/2	
122	Z259	O'er the moor among the heather	vn, cont	1794–5	XXXII/2	
122ter	Z260	O'er the moor among the heather	vn, vc, kbd	1802–3	XXXII/5	
123	Z331	The tears I shed	vn, cont	1794–5	XXXII/2	
124	Z365	The wee wee man	vn, cont	1794–5	XXXII/2	
124bis	Z366	The wee wee man	vn, vc, kbd	1801	XXXII/3	
125	Z250	Nithsdall's welcome hame	vn, cont	1794–5	XXXII/2	
126	Z23	Bid me not forget	vn, cont	1794–5	XXXII/2	
127	Z177	Lady Randolph's complaint	vn, cont	1794–5	XXXII/2	
128	Z308	The shepherd's wife	vn, cont	1794–5	XXXII/2	
128bis	Z309	The shepherd's wife	vn, vc, kbd	1801	XXXII/3	
129	Z363	The weary pund o' tow	vn, cont	1794–5	XXXII/2	
129bis	Z364	The weary pund o' tow	vn, vc, kbd	1801	XXXII/3	
130	Z341	The tither morn	vn, cont	1794–5	XXXII/2	
131	Z1	Ae fond kiss	vn, cont	1794–5	XXXII/2	
132	Z160	Jenny drinks nae water	vn, cont	1794–5	XXXII/2	

Hob.XXXIa	*NG*	*Title*	*Accompaniment*	*Date*	*JHW*	*Other edn(s)*
133	Z355	The vain pursuit	vn, cont	1794–5	XXXII/2	
134	Z368	What can a young lassie do	vn, cont	1794–5	XXXII/2	
134bis	Z368	What can a young lassie do (with chor)	vn, vc, kbd	1801	XXXII/3	
135	Z289	The rose bud	vn, cont	1794–5	XXXII/2	
136	Z75	Dear Silvia	vn, cont	1794–5	XXXII/2	
137	Z316	The slave's lament	vn, cont	1794–5	XXXII/2	
138	Z76	The death of a linnet	vn, cont	1794–5	XXXII/2	
138bis	Z77	The death of a linnet (duet)	vn, vc, kbd	1801	XXXII/3	
139	Z82	Donald and Flora	vn, cont	1794–5	XXXII/2	
139bis	Z83	Donald and Flora	vn, vc, kbd	1802–3	XXXII/5	
140	Z145	I canna come ilke day to woo	vn, cont	1794–5	XXXII/2	
140bis	Z146	I canna come ilke day to woo	vn, vc, kbd	1801	XXXII/3	
141	Z143	Hughie Graham	vn, cont	1794–5	XXXII/2	
142	Z264	On a bank of flowers	vn, cont	1794–5	XXXII/2	
143	Z227	Morag	vn, cont	1794–5	XXXII/2	
143bis	Z228	Morag	vn, vc, kbd	1801	XXXII/3	
144	Z69	A country lassie	vn, cont	1794–5	XXXII/2	
145	Z322	Strathallan's lament	vn, cont	1794–5	XXXII/2	
145bis	Z323	Strathallan's lament	vn, vc, kbd	1801	XXXII/3	
146	Z335	Tho' for sev'n years and mair	vn, cont	1794–5	XXXII/2	
147	Z20	Bess and her spinning wheel	vn, cont	1794–5	XXXII/2	
148	Z173	Kellyburn Braes	vn, cont	1794–5	XXXII/2	
148bis	Z174	Kellyburn Braes	vn, vc, kbd	1801	XXXII/3	
149	Z257	O'er the hills and far away	vn, cont	1794–5	XXXII/2	
149bis	Z258	O'er the hills and far away (with chor)	vn, vc, kbd	1801	XXXII/3	
150	Z324	Strephon and Lydia	vn, cont	1794–5	XXXII/2	
151	Z265	On Ettrick banks	vn, vc, kpd	1800	XXXII/3	
152	Z86	Down the burn Davie	vn, vc, kpd	1800	XXXII/3	
153	Z378	William and Margret	vn, vc, kpd	1800	XXXII/3	
154	Z169	Johnny's gray breeks	vn, vc, kpd	1800	XXXII/3	
155	Z385	Woes my heart that we shou'd sunder (duet)	vn, vc, kpd	1800	XXXII/3	
156	Z99	Fee him, father	vn, vc, kpd	1800	XXXII/3	
157	Z13	Ay waking, O!	vn, vc, kpd	1800	XXXII/3	

Hob.XXXIa	*NG*	*Title*	*Accompaniment*	*Date*	*JHW*	*Other edn(s)*
158	Z202	The looking glass	vn, vc, kpd	1801	XXXII/3	
159	Z136	Highland Mary	vn, vc, kpd	1800	XXXII/3	
160	Z185	The lass of Patie's mill	vn, vc, kpd	1800	XXXII/3	
160bis	Z186	The lass of Patie's mill (duet)	vn, vc, kpd	1804	XXXII/5	
161	Z282	Queen Mary's lamentation	vn, vc, kpd	1800	XXXII/3	
162	Z29	The blathrie o't	vn, vc, kpd	1800	XXXII/3	
163	Z199	Logan water	vn, vc, kpd	1800	XXXII/3	
164	Z3	An thou wert mine ain thing	vn, vc, kpd	1800	XXXII/3	
164bis	Z4	An thou wert mine ain thing	vn, vc, kpd	1804	XXXII/5	
165	Z292	Rothiemurche's rant	vn, vc, kpd	1800	XXXII/3	
166	Z237	My dearie if thou die	vn, vc, kpd	1800	XXXII/3	
167	Z271	Peggy, I must love thee (duet)	vn, vc, kpd	1801	XXXII/3	
168	Z10	Auld Robin Gray	vn, vc, kpd	1800	XXXII/3	
169	Z175	Killicrankie	vn, vc, kpd	1801	XXXII/3	
170	Z55	The broom of Cowdenknows (with chor)	vn, vc, kpd	1800	XXXII/3	
171	Z15	Banncoks o' barley meal	vn, vc, kpd	1801	XXXII/3	UCCP 1984
172	Z47	Bonny Jean	vn, vc, kpd	1800	XXXII/3	
173	Z301	Sensibility	vn, vc, kpd	1800	XXXII/3	
174	Z135	Hey tutti taiti	vn, vc, kpd	1801	XXXII/3	UCCP 1984
175	Z201	The lone vale	vn, vc, kpd	1801	XXXII/3	
176	Z37	The blue bells of Scotland	vn, vc, kpd	1801–2	XXXII/3	
177	Z157	I wish my love were in a myre	vn, vc, kpd	1800	XXXII/3	
178	Z21	Bessy Bell and Mary Gray	vn, vc, kpd	1800	XXXII/3	
178bis	Z22	Bessy Bell and Mary Gray	vn, vc, kpd	1804	XXXII/5	
179	Z111	Galashiels	vn, vc, kpd	1800	XXXII/3	
180	Z328	Tak' your auld cloak about ye	vn, vc, kpd	1800	XXXII/3	
180bis	Z329	Tak' your auld cloak about ye	vn, vc, kpd	1804	XXXII/5	
181	Z339	Thro' the wood, laddie	vn, vc, kpd	1800	XXXII/3	
182	Z205	Macpherson's farewell (with chor)	vn, vc, kpd	1801	XXXII/3	
183	Z274	Pinkie house	vn, vc, kpd	1800	XXXII/3	
184	Z8	The auld gudeman	vn, vc, kpd	1801	XXXII/3	UCCP 1984
185	Z299	Scornfu' Nancy	vn, vc, kpd	1800	XXXII/3	
185bis	Z300	Scornfu' Nancy	vn, vc, kpd	1804	XXXII/5	

Hob.XXXIa	*NG*	*Title*	*Accompaniment*	*Date*	*JHW*	*Other edn(s)*
186	Z332	Tears that must ever fall	vn, vc, kpd	1801	XXXII/3	UCCP 1984
187	Z26	The birks of Invermay	vn, vc, kpd	1801	XXXII/3	
187bis	Z27	The birks of Invermay	vn, vc, kpd	1802–3	XXXII/5	
188	Z94	The ewe-bughts	vn, vc, kpd	1801	XXXII/3	
189	Z234	My apron deary	vn, vc, kpd	1801	XXXII/3	
189bis	Z235	My apron deary	vn, vc, kpd	1802–3	XXXII/5	
190bis	Z198	Lochaber	vn, vc, kpd	1804	XXXII/5	
191	Z290	Roslin Castle	vn, vc, kpd	1801	XXXII/3	
191bis	Z291	Roslin Castle	vn, vc, kpd	1802–3	XXXII/5	
192	Z11	Auld Rob Morris (duet)	vn, vc, kpd	1801	XXXII/3	
193	Z70	Craigieburn Wood	vn, vc, kpd	1801	XXXII/3	
194	Z242	My love she's but a lassie yet	vn, vc, kpd	1801	XXXII/3	
195	Z12	The auld wife ayont the fire	vn, vc, kpd	1801	XXXII/3	
196	Z117	Gil Morris	vn, vc, kpd	1801	XXXII/3	
198	Z325	The sutor's daughter (duet)	vn, vc, kpd	1801	XXXII/3	
199	Z187	The last time I came o'er the muir	vn, vc, kpd	1801	XXXII/3	
199bis	Z188	The last time I came o'er the muir	vn, vc, kpd	1802–3	XXXII/5	
200	Z48	The braes of Ballenden	vn, vc, kpd	1801	XXXII/3	
200bis	Z49	The braes of Ballenden	vn, vc, kpd	1802–3	XXXII/5	
201	Z331	The tears of Caledonia	vn, vc, kpd	1801	XXXII/3	
202	Z286	Robin Adair (duet)	vn, vc, kpd	1801	XXXII/3	UCCP 1984
203bis	Z92	Erin-go-bragh	vn, vc, kpd	1802–3	XXXII/5	
204	Z56	The bush aboon Traquair (duet)	vn, vc, kpd	1802–3	XXXII/5	
205	Z154	I'll never leave thee	vn, vc, kpd	1802–3	XXXII/5	
206	Z349	Tweedside (duet)	vn, vc, kpd	1802–3	XXXII/5	
207	Z51	The braes of Yarrow	vn, vc, kpd	1802–3	XXXII/5	
208	Z313	The silken snood	vn, vc, kpd	1802–3	XXXII/5	
209	Z184	The lass of Lochroyan	vn, vc, kpd	1802–3	XXXII/5	
210	Z204	Low down in the broom	vn, vc, kpd	1802–3	XXXII/5	
211	Z392	The yellow hair'd laddie (duet)	vn, vc, kpd	1802–3	XXXII/5	
212	Z106	The flowers of the forest	vn, vc, kpd	1802–3	XXXII/5	
213	Z65	The collier's bonny lassie	vn, vc, kpd	1802–3	XXXII/5	
214	Z358	Waly, waly	vn, vc, kpd	1802–3	XXXII/5	

Hob.XXXIa	NG	Title	Accompaniment	Date	JHW	Other edn(s)
214bis	Z359	Waly, waly	vn, vc, kpd	1801	XXXII/3	
215	Z195	Lewie Gordon	vn, vc, kpd	1802–3	XXXII/5	
216	Z68	Corn riggs (duet)	vn, vc, kpd	1802–3	XXXII/5	
217	Z81	Donald	vn, vc, kpd	1802–3	XXXII/5	UCCP 1984
218	Z9	Auld lang syne	vn, vc, kpd	1802–3	XXXII/5	
219	Z310	She rose and loot me in	vn, vc, kpd	1802–3	XXXII/5	
219bis	Z311	She rose and loot me in	vn, vc, kpd	1801	XXXII/3	
220	Z172	Katherine Ogie	vn, vc, kpd	1802–3	XXXII/5	
221	Z211	The maid that tends the goats	vn, vc, kpd	1802–3	XXXII/5	
221bis	Z212	The maid that tends the goats	vn, vc, kpd	1801	XXXII/3	
222	Z107	For the lack of gold	vn, vc, kpd	1802–3	XXXII/5	
223	Z294	Sae merry as we ha'e been	vn, vc, kpd	1802–3	XXXII/5	
224	Z57	Captain O'Kain	vn, vc, kpd	1802–3	XXXII/4	
225	Z116	Gilderoy (duet)	vn, vc, kpd	1802–3	XXXII/5	
227	Z283	Rattling roaring Willy	vn, vc, kpd	1801	XXXII/3	
228	Z268	Oran Gaoil (duet)	vn, vc, kpd	1801	XXXII/3	
229	Z78	Deil tak the wars	vn, vc, kpd	1801	XXXII/3	
230	Z276	The poet's ain Jean	vn, vc, kpd	1801	XXXII/3	
230bis	Z277	The poet's ain Jean	vn, vc, kpd	1804	XXXII/5	
231	Z158	A jacobite aire	vn, vc, kpd	1801	XXXII/3	
233	Z351	Up and war them a' Willie	vn, vc, kpd	1801	XXXII/3	
234	Z89	The east Neuk o' Fife	vn, vc, kpd	1801	XXXII/3	
235	Z180	Langolee	vn, vc, kpd	1801	XXXII/3	
236	Z98	Fair Helen of Kirkconnell	vn, vc, kpd	1804	XXXII/4	
237	Z140	Hooly and fairly	vn, vc, kpd	1801	XXXII/3	
241	Z270	Pat and Kate	vn, vc, kpd	1803	XXXII/4	
242	Z232	Muirland Willy (with chor)	vn, vc, kpd	1801	XXXII/3	
243	Z130	The happy topers (with chor)	vn, vc, kpd	1801	XXXII/3	
244	Z367	What ails this heart of mine (duet)	vn, vc, kpd	1804	XXXII/4	
245	Z384	The wish	vn, vc, kpd	1801	XXXII/3	
246	Z39	The boatman	vn, vc, kpd	1801	XXXII/3	
248	Z263	The old highland laddie	vn, vc, kpd	1801	XXXII/3	
249	Z266	Oonagh	vn, vc, kpd	1801	XXXII/3	

Hob.XXXIa	NG	Title	Accompaniment	Date	JHW	Other edn(s)
250	Z315	Sir Patrick Spence	vn, vc, kpd	1803	XXXII/4	
252	Z161	Jenny's bawbee	vn, vc, kpd	1801	XXXII/3	
255	Z267	Open the door	vn, vc, kpd	1804	XXXII/5	
256	Z144	The humours o' glen	vn, vc, kpd	1802–3	XXXII/5	
257	Z133	Here awa', there awa'	vn, vc, kpd	1802–3	XXXII/5	
258	Z240	My jo Janet	vn, vc, kpd	1804	XXXII/5	
259	Z74	The day returns (duet)	vn, vc, kpd	1804	XXXII/5	
260	Z314	The siller crown	vn, vc, kpd	1804	XXXII/5	
261	Z326	Sweet Annie	vn, vc, kpd	1802–3	XXXII/5	
262	Z241	My lodging is on the cold ground	vn, vc, kpd	1802–3	XXXII/5	
263	Z163	Jingling Jonnie	vn, vc, kpd	1801	XXXII/3	
264	Z338	The three captains	vn, vc, kpd	1803	XXXII/4	
265	Z278	Polwarth on the Green (duet)	vn, vc, kpd	1801	XXXII/3	
272	Z182	Lassie wi' the gowden hair	vn, vc, kpd	1803	XXXII/4	

Hob.XXXIb	NG	Title	Accompaniment	Date	JHW	Other edn(s)
1	Z63	Codiad yr hedydd	vn, vc, kpd	1803	XXXII/4	UCCP 1984
2	Z119	Gorhoffedd gwyr Harlech	vn, vc, kpd	1803	XXXII/4	UCCP 1984
3	Z346	Toriad y dydd	vn, vc, kpd	1803	XXXII/4	
4	Z72	Dafydd y garreg wen	vn, vc, kpd	1804	XXXII/4	UCCP 1984
5	Z214	Mantell Siani	vn, vc, kpd	1803	XXXII/4	
6	Z220	Mentra Gwen (duet)	vn, vc, kpd	1803	XXXII/4	
7	Z197	Llwyn Onn	vn, vc, kpd	1803	XXXII/4	UCCP 1984
8	Z285	Rhyfelgyrch Cadpen Morgan	vn, vc, kpd	1803	XXXII/4	
9	Z5	Ar hyd y nos (duet)	vn, vc, kpd	1803	XXXII/4	UCCP 1984
10	Z350	Twll yn ei boch	vn, vc, kpd	1803	XXXII/4	
11	Z137	Hob y deri dando	vn, vc, kpd	1803	XXXII/4	
12	Z62	Codiad yr haul (duet)	vn, vc, kpd	1803	XXXII/4	
13	Z100	Ffarwel Ffranses	vn, vc, kpd	1804	XXXII/4	
14	Z85	Dowch i'r frwydr	vn, vc, kpd	1803	XXXII/4	
15	Z127	Griseil ground	vn, vc, kpd	1803	XXXII/4	

Hob.XXXIb	*NG*	*Title*	*Accompaniment*	*Date*	*JHW*	*Other edn(s)*
16	Z138	Hob y deri dando	vn, vc, kpd	1804	XXXII/4	
17	Z348	Tros y garreg	vn, vc, kpd	1804	XXXII/4	
18	Z345	Tôn y ceiliog du (duet)	vn, vc, kpd	1804	XXXII/4	
19	Z388	Wyres Ned Puw	vn, vc, kpd	1804	XXXII/4	
20	Z93	Eryri wen	vn, vc, kpd	1804	XXXII/4	
21	Z67	The Cornish May song	vn, vc, kpd	1803	XXXII/4	
22	Z269	Pant corlan yr ŵyn	vn, vc, kpd	1804	XXXII/4	
23	Z33	Blodau Llundain (duet)	vn, vc, kpd	1804	XXXII/4	
24	Z393	Y gadlys (duet)	vn, vc, kpd	1803	XXXII/4	
25	Z389	Y bardd yn ei awen	vn, vc, kpd	1804	XXXII/4	
26	Z58	Castell Towyn	vn, vc, kpd	1803	XXXII/4	
27	Z91	Erddigan caer Y Waun	vn, vc, kpd	1803	XXXII/4	
28	Z139	Hoffedd Hywel ab Owen Gwynedd	vn, vc, kpd	1804	XXXII/4	
29	Z251	Nos galan	vn, vc, kpd	1803	XXXII/4	
30	Z35	Blodau'r grug	vn, vc, kpd	1803	XXXII/4	
31	Z233	Mwynen Cynwyd	vn, vc, kpd	1804	XXXII/4	
32	Z390	Y Cymry dedwydd	vn, vc, kpd	1804	XXXII/4	
33	Z131	Hela'r ysgyfarnog	vn, vc, kpd	1804	XXXII/4	
34	Z80	Digan y pibydd coch	vn, vc, kpd	1803	XXXII/4	
35	Z34	Blodau'r drain	vn, vc, kpd	1803	XXXII/4	
36	Z213	Malltraeth	vn, vc, kpd	1804	XXXII/4	
37	Z398	Yr hen erddigan	vn, vc, kpd	1803	XXXII/4	
38	Z284	Reged	vn, vc, kpd	1804	XXXII/4	
39	Z61	Cerdd yr hen wr o'r coed	vn, vc, kpd	1804	XXXII/4	
40	Z101	Ffarwel ieuenctid	vn, vc, kpd	1804	XXXII/4	
41	Z347	Troaid y droell (duet)	vn, vc, kpd	1804	XXXII/4	
42	Z129	Happiness lost	vn, vc, kpd	1804	XXXII/4	
43a	Z178	The lamentation of Britain (duet)	vn, vc, kpd	1803	XXXII/4	
43b	Z179	The lamentation of Cambria (duet)	vn, vc, kpd	1804	XXXII/4	
44	Z327	The sweet melody of North Wales	vn, vc, kpd	1803	XXXII/4	
45	Z176	Lady's Owen's delight	vn, vc, kpd	1803	XXXII/4	
46	Z383	Winifreda (duet)	vn, vc, kpd	1803	XXXII/4	
47	Z381	The willow hymn	vn, vc, kpd	1803	XXXII/4	
48	Z2	The allurement of love	vn, vc, kpd	1804	XXXII/4	

Hob.XXXIb	*NG*	*Title*	*Accompaniment*	*Date*	*JHW*	*Other edn(s)*
49	Z216	The marsh of Rhuddlan	vn, vc, kpd	1804	XXXII/4	
50	Z84	The door clapper (duet)	vn, vc, kpd	1804	XXXII/4	
51	Z54	The Britons	vn, vc, kpd	1804	XXXII/4	
52	Z281	The pursuit of love	vn, vc, kpd	1804	XXXII/4	
53	Z279	The poor pedlar	vn, vc, kpd	1804	XXXII/4	
54	Z36	The blossom of the honey suckle	vn, vc, kpd	1804	XXXII/4	
55	Z6	Aria di guerra e vittoria	vn, vc, kpd	1804	XXXII/4	
56	Z19	The bend of the horse shoe	vn, vc, kpd	1804	XXXII/4	
57	Z181	La partenza dal paese e dalli amici	vn, vc, kpd	1804	XXXII/4	
58	Z103	The flower of North Wales	vn, vc, kpd	1804	XXXII/4	
59	Z79	The departure of the king	vn, vc, kpd	1804	XXXII/4	
60	Z249	The new year's gift	vn, vc, kpd	1804	XXXII/4	

Hob.XXXIc	*NG*	*Original work; composer*	*Date*	*JHW*	*Other edn(s)*
1		Vias tuas Domine (chor); gradual from 1576 by unknown composer			
3	Fapp2:1	Vi miro fiso (S); Dittersdorf, L'Arcifanfano re de matti	1777		
4	Fapp2:3	Se provasse un pocolino (S); Anfossi, La forza delle donne	1780		
5	Fapp2:4	Ah crudel, poi ché lo brami (S); Gazzaniga, La vendemmia	1780		HMP 1961
6	Fapp2:6	Gelosia d'amore è figlia (S); Salieri, La scuola de' gelosi	1780		
7	Fapp2:7	Si promette facilmente (S); Anfossi, La finta giardiniera	1780		
8	Fapp2:8	Vorrei punirti indegno (S); Anfossi, La finta giardiniera	1780		
9	Fapp2:9	Non ama la vita (S); Anfossi, Isabella e Rodrigo	1781		
10	Fapp2:10	Che tortora (S); Piccinni, Gli stravaganti	1781		
11	Fapp2:11	Una semplice agnelletta (S); Piccinni, Gli stravaganti	1781		
12	Fapp2:14	Deh frenate i mesti accenti (S); Anfossi, Il curioso indiscreto	1782		
13	Fapp2:18	Se voi foste un cavaliere (S); Cimarosa, I due supposti conti	1789		
14	Fapp2:20	Silenzio, miei signori (T or B); Cimarosa, L'impresario in angustie	1790		
15	Fapp2:17	Se palpitar degg'io (S); Prati, La vendetta di Nino	1788		
16	Happ:1–12	12 Sentimental Catches and Glees (SSS or TTT, kbd or harp); melodies credited to Earl of Abingdon	1795	XXIX/2	
17	Gapp1:2	The Lady's Looking-glass (SSS or TTT); Earl of Abingdon	1791-5	XXIX/1	

Hoboken XXXII: pasticcios

Hoboken lists four works in this section; nos. 2–4 are stage works that include adaptations of music by Haydn. The first work, however, includes music specially composed by Haydn.

Hob.XXXII	*NG*	*Title*	*Role; opera*	*Date*	*JHW*	*Other edn(s)*
1a	F15	Son due ore che giro (recit)	Pedrillo (B); *La Circe*	1789	XXVI/2	Bartha and Somfai; lib facs *HYB* 22
1b	F15	Son pietoso, son bonina (aria)	Lindora (S); *La Circe*	1789	XXVI/2	D 1959; lib facs *HYB* 22
1c	F15	Lavatevi presto	Teodoro (T), Brunoro (T), and Corado (B); *La Circe*	1789	XXVI/2	UCCP 1982; lib facs *HYB* 22

APPENDIX 2

TEXT INCIPITS

The following alphabetical list includes text incipits of individual movements in Haydn's vocal works cross referenced to the Hoboken catalogue. Sacred works in Latin, folksong settings, revisions of arias by other composers, and recitatives are not included.

Incipit	*Hob. number*
Ach! das Ungewitter naht	XXI:3, Summer
Achieved is the glorious work	XXI:2, Part 2
Ad acquistar già volo	XXVIII:6, Act 2
Ad un guardo, a un cenno solo	XXVIII:11, Act 1
A fatti tuoi badar tu puoi	XXVIII:3, Act 2
Ah che divenni stupida	XXVIII:8, Act 1
Ah, che in van per me pietoso	XXVIII:9, Part 2
Ah gran Dio	XXI:1, Part 1
Ah me, how scanty is my store!	XXVIa:36
Ah non ferir	XXVIII:12, Act 3
Ah non lasciarmi	XXXIc:16
Ah se dire io vi potessi	XXVIII:11, Act 1
Ah se tu vuoi, ch'io viva	XXVIII:10, Act 3
Ah si plachi il fiero Nume	XXVIII:12, Act 2
Ah, sposo infelice!	XXVIII:13, Act 3
Ah tu m'ascolta	XXI:1, Part 1
Ah vedrai, bell'idol mio	XXVIII:1
Al comando tua lunatico	XXVIII:7, Act 2
Alles ging für mich verloren	XXVIIb:24
All' Kummer Gram und Schmerz	XXIXb:A, Act 1
Als einst mit Weibes Schönheit	XXVIa:44
Al tuo seno fortunato	XXVIII:13, Act 3
Amico! Eccoci dunque	XXVIII:6, Act 3
Amore del mio petto	XXVIII:3, Act 1
Andiamo, amiche, andiamo	XXVIII:13, Act 4
And the spirit of God moved upon the face of the waters	XXI:2, Part 1
anguish of my bursting heart, The	XXVIa:28
Animo risoluto	XXVIII:8, Act 2
Anna, m'ascolta!	XXI:1, Part 1
Apri pur, mia dea terrestre	XXVIII:2; Act 2
Aspettare e non venire	XXVIIb:17
Astri che in ciel splendete	XXVIII:12, Act 3
A trionfar t'invita	XXVIII:8, Act 1
Auch die sprödeste der Schönen	XXVIa:18
Auf starkem Fittiche schwinget	XXI:2, Part 2
Aure chete, verdi allori	XXVIII:11, Act 2
Ausgesandt vom Strahlenthrone	XXX:5b
Awake the harp	XXI:2, Part 1
Bald wehen uns des Frühlings Lüfte	XXVIa:47
Befehlt doch draußen still zu schweigen	XXVIIb:4
Begli occhi vezzosi	XXVIII:7, Act 1
Beherzigt doch das Diktum	XXVIIb:16
Beim Schmerz, der dieses Herz durchwühlet	XXVIa:37

Incipit	*Hob. number*
Bekomm i nur den Stän	XXIXb:A, Act 1
Bella dea	XXVIII:10, Act 1
Bella sera ed aure grate	XXVIII:5, Act 1
Bell'ombra gradita	XXVIII:4, Act 1
Benché gema un'alma oppressa	XXVIII:8, Act 3
Beschattet von blühenden Ästen	XXVIa:12
Bevi, bevi in questa tazza	XXVIII:13, Act 4
Blest be the name of Jacob's god	XXIII: Nachtrag
Blest leader!	XXVIb:4
Burlottino, mio carino	XXVIII:4, Act 2
By thee with bliss, O bounteous Lord	XXI:2, Part 3
Cara, è vero, io son tiranno	XXVIII:12, Act 2
Cara, sarò fedele	XXVIII:12, Act 1
Cara speme! Alme di scoglio	XXVIII:13, Act 1
Care spiagge, selve, addio	XXVIII:8, Act 2
Caro Volpino amabile	XXVIII:3, Act 1
Castagno, castagna	XXVIII:6, Act 1
Che bevanda, che liquore!	XXVIII:6, Act 1
Che burrasca, che tempesta	XXVIII:8, Act 1
Che imbroglio è questo!	XXVIII:5, Act 1
Che mondo amabile	XXVIII:7, Act 2
Che sian i Calandri filosofi pazzi	XXVIII:6, Act 1
Che vi par? Son io gentile?	XXVIII:4, Act 2
Che visino delicato	XXVIII:2, Act 1
Che vive amante, so che delira	XXIVb:13
Chi nel cammin d'onore	XXVIII:9, Part 1
Chi s'impaccia di moglie cittadina	XXVIII:5, Act 1
Chi spira e non spera	XXVIII:13, Act 3
Coll'amoroso foco	XXVIII:10, Act 1
Colla presente scrittura privata	XXVIII:3; Act 2
Come il foco allo splendoro	XXVIII:13, Act 1
Come il vapor s'ascende	XXVIII:9, Part 2
Come in sogno un stuol m'apparve	XXI:1, Part 2
Come piglia sì bene la mira	XXVIII:5, Act 1
Come se a voi parlasse	XXI:1, Part 2
Compatite la vecchiezza	XXVIII:4, Act 1
Con un tenero sospiro	XXVIII:8, Act 1
Cosa vedo! cosa sento!	XXVIII:11, Act 2
Costretta a piangere dolente	XXIVb:1
Da che penso a maritarmi	XXIVb:16
Da ist die Katz	XXIXb:2, Act 1
Dal mondo della Luna	XXVIII:7, Act 3
D'Angelica il nome!	XXVIII:11, Act 1
Dann bricht der grosse Morgen an	XXI:3, Winter
Das Leben, das Leben ist ein Traum!	XXVIa:21
Das nenn' ich einen Edelmann	XXVIIb:2
Deh! Se in ciel pietade avete	XXVIII:6, Act 1
Deh soccorri un infelice	XXVIII:10, Act 1
Dein kleinster Feind ist der	XXVIIb:36
Dei pietosi	XXVIII:12, Act 3
Del caro sposo	XXI:1, Part 1
Dell'amor mio fedele	XXVIII:10, Act 2

Incipit	*Hob. number*
Dell'estreme sue voci dolenti	XXVIII:11, Act 3
Del mio core il voto estremo	XXVIII:13, Act 2
Dem Druck' erlieget die Natur	XXI:3, Summer
Denkst du auch so innig meiner	XXVIa:46
Den Strikrok solt ich gar ablegen	XXIXb:A, Act 2
Der Jüngling hofft	XXVb:3
Der Mann, der ist ein Hexenmeister	XXIXb:A, Act 2
Der Morgen graut, es ruft der Hahn	XXX:5c
Der muntre Hirt versammelt	XXI:3, Summer
Despairing, cursing rage	XXI:2, Part 1
Des reichen Hiesels Haus, das brennt	XXIXb:A, Act 1
Dica pure chi vuol dire	XXIVb:8
Dice benissimo, chi si marita	XXIVb:5
Dictamina mea	XXIVa:6
Die düstren Wolken trennen sich	XXI:3, Summer
Die ganze Welt will glücklich sein	XXVIa:38
Die Himmel erzählen die Ehre Gottes	XXI:2, Part 1
Die Seele wachet auf	XXI:3, Summer
Dille che un infelice	XXVIII:11, Act 2
Di questo audace ferro	XXVIII:10, Act 2
Dir danken wir, was uns ergötz	XXI:3, Summer
Dir nah' ich mich	XXVIa:17
Discendi, Amor pietoso	XXVIII:4, Act 3
Dove fuggo, ove m'ascondo	XXVIII:8, Act 2
Dove, oh dio	XXVIII:10, Act 1
Dove sei, mio bel tesoro	XXVIb:2
Dove son? Che miro intorno?	XXVIII:12, Act 1
Du bist's, dem Ruhm und Ehre	XXVc:8
Du, merke dir die Lehre	XXVIIb:11
D'una sposa meschinella	XXIVb:2
Dunque, oh Dio	XXI:1, Part 2
Du sollst an einem Gott glauben	XXVIIa:1
Du sollst den Namen Gottes nicht eitel nennen	XXVIIa:2
Du sollst kein falsch Zeugnis geben	XXVIIa:8
Du sollst nicht begehren deines Nächsten Gut	XXVIIa:10
Du sollst nicht begehren deines Nächsten Weib	XXVIIa:9
Du sollst nicht stehlen	XXVIIa:7
Du sollst nicht töten	XXVIIa:5
Du sollst nicht Unkeuschheit treiben	XXVIIa:6
Du sollst Sonn- und Feiertag heiligen	XXVIIa:3
Du sollst Vater und Mutter verehren	XXVIIa:4
È amore di natura	XXVIII:10, Act 1
Ecco spiano	XXVIII:11, Act 2
Ecco un splendido banchetto	XXVIII:6, Act 3
Ehre, Lob und Preis sei dir	XXI:3, Spring
Eilt, ihr Schäfer, aus den Gründen	XXVIa:8
Ein einzig böses Weib	XXVIIb:23
Ein Herr, der Narren hält	XXVIIb:35
Ein jeder bleib bei einem Stand	XXVIIb:3
Ein kleines Haus, von Nußgesträuch umgrenzt	XXVIa:45
Ein Liedchen vom Lieben	XXVIa:7
Ein Mädchen, das auf Ehre hielt	XXI:3, Winter

Incipit	*Hob. number*
Ein' Magd, ein' Dienerin Maria	XXIIId:1
Ein Narr trifft allemal	XXVIIb:34
È in ordine la festa	XXVIII:6, Act 2
Ein Tag, der allen Freude bringt	XXIXb:2
Ein verliebter Rauchfangkehrer	XXIXb:A, Act 1
Ein weises Herz und guter Mut	XXVIIb:31
È la pompa un grand'imbroglio	XXVIII:5, Act 2
Entfernt von Gram und Sorgen	XXVIa:10
Entflohn ist nun der Schlummer	XXIXb:2
envious snow, The	XXXIc:16
Erblickke hier, betörter Mensch	XXI:3, Winter
Er ist nicht mehr	XX/2
Erschütert wankt die Erde	XXI:3, Summer
Es ist umsonst	XXVIIb:18
Es ist vollbracht	XX/2
Es stecket Ja im linken	XXVIIb:14
Ewiger, mächtiger, gütiger Gott!	XXI:3, Spring
Ey, wer hat' ihm das Ding gedenckt	XXIIId:G1
Farewell my flocks	XXXIc:16
Far from this throbbing bosom haste	XXVIa:29
Faulheit, endlich muß ich dir	XXVIa:22
Favorisca la sua bella mano	XXVIII:4, Act 3
Ferma il piede, o principessa!	XXVIII:13, Act 1
Fiera strage dell'indegno	XXVIII:4, Act 1
Filomena abbandonata	XXVIII:13, Act 1
Finché circola il vigore	XXVIII:13, Act 2
Fliehe, wenn dein Wohl dir heilig ist	XXVIIb:25
Fra cetre e cembali ti sposerò	XXVIII:4, Act 1
Frau, hier siehe deinen Sohn, un du, siehe deine Mutter!	XX/2
Fra un dolce deliro	XXVIII:9, Part 1
Freunde, Wasser machet stumm	XXVc:4
Freund! ich bitte, hüte dich	XXVc:6
Funesto orror di morte	XXIVa:7
Fürwahr, ich sag es dir: Heute wirst du bei mir im Paradiese sein	XX/2
Geh, sag mir nur	XXVIIb:41
Giacché il pietoso amico	XXVIII:9, Part 2
Già la morte in manto nero	XXXVIII:8, Act 2
Già mi sembra di sentire	XXVIII:10, Act 1
Già si vede i vezzi e vanti	XXVIII:4, Act 2
Gott erhalte Franz den Kaiser	XXVIa:43
Gott im Herzen	XXVIIb:44
Graceful consort! At thy side	XXI:2, Part 3
Grand'Eroe, del mondo onore	XXIVa:2
Groß willst du und auch artig sein?	XXVIIb:5
Guarda qui che lo vedrai	XXVa:1
Ha, die wird erwischt! ich wette	XXIXb:A, Act 2
Ha gl'occhi brillanti	XXVIII:4, Act 2
Hail to the myrtle shade	XXXIc:16
Halt dein Maul! und flenn mir nicht	XXIXb:2, Act 2
Hark! The wild uproar of the winds	XXIVa:8
Hark! What I tell to thee	XXVIa:41
heavens are telling the glory of God, The	XXI:2, Part 1

Incipit	*Hob. number*
Herr! der du mir das Leben	XXVc:9
Herst Nachbä, hä, sag mir was heut	XXIIId:3
Heut fühl ich der Armut Schwere	XXIXb:2
Heysa, heysa, heysa, sa, sa	XXIXb:A, Act 2
Hier liegt Hans Lau	XXVIIb:19
Hier sein Grab	XXVIa:24
Hier sieht der Wandrer nun	XXI:3, Winter
High on the giddy bending mast	XXVIa:31
Hin ist alle meine Kraft	XXVc:5
Holder Gattin! Dir zur Seite	XXI:2, Part 3
Ho promesso oprar destrezza	XXVIII:6, Act 2
Hör auf, meines armes Herz	XXVIa:5
Höre, Mädchen, meine Bitte!	XXVIIb:6
Hört! das laute Getön!	XXI:3, Autumn
Hört! Die winde furchtbar heulen	XXIVa:8
Ho tesa la rete	XXVIII:5, Act 2
Ho un tumore in un ginocchio	XXVIII:5, Act 2
Ho veduto una ragazza	XXVIII:7, Act 1
Ho veduto un buon marito	XXVIII:7, Act 1
Ho veduto dall'amante	XXVIII:7, Act 1
Ho viaggiato in Francia, in Spagna	XXVIII:11, Act 1
How oft, instinct with warmth divine	XXIII: Nachtrag
Ich bin vernügt, will ich was mehr	XXVIa:20
Ich dich beneiden?	XXVIIb:22
I fruitless mourn	XXXIc:16
Ihr mißvergnügten Stunden	XXVIa:9
Ihr Schönen aus der Stadt	XXI:3, Autumn
Il guerrier con armi avvolto	XXVIII:6, Act 2
Il lavorar l'è pur la brutta cosa	XXVIII:11, Act 1
Ille potens sui laetusque deget	XXVIIb:10
Il meglio mio carattere	XXIVb:17
Il pensier sta negli oggetti	XXVIII:13, Act 1
Il Profeta Maometto	XXVIII:6, Act 2
Inbrunst, Zärtlichkeit	XXVc:1
Infelice sventurata, sono oppressa	XXIVb:15
Infelici ombre dolenti	XXVIII:13, Act 4
In holder Anmut steh'n	XXI:2, Part 2
In native worth and honour clad	XXI:2, Part 2
In thee I bear so dear a part	XXVIa:33
In un mar d'acerbe pene	XXVIII:13, Act 2
Invan lo chiedi, amico	XXI:1, Part 2
In Wolken, hoch emporgetragen	XXIXb:2
Io non oso alzar	XXI:1, Part 2
Io son poverino	XXVIII:8, Act 1
Io sposar l'empio tiranno	XXVIII:2, Act 1
Ist Gott mein Schutz	XXVIIb:8
Ja, Vetter, ja	XXVb:1
Jeder meint, der Gegenstand	XXVIa:13
Jeder prüfe seine Stärke!	XXVIIb:32
Je höher Stand, je mehr Gefahr	XXVIIb:42
Jesus rufet: Ach, mich dürstet!	XX/2
Jezt bin ich, was ich war	XXIXb:A, Act 2

Appendix 2

Incipit	*Hob. number*
Juhe, juhe! der Wein ist da	XXI:3, Autumn
Kaum seh' ich den Donner die Himmel umziehen	XXVIIb:27
Kein Unglük kann stärker betrüben	XXIXb:A, Act 1
Kenne Gott, die Welt und dich	XXVIIb:13
Know then this truth	XXXIc:16
Knurre, schnurre, knurre	XXI:3, Winter
Komm, holder Lenz!	XXI:3, Spring
La beltà, che m'innamora	XXVIII:1
Lachet nicht, Mädchen	XXVIa:14
La giustizia in cor regina	XXVIII:13
La mia bella m'ha detto di no	XXVIII:11, Act 1
La mia pace, oh Dio, perdei	XXIVb:19
La moglie quando è buona è quella	XXIVb:18
L'amore è un gran briccone	XXVIII:6, Act 1
Langweiliger Besuch macht Zeit und Zimmer enger	XXVIIb:43
La ragazza col vecchione	XXVIII:7, Act 1
Lauf geschwind hol mir Pomade her	XXIXb:A, Act 1
L'augusto Prence serba a noi Giove	XXIVa:2
Lavatevi presto, vedete quel vaso	XXXII:1
Lebe, liebe, trinke	XXVc:3
Leiser nannt' ich deinen Namen	XXVIa:3
Licht und Leben sind geschwächet	XXI:3, Winter
Long life shall Israel's king behold	XXIII: Nachtrag
Lord, th'almighty Monarch, spake	XXIII: Nachtrag
Love, free as air	XXXIc:16
Mai non sia inulto	XXVIII:13, Act 2
Mai per te stella rubella	XXIVa:2
Maker of all! Be Thou my guard	XXIII: Nachtrag
Maria Jungfrau rein, du liebste Mutter mein	Hob. deest; see entry
marv'llous work beholds amazed, The	XXI:2, Part 1
Massima filosofica	XXVIII:8, Act 2
Mehr als zwanzig Jahr' Vermählte	XXIXb:2
Mein Gott, mein Gott, warum hast du mich verlassen?	XX/2
Mia dica, il mio signore	XXVIII:10, Act 1
Miei pensieri, dove siete?	XXVIII:11, Act 3
Mi fanno ridere	XXVIII:7, Act 1
Mille lampi d'accese faville	XXVIII:11, Act 2
Mi sembra un sogno	XXVIII:6, Act 1
Mi sento languire	XXVIII:13, Act 4
Miseri affetti miei	XXVIII:10, Act 1
Mit Staunen sieht das Wunderwerk	XXI:2, Part 1
Mit Würd' und Hoheit angetan	XXI:2, Part 2
Most beautiful appear	XXI:2, Part 2
Mutter Gottes, mir erlaube	XXIIId:2
My mother bids me bind my hair	XXVIa:27
Nackt ward ich zur Welt geboren	XXVIIb:15
Nä, nä, nä, s'Haus gib i nit her	XXIXb:A, Act 1
Natur gab Stieren Hörner	XXVb:4
Navicella da vento agitata	XXX:1
Nel mille settecento	XXVIII:5, Act 2
Nel solitario speco	XXVIII:11, Act 2
Nicht fressen, nicht sauffen	XXIXb:A, Act 2

Incipit	*Hob. number*
Nie wich ich dem zu schaden suchen	XXVIIb:26
Nimm dies kleine Angedenken	XXVIa:40
Noi pariamo Santarelli	XXVIII:6, Act 1
Non aver di me sospetto	XXVIII:7, Act 2
Non chymaeras somniatis	XXIVa:6
Non ò genio con amore	XXX:1
Non parmi esser fra gl'uomini	XXI:1, Part 2
Non partir, bell'idol mio	XXIVa:10
Non partir, mia bella face	XXVIII:11, Act 1
Non piangete, putte care	XXVIII:6, Act 2
Non s'innalza, non stride sdegnosa	XXVIII:8, Act 1
Non sparate	XXVIII:8, Act 1
Non turbar quand'io mi lagno	XXVIII:9, Part 2
Non v'è chi mi aiuta	XXVIII:2, Act 2
Non v'è rimedio	XXVIII:5, Act 1
Non vi sdegnate, mia Signorina	XXVIII:10, Act 2
Nor can I think my suit is vain	XXIVa:9
Now heav'n in all her glory shone	XXI:2, Part 2
Now the dancing sunbeams play	XXVIa:25
Now vanish before the holy beams	XXI:2, Part 1
Nume, che al mare	XXVIII:4, Act 3
Nun beut die Flur das frische Grün	XXI:2, Part 1
Nun endt't sich der Kummer	XXIXb:A, Act 2
Nun scheint in vollem Glanze	XXI:2, Part 2
Nun schwanden vor dem heiligen Strahle	XXI:2, Part 1
O beatus incolatus!	XXIVa:6
Ob ich morgen leben wurde	XXVIIb:28
O Caelites, vos invocamus	XXIVa:6
Odi le nostre voci	XXI:1, Part 1
Odio, furor, dispetto	XXVIII:12, Act 2
O ever beauteous	XXXIc:16
O Fleiß, o edler Fleiß, von dir kommt alles Heil	XXI:3, Autumn
O fließ, ja wallend fließ in Zähren	XXVIa:19
O gebt mir doch ein Stükkel Brod!	XXIXb:A, Act 2
Oh che gusto!	XXVIII:8, Act 2
Oh, che orrore!	XXVIII:13, Act 4
O let me in th'accepted hour	XXIII: Nachtrag
O liebes Mädchen, höre mich	XXVIa:15
O Luna lucente	XXVIII:7, Act 1
Ombra del caro bene	XXVIII:10, Act 2
Ombre insepolte	XXVIII:11, Act 2
O meiner Augen Weide	XXIXb:A, Act 1
On mighty pens uplifted soars	XXI:2, Part 2
O piglia questa!	XXVIII:5, Act 1
O pii Patres Patriae!	XXIVa:6
O poter dell'armonia!	XXVIII:13, Act 1
Or gli affanni son svaniti	XXVIII:6, Act 3
Or vicina a te, mio cuore	XXVIII:6, Act 2
O say what is, that thing call'd light	XXXIc:16
O Sonne, Heil!	XXI:3, Summer
O stelle dich, Narziß, doch morgen bei mir ein!	XXVIIb:1
O tuneful voice!	XXVIa:42

Incipit	Hob. number
O Vater hört!	XXIXb:A, Act 2
O wie lieblich ist der Anblick	XXI:3, Spring
O wollte doch der Mensch	XXVIIb:7
O wunderbare Harmonie	XXVc:2
Palpita ad ogni istante	XXVIII:11, Act 1
Partirò, ma pensa, ingrato	XXVIII:12, Act 2
Parto. Ma, oh dio, non posso	XXVIII:11, Act 1
Perché se tanti siete	XXIVa:10
Perché stupisci tanto	XXVIII:1
Per pietà vezzosi rai	XXVIII:8, Act 2
Per quel che ha mal di stomaco	XXVIII:3, Act 1
Per te m'accese amore	XXVIII:10, Act 1
Pescatori, pescatrici	XXVIII:4, Act 2
Philint stand jüngst von Babetts Tür	XXVIa:4
Pietà di me, benigni Dei	XXVb:5
Pietà d'un'infelice	XXI:1, Part 1
Più la belva nel bosco non freme	XXVIII:10, Act 2
Placidi ruscelletti	XXVIII:10, Act 1
Potz tausend säfferment!	XXIXb:A, Act 1
Prence amato	XXVIII:12, Act 2
Prendiamo, fratelli	XXVIII:7, Act 1
Presto rispondi, indegno	XXVIII:11, Act 1
Principessa a voi mi prostro	XXVIII:4, Act 1
Qualche volta non fa male	XXVIII:7, Act 2
Qual contento	XXVIII:11, Act 2
Qual destra omicida la morte	XXIVb:10
Qual felice nocchier	XXI:1, Part 2
Quando la rosa non ha più spine	XXIVb:3
Quando mi dona un cenno	XXI:1, Part 1
Quando viene a far l'amore	XXVIII:5, Act 1
Quanta gente che sospira	XXVIII:7, Act 2
Quanti son di questa polvere	XXVIII:3, Act 1
Quanto affetto mi sorprende!	XXVIII:6, Act 1
Quanto più diletta	XXVIII:10, Act 3
Quel silenzio e quelli pianti	XXVIII:10, Act 2
Quel tuo visetto amabile	XXVIII:11, Act 2
Questa è un'altra novità	XXVIII:3, Act 1
Questa mano e questo cuore	XXVIII:4, Act 3
Questi torti, questi affronti	XXVIII:10, Act 1
Quivi in un seren gentile	XXVIII:6, Act 2
Ragazzaccie, che senza cervello	XXVIII:3, Act 2
Ragion nell'alma siede	XXVIII:7, Act 1
Recida il ferro istesso	XXVIII:10, Act 2
Rerum, quas perpendimus	XXIVa:6
Rollend in schäumenden Wellen	XXI:2, Part 1
Rolling in foaming billows	XXI:2, Part 1
Rosina, vezzosina	XXVIII:8, Act 3
Salamelica, Semprugna cara	XXVIII:3, Act 3
Salva, salva … aiuto, aiuto	XXVIII:10, Act 1
Sangue d'un ginocchio storto!	XXVIII:6, Act 1
Saper vorrei se m'ami	XXVa:2
Sappi, che la bellezza	XXVIII:10, Act 2

Incipit	*Hob. number*
Saure Arbeit! Mädchen fangen	XXIXb:A, Act 2
Scellerata, mancatrice	XXVIII:2, Act 1
Scenda propizio un raggio	XXIVa:4
Schaft mir Bier und Brandtewein	XXIXb:A, Act 2
Schon eilet froh der Ackermann	XXI:3, Spring
Schon fesselt Lieb' und Ehre mich	XXVIa:23
season comes when first we met, The	XXVIa:26
Se credesse che un visetto	XXX:1
Se da' begli occhi tuoi	XXVIII:10, Act 2
Se dal suo braccio oppresso	XXVIII:12, Act 1
S'egli è vero, che dagli astri	XXVIII:6, Act 3
Sehr nützlich ist uns oft ein Feind	XXVIIb:39
Seht auf die breiten Wiesen hin!	XXI:3, Autumn
Sei uns gnädig, milder Himmel!	XXI:3, Spring
Se la mia stella	XXVIII:7, Act 2
Se lo comanda	XXVIII:7, Act 2
Sembra che in questo giorno	XXIVa:3
Se men gentile	XXVIII:1
Se non mi credi	XXX:1
Se non piange un'infelice	XXVIII:9, Part 1
Se non son bella tanto	XXX:1
Senti, al buio pian, pianino	XXVIII:6, Act 2
Se ogni giorno, Prence invitto	XXIVa:4
Se pietade avete, o Numi	XXVIII:12, Act 1
Se te mi sprezzi, ingrata	XXIVb:14
Se tu seguir mi vuoi	XXVIII:12, Act 1
She never told her love	XXVIa:34
Siam femmine buonine	XXVIII:6, Act 1
Sie hat das Auge, die Hand	XXVb:2
Sie steiget herauf die Sonne	XXI:3, Summer
Signor mio	XXVIII:2, Act 2
Signor Sempronio	XXVIII:3, Act 3
Signor voi sapete	XXIVb:7
Si jamais je prends un époux	XXX:4
Singt dem Herren alle Stimme	XXI:2, Part 3
Sing the Lord ye voices all	XXI:2, Part 3
Si obtrudat ultimam	XXIVa:6
Soavi zeffiri	XXVIII:4, Act 3
So che una bestia sei	XXVIII:8, Act 1
So far la semplicetta	XXVIII:4, Act 1
So lang, ach, schon so lang	XXVIa:11
Sollt' ich voller Sorg' und Pein	XXVIa:6
Solo e pensoso i più deserti campi	XXIVb:20
So lohnet die Natur den Fleiß	XXI:3, Autumn
Some kind angel	XXXIc:16
Son confuso e stupefatto	XXVIII:11, Act 3
Son disperato	XXVIII:5, Act 1
Son fanciulla da marito	XXVIII:7, Act 1
Son finite le tue pene	XXVIII:13, Act 4
Sono Alcina, e sono ancora un visino	XXIVb:9
Sono contenta appieno	XXVIII:9, Part 2
Son pietosa, son bonina	XXXII:1b

Incipit	*Hob. number*
Son quest'occhi un stral d'amore	XXVIII:6, Act 2
Son vecchio, son furbo	XXVIII:4, Act 2
So war der Mensch zu allen Zeiten	XXVIIb:30
Stimmt an die Saiten	XXI:2, Part 1
Sudò il guerriero	XXI:1, Part 1
Svanisce in un momento	XXI:1, Part 2
Teco lo guida al campo	XXVIII:12, Act 2
Temerario! senti e trema	XXVIII:11, Act 1
Tergi i vezzosi rai	XXVIII:1
Thy great endeavours to increase	XXIVa:9
Thy voice o Harmony	XXVIIb:46
Ti miro fisso fisso	XXVIII:4, Act 1
Tira, tira; viene, viene	XXVIII:4, Act 1
Tod ist ein langer Schlaf	XXVIIb:21
Torna pure al caro bene	XXVIII:12, Act 3
Tornate pur mia bella	XXIVb:22
To wander alone	XXVIa:32
Trachten will nicht auf Erden	XXVIa:39
Tra tuoni, lampi e fulmini	XXVIII:4, Act 1
Trema, tiran regnante	XXX:1
Trinche vaine allegramente	XXVIII:5, Act 2
Trionfi oggi pietà	XXVIII:13, Act 4
Triumph, dem Gott der Götter	XXIXb:2
Triumph dir Haldane	XXX:5a
Trust not too much that entrancing face	XXXIc:17
Tu mi piaci, ed io ti bramo	XXX:1
Tu mi sprezzi	XXVIII:12, Act 2
Turk was a faithful dog	XXVIIb:45
Tu sposarti alla Sandrina?	XXVIII:5, Act 2
Tutto il giorno pista	XXVIII:3, Act 1
Una donna come me	XXVIII:7, Act 1
Un avaro suda e pena	XXVIII:7, Act 2
Un certo ruscelletto	XXVIII:7, Act 3
Un certo tutore in Francia vi fu	XXVIII:3, Act 2
Un cor sì tenero in petto forte	XXIVb:11
Und der Geist Gottes schwebte auf der Fläche der Wasser	XX1:2, Part 1
Und hörst du, kleine Phyllis	XXVIa:1
Un poco di denaro	XXVIII:7, Act 1
Uns leite deine Hand, o Gott!	XXI:3, Winter
Uomo felice	XXVIII:7, Act 2
Urli orrendi, disperati	XXVIII:13, Act 4
Vado adagio, signorina	XXIVb:12
Vado a pugnar contento	XXVIII:12, Act 1
Vado, vado; volo, volo	XXVIII:7, Act 1
Vanne ... fuggi ... traditore!	XXVIII:10, Act 1
Varca il mar di sponda in sponda	XXVIII:4, Act 1
Vater, in deine Hände empfehle ich meinen Geist	XX/2
Vater, vergib, denn sie wissen nicht, was sie tun	XX/2
Verdammtes Mädel!	XXIXb:A, Act 2
Verzweiflung, Wut und Schrecken	XXI:2, Part 1
Vi cerca il fratello	XXVIII:4, Act 2
Vieni amato Orfeo	XXVIII:13, Act 4

Incipit	*Hob. number*
Virtus inter ardua	XXIVa:6
Vittoria, vittoria!	XXVIII:11, Act 2
Voglio amar e vuò scherzare	XXVIII:4, Act 1
Voglio goder contenta	XXVIII:4, Act 1
Voi lo sapete	XXVIII:7, Act 2
Volgi pure ad altr'oggetto	XXVIII:10, Act 2
Vollendet ist das grosse Werk	XXI:2, Part 2
Von allen Sterblichen auf Erden	XXVIa:36bis
Von deinem Segensmahle	XXI:3, Spring
Von deiner Güt', o Herr	XXI:2, Part 2
Von oben winkt der helle Stern	XXI:3, Summer
Was durch seine Blüte der Lenz zuerst versprach	XXI:3, Autumn
Was fang i armer Wurstel an?	XXIXb:A, Act 1
Was hilft Gesetz	XXVIIb:38
Was ist mein Stand	XXVc:7
Was meine matte Brust bekränket	Hob. deest; see entry
Wein, Bad und Liebe	XXVIIb:33
Weißt du, mein kleines Mägdelein	XXVIa:2
Welche Labung für die Sinne	XXI:3, Summer
Wenn am weiten Firmamente	XXIXb:2
Wer leichtlich zürnt	XXVIIb:37
Wer Lust zu lernen hat	XXVIIb:40
Wer Schwache leiten will	XXVII:12
What art expresses	XXVIb:3
What though no high descent I claim	XXVIa:36
Where shall a hapless lover	XXXIc:16
While hollow burst the rushing winds	XXVIa:30
Why asks my fair one if I love?	XXVIa:35
Wie wallet mein Herze	XXIXb:A, Act 2
Wir grausam, Dorilis	XXVIIb:9
Wir manche schliefen hier mit Ehren	XXVIIb:20
With verdure clad the fields appear	XXI:2, Part 2
Wüßt' ich, wüßt' ich	XXVIa:16
Ye little loves	XXXIc:16
Zwischen Gott und unsern Sinnen	XXVIIb:29